PHILIP'S NAVIGATOR®

Camping and Caravanning

Atlas of Britain

www.philips-maps.co.uk

First published in 2014 by Philip's,
a division of Octopus Publishing Group Ltd
www.octopusbooks.co.uk
Carmelite House
50 Victoria Embankment
London EC4Y 0DZ
An Hachette UK Company
www.hachette.co.uk

Third edition 2019
Second impression 2020

ISBN 978-1-84907-509-1

Cartography by Philip's
Copyright © 2019 Philip's

This product includes mapping data licensed
from Ordnance Survey®, with the permission of
the Controller of Her Majesty's Stationery Office.
© Crown copyright 2019. All rights reserved.
Licence number 100011710

Data for the caravan sites provided by
The Camping and Caravanning Club.

Information for the selection of Wildlife Trust nature reserves
provided by The Wildlife Trusts.

Information for National Parks, Areas of Outstanding Natural Beauty,
National Trails and Country Parks in Wales supplied by the
Countryside Council for Wales.

Information for National Parks, Areas of Outstanding Natural Beauty,
National Trails and Country Parks in England supplied by Natural
England. Data for Regional Parks, Long Distance Footpaths and
Country Parks in Scotland provided by Scottish Natural Heritage.

Information for Forest Parks supplied
by the Forestry Commission

Information for the RSPB reserves provided by the RSPB

Gaelic name forms used in the Western Isles provided by
Comhairle nan Eilean.

Data for the National Nature Reserves in England provided by Natural
England. Data for the National Nature Reserves in Wales provided
by Countryside Council for Wales. Darparwyd data'n ymwneud â
Gwarchodfeydd Natur Cenedlaethol Cymru gan Gyngor Cefn Gwlad
Cymru.

Information on the location of National Nature Reserves in Scotland
was provided by Scottish Natural Heritage.

Data for National Scenic Areas in Scotland provided by the Scottish
Executive Office. Crown copyright material is reproduced with the
permission of the Controller of HMSO and the Queen's Printer for
Scotland. Licence number C02W0003960.

Photographic acknowledgements
Front cover and title page: The A835 road with view towards
Ullapool and Loch Broom • David Robertson / Alamy
Back cover top: Jim Holden / Alamy
Back cover bottom: Camping and Caravanning Club

Printed in China

Contents

II Key to map symbols

III Our great camp sites, your great experiences

VIII Route planning maps

XIV Distances and journey times

1 Road maps of Britain

315 Urban approach maps

315 Bristol *approaches*	**320** Glasgow *approaches*	**327** Manchester *approaches*
316 Birmingham *approaches*	**321** Leeds *approaches*	**328** Newcastle *approaches*
318 Cardiff *approaches*	**322** London *approaches*	**329** Nottingham *approaches*
319 Edinburgh *approaches*	**326** Liverpool *approaches*	**330** Sheffield *approaches*

331 Town plans

331 Aberdeen, Aberystwyth, Ashford, Ayr, Bangor, Barrow-in-Furness, Bath, Berwick-upon-Tweed

332 Birmingham, Blackpool, Bournemouth, Bradford, Brighton, Bristol, Bury St Edmunds

333 Cambridge, Canterbury, Cardiff, Carlisle, Chelmsford, Cheltenham, Chester, Chichester, Colchester

334 Coventry, Derby, Dorchester, Dumfries, Dundee, Durham, Edinburgh, Exeter

335 Fort William, Glasgow, Gloucester, Grimsby, Hanley, Harrogate, Holyhead, Hull

336 Inverness, Ipswich, Kendal, King's Lynn, Leeds, Lancaster, Leicester, Lewes

337 Lincoln, Liverpool, Llandudno, Llanelli, Luton, Macclesfield, Manchester

338 London

340 Maidstone, Merthyr Tydfil, Middlesbrough, Milton Keynes, Newcastle, Newport, Newquay, Newtown, Northampton

341 Norwich, Nottingham, Oban, Oxford, Perth, Peterborough, Plymouth, Poole, Portsmouth

342 Preston, Reading, St Andrews, Salisbury, Scarborough, Shrewsbury, Sheffield, Southampton

343 Southend-on-Sea, Stirling, Stoke, Stratford-upon-Avon, Sunderland, Swansea, Swindon, Taunton, Telford

344 Torquay, Truro, Wick, Winchester, Windsor, Wolverhampton, Worcester, Wrexham, York

345 Index to town plans

361 Index to road maps of Britain

402 County and unitary authority boundaries

Road map symbols

Motorway

Motorway junctions – full access, restricted access

Toll motorway

Motorway service area

Motorway under construction

Primary route – dual, single carriageway, services
– under construction, narrow

Primary destination

Numbered junctions – full, restricted access

A road – dual, single carriageway
– under construction, narrow

B road – dual, single carriageway
– under construction, narrow

Minor road – dual, single carriageway

Drive or track

Urban side roads (height, weight and width restrictions not shown)

Height restriction, width restriction – feet and inches

Tunnel, weight restriction – tonnes

Distance in miles

Roundabout, multi-level junction,

Toll, steep gradient – points downhill

National trail – England and Wales

Long distance footpath – Scotland

Railway with station, level crossing, tunnel

Preserved railway with level crossing, station, tunnel

Tramway

National boundary

County or unitary authority boundary

Car ferry, catamaran

Passenger ferry, catamaran

Hovercraft

Internal ferry – car, passenger

Principal airport, other airport or airfield

Area of outstanding natural beauty, National Forest – England and Wales, Forest park, National park, National scenic area – Scotland, Regional park

Woodland

Beach – sand, shingle

Navigable river or canal

Lock, flight of locks, canal bridge number

Caravan or camping sites
– CCC* Club Site, Ready Camp Site, Camping in the Forest Site
– CCC Certificated Site, Listed Site
*Categories defined by The Camping and Caravanning Club of Great Britain

Viewpoint, park and ride, spot height – in metres

Linear antiquity

Adjoining page number, OS National Grid reference – see page 402

Tourist information

BYLAND ABBEY ✠	Abbey or priory
WOODHENGE 🏛	Ancient monument
SEALIFE CENTRE 🐬	Aquarium or dolphinarium
CITY MUSEUM AND ART GALLERY 🏛	Art collection or museum
TATE ST IVES 🏛	Art gallery
1644 ⚔	Battle site and date
ABBOTSBURY SWANNERY 🦅	Bird sanctuary or aviary
BAMBURGH CASTLE 🏰	Castle
YORK MINSTER ✝	Cathedral
SANDHAM MEMORIAL CHAPEL ⛪	Church of interest
SEVEN SISTERS 🌲	Country park – England and Wales
LOCHORE MEADOWS 🌲	– Scotland
ROYAL BATH & WEST SHOWGROUND 🐄	County show ground
MONK PARK FARM 🐖	Farm park
HILLIER GARDENS AND ARBORETUM ❀	Garden, arboretum
ST ANDREWS ⛳	Golf course – 18-hole
TYNTESFIELD 🏠	Historic house
SS GREAT BRITAIN ⛴	Historic ship
HATFIELD HOUSE 🏰	House and garden
CUMBERLAND PENCIL MUSEUM 🏛	Museum
MUSEUM OF DARTMOOR LIFE	– Local
NAT MARITIME MUSEUM ◇	– Maritime or military

⚓	Marina
SILVERSTONE 🏁	Motor racing circuit
	Nature reserves
HOLTON HEATH	– National nature reserve
BOYTON MARSHES RSPB	– RSPB reserve
DRAYCOTT SLEIGHTS	– Wildlife Trust reserve
Ꝥ	Picnic area
WEST SOMERSET RAILWAY 🚂	Preserved railway
THIRSK 🏇	Racecourse
LEAHILL TURRET	Roman antiquity
THRIGBY HALL 🦁	Safari park
FREEPORT BRAINTREE 🛍	Shopping village
MILLENNIUM STADIUM 🏟	Sports venue
ALTON TOWERS 🎡	Theme park
	Tourist information centres
i	– open all year
i	– open seasonally
NATIONAL RAILWAY MUSEUM	Transport collection
LEVANT MINE 🌐	World heritage site
HELMSLEY △	Youth hostel
MARWELL 🐘	Zoo
SUTTON BANK VISITOR CENTRE ∴	Other place
GLENFIDDICH DISTILLERY ◆	of interest

Approach map symbols

Motorway

Toll motorway

Motorway junction – full, restricted access

Service area

Under construction

Primary route – dual, single carriageway

Service area

Multi-level junction

roundabout

Under construction

A road – dual, single carriageway

B road – dual, single carriageway

Minor road – dual, single carriageway

Ring road

Distance in miles

Railway with station

Tramway with station

Underground or metro station

Congestion charge area

Road map scale 1:100 000 • 1cm = 1km • 1 inch = 1.58 miles

0   1   2   3   4   5 km

0   1   2   3 miles

Road map scale (Isle of Man and parts of Scotland)
1:200 000 • 1cm = 2km • 1 inch = 3.15 miles

0 1 2 3 4 5 6 7 8 9 10 km

0   1   2   3   4   5   6 miles

Load and vehicle restrictions – please read

Any information on height, width and weight restrictions in the UK as noted on pages 1–314 of this atlas has been derived from the relevant OS material used to compile this atlas. Any information on height, width and weight restrictions on the Isle of Man has been derived from the relevant information as supplied by the Isle of Man Highways Department. Where a warning sign is displayed, any height obstructions, including but not limited to low bridges and overhead cables, are shown in the atlas where such obstructions cross navigable roads selected for inclusion. Height restrictions lower than 16'6" and width restrictions narrower than 13 feet, are all shown in 3 inch multiples and have been rounded down where necessary. Weight restrictions indicate weak bridges and the maximum gross weight which could be supported is shown in tonnes. While every effort has been made to include all relevant and accurate information, due to limitations of scale a single symbol may be used to indicate more than one feature and it is not possible to show restrictions on urban side roads.

OUR CAMPSITES, YOUR GREAT EXPERIENCES

The **Camping** and **Caravanning Club**
The Friendly Club

campingandcaravanningclub.co.uk

READY Camp
FROM THE CAMPING AND CARAVANNING CLUB

www.readycamp.co.uk

CAMPING IN THE FOREST

www.campingintheforest.co.uk

Symbols explained

Understanding Club pitches

- G A grass-only pitch with no electric hook-up or other services.
- J A large grass-only pitch with no electric hook-up, where the unit measures more than 5m x 9m.
- GWE A grass pitch with electric hook-up.
- HWE A hardstanding pitch with electric hook-up.
- JWE A large pitch with electric hook-up for units that measure more than 5m x 9m.
- SS A hardstanding pitch with electric hook-up plus fresh water and waste drainage. Some pitches may also have TV hook-up points.

Other symbols

- Touring caravans
- Motorhomes
- Trailer tents and folding campers
- Tents
- Camping Pods or Dens
- HH Holiday Homes and Exclusive Lodges
- ACC Alternative Accommodation/Self-catering
- SP Seasonal Pitches
- SF Storage facilities
- ! Difficult access or a difficult approach
- Open site
- Well-sheltered site
- Coastal
- Sea/loch view
- Dedicated accessible facilities
- Some accessible facilities
- No dedicated accessible facilities
- Parent and baby room
- Mother and baby room
- Family shower room
- Backpacker facilities
- WC Toilet
- Showers
- Washbasins
- Dishwashing facilities
- Washing machines
- Drying room
- MHS Motorhome Stop-off
- Shop
- FF Ice pack freezing
- Gas cylinders
- Battery charging
- Recreation hall
- TV Television room (not for hire)
- Wireless internet provider is Infinium
- Wireless internet
- Children's play area
- Ball games
- Swimming pool
- Boating
- Fishing facilities
- Tennis
- Restaurant
- Pets welcome
- Designated dog walk
- PH1 Pub within one mile
- RC Ready Camp
- Don't use SatNav - see directions online use campingandcaravanningclub.co.uk/bookasite

Camping in the Forest site specific symbols

- Public transport
- Pets not permitted

Club Site Map Key
- ● Club Site
- ● Camping in the Forest Site

Map labels: INVEREWE, DINGWALL, NAIRN, ROSEMARKIE, SPEYSIDE, SKYE, LOCH NESS SHORES, GLENMORE, TARLAND, ABERDEEN, GLENCOE, DUNDEE, OBAN, COBLELAND, SCONE, CASHEL, LUSS, MILARROCHY BAY, DUNBAR, GLASGOW, EDINBURGH, KILMARNOCK, LAUDER, BEADNELL BAY, AYR, JEDBURGH, DUNSTAN HILL, CULZEAN CASTLE, MOFFAT, DUMFRIES, BELLINGHAM, NEWCASTLE, STRANRAER, HALTWHISTLE, LARNE, CARLISLE, BELFAST, DERWENTWATER, KESWICK, BARNARD CASTLE, DELAMONT COUNTRY PARK, RAVENGLASS, KENDAL, WINDERMERE, SCARBOROUGH, DOUGLAS, BRAITHWAITE FOLD, SLINGSBY, SHERIFF HUTTON, BOROUGHBRIDGE, YORK, DUBLIN, CLITHEROE, LEEDS, HULL, BLACKPOOL, CHORLEY, HUDDERSFIELD, SCUNTHORPE, SOUTHPORT, CROWDEN, LIVERPOOL, MANCHESTER, SHEFFIELD, DELAMERE FOREST, HAYFIELD, LINCOLN, MABLETHORPE, HOLYHEAD, CHESTER, BAKEWELL, TEVERSAL, WOODHALL SPA, WREXHAM, LEEK, ASHBOURNE, BOSTON, LLANYSTUMDWY, BALA, STOKE, DERBY, NOTTINGHAM, OSWESTRY, ALTON, THE STAR, SANDRINGHAM, WEST RUNTON, EBURY HILL, CANNOCK CHASE, CONKERS, ABERYSTWYTH, DRAYTON MANOR, KINGSBURY WATER PARK, PETERBOROUGH, NORWICH, WOLVERHAMPTON, BIRMINGHAM, KESSINGLAND, WYESIDE, WOLVERLEY, CLENT HILLS, HUNTINGDON, CARDIGAN BAY, ST NEOTS, CAMBRIDGE, IPSWICH, RHANDIRMWYN, BLACKMORE, HEREFORD, POLSTEAD, ST DAVIDS, WINCHCOMBE, CHIPPING NORTON, COLCHESTER, BRACELANDS, OXFORD, HERTFORD, KELVEDON HATCH, SWANSEA, THEOBALDS PARK, CARDIFF, BRISTOL, POSTERN HILL, LONDON, WALTON-ON-THAMES, DEVIZES, CHERTSEY, OLDBURY HILL, CANTERBURY, LYNTON, MINEHEAD, CHEDDAR, BASINGSTOKE, HORSLEY, FOLKESTONE, UMBERLEIGH, TAUNTON, SALISBURY, CROWBOROUGH, CHICHESTER, GRAFFHAM, BUDE, CHARMOUTH, VERWOOD, SLINDON, MORETON, ADGESTONE, NORMAN'S BAY, EXETER, CORFE CASTLE, TREGURRIAN, TAVISTOCK, TORQUAY, DARTMOUTH, SLAPTON SANDS, ST IVES, VERYAN, CALIFORNIA CROSS, SENNEN COVE

NEW FOREST SITES
Aldridge Hill; Ashurst
Denny Wood & Matley Wood; Hollands Wood
Holmsley; Ocknell & Longbeech
Roundhill; Setthorns

Club Site Philip's Map Key

 Club Site – we have over 100 camp sites across the UK. See them listed over the next 4 pages and within the maps.

 Ready Camp – pre-erected glamping tents in over 45 locations across the UK.

 Camping in the Forest Site – the Club works with the Forestry Commission to run these 16 sites in Britain's forest woodlands.

 Certificated Site – nearly 1,400 smaller sites, accepting up to 5 caravans or motorhomes, plus tents – space permitting – they are exclusive to Club members only.

 Listed Site – these can range from huge holiday parks with entertainment to quiet commercial sites. The Club does not approve or recommend any of these sites.

The Camping and Caravanning Club
The Friendly Club

SCOTLAND

Culzean Castle Club Site
Culzean, Maybole, Ayrshire
KA19 8JX
Tel: 01655 760627
Map reference:
Pg: 256 Grid Ref: G6
Open: 1 Apr – 4 Nov 2019
Pitches: 90

Dingwall Club Site
Jubilee Park Road, Dingwall,
Highlands IV15 9QZ
Tel: 01349 862236
Map reference:
Pg: 300 Grid Ref: D5
Open: 1 Apr – 28 Oct 2019
Pitches: 83

Dunbar Club Site
Oxwellmains, Dunbar,
East Lothian EH42 1WG
Tel: 01368 866881
Map reference:
Pg: 282 Grid Ref: F4
Open: 1 Apr – 4 Nov 2019
Pitches: 90

Glencoe Club Site
Glencoe, Ballachulish, Argyll
PH49 4LA
Tel: 01855 811397
Map reference:
Pg: 284 Grid Ref: B5
Open: 1 Apr – 28 Oct 2019
Pitches: 102

Inverewe Gardens Club Site
Poolewe, Achnasheen, Highlands
IV22 2LF
Tel: 01445 781249
Map reference:
Pg: 307 Grid Ref: L3
Open: 1 Apr – 28 Oct 2019
Pitches: 55

Jedburgh Club Site
Elliot Park, Jedburgh, Borders
TD8 6EF
Tel: 01835 863393
Map reference:
Pg: 262 Grid Ref: E5
Open: 1 Apr – 4 Nov 2019
Pitches: 50

Lauder Club Site
Carfraemill, Oxton, Lauder,
Borders TD2 6RA
Tel: 01578 750697
Map reference:
Pg: 271 Grid Ref: E10
Open: 1 Apr – 4 Nov 2019
Pitches: 60

Loch Ness Shores Club Site
Lower Foyers, Highland IV2 6YH
Tel: 01456 486333
Map reference:
Pg: 300 Grid Ref: G4
Open: All year
Pitches: 99

Luss Club Site
Luss, Loch Lomond, Alexandria,
Nr Glasgow, Scotland G83 8NT
Tel: 01436 860658
Map reference:
Pg: 277 Grid Ref: C7
Open: 1 Apr – 28 Oct 2019
Pitches: 90
Note: Member only Caravans
and Motorhomes

Milarrochy Bay Club Site
Milarrochy Bay, Balmaha,
Nr Drymen, Glasgow G63 0AL
Tel: 01360 870236
Map reference:
Pg: 277 Grid Ref: C8
Open: 1 Apr – 4 Nov 2019
Pitches: 150

Moffat Club Site
Hammerlands, Moffat
DG10 9QL
Tel: 01683 220436
Map reference:
Pg: 248 Grid Ref: C3
Open: All year
Pitches: 180

Nairn Club Site
Delnies Wood, Nairn, Inverness,
Morayshire IV12 5NX
Tel: 01667 455281
Map reference:
Pg: 301 Grid Ref: D8
Open: 1 Mar – 28 Oct 2019
Pitches: 75

Oban Club Site
Barcaldine by Connel, Argyll
PA37 1SG
Tel: 01631 720348
Map reference:
Pg: 284 Grid Ref: C3
Open: 1 Apr – 28 Oct 2019
Pitches: 75

Rosemarkie Club Site
Ness Road East, Rosemarkie,
Fortrose, Highlands IV10 8SE
Tel: 01381 621117
Map reference:
Pg: 301 Grid Ref: D7
Open: 1 Apr – 28 Oct 2019
Pitches: 60

Scone Club Site
Scone Palace Caravan Park,
Scone, Tayside PH2 6BB
Tel: 01738 552323
Map reference:
Pg: 286 Grid Ref: E5
Open: 1 Mar – 2 Jan 2020
Pitches: 120

Skye Club Site
Loch Greshornish, Bovre, Arnisort,
Edinbane, Portree, Isle of Skye
IV51 9PS
Tel: 01470 582230
Map reference:
Pg: 298 Grid Ref: D3
Open: 1 Apr – 6 Oct 2019
Pitches: 105

Speyside Club Site
Archiestown, Aberlour,
Moray AB38 9SL
Tel: 01340 810414
Map reference:
Pg: 302 Grid Ref: E2
Open: 1 Apr – 30 Sep 2019
Pitches: 75

Tarland by Deeside Club Site
Tarland by Aboyne,
Aberdeenshire AB34 4UP
Tel: 01339 881388
Map reference:
Pg: 292 Grid Ref: C6
Open: 1 Mar – 28 Oct 2019
Pitches: 52

NORTHERN IRELAND

Delamont Country Park Club Site
Downpatrick Road, Killyleagh,
Northern Ireland BT30 9TZ
Tel: 028 4482 1833
Map reference:
Pg: N/A Grid Ref: N/A
Open: 7 Mar – 28 Oct 2019
Pitches: 63

NORTHERN ENGLAND

Barnard Castle Club Site
Dockenflatts Lane, Lartington,
Barnard Castle, County Durham
DL12 9DG
Tel: 01833 630228
Map reference:
Pg: 223 Grid Ref: B10
Open: 1 Mar – 4 Nov 2019
Pitches: 90

Beadnell Bay Club Site
Beadnell, Chathill,
Northumberland NE67 5BX
Tel: 01665 720586
Map reference:
Pg: 264 Grid Ref: D6
Open: 1 Apr – 4 Nov 2019
Pitches: 150

Bellingham Club Site
Brown Rigg, Bellingham, Hexham,
Northumberland NE48 2JY
Tel: 01434 220175
Map reference:
Pg: 251 Grid Ref: G8
Open: 1 Mar – 5 Jan 2020
Pitches: 70

Boroughbridge Club Site
Bar Lane, Roecliffe,
Boroughbridge, North Yorkshire
YO51 9LS
Tel: 01423 322683
Map reference:
Pg: 215 Grid Ref: F7
Open: All year
Pitches: 85

Braithwaite Fold Club Site
Glebe Rd, Bowness-On-
Windermere, Cumbria
LA23 3HB
Tel: 01539 442177
Map reference:
Pg: 221 Grid Ref: F7
Open: 1 Feb – 2 Jan 2020
Pitches: 65

Clitheroe Club Site
Edisford Road, Clitheroe,
Lancashire BB7 3LA
Tel: 01200 425294
Map reference:
Pg: 203 Grid Ref: E10
Open: 21 Feb – 28 Oct 2019
Pitches: 80

Derwentwater Club Site
Crow Park Road, Keswick,
Cumbria CA12 5EN
Tel: 01768 772579
Map reference:
Pg: 229 Grid Ref: G11
Open: 21 Feb – 2 Jan 2020
Pitches: 50

Dunstan Hill Club Site
Alnwick, Northumberland,
NE66 3TQ
Tel: 01665 576310
Map reference:
Pg: 264 Grid Ref: E6
Open: 1 Apr – 4 Nov 2019
Pitches: 150

Haltwhistle Club Site
Burnfoot Park Village,
Haltwhistle, Northumberland
NE49 0JP
Tel: 01434 320106
Map reference:
Pg: 240 Grid Ref: E5
Open: 1 Apr – 4 Nov 2019
Pitches: 50

Kendal Club Site
Millcrest, Shap Road, Kendal,
Cumbria LA9 6NY
Tel: 01539 741363
Map reference:
Pg: 221 Grid Ref: G10
Open: 1 Apr – 4 Nov 2019
Pitches: 50

Keswick Club Site
Crow Park Road, Keswick,
Cumbria CA12 5EP
Tel: 01768 772392
Map reference:
Pg: 229 Grid Ref: G11
Open: All year
Pitches: 250

Ravenglass Club Site
Ravenglass, Cumbria CA18 1SR
Tel: 01229 717250
Map reference:
Pg: 219 Grid Ref: F11
Open: 7 Feb – 4 Nov 2019
Pitches: 75

Scarborough Club Site
Field Lane, Burniston Road,
Scarborough, North Yorkshire
YO13 0DA
Tel: 01723 366212
Map reference:
Pg: 227 Grid Ref: G10
Open: 1 Apr – 4 Nov 2019
Pitches: 300

Sheriff Hutton Club Site
Bracken Hill, Sheriff Hutton,
North Yorkshire YO60 6QG
Tel: 01347 878660
Map reference:
Pg: 216 Grid Ref: F2
Open: 1 Apr – 4 Nov 2019
Pitches: 90

Slingsby Club Site
Railway Street, Slingsby,
North Yorkshire YO62 4AN
Tel: 01653 628335
Map reference:
Pg: 216 Grid Ref: D4
Open: 1 Apr – 4 Nov 2019
Pitches: 60

Windermere Club Site

Ashes Lane, Staveley, Kendal,
Cumbria LA8 9JS
Tel: 01539 821119
Map reference:
Pg: 221 Grid Ref: F9
Open: 7 Mar 2019 – 6 Jan 2020
Pitches: 250

WALES

Bala Club Site

Crynierth Caravan Park,
Cefn-Ddwysarn, Bala,
Gwynned LL23 7LN
Tel: 01678 530324
Map reference:
Pg: 147 Grid Ref: B9
Open: 1 Apr – 4 Nov 2019
Pitches: 50

Cardigan Bay Club Site

Llwynhelyg, Cross Inn, Llandysul,
Ceredigion SA44 6LW
Tel: 01545 560029
Map reference:
Pg: 111 Grid Ref: F7
Open: 21 Mar – 4 Nov 2019
Pitches: 90

Llanystumdwy Club Site

Tyddyn Sianel, Llanystumdwy,
Criccieth, Gwynedd LL52 0LS
Tel: 01766 522855
Map reference:
Pg: 145 Grid Ref: B9
Open: 1 Apr – 30 Sep 2019
Pitches: 70

Rhandirmwyn Club Site

Llandovery, Carmarthenshire
SA20 0NT
Tel: 01550 760257
Pg: 94 Grid Ref: C5
Open: 1 Apr – 4 Nov 2019
Pitches: 90

St David's Club Site

Dwr Cwmwdig, Berea, St David's,
Haverfordwest, Pembrokeshire
SA62 6DW
Tel: 01348 831376
Map reference:
Pg: 90 Grid Ref: E6
Open: 11 Apr – 30 Sep 2019
Pitches: 40

Wyeside Club Site

Rhayader, Powys LD6 5LB
Tel: 01597 81018
Map reference:
Pg: 113 Grid Ref: D9
Open: 1 Apr – 2 Nov 2019
Pitches: 60

CENTRAL ENGLAND

Alton, The Star Club Site

Cotton, Stoke-on-Trent,
Staffordshire ST10 3DW
Tel: 01538 702219
Map reference:
Pg: 169 Grid Ref: F9
Open: 1 Mar – 4 Nov 2019
Pitches: 195

Ashbourne Club Site

Belper Road (A517), Hulland
Ward, Bradley Nr Ashbourne,
Derbyshire DE6 3EN
Tel: 01335 370855
Map reference:
Pg: 170 Grid Ref: F2
Open: 1 Apr – 3 Nov 2019
Pitches: 70

Bakewell Club Site

Hopping Lane, Youlgreave,
Bakewell, Derbyshire
DE45 1NA
Tel: 01629 636555
Map reference:
Pg: 170 Grid Ref: C2
Open: 1 Apr – 4 Nov 2019
Pitches: 100

Blackmore Club Site

No.2, Hanley Swan,
Worcestershire WR8 0EE
Tel: 01684 310280
Map reference:
Pg: 98 Grid Ref: C6
Open: All year
Pitches: 180

Cannock Chase Club Site

Old Youth Hostel, Wandon,
Rugeley, Staffordshire WS15 1QW
Tel: 01889 582166
Map reference:
Pg: 151 Grid Ref: G10
Open: 1 Apr – 4 Nov 2019
Pitches: 60

Chipping Norton Club Site

Chipping Norton Road,
Chadlington, Chipping Norton,
Oxfordshire OX7 3PE
Tel: 01608 641993
Map reference:
Pg: 100 Grid Ref: G6
Open: 1 Apr – 4 Nov 2019
Pitches: 105

Clent Hills Club Site

Fieldhouse Lane, Romsley,
Halesowen, West Midlands
B62 0NH
Tel: 01562 710015
Map reference:
Pg: 117 Grid Ref: B9
Open: 1 Apr – 4 Nov 2019
Pitches: 95

Conkers, National Forest Club Site

50 Bath Lane, Moira, Swadlincote,
Derbyshire DE12 6BD
Tel: 01283 224925
Map reference:
Pg: 152 Grid Ref: F6
Open: All year
Pitches: 90

Crowden Club Site

Woodhead Road, Crowden,
Glossop SK13 1HZ
Tel: 01457 866057
Map reference:
Pg: 185 Grid Ref: B9
Open: 1 Apr – 4 Nov 2019
Pitches: 45

Delamere Forest Club Site

Station Road, Delamere,
Northwich, Cheshire CW8 2HZ
Tel: 01606 889231
Map reference:
Pg: 183 Grid Ref: G8
Open: All year
Pitches: 80

Drayton Manor Club Site

Drayton Manor, Nr Tamworth,
Staffordshire B78 3TW
Tel: 01827 260617
Map reference:
Pg: 134 Grid Ref: C3
Open: 7 Feb – 4 Nov 2019
Pitches: 90

Ebury Hill Club Site

Ring Bank, Haughton, Shrewsbury
SY4 4GB
Tel: 01743 709334
Map reference:
Pg: 149 Grid Ref: F10
Open: 1 Apr – 4 Nov 2019
Pitches: 100

Hayfield Club Site

Kinder Road, Hayfield, High Peak,
Derbyshire SK22 2LE
Tel: 01663 745394
Map reference:
Pg: 185 Grid Ref: D8
Open: 1 Apr – 4 Nov 2019
Pitches: 90

Hereford Club Site

The Millpond, Little Tarrington,
Hereford HR1 4JA
Tel: 01432 890243
Map reference:
Pg: 98 Grid Ref: C2
Open: 8 Mar – 3 Nov 2019
Pitches: 102

Kingsbury Water Park Club Site

Bodymoor Heath Lane, Sutton
Coldfield, West Mids B76 0DY
Tel: 01827 874101
Map reference:
Pg: 134 Grid Ref: D3
Open: All year
Pitches: 150

Leek Club Site

Blackshaw Grange, Blackshaw
Moor, Leek, Staffordshire ST13 8TL
Tel: 01538 300285
Map reference:
Pg: 169 Grid Ref: D8
Open: 1 Apr – 4 Nov 2019
Pitches: 70

Mablethorpe Club Site

Highfield, 120 Church Lane,
Mablethorpe, Lincolnshire
LN12 2NU
Tel: 01507 472374
Map reference:
Pg: 191 Grid Ref: E7
Open: 1 Apr – 4 Nov 2019
Pitches: 105

Oswestry Club Site

Cranberry Moss Kinnerley,
Oswestry, Shropshire SY10 8DY
Tel: 01743 741118
Map reference:
Pg: 149 Grid Ref: E7
Open: All year
Pitches: 65

Oxford Club Site

426 Abingdon Road,
Oxford OX1 4XG
Tel: 01865 244088
Map reference:
Pg: 83 Grid Ref: E8
Open: All year
Pitches: 85

Teversal Club Site

Silverhill Lane, Teversal,
Notts NG17 3JJ
Tel: 01623 551838
Map reference:
Pg: 171 Grid Ref: C7
Open: All year
Pitches: 126

Winchcombe Club Site

Brooklands Farm, Alderton,
Nr Tewkesbury, Gloucestershire
GL20 8NX
Tel: 01242 620259
Map reference:
Pg: 99 Grid Ref: E10
Open: 7 Mar 2019 – 6 Jan 2020
Pitches: 84

Wolverley Club Site

Brown Westhead Park, Wolverley,
Nr Kidderminster, Worcestershire
DY10 3PX
Tel: 01562 850909
Map reference:
Pg: 116 Grid Ref: B6
Open: 7 Mar – 4 Nov 2019
Pitches: 105

Woodhall Spa Club Site

Wellsyke Lane, Kirkby-on-Bain,
Woodhall Spa, Lincolnshire LN10
6YU
Tel: 01526 352911
Map reference:
Pg: 174 Grid Ref: C2
Open: 1 Apr – 4 Nov 2019
Pitches: 90

EAST ANGLIA

Cambridge Club Site

19 Cabbage Moor, Great Shelford,
Cambridgeshire CB22 5NB
Tel: 01223 841185
Map reference:
Pg: 123 Grid Ref: G9
Open: 1 Apr – 4 Nov 2019
Pitches: 120

Kessingland Club Site

Whites Lane, Kessingland, Nr
Lowestoft, Suffolk NR33 7TF
Tel: 01502 742040
Map reference:
Pg: 143 Grid Ref: F10
Open: 1 Apr – 30 Sep 2019
Pitches: 90

Norwich Club Site

Martineau Lane, Norwich,
Norfolk NR1 2HX
Tel: 01603 620060
Map reference:
Pg: 142 Grid Ref: B4
Open: 1 Apr – 4 Nov 2019
Pitches: 50

Polstead Club Site

Holt Road, Bower House Tye,
Polstead, Suffolk CO6 5BZ
Tel: 01787 211969
Map reference:
Pg: 107 Grid Ref: C9
Open: 15 Feb – 6 Jan 2020
Pitches: 60

St Neots Club Site
Hardwick Road, Eynesbury,
St Neots, Cambridgeshire
PE19 2PR
Tel: 01480 474404
Map reference:
Pg: 122 Grid Ref: F3
Open: 1 Apr – 4 Nov 2019
Pitches: 180

Sandringham Club Site
The Sandringham Estate, Double
Lodges, Sandringham, Norfolk
PE35 6EA
Tel: 01485 542555
Map reference:
Pg: 158 Grid Ref: D3
Open: 14 Feb 2019 – 6 Jan 2020
Pitches: 275

West Runton Club Site
Holgate Lane, West Runton,
Cromer, Norfolk NR27 9NW
Tel: 01263 837544
Map reference:
Pg: 177 Grid Ref: E11
Open: 1 Apr – 4 Nov 2019
Pitches: 200

SOUTH EAST ENGLAND

Adgestone Club Site
Lower Road, Adgestone,
Isle of Wight PO36 0HL
Tel: 01983 403432
Map reference:
Pg: 21 Grid Ref: D7
Open: 11 Apr – 30 Sep 2019
Pitches: 270

Canterbury Club Site
Bekesbourne Lane, Canterbury,
Kent CT3 4AB
Tel: 01227 463216
Map reference:
Pg: 55 Grid Ref: B7
Open: All year
Pitches: 150

Chertsey Club Site
Bridge Road, Chertsey, Surrey
KT16 8JX
Tel: 01932 562405
Map reference:
Pg: 66 Grid Ref: F5
Open: All year
Pitches: 150

Chichester Club Site
345 Main Road, Southbourne,
Hampshire PO10 8JH
Tel: 01243 373202
Map reference:
Pg: 34 Grid Ref: F3
Open: 1 Feb – 18 Nov 2019
Pitches: 58

Crowborough Club Site
Goldsmith Recreation Ground,
Bridge Road, Crowborough,
Sussex TN6 2TN
Tel: 01892 664827
Map reference:
Pg: 52 Grid Ref: G4
Open: 1 Apr – 4 Nov 2019
Pitches: 90

Folkestone Club Site
The Warren, Folkestone,
Kent CT19 6NQ
Tel: 01303 255093
Map reference:
Pg: 55 Grid Ref: F8
Open: 1 Apr – 4 Nov 2019
Pitches: 60

Graffham Club Site
Great Bury, Graffham, Petworth,
West Sussex GU28 0QF
Tel: 01798 867476
Map reference:
Pg: 34 Grid Ref: D6
Open: 1 Apr – 4 Nov 2019
Pitches: 90

Hertford Club Site
Mangrove Road (Not Ball Park),
Hertford, Hertfordshire SG13 8AJ
Tel: 01992 586696
Map reference:
Pg: 86 Grid Ref: C4
Open: All year
Pitches: 250

Horsley Club Site
Ockham Road North, West
Horsley, Surrey KT24 6PE
Tel: 01483 283273
Map reference:
Pg: 50 Grid Ref: B5
Open: 1 Apr – 4 Nov 2019
Pitches: 130

Kelvedon Hatch Club Site
Warren Lane, Doddinghurst,
Brentwood, Essex CM15 0JG
Tel: 01277 372773
Map reference:
Pg: 87 Grid Ref: F9
Open: 1 Apr – 4 Nov 2019
Pitches: 90

Normans Bay Club Site
Normans Bay, Pevensey,
East Sussex BN24 6PR
Tel: 01323 761190
Map reference:
Pg: 37 Grid Ref: F11
Open: 1 Apr – 4 Nov 2019
Pitches: 200

Oldbury Hill Club Site
Styants Bottom, Seal, Sevenoaks,
Kent TN15 0ET
Tel: 01732 762728
Map reference:
Pg: 52 Grid Ref: B5
Open: 1 Apr – 4 Nov 2019
Pitches: 60

Slindon Club Site
Slindon Park, Nr Arundel,
Sussex BN18 0RG
Tel: 01243 814387
Map reference:
Pg: 35 Grid Ref: F7
Open: 1 Apr – 30 Sep 2019
Pitches: 40

Theobalds Park Club Site
Bulls Cross Ride, Waltham Cross,
Hertfordshire EN7 5HS
Tel: 01992 620604
Map reference:
Pg: 86 Grid Ref: E4
Open: All year
Pitches: 90

Walton on Thames Club Site
Fieldcommon Lane, Walton on
Thames, Surrey KT12 3QG
Tel: 01932 220392
Map reference:
Pg: 66 Grid Ref: F6
Open: 1 Apr – 4 Nov 2019
Pitches: 115
Note: Members Only Site

SOUTH WEST ENGLAND

Bude Club Site
Gillards Moor, St Gennys, Bude,
Cornwall EX23 0BG
Tel: 01840 230650
Map reference:
Pg: 11 Grid Ref: C9
Open: 11 Apr – 30 Sep 2019
Pitches: 100

California Cross Club Site
Modbury, Ivybridge, Devon PL21 0SG
Tel: 01548 821297
Map reference:
Pg: 8 Grid Ref: E4
Open: 11 Apr – 30 Sep 2019
Pitches: 80

Charmouth Club Site
Monkton Wyld Farm, Scotts Lane,
Nr Charmouth, Dorset DT6 6DB
Tel: 01297 32965
Map reference:
Pg: 16 Grid Ref: B2
Open: 15 Mar – 4 Nov 2019
Pitches: 150

Cheddar, Mendip Heights Club Site
Mendip Heights, Townsend,
Priddy Wells, Somerset BA5 3BP
Tel: 01749 870241
Map reference:
Pg: 44 Grid Ref: C4
Open: 15 Mar 2019 – 5 Jan 2020
Pitches: 90

Corfe Castle Club Site
Bucknowle, Wareham,
Dorset BH20 5PQ
Tel: 01929 480280
Map reference:
Pg: 18 Grid Ref: E4
Open: 1 Mar – 3 Nov 2019
Pitches: 80

Dartmouth Club Site
Stoke Fleming, Dartmouth,
Devon TQ6 0RF
Tel: 01803 770253
Map reference:
Pg: 9 Grid Ref: F7
Open: 1 Apr – 4 Nov 2019
Pitches: 90

Devizes Club Site
Spout Lane, Nr Seend, Melksham,
Wiltshire SN12 6RN
Tel: 01380 828839
Map reference:
Pg: 62 Grid Ref: G2
Open: All year
Pitches: 90

Lynton Club Site
Lydiate Lane, Caffyn's Cross,
Lynton, Devon EX35 6JS
Tel: 01598 752379
Map reference:
Pg: 41 Grid Ref: D8
Open: 1 Apr – 30 Sep 2019
Pitches: 105

Minehead Club Site
Hill Road, North Hill, Minehead
Somerset TA24 5LB
Tel: 01643 704138
Map reference:
Pg: 42 Grid Ref: D3
Open: 11 Apr – 30 Sep 2019
Pitches: 60

Moreton Club Site
Station Road, Moreton,
Dorchester, Dorset DT2 8BB
Tel: 01305 853801
Map reference:
Pg: 17 Grid Ref: D11
Open: 1 Apr – 4 Nov 2019
Pitches: 120

Salisbury Club Site
Hudson's Field, Castle Road,
Salisbury, Wiltshire SP1 3SA
Tel: 01722 320713
Map reference:
Pg: 46 Grid Ref: G6
Open: 1 Apr 2019 – 3 Jan 2020
Pitches: 150

Sennen Cove Club Site
Higher Tregiffian Farm,
St Buryan, Penzance,
Cornwall TR19 6JB
Tel: 01736 871588
Map reference:
Pg: 1 Grid Ref: D3
Open: 1 Apr – 4 Nov 2019
Pitches: 72

Slapton Sands Club Site
Middle Grounds, Slapton,
Kingsbridge, Devon TQ7 2QW
Tel: 01548 580538
Map reference:
Pg: 8 Grid Ref: G6
Open: 1 Apr – 4 Nov 2019
Pitches: 115
Note: Member-only caravans

Tavistock Club Site
Higher Longford, Moorshop,
Devon PL19 9LQ
Tel: 01822 618672
Map reference:
Pg: 12 Grid Ref: G6
Open: All year
Pitches: 80

Tregurrian Club Site
Nr Newquay, Cornwall TR8 4AE
Tel: 01637 860448
Map reference:
Pg: 4 Grid Ref: B6
Open: 7 Mar – 4 Nov 2019
Pitches: 90

Umberleigh Club Site
Over Weir, Umberleigh,
Devon EX37 9DU
Tel: 01769 560009
Map reference:
Pg: 25 Grid Ref: C10
Open: 1 Apr – 30 Sep 2019
Pitches: 60

Verwood Club Site
Sutton Hill, Woodlands,
Wimborne, Dorset BH21 8NQ
Tel: 01202 822763
Map reference:
Pg: 31 Grid Ref: F9
Open: 1 Apr – 4 Nov 2019
Pitches: 150

Veryan Club Site
Tretheake, Veryan, Truro, Cornwall TR2 5PP
Tel: 01872 501658
Map reference:
Pg: 5 Grid Ref: G8
Open: 1 Apr – 30 Sep 2019
Pitches: 150

CAMPING IN THE FOREST

NEW FOREST

Aldridge Hill CITF Site
Brockenhurst, Hampshire SO42 7QD
Tel: 01590 623152
Map reference:
Pg: 32 Grid Ref: G3
Open: 23 May – 3 Jun; 27 Jun – 9 Sep 2019
Pitches: 170

Ashurst CITF Site
Lyndhurst Road, Ashurst, Hampshire SO40 7AR
Tel: 02380 292097
Map reference:
Pg: 32 Grid Ref: F4
Open: 11 Apr – 30 Sep 2019
Pitches: 280

Denny and Matley Wood CITF Sites
Beaulieu Road, Lyndhurst, Hampshire SO43 7FZ
Tel: 02380 293144
Map reference:
Pg: 32 Grid Ref: F4
Open: 11 Apr – 30 Sep 2019
Pitches: 240

Denny Wood

Matley Wood

Hollands Wood CITF Site
Lyndhurst Road, Brockenhurst, Hampshire SO42 7QH
Tel: 01590 622967
Map reference:
Pg: 32 Grid Ref: G4
Open: 11 Apr – 30 Sep 2019
Pitches: 600

Holmsley CITF Site
Forest Road, Thorney Hill, Bransgore, Christchurch, Dorset BH23 7EQ
Tel: 01425 674502
Map reference:
Pg: 19 Grid Ref: B10
Open: 11 Apr – 28 Oct 2019
Pitches: 600

Ocknell and Longbeech CITF Sites
Fritham, Hampshire SO43 7HH
Tel: 02380 812740
Map reference:
Pg: 32 Grid Ref: E2
Open: 11 Apr – 30 Sep 2019
Pitches: 480

Ocknell

Longbeech

Roundhill CITF Site
Beaulieu Road, Brockenhurst, Hampshire SO42 7QL
Tel: 01590 624344
Map reference:
Pg: 32 Grid Ref: G4
Open: 11 Apr – 30 Sep 2019
Pitches: 500

Setthorns CITF Site
Wooton, New Milton, Hampshire BH25 5WA
Tel: 01590 681020
Map reference:
Pg: 32 Grid Ref: G3
Open: All year
Pitches: 235

SAVERNAKE FOREST

Postern Hill CITF Site
Postern Hill, Marlborough, Wiltshire SN8 4ND
Tel: 01672 515195
Map reference:
Pg: 63 Grid Ref: F7
Open: All Year
Pitches: 170

FOREST OF DEAN

Bracelands CITF Site
Bracelands Drive, Christchurch, Coleford, Gloucester GL16 7NP
Tel: 01594 837258
Map reference:
Pg: 79 Grid Ref: C9
Open: All year
Pitches: 520

SHERWOOD FOREST

Sherwood Pines CITF Site
COMING SOON

LOCH LOMOND AND TROSSACHS NATIONAL PARK

Cashel CITF Site
Rowardennan G63 0AW
Tel: 01360 870234
Map reference:
Pg: 277 Grid Ref: C7
Open: 1 Mar – 21 Oct 2019
Pitches: 168

Cobleland CITF Site
Station Road, Gartmore, Stirlingshire FK8 3RR
Tel: 01877 382392
Map reference:
Pg: 277 Grid Ref: B10
Open: 11 Apr – 21 Oct 2019
Pitches: 126

CAIRNGORMS NATIONAL PARK

Glenmore CITF Site
Aviemore, Inverness-shire PH22 1QU
01479 861271
Map reference:
Pg: 291 Grid Ref: C11
Open: All Year
Pitches: 206

Scale 1:1 000 000   1cm = 10km   1 inch = 15.78 miles

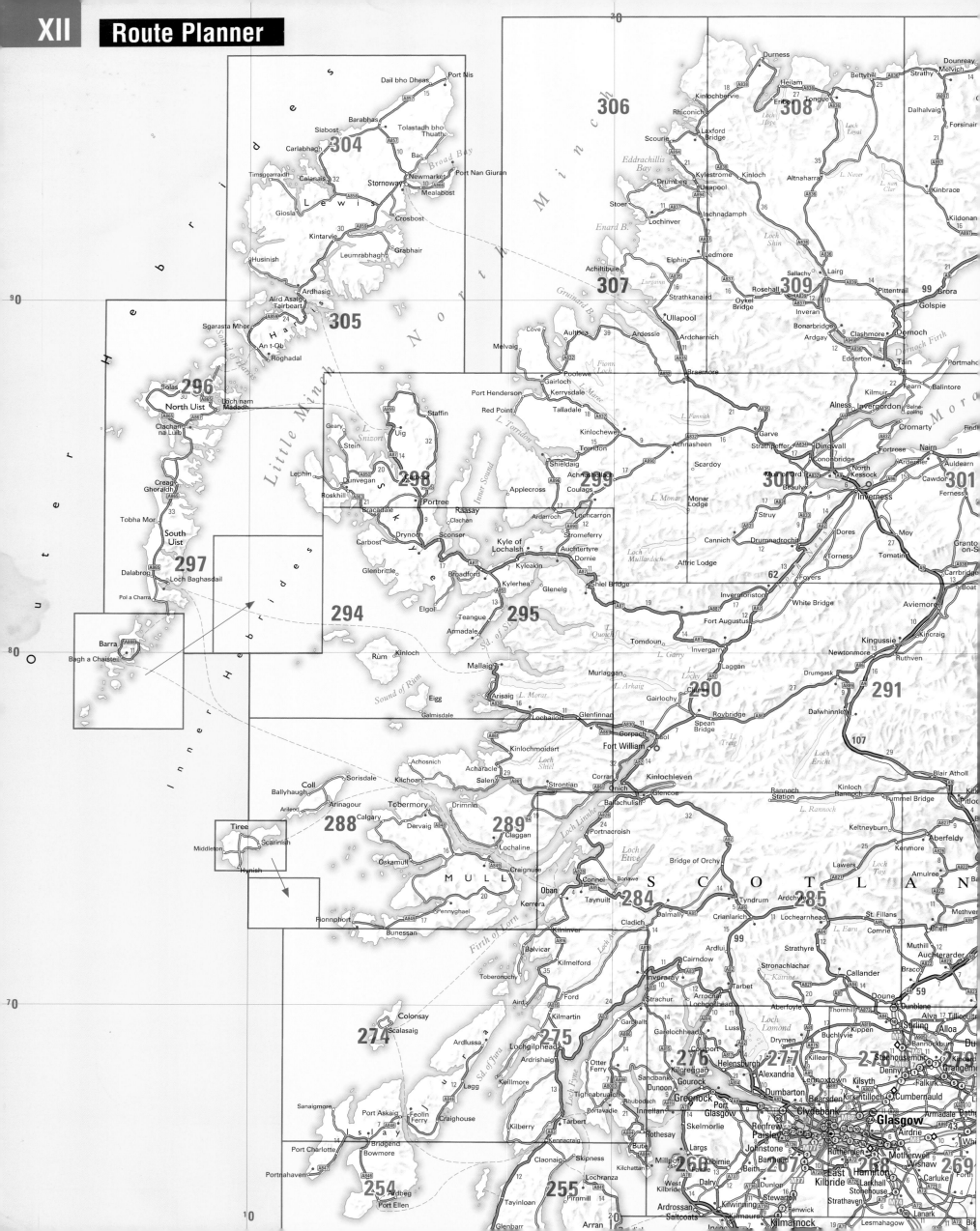

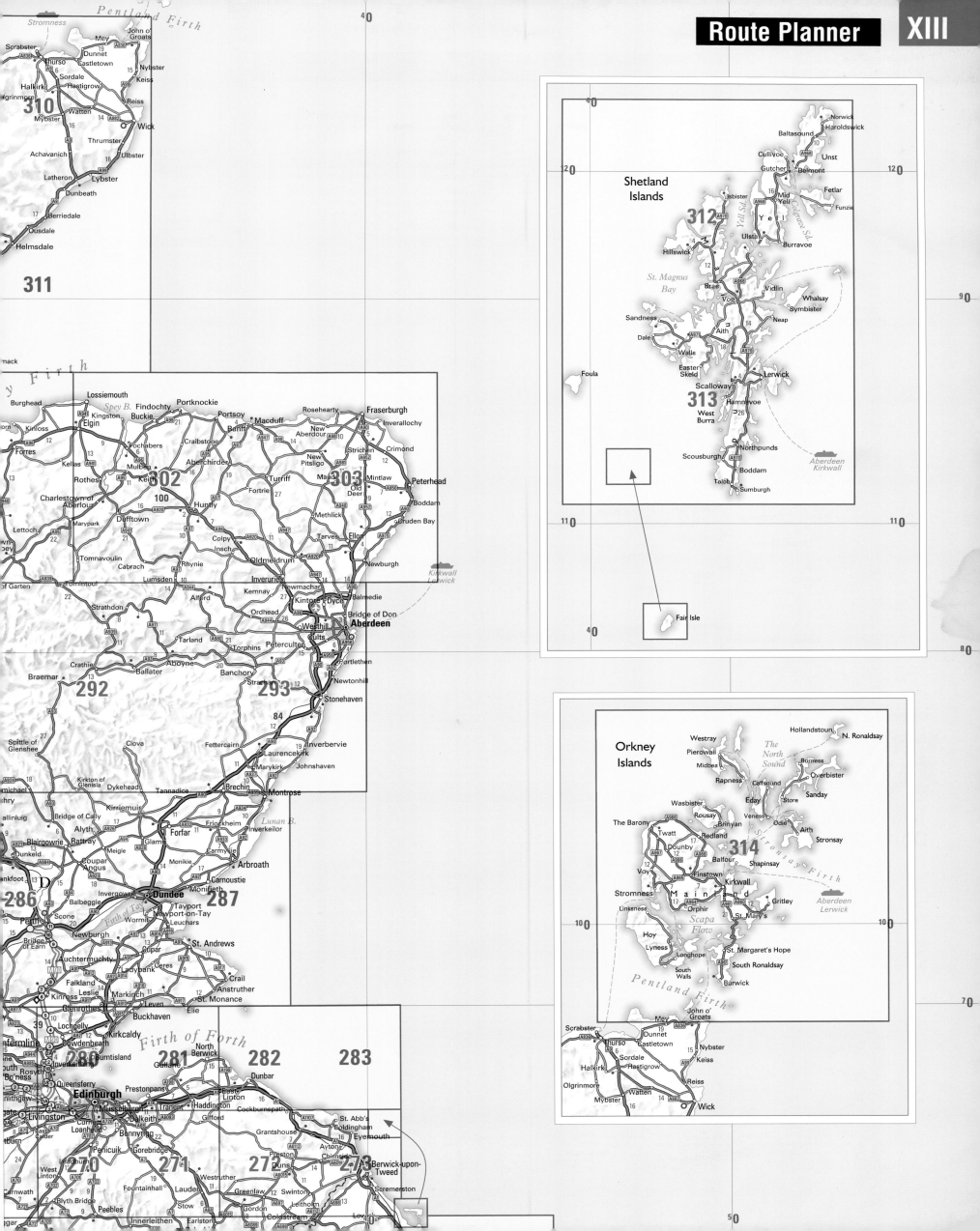

Distances and journey times

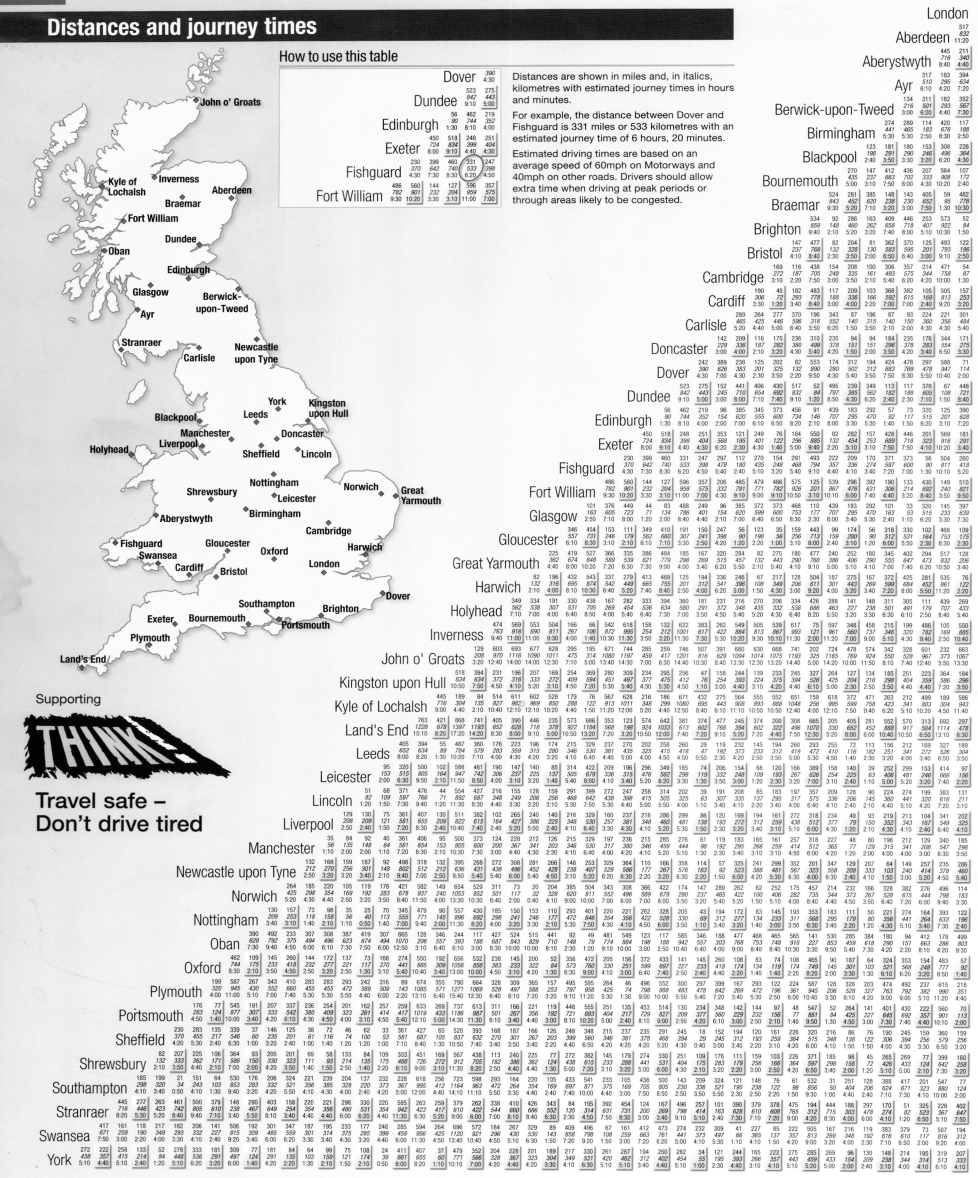

How to use this table

Distances are shown in miles and, in italics, kilometres with estimated journey times in hours and minutes.

For example, the distance between Dover and Fishguard is 331 miles or 533 kilometres with an estimated journey time of 6 hours, 20 minutes.

Estimated driving times are based on an average speed of 60mph on Motorways and 40mph on other roads. Drivers should allow extra time when driving at peak periods or through areas likely to be congested.

Supporting

THINK!

Travel safe –
Don't drive tired

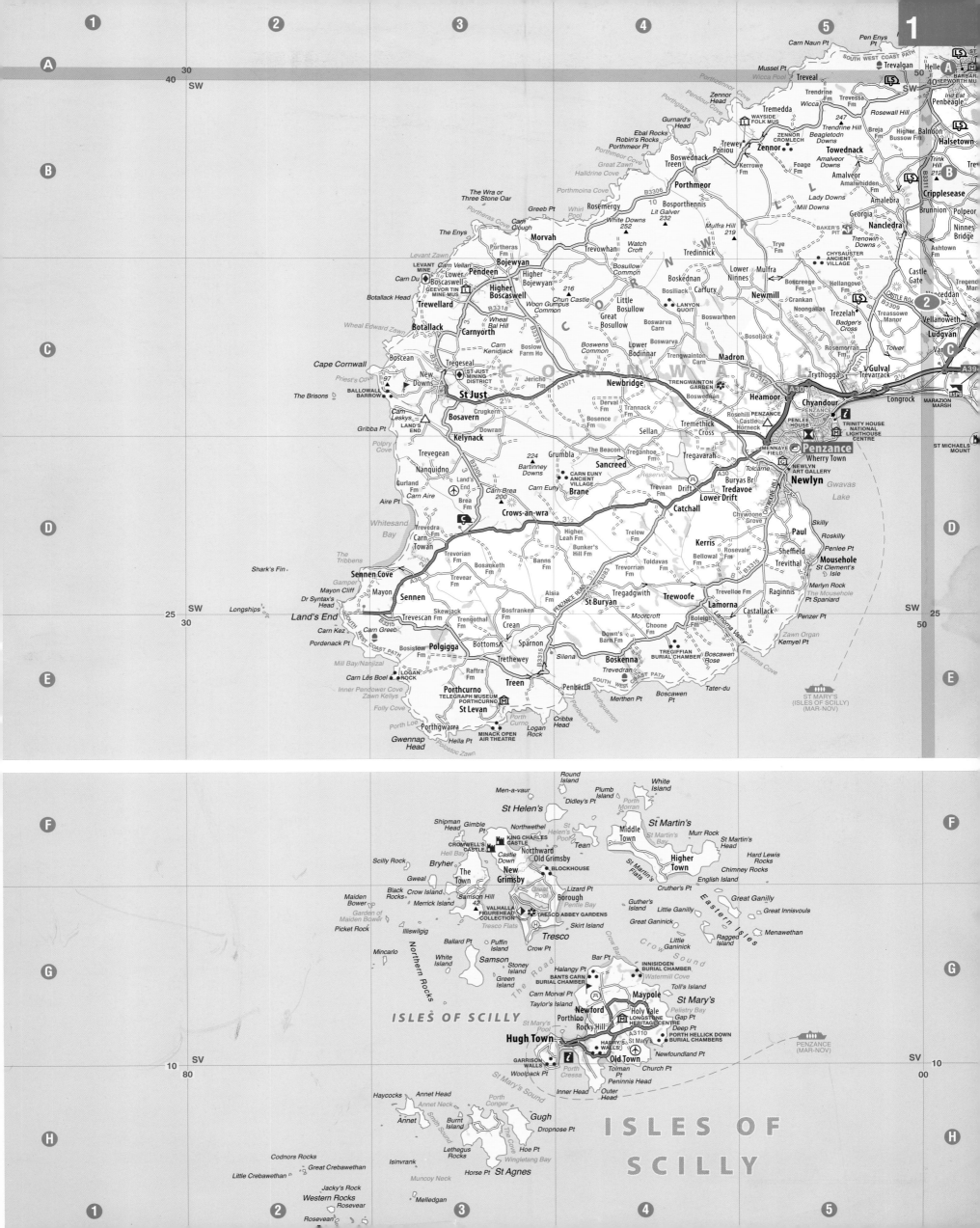

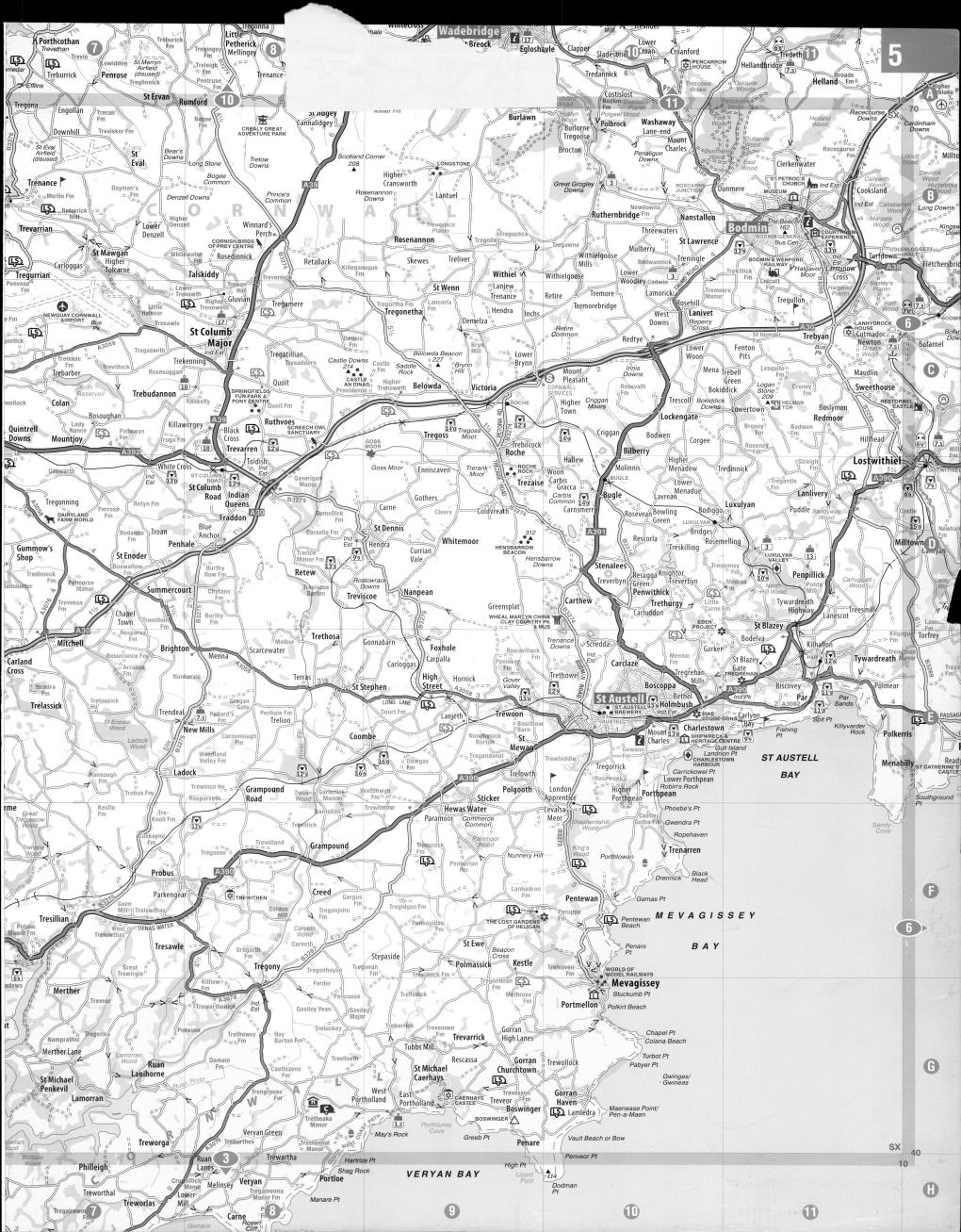

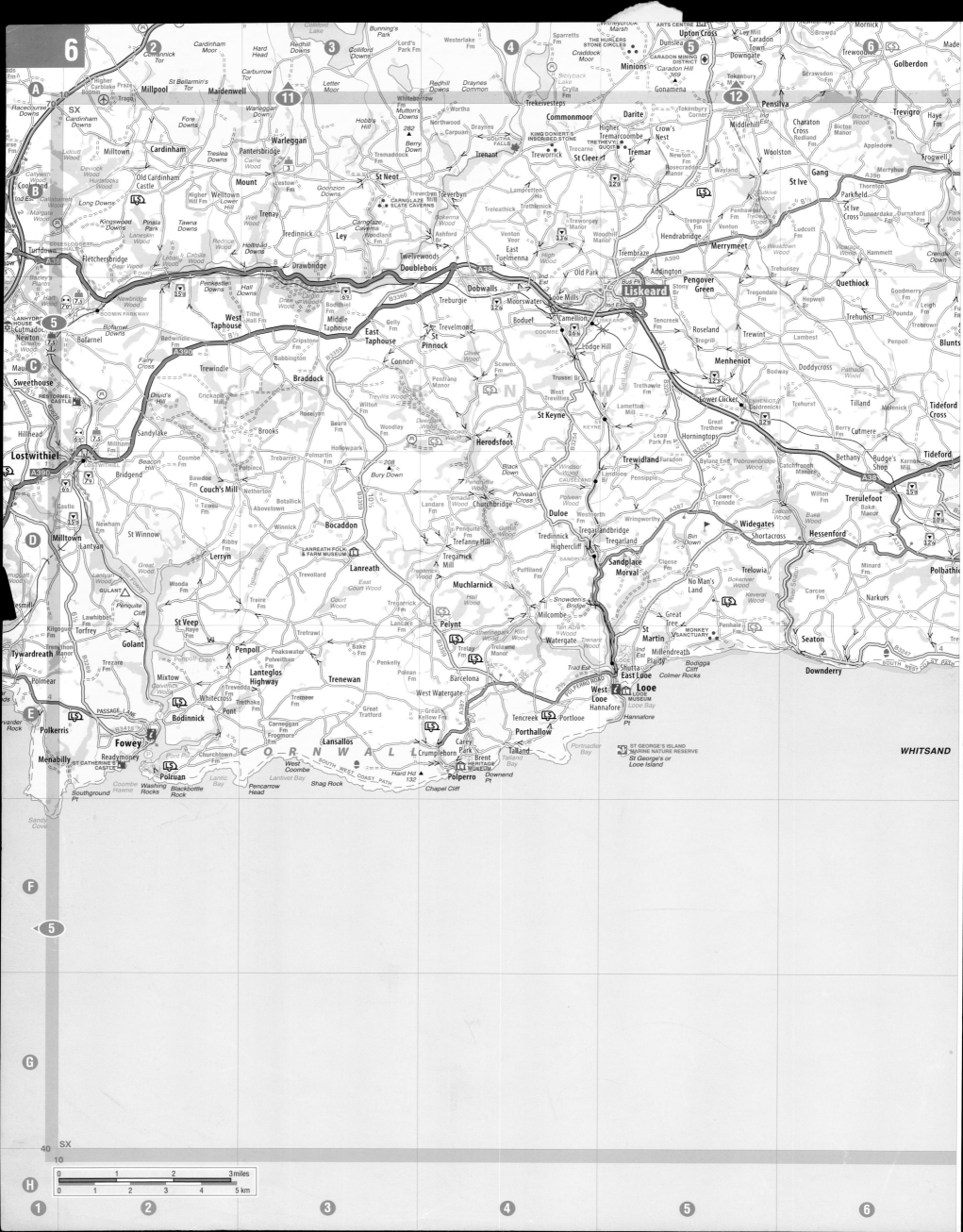

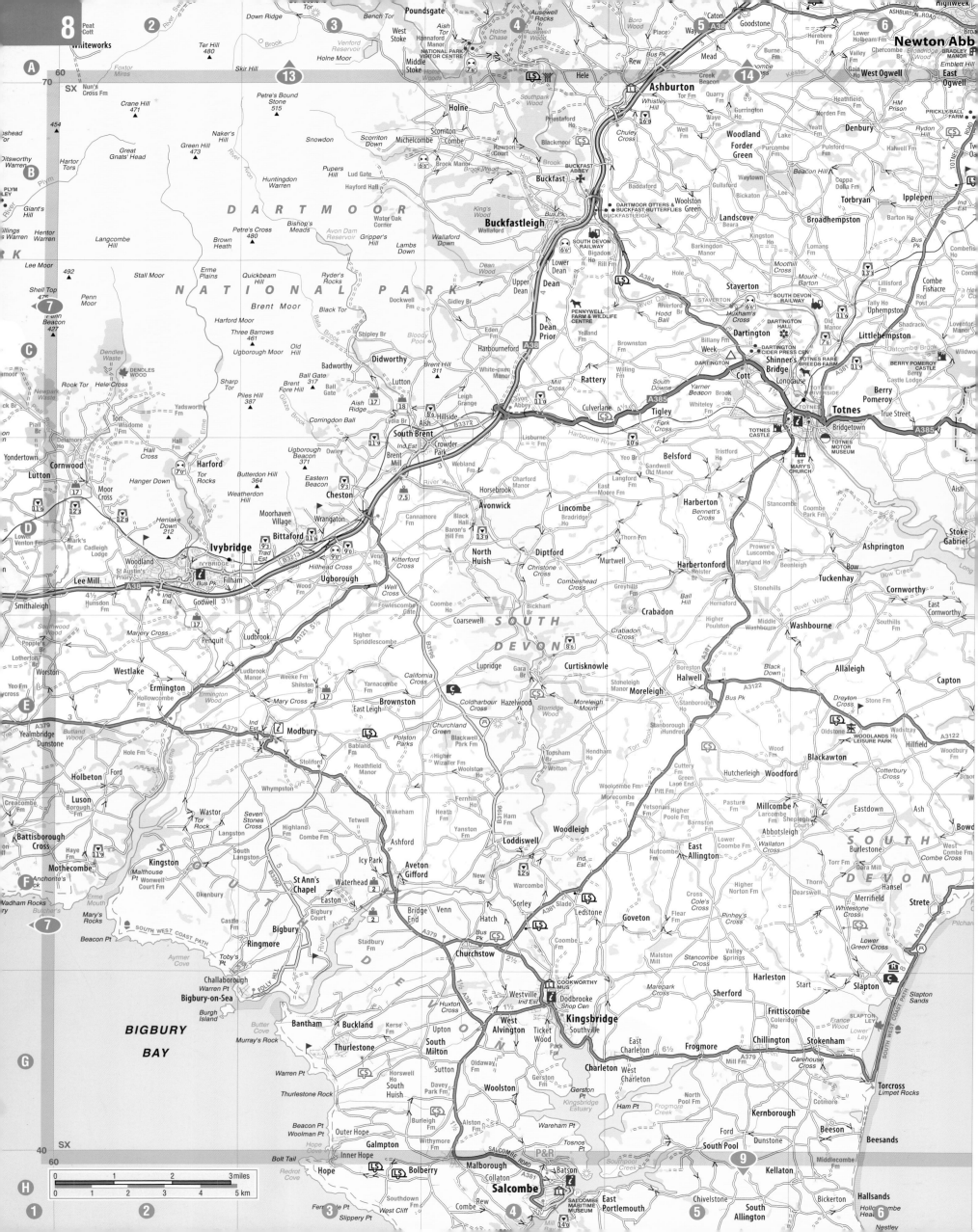

80
00 SW

A

B

C

D

The Island
Tintagel Head
Glebe
Dunderhole Pt
TINTAGEL
Penhallic Pt

T
Trebarw
Stra

Gull Rock
Port
William
Dennis Pt
Backways Cove
Start Pt
T

E

Trerubies
Cove
Tregardock
Cliff
Jacket's Pt
Crookmoyle Rock
Delabole Pt
Port
Isaac Bay
Barrett's Zawn
Ranie Pt
Dannonchapel
Wes

Varley
Head
Kellan
Head
Scarnor
Lobber
Pt
Tresungers
Pt
Newland
Rumps
Pt
The Mouls
Com
Head
Doyden
Pt
Reedy
Cliff
Port Quin Bay
Port
Isaac
Port Gaverne
Trewetha
Treore
Pentire Pt
Pentire
Fm
Carnweather
Pt
Trevan
Pt
Port Quin
Pentireglaze
Haven
Porteath
Scarrabine
Fm
LONG CROSS
VICTORIAN GDNS
Trelights
Pendoggett
Gulland Rock
Padstow Bay
New Polzeath
Hayle Bay
Trenant
Carruan
Plain
Street
St
Endellion
Poltreworgey
Pepper
Hole
Stepper Pt
The
Narrows
Polzeath
Shilla
Mill
Gunvenna
Pennytinney
Trelill

F

Butter Hole
Daymer
Bay
Trebetherick
Trewiston
Fm
Trevanger
Treglyn Down
Tregellist
Trevine
Trewethern
Trequite
St Kew
Gunver
Head
Harbour
Cove
Trebetherick
Gun
Pt
Pityme
Trevan
St Minver
Tredrizzick
Trevrick
Trewoon
Trevose Head
Merope Rocks
Round Hole
Mother Ivey's
or Polventon Bay
Porthmissen
Bridge
Trevone
Bay
Round
Hole
PRIDEAUX
PLACE
Rock
Splatt
Penmayne
Treglyn
Fm
Rooke Fm
Chapel
Amble
Carclaze
Fm
Trewethern
St Kew
Stinking Cove
Dinas Head
Quies
Harlyn
Bay
Trethillick
Crugmeer
Stoptide
Tresfrea
Fm
Blakes
Keiro
Penpont Fm
Hendra
Trevone
Harlyn
Treator
Porthilly
Cove
Porthilly
Lower
Amble
Trewornan
Tregorden
St Kew
Highway
Trevisqui
Manor
Booby's Bay
Constantine
Bay
Padstow
MUSEUM
Town Bar
Porthilly
Trevelver
Gutt Bridge
Kelly
Trehevan
Fm
Cro
Hil
Treyarnon Pt
Padstow
Ind Est
NATIONAL
LOBSTER HATCHERY
Caint
Cove
River Camel
Tregunna
Rocksea
Fm
Dinham's
Br
Trethias Island
Warren Cove
TREYARNON
BAY
Windmill
Dinas
Dennis
Hill
Oldtown
Cove
Burniere
Bodieve
Three
Holes Cross
Treg
Pepper Cove
Fox Cove
Treyarnon
Towan
Trewithen
Fm
Sea
Mills
Oldtown
Tregonce
Trevorrick
Trevanson
Ball
St Mabyn
Minnows Islands
Will's Rock
Trehemborne
Carnevas
Trevorrick
St Merryn
Highlanes
Burgois
Trevilgus
Fm
Bodellick
Edmonton
Dunveth
Ind Est
Hingham
Mill
Trevilder

G

Shop
Trevean
Tregonna
Penhale
Whitecross
Wadebridge
Trenant
Egloshayle
Lower
Croan
Croanford
Porthcothan
Bay
Trescore Islands
Porthcothan
Trevethan
Treburrick
Tregingey
Little
Petherick
Mellingey
ROYAL CORNWALL
SHOWGROUND
St Breock
Clapper
Sladesbridge
PENCARR
HOUSE
Porth Mear
High Cove
Trevemedar
Treburrick
Penrose
Lewidden
Lane
St Merryn
Airfield
(disused)
Treglinnick
Tregonce
Fm
Trelow
Treven
St Issey
Trevance
Trelyll
Fm
Tredinnick
Polmorla
Treraven
Trescowe
Brake
Park
Tredannick
Park Head
Diggory's Island
Effins
Tregona
gollan
Trerair
Fm
Bogee
Fm
Trenance
Blable
Ho
Hay
Pengelly
Fm
Bishop's
Wood
Costislost
Costislost
Bozion
Plantn
Polgeel Wood

70 SW
80

H

Queen Bess Rock
REDRUTHEN STEPS
Tregona
Downhill
Trevisker Fm
St Eval
Airfield
(disused)
Bear's
Downs
Long Stone
St Ervan
Rumford
Tredruston
Fm
Pentruse
Trenance
St Jidgey
Cannalidgey
Pawton
Manor Fm
urlawn
Burlorne
Tregoose
Washaway
Lane-end
Mount
Charles
CREALY GREAT
ADVENTURE PARK
Trelow
Downs
Scotland Corner
208
Higher
Cranworth
Brocton
Penaligon
Downs
BOSCARN

1

0   1   2   3 miles
0   1   2   3   4   5 km

2
Trenance Pt

3
St
Eval
Bogee
Common

4

5

6
Great Grogley
A 3

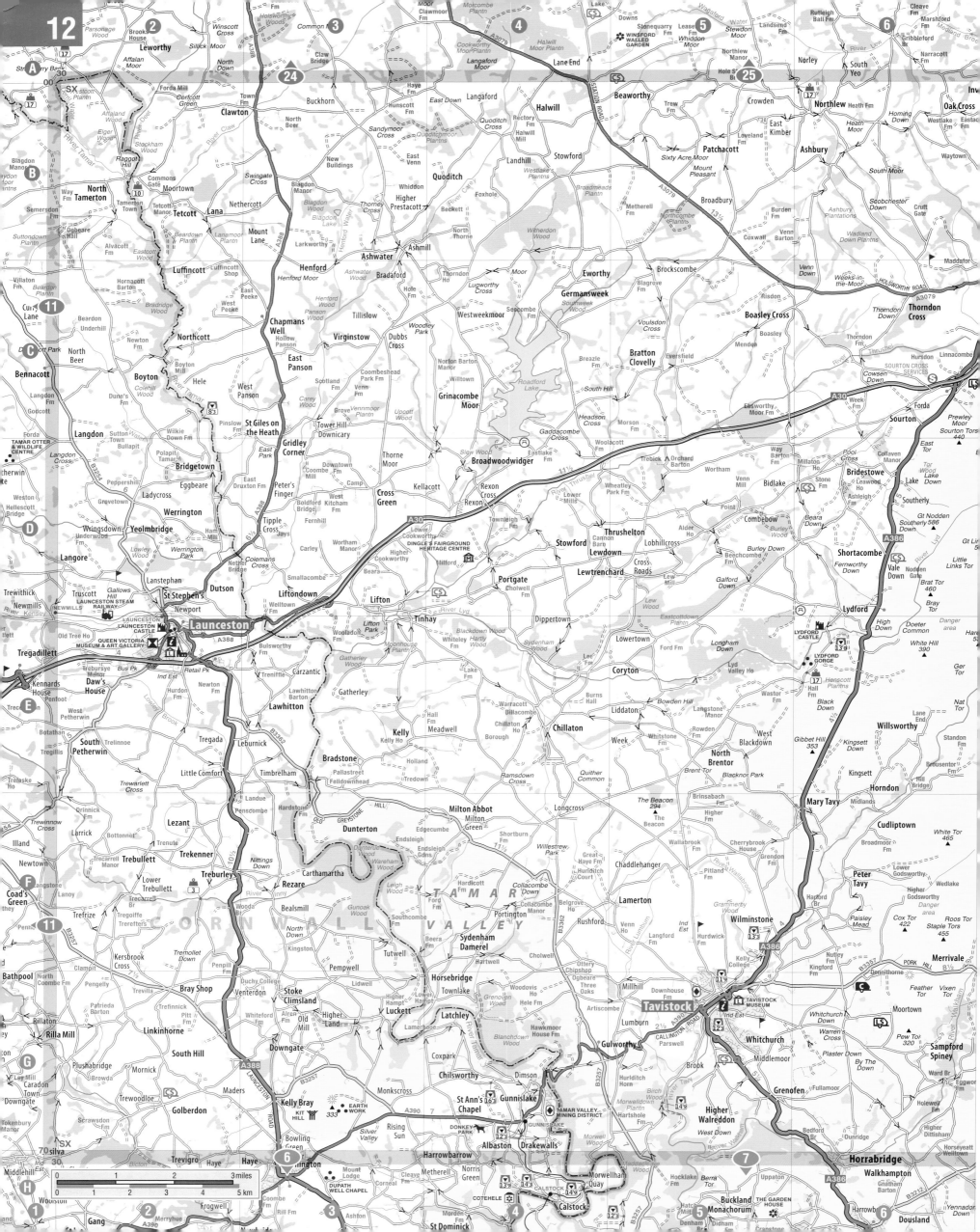

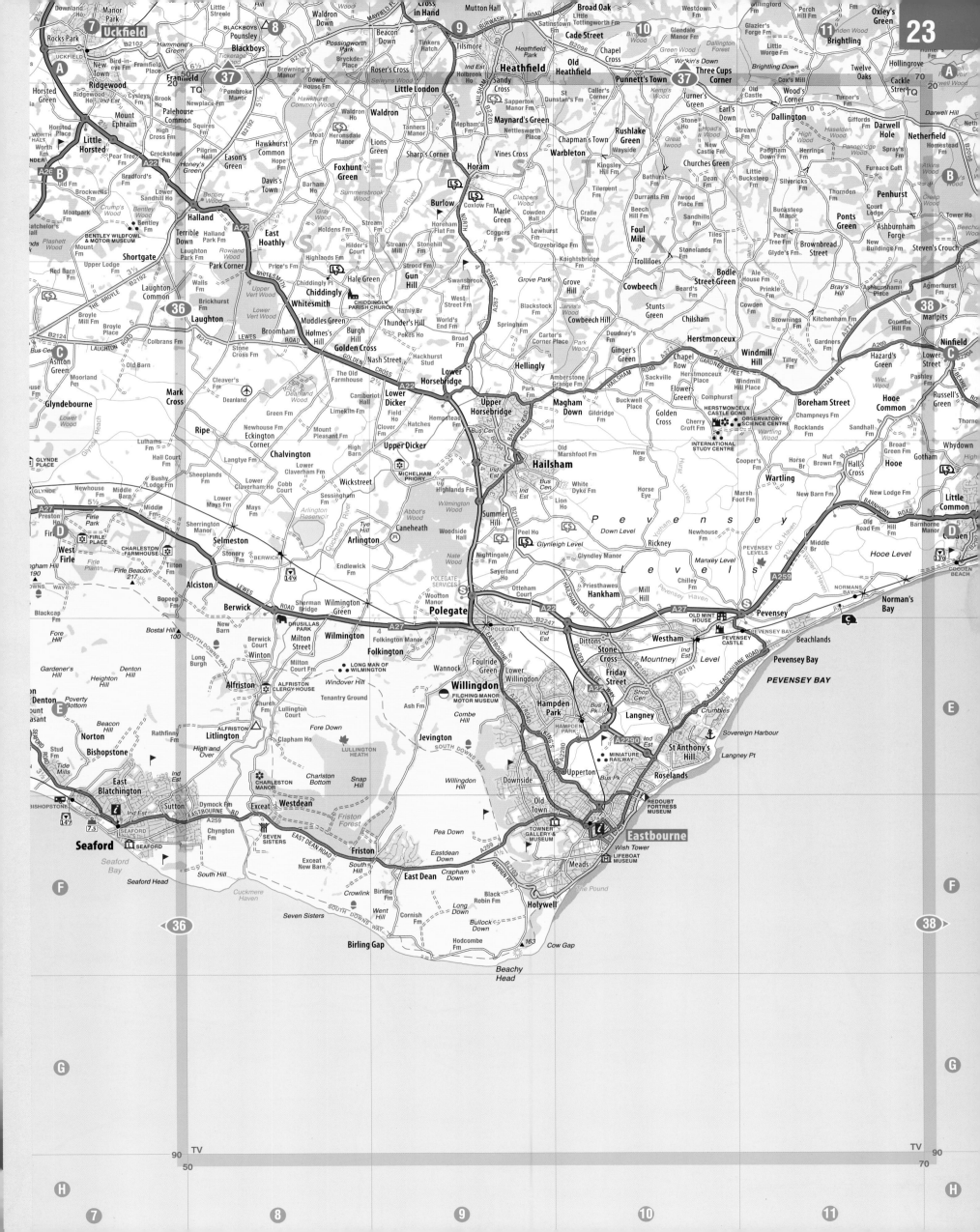

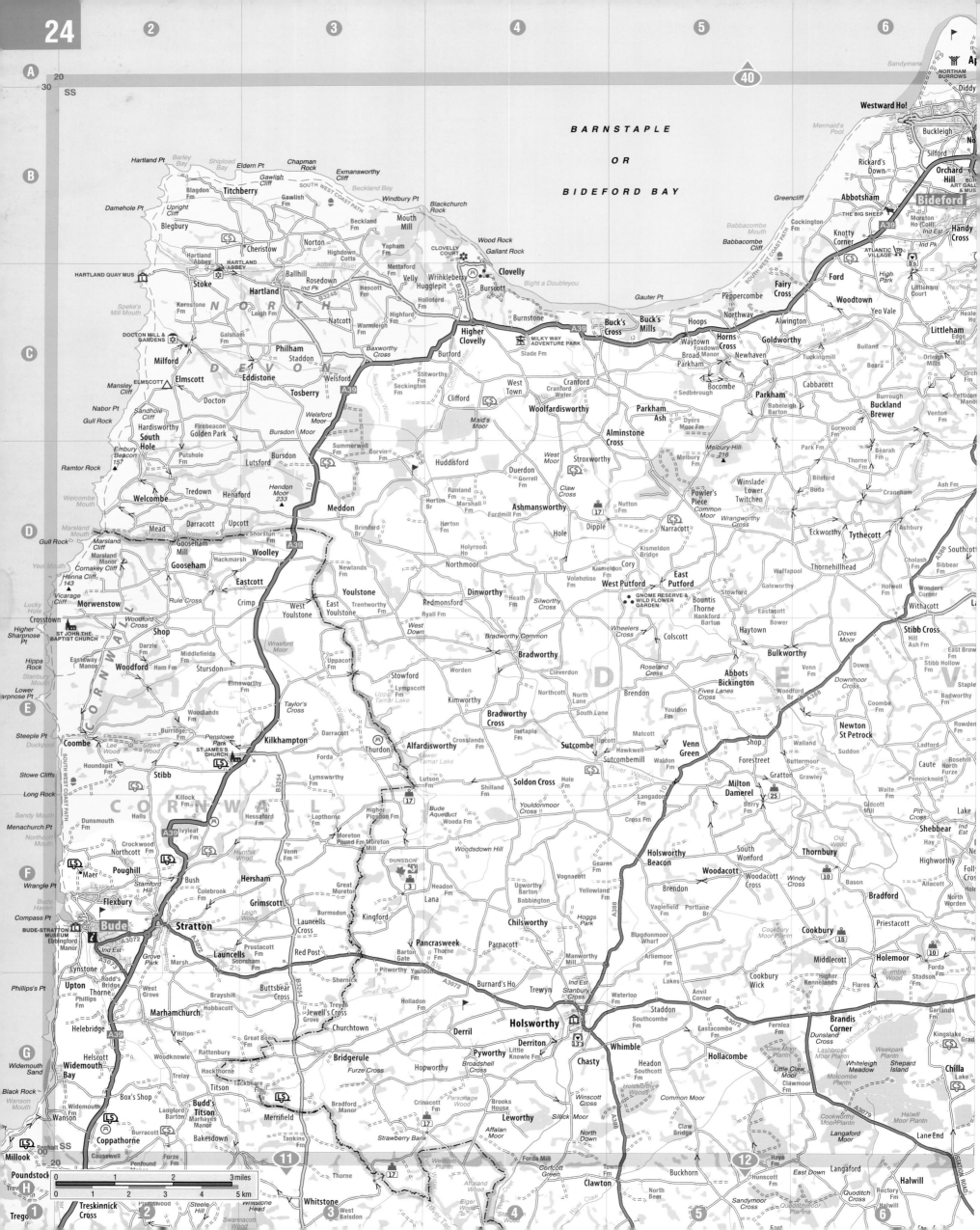

Heasley Mill
South Wood
Barcombe Down
Holywell Cross
Balls
Wheatclose Cross
Tarr Steps
Ashway Side
Mounsey Hill
374
South Hill
Broford Fm
Kents Fm
Chilly Bridge
Daws Fm
Redcross
Lyncombe
Cloggs Fm
Lyshwell Fm
Hawkridge Common
Hawkridge
Hawkridge Ridge
Hollowcombe
Shircombe Fm
Steep Head
Brinsworthy
Twitchen Mill
Twitchen
Cussacombe Gate
Molland Common
Halscombe Fm
High Bullen Fm
Millbrook
Pitt Fm
Pulham Fm
Pulsworthy Fm
Kerswell Fm
Anstey Gate
Whiterocks Down
Draydon Fm
Mounsey Castle
Marsh Hill Ho
Court Down
316
Nadrid Fm
Stony Br
West Park
North Molton
Luckworthy
Smallacombe
West Anstey Common
Wheatlands Fm
Coombe
Burcombe
Sannacott Fm
Waterbrooks Fm
Bickingcott
Champson
Molland
Stone
Gourte Fm
Five Cross Ways
Old Berry Fm
Louisa Gate
Snurridge
South Cockerham
Limeslake Fm
Woodland Fm
West Anstey
Two Moor Ways
Higher Town
Rhyll Manor
Cawkett Fm
Dulverton
Three Gates Cross
Hele Br
Jury Road
Pixton Park
Bury Castle
Hacche Moor
East Marsh
Great Woods
Abbotts Park
Beere Fm
Armer Wood
Battleton
Beasley Fm
Bicknor Fm
Mornacott
Reach
Veraby
Yeo Fm
River Yeo
Bottreaux Mill
Waddicombe
Ridlers Fm
Beer Moors
Common Moors
Bus Pk
Johnstone Moors
Hall Fm
New Park Fm
Wester New Moor
Cuckoo Fm
Yeo Mill
East Anstey
Venn Fm
Allers Wood
Weir Ho
Quince Honey Farm
Rawstone Moors
Whitechapel Moors
Ashill Fm
Brushford
Hulverton Hill
South Molton
Mole Br
Gorton Hill
Bish Mill
Garliford
Combsland Cross
Wester Bullaford Moor
Hawkwell Fm
Higher Radnidge Moor
Oldways End
Nightcott
Langaller Fm
Croft Fm
Stone
Newtown
Smallacombe Moors
White Moor
Den Brook
Exebridge
Grilstone
Hall Park
Little Hill
Paul's Moor
Luckett Moor
Thorne Fm
Parsonage Fm
Bishops Nympton
Ford Fm
Whitmoor Fm
Whitefield Fm
Shapcott Barton
Tucker's Moor
Hele Manor Fm
Surridge Fm
Highleigh
Blights Fm
Broomhouse Fm
George Nympton
Culverhill Fm
Trayne Fm
Crosse Fm
Park
Avercombe
Crooked Oak
Ash Mill
Woods
Luckett Fm
East Knowstone
Little Oak Fm
Combe Water
East Loosemoor
Benshayes Fm
Rows Fm
Alswear
Pitt Fm
Hilltown
Nutshill Fm
Pearchay Fm
Eastacott Fm
Knowstone
Side Moor
Beaple's Hill
Beaple's Moor
Roachill
Ford Fm
Oakfordbridge
Westbrook Fm
Littlewood Fm
Jose's Cross
Cleave Fm
Westacott Fm
Rowcliffe Fm
Mariansleigh
Munson Fm
Rose Ash
Nutcombe Fm
Fanny's Cross
Nethercott Manor Fm
Hares Down
Middle Hill Fm
Bickham Moor
South Esworthy Fm
Upcott Fm
Holme Place
Oakford
Manor House
Stuckeridge Ho
Westbrook Wood
Chain Br
Broomham Moor
Huxford Fm
Cherridge
Odam Br
Romansleigh
Manor Fm
Batsworthy Cross
Batsworthy
Hares Down Cross
Fox Brake
Rackenford Moor
Great Wood
Spurway Mill
Westcott Fm
Nethercott Fm
Chample's Fm
Hangman's Hill Cross
Iron Mill Stream
River Exe
Smiths
Hummacott
Odam Barton
Langley
Meshaw
Narracott
Meshaw Barton
Burcombe
Ash Moor
Frankhill Fm
Rackenford Manor
Sydeham Fm
Stoodleigh Beacon
301
Wasprey Fm
Thorne Fm
Coleford Bottom
Stoodleighmoor
East Stoodleigh Barton
Carscombe
Quoit-at-Cross
Dryhill
Stoodleigh
Exe Valley
King's Nympton
Great Lightleigh
Garland Cross
Great Odham Moor Plantn
Batney Fm
Heath Fm
Creacombe
Parsonage Cross
Nutcott
Rackenford Fm
Little Fm
Broadmead Fm
Willicroft Moor
Waddington
West Garland Fm
Waterloo Fm
Huntacott Water
Burrow Cross
Gidley Cross
Crowdhole
Rackenford
Bulworthy Fm
Willicroft Fm
Stoneland Fm
Slade Fm
Wheadon Fm
Wilson Fm
Mogworthy
Rifton Moor
Diptford Fm
Gibbett Moor Fm
Haydon Fm
Hatherland
Cadbury Barton
Week
Broadridge Fm
Rowden Fm
Leat Fm
Bradford Mill
Queen Dart
Ford Down
Colleton Hall
Horestone
Emerleigh
Moorhayes
Wixon Fm
Hole Fm
Lutworthy
Horseford Fm
Hellinghayes Fm
Stanterton
Beacon
Kempland Fm
Bealy Court
Cuddenhay Fm
Stone Fm
River Dart
Down Cross
Rose Moor
Witheridge Moor
Great Moor
Holmead Fm
Deepaller
Loxbeare
Courtenay Pitt
Parsonage Fm
Horridge Moor
Benley Cross
Holland Fm
Dart Raffe Fm
Hole Fm
South Coombe
Washfield
Marsh Fm
New Br
Ind Est
Witheridge Moor Fm
Templeton Bridge
Lurley
Harpridge
Velvains
Chulmleigh
Huntacott
Edgiford Cross
Winswood Moor
Affeton Moor
Town Moor
Witheridge
Charnaford Fm
Nomansland
Cleave Fm
Templeton
Court
Calverleigh
Palmers
Sydham
Chapner Fm
Summer Fm
West Bradley
Lower Farleigh
Savourys
Stonemill Fm
East Cheldon Fm
West Worlington
East Worlington
Drayford
Stretch Down
Westway Fm
Kelly Fm
Partridge Fm
Bradleigh Down
Higher Farleigh
Coombehayes
Moortown
Cheldon
Moor Barton Fm
Gogland Manor
Mudford Gates
The Old Rectory
Longdrag Hill
Hollow Tree Cross
East Leigh
Chawleigh
Leigh
Cobley Fm
Coombe Fm
Thelbridge Barton
Stourton Barton
Washford Moor
Henceford Moor
Deptford Fm
Wood Fm
Cruwys Morchard
Wayland
Hensleigh Ho
Cotteylands
St Peter's Church
Withleigh
Eggesford Station
Labbett's Cross
D E V O N
Thelbridge Cross
Washford Pyne
Beer Fm
Little Heath
Old Ford
Thorne Fm
Mogridge Fm
Southcott
North Lake Fm
Yeatheridge Fm
Billhole Fm
Puddington
Pennymoor
East Ruckham
Down Fm
Lodge Hill Fm
Handsford Fm
Denridge Fm
Canns Mill Bridge
Pyne Fm
Littleborough
Yowlestone Ho
Hill Fm
Coombeland
Ashley
Filleigh
Forches Cross
River Dalch
Stickeridge
Westway
Way Village
Chenson Fm
Tonyfield Fm
Nymet Br
Hole
Mear Fm
Black Dog
Puddington Bottom
Sunnybrook Fm
Trundlemoor Fm
Marshay Fm
Cotton Fm
Meadhayes Fm
Little Silver
Well Fm
Way
Hawkridge Fm
Bowerthy Wood
Broadridge Fm
Eastington
Lane End Fm
Hill Barton
Berry Castle
Tridley Foot
Edbury Fm
Well Town
Eggesford
Higher Park
Hele Fm
Nymet Ho
Calves Br
Beech Hill
Emlett Hill
Partridge Hole
Upham Fm
Haydon Fm
Higher Pitt Fm
East Barton
River Taw
Nymet Rowland
Lapford
Lapford Cross
Redhill
Morchard Bishop
Woolfardisworthy
Park
Greenhill Cross
Poughill
Court Place
Upham
Captain's Fm
Cadeleigh
Devon Rail Centre
Bickleigh Mill
Rudge Rew
Middlecott
Barton Ho
South Emlett
Hollyford Fm
New House Fm
Marsh Fm
Redyeates Fm
Hayne
East Court
Coldridge
Rudge
Farthing Park
Kennerleigh
Down Fm
Rookbeare Fm
Cadeleigh Court
Scotland
Stockleigh English
Wolland Fm
Round Hill
Bickleigh Castle
Bickleigh
Aller Br
Gillscott Fm
Frost
Carrhouse
Moor Fm
Welland Down
Splitwell Cross
White Cross
Weeke
Oldborough
Stockleigh Court
Cheriton Fitzpaine
Way Fm
Perry Fm
West Leigh
Birch Fm
Stopgate Cross
Bradiford Fm
Sharland Fm
Venn
Rolstone Barton
Burridge Fm
Vellake
Prowse
Forde Cross
Pitt Fm
East Leigh
Leigh Cross
Morchard Road
Gays Fm
Dowrich Ho
Perry
Cadbury
Cadbury Castle
Chitterley
Middle Yeo Fm
Thorne Fm
Morchard Road
Dowrich Fm
East Village
Heath Fm
North Coombe
Fursdon House
Pitt Fm
Hole Fm
Zeal Monachorum
Down St Mary
Ash Bullayne
Beacon Cross
Thelbridge Br
Cheriton Cross
East Coombe
Higher Coombe
Bus Cen
Newbuildings
Clampitt
Bawdenhayes
Upton Hellions
Raddons Hills
235
Bidwell
Gillhouse Fm
Oak Tree Fm
Lammacott Fm
Clannaborough Cross
Frleatons Fm
Ash Brook
Copplestone
Bewsley Fm
Sturridge
Westwood Fm
Lower Creedy
Stockleigh Pomeroy
Reeve Castle
Great Beere Moor
Burston
Serstone Fm
Sutton Fm
Beers Hill
Copplestone
Elston
Woolsgrove
West Sandford
Sandford
Chapel Fm
Lynch Fm
Ford Cross
Nichols Nymet Ho
Brandirons Corner
Bradley Fm
Uppincott
Raddon Court
Up Exe
Nichols Nymet Cross
Hampson
Bow
Coplestone Ho
Knowle
Priestcombe Fm
Long Barn
Creedy Br
Wood Fm
Thorverton
Raddon
Appledore Fm
Walson Barton
Ford Fm
Coleford
South Coombe
Coombe Ho
Pounds Hill
Shobrooke Park
Shobrooke
Efford
Berrysbridge
Broadnymett Moor
Glebe Ho
Nymet Tracey
Thorne
Penstone
Hollacombe Cross
Hollacombe
The Collegiate Church of the Holy Cross
Crediton
Downes Head
Westacott Cotts
Shobrooke Mill Fm
Yendacott Manor
Yellowford
Heathfield
Willowpark
Nether Exe
Newcott
Colebrooke
Barn Fm
Stairhill Fm
Park
Shute
Sweetham
Lake Fm
Nettacott
Norton Fm
Brampford Speke
Rewe
Itton Moor
Crocks Cross
Yeoford
Neopardy
Gunstone Ho
Denbury Fm
Salmonhutch
Crediton
Trad Est
Fordton
Hookway
Winscott Barton
Jackmoor
Newton St Cyres
Burrow Fm
Bowbeer
Grange
Hillerton
Gunstone Ho
Venny
Yeoton
Culvery Bridge
Trobridge
Smallbrook
Newton
Newton Ho
Bidwell Barton
Pye Corner
Ley
Stoke Canon
River Culm
A396
A361
A377
A3072
A399
B3227
B3226
B3137
B3042
B3096
B3220
River Mole
River Dart
River Exe
River Yeo
River Creedy
Little Dart
Exe
0 1 2 3 miles
0 1 2 3 4 5 km
SS
41
42
25
13
14

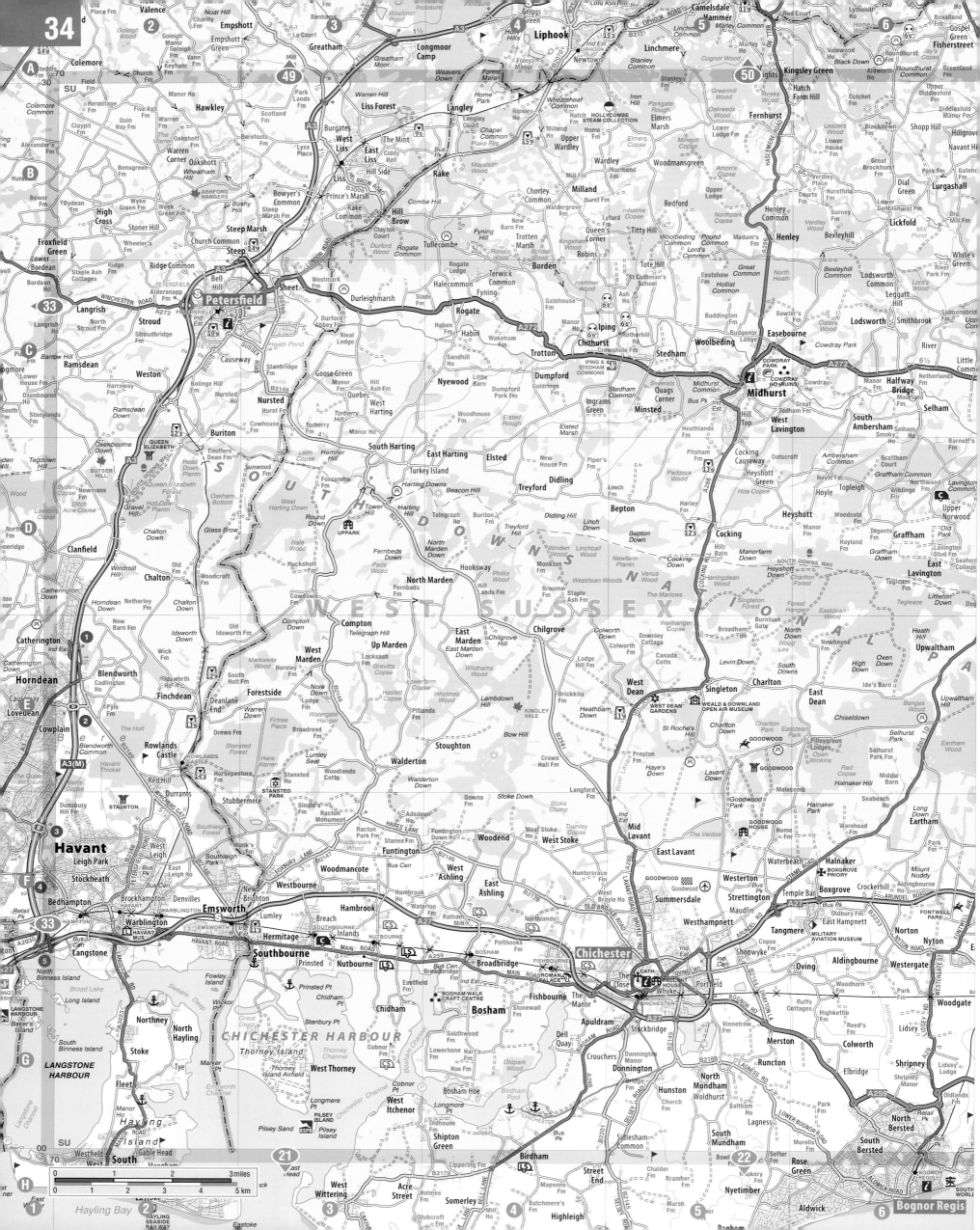

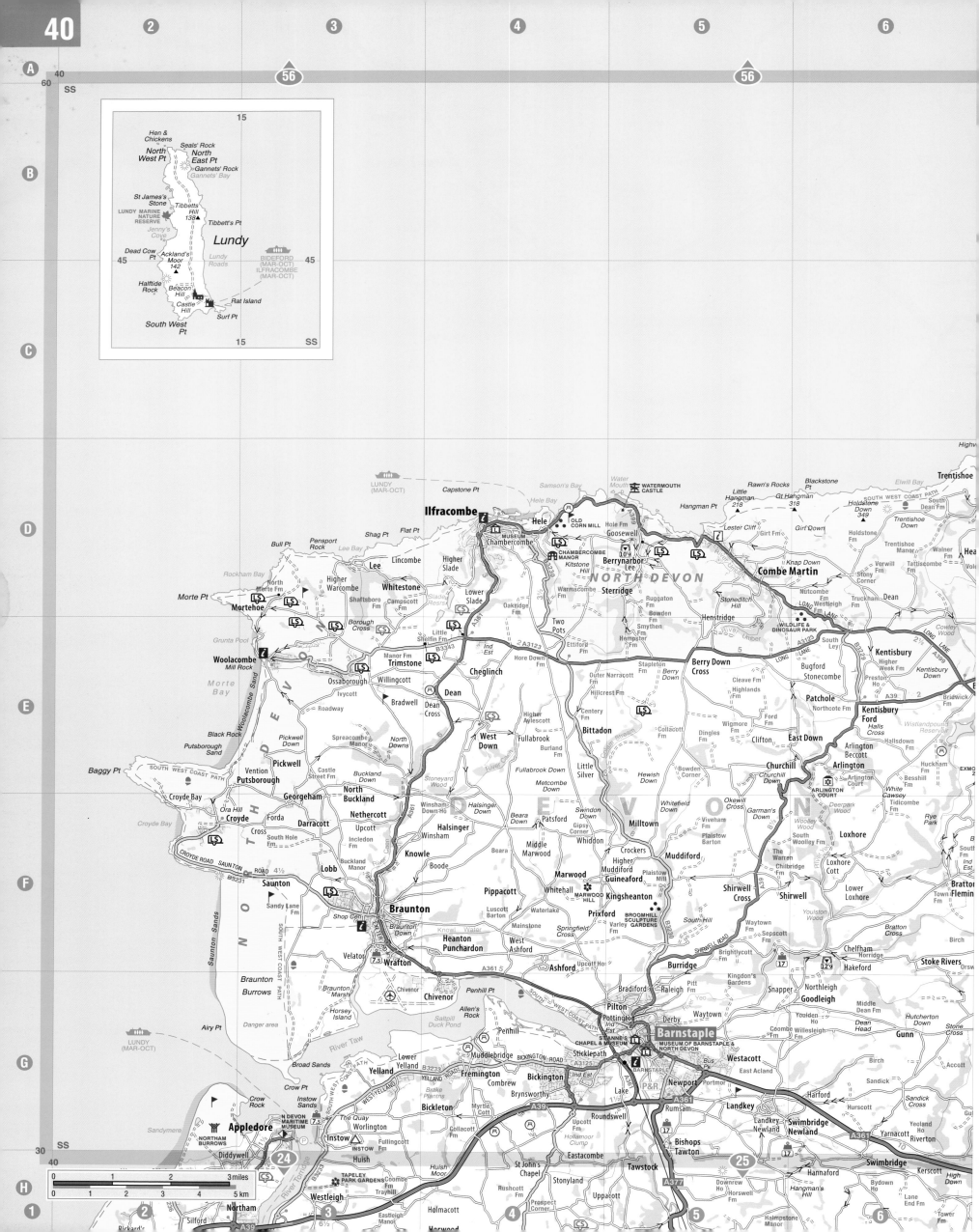

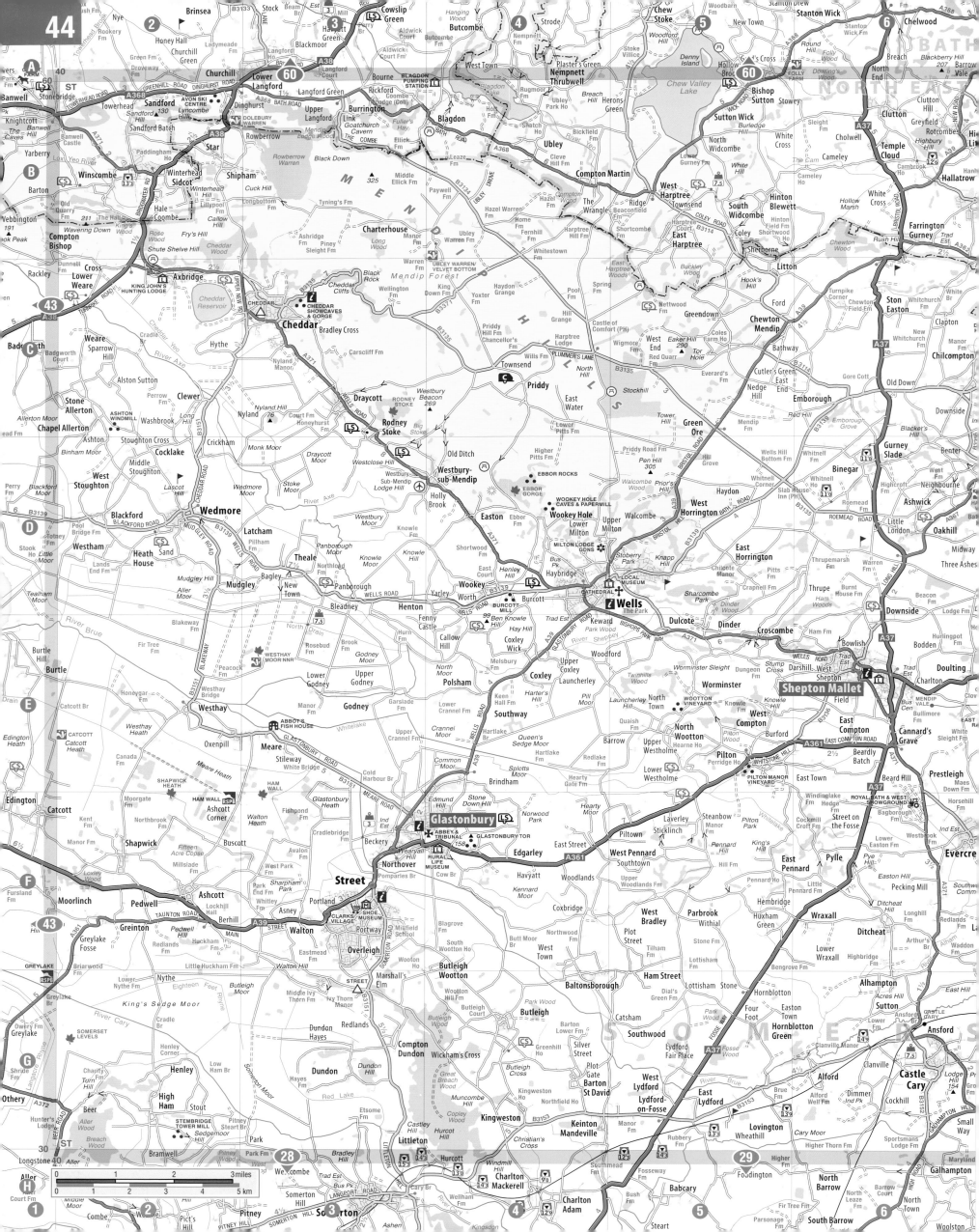

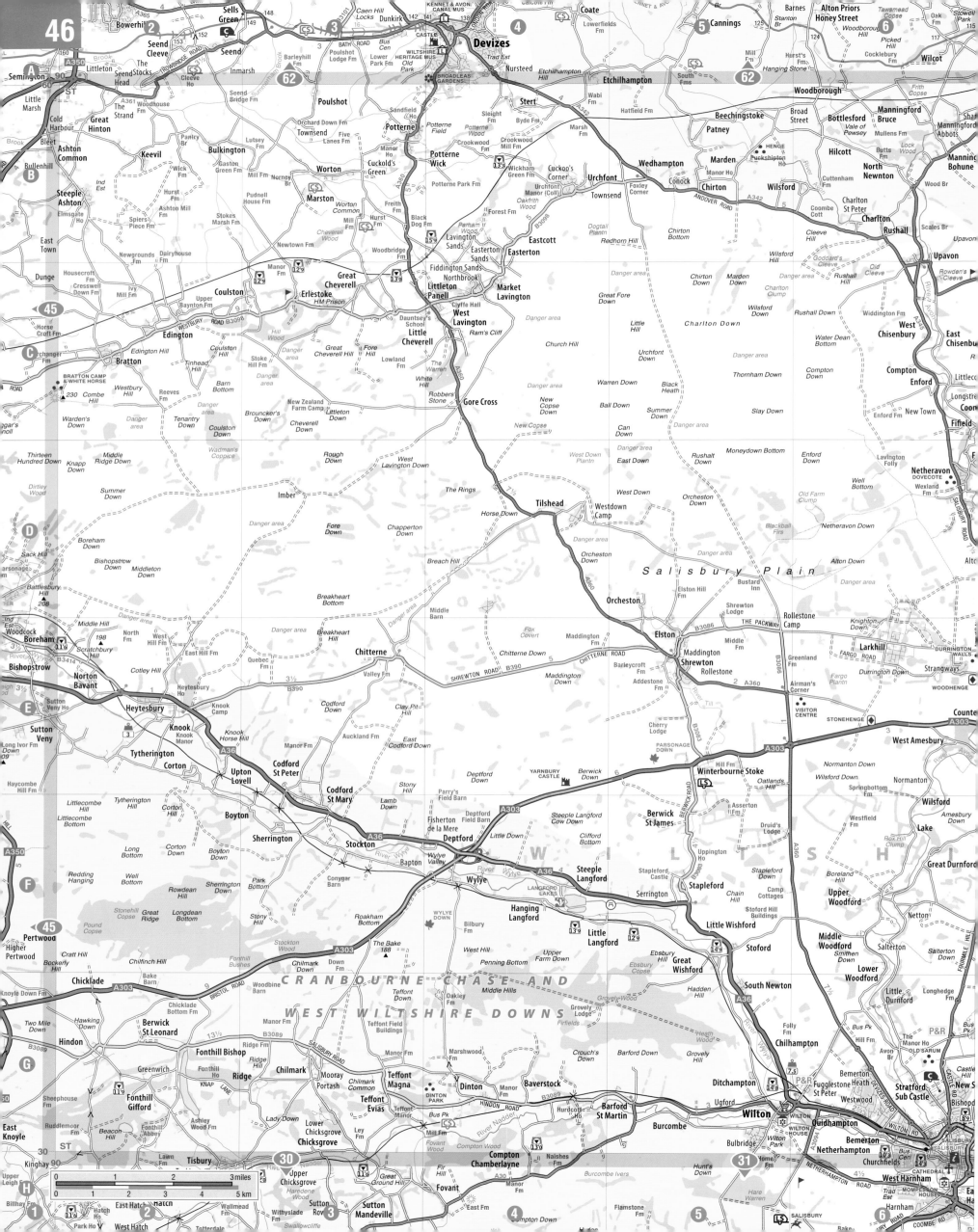

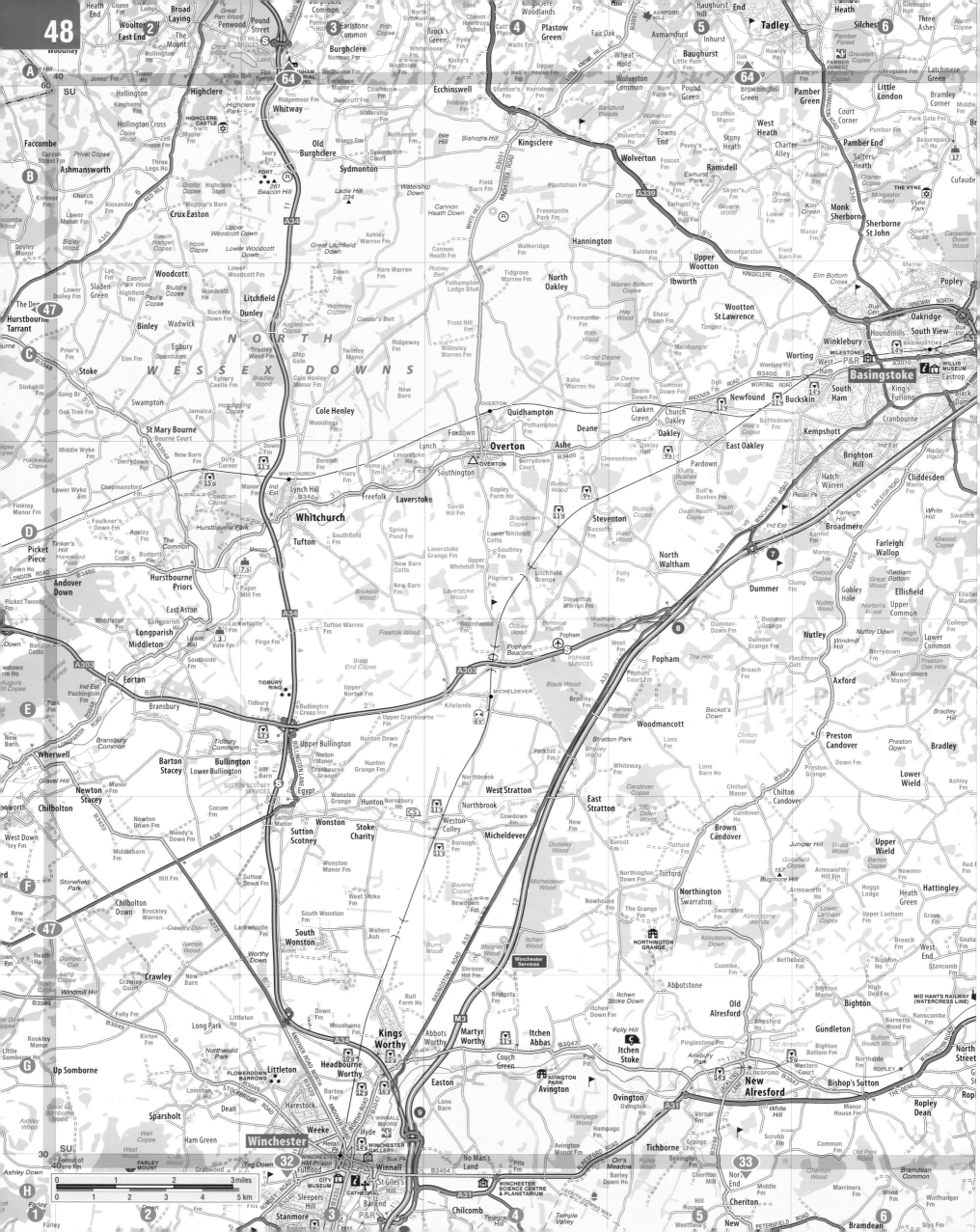

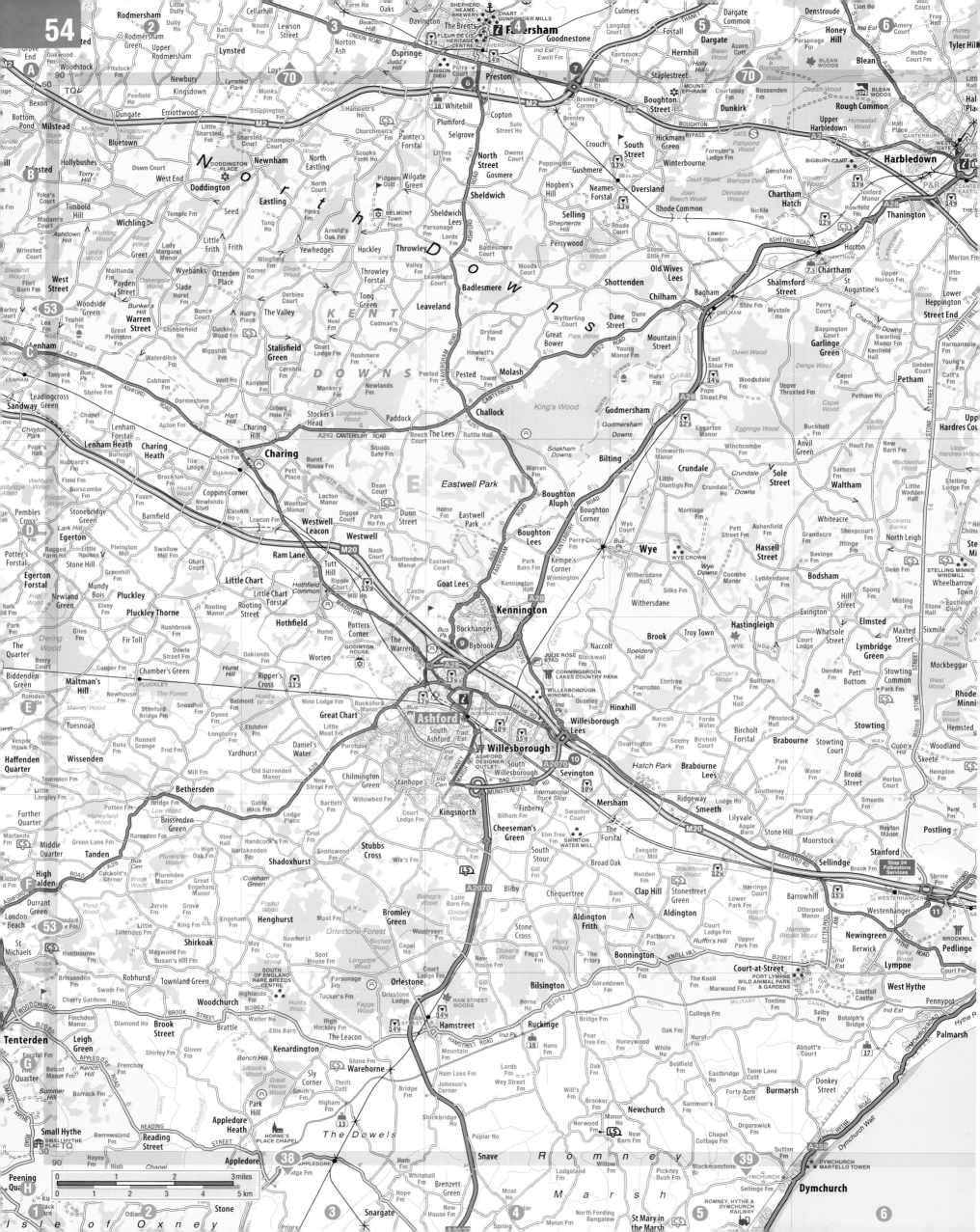

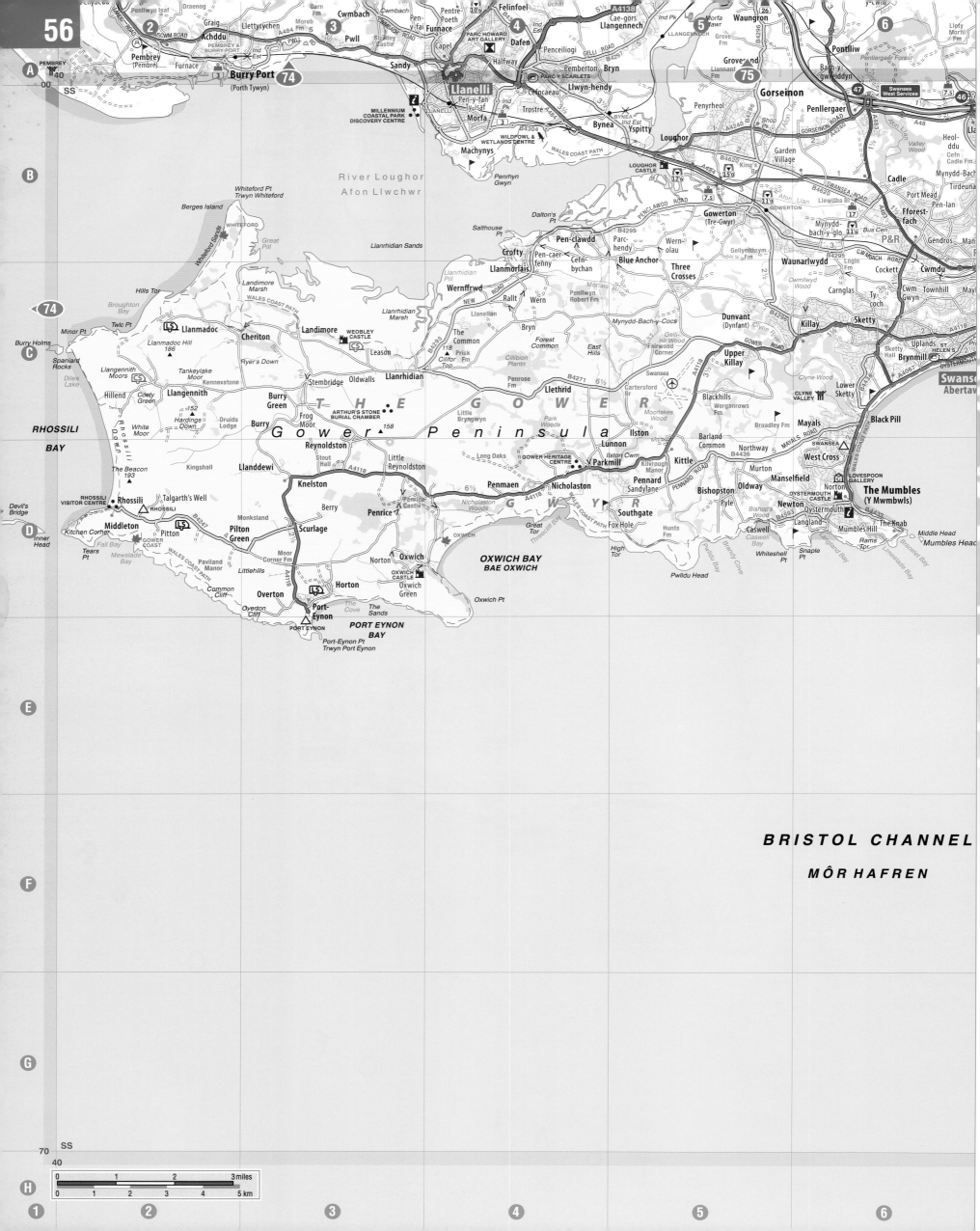

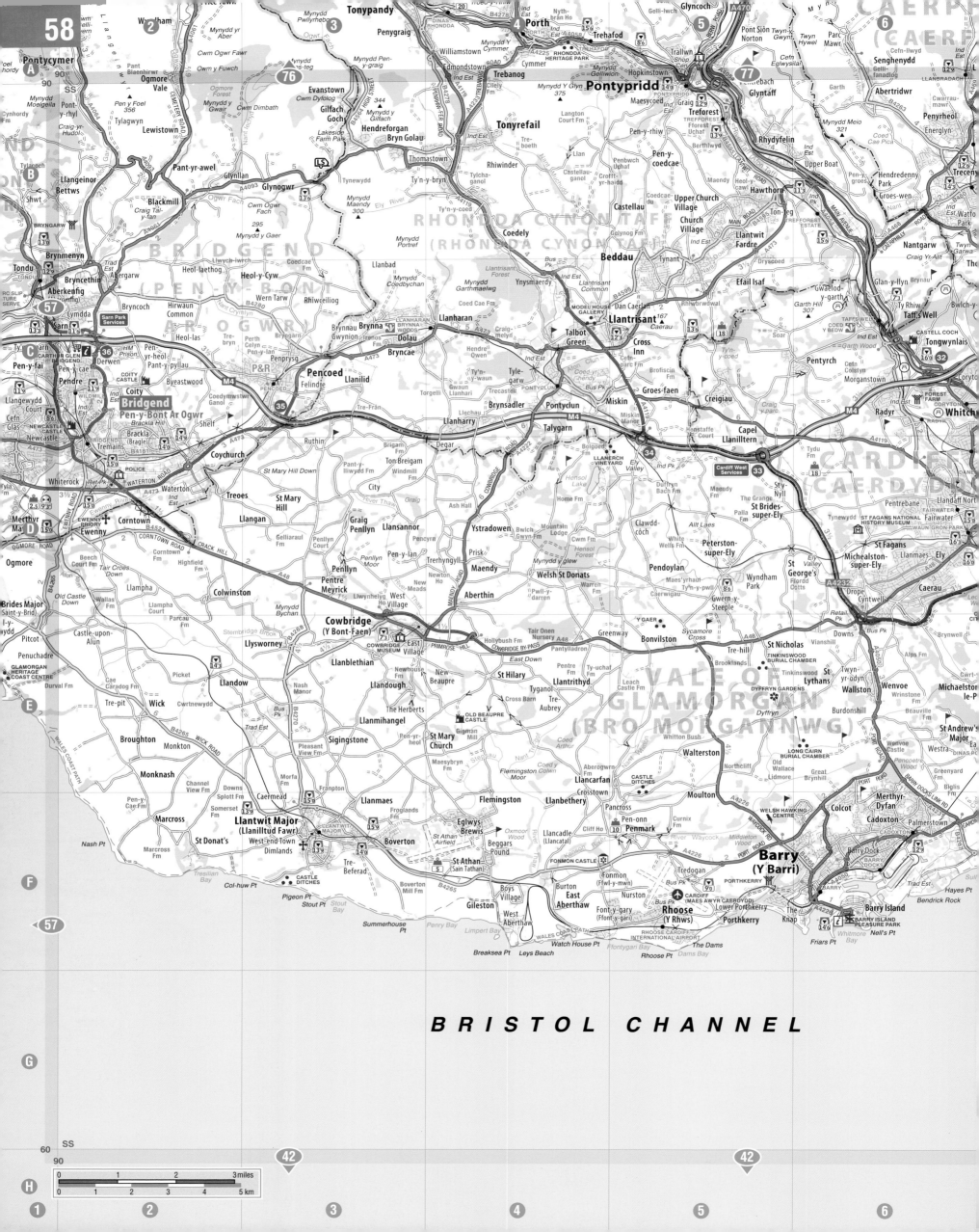

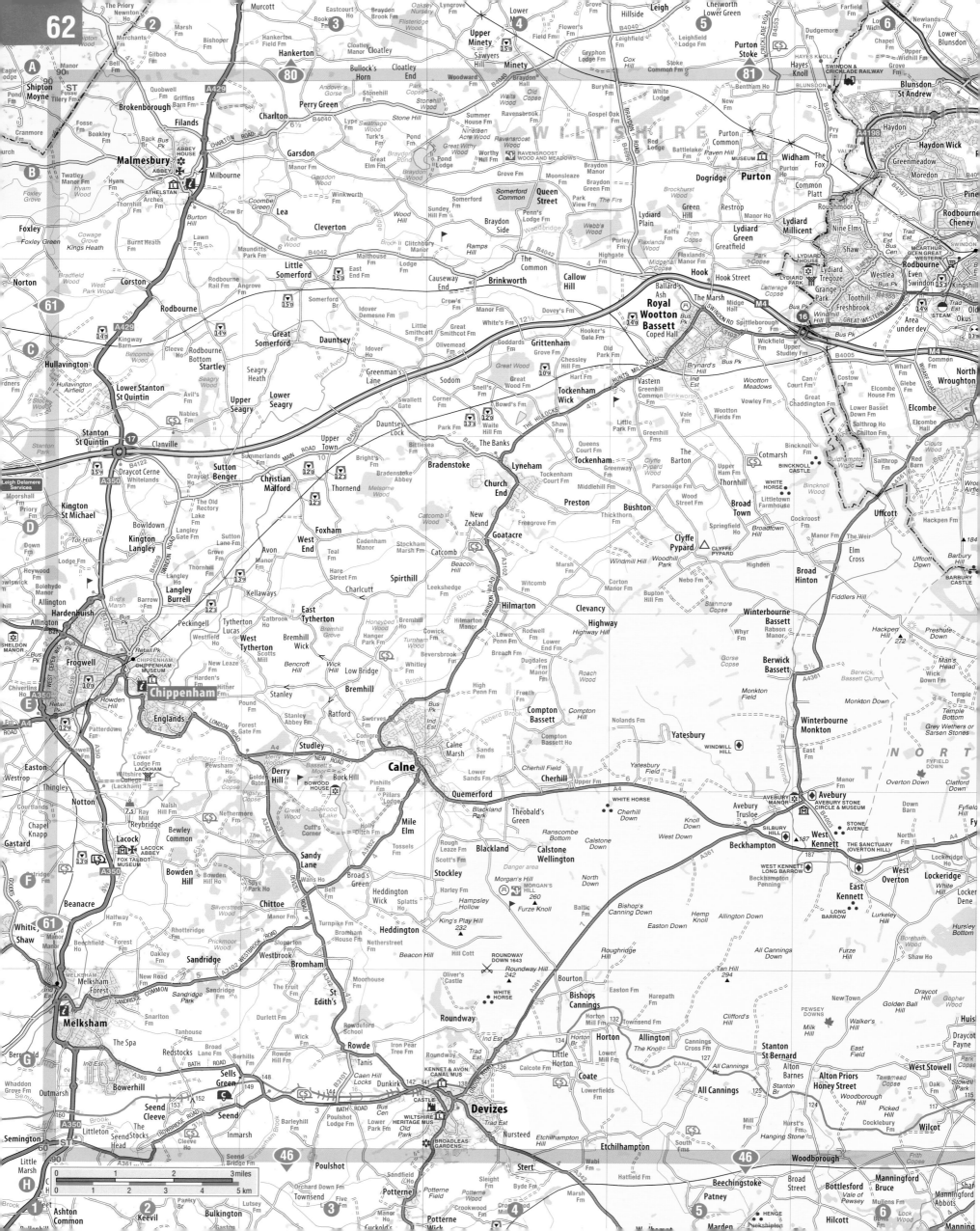

ST BRIDES BAY

BAIE SAIN FFRAID

PEMBROKESHIRE COAST

NATIONAL PARK

Milford Haven
Aberdaugleddyf

Milford Haven
Aberdaugleddau

PEMBROKESHIRE

COAST NATIONAL PARK

0 1 2 3miles
0 1 2 3 4 5 km

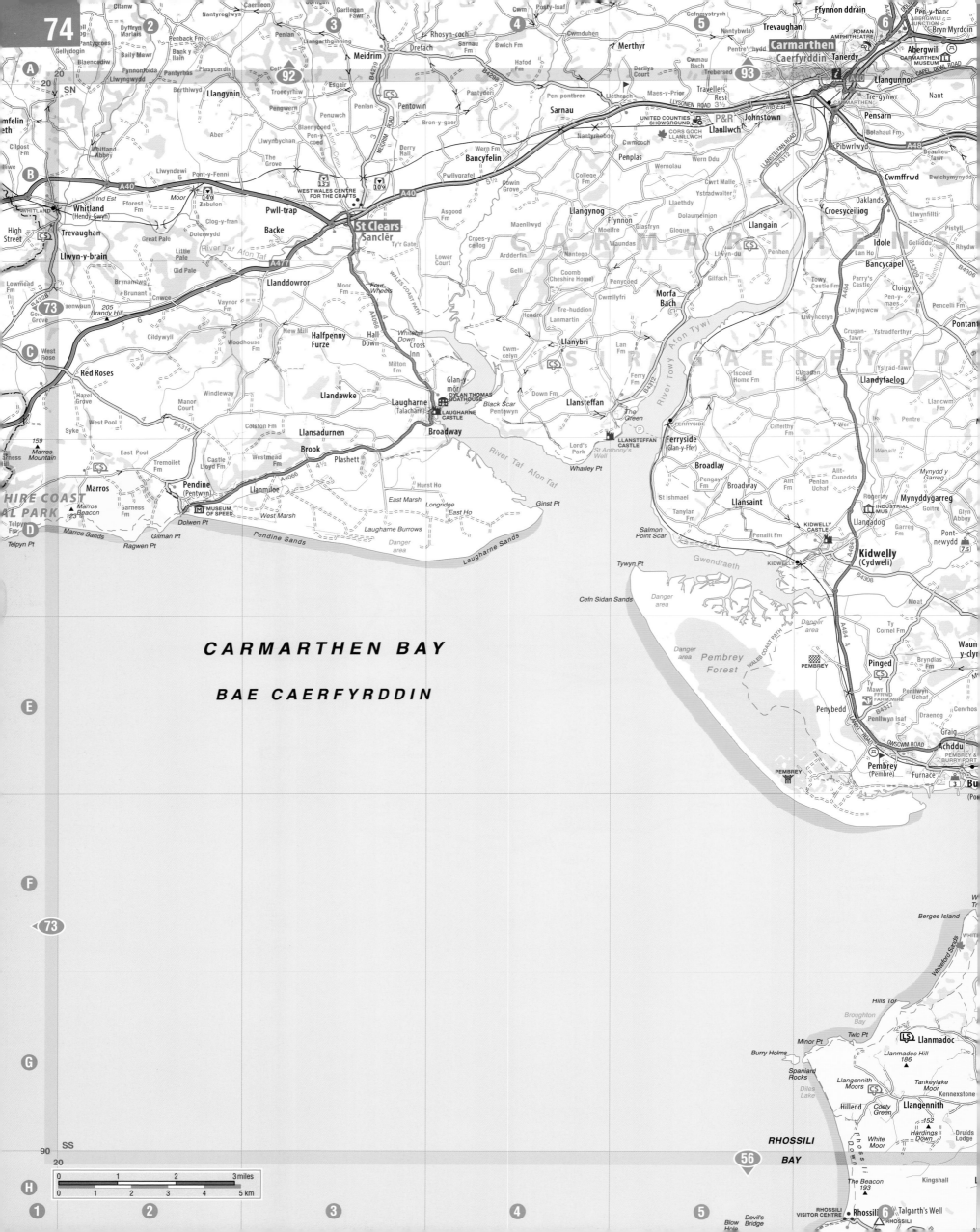

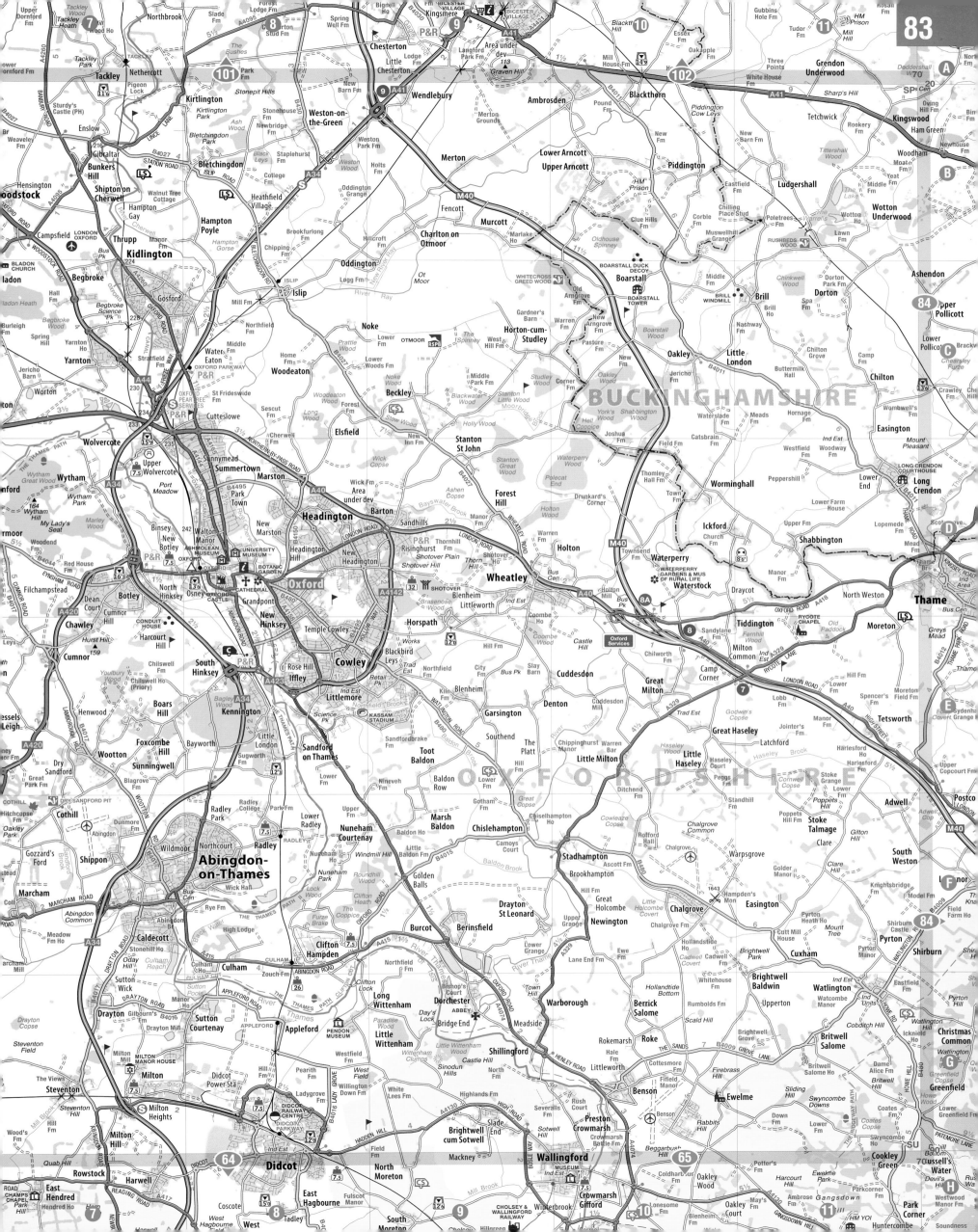

IRISH SEA

MÔR IWERDDON

ST BRIDES BAY

BAIE SAIN FFRAID

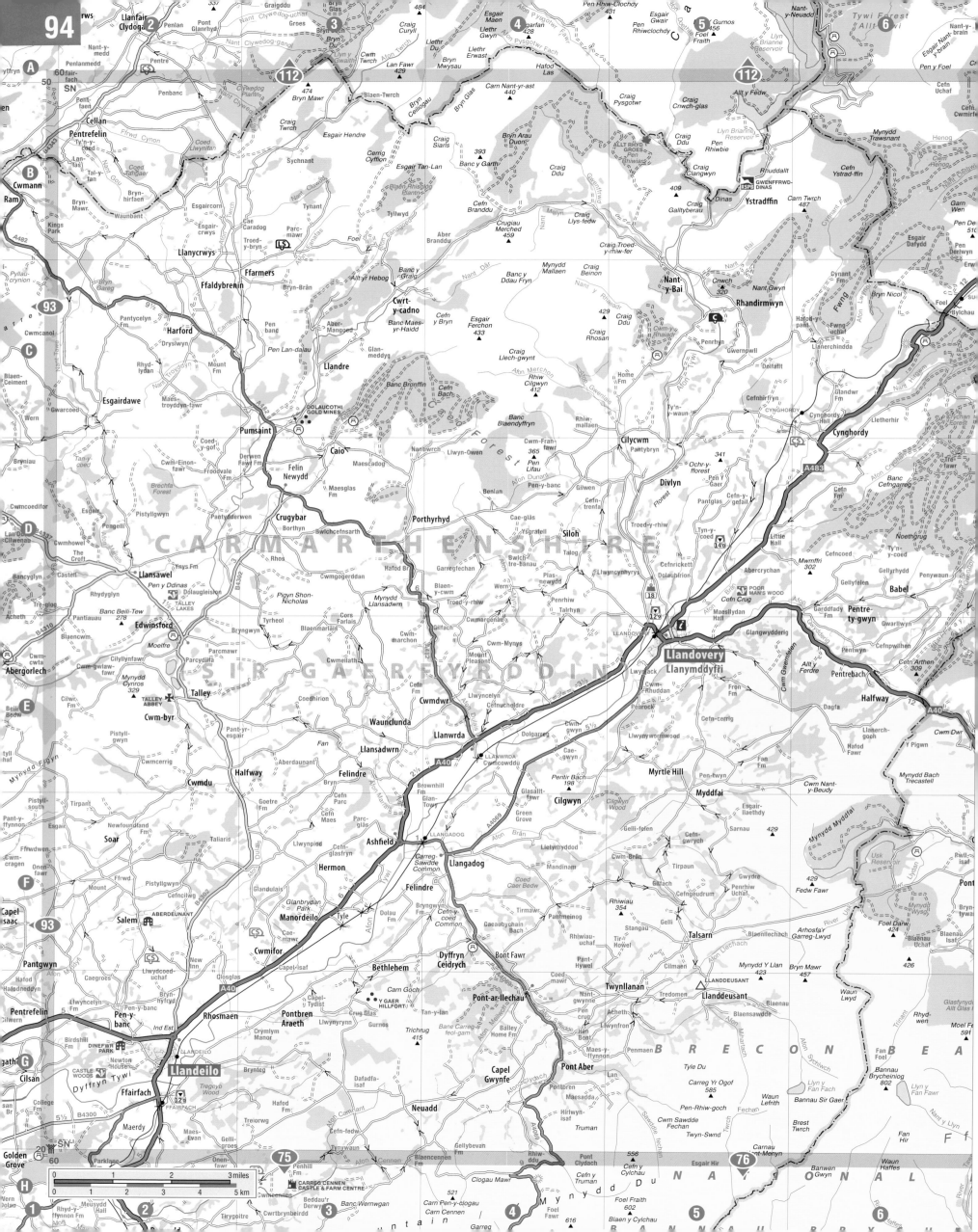

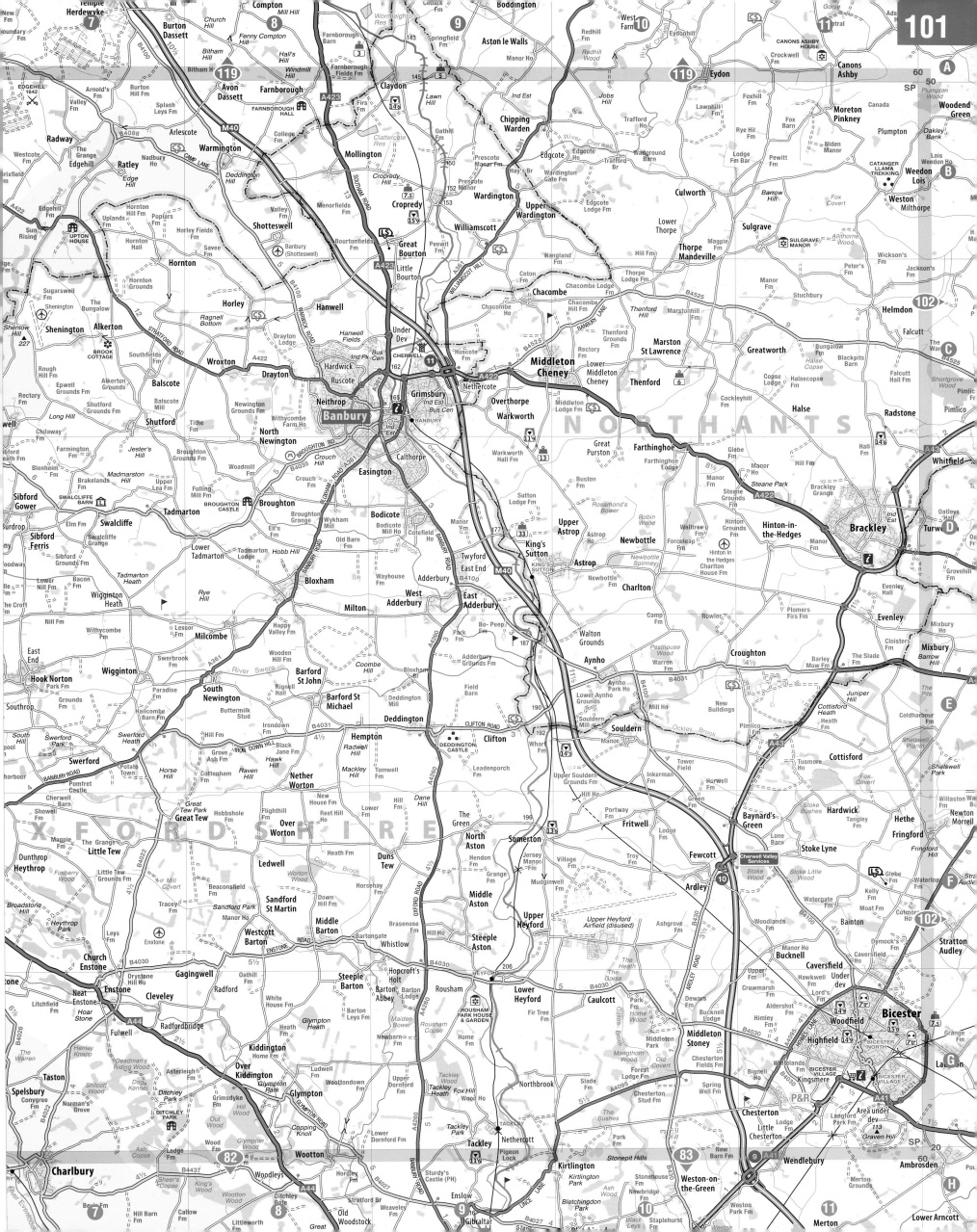

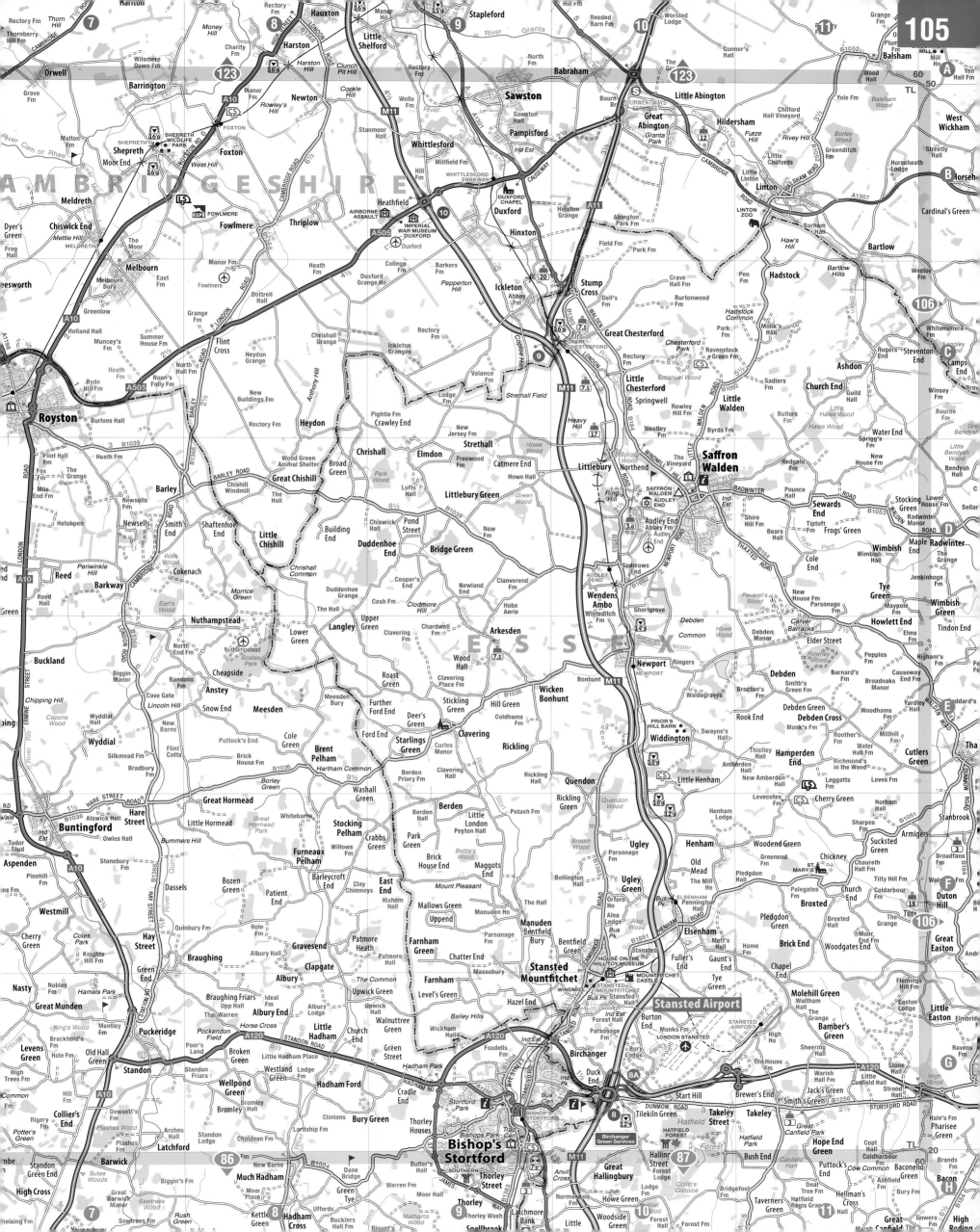

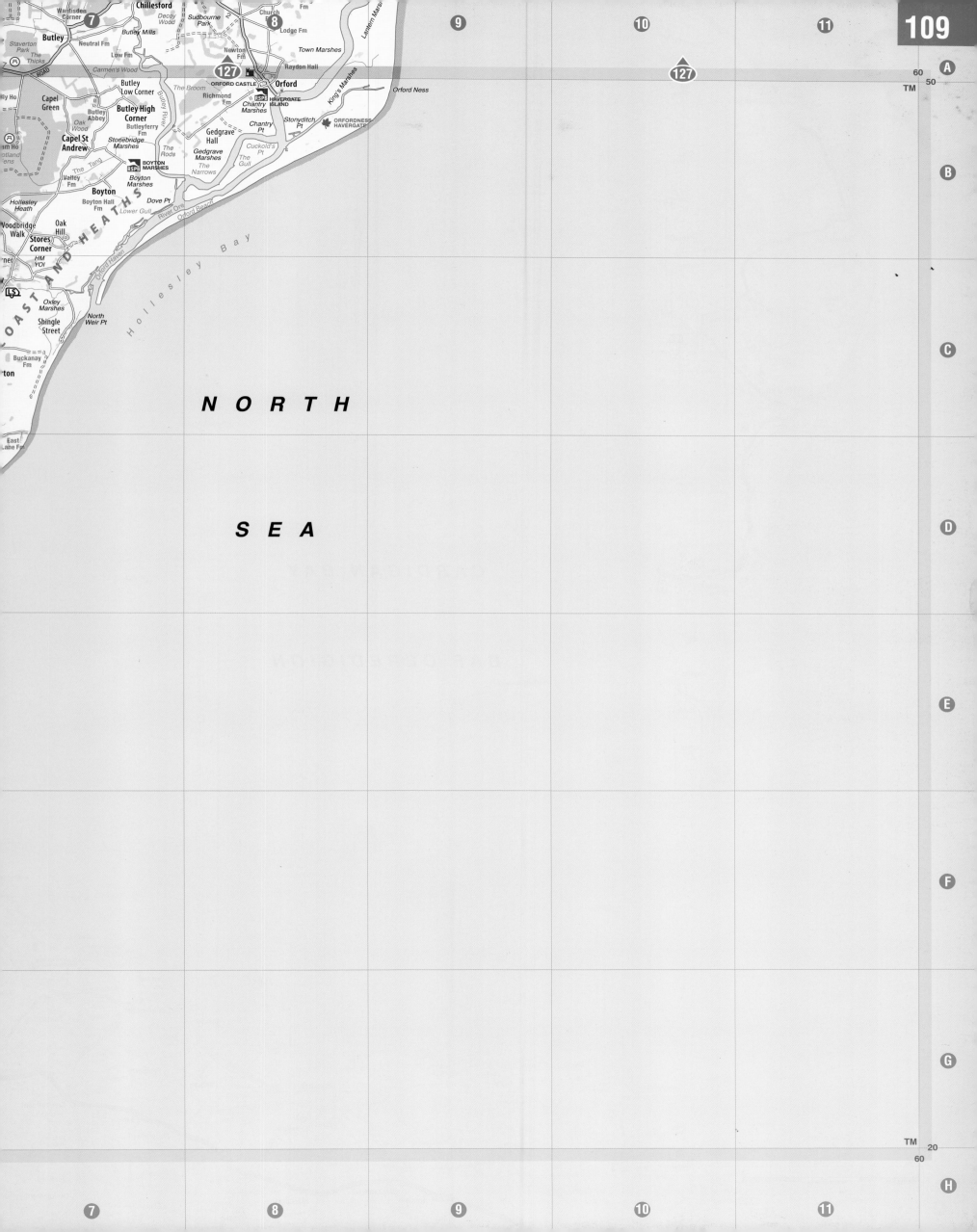

N O R T H

S E A

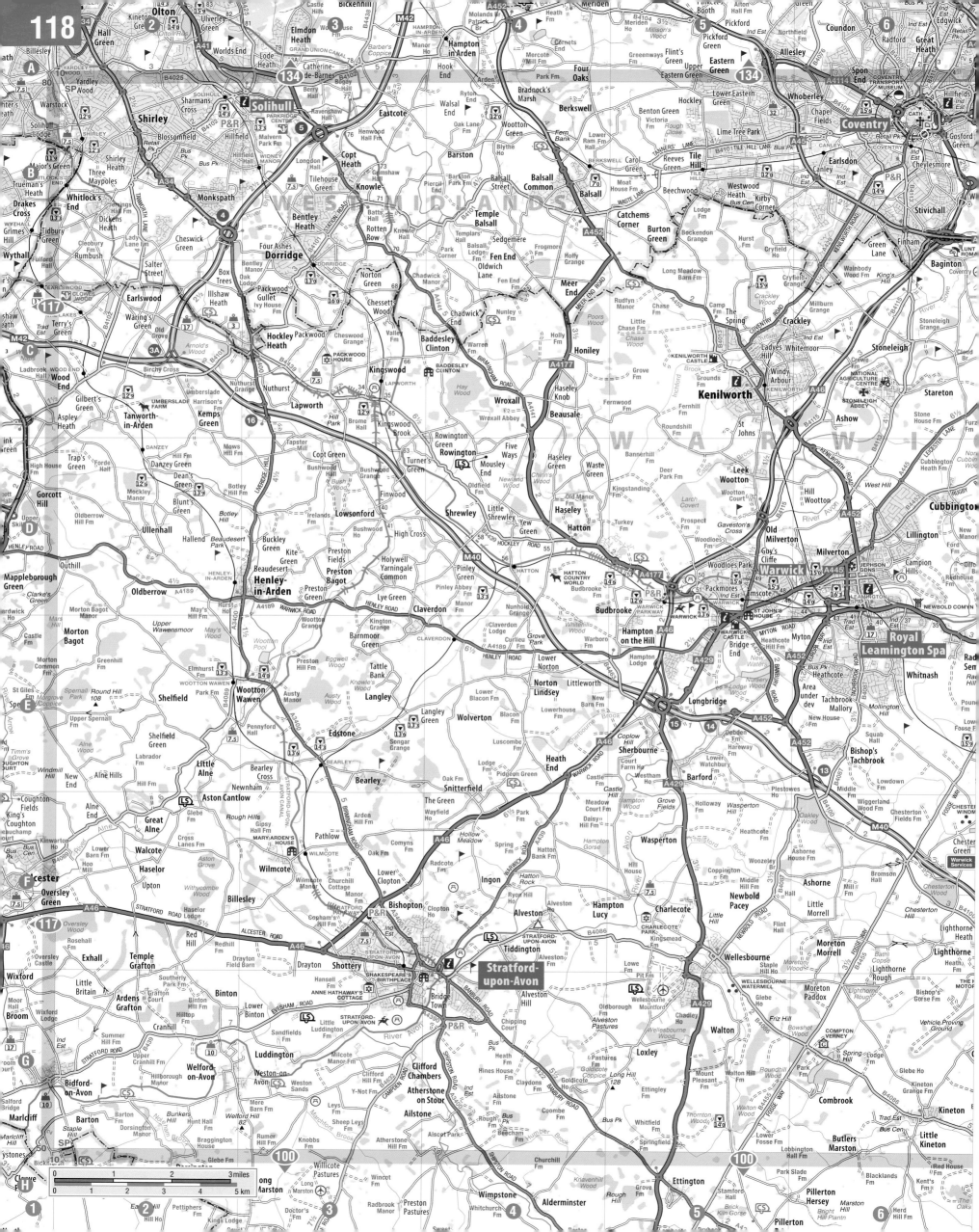

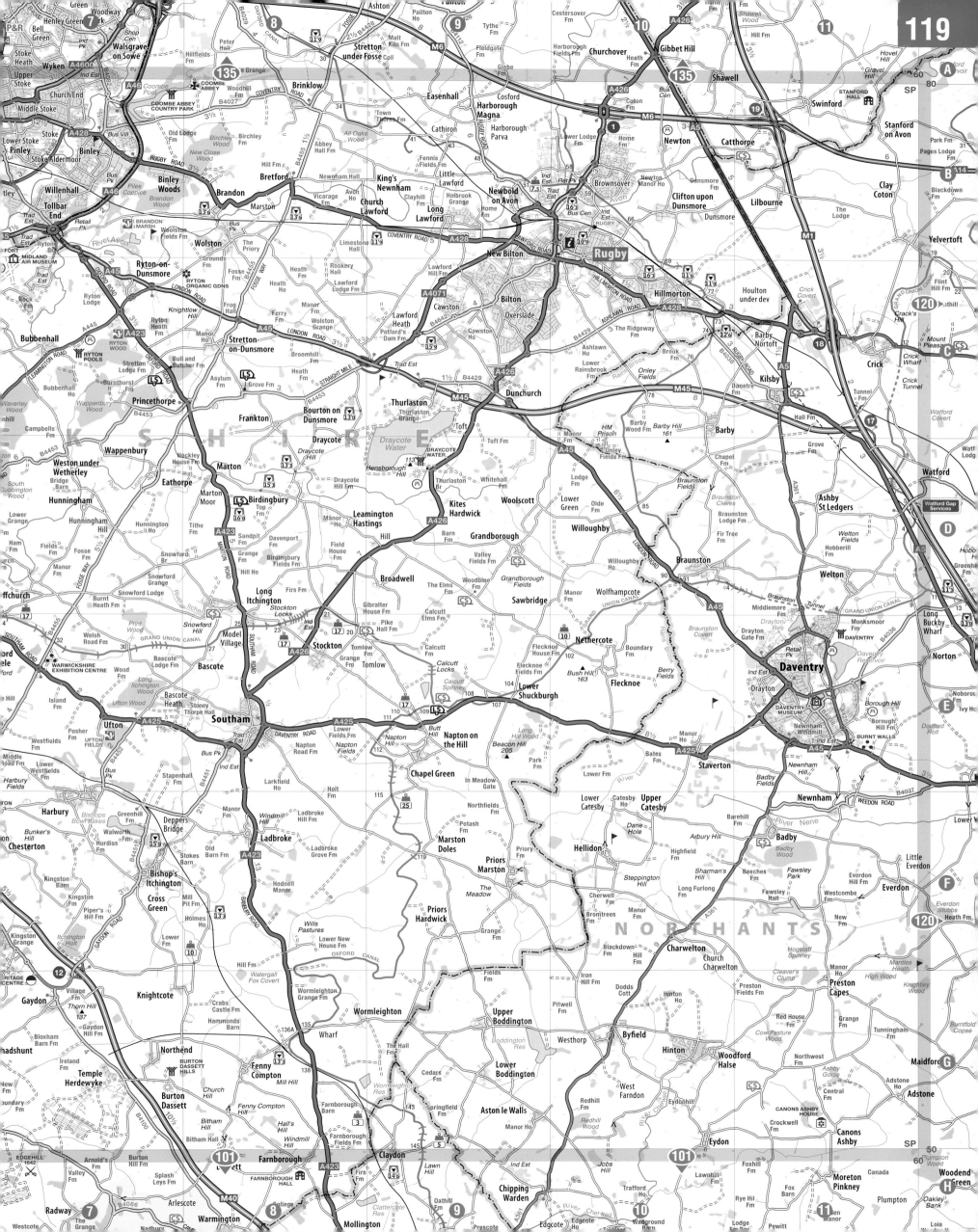

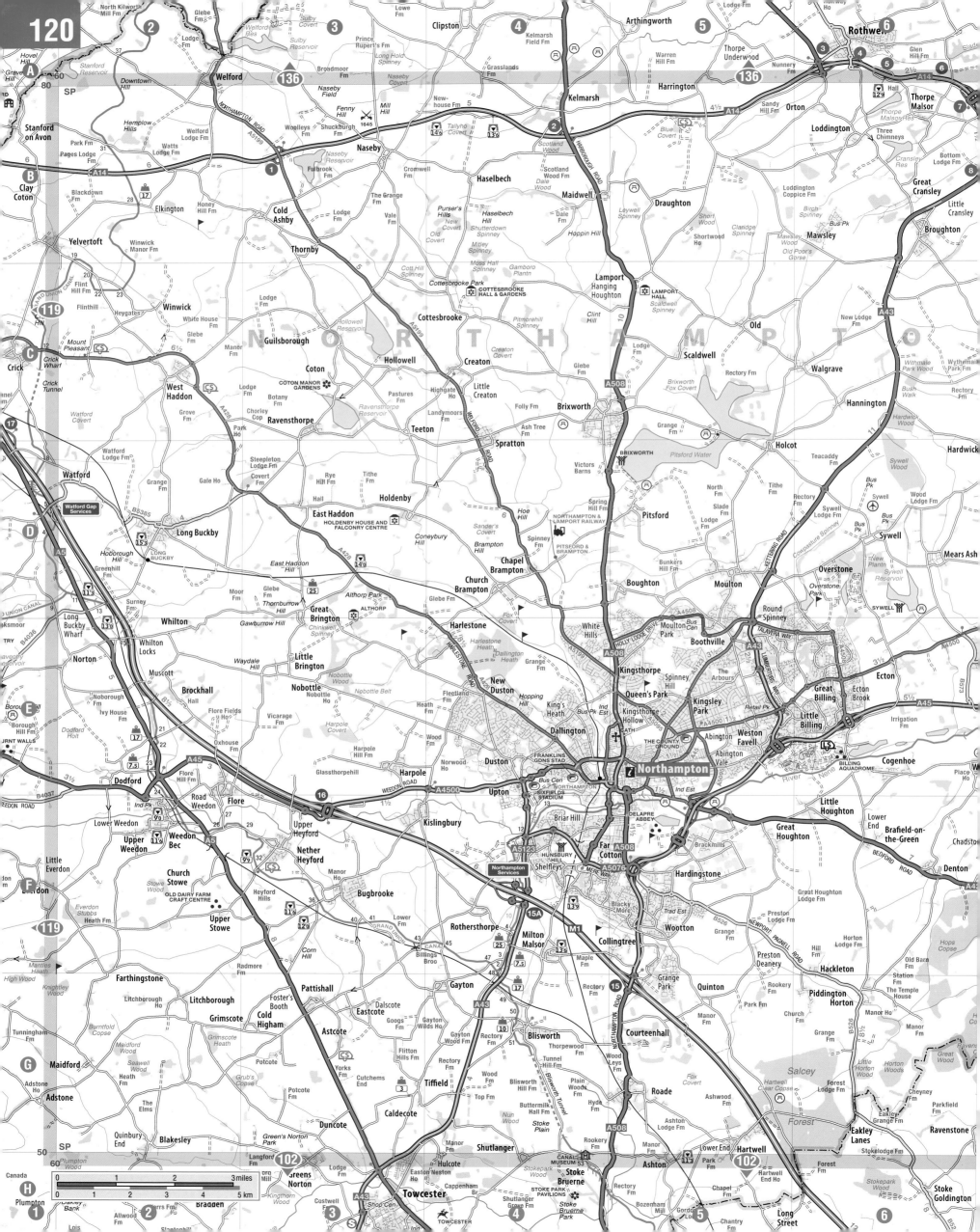

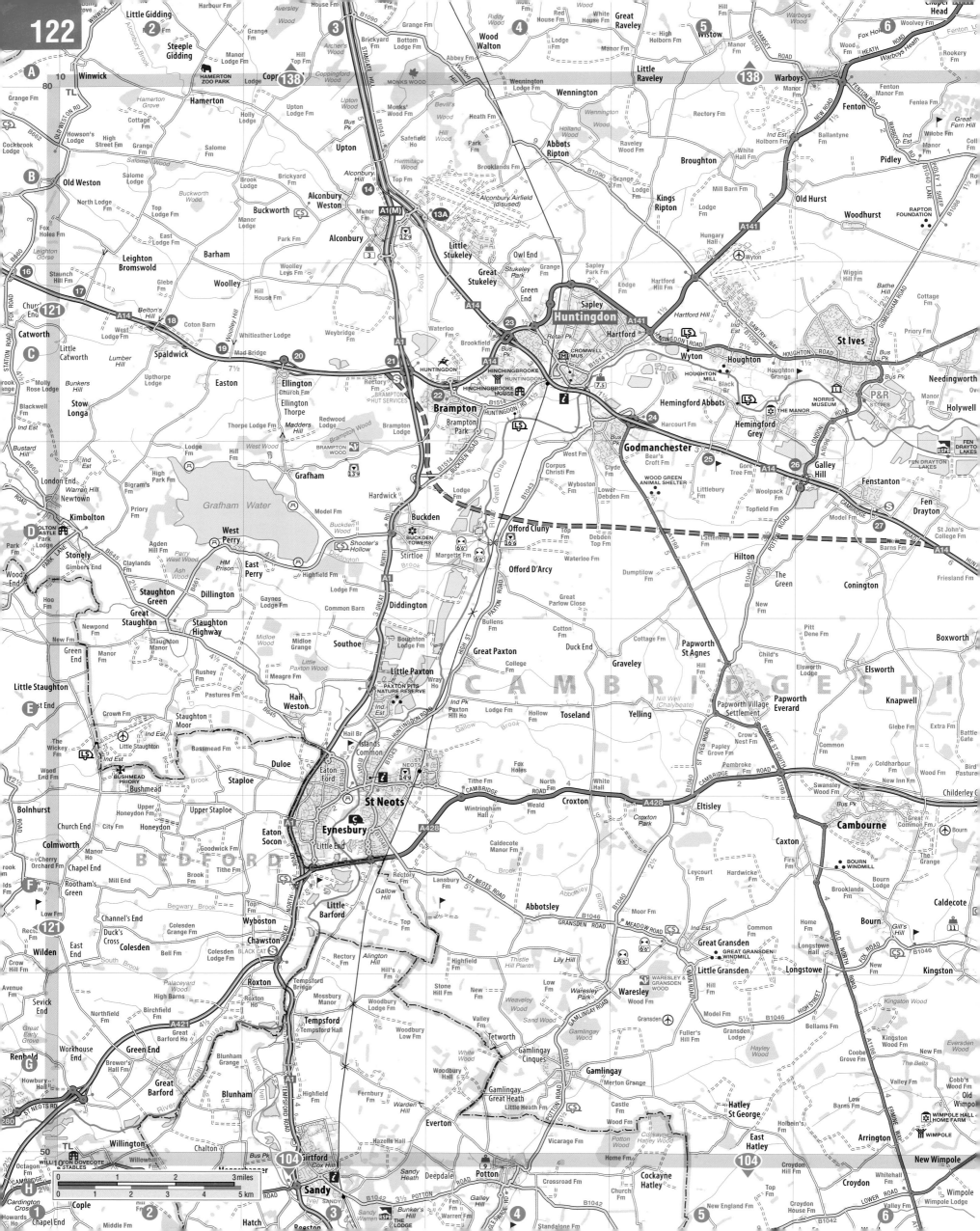

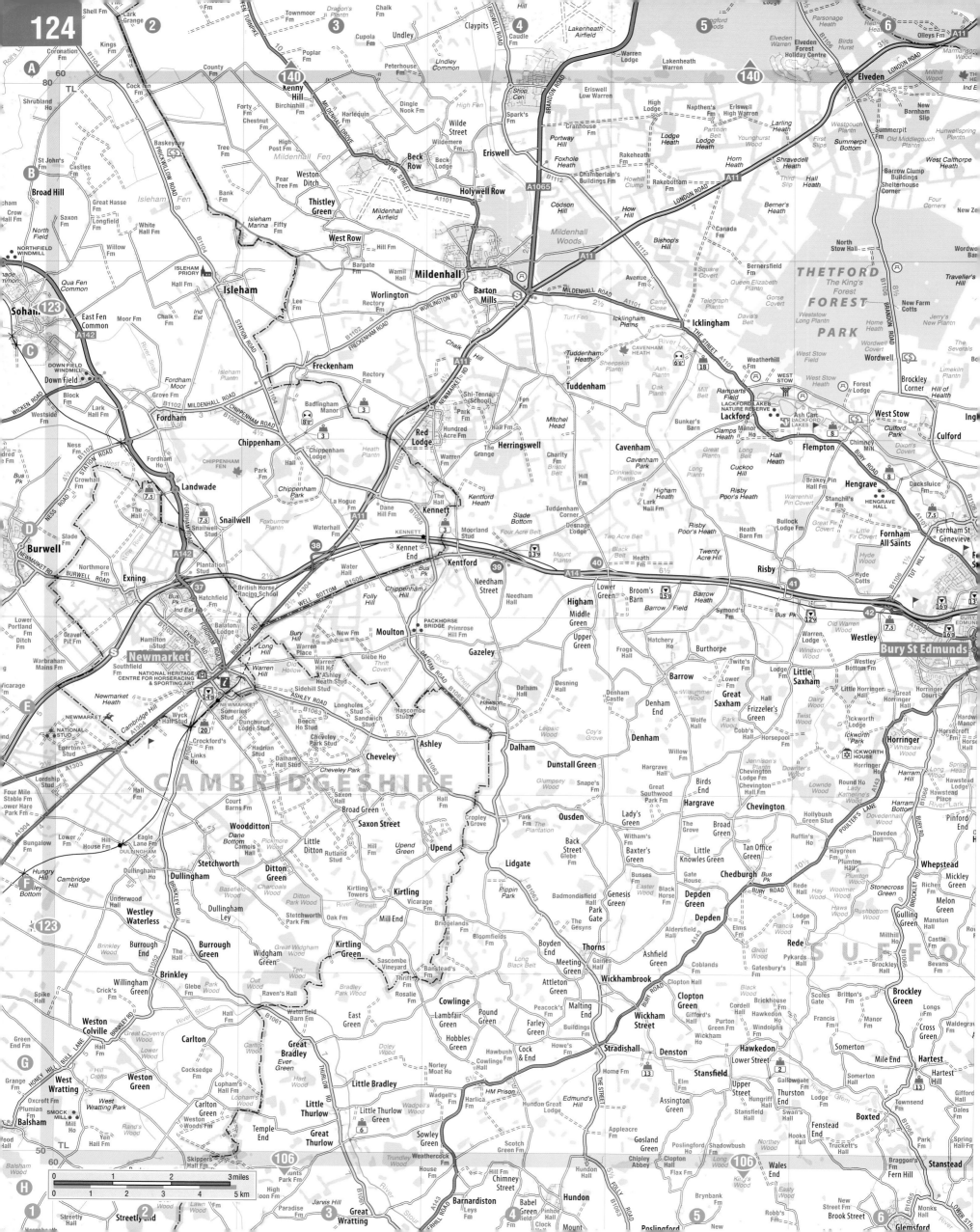

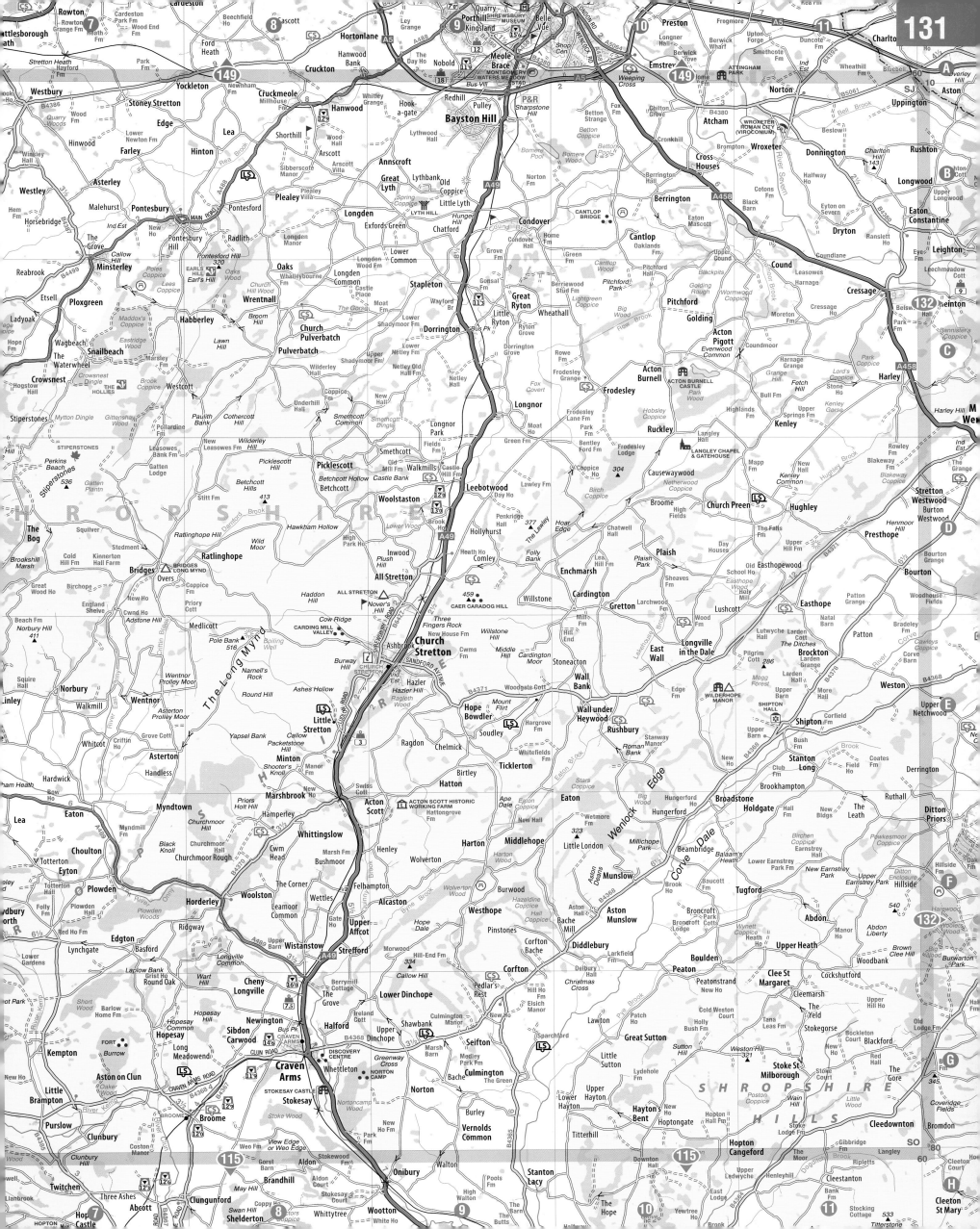

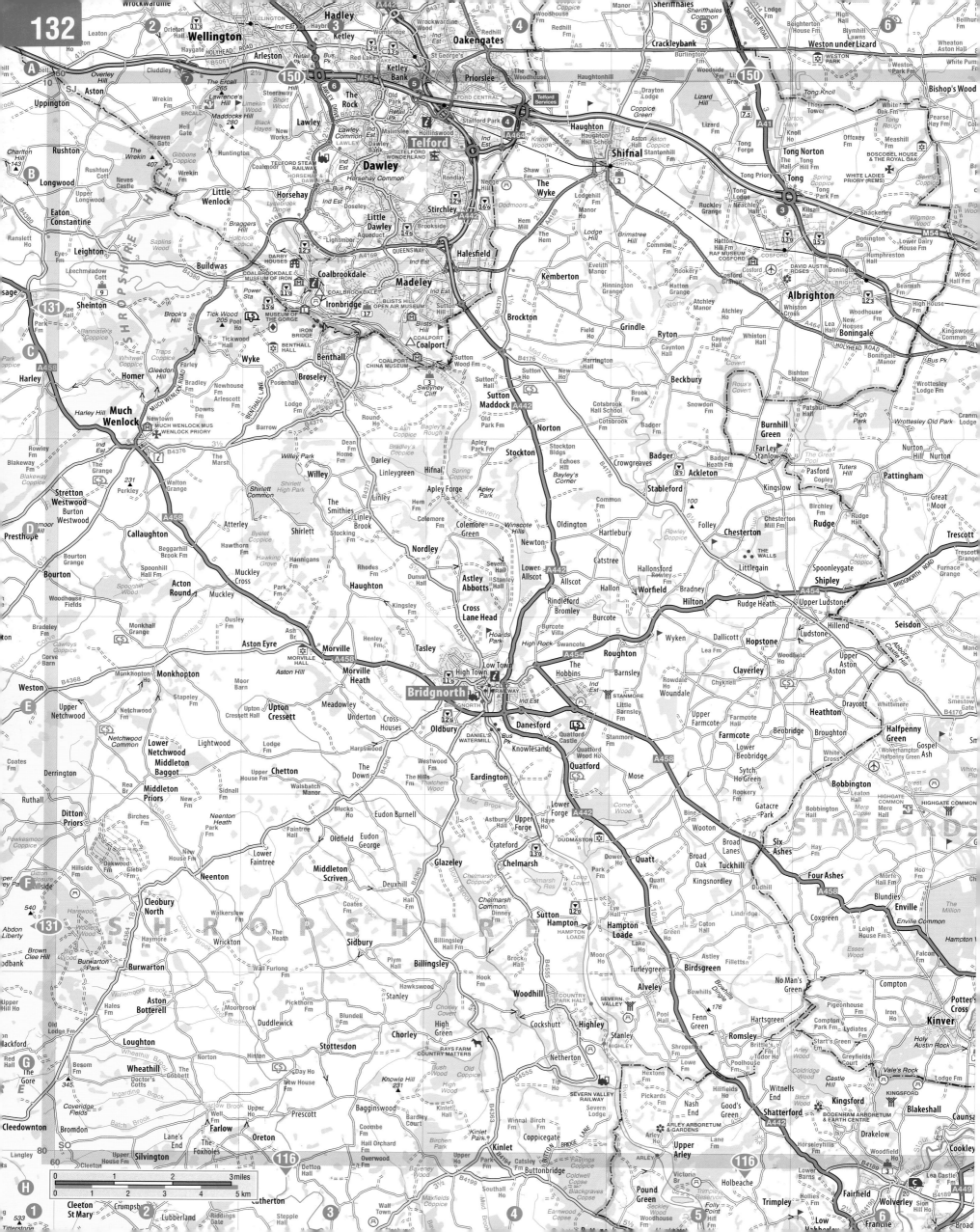

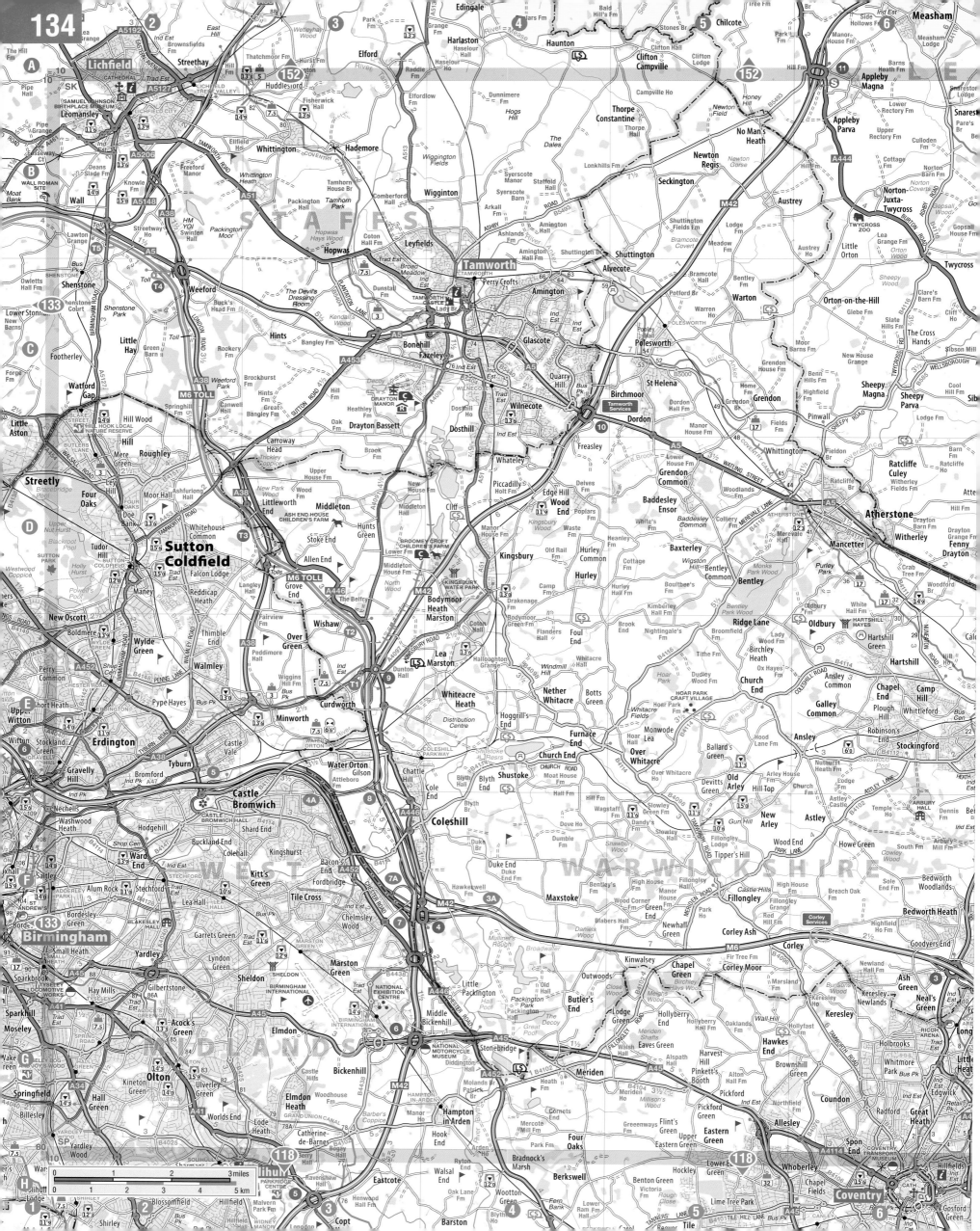

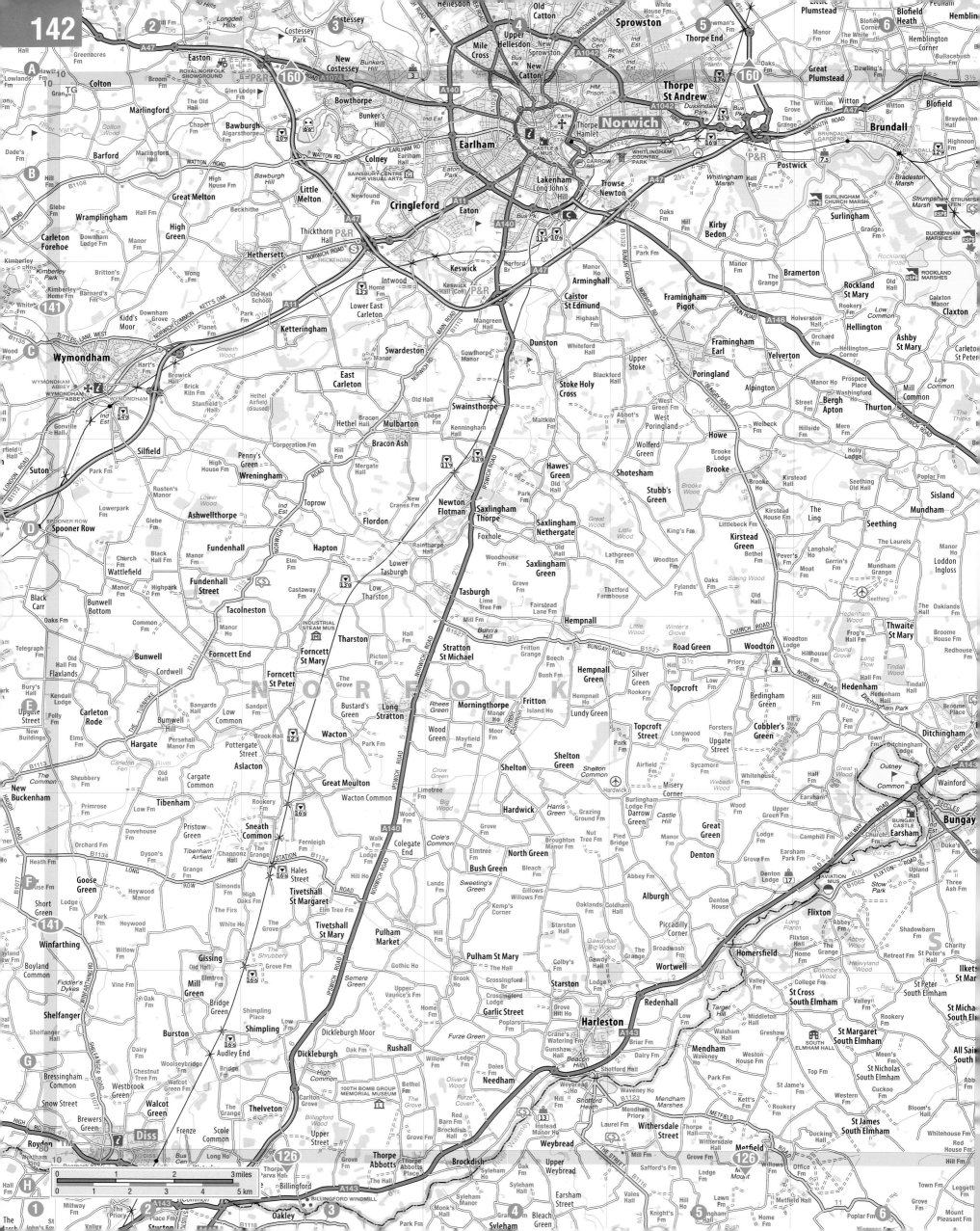

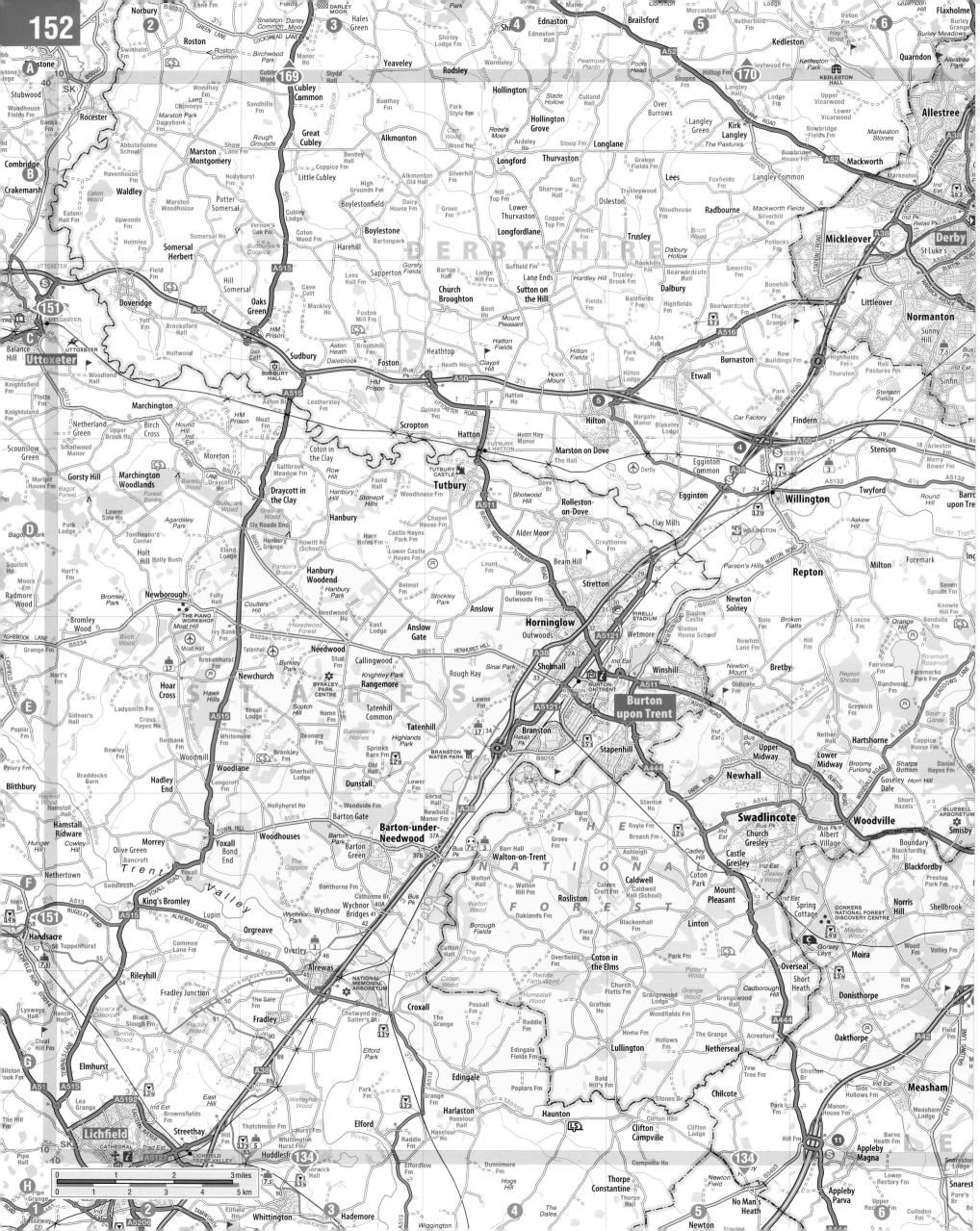

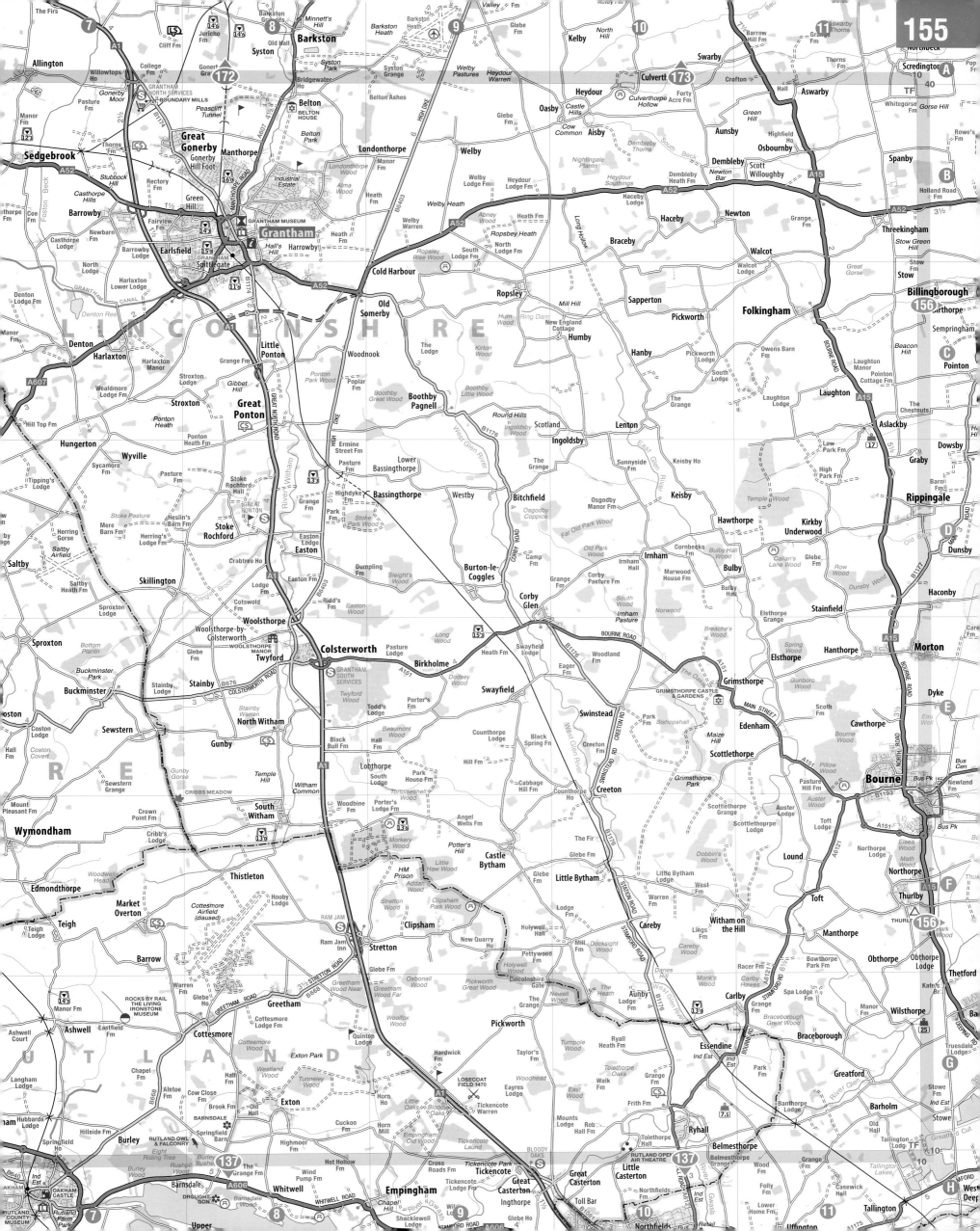

CAERNARFON

BAY

BAE CAERNARFON

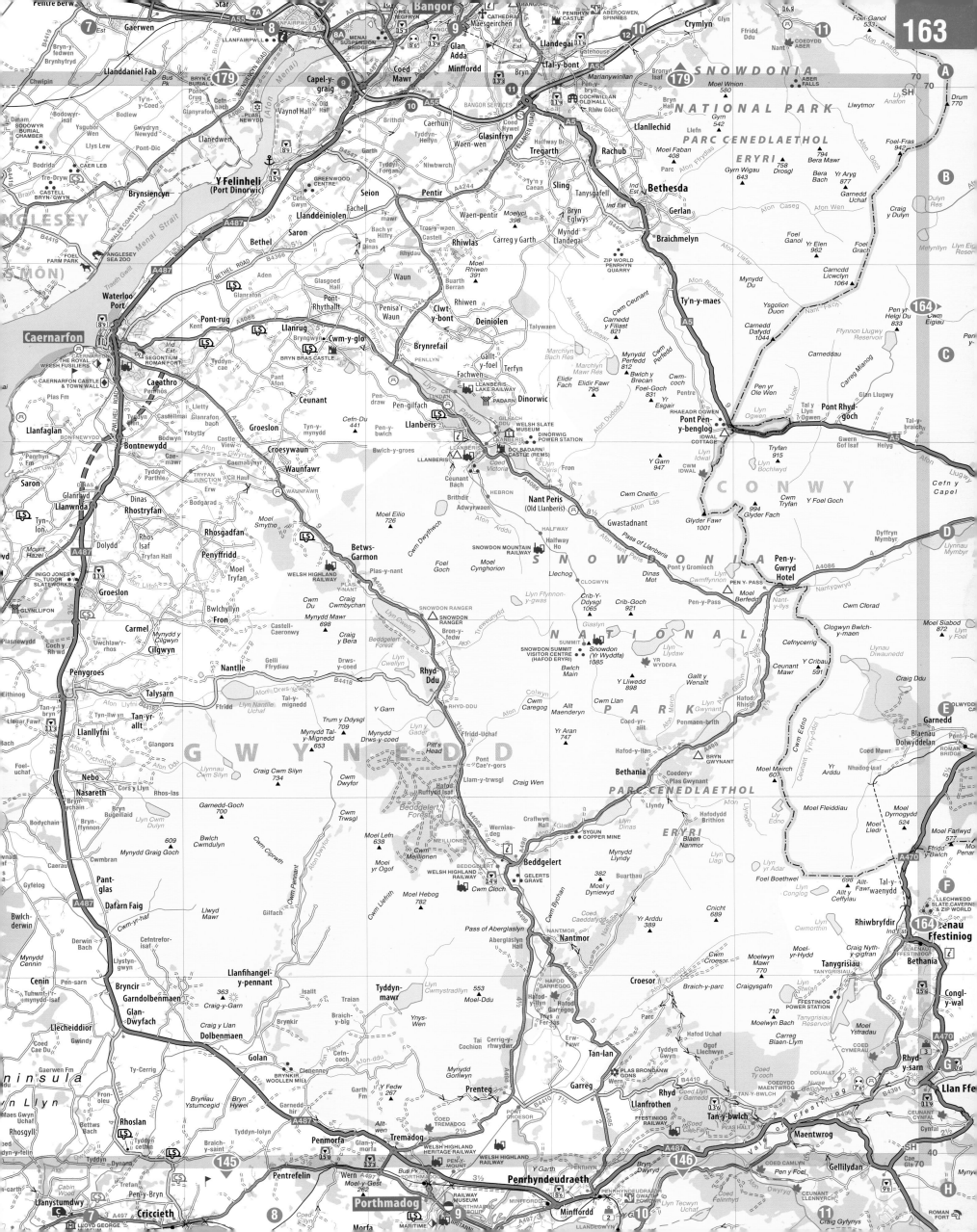

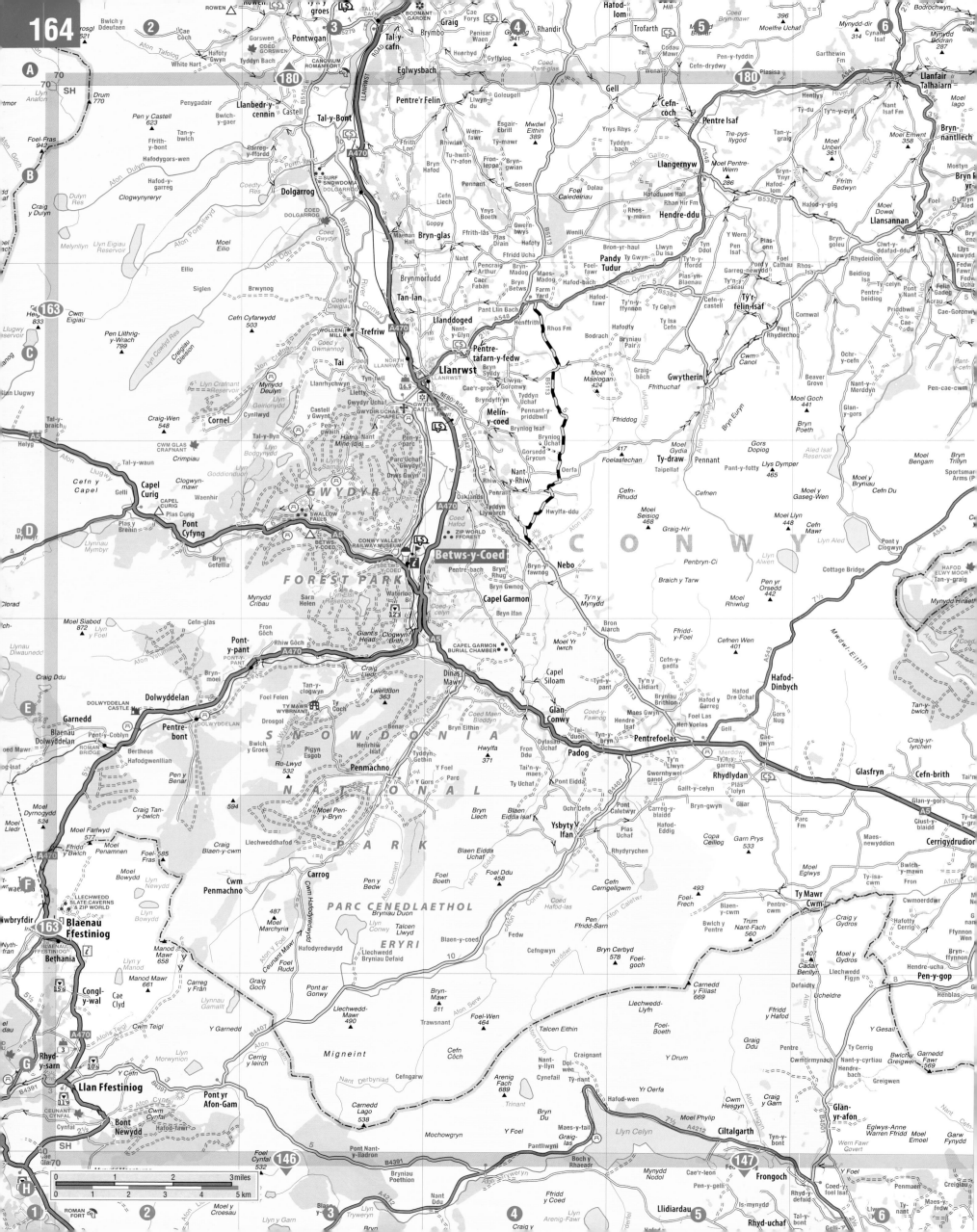

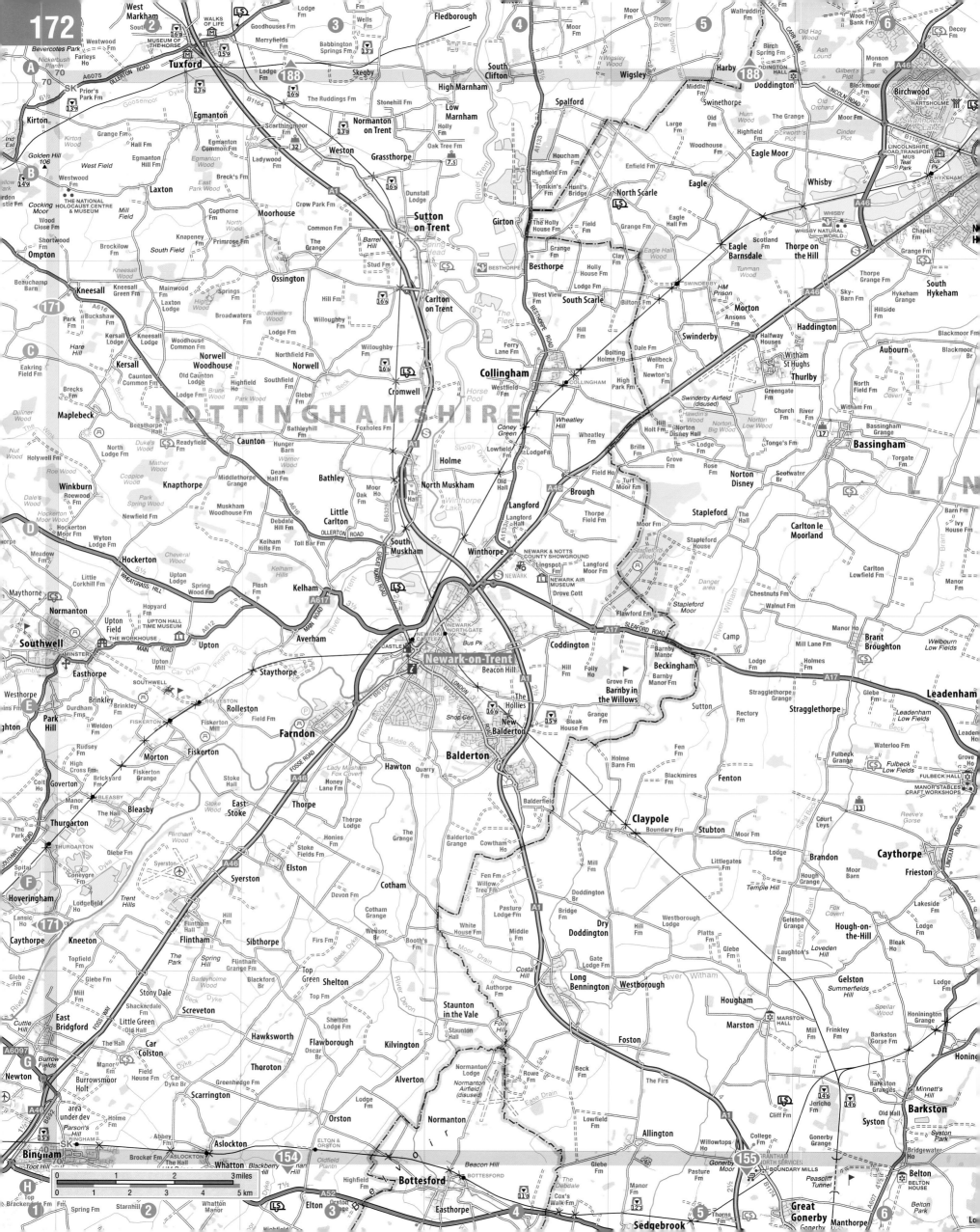

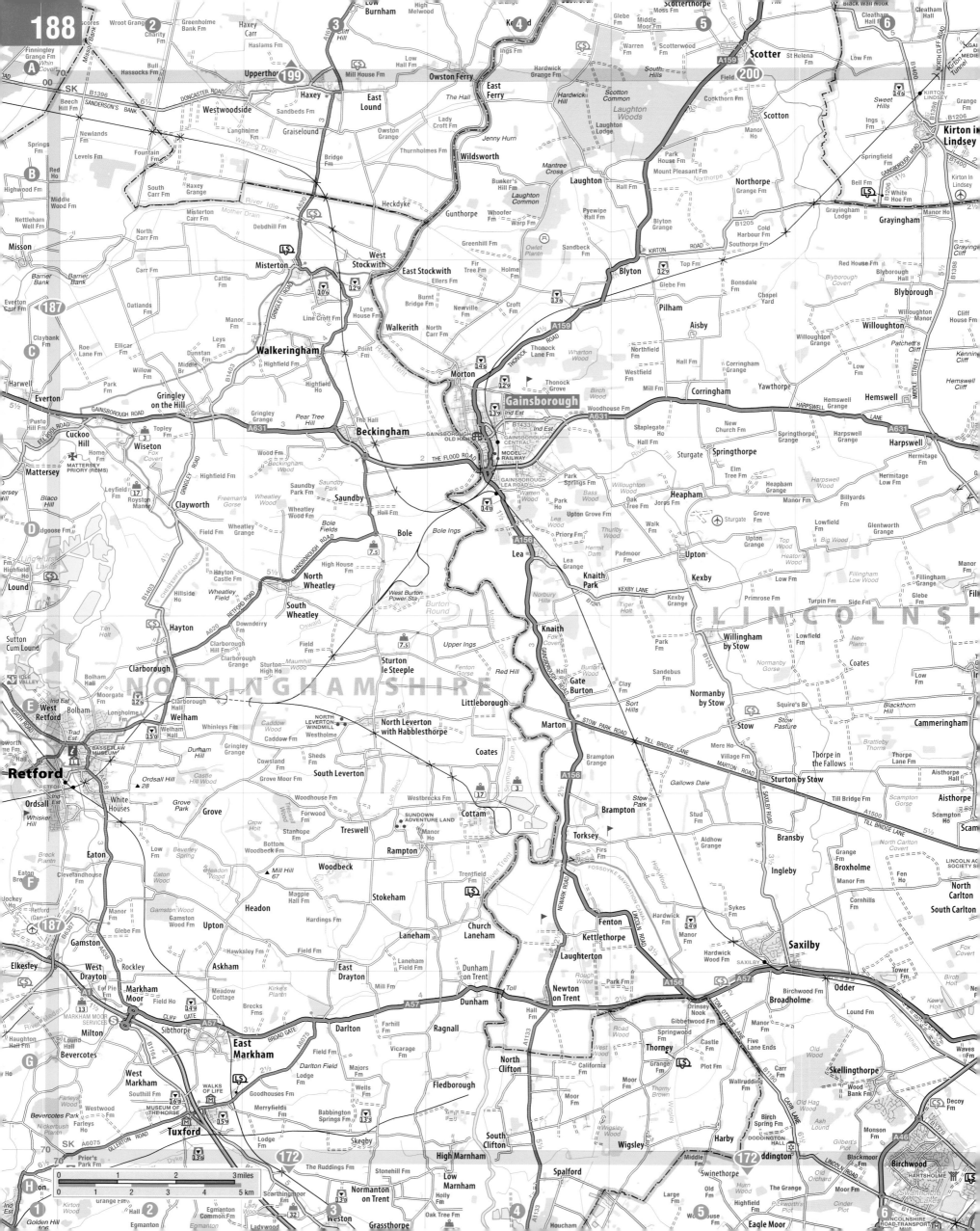

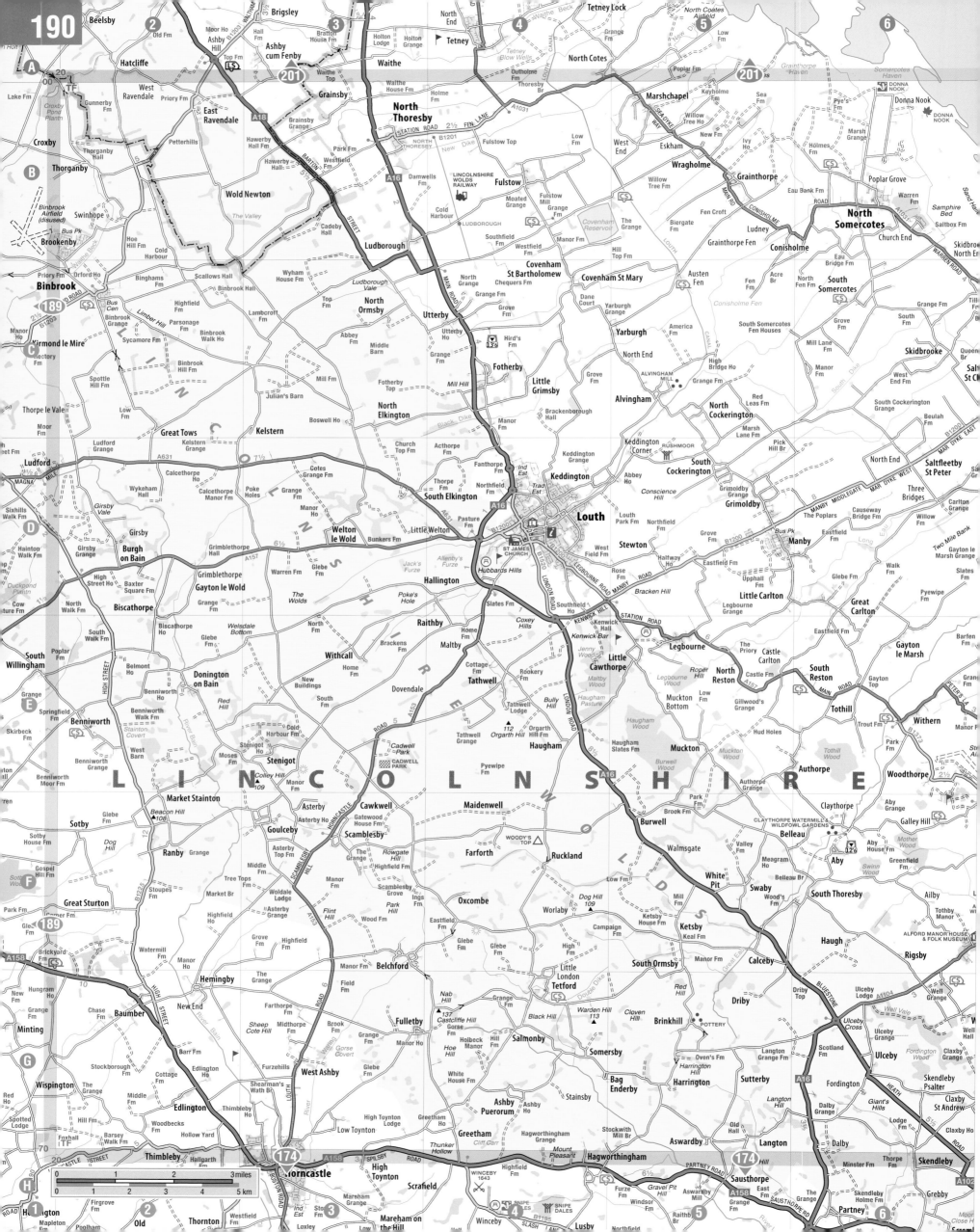

N O R T H

S E A

Saltfleet

Rimac

Saltfleetby
All Saints

Theddlethorpe
St Helen

Theddlethorpe
All Saints

Gayton
Engine

North End

Will Row

Meers
Bridge

Westfield
Fm

Meers
Bank

Mablethorpe

FUN FAIR

Poplar
Fm

Strubby
Grange

Earl's Br

Grange
Fm

Trusthorpe

Willow
Fm

Bamber's Br

Strubby

Thorpe

Trusthorpe
Hall

Sutton on Sea

Maltby le Marsh

Manor Ho

Sandilands

Poplar
Lodge Fm

Mill Hill

Beesby

Abbey Fm

Beesby
Grange

Manor
Fm

Hagnaby

Washdyke
Br

Hannah

Sea Bank
Fm

Saleby

America
Fm

Cob Hill

Glebe
Fm

Priory
Fm

Markby

College
Fm

The Grange

Asserby
Turn

Asserby

Willow
Fm

Black
House Fm

Thorethorpe

Bilsby

Dryby
Fm

Wold
Sea Fm

Moat Ho

Huttoft

Manor
Fm

Anderby Creek

The Grange

The Manor

Alford

Bilsby Field

Thurlby

Anderby

Wolla Bank

Farlesthorpe Fen

ON YOUR
MARQUES

Mumby

Manor Ho

Langham
Fm

Manor
Fm

Chapel Six Marshes

Farlesthorpe

School Fm

Mill Hill

Authorpe
Row

Cumberworth

Cherry
Fm

Mickleberry
Hill

Chapman's
Fm

Chapel Pt

Mawthorpe

Bonthorpe

Helsey

Croft Fm

Manor
Fm

Listoft

Chapel St Leonards

Willoughby

Poplar
Fm

Hogsthorpe

Claxby

Willoughby High
Drain

Willoughby
Wood

Hogsbeck
Ho

Sloothby

Burlands Beck

Howlet
Ho

Slackholme
End

Hope
Fm

Beeches
Fm

HARDY'S
ANIMAL FARM

Hasthorpe

175

175

Welton
High Wood

Welbourne Fm

TF 70

Highfield Fm

Thwaite
Hall

Habertoft

Ingoldmells

Candlesby
Hill

Boothby
Hall

Addlethorpe

FANTASY ISLAND

**Welton
le Marsh**

Boothby

Ingoldmells Pt

ISLE OF MAN

Scale 1:200,000

POINT OF AYRE

AYRES VISITOR
CENTRE & NATURE
TRAIL

Rue Pt.
The Ayres

CRONK Y BING
10.0   A10   10.0   Glentruan
The Lhen   B2   Dhowin   A17   Cranstal
A10   A19   B6   Bride

B3   Andreas   A9

MANX CROSSES   Jurby   JURBY
South   East   MANX
Jurby Head   Sandygate   CROSSES   Regaby   B7
Ballasalla   Jurby   A14   A17   St   A13   Dhoor
West   Judes   B14   RAMSEY BAY
The Cronk   7.5   CLOSE SARTFIELD   GROVE
3.0   CURRAGHS   MUSEUM   Ramsey
WILDLIFE PARK   A3   MANX ELECTRIC
3.0   Sulby   Churchtown   RAILWAY
Orrisdale   Ballaugh   T.T. Course   Glen   Port e Vullen
Auldyn
Rhencullen   A15   Maughold
Ravensdale   A18 T.T. Course   Dreemskerry   Maughold Head
MANX CROSSES   Kirk   Sulby   Ballajora   MANX CROSSES
Michael   565   7.5
NORTH
COOILDARRY   7.0   BARRULE   Corrany
Ballaleigh   Glen Mona
CELTIC CRAFT   Cornaa
CENTRE   Snaefell   9
Barregarrow   B10   621   14   Dhoon
Druidale   MURRAYS   SNAEFELL   Agneash
MOTORCYCLE MUSEUM   MOUNTAIN   LAXEY WHEEL
Knocksharry   A4   7.0   RAILWAY   AND MINES
Cronk-y-Voddy   544   Ballaquine   Bulgham Bay
3.0   7.0   Laxey   16.6
MANX TRANSPORT MUSEUM   487   SNAEFELL   LAXEY   Old Laxey
St Patrick's I.   COLDEN   BALLALHEANNAGH   WOOLLEN MILLS   Laxey Head
PEEL   GARDENS   12.3   Fairy Cottage   Laxey Bay
Peel   A20   Ballacannel
HOUSE OF MANANNAN   TYNWALD   Creg-ny-Baa   B12   Baldrine
Contrary Head   CRAFT CENTRE   Baldwin   A21   Clay Head
KIPPER MUSEUM   TYNWALD HILL   B22   B20
A1   St John's   Greeba   7.5
Patrick   A30   T.T. Course   A23   Course
333   Crosby   7.5   MANX CROSSES
Glenmaye   Lower Foxdale   Glen Vine   3.5   GROUDLE GLEN
A1   Strang   Onchan   RAILWAY
Dalby Pt.   DALBY   A24   Union Mills   Tromode   7.5
MOUNTAIN   B35   ONCHAN PLEASURE PARK
Dalby   Foxdale   Eairy   Braaid   7.5   Douglas
Niarbyl   483   B36   Cooil   3.0   Douglas Head
Niarbyl Bay   SOUTH   A3   Spring   CAMERA OBSCURA
14   BARRULE   Close   222   Valley
Clark   B37   A5   7.5   Ellenbrook   Head
Lingague   Ronague   St Mark's   A6
Ballamodha   B30   Newtown   11   Ballaveare   Little Ness
Surby   Grenaby   A25   ISLE OF MAN
Bradda   Colby   A34   12.0   STEAM RAILWAY
Bradda Head   Ballabeg   RUSHEN   Ballasalla   Santon Head
Port Erin   A7   ABBEY   Port
RAILWAY MUS   Ballasalla   ISLE OF MAN   Greenaugh
The Howe   Four Roads   BILLOWN   Derbyhaven
Cregneash   A5   5   Castletown   NAUTICAL   St Michael's I.
CASTLE RUSHEN   MUS
CREGNEASH VILLAGE   Port   SCARLETT   OLD
FOLK MUSEUM   St Mary   12.5   VISITOR CENTRE   HOUSE OF KEYS
128   Scarlett   Dreswick Pt.
Calf of Man   Point
Spanish Head   HEYSHAM
Chicken Rock   LARNE
(TT race period only)
LIVERPOOL
(March-Nov)
BIRKENHEAD
(Nov-March)
BELFAST
(April-Sept)
DUBLIN
(April-Sept, & Christmas)

0   2   4   6 miles
0   2   4   6   8   10 km

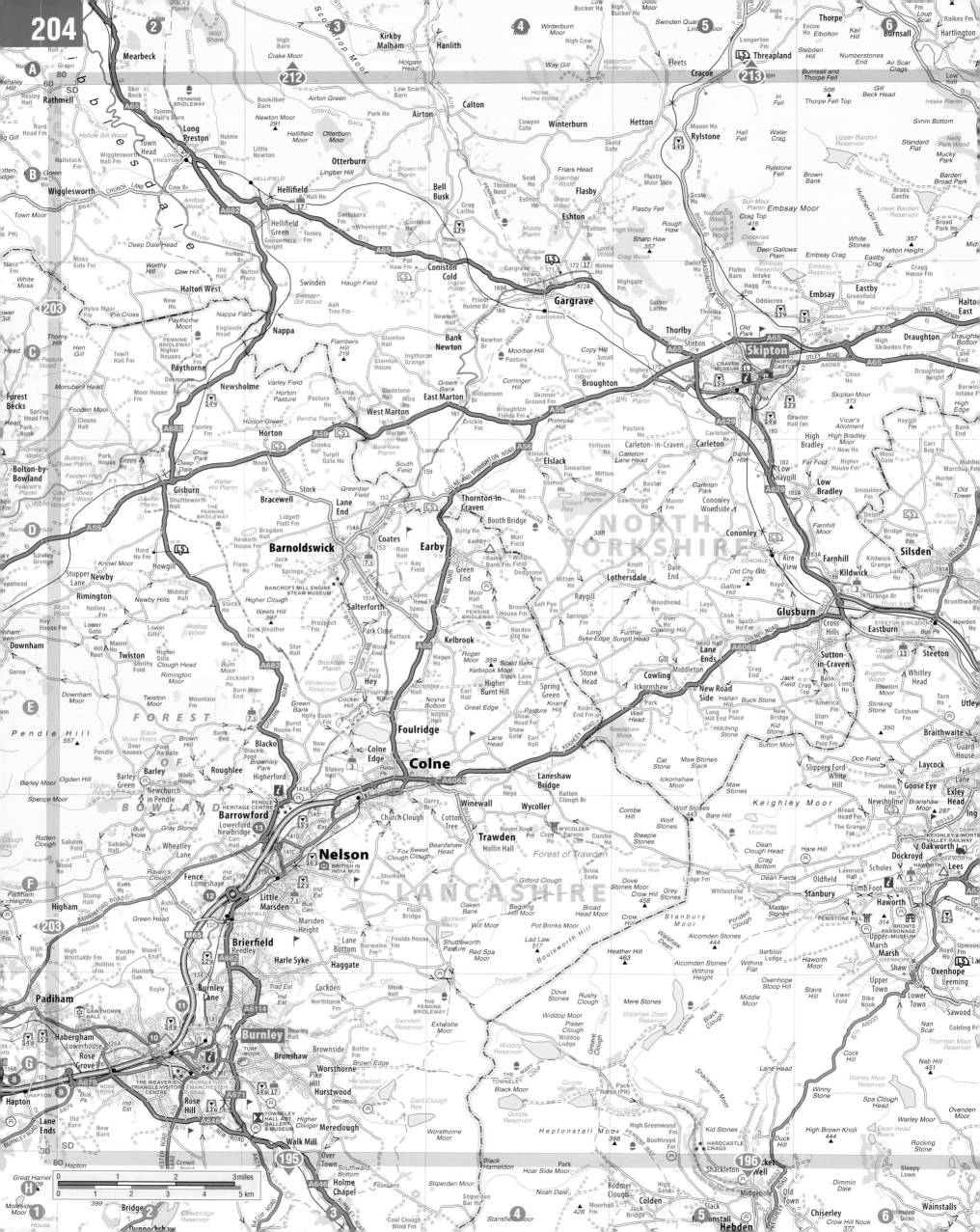

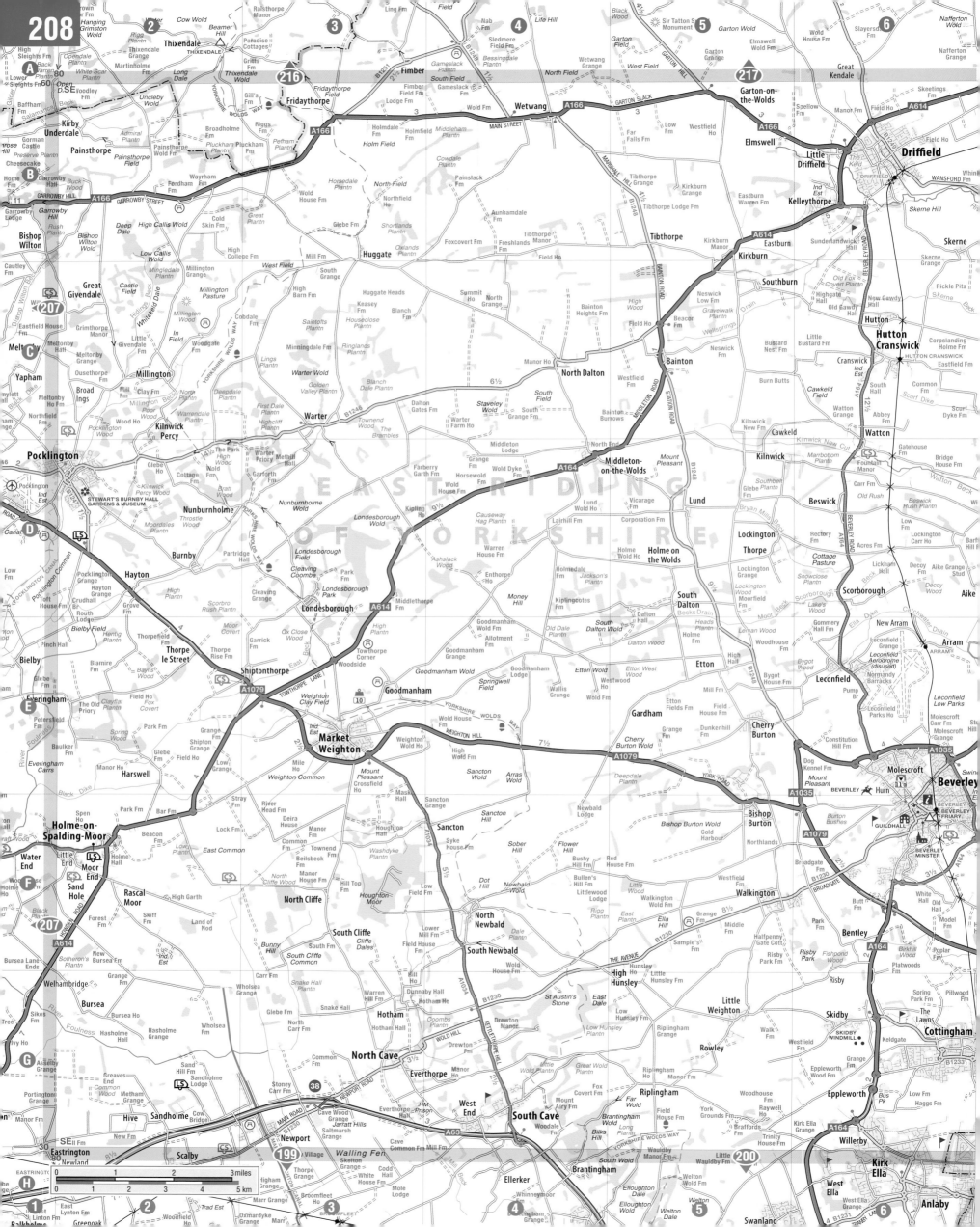

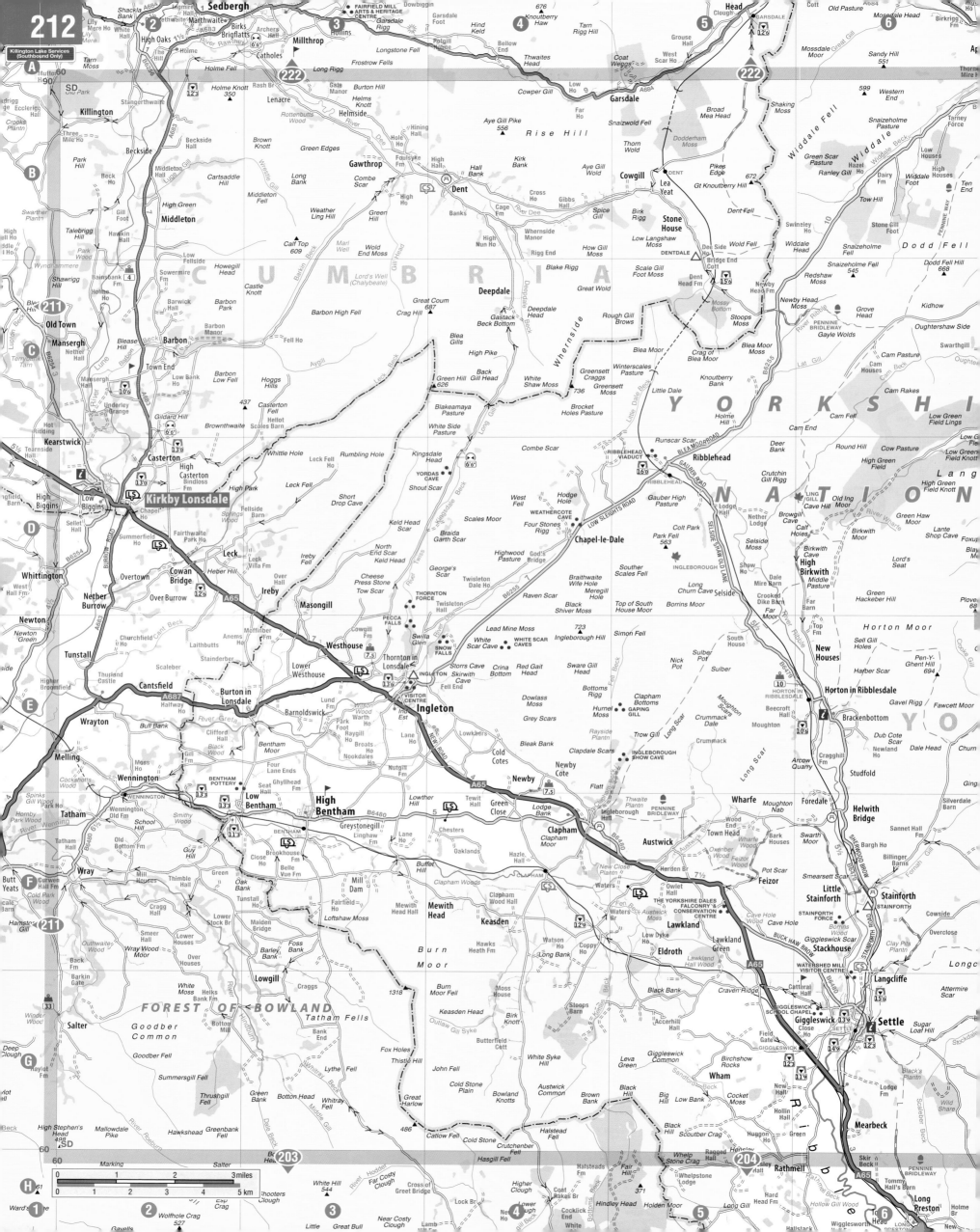

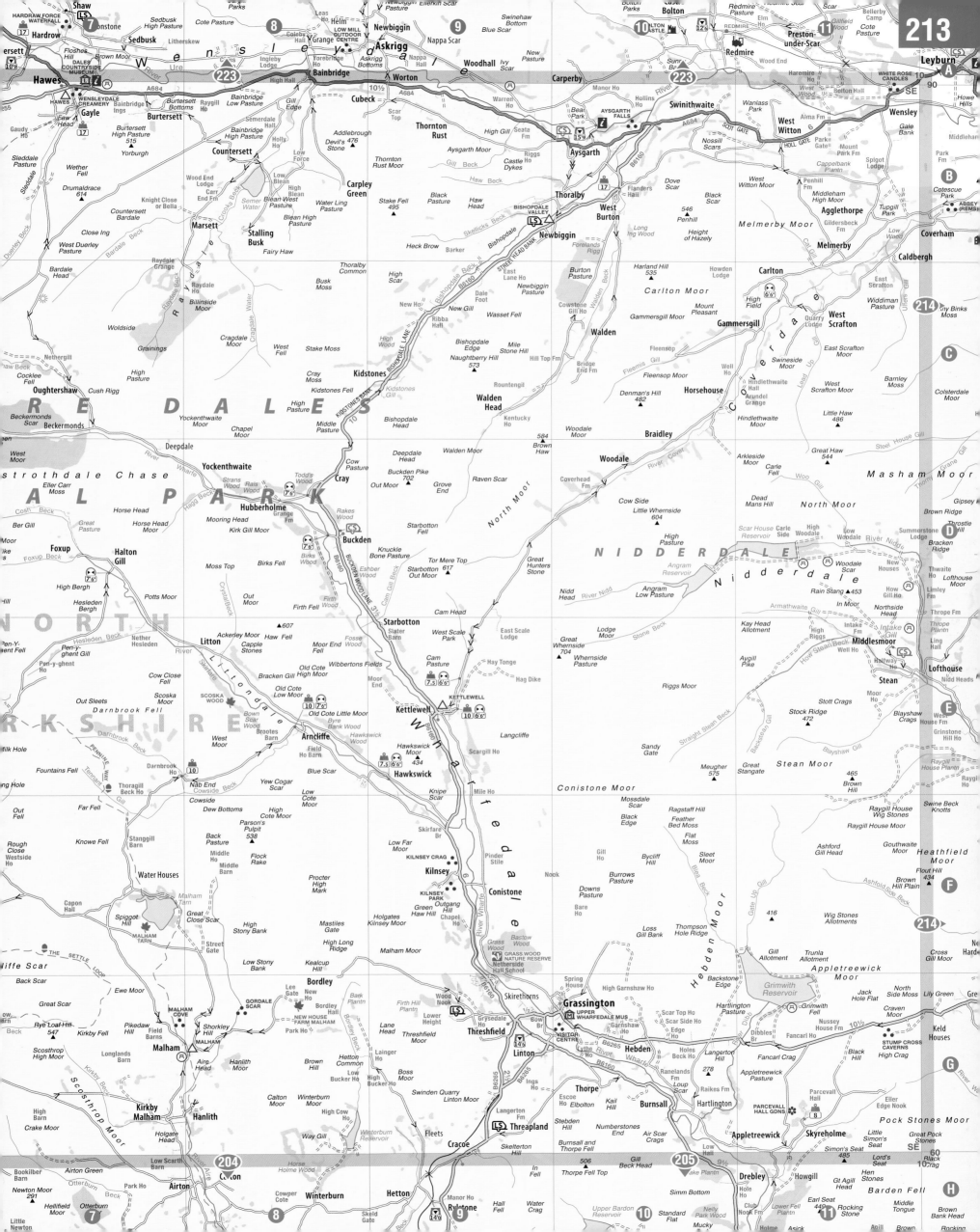

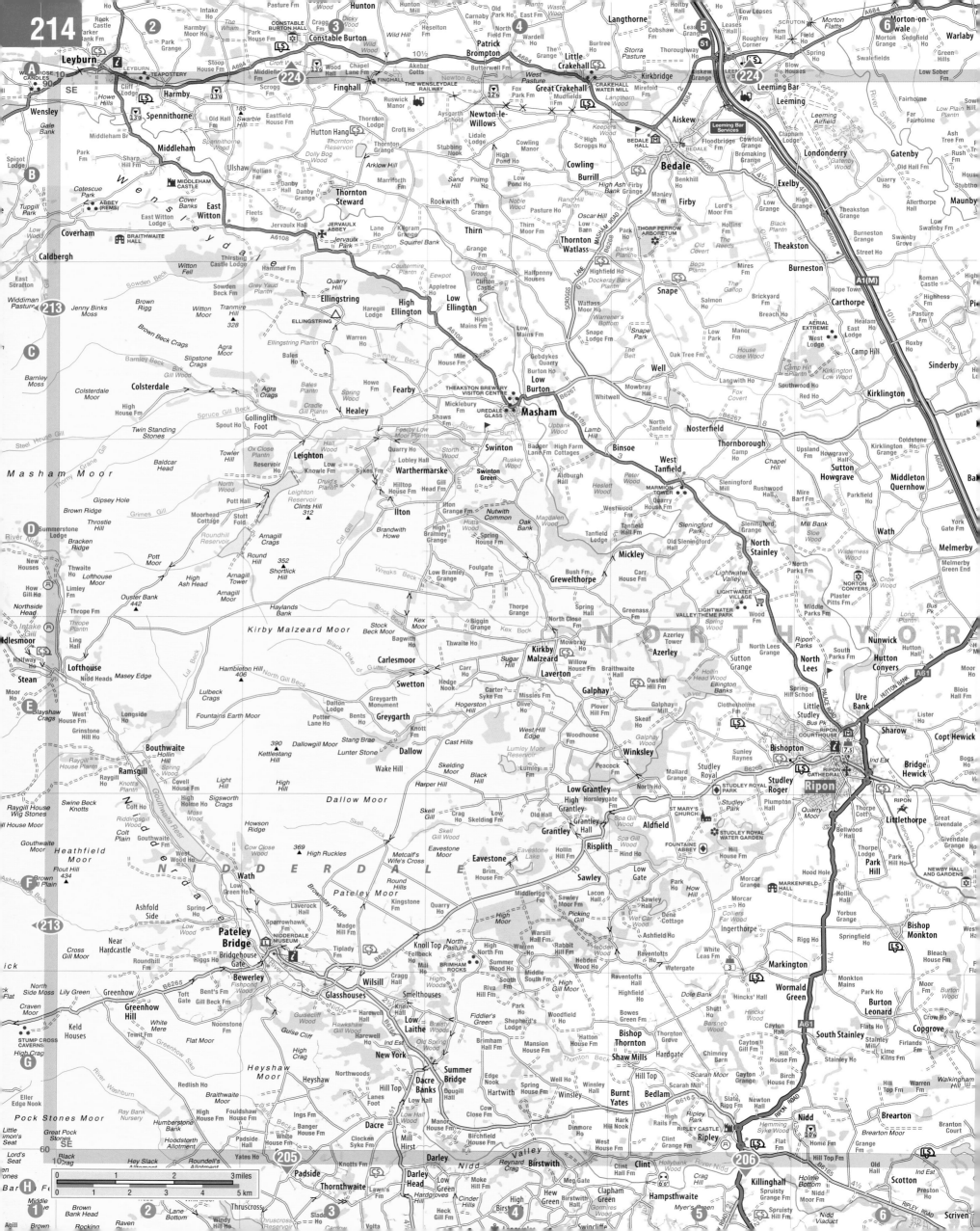

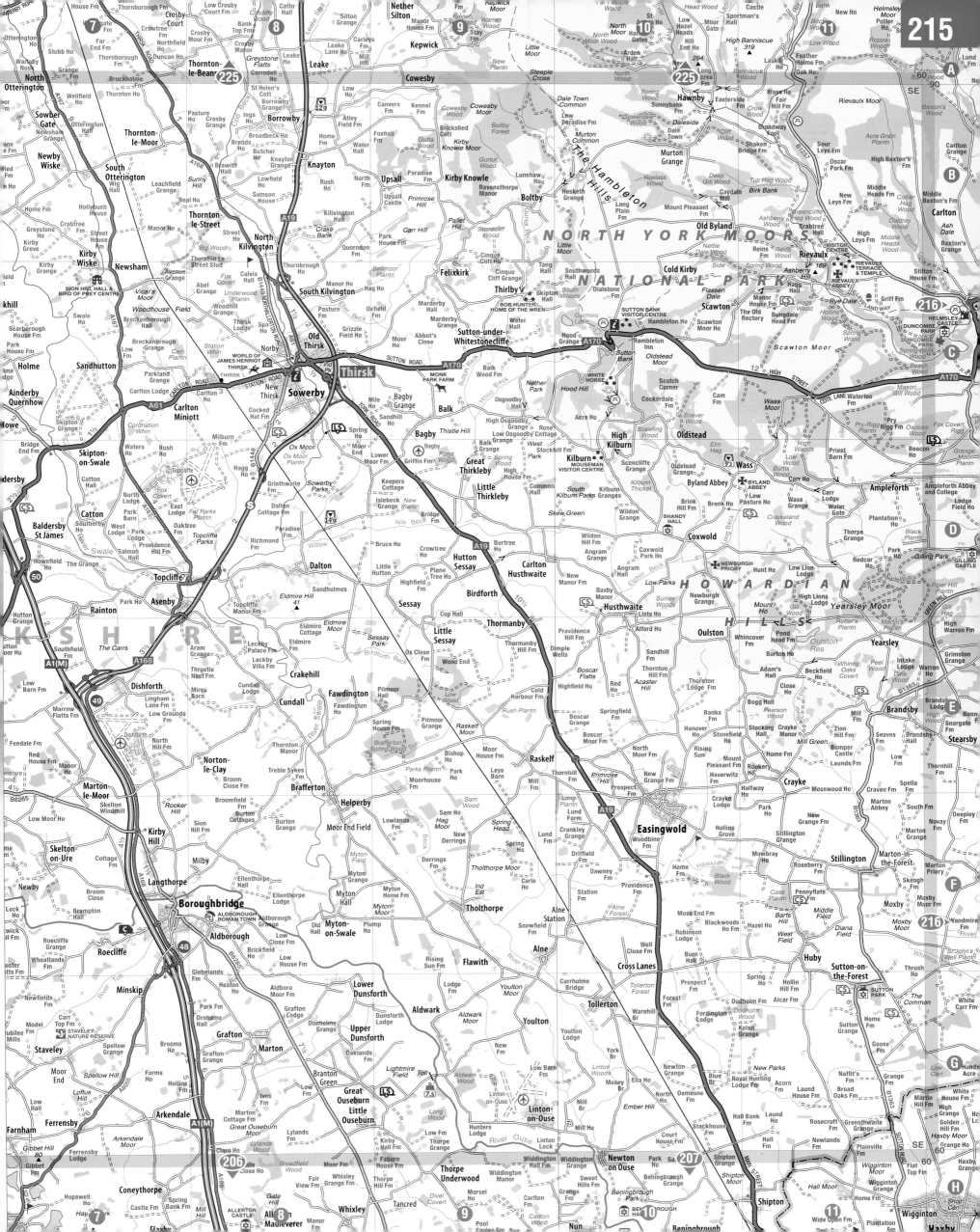

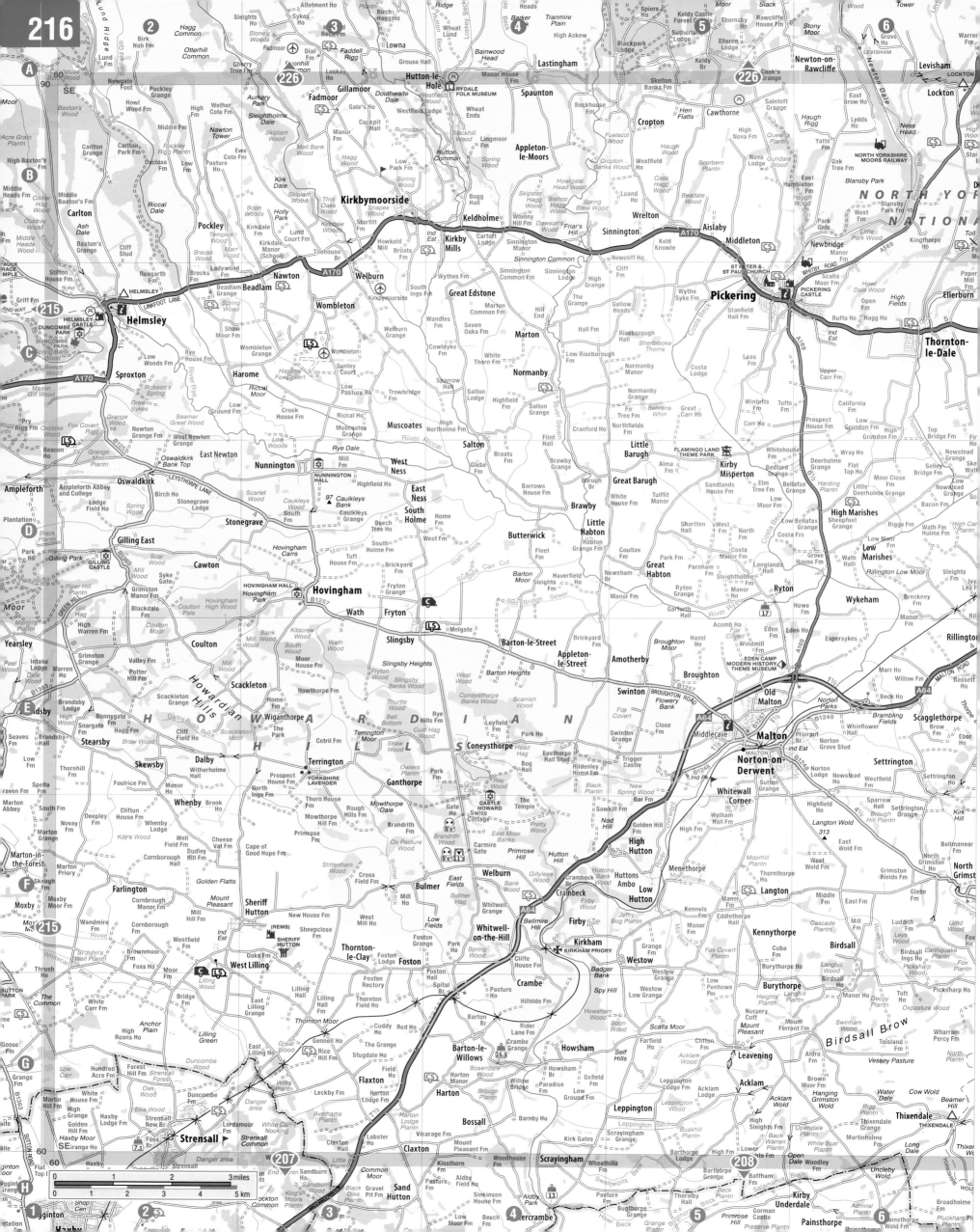

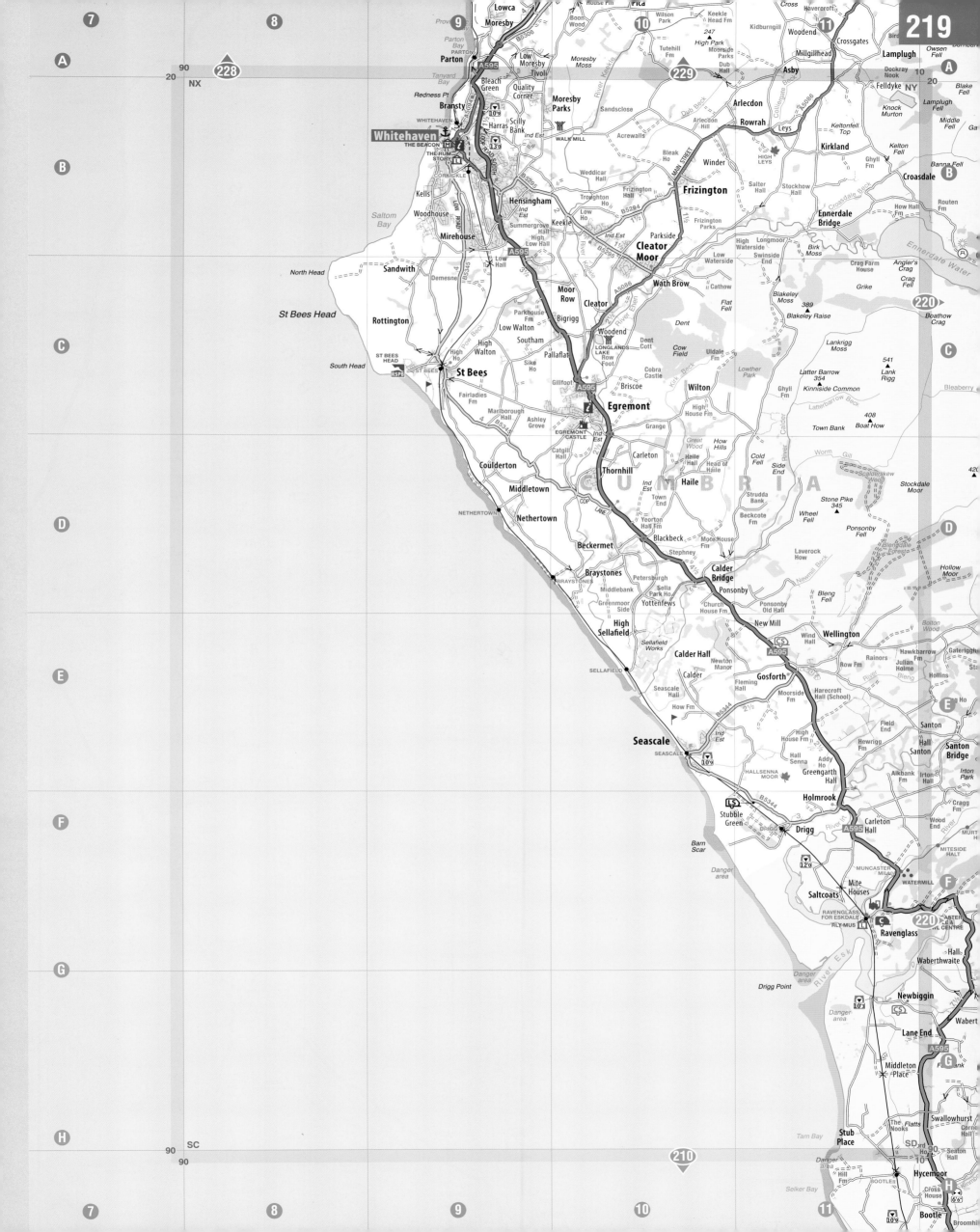

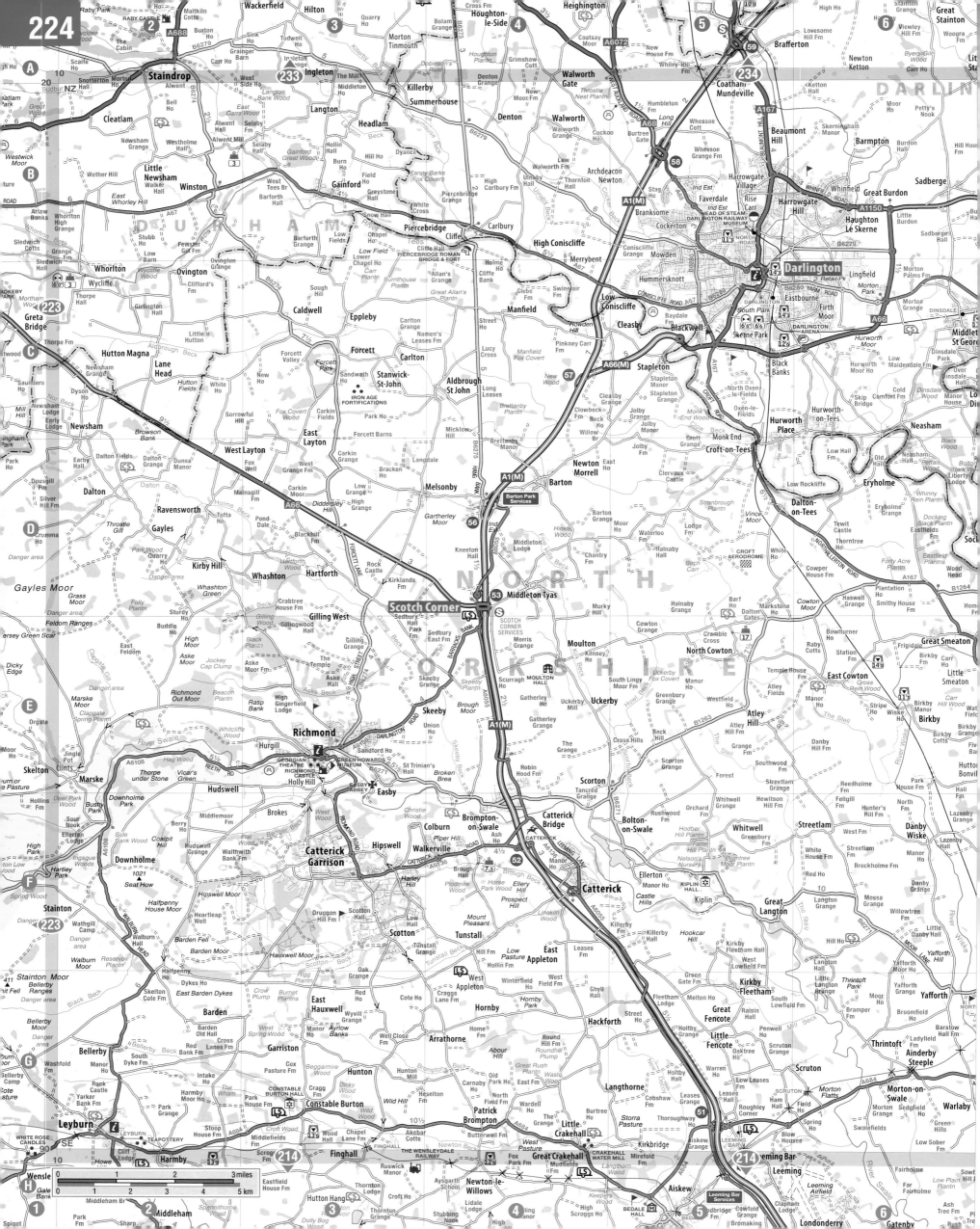

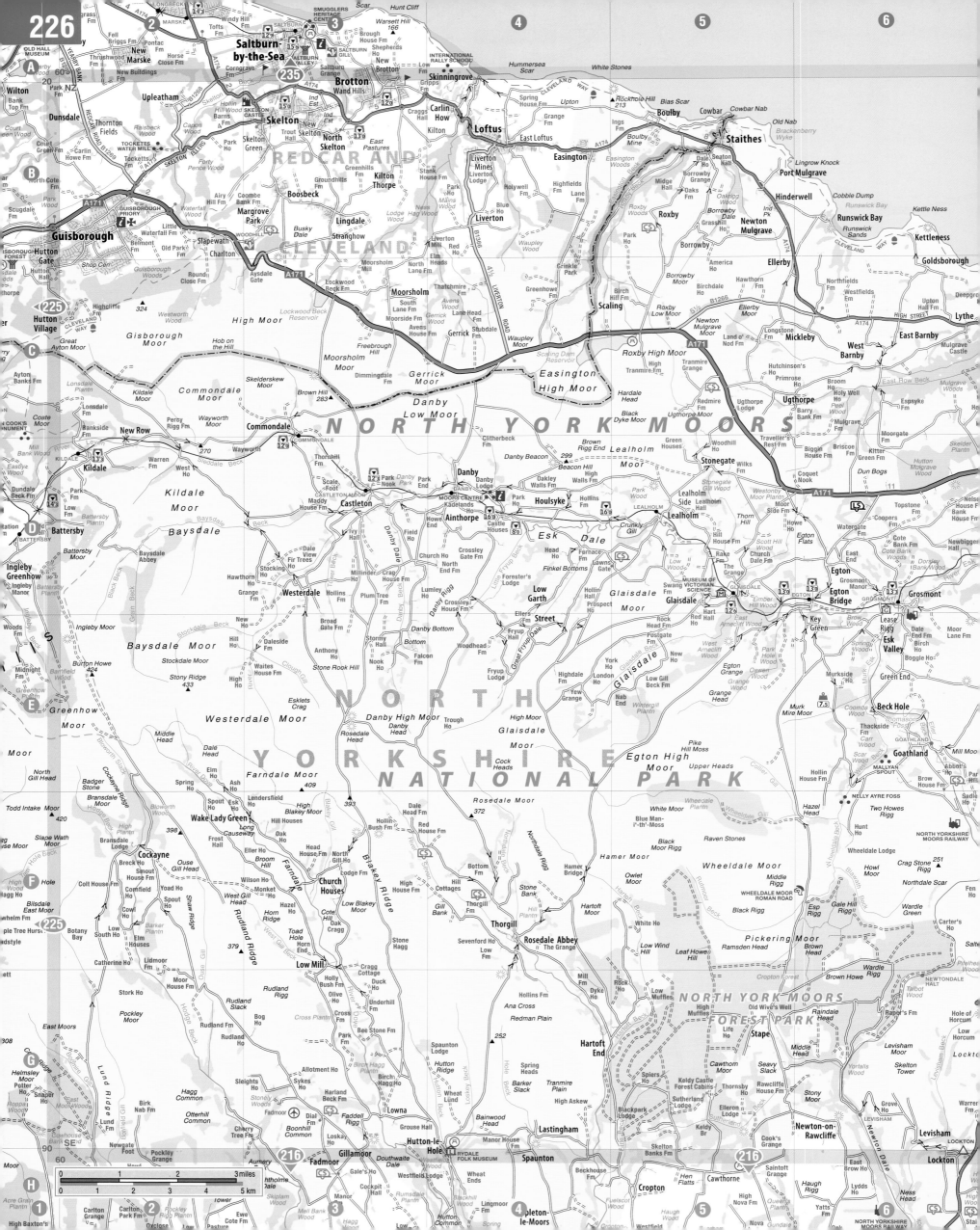

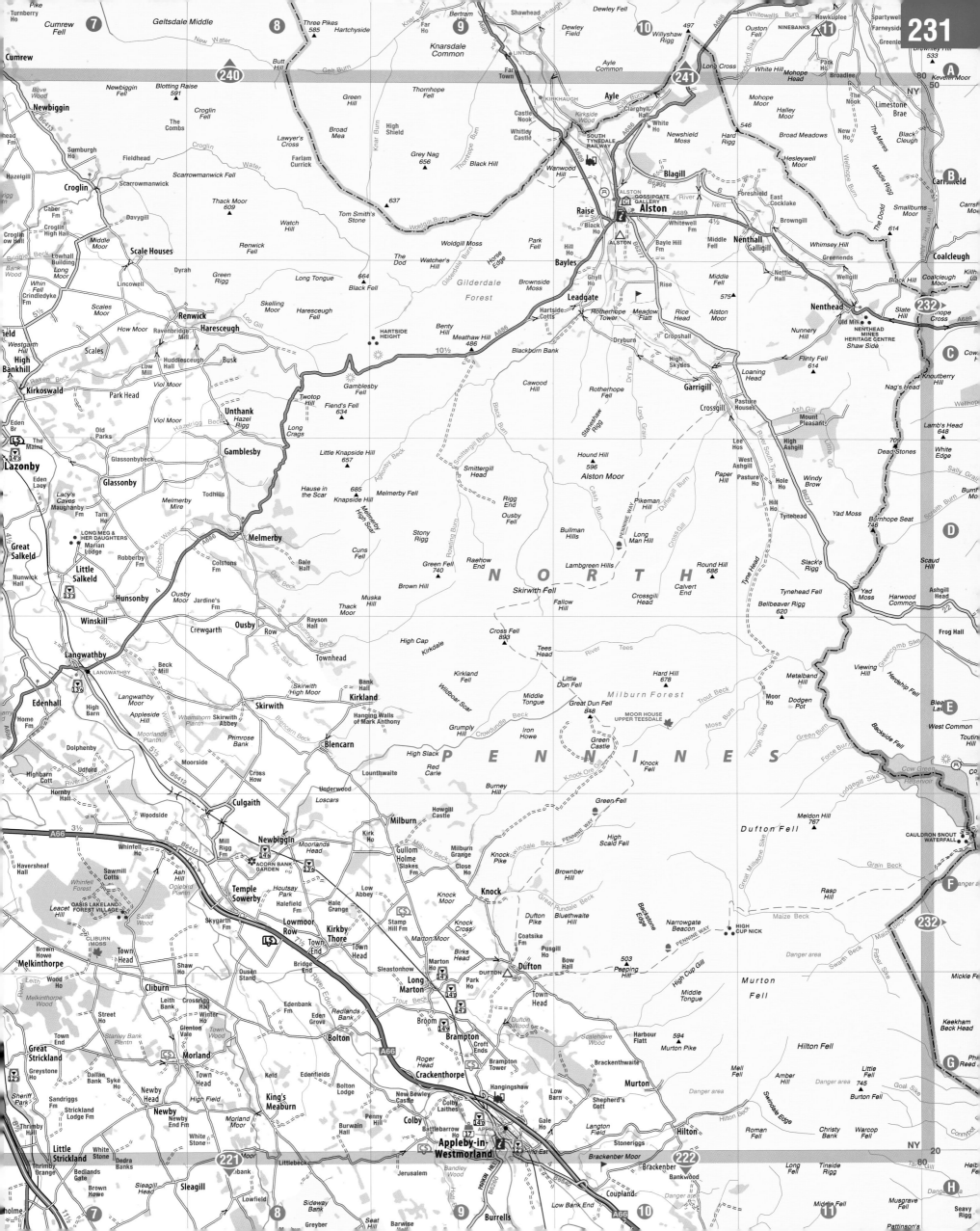

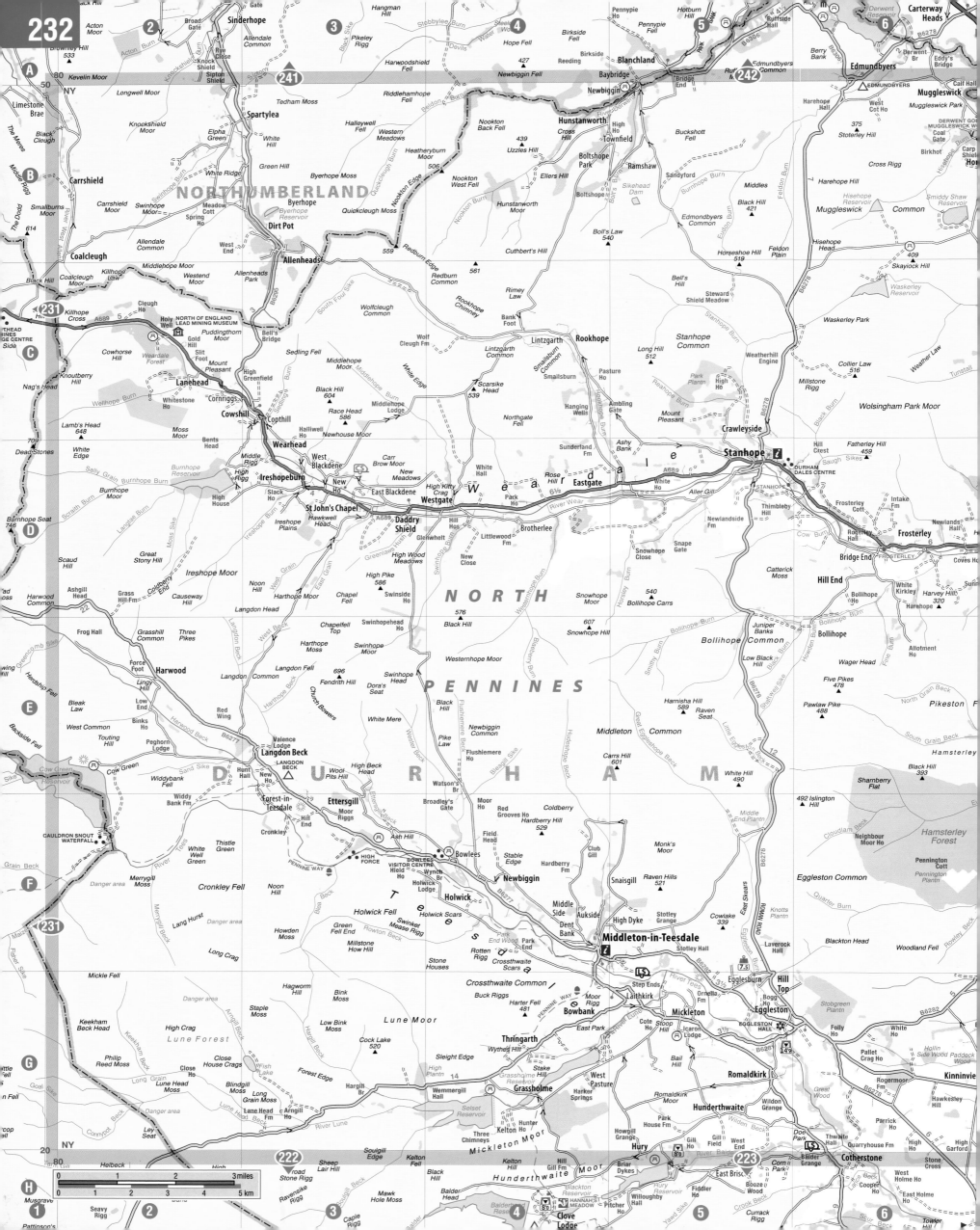

NORTH SEA

TEES BAY

Redcar

Saltburn-by-the-Sea

Marske-by-the-Sea

Dormanstown

Coatham

Warrenby

Westfield

Kirkleatham

Yearby

New Marske

Lazenby

Wilton

Dunsdale

Upleatham

Skelton

Brotton

Skinningrove

Loftus

Staithes

Boulby

East Loftus

Carlin How

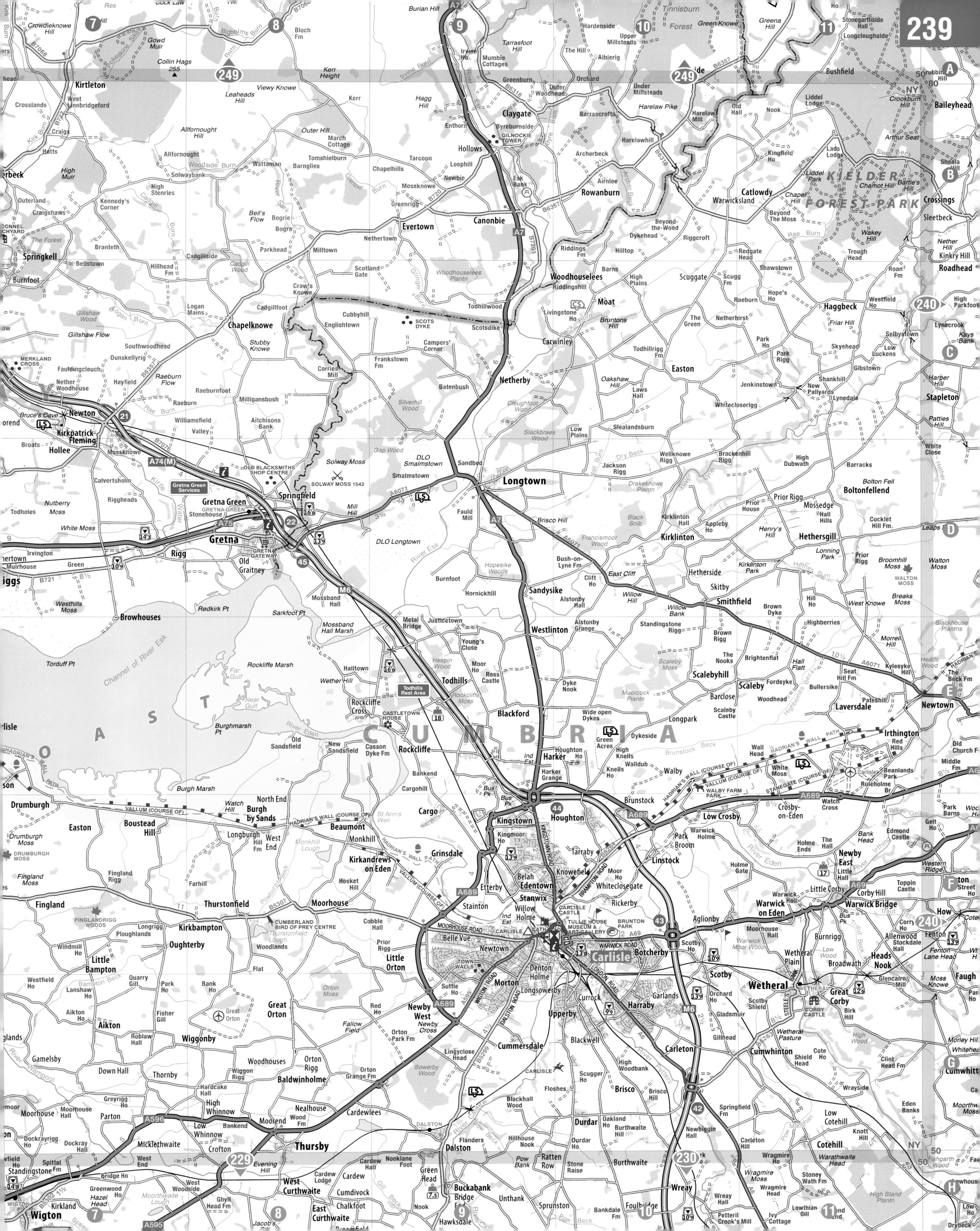
Kirtleton
Crowdieknowe Hill
Bloch Fm
Burian Hill
Tinnisburn Forest
Greena Hill
Stonegarthside Hall
Longcleughside
Collin Hags 255
Kerr Height
Mumbie Cottages
Tarrasfoot Hill
Hardenside
Upper Millsteads
Bushfield
Baileyhead
Crosslands
West Kirtlebridgeford
Allfornought Hill
Outer Hill
March Cottage
Claygate
Under Millsteads
Harelaw Pike
Liddel Lodge
Crookburn Hill
Craigs
Hollows
Gilnockie Tower
Byreburnside
Barrascrofts
Harelawhill
Arthur Seat
High Muir
Tomshielburn
Barnglies
Chapelhills
Tarcoon
Loophill
Archerbeck
Kingfield Ho
Lads Lodge
Sheala Hill
Kielder Forest Park
Newbie
Esk Bank
Rowanburn
Catlowdy
Warwicksland
Chapel Hill
Crossings
Sleetbeck
Outerland
Craigshaws
Kennedy's Corner
High Stenries
Greenrigg
Evertown
Canonbie
Beyond the Moss
Springkell
Branteth
Bellstown
Burnfoot
Parkhead
Milltown
Nethertown
Cadgillside
Riddings Fm
Hilltop
Dykehead
Riggcroft
Redgate Head
Shawstown
Trough Head
Kinkry Hill
Roadhead
Hillhead Fm
Scotland Gate
Woodhouselees Plantn
Woodhouselees
Riddingshill
High Plains
Scuggate
Raeburn
Hope's Ho
Haggbeck
Westfield Ho
High Parkfoot
Cadgillfoot
Chapelknowe
Cubbyhill
Englishtown
Scots Dyke
Todhillwood
Scotsdike
Moat
Livingstone Ho
Bruntons Hill
The Green
Netherhirst
Friar Hill
Lynecrook
Kays Bank
Gillshaw Flow
Southwoodhead
Dunskellyrig
Campers' Corner
Frankstown Fm
Carwinley
Todhillrigg Fm
Park Ho
Park Rigg
Skyehead
Low Luckens
Gibstown
Selbystown
Merkland Cross
Corries Mill
Batenbush
Netherby
Easton
Jenkinstown
Shankhill
New Pallyards
Lynedale
Stapleton
Harper Hill
Newton
Kirkpatrick-Fleming
Hollee
Raeburnfoot
Milligansbush
Silverhill Wood
Oakshaw Hill
Laws Hall
Whitecloserigg
Patties Hill
Aitchisons Bank
Cleughfoot Wood
Slealandsburn
Low Plains
Slackbraes Wood
White Close
Solway Moss
DLO Smalmstown
Smalmstown
Sandbed
Longtown
Jackson Rigg
Wellknowe Rigg
Brackenhill Rigg
High Dubwath
Barracks
Bolton Fell
Boltonfellend
Calvertsholm
Old Blacksmiths Shop Centre
Solway Moss 1542
Drakeknowe Plantn
Prior Rigg
Mossedge
Riggheads
Gretna Green Services
Gretna Green
Springfield
Mill Hill
Fauld Mill
Brisco Hill
Black Snib
Kirklinton Hall
Appleby Ho
Henry's Hill
Hethersgill
Cocklet Hill Fm
Leaps
Todholes
Nutberry Moss
White Moss
Gretna
Rigg
Gretna Gateway
DLO Longtown
Francismoor Wood
Kirklinton
Lonning Park
Prior Rigg
Broomhill Moss
Walton Moss
Irvington
Muirhouse
Old Graitney
River Esk
Hopesike Woods
Bush-on-Lyne Fm
East Cliff
Hetherside
Kirklinton Park
Westhills Moss
Browhouses
Redkirk Pt
Sarkfoot Pt
Mossband Hall
Burnfoot
Hornickhill
Sandysike
Cliff Ho
Skitby
Smithfield
Willow Hill
Willow Bank
Brown Dyke
Breaks Moss
West Knowe
Mossband Hall Marsh
Metal Bridge
Justicetown
Westlinton
Alstonby Grange
Standingstone Rigg
Highberries
Blackhouse Plantns
Torduff Pt
Rockliffe Marsh
Channel of River Esk
Young's Close
Brown Rigg
Morrell Hill
Hespin Wood
The Nooks
Brightenflat
Hall Flatt
Kylesyke Hill
Halltown
Moor Ho
Ross Castle
Scaleby Moss
Wether Hill
Todhills Rest Area
Todhills
Scalebyhill
Seat Hill Fm
Scaleby
Fordsyke
Bullersike
The Beck Fm
Rockliffe Cross
Castletown House
Dyke Nook
Moorcock Plantn
Barclose
Woodhead
Pateshill
Laversdale
Newtown
Blackford
Wide open Dykes
Scaleby Castle
Longpark
Irthington
Burghmarsh Pt
Old Sandsfield
New Sandsfield
Casson Dyke Fm
Rockcliffe
Cumbria
Green Acres
Dykeside
Brunstock Beck
Wall Head
Red Hills
Old Church Fm
Houghton Ho
Harker
High Knells
Hadrian's Wall (course of)
White Moss
Middle Fm
Drumburgh
Burgh Marsh
Watch Hill
North End
Burgh by Sands
Bankend
Cargohill
Harker Grange
Walldub
Walby
Vallum (course of)
Walby Farm Park
Carlisle
Beanlands Park
Ruleholme Br
Stanegate (course of)
Easton
Boustead Hill
Beaumont
St Ann's Well
Cargo
Kingstown
Houghton
Brunstock
Crosby-on-Eden
Watch Close
Low Crosby
Park Barns
Drumburgh Moss
Longburgh
Hill Fm
West End
Monkhill
Monkhill Lough
Grinsdale
Kingmoor Ho
Tarraby
Park Broom
Warwick Holme
Holme Ends
The Hall
Bank Head
Edmond Castle
Newby East
Little Hill
Linstock
Holme Gate
Western Ridge
Finglandrigg Moss
Fingland Moss
Fingland Rigg
Farmhill
Kirkandrews on Eden
Hosket Hill
Etterby
Belah
Edentown
Knowefield
Moor Ho
Whiteclosegate
Little Corby
Corby Hill
Toppin Castle
Fingland
Thurstonfield
Moorhouse
Stainton
Stanwix
Willow Holme
Carlisle Castle
Rickerby
Warwick Hall
Warwick on Eden
Warwick Bridge
Finglandrigg Woods
Longrigg
Ploughlands
Kirkbampton
Cumberland Bird of Prey Centre
Thurstonfield Lough
Cobble Hall
Ind Est
Tullie House Museum & Art Gallery
Brunton Park
Aglionby
Moorhouse Hall
Allenwood
Fenton
Burnrigg
Windmill Ho
Little Bampton
Oughterby
Woodlands
Prior Rigg
Little Orton
Belle Vue
Newtown
Botcherby
Scotby Ho
Warwick Moor Wood
Wetheral Plain
Low Wood
Broadwath
Heads Nook
Stockdale Hall
Fenton Lane Head
Westfield Ho
Lanshaw Ho
Quarry Gill
Park Ho
Bank Ho
Flat
Orton Moss
Suttle Ho
Morton
Denton Holme
Longsowerby
Currock
Harraby
Garlands
Scotby
Wetheral
Glencairn Mill
Moss Knowe
Faugh
Aikton Ho
Aikton
Fisher Gill
Great Orton
Red Ho
Newby West
Newby Cross
Upperby
Orchard Ho
Gladsmuir
Scotby Shield
Great Corby
Corby Castle
Birk Hill
Roblaw Hall
Wiggonby
Fallow Field
Orton Park Fm
Cummersdale
Blackwell
Wetheral Pasture
Gillhead
Carleton
Cumwhinton
Shield Head
Cote Ho
High Wood
Morley Hill
Gamelsby
River Wampool
Down Hall
Thornby
Woodhouses
Wiggon Rigg
Orton Rigg
Baldwinholme
Orton Grange Fm
Lingyclose Head
Sowerby Wood
Carlisle
Scugger Ho
High Woodbank
Brisco
Brisco Hill
Clint Head Fm
Cumwhitton
Hardcake Hall
High Whinnow
Greyrigg Ho
Parton
Moorhouse Hall
Moorhouse
Nealhouse
Cardewlees
Blackhall Wood
Floshes
Wrayside
Eden Banks
Moorthwaite Moss
Dockrayrigg Ho
Dockray Hall
Low Whinnow
Bankend
Moorend
Wood Fm
Dalston
Oakland Ho
Burthwaite Hill
Durdar
Springfield Fm
Low Cotehill
Micklethwaite
Crofton
Thursby
Flanders
Hillhouse Nook
Durdar Ho
Newbiggin Hall
Carleton Ho
Knott Hill
Cotehill
Standingstone
Spittal Fm
West End
Evening Hill
Cardew Hall
Nooklane Foot
Green Head
Pow Bank
Ratten Row
Stone Raise
Burthwaite
Wragmire Ho
Warathwaite Head
Fishgarth Fm
Bridge Ho
West Woodside
Moorthwaite Lough
Cardew Lodge
Cardew
Buckabank
Bridge End
Unthank
Sprunston
Wreay
Wragmire Moss
Stoney Wath Fm
Wragmire Head
Wreay Hall
High Stand Plantn
Wigton
Kirkland
Greenwood Ho
Hazel Head
Ghyll Head Fm
West Curthwaite
Cumdivock
Chalkfoot
East Curthwaite
Hawksdale
Bankdale Fm
Foulbridge
Petteril Crook's Mill
Ivy Cottage
Lowthian Gill
Dryebeck
A7
A74(M)
A75
A6071
B7076
M6
A689
A69
A595
A596
A6
B5299
B5307
B6357
B6318
B721
B722
B7068
B5302
249
240
229
230

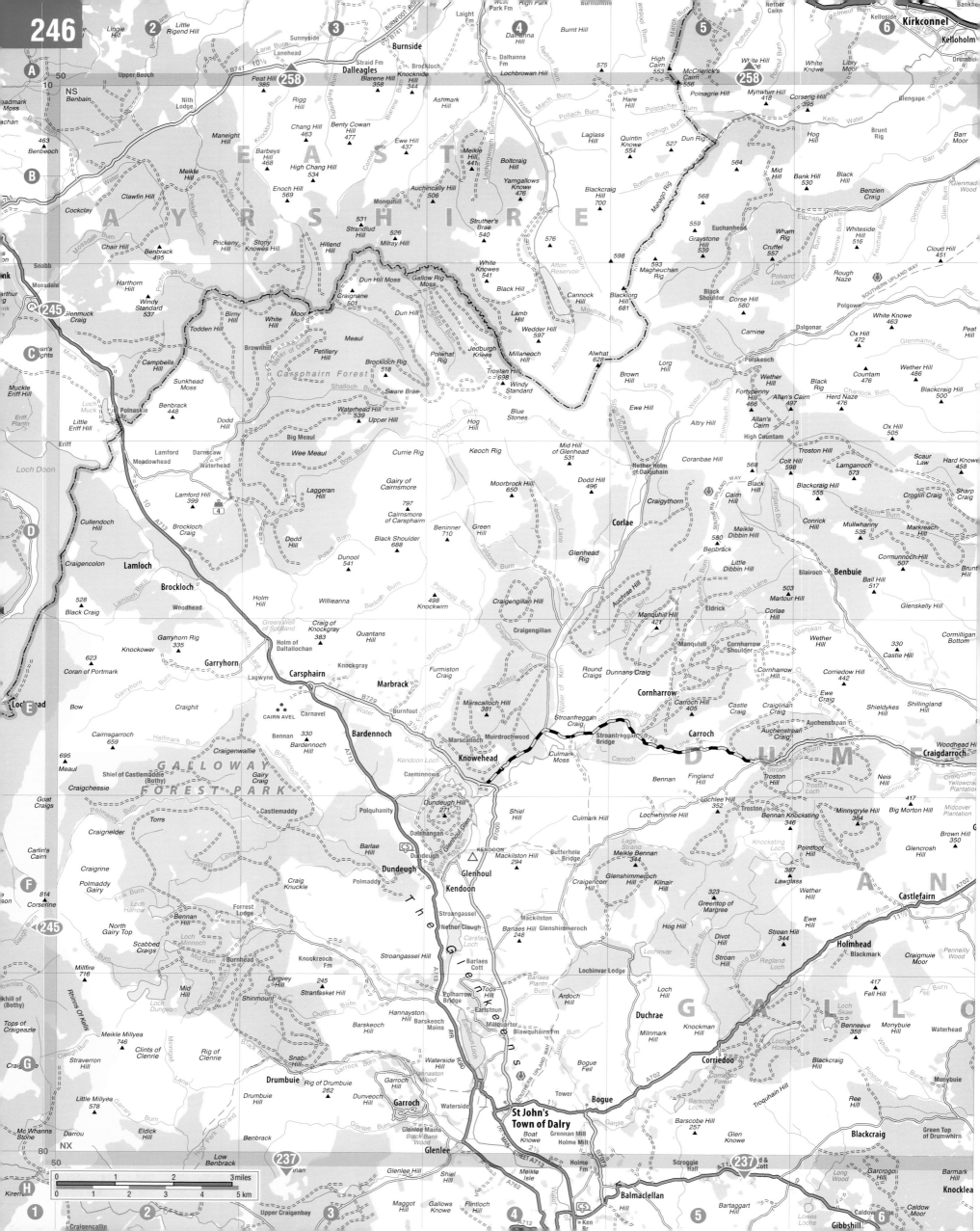

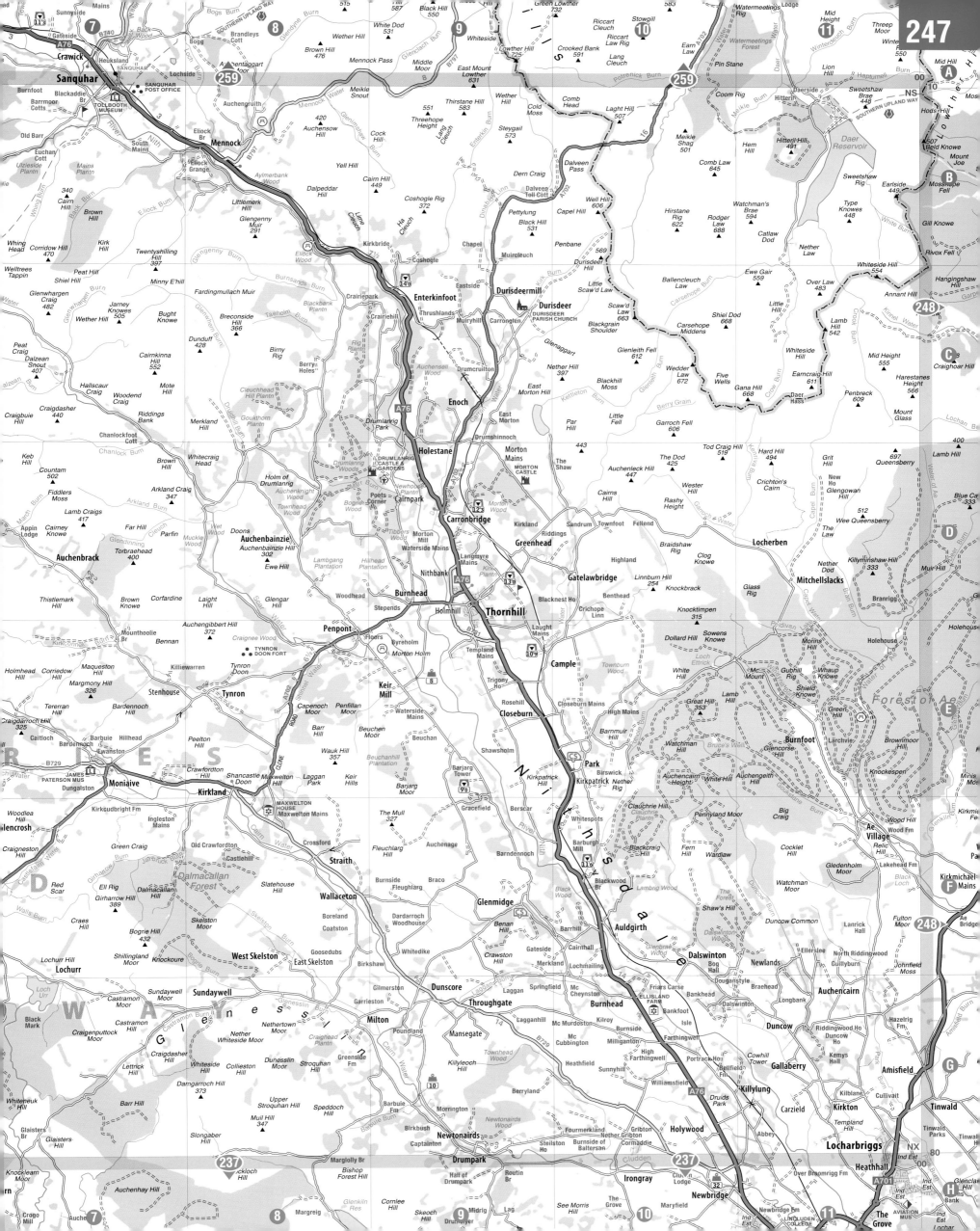

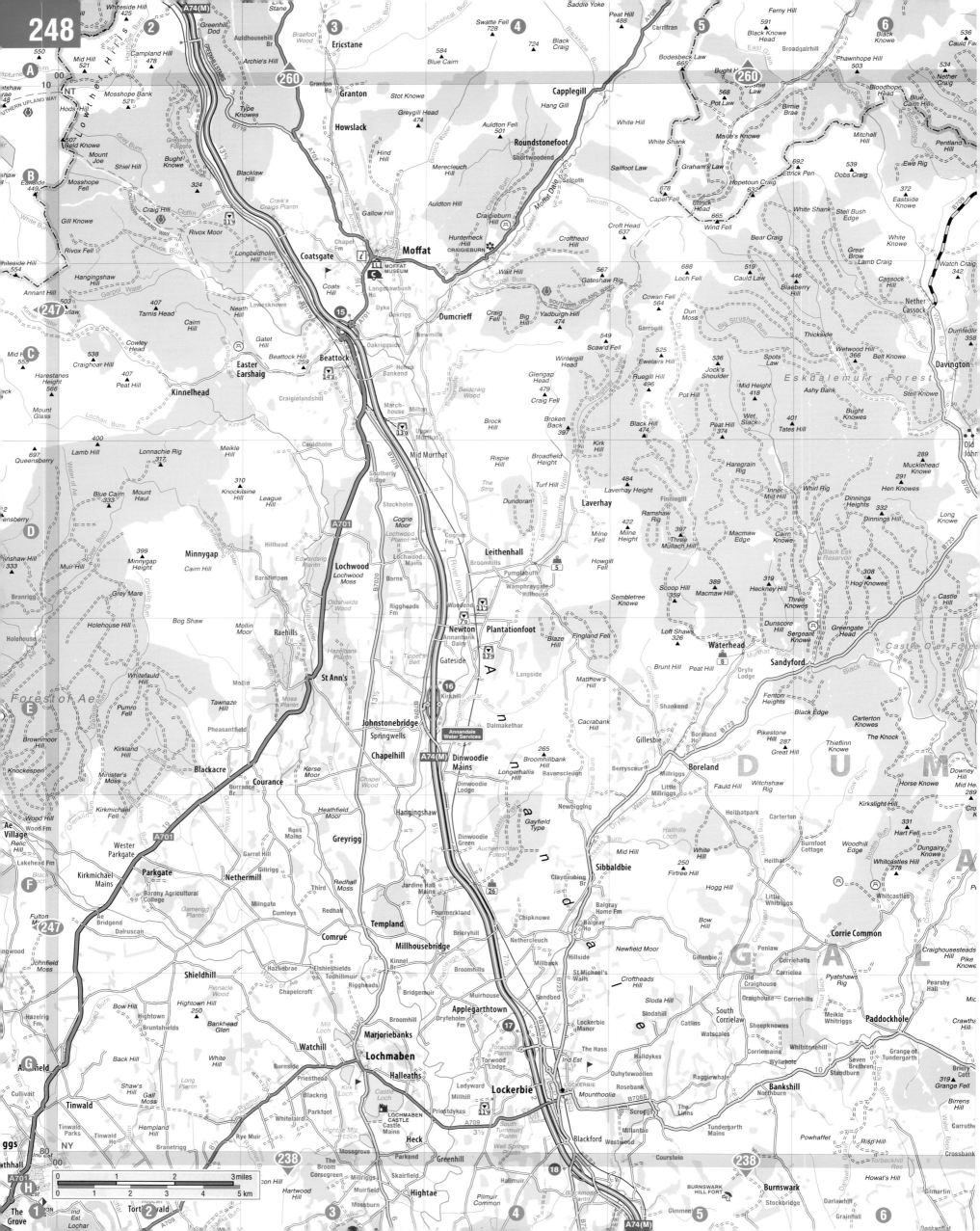

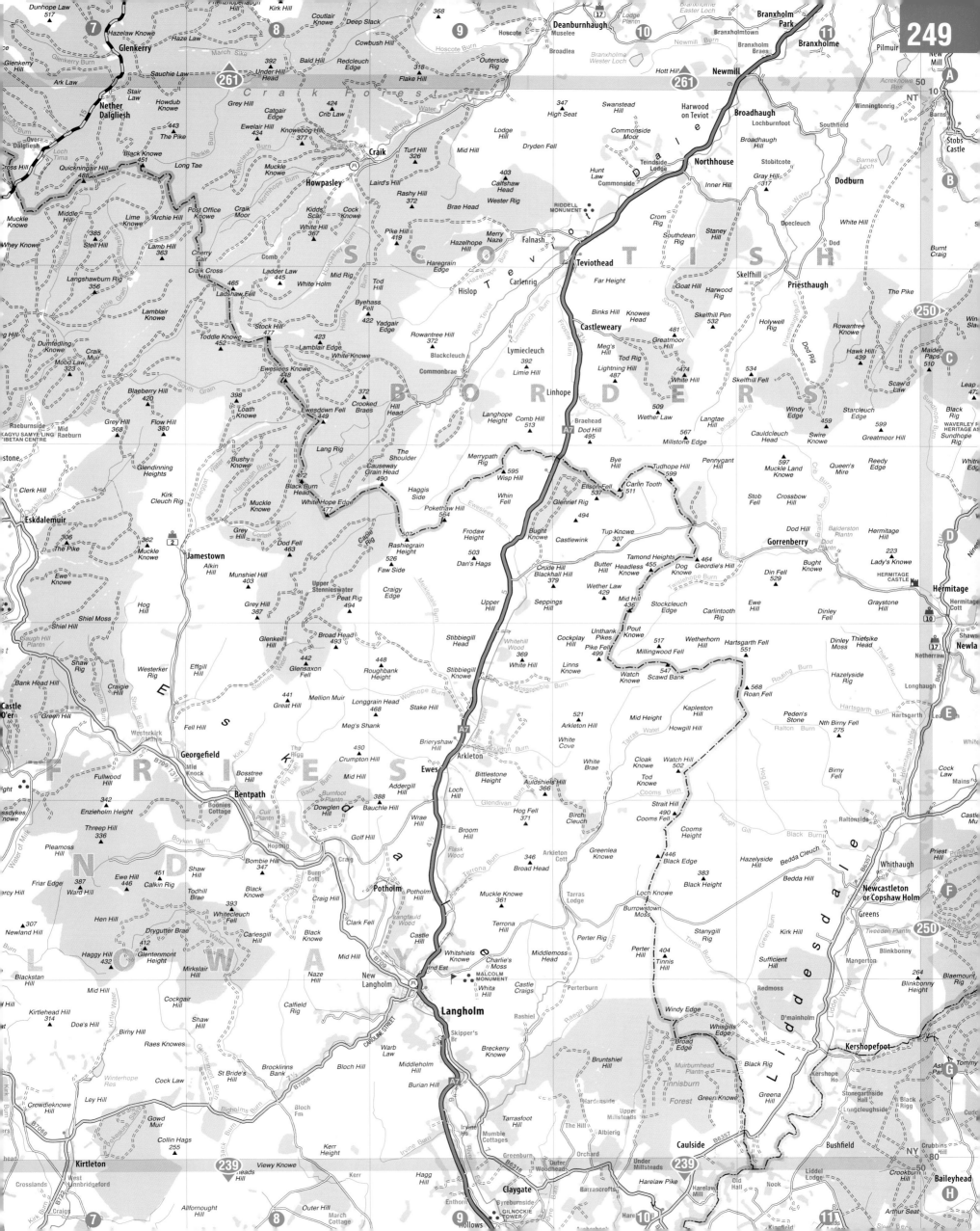

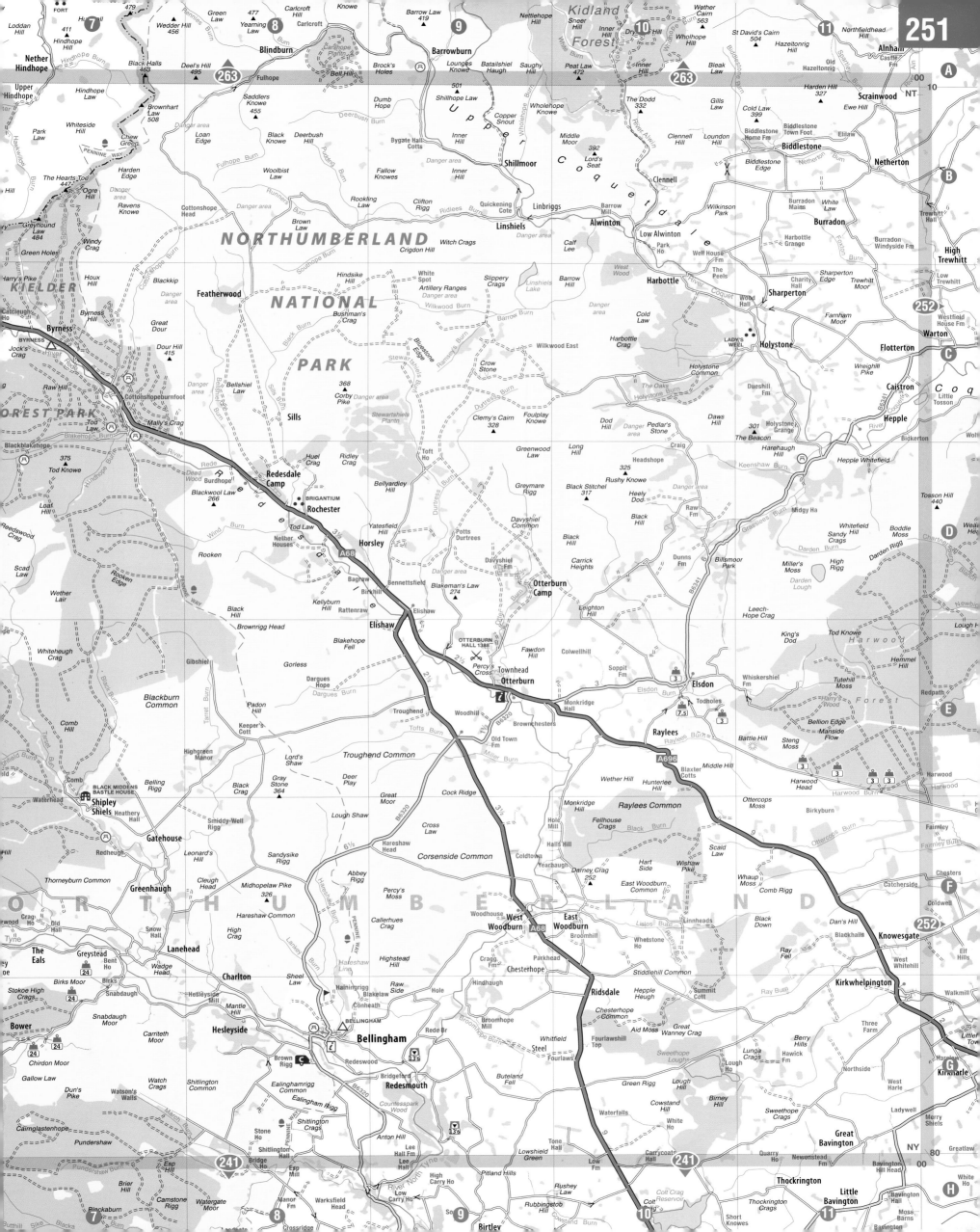

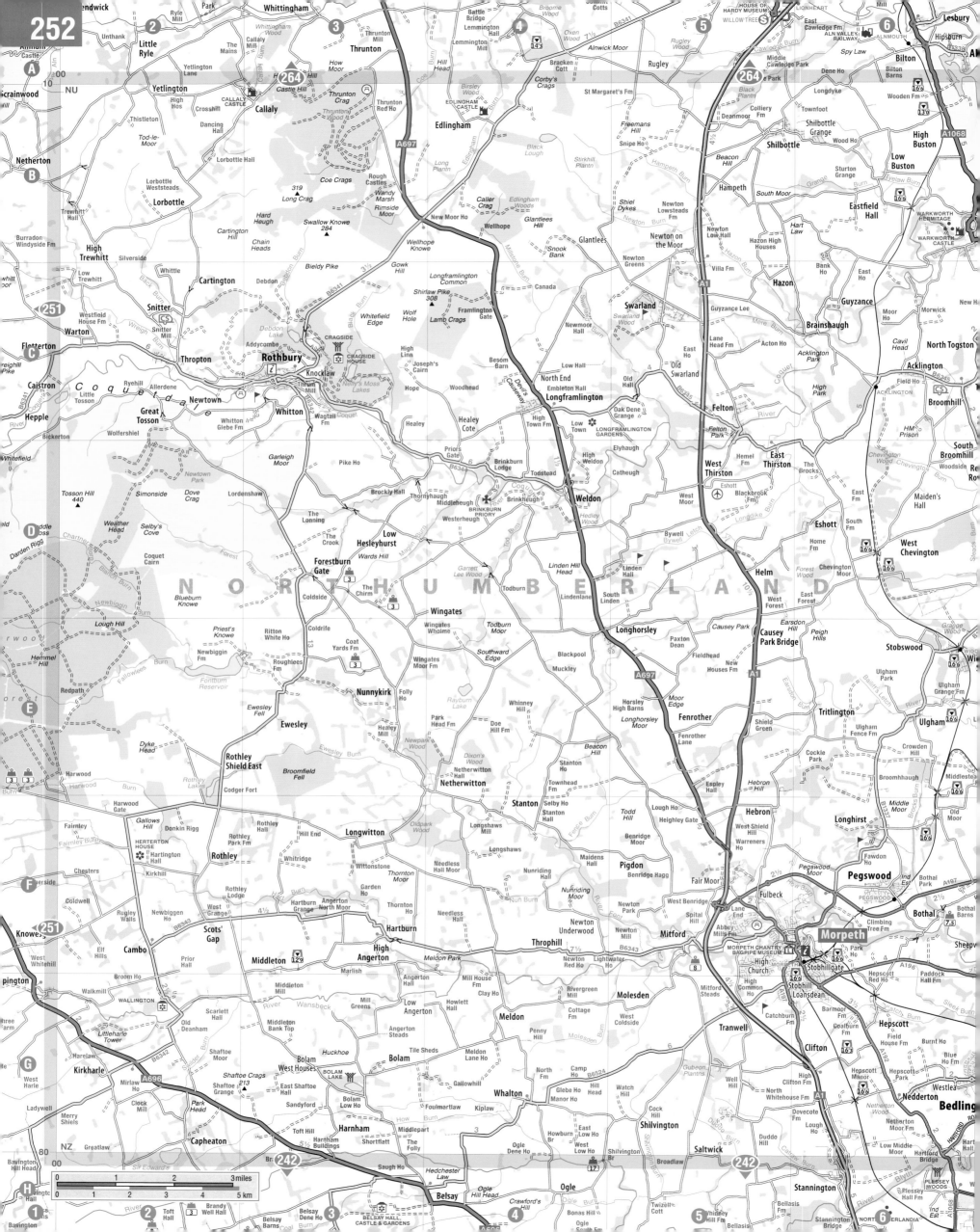

7 8 9 10 11

A

B

C

D

E

F

G

H

N O R T H

S E A

Marden Rocks

Alnmouth Bay

265   265   50
NU   10

Birling

Warkworth

Warkworth Harbour

Pan Pt   *Wellhaugh Pt*

Gloster Hill   *Coquet Island*

Amble   High Hauxley

Moorhouse Fm

Togston Hall   Low Hauxley   HAUXLEY

Radcliffe

Togston Barns

A1068   Togston East Fm

Togston

Danger area   *Ladyburn Lake*

Hadston   DRURIDGE BAY

Whitefield Ho   *Druridge Bay*

Chibburn Fm

High Chibburn

Widdrington

Hemscott Hill

A1068

RINGTON

ldrington Station   Highthorn   Cresswell

Warkworthlane Cott

North inton Fm   Hagg House

Ellington

Linton   Cresswell Home Fm

Lynemouth

East Moor Fm

Potland Fm

Works

QUEEN ELIZABETH II   Woodhorn

A189

WOODHORN COLLIERY MUS   WOODHORN CHURCH MUS

A1068   Bus Cen

Woodbridge

Ashington   Newbiggin-by-the-Sea

Hirst   *Newbiggin Bay*

North Seaton

Ind Est

WANSBECK   North Seaton Colliery

Stakeford   *Wansbeck*

West Sleekburn

STAKEFORD LANE

Guide Post   Bus Cen

Scotland Gate   Bomarsund   Cambois

Choppington   East Sleekburn

Bedlington Station   Mount Pleasant Fm   North Blyth

3

B1331   STEAD   A193

Bebside   Cowpen   Blyth

CHURCH LANE

Humford Mill   Isabella Pit

A189   ford   BEDLINGTON

NORTON ROAD

East Hartford   Newsh   243   South Beach

Low Horton Fm   SOUTH NE   243

West Hartford Fm   New Delaval   A1061   Gloucester Lodge Fm

Laverock Hall   South Newsham

Shankhouse   LAVEROCK HALL ROAD

NZ   80   50

7 8 9 10 11

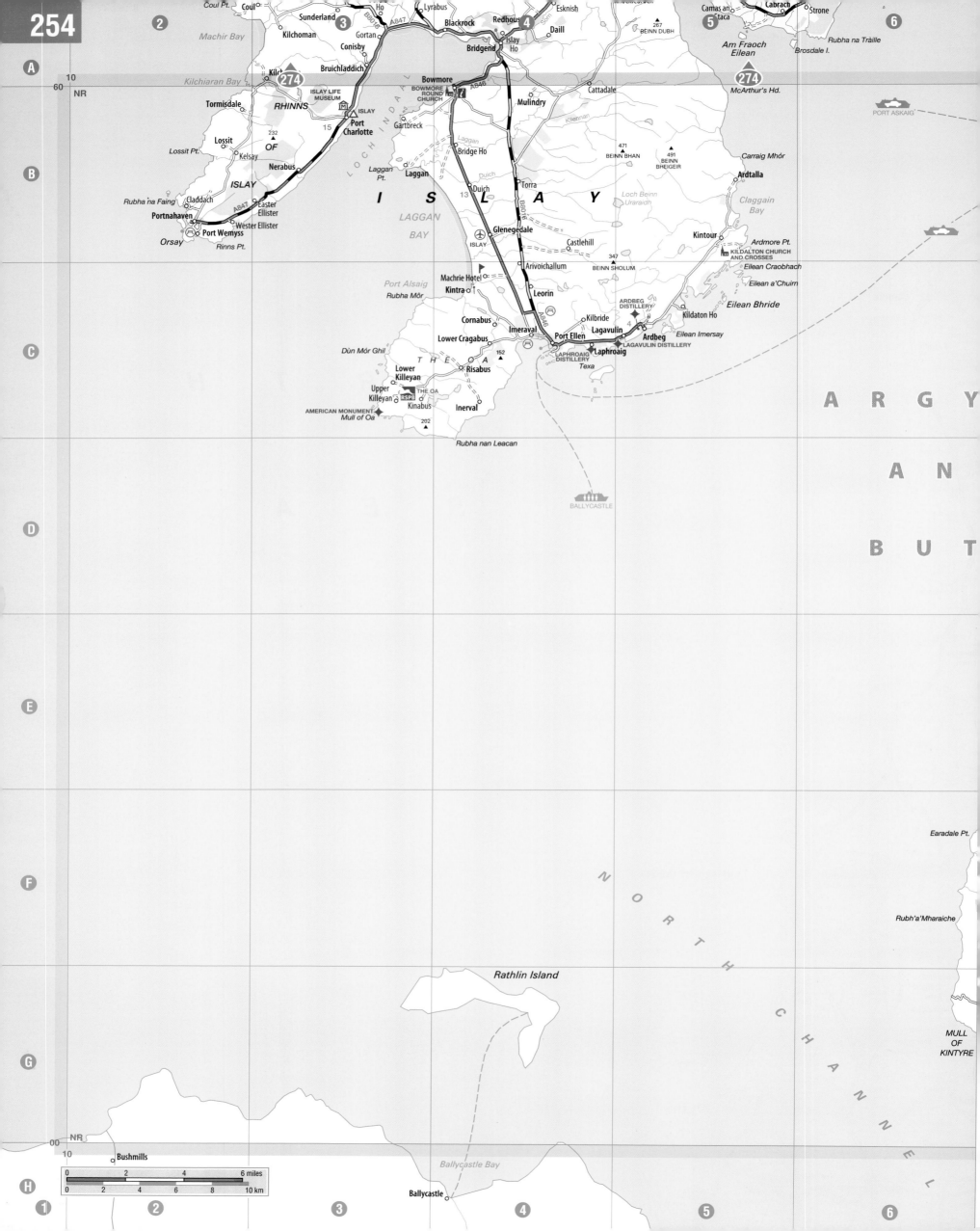

Čoul Pt. Coul
Sunderland
Kilchoman
Gortan
Conisby
Bruichladdich
Kilc
RHINNS
Tormisdale
ISLAY LIFE MUSEUM
ISLAY
Port Charlotte
Lossit
Lossit Pt.
Kelsay
Nerabus
ISLAY
OF
Rubha na Faing
Claddach
Easter Ellister
Portnahaven
Wester Ellister
Port Wemyss
Orsay
Rinns Pt.

Lyrabus
Blackrock
Redhous
Esknish
Bridgend
Islay Ho
Bowmore
BOWMORE ROUND CHURCH
Mulindry
Cattadale
McArthur's Hd.

Daill
BEINN DUBH
Camas an taca
Cabrach
Strone
Rubha na Tràille
Brosdale I.
Am Fraoch Eilean
PORT ASKAIG

Machir Bay
Kilchiaran Bay
10
60
NR

274
274

Bridge Ho
Laggan Pt.
Laggan
Duich
Torra
BEINN BHAN
BEINN BHEIGEIR
Carraig Mhór
Ardtalla
Claggain Bay
ISLAY
Duich
Glenegedale
Loch Beinn Uraraidh
Kintour
LAGGAN BAY
ISLAY
Castlehill
Arivoichallum
BEINN SHOLUM
KILDALTON CHURCH AND CROSSES
Ardmore Pt.
Machrie Hotel
Kintra
Leorin
Kilbride
ARDBEG DISTILLERY
Kildaton Ho
Eilean Craobhach
Eilean a'Chuirn
Eilean Bhride
Cornabus
Lower Cragabus
Imeraval
Port Ellen
Lagavulin
Ardbeg
LAGAVULIN DISTILLERY
Eilean Imersay
Dùn Mór Ghil
THE OA
Risabus
LAPHROAIG DISTILLERY
Laphroaig
Texa
Lower Killeyan
Upper Killeyan
RSPB
THE OA
Kinabus
Inerval
AMERICAN MONUMENT
Mull of Oa
Rubha Mòr
Port Alsaig

A R G Y
A N
B U T

BALLYCASTLE

Earadale Pt.

N O R T H   C H A N N E L

Rubh'a'Mharaiche

Rathlin Island

MULL OF KINTYRE

NR
00
10
Bushmills

Ballycastle Bay
Ballycastle

0		2		4		6 miles
0	2	4	6	8		10 km

Kilberry
SCULPTURED STONES
Torinturk
Rhu
Ardlamont Pt.
Rothesay
Ardroscadale
Upper Ardroscadale
Straad
Woodend Ho.
Kennacraig
CNOC
A'BHAILESHIOS
422
Rubha Leathan
Northpark
Midpark
Scalpsie
ISLAND
Carse Ho.
Dunmore
Redhouse
Kerry
Kerrylamont
Ardpatrick
Kilchamaig
Whitehouse
Inchmarnock
Loch Quien
MOUNT STUART HOUSE AND GARDEN
Ardpatrick Ho.
Portachoillan
Gartnagrenach
Glenreasdell Mains
Skipness
254
Ardscalpsie Pt.
Loch Fad
Piperhall
OF
Eilean Tráighe
Ronachan Pt.
Clachan
CRUACH NAM FIADH
SKIPNESS CASTLE
Skipness Pt.
Skipness Bay
Kingarth
BUTE
Ardpatrick Pt.
Ronachan Ho.
Claonaig
Claonaig Bay
Garroch Hd.
Kilchattan Bay
Eilean Garbh
West Tarbert Bay
Balochroy
Crossaig Glen
TARBET (Oct-Mar)
SOUND OF BUTE
ST BLANE'S CHAPEL
157
Loch Garasdale
Crossaig
(April-Oct)
Cock of Arran
Tarbert
Ardaily
Gigha Island
Ardminish
CRUACH MHIC GOUGAN
248
Cour
Catacol Bay
LOCHRANZA CASTLE
Lochranza
Millstone Pt.
Achamore Gardens
Rhunahaorine
Gortinanane
BEINN BHREAC
241
Cour Bay
Catacol
Fairhaven
ISLE OF ARRAN DISTILLERY
444
266
Gigalum I.
Tayinloan
CNOC NAN CRAOBH
322
Auchenbreck
Grogport
Whitefarland
570
MEALL NAN DAMH
NORTH
Cara Island
Killean
Braids
CRUACH MHIC-AN T-SAOIR
364
Thundergay
573
Sannox
14
Sannox Bay
Beacharr
Achaglass
CRUACH NAN GABHAR
364
Brackley
Pirnmill
Loch Tanna
859
Glen Sannox
ARRAN
Corrie
Muasdale
Rhonadale
Carradale
Port Righ
Imachar
721
BEINN BHARRAIN
798
CIR MHÒR
BEINN TARSUINN
825
874
GOAT FELL
ISLE
Corrie
NORTH
Glenacardoch Pt.
Amod
BEINN BHREAC
426
Bridgend
Waterfoot
Balliekine
Merkland
Belloch
Torrisdale-Square
Torrisdale Castle
Carradale Pt.
Dougarie
Glen Iorsa
Machrie Water
BRODICK
Glenrosa
OF
BRODICK CASTLE
Brodick Bay
AYRSHIRE
Glenbarr
CLAN MACALISTER CENTRE
Killegruer
BEINN AN TUIRC
454
Carradale Bay
228
Auchencar
Glen Rosa
ISLE OF ARRAN HERITAGE MUSEUM
Brodick
Strathwhillan
North Corriegills
Cleongart
Saddell Glen
Auchagallon
A'CHRUACH
512
Glenloig
Glen Cloy
South Corriegills
Bellochantuy
Bellochantuy Bay
SADDELL ABBEY
Saddell
Saddell Ho.
Machrie
ARRAN
Clauchlands Pt.
Killocraw
Corrylach
A'CHRUACH
341
Tormore
MACHRIE MOOR STANDING STONES
503
Blairbeg
Margnaheglish
Lamlash
Lamlash Bay
Holy Island
Kilpatrick
Westport
Kilchenzie
Skeroblingarry
SGREADAN HILL
397
Ugadale
KING'S CAVE
Balmichael
Cordon
CAMPBELTOWN (May-Sept Sat only)
Glenlussa Ho.
Kilkeddan
Black Bay
Shiskine
Birchburn
North Feorline
314
Tangy Loch
Tangy
Glenlussa
Peninver
Ardnacross Bay
Drumadoon Pt.
Torbeg
Blackwaterfoot
Drumadoon Bay
KILPATRICK DUN
TIGHVEIN
458
Auchencairn
Knockenkelly
Kingscross Pt.
Kingscross
West Darlochan
Kilmichael
CAMPBELTOWN
Drumore
CAMPBELTOWN HERITAGE CENTRE
Low Smerby
Corriecravie Moor
Glenree
Clachaig
Auchareoch
North Kiscadale
South Kiscadale
Whiting Bay
Machrihanish Bay
Machrihanish
Trodigal
Campbeltown
Campbeltown Loch
Island Davaar
DAVAAR ISLAND CAVE PAINTING
Corriecravie
Brown Hd.
CARN BAN
GLENASHDALE FALLS
Largymore
Largymeanoch
256
Ballygroggan
Drumlemble
Stewarton
Moy
BUCKHOUSE
Kilkerran
Kildalloig
ARDROSSAN (May-Sept)
BRODICK (May-Sept, Sat only)
Sliddery
Lagg
Largybeg
Dippin
High Tirfergus
Knocknaha
BEINN GHUILEAN
352
Achinhoan Hd.
Shannochie
Levencorroch
Dippin Head
385
THE SLATE
Lochorodale
Woodbank
BALLYCASTLE
TORRYLINN CAIRN
Kilmory
Bennan
244
446
CNOC MOY
Largiebaan
CNOC ODHAR
277
Feochaig
Johnston's Pt.
Bennan Hd.
Kildonan
Sound of Pladda
Strone
North Carrine
Keprigan
Knockstapplemore
Polliwilline
Pladda
Carskiey
Southend
Macharioch
Mill Park
Polliwilline Bay
Rubha Chlachan
Brunerican Bay
Cove Pt.
Sheep I.
123
Sanda Island
NS 00 10
338
Ailsa Craig

FIRTH

OF

CLYDE

Isle
of
Arran

NORTH
AYRSHIRE

Saltcoats

BRODICK
CAMPBELTOWN
(May-Sept only)

ARDROSSAN HARBOUR
NORTH AYRSHIRE TOWN
South Bay
NORTH AYRSHIRE MUSEUM
Outer Nebbock

Merkland
Glenshant Hill
Maol Donn 368
Glen Rosa
Creag Rosa
Torr Breac
Glenrosa
Glen Shurig
Merkland Wood
Merkland Pt
Port nam Balach
Cladach
Old Quay
BRODICK CASTLE
BRODICK
Wine Port
Port nam Balach
THE STRING
ISLE OF ARRAN HERITAGE MUSEUM
Brodick
Glen City
Glen Cloy
Gaoithe
Glen Ormidale
Sgiath Bhán
Strathwhillan
Corriegills Pt
North Corriegills
Fairy Glen
South Corriegills
Dun Dubh
Clauchland Hills
Clauchlands Fm
Clauchlands Pt
Kerr's Port
Hamilton Isle
Cnoc Dubh
Meall Buidhe
Cnoc Creac
Margnaheglish
Clauchlands
Blairbeg
Benlister Glen
Benlister Burn
Lamlash
Mullach Beag
Holy Island
The Ross ▲ 311
Monamore Br
Cordon
White Pt
CAMPBELTOWN
(May-Sept Sat only)
Monamore Glen
Gortonallister
314 ▲ Mullach Mor
Pillar Rock Pt
The Knowe Fm
Cnoc Dubh
Urie Loch
Auchencairn
Kingscross Pt
Knockenkelly
Kingscross
Sandbraes
Dhvein
Glas Choirein
Borrach
North Kiscadale
Cnoc Donn
Cnoc an Fheidh
Cnoc Mòr
South Kiscadale
Whiting Bay
GLENASHDALE FALLS
Glenashdale Burn
Auchareoch
Largymore
Torr bh Mòr
Kilmory Water
Cnoc na Garbad
Cnoc na Comhairle
Largymeanoch
Cnoc Craobhach
Largybeg
Largybeg Pt
Port na Gaillin
Torr a' Fannain
Margenaish Fm
Levencorroch Hill
Dippin Head
Dippin
Southbank
East Bennan
Levencorroch
Auchenhew
Drumla
Porta Leacach
West Bennan
Porta Buidhe
Kildonan
Port a'Ghillie Ghlais
Port Dearg
STRUEY ROCKS
Bennan Head
Sound of Pladda
Pladda

Dur
Broad Craig

CULZEAN CASTLE
Culzean Bay
Glasson Rock
Barwhin Pt
Maidenhead Bay
Morriston
Port Murray
Balvaird
Thoma
Birniehill
A719

NS
00
40
255
266
255
255
244
244
NS
00
10

0   1   2   3miles
0 1 2 3 4 5 km

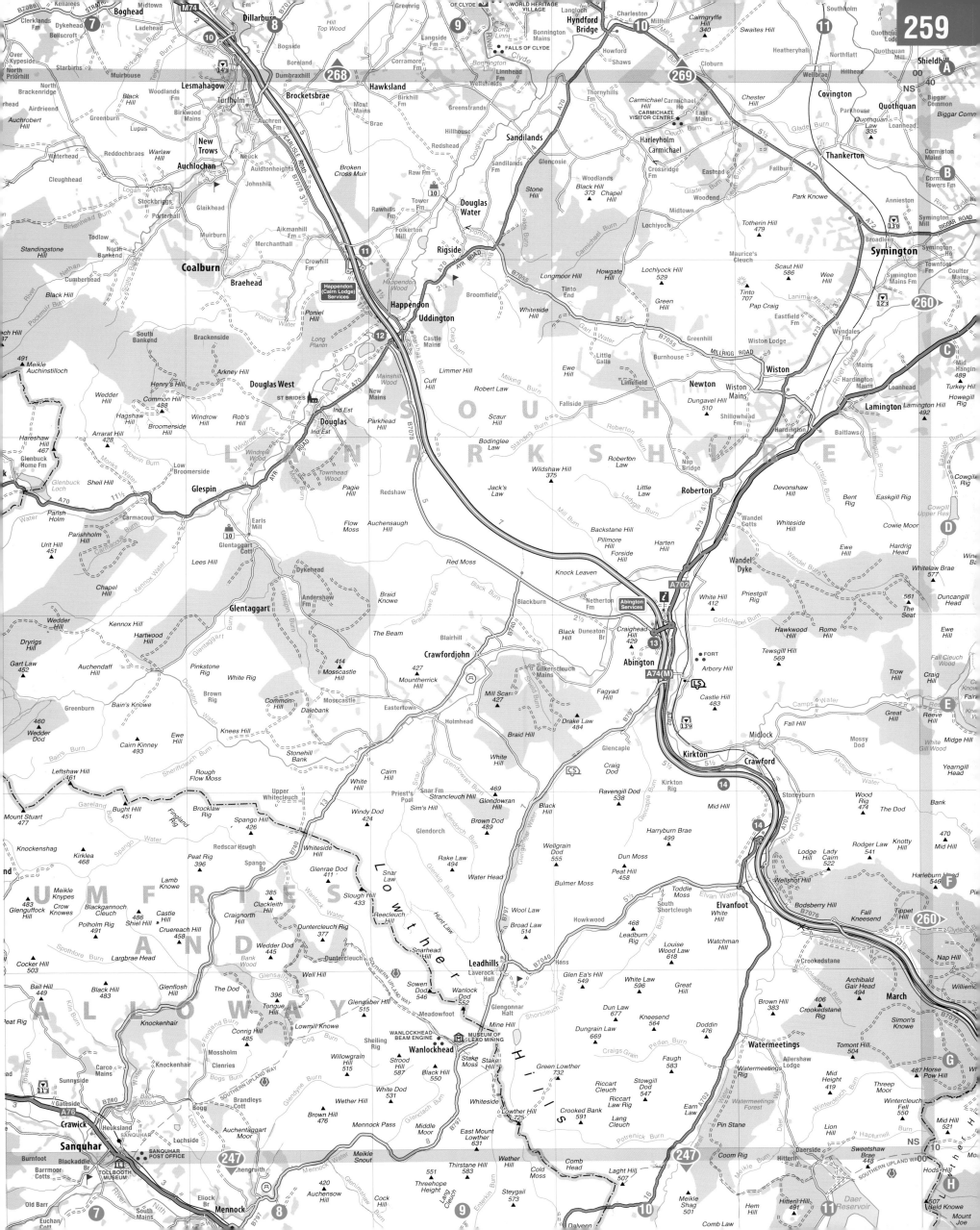

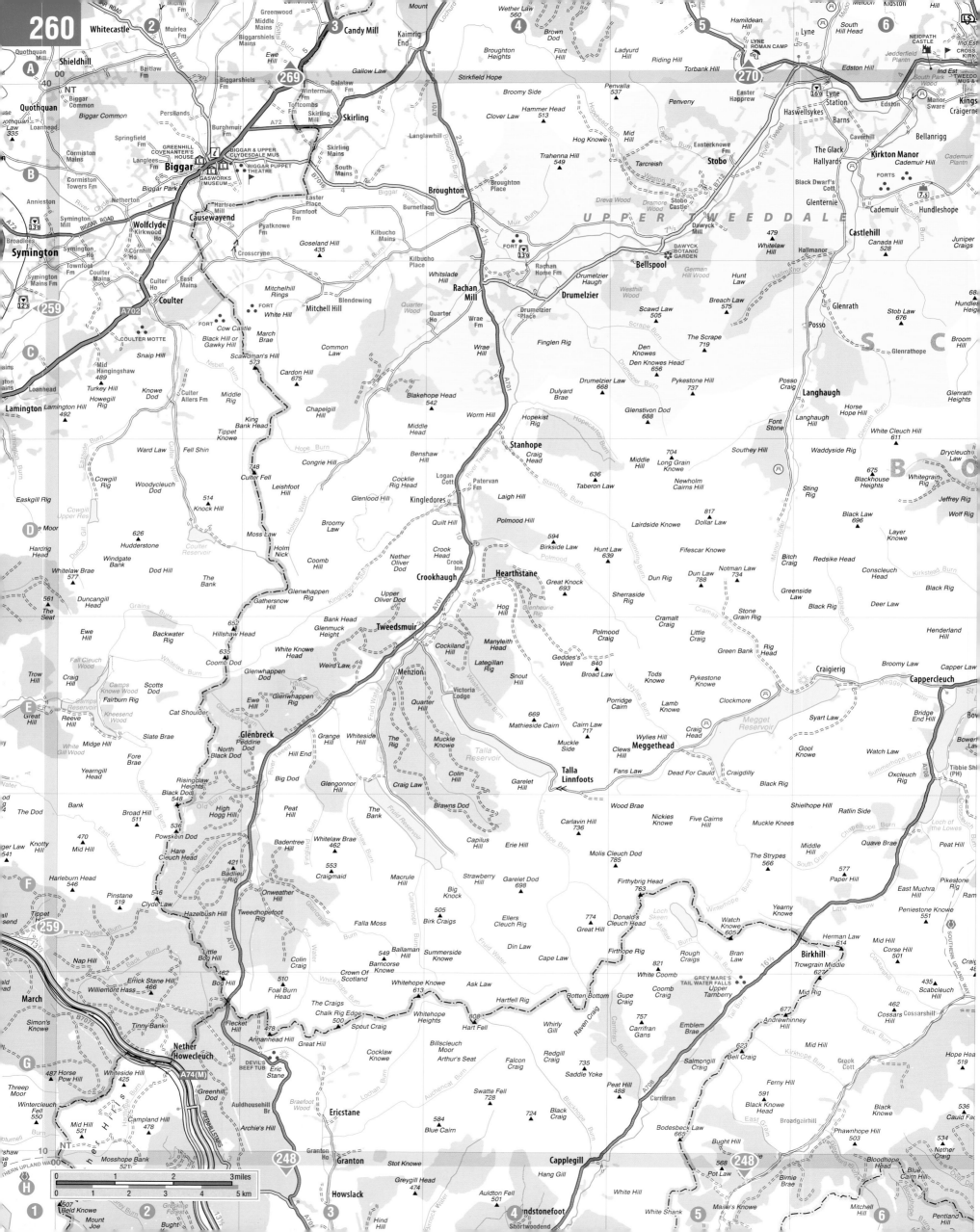

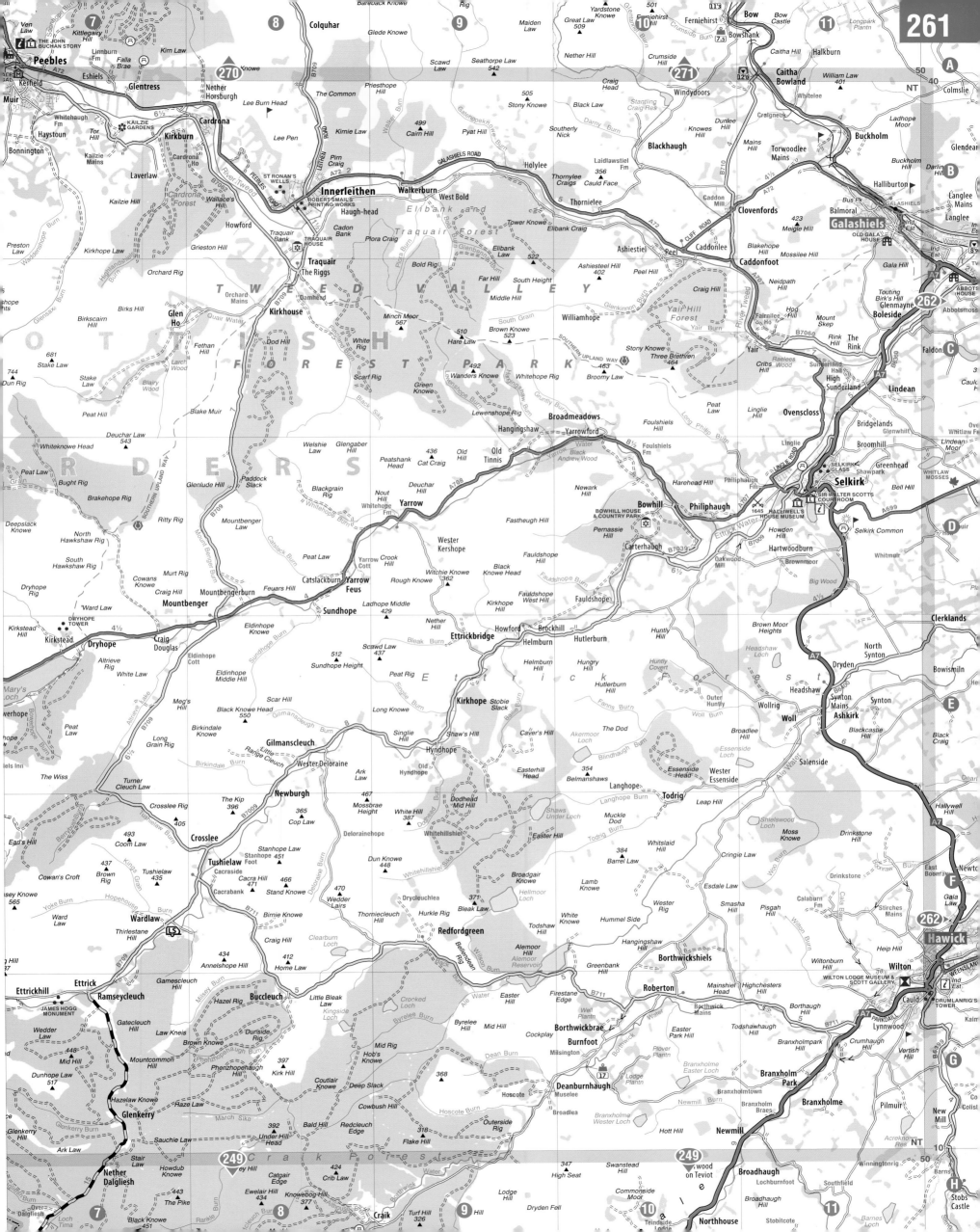

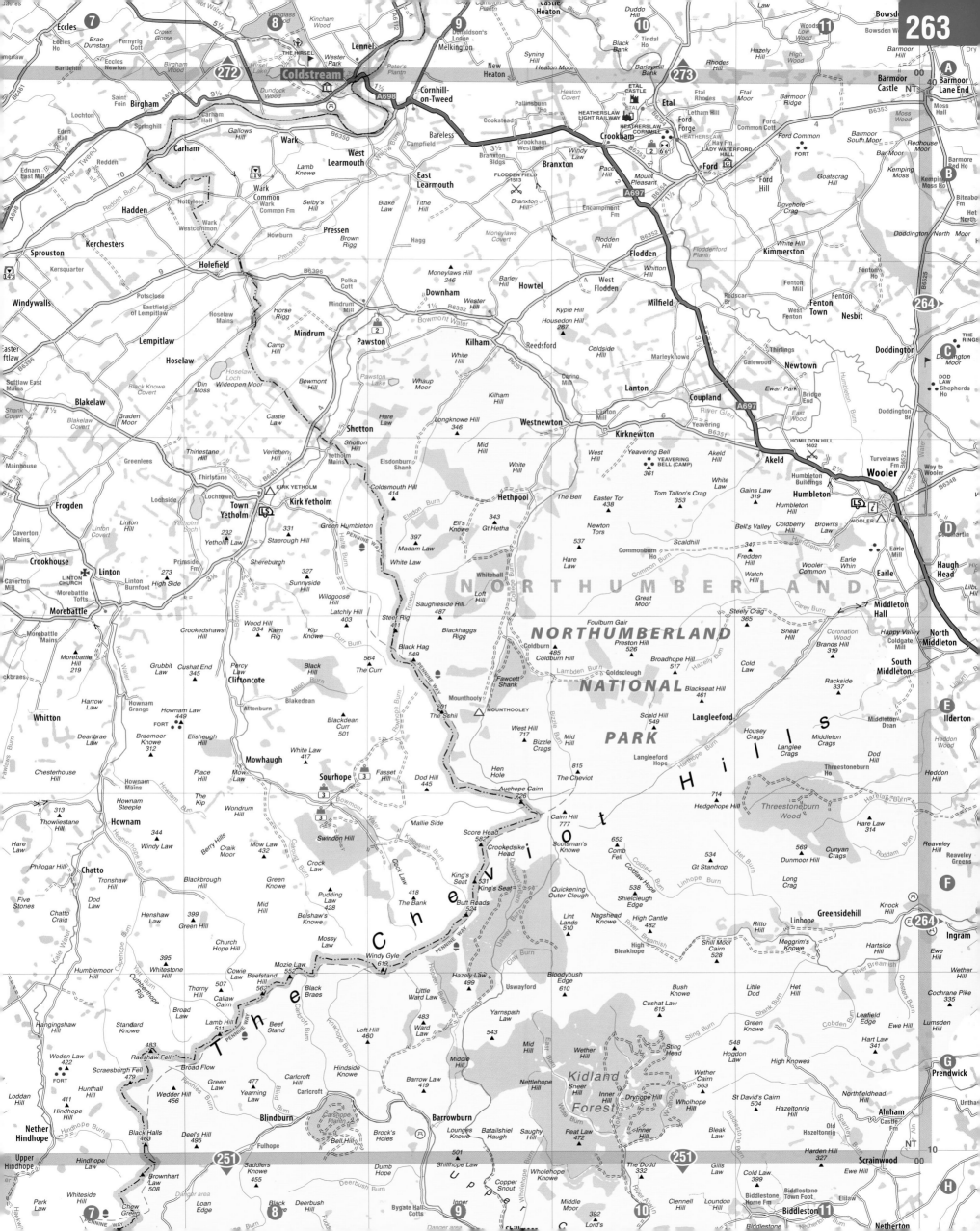

7   8   9   10   11

ngstone

ar

ton Pt

*Embleton
Bay*

Castle Pt
DUNSTANBURGH
CASTLE
*Queen
Margaret's Cove*

N O R T H

S E A

Craster

Cullernose Pt

Howick

Rumbling Kern

Red
Stead

*Howick
Haven*

Sugar Sands

Low
Stead

Howdiemont Sands

houghton

Red Ends

Boulmer

*Boulmer
Haven*

ield
o

Seaton Pt

Marden Rocks

mouth

*Alnmouth
Bay*

253   253

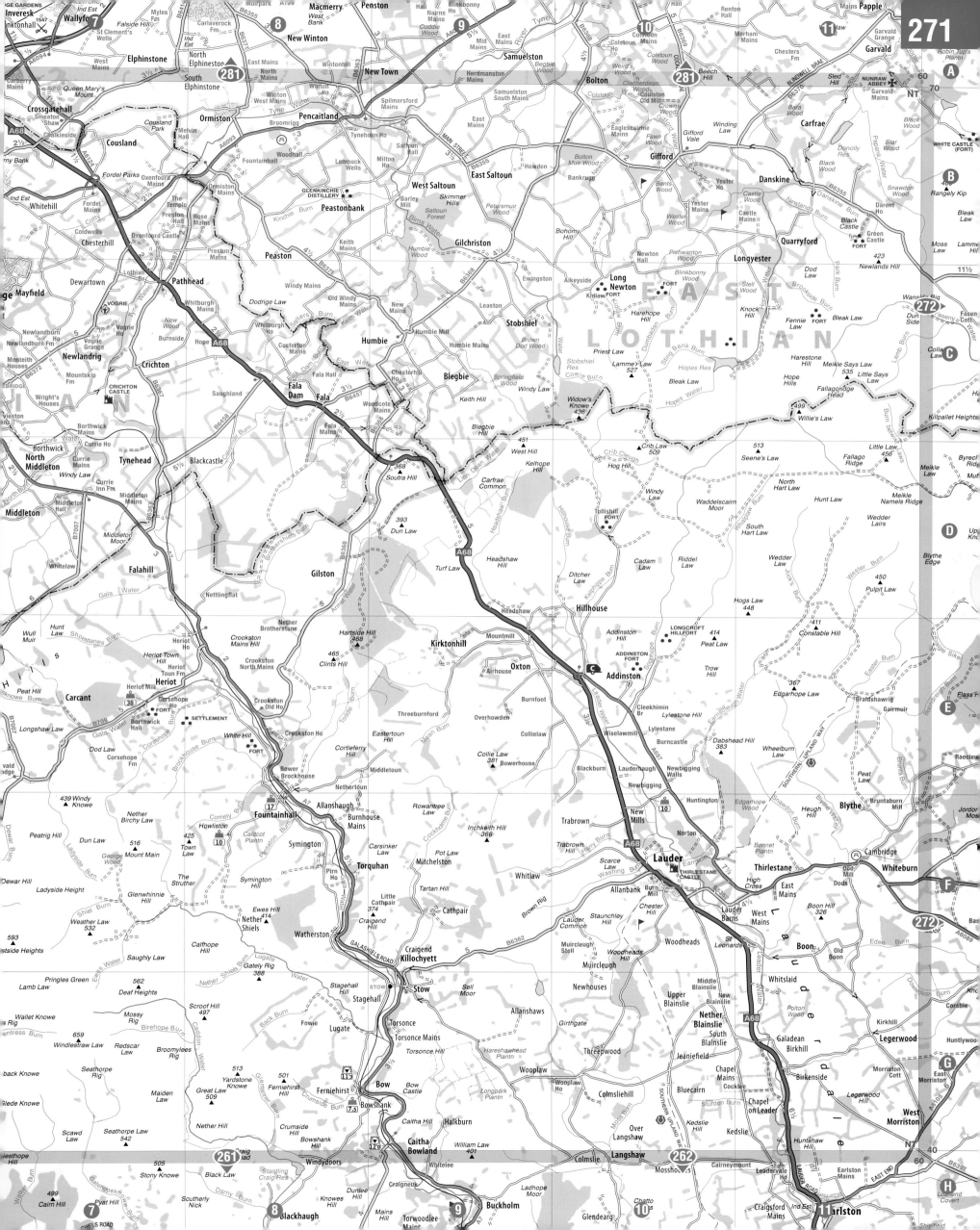

A

IONA ABBEY AND CATHEDRAL
IONA HERITAGE CENTRE
ST COLUMBA EXHIBITION
& WELCOME CENTRE
Torrans
BEINN NA CROISE

Stac an
Aoineidh
Iona
Aridhglas
Kintra
Achnahard
Knokan
18
BROLASS
Leidle
Loch B
Glenbyre

Baile Mor
Eorabus
Lower
Ardtun
Lee
376
Carsaig

Fionnphort
Fidden
Tiraghoil
Bunessan
Loch
376
Glenbyre
Loch B

A849

Slogneach

288

CRUACHAN MIN
Carsaig
Bay
Rubha
Dubh

Erraid
Knockvologan
ROSS OF MULL
Uisken
Scoor
289
CARSAIG ARCHES

Soa I.
Ardalanish
Ardchiavaig
Malcolm's Pt.

NM

Eilean a'Chalmain
125
Rubha nam
Braithrean

Rubh Ardalanish

B

Torran Rocks

C

OBAN

Dubh Artach

Rubh'a'Geadha

Kiloran Bay
Balnahard

Uragaig

KILORAN GARDENS
Kiloran

Kilchattan
136

COLONSAY
Scalasaig

B8086
B8087
B8085

D

Loch Staosnaig

Glendel

Corpach Bay

BEINN BI

Ardskenish
Garvard
Rubha Dubh

Balerominor

Shian Bay
453
RAINBERG
MOR

PRIORY

Dubh Eilean
Oronsay

318
R

Eilean nan Ron

Shian
Loch Righ
Mòr

Loch Tarbert

E

Rubh'an t-Sàilein

Rubha Lang-aoinidh

U

F

Rubha Bholsa
Rubha a'Mhail

Nave Island
Ardnave Pt.
364
SGARBH
BREAC

JURA

439
Loch Lesgamaill
Lagg

Carraig Bhan
Ardnave
Kilnave
Killinallan
Gortantaoid
316
Bunnahabhain
BUNNAHABHAIN
DISTILLERY

785
755
PAPS OF JURA
Loch an Aircill

An Clachan
Garra
Eallabus
Loch a Chnuic
Bhric
Cnocbreac
JURA FOREST
Ardmenish
An Dùnan

Sanaigmore
Leckgruinart
Loch Gruinart
SOUND
Corran

Gleann Astaile
Leargybreck
Knockrome
Lowlandman's
Bay

Braigo
Smaull
Ballinaby
Carnduncan
LOCH
GRUINART
RSPB
LOCH GRUINART NATURE
RESERVE VISITORS CENTRE
CAOL ILA DISTILLERY
Caol Ila
Port Askaig
FINLAGGAN
CENTRE
Keills
561
Ardfernal
Keils

Aoradh
Craigens
Tighnacachla
Bafole
8
Loch
Ballygrant
Lossit Lodge
Kilmeny
OF
342
BRAT BHEINN
Craighouse
ISLE OF JURA
DISTILLERY
Small Isles

Saligo Bay
Saligo
Loch
Gorm
Foreland
Ho
Lyrabus
ISLAY
Esknish
Knockfearoch
Ballygrant
A846
Loch
Finlaggan
Loch
Cam
8
Gleann Ullibh
A846
Cabrach
Strone
Crackaig

Coul Pt.
Coull
Sunderland
Gortan
B8018
A847
Blackrock
Redhouses
Daill
267
BEINN DUBH
Camas an
Staca
Rubha na Tràille
Brosdale I.

Machir Bay
Kilchoman
Conisby
Bridgend
Islay
Ho
Am Fraoch
Eilean

Kilchiaran
Bruichladdich
Bowmore
BOWMORE
ROUND CHURCH
A846
Cattadale
's Hd.

Kilchiaran Bay
254
ISLAY LIFE
MUSEUM
Mulindry
254

NR

Tormisdale
RHINS
OF
ISLAY
ISLAY
Port Charlotte
Gartbreck
Laggan

Lossit Pt.
Kelsay
Bridge Ho
471
BEINN BHAN
491
BEINN
Carraig Mhór

0   2   4   6 miles
0 2 4 6 8 10 km

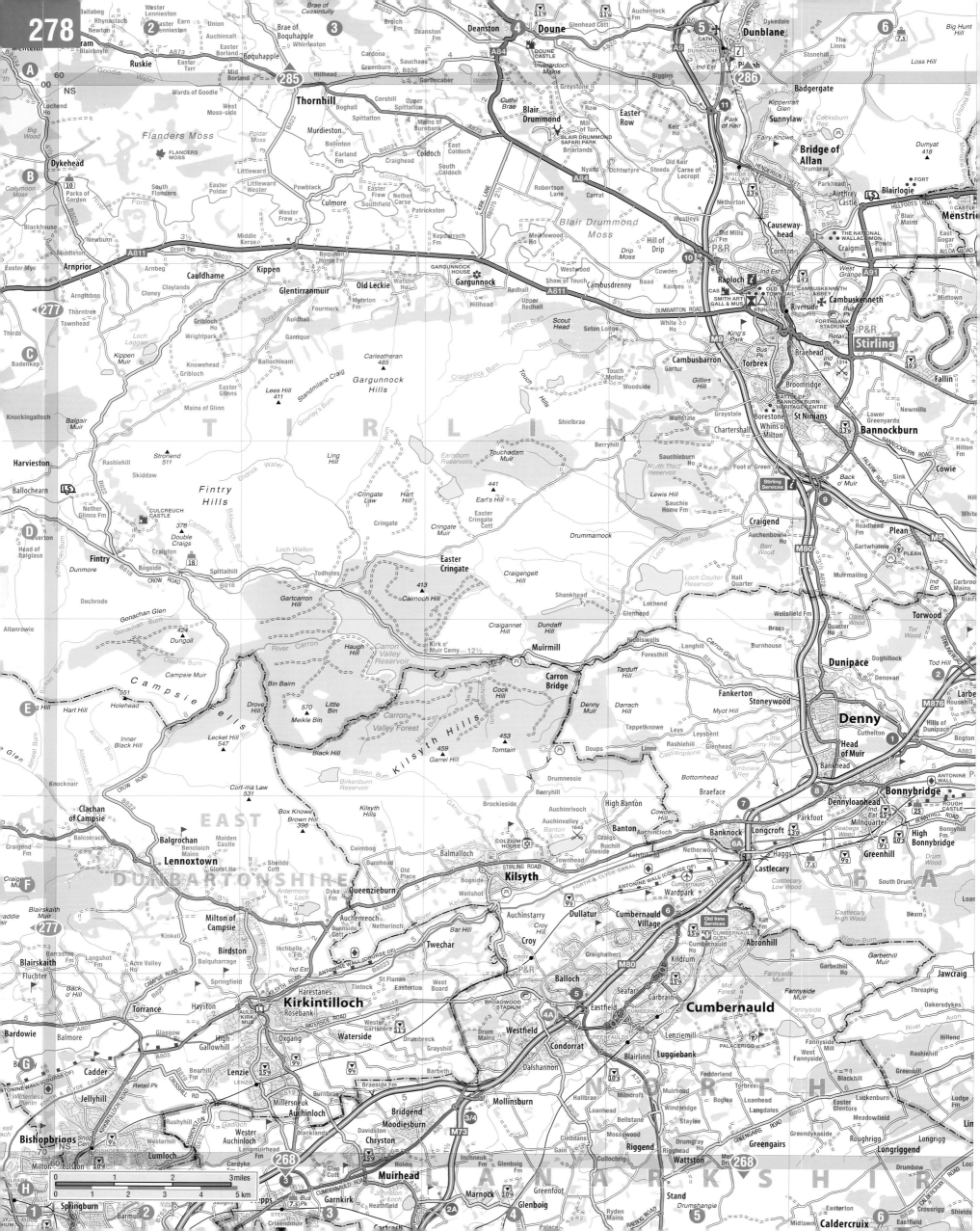

NORTH

SEA

EAST

LOTHIAN

A

10
00
NT

B

Lumsdaine

Coldingham Loch

St Abb's Head

Horsecastle Bay

C

D

E

F

G

Fast Castle
Head   Wheat Stack

Telegraph
Hill   FAST
CASTLE

NT
70
10

273

Oatlee Hill   St Abb's Head

273

Dowlaw Burn

Lumsdaine   ST ABB'S HEAD

Horsecastle Bay

Coldingham
Common   Lumsdaine
Moor   Coldingham Loch   SETTLEMENT   Mire
Loch

7   Bell
Hill

Cross
Law   8   9   10   11

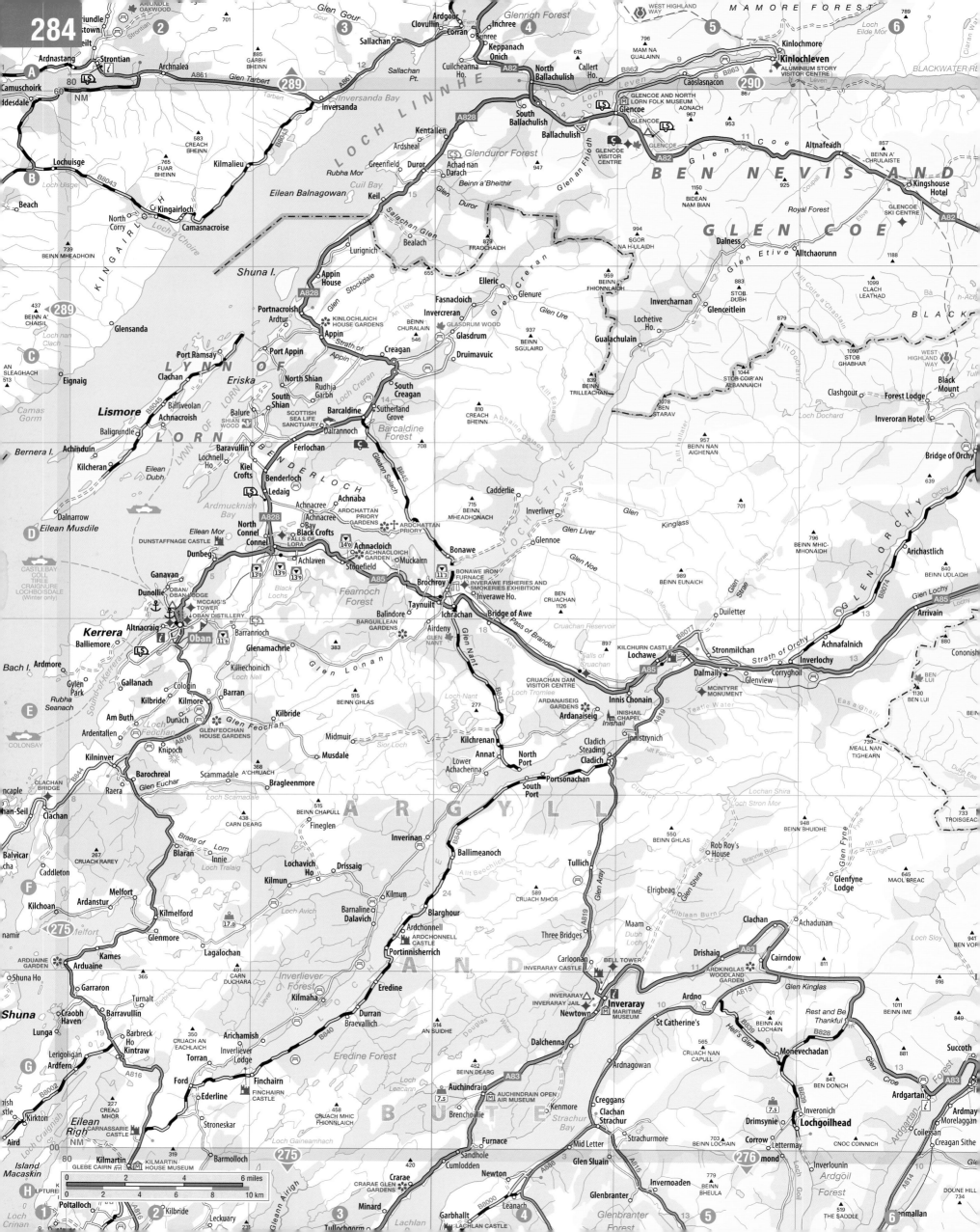

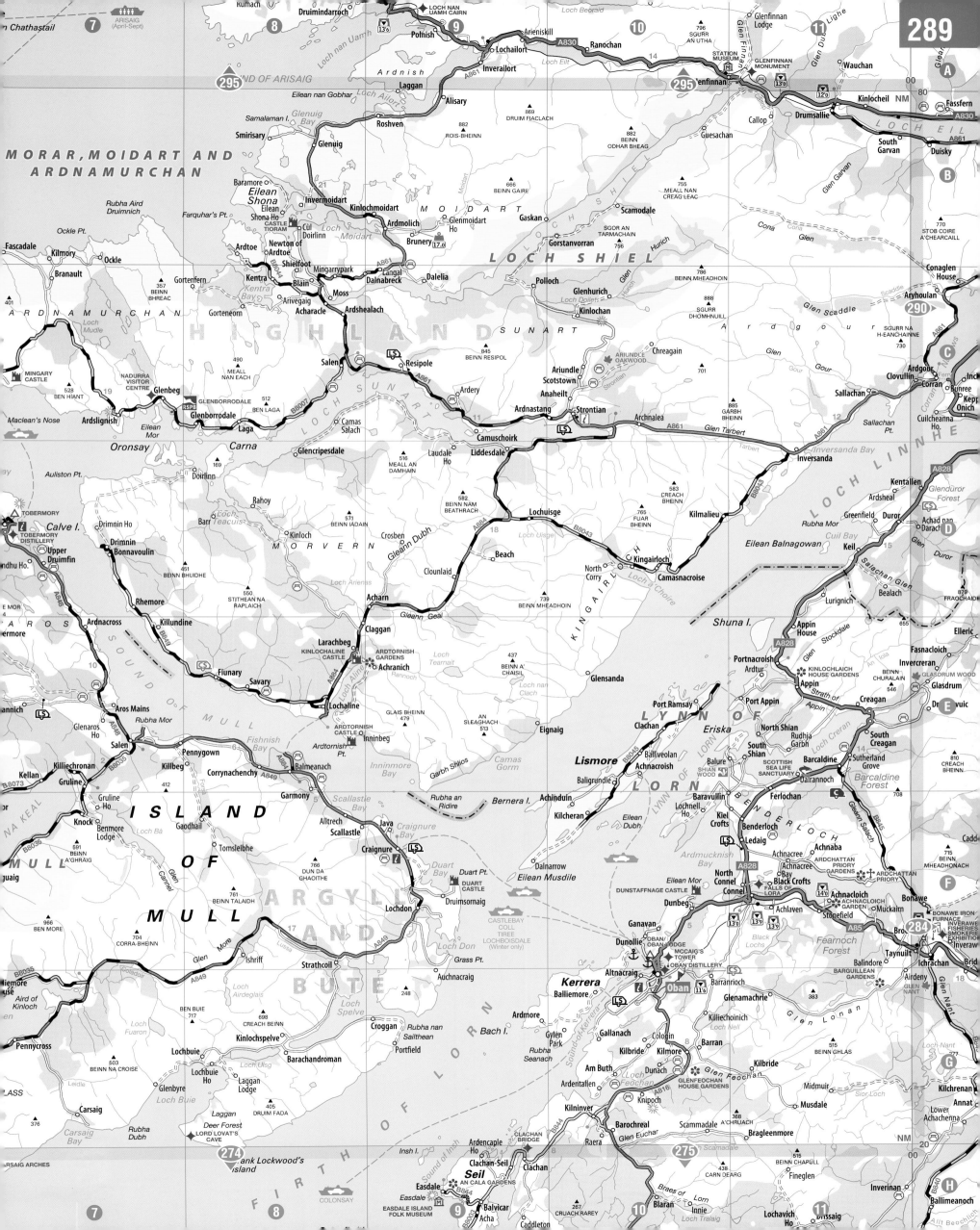

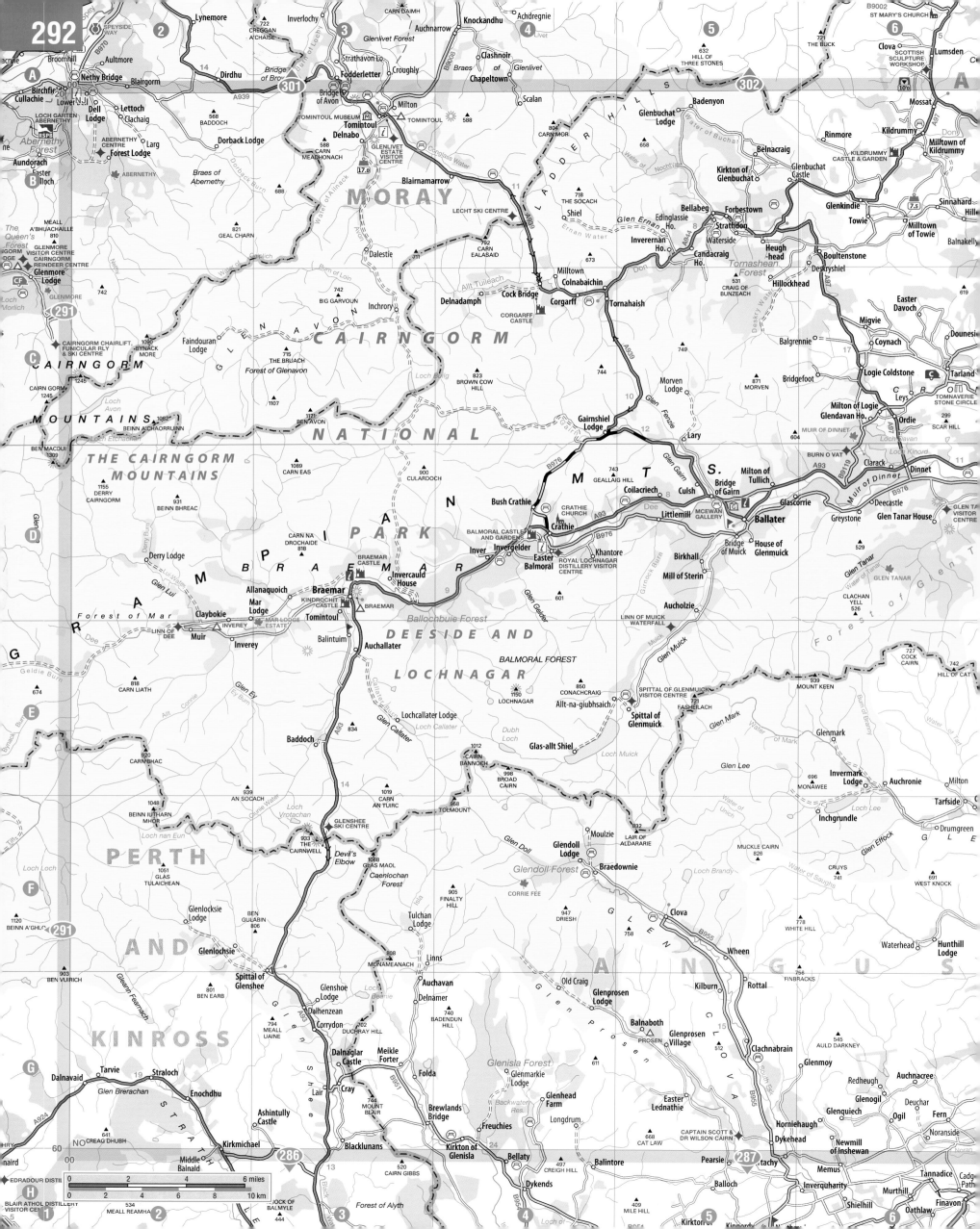

Ramasaig
Roag
Feorlig
Balmeanach
Vatten
Loch Connan
Glengrasco
Sluggans
Tormore
Torvaig
Shul
THE AROS
EXPERIENCE
Portree
Inve
Hoe Rape
Orbost
Harlosh
Greep
Macleod's
Tables
488
HEALABHAL BHEAG
Heatherfield
417
Peni
Peinmore
ISLAND
Balmore
Ose
Eabost
West
Eabost
Bracadale
Totardor
Loch Duagrich
Glenmore
Mugeary
Conord
Hoe Point
NG
00
40
Geodha Mor
Harlosh I.
Tarner I.
Ullinish
Loch Bracadale
Struan
Coillore
Loch
Wiay
Oronsay
Gesto
Ho
Portnalong
ROINEVAL
439
Idrigill Point
MACLEOD'S MAIDENS
Ardtreck
Rubha
nan Clach
Fiskavaig
Fernilea
TALISKER
DISTILLERY
Carbost
Drynoch
Crossal
ARNAVAL
369
Satran
Merkadale
Talisker Bay
Gleann Oraid
Sligachan
Hotel
297
Talisker
Glen Brittle
Forest
Eynort
Grula
SGURR NAN
GILLEAN
964
Glen Sligachan
BEINN BHREAC
445
459
THE
Loch Eynort
SGURR
A'GHREADAIDH
973
Kraiknish
GLENBRITTLE
CUILLIN HILLS
HI
Glenbrittle House
992
SGURR
ALASDAIR
Loch
Coruisk
Bualintur
Culnaneam
924
SGURR
NAN EAG
Rubh an Dunain
Soay Sound
Soay
Mol-chlach
PRINCE CH
BOA

Canna
Garrisdale Pt.
A'Chill
Rubha Shamhnan Insir
Canna Harbour
Sanday
Sound of Canna
Kilmory
MALLAIG
(Sun only)
Guirdil
Bay
Kilmory Glen
Kinloch Glen
Rubha na Roinne
A'Bhrideanach
388
Kinloch
Loch Scresort
Oigh-sgeir
571
ORVAL
RÙM
RÙM
KINLOCH
CASTLE
Rubha Port
na Caranean
Schooner Pt.
Harris
Glen Harris
812
ASKIVAL
Rubha Sgorr an t-Snidhe
781
AINSHVAL
Rubha nam
Meirleach
Bay of Laig
Cleadale
Rubha an
Fhasaidh
Laig
Eigg
Rubha Sgorr an t-Snidhe
Sandavore
393
AN SGURR
Kildon
Galmisdal
Eilea
Eilean nan Each
Gallanach
137
Port Mor
Muck

0   2   4   6 miles
0   2   4   6   8   10 km

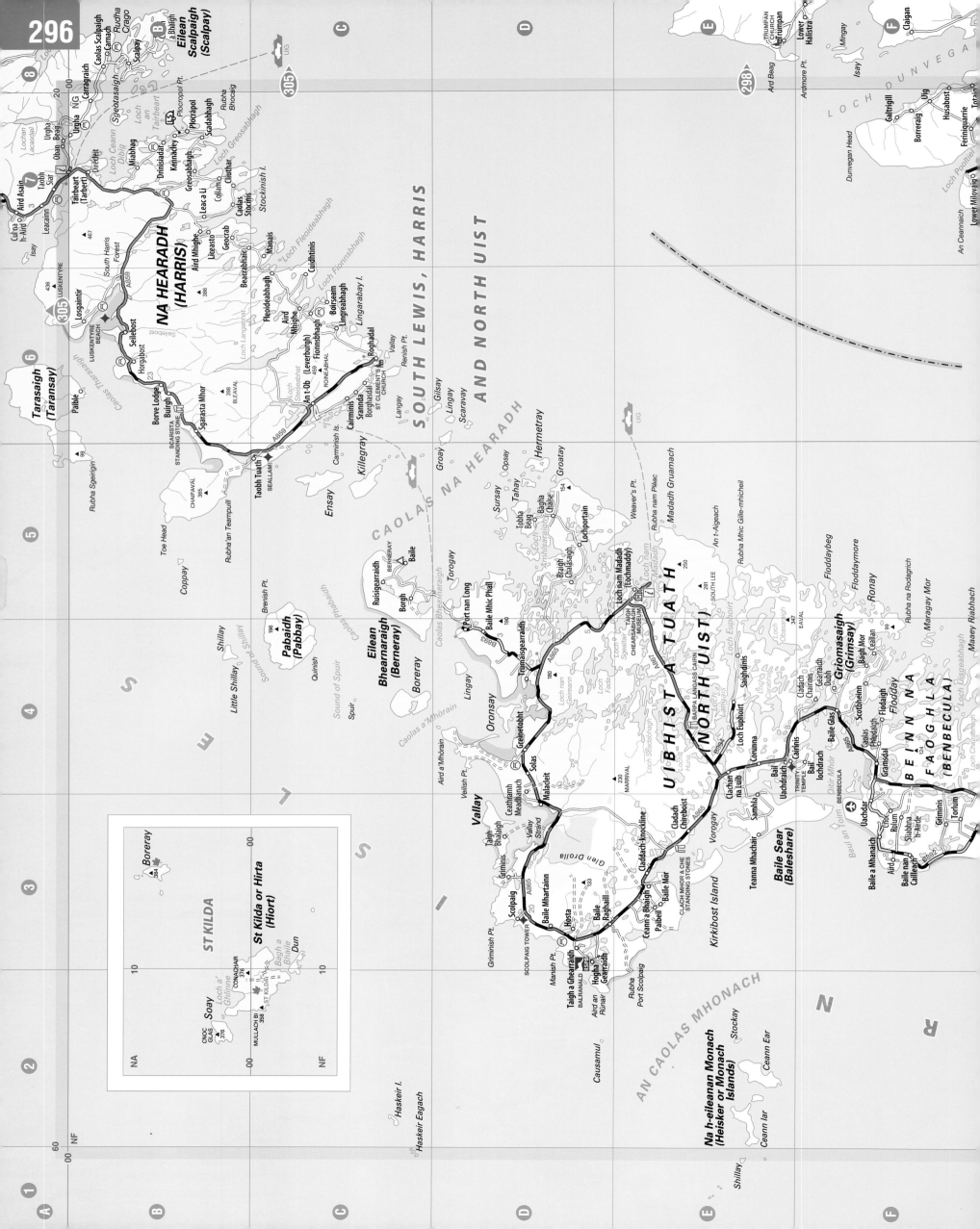

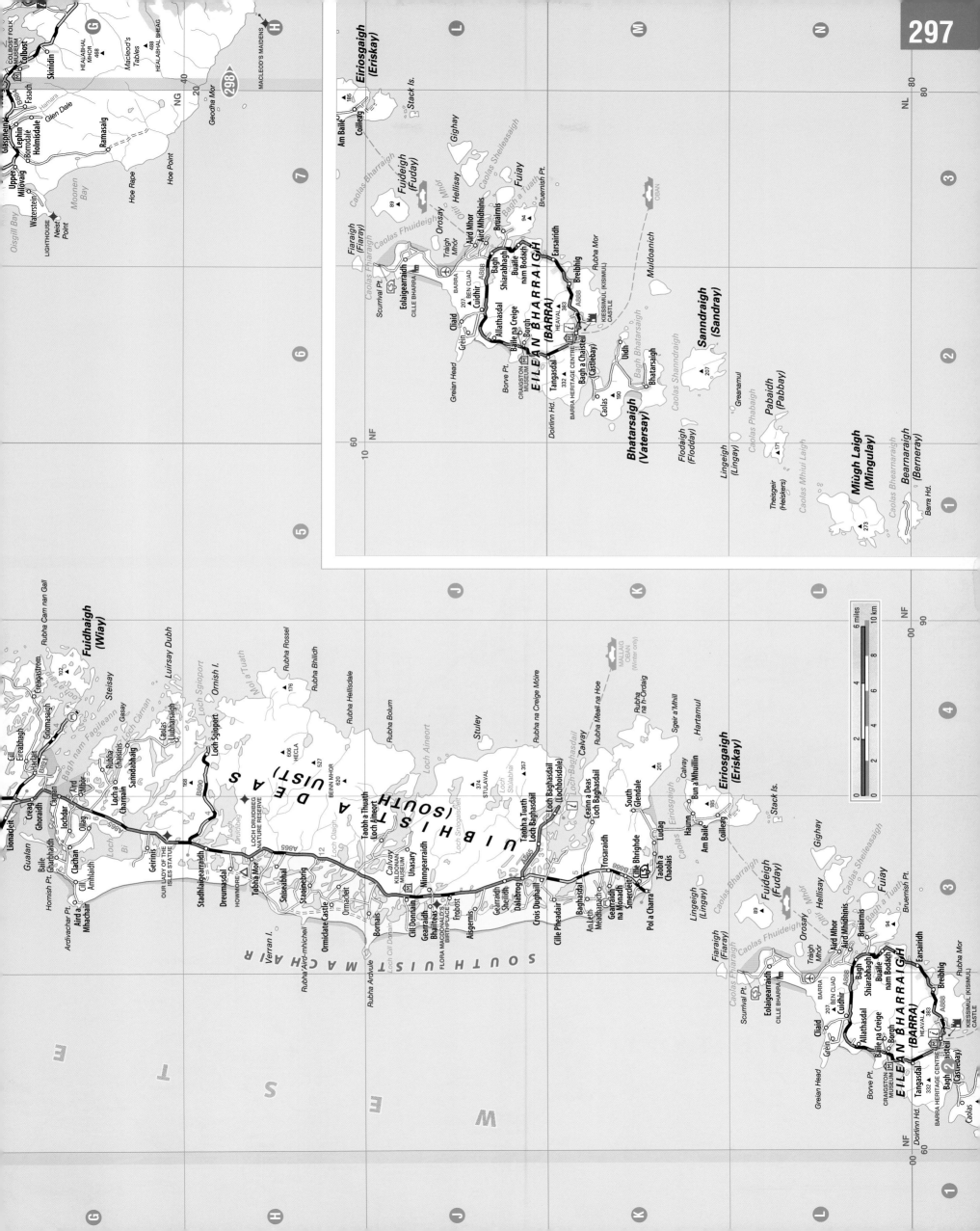

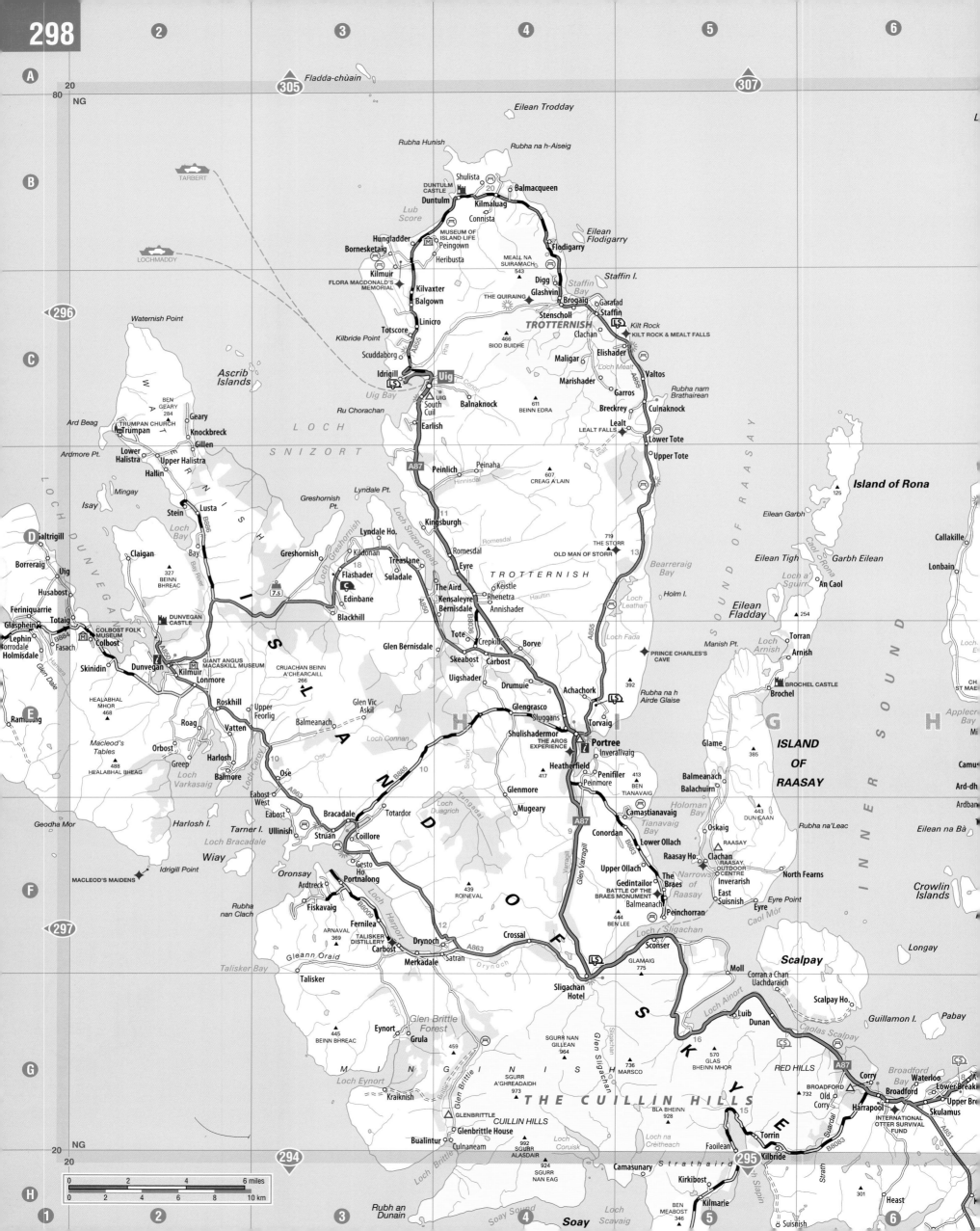

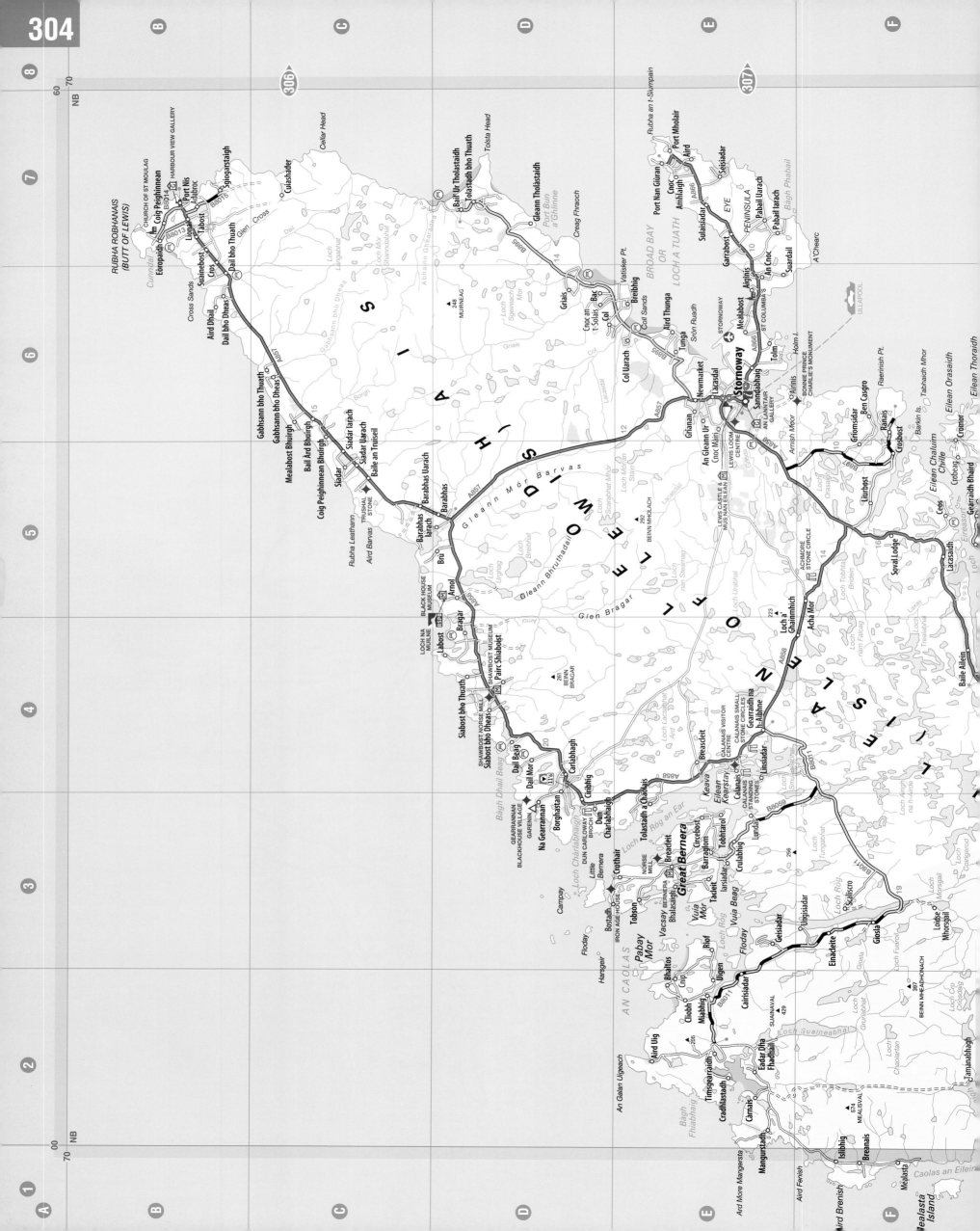

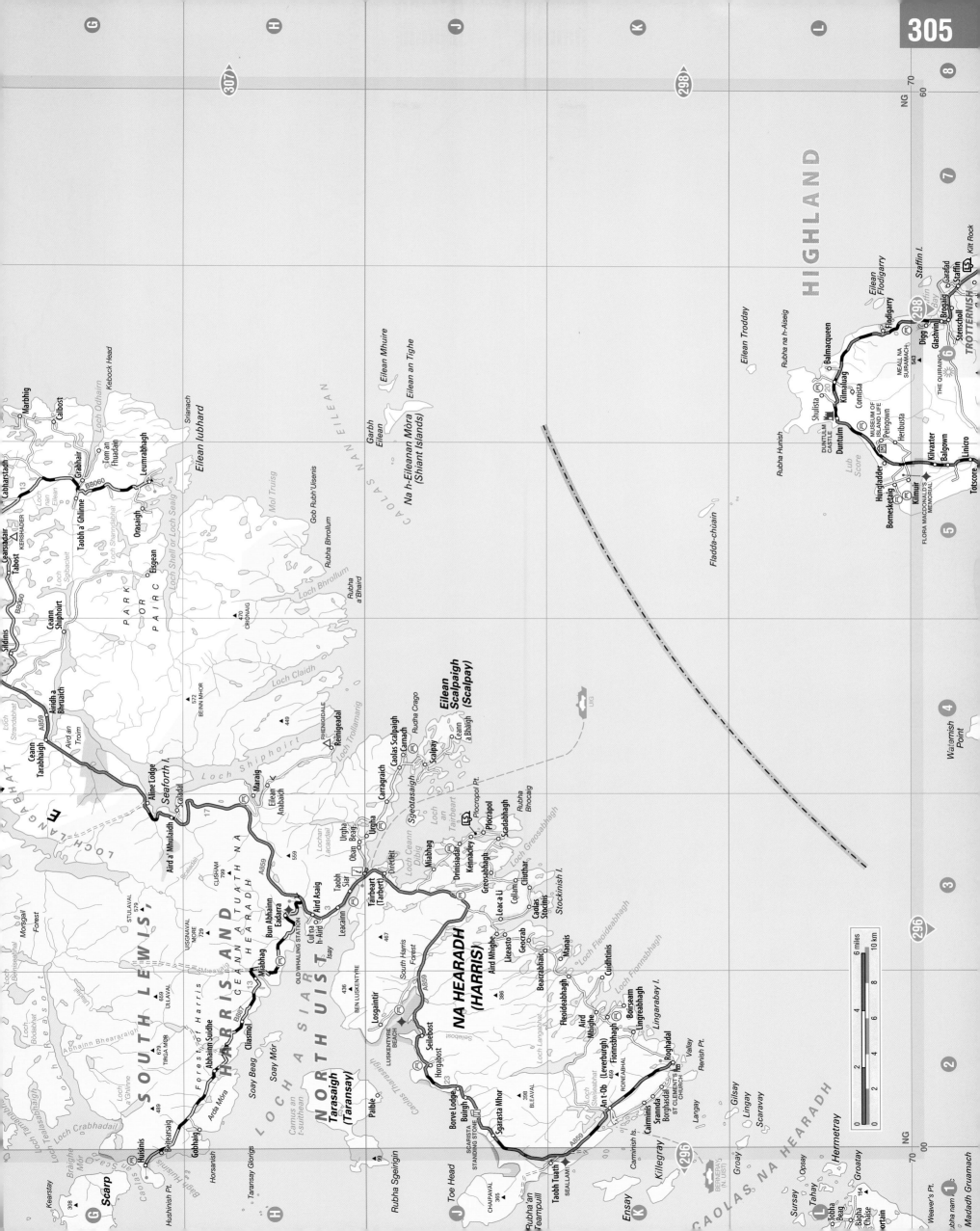

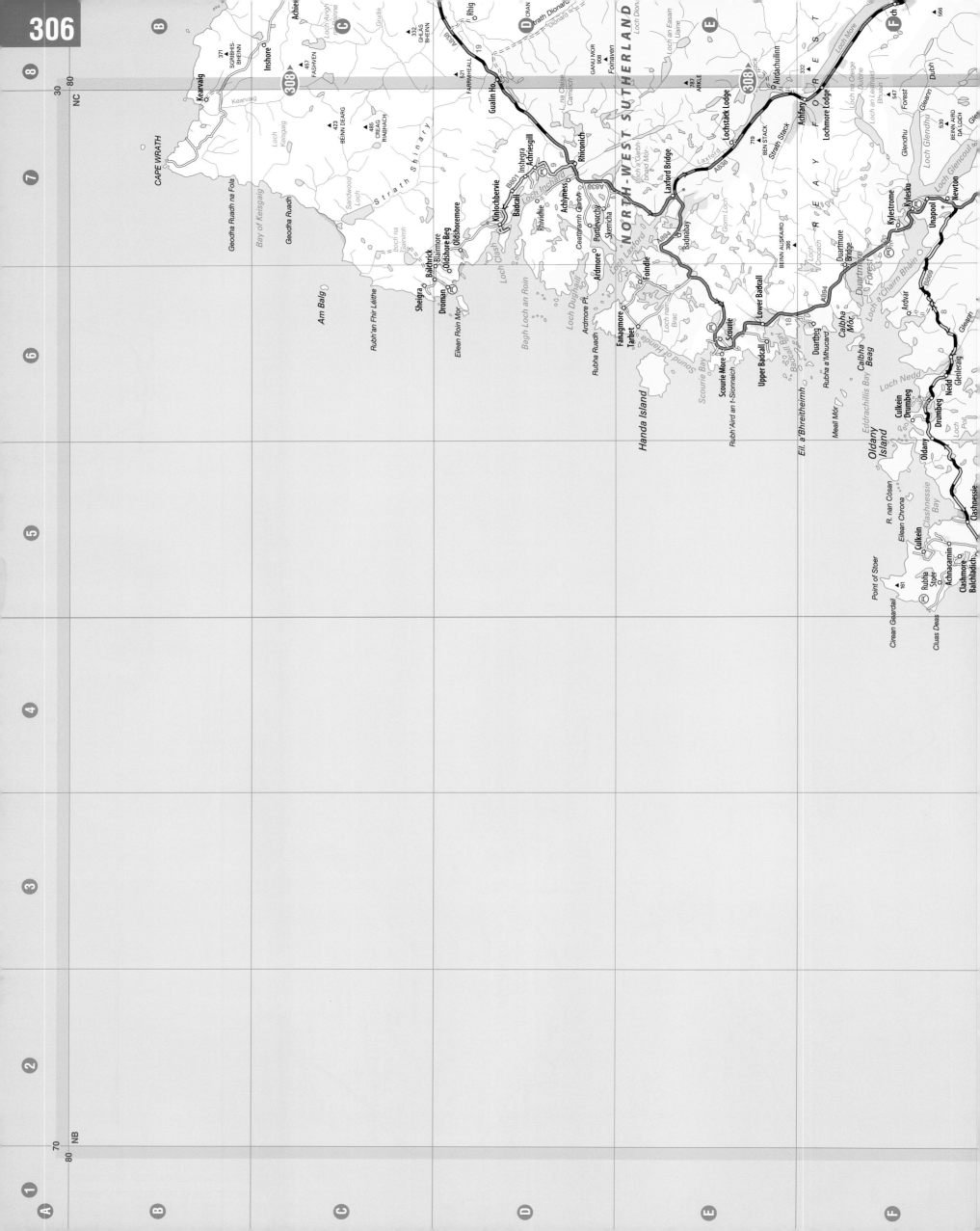

NORTH-WEST SUTHERLAND

CAPE WRATH

Kearvaig
Kearvaig
Inshore
SGRIBHIS-BHEINN 371
FASHVEN 457
GHLAS BHEINN 332
Achiemore
Rhig

Strath Dionard

CRAN

Loch Dionard

Loch an Easain Uaine

Foinaven

GANU MOR 908

FARRMHEALL 571

Gualin Ho.

A838

19

Inshegra
Achriesgill
Rhiconich
Badcall
Kinlochbervie
B801
Loch Inchard
Rhividhe
Achlyness
Skerricha
Ceathramh Garbh
Portlevorachy

Oldshoremore
Oldshore Beg
Blairmore
Balchrick
Droman
Sheigra

Ardmore

Rubha Ruadh
Ardmore Pt.

Loch Clash
Loch Dughaill

Loch na Gainmh

Eilean Roin Mor

Rubh'an Fhir Léithe

Am Balg

Bagh Loch an Roin

Sandwood Loch

Loch Keisgaig

Geodha Ruadh

Geodha Ruadh na Fola

Bay of Keisgaig

Strath Shinary

Loch Laxford

BEN STACK 719
Strath Stack

Loch a'Garbh-bhaid Mór

Laxford Bridge

Lochstack Lodge
Lochmore Lodge

308

Airdachuilinn
ARKLE 787
332

FOREST

Loch More

Achfary

566

530

BENN AIRD DA LOCH

547

Glendhu
Loch Glendhu
Forest

R E A Y

Loch a'Chairn Bhàin

Kylesku
Kylestrome

Newton
Unapool

Loch Glencoul

Loch Beag

BENN AUSKAIRD 386

Duartmore Forest
Duartmore Bridge

Calbha Mór
Calbha Beag

Duartbeg
Rubha a'Mhucard

A894

Lower Badcall
Upper Badcall

Scourie
Scourie More
18

Foindle
Badnabay

A838

A894

Badcall

Loch Crocach

Loch nan Brac

Fanagmore
Tarbet

Sound of Handa

Handa Island

Scourie Bay

Rubh'Aird an t-Sionnaich

Eil. a'Bhreitheimh

Eddrachillis Bay

Meall Mór

Ardvar

Oldany Island

Loch Nedd

Culkein Drumbeg

Nedd
Drumbeg
Oldany

Loch Poll

Point of Stoer
161
Rubha Stoer

R. nan Còsan
Eilean Chrona

Glenleraig
Glenann

Ardvar

Clashnessie Bay

Culkein
Achnacarnin
Clashmore
Balchladich

Cirean Geardail
Cluas Deas

Clashnessie

CR

ch

NC 80
30

NB 70
80

NC 30

NB 80

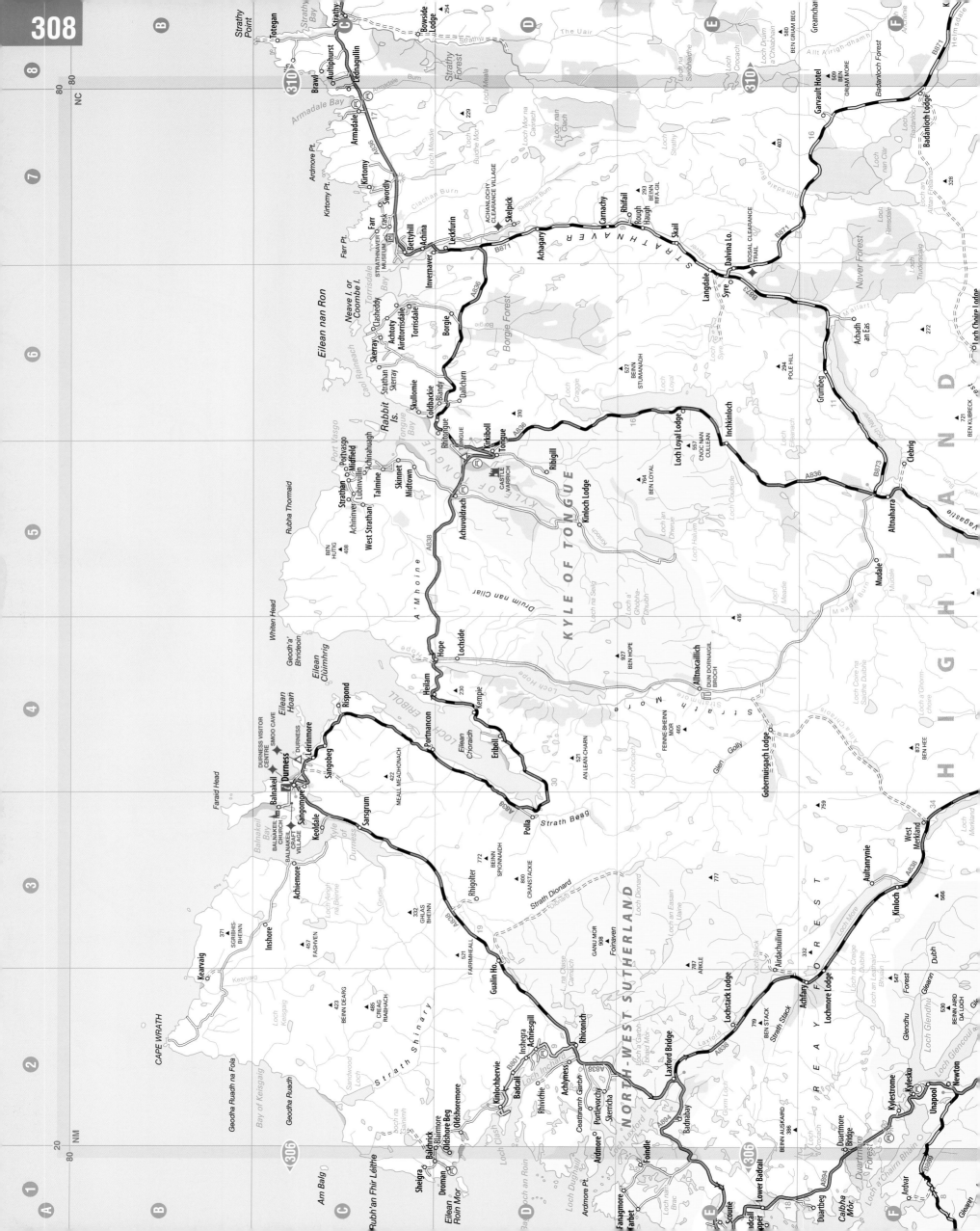

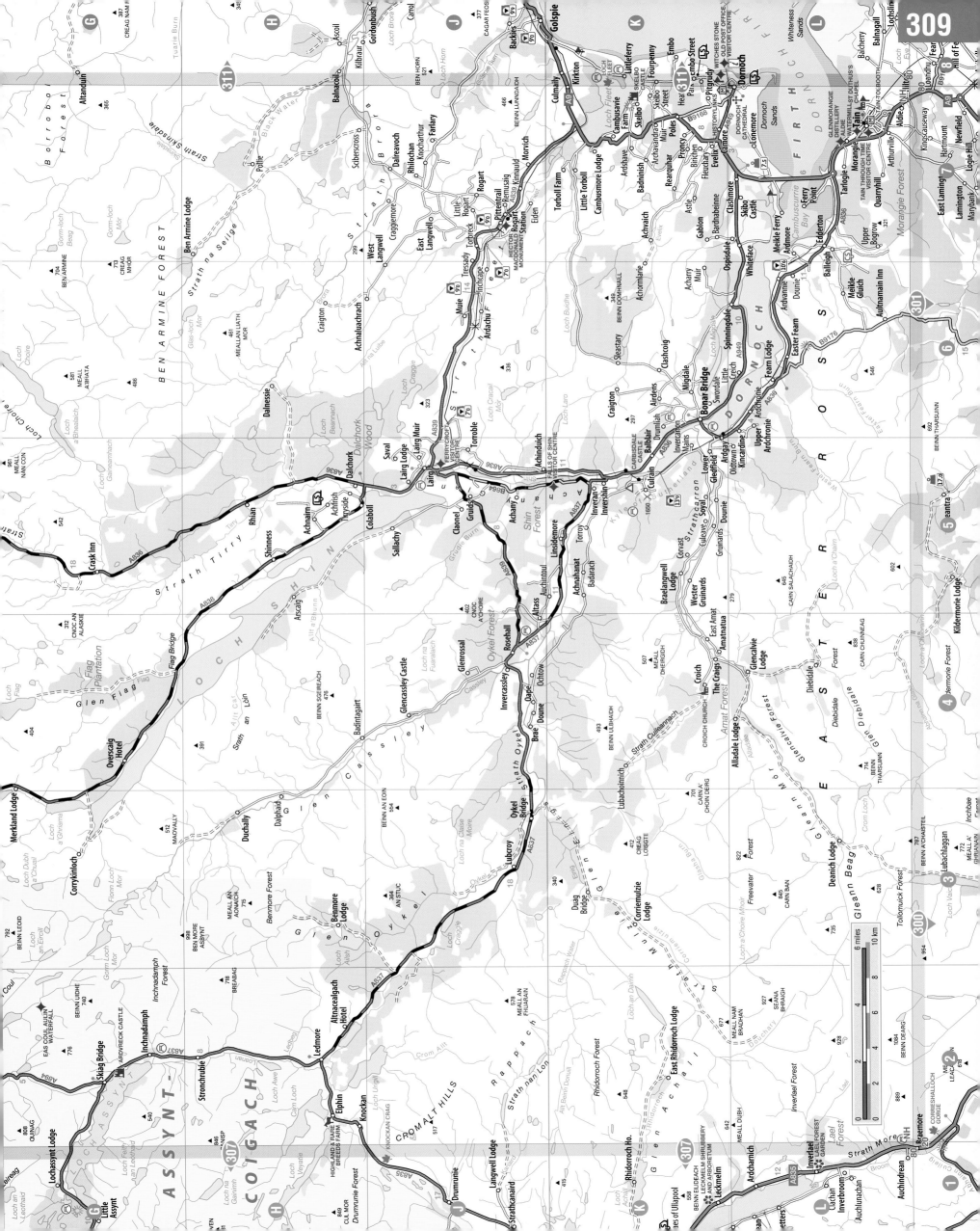

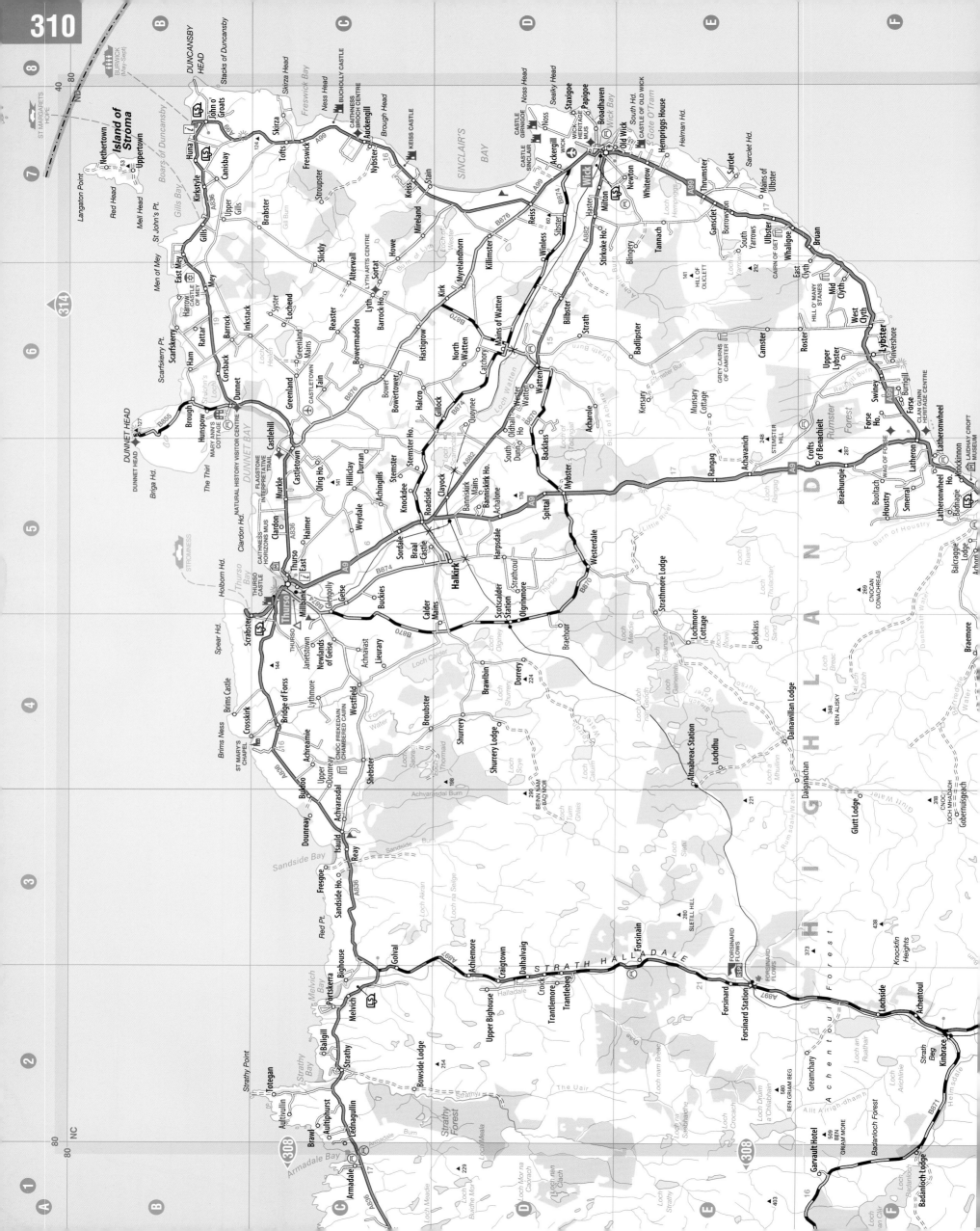

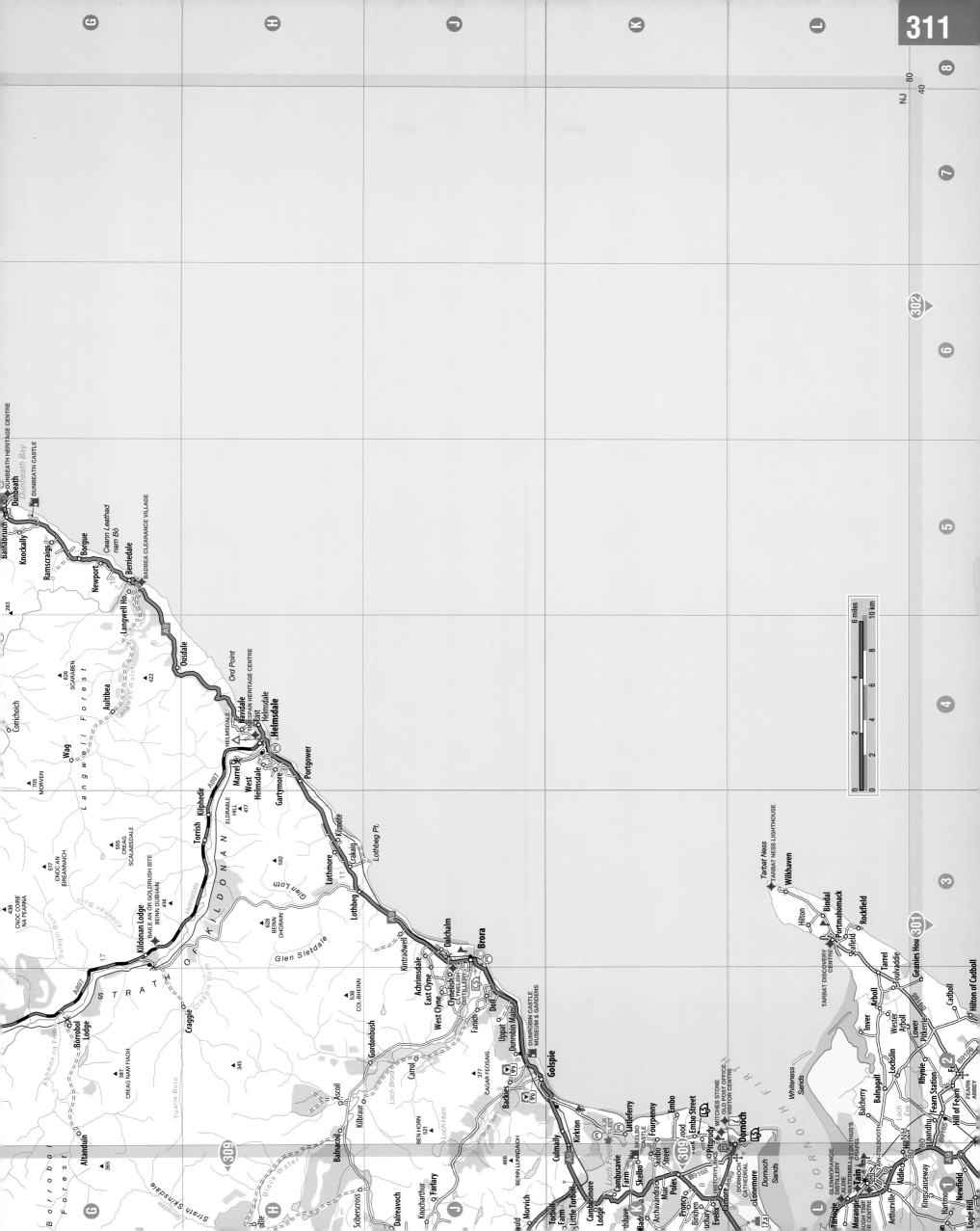

G H J K L

8

7

6

302

5

4

3

2

1

Dunbeath Bay
DUNBEATH HERITAGE CENTRE
DUNBEATH CASTLE
Dunbeath
Balnabruich
Knockally
Ramscraigs
Borgue
Ceann Leathad nam Bò
Newport
Langwell Ho.
Berriedale
BADBEA CLEARANCE VILLAGE
283
SCARABEN
626
MORVEN
705
Corrichoich
Wag
Langwell Forest
Aultibea
Ousdale
Ord Point
A9
CNOC AN EIREANNAICH
517
CREAG SCALABSDALE
555
BEINN DUBHAIN
414
Kildonan Lodge
BAILE AN OR GOLDRUSH SITE
CNOC COIRE NA PEARNA
438
Borrobol Lodge
A897
17
STRATH OF KILDONAN
Helmsdale Burn
Helmsdale
HELMSDALE
TIMESPAN HERITAGE CENTRE
Navidale
East Helmsdale
Marrel
West Helmsdale
A897
Torrish
Kilphedir
ELDRABLE HILL 417
Gartymore
Portgower
BEINN DHORAIN
628
Lothmore
11
Kintradwell
Cakaig
Kilmote
Lothbeg Pt.
Lothbeg
A9
Glen Loch
Glen Sletdale
592
COL-BHEINN
538
Achrimsdale
East Clyne
West Clyne
Clynelish
CLYNELISH DISTILLERY
Dalchalm
Brora
Doll
Fleuchary
Uppat
Dunrobin Mains
DUNROBIN CASTLE MUSEUM & GARDENS
Craggie
Gordonbush
345
Carrol
Ascoil
CAGAR FEOSAIG
377
Backies
A9
Golspie
BEN HORN 521
Kilbraur
Balnacoil
Kinbrace
Loch Brora
Loch Horn
Loch Lundie
387
CREAG NAM FIADH
Altanduin
365
Abhainn na Frithe
Borrobol Forest
A897
Strath Skinsdale
Tuarie Burn
Suisgill Burn
Kildonan Burn
Borrobol Forest
Skinsdale
Strath Brora
Black Water
Culmaily
BEINN LUNNDAIDH
466
Kirkton
Loch Fleet
A9
309
A839
Skelbo
SKELBO CASTLE
Skelbo Street
Littleferry
Fourpenny
Embo
Embo Street
WITCHES STONE
OLD POST OFFICE
VISITOR CENTRE
Dornoch
DORNOCH CATHEDRAL
Whiteness Sands
HISTORYLINKS
Pitgrudy
Proncy
Evelix
Cuthill
Poles
B9168
Dornoch Sands
Dornoch Firth
Tarbat Ness
TARBAT NESS LIGHTHOUSE
Wilkhaven
Portmahomack
TARBAT DISCOVERY CENTRE
Tarrel
Rockfield
Hilton
Bindal
301
Geanies Hou
Arboll
Inver
Lower Arboll
West Arboll
Loch Eye
Cadboll
Hilton of Cadboll
NH
80
40
NJ
40
80
302

6 miles
10 km
8
6
4
2
0
4
2
0
2
4
6
8
0

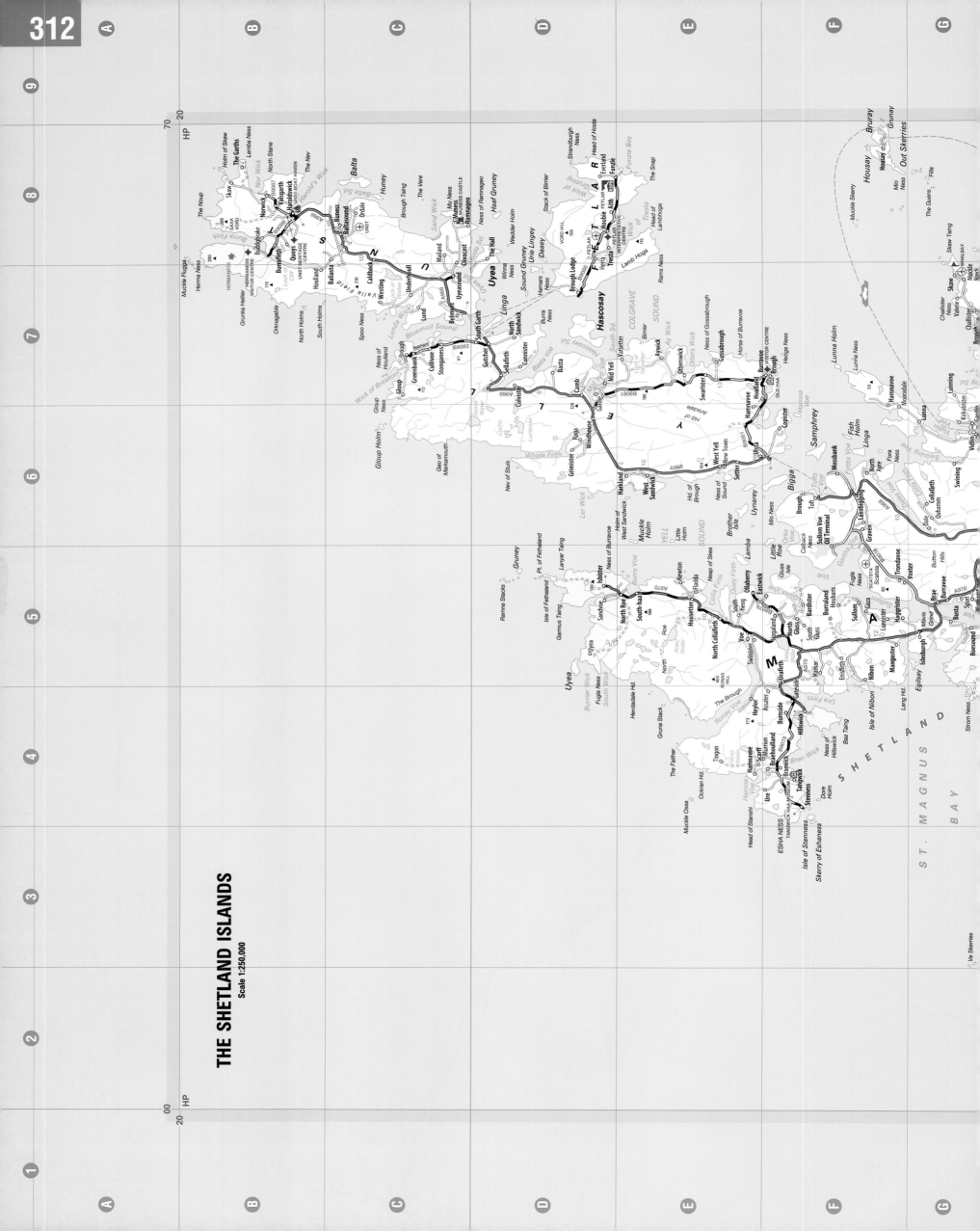

THE SHETLAND ISLANDS

Scale 1:250,000

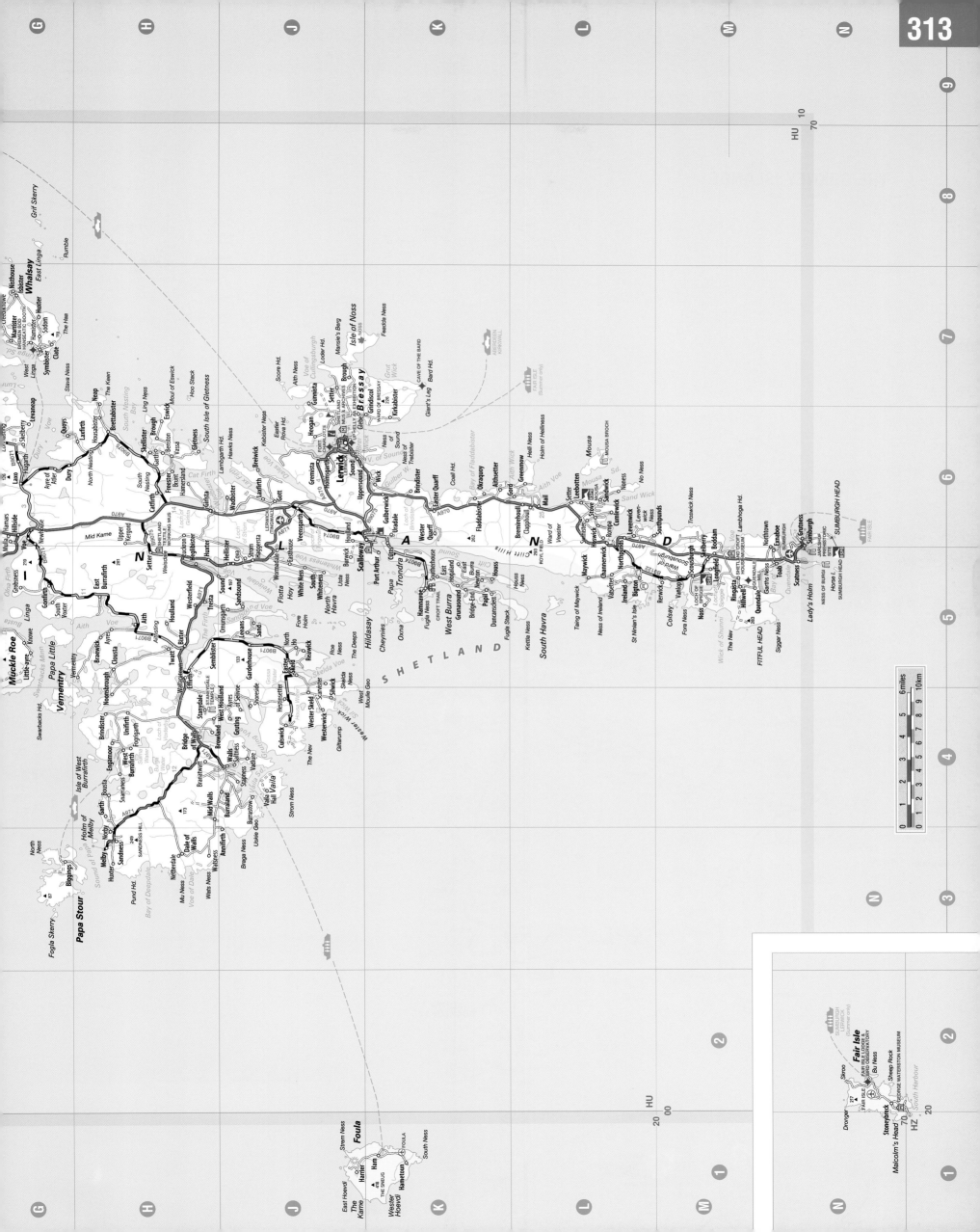

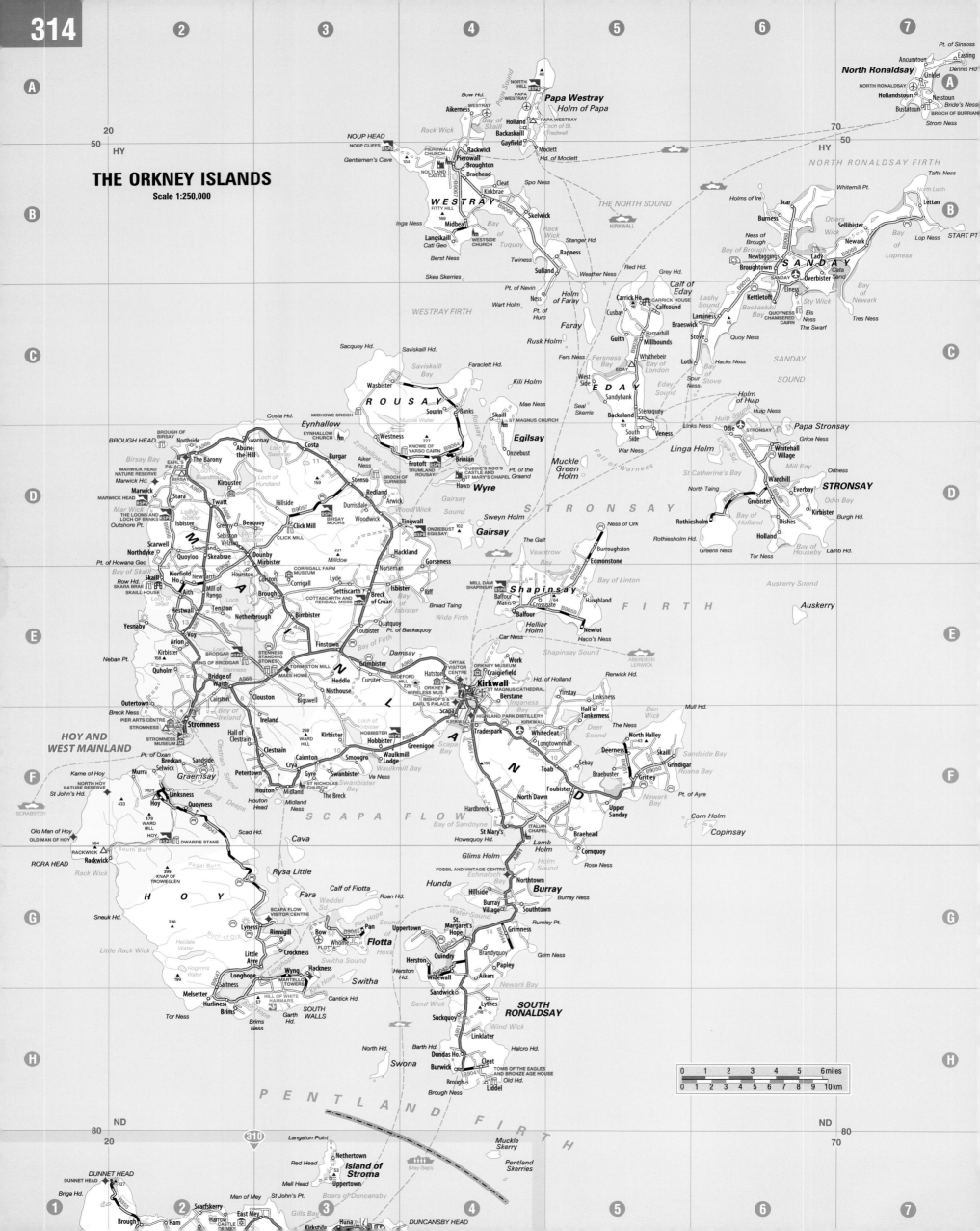

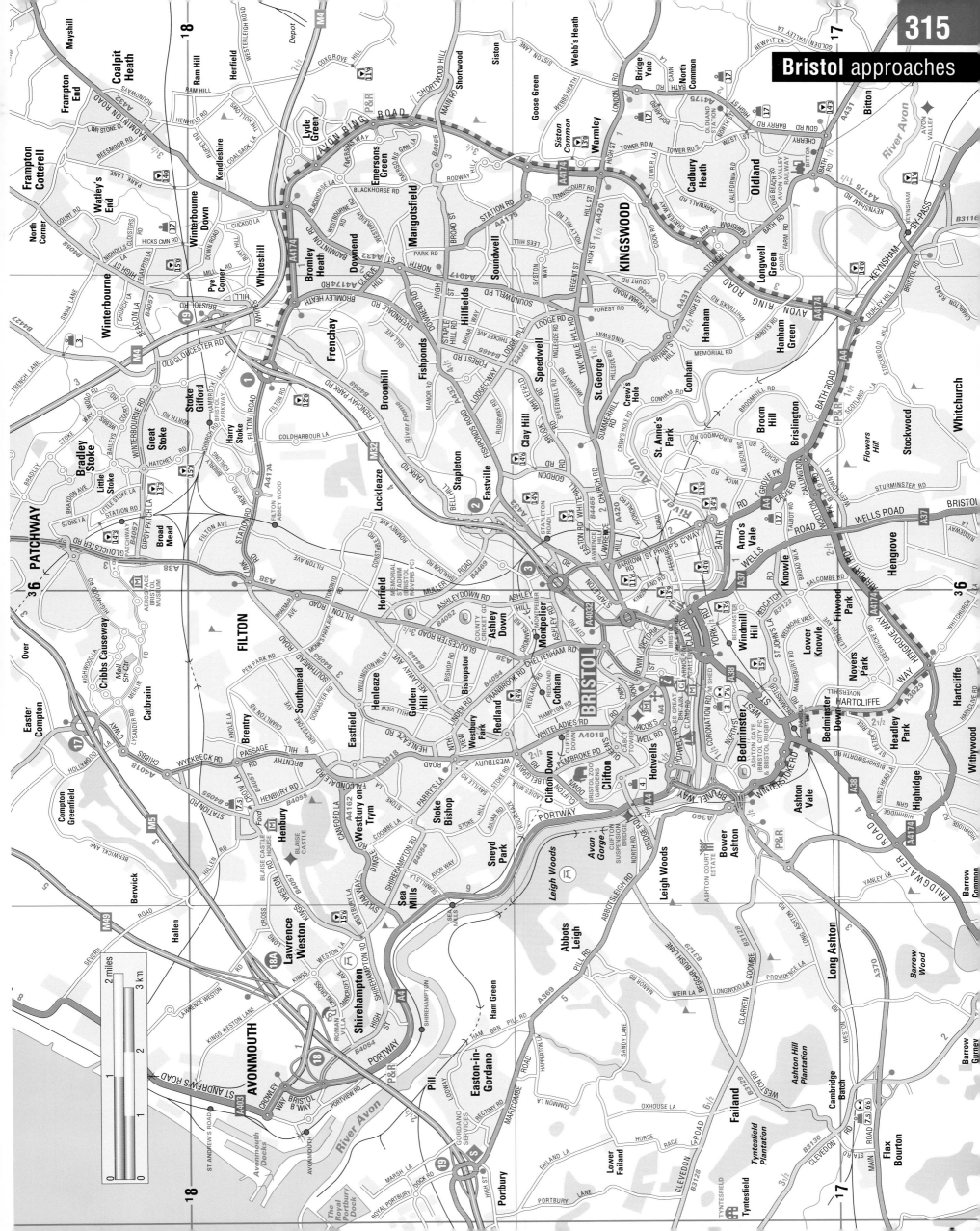

Pentland Hills

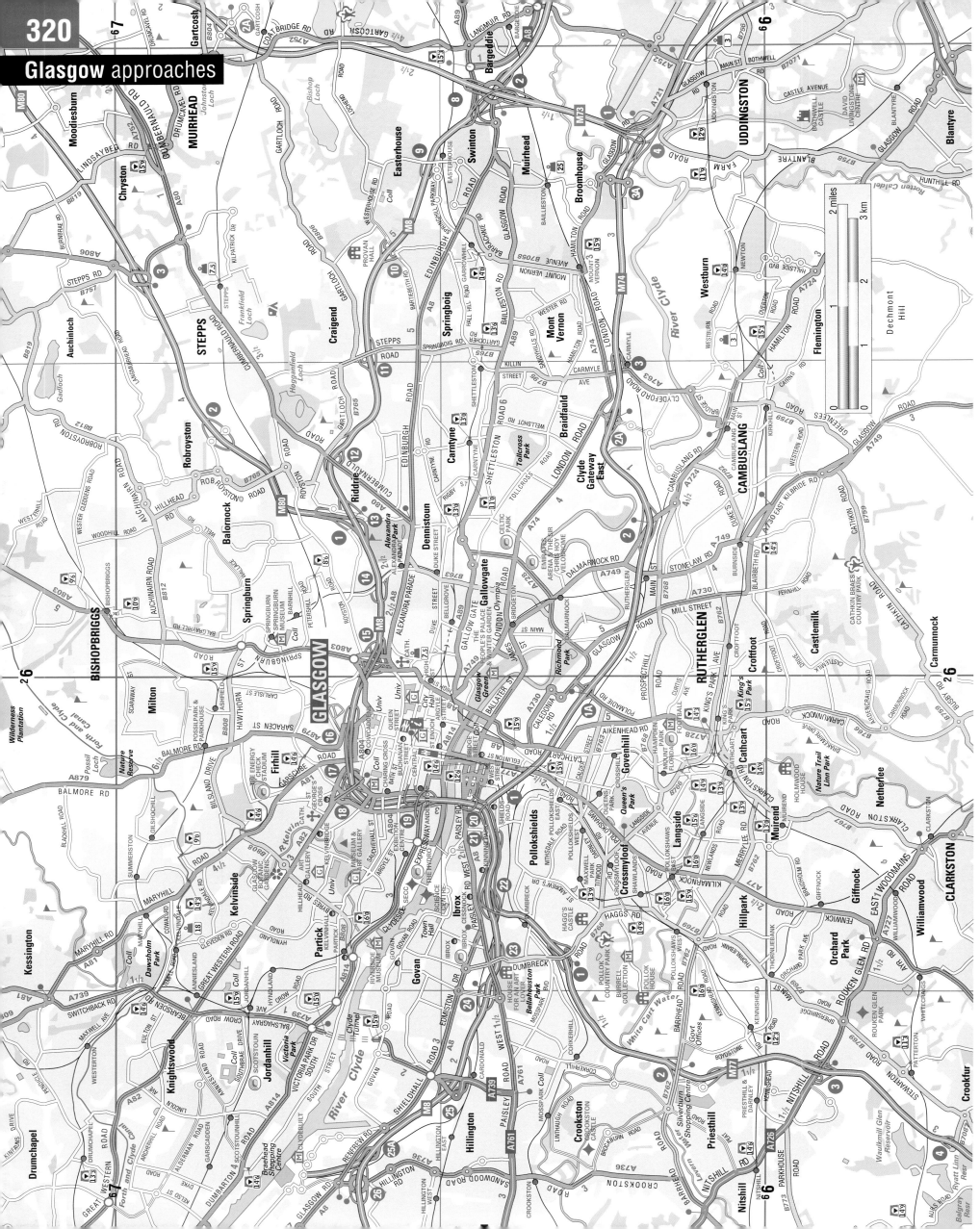

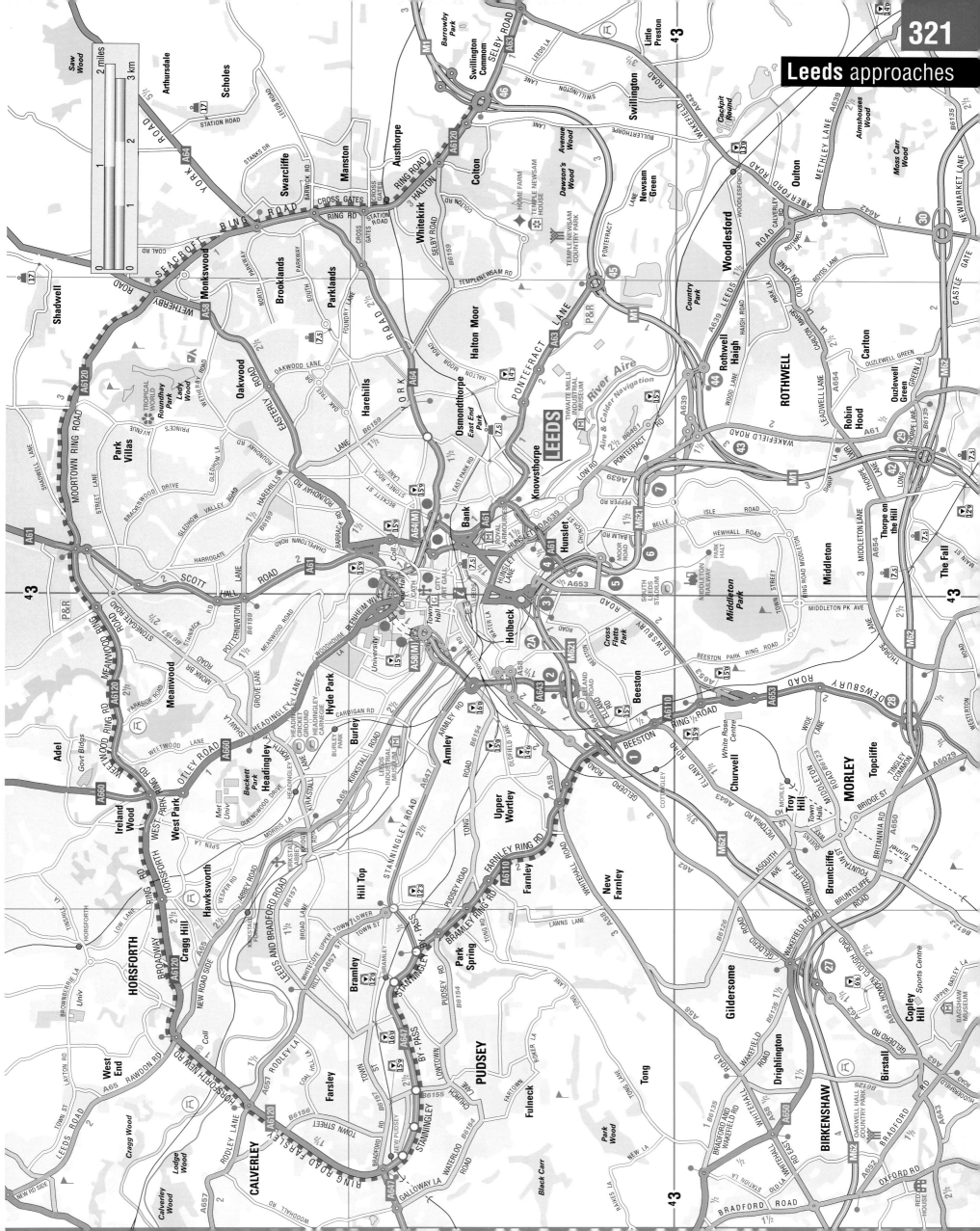

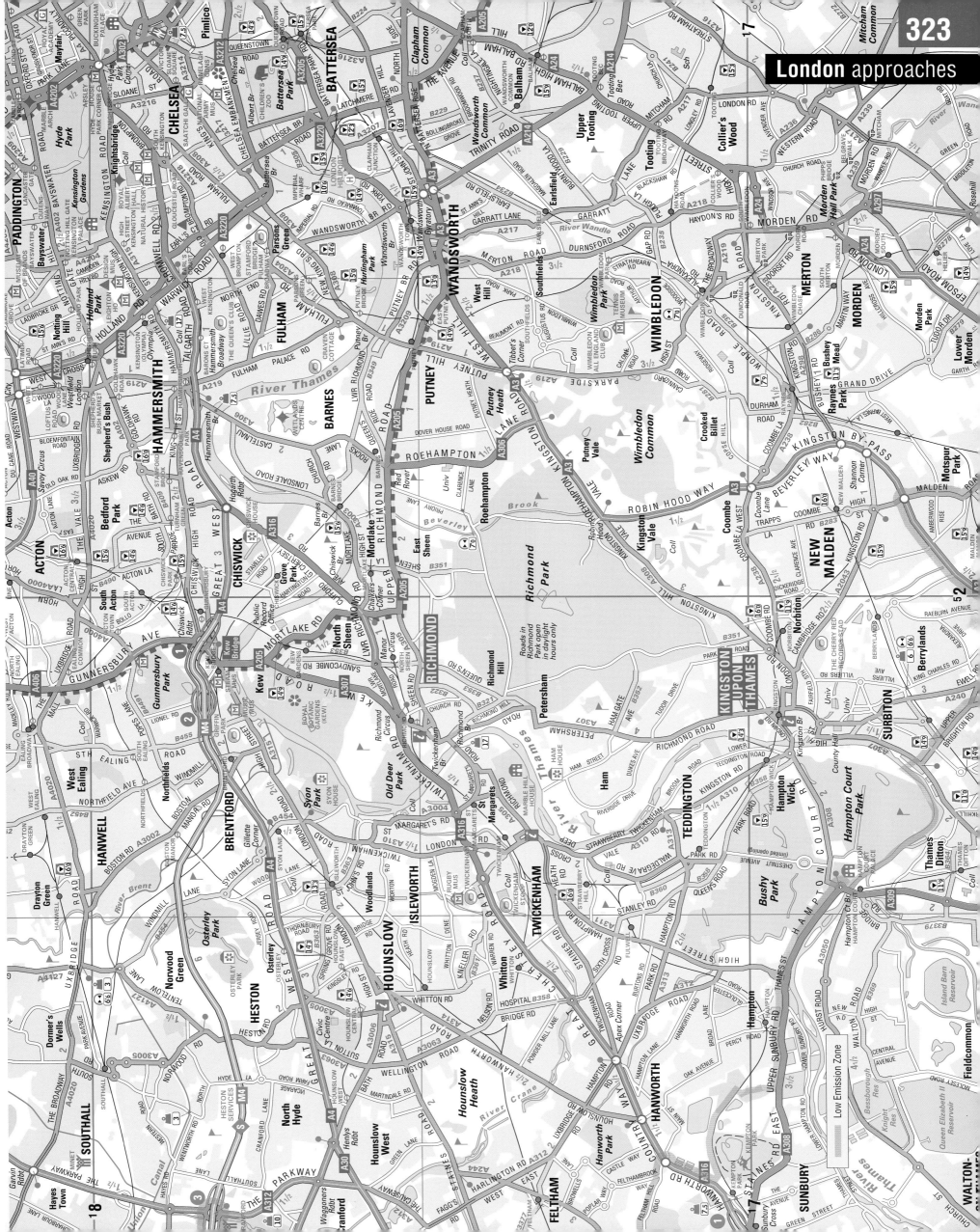

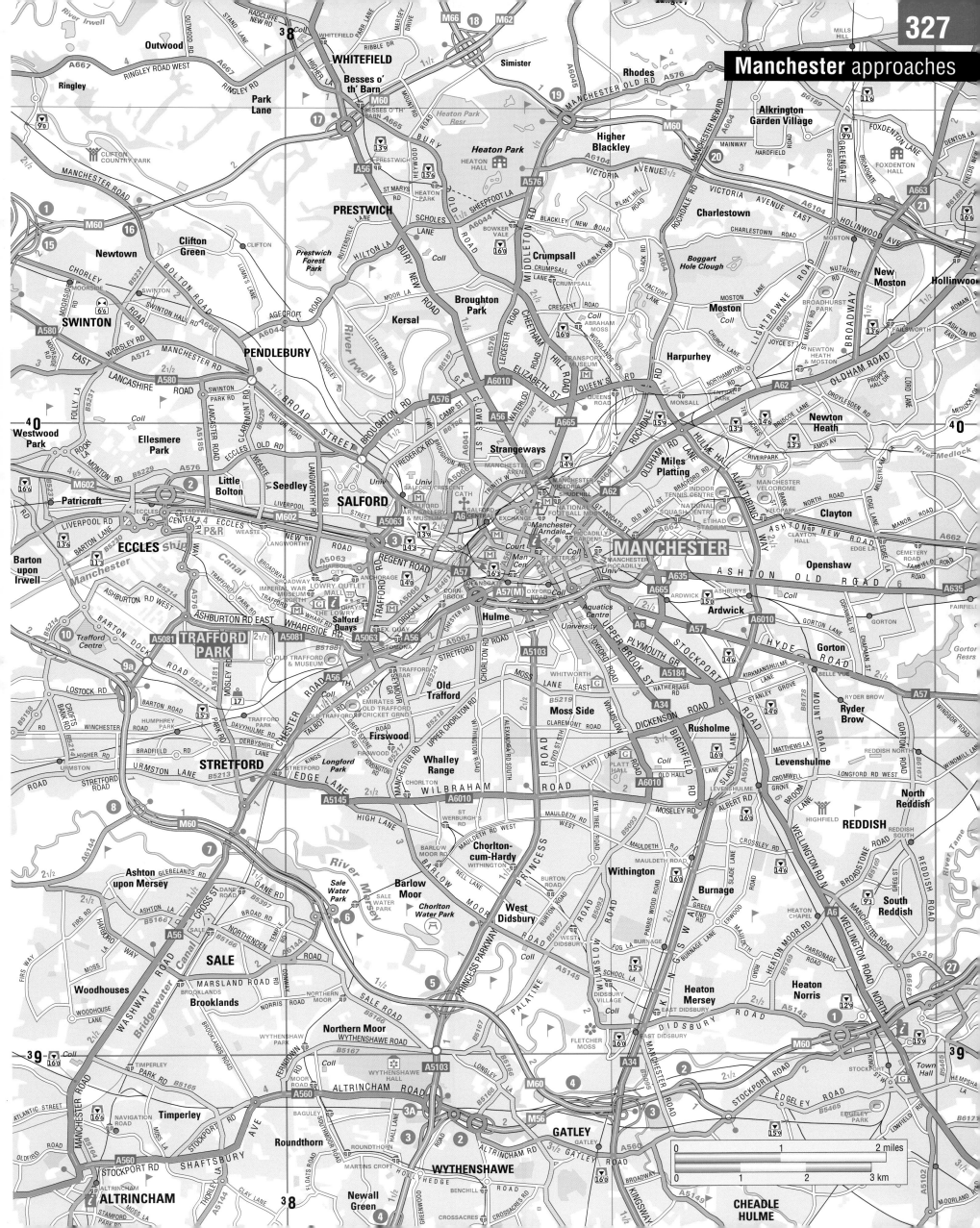

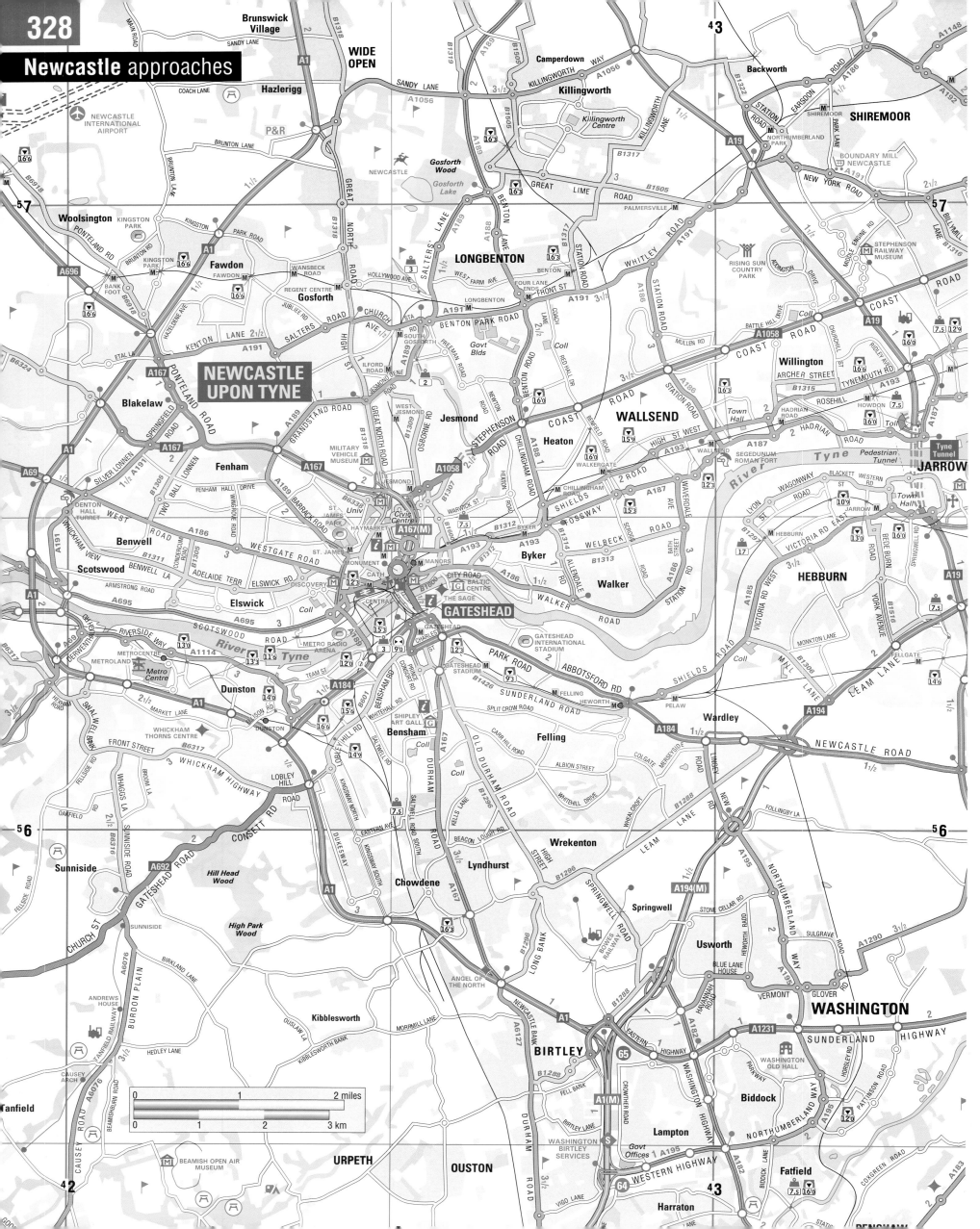

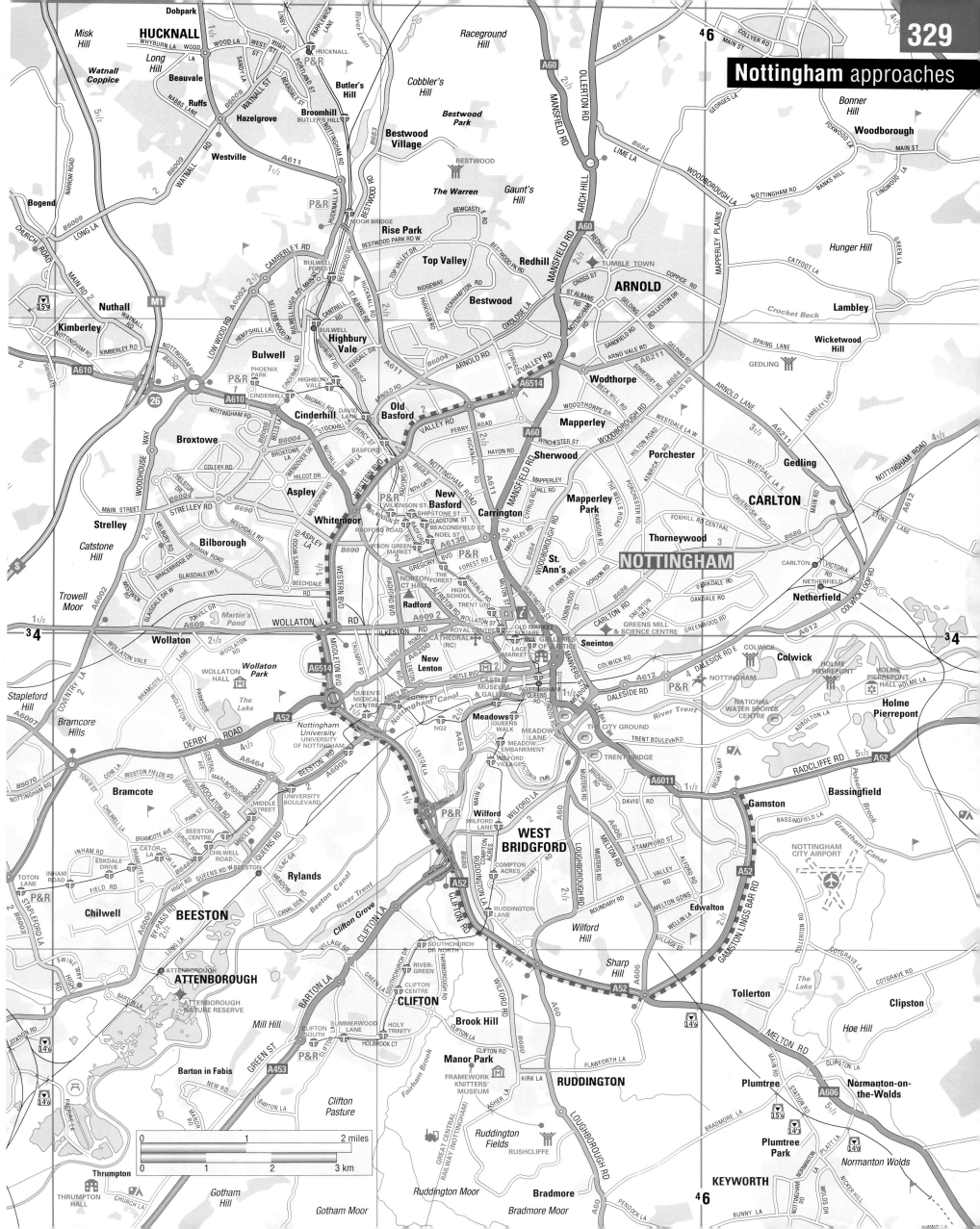

Town plan symbols

	Motorway
	Primary route – dual, single carriageway
	A road – dual, single carriageway
	B road – dual, single carriageway
	Minor through road
	One-way street
	Pedestrian roads
	Shopping streets
	Railway with station
	Tramway with station
	Underground or Metro station
H	Hospital
P	Parking
	Police, Post Office
	Shopmobility
▲	Youth hostel
	Bus or railway station building
	Shopping precinct or retail park
	Park
	Congestion charge zone

✠	Abbey or cathedral
	Ancient monument
	Aquarium
	Art gallery
	Bird collection or aviary
	Building of interest
	Castle
	Church of interest
	Cinema
	Garden
	Historic ship
	House
	House and garden
	Museum
	Preserved railway
	Roman antiquity
	Safari park
	Theatre
ℹ	Tourist information centre
	Zoo
✦	Other place of interest

Aberdeen

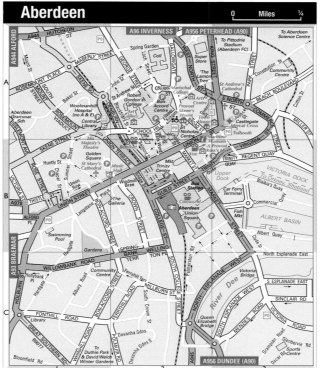

Aberystwyth

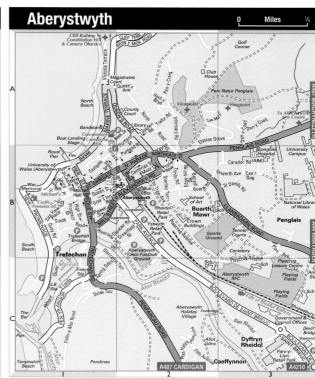

Ashford

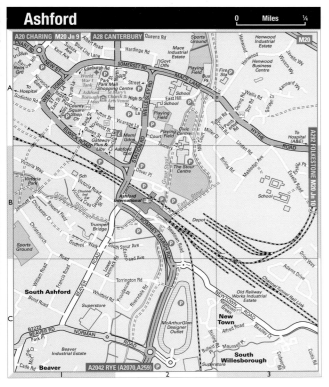

Ayr

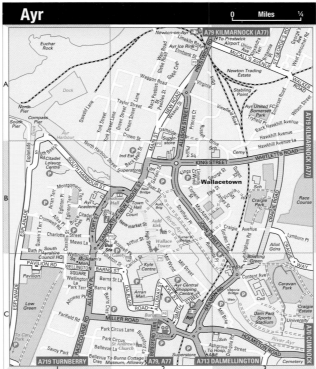

Bangor

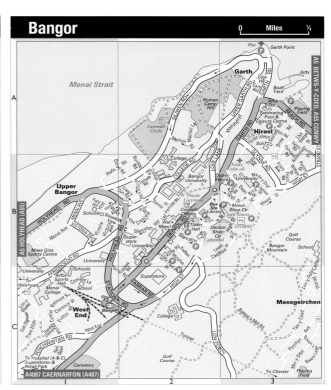

Barrow-in-Furness

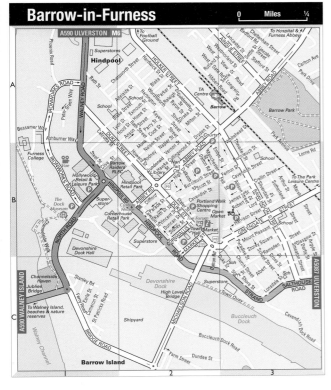

Bath

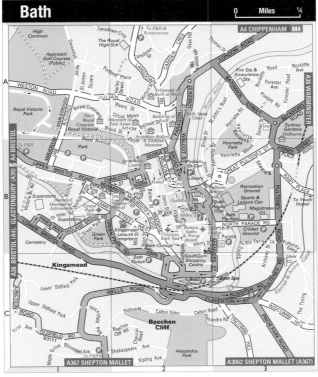

Berwick-upon-Tweed

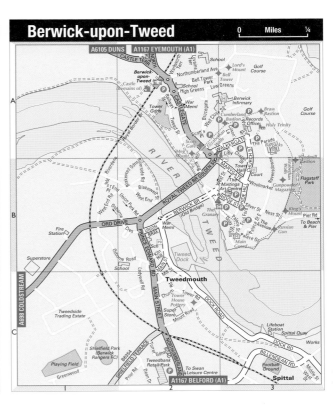

332

Birmingham page 133 ● **Blackpool** page 202 ● **Bournemouth** page 19 ● **Bradford** page 205 ● **Brighton** page 36 ● **Bristol** page 60 ● **Bury St Edmunds** page 125

Birmingham

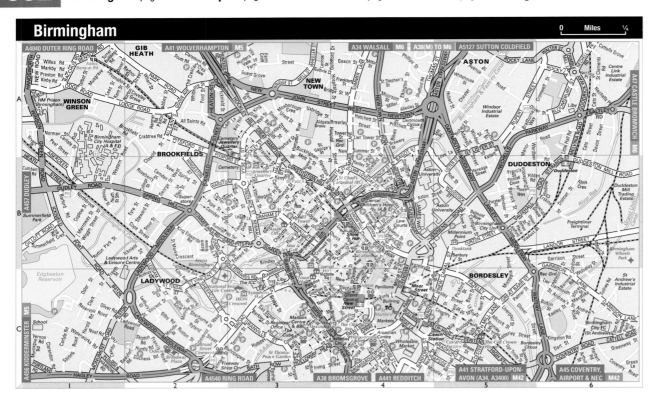

Blackpool

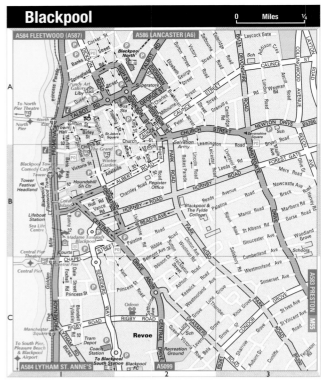

Bournemouth

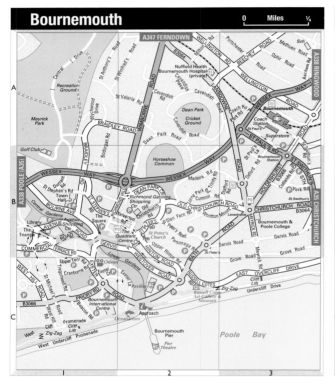

Bradford

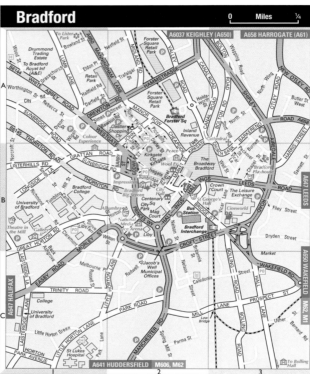

Brighton

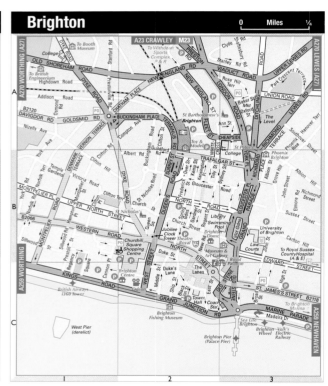

Bristol

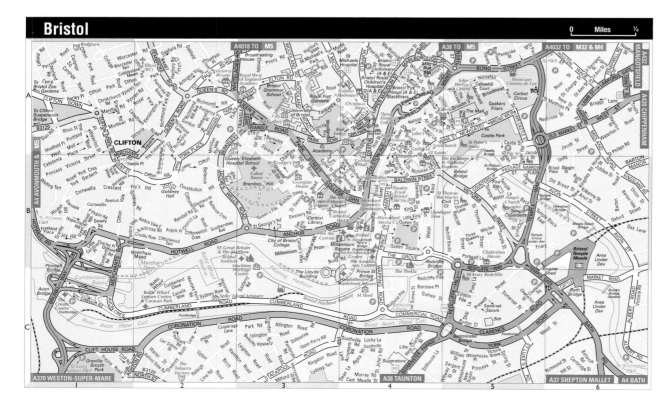

Bury St Edmunds

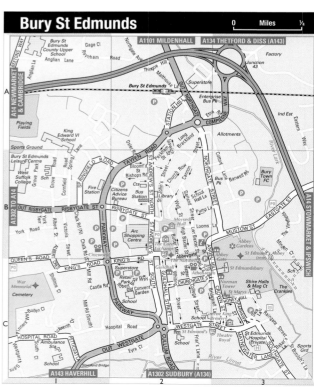

Cambridge page 123 • **Canterbury** page 54 • **Cardiff** page 59 • **Carlisle** page 239 • **Chelmsford** page 88 • **Cheltenham** page 99 • **Chester** page 166 • **Chichester** page 22 • **Colchester** page 107

333

Cambridge

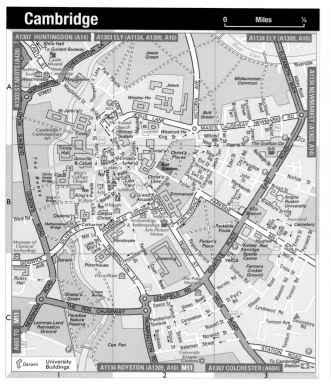

Canterbury

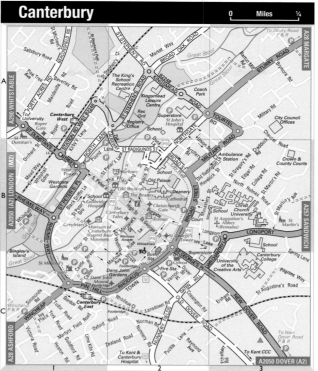

Cardiff / Caerdydd

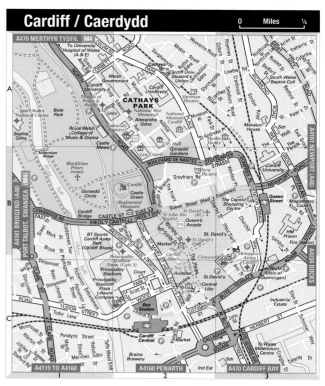

Carlisle

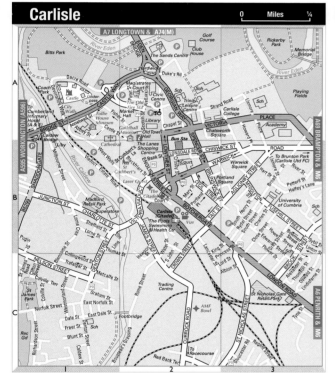

Chelmsford

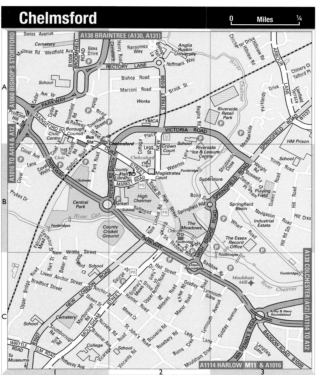

Cheltenham

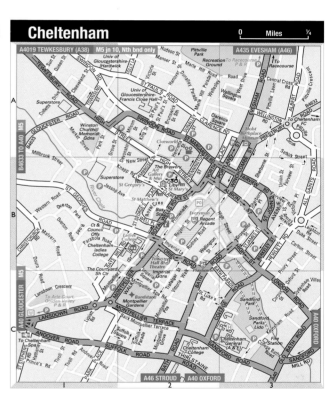

Chester

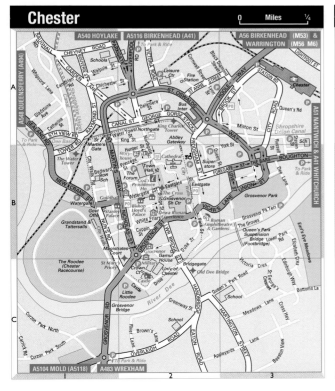

Chichester

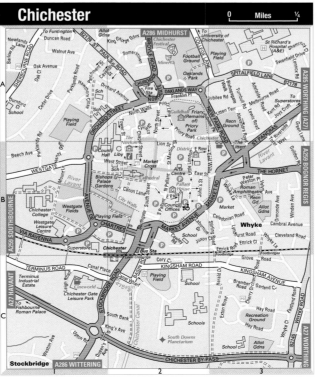

Colchester

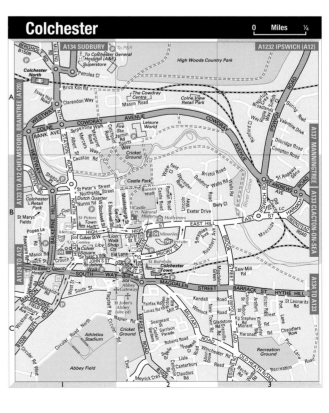

Coventry
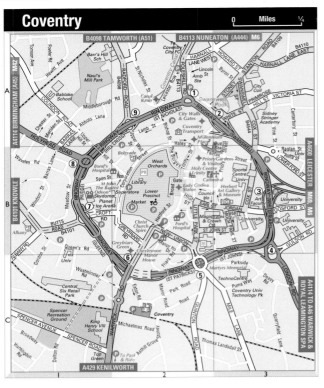

Derby
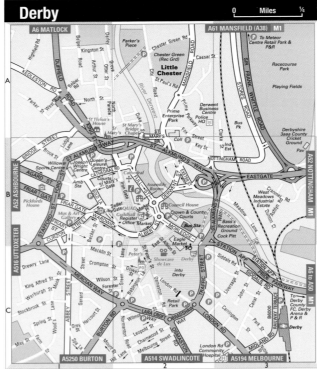

Dorchester
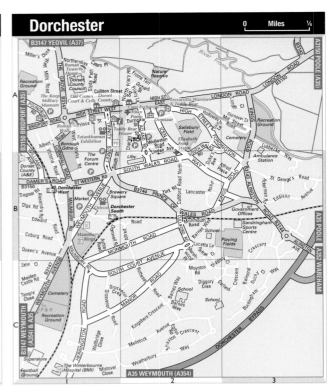

Dumfries
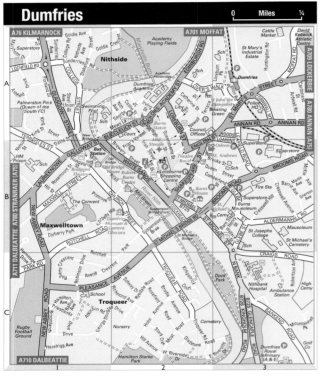

Dundee
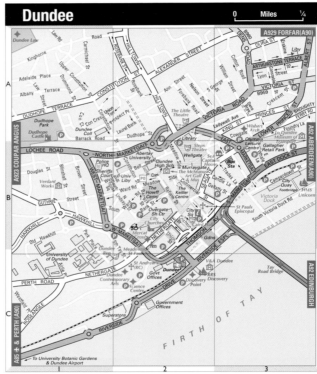

Durham
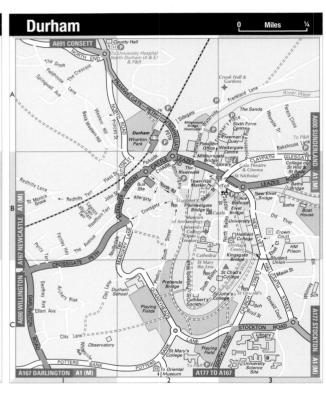

Edinburgh
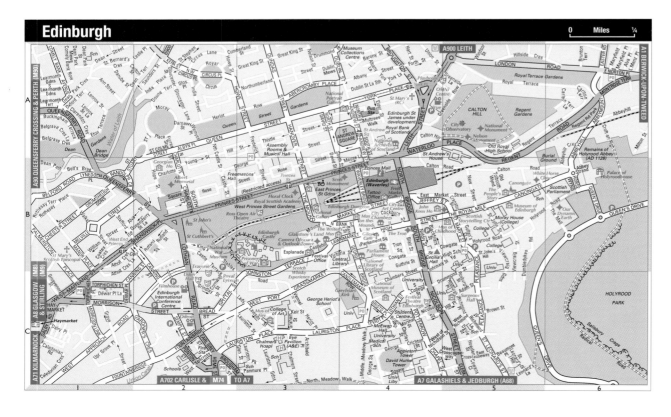

Exeter
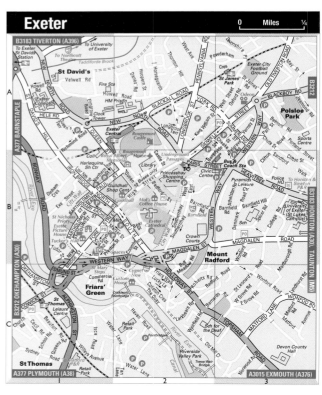

Fort William page 290 ● **Glasgow** page 267 ● **Gloucester** page 80 ● **Grimsby** page 201 ● **Hanley (Stoke-on-Tent)** page 168 ● **Harrogate** page 206 ● **Holyhead** page 178 ● **Hull** page 200

335

Fort William

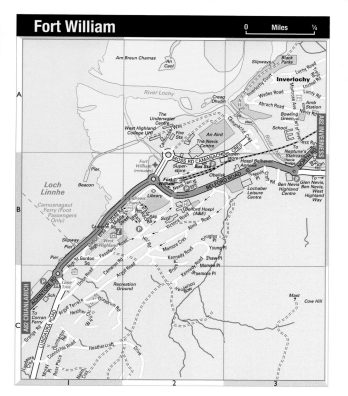

Glasgow

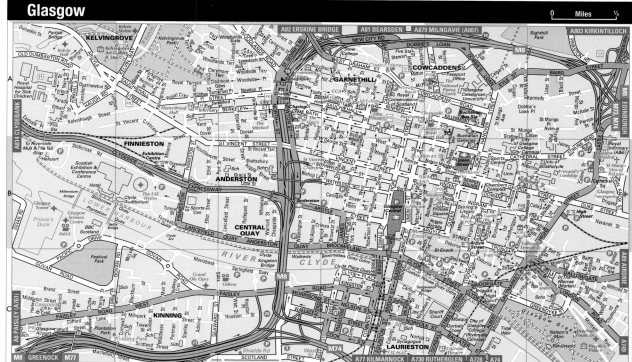

Gloucester

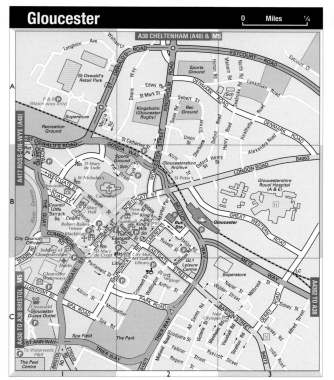

Grimsby

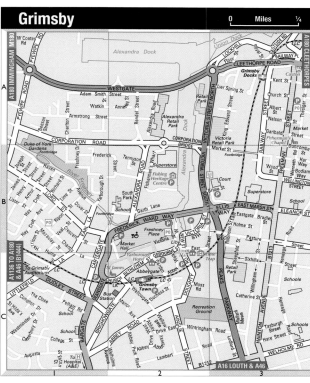

Hanley (Stoke-on-Trent)

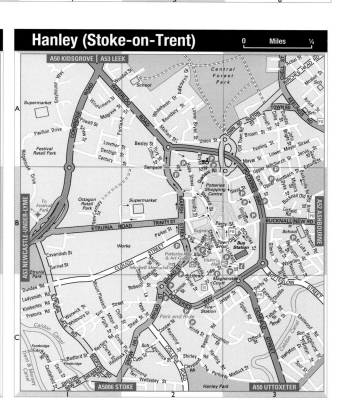

Harrogate

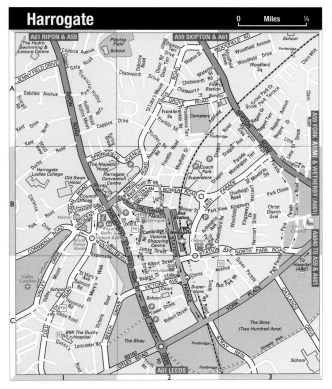

Holyhead / Caergybi

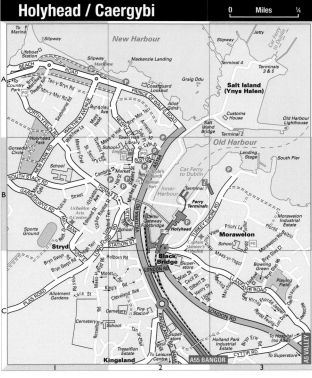

Hull

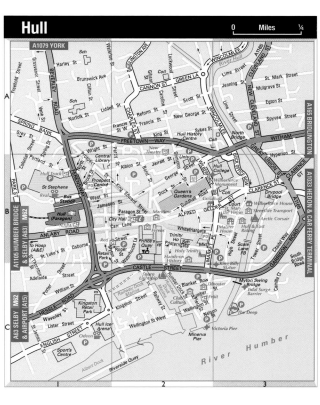

336

Inverness page 300 • **Ipswich** page 108 • **Kendal** page 221 • **King's Lynn** page 158 • **Leeds** page 205 • **Lancaster** page 211 • **Leicester** page 135 • **Lewes** page 36

Inverness

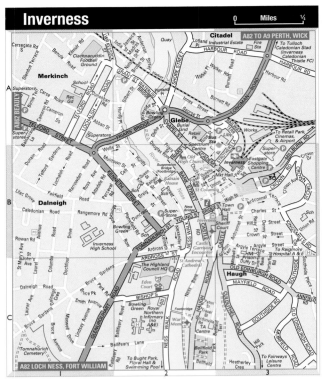

Ipswich

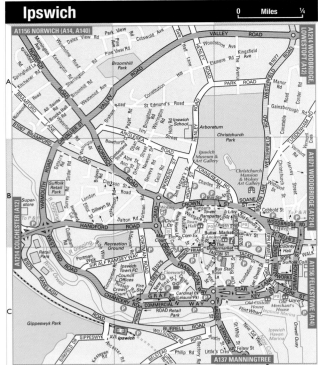

Kendal

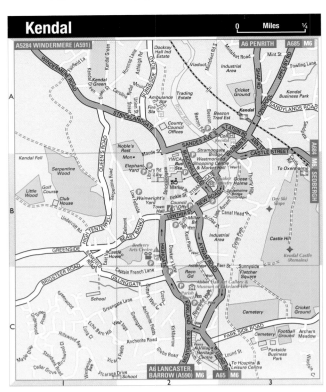

King's Lynn

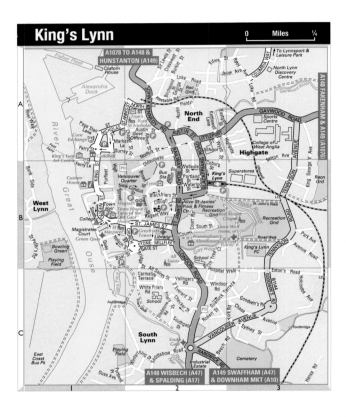

Leeds

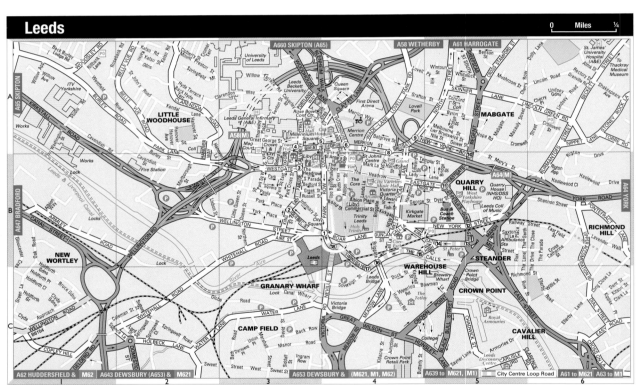

Lancaster

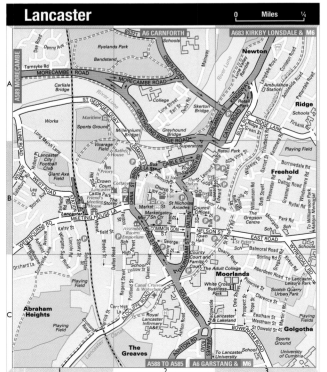

Leicester

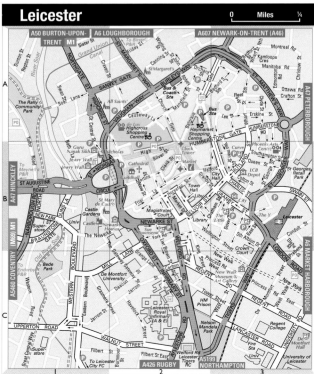

Lewes

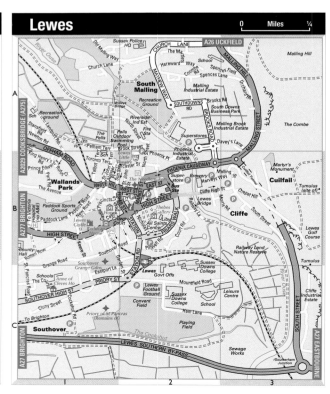

Lincoln

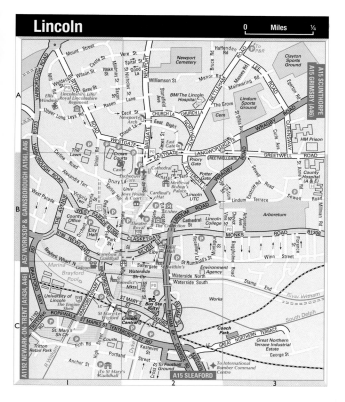

Liverpool

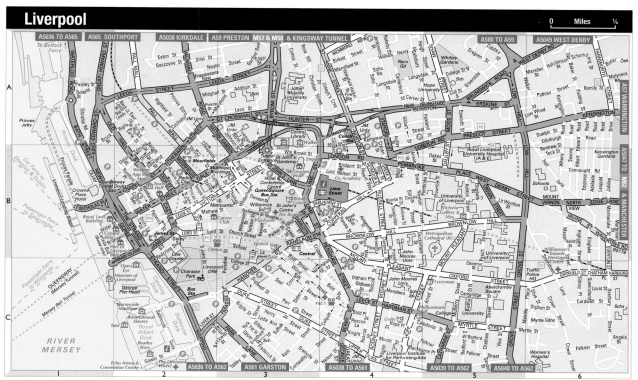

Llandudno

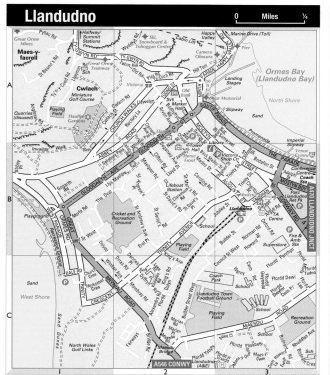

Llanelli

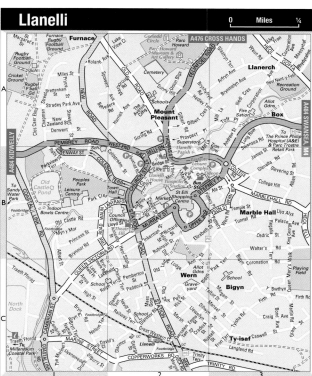

Luton

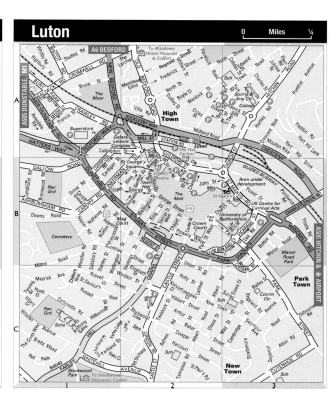

Macclesfield

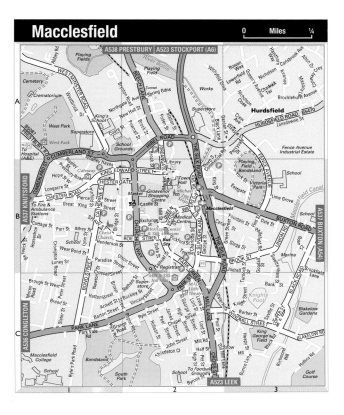

Manchester

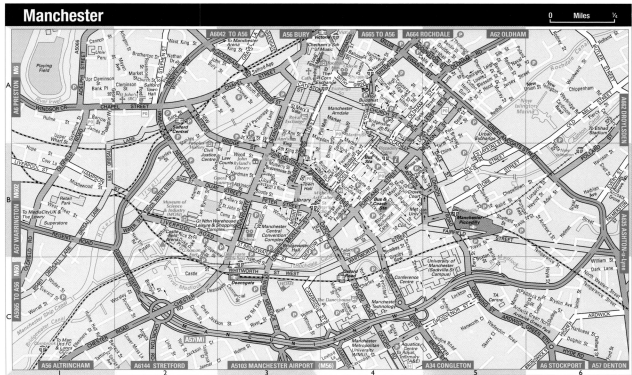

Maidstone

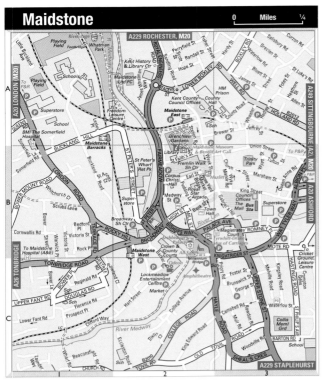

Merthyr Tydfil / Merthyr Tudful

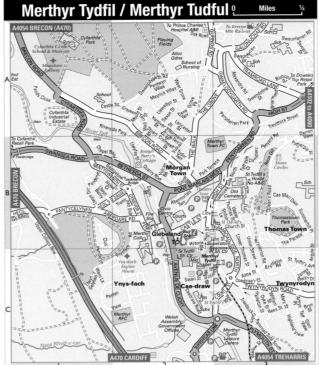

Middlesbrough

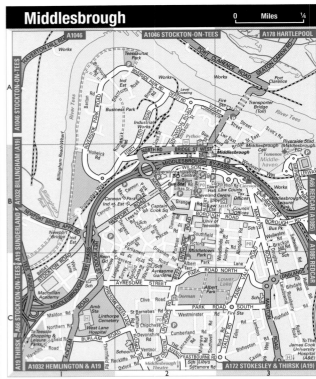

Milton Keynes

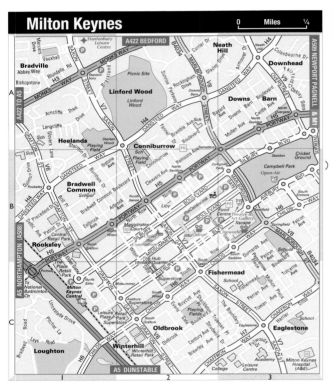

Newcastle upon Tyne

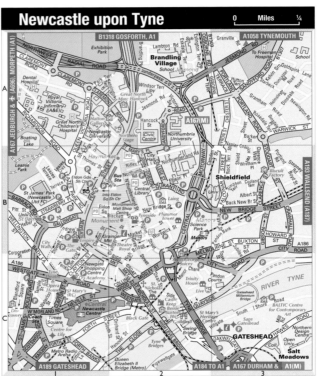

Newport / Casnewydd

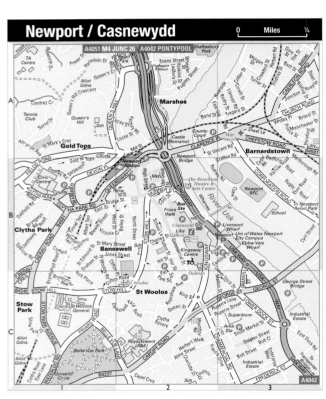

Newquay

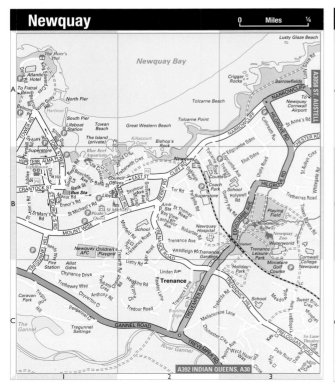

Newtown / Y Drenewydd

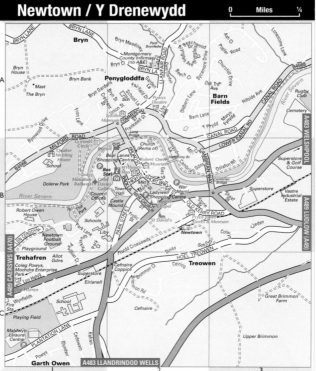

Northampton

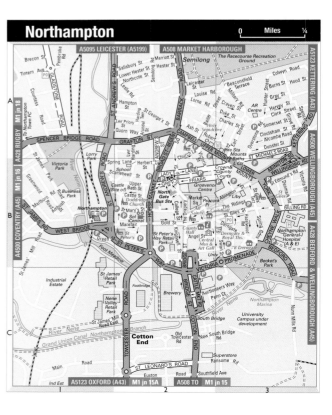

Norwich page 142 ● **Nottingham** page 153 ● **Oban** page 289 ● **Oxford** page 83 ● **Perth** page 286 ● **Peterborough** page 138 ● **Plymouth** page 7 ● **Poole** page 18 ● **Portsmouth** page 21

341

Norwich

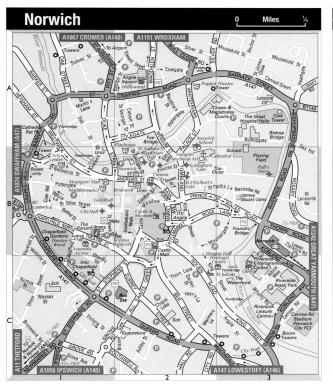

Nottingham

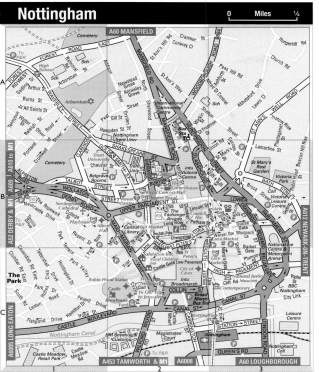

Oban

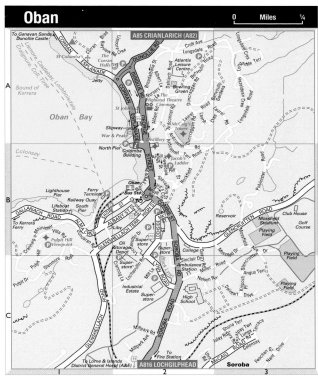

Oxford

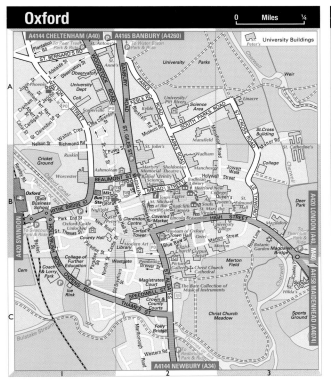

Perth

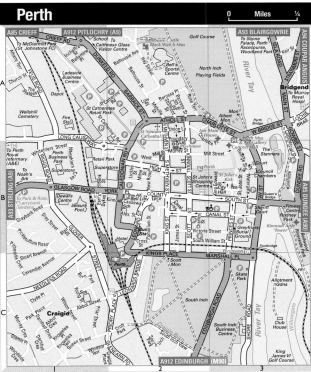

Peterborough

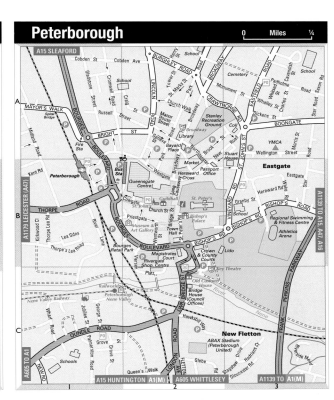

Plymouth

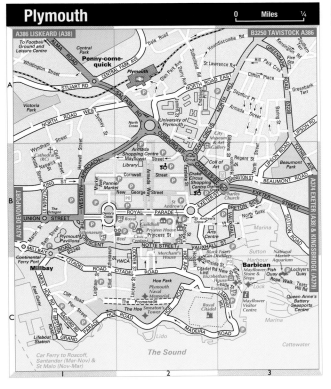

Poole

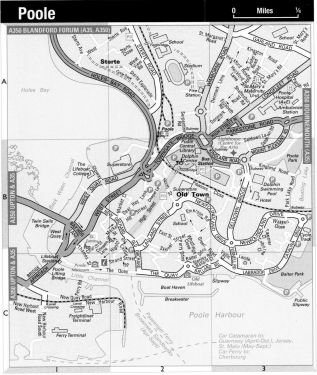

Portsmouth

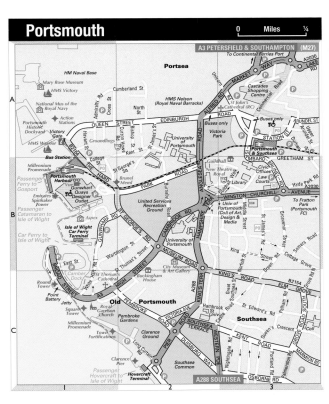

342

Preston page 194 ● **Reading** page 65 ● **St Andrews** page 287 ● **Salisbury** page 31 ● **Scarborough** page 217 ● **Shrewsbury** page 149 ● **Sheffield** page 186 ● **Southampton** page 32

Preston

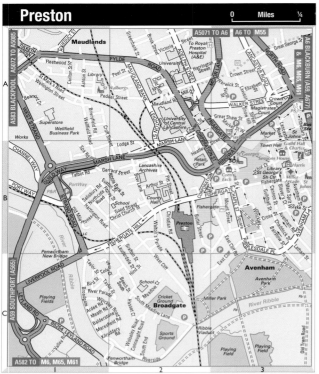

Reading

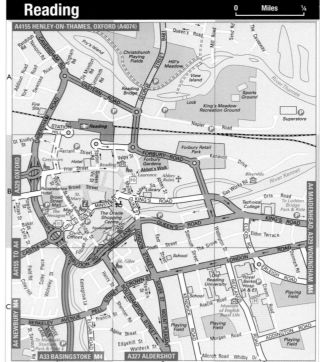

St Andrews

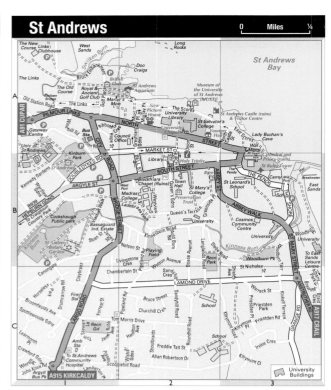

Salisbury

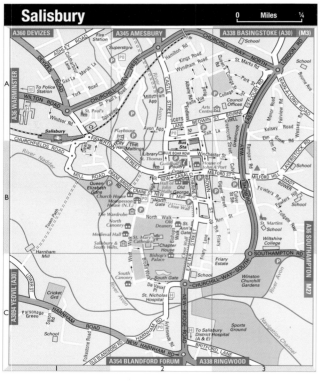

Scarborough

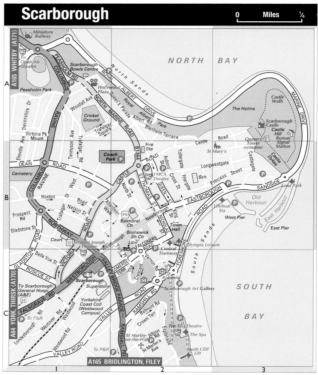

Shrewsbury

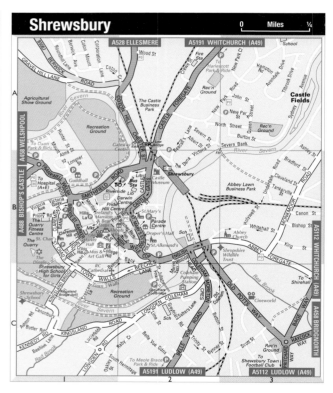

Sheffield

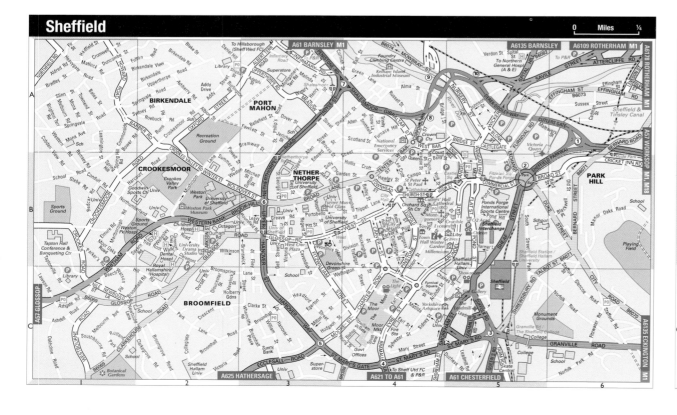

Southampton

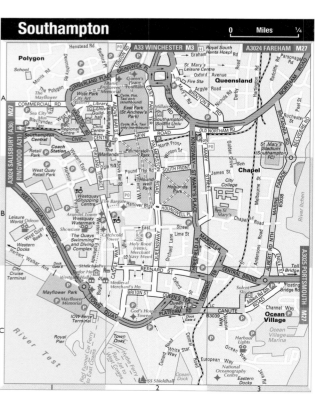

Southend page 69 ● **Stirling** page 278 ● **Stoke** page 168 ● **Stratford-upon-Avon** page 118 ● **Sunderland** page 243 ● **Swansea** page 56 ● **Swindon** page 63 ● **Taunton** page 28 ● **Telford** page 132

343

Southend-on-Sea

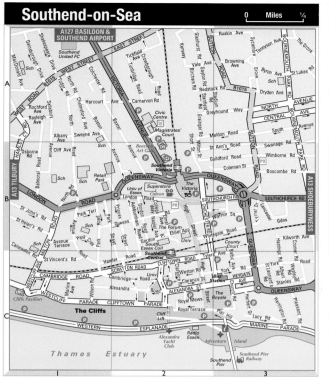

Stirling

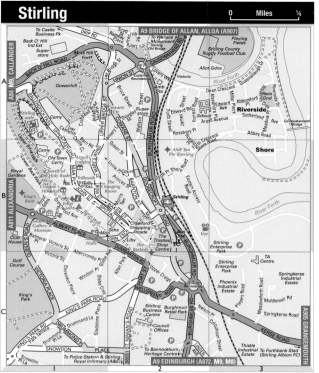

Stoke

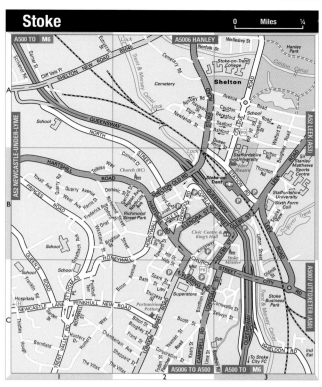

Stratford-upon-Avon

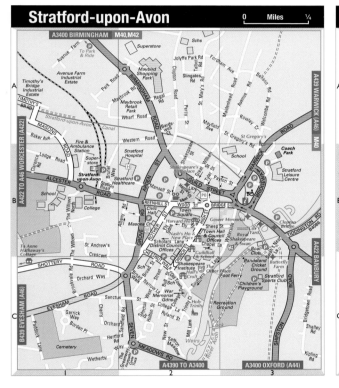

Sunderland

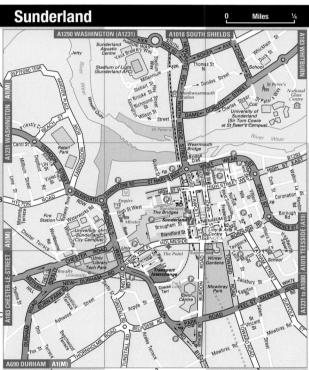

Swansea / Abertawe

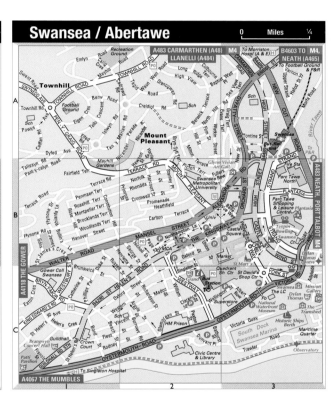

Swindon

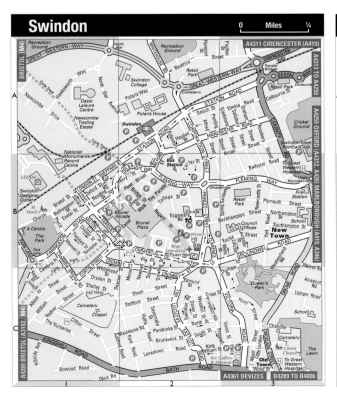

Taunton

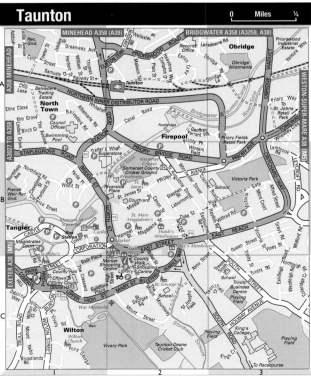

Telford

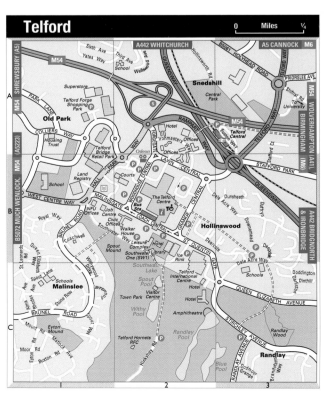

344

Torquay page 9 • Truro page 4 • Wick page 310 • Winchester page 33 • Windsor page 66 • Wolverhampton page 133 • Worcester page 117 • Wrexham page 166 • York page 207

Torquay

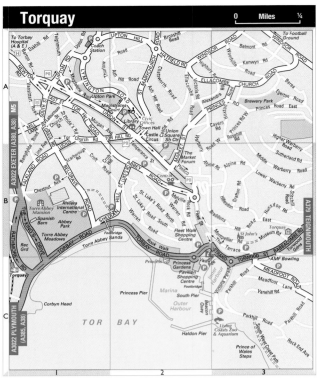

Truro

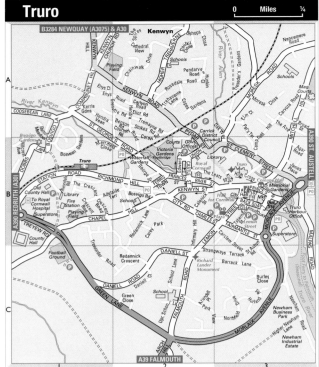

Wick

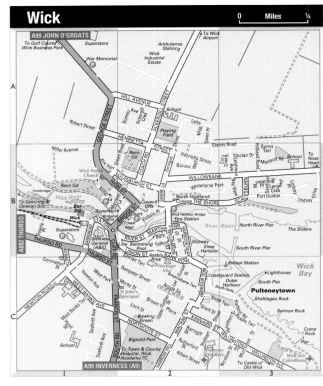

Winchester

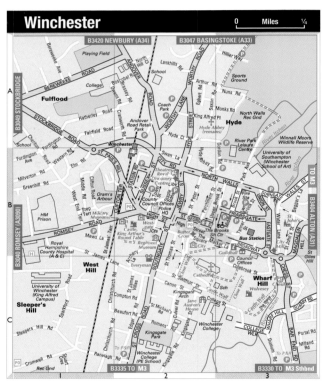

Windsor

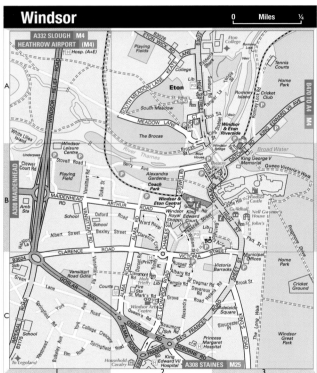

Wolverhampton

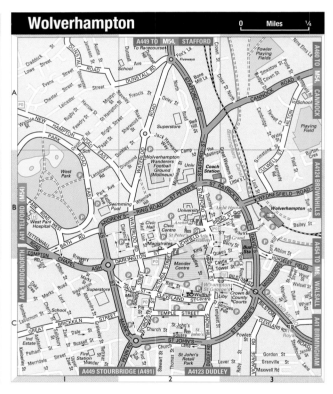

Worcester

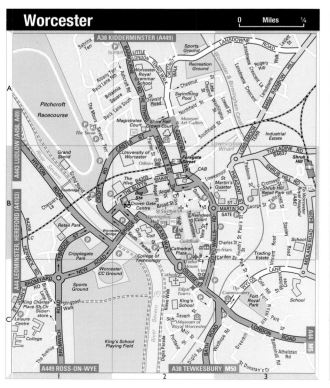

Wrexham / Wrecsam

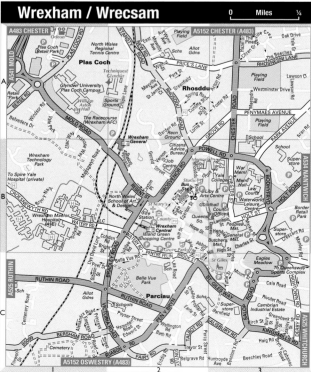

York

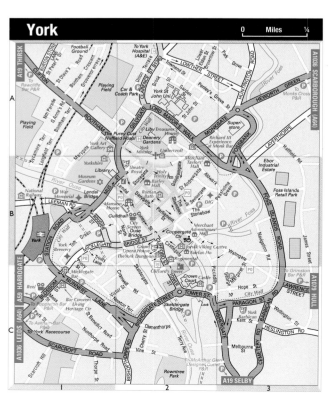

Town plan indexes

Aberdeen 331

Aberdeen ⇌ B2
Aberdeen Grammar School A1
Academy, The B2
Albert Basin B3
Albert Quay B3
Albury Rd C1
Alford Pl B1
Art Gallery 🏛 A2
Arts Centre A2
Back Wynd A2
Baker St A1
Beach Blvd. A3
Belmont ⊞ B2
Belmont St B2
Berry St A2
Blackfriars St A2
Blaikie's Quay B3
Bloomfield Rd. C1
Bon Accord Centre A2
Bon-Accord St B1/C1
Bridge St B2
Broad St A2
Bus Station B2
Car Ferry Terminal B3
Castlegate A2
Central Library A1
Chapel St B1
Cineworld 🎬 B2
Clyde St B3
College. A2
College St B2
Commerce St A2
Commercial Quay B3
Community Ctr A3/C1
Constitution St A3
Cotton St A3
Crown St B2
Denburn Rd. A2
Devanha Gdns C2
Devanha Gdns South C2
East North St. A3
Esslemont Ave A1
Ferryhill Rd C2
Ferryhill Terr. C2
Fish Market B3
Fonthill Rd. C1
Galleria, The B1
Gallowgate A2
George St. A2
Glenbervie Rd C3
Golden Sq B1
Grampian Rd C3
Great Southern Rd. C1
Guild St B2
Hardgate B1/C1
His Majesty's 🎭 A1
Holburn St C1
Hollybank Pl C1
Huntly St B1
Hutcheon St A1
Information Ctr ⓘ
John St. A2
Justice St A2
King St A2
Langstane Pl B1
Lemon Tree, The A2
Library C1
Loch St A2
Maberly St. A1
Marischal College 🏛 A2
Maritime Museum & Provost Ross's Ho 🏛 B2
Market B2
Market St. B2/B3
Menzies Rd C3
Mercat Cross ✦ A3
Millburn St. C2
Miller St. B3
Mount St A1
Music Hall 🎭 B1
North Esp East C3
North Esp West. C3
Oscar Rd. C3
Palmerston Rd C2
Park St A3
Police Station 🏢 A2
Polmuir Rd. C2
Post Office 🏣 A1/A2/A3/B1/C3
Provost Skene's Ho 🏛 A2
Queen Elizabeth Br C2
Queen St A2
Regent Quay B3
Regent Road A3
Robert Gordon's Coll. A2
Rose St. B1
Rosemount Pl A1
Rosemount Viaduct A1
St Andrew A2
St Andrew's Cathedral ✝ A3
St Mary's Cathedral ✝ B1
St Nicholas Centre A2
St Nicholas St A2
School Hill A2
Sinclair Rd. C3
Skene Sq A1
Skene St. B1
South College St. C2
South Crown St. C2
South Esp East C3
South Esp West. C3
South Mount St. A1
Sports Centre C3
Spring Garden A2
Springbank Terr. C1
Summer St. B1
Superstore B2
Swimming Pool C3
Thistle St. B1
Tolbooth 🏛 A2
Town House 🏛 A2
Trinity Centre B2
Trinity Quay B3
Union Row B1
Union Square B2
Union St. B1/B2
Upper Dock B3
Upper Kirkgate A2
Victoria Bridge C3
Victoria Dock B3
Victoria Rd C3
Victoria St. B2
Virginia St A3
Vue 🎬 B2
Wellington Pl B1
West North St A2
Whinhill Rd C1
Willowbank Rd C1
Windmill Brae. B2
Woolmanhill Hosp [H] A1

Aberystwyth 331

Aberystwyth Holiday Village C2
Aberystwyth Library and Ceredigion Archives C1
Aberystwyth ⇌ B2
Aberystwyth RFC C1
Aberystwyth Sta ⇌ B2
Aberystwyth Town Football Ground B2
Alexandra Rd B2
Ambulance Station C3
Baker St. B2
Banadl Rd C1
Bandstand B1
Bar, The C1
Bath St B1
Boat Landing Stage A1
Bridge St B2
Bronglais Hospital [H] C3
Bryn-y-Mor Rd A2
Buarth Rd. B2
Bus Station B2
Cae Melyn A2
Cae'r-Gog A2
Cambrian St B2
Caradoc Rd B3
Caravan Site C2
Castle (Remains of) 🏛 B1
Castle St. B1
Cemetery B1
Ceredigion Mus 🏛 B2
Chalybeate St B1
Cliff Terr. A1
Club House A2
Commodore 🎬 C1
County Court. B2
Crown Buildings. B2
Dan-y-Coed A3
Dinas Terr. C1
Eastgate. B1
Edge-hill Rd C1
Elm Tree Ave C2
Elysian Gr. C1
Felin-y-Mor Rd. C1
Fifth Ave. C2
Fire Station C2
Glanrafon Terr C1
Glan Rheidol B2
Glyndwr Rd C1
Golf Course A3
Government & Council Offices. C3
Gray's Inn Rd. B1
Great Darkgate St. B1
Greenfield St. C1
Heol-y-Bryn A2
High St. B1
Infirmary Rd. C1
Information Ctr ⓘ B1
Iorwerth Ave. B3
King St. B1
Lauraplace B1
Lifeboat Station B1
Llanbadarn Rd C1
Loveden Rd C1
Magistrates Court B1
Marina B1
Marine Terr. A1
Market Hall B1
Mill St. B1
Moor La. B1
National Library of Wales B3
New Promenade. A1
New St. B1
North Beach B1
North Parade B1
North Rd. B2
Northgate St. B1
Parc Natur Penglais. A3
Parc-y-Llyn Retail Pk C3
Park Ave. B2
Pavillion. A2
Pen-y-Craig A2
Pen-yr-angor C1
Pendinas C1
Penglais Rd. B3
Penrheidol C2
Pier St. B1
Plas Ave B2
Plas Helyg B2
Plascrug Ave. B2/C3
Plascrug Leisure Ctr C2
Police Station 🏢 ⓘ C1
Poplar Row B2
Portland Rd. B1
Portland St. B2
Powell St B1
Prospect St B1
Quay Rd. B1
Queen St. B1
Queen's Ave. B2
Queen's Rd B1
Rheidol Retail Park C2
Riverside Terr. C1
St Davids Rd B2
St Michael's ✝ B1
School of Art. B2
Seaview Pl. B1
Shopmobility B1
South Beach B1
South Rd B1
Sports Ground B2
Spring Gdns. C1
Stanley Terr. C1
Superstore B1/B2
Superstore B2/B3
Swimming Pool & L Ctr C1
Tanybwlch Beach. C1
Tennis Courts B3
Terrace Rd. B1
Trefechan Bridge B1
Trefechan Rd. C2
Trefor Rd A2
Trinity Rd B2
University Campus. B3
University of Wales (Aberystwyth) B3
Vale of Rheidol Railway ⇌ C3
Vaynor St. B2
Victoria Terr. A1
Viewpoint ✦ A2
Viewpoint ✦ A2
War Memorial. B1
Wharf Quay C1
Y Lanfa C1
Ystwyth Retail Park. C1

Ashford 331

Adams Drive C3
Albert Rd. C2
Alfred Rd C2
Apsley St A1
Ashford Borough Museum 🏛 A1
Ashford College C2
Ashford International Station ⇌ A2
Bank St. B1
Barrowhill Gdns A1
Beaver Industrial Est. C1
Beaver Rd C1
Beazley Ct C3
Birling Rd. B3
Blue Line La. A1
Bond Rd B2
Bowens Field A1
Bulleid Pl. C2
Business Park A2
Cade Rd C1
Chart Rd. A1
Chichester Cl B1
Christchurch Rd B2
Chunnel Industrial Estate. A2
Church Rd A1
Civic Centre. A2
County Square Shopping Centre A1
Croft Rd. A3
Cudworth Rd A2
Curtis Rd. C2
Dering Rd. A1
Dover Pl. A1
Drum La A1
East Hill A2
East St A1
Eastmead Ave B2
Edinburgh Rd C2
Elwick Rd B1
Essella Pk B3
Essella Rd B3
Fire Sta. A3
Forge La. A1
Francis Rd C1
Gateway Plus and Library B1
George St. B1
Godfrey Walk B1
Gordon Cl. A3
Government Offices A2
Hardinge Rd A1
Henwood A2
Henwood Bsns Centre A3
Henwood Ind Est A3
High St. A1
Hythe Rd C2
Information Ctr ⓘ A1
Javelin Way A3
Jemmett Rd. B1
Kennard Way. A3
Kent Ave. A1
Linden Rd. A2
Lower Denmark Rd C1
Mabledon Ave. B3
Mace Industrial Estate A2
Mace La. A2
Maunsell Pl. A3
McArthurGlen Designer Outlet C2
Memorial Gdns A2
Mill Ct. A2
Miller Cl. A2
Mortimer Cl. A2
New St A1
Newtown Green C2
Newtown Rd B2/C3
Norman Rd C2
North St A2
Norwood Gdns B1
Norwood St A1
Old Railway Works Industrial Estate. C3
Orion Way C3
Pk Mall Shopping Ctr. A1
Park Pl C1
Park St A1/A2
Pemberton Rd. A3
Police Station 🏢 B1
Post Office 🏣 A1/A3
Providence St. B1
Queen St. A1
Queens Rd A2
Regents Pl A1
Riversdale Rd C2
Romney Marsh Rd B2
St John's La. A1
St Mary's Church & Arts Venue 🎭 A1
Somerset Rd A2
South Stour Ave B2
Star Rd A3
Station Rd B2
Stirling Rd C2
Stour Centre, The. B2
Sussex Ave. A2
Tannery La. C2
Torrington Rd C2
Trumper Bridge B1
Tufton Rd. B1
Tufton St. A1
Vicarage La A2
Victoria Cres. B1
Victoria Park. C1
Victoria Way B1
Wallis Rd. A2
Wellesley Rd A2
West St. B1
Whitfeld Rd A3
William Rd. C1

Ayr 331

Ailsa Pl C1
Alexandra Terr A3
Allison St B2
Alloway Pk. C1
Alloway Pl C1
Alloway St B2
Arran Mall C2
Arran Terr B1
Arthur St B2
Ashgrove St. C2
Auld Brig B2
Auld Kirk ⛪ A2
Ayr ⇌ C2
Ayr Academy B1
Ayr Central Sh Ctr. C2
Ayr Harbour. A1
Ayr Ice Rink C3
Ayr United FC A3
Back Hawkhill Ave A3
Back Main St. B2
Back Peebles St. A2
Barns Cres. C1
Barns Pk. C1
Barns St. C2
Barns Street La. B1
Bath Pl B1
Bellevue Cres C1
Bellevue La. C1
Beresford La. C2
Beresford Terr. C2
Boswell St. B1
Britannia Pl. A3
Bruce Cres. B1
Bus Sta. B2
Carrick St. B2
Cassillis St. C1
Cathcart St B1
Charlotte St. B2
Citadel Leisure Ctr. B1
Citadel Pl. B1
Compass Pier A1
Content Ave. C3
Content St. C2
Craigie Ave B3
Craigie Rd. B3
Craigie Way. C3
Cromwell Rd B2
Crown St A2
Dalblair Rd. C2
Dam Park Sports Stadium A3
Damside. B2
Dongola Rd C2
Eglinton Pl. B1
Eglinton Terr. B1
Elba St C2
Elmbank St. A2
Esplanade B1
Euchar Rock C1
Farifield Rd C1
Fort St. B1
Fothringham Rd C2
Fullarton St C1
Gaiety 🎭 B2
Garden St. B1
George St. B2
George's Ave A3
Glebe Cres. A2
Glebe Rd A2
Gorden Terr. B3
Green St. C2
Green Street La C2
Hawkhill Ave C3
Hawkhill Avenue La B3
High St B2
Holmston Rd. C3
Information Ctr ⓘ B1
James St A2
John St. B2
King St A2
Kings Ct A2
Kyle Centre C2
Kyle St B2
Library C2
Limekiln Rd. A2
Limonds Wynd B2
Lymburn Pl B3
Macadam Pl B2
Main St. B2
Mcadam's Monument C1
Mccall's Ave A3
Mews La. A3
Mill Brae. C1
Mill St. C2
Mill Wynd. C2
Miller Rd C2
Montgomerie Terr. B1
New Bridge B2
New Bridge St. B2
New Rd. A2
Newmarket St. B2
North Harbour St B1
North Pier A1
Odeon 🎬 C2
Oswald La C1
Park Circus C1
Park Circus La. C1
Park Terr C1
Pavilion Rd B1
Peebles St. A2
Philip Sq. A2
Police Station 🏢 B2
Post Office 🏣 A2/B2
Prestwick Rd. B1
Princes Ct C2
Queen St B3
Queen's Terr. B1
Racecourse Rd C1
River St. B2
Riverside Pl. B2
Russell St B2
St Andrews Church ⛪ C2
St George's Rd A3
Sandgate. B2
Savoy Park. C1
Smith St. C2
Somerset Rd A3
South Beach Rd B1
South Harbour St. B1
South Pier A1
Station Rd C2
Strathayr Pl. B3
Superstore A2/B2
Taylor St. B3
Town Hall. B1
Tryfield Pl C3
Turner's Bridge B2
Union Ave. C3
Victoria Bridge C3
Victoria St. B2
Viewfield Rd A3
Virginia Gdns A2
Waggon Rd A2
Walker Rd C3
Wallace Tower ✦ B2
Weaver St B2
Weir Rd. C2
Wellington La C1
Wellington Sq. C1
West Sanouhar Rd A3
Whitletts Rd A3
Wilson St A2
York St A1
York Street La B1

Bangor 331

Abbey Rd C2
Albert St. C3
Ambrose St A3
Ambulance Station A3
Arfon Sports Hall C1
Ashley Rd B3
Bangor Mountain B3
Bangor Station ⇌ C1
Bangor University C1
Beach Rd C1
Belmont St C1
Bishop's Mill Rd B2
Boat Yard C1
Brick St B2
Buckley Rd. B2
Bus Station B2
Caellepa B2
Caernarfon Rd C1
Cathedral ✝ B2
Cemetery A3
Clarence St A1
Clock Tower ✦ B3
College B2/C2
College La C2
College Rd B2
Convent La. C1
Council Offices B2
Craig y Don Rd. B2
Crescent, The B2
Dean St. A3
Deiniol Rd B2
Deiniol Shopping Ctr. B2
Deiniol St. B2
Edge Hill. A3
Euston Rd C1
Fairview Rd A3
Farrar Rd C2
Ffordd Cynfal C3
Ffordd Islwyn C3
Ffordd y Castell C3
Ffriddoedd Rd. B1
Field St. A3
Fountain St. A3
Friars Ave. B3
Friars Rd B3
Friary (Site of) ✦ B3
Gardd Deman C2
Garth Hill A3
Garth Point B3
Garth Rd. A3
Glanrafon B2
Glanrafon Hill B2
Glynne Rd B2
Golf Course A2
Golf Course C2
Gorad Rd C3
Gorsedd Circle 🏛 B2
Gwern Las C1
Heol Dewi C1
High St B3/C2
Hill St B2
Holyhead Rd B1
Hwfa Rd B2
Information Ctr ⓘ B2
James St B2
Library B2
Llys Emrys A3
Lon Ogwen C1
Lon-Pobty C1
Lon-y-Felin C1
Lon-y-Glyder C1
Love La. C1
Lower Penrallt Rd B2
Lower St. C2
Maes Glas Sports Ctr B1
Maes-y-Dref B3
Maeshyfryd A3
Meirion La. A3
Meirion Rd. A3
Menai Ave. B1
Menai College. C1
Menai Shopping Ctr. B3
Min-y-Ddol C3
Minafon C3
Mount Sq A3
Mount St A3
Nant Tait Centre C2
Napier St A3
Nelson St C1
North Rd B2
Open Market B2
Orme Rd. A3
Parc Victoria. A2
Penchwintan Rd C1
Penlon Gr. A3
Penrhyn Ave A3
Pier A1
Police Station 🏢 B2
Post Office 🏣 B2/B3/C1/C3
Prince's Rd B2
Queen's Terr. B3
Sackville Rd C2
St Paul's St B2
Seion St. B2
Seiriol Rd A3
Siliwen Rd A1
Snowdon View B1
Station Rd C1
STORIEL 🏛 B2
Strand St B3
Superstore B3/C2
Swimming Pool and Leisure Centre A3
Tan-y-Coed C3
Tegid Rd. A3
Temple Rd B2
Theatr Gwynedd 🎭 B2
Totton Rd. A3
Town Hall. B2
Treflan C3
Trem Elidir. C1
Upper Garth Rd. A3
Victoria Rd. B2
Victoria Dr. A3
Victoria St. B2
Vron St. C3
Well St. B3
West End C1
William St B2

Barrow-in-Furness 331

Abbey Rd A3/B2
Adelaide St. A2
Ainslie St A2
Albert St. C3
Allison St A2
Anson St. A2
Argyle St C3
Arthur St A2
Ashburner Way A1
Barrow Park C3
Barrow Raiders RLFC B1
Barrow Station ⇌ B2
Bath St A1/B2
Bedford Rd A3
Bessamer Way A1
Blake St A1/A2
Bridge Rd. C2
Buccleuch Dock C3
Buccleuch Dock Rd. C2/C3
Buccleuch St. B2/B3
Byron St A2
Calcutta St A1
Cameron St. A2
Carlton Ave A3
Cavendish Dock Rd C3
Cavendish St. B2/B3
Channelside Haven C1
Channelside Walk B1
Chatsworth St A2
Cheltenham St. A2
Church St. B2
Clifford St. A2
Clive St. B2
Collingwood St. A2
Cook St. A2
Cornerhouse Retail Pk B2
Cornwallis St A2
Courts B2
Crellin St. B2
Cross St A2
Dalkeith St B2
Dalton Rd. B2/C2
Derby St. C2
Devonshire Dock C2
Devonshire Dock Hall B1
Dock Museum, The B1
Drake St. A2
Dryden St. A3
Duke St. A1/B2/C3
Duncan St. A2
Dundee St. A3
Dundonald St. A2
Earle St. C1
Emlyn St. A3
Exmouth St. C2
Farm St. A2
Fell St. B2
Fenton St. C2
Ferry Rd. C1
Fire Station B2
First Ave. C1
Forster St A3
Furness College C1
Glasgow St. A2
Goldsmith St. A2
Greengate St. C2
Hardwick St. A2
Harrison St. A2
Hartington St. A2
Hawke St. A2
Hibbert Rd. C2
High Level Bridge B1
High St. B2
Hindpool Rd. A1
Hindpool Retail Park. B1
Holker St. A2
Hollywood Ret & L Pk B1
Hood St A2
Howard St B2
Howe St A2
Information Ctr ⓘ B2
Ironworks Rd. A1/B1
James St B3
Jubilee Bridge C1
Keith St B2
Keyes St A3
Lancaster St B2
Lawson St B2
Library B2
Lincoln St. B2
Longreins Rd. C3
Lord St B2
Lorne Rd B3
Lyon St A2
Manchester St B2
Market B2
Market St. B2
Marsh St. B2
Michaelson Rd C2
Milton St B2
Monk St B2
Mount Pleasant B2
Nan Tait Centre C2
Napier St A3
Nelson St C1
North Rd B2
Open Market B2
Orme Rd. A3
Parade St B2
Paradise St B3
Park Ave. A3
Park Dr. A3
Parker St A2
Parry St A2
Peter Green Way A1
Phoenix Rd B2
Police Station 🏢 B2
Portland Walk Sh Ctr A2
Raleigh St B2
Ramsden St B3
Rawlinson St B3
Robert St B2
Rodney St B2
Rutland St A2
St Patricks Rd C1
Salthouse Rd B3
School St B3
Scott St B2
Settle St A3
Shore St B1
Sidney St B2
Silverdale St B3
Slater St B3
Smeaton St B3
Stafford St A2
Stanley Rd C1
Stark St B1
Steel St B1
Storey Sq C3
Strand C3
Superstore A1/B1/C3
Sutherland St B2
TA Centre B3
Thwaite St B2
Town Hall. B2
Town Quay C3
Vernon St B2
Vincent St B2
Vue Cinema 🎬 A1
Walney Rd A1
West Gate Rd C2
West View Rd A3
Westmorland St A2
Whitehead St A2
Wordsworth St A2

Bath 331

Alexandra Park B2
Alexandra Rd. C2
Ambulance Station A3
Approach Golf Courses (Public) A1
Archway St C3
Assembly Rooms & Fashion Museum 🏛 A2
Avon St. B2
Barton St B2
Bath Abbey ✝ B2
Bath Aqua Glass 🏛 B2
Bath College B2
Bath Rugby Club B3
Bath Spa Station ⇌ C2
Bathwick St. A3
Beckford Road A3
Beechen Cliff Rd. C2
Bennett St. A2
Bloomfield Ave. C1
Broad Quay B2
Broad St. B2
Brock St. A2
Building of Bath Museum 🏛 A2
Bus Station C2
Calton Gdns. C2
Calton Rd. C2
Camden Cr. A2
Cavendish Rd. A1
Cemetery B1
Charlotte St. B2
Chaucer Rd. C2
Cheap St. B2
Circus Mews A2
Claverton St. C2
Corn St. C2
Cricket Ground A3
Daniel St. A3
Edward St. A2
Ferry La. B2
Fire Station B2
First Ave. A3
Forester Ave. A3
Forester Rd. A3
Gays Hill A2
George St. B2
Great Pulteney St. B3
Green Park B1
Green Park Rd. B2
Green Park Station ⇌ B1
Grove St. A2
Guildhall 🏛 A2
Harley St. A2
Hayesfield Park C1
Henrietta Gdns A3
Henrietta Mews B3
Henrietta Park A3
Henrietta Rd A3
Henrietta St. B2
Henry St. B2
Herschel Museum of Astronomy 🏛 B1
High Common A1
Holburne Museum 🏛 A3
Holloway C2
Information Ctr ⓘ B2
James St West B1
Jane Austen Centre 🏛 B2
Julian Rd A1
Junction Rd. A1
Kingsmead Leisure Complex B2
Kipling Ave C1
Lansdown Cr. A1
Lansdown Gr. A2
Lansdown Rd. A2
Library B2
London Rd A3
London St. A2
Lower Bristol Rd C1
Lower Oldfield Park. C1
Lyncombe Hill C3
Magistrates' Court. B2
Manvers St. B3
Maple Gr C2
Margaret's Hill A2
Marlborough Bldgs A1
Marlborough La B1
Midland Bridge Rd B1
Milk St B2
Milsom St B2
Monmouth St B2
Morford St A2
Museum of Bath at Work 🏛 A2
Museum of East Asian Art 🏛 A2
New King St. B1
No 1 Royal Cres 🏛 A1
North Rd C3
North Parade Rd. B3
Oldfield Rd. C2
Paragon. A2
Pines Way B1
Podium Shopping Ctr A2
Police Station 🏢 B3
Portland Pl. A2
Postal Museum 🏛 B2
Powlett Rd. A3
Prior Park Rd. C3
Pulteney Bridge ✦ B2
Pulteney Gdns. B3
Pulteney Rd. B3/C3
Queen Sq B2
Raby Pl. B3
Recreation Ground B3
Rivers St. A2
Rockliffe Ave A3
Rockliffe Rd. A3
Roman Baths & Pump Room 🏛 B2
Rossiter Rd C3
Royal Ave. A1
Royal Cr. A1
Royal High School, The A1
Royal Victoria Park A1
St James Sq B1
St John's Rd. A3
Sally Lunn's House ✦ B2
Shakespeare Ave C2
Shopmobility B2
South Pde B3
SouthGate Shopping Centre B2
Sports & Leisure Ctr B3
Spring Gdns B2
Stall St. B2
Stanier Rd B1
Superstore B1
Sydney Gdns A3
Sydney Pl. A3
Sydney Rd. B3
Theatre Royal 🎭 B2
Thermae Bath Spa ✦ B2
Thomas St A3
Tyning, The A3
Union St B2
University A3
Upper Bristol Rd. A1
Upper Oldfield Park. C1
Victoria Art Gallery 🏛 B2
Victoria Bridge Rd B1
Walcot St. B2
Wells Rd. C1
Westgate Buildings B2
Westgate St. B2
Weston Rd A1
Widcombe Hill C3

Berwick-upon-Tweed 331

Berwick-upon-Tweed ⇌ A2
Billendean Rd. C3
Blakewell Gdns B2
Blakewell Rd B2
Brass Bastion ✦ A3
Bridge St B3
Brucegate St. B2
Castle (Remains of) ✦ A2
Castle Terr. A2
Castlegate A2
Chapel St. C2
Church Rd. C2
Church St. B3
Court A2
Coxon's La A3
Cumberland Bastion ✦ A3
Dean Dr C2
Dock Rd. C2
Elizabethan Walls A2/B3
Fire Station B1
Flagstaff Park. C3
Football Ground C3
Foul Ford B2
Golden Sq A2
Golf Course A3
Granary, The ✦ B3
Greenwood C1
Gunpowder Magazine ✦ B3
Hide Hill B3
High Greens A2
Holy Trinity ⛪ A3
Information Ctr ⓘ B2
Kiln Hill B3
King's Mount ✦ B3
Ladywell Rd C2
Library A2
Lifeboat Station A3
Lord's Mount ✦ A3
Lovaine Terr B2
Low Greens A2
Main Guard 🏛 B3
Main St. A2
Maltings Art Ctr, The B3
Marygate A2
Meg's Mount ✦ A2
Middle St. C3
Mill St. C2
Mount Rd. C2
Museum 🏛 B3
Ness St B3
North Rd A2
Northumberland Ave. A2
Northumberland Rd B1
Osborne Cr B2
Osborne Rd. B1
Palace Gr. B3
Palace St B3
Palace St East B3
Parade, The A3
Pier Rd C1
Playing Field C1
Police Station 🏢 B2
Post Office 🏣 B2/B3
Prince Edward Rd B2
Prior Rd. B3
Quay Walls B3
Railway St. B2
Ravensdowne B3
Records Office A2
Riverdene B3
Riverside Rd A2
Royal Border Br B2
Royal Tweed Br B2
Russian Gun ✦ B3
Scots Gate ✦ A2
Scott's Pl A2
Shielfield Park (Berwick Rangers FC) C1
Shielfield Terr. C2
Silver St. B3
Spittal Quay. C3
Superstore B1/C1/C2
Tower Gdns A2
Tower Ho Pottery ✦ C2
Tower Rd C2
Town Hall. B3
Turret Gdns. C2
Tweedbank Retail Pk. C2
Tweed Dock. B2
Tweed St B2
Tweedside Trading Estate. C1
Union Brae. C1
Union Park Rd C2
Walkergate B2
Wallace Gr. C2
War Memorial. A2
War Memorial. B3
Warkworth Terr. C2
Well Close Sq. A2
West End B1
West End Rd B1
West St. B3
West St. C2
Windmill Bastion ✦ B3
Woolmarket B3
Works C3

Birmingham 332

Abbey St. A2
Aberdeen St A1
Acorn Gr. A2
Adams St A5
Adderley St. C5
Albert St. B4
Albion St A2
Alcester St. C5
Aldgate Gr A2
All Saint's St A2

All Saints Rd A2
Allcock St C5
Allesley St A4
Allison St C4
Alma Cr B6
Alston Rd C1
Arcadian Centre C4
Arena Birmingham C2
Arthur St C6
Assay Office B3
Aston Expressway A5
Aston St B4
Aston University B4/B5
Avenue Rd A5
Bacchus Rd A1
Bagot St B4
Banbury St B5
Barford Rd B1
Barford St C4
Barn St C5
Barnwell Rd C6
Barr St A3
Barrack St B5
Barwick St B4
Bath Row C3
Beaufort Rd C1
Belmont Row B5
Benson Rd A1
Berkley St C3
Bexhill Gr C3
Birchall St C5
Birmingham City FC C6
Birmingham City Hospital (A&E) A1
Birmingham City Univ B3
Birmingham Wheels Park B6
Bishopsgate St C3
Blews St A4
Bloomsbury St A6
Blucher St C3
Bordesley St C4
Bowyer St C5
Bradburne Way A5
Bradford St C5
Branston St A3
Brearley St A4
Brewery St A4
Bridge St A3
Bridge St C3
Bridge St West A4
Brindley Dr B3
Broad St C3
Broad St Cineworld C2
Broadway Plaza C2
Bromley St C5
Bromsgrove St C4
Brookfield Rd A2
Browning St C2
Bryant St A1
BT Tower B3
Buckingham St A3
Bull St B4
Bull St B4
Bullring C4
Cambridge St C3
Camden Dr B3
Camden St B2
Cannon St C4
Cardigan St B5
Carlisle St A1
Carlyle Rd C1
Caroline St B3
Carver St B2
Cato St A6
Cattell Rd C6
Cattells Gr A6
Cawdor Cr C1
Cecil St B4
Cemetery A2/B2
Cemetery La A2
Ctr Link Industrial Est A6
Charlotte St B3
Cheapside C4
Chester St A5
Children's Hospital (A&E) B4
Church St B4
Claremont Rd A2
Clarendon Rd C1
Clark St C1
Clement St B3
Clissold St B2
Cliveland St B4
Coach Station C5
College St B2
Colmore Circus B4
Colmore Row B4
Commercial St C3
Constitution Hill B3
Convention Ctr, The C3
Cope St B2
Coplow St B1
Corporation St C4
Council House B3
County Court B4
Coveley Gr A2
Coventry Rd C6
Coventry St C5
Cox St B3
Crabtree Rd A2
Cregoe St C3
Crescent Ave A2
Crescent Theatre C3
Crescent, The A2
Cromwell St A6
Cromwell St B3
Cube, The C3
Curzon St B5
Custard Factory C5
Cuthbert Rd B1
Dale End B4
Dart St C6
Dartmouth Circus A4
Dartmouth Middleway A5
Dental Hospital B4
Deritend C5
Devon St A6
Devonshire St A1
Digbeth High St C4
Dolman St B6
Dover St A1
Duchess Rd C2
Duddeston B6
Duddeston Manor Rd B5
Duddeston Mill Rd B6
Duddeston Mill Trading Estate B6
Dudley Rd B1
Edmund St B3
Edward St B3
Elkington St A4
Ellen St B2
Ellis St C3
Erskine St B6
Essex St C4
Eyre St B2
Farm Croft A3
Farm St A3
Fazeley St B4/C5
Felstead Way B5
Finstall Cl B5
Five Ways C2
Fiveway Shopping Ctr C2
Fleet St B3
Floodgate St C5
Ford St A2
Fore St C4
Forster St B5
Francis Rd C2
Francis St B5
Frankfort St A4
Frederick St B3
Freeth St C1
Freightliner Terminal B6
Garrison La C6
Garrison St B6
Gas St C3
Geach St A4
George St B3
George St West B2
Gibb St C5
Gilby Rd C2
Gillott Rd B1
Glover St C5
Goode Ave A2
Goodrick Way A6
Gordon St B6
Graham St B3
Grand Central C4
Granville St C3
Gray St C6
Great Barr St C5
Great Charles St Queensway B3
Great Francis St B6
Great Hampton Row A3
Great Hampton St A3
Great King St A3
Great Lister St A5
Great Tindal St C2
Green La C6
Green St C5
Greenway St C6
Grosvenor St West C2
Guest Gr A3
Guild Cl C2
Guildford Dr A4
Guthrie Cl A3
Hagley Rd C1
Hall St B3
Hampton St A3
Handsworth New Rd A1
Hanley St B4
Harford St A3
Harmer Rd A2
Harold Rd C1
Hatchett St A4
Heath Mill La C5
Heath St B1
Heath St South B1
Heaton St A2
Heneage St B5
Henrietta St B4
Herbert Rd C6
High St C4
High St C5
Hilden Rd B5
Hill St C3/C4
Hindlow Cl B6
Hingeston St B2
Hippodrome Theatre C4
HM Prison A1
Hockley Circus A2
Hockley Hill A3
Hockley St A3
Holliday St C3
Holloway Circus C4
Holloway Head C3
Holt St B5
Hooper St B1
Horse Fair C4
Hospital St A4
Howard St B3
Howe St B5
Hubert St A5
Hunters Rd A2
Hunters Vale A3
Huntly Rd C2
Hurst St C4
Icknield Port Rd B1
Icknield Sq B2
Icknield St A2/B2
IKON C3
Information Ctr C3
Inge St C4
Irving St C3
James Watt Queensway B4
Jennens Rd B5
Jewellery Quarter A3
Jewellery Quarter Museum B3
John Bright St C4
Keeley St C6
Kellett Rd B5
Kent St C4
Kenyon St B3
Key Hill A3
Kilby Ave C2
King Edwards Rd B2
King Edwards Rd C3
Kingston Rd C6
Kirby Rd A1
Ladywood Arts & Leisure Ctr B1
Ladywood Middleway C2/C3
Ladywood Rd C1
Lancaster St B4
Landor St B6
Law Courts B4
Lawford Cl B5
Lawley Middleway B5
Ledbury Cl C2
Ledsam St B2
Lees St A1
Legge La B3
Lennox St A3
Library A6/C3
Lighthorne Ave B2
Link Rd B1
Lionel St B3
Lister St B5
Little Ann St C5
Little Hall Rd A6
Liverpool St C5
Livery St B3/B4
Lodge Rd A1
Lord St A5
Love La A5
Loveday St B4
Lower Dartmouth St C6
Lower Loveday St B4
Lower Tower St A4
Lower Trinity St C5
Ludgate Hill B3
Mailbox Centre & BBC C3
Margaret St B3
Markby Rd A1
Marroway St B1
Maxstoke St C6
Melvina Rd A6
Meriden St C4
Metropolitan (RC) B4
Midland St B6
Milk St C5
Mill St A5
Millennium Point B5
Miller St A4
Milton St A4
Moat La C4
Montague Rd C1
Montague St C5
Monument Rd C1
Moor St Queensway C4
Moor Street C4
Moorsom St A4
Morville St C2
Mosborough Cr A3
Moseley St C4
Mott St B3
Mus & Art Gallery B3
Musgrave Rd A1
National Sea Life Centre C3
Navigation St C3
Nechell's Park Rd A6
Nechells Parkway B5
Nechells Pl A6
New Alexandra C3
New Bartholomew St C4
New Canal St C5
New John St West A3
New Spring St B2
New St C4
New Street C4
New Summer St A4
New Town Row A4
Newhall Hill B3
Newhall St B3
Newton St B4
Newtown A4
Noel Rd C1
Norman St A1
Northbrook St B1
Northwood St B3
Norton St A2
Odeon C2
Old Crown House C5
Old Rep Theatre, The C4
Old Snow Hill B4
Oliver Rd C1
Oliver St A5
Osler St C1
Oxford St C5
Palmer St C5
Paradise Circus Queensway C3
Paradise St C3
Park Rd A2
Park St C4
Pavilions C4
Paxton Rd A2
Peel St A1
Pershore St C4
Phillips St A4
Pickford St C5
Pinfold St C4
Pitsford St A2
Plough & Harrow Rd C1
Police Station A4/B4/C2/C4
Pope St B2
Portland Rd C1
Post Office A5/B1/B3/B4/B5/C2/C3/C5
Preston Rd A1
Price St B4
Princip St B4
Printing House St B4
Priory Queensway B4
Pritchett St A4
Proctor St A5
Radnor St A2
Rea St C4
Regent Pl B3
Register Office C3
Repertory Theatre C3
Reservoir Rd C1
Richard St A5
River St C5
Rocky La A5/A6
Rodney Cl C2
Roseberry St B2
Rotton Park St B1
Rupert St A5
Ruston St C2
Ryland St C2
St Andrew's Ind Est C6
St Andrew's Rd C6
St Andrew's St C6
St Bolton St C6
St Chads B4
St Chads Queensway B4
St Clements Rd A6
St George's St A3
St James Pl B5
St Marks Cr B2
St Martin's C4
St Paul's B3
St Paul's B3
St Paul's Sq B3
St Philip's B4
St Stephen's St A4
St Thomas' Peace Garden C3
St Vincent St C2
Saltley Rd A6
Sand Pits Pde B3
Severn St C3
Shadwell St B4
Sheepcote St C2
Shefford Rd A4
Sherborne St C2
Shylton's Croft C2
Skipton Rd C2
Smallbrook Queensway C4
Smith St A3
Snow Hill B4
Snow Hill Queensway B4
Soho, Benson Rd A1
South Rd A2
Spencer St B3
Spring Hill B2
Staniforth St B4
Station St C4
Steelhouse La B4
Stephenson St C4
Steward St B2
Stirling Rd C1
Stour St B2
Suffolk St Queensway C3
Summer Hill Rd B2
Summer Hill St B2
Summer Hill Terr B2
Summer La A4
Summer Row B3
Summerfield Cr B1
Summerfield Park B1
Superstore B2
Sutton St C3
Swallow St C3
Sydney Rd C6
Symphony Hall C3
Talbot St A1
Temple Row C4
Temple St C4
Templefield St C6
Tenby St B3
Tenby St North B2
Tennant St C2/C3
Thimble Mill La A6
Thinktank (Science & Discovery) B5
Thomas St A4
Thorpe St C4
Tilton Rd C6
Tower St A4
Town Hall C3
Trent St C5
Turner's Buildings A1
Unett St A3
Union Terr B5
Upper Trinity St C5
Uxbridge St A3
Vauxhall Gr B5
Vauxhall Rd B5
Vernon Rd C1
Vesey St B4
Viaduct St B5
Victoria Sq C3
Villa St A3
Vittoria St B3
Vyse St B3
Walter St A6
Wardlow Rd A5
Warstone La B2
Washington St C3
Water St B3
Waterworks Rd C1
Watery La C5
Well St A3
Western Rd B1
Wharf St A2
Wheeler St A3
Whitehouse St A5
Whitmore St A2
Whittall St B4
Wholesale Market C4
Wiggin St B1
Willes Rd A1
Windsor Industrial Est A5
Windsor St A5
Windsor St B5
Winson Green Rd A1
Witton St C6
Wolseley St C6
Woodcock St B5

Blackpool 332

Abingdon St A1
Addison Cr A3
Adelaide St B1
Albert Rd B2
Alfred St B2
Ascot Rd A3
Ashton Rd C2
Auburn Gr C3
Bank Hey St B1
Banks St A1
Beech Ave A3
Bela Gr C2
Belmont Ave B2
Birley St A1
Blackpool & Fleetwood Tram B1
Blackpool & the Fylde College B2
Blackpool FC C2
Blackpool North A2
Blackpool Tower B1
Blundell St C1
Bonny St B1
Breck Rd B3
Bryan Rd A3
Buchanan St A2
Bus Station A2
Cambridge Rd A3
Caunce St A2/A3
Central Dr B1/C2
Central Pier C1
Central Pier C1
Central Pier Theatre C1
Chapel St C1
Charles St A2
Charnley Rd B2
Church St A1/A2
Clinton Ave B2
Coach Station A2/C1
Cocker St A1
Coleridge Rd A3
Collingwood Ave A3
Comedy Carpet B1
Condor Gr C3
Cookson St A2
Coronation St B1
Corporation St A1
Courts B1
Cumberland Ave B3
Cunliffe Rd C3
Dale St C1
Devonshire Rd A3
Devonshire Sq A3
Dickson Rd A1
Elizabeth St A2
Ferguson Rd C3
Forest Gate B3
Foxhall Rd C1
Freckleton St C2
George St A2
Gloucester Ave B3
Golden Mile, The C1
Gorse Rd B3
Gorton St A2
Grand Theatre, The B1
Granville Rd A2
Grasmere Rd C2
Grosvenor St A2
Grundy Art Gallery A1
Harvey Rd B3
Hornby Rd B2
Houndshill Sh Ctr B1
Hull Rd B1
Ibbison Ct C2
Information Ctr A1
Kent Rd C2
Keswick Rd C2
King St A2
Knox Gr C3
Laycock Gate A3
Layton Rd A3
Leamington Rd B2
Leeds Rd B3
Leicester Rd B2
Levens Gr C2
Library A1
Lifeboat Station B1
Lincoln Rd B2
Liverpool Rd B3
Livingstone Rd B2
London Rd A3
Lune Gr C2
Lytham Rd C1
Madame Tussaud's Blackpool B1
Manchester Sq C1
Manor Rd B3
Maple Ave B3
Market St A1
Marlboro Rd B3
Mere Rd B3
Milbourne St A2
Newcastle Ave B3
Newton Dr A3
North Pier A1
North Pier A1
North Pier Theatre A1
Odeon C2
Olive Gr B3
Palatine Rd B2
Park Rd B2/C3
Peter St A2
Police Station B1
Post Office A1/A3/B1/B2
Princess Pde A1
Princess St C1/C2
Promenade A1/C1
Queen St A1
Queen Victoria Rd C2
Raikes Pde B2
Reads Ave B2
Regent Rd B2
Register Office B2
Ribble Rd B2
Rigby Rd C1/C2
Ripon Rd B3
St Albans Rd B3
St Ives Ave C3
St John's Square A1
St Vincent Ave C3
Salisbury Rd B3
Salthouse Ave C2
Salvation Army Centre A2
Sands Way C2
Sea Life Centre B1
Seasiders Way C1
Selbourne Rd A2
Sharrow Gr C3
Somerset Ave C3
South King St B2
Springfield Rd A1
Sutton Pl B2
Talbot Rd A1/A2
Thornber Gr C2
Topping St A1
Tower B1
Town Hall A1
Tram Depot C1
Tyldesley Rd C1
Vance Rd B1
Victoria St B1
Victory Rd A2
Wayman Rd A3
Westmorland Ave C2/C3
Whitegate Dr B3
Winter Gardens Theatre B1
Woodland Gr B3
Woolman Rd B2

Bournemouth 332

Ascham Rd A3
Avenue Rd B1
Ave Shopping Centre B1
Bath Rd C2
Beacon Rd C1
Beechey Rd A3
Bodorgan Rd B1
Bourne Ave B1
Bournemouth A3
Bournemouth & Poole College B3
Bournemouth Int Ctr C1
Bournemouth Pier C2
Bournemouth Sta B3
Braidley Rd A1
Cavendish Place A2
Cavendish Rd A2
Central Drive A1
Central Gdns B1
Christchurch Rd B3
Cliff Lift C1/C3
Coach House Pl A3
Coach Station A3
Commercial Rd B1
Cotlands Rd B3
Cranborne Rd C1
Cricket Ground A2
Cumnor Rd B2
Dean Park A2
Dean Park Cr B2
Dean Park Rd A2
Durrant Rd B1
East Overcliff Dr C3
Exeter Cr C1
Exeter La C2
Exeter Rd C1
Gervis Place B1
Gervis Rd B3
Glen Fern Rd B2
Golf Club B1
Grove Rd B3
Hinton Rd C2
Holdenhurst Rd B3
Horseshoe Common B2
Information Ctr C2
Lansdowne B3
Lansdowne Rd A2
Lorne Park Rd B2
Lower Gdns B1/C2
Madeira Rd B2
Methuen Rd A3
Meyrick Park A1
Meyrick Rd B3
Milton Rd A2
Nuffield Health Bournemouth Hospital (private) A2
Oceanarium C2
Odeon Cinema C2
Old Christchurch Rd B2
Ophir Rd A3
Oxford Rd B3
Park Rd A3
Parsonage Rd B2
Pavilion C2
Pier Approach C2
Pier Theatre C2
Police Station A3/B3
Portchester Rd A3
Post Office B1/B3
Priory Rd C1
Quadrant, The B2
Recreation Ground A1
Richmond Gardens Shopping Centre B2
Richmond Hill Rd B1
Russell-Cotes Art Gallery & Museum C2
Russell Cotes Rd C2
St Anthony's Rd A1
St Michael's Rd C1
St Paul's A3
St Paul's La B3
St Paul's Rd A3
St Peter's B2
St Peter's B2
St Peter's Rd B2
St Stephen's Rd B1/B2
St Swithun's B3
St Swithun's Rd B3
St Swithun's Rd South B3
St Valerie Rd A2
St Winifred's Rd A2
Square, The B1
Stafford Rd B3
Terrace Rd B1
Town Hall B1
Tregonwell Rd C1
Triangle, The B1
Trinity Rd B2
Undercliff Drive C3
Upper Hinton Rd B2
Upper Terr Rd C1
Wellington Rd A2/A3
Wessex Way A3/B1/B2
West Cliff Promenade C1
West Hill Rd C1
West Undercliff Prom C1
Westover Rd B2
Wimborne Rd A2
Wootton Mount B2
Wychwood Dr A1
Yelverton Rd B2
York Rd B3
Zig-Zag Walks C1/C3

Bradford 332

Alhambra B2
Back Ashgrove B1
Barkerend Rd A3
Barnard Rd C3
Barry St B2
Bolling Rd C3
Bolton Rd A3
Bowland St A1
Bradford Big Screen B2
Bradford College B1
Bradford Forster Square A2
Bradford Interchange B3
Bradford Playhouse B3
Bridge St B2
Britannia St B2
Broadway Bradford, The B2
Burnett St B3
Bus Station B2
Butler St West A3
Caledonia St C2
Canal Rd A2
Carlton St B1
Cathedral A3
Centenary Sq B2
Chapel St B3
Cheapside A2
Church Bank B3
Cineworld B3
City Hall B2
City Rd A1
Claremont B1
Colour Experience B1
Croft St B2
Crown Court B3
Darfield St A1
Darley St A2
Drewton Rd A1
Drummond Trading Estate A1
Dryden St B3
Dyson St A1
Easby Rd C1
East Parade B3
Eldon Pl A1
Filey St B3
Forster Square Retail Park A2
Gallery II B1
Garnett St B3
Godwin St B2
Gracechurch St A1
Grattan Rd B1
Great Horton Rd B1/B2
Grove Terr B1
Hall Ings B2
Hall La C3
Hallfield Rd A1
Hammstrasse A2
Harris St B3
Holdsworth St A2
Ice Arena B2
Impressions B2
Information Ctr B2
Inland Revenue A2
Ivegate B2
Jacob's Well Municipal Offices B2
James St A2
John St A2
Kirkgate B2
Kirkgate Centre B2
Laisteridge La C1
Leeds Rd B3
L Exchange, The B3
Library B1/B2
Listerhills Rd B1
Little Horton Gn C1
Little Horton La C1
Longside La B1
Lower Kirkgate B2
Lumb La A1
Magistrates Court B2
Manchester Rd C2
Manningham La A1
Manor Row A2
Market C3
Market St B2
Melbourne Place C1
Midland Rd A2
Mill La C2
Morley St B1
National Media B2
Nelson St B2/C2
Nesfield St A2
New Otley Rd A3
Norcroft St B1
North Parade A2
North St A3
North Wing A3
Oastler Shopping Ctr A2
Otley Rd A3
Park Ave C1
Park La C1
Park Rd C2
Parma St C2
Peace Museum B2
Peckover St B3
Piccadilly A2
Police Station C2
Post Office A2/B1/B2/C3
Princes Way B2
Prospect St C3
Radwell Drive C2
Rawson Rd A1
Rebecca St A1
Richmond Rd B1
Russell St C1
St George's Hall B2
St Lukes Hospital C1
Shipley Airedale Rd A3/B3
Shopmobility A2
Simes St A1
Smith St B1
Spring Mill St C2
Stott Hill A3
Sunbridge Rd A1/B1/B2
Theatre in the Mill B1
Thornton Rd A1/B1
Trafalgar St A2
Trinity Rd C1
Tumbling Hill St B1
Tyrrel St B2
Univ of Bradford B1/C1
Usher St C3
Valley Rd A2
Vicar La B3
Wakefield Rd C3
Wapping Rd A3
Well St B3
Westgate A1
White Abbey Rd A1
Wigan Rd A1
Wilton St B1
Wood St A1
Wool Exchange B2
Worthington St A1

Brighton 332

Addison Rd A1
Albert Rd B2
Albion Hill B3
Albion St B3
Ann St A3
Baker St A3
Black Lion St C2
Brighton A2
Brighton Centre C2
Brighton Fishing Museum C2
Brighton Pier (Palace Pier) C3
Brighton Wheel C3
British Airways i360 Tower C1
Broad St C3
Buckingham Pl A2
Buckingham Rd B2
Cannon Pl C1
Carlton Hill B3
Chatham Pl A1
Cheapside A3
Church St B2
Churchill Square Shopping Centre B2
Clifton Hill B1
Clifton Pl B1
Clifton Rd B1
Clifton St A2
Clifton Terr B1
Clyde Rd A3
Coach Station C3
Compton Ave A2
Davigdor Rd A1
Denmark Terr B1
Ditchling Rd A3
Dome B2
Duke St B2
Duke's La C2
Dyke Rd A1/B2
East St C2
Edward St B3
Elmore Rd B3
Fleet St A2
Frederick St B2
Gardner St B2
Gloucester Pl B3
Gloucester Rd B2
Goldsmid Rd A1
Grand Junction Rd C2
Grand Pde B3
Grove Hill B3
Guildford St A2
Hampton Pl B1
Hanover Terr A3
High St C3
Highdown Rd A1
Information Ctr C2
John St B3
Jubilee Clock Tower B2
Kemp St B2
Kensington Pl B2
Kings Rd C1
Lanes, The C2
Law Courts B3
Lewes Rd A3
Library B2
London Rd A3
Madeira Dr C3
Marine Pde C3
Middle St C2
Montpelier Pl B1
Montpelier Rd B1
Montpelier St B1
Mus & Art Gallery B3
New England Rd A2
New England St A2
New Rd B2
Nizells Ave A1
Norfolk Rd B1
Norfolk Terr B1
North Rd B2
North St B2
Odeon C2
Old Shoreham Rd A1
Old Steine C3
Osmond Rd A1
Over St B2
Oxford St A3
Park Crescent Terr A3
Phoenix Brighton B3
Phoenix Rise A3
Police Station B3
Post Office A1/A3/C3
Preston Rd A2
Preston St B1
Prestonville Rd A1
Queen's Rd B2
Queen Sq B2
Regency Sq C1
Regent St B2
Richmond Pl B3
Richmond St B3
Richmond Terr A3
Rose Hill Terr A3
Royal Pavilion B2
St Bartholomew's A3
St James's St C3
St Nicholas Rd B2
St Nicholas' B2
St Peter's A3
Sea Life Brighton C3
Shaftesbury Rd A3
Ship St C2
Sillwood Rd B1
Sillwood St B1
Southover St A3
Spring Gdns B2
Stanford Rd A1
Stanley Rd A3
Surrey St B2
Sussex St B3
Swimming Pool B3
Sydney St B3
Temple Gdns B1
Terminus Rd A2
Theatre Royal B2
Tidy St B2
Town Hall C2
Toy & Model Mus A2
Trafalgar St B2
Union Rd A3
University of Brighton B3
Upper Lewes Rd A3
Upper North St B1
Viaduct Rd A3
Victoria Gdns B3
Victoria Rd B1
Volk's Electric Railway C3
West Pier (derelict) C1
West St C2
Western Rd B1
Whitecross St B2
York Ave B1
York Pl B3
York Rd B1

Bristol 332

Acramans Rd C4
Albert Rd C6
Alfred Hill A4
All Saint's St A4
All Saints' B4
Allington Rd C3
Alpha Rd C4
Ambra Vale B1
Ambra Vale East B2
Ambrose Rd B2
Amphitheatre & Waterfront Sq C4
Anchor Rd B3
Anvil St B6
Arcade, The A5
Architecture Centre, The B4
Argyle Pl B2
Arlington Villas A2
Arnolfini Arts Centre, The B4
Art Gallery A3
Ashton Gate Rd C2
Ashton Rd C1
Avon Bridge C1
Avon Cr C1
Avon St B6
Baldwin St B4
Baltic Wharf C2
Baltic Wharf Leisure Ctr & Caravan Pk C2
Baltic Wharf Marina C2
Barossa Pl C4
Barton Manor B6
Barton Rd B6
Barton Vale B6
Bath Rd C6
Bathurst Basin C4
Bathurst Parade C4
Beauley Rd C3
Bedminster Bridge C5
Bedminster Parade C4
Bellevue B2
Bellevue Cr B2
Bellevue Rd C6
Berkeley Pl A2
Berkeley Sq A3
Birch Rd C2
Blackfriars A4
Bond St A5
Braggs La A6
Brandon Hill B3
Brandon Steep B3
Bristol Aquarium B4
Bristol Bridge B5
Bristol Cath (CE) B3
Bristol Eye Hosp (A&E) A4
Bristol Grammar School A3
Bristol Harbour Railway C3
Bristol Royal Children's Hospital A4
Bristol Royal Infirmary (A&E) A4

Bristol Temple Meads
Station ⇌ B6
Broad Plain B6
Broad Quay B4
Broad St B4
Broad Weir A5
Broadcasting House . . A3
Broadmead A5
Brunel Institute ◆ . . . C1
Brunel Way C1
Brunswick Sq A5
Burton Cl C5
Bus Station A4
Butts Rd B3
Cabot Circus B3
Cabot Tower ◆ C3
Caledonia Pl C1
Callowhill Ct A5
Cambridge St C6
Camden Rd C3
Camp Rd A2
Canada Way C2
Cannon St A4
Canon's Way B3
Cantock's Cl A1
Canynge Rd A1
Canynge Sq A1
Castle Park B4
Castle St B4
Cathedral Walk B3
Catherine Meade St . . C4
Cattle Market Rd C5
Central Library B3
Charles Pl B3
Charlotte St B3
Charlotte St South . . . B3
Chatterton House ⌂ . B5
Chatterton Sq C5
Chatterton St C5
Cheese La B5
Christchurch ⌂ A4
Christchurch Rd A1
Christmas Steps ◆ . . . A3
Church La B2/B5
Church St B5
City Museum ⌂ A3
City of Bristol College . B4
Civil and Family
 Justice Centre B5
Clare St B4
Clarence Rd C5
Cliff Rd C1
Clift House Rd C1
Clifton Cath (RC) † . . . A1
Clifton Down A1
Clifton Down Rd A1
Clifton Hill B2
Clifton Park A1/A2
Clifton Park Rd A1
Clifton Rd B2
Clifton Vale B1
Cliftonwood Cr B2
Cliftonwood Rd B2
Cliftonwood Terr B1
Cobblestone Mews . . A1
College Green B3
College Rd A1
College St B3
Colston
 Almshouses ⌂ A4
Colston Ave B4
Colston Hall ♺ B4
Colston Parade C5
Colston St B3
Commercial Rd C4
Constitution Hill B2
Cooperage La C2
Corn St B4
Cornwallis Ave B1
Cornwallis Cr B1
Coronation Rd C2/C4
Council House ⌂ B3
Counterslip B5
Create Centre, The ◆ . C1
Crosby Row B2
Crown Court A4
Culver St B3
Cumberland Basin . . . C1
Cumberland Cl C1
Cumberland Rd . . . C2/C3
Dean La C4
Deanery Rd B3
Denmark St B3
Dowry Sq B1
Eaton Cr A1
Elmdale Rd A3
Elton Rd A4
Eugene St A4/A6
Exchange and
 St Nicholas' Mkts,
 The ⌂ B4
Fairfax St B5
Fire Station B5
Floating Harbour C3
Fosseway, The A1
Foster Almshouses ⌂ A4
Frayne Rd C1
Frederick Pl B1
Freeland Pl B1
Friary B5
Frogmore St B3
Fry's Hill B2
Gas Lane B6
Gasferry Rd C3
Georgian House ⌂ . . . B3
Glendale B1
Glentworth Rd B1
Gloucester St A1
Goldney Hall B1
Goldney Rd B1
Gordon Rd A1
Granby Hill B1
Grange Rd A1
Great Ann St A6
Great George Rd B3
Great George St . . A6/B3
Green St North B1
Green St South B1
Greenay Bush La C1
Greenbank Rd C2

Greville Smyth Park . . C1
Grove, The B4
Guildhall ⌂ B4
Guinea St C4
Hamilton Rd C1
Hanover Pl C2
Harley Pl A1
Haymarket A4
Hensman's Hill B1
High St B4
Highbury Villas A3
Hill St C5
Hill St C6
Hippodrome ♺ B4
Hopechapel Hill B1
Horfield Rd A3
Horsefair, The A5
Horton St B6
Host St B4
Hotwell Rd B1/C1
Houlton St A6
Howard Rd C3
IMAX Cinema ♺ B4
Information Ctr ⓘ . . . B4
Islington Rd C2
Jacob St A5/A6
Jacob's Wells Rd B1
John Carr's Terr B2
John Wesley's
 Chapel ⌂ A5
Joy Hill B1
Jubilee St B6
Kensington Pl A1
Kilkenny St A6
King St B4
Kingsland Rd B6
Kingston Rd C3
Lamb St A6
Lansdown Rd A1
Lawford St A6
Lawfords Gate A6
Leighton Rd C3
Lewins Mead A4
Lime Rd C2
Litfield Rd A1
Little Ann St A6
Little Caroline Pl C1
Little George St A6
Little King St B4
Llandoger Trow ⌂ . . . B4
Lloyd's Building, The . . C3
Lodge St A4
Lord Mayor's Chapel,
 The ⌂ B3
Lower Castle St A5
Lower Church La A3
Lower Clifton Hill B2
Lower Guinea St C4
Lower Lamb St B3
Lower Maudlin St A4
Lower Park Rd A4
Lower Sidney St C2
Lucky La C4
Lydstep Terr C3
M Shed ⌂ C4
Magistrates' Court . . . B4
Mall (Galleries
 Shopping Ctr), The . A5
Mall, The A1
Manilla Rd A1
Mardyke Ferry Rd . . . C2
Maritime Heritage
 Centre ⌂ C2
Marlborough Hill A4
Marlborough St A4
Marsh St B4
Mead St C5
Merchant Dock C2
Merchant Seamen's
 Almshouses ⌂ B4
Merchant St A5
Merchants Rd A1
Merchants Rd C1
Meridian Pl A1
Meridian Vale A1
Merrywood Rd C3
Midland Rd A6
Milford St C3
Millennium Prom B3
Millennium Sq B3
Mitchell La B5
Mortimer Rd A1
Murray Rd A2
Myrtle Rd A3
Narrow Plain B5
Narrow Quay B4
Nelson St B4
New Charlotte St C4
New Kingsley Rd B6
New Queen St C5
New St A6
Newgate A5
Newton St A6
Norland Rd B1
North St C2
O2 Academy B3
Oakfield Gr A1
Oakfield Pl A1
Oakfield Rd A1
Old Bread St B6
Old Market St A6
Old Park Hill A4
Oldfield Rd B1
Orchard Ave B4
Orchard La B4
Orchard St B4
Osborne Rd C3
Oxford St B6
Park Pl A2
Park Rd C3
Park Row A3
Park St A3
Passage St B5
Pembroke Gr A2
Pembroke Rd A2
Pembroke St A5
Penn St A5
Pennywell Rd A6

Percival Rd A1
Pero's Bridge B4
Perry Rd A4
Phipps St C2
Pip 'n' Jay ⌂ B5
Plimsoll Bridge B1
Polygon Rd B1
Portland St A1
Portwall La B5
Post Office ⌂ . . . A1/A3/A5/
 . . . . B1/B4/C4/C5
Prewett St C5
Prince St B4
Prince St Bridge C4
Princess St C4
Princess Victoria St . . . B1
Priory Rd A4
Pump La B5
QEH Theatre ♺ A2
Quakers Friars A5
Quay St A4
Queen Charlotte St . . . B4
Queen Elizabeth
 Hospital School . . . B2
Queen Sq B4
Queen St A5
Queen's Ave A3
Queen's Parade B3
Queen's Rd A2/A3
Raleigh Rd C2
Randall Rd B2
Red Lodge ⌂ A4
Redcliffe Backs B5
Redcliffe Bridge B4
Redcliffe Hill C5
Redcliffe Parade C5
Redcliffe St B5
Redcliffe Way B5
Redcross St A6
Redgrave Theatre ♺ . . A1
Regent St B1
Richmond Hill A2
Richmond Hill Ave . . . A2
Richmond La A2
Richmond Park Rd . . . A2
Richmond St C6
Richmond Terr A2
River St A6
Rownham Mead B2
Royal Fort Rd A3
Royal Park A2
Royal West of England
 Academy ⌂ A3
Royal York Cr B1
Royal York Villas B1
Rupert St A4
Russ St B6
St Andrew's Walk B1
St George's ⌂ B3
St George's Rd B3
St James ⌂ A4
St John's ⌂ A4
St John's Rd C4
St Luke's Rd C5
St Mary Redcliffe ⌂ . . C5
St Matthias Park A6
St Michael's Hill A3
St Michael's Hosp ⌂ . A4
St Michael's Park A3
St Nicholas St B4
St Paul St A5
St Paul's Rd A2
St Peter's (ruin) ⌂ . . . A5
St Philip's Bridge B5
St Philips Rd A6
St Stephen's ⌂ B4
St Stephen's St B4
St Thomas St B5
St Thomas the
 Martyr ⌂ B5
Sandford Rd B1
Sargent St C5
Saville Pl B1
Ship La C5
Shopmobility A5
Showcase Cinema
 de Lux ♺ A5
Silver St A4
Sion Hill B1
Small St A4
Smeaton Rd C1
Somerset Sq C5
Somerset St C5
Southernhay Ave B2
Southville Rd C4
Spike Island
 Artspace ⌂ C2
Spring St C4
Superstore C4
SS Great Britain and
 the Matthew ◆ B2
Stackpool Rd C3
Staight St B6
Stillhouse La C4
Sydney Row C2
Tankard's Cl A3
Temple Back B5
Temple Back East B5
Temple Bridge B5
Temple Church ⌂ B5
Temple Circus B5
Temple Gate C5
Temple St B5
Temple Way B5
Terrell St A4
Theatre Royal
 (Bristol Old Vic) ♺ . . B4
Thekla ⌂ B4
Thomas La B5
Three Kings of
 Cologne ⌂ C2
Three Queens La B5
Tobacco Factory,
 The ♺ C2
Tower Hill B5
Tower La A4
Trenchard St A4
Triangle South A3
Triangle West A3

Trinity Rd A6
Trinity St A6
Tyndall Ave A3
Union St A5
Union St B6
Unity St A1
Unity St B3
University of Bristol . . A3
University Rd A3
Upper Byron Pl A3
Upper Maudlin St A4
Upper Perry Hill C3
Upton Rd C2
Valentine Bridge B6
Victoria Gr C1
Victoria Rd A6
Victoria Rooms ⌂ . . . A2
Victoria Sq A1
Victoria St B5
Vyvyan Rd A1
Vyvyan Terr A1
Wade St A6
Walter St C3
Wapping Rd C4
Water La B5
Waterloo Rd A6
Waterloo St A1
Waterloo St A6
Watershed Media
 Centre ◆ B4
We the Curious ◆ . . . B3
Welling Terr A1
Welsh Back B4
West Mall A1
West St A6
Westfield Pl A1
Wetherell Pl A1
Whitehouse Pl C5
Whitehouse St C5
Whiteladies Rd A1
Whitson St A4
William St C5
Willway St C5
Windsor Pl A1
Wine St A4
Woodland Rd A3
Woodland Rise A3
Worcester Rd A1
Worcester Terr A1
YHA ▲ B4
York Gdns B1
York Pl A1
York Rd C5

Bury St Edmunds 332

Abbey Gardens ❀⌂ . . B3
Abbey Gate ⌂ B3
Abbeygate St B2
Albert Cr B1
Albert St B1
Ambulance Sta C1
Angel Hill B2
Angel La B2
Anglian Lane A1
Arc Shopping Centre . . B2
Athenaeum ⌂ B2
Baker's La C3
Barwell Rd A3
Beetons Way A1
Bishops Rd C2
Bloomfield St B2
Bridewell La C1
Bullen Cl C1
Bury St Edmunds ⌂ . . B3
Bury St Edmunds County
 Upper School A1
Bury St Edmunds
 Leisure Ctr. B1
Bury Town FC B2
Bus Station B2
Business Park B3
Butter Mkt. B2
Cannon St B2
Castle Rd C1
Cemetery A2
Chalk Rd (N) B1
Chalk Rd (S) B1
Church Row B2
Churchgate St C2
Cineworld ♺ B1
Citizens Advice
 Bureau B2
College St C2
Compiegne Way A3
Corn Exchange, The ♺ B2
Cornfield Rd B1
Cotton Lane B2
Courts B2
Covent Garden C2
Crown St B2
Cullum Rd C2
Eastern Way A3
Eastgate St B3
Enterprise Bsns Park . . A2
Etna Rd A3
Eyre Cl C2
Fire Station B1
Friar's Lane C2
Gage Cl A1
Garland St B2
Greene King
 Brewery ⌂ C2
Grove Park B1
Grove Rd B1
Guildhall ⌂ C2
Guildhall St C2
Hatter St C2
High Baxter St B2
Honey Hill C2
Hospital Rd C1/C2
Ickworth Dr C1
Industrial Estate A3
Information Ctr ⓘ . . . B2
Ipswich St B2
Junction 43 . . . . A2
King Edward VI Sch . . . A1
King's Rd C1/B2
Library B1
Long Brackland A2

Looms La B2
Lower Baxter St B2
Malthouse La C3
Maynewater La C3
Mill Rd C1
Mill Rd (South) C1
Minden Close B2
Moyses Hall ⌂ B2
Mustow St B3
Norman Tower ⌂ C2
Northgate Ave. A2
Northgate St B2
Nutshell, The ⌂ B2
Osier Rd A2
Out Northgate. A2
Out Risbygate B1
Out Westgate C1
Parkway B1/C2
Peckham St B2
Petticoat La B2
Pinners Way C1
Police Station ⌂ B2
Post Office ⌂ B2/B3
Pump La B2
Queen's Rd B1
Raingate St C2
Raynham Rd A1
Retail Park C2
Risbygate St B1/B2
Robert Boby Way C1
St Andrew's St North . . B2
St Andrew's St South . . B2
St Botolph's La C2
St Edmund's
 Abbey (Remains) ◆ . B3
St Edmunds Hospital
 (private) ⌂ C3
St Edmundsbury † . . . C3
St John's St B2
St Marys ⌂ C2
School Hall La B2
Shillitoe Cl A1
Shire Halls &
 Magistrates Ct C2
South Cl C2
Southgate St C3
Sparhawk St C3
Spring Lane B1
Springfield St A2
Station Hill A2
Swan La B2
Tayfen Rd A2
Theatre Royal ♺ C2
Thingoe Hill A2
Victoria St B1
Vinefields, The B3
War Memorial ◆ C1
Well St B2
West Suffolk College. . B1
Westgarth Gdns C1
Westgate St C2
Whiting St C2
York Rd B1
York Terr B1

Cambridge 333

Abbey Rd A3
ADC ♺ A2
Anglia Ruskin Univ . . . B3
Archaeology &
 Anthropology ⌂ . . . B2
Arts Picture House ♺ . B2
Arts Theatre ♺ B1
Auckland Rd A3
Backs, The B1
Bateman St C2
Benet St B1
Bradmore St B3
Bridge St A1
Broad St B3
Brookside C2
Brunswick Terr A3
Burleigh St B3
Bus Station B2
Butt Green A2
Cambridge
 Contemporary Art
 Gallery ⌂ B1
Castle Mound ⌂ A1
Castle St A1
Cemetery A3
Chesterton La A1
Christ's (Coll) B2
Christ's Lane B2
Christ's Pieces B2
City Rd B3
Clare (Coll) B1
Clarendon St B2
Coe Fen C1
Corn Exchange, The ♺ B1
Corpus Christi (Coll) . . B1
Court A3
Cross St C2
Crusoe Bridge C1
Darwin (Coll) C1
Devonshire Rd C3
Downing (Coll) B2
Downing St B2
Earl St B2
East Rd B3
Eden St B3
Elizabeth Way A3
Elm St B2
Emery St B3
Emmanuel (Coll) B2
Emmanuel Rd B2
Emmanuel St B2
Fair St A3
Fen Causeway, The . . C1
Fenner's Cricket Gd . . C3
Fire Station B3
Fitzroy St B3
Fitzwilliam Mus ⌂ . . . C2
Fitzwilliam St C2
Garret Hostel Bridge . . B1
Glisson Rd C3
Gonville & Caius (Coll) B1

Gonville Place C2
Grafton Centre, The . . A3
Grand Arcade B2
Green St B1
Gresham Rd C3
Guest Rd B3
Guildhall ⌂ B1
Harvey Rd C2
Hills Rd C2
Hobson St B2
Hughes Hall (Coll) . . . B3
Information Ctr ⓘ . . . B2
James St B3
Jesus (Coll) A2
Jesus Green A2
Jesus La A2
Jesus Terr B3
John St B3
Kelsey Kerridge
 Sports Centre B3
Kettle's Yard ⌂ A1
King's Bridge B1
King's (Coll) B1
King's Coll Chapel ✝ . . B1
King's Parade B1
Lammas Land Rec Gd . C1
Lensfield Rd C2
Library A3
Lion Yard B2
Little St Mary's La B1
Lyndewod Rd C3
Magdalene (Coll) A1
Magdalene St A1
Maid's Causeway A3
Malcolm St A2
Market Hill B1
Market St B1
Mathematical Bridge . B1
Mawson Rd C3
Midsummer Common . A3
Mill La B1
Mill Rd B3
Mill St C3
Mumford
 (Theatre) ♺ B3
Mus of Cambridge ⌂ . A1
Museum of Classical
 Archeology ⌂ C1
Napier St A3
New Square A2
Newmarket Rd A3
Newnham Rd C1
Norfolk St B3
Northampton St A1
Norwich St C2
Orchard St B2
Panton St C2
Paradise Nature
 Reserve C1
Paradise St B3
Park Parade A1
Park St A2
Park Terr B2
Parker St B2
Parker's Piece B2
Parkside B3
Parkside Pools B3
Parsonage St A3
Pembroke Terr C2
Pembroke (Coll) B2
Pembroke St B2
Perowne St B3
Peterhouse (Coll) C1
Petty Cury B2
Polar Museum, The ⌂ . C2
Police Station ⌂ B3
Post Office ⌂ . . . A1/A3/B2/
 . . . . B3/C1/C2/C3
Queen's La B1
Queen's Rd B1
Queens' (Coll) B1
Regent St B2
Regent Terr B2
Ridley Hall (Coll) C1
Riverside A3
Round Church, The ⌂ . A1
Russell St C3
St Andrew's St B2
St Benet's ⌂ B1
St Catharine's (Coll) . . B1
St Eligius St C3
St John's (Coll) A1
St Mary's ⌂ B1
St Paul's Rd C3
Saxon St C2
Sedgwick Mus ⌂ B2
Sheep's Green C1
Shire Hall A1
Sidgwick Ave C1
Sidney St B2
Sidney Sussex (Coll) . . B2
Silver St B1
Station Rd C3
Tenison Ave C3
Tenison Rd C3
Tennis Court Rd B2
Thompson's La A1
Trinity (Coll) A1
Trinity Hall (Coll) B1
Trinity St B1
Trumpington Rd C1
Trumpington St B1
Union Rd C2
University Botanic
 Gardens ⌂ C2
Victoria Ave A2
Victoria St B2
Warkworth St B3
Warkworth Terr B3
Wesley House (Coll) . . A2
West Rd B1
Westcott House (Coll) . A2
Westminster (Coll) . . . A1
Whipple ⌂ B2
Willis Rd B3
Willow Walk A2
YMCA C3

Canterbury 333

Artillery St B2
Barton Mill Rd A3
Beaconsfield Rd A1
Beaney ⌂ B2
Beverley Rd A1
Bingley's Island B1
Black Griffin La B1
Broad Oak Rd A2
Broad St B2
Brymore Rd A3
Burgate B2
Bus Station B2
Canterbury College . . C3
Canterbury East ⇌ . . . C1
Canterbury Tales,
 The ◆ B2
Canterbury West ⇌ . . . A1
Castle C1
Castle Row C1
Castle St C1
Cathedral † B2
Causeway, The A2
Chaucer Rd A3
Christ Church Univ. . . B3
Christchurch Gate ⌂ . B2
City Council Offices . . . A3
City Wall A2
Coach Park A2
College Rd B3
Cossington Rd C2
Court A2
Craddock Rd A3
Crown & County
 Courts B3
Dane John Gdns C2
Dane John Mound ◆ . . C1
Deanery B2
Dover St C2
Duck La B2
Eastbridge Hosp ⌂ . . B2
Edgar Rd B3
Ersham Rd C3
Ethelbert Rd C3
Fire Station C2
Forty Acres Rd A1
Friars, The B2
Gordon Rd C1
Greyfriars ◆ B1
Guildford St B1
Havelock St B2
Heaton Rd C1
High St B2
Information Ctr ⓘ . A2/B2
Ivy La B2
Ivy Pl C1
King St B2
King's School B2
King's School Rec Ctr,
 The A2
Kingsmead Leisure CtrA2
Kingsmead Rd A2
Kirby's La B1
Lansdown Rd C2
Lime Kiln Rd C1
Longport B3
Lower Chantry La C3
Mandeville Rd A1
Market Way A2
Marlowe Arcade B2
Marlowe Ave C2
Marlowe Theatre ♺ . . B2
Martyrs Field Rd C1
Mead Way B1
Military Rd B2
Monastery St B2
Mus of Canterbury
 (Rupert Bear Mus) ⌂ B1
New Dover Rd C3
Norman Rd C2
North Holmes Rd B3
North La B1
Northgate A2
Nunnery Fields C2
Nunnery Rd C2
Oaten Hill C2
Odeon Cinema ♺ B2
Old Dover Rd C2
Old Palace B2
Old Ruttington La B2
Old Weavers ⌂ B2
Orchard St B1
Oxford Rd C1
Palace St B2
Pilgrims Way C3
Pin Hill C1
Pine Tree Ave A1
Police Station ⌂ B2
Post Office ⌂ B2
Pound La B1
Puckle La C2
Raymond Ave C1
Recreation Ground . . . A2
Registry Office B2
Rheims Way B1
Rhodaus Cl C2
Rhodaus Town C2
Roman Museum ⌂ . . . B3
Roper Gateway A1
Roper Rd A1
Rose La B2
Shopmobility C2
St Augustine's Abbey
 (remains) † B3
St Augustine's Rd C3
St Dunstan's ⌂ A1
St Dunstan's St A1
St George's Pl C2
St George's Tower ◆ . . B2
St Gregory's ⌂ B3
St John's Hospital ⌂ . A2
St Margaret's St B2
St Martin's ⌂ B3
St Martin's Ave B3
St Martin's Rd B3
St Michael's Rd C1
St Mildred's ⌂ C1
St Peter's Gr B1

St Peter's La B2
St Peter's Pl B1
St Peter's St B1
St Radigunds St A2
St Stephen's Ct A1
St Stephen's Path A1
St Stephen's Rd A1
Salisbury Rd A1
Simmonds Rd C1
Spring La C3
Station Rd West B1
Stour St B1
Sturry Rd A3
Tourtel Rd A3
Tudor Rd C1
Union St B2
University for the
 Creative Arts C3
Vernon Pl C1
Victoria Rd C1
Watling St B2
Westgate Gdns B1
Whitefriars B2
Whitehall Gdns B1
Whitehall Rd B1
Wincheap C1
York Rd C1
Zealand Rd C2

Cardiff Caerdydd 333

Adam St B3
Alexandra Gdns A2
Allerton St C1
Arran St A3
ATRiuM (Univ of
 Glamorgan). C3
Beauchamp St. C1
Bedford St A3
Blackfriars Priory
 (rems) ⌂ B2
Boulevard De Nantes . B2
Brains Brewery C2
Brook St B1
BT Sports Cardiff Arms
 Park (Cardiff Blues) . B1
Bus Station C2
Bute Park A1
Bute St C2
Bute Terr C3
Callaghan Sq C2/C3
Capitol Sh Ctr, The . . . B3
Cardiff Bridge B1
Cardiff Castle ⌂ B2
Cardiff Central ⇌ C2
Cardiff Story, The ⌂ . . B2
Cardiff Univ . . . A1/A2/B3
Cardiff University
 Student's Union . . . A2
Caroline St C2
Castle Green A2
Castle Mews A1
Castle St (Heol y
 Castell) B2
Cathays Station ⇌ . . . A3
Celerity Drive C3
Central Library C2
Central Sq C2
Charles St (Heol Siarl) B3
Churchill Way B3
City Hall ⌂ A2
Clare Rd C1
Clare St C1
Coburn St A3
Coldstream Terr B1
College Rd A1
Colum Rd A1
Court A3
Court Rd C1
Craiglee Drive C3
Cranbrook St A3
Customhouse St C2
Cyfartha St A3
Despenser Place C1
Despenser St C1
Dinas St C2
Duke St (Heol y Dug) . B2
Dumfries Place B3
East Grove A3
Ellen St C3
Fire Station A3
Fitzalan Place B3
Gloucester St C1
Glynrhondda St A2
Gordon Rd A3
Gorsedd Gdns A2
Green St B1
Greyfriars Rd B2
Hafod St C1
Hayes, The C2
Herbert St C3
High St B2
HM Prison B3
Industrial Estate. C3
John St C2
Jubilee St C1
King Edward VII Ave . . A1
Kingsway (Ffordd y
 Brenin) B2
Knox Rd B3
Law Courts A2
Llanbleddian Gdns . . . A2
Llantwit St A2
Lloyd George Ave . . . C3
Lower Cathedral Rd . . B1
Lowther Rd A3
Magistrates Court . . . B3
Mansion House A3
Mardy St C1
Mark St B1
Market B2
Mary Ann St C3
Merches Gdns C1
Mill La C2

Millennium Bridge . . . B1
Miskin St A2
Monmouth St C1
Motorpoint Arena
 Cardiff C3
Museum Ave A2
Museum Place A2
National Museum
 Cardiff ⌂ A2
National War Meml ◆ . A2
Neville Place B1
New Theatre ♺ B2
Newport Rd B3
Northcote La A3
Northcote St A3
Parade, The A3
Park Grove A2
Park Place A2
Park St C2
Penarth Rd C2
Pendyris St C1
Plantagenet St C1
Post Office B3
Principality Plaza
 Leisure Complex ♺ . C3
Principality Stadium . . C1
Principality Stadium
 Tours (Gate 3) ◆ . . . B2
Quay St B2
Queen's Arcade B2
Queen Anne Sq A1
Queen St (Heol y
 Frenhines) B2
Queen St Station ⇌ . . . B3
Regimental
 Museums ⌂ B2
Rhymney St A3
Richmond Rd A3
Royal Welsh College of
 Music and Drama . . A1
Russell St A3
Ruthin Gdns A2
St Andrews Place A2
St David's ⌂ B2
St David's Hall ♺ B2
St John the Baptist ⌂ . B2
St Mary St (Heol
 Eglwys Fair) B2
St Peter's St A3
Salisbury Rd A3
Sandon St B3
Schooner Way C3
Scott Rd C2
Scott St C2
Senghennydd Rd A2
Sherman Theatre ♺ . . A2
Sophia Gardens A1
South Wales Baptist
 College. A3
Sport Wales
 National Ctr ◆ A1
Stafford Rd C1
Station Terr B3
Stuttgarter Strasse . . B2
Sussex St C1
Taffs Mead Emb C1
Talworth St A3
Temple of Peace &
 Health ◆ A1
Treharris St A3
Trinity St B2
Tudor La C1
Tudor St C1
Walk, The A3
Welsh Government . . . A1
West Grove A3
Westgate St
 (Heol y Porth) B2
Windsor Place B3
Womanby St B2
Wood St C2
Working St B2
Wyeverne Rd A2

Carlisle 333

Abbey St A1
Aglionby St B3
Albion St C3
Alexander St B3
AMF Bowl ♺ C2
Annetwell St A1
Bank St B2
Bitts Park A1
Blackfriars St B2
Blencome St C1
Blunt St C1
Botchergate C2
Boustead's Grassing . . C2
Bowman St B3
Bridge St A1
Broad St B3
Brook St C3
Brunswick St B2
Bus Station B2
Caldew Bridge A1
Caldew St C1
Carlisle
 (Citadel) Station ⇌ . B2
Carlisle College A2
Castle ⌂ A1
Castle St A1
Castle Way A1
Cathedral † A2
Cecil St B3
Chapel St A2
Charles St B3
Charlotte St B2
Chatsworth Square . . A2
Chiswick St B3
Citadel, The ◆ B2
City Walls A1
Civic Centre A2
Clifton St C1
Close St B3
Collingwood St C2
Colville St C2
Colville Terr. C2
Court B2

Court St B2
Crosby St B2
Crown St C2
Currock Rd C2
Dacre Rd A1
Dale St C1
Denton St C1
Devonshire Walk A1
Duke's Rd A2
East Dale St C1
East Norfolk St C1
Eden Bridge A2
Edward St B3
Elm St B1
English St B2
Fire Station A2
Fisher St A1
Flower St B3
Freer St C1
Fusehill St B3
Georgian Way A2
Gloucester Rd C3
Golf Course A2
Graham St C1
Grey St B3
Guildhall Museum 🏛 A2
Halfey's La B3
Hardwicke Circus A2
Hart St B3
Hewson St C2
Howard Pl A3
Howe St B3
Information Ctr ℹ A2
James St B2
Junction St B1
King St B2
Lancaster St B2
Lanes Shopping Ctr, The B2
Laser Quest ✦ B2
Library A2/B1
Lime St B1
Lindisfarne St C3
Linton St B3
Lismore Pl A3
Lismore St B3
London Rd C3
Lonsdale Rd B2
Lord St C3
Lorne Cres B1
Lorne St B1
Lowther St B2
Madford Retail Park B1
Magistrates' Ct A2
Market Hall A2
Mary St B2
Memorial Bridge A3
Metcalfe St C1
Milbourne St B1
Myddleton St B3
Nelson St C1
Norfolk St C1
Old Fire Sta, The 🎭 A2
Old Town Hall A2
Oswald St C3
Peter St A2
Petteril St B3
Pools B2
Portland Pl B2
Portland Sq B2
Post Office ✉ A2/B2/B3/C1/C3
Princess St C2
Pugin St B1
Red Bank Terr C2
Regent St C3
Richardson St C1
Rickerby Park A3
Rickergate A2
River St B3
Rome St C2
Rydal St B3
Shopmobility A2
St Cuthbert's ⛪ B2
St Cuthbert's La B2
St James' Park C1
St James' Rd C1
St Nicholas Gate Retail Park C3
St Nicholas St C3
Sands Centre, The A2
Scotch St A2
Shaddongate B1
Sheffield St B1
South Henry St B3
South John St C2
South St B3
Spencer St B2
Strand Rd A2
Superstore B1
Sybil St B3
Tait St B2
Thomas St B1
Thomson St C3
Trafalgar St C1
Trinity Leisure Centre A2
Tullie House Museum 🏛 A1
Tyne St C3
University of Cumbria B3
Viaduct Estate Rd B1
Victoria Pl A2
Victoria Viaduct B2
Vue 🎦 B2
Warwick Rd B2
Warwick Sq B3
Water St B2
West Walls B1
Westmorland St C1

Chelmsford 333

Anchor St C1
Anglia Ruskin Univ A2
Arbour La A3
Baddow Rd B2/C3
Baker St C1
Barrack Sq B2
Bellmead B2
Bishop Hall La A2
Bishop Rd A2
Bond St B2
Boswells Dr B3
Bouverie Rd C2
Bradford St C1
Braemar Ave C1
Brook St A2
Broomfield Rd A1
Burns Cres C2
Bus Station B1
Can Bridge Way B2
Cedar Ave A1
Cedar Ave West A1
Cemetery A1
Cemetery A2
Cemetery C1
Central Park B1
Chelmsford ✝ B2
Chelmsford ⇌ A1
Chichester Dr A3
Chinery Cl A3
Civic Centre A1
Civic Theatre 🎭 B1
College C1
Cottage Pl A2
County Cricket Gr B2
County Hall B2
Coval Ave B1
Coval La B1
Coval Wells B1
Crown Court B2
Duke St B2
Elm Rd C1
Elms Dr A1
Essex Record Office, The B3
Fairfield Rd B1
Falcons Mead B1
George St C2
Glebe Rd A1
Godfrey's Mews C2
Goldlay Ave C3
Goldlay Rd C2
Grove Rd C2
Hall St C2
Hamlet Rd C2
Hart St C1
Henry Rd A2
High Bridge Rd B2
High Chelmer Shopping Ctr B2
High St B2
Hill Cres B3
Hill Rd B3
Hill Rd Sth B3
Hillview Rd A3
HM Prison A3
Hoffmans Way A2
Hospital Ⓗ B2
Lady La C2
Langdale Gdns C3
Legg St B2
Library B2
Lionfield Terr A3
Lower Anchor St C1
Lynmouth Ave C2
Lynmouth Gdns C3
Magistrates Court B2
Maltese Rd A1
Manor Rd C2
Marconi Rd A2
Market B2
Market Rd B2
Marlborough Rd C1
Meadows Sh Ctr, The B2
Meadowside A3
Mews Ct C2
Mildmay Rd C2
Moulsham Dr C2
Moulsham Mill ✦ C3
Moulsham St C1/C2
Navigation Rd B3
New London Rd B2/C1
New St A2/B2
New Writtle St C1
Nursery Rd C2
Orchard St C2
Odeon 🎦 B2
Park Rd B1
Parker Rd C2
Parklands Dr A3
Parkway A1/B1/B2
Police Station 🚓 A2
Post Office ✉ B2/C2
Primrose Hill A1
Prykes Dr B1
Queen St C1
Queen's Rd B3
Railway St A1
Rainsford Rd A1
Ransomes Way A2
Rectory La A2
Regina Rd A2
Riverside Ice & Leisure Ctr B2
Riverside Retail Park A3
Rosebery Rd C2
Rothesay Ave C1
St John's Rd C2
Sandringham Pl B3
Seymour St B1
Shrublands Cl B3
Southborough Rd C1
Springfield Basin B3
Springfield Rd A3/B2/B3
Stapleford Cl C1
Superstore B2
Swiss Ave A1
Telford Pl A3
Tindal St B2
Townfield St A1
Trinity Rd B3
University B1
Upper Bridge Rd C1
Upper Roman Rd C2
Van Dieman's Rd C3
Viaduct Rd B1
Vicarage Rd C1
Victoria Rd A2
Victoria Rd South B2
Vincents Rd C2
Waterloo La B2
Weight Rd B3
Westfield Ave A1
Wharf Rd B3
Writtle Rd C1
YMCA A2
York Rd C1

Cheltenham 333

Albert Rd A3
Albion St B3
All Saints Rd B3
Ambrose St B2
Andover Rd C1
Art Gallery & Mus 🏛 B2
Back Montpellier Terr C2
Bandstand ✦ C2
Bath Pde B2
Bath Rd C2
Bays Hill Rd C1
Bennington St B2
Berkeley St B3
Brewery, The A2
Brunswick St South A2
Bus Station B2
Carlton St B3
Central Cross Road A3
Cheltenham College C2
Cheltenham FC A3
Cheltenham General (A&E) Ⓗ C3
Cheltenham Ladies College B2
Christchurch Rd B1
Cineworld 🎦 A2
Clarence Rd A2
Clarence Sq A2
Clarence St B2
Cleeveland St A1
College Baths Road C3
College Rd C2
Colletts Dr A1
Corpus St C3
Council Office B1
Court B1
Devonshire St A2
Douro Rd B1
Duke St B3
Dunalley Pde A2
Dunalley St A2
Everyman 🎭 B2
Evesham Rd A3
Fairview Rd B3
Fairview St B3
Fire Station C3
Folly La A2
Gloucester Rd A1
Grosvenor St B3
Grove St A1
Hanover St A2
Hatherley St C1
Henrietta St A2
Hewlett Rd B3
High St B2/B3
Holst Birthplace Museum 🏛 A3
Hudson St A2
Imperial Gdns C2
Imperial La B2
Imperial Sq C2
Information Ctr ℹ B2
Keynsham Rd C3
King St A2
Knapp Rd B2
Ladies College 🏠 B2
Lansdown Cr C1
Lansdown Rd C1
Leighton Rd B3
Library B2
London Rd C3
Lypiatt Rd C1
Malvern Rd B1
Manser St A2
Market St A1
Marle Hill Parade A2
Marle Hill Rd A2
Millbrook St A1
Milsom St A2
Montpellier Gdns C2
Montpellier Gr C2
Montpellier Parade C2
Montpellier Spa Rd C2
Montpellier St C1
Montpellier Terr C2
Montpellier Walk C2
New St B2
North Pl B2
Old Bath Rd C3
Oriel Rd B2
Overton Park Rd B1
Overton Rd B1
Oxford St C3
Parabola Rd B1
Park Pl C1
Park St A1
Pittville Circus A3
Pittville Cr A3
Pittville Lawn A3
Pittville Park A2
Playhouse 🎭 B2
Police Station 🚓 C1
Portland St B3
Prestbury Rd A3
Prince's Rd C1
Priory St B3
Promenade B2
Queen St A1
Recreation Ground A2
Regent Arcade B2
Regent St B2
Rodney Rd B2
Royal Cr B2
Royal Wells Rd B2
St George's Pl B2
St Georges Rd B1
St Gregory's ⛪ B2
St James St B3
St John's Ave B3
St Luke's Rd C2
St Margarets Rd A2
St Mary's ⛪ B2
St Matthew's ⛪ B2
St Paul's La A2
St Paul's Rd A2
St Paul's St A2
St Stephen's Rd C1
Sandford Parks Lido C3
Sandford Mill Road C3
Sandford Park C3
Sandford Rd C2
Selkirk St A3
Sherborne Pl B3
Sherborne St B3
Shopmobility B2
Suffolk Parade C2
Suffolk Rd C1
Suffolk Sq C1
Sun St A1
Swindon Rd B2
Sydenham Villas Rd C3
Tewkesbury Rd A1
The Courtyard B1
Thirlstaine Rd C2
Tivoli Rd C1
Tivoli St C1
Town Hall & Theatre 🎭 B2
Townsend St A1
Trafalgar St C2
Union St B3
Univ of Gloucestershire (Francis Cl Hall) A2
Univ of Gloucestershire (Hardwick) A1
Victoria Pl B3
Victoria St A2
Vittoria Walk C2
Wel Pl B2
Wellesley Rd A2
Wellington Rd A3
Wellington Sq A3
Wellington St B2
West Drive A3
Western Rd B1
Winchcombe St B3
Winston Churchill Memorial Gardens ✿ A1

Chester 333

Abbey Gateway A2
Appleyards La C3
Bars, The B3
Bedward Row B1
Beeston View C3
Bishop Lloyd's Pal 🏠 B2
Black Diamond St A2
Bottoms La C3
Boughton B3
Bouverie St A1
Bus Interchange A2
Bridge St B2
Bridgegate C2
Brook St A3
Brown's La C2
Cambrian Rd A1
Canal St A2
Carrick Rd C1
Castle 🏰 C2
Castle Dr C2
Cathedral ✝ B2
Catherine St A1
Chester ⇌ A3
Cheyney Rd A1
Chichester St A1
City Rd A3
City Walls B1/B2
City Walls Rd B1
Cornwall St A2
County Hall C2
Cross Hey C3
Cross, The ✦ B2
Crown Ct C2
Cuppin St B2
Curzon Park North C1
Curzon Park South C1
Dee Basin A1
Dee La B3
Delamere St A2
Dewa Roman Experience 🏛 B2
Duke St B2
Eastgate B2
Eastgate St B2
Eaton Rd C2
Edinburgh Way C3
Elizabeth Cr B3
Fire Station A2
Foregate St B2
Forum, The B2
Frodsham St B2
Gamul House B2
Garden La A1
George St A2
Gladstone Ave A1
God's Providence House 🏠 B2
Gorse Stacks A2
Greenway St C2
Grosvenor Bridge C1
Grosvenor Museum 🏛 B2
Grosvenor Park B3
Grosvenor Park Terr C1
Grosvenor Sh Ctr B2
Grosvenor St B2
Groves Rd B3
Groves, The B3
Guildhall Museum 🏛 B1
Handbridge C2
Hartington St C3
Hoole Way A2
Hunter St B2
Information Ctr ℹ B2
King Charles' Tower ✦ A2
King St A2
Leisure Centre A2
Library B2
Lightfoot St A3
Little Roodee C2
Liverpool Rd A2
Love St B3
Lower Bridge St B2
Lower Park Rd B3
Lyon St A2
Magistrates Court B2
Meadows La C3
Meadows, The B3
Military Museum 🏛 C2
Milton St A3
New Crane St B1
Nicholas St B2
Northgate A2
Northgate St A2
Nun's Rd B1
Old Dee Bridge ✦ C2
Overleigh Rd C2
Park St B2
Police Station 🚓 B2
Post Office ✉ A2/A3/B2
Princess St B2
Queen St B2
Queen's Park Rd C3
Queen's Rd A3
Race Course B1
Raymond St A1
River La C2
Roman Amphitheatre & Gardens 🏟 B2
Roodee (Chester Racecourse), The B1
Russell St A3
St Anne St A2
St George's Cr C3
St Martin's Gate A1
St Martin's Way B1
St Mary's Priory ✦ B2
St Oswalds Way A2
Saughall Rd A1
Sealand Rd A1
South View Rd A1
Stanley Palace 🏠 B1
Station Rd A3
Steven St A3
Storyhouse 🎭 B2
Superstore B2
Tower Rd B1
Town Hall B2
Union St B3
University of Chester C2
Vicar's La B2
Victoria Cr C3
Victoria Rd A2
Walpole St A1
Water Tower St A1
Water Tower, The ✦ B1
Watergate B1
Watergate St B2
Whipcord La A1
White Friars B2
York St B3

Chichester 333

Adelaide Rd A3
Alexandra Rd A3
Arts Centre B2
Ave de Chartres B1/B2
Barlow Rd A1
Basin Rd C2
Beech Ave B1
Bishops Palace Gardens B2
Bishopsgate Walk A3
Bramber Rd C3
Broyle Rd A2
Bus Station B2
Caledonian Rd B3
Cambrai Ave B3
Canal Pl C1
Canal Wharf C2
Canon La B2
Cathedral ✝ B2
Cavendish St A1
Cawley Rd B2
Cedar Dr A1
Chapel St A2
Cherry Orchard Rd C3
Chichester ⇌ B2
Chichester By-Pass C2/C3
Chichester Coll B1
Chichester Cinema 🎦 B3
Chichester Festival 🎭 A2
Chichester Gate Leisure Park C1
Churchside A2
Cineworld 🎦 C1
City Walls B2
Cleveland Rd B3
College La A2
Cory Cl C2
Council Offices B2
County Hall B2
District 🏛 B2
Duncan Rd A1
Durnford Cl A1
East Pallant B2
East Row B2
East St B2
East Walls B3
Eastland Rd C3
Ettrick Cl B3
Ettrick Rd B3
Exton Rd C3
Fire Station A2
Football Ground A2
Franklin Pl A2
Friary (Rems of) A2
Garland Cl C3
Green La A3
Grove Rd C3
Guilden Rd B3
Guildhall 🏛 A2
Hawthorn Cl A1
Hay Rd C3
Henty Gdns B1
Herald Dr C3
Hornet, The B3
Information Ctr ℹ B2
John's St B2
Joys Croft A3
Jubilee Pk A3
Jubilee Rd A3
Juxon Cl B2
Kent Rd A3
King George Gdns A2
King's Ave C2
Kingsham Ave C3
Kingsham Rd C2
Laburnum Gr B2
Leigh Rd C1
Lennox Rd A3
Lewis Rd A3
Library B2
Lion St B2
Litten Terr A3
Litten, The A3
Little London B2
Lyndhurst Rd B3
Market B3
Market Ave B2
Market Cross B2
Market Rd B3
Melbourne Rd A3
Minerva 🎭 A2
Mount La B1
New Park Rd A3
Newlands La A1
North Pallant B2
North St A2
North Walls A2
Northgate A2
Novium, The 🏛 B2
Oak Ave A1
Oak Cl A1
Oaklands Park A2
Oaklands Way A2
Orchard Ave A1
Orchard St A1
Ormonde Ave B3
Pallant House 🖼 B2
Parchment St A1
Parklands Rd A1/B1
Peter Weston Pl B3
Police Station 🚓 C2
Post Office ✉ A1/B2/C3
Priory La A2
Priory Park A2
Priory Rd A2
Queen's Ave C1
Riverside A3
Roman Amphitheatre B3
St Cyriacs A2
St Martins' St B2
St Pancras A3
St Paul's Rd A2
St Richard's Hospital (A&E) Ⓗ A3
Shamrock Cl A3
Sherbourne Rd A1
Somerstown A2
South Bank C2
South Downs Planetarium ✦ C2
South Pallant B2
South St B2
Southgate B2
Spitalfield La A3
Stirling Rd B3
Stockbridge Rd C1/C2
Swanfield Dr A3
Terminus Ind Est C1
Tower St A2
Tozer Way A3
Turnbull Rd A3
Upton Rd C1
Velyn Ave B3
Via Ravenna B1
Walnut Ave A1
West St B2
Westgate B1
Westgate Fields B1
Westgate Leisure Ctr B1
Weston Ave C1
Whyke Cl C3
Whyke La B3
Whyke Rd C3
Winden Ave B3

Colchester 333

Abbey Gateway ✝ C2
Albert St A1
Albion Grove C2
Alexandra Rd C1
Artillery St C3
Arts Centre 🖼 B1
Balkerne Hill B1
Barrack St C3
Beaconsfield Rd C1
Beche Rd C3
Bergholt Rd A1
Bourne Rd C3
Brick Kiln Rd A1
Brigade Gr C2
Bristol Rd B2
Broadlands Way A3
Brook St B3
Bury Cl B2
Bus Sta C2
Butt Rd C1
Campion Rd C2
Cannon St C3
Canterbury Rd C2
Captain Gardens C2
Castle 🏰 B2
Castle Park B2
Castle Rd B2
Catchpool Rd A1
Causton Rd B1
Chandlers Row C3
Circular Rd East C2
Circular Rd North C1
Circular Rd West C1
Clarendon Way A1
Claudius Rd C2
Colchester ⇌ A1
Colchester Camp Abbey Field C1
Colchester Retail Park B1
Colchester Town ⇌ C2
Colne Bank Ave A1
Colne View Retail Pk A2
Compton Rd A3
Cowdray Ave A1/A2
Cowdray Centre, The A2
Crouch St B1
Crowhurst Rd B1
Culver Square Shopping Centre B1
Culver St East B2
Culver St West B1
Dilbridge Rd A3
East Hill B2
East St B3
East Stockwell St B1
Eld La B1
Essex Hall Rd A1
Exeter Dr B2
Fairfax Rd C2
Fire Station A2
Firstsite 🖼 B2
Flagstaff Rd C1
Garrison Parade C2
George St B2
Gladstone Rd C2
Golden Noble Hill C2
Goring Rd A3
Granville Rd C3
Greenstead Rd B3
Guildford Rd B2
Harsnett Rd C3
Harwich Rd B3
Head St B1
High St B1/B2
High Woods Country Park A2
Hollytrees 🏛 B2
Hyderabad Cl C2
Hythe Hill C3
Information Ctr ℹ B2
Jarmin Rd A2
Kendall Rd C2
Kimberley Rd C3
King Stephen Rd C3
Leisure World A2
Library B1
Lincoln Way B2
Lion Walk Shopping Centre B1
Lisle Rd C2
Lucas Rd C2
Magdalen Green C3
Magdalen St C2
Maidenburgh St B2
Maldon Rd C1
Manor Rd B1
Margaret Rd A1
Mason Rd A2
Mercers Way A1
Mercury 🎭 B1
Mersea Rd C2
Meyrick Cr C2
Mile End Rd A1
Military Rd C2
Mill St C2
Minories 🖼 B2
Moorside B3
Morant Rd C3
Napier Rd C2
Natural History 🏛 B2
New Town Rd C2
Norfolk Cr A3
North Hill B1
North Station Rd A1
Northgate St B1
Nunns Rd B1
Odeon 🎦 B1
Old Coach Rd B3
Old Heath Rd C3
Osborne St B2
Petrolea Cl A1
Police Station 🚓 C1
Popes La B1
Port La C3
Post Office ✉ B2/C1
Priory St B2
Queen St B2
Rawstorn Rd B1
Rebon St C3
Recreation Rd C3
Ripple Way A3
Roberts Rd C2
Roman Rd B2
Roman Wall B2
Romford Cl A3
Rosebery Ave B2
St Andrews Ave B3
St Andrews Gdns B3
St Botolph St B2
St Botolphs ⛪ B2
St John's Abbey (site of) ✝ C2
St John's St B1
St Johns Walk Shopping Centre B1
St Leonards Rd C3
St Marys Fields B1
St Peter's St B1
St Peters ⛪ B1
Salisbury Ave C1
Saw Mill Rd C3
Sergeant St C2
Serpentine Walk A1
Sheepen Pl B1
Sheepen Rd B1
Sir Isaac's Walk B1
Smythies Ave B2
South St C1
South Way C1
Sports Way A2
Suffolk Cl A3
Superstore A1
Town Hall B1
Valentine Dr A3
Victor Rd C3
Wakefield Cl B2
Wellesley Rd C1
Wells Rd B2/B3
West St C1
West Stockwell St B1
Weston Rd C3
Westway A1
Wickham Rd C1
Wimpole Rd C3
Winchester Rd C2
Winnock Rd C2
Worcester Rd B2

Coventry 334

Abbots La A1
Albany 🎭 B1
Albany Rd B1
Alma St B3
Ambulance Sta A2
Art Faculty B3
Asthill Grove C2
Bablake School A1
Barras La A1/B1
Barr's Hill School A1
Belgrade 🎭 B2
Bishop St A2
Bond's Hospital 🏠 B1
Broad Gate B2
Broadway C1
Burges, The B2
Bus Station A3
Butts Radial B1
Byron St A3
Canal Basin ✦ A2
Canterbury St A3
Cathedral ✝ B3
Central Six Retail Pk C1
Chester St A1
Cheylesmore Manor House 🏠 B2
Christ Church Spire ✦ B2
City Coll A3
City Walls & Gates ✦ A2
Corporation St B2
Council House B2
Coundon Rd A1
Coventry Station ⇌ C2
Coventry Transport Museum 🏛 A2
Coventry University Technology Park C3
Cox St A3
Croft Rd B1
Dalton Rd C1
Deasy Rd C3
Earl St B2
Eaton Rd C2
Fairfax St B2
Foleshill Rd A2
Ford's Hospital 🏠 B2
Fowler Rd A1
Friars Rd C2
Gordon St C1
Gosford St B3
Greyfriars Green ✦ B2
Greyfriars Rd B2
Gulson Rd B3
Hales St A2
Harnall Lane East A3
Harnall Lane West A2
Herbert Art Gallery & Museum 🖼 B3
Hertford St B2
Hewitt Ave A1
High St B2
Hill St B1
Holy Trinity ⛪ B2
Holyhead Rd A1
Howard St A3
Huntingdon Rd C1
Information Ctr ℹ B2
Jordan Well B3
King Henry VIII Sch C1
Lady Godiva Statue ✦ B2
Lamb St A2
Leicester Row A2
Library B2
Lincoln St A2
Little Park St B2
London Rd C3
Lower Ford St B3
Lower Prec Shop Ctr B2
Magistrates & Crown Courts B2
Manor House Drive B2
Manor Rd C2
Market B2
Martyrs Memorial ✦ C2
Meadow St B1
Meriden St A1
Michaelmas Rd C2
Middleborough Rd A1
Mile La C3
Millennium Place ✦ A2
Much Park St B3
Naul's Mill Park A1
New Union B2
Odeon 🎦 B1
Park Rd C2
Parkside C3
Planet Ice Arena B1
Post Office ✉ B2
Primrose Hill St A3
Priory Gardens & Visitor Centre B2
Priory St B3
Puma Way C3
Quarryfield La C3
Queen's Rd B1
Quinton Rd C2
Radford Rd A2
Raglan St B3
Ringway (Hill Cross) A1
Ringway (Queens) B1
Ringway (Rudge) B1
Ringway (St Johns) B3
Ringway (St Nicholas) A2
Ringway (St Patricks) C2
Ringway (Swanswell) A2
Ringway (Whitefriars) B3
St John St B2
St John the Baptist ⛪ B2
St Nicholas St A2
Sidney Stringer Acad A3
Skydome B1
Spencer Ave C1
Spencer Rec Gnd C1
Spencer Rd C1
Spon St B1
Sports Centre B3
Stoney Rd C2
Stoney Stanton Rd A3
Superstore B2
Swanswell Pool A3
Technocentre C3
Thomas Landsdail St C2
Tomson Ave A1
Top Green C1
Trinity St B2
University B3
University Sports Ctr B3
Upper Hill St A1
Upper Well St A2
Victoria St A3
Vine St A3
Warwick Rd C2
Waveley Rd B1
West Orchards Shopping Centre B2
Westminster Rd C1
White St A3
Windsor St B1

Derby 334

Abbey St C1
Agard St B1
Albert St B2
Albion St B2
Ambulance Station B1
Arthur St A1
Ashlyn Rd B3
Assembly Rooms 🏢 B2
Babington La C2
Becket St B1
Belper Rd A1
Bold La B1
Bradshaw Way C2
Bradshaw Way Retail Park C2
Bridge St B1
Brook St B1
Burton Rd C1
Bus Station B2
Business Park A3
Caesar St A2
Canal St C3
Carrington St C3
Cathedral ✝ B2
Cathedral Rd B1
Charnwood St C2
Chester Green Rd A2
City Rd A2
Clarke St A3
Cock Pitt B3
Council House 🏢 B2
Courts B1
Cranmer Rd B3
Crompton St C1
Crown & County Courts B2
Curzon St B1
Darley Grove A1
Derby ⇌ C3
Derby 🎭 C2
Derbyshire 3aaa County Cricket Ground B3
Derwent Business Ctr A2
Derwent St B2
Drewry La C1
Duffield Rd A1
Duke St A2
Dunton Cl B3
Eagle Market C2
East St B2
Eastgate B3
Exeter St B2
Farm St C1
Ford St B1
Forester St C1
Fox St A2
Friar Gate B1
Friary St B1
Full St B2
Gerard St C1
Gower St C2
Green La C2
Grey St C1
Guildhall 🏢 B2
Harcourt St C1
Highfield Rd A1
Hill La C2
Information Ctr ℹ B2
intu Derby C2
Iron Gate B2
John St C3
Joseph Wright Centre B1
Kedleston Rd A1
Key St B2
King Alfred St C1
King St A1
Kingston St A1
Lara Croft Way C2
Leopold St C2
Library B1
Liversage St C3
Lodge La B1
London Rd C2
London Rd Community Hospital Ⓗ C2
Macklin St C1
Mansfield Rd A2
Market B2
Market Pl B2
May St C1
Meadow La B3
Melbourne St C2
Mercian Way C1
Midland Rd C3
Monk St C1
Morledge B2
Mount St C1

Mus & Art Gallery . . B1
Noble St . . C3
North Parade . . A1
North St . . C2
Nottingham Rd. . . B3
Osmaston Rd. . . A1
Otter St . . A1
Park St . . C3
Parker St . . A1
Pickfords House . . B1
Police HQ . . C2
Police Station . . B2
Post Office . . A1/A2/B1/C2/C3
Pride Parkway . . C3
Prime Enterprise Park . . A2
Prime Parkway . . A2
QUAD . . B2
Queens Leisure Ctr . . A3
Racecourse Park . . A3
Railway Terr . . B2
Register Office . . B2
Sadler Gate . . B1
St Alkmund's Way . . B1/B2
St Helens House . . A1
St Mary's . . A1
St Mary's Bridge . . A1
St Mary's Bridge Chapel . . A1
St Mary's Gate . . B1
St Paul's Rd . . A1
St Peter's . . C2
St Peter's St . . C2
Showcase De Lux . . A1
Siddals Rd . . C2
Sir Frank Whittle Rd . . A3
Spa La. . . C1
Spring St . . C1
Stafford St . . B1
Station Approach. . . C3
Stockbrook St. . . C1
Stores Rd . . A3
Traffic St . . C2
Wardwick . . B1
Werburgh St . . C1
West Ave . . A1
West Meadows Ind Est . . B3
Wharf Rd . . A2
Wilmot St . . C1
Wilson St . . C1
Wood's La . . C1

Dorchester 334
Ackerman Rd. . . B3
Acland Rd . . B2
Albert Rd . . A1
Alexandra Rd. . . B1
Alfred Place . . B3
Alfred Rd . . B2
Alington Ave . . B3
Alington Rd . . B3
Ambulance Station . . B1
Ashley Rd . . B1
Balmoral Cres . . A3
Barnes Way . . B2/C2
Borough Gdns . . A1
Brewery Sq . . B2
Bridport Rd . . A1
Buckingham Way . . C3
Caters Place . . A1
Cemetery . . A3/C1
Charles St . . A2
Coburg Rd . . A2
Colliton St . . A1
Cornwall Rd. . . A1
Cromwell Rd. . . B1
Culliford Rd. . . B2
Culliford Rd North . . B2
Dagmar Rd. . . B1
Damer's Rd . . B1
Diggory Cres . . C2
Dinosaur Museum . . A2
Dorchester Bypass . . C1
Dorchester South Station . . B1
Dorchester West Station . . B1
Dorset County (A&E) . . A1
Dorset County Council Offices . . A1
Dorset County Mus . . B1
Duchy Close . . C3
Duke's Ave. . . A1
Durngate St . . A2
Durnover Court . . A3
Eddison Ave. . . B1
Edward Rd . . B1
Egdon Rd . . C2
Elizabeth Frink Statue . . B2
Farfrae Cres . . B2
Forum Centre, The . . B1
Friary Hill. . . A2
Friary Lane . . A2
Frome Terr . . A2
Garland Cres . . C3
Glyde Path Rd . . A1
Government Offices . . C1
Grosvenor Cres. . . C1
Grosvenor Rd . . C1
Grove, The. . . A1
Gt Western Rd. . . C1
Herrington Rd. . . C1
High St East. . . A2
High St Fordington . . A2
High Street West . . A1
Holloway Rd . . A2
Icen Way . . A2
Keep Military Museum, The . . A1
Kings Rd. . . A3/B3
Kingsbere Cres. . . C2
Lancaster Rd. . . B2
Library . . B1
Lime Cl . . A3
Linden Ave . . B3
London Cl. . . A3
London Rd . . A2/A3

Lubbecke Way. . . A3
Lucetta La . . B2
Maiden Castle Rd . . C1
Manor Rd . . C2
Market . . B1
Marshwood Pl. . . B2
Maumbury Rd . . B2
Maumbury Rings . . B1
Mellstock Ave . . C2
Mill St . . A1
Miller's Cl . . A1
Mistover Cl . . C1
Monmouth Rd. . . B1/B2
Moynton Rd. . . C2
Nature Reserve. . . A2
North Sq. . . A2
Northernhay . . A1
Odeon . . B1
Old Crown Court & Cells . . A1
Olga Rd. . . A1
Orchard St . . A2
Police Station . . A1
Post Office . . A1
Pound Lane . . A2
Poundbury Rd. . . A1
Prince of Wales Rd. . . B2
Prince's St . . B2
Queen's Ave. . . B1
Roman Town House . . A1
Roman Wall . . A1
Rothesay Rd . . C2
St George's Rd . . B3
Salisbury Field . . A2
Sandringham Sports Centre . . B3
Shaston Cres. . . C2
Smokey Hole La . . B2
South Court Ave . . C1
South St . . A2
South Walks Rd. . . B2
Superstore . . C3
Teddy Bear House . . A1
Temple Cl. . . C1
Terracotta Warriors & Teddy Bear Mus . . A1
Town Hall . . A1
Town Pump . . A1
Trinity St . . B1
Tutankhamun Ex . . B1
Victoria Rd . . B1
Weatherbury Way . . C1
Wellbridge Cl . . C1
West Mills Rd . . A1
West Walks Rd . . A1
Weymouth Ave . . C1
Williams Ave . . B1
Winterbourne (BMI)
Wollaston Rd. . . C1
York Rd. . . B2

Dumfries 334
Academy St . . A2
Aldermanhill Rd . . B3
Ambulance Station . . C3
Annan Rd . . A3
Ardwall Rd. . . A3
Ashfield Dr . . A2
Atkinson Rd . . C1
Averill Cres . . C1
Balliol Ave . . C1
Bank St . . B2
Bankend Rd. . . C3
Barn Slaps . . B3
Barrie Ave . . C3
Beech Ave . . A1
Bowling Green . . B1
Brewery St. . . B2
Bridgend Theatre . . A1
Brodie Ave . . C1
Brooke St. . . B2
Broomlands Dr . . C1
Brooms Rd. . . B3
Buccleuch St . . B2
Burns House . . B2
Burns Mausoleum . . B3
Burns St. . . B3
Burns Statue . . B1
Bus Station . . B1
Cardoness St. . . A1
Castle St. . . A1
Catherine St . . B1
Cattle Market . . B1
Cemetery . . A1
Cemetery. . . C3
Church Cres . . B1
Church St. . . B2
College Rd . . A1
College St . . A1
Convent, The. . . A1
Corbelly Hill . . B1
Corberry Park . . B1
Cornwall Mt. . . A3
Council Offices . . A2
Court . . B2
Craigs Rd . . C3
Cresswell Ave . . B3
Cresswell Hill . . B3
Cumberland St . . B3
David Keswick Athletic Centre . . C3
David St . . B1
Dock Park . . C2
Dockhead . . B2
Dumfries . . B1
Dumfries Academy . . A2
Dumfries Museum & Camera Obscura . . B2
Dumfries Royal Infirmary (A&E) . . C3
East Riverside Dr . . C3
Edinburgh Rd . . A2
English St. . . B2
Fire Station . . B3
Friar's Vennel . . A2
Galloway St . . A1
George Douglas Dr . . C1
George St. . . A2

Gladstone Rd. . . C2
Glasgow St. . . A1
Glebe St . . B3
Glencaple Rd . . C2
Goldie Ave . . A1
Goldie Cres . . A1
Golf Course . . C3
Greyfriars . . A2
Grierson Ave . . B3
Hamilton Ave . . C1
Hamilton Starke Park . . C2
Hazelrigg Ave . . C1
Henry St . . B3
Hermitage Dr . . C1
High Cemetery . . C3
High St . . A2
Hill Ave . . C2
Hill St . . B1
HM Prison . . B1
Holm Ave . . C2
Hoods Loaning . . A3
Howgate St . . B1
Huntingdon Rd . . A1
Information Ctr . . B2
Irish St . . B2
Irving St . . A2
King St . . A1
Kingholm Rd . . C3
Kirkpatrick Ct . . C1
Laurieknowe . . B1
Leafield Rd . . B3
Library . . A2
Lochfield Rd . . A1
Loreburn Pk . . B2
Loreburn St . . B2
Loreburne Shopping Ctr. . . B2
Lover's Walk . . A2
Martin Ave . . B3
Maryholm Dr . . A1
Mausoleum . . B3
Maxwell St . . B3
McKie Ave . . A3
Mews La . . A3
Mid Steeple . . B2
Mill Green . . B2
Mill Rd . . B1
Moat Rd . . C2
Moffat Rd. . . A3
Mountainhall Pk. . . C2
Nelson St . . B1
New Abbey Rd. . . B1/C1
New Bridge . . B1
Newall Terr . . A2
Nith Ave . . A2
Nith Bank . . C2
Nithbank Hospital . . C3
Nithside Ave . . A1
Odeon . . B2
Old Bridge . . B1
Old Bridge House . . B1
Palmerston Park (Queen of the South FC) . . A1
Park Rd. . . C1
Pleasance Ave. . . C1
Police HQ . . A3
Police Station . . A2
Portland Dr . . A1
Post Office . . B1/B2/B3/B3
Priestlands Dr. . . C1
Primrose St . . B1
Queen St . . B3
Queensberry St . . A2
Rae St . . A2
Richmond Ave . . C1
Roberts Cres . . C1
Robertson Ave . . C1
Robinson Dr . . C1
Rosefield Rd . . C2
Rosemount St . . B1
Rotchell Park . . C1
Rotchell Rd . . C1
Rugby Football Gd . . C1
Ryedale Rd. . . C2
St Andrews . . B2
St John the Evangelist . . A2
St Josephs College . . B3
St Mary's Ind Est . . A3
St Mary's St . . B3
St Michael St . . B2
St Michael's St . . B2
St Michael's Bridge . . B2
St Michael's Bridge Rd . . B2
St Michael's Cemetery . . B3
Shakespeare St . . B2
Solway Dr . . C2
Stakeford St . . A1
Stark Cres . . C2
Station Rd . . B1
Steel Ave . . A1
Sunderries Ave . . A1
Sunderries Rd . . A1
Superstore . . B3
Suspension Brae . . B2
Swimming Pool . . A1
Terregles St . . A1
Theatre Royal . . B2
Troqueer Rd . . C1
Union St . . A1
Wallace St . . B1
Welldale . . B2
West Riverside Dr . . C2
White Sands . . B2

Dundee 334
Abertay University . . B2
Adelaide Pl . . A1
Airlie Pl . . C1
Albany Terr . . A1
Albert St . . A3
Alexander St . . A2
Ann St . . A2
Arthurstone Terr . . A3
Bank St . . B2
Barrack Rd. . . A1
Barrack St . . B2

Bell St. . . B2
Blinshall St . . B1
Broughty Ferry Rd . . A3
Brown St . . B1
Bus Station . . A2
Caird Hall . . B2
Camperdown St . . B3
Candle La. . . B3
Carmichael St . . A1
City Churches . . B2
City Quay . . B3
City Sq . . B2
Commercial St . . B2
Constable St . . A3
Constitution Cres. . . A1
Constitution Ct . . A1
Constitution St . . A1/B2
Cotton Rd. . . A2
Courthouse Sq . . B1
Cowgate . . B2
Crescent St . . A3
Crichton St . . B2
Dens Brae . . A3
Dens Rd . . A2
Discovery Point . . C2
Douglas St . . B1
Drummond St . . A1
Dudhope Castle . . A1
Dudhope St . . A2
Dudhope Terr . . A1
Dundee . . C2
Dundee Contemporary Arts . . C2
Dundee High School . . B2
Dundee Law . . A1
Dundee Repertory . . C2
Dunhope Park . . A1
Dura St . . A3
East Dock St . . B3
East Marketgait . . B3
East Whale La . . B3
Erskine St . . A3
Euclid Cr . . B2
Forebank Rd . . A2
Foundry La . . A2
Gallagher Retail Park . . A3
Gellatly St . . B2
Government Offices . . C2
Guthrie St . . B1
Hawkhill . . C1
Hilltown . . A2
HMS Unicorn . . B3
Howff Cemetery, The . . B2
Information Ctr . . B2
Keiller Shopping Ctr . . B2
Keiller Ctr, The. . . B2
King St . . A3
Kinghorne Rd . . A1
Ladywell Ave . . A2
Laurel Bank . . A2
Law Rd . . A1
Law St . . A2
Library . . A2/A3
Library and Steps Theatre . . A2
Little Theatre, The . . A2
Lochee Rd . . B1
Lower Princes St . . A3
Lyon St . . A3
McManus Art Gallery & Museum, The . . B2
Meadow Side . . B2
Meadowside St Pauls . . B2
Mercat Cross . . B2
Murraygate . . B2
Nelson St . . A2
Nethergate . . B2/C1
North Lindsay St . . B2
North Marketgait . . B2
Old Hawkhill . . B1
Olympia Leisure Ctr. . . B3
Overgate Shopping Centre . . B2
Park Pl . . C1
Perth Rd . . C1
Police Station . . B1
Post Office . . B2
Princes St . . A3
Prospect Pl . . A2
Reform St . . B2
Riverside Dr . . C2
Riverside Esplanade . . C2
Roseangle . . C1
Rosebank St . . A1
RRS Discovery . . C2
St Andrew's . . C2
St Pauls Episcopal † . . B2
Science Centre . . C2
Seagate . . B2
Sheriffs Court . . B1
Shopmobility . . B2
South George St . . A2
South Marketgait . . B3
South Tay St . . C2
South Victoria Dock Road . . B3
South Ward Rd . . B2
Tay Road Bridge . . C3
Thomson Ave . . A3
Trades La . . B3
Union St . . B2
Union Terr . . A1
University Library . . C2
University of Dundee . . C1
Upper Constitution St . . A1
Verdant Works . . B1
V&A Dundee . . C2
Victoria Dock . . B3
Victoria Rd. . . B2
Victoria St . . A3
Ward Rd . . B1
Wellgate . . B2
West Bell St . . B1
West Marketgait . . B1/B2
Westfield Pl. . . C1
William St . . A3
Wishart Arch . . A3

Durham 334
Alexander Cr. . . B2
Allergate . . C1
Archery Rise . . C1
Avenue, The . . A1
Back Western Hill. . . A1
Bakehouse La . . B3
Baths . . B3
Baths Bridge . . B3
Boat House . . B3
Bowling . . A2
Boyd St . . B3
Bus Station . . B2
Castle . . B2
Castle Chare . . B2
Cathedral † . . B2
Church St. . . C3
Clay La . . C1
Claypath. . . B2
College of St Hild & St Bede . . A3
County Hall . . A1
County Hospital . . C1
Crescent, The . . A1
Crook Hall & Gardens . . A2
Crossgate . . B2
Crossgate Peth. . . C1
Crown Court . . B2
Darlington Rd . . C1
Durham . . A2
Durham School. . . C2
Durham University Science Site . . C3
Ellam Ave . . C1
Elvet Bridge . . B3
Elvet Court. . . B3
Farnley Hey . . A1
Ferens Cl . . A3
Fieldhouse La . . A1
Flass St . . C1
Framwelgate Bridge . . B2
Framwelgate . . A2
Framwelgate Peth . . A2
Framwelgate Waterside . . A3
Frankland La . . A3
Freeman's Pl . . A3
Freeman's Quay L Ctr . . A3
Gala Theatre & Cinema . . B3
Geoffrey Ave . . C1
Gilesgate . . B3
Grey College . . C2
Grove, The. . . A1
Hallgarth St. . . C3
Hatfield College . . B2
Hawthorn Terr . . B1
Heritage Centre . . B3
HM Prison . . B1
Information Ctr . . B2
John St. . . B1
Kingsgate Bridge . . B3
Laburnum Terr . . B1
Lawson Terr . . B1
Leazes Rd . . B2/B3
Library . . B1
Library . . B3
Margery La . . C2
Market . . B2
Mavin St . . C3
Millburngate . . B2
Millburngate Bridge . . B2
Millennium Bridge (foot/cycle) . . A2
Mountjoy Research Centre . . C2
Museum of Archaeology . . B2
Nevilledale Terr . . B1
New Elvet . . B3
New Elvet Bridge . . B3
North Bailey . . B2
North End . . A1
North Rd . . A1/B2
Observatory . . C1
Old Elvet. . . B3
Open Treasure . . B2
Oriental Museum . . C2
Oswald Court . . C3
Parkside. . . C3
Passport Office . . A2
Percy Terr . . B1
Pimlico. . . C2
Police Station . . B3
Post Office . . A1/B2
Potters Bank . . C1/C2
Prebends Bridge . . C2
Prebends Walk . . C2
Prince Bishops Shopping Centre . . B3
Princes St . . A2
Providence Row . . A3
Quarryheads La . . C2
Redhills La . . B1
Redhills Terr . . B1
Riverwalk, The . . B2
Saddler St . . B3
St Chad's College . . C3
St Cuthbert's Society . . C2
St John's College . . C2
St Margaret's . . B2
St Mary the Less . . C2
St Mary's College . . C2
St Monica Grove . . B1
St Nicholas' . . B2
St Oswald's . . C3
Sands, The. . . A3
Shopmobility . . B3
Sidegate . . A2
Silver St . . B2
Sixth Form College . . C1
South Bailey . . C2
South Rd . . C2
South St . . B2
Springwell Ave . . A1
Stockton St . . C3
Student Union. . . B3
Sutton St . . B2

Town Hall . . B2
University Arts Block . . B3
University College . . B2
Walkergate Centre . . B3
Wearside Dr . . A3
Western Hill . . A1
Wharton Park . . A1
Whinney Hill . . C3
Whitehouse Ave . . C1
YHA . . C3

Edinburgh 334
Abbey Strand . . B6
Abbeyhill . . B6
Abbeyhill Cr. . . B6
Abbeymount . . B6
Abercromby Pl . . A4
Adam St . . C5
Albany La . . A4
Albany St . . A4
Albert Memorial . . B2
Albyn Pl . . A3
Alva Pl. . . A6
Alva St . . B2
Ann St . . A2
Appleton Tower . . C4
Archibald Pl . . C3
Assembly Rooms & Musical Hall . . A3
Atholl Crescent. . . B2
Atholl Crescent La . . C2
Bank St . . B4
Barony St . . A4
Beaumont Pl . . C5
Belford Rd . . B1
Belgrave Cr . . A1
Belgrave Crescent La . . A1
Bell's Brae . . A1
Blackfriars St . . B4
Blair St . . B4
Bread St . . C2
Bristo Pl . . C4
Bristo Sq . . C4
Brougham St . . C3
Broughton St . . A4
Brown St . . C4
Brunton Terr . . A6
Buckingham Terr . . A1
Burial Ground . . A6
Bus Station . . A4
Caledonian Cr . . C1
Caledonian Rd . . C1
Calton Hill . . A4
Calton Hill . . A4
Calton Rd . . B4
Camera Obscura & Outlook Tower . . B3
Candlemaker Row . . C4
Canning St . . B2
Canongate . . B5
Canongate . . B5
Carlton St . . A2
Carlton Terr . . A6
Carlton Terrace La . . A6
Castle . . B3
Castle Terr . . B3
Castlehill . . B3
Central Library . . B4
Chalmers Hospital . . C3
Chalmers St . . C3
Chambers St . . C4
Chapel St . . C4
Charles St . . C4
Charlotte Sq . . B2
Chester St . . B1
Circus La . . A3
Circus Pl. . . A3
City Art Centre . . B4
City Chambers . . B4
City Observatory . . A5
Clarendon Cr . . A1
Clerk St . . C5
Coates Cr . . B2
Cockburn St . . B4
College of Art . . C3
Comely Bank Ave . . A1
Comely Bank Row. . . A1
Cornwall St . . C2
Cowans Cl . . C5
Cowgate . . B4
Cranston St . . B5
Crichton St . . C4
Croft-An-Righ . . A6
Cumberland St . . A3
Dalry Pl . . C1
Dalry Rd . . C1
Danube St . . A2
Darnaway St . . A2
David Hume Tower . . C4
Davie St . . C5
Dean Bridge . . A2
Dean Gdns . . A2
Dean Park Cr . . A1
Dean Park Mews . . A1
Dean Park St . . A1
Dean Path . . B1
Dean St . . A2
Dean Terr . . A2
Dewar Pl . . C1
Dewar Place La . . C1
Doune Terr . . A2
Drummond Pl . . A4
Drummond St . . C5
Drumsheugh Gdns . . B1
Dublin Mews . . A3
Dublin St . . A4
Dublin Street Lane South . . A4
Dumbiedykes Rd . . B5
Dundas St . . A3
Earl Grey St . . C2
East Crosscauseway . . C5
East Market St . . B4
East Norton Pl . . A6
East Princes St Gdns . . B3
Easter Rd . . A6
Edinburgh (Waverley) . . B4
Edinburgh Castle . . B3

Edinburgh Dungeon . . B4
Edinburgh International Conference Ctr. . . C2
Elder St . . A4
Esplanade . . B3
Eton Terr . . A2
Eye Pavilion . . C3
Festival Theatre Edinburgh . . C5
Filmhouse . . C2
Floral Clock . . B3
Forres St . . A3
Forth St . . A4
Fountainbridge . . C2
Frederick St . . A3
Fruit Market . . B4
Gardner's Cr. . . C2
George Heriot's School . . C3
George IV Bridge . . B4
George Sq . . C4
George Square La . . C4
George St . . A3
Georgian House . . B2
Gladstone's Land . . B3
Glen St . . C3
Gloucester La . . A2
Gloucester Pl . . A2
Gloucester St . . A2
Graham St . . C1
Grassmarket . . C3
Great King St . . A3
Great Stuart . . B1
Greenside La . . A5
Greenside Row . . A5
Greyfriars Kirk . . C4
Grindlay St . . C2
Grosvenor St . . C1
Grove St . . C1
Gullan's Cl . . B5
Guthrie St . . B4
Hanover St . . A3
Hart St . . A4
Haymarket . . C1
Haymarket Station . . C1
Heriot Pl. . . C3
Heriot Row . . A2
High School Yard . . B5
High St . . B4
Hill Pl . . C5
Hill St . . A2
Hillside Cr . . A5
Holyrood Park . . B6
Holyrood Rd . . B5
Holyrood Abbey, remains of (AD 1128) . . A6
Home St . . C2
Hope St . . B2
Horse Wynd . . B6
Howden St . . C5
Howe St . . A3
India Pl . . A2
India St . . A2
Infirmary St . . B4
Information Ctr . . B4
Jeffrey St . . B4
John Knox House . . B4
Johnston Terr . . C3
Keir St . . C3
Kerr St . . A2
King's Stables Rd . . B2
Lady Lawson St . . C3
Lauriston Gdns . . C3
Lauriston Park . . C3
Lauriston Pl . . C3
Lauriston St . . C3
Lawnmarket . . B3
Learmonth Gdns. . . A1
Learmonth Terr . . A1
Leith St . . A4
Lennox St . . A1
Lennox St La . . A1
Leslie Pl . . A2
London Rd . . A5
Lothian Rd . . B2
Lothian St . . C4
Lower Menz Pl . . A6
Lynedoch Pl. . . B1
Mall, The . . B6
Manor Pl . . B1
Market St . . B4
Marshall St . . C4
Maryfield. . . A6
Maryfield Pl . . A6
McEwan Hall . . C4
Medical School. . . C4
Melville St . . B1
Meuse La . . B4
Middle Meadow Walk . . C4
Milton St . . A6
Montrose Terr. . . A6
Moray House (coll) . . B5
Moray Place . . A2
Morrison Link . . C1
Morrison St . . C1
Mound Pl . . B3
Mound, The. . . B3
Multrees Walk . . A4
Mus Collections Ctr . . A4
Mus of Childhood . . B4
Mus of Edinburgh . . B5
Museum of Fire . . C3
Mus on the Mound . . B4
National Archives of Scotland . . A4
National Museum of Scotland . . C4
National Gallery . . B3
National Library of Scotland . . B4
National Monument . . A5
National Portrait Gallery . . A4
Nelson Monument . . A5
Nelson St . . A4
New St . . B5
Nicolson Sq . . C5
Nicolson St . . C4
Niddry St . . B4

West End Princess St . . B1
West Maitland St . . C1
West of Nicholson St . . C4
West Port. . . C2
West Princes St Gdns . . B3
West Richmond St . . C5
West Tollcross . . C2
White Horse Cl . . B5
William St . . B1
Windsor St . . A5
Writer's Mus, The . . B4
York La . . A4
York Pl . . A4
Young St. . . B2

Exeter 334
Alphington St . . C1
Athelstan Rd . . B3
Bampfylde St . . B2
Barnardo Rd . . C2
Barnfield Hill. . . B3
Barnfield Rd . . B2/B3
Barnfield Theatre . . B3
Bartholomew St East. . . B1
Bartholomew St West. . . B1
Bear St. . . C2
Beaufort Rd . . C1
Bedford St . . B2
Belgrave Rd . . A3
Belmont Rd . . A3
Blackall Rd . . A2
Blackboy Rd . . A3
Bonhay Rd . . B1
Bull Meadow Rd . . C2
Bus & Coach Sta . . B3
Castle St . . B2
Cecil Rd . . C1
Cheeke St . . A3
Church Rd . . C1
Chute St . . A3
City Wall . . B1/B2
Civic Centre . . B2
Clifton Rd . . B3
Clifton St . . B3
Clock Tower . . B1
College Rd . . B3
Colleton Cr . . C2
Commercial Rd . . C1
Coombe St . . C2
Cowick St . . C1
Crown Courts . . B2
Custom House . . C2
Cygnet New Theatre . . C2
Danes' Rd . . A2
Denmark Rd . . B3
Devon County Hall . . C3
Devonshire Pl . . A3
Dinham Cres . . B1
East Grove Rd . . C3
Edmund St . . C1
Elmgrove Rd . . A1
Exe St . . B1
Exeter Cathedral † . . B2
Exeter Central Sta . . A1
Exeter City Football Ground . . A3
Exeter College . . B2
Exeter Picture Ho . . B1
Fire Station . . A1
Fore St . . C2
Friars Walk . . C2
Guildhall . . B2
Guildhall Shopping Ctr . . B2
Harlequins Shopping Ctr. . . B1
Haven Rd . . C2
Heavitree Rd . . B3
Hele Rd . . A1
High St . . B2
HM Prison . . A2
Holloway St . . C2
Hoopern St . . A2
Horseguards . . A3
Howell Rd . . A1
Information Ctr . . B3
Iron Bridge . . B1
Isca Rd . . C1
Jesmond Rd . . A3
King St . . B1
King William St . . A2
Larkbeare Rd . . C2
Leisure Centre . . C1
Library . . B2
Longbrook St . . A2
Longbrook Terr . . A2
Lower North St . . B1
Lucky La. . . C2
Lyndhurst Rd . . C3
Magdalen Rd . . C3
Magdalen St . . C2
Market . . B2
Market St . . B2
Marlborough Rd . . C3
Mary Arches St . . B1
Matford Ave . . C2
Matford La . . C3
Matford Rd . . C3
May St . . A3
Mol's Coffee House . . B2
New Bridge St . . B1
New North Rd . . A1/A2
North St . . B2
Northernhay St . . B1
Norwood Ave . . C3
Odeon . . B3
Okehampton St . . C1
Old Mill Cl . . C2
Old Tiverton Rd . . A3
Oxford Rd . . A3
Paris St . . B2
Parr St . . A3
Paul St . . B2
Pennsylvania Rd . . A2
Police HQ . . B3
Portland Street. . . A3

350 Fort William • Glasgow • Gloucester • Grimsby • Hanley (Stoke-on-Trent) • Harrogate

Post Office A3/B2/B3/C1
Powderham Cr A3
Preston St B1
Princesshay Sh Ctr B2
Pyramids Leisure Ctr B3
Quay, The C2
Queen St A1
Queen's Terr A1
Queens Rd C1
Radford Rd C2
Richmond Rd A1
Roberts Rd C2
Rougemont Castle A2
Rougemont House B2
Royal Albert Memorial Museum B2
St David's Hill A1
St James' Pk Sta A3
St James' Rd A3
St Leonard's Rd C3
St Mary Steps C1
St Nicholas Priory B1
St Thomas Station C1
Sandford Walk B3
School for the Deaf C2
School Rd C1
Sidwell St A2
Smythen St B1
South St B2
Southernhay East B2
Southernhay West B2
Spacex Gallery B1
Spicer Rd B3
Sports Centre A3
Summerland St A3
Sydney Rd C1
Tan La C2
Thornton Hill A2
Topsham Rd C3
Tucker's Hall B1
Tudor St B1
Underground Passages B2
University of Exeter (St Luke's Campus) B3
Velwell Rd A1
Verney St A3
Water La C1/C2
Weirfield Rd C2
Well St A3
West Ave A2
West Grove Rd C3
Western Way A3/B1/B2
Willeys Ave C1
Wonford Rd B3/C3
York Rd A2

Fort William 335

Abrach Rd A3
Achintore Rd C1
Alma Rd B2
Am Breun Chamas A2
Ambulance Station A3
An Aird A2
Argyll Rd C1
Argyll Terr C1
Bank St B2
Belford Hospital B2
Ben Nevis Highland Centre B3
Black Parks A3
Braemore Pl C2
Bruce Pl C2
Bus Station B2
Camanachd Cr A3/B2
Cameron Rd C1
Cameron Sq B1
Carmichael Way A2
Claggan Rd B3
Connochie Rd C1
Cow Hill C3
Creag Dhubh A2
Croft Rd B3
Douglas Pl B2
Dudley Rd B2
Dumbarton Rd C1
Earl of Inverness Rd A3
Fassifern Rd B1
Fire Station A2
Fort William B2
Fort William (Remains) B2
Glasdrum Rd C1
Glen Nevis Pl B3
Gordon Sq B1
Grange Rd C1
Heathercroft Dr C1
Heather Croft Rd C1
Henderson Row C2
High St B1
Hill Rd B2
Hosp Belhaven Annexe B3
Information Ctr A3
Inverlochy Ct A3
Kennedy Rd B2/C2
Library B2
Lime Tree Gallery C1
Linnhe Rd B1
Lochaber Leisure Ctr B3
Lochiel Rd A3
Lochy Rd A3
Lundavra Cres C1
Lundavra Rd C1
Lundy Rd A3
Mamore Cr B2
Mary St B2
Middle St B1
Montrose Ave A3
Moray Pl C1
Morven Pl C2
Moss Rd B2
Nairn Cres C1
Nevis Bridge B3
Nevis Centre, The A2
Nevis Rd A3
Nevis Terr B2
North Rd B3
Obelisk B2
Parade Rd B2
Police Station C1
Post Office A3/B2
Ross Pl B1
St Andrews B2
Shaw Pl B2
Station Brae B1
Superstore B3
Treig Rd A3
Underwater Ctr, The A2
Union Rd C1
Victoria Rd B2
Wades Rd A3
West Highland B1
West Highland College UHI A2
Young Pl B2

Glasgow 335

Admiral St C2
Albert Bridge C5
Albion St B5
Anderston B3
Anderston Quay B3
Argyle Arcade B5
Argyle St A1/A2/B3/B4/B5
Argyle Street B5
Arlington St A3
Arts Centre B3
Ashley St A3
Bain St C6
Baird St A6
Baliol St A3
Ballater St C5
Barras (Market), The C6
Bath St A3
BBC Scotland B1
Bell St C6
Bell's Bridge B1
Bentinck St A2
Berkeley St A3
Bishop La B3
Black St A6
Blackburn St C2
Blackfriars St B6
Blantyre St A1
Blythswood Sq A4
Blythswood St B4
Bothwell St B4
Brand St C1
Breadalbane St A2
Bridge St C4
Bridge St C4
Bridgegate C5
Briggait C5
Broomielaw B4
Broomielaw Quay Gdns B3
Brown St B4
Brunswick St B5
Buccleuch St A3
Buchanan Bus Station A5
Buchanan Galleries A5
Buchanan St B5
Buchanan St B5
Cadogan St B4
Caledonian University A5
Calgary St A5
Cambridge St A4
Canal St A5
Candleriggs B5
Carlton Pl C4
Carnarvon St A3
Carrick St B4
Castle St B6
Cathedral Sq B6
Cathedral St B5
Ctr for Contemporary Arts A4
Centre St C4
Cessnock C1
Cessnock St C1
Charing Cross A3
Charlotte St C6
Cheapside St B3
Cineworld A5
Citizens' Theatre C5
City Chambers Complex B5
City Halls B5
City of Glasgow Coll (City Campus) B5
City of Glasgow Coll (Riverside Campus) C5
Clairmont Gdns A2
Claremont St A2
Claremont Terr A2
Claythorne St C6
Cleveland St A3
Clifford La C1
Clifford St C1
Clifton Pl A2
Clifton St A2
Clutha St C1
Clyde Arc B2
Clyde Auditorium B2
Clyde Pl C4
Clyde Place Quay C4
Clyde St C5
Clyde Walkway C3
Clydeside Expressway B2
Coburg St C4
Cochrane St B5
College St B6
Collins St B6
Commerce St C4
Cook St C4
Cornwall St C1
Couper St A5
Cowcaddens A4
Cowcaddens Rd A4
Crimea St B3
Custom Ho Quay Gdns C4
Dalhousie St A4
Dental Hospital A4
Derby St A2
Dobbie's Loan A4/A5
Dobbie's Loan Pl A5
Dorset St A3
Douglas St B4
Doulton Fountain C6
Dover St A2
Drury St B4
Drygate B6
Duke St B6
Dunaskin St A1
Dunblane St A4
Dundas St B5
Dunlop St C5
East Campbell St C6
Eastvale Pl A1
Eglinton St C4
Elderslie St A3
Elliot St B2
Elmbank St A3
Esmond St A1
Exhibition Centre B2
Eye Infirmary A2
Festival Park C1
Film Theatre A4
Finnieston Quay B2
Finnieston St B2
Fire Station C6
Florence St C5
Fox St C5
Gallowgate C6
Garnet St A3
Garnethill St A4
Garscube Rd A4
George Sq B5
George St B5
George V Bridge C4
Gilbert St A1
Glasgow Bridge C4
Glasgow Cathedral B6
Glasgow Central B4
Glasgow Green C6
Glasgow Necropolis B6
Glasgow Royal Concert Hall A5
Glasgow Science Centre B1
Glasgow Tower B1
Glassford St B5
Glebe St A6
Gorbals Cross C5
Gorbals St C5
Gordon St B4
Govan Rd B1/C1/C2
Grace St B3
Grafton Pl A5
Grand Ole Opry C2
Grant St A3
Granville St A3
Gray St A2
Greendyke St C6
Grey Eagle St B7
Harley St C1
Harvie St C1
Haugh Rd A1
Havanah St B6
Heliport B1
Henry Wood Hall A2
High Court C5
High St B6
High Street B6
Hill St A3
Holland St A3
Holm St B4
Hope St A5
Houldsworth St B2
Houston Pl C3
Houston St C3
Howard St C5
Hunter St C6
Hutcheson St B5
Hydepark St B3
Imax Cinema B1
India St A3
Information Ctr B5
Ingram St B5
Jamaica St B4
James Watt St B4
John Knox St B6
John St B5
Kelvin Hall A1
Kelvin Statue A2
Kelvin Way A2
Kelvingrove Art Gallery & Museum A1
Kelvingrove Park A2
Kelvingrove St A2
Kelvinhaugh St A1
Kennedy St A6
Kent Rd A2
Killermont St A5
King St B5
King's, The A3
Kingston Bridge C3
Kingston St C4
Kinning Park C2
Kyle St A5
Lancefield Quay B2
Lancefield St B3
Langshot St C1
Lendel Pl C1
Lighthouse, The B4
Lister St A6
Little St B3
London Rd C6
Lorne St C1
Lower Harbour B1
Lumsden St A1
Lymburn St A1
Lyndoch Cr A3
Lynedoch Pl A3
Lynedoch St A3
Maclellan St C1
Mair St C2
Maitland St A4
Mansell St C7
Mavisbank Gdns C2
Mcalpine St B3
Mcaslin St A6
McLean Sq C2
McLellan Gallery A4
McPhater St A4
Merchants' House B5
Middlesex St C2
Middleton St C1
Midland St B4
Miller St B5
Millennium Bridge B1
Millroad St C6
Milnpark St C2
Milton St A4
Minerva St B2
Mitchell Library, The A3
Mitchell St West B4
Mitchell Theatre, The A3
Modern Art Gallery B5
Moir St C6
Molendinar St C6
Moncur St C6
Montieth Row C6
Montrose St B5
Morrison St C3
Mosque C5
Nairn St A1
National Piping Centre, The A5
Nelson Mandela Sq B5
Nelson St C4
Nelson's Monument C6
New City Rd A4
Newton Pl A3
Newton St A3
Nicholson St C4
Nile St B5
Norfolk Court C4
Norfolk St C4
North Frederick St B5
North Hanover St B5
North Portland St B6
North St A3
North Wallace St A5
O2 ABC A4
O2 Academy C4
Odeon C3
Old Dumbarton Rd A1
Osborne St B5/C5
Oswald St B4
Overnewton St A1
Oxford St C4
Pacific Dr B1
Paisley Rd C3
Paisley Rd West C1
Park Circus A2
Park Gdns A2
Park St South A2
Park Terr A2
Parkgrove Terr A2
Parnie St C5
Parson St A6
Partick Bridge A1
Passport Office A5
Pavilion Theatre A4
Pembroke St A3
People's Palace C6
Pinkston Rd A6
Pitt St A4/B4
Plantation Park C1
Plantation Quay B1
Police Station A4/A6
Port Dundas Rd A5
Port St B2
Portman St C2
Prince's Dock B1
Princes Sq B5
Provand's Lordship B6
Queen St B5
Queen Street B5
Ramshorn B5
Renfrew St A3/A4
Renton St A5
Richmond St B5
Robertson St B4
Rose St A4
Rottenrow B5
Royal Concert Hall A5
Royal Conservatoire of Scotland A4
Royal Cr A2
Royal Exchange Sq B5
Royal Highland Fusiliers Museum A3
Royal Hospital For Sick Children A1
Royal Infirmary B6
Royal Terr A2
Rutland Cr C2
St Andrew's C6
St Andrew's (RC) C5
St Andrew's St C5
St Enoch B5
St Enoch Shopping Ctr B5
St Enoch Sq B4
St George's Rd A3
St James Rd B6
St Kent St C6
St Mungo Ave A5/A6
St Mungo Museum of Religious Life B6
St Mungo Pl A6
St Vincent Cr A2
St Vincent Pl B5
St Vincent St B3/B4
St Vincent Street Church B4
St Vincent Terr B3
Saltmarket C5
Sandyford Pl A3
Sauchiehall St A2/A4
School of Art A4
Sclater St B7
Scotland St C2
Scott St A4
Scottish Exhibition & Conference Centre B1
Seaward St C2
Shaftesbury St B3
Sheriff Court C5
Shields Rd C3
Shopmobility A5
Shuttle St B6
Sighthill Park A6
Somerset Pl A2
South Portland St C4
Springburn Rd A6
Springfield Quay C3
SSE Hydro The B2
Stanley St C2
Stevenson St C6
Stewart St A4
Stirling Rd B6
Stirling's Library B5
Stobcross Quay B1
Stobcross Rd B1
Stock Exchange B5
Stockwell Pl C5
Stockwell St B5
Stow College A4
Sussex St C2
Synagogues A3/C4
Taylor Pl A6
Tenement House A3
Teviot St A1
Theatre Royal A4
Tolbooth Steeple & Mercat Cross C6
Tower St C2
Trades House B5
Tradeston St C4
Transport Museum A1
Tron C5
Trongate B5
Tunnel St B2
Turnbull St C5
Union St B4
Univ of Strathclyde B6
Victoria Bridge C5
Virginia St B5
Wallace St C3
Walls St B6
Walmer Cr C1
Warrock St B3
Washington St B3
Waterloo St B4
Watson St B6
Watt St C3
Wellington St B4
West Campbell St B4
West George St B4
West Graham St A4
West Greenhill Pl B2
West Regent St A4
West Regent St B4
West St C4
West St C4
Whitehall St B3
Wilkes St C7
Wilson St B5
Woodlands Gate A3
Woodlands Rd A3
Woodlands Terr A2
Woodside Pl A3
Woodside Terr A3
York St B4
Yorkhill Pde A1
Yorkhill St A1

Gloucester 335

Albion St C1
Alexandra Rd B3
Alfred St C3
All Saints Rd C2
Alvin St B2
Arthur St C2
Barrack Square B1
Barton St C2
Blackfriars B1
Blenheim Rd C2
Bristol Rd C1
Brunswick Rd C2
Bruton Way B2
Bus Station B2
Cineworld C1
City Council Offices B1
City Mus, Art Gall & Library B2
Clarence St B2
Commercial Rd B1
Council Offices C1
Courts B1
Cromwell St C2
Deans Way A2
Denmark Rd A3
Derby Rd C3
Docks C1
Eastgate St B2
Eastgate, The B1
Edwy Pde A2
Estcourt Cl A3
Estcourt Rd A3
Falkner St C2
GL1 Leisure Centre C2
Gloucester Cath B1
Gloucester Life B1
Gloucester Quays Outlet C1
Gloucester Station B2
Gloucester Waterways C1
Gloucestershire Archive B2
Gloucestershire Royal Hospital (A&E) B3
Goodyere St C2
Gouda Way A1
Great Western Rd B3
Guildhall B2
Heathville Rd A3
Henry Rd B3
Henry St B2
Hinton Rd A2
India Rd C3
Information Ctr B1
Jersey Rd C3
King's C2
King's Walk Sh Ctr B2
Kingsholm (Gloucester Rugby) A2
Kingsholm Rd A2
Lansdown Rd A3
Library C2
Llanthony Rd C1
London Rd B3
Longhorn Ave A1
Longsmith St B1
Malvern Rd A3
Market B2
Market Pde B2
Mercia Rd A1
Metz Way C3
Midland Rd C2
Millbrook St C3
Montpellier C1
Napier St C3
Nettleton Rd C2
New Inn B2
New Olympus C3
North Rd A3
Northgate St B2
Oxford Rd A2
Oxford St B2
Park & Ride Gloucester A1
Park Rd C2
Park St B2
Park, The C2
Parliament St C1
Peel Centre, The C1
Pitt St B1
Police Station C3
Post Office B2
Quay St B1
Quay, The B1
Recreation Gd A1/A2
Regent St C2
Robert Raikes Ho B1
Royal Oak Rd B1
Russell St B2
Ryecroft St C2
St Aldate St B2
St Ann Way C1
St Catherine St A2
St Mark St A2
St Mary de Crypt B1
St Mary de Lode B1
St Nicholas's B1
St Oswald's Rd A1
St Oswald's Retail Pk A1
St Peter's B2
Seabroke Rd A3
Sebert St A2
Severn Rd C1
Sherborne St B2
Shire Hall B1
Sidney St C3
Soldiers of Gloucestershire B1
Southgate St B1/C1
Spa Field C1
Spa Rd C1
Sports Ground A2/B2
Station Rd B2
Stratton Rd C3
Stroud Rd C1
Superstore A1
Swan Rd A2
Trier Way C1/C2
Union St A2
Vauxhall Rd C3
Victoria St C2
Walham Lane A1
Wellington St C2
Westgate Retail Park B1
Westgate St B1
Widden St C2
Worcester St B2

Grimsby 335

Abbey Drive East C2
Abbey Drive West C2
Abbey Park Rd C2
Abbey Rd C2
Abbey Walk C2
Abbeygate Sh Ctr C2
Abbotsway C2
Adam Smith St A1/A2
Ainslie St C2
Albert St A3
Alexandra Dock A2/B2
Alexandra Rd A2/B2
Alexandra Retail Park A2
Annesley St A2
Armstrong St A1
Arthur St B1
Augusta St C1
Bargate C1
Beeson St A1
Bethlehem St C2
Bodiam Way B3
Bradley St B3
Brighowgate C1/C2
Bus Station C2
Canterbury Dr C1
Cartergate B1/C1
Catherine St C3
Caxton A3
Chantry La B1
Charlton St A1
Church La C2
Church St A3
Cleethorpe Rd A3
Close, The C1
College St C1
Compton Dr C1
Corporation Bridge A2
Corporation Rd A1
Court B3
Crescent St B1
Deansgate C1
Doughty Rd C2
Dover St B1
Duchess St C2
Dudley St C1
Duke of York Gardens B1
Duncombe St B3
Earl La B1
East Marsh St B3
East St B2
Eastgate B3
Eastside Rd A3
Eaton Ct C1
Eleanor St B3
Ellis Way B3
Fisherman's Chapel A3
Fisherman's Wharf B2
Fishing Heritage Centre B2
Flour Sq A3
Frederick St B1
Frederick Ward Way B2
Freeman St A3/B3
Freshney Dr B1
Freshney Pl B2
Garden St C2
Garibaldi St A3
Garth La B2
Grime St B3
Grimsby Docks Sta A3
Grimsby Town Sta C2
Hainton Ave C3
Har Way B3
Hare St C3
Harrison St B1
Haven Ave B1
Hay Croft Ave B1
Hay Croft St B1
Heneage Rd B3/C3
Henry St B1
Holme St B3
Hume St C1
James St B1
Joseph St B1
Kent St A3
King Edward St A3
Lambert Rd C2
Library B2
Lime St B1
Lister St B1
Littlefield La C1
Lockhill A3
Lord St B1
Lower Spring St A3
Ludford St C3
Macaulay St B1
Mallard Mews C3
Manor Ave C2
Market A3
Market Hall B2
Market St B3
Moss Rd C2
Nelson St A3
New St B2
Osbourne St B2
Pasture St B3
Peaks Parkway C3
Pelham Rd C1
Police Station B3
Post Office B1/B2
Pyewipe Rd A1
Railway Pl A3
Railway St A3
Recreation Ground C2
Rendel St A2
Retail Park A2/B3
Richard St B1
Ripon St B1
Robinson St East B3
Royal St A3
St Hilda's Ave C1
St James C2
Sheepfold St B3/C3
Shopmobility B2
Sixhills St C3
South Park B2
Superstore B3/B2
Tasburgh St C3
Tennyson St B2
Thesiger St A3
Time Trap C2
Town Hall B2
Veal St B1
Victoria Retail Park A3
Victoria St North A2
Victoria St South B2
Victoria St West B2
Watkin St A1
Welholme Ave C2
Welholme Rd C3
Wellington St B3
Wellowgate C2
Werneth Rd B3
West Coates Rd A1
Westgate A2
Westminster Dr C1
Willingham St C3
Wintringham Rd C2
Wood St B3
Yarborough Dr B1
Yarborough Hotel C2

Hanley 335

Acton St A3
Albion St B2
Argyle St C1
Ashbourne Gr A2
Avoca St A3
Baskerville Rd B3
Bedford Rd C1
Bedford St C1
Bethesda St B2
Bexley St A2
Birches Head Rd A3
Botteslow St C3
Boundary St A2
Broad St C2
Broom St A3
Bryan St A2
Bucknall New Rd B3
Bucknall Old Rd B3
Bus Station B3
Cannon St C2
Castlefield St C1
Cavendish St B1
Central Forest Pk A2
Charles St B3
Cheapside B2
Chell St A3
Clarke St C1
Cleveland Rd C2
Clifford St C3
Clough St B2
Clyde St C1
College Rd C2
Cooper St C2
Corbridge Rd A1
Cutts St C2
Davis St C1
Denbigh St A1
Derby St C3
Dilke St A3
Dundas St A3
Dundee Rd C1
Dyke St B3
Eastwood Rd C3
Eaton St A3
Etruria Park B1
Etruria Rd B1
Etruria Vale Rd C1
Festing St A3
Festival Retail Park A1
Fire Station C2
Foundry St B2
Franklyn St C3
Garnet St B1
Garth St B3
George St A3
Gilman St B3
Glass St B3
Goodson St B3
Greyhound Way A1
Grove Pl C1
Hampton St C3
Hanley Park C2
Hanley Park C2
Harding Rd C2
Hassall St B3
Havelock Pl C1
Hazlehurst St C3
Hinde St C2
Hope St B2
Houghton St C2
Hulton St A3
Information Ctr B3
Jasper St C2
Jervis St A3
John Bright St A3
John St B2
Keelings Rd A3
Kimberley Rd C1
Ladysmith Rd C1
Lawrence St C2
Leek Rd C3
Library C2
Lichfield St C3
Linfield Rd B3
Loftus St A2
Lower Bedford St C1
Lower Bryan St A2
Lower Mayer St A3
Lowther St A1
Magistrates Court C2
Malham St A2
Marsh St B2
Matlock St C3
Mayer St A3
Milton St C1
Mitchell Memorial Theatre B2
Morley St B2
Moston St A3
Mount Pleasant C1
Mulgrave St A1
Mynors St B3
Nelson Pl B3
New Century St B1
Octagon Retail Park B1
Ogden Rd C3
Old Hall St B3
Old Town Rd A3
Pall Mall B2
Palmerston St C3
Park and Ride C2
Parker St B2
Parkway, The C2
Pavilion Dr A1
Pelham St C3
Percy St B2
Piccadilly B2
Picton St B3
Plough St A3
Police Station C2
Portland St A1
Post Office A3/B3/C3
Potteries Museum & Art Gallery B2
Potteries Sh Ctr B2
Potteries Way C2
Powell St A1
Pretoria Rd C1
Quadrant Rd B2
Ranelagh St C2
Raymond St C2
Rectory Rd C1
Regent Rd C2
Regent Theatre B2
Richmond Terr C2
Ridgehouse Dr A1
Robson St C2
St Ann St B3
St Luke St B3
Sampson St B2
Shaw St A1
Sheaf St C2
Shearer St C1
Shelton New Rd C1
Shirley Rd C2
Slippery La B2
Snow Hill C2
Spur St C3
Stafford St B2
Statham St B2
Stubbs La C3
Sun St C1
Supermarket A1/B2
Talbot St C3
Town Hall B2
Town Rd A3
Trinity St B2
Union St A2
Upper Hillchurch St A3
Upper Huntbach St B3
Victoria Hall Theatre B3
Warner St C2
Warwick St C1
Waterloo Rd A1
Waterloo St B3
Well St B3
Wellesley St C2
Wellington Rd B3
Wellington St B3
Whitehaven Dr A2
Whitmore St C1
Windermere St A1
Woodall St A1
Yates St C2
York St A2

Harrogate 335

Albert St C2
Alexandra Rd B2
Arthington Ave B2
Ashfield Rd A2
Back Cheltenham Mount B2
Beech Grove C1
Belmont Rd C1
Bilton Dr A2
BMI The Duchy Hospital C1
Bower Rd B2
Bower St B2
Bus Station B2
Cambridge Rd B2
Cambridge St B2
Cemetery A2
Chatsworth Grove A2
Chatsworth Pl A2
Chatsworth Rd A2
Chelmsford Rd B3
Cheltenham Cr B2
Cheltenham Mt B2
Cheltenham Pde B2
Christ Church B3
Christ Church Oval B3
Chudleigh Rd B3
Clarence Dr B1
Claro Rd A3
Claro Way A3
Coach Park B2
Coach Rd B3
Cold Bath Rd C1
Commercial St B2
Coppice Ave A1
Coppice Dr A1
Coppice Gate A1
Cornwall Rd B1
Council Offices B1
Crescent Gdns B1
Crescent Rd B1
Dawson Terr A2
Devonshire Pl B3
Dixon Rd A2
Dixon Terr A2
Dragon Ave B3
Dragon Parade B2
Dragon Rd B2
Duchy Rd B1
East Parade B2
East Park Rd C3
Esplanade B1
Everyman B2
Fire Station A2
Franklin Mount A2
Franklin Rd B2
Franklin Square A2
Glebe Rd C1
Grove Park Ct A3
Grove Park Terr A3
Grove Rd A2
Hampsthwaite Rd A1
Harcourt Dr B3
Harcourt Rd B3
Harrogate B2
Harrogate Convention Centre B1
Harrogate Justice Centre (Magistrates' and County Courts) C2
Harrogate Ladies Coll B1
Harrogate Theatre B2
Heywood Rd C1
Hollins Cr A1
Hollins Mews A1
Hollins Rd A1
Hydro Leisure Ctr, The A1
Information Ctr B1
James St B2
Jenny Field Dr A1
John St B2
Kent Dr A1
Kent Rd A1
Kings Rd A2
Kingsway B3
Kingsway Dr B3
Lancaster Rd C1
Leeds Rd C2
Lime Grove B3
Lime St A3
Mayfield Grove B2
Mercer B1
Montpellier Hill B1
Mornington Cr A3
Mornington Terr B3
Mowbray Sq B3
North Park Rd B3
Oakdale Ave A1
Oatlands Dr C3
Odeon B2
Osborne Rd A2
Otley Rd C2
Oxford St B2
Parade, The B2
Park Chase B3
Park Parade B3
Park View B2
Parliament St B1
Police Station C3
Post Office B2/C1

Holyhead • Hull • Inverness • Ipswich • Kendal • King's Lynn • Lancaster 351

Providence Terr A2
Queen Parade C3
Queen's Rd C1
Raglan St C2
Regent Ave A3
Regent Grove A3
Regent Parade A3
Regent St A3
Regent Terr A3
Ripon Rd A1
Robert St C2
Royal Baths & Turkish Baths B1
Royal Pump Room B1
St Luke's Mount A2
St Mary's Ave C1
St Mary's Walk C1
Scargill Rd A1
Skipton Rd A3
Skipton St A2
Slingsby Walk C3
South Park Rd C2
Spring Grove A1
Springfield Ave B1
Station Ave B2
Station Parade B2
Stray Rein C3
Stray, The C2/C3
Studley Rd A2
Superstore B2/C1
Swan Rd B1
Tower St C2
Trinity Rd C2
Union St B2
Valley Dr C1
Valley Gardens C1
Valley Mount C1
Victoria Ave C2
Victoria Rd C1
Victoria Shopping Ctr B2
Waterloo St A2
West Park C2
West Park St C2
Wood View A1
Woodfield Ave A3
Woodfield Dr A3
Woodfield Grove A3
Woodfield Rd A3
Woodfield Square A3
Woodside B3
York Pl C3
York Rd B1

Holyhead Caergybi 335

Armenia St A2
Arthur St C2
Beach Rd A1
Boston St B2
Bowling Green C3
Bryn Erw Rd C3
Bryn Glas Cl C3
Bryn Glas Rd C3
Bryn Gwyn Rd C1
Bryn Marchog A1
Bryn Mor Terr A2
Bryngoleu Ave A1
Cae Braenar C3
Cambria St B1
Captain Skinner's Obelisk B2
Cecil St C2
Celtic Gateway Footbridge B2
Cemetery C1/C2
Cleveland Ave C2
Coastguard Lookout A2
Court B2
Customs House A3
Cybi Pl A2
Cyttir Rd C3
Edmund St B1
Empire B2
Ferry Terminals B2
Ffordd Beibio B3
Ffordd Feurig C3
Ffordd Hirnos C3
Ffordd Jasper C3
Ffordd Tudur B3
Fire Station C2
Garreglwyd Rd B1
Gilbert St C2
Gorsedd Circle B1
Gwelfor Ave A1
Harbour View B3
Henry St C2
High Terr C1
Hill St B2
Holborn Rd C2
Holland Park Ind Est C3
Holyhead Park B1
Holyhead Station B2
Information Ctr B2
King's Rd C2
Kingsland Rd C2
Lewascote C3
Library B2
Lifeboat Station A1
Llanfawr Cl C3
Llanfawr Rd C3
Lligwy St C2
Lon Deg C3
London Rd C3
Longford Rd B1
Longford Terr B1
Maes Cybi B1
Maes Hedd A1
Maes-Hyfryd Rd C1
Maes-y-Dref B1
Maes-yr-Haf A2/B1
Maes-yr-Ysgol C3
Marchog C3
Marina A1
Maritime Museum A1
Market B2
Market St B2
Mill Bank B1
Min-y-Mor Rd A1
Morawelon Ind Est B3
Morawelon Rd B3
Moreton Rd C1
New Park Rd B1
Newry St A2
Old Harbour Lighthouse A3
Plas Rd C1
Police Station B2
Porth-y-Felin Rd A1
Post Office A1/B2/B3
Prince of Wales Rd A2
Priory La B3
Pump St C1
Queens Park B1
Reseifion Rd C1
Rock St B1
Roman Fort B2
St Cybi St B2
St Cybi's Church B2
St Seiriol's Cl B1
Salt Island Bridge A2
Seabourne Rd A1
South Stack Rd B1
Sports Ground B1
Stanley St B2
Station St B2
Superstore C2
Tan-y-Bryn Rd A1
Tan-yr-Efail C2
Tara St C1
Thomas St B1
Town Hall A2
Treseifion Estate C2
Turkey Shore Rd B2
Ucheldre Arts Ctr B1
Ucheldre Ave B1
Upper Baptist St B1
Victoria Rd B2
Victoria Terr B2
Vulcan St B1
Walthew Ave A1
Walthew La A1
Wian St C2

Hull 335

Adelaide St C1
Albert Dock C1
Albion St B2
Alfred Gelder St B2
Anlaby Rd B1
Arctic Corsair B3
Beverley Rd A1
Blanket Row C2
Bond St B2
Bridlington Ave A2
Brook St B1
Brunswick Ave A1
Bus Station B1
Camilla Cl C3
Cannon St A2
Caroline St A2
Carr La B2
Castle St C2
Central Library B1
Charles St A2
Citadel Way B3
City Hall B2
City Hall Theatre B2
Clarence St B3
Cleveland St A3
Clifton St A1
Club Culture C2
Colonial St B1
Court B2
Deep, The C3
Dinostar C2
Dock Office Row B3
Dock St B2
Drypool Bridge B3
Egton St A3
English St C1
Ferens Gallery B2
Ferensway B1
Francis St A2
Francis St West A2
Freehold St A1
Freetown Way A2
Früit Theatre C2
Garrison Rd B3
George St B2
Gibson St A2
Great Thornton St B1
Great Union St A3
Green La A2
Grey St A1
Grimston St B2
Grosvenor St A1
Guildhall B2
Guildhall Rd B2
Hands-on History B2
Harley St A1
Hessle Rd C1
High St B3
Holy Trinity B2
Hull (Paragon) Sta B1
Hull & East Riding Museum B3
Hull Ice Arena C1
Hull College B3
Hull History Centre A2
Hull Truck Theatre B1
Humber Dock Marina C2
Humber Dock St C2
Humber St C2
Hyperion St A3
Information Ctr B2
Jameson St B1
Jarratt St B2
Jenning St A3
King Billy Statue C2
King Edward St B2
King St A2
Kingston Retail Park C1
Kingston St C2
Liddell St A1
Lime St A3
Lister St C1
Lockwood St A2
Maister House B3
Maritime Museum B2
Market B2
Market Place B2
Minerva Pier C2
Mulgrave St A3
Myton Swing Bridge C3
Myton St B1
NAPA (Northern Acad of Performing Arts) B1
Nelson St C2
New Cleveland St A3
New George St A2
New Theatre A2
Norfolk St A1
North Bridge A3
North St B1
Odeon C1
Old Harbour C3
Osborne St B1
Paragon St B2
Park St B1
Percy St A2
Pier St C2
Police Station B1
Porter St C1
Portland St B1
Post Office B1/B2
Posterngate B2
Prince's Quay B2
Prospect Centre B1
Prospect St B1
Queen's Gdns B2
Railway Dock Marina C2
Railway St C2
Real B1
Red Gallery B1
Reform St A2
Retail Park B1
Riverside Quay C2
Roper St B2
St James St C1
St Luke's St B1
St Mark St A3
St Mary the Virgin B3
St Stephens Sh Ctr B1
Scale Lane Footbridge B3
Scott St A2
South Bridge Rd B3
Sport's Centre C1
Spring Bank A1
Spring St B1
Spurn Lightship C2
Spyvee St A3
Streetlife Transport Museum B3
Sykes St A2
Tidal Surge Barrier C3
Tower St B3
Trinity House B2
University B2
Vane St A1
Victoria Pier C2
Waterhouse La B2
Waterloo St A1
Waverley St C1
Wellington St C2
Wellington St West C2
West St B1
Whitefriargate B2
Wilberforce Dr B2
Wilberforce House B3
Wilberforce Monument B3
William St C1
Wincolmlee A3
Witham A3
Wright St A1

Inverness 336

Abban St A1
Academy St B2
Alexander Pl B2
Anderson St A2
Annfield Rd C3
Ardconnel St B3
Ardconnel Terr B3
Ardross Pl B2
Ardross St B2
Argyle St B3
Argyle Terr B3
Attadale Rd B1
Ballifeary La C2
Ballifeary Rd C1/C2
Balnacraig La A1
Balnain House B2
Balnain St B2
Bank St B2
Bellfield Park C2
Bellfield Terr C3
Benula Rd A1
Birnie Terr A1
Bishop's Rd C2
Bowling Green B2
Bridge St B2
Brown St A2
Bruce Ave C1
Bruce Gdns C1
Bruce Pk C1
Burial Ground A2
Burnett Rd A3
Bus Station B3
Caledonian Rd B1
Cameron Rd A1
Cameron Sq A1
Carse Rd A1
Carsegate Rd Sth A1
Castle Garrison Encounter B2
Castle Rd B2
Castle St B3
Celt St B2
Chapel St A2
Charles St B3
Church St B2
Clachnacuddin Football Ground A1
Columba Rd B1/C1
Crown Ave B3
Crown Circus B3
Crown Dr B3
Crown Rd B3
Crown St B3
Culduthel Rd C3
Dalneigh Cres C1
Dalneigh Rd C1
Denny St B3
Dochfour Dr B1/C1
Douglas Row B2
Duffy Dr C3
Dunabban Rd A1
Dunain Rd B1
Duncraig St B2
Eastgate Shopping Ctr B3
Eden Court C2
Fairfield Rd B1
Falcon Sq B3
Fire Station A3
Fraser St B2
Fraser St C2
Friars' Bridge A2
Friars' La B2
Friars' St A2
George St A2
Gilbert St A2
Glebe St A2
Glendoe Terr A1
Glenurquhart Rd C1
Gordon Terrace B3
Gordonville Rd C2
Grant St A2
Greig St B2
Harbour Rd A3
Harrowden Rd B1
Haugh Rd C2
Heatherley Cres C3
High St B3
Highland Council HQ, The C2
Hill Park C3
Hill St B3
HM Prison B3
Huntly Pl A2
Huntly St B2
India St A2
Industrial Estate A3
Information Ctr B2
Innes St A2
Inverness B3
Inverness High Sch B1
Inverness Museum B2
Jamaica St A2
Kenneth St B2
Kilmuir Rd A1
King St B2
Kingsmills Rd B3
Laurel Ave B1/C1
Library A3
Lilac Gr B1
Lindsay Ave C1
Lochalsh Rd A1/B1
Longman Rd A3
Lotland Pl A2
Lower Kessock St A1
Madras St A2
Market Hall B3
Maxwell Dr C1
Mayfield Rd C3
Millburn Rd B3
Mitchell's La C3
Montague Row B2
Muirfield Rd C3
Muirtown St B1
Nelson St A2
Ness Bank C2
Ness Bridge B2
Ness Walk B2/C2
Old Edinburgh Rd C3
Old High Church B2
Park Rd C1
Paton St C2
Perceval Rd B1
Planefield Rd B2
Police Station A3
Porterfield Bank C3
Porterfield Rd C3
Portland Pl A2
Post Office A2/B1/B2
Queen St B2
Queensgate B2
Railway Terr A3
Rangemore Rd B1
Reay St B3
Riverside St A2
Rose St A2
Ross Ave B1
Rowan Rd B1
Royal Northern Infirmary C2
St Andrew's Cath C2
St Columba B2
St John's Ave C1
St Mary's Ave C1
Sheriff Court B3
Shore St A2
Smith Ave C1
Southside Pl C3
Southside Rd C3
Spectrum Centre B2
Strothers La B3
Superstore A1/B2
TA Centre C2
Telford Gdns B1
Telford Rd A1
Telford St A1
Tomnahurich Cemetery C1
Tomnahurich St B2
Town Hall B3
Union Rd B3
Union St B3
Walker Pl A2
Walker Rd A3
War Memorial C2
Waterloo Bridge A2
Wells St B1
Young St B2

Ipswich 336

Alderman Rd B2
All Saints' Rd A1
Alpe St B2
Ancaster Rd C1
Ancient House B3
Anglesea Rd B2
Ann St B2
Arboretum A2
Austin St C2
Avenue, The A3
Belstead Rd C2
Berners St B2
Bibb Way B1
Birkfield Dr C1
Black Horse La B2
Bolton La B3
Bond St C3
Bowthorpe Cl B2
Bramford La A1
Bramford Rd A1
Bridge St C2
Brookfield Rd A1
Brooks Hall Rd A1
Broomhill A2
Broomhill Rd A1
Broughton Rd A2
Bulwer Rd B1
Burrell Rd C2
Bus Station B3
Butter Market B2
Buttermarket Shopping Centre, The B3
Cardinal Park Leisure Park C2
Carr St B3
Cecil Rd B2
Cecilia St C2
Chancery Rd C2
Charles St B2
Chevallier St A1
Christchurch Mansion & Wolsey Art Gallery B3
Christchurch Park A3
Christchurch St B3
Cineworld C2
Civic Centre B2
Civic Dr B2
Clarkson St B1
Cobbold St B3
Commercial Rd C2
Constable Rd A3
Constantine Rd C1
Constitution Hill A2
Corder Rd A3
Corn Exchange B2
Cotswold Ave A2
Council Offices C2
County Hall B3
Crown Court C2
Crown St B2
Cullingham Rd B1
Cumberland St B2
Curriers La B2
Dale Hall La A2
Dales View Rd A1
Dalton Rd B2
Dillwyn St B1
Elliot St B1
Elm St B2
Elsmere Rd A3
Falcon St C2
Felaw St C3
Flint Wharf C3
Fonnereau Rd B2
Fore St C3
Foundation St C3
Franciscan Way C2
Friars St C2
Gainsborough Rd A3
Gatacre Rd B1
Geneva Rd B2
Gippeswyk Ave C1
Gippeswyk Park C1
Grafton Way C2
Graham Rd A1
Great Whip St C3
Grimwade St C3
Handford Cut B1
Handford Rd B1
Henley Rd A2
Hervey St B3
High St B2
Holly Rd A2
Information Ctr B3
Ipswich Haven Marina C3
Ipswich Museum & Art Gallery B2
Ipswich School A2
Ipswich Station C2
Ipswich Town FC (Portman Road) C2
Ivry St A2
Kensington Rd A1
Kesteven Rd C1
Key St C3
Kingsfield Ave A3
Kitchener Rd A1
Little's Cr C2
London Rd B1
Low Brook St C3
Lower Orwell St C3
Luther Rd C2
Magistrates Court B2
Manor Rd A3
Mornington Ave A1
Museum St B2
Neale St B3
New Cardinal St C2
New Cut East C3
New Cut West C3
New Wolsey C2
Newson St B2
Norwich Rd A1/B1
Oban St B2
Old Custom House C3
Old Foundry Rd B3
Old Merchant's Ho C3
Orford St B2
Paget Rd A2
Park Rd A3
Park View Rd A2
Peter's St C2
Philip Rd C2
Pine Ave A2
Pine View Rd A2
Police Station B2
Portman Rd B2
Portman Walk C1
Post Office B2
Princes St C2
Prospect St B1
Queen St B2
Ranelagh Rd C1
Recreation Ground B1
Rectory Rd C2
Regent Theatre B3
Retail Park C1
Retail Park C2
Richmond Rd A1
Rope Walk C3
Rose La C2
Russell Rd C2
St Edmund's Rd A2
St George's St B2
St Helen's St B3
Sherrington Rd A1
Shopmobility B2
Silent St C2
Sir Alf Ramsey Way C1
Sirdar Rd B1
Soane St B3
Springfield La A1
Star La C3
Stevenson Rd B1
Suffolk College C3
Suffolk Retail Park B1
Superstore B1
Surrey Rd B1
Tacket St C3
Tavern St B3
Tower Ramparts B2
Tower Ramparts Shopping Centre B2
Tower St B3
Town Hall B2
Tuddenham Rd A3
University C3
Upper Brook St B3
Upper Orwell St B3
Valley Rd A2
Vermont Cr B3
Vermont Rd B3
Vernon St C3
Warrington Rd A2
Waterloo Rd A1
Waterworks St C3
Wellington St B1
West End Rd B1
Westerfield Rd A3
Westgate St B2
Westholme Rd A1
Westwood Ave A1
Willoughby Rd C2
Withipoll St B3
Woodbridge Rd B3
Woodstone Ave A3
Yarmouth Rd B1

Kendal 336

Abbot Hall Art Gallery & Museum of Lakeland Life C2
Ambulance Station A2
Anchorite Fields C2
Anchorite Rd C2
Ann St A3
Appleby Rd A3
Archers Meadow C3
Ashleigh Rd A2
Aynam Rd B2
Bankfield Rd B1
Beast Banks B2
Beezon Fields A2
Beezon Rd A2
Beezon Trad Est A3
Belmont B2
Birchwood Cl C1
Blackhall Rd B2
Brewery Arts Ctr B2
Bridge St B2
Brigsteer Rd C1
Burneside Rd A2
Bus Station B2
Buttery Well La C2
Canal Head North B3
Captain French La C2
Caroline St A2
Castle Hill B3
Castle Howe B2
Castle Rd B3
Castle St A3/B3
Cedar Gr C1
Council Offices B2
County Council Offices A2
Cricket Ground A3
Cricket Ground C3
Cross La C2
Dockray Hall Ind Est A2
Dowker's La B2
Dry Ski Slope B3
East View B1
Echo Barn Hill C1
Elephant Yard B2
Fairfield La A1
Finkle St B2
Fire Station A2
Fletcher Square C3
Football Ground C3
Fowling La A3
Gillinggate C2
Glebe Rd C2
Golf Course B1
Goose Holme B3
Gooseholme Bridge B3
Green St A1
Greengate C2
Greengate La C1/C2
Greenside B1
Greenwood C1
Gulfs Rd B2
High Tenterfell B1
Highgate B2
Hillswood Ave C1
Horncop La A2
Information Ctr B2
Kendal A3
Kendal Business Park A3
Kendal Castle (Remains) B3
Kendal Fell B1
Kendal Green A1
Kendal Station A3
Kent Pl B2
Kirkbarrow C2
Kirkland C2
Library B2
Library Rd B2
Little Aynam B3
Little Wood B3
Long Cl C1
Longpool A3
Lound Rd C3
Lound St C3
Low Fellside B2
Lowther St B2
Maple Dr C1
Market Pl B2
Maude St B2
Miller Bridge B2
Milnthorpe Rd C2
Mint St A3
Mintsfeet Rd A3
Mintsfeet Rd South A2
New Rd B2
Noble's Rest B2
Parish Church C2
Park Side Rd C3
Parkside Bsns Park C3
Parr St B3
Police Station A2
Post Office A3/B2
Quaker Tapestry B2
Queen's Rd B1
Riverside Walk C2
Rydal Mount A2
Sandes Ave A2
Sandgate A3
Sandylands Rd A3
Serpentine Rd B1
Serpentine Wood B1
Shap Rd A3
South Rd C2
Stainbank Rd C1
Station Rd A3
Stramongate B2
Stramongate Bridge B2
Stricklandgate A2/B2
Sunnyside C3
Thorny Hills B3
Town Hall B2
Undercliff Rd B1
Underwood C1
Union St A2
Vicar's Fields C2
Vicarage Dr C1/C2
Wainwright's Yard B2
Wasdale Cl C3
Well Ings C2
Westmorland Shopping Centre & Market Hall B2
Westwood Ave C1
Wildman St A3
Windermere Rd A1
YHA B2
YWCA B2

King's Lynn 336

Albert St A2
Albion St B2
Alive St James' Swimming Pool B2
All Saints B2
All Saints St B2
Austin Fields A2
Austin St A2
Avenue Rd B3
Bank Side B1
Beech Rd C2
Birch Tree Cl B2
Birchwood St A2
Blackfriars Rd B2
Blackfriars St B2
Boal St B1
Bridge St B2
Broad St B2
Broad Walk B2
Burkitt St A2
Bus Station A2
Carmelite Terr C2
Chapel St A2
Chase Ave C3
Checker St C2
Church St B2
Clough La B2
Coburg St B2
College of West Anglia A3
Columbia Way A3
Corn Exchange A1
County Court Rd B2
Cresswell St A2
Custom House A1
East Coast Bsns Park C1
Eastgate St A2
Edma St A2
Exton's Rd C3
Ferry La B1
Ferry St A1
Framingham's Almshouses B2
Friars St C2
Friars Walk C2
Gaywood Rd A3
George St A2
Gladstone Rd C2
Goodwin's Rd C3
Green Quay B1
Greyfriars' Tower B2
Guanock Terr C2
Guildhall A1
Hansa Rd C3
Hardwick Rd C2
Hextable Rd A2
High St B1
Holcombe Ave C3
Hospital Walk C2
Information Ctr B1
John Kennedy Rd A2
Kettlewell Lane A2
King George V Ave B3
King St B1
King's Lynn Art Ctr A1
King's Lynn FC B3
King's Lynn Station B2
Library B2
Littleport St A2
Loke Rd A2
London Rd B2
Lynn Museum B2
Magistrates Court B1
Majestic B2
Market La A1
Millfleet B2
Milton Ave A3
Nar Valley Walk C2
Nelson St B1
New Conduit St B2
Norfolk St A2
North Lynn Discovery Centre A3
North St A2
Oldsunway B2
Ouse Ave C1
Page Stair Lane A1
Park Ave B3
Police Station B2
Portland Pl C1
Portland St B2
Purfleet B1
Queen St B1
Raby Ave A3
Railway Rd A2
Red Mount Chapel B3
Regent Way B2
River Walk A1
Robert St C2
Saddlebow Rd C2
Shopmobility B2
St Ann's St A1
St James St B2
St James' Rd B2
St John's Walk B3
St Margaret's B1
St Nicholas A2
St Nicholas St A1
St Peter's Rd B1
Sir Lewis St A2
Smith Ave A3
South Everard St C2
South Gate C2
South Quay B1
South St B2
Southgate St C2
Stonegate St B2
Surrey St A1
Sydney St C3
Tennyson Ave B3
Tennyson Rd B3
Tower St B2
Town Hall B1
Town Ho & Tales of the Old Gaol House B1
Town Wall (Remains) B3
True's Yard Mus A2
Valingers Rd C2
Vancouver Ave C2
Vancouver Quarter B2
Waterloo St B2
Wellesley St B2
White Friars Rd C2
Windsor Rd C2
Winfarthing St C2
Wyatt St A2
York Rd C3

Lancaster 336

Aberdeen Rd C3
Adult College, The C3
Aldcliffe Rd C2
Alfred St B3
Ambleside Rd A3
Ambulance Sta A3
Ashfield Ave B1
Ashton Rd C2
Assembly Rooms Emporium B2
Balmoral Rd B3
Bath House B2
Bath Mill La B3
Bath St B3
Blades St B1
Borrowdale Rd B3
Bowerham Rd C3
Brewery La B2
Bridge La B2
Brook St C1
Bulk Rd A3
Bulk St B2
Bus Station B2
Cable St B2
Canal Cruises & Waterbus C2
Carlisle Bridge A1
Carr House La C2
Castle B1
Castle Park B1
Caton Rd A3
China St B2
Church St B2
City Museum B2
Clarence St C3
Common Gdn St B2
Coniston Rd A3
Cottage Museum B2
Council Offices B2
County Court and Family Court B2
Cromwell Rd C1
Crown Court B1
Dale St C3
Dallas Rd B1/C1
Dalton Rd B3
Dalton Sq B2
Damside St B2
De Vitre St B3
Dee Rd A1
Denny Ave A1
Derby Rd A2
Dukes, The B2
Earl St A2
East Rd B3
Eastham St C3
Edward St B3
Fairfield Rd B1
Fenton St B2
Firbank Rd A3
Fire Station B2
Friend's Meeting Ho B1
Garnet St B3
George St B2
Giant Axe Field B1
Grand B2
Grasmere Rd B3
Greaves Rd C2
Green St A3
Gregson Centre, The B3
Gregson Rd C3
Greyhound Bridge A2
Greyhound Bridge Rd A2
High St B2
Hill Side B1
Hope St C3
Hubert Pl B1
Information Ctr B2
Kelsy St B1
Kentmere Rd B3
King St B2
Kingsway A3
Kirkes Rd C3
Lancaster & Lakeland C3
Lancaster City Football Club B1
Lancaster Station B1
Langdale Rd A3
Ley Ct B1
Library B2
Lincoln Rd B1
Lindow St C2
Lodge St B2
Long Marsh La B1
Lune Rd A1
Lune St A2
Lune Valley Ramble A3
Mainway A2
Maritime Museum A1
Marketgate Sh Ctr B2
Market St B2
Meadowside C2
Meeting House La B1
Millennium Bridge A2
Moor La B2
Moorgate B3
Morecambe Rd A1/A2
Nelson St B2
North Rd B2
Orchard La C1
Owen Rd A2
Park Rd B3
Parliament St A3
Patterdale Rd A3
Penny St B2
Police Station B2
Portland St C2
Post Office B2
Primrose St C3
Priory B1
Prospect St C3
Quarry Rd B3
Queen St C2
Regent St C2
Ridge La A3
Ridge St A3
Royal Lancaster Infirmary (A&E) C2
Rydal Rd B3
Ryelands Park A1
St Georges Quay A1
St John's B2
St Leonard's Gate B2
St Martin's Rd C3
St Nicholas Arcades Shopping Centre B2
St Oswald St C3
St Peter's B3
St Peter's Rd B3
Salisbury Rd B1
Scotch Quarry Urban Park C3
Sibsey St B1
Skerton Bridge A2
South Rd C2
Station Rd B1
Stirling Rd C3
Storey Ave B1
Sunnyside La C1
Sylvester St C1
Tarnsyke Rd A1
Thurnham St C2
Town Hall B2
Troutbeck Rd B3
Ulleswater Rd B3
University of Cumbria C3
Vicarage Field B1
Vue B2
West Rd B1
Westbourne Dr C1
Westbourne Rd B1
Westham St C3
Wheatfield St B1
White Cross Bsns Park C2

Vine St C5
Wakefield St A4
Walker Art Gallery ⌂ .A3
Walker St A6
Wapping C5
Water St B1/B2
Waterloo Rd B3
Wavertree Rd B6
West Derby Rd B5
West Derby St B5
Western Approaches
War Museum ⌂ B2
Whitechapel B3
Whitley Gdns A5
William Brown St B3
William Henry St A4
Williamson Sq B3
Williamson St B3
Williamson's Tunnels
Heritage Centre ✦ . .C6
Women's Hospital H . .B3
Wood St B3
World Museum,
Liverpool A3
York St C3

Llandudno 337

Abbey Pl B1
Abbey Rd B1
Adelphi St B2
Alexandra Rd C2
Anglesey Rd. A1
Argyll Rd A2
Arvon Ave. A2
Atlee Cl. C3
Augusta St. B2
Back Madoc St B2
Bodafon St. B2
Bodhyfryd Rd A2
Bodnant Cr B2
Bodnant Rd C2
Bridge Rd. B3
Bryniau Rd. B3
Builder St B3
Builder St West. A2
Cabin Lift. A2
Camera Obscura ✦ . .A3
Caroline Rd C2
Chapel St A2
Charlton St A2
Church Cr C1
Church Walks B2
Claremont Rd B2
Clement Ave A2
Clifton Rd. A2
Clonmel St. B3
Coach Station B3
Conway Rd C3
Council St West C3
Cricket and Rec Gd. . . .A2
Cwlach Rd A2
Cwlach St. A1
Cwm Howard La C3
Cwm Pl C3
Cwm Rd C3
Dale Rd. C1
Deganwy Ave. C2
Denness Pl. C2
Dinas Rd. C2
Dolydd B1
Erol Pl. B1
Ewloe Dr. C3
Fairways C3
Fford Dewi C3
Fford Dulyn C3
Fford Dwyfor C3
Fford Elisabeth. C3
Fford Gwynedd. C3
Fford Las C3
Fford Morfa C3
Fford Penrhyn C3
Fford Tudno C3
Fford yr Orsedd C3
Fford Ysbyty C3
Fire & Ambulance Sta .B3
Garage St B3
George St. B2
Gloddaeth Ave B2
Gloddaeth St B2
Gogarth Rd B1
Great Orme Mines ✦ .A1
Great Ormes Rd A1
Great Orme
Tramway ✦ A2
Happy Valley A2
Happy Valley Rd A2
Haulfre Gardens ❀ . . .A1
Herkomer Cr C1
Hill Terr B2
Home Front Mus ⌂ . . .B1
Hospice B2
Howard Rd. B1
Information Ctr Z B2
Invalids' Walk B1
James St B2
Jubilee St B3
King's Ave C2
King's Rd C2
Knowles Rd C2
Lees Rd. C2
Library B2
Lifeboat Station B2
Llandudno H B2
Llandudno (A&E) H . .B2
Llandudno Station ₹ . .B3
Llandudno Town
Football Ground A2
Llewelyn Ave A2
Lloyd St B2
Lloyd St West. B1
Llwynon Rd A1
Llys Maelgwn B1
Madoc St B2
Maelgwn Rd B2
Maes-y-Cwm B2
Maes-y-Orsedd C2
Maesdu Bridge C2/C3
Maesdu Rd C2/C3
Marian Pl B2

Marian Rd C2
Marine Drive (Toll) . . .A3
Market Hall B2
Market St. B2
Miniature Golf Course .A1
Morfa Rd B1
Mostyn ⌂ B3
Mostyn Broadway B3
Mostyn St. B3
Mowbray Rd C2
New St A2
Norman Rd B3
North Parade A2
North Wales Golf
Links. C1
Old Bank Gallery ⌂ . . .A2
Old Rd. A2
Oval, The B1
Oxford Rd. B3
Parade, The B3
Parc Llandudno
Retail Park. B3
Pier ✦ A3
Plas Rd B2
Police Station ◆ B3
Post Office ⊞ B3
Promenade A3
Pyllau Rd B1
Rectory La C2
Rhuddlan Ave C3
St Andrew's Ave B2
St Andrew's Pl. B2
St Beuno's Rd A1
St David's Pl B2
St David's Rd B2
St George's Pl A3
St Mary's Rd B2
St Seriol's Rd B2
Salisbury Pass B1
Salisbury Rd B2
Somerset St B3
South Parade B3
Stephen St. B3
TA Centre. B3
Tabor Hill A2
Town Hall. B2
Trinity Ave B1
Trinity Cres C1
Trinity Sq. B2
Tudno St. A2
Ty-Coch Rd C3
Ty-Gwyn Rd A1/A2
Ty'n-y-Coed Rd A1
Vaughan St B3
Victoria Shopping Ctr .B3
Victoria ⌂ A2
War Memorial ✦ A2
Werny Wylan C3
West Parade B1
Whiston Pass A2
Winllan Ave. C2
Wyddfyd Rd A2
York Rd. A2

Llanelli 337

Alban Rd. B3
Albert St B2
Als St. B3
Amos St B2
Andrew St A3
Ann St. A2
Annesley St B2
Arfryn Ave A3
Avenue Cilfig, The A2
Belvedere Rd. A1
Bigyn Park Terr. C3
Bigyn Rd. C3
Bond Ave C3
Brettenham St A1
Bridge St B2
Bryn Pl C1
Bryn Rd. C1
Bryn Terr C1
Bryn-More Rd. C1
Brynhyfryd Rd. A2
Brynmelyn Ave A3
Brynmor Rd B1
Burry St B2
Bus Station B2
Caersalem Terr. C1
Cambrian St C1
Caswell St B1
Cedric St B3
Cemetery A2
Chapman St. A1
Charles Terr C2
Church St. B2
Clos Caer Elms A1
Clos Sant Paul. A1
Coastal Link Rd B1/C1
Coldstream St B2
Coleshill Terr B1
College Hill B2
College Sq. B3
Copperworks Rd. C2
Coronation Rd. A3
Corporation Ave. A3
Council Offices B2
Court B2
Cowell St B2
Cradock St. C2
Craig Ave A2
Cricket Ground A1
Derwent St B2
Dillwyn St C1
Druce St C1
Eastgate Leisure
Complex ✦ B2
Elizabeth St. B2
Emma St A2
Erw Rd B1
Felinfoel Rd. A3
Fire Station A3
Firth Rd C3
Fron Terr C2
Furnace Rugby
Football Ground A2
Gelli-On C3
George St. C2

Gilbert Cres. A2
Gilbert Rd A2
Glanmor Rd C2
Glanmor Terr. C2
Glasfryn Terr. A3
Glenalla Rd B3
Glevering St B3
Goring Rd. A3
Gorsedd Circle ⌂ A2
Grant St C3
Graveyard C2
Great Western Cl C2
Greenway St B1
Hall St B2
Harries Ave A2
Hedley Terr A2
Heol Elli B3
Heol Goffa A3
Heol Nant-y-Felin B2
Heol Siloh B2
Hick St C2
High St. C1
Indoor Bowls Centre . .B1
Inkerman St. B2
Island Pl B3
James St B3
John St. B2
King George Ave. B3
Lake View Cl A2
Lakefield Pl C1
Lakefield Rd C1
Langland Rd C3
Leisure Centre B1
Library B2
Llanelli House ⌂ B2
Llanelli Parish
Church B2
Llanelli Station ₹ C2
Llewellyn St C1
Lliedi Cres A3
Lloyd St B2
Llys Alys B3
Llys Fran. A3
Llysnewedd C1
Long Row A3
Maes Gors A3
Maesyrhaf A3
Mansel St. B2
Marblehall Rd B3
Marborough Rd A3
Margam St C3
Marged St C2
Marine St B2
Mariners, The C1
Market B2
Market St. B2
Marsh St. C2
Martin Rd. C3
Miles St B2
Mill La. A3/B2
Mincing La. C2
Murray St. B2
Myn y Mor C1
Nathan St. C1
Nelson Terr C2
Nevill St B2
New Dock Rd C2
New Rd A1
New Zealand St. A1
Odeon ⌂ B2
Old Lodge A2
Old Rd. A2
Paddock St C2
Palace Ave. B3
Parc Howard A2
Parc Howard Museum &
Art Gallery ⌂ A2
Park Cres B1
Park St B1
Parkview Terr B1
Pemberton St C2
Pembrey Rd. A1
Peoples Park. B1
Police Station ◆ B2/C2
Post Office ⊞ B2/C2
Pottery Pl B3
Pottery St B3
Princess St B1
Prospect Pl A2
Pryce St A1
Queen Mary's Walk . . .C3
Queen Victoria Rd C2
Raby St B1
Railway Terr C1
Ralph St B2
Ralph Terr C1
Regalia Terr B3
Rhydyrafon A3
Richard St C2
Robinson St B1
Roland Ave A1
Russell St B2
St David's Cl A2
St Elli Shopping Ctr . . .B2
St Margaret's Dr A1
Spowart Ave A1
Station Rd B2/C2
Stepney Pl B2
Stepney St B2
Stewart St A1
Stradey Park Ave A1
Sunny Hill A2
Superstore A2
Swansea Rd C3
Talbot St C3
Temple St. B3
Thomas St B2
Tinopolos
TV Studios ✦ B2
Toft Pl A3
Town Hall B2
Traeth Ffordd C1
Trinity Rd C2
Trinity Terr C1
Tunnel Rd C3
Tyisha Rd B2
Union Blgs A2
Upper Robinson St. . . .A2
Vauxhall St C2

London 338

Abbey Orchard St. E4
Abbey St. E8
Abchurch La D7
Abingdon St E5
Achilles Way. D3
Acton St. B5
Addington St E5
Air St. D4
Albany St B3
Albemarle St D4
Albert Embankment . . .F5
Alberta St F6
Aldenham St A4
Alderney St F3
Aldersgate St C7
Aldford St D3
Aldgate ⊖ C8
Aldgate High St. C8
Aldwych. C5
Allsop Pl. B2
Alscot Rd E8
Amwell St. B6
Andrew Borde St C4
Angel ⊖ A6
Appold St C8
Argyle Sq. B5
Argyle St B5
Argyll St C3
Arnold Circus B8
Artillery La C8
Artillery Row E4
Ashbridge St B2
Association of
Photographers
Gallery ⌂ B7
Baker St ⊖ B2
Baker St. B2
Balaclava Rd F8
Balcombe St B2
Baldwin's Gdns C6
Balfour St. F7
Baltic St C7
Bank ⊖ C7
Bank Museum ⌂ C7
Bank of England ⌂ . . .C7
Bankside D7
Bankside Gallery ⌂ . . .D6
Banner St. C7
Barbican ⊖ C7
Barbican Centre
for Arts, The C7
Barbican Gallery ⌂ . . .C7
Basil St E2
Bastwick St C7
Bateman's Row. B8
Bath St B7
Bath Terr E7
Bayley St C4
Baylis Rd E6
Bayswater Rd. D2
Beak St D4
Beauchamp Pl. E2
Bedford Row C5
Bedford Sq. C4
Bedford St D5
Bedford Way B4
Beech St. C7
Belgrave Pl. E3
Belgrave Rd. F4
Belgrave Sq. E3
Bell La C8
Belvedere Rd. D5
Berkeley Sq D3
Berkeley St D3
Bermondsey St E8
Bernard St. B5
Berners Pl C4
Berners St C4
Berwick St C4
Bessborough St F4
Bethnal Green Rd B8
Bevenden St B7
Bevis Marks. C8
BFI (British Film
Institute) ⌂ D5
BFI London
IMAX Cinema ⌂ D5
Bidborough St. B5
Binney St C3
Birdcage Walk E4
Bishopsgate C8
Black Prince Rd F5
Blackfriars ⊖ D6
Blackfriars Bridge D6
Blackfriars Rd. D6
Blandford St C2
Blomfield St C7
Bloomsbury St C4
Bloomsbury Way C5
Bolton St D3
Bond St ⊖ C3
Borough ⊖ E7
Borough High St E7
Borough Rd E7
Boswell St C5
Bourne St. F3
Bow St C5
Bowling Green La. B6
Brad St D6
Brandon St F7
Bressenden Pl. E4
Brewer St D4
Brick St D3
Bridge St E5
Britannia Walk B7
British Film Institute
(BFI) ⌂ D5
British Library ⌂ B4
British Museum ⌂ C5
Britton St B6

Broad Sanctuary E4
Broadley St C2
Broadway. E4
Brompton Rd. E2
Brompton Sq. E2
Brook Dr. F6
Brook St D3
Brown St C2
Brunswick Pl. B7
Brunswick Sh Ctr, The .B5
Brushfield St C8
Bruton St. D3
Bryanston St C2
BT Centre. C6
Buckingham Gate. E4
Buckingham Palace ⌂ .E4
Buckingham Palace Rd .F3
Bunhill Row B7
Byward St D8
Cabinet War Rooms &
Churchill Museum ⌂ .E4
Cadogan La E3
Cadogan Pl E3
Cadogan Sq F2
Cadogan St F2
Cale St F2
Caledonian Rd A5
Calshot St A5
Calthorpe St B6
Calvert Ave B8
Cambridge Circus C4
Cambridge Sq. C2
Cambridge St. F3
Camomile St C8
Cannon St. D7
Cannon St ⊖ D7
Capland St B1
Carey St C6
Carlisle La E5
Carlisle Pl F4
Carlton House Terr D4
Carmelite St D6
Carnaby St C4
Carter La C6
Carthusian St C7
Cartwright Gdns. B5
Castle Baynard St D6
Cavendish Pl C3
Cavendish Sq C3
Caxton Hall E4
Caxton St. E4
Central St. B7
Chalton St. B4
Chancery Lane ⊖ C6
Chapel St B2
Chapel St E3
Charing Cross ⊖ D5
Charing Cross Rd C4
Charles II St D4
Charles Sq. B7
Charles St D3
Charlotte Rd B8
Charlotte St C4
Chart St B7
Charterhouse Sq C6
Charterhouse St C6
Chatham St F7
Cheapside C7
Chenies St C4
Chesham St E3
Chester Sq. F3
Chester Way F6
Chesterfield Hill. D3
Cheval Pl E2
Chiltern St C3
Chiswell St C7
Church St. B2
City Garden Row. A6
City Rd B7
City Thameslink ₹ C6
City University, The . . .B6
Claremont Sq. A6
Clarendon St F3
Clarges St D3
Clerkenwell Cl B6
Clerkenwell Green. B6
Clerkenwell Rd B6
Cleveland St C4
Clifford St D4
Clink Prison Mus ⌂ . . .D7
Cliveden Pl F3
Clock Museum ⌂ C7
Club Row B8
Cockspur St D4
Coleman St C7
Columbia Rd. B8
Commercial Rd. C8
Commercial St C8
Compton St B6
Conduit St. D3
Congreve St F7
Connaught Sq. C2
Connaught St C2
Constitution Hill. E3
Copperfield St E7
Coptic St. C5
Cornhill C7
Cornwall Rd. D6
Coronet St B8
County St. E7
Courtauld Gallery ⌂ . . .D5
Courtenay St F6
Covent Garden ⊖ D5
Covent Garden ✦ D5
Cowcross St C6
Cowper St B7
Crampton St. F7
Cranbourn St D5
Craven St D5
Crawford Pl C2
Crawford St C2
Creechurch La C8
Cricket Museum ⌂ . . .B1
Cromer St B5
Cromwell Rd F1
Crosby Row E7
Crucifix La E8
Cumberland Gate. C2
Cumberland Gate F3
Cumberland Mkt B3

Cumberland Terr A3
Cuming Mus ⌂ F7
Curtain Rd B8
Curzon St D3
Cut, The E6
D'arblay St C4
Dante Rd F6
Davies St D3
Dean St. C4
Deluxe Gallery ⌂ B8
Denbigh Pl. F4
Denmark St C4
Dering St C3
Devonshire St C3
Diana, Princess of Wales
Memorial Garden ✦ .D1
Diana, Princess of Wales
Memorial Walk E4
Dingley Rd B7
Dorset St C2
Doughty St B5
Douglas St F4
Dover St D3
Downing St E5
Draycott Avenue. F2
Draycott Pl F2
Druid St E8
Drummond St B4
Drury La C5
Drysdale St B8
Duchess St C3
Dufferin St C7
Duke of Wellington Pl . .E3
Duke St. C3/D3
Duke St Hill D7
Duke's Pl. C8
Duncannon St D5
Dunton Rd F8
East Rd B7
East St F7
Eastcastle St C4
Eastcheap D8
Eastman Dental
Hospital H B5
Eaton Gate. F3
Eaton Pl E3
Eaton Sq F3
Eaton Terr F3
Ebury Bridge. F3
Ebury Bridge Rd F3
Eccleston Bridge F3
Eccleston Sq F3
Eccleston St F3
Edgware Rd C2
Edgware Rd ⊖ C2
Egerton Gdns F2
Eldon St C7
Elephant & Castle ₹ . . .F7
Elephant and
Castle ⊖ E6
Elephant Rd. F7
Elizabeth Bridge. F3
Elizabeth St F3
Elm Tree Rd B1
Elystan Pl F2
Elystan St F2
Endell St C5
Endsleigh Pl B4
Enid St E8
Ennismore Gdns. E2
Erasmus St F4
Euston ⊖₹ B4
Euston Rd. B4
Euston Square ⊖ B4
Evelina Children's
Hospital E7
Eversholt St A4
Exhibition Rd. E1
Exmouth Market. B6
Fair St. E8
Falmouth Rd E7
Fann St C7
Farringdon ⊖₹ C6
Farringdon Rd. C6
Farringdon St C6
Featherstone St B7
Fenchurch St D8
Fenchurch St ₹ D8
Fetter La C6
Finsbury Circus C7
Finsbury Pavement. C7
Finsbury Sq C7
Fitzalan St F6
Fitzmaurice Pl D3
Fleet St C6
Fleming Laboratory
Museum ⌂ C2
Floral St. D5
Florence Nightingale
Museum ⌂ E5
Folgate St. C8
Fore St C7
Foster La C7
Francis St F4
Frazier St E6
Freemason's Hall C5
Friday St. C7
Fulham Rd F1
Gainsford St E8
Garden Row. E6
Gee St. B7
Geological Mus ⌂ E1
George Row. E9
George St. C2
Gerrard St D4
Gibson St E6
Giltspur St C6
Glasshouse St D4
Glasshouse Walk F5
Gloucester Pl C2
Gloucester St F4
Golden Hinde ⌂ D7
Golden La. C7
Goodge St ⊖ C4
Gordon Sq B4
Gordon Hospital H. . . .F4

Goswell Rd. B6
Gough St B5
Goulston St C8
Gower St B4
Gracechurch St D7
Grafton Way B4
Graham Terr F3
Grange Rd E8
Grange Walk E8
Gray's Inn Rd B5
Great College St E5
Great Cumberland Pl. . .C2
Great Dover St E7
Great Eastern St B8
Great Guildford St D7
Great Marlborough St .C4
Great Ormond Street
Children's Hospital H .B5
Great Percy St B5
Great Peter St E4
Great Portland St ⊖ . . .B3
Great Portland St B3
Great Queen St C5
Great Russell St C4
Great Scotland Yd D5
Great Smith St E4
Great Suffolk St D6/E7
Great Titchfield St C4
Great Tower St D8
Great Windmill St D4
Greek St C4
Green Park ⊖ D4
Green St. D3
Greencoat Pl F4
Greenwich Hosp Sch. . .E4
Greet St B5/C6
Grenville St B5
Gresham St C7
Greville St C6
Grosvenor Cres. E3
Grosvenor Gdns E3
Grosvenor Pl E3
Grosvenor Sq D3
Grosvenor St D3
Grove End Rd B1
Guards Museum
and Chapel E4
Guildhall Art Gallery
⌂ C7
Guilford St B5
Guy's Hospital H D7
Haberdasher St B7
Hackney Rd B8
Half Moon St D3
Halkin St E3
Hall Pl B1
Hall St B6
Hallam St C3
Hamilton Place D3
Hampstead Rd B4
Hanover Sq C3
Hans Cres E2
Hans Rd E2
Hanway St C4
Hardwick St. B6
Harewood Ave. B2
Harley St C3
Harper Rd E7
Harrington Rd F1
Harrison St B5
Harrowby St C2
Hasker St F2
Hastings St B5
Hatfields D6
Hay's Galleria D8
Hay's Mews D3
Hayles St F6
Haymarket. D4
Hayne St. C6
Hayward Gallery ⌂ D5
Helmet Row B7
Herbrand St B5
Hercules Rd. E5
Hertford St D3
Heygate St F7
High Holborn C5
Hill St D3
HMS Belfast ⌂ D8
Hobart Pl E3
Holborn ⊖ C6
Holborn C6
Holborn Viaduct. C6
Holland St D6
Holmes Mus ⌂ B2
Holywell La. B8
Horse Guards' Rd D4
Horseferry Rd F4
Houndsditch C8
Houses of
Parliament ⌂ E5
Howland St C4
Hoxton Sq B8
Hoxton St B8
Hugh St F3
Hunter St B5
Hunterian Mus ⌂ C5
Hyde Park D2
Hyde Park Cres C2
Hyde Park St C2
Imperial Coll London. .E1
Imperial College Rd. . . .E1
Imperial War Mus ⌂ . . .E6
Inner Circle B3
Institute of Archaeology
(London Univ). B4
Ironmonger Row B7
Jacob St. E9
Jamaica Rd E8
James St C3
James St D5
Jermyn St D4
Jockey's Fields C5
John Carpenter St D6
John Fisher St D9
John Islip St F4
John St B5
Jonathan St F5
Judd St B5

Minories C8
Monck St E4
Monkton St F6
Monmouth St C5
Monmouth St C5
Montagu Pl C2
Montagu Sq. C2
Montague Pl. C4
Montague St C5
Montpelier St E2
Montpelier Walk. E2
Monument ⊖ D7
Monument St D7
Monument, The ✦ D7
Moor La C7
Moorfields C7
Moorfields Eye
Hospital H B7
Moorgate. C7
Moorgate ⊖ C7
Moreland St B6
Morley St E6
Mortimer St C4
Mossop St F2
Mount Pleasant B6
Mount St D3
Murray St A5
Mus of Gdn History ⌂ .E5
Museum of London ⌂ .C7
Museum St C5
Myddelton Sq B6
Myddelton St B6
National Gallery ⌂ D4
National Hospital H . . .B5
National Portrait
Gallery ⌂ D4
Natural History
Museum ⌂ E1
Neal St C5
Nelson's Column ✦ . . .D5
Neville St F1
New Bond St C3/D3
New Bridge St C6
New Cavendish St. C3
New Change C7
New Fetter La C6
New Inn Yard B8
New Kent Rd F7
New North Rd A7
New Oxford St C4
New Scotland Yard E5
New Sq C6
Newburn St F5
Newgate St C6
Newington Butts F6
Newington Cswy. E7
Newton St C5
Nile St. B7
Noble St. C7
Noel St C4
Norfolk Cres C2
Norfolk Sq. C1
North Audley St D3
North Carriage Dr D2
North Cres C4
North Ride. D2
North Row D3
North Wharf Rd C1
Northampton Sq. B6
Northington St B5
Northumberland Ave . .D5
Norton Folgate. C8
Nottingham Pl C3
Old Bailey C6
Old Broad St C7
Old Brompton Rd F1
Old Compton St C4
Old County Hall. E5
Old Gloucester St C5
Old Jamaica Rd E9
Old Kent Rd F8
Old King Edward St C7
Old Marylebone Rd C2
Old Montague St C9
Old Nichol St B8
Old Paradise St F5
Old Spitalfields Mkt. . . .C8
Old St B7
Old St ⊖₹ B7
Old Vic ✦ E6
Onslow Gdns F1
Onslow Sq F1
Ontario St E6
Open Air Theatre ✦ . . .B3
Operating Theatre
Museum ⌂ D7
Orange St D4
Orchard St C3
Ossulston St A4
Outer Circle. B2
Ovington Sq. E2
Oxford Circus ⊖ C4
Oxford St C3/C4
Paddington ⊖₹ C1
Paddington Green
Hospital H. C1
Paddington St C3
Page's Walk E8
Palace Ave E4
Pall Mall D4
Pall Mall East D4
Pancras Rd A5
Panton St D4
Paris Gdn D6
Park Cres B3
Park La D3
Park Rd. B2
Park St D3
Park St D7
Parker St C5
Parliament Sq. E5
Parliament St E5
Paternoster Sq C6
Paul St B7
Pear Tree St. B6
Pelham Cres F2
Pelham St F1
Penfold St C2
Penton Pl F6
Penton Rise B5
Penton St A6

Pentonville Rd A5/A6
Percival St B6
Petticoat La
  (Middlesex St) C8
Petty France E4
Phoenix Pl B5
Phoenix Rd A4
Photo Gallery 🏛 D4
Piccadilly D3
Piccadilly Circus ⊖ D4
Pilgrimage St E7
Pimlico F4
Pimlico Rd F3
Pitfield St B8
Pollock's Toy Mus 🏛 A4
Polygon Rd A4
Pont St E2
Porchester Pl C2
Portland Pl C3
Portman Mews C3
Portman Sq C3
Portman St C2
Portugal St C5
Postal Mus, The B5
Poultry C7
Praed St C1
Primrose St C8
Prince Consort Rd E1
Prince's Gdns E1
Princes St C7
Procter St C5
Provost St B7
Quaker St C8
Queen Anne St C3
Queen Elizabeth Hall
  🎭 D5
Queen Elizabeth St. E8
Queen Sq B5
Queen St D7
Queen Street Pl D7
Queen Victoria St. D6
Queens Gallery 🏛 E4
Queensberry Pl. F1
Quilter St B9
Radnor St B7
Rathbone Pl. C4
Rawlings St F2
Rawstone St. B6
Red Lion Sq C5
Red Lion St C5
Redchurch St B8
Redcross Way D7
Reedworth St F6
Regency St F4
Regent Sq B5
Regent St C4
Regent's Park B3
Richmond Terr E5
Ridgmount St C4
Riley Rd E8
Rivington St B8
Robert St B3
Rochester Row F4
Rockingham St E7
Rodney St F7
Rolls Rd F8
Ropemaker St C7
Rosebery Ave B6
Rossmore Rd. B2
Rothsay St E8
Rotten Row E2
Roupell St D6
Royal Acad of Arts 🏛. D4
Royal Academy of
  Dramatic Art B4
Royal Acad of Music. B3
Royal Albert Hall 🎭 E1
Royal Artillery
  Memorial ✦ E2
Royal Brompton
  Hospital Ⓗ F1/F2
Royal Coll of Nursing. C3
Royal Coll of Surgeons C5
Royal Festival Hall 🎭 D5
Royal London Hospital
  for Integrated
  Medicine Ⓗ C5
Royal Marsden Hosp Ⓗ F1
Royal National
  Theatre 🎭 D6
Royal National Throat,
  Nose and Ear Hosp Ⓗ B5
Royal Opera House 🎭 D5
Rushworth St E6
Russell Sq B4
Russell Square ⊖ B5
Rutland Gate. E2
Sackville St D4
Sadlers Wells 🎭 B6
Saffron Hill C6
St Alban's St D4
St Andrew St C6
St Barnabas St F3
St Bartholomew's
  Hospital Ⓗ C6
St Botolph St C8
St Bride St C6
St George's Circus F6
St George's Dr. F4
St George's Rd E6
St George's Sq F4
St Giles High St C4
St James's Palace 🏛. D4
St James's Park ⊖ D4
St James's St D4
St John St B6
St John's Wood St. B1
St Margaret St. E5
St Mark's Hosp Ⓗ B6
St Martin's La D5
St Martin's Le Grand C7
St Mary Axe C8
St Mary's Hosp Ⓗ C1
St Pancras Int ≋ A5
St Paul's C7
St Paul's Cath †. C7
St Paul's Churchyard. C6
St Thomas St D7
St Thomas' Hosp Ⓗ E5

Sancroft St F5
Savile Row D4
Savoy Pl D5
Savoy St D5
School of Hygiene &
  Tropical Medicine C4
Science Mus 🏛 E1
Scrutton St B8
Sekforde St B6
Serpentine Gallery 🏛 E1
Serpentine Rd. D2
Seven Dials C5
Seward St B6
Seymour Pl C2
Seymour St C2
Shad Thames D8/E8
Shaftesbury Ave D4
Shakespeare's Globe
  Theatre 🎭 D7
Shepherd Market D3
Sherwood St D4
Shoe La C6
Shoreditch High St. B8
Shoreditch High St ⊖ B8
Shorts Gdns. C5
Shouldham St C2
Sidmouth St B5
Silk St C7
Sir John Soane's
  Museum 🏛 C5
Skinner St B6
Sloane Ave. F2
Sloane St F2
Sloane Square ⊖ F2
Sloane St E2
Snow Hill C6
Soho Sq C4
Somerset House 🏛 D5
South Audley St D3
South Carriage Dr E2
South Eaton Pl F3
South Kensington ⊖ F1
South Molton St C3
South Parade F1
South Pl C7
South St D3
South Terr F2
South Wharf Rd C1
Southampton Row C5
Southampton St D5
Southwark ⊖ D6
Southwark Bridge D7
Southwark Bridge Rd D7
Southwark Cath † D7
Southwark Park Rd D7
Southwark St D7
Spa Rd E8
Speakers' Corner D2
Spencer St B6
Spital Sq C8
Spring St C1
Stamford St D6
Stanhope St B4
Stanhope Terr. D1
Stephenson Way. B4
Stock Exchange C6
Stoney St D7
Strand D5
Strathearn Pl D2
Stratton St D3
Sumner St D6
Sussex Gdns C1
Sussex Pl C1
Sussex Pl D1
Sussex Sq F3
Sutton's Way B7
Swan St E7
Swanfield St B8
Swinton St B5
Sydney Pl F1
Sydney St F2
Tabard St E7
Tabernacle St B7
Tachbrook St. F4
Tanner St E8
Tate Britain 🏛 F5
Tate Modern 🏛 D7
Tavistock Pl. B4
Tavistock Sq B4
Tea & Coffee Mus 🏛 D7
Temple ⊖ D6
Temple † D6
Temple Ave D6
Temple Pl D5
Terminus Pl. E3
Thayer St C3
Theobald's Rd. C5
Thorney St F5
Threadneedle St. C7
Throgmorton St C7
Thurloe Pl F1
Thurloe Sq F1
Tonbridge St B5
Tooley St D8
Torrington Pl. B4
Tothill St E4
Tottenham Court Rd B4
Tottenham Ct Rd ⊖ C4
Tottenham St C4
Tower Bridge ✦ D8
Tower Bridge App. D8
Tower Bridge Rd. E8
Tower Hill D8
Tower Hill ⊖ D8
Tower of London,
  The ✦ D8
Toynbee St C8
Trafalgar Square D4
Trinity Sq D8
Trinity St E7
Trocadero Centre. D4
Tudor St D6
Turin St B9
Turnmill St C6
Tyers St F5
Ufford St E6
Union St D6
University Coll Hosp Ⓗ B4
University of London. C4
Univ of Westminster B4
University St B4

Upper Belgrave St E3
Upper Berkeley St C2
Upper Brook St D2
Upper Grosvenor St. D2
Upper Ground D6
Upper Montague St C2
Upper St Martin's La D5
Upper Thames St D7
Upper Wimpole St C3
Upper Woburn Pl B4
Vauxhall Bridge Rd. F4
Vauxhall St F5
Vere St C3
Vernon Pl C5
Vestry St B7
Victoria ⊖ E3
Victoria and
  Albert Mus 🏛 E1
Victoria Coach Sta F3
Victoria Embankment D5
Victoria Pl Sh Ctr E4
Victoria St E4
Villiers St D5
Vincent Sq. F4
Vinopolis City of
  Wine D7
Virginia Rd. B8
Wakley St B6
Walbrook C7
Walcot Sq F6
Wallace Collection 🏛 C3
Walnut Tree Walk. F6
Walton St F2
Walworth Rd F7
Wardour St C4/D4
Warner St. B6
Warren St ⊖ B4
Warren St B4
Warwick Sq F4
Warwick Way F3
Waterloo ≋⊖ D6
Waterloo Bridge. D5
Waterloo East ≋ D6
Waterloo Rd D6
Watling St C7
Webber St E6
Welbeck St C3
Wellington Arch ✦ E3
Wellington Mus 🏛 E3
Wellington Rd. B2
Wellington Row B9
Wells St C4
Wenlock St A7
Wentworth St C8
West Carriage Dr D2
West Smithfield C6
West Sq F6
Westbourne St. D1
Westbourne Terr. C1
Westminster ⊖ E5
Westminster Abbey † E5
Westminster Bridge E5
Westminster Bridge
  Rd E6
Westminster
  Cathedral (RC) † E4
Westminster City Hall E4
Westminster Hall 🏛 E5
Weymouth St. C3
Wharf Rd A7
Wharton St. B5
Whitcomb St D4
White Cube 🏛 B8
White Lion Hill D7
White Lion St. A6
Whitechapel Rd C9
Whitecross St B7
Whitefriars St C6
Whitehall D5
Whitehall Pl. D5
Wigmore Hall C3
Wigmore St C3
William IV St D5
Willow Walk F8
Wilmington Sq B6
Wilson St C7
Wilton Cres E3
Wilton Rd F4
Wimpole St C3
Winchester St F3
Wincott St F6
Windmill Walk D6
Woburn Pl B5
Woburn Sq B4
Wood St C7
Woodbridge St B6
Wootton St D6
Wormwood St C8
Worship St B7
Wren St B5
Wynyatt St B6
York Rd E5
York St C2
York Terrace East. B3
York Terrace West B3
York Way A5

Bury Park Rd A1
Bute St B2
Buxton Rd B2
Cambridge St C3
Cardiff Grove C1
Cardiff Rd B1
Cardigan St B2
Castle St B2/C2
Chapel St C2
Charles St A3
Chase St A2
Cheapside B2
Chequer St C2
Chiltern Rise C1
Church St B2/B3
Cobden St A3
College. A3
Collingdon St A1
Community Centre A3
Concorde St A3
Corncastle Rd. C1
Cowper St C2
Crawley Green Rd. A3
Crawley Rd A1
Crescent Rd A1
Crescent Rise A1
Cromwell Rd A1
Cross St A2
Cross Way, The. C1
Crown Court B2
Cumberland St B2
Cutenhoe Rd C3
Dallow Rd. B1
Downs Rd. A1
Dudley St. A2
Duke St B2
Dumfries St B1
Dunstable Place. C1
Dunstable Rd A1/B1
Edward St A3
Elizabeth St C2
Essex Cl C1
Farley Hill C1
Farley Lodge C1
Flowers Way B2
Francis St. A1
Frederick St A2
Galaxy L Complex A2
George St B2
George St West B2
Gordon St B2
Grove Rd B1
Guildford St. A2
Haddon Rd. A3
Harcourt St C1
Hart Hill Drive A3
Hart Hill Lane A3
Hartley Rd A3
Hastings St B2
Hatters Way. A1
Havelock Rd A2
Hibbert St C2
High Town Rd A2
Highbury Rd A1
Hightown Community
  Sports & Arts Centre A3
Hillary Cres. C1
Hillborough Rd. C1
Hitchin Rd A3
Holly St. C2
Holm. A2
Hucklesby Way A2
Hunts Cl C1
Inkerman St B2
John St. B2
Jubilee St A3
Kelvin Cl. C2
King St B2
Kingsland Rd. C2
Larches, The. A2
Latimer Rd. C2
Lawn Gdns C1
Lea Rd. B3
Library B2
Library Rd B2
Library Theatre 🎭 B2
Liverpool Rd. A1
London Rd C2
Luton Station ≋ A2
Lyndhurst Rd. C1
Magistrates Court B2
Mall, The B2
Manchester St B2
Manor Rd B3
Manor Road Park B3
May St. A2
Meyrick Ave. C1
Midland Rd. A2
Mill St A2
Milton Rd C1
Moor St A1
Moor, The A1
Moorland Gdns A1
Moulton Rise. A3
Napier Rd. B1
New Bedford Rd A1
New Town St C2
North St A2
Old Bedford Rd. A2
Old Orchard. C3
Osbourne Rd C3
Oxen Rd A3
Park Sq. B2
Park St B3/C3
Park St West C2
Park Viaduct B3
Parkland Drive. C1
Police Station 🔲. A2
Pomfret Ave A3
Pondwicks Rd. B3
Post Office ⊠ A1/B2
Power Court B3
Princess St B1
Red Rails C1
Regent St B1
Reginald St A2
Rothesay Rd B1
Russell Rise B1

Russell St. C1
St Ann's Rd A3
St George's Square B2
St Mary's ⛪ B3
St Marys Rd B3
St Paul's Rd B1
St Saviour's Cres C1
Salisbury Rd. B1
Seymour Ave. C3
Seymour Rd. C3
Silver St. B2
South Rd. C2
Stanley St. B1
Station Rd A2
Stockwood Cres. C1
Stockwood Park. C1
Strathmore Ave B2
Stuart St. B2
Studley Rd. A1
Surrey St C3
Sutherland Place. C1
Tavistock St. C2
Taylor St. A3
Telford Way A1
Tennyson Rd C2
Tenzing Grove. C1
Thistle Rd. B3
Town Hall. B2
Townsley Cl C2
UK Centre for
  Carnival Arts ✦ B3
Union St B2
Univ of Bedfordshire. B3
Upper George St. B2
Vicarage St B3
Villa Rd. A2
Waldeck Rd. A1
Wardown Ho Mus &
  Gallery 🏛 A2
Wellington St B1/B2
Wenlock St. A1
Whitby Rd A1
Whitehill Ave. C1
William St A2
Wilsden Ave. C1
Windmill Rd. B3
Windsor St C2
Winston Rd. B1
York St A3

Macclesfield 337
108 Steps. B2
Abbey Rd B1
Alton Dr A1
Armett St C1
Athey St. B1
Bank St. C3
Barber St. C1
Barton St C1
Beech La B1
Beswick St. B1
Black La A2
Black Rd C3
Blakelow Gardens C3
Blakelow Rd C3
Bond St. B1/C1
Bread St C2
Bridge St. B2
Brock St A2
Brocklehurst Ave. A3
Brook St. B3
Brookfield La B3
Brough St West C1
Brown St C1
Brynton Rd A2
Buckley St. C2
Bus Station B2
Buxton Rd B3
Byrons St. C2
Canal St B3
Carlsbrook Ave. B1
Castle St B2
Catherine St B1
Cemetery. A1
Chadwick Terr. A2
Chapel St. C2
Charlotte St. C1
Chester Rd. B1
Chestergate B2
Christ Church ⛪ B1
Churchill Way A2
Coare St A1
Commercial Rd. B2
Conway Cres A3
Copper St. C3
Cottage St. B2
Crematorium A1
Crew Ave. A1
Crompton Rd. B1/C1
Cross St C1
Crossall St C1
Cumberland St A1/B1
Dale St. C3
Duke St. B2
Eastgate. B2
Exchange St B2
Fence Ave B3
Fence Ave Ind Est A3
Flint St A2
Foden St. A3
Fountain St B3
Garden St. A3
Gas Rd A2
Gateway Gallery ✦ B1
George St. B2
Glegg St. B2
Golf Course A3
Goodall St. B1
Grange Rd C1
Great King St B1
Green St. B3
Grosvenor Sh Ctr B2
Gunco La C2
Half St. B2
Hallefield Rd. B3
Hatton St C1
Hawthorn Way A3
Heapy St. C3
Henderson St B1

Heritage Centre & Silk
  Museum 🏛 B2
Hibel Rd. A2
High St. C2
Hobson St C2
Hollins Rd. C3
Hope St West. B1
Horseshoe Dr B1
Hurdsfield Rd A3
Information Ctr ℹ B2
James St C3
Jodrell St. B3
John St. C2
Jordangate B2
King Edward St B2
King George's Field. C3
King St. B2
King's School A1
Knight Pool C3
Knight St C3
Lansdowne St. A3
Library B2
Lime Gr. B1
Loney St B1
Longacre St. B1
Lord St C2
Lowe St. C2
Lowerfield Rd. A3
Lyon St B1
Macclesfield College. C1
Macclesfield Sta ≋ B2
MADS Little
  Theatre 🎭 C2
Marina B3
Market B2
Market Pl B2
Masons La A3
Mill Rd. C2
Mill St. B2
Moran Rd. C1
New Hall St C1
Newton St C1
Nicholson Ave. A3
Nicholson Cl A3
Northgate Ave. A2
Old Mill La C2
Paradise Mill 🏛 B1
Paradise St B1
Park Green B2
Park La C1
Park Rd. C2
Park St C2
Park Vale Rd A2
Parr St. C2
Peel St. C2
Percyvale St. A1
Peter St. C1
Pickford St. B2
Pierce St. B1
Pinfold St. A3
Pitt St C2
Police Station 🔲 B2
Pool St. B2
Poplar Rd C2
Post Office ⊠ B2
Pownall St. B2
Prestbury Rd. A1/B1
Queen Victoria St. A3
Queen's Ave. A3
Registrar. B2
Richmond Hill. C3
Riseley St. B1
Roan Ct. B2
Roe St. B2
Rowan Way A2
Ryle St. C2
Ryle's Park Rd. C2
St George's St. C2
St Michael's ⛪ B2
Samuel St. B2
Saville St C1
Shaw St. B1
Silk Rd, The. A2/B2
Slater St. B2
Snow Hill. C1
South Park. C1
Spring Gdns. A2
Statham St. B2
Station St. B3
Steeple St. A3
Sunderland St. B2
Superstore A1/A2/C2
Swettenham St. B2
Thistleton Cl C2
Thorp St. B2
Town Hall. B2
Townley St. B2
Turnock St. C2
Union Rd B3
Union St. B2
Victoria Park. B3
Vincent St C2
Waters Green B2
Waterside. B2
West Bond St. B1
West Park B1
West Park Museum 🏛 A1
Westbrook Dr A1
Westminster Rd. A1
Whalley Hayes B1
Windmill St B2
Withyfold Dr A2
York St B1

Maidstone 340
Albion Pl B3
All Saints ⛪ C2
Allen St. A3
Amphitheatre ✦ C2
Archbishop's
  Palace B2
Bank St. B2
Barker Rd. C2
Barton Rd. C2
Beaconsfield Rd. C1
Bedford Pl. A1
Bishops Way B2
Bluett St. A3

BMI The Somerfield
  Hospital Ⓗ C1
Bower La C1
Bower Mount Rd. B1
Bower Pl. C1
Bower St. B1
Boxley Rd. A3
Brenchley Gardens A2
Brewer St. B3
Broadway. B2
Broadway Sh Ctr. B2
Brunswick St. C3
Buckland Hill A1
Buckland Rd. B1
Bus Station B3
Campbell Rd. C3
Church Rd. A3
Church St. B3
Cinema 🎬 B2
Clifford Way C1/C2
College Ave. C2
College Rd. C2
Collis Memorial Gdn B2
Cornwallis Rd. B1
Corpus Christi Hall. B2
Council Offices. B2
County Hall. A3
County Rd. A3
Crompton Gdns. B1
Crown & County
  Courts. A2
Curzon Rd. A3
Dixon Cl C2
Douglas Rd. C1
Earl St. B2
Eccleston Rd. C2
Fairmeadow B2
Fisher St. A3
Florence Rd. C1
Foley St. A3
Foster St. C2
Freedom L Ctr. A1/A2
Fremlin Walk Sh Ctr. B2
Gabriel's Hill B3
George St. A2
Grecian St. A3
Hardy St. A2
Hart St. C2
Hastings Rd. C1
Hayle Rd. C2
Hazlitt 🎭 B2
Heathorn St. A3
Hedley St. A3
High St. B2
HM Prison A3
Holland Rd. A3
Hope St. A3
Information Ctr ℹ B2
James St. A3
James Whatman Way B2
Jeffrey St. A3
Kent County Council
  Offices A2
Kent History & Liby Ctr A2
King Edward Rd C2
King St B2
Kingsley Rd C2
Knightrider St. C2
Launder Way. A1
Lesley Pl. A1
Library B2
Little Buckland Ave. A1
Lockmeadow Leisure
  Complex. B2
London Rd. B1
Lower Boxley Rd. A2
Lower Fant Rd. C1
Magistrates Court B2
Maidstone Barracks
  Station ≋ A1
Maidstone East Sta ≋ A2
Maidstone Museum &
  Bentlif Art Gall B2
Maidstone Utd FC. C2
Maidstone West Sta ≋ B2
Mall, The B2
Market A2
Market Buildings B2
Marsham St. B3
Medway St. B2
Melville Rd. C3
Mill St. B2
Millennium Bridge. B2
Mote Rd. B3
Muir Rd. A3
Old Tovil Rd. C2
Palace Ave. B2
Perryfield St. A2
Police Station 🔲. B2
Post Office ⊠ B2/C2
Priory Rd. C1
Prospect Pl. C1
Pudding La. B2
Queen Anne Rd B3
Queens Rd. A1
Randall St. A2
Rawdon Rd. C2
Reginald St. A3
Riverstage B2
Rock Pl. B1
Rocky Hill B1
Romney Pl. B3
Rose Yard. B2
Rowland Cl C1
Royal Engineers' Rd. A2
Royal Star Arcade B2
St Annes St C1
St Faith's St. B2
St Luke's Rd. A3
St Peter St B2
St Peter's Bridge B2
St Peter's Wharf Retail
  Park B2
St Philip's Ave. C3
Salisbury Rd. A3
Sandling Rd. A2
Scott St. A3
Scrubs La. B3
Sheal's Cres B3
Somerfield La. B1

Somerfield Rd. B1
Staceys St. A2
Station Rd A2
Superstore A1/B2/B3
Terrace Rd. C1
Tonbridge Rd C1
Tovil Rd. C2
Town Hall. B2
Trinity Park B2
Tufton St. B3
Tyrwhitt-Drake Mus
  of Carriages 🏛 B2
Union St. B3
Upper Fant Rd. C1
Upper Stone St C2
Victoria St. B1
Warwick Pl. B1
Wat Tyler Way B3
Waterloo St. C2
Waterlow Rd. A3
Week St. B2
Well Rd. B1
Westree Rd. C1
Wharf Rd. C2
Whatman Park A1
Wheeler St. A3
Whitchurch Cl. B1
Woodville Rd. C3
Wyatt St. B3
Wyke Manor Rd. B3

Manchester 337
Adair St B3
Addington St. A5
Adelphi St A1
Albert Sq. B3
Albion St C3
Ancoats Gr. B6
Ancoats Gr North B6
Angela St C1
Aquatics Centre C4
Ardwick Green North C5
Ardwick Green Park. C5
Ardwick Green South C5
Arlington St A2
Artillery St. B3
Arundel St C2
Atherton St B2
Atkinson St. B3
Aytoun St B4
Back Piccadilly A4
Baird St B5
Balloon St A4
Bank Pl. A1
Baring St B5
Barrack St C1
Barrow St A1
Bendix St A5
Bengal St. A5
Berry St. C5
Blackfriars Rd. A3
Blackfriars St. A3
Blantyre St. C2
Bloom St A4
Blossom St. A5
Boad St. B5
Bombay St. C4
Booth St B3
Booth St. B4
Bootle St B3
Brazennose St. B3
Brewer St. A5
Bridge St B3
Bridgewater Hall B3
Bridgewater Pl A4
Bridgewater St B2
Brook St. C4
Brotherton Dr. C1
Brown St B3
Brown St. A4
Brunswick St. C6
Brydon Ave. C6
Buddhist Centre A4
Bury St A1
Bus & Coach Station B4
Bus Station A6
Butler St. A6
Buxton St C5
Byrom St B3
Cable St A5
Cambridge St C3/C4
Camp St B3
Canal St B4
Cannon St A4
Cardroom Rd. A6
Carruthers St. A6
Castle St. B2
Castlefield Arena C2
Cateaton St A3
Cathedral † A3
Cavendish St C4
Chapel St. A1/A3
Chapeltown St. B5
Charles St. C4
Charlotte St. B4
Chatham St. B4
Chepstow St. C3
Chester Rd. C1/C2
Chester St C4
Chetham's Sch of
  Music A3
China La. B5
Chippenham Rd. A6
Chorlton Rd. C1
Chorlton St. B4
Church St. A4
Church St. A6
City Park A4
City Rd East. C4
Civil Justice Centre B2
Cleminson St. A1
Clowes St. A3
College Land. A3
Collier St A2
Commercial St. C3
Conference Centre C4
Cooper St. B4
Copperas St. A4

Corn Exchange, The. A4
Cornbrook ⊖ C1
Cornell St A5
Corporation St A4
Cotter St C6
Cotton St A5
Cow La. B1
Cross St B3
Crown Court B4
Crown St C2
Dalberg St C6
Dale St A4/B4
Dancehouse, The 🎭 C4
Dantzic St A4
Dark La. C6
Dawson St B2
Dean St A5
Deansgate. A3/B3/C2
Deansgate
  Castlefield ⊖ C3
Deansgate Station ≋ C3
Dolphin St C6
Downing St C5
Ducie St B5
Duke Pl. B2
Duke St B2
Durling St C6
East Ordsall La A2/B1
Edge St. A4
Egerton St. C2
Ellesmere St C1
Everard St. C1
Every St. B6
Exchange Sq ⊖ A4
Fairfield St. B5
Faulkner St B4
Fennel St. A3
Ford St C2
Ford St. C6
Fountain St B4
Frederick St A2
Gartside St. B2
Gaythorne St. A1
George Leigh St A5
George St. B4
Gore St. A2
Goulden St. A5
Granby Row B4
Gravel La A3
Great St. B6
Great Ancoats St A5
Great Bridgewater St B3
Great George St A1
Great Jackson St C2
Great Marlborough St C4
Great Northern
  Warehouse Leisure &
  Shopping Complex B3
Greengate A3
Grosvenor St. C5
Gun St. A5
Hadrian Ave. B6
Hall St. B3
Hampson St. B1
Hanover St. A4
Hanworth Cl. C5
Hardman St. B3
Harkness St. C6
Harrison St. B6
Hart St. B4
Helmet St. B6
Henry St. A5
Heyrod St. B6
High St. A4
Higher Ardwick. C5
Hilton St. A4/A5
Holland St. A6
HOME ✦ C3
Hood St. A5
Hope St. B1
Hope St. B4
Houldsworth St A5
Hoyle St. C6
Hulme Hall Rd C1
Hulme St. A1
Hulme St. C3
Hyde Rd. C6
Information Ctr ℹ B4
Irwell St. A1
Islington Way. A1
Jackson Cr. C2
Jackson's Row B3
James St. A1
Jenner Cl. C3
Jersey St A5
John Dalton St B3
John Ryland's Liby 🏛 B3
John St. A2
Kennedy St B3
Kincardine Rd. C5
King St A2
King St West A3
Law Courts B3
Laystall St. B5
Lever St A4
Library B3
Linby St C2
Little Lever St A4
Liverpool Rd B1
Liverpool St. B1
Lloyd St B3
Lockton Cl. C5
London Rd B5
Long Millgate A3
Longacre St. B6
Loom St A5
Lower Byrom St B2
Lower Mosley St. B3
Lower Moss La C2
Lower Ormond St C4
Loxford St. C4
Luna St. A5
Major St. B4
Manchester Arndale A4
Manchester
  Art Gallery 🏛 B3
Manchester Central
  Convention Complex. B3

Merthyr Tydfil • Middlesbrough • Milton Keynes • Newcastle upon Tyne • Newport • Newquay 355

Manchester Metropolitan University (MMU) B4/C4
Manchester Piccadilly Station B5
Manchester Technology Centre C4
Mancunian Way C3
Manor St C5
Marble St A4
Market St A2
Market St A4
Market St A4
Marsden St A3
Marshall St A5
Mayan Ave A2
Medlock St C3
Middlewood St B1
Miller St A4
Minshull St B4
Mosley St A4
Mount St B3
Mulberry St B3
Murray St A5
Museum of Science & Industry (MOSI) B2
Nathan Dr A2
National Football Museum A4
Naval St A5
New Bailey St A2
New Elm Rd B2
New Islington A6
New Islington Sta B6
New Quay St B2
New Union St A6
Newgate St A4
Newton St A5
Nicholas St B4
North Western St C6
Oak St A4
Odeon A4/B3
Old Mill St A6
Oldfield Rd A1/C1
Oldham Rd A5
Oldham St A4
Opera House B3
Ordsall La C1
Oxford Rd C4
Oxford Rd C4
Oxford St B4
Paddock St C6
Palace Theatre B4
Pall Mall A3
Palmerston St B6
Parker St B4
Peak St B5
Penfield Cl C5
Peoples' History Museum B2
Peru St A1
Peter St B3
Piccadilly A4
Piccadilly B5
Piccadilly Gdns B4
Piercy St A6
Poland St A5
Police Station B3/B5
Pollard St B6
Port St A5
Portland St B4
Portugal St East B5
Post Office A1/A2/A4/A5/B3/B4
Potato Wharf B2
Princess St B3/C4
Pritchard St C4
Quay St A2
Quay St B2
Queen St B3
Radium St A5
Redhill St A5
Regent Rd B1
Retail Park A5
Rice St B2
Richmond St B4
River St C3
Roby St B5
Rodney St A6
Roman Fort B2
Rosamond St A2
Royal Exchange A3
Sackville St B4
St Andrew's St B6
St Ann St A3
St Ann's A3
St George's Ave C1
St James St B4
St John St B3
St John's Cath (RC) A2
St Mary's B3
St Mary's Gate A3
St Mary's Parsonage A3
St Peter's Sq B3
St Stephen St A2
Salford Approach A3
Salford Central A2
Sheffield St B5
Sherratt St A5
Shopmobility A4
Shudehill A4
Shudehill A4
Sidney St C4
Silk St A5
Silver St B4
Skerry Cl C5
Snell St B6
South King St B3
Sparkle St B5
Spear St A4
Spring Gdns A4
Stanley St A2/B2
Store St B5
Superstore B1
Swan St A4
Tariff St B5
Tatton St C1
Temperance St B6/C6
Thirsk St C6
Thomas St A4
Thompson St A5
Tib La B3
Tib St A4
Town Hall (Manchester) B3
Town Hall (Salford) A2
Trafford St C3
Travis St B5
Trinity Way A2
Turner St A4
Union St C6
University of Manchester (Sackville Street Campus) C5
University of Salford A1
Upper Brook St C5
Upper Cleminson St A1
Upper Wharf St A1
Urban Exchange A5
Vesta St B6
Victoria A4
Victoria Station A4
Wadesdon Rd C5
Water St B2
Watson St B3
West Fleet St B1
West King St A2
West Mosley St B4
Weybridge Rd A6
Whitworth St B4
Whitworth St West C3
William St A2
William St C6
Wilmott St C3
Windmill St B3
Windsor Cr A1
Withy Gr A4
Woden St C1
Wood St B3
Woodward St A6
Worrall St C1
Worsley St C2
York St B4
York St C2
York St C4

Merthyr Tydfil
Merthyr Tudful 340

Aberdare Rd B2
Abermorlais Terr B2
Alexandra Rd A3
Alma St C3
Arfryn Pl C3
Argyle St C3
Avenue De Clichy C2
Beacons Pl Sh Ctr C2
Bethesda St B2
Bishops Gr A3
Brecon Rd A1/B2
Briarmead A3
Bryn St C3
Bryntirion Rd B3/C3
Bus Station B2
Cae Mari Dwn B3
Caedraw Rd C2
Castle Sq A1
Castle St B2
Chapel C2
Chapel Bank B1
Church St B3
Civic Centre B2
Clos Penderyn B1
Coedcae'r Ct C3
County and Crown Courts B2
Court St C3
Cromwell St B2
Cyfarthfa Castle School and Museum A1
Cyfarthfa Ind Est A1
Cyfarthfa Park A1
Cyfarthfa Rd A1
Dane St A2
Dane Terr A2
Danyparc B3
Darren View A3
Dixon St B2
Dyke St C3
Dynevor St B2
Elwyn Dr C3
Fire Station B2
Fothergill St B3
Galonuchaf Rd A3
Garth St B2
Georgetown B2
Grawen Terr A2
Grove Pk A2
Grove, The A2
Gurnos Rd A2
Gwaelodygarth Rd A2/A3
Gwaunfarren Gr A3
Gwaunfarren Rd A3
Gwendoline St A3
Hampton St C3
Hanover St A2
Heol S O Davies B1
Heol-Gerrig B1
High St A3/B2/B3/C2
Highland View C3
Howell Cl B1
Information Ctr B2
Jackson's Bridge B2
James St C3
John St B3
Joseph Parry's Cott B2
Lancaster St A2
Library B2
Llewellyn St A2
Llwyfen St B2
Llwyn Berry B1
Llwyn Dic Penderyn B1
Llwyn-y-Gelynen C1
Lower Thomas St B3
Market C2
Mary St C3
Masonic St C2
Merthyr College B2
Merthyr RFC C2
Merthyr Town FC B3
Merthyr Tydfil Leisure Ctr C3
Merthyr Tydfil Sta C3
Meyrick Villas A2
Miniature Railway A1
Mount St A2
Nantygwenith St B1
Norman Terr B2
Oak Rd A2
Old Cemetery B3
Pandy Cl A1
Pantycelynen B1
Parade, The B3
Park Terr B2
Penlan View C2
Penry St B2
Pentwyn Villas A2
Penyard Rd B3
Penydarren Park A3
Penydarren Rd B3
Plymouth St C3
Police Station C2
Pont Marlais West B2
Post Office B2
Quarry Row B2
Queen's Rd B3
Rees St C3
Rhydycar Link C2
Riverside Park A1
St David's B3
St Tydfil's C2
St Tydfil's Ave C3
St Tydfil's Hospital (No A&E) B3
St Tydfil's Sq Sh Ctr C2
Saxon St A2
School of Nursing A2
Seward St A3
Shiloh La B3
Stone Circles B3
Stuart St A2
Summerhill Pl B3
Superstore B3
Swan St C2
Swansea Rd B1
Taff Glen View C3
Taff Vale Ct B3
Theatre Soar B2
Thomastown Park B3
Tramroad La A3
Tramroad Side B2
Tramroad Side North B3
Tramroad Side South C3
Trevithick Gdns C3
Trevithick St A3
Tudor Terr B2
Twynyrodyn Rd C3
Union St B3
Upper Colliers Row B1
Upper Thomas St B3
Victoria St B2
Vue C3
Vulcan Rd B2
Walk, The B2
Warlow St C3
Well St A2
Welsh Assembly Government Offices C2
Wern La C1
West Gr A2
William St C3
Yew St C3
Ynysfach Engine Ho C2
Ynysfach Rd C2

Middlesbrough 340

Abingdon Rd C3
Acklam Rd C1
Albert Park C3
Albert Rd B2
Albert Terr C2
Ambulance Station C1
Aubrey St C3
Avenue, The C2
Ayresome Gdns C2
Ayresome Green La C1
Ayresome St C2
Barton Rd A1
Bilsdale Rd C3
Bishopton Rd C3
Borough Rd B2/B3
Bowes Rd A2
Breckon Hill Rd B3
Bridge St East B3
Bridge St West B2
Brighouse Rd A1
Burlam Rd C1
Bus Station B2
Cannon Park B1
Cannon Park Way B2
Cannon St B1
Captain Cook Sq B2
Carlow St C1
Castle Way C3
Chipchase Rd C2
Cineworld B3
Cleveland Centre B2
Clive Rd C2
Commercial St A2
Corporation Rd B2
Costa St C2
Council Offices B3
Crescent Rd C2
Crescent, The C2
Cumberland Rd C2
Depot Rd A2
Derwent St B2
Devonshire Rd C2
Diamond Rd B2
Dorman Museum C2
Douglas St B3
Eastbourne Rd C2
Eden Rd C3
Fire Sta A3
Forty Foot Rd A2
Gilkes St B2
Gosford St A2
Grange Rd B2
Gresham Rd B2
Harehills Rd C1
Harford St C2
Hartington Rd B2
Haverton Hill Rd A1
Hey Wood St B1
Highfield Rd C3
Hillstreet Centre B2
Holwick Rd B1
Hutton Rd C3
Ironmasters Way B1
Lambton Rd C3
Lancaster Rd C2
Lansdowne Rd C3
Latham Rd C2
Law Courts B2/B3
Lees Rd B2
Leeway B3
Library B2/C2
Linthorpe Cemetery C1
Linthorpe Rd B2
Lloyd St B2
Longford St C2
Longlands Rd C3
Lower East St A3
Lower Lake C3
Macmillan Academy C1
Maldon Rd C1
Manor St B2
Marsh St B2
Marton Rd B3
Middlehaven B3
Middlesbrough By-Pass B2/C1
Middlesbrough Coll B3
Middlesbrough L Park B3
Middlesbrough Sta B2
Middletown Park C2
MIMA B3
Mulgrave Rd C2
Newport Bridge B1
Newport Bridge Approach Rd B1
Newport Rd B2
North Ormesby Rd B3
North Rd B2
Northern Rd C1
Outram St B2
Oxford Rd C2
Park La C2
Park Rd North C2
Park Rd South C2
Park Vale Rd C3
Parliament Rd B1
Police Station A2
Port Clarence Rd A3
Portman St B2
Post Office B3/C1/C2
Princes Rd B2
Python A2
Riverside Park Rd A1
Riverside Stadium (Middlesbrough FC) B3
Rockliffe Rd C2
Romaldkirk Rd B1
Roman Rd C2
Roseberry Rd C3
St Barnabas' Rd C2
St Paul's Rd B2
Saltwells Rd B3
Scott's Rd A3
Seaton Carew Rd A3
Shepherdson Way B3
Shopmobility B2
Snowdon Rd A2
South West Ironmasters Park B1
Southfield Rd B2
Southwell Rd C2
Springfield Rd C1
Startforth Rd A2
Stockton Rd C1
Stockton St A2
Superstore B2
Surrey St C2
Sycamore Rd C2
Tax Offices B3
Tees Viaduct C1
Teessaurus Park A2
Teesside Tertiary Coll C3
Temenos B3
Thornfield Rd C1
Town Hall B2
Transporter Bridge (Toll) A3
Union St B2
University of Teesside B2
Upper Lake C2
Valley Rd C3
Ventnor Rd C2
Victoria Rd B2
Vulcan St A2
Warwick St C2
Wellesley Rd B3
West La C1
West Lane Hospital C1
Westminster Rd C2
Wilson St B2
Windward Way B3
Woodlands Rd B2
York Rd C3

Milton Keynes 340

Abbey Way A1
Arbrook Ave B1
Armourer Dr A3
Arncliffe Dr A1
Avebury C2
Avebury Blvd C2
Bankfield B3
Bayard Ave A2
Belvedere A2
Bishopstone A1
Blundells Rd A1
Boundary, The C3
Boycott Ave C2
Bradwell Comm Blvd B1
Bradwell Rd C1
Bramble Ave A2
Brearley Ave C2
Breckland A1
Brill Place B1
Burnham Dr B1
Campbell Park B3
Cantle Ave A3
Central Retail Park C1
Century Ave C2
Chaffron Way C3
Childs Way C1
Christ the Cornerstone B2
Cineworld B2
Civic Offices B2
Cleavers Ave B2
Colesbourne Dr A3
Conniburrow Blvd B2
Currier Dr A2
Dansteed Way A2/A3/B1
Deltic Ave B1
Downs Barn B2
Downs Barn Blvd A3
Eaglestone C3
Eelbrook Ave B1
Elder Gate B1
Evans Gate C2
Fairford Cr A3
Falcon Ave B3
Fennel Dr A2
Fishermead Blvd C3
Food Centre B3
Fulwoods Dr C3
Glazier Dr A2
Glovers La A1
Grafton Gate C1
Grafton St A1/C2
Gurnards Ave B3
Harrier Dr C3
The Hub Leisure Quarter B2/C2
Ibstone Ave B1
intu Milton Keynes B2
Langcliffe Dr A1
Leisure Centre C3
Leisure Plaza C1
Leys Rd C1
Library B2
Linceslade Grove C1
Linford Wood A2
Magistrates Court B2
Marlborough Gate B3
Marlborough St A2/B3
Mercers Dr A1
Midsummer C2
Midsummer Blvd B2
Milton Keynes Central C1
Milton Keynes Hospital (A&E) C3
Monks Way A1
Mullen Ave A3
Mullion Pl C3
Neath Hill A3
North Elder C1
North Grafton B1
North Overgate A3
North Row B2
North Saxon B2
North Secklow B2
North Skeldon A3
North Witan B1
Oakley Gdns A3
Odeon B2
Oldbrook Blvd C2
Open-Air Theatre B3
Overgate A3
Overstreet A3
Patriot Dr B1
Pencarrow Pl B3
Penryn Ave B3
Perran Ave C3
Pitcher La C1
Place Retail Park, The C1
Police Station B2
Portway B2
Post Office A2/B2/B3
Precedent Dr B1
Quinton Dr B1
Ramsons Ave B2
Retail Park C2
Rockingham Dr A2
Rooksley B1
Saxon Gate B2
Saxon St A1/C3
Secklow Gate B2
Shackleton Pl C2
Shopmobility B2
Silbury Blvd B2
Skeldon A3
South Enmore B3
South Grafton C2
South Row C2
South Saxon C2
South Secklow B3
South Witan C2
Springfield B3
Stainton Dr A1/B1
Stanton Wood A1
Stantonbury A1
Stantonbury Leisure Ctr A1
Strudwick Dr C2
Sunrise Parkway A2
Superstore C1/C2
Theatre & Art Gallery B3
theCentre:mk B2
Tolcarne Ave C3
Towan Ave C3
Trueman Pl C2
Vauxhall A1
Winterhill Retail Park C2
Witan Gate B2
Xscape B3

Newcastle upon Tyne 340

Albert St B3
Argyle St B3
Back New Bridge St B3
BALTIC Centre for Contemporary Art C3
Barker St A3
Barrack Rd B1
Bath La B1
Bessie Surtees Ho C2
Bigg Market C2
Biscuit Factory B3
Black Gate C2
Blackett St B2
Blandford Sq C1
Boating Lake A1
Boyd St B3
Brandling Park A2
Bus Station B2
Buxton St B3
Byron St A3
Camden St B2
Castle Keep C2
Central C1
Central Library B2
Central Motorway B2
Chester St A3
City Hall B2
City Rd B3/C3
City Walls C1
Civic Centre A2
Claremont Rd A1
Clarence St B3
Clarence Walk B3
Clayton St C1/B1
Clayton St West C1
Close, The C2
Coach Station C1
College St B2
Collingwood St C2
Copland Terr B3
Coppice Way B3
Corporation St B1
Courts C3
Crawhall Rd B3
Dean St C2
Dental Hospital A1
Dinsdale Pl A3
Dinsdale Rd A3
Discovery C1
Doncaster Rd A3
Durant Rd B2
Eldon Sq B1
Ellison Pl B2
Empire B1
Eskdale Terr A2
Eslington Terr A2
Exhibition Park A1
Falconar St B3
Fenkle St C1
Forth Banks C1
Forth St C1
Gallowgate B1
Gate, The B1
Gateshead Millennium Bridge C3
Gibson St B3
Goldspink La A3
Grainger Market B2
Grainger St B2
Grantham Rd A3
Granville Rd A3
Great North Children's Hospital A1
Great North Mus:Hancock A2
Grey St B2
Groat Market C2
Guildhall C2
Hancock St A2
Hanover St C2
Hatton Gallery A1
Hawks Rd C3
Haymarket B2
Heber St B1
Helmsley Rd A3
High Bridge B2
High Level Bridge C2
Hillgate C3
Howard St B3
Hutton Terr A3
Information Ctr C3
intu Eldon Sq Sh Ctr B2
Jesmond A2
Jesmond Rd A2/A3
John Dobson St B2
John George Joicey Museum C2
Jubilee Rd B3
Kelvin Gr A3
Kensington Terr A2
Laing Gallery B2
Lambton Rd A2
Leazes Cr B1
Leazes La B1
Leazes Park B1
Leazes Park Rd B1
Leazes Terr B1
Library A2
Live C2
Low Friar St C1
Manor Chare C2
Manors B2
Manors Station B2
Market St B2
Melbourne St B2
Mill Rd C3
Monument B2
Monument Mall Shopping Ctr B2
Morpeth St A2
Mosley St C2
Napier St A3
New Bridge St B2/B3
Newcastle Central Station C1
Newcastle University A1
Newgate Shopping Ctr C1
Newgate St B1
Newington Rd A3
Northern Design Ctr C3
Northern Stage Theatre A2
Northumberland Rd B2
Northumberland St B2
Northumbria Univ A2
Northwest Radial Rd A1
O2 Academy C1
Oakwellgate C3
Open Univ C3
Orchard St C2
Osborne Rd A2
Osborne Terr A3
Pandon C3
Pandon Bank B3
Park Terr A1
Percy St B1
Pilgrim St B2
Pipewellgate C2
Pitt St B1
Plummer Tower A2
Police Station B1
Portland Rd A3/B3
Portland Terr A3
Post Office B1/B2
Pottery La C1
Prudhoe Pl B1
Prudhoe St B1
Quayside C2
Queen Elizabeth II Bridge C2
Queen Victoria Rd A1
Richardson Rd A1
Ridley Pl B2
Rock Terr B3
Rosedale Terr A3
Royal Victoria Infirmary A1
Sage Gateshead C3
St Andrew's St B1
St James B1
St James' Blvd C1
St James' Park (Newcastle Utd FC) B1
St Mary's Heritage Centre C3
St Mary's (RC) C1
St Mary's Place B2
St Nicholas C2
St Nicholas St C2
St Thomas' St B1
Sandyford Rd A2/A3
Science Park B2
Shield St B3
Shieldfield B3
Shopmobility B1
Side, The C2
Simpson Terr B3
South Shore Rd C3
South St C1
Starbeck Ave A3
Stepney Rd B3
Stoddart St B3
Stowell St B1
Strawberry Pl B1
Swing Bridge C2
Temple St C1
Terrace Pl B1
Theatre Royal B2
Times Sq C1
Tower St B3
Trinity House C2
Tyne Bridge C2
Tyne Bridges C2
Tyne Theatre & Opera House C1
Tyneside B2
Victoria Sq A2
Warwick St A3
Waterloo St C1
Wellington St B1
Westgate Rd C1/C2
Windsor Terr A2
Worswick St B2
Wretham Pl B3

Newport
Casnewydd 340

Albert Terr B1
Allt-yr-Yn Ave A1
Alma St C2
Ambulance Station C3
Bailey St B2
Barrack Hill A2
Bath St A3
Bedford Rd B3
Belle Vue La C1
Belle Vue Park C1
Bishop St A3
Blewitt St B1
Bolt Cl C3
Bolt St C3
Bond St A2
Bosworth Dr A1
Bridge St B1
Bristol St A3
Bryngwyn Rd B1
Brynhyfryd Ave C1
Brynhyfryd Rd C1
Bus Station B2
Caerau Cres C1
Caerau Rd B1
Caerleon Rd A3
Capel Cres C2
Cardiff Rd C2
Caroline St B3
Castle (Remains) A2
Cedar Rd B3
Charles St B2
Charlotte Dr C2
Chepstow Rd A3
Church Rd A3
Cineworld B2
Civic Centre B1
Clarence Pl A2
Clifton Pl B1
Clifton Rd C1
Clyffard Cres B1
Clytha Park Rd B1
Clytha Sq C2
Coldra Rd C1
Collier St A3
Colne St B3
Comfrey Cl A1
Commercial Rd C3
Commercial St B2
Corelli St A3
Corn St B2
Corporation Rd B3
Coulson Cl C2
County Court A2
Courts A1
Courts B1
Crawford St A3
Cyril St B3
Dean St A3
Devon Pl B1
Dewsland Park Rd C2
Dolman B2
Dolphin St C3
East Dock Rd C3
East St B1
East Usk Rd A3
Ebbw Vale Wharf B3
Emlyn St B2
Enterprise Way C3
Eton Rd B3
Evans St A2
Factory Rd A2
Fields Rd B1
Francis Dr C2
Frederick St C3
Friars Rd C1
Friars Walk B2
Gaer La C1
George St C3
George Street Bridge C3
Godfrey Rd B1
Gold Tops B1
Gore St A3
Gorsedd Circle C1
Grafton Rd A3
Graham St B1
Granville St C3
Harlequin Dr A1
Harrow Rd B3
Herbert Rd A3
Herbert Walk C2
Hereford St A3
High St B2
Hill St B2
Hoskins St A2
Information Ctr B2
Ivor St B2
Jones St B1
Junction Rd A3
Keynshaw Ave C2
King St C2
Kingsway B2
Kingsway Centre B2
Ledbury Dr A2
Library A3
Library, Museum & Art Gallery B2
Liverpool Wharf B3
Llanthewy Rd B1
Llanvair Rd A3
Locke St A2
Lower Dock St C3
Lucas St A2
Manchester St A3
Market B2
Marlborough Rd B3
Mellon St C3
Mill St A2
Morgan St A3
Mountjoy Rd C2
Newport Bridge A2
Newport Ctr B2
Newport RFC B3
Newport Station B2
North St B2
Oakfield Rd B1
Park Sq C2
Police Station A3/C2
Post Office B2/C3
Power St A1
Prince St A3
Pugsley St A2
Queen St C2
Queen's Cl A1
Queen's Hill A1
Queen's Hill Cres A1
Queensway B2
Railway St B2
Riverfront Theatre & Arts Centre, The B2
Riverside A3
Rodney Rd B2
Royal Gwent (A&E) C2
Rudry St A3
Rugby Rd B3
Ruperra La C3
Ruperra St C3
St Edmund St B1
St Mark's Cres A1
St Mary St B1
St Vincent Rd A3
St Woolos C2
St Woolos General (no A&E) C1
St Woolos Rd B1
School La B2
Serpentine Rd B1
Shaftesbury Park A2
Sheaf La A3
Skinner St B2
Sorrel Dr A1
South Market St C3
Spencer Rd B1
Stow Hill B2/C1/C2
Stow Park Ave C1
Stow Park Dr C1
TA Centre A1
Talbot St B2
Tennis Club A1
Tregare St A3
Trostrey St A3
Tunnel Terr B1
Turner St A3
Univ of Wales Newport City Campus B3
Upper Dock St B2
Usk St A3
Usk Way B3/C3
Victoria Cr B1
War Memorial A3
Waterloo Rd C1
West St B1
Wharves B2
Wheeler St A2
Whitby Pl A3
Windsor Terr B1
York Pl C1

Newquay 340

Agar Rd B2
Alma Pl B1
Ambulance Station B2
Anthony Rd C1
Atlantic Hotel A1
Bank St B1
Barrowfields A3
Bay View Terr B2
Beach Rd B1
Beachfield Ave B1
Beacon Rd A1
Belmont Pl A1
Berry Rd B2
Blue Reef Aquarium B1
Boating Lake C2
Bus Station B1
Chapel Hill B1
Chester Rd A3
Cheviot Rd C1/C2
Chichester Cres C2
Chynance Dr C1
Chyverton Cl C1
Cliff Rd B2
Coach Park B2
Colvreath Rd A3
Cornwall College Newquay B3
Council Offices B1
Crantock St B1
Crescent, The B1
Criggar Rocks A3
Dale Cl C3
Dale Rd C3
Dane Rd A1
East St B2
Edgcumbe Ave B3
Edgcumbe Gdns B3
Eliot Gdns B3
Elm Cl C3
Ennor's Rd B1
Fernhill Rd B1
Fire Station B1
Fore St B1
Gannel Rd C2
Golf Driving Range B3
Gover La B1
Great Western Beach A2
Grosvenor Ave B2
Harbour A1
Hawkins Rd C2
Headleigh Rd B2
Hilgrove Rd A3/B3
Holywell Rd B3
Hope Terr B1
Huer's Hut, The A1
Information Ctr B1
Island Cres B2
Jubilee St B1
Kew Cl C3
Killacourt Cove A2
King Edward Cres A1
Lanhenvor Ave B2
Library B1
Lifeboat Station A1
Lighthouse B1
Linden Ave C2
Listry Rd C2
Lusty Glaze Beach A3
Lusty Glaze Rd A3
Manor Rd B1
Marcus Hill B2
Mayfield Rd B2
Meadowside C3
Mellanvrane La C2
Michell Ave B2
Miniature Golf Course C3
Miniature Railway B3
Mount Wise B1
Mowhay Cl C3
Narrowcliff A3
Newquay B2
Newquay Hospital B2
Newquay Town Football Ground B1
Newquay Zoo B3
North Pier A1
North Quay Hill A1
Oakleigh Terr B2
Pargolla Rd B2
Pendragon Cres C3
Pengannel Cl C1
Penina Ave C3
Pirate's Quest B1
Police Sta & Courts B2
Post Office B1/B2
Quarry Park Rd B3
Rawley La C2
Reeds Way B1
Robartes Rd B2
St Anne's Rd A3
St Aubyn Cres B3
St George's Rd B1
St John's Rd B1
St Mary's Rd B1
St Michael's B1
St Michael's Rd B1
St Thomas' Rd B2
Seymour Ave B2
South Pier A1
South Quay Hill A1
Superstore B2
Sweet Briar Cres C3

Sydney Rd A1
Tolcarne Beach. A2
Tolcarne Point A2
Tolcarne Rd B2
Tor Rd B2
Towan Beach. A1
Towan Blystra Rd B2
Tower Rd B2
Trebarwith Cres B2
Tredour Rd C2
Treforda Rd C3
Tregoss Rd. B2
Tregunnel Hill. B1/C1
Tregunnel Saltings . . .C1
Trelawney Rd C2
Treloggan La C3
Treloggan Rd. C3
Trembath Cres B2
Trenance Ave B2
Trenance Gardens B2
Trenance La. B2
Trenance Leisure Park B3
Trenance Rd B2
Trenarth Rd B2
Treninnick Hill B2
Tretherras Rd C1
Trethewey Way. C1
Trevemper Rd B3
Ulalia Rd. B3
Vivian Cl. B3
Waterworld. B3
Whitegate Rd A3
Wych Hazel Way A2

Newtown
Y Drenewydd   340

Ash Cl A3
Back La. B2
Baptist Chapel ♦ B2
Barn La. B2
Bear Lanes Sh Ctr. . . .B2
Beech Cl. B3
Beechwood Dr A3
Brimmon Cl. C2
Brimmon Rd C2
Broad St. B2
Bryn Bank A1
Bryn Cl A2
Bryn Gdns B1
Bryn House A2
Bryn La. A1/A2
Bryn Meadows A2
Bryn St A2
Bryn, The A2
Brynglais Ave A2
Brynglais Cl. A2
Bus Station B2
Byrnwood Dr A1
Cambrian Bridge A2
Cambrian Gdns A2
Cambrian Way. A2
Canal Rd. B2
Castle Mound B2
Cedewain C1
Cefnaire. C2
Cefnaire Coppice C2
Ceiriog C2
Cemetery. A2
Church (Remains of) . .B2
Churchill Dr. A3
Cledan B3
Colwyn B3
Commercial St B2
Council Offices. B1
Crescent St A3
Cwm Llanfair. B2
Dinas B2
Dolafon Rd C1
Dolerw Park B1
Dolfor Rd C1
Eirianell C1
Fairfield Dr A3
Fforddd Croesawdy . . .C2
Fire Station A3
Frankwell St A2
Frolic St B2
Fron La. A1
Garden La B2
Gas St B2
Glyndwr C1
Golwgydre La C1
Gorsedd Circle ♦ B1
Great Brimmon Farm. .C3
Hafren B2
Halfpenny Bridge. B2
High St B2
Hillside Ave A3
Hoel Treowen C2
Information Ctr ⅈ B2
Kerry Rd. C1
Ladywell Shopping Ctr B2
Library B1
Llanfair Rd C2
Llanidloes Rd C1
Llys Ifor B2
Lon Cerddyn A3
Lon Helyg. A2
Lonesome La A3
Long Bridge. B2
Lower Canal Rd. B2
Maldwyn Leisure Ctr. .B2
Market B1
Market St. B2
Milford Rd C3
Mill Cl C1
Miniature Railway ♦ . .A1
Montgomery County
  Infirmary Ⓗ A2
Mwyn Fynydd A3
New Church St B2
New Rd. B2
Newtown Football Gd .C1
Newtown Station ≄ . . .B1
Oak Tree Ave A1
Old Kerry Rd B2
Oldbarn La. C3
Oriel Davies Gallery ♦.B1
Park Cl B3
Park La. B1

Park St B2
Park, The B1
Parklands B1
Pavillion Ct C1
Plantation La. C1
Police Station ▣ B1
Pont Brynfedw A2
Pool Rd. B3
Poplar Rd. A3
Post Office ⓟ B2
Powys. C1
Powys Theatre ♥ A2
Pryce Jones Stores &
  Museum B2
Quaker Meeting Ho ♦ .B1
Regent B2
Robert Owen House. . .B1
Robert Owen Mus ♦ . .B2
Rugby Club A3
St David's B2
School La. B2
Sheaf St B3
Short Bridge St. B2
Stone St B2
Superstore B3/C1
Sycamore Dr A1
Textile Museum ♦ B2
Town Hall. B2
Union St B2
Upper Brimmon C3
Vastre Industrial Est . .B3
War Memorial B2
WHSmith Museum ♦ . .B2
Wynfields C1
Y Ffrydd A3

Northampton   340

78 Derngate ♦ B3
Abington Sq B3
Abington St B3
Alcombe Rd A3
All Saints' ♦ B2
Ambush St B1
Angel St B2
AR Centre A3
Arundel St A2
Ash St C2
Auctioneers Way C2
Bailiff St. A2
Barrack Rd. A2
Beaconsfield Terr A3
Becket's Park C3
Bedford Rd B3
Billing Rd B3
Brecon St. A1
Brewery C2
Bridge St C2
Broad St. B2
Burns St A3
Bus Station B2
Campbell St. A2
Castle (Site of) B2
Castle St. B2
Cattle Market Rd B2
Central Museum &
  Art Gallery ♦ B2
Charles St A3
Cheyne Walk B2
Church La A2
Clare St A3
Cloutsham St. A3
College St B2
Colwyn Rd A3
Cotton End. C2
Countess Rd A1
Court A2
Craven St A3
Crown & County
  Courts B3
Denmark Rd A3
Derngate. B3
Derngate & Royal
  Theatres ♥ B3
Doddridge Church ♦ . .B2
Drapery, The B2
Duke St. A3
Dunster St A3
Earl St. A3
Euston Rd. C2
Fire Station B2
Foot Meadow B2
Gladstone Rd A1
Gold St. B2
Grafton St A2
Gray St A1
Green St. B1
Greenwood Rd B2
Greyfriars B2
Grosvenor Centre B2
Grove Rd A3
Guildhall ♦ B2
Hampton St A2
Harding Terr A2
Hazelwood Rd B3
Herbert St B2
Hervey St A2
Hester St A2
Holy Sepulchre ♦ A2
Hood St A3
Horse Market B2
Hunter St A3
Information Ctr ⅈ B2
Kettering Rd A3
Kingswell St B2
Lady's La B2
Leicester St A3
Library B2
Lorne Rd A2
Louise Rd A1
Lower Harding St. A2
Lower Hester St. A2
Lower Mounts B3
Lower Priory St. A2
Main Rd B2
Marefair. B2
Market Sq B2

Marlboro Rd B1
Marriott St. A3
Military Rd A3
Mounts Baths L Ctr. . .A3
Nene Valley Retail Pk. .C2
New South Bridge St. .C2
Northampton General
  Hospital (A&E) Ⓗ . . .B1
Northampton Marina . .C3
Northampton Sta ≄ . . .B1
Northcote St A1
Nunn Mills Rd C3
Old Towcester Rd C2
Overstone Rd A3
Peacock Pl. B2
Pembroke Rd A1
Penn Court A2
Police Station ▣ B3
Post Office ⓟ A1/B3
Quorn Way. A2
Ransome Rd C3
Regent Sq B2
Ridings, The B3
Robert St A3
St Andrew's Rd B1
St Andrew's St B2
St Edmund's Rd B3
St George's St B2
St Giles B3
St Giles St B3
St Giles' Terr B3
St James La. B1
St James Park Rd B1
St James Retail Park . .B1
St James Rd. B1
St James' Mill Rd B1
St James' Mill Rd East.C1
St Leonard's Rd C2
St Mary's St B2
St Michael's Rd A3
St Peter's Way
  Shopping Precinct. . .B2
St Peter's Way. B2
Salisbury St A1
Scarletwell St B2
Semilong Rd A2
Sheep St B2
Sol Central
  (Leisure Ctr) B2
Somerset St A3
South Bridge. C2
Southfield Ave C2
Spencer Bridge Rd. . . .A1
Spencer Rd A2
Spring Gdns B3
Spring La A2
Superstore A3
Swan St B3
Tintern Ave A1
Towcester Rd C2
Upper Bath St B2
Upper Mounts A2
Victoria Park. A3
Victoria Promenade . . .B2
Victoria Rd A3
Victoria St A2
Wellingborough Rd . . .B1
West Bridge. B1
York Rd B3

Norwich   341

Albion Way C3
All Saints Green C2
Anchor St. A3
Anglia Sq A2
Argyle St C3
Arts Centre ♥ B1
Ashby St C2
Assembly House ♦ B1
Bank Plain. B2
Barker St A1
Barn Rd B1
Barrack St A3
Ber St C2
Bethel St B1
Bishop Bridge A3
Bishopbridge Rd. A3
Bishopgate B3
Blackfriars St A2
Botolph St A2
Bracondale C2
Brazen Gate. C2
Bridewell ♦ B2
Brunswick Rd C1
Bull Close Rd. A2
Bus Station C2
Calvert St A2
Cannell Green. A3
Carrow Rd C3
Castle & Museum ♦▥♦ .B2
Castle Mall B2
Castle Meadow B2
Cathedral † B2
Cathedral Retail Park . .A1
Cattlemarket St B2
Chantry Rd. C1
Chapel Loke C2
Chapelfield East C1
Chapelfield Gdns C1
Chapelfield North B1
Chapelfield Rd C1
Cinema City ♥ B2
City Hall B1
City Rd C2
City Wall C1/C3
Close, The. B2/B3
Colegate A2
Coslany St A1
Cow Hill B1
Cow Tower A3
Cowgate. A2
Crown & Magistrates'
  Courts B2
Dragon Hall Heritage
  Centre ♦ C3
Duke St. B1
Edward St A2
Elm Hill B2
Erpingham Gate ♦ B2

Fishergate. A2
Forum, The B1
Foundry Bridge B3
Fye Bridge A2
Garden St C2
Gas Hill. B3
Gentlemans Walk B1
Grapes Hill. B1
Great Hosp Halls, The .A3
Grove Ave. C1
Grove Rd C1
Guildhall ♦ B1
Gurney Rd A3
Hall Rd C2
Heathgate A3
Heigham St A1
Hollywood ♥ A2
Horn's La C2
Hungate Medieval
  Art ♦ B2
Information Ctr ⅈ B1
intu Chapelfield C1
Ipswich Rd C1
ITV Anglia. B3
James Stuart Gdns . . .B3
King St B2
King St C3
Koblenz Ave. C3
Leisure Centre A3
Library B1
London St B2
Lower Clarence Rd. . . .B3
Maddermarket ♥ B1
Magdalen St A2
Mariners La. C2
Market B1
Market Ave B2
Mountergate. B3
Mousehold St A3
Newmarket Rd C1
Norfolk St C1
Norwich City FC C3
Norwich Gallery ♦ B2
Norwich School ♦ B2
Norwich Station ≄ B3
Oak St A1
Odeon ♥ B1
Palace St B2
Pitt St A2
Playhouse ♥ B2
Police Station ▣ C2
Post Office ⓟ
  . . . . .A2/B2/B3/C1
Pottergate. B1
Prince of Wales Rd. . . .B2
Princes St B2
Pull's Ferry ♦ B3
Puppet Theatre ♥ A2
Queen St B2
Queens Rd C2
RC Cathedral † B1
Recorder Rd B3
Riverside
  Entertainment Ctr . .C3
Riverside Leisure Ctr. .C3
Riverside Rd B3
Riverside Retail Park. . .C3
Rosary Rd B3
Rose La. B2
Rouen Rd C2
St Andrews St B2
St Augustines St A2
St Benedicts St B1
St Ethelbert's Gate ♦ .B2
St Faiths La B3
St Georges St A2
St Giles St B1
St James Cl. A3
St Julians C2
St Leonards Rd A3
St Martin's La A1
St Peter Mancroft † . . .B1
St Peters St B1
St Stephens Rd. C1
St Stephens St. C1
Shopmobility B1
Silver Rd. A3
Silver St A2
Southwell Rd. C2
St. Andrew's &
  Blackfriars' Hall ♦ . .B2
Strangers' Hall ♦ B1
Superstore C2
Surrey St C2
Sussex St A2
Theatre Royal ♥ B1
Theatre St B1
Thorn La. C2
Thorpe Rd B3
Tombland B2
Union St C1
Vauxhall St B1
Victoria St C1
Vue ♥ B2
Walpole St C1
Waterfront, The C3
Wensum St B2
Wessex St C1
Westwick St A1
Wherry Rd C3
Whitefriars A2
Willow La B1

Nottingham   341

Abbotsford Dr. A3
Addison St A1
Albert Hall ♦ B1
Alfred St Central A3
Alfreton Rd A1
All Saints St A1
Annesley Rd C3
Arboretum ❀ A1
Arboretum St A1
Arthur St A1
Arts Theatre ♥ B3
Ashforth St A2
Balmoral Rd A1
Barker Gate B3
Bath St B3

BBC Nottingham. C3
Beacon Hill Rise B3
Belgrave Rooms B1
Bellar Gate B3
Belward St. B3
Brewhouse Yard ♦ C2
Broad Marsh Bus Sta. .C2
Broad St. B3
Brook St B3
Burns St A1
Burton St B2
Bus Station C2
Canal St. C2
Carlton St. B3
Carrington St C2
Castle ▥ C2
Castle Blvd. C1
Castle Gate C2
Castle Meadow Rd C1
Castle Meadow
  Retail Pk. C1
Castle Rd. C2
Castle Wharf. C2
Cavendish Rd East C1
Cemetery. A1/B1
Chaucer St B2
Cheapside. B2
Church Rd A3
City Link. C3
City of Caves ♦ C2
Clarendon St B1
Cliff Rd C3
Clumber Rd East. C1
Clumber St B2
College St B1
Collin St C2
Contemporary ♦ C3
Conway St C3
Cornerhouse, The ♥ . . .B2
Council House ♦ B2
Cranbrook St B3
Cranmer St A2
Cromwell St B1
Curzon St B3
Derby Rd B1
Dryden St A2
Exchange Ctr, The B2
Fishpond Dr C1
Fletcher Gate B3
Forest Rd East. A1
Forest Rd West. A1
Friar La. C2
Gedling Gr A2
Gedling St B3
George St B3
Gill St A2
Glasshouse St B2
Goldsmith St B2
Goose Gate B3
Great Freeman St A2
Guildhall ♦ B2
Hamilton Dr. C1
Hampden St. A1
Heathcote St B3
High Pavement C3
High School ⅈ A1
HM Revenue &
  Customs. B1
Holles Cr C1
Hope Dr C1
Hungerhill Rd A3
Huntingdon Dr A1
Huntingdon St. A2
Information Ctr ⅈ B2
Instow Rise A3
International Com Ctr .A2
intu Broadmarsh. C2
intu Victoria Centre. . .B2
Kent St B3
King St. B2
Lace Market ≄ B3
Lace Mkt Theatre ♥ . . .C3
Lamartine St B3
Leisure Ctr. C3
Lenton Rd C1
Lewis Cl A3
Lincoln St B2
London Rd C3
Long Row B2
Low Pavement C2
Lower Parliament St . .B3
Magistrates' Court. C2
Maid Marian Way B2
Mansfield Rd. A2/B2
Middle Hill C2
Milton St B2
Mount St C2
National Ice Centre &
  Motorpoint Arena. . .C3
National Justice
  Museum ♦ C3
Newcastle Dr. B1
Newstead Gr A1
North Sherwood St . . .A2
Nottingham Arena C3
Nottingham Cath † B2
Nottingham College . . .B2
Nottingham Station ≄.C3
Nottingham Station . . .C3
Nottingham Trent
  University A2/B2
Old Market Square ≄ . .B2
Oliver St A1
Park Dr C1
Park Row B1
Park Terr B1
Park Valley C1
Park, The C1
Peas Hill Rd A2
Peel St A1
Pelham St B2
Peveril Dr C1
Plantagenet St A3
Playhouse Theatre ♥ . .B1
Plumptre St C3
Police Station ▣ . . .B1/B2
Poplar St C3
Portland Rd. C1
Post Office ⓟ C1
Queen's Rd C3

Raleigh St A1
Regent St B1
Rick St B3
Robin Hood St B3
Robin Hood Statue ♦ .C2
Ropewalk, The B1
Royal Centre ♥ B2
Royal Children Inn ♦ . .B1
Royal Concert Hall ♥ . .B2
St Ann's Hill Rd A2
St Ann's Way A2
St Ann's Well Rd A3
St James' St B2
St Mark's St A3
St Mary's Rest Garden .B3
St Mary's Gate B3
St Nicholas † C2
St Peter's St C2
St Peter's Gate C2
Salutation Inn ♦ C2
Shakespeare St A2
Shelton St A2
Shopmobility B2
South Pde B2
South Rd C1
South Sherwood St B2
Stanford St C2
Station Street ≄ C2
Stoney St B3
Talbot St B1
Tattershall Dr C1
Tennis Dr B1
Tennyson St A1
Theatre Royal ♥ B2
Trent St C3
Trent University ≄ B2
Union Rd A3
Upper Parliament St . .B2
Victoria Leisure Ctr . . .B3
Victoria Park. A3
Victoria St B2
Walter St A1
Warser Gate B3
Watkin St A2
Waverley St A1
Wheeler Gate B2
Wilford Rd C2
Wilford St C2
Wollaton St B1
Woodborough Rd. A2
Woolpack La B3
Ye Old Trip to
  Jerusalem ♦ C2
York St A2

Oban   341

Aird's Cres. B2
Albany St B2
Albert La A2
Albert Rd A2
Alma Cres B3
Ambulance Station . . .C2
Angus Terr. A2
Ardconnel Rd A2
Ardconnel Terr. A2
Argyll Sq B2
Argyll St B2
Atlantis Leisure Ctr . . .A2
Bayview Rd A1
Benvoulin Rd. A1
Bowling Green A1
Breadalbane St B2
Bus Station B2
Campbell St. B2
College. B2
Colonsay Terr B3
Columba Building B2
Combie St B2
Corran Brae. A1
Corran Esplanade . .A1/A2
Corran Halls, The ♥. . . .A2
Court B2
Crannaig-a-
  Mhinister B1
Crannog La C2
Croft Ave B3
Dalintart Dr C3
Dalriach Rd A2
Distillery ♦ B2
Drummore Rd. C2
Duncraggan Rd. A2
Dunollie Rd A2
Dunuaran Rd B1
Feochan Gr C2
Ferry Terminal B1
Gallanach Rd. B1
George St B2
Glencruitten Dr C3
Glencruitten Rd B3
Glenmore Rd C1
Glenshellach Rd B1
Glenshellach Terr B2
Hazeldean Cres B2
High St B2
Highland Theatre
  Cinema, The ♥ A2
Hill St B2
Industrial Estate. C2
Information Ctr ⅈ B2
Islay Rd B3
Jacob's Ladder ♦ B2
Jura Rd B3
Knipoch Pl. C3
Laurel Cres A2
Laurel Rd A2/A3
Library B1
Lifeboat Station B1
Lighthouse Pier A1
Lismore Cres. A2
Lochavullin Dr C2
Lochavullin Rd C2
Lochside St C2
Longsdale Cres A3
Longsdale Rd A2/A3
Longsdale Terr A3
Lunga Rd A3
Lynn Rd C2
Market St B2
McCaig Rd C3
McCaig's Tower ♦ A2

Oxford   341

Adelaide St A1
Albert St. A1
All Souls (Coll) B2
Ashmolean Mus ▥ B1
Balliol (Coll) B2
Banbury Rd A2
Bate Collection of
  Musical
  Instruments ▥ C2
Beaumont St B1
Becket St B1
Blackhall Rd A1
Blue Boar St B2
Bodleian Library ♦ B2
Botanic Garden ❀ B3
Brasenose (Coll) B2
Brewer St C2
Broad St B2
Burton-Taylor
  Theatre ♥ B2
Bus Station B1
Canal St A1
Cardigan St A1
Carfax Tower. B2
Castle ▥ B1
Castle St. B1
Catte St B2
Cemetery. A1
Christ Church (Coll) . . .B2
Christ Church Cath † . .C2
Christ Church Mdw . . .C2
Clarendon Centre B2
Coach & Lorry Park . . .A1
College. B3
Coll of Further Ed. C1
Cornmarket St B2
Corpus Christi (Coll) . . .B2
County Hall B1
Covered Market B2
Cowley Pl. C3
Cranham St A1
Cranham Terr A1
Cricket Ground B1
Crown & County
  Courts C2
Deer Park. C2
Exeter (Coll). B2
Folly Bridge C2
George St B1
Great Clarendon St . . .A1
Hart St A1
Hertford (Coll) B2
High St B2
Hollybush Row B1
Holywell St B2
Hythe Bridge St B1
Ice Rink C1
Information Ctr ⅈ B2
Jericho St A1
Jesus (Coll) B2
Jowett Walk B3
Juxon St A1
Keble (Coll) A2
Keble Rd. A2
Library B3
Linacre (Coll) A3
Lincoln (Coll) B2
Little Clarendon St A1
Longwall St B3
Magdalen (Coll) B3
Magdalen Bridge B3
Magdalen St B2
Magistrate's Court. C1
Manor Rd B3
Mansfield (Coll) A2
Mansfield Rd. A2
Market B2
Marlborough Rd C2
Martyrs' Memorial ♦ . .B2
Merton (Coll) B3
Merton Field B3
Merton St B2
Mus of Modern Art ▥ .B2
Museum of Oxford ▥ . .B2
Museum Rd A2
New College (Coll) B3
New Inn Hall St B1
New Rd B1
New Theatre ♥ B2

Perth   341

AK Bell Library B2
Abbot Cres. C1
Abbot St C1
Albany Terr A1
Albert Monument. A2
Alexandra St B2
Atholl St A2
Balhousie Ave A2
Balhousie Castle Black
  Watch Museum ▥ . . .A2
Balhousie St A2
Ballantine Pl A1
Barossa Pl A2
Barossa St A2
Barrack St A2
Bell's Sports Centre. . .A1
Bellwood B3
Blair St A1
Burn Park. C1
Bus Station B2
Caledonian Rd B2
Canal Cres. B2
Canal St B3
Cavendish Ave. C1
Charles St B2
Charlotte Pl. A2
Charlotte St A2
Church St A1
City Hall B2
Club House A1
Clyde Pl. C1
Commercial St A3
Concert Hall ♦ B3
Council Chambers B2
County Pl B2
Court B3
Craigie Pl C2
Crieff Rd A1
Croft Park. A1
Cross St C2
Darnhall Cres C1
Darnhall Dr C1
Dewars Centre B1
Dundee Rd B3
Dunkeld Rd A1
Earl's Dykes B1
Edinburgh Rd C3
Elibank St C1
Fair Maid's House ♦ . . .A2
Fergusson ▥ B2
Feus Rd A1
Fire Station B1
Fitness Centre B3
Foundry La A2
Friar St C1
George St B3

Peterborough   341

ABAX Stadium
  (Peterborough
  United). C2
Athletics Arena. B3
Bishop's Palace ▥ B2
Bishop's Rd B2/B3
Boongate. A3
Bourges Boulevard . . .A1
Bourges Retail Pk .B1/B2
Bridge House
  (Council Offices). . . .C2
Bridge St B2
Bright St. A1
Broadway. A2
Broadway ♥ A2
Brook St A2
Burghley Rd A2
Bus Station A2
Cavendish St A3

Nuffield (Coll) B1
Observatory A1
Observatory St A1
Odeon ♥ B1/B2
Old Fire Station B1
Old Greyfriars St C2
Oriel (Coll) B2
Oxford Station ≄ B1
Oxford University
  Research Centres . . .A1
Oxpens Rd C1
Paradise Sq C1
Paradise St B1
Park End St B1
Parks Rd A2/B2
Pembroke (Coll) C2
Phoenix ♥ A1
Picture Gallery ▥ B3
Plantation Rd A1
Playhouse ♥ B2
Post Office ⓟ A1/B2
Pulpit Dr. C1
Pulpit Hill. C1
Pulpit Hill
  Viewpoint ♦ B1
Quarry Rd. C2
Queen's Park Pl B2
Railway Quay. C1
Rockfield Rd B2
St Columba's † A1
St John's † A2
Scalpay Terr A2
Shore St A2
Shuna Terr. A1
Sinclair Dr A2
Soroba Rd B2/C2
South Pier A2
Stevenson St B2
Tweedale St B2
Ulva Rd A2
Villa Rd. B3
War & Peace ▥ A1

Glamis Pl C1
Glasgow Rd B1
Glenearn Rd C2
Glover St B1/C1
Golf Course. A3
Gowrie St A3
Gray St B1
Graybank Rd A1
Greyfriars Burial Grnd B3
Hay St A1
High St B2/B3
Hotel B2
Inchaffray St A1
Industrial/Retail Park. .B1
Information Ctr ⅈ B2
Isla Rd A3
James St B3
Keir St A3
King Edward St B2
King James VI Golf
  Course C3
King St C2
Kings Pl C1
Kinnoull Aisle
  'Tower' ♦ B3
Kinnoull Causeway . . .B2
Kinnoull St. B2
Knowelea Pl C1
Knowelea Terr. C1
Ladeside Business Ctr. .A1
Leisure Pool B1
Leonard St B2
Lickley St A2
Lochie Brae A3
Long Causeway A1
Low St. A2
Main St A3
Marshall Pl C2
Melville St A2
Mill St A2
Milne St. B1
Murray Cres. C2
Murray St B2
Needless Rd C1
New Rd. B2
North Inch A2
North Methven St A2
Park Pl C2
Perth ≄ B2
Perth Bridge A3
Perth Business Park . .B1
Perth Museum &
  Art Gallery ▥ B3
Perth Station ≄ B2
Pickletullum Rd. B1
Pitheavlis Cres C1
Playhouse ♥ B2
Police Station ▣ A2
Pomarium St B1
Post Office ⓟ B2/C2
Princes St B3
Priory Pl C1
Queen St C2
Queen's Bridge. B3
Riggs Rd. B1
Riverside B3
Riverside Park A3
Rodney Park C2
Rose Terr A2
St Catherine's Rd . .A1/A2
St Catherines Ret Pk . .A2
St John St B3
St John's Kirk † B3
St John's Shopping Ctr B2
St Leonards Bridge . . .C2
St Ninians Cathedral †A2
Scott Monument. A2
Scott St B2
Sheriff Court. B3
Shore Rd C3
Skate Park C3
South Inch C3
South Inch Bsns Ctr. . .C3
South Inch Park C2
South Inch View C2
South Methven St B2
South St B3
South William St B3
Stables, The A1
Stanners, The A3
Stormont St A2
Strathmore St A3
Stuart Ave C1
Superstore B1/B2
Tay St B3
Union La. B2
Victoria St B2
Watergate B3
Wellshill Cemetery . . .A1
West Bridge St A3
West Mill St B2
Whitefriers Cres B1
Whitefriers St. B1
Wilson St C1
Windsor Terr. C1
Woodside Cres C1
York Pl B1
Young St C1

Charles St ... A3
Church St ... B2
Church Walk ... B2
Cobden Ave ... A1
Cobden St ... A1
Cowgate ... B2
Craig St ... A1
Crawthorne Rd ... A1
Cromwell Rd ... A1
Dickens Rd ... A3
Eastfield Rd ... A3
Eastgate ... A1
Fire Station ... A1
Fletton Ave ... C2
Frank Perkins
 Parkway ... C3
Geneva St ... A1
George St ... C1
Gladstone St ... A1
Glebe Rd ... B3
Gloucester Rd ... C1
Granby St ... B3
Grove St ... A1
Guildhall ... B2
Hadrians Ct ... C3
Hawksbill Way ... B2
Henry St ... A1
Hereward Cross (Sh) ... B2
Hereward Rd ... B2
Information Ctr ... B2
Jubilee St ... C2
Kent Rd ... B1
Key Theatre ... C2
Kirkwood Cl ... B1
Lea Gdns ... B1
Library ... A1
Lincoln Rd ... A2
London Rd ... A1
Long Causeway ... B2
Lower Bridge St ... B2
Magistrates Court ... C1
Manor House St ... A1
Mayor's Walk ... A1
Midland Rd ... A1
Monument St ... A1
Morris St ... A3
Mus & Art Gallery ... B2
Nene Valley Railway ... C1
New Rd ... A2
New Rd ... C1
Northminster ... A2
Old Customs House ... C2
Oundle Rd ... C1
Padholme Rd ... A3
Palmerston Rd ... C1
Park Rd ... A2
Passport Office ... A2
Peterborough Nene
 Valley ... C3
Peterborough Sta ... B2
Police Station ... B2
Post Office ... A3/B1/B2/B3/C1
Priestgate ... B2
Queen's Walk ... C2
Queensgate Centre ... B2
Railworld ... C3
Regional Swimming &
 Fitness Centre ... B3
River La ... B2
Rivergate Sh Ctr ... B2
Riverside Mead ... C1
Russell St ... A1
St John's ... A3
St John's St ... A3
St Marks St ... A2
St Peter's ... B2
St Peter's Rd ... B2
Saxon Rd ... A1
Spital Bridge ... A1
Stagshaw Dr ... C3
Star Rd ... A3
Thorpe Lea Rd ... B1
Thorpe Rd ... B1
Thorpe's Lea Rd ... B1
Tower St ... A2
Town Hall ... B2
Viersen Platz ... B2
Vineyard Rd ... B3
Wake Rd ... A3
Wellington St ... A3
Wentworth St ... B2
Westgate ... B2
Whalley St ... A3
Wharf Rd ... A3
Whitsed St ... A3
YMCA ... B1

Plymouth 341
Alma Rd ... A1
Anstis St ... A1
Armada Shop Ctr ... A2
Armada St ... A1
Armada Way ... B2
Arts Centre ... B2
Athenaeum ... B1
Athenaeum St ... C1
Barbican ... C3
Baring St ... A3
Bath St ... B1
Beaumont Park ... B3
Beaumont Rd ... B3
Black Friars Gin
 Distillery ... C2
Breton Side ... B3
Castle St ... C3
Cathedral (RC) ... A1
Cecil St ... A1
Central Park ... A1
Central Park Ave ... A1
Charles Church ... B3
Charles Cross ... B3
Charles St ... B2

Cliff Rd ... C1
Clifton Pl ... A3
Cobourg St ... A2
College of Art ... A2
Colborne Cl ... B3
Continental Ferry Port ... B1
Cornwall St ... B2
Crescent, The ... B1
Dale Rd ... A2
Deptford Pl ... A2
Derry Ave ... A1
Derry's Cross ... B2
Drake Circus ... B2
Drake Cir Sh Ctr ... B2
Eastlake St ... B2
Ebrington St ... B3
Elizabethan House ... B3
Elliot St ... C1
Endsleigh Pl ... A2
Exeter St ... B3
Fire Station ... A3
Fish Quay ... C3
Gibbons St ... A3
Glen Park Ave ... A1
Grand Pde ... C1
Great Western Rd ... C1
Greenbank Rd ... A3
Greenbank Terr ... A3
Guildhall ... B2
Hampton St ... B3
Harwell St ... A2
Hill Park Cr ... A2
Hoe Approach ... B2
Hoe Rd ... C2
Hoe, The ... C2
Hoegate St ... C2
Houndiscombe Rd ... A2
Information Ctr ... C3
James St ... A2
Kensington Rd ... A3
King St ... B1
Lambhay Hill ... C3
Leigham St ... C1
Library ... B2
Lipson Rd ... A3/B3
Lockyer St ... C2
Lockyers Quay ... C3
Madeira Rd ... C2
Marina ... C3
Market Ave ... B1
Martin St ... B1
Mayflower St ... B2
Mayflower Stone &
 Steps ... C3
Mayflower Visitor
 Centre ... C3
Merchant's House ... B2
Millbay Rd ... C1
National Marine
 Aquarium ... C3
Neswick St ... A1
New George St ... B2
New St ... C3
North Cross ... A2
North Hill ... A3
North Quay ... B2
North Rd East ... A2
North Rd West ... A1
North St ... B3
Notte St ... B2
Octagon, The ... B1
Octagon St ... B1
Pannier Market ... B1
Pennycomequick ... A2
Pier St ... C1
Plymouth Naval
 Memorial ... C2
Plymouth Pavilions ... B1
Plymouth Station ... A2
Police Station ... B3
Post Office ... B2
Princess St ... B2
Promenade, The ... C2
Prysten House ... B2
Queen Anne's Battery
 Seasports Centre ... C3
Radford Rd ... C2
Reel ... B2
Regent St ... B3
Rope Walk ... C3
Royal Citadel ... C3
Royal Pde ... B2
Royal Theatre ... B2
St Andrew's ... B2
St Andrew's Cross ... B2
St Andrew's St ... B2
St Lawrence Rd ... A2
Saltash Rd ... A1
Shopmobility ... B2
Smeaton's Tower ... C2
Southern Terr ... A3
Southside St ... C2
Stuart Rd ... A1
Sutherland Rd ... A2
Sutton Rd ... B3
Sydney St ... A1
Teats Hill Rd ... C3
Tothill Ave ... B3
Union St ... B1
Univ of Plymouth ... A2
Vauxhall St ... B2/3
Victoria Park ... A1
West Hoe Rd ... C1
Western Approach ... B1
Whittington St ... A1
Wyndham St ... A1
YMCA ... B2
YWCA ... C2

Poole 341
Ambulance Station ... A3
Baiater Gdns ... C2
Baiter Park ... C2
Ballard Cl ... C2
Ballard Rd ... C2
Bay Hog La ... B1
Bridge Approach ... C1
Bus Station ... B2
Castle St ... B2
Catalina Dr ... B3

Chapel La ... B2
Church St ... B1
Cinnamon La ... B1
Colborne Cl ... B3
Dear Hay La ... B2
Denmark La ... A3
Denmark Rd ... A3
Dolphin Ctr ... B2
East St ... B2
Elizabeth Rd ... A3
Emerson Rd ... B2
Ferry Rd ... C1
Ferry Terminal ... C1
Fire Station ... A2
Freightliner Terminal ... C1
Furnell Rd ... C2
Garland Rd ... A3
Green Rd ... B2
Heckford La ... A3
Heckford Rd ... A3
High St ... B2
High St North ... A3
Hill St ... A2
Holes Bay Rd ... A1
Hospital (A&E) ... A2
Information Ctr ... C2
Kingland Rd ... B3
Kingston Rd ... A3
Labrador Dr ... C3
Lagland St ... B2
Lander Cl ... B3
Lifeboat College, The ... B2
Lighthouse – Poole
 Centre for the Arts ... B3
Longfleet Rd ... A3
Maple Rd ... A3
Market Cl ... B2
Market St ... B2
Mount Pleasant Rd ... B3
New Harbour Rd ... C1
New Harbour Rd South ... C1
New Harbour Rd West ... C1
New Orchard ... B2
New Quay Rd ... C1
New St ... B2
Newfoundland Dr ... B2
North St ... B2
Old Lifeboat ... C1
Old Orchard ... B2
Parish Rd ... A2
Park Lake Rd ... B3
Parkstone Rd ... A3
Perry Gdns ... B2
Pitwines Cl ... B2
Police Station ... A2
Poole Central Library ... B2
Poole Lifting Bridge ... C1
Poole Park ... B2
Poole Station ... B2
Poole Museum ... C1
Post Office ... A2/B2
Quay, The ... C2
St John's Rd ... A3
St Margaret's Rd ... A2
St Mary's Maternity
 Unit ... A3
St Mary's Rd ... A3
Seldown Bridge ... B3
Seldown La ... B3
Seldown Rd ... B3
Serpentine La ... B2
Shaftesbury Rd ... A3
Skinner St ... B2
Slipway ... B1
Stanley Rd ... C2
Sterte Ave ... A2
Sterte Ave West ... A1
Sterte Cl ... A2
Sterte Esplanade ... A2
Sterte Rd ... A2
Strand St ... C2
Swimming Pool ... B3
Taverner Cl ... B3
Thames St ... B1
Towngate Bridge ... B2
Vallis Cl ... B3
Waldren Cl ... B3
West Quay ... C1
West Quay Rd ... B1
West St ... C1
West View Rd ... A2
Whatleigh Cl ... B2
Wimborne Rd ... A3

Portsmouth 341
Action Stations ... A1
Admiralty Rd ... A1
Alfred Rd ... A2
Anglesea Rd ... B2
Arundel St ... B3
Aspex ... C1
Bishop St ... A1
Broad St ... C1
Buckingham House ... C2
Burnaby Rd ... B2
Bus Station ... C1
Camber Dock ... C1
Cambridge Rd ... B2
Car Ferry to Isle of
 Wight ... C1
Cascades Sh Ctr ... A3
Castle Rd ... C3
City Museum & Art
 Gallery ... B2
Civic Offices ... A3
Clarence Pier ... C2
College St ... C3
Commercial Rd ... A3
Cottage Gr ... C3
Cross St ... B1
Cumberland St ... B1
Duisburg Way ... C2
Durham St ... A3
East St ... B1
Edinburgh Rd ... B2
Elm Gr ... C3
Emirates Spinnaker
 Tower ... C1
Great Southsea St ... C3

Green Rd ... B3
Greetham St ... B3
Grosvenor St ... B3
Groundlings ... A2
Grove Rd North ... B3
Grove Rd South ... C3
Guildhall ... B3
Guildhall Walk ... B3
Gunwharf Quays
 Designer Outlet ... B1
Gunwharf Rd ... B1
Hambrook St ... C2
Hampshire Terr ... B2
Hanover St ... A1
Hard, The ... B1
High St ... C2
HM Naval Base ... A1
HMS Nelson (Royal
 Naval Barracks) ... A1
HMS Victory ... A1
HMS Warrior ... B1
Hovercraft Terminal ... C2
Hyde Park Rd ... B3
Information Ctr ... A1/B3
Isambard Brunel Rd ... B3
Isle of Wight Car Ferry
 Terminal ... C1
Kent Rd ... C3
Kent St ... A2
King St ... B2
King's Rd ... C2
King's Terr ... C2
Lake Rd ... A3
Law Courts ... B3
Library ... B3
Long Curtain Rd ... C2
Market Way ... A3
Marmion Rd ... C3
Mary Rose Museum ... A1
Middle St ... B3
Millennium Prom ... B1/C1
Museum Rd ... B2
National Museum of the
 Royal Navy ... A1
Naval Recreation Gd ... C2
Nightingale Rd ... C2
Norfolk St ... B3
North St ... A1
Osborne Rd ... C3
Park Rd ... B2
Passenger Catamaran
 to Isle of Wight ... B1
Passenger Ferry to
 Gosport ... B1
Pelham Rd ... B3
Pembroke Gdns ... C2
Pier Rd ... C2
Point Battery ... C1
Police Station ... B3
Portsmouth & Southsea
 Station ... B3
Portsmouth Harbour
 Station ... B1
Portsmouth Historic
 Dockyard ... A1
Post Office ... A3/B1/B3
Queen St ... A1
Queen's Cr ... C3
Round Tower ... C1
Royal Garrison
 Church ... C2
St Edward's Rd ... C3
St George's Rd ... B2
St George's Sq ... B2
St George's Way ... B2
St James's Rd ... B3
St James's St ... C2
St John's Cath (RC) ... B3
St Thomas's Cath ... C2
St Thomas's St ... C2
Shopmobility ... A3/B1
Somers Rd ... B3
Southsea Common ... C2
Southsea Terr ... C2
Square Tower ... C1
Station St ... A3
Town Fortifications ... C1
Unicorn Rd ... A2
United Services
 Recreation Ground ... B2
University of
 Portsmouth ... A2/B2
University of Portsmouth
 – College of Art, Design
 & Media ... A3
Upper Arundel St ... A3
Victoria Ave ... C2
Victoria Park ... A2
Victory Gate ... A1
Vue ... B1
Warblington St ... B1
Western Pde ... C2
White Hart Rd ... C1
Winston Churchill Ave ... B3

Preston 342
Adelphi St ... A2
Anchor Ct ... B3
Aqueduct St ... A1
Ardee Rd ... C1
Arthur St ... A1
Ashton St ... A1
Avenham La ... B2
Avenham Park ... C3
Avenham Rd ... B3
Bairstow St ... B2
Balderstone Rd ... C1
Beamont Dr ... A1
Beech St South ... C1
Bird St ... C1
Bow La ... B2
Brierfield Rd ... A1
Broadgate ... C2
Brook St ... A2
Bus Station ... A3
Butler St ... B2
Cannon St ... B2
Carlton St ... A1

Chaddock St ... B3
Channel Way ... B1
Chapel St ... B2
Christ Church St ... B2
Christian Rd ... A1
Cold Bath St ... C1
Coleman Ct ... C1
Connaught Rd ... C2
Corn Exchange ... B2
Corporation St ... A2/B2
County Hall ... B2
Cricket Ground ... A1
Croft St ... A1
Cross St ... B3
Crown Court ... A2
Crown St ... A2
East Cliff ... C3
East Cliff Rd ... B3
Edward St ... A3
Elizabeth St ... A3
Euston St ... A3
Fishergate ... B2/B3
Fishergate Hill ... B2
Fishergate
 Shopping Centre ... B2
Fitzroy St ... B1
Fleetwood St ... A1
Friargate ... A2
Fylde Rd ... A1/A2
Gerrard St ... B2
Glover's Ct ... B3
Good St ... A2
Grafton St ... C2
Great George St ... A3
Great Shaw St ... A3
Greenbank St ... A3
Guild Way ... B1
Guild Hall and
 Charter ... B3
Guildhall St ... B3
Harrington St ... A2
Harris Museum ... B3
Hartington Rd ... C3
Hasset Cl ... C2
Heatley St ... A2
Hind St ... C2
Information Ctr ... B3
Kilruddery Rd ... C1
Lancashire Archives ... B2
Lancaster Rd ... A3/B3
Latham St ... A3
Lauderdale St ... C2
Lawson St ... A3
Leighton St ... A1
Leyland Rd ... C1
Library ... A1
Library ... A3
Liverpool Rd ... C1
Lodge St ... A2
Lune St ... B2
Magistrate's Court ... A3
Main Sprit West ... B3
Maresfield Rd ... C1
Market St West ... A3
Market St ... B1/B2
Maudland Bank ... A1
Maudland Rd ... A1
Meadow Ct ... C2
Meath Rd ... C1
Mill Hill ... A3
Miller Arcade ... B3
Miller St ... A3
Moor La ... A2
Mount St ... B3
North Rd ... A3
North Rd ... C1
North St ... A3
Northcote Rd ... B1
Old Milestones ... B1
Old Tram Rd ... C3
Pedder St ... A1/A2
Peel St ... A2
Penwortham Bridge ... C2
Penwortham New
 Bridge ... C1
Pitt St ... A2
Playhouse ... A3
Police Station ... A3
Port Way ... B1
Preston Station ... B2
Retail Park ... A2
Ribble Bank St ... B2
Ribble Viaduct ... C2
Ribblesdale Pl ... B3
Ringway ... A3
River Parade ... B1
Riverside ... B1
St George's Sh Ctr ... B2
St Georges ... B2
St Johns ... B3
St Johns Shopping Ctr ... A3
St Mark's St ... A1
St Walburges Rd ... A1
Salisbury Rd ... C1
Sessions House ... B2
Snow Hill ... A3
South End ... C2
South Meadow La ... C1
Spa Rd ... A1
Sports Ground ... C1
Strand Rd ... B1
Syke St ... A3
Talbot Rd ... C1
Taylor St ... C1
Tithebarn St ... A3
Town Hall ... B2
Tulketh Brow ... A1
University of
 Central Lancashire ... A2
Valley Rd ... C1
Victoria St ... A1
Walker St ... A3
Walton's Parade ... B3
Warwick St ... A3
Wellfield Bsns Park ... A1
Wellfield Rd ... A1
Wellington St ... A1
West Cliff ... B2
West Strand ... B1
Winckley Rd ... C1

Winckley Square ... B3
Zinzan St ... B2

Reading 342
Abbey Ruins ... B2
Abbey Sq ... B2
Abbot's Walk ... B2
Acacia Rd ... C2
Addington Rd ... C3
Addison Rd ... A1
Allcroft Rd ... C3
Alpine St ... C2
Baker St ... B1
Berkeley Ave ... C1
Bridge St ... B1
Brigham Rd ... A1
Broad St ... B2
Broad Street Mall ... B2
Carey St ... B1
Castle Hill ... C1
Castle St ... B1
Causeway, The ... A3
Caversham Rd ... A1
Christchurch
 Playing Fields ... A2
Civic Offices ... B2
Coley Hill ... C1
Coley Pl ... C2
Craven Rd ... C3
Crown St ... C2
De Montfort Rd ... A1
Denmark Rd ... C3
Duke St ... B2
East St ... C2
Edgehill St ... C2
Eldon Rd ... C3
Eldon Terr ... C3
Elgar Rd ... C1
Erleigh Rd ... C3
Field Rd ... C1
Fire Station ... B3
Fobney St ... C2
Forbury Gdns ... B2
Forbury Rd ... B2
Forbury Retail Park ... B2
Francis St ... C1
Friar St ... B1
Garrard St ... B1
Gas Works Rd ... B3
George St ... A1
Great Knollys St ... B1
Greyfriars ... B1
Grove, The ... B2
Gun St ... B1
Henry St ... C1
Hexagon Theatre,
 The ... B1
Hill's Meadow ... A2
Howard St ... C1
Information Ctr ... B1
Inner Distribution Rd ... B1
Katesgrove La ... C1
Kenavon Dr ... B3
Kendrick Rd ... C2
King's Meadow
 Recreation Ground ... A3
King's Rd ... B2
Library ... B2
London Rd ... C3
London St ... B2
Lynmouth Rd ... A1
Magistrate's Court ... B1
Market Pl ... B2
Mill La ... C2
Mill Rd ... A3
Minster St ... B1
Morgan Rd ... C3
Mount Pleasant ... C2
Museum of English
 Rural Life ... C3
Napier Rd ... A2
Newark St ... C2
Newport Rd ... A1
Old Reading
 University ... C3
Oracle Shopping
 Centre, The ... B1
Orts Rd ... B3
Pell St ... C2
Queen Victoria St ... B2
Queen's Rd ... A2
Queen's Rd ... B2
Randolph Rd ... A1
Reading Bridge ... A2
Reading Station ... A1
Redlands Rd ... C3
Renaissance Hotel ... A1
Riverside
 Museum ... A2
Rose Kiln La ... C1
Royal Berks
 Hospital (A&E) ... C3
St Giles ... C2
St Laurence ... B2
St Mary's ... B1
St Mary's Butts ... B1
St Saviour's Rd ... C1
Send Rd ... A3
Sherman Rd ... C2
Sidmouth St ... B2
Silver St ... C2
South St ... B2
Southampton St ... C2
Station Hill ... A1
Station Rd ... B1
Superstore ... A2
Swansea Rd ... A1
Technical College ... A3
Valpy St ... B2
Vastern Rd ... A1
Vue ... B2
Waldeck St ... C2
Watlington St ... B3
West St ... B1
Whitby Dr ... C3
Wolseley St ... C1

York Rd ... A1
Zinzan St ... B2

St Andrews 342
Abbey St ... B3
Abbey Walk ... B3
Abbotsford Cres ... A3
Albany Pk ... C3
Allan Robertson Dr ... C1
Ambulance Station ... C1
Anstruther Rd ... C1
Argyle St ... B1
Argyll Business Park ... C1
Auld Burn Rd ... B2
Bassaguard Ind Est ... B1
Bell St ... B2
Blackfriars Chapel
 (Ruins) ... B2
Boase Ave ... B2
Braid Cres ... C3
Brewster Pl ... C3
Bridge St ... B1
British Golf Mus ... A1
Broomfaulds Ave ... C1
Bruce Embankment ... A1
Bruce St ... C2
Bus Station ... A1
Byre ... B2
Canongate ... C1
Cathedral and Priory
 (Ruins) ... A3
Cemetery ... A3
Chamberlain St ... C1
Church St ... B2
Churchill Cres ... C2
City Rd ... A1
Claybraes ... C1
Cockshaugh Public Pk ... B1
Cosmos Com Centre ... A3
Council Office ... A2
Crawford Gdns ... C1
Doubledykes Rd ... B1
Drumcarrow Rd ... C1
East Sands ... B3
East Scores ... A3
Fire Station ... C1
Forrest St ... C1
Fraser Ave ... C1
Freddie Tait St ... C2
Gateway Centre ... A1
Glebe Rd ... B3
Golf Pl ... A1
Grange Rd ... C2
Greenside Pl ... B2
Greyfriars Gdns ... B2
Hamilton Ave ... C2
Hepburn Gdns ... B1
Holy Trinity ... B2
Horseleys Park ... C1
Information Ctr ... B2
Irvine Cres ... C3
James Robb Ave ... C1
James St ... B1
John Knox Rd ... C2
Kennedy Gdns ... B1
Kilrymont Cl ... C3
Kilrymont Pl ... C3
Kilrymont Rd ... C3
Kinburn Park ... B1
Kinkell Terr ... C3
Kinnesburn Rd ... B2
Ladebanks Walk ... B2
Lady Buchan's Cave ... A3
Lamberton Pl ... C3
Lamond Dr ... C2
Langlands Rd ... C2
Largo Rd ... C1
Learmonth Pl ... C2
Library ... B2
Links Clubhouse ... A1
Links, The ... A2
Livingstone Cres ... B2
Long Rocks ... A2
Madras College ... B2
Market St ... B2
Martyr's Monument ... A1
Murray Pk ... C1
Murray Pl ... B2
Mus of the Univ of St
 Andrews (MUSA) ... A1
Nelson St ... C2
New Course, The ... A1
New Picture House ... B2
North Castle St ... B3
North St ... B2
Old Course, The ... A1
Old Station Rd ... B1
Pends, The ... B3
Pilmour Links ... A1
Pipeland Rd ... C2/C3
Police Station ... A2/C1
Post Office ... C2
Preservation Trust ... B2
Priestden Pk ... C3
Priestden Pl ... C3
Priestden Rd ... C3
Queen's Gdns ... B2
Queen's Terr ... B2
Roundhill Rd ... C3
Royal & Ancient
 Golf Club ... A1
St Andrews ... B3
St Andrews
 Aquarium ... A2
St Andrews Botanic
 Garden ... C2
St Andrews Castle
 (Ruins) & Visitor
 Centre ... A3
St Leonard's School ... B3
St Mary's College ... B2
St Nicholas St ... C3
St Rules Tower ... B3
St Salvator's College ... B2
Sandyford Cres ... C2
Sandyhill Rd ... C2
Scooniehill Rd ... C3
Scores, The ... A2

Shields Ave ... C3
Shoolbraids ... C3
Shore, The ... B3
Sloan St ... B2
South St ... B2
Spottiswoode Gdns ... C1
Station Rd ... B1
Swilcen Bridge ... A1
Tom Morris Dr ... C1
Tom Stewart La ... C1
Town Hall ... B2
Union St ... B2
University Chapel ... A1
University Library ... B2
Univ of St Andrews ... A1
Viaduct Walk ... B1
War Memorial ... A2
Wardlaw Gdns ... B1
Warrack St ... C2
Watson Ave ... B2
West Port ... B2
West Sands ... A1
Westview ... B2
Windmill Rd ... B2
Winram Pl ... C2
Wishart Gdns ... C2
Woodburn Pk ... B3
Woodburn Pl ... B3
Woodburn Terr ... B3
Younger Hall ... A2

Salisbury 342
Albany Rd ... A2
Arts Centre ... A1
Ashley Rd ... A1
Avon Approach ... A2
Ayleswade Rd ... C2
Bedwin St ... A2
Belle Vue ... C1
Bishop's Palace ... C2
Bishops Walk ... B2
Blue Boar Row ... B2
Bourne Ave ... A3
Bourne Hill ... A2
Britford La ... C2
Broad Walk ... C1
Brown St ... B2
Bus Station ... B2
Castle St ... A2
Catherine St ... B2
Chapter House ... B2
Church House ... A2
Churchfields Rd ... B1
Churchill Way East ... A3
Churchill Way North ... A3
Churchill Way South ... C2
Churchill Way West ... A1
City Hall ... B1
Close Wall ... C2
Coldharbour La ... A1
College St ... A3
Council Offices ... A3
Court ... A1
Crane Bridge Rd ... B1
Crane St ... B2
Cricket Ground ... C1
Culver St South ... B2
De Vaux Pl ... C2
Devizes Rd ... A1
Dews Rd ... B1
Elm Grove ... B3
Elm Grove Rd ... A3
Endless St ... A2
Estcourt Rd ... A3
Exeter St ... C2
Fairview Rd ... A3
Fire Station ... C1
Fisherton St ... B1
Folkestone Rd ... C1
Fowlers Hill ... B3
Fowlers Rd ... B3
Friary Estate ... C3
Friary La ... C2
Friary, The ... C2
Gas La ... B1
Gigant St ... B2
Greencroft ... B3
Greencroft St ... A3
Guildhall ... B2
Hall of John Halle ... B2
Hamilton Rd ... A1
Harnham Mill ... C1
Harnham Rd ... C1/C2
High St ... B2
Hospital ... A1
Ho of John A'Port ... B2
Information Ctr ... B2
Kelsey Rd ... A3
King's Rd ... A2
Laverstock Rd ... B3
Library ... B2
London Rd ... A3
Lower St ... C1
Maltings, The ... B1
Manor Rd ... A3
Marsh La ... A1
Medieval Hall ... C2
Milford Hill ... B3
Milford St ... B2
Mill Rd ... B1
Millstream Approach ... A2
Mompesson House
 (NT) ... B2
New Bridge Rd ... C2
New Canal ... B2
New Harnham Rd ... C2
New St ... B2
North Canonry ... C2
North Gate ... B2
North Walk ... B2
Old Blandford Rd ... C1
Old Deanery ... B2
Old George Hall ... B2
Park St ... B3
Parsonage Green ... C1
Playhouse Theatre ... B1
Post Office ... A2/B2/C2
Poultry Cross ... B2
Queen Elizabeth Gdns ... B1

Queen's Rd ... A3
Rampart Rd ... B3
St Ann St ... B2
St Ann's Gate ... B2
St Marks Rd ... A3
St Martins ... B3
St Mary's Cathedral ... B2
St Nicholas Hospital ... C2
St Paul's ... A1
St Paul's Rd ... A1
St Thomas ... B2
Salisbury & South
 Wiltshire Museum ... B2
Salisbury Station ... A1
Salt La ... A3
Saxon Rd ... C1
Scots La ... A2
Shady Bower ... B3
South Canonry ... C2
South Gate ... C2
Southampton Rd ... B2
Spire View ... A1
Sports Ground ... C3
Tollgate Rd ... B3
Town Path ... B1
Wain-a-Long Rd ... A3
Wardrobe, The ... B2
Wessex Rd ... A3
West Walk ... C2
Wilton Rd ... A1
Wiltshire College ... A1
Winchester St ... B2
Windsor Rd ... A1
Winston Churchill
 Gdns ... C3
Wyndham Rd ... A2
YHA ... B3
York Rd ... A1

Scarborough 342
Aberdeen Walk ... B2
Albert Rd ... A2
Albion Rd ... C2
Auborough St ... B2
Balmoral Ctr ... C2
Belle Vue St ... C1
Belmont Rd ... C2
Blenheim Terrace ... A2
Brunswick Shop Ctr ... B2
Castle Dykes ... B3
Castle Hill ... A3
Castle Rd ... A2
Castle Walls ... A3
Castlegate ... B3
Cemetery ... C1
Central Tramway ... B2
Coach Park ... A2
Columbus Ravine ... A1
Court ... B1
Crescent, The ... B2
Cricket Ground ... C1
Cross St ... B2
Crown Terr ... B2
Dean Rd ... A1
Devonshire Dr ... A1
East Harbour ... B3
East Pier ... B3
Eastborough ... B2
Elmville Ave ... A1
Esplanade ... C2
Falconers Rd ... B2
Falsgrave Rd ... C1
Fire Station ... B1
Foreshore Rd ... B3
Friargate ... B2
Gladstone Rd ... B1
Gladstone St ... B1
Hollywood Plaza ... A1
Holms, The ... A3
Hoxton Rd ... A2
King St ... B2
Library ... B2
Lifeboat Station ... B3
Londesborough Rd ... C1
Longwestgate ... B3
Marine Dr ... A3
Luna Park ... B3
Miniature Railway ... A1
Nelson St ... B1
Newborough ... B2
Nicolas St ... B2
North Marine Rd ... A1
North St ... B2
Northway ... B1
Old Harbour ... B3
Olympia Leisure ... B2
Peasholm Park ... A1
Peasholm Rd ... A1
Police Station ... B1
Post Office ... B2
Princess St ... B3
Prospect Rd ... C1
Queen St ... B2
Queen's Parade ... A2
Queen's Tower
 (Remains) ... A3
Ramshill Rd ... C2
Roman Signal Sta ... A3
Roscoe St ... C1
Rotunda Museum ... C2
Royal Albert Dr ... A2
Royal Albert Park ... A2
St Martin-on-
 the-Hill ... C2
St Martin's Ave ... C2
St Mary's ... B3
St Thomas St ... B2
Sandside ... B3
Scarborough Station ... C1
Scarborough
 Art Gallery ... C2
Scarborough
 Bowls Centre ... A1
Scarborough Castle ... A3
Shopmobility ... B2
Somerset Terr ... C2
South Cliff Lift ... C2
Spa Theatre, The ... C2
Spa, The ... C2

358 Sheffield • Shrewsbury • Southampton • Southend-on-Sea • Stirling • Stoke • Stratford-upon-Avon

Stephen Joseph Theatre . . . C1
Tennyson Ave . . . B1
Tollergate . . . B2
Town Hall . . . B2
Trafalgar Rd . . . B1
Trafalgar Square . . . A1
Trafalgar St West . . . B1
Valley Bridge Parade . C2
Valley Rd . . . C1
Vernon Rd . . . C2
Victoria Park Mount . A1
Victoria Rd . . . B1
West Pier . . . B3
Westborough . . . C1
Westover Rd . . . C1
Westwood . . . C1
Woodall Ave . . . A1
YMCA Theatre . . . B2
York Pl . . . B2
Yorkshire Coast College (Westwood Campus) . C1

Sheffield 342

Addy Dr . . . A2
Addy St . . . A2
Adelphi St . . . A3
Albert Terrace Rd . . . A3
Albion St . . . A2
Aldred Rd . . . A1
Allen St . . . A4
Alma St . . . A4
Angel St . . . B5
Arundel Gate . . . B5
Arundel St . . . C4
Ashberry Rd . . . A2
Ashdell Rd . . . C1
Ashgate Rd . . . C1
Athletics Centre . . . B2
Attercliffe Rd . . . A6
Bailey St . . . B4
Ball St . . . A4
Balm Green . . . B4
Bank St . . . B4
Barber Rd . . . A2
Bard St . . . B5
Barker's Pool . . . B4
Bates St . . . A1
Beech Hill Rd . . . C1
Beet St . . . B3
Bellefield St . . . A3
Bernard Rd . . . A6
Bernard St . . . B6
Birkendale . . . A2
Birkendale Rd . . . A2
Birkendale View . . . A1
Bishop St . . . C4
Blackwell Pl . . . B6
Blake St . . . A2
Blonk St . . . A5
Bolsover St . . . B2
Botanical Gdns . . . C1
Bower Rd . . . A1
Bradley St . . . A1
Bramall La . . . C4
Bramwell St . . . A3
Bridge St . . . A4/A5
Brighton Terrace Rd . A1
Broad La . . . B3
Broad St . . . B6
Brocco St . . . A3
Brook Hill . . . B3
Broomfield Rd . . . C1
Broomgrove Rd . . . C2
Broomhall Pl . . . C3
Broomhall Rd . . . C2
Broomhall St . . . C3
Broomspring La . . . C2
Brown St . . . C5
Brunswick St . . . B3
Burgess St . . . B4
Burlington St . . . A2
Burns Rd . . . A2
Cadman St . . . A6
Cambridge St . . . B4
Campo La . . . B4
Carver St . . . B4
Castle Square . . . B5
Castlegate . . . A5
Cathedral . . . B4
Cathedral (RC) . . . B4
Cavendish St . . . B3
Charles St . . . C4
Charter Row . . . C4
Children's Hospital . B2
Church St . . . B4
City Hall . . . B4
City Hall . . . B4
City Rd . . . C6
Claremont Cr . . . B2
Claremont Pl . . . B2
Clarke St . . . C3
Clarkegrove Rd . . . C2
Clarkehouse Rd . . . C1
Clarkson St . . . B2
Cobden View Rd . . . A1
Collegiate Cr . . . C2
Commercial St . . . B5
Commonside . . . A1
Conduit Rd . . . B1
Cornish St . . . A3
Corporation St . . . A4
Court . . . B4
Cricket Inn Rd . . . B6
Cromwell St . . . A1
Crookes Rd . . . B1
Crookes Valley Park . . B2
Crookes Valley Rd . . . B2
Crookesmoor Rd . . . A2
Crown Court . . . A4
Crucible Theatre . . . B5
Cutlers' Hall . . . B4
Cutlers Gate . . . A6
Daniel Hill . . . A2
Dental Hospital . . . B2
Derek Dooley Way . . . A5
Devonshire Green . . . B3
Devonshire St . . . B3
Division St . . . B4
Dorset St . . . C2
Dover St . . . A3
Duchess Rd . . . C5
Duke St . . . B5
Duncombe St . . . A1
Durham Rd . . . B2
Earl St . . . C4
Earl Way . . . C4
Ecclesall Rd . . . C3
Edward St . . . B3
Effingham Rd . . . A6
Effingham St . . . A6
Egerton St . . . C3
Eldon St . . . B3
Elmore Rd . . . B1
Exchange St . . . B5
Eyre St . . . C4
Fargate . . . B4
Farm Rd . . . C5
Fawcett St . . . A3
Filey St . . . B3
Fir St . . . A1
Fire Station . . . C4
Fitzalan Sq/ Ponds Forge . . . B5
Fitzwater Rd . . . C6
Fitzwilliam Gate . . . C4
Fitzwilliam St . . . B3
Flat St . . . B5
Foley St . . . A6
Foundry Climbing Ctr . A4
Fulton Rd . . . A1
Furnace Hill . . . A4
Furnival Rd . . . A5
Furnival Sq . . . C4
Furnival St . . . C4
Garden St . . . B3
Gell St . . . B3
Gibraltar St . . . A4
Glebe Rd . . . B1
Glencoe Rd . . . C6
Glossop Rd . . . B2/B3/C1
Gloucester St . . . C2
Government Offices . . C4
Granville Rd . . . C6
Granville Rd / The Sheffield College . . . C5
Graves Gallery . . . B5
Greave Rd . . . B3
Green La . . . A4
Hadfield St . . . A1
Hanover St . . . C3
Hanover Way . . . C3
Harcourt Rd . . . B1
Harmer La . . . B5
Havelock St . . . C2
Hawley St . . . B4
Haymarket . . . B5
Headford St . . . C3
Heavygate Rd . . . A1
Henry St . . . A3
High St . . . B4
Hodgson St . . . C3
Holberry Gdns . . . C2
Hollis Croft . . . B4
Holly St . . . B4
Hounsfield Rd . . . B3
Howard Rd . . . A1
Hoyle St . . . A3
Hyde Park . . . A6
Infirmary Rd . . . A3
Infirmary Rd . . . A3
Information Ctr . . . B4
Jericho St . . . A3
Johnson St . . . A5
Kelham Island Industrial Museum . . . A4
Lawson Rd . . . C1
Leadmill Rd . . . C5
Leadmill St . . . C5
Leadmill, The . . . C5
Leamington St . . . A1
Leavy Rd . . . B3
Lee Croft . . . B4
Leopold St . . . B4
Leveson St . . . A6
Library . . . A2/B5/C1
Light, The . . . C4
Lyceum Theatre . . . B5
Malinda St . . . A3
Maltravers St . . . A5
Manor Oaks Rd . . . B6
Mappin St . . . B3
Marlborough Rd . . . B1
Mary St . . . C4
Matilda St . . . C4
Matlock Rd . . . A1
Meadow St . . . A3
Melbourn Rd . . . A1
Melbourne Ave . . . C1
Millennium Galleries . . . B5
Milton St . . . C3
Mitchell St . . . B3
Mona Ave . . . A1
Mona Rd . . . A1
Montgomery Terr Rd . A3
Montgomery Theatre . . . B4
Monument Grounds . . C6
Moor Oaks Rd . . . B1
Moor, The . . . C4
Moor, The . . . C4
Moor Market . . . C4
Moore St . . . C3
Mowbray St . . . A4
Mushroom La . . . B2
National Emergency Service . . . A4
Netherthorpe Rd . . . B3
Netherthorpe Rd . . . B3
Newbould La . . . C1
Nile St . . . C1
Norfolk Park Rd . . . C6
Norfolk Rd . . . C6
Norfolk St . . . B4
North Church St . . . B4
Northfield Rd . . . A1
Northumberland Rd . . B1
Nursery St . . . A5
O2 Academy . . . B5
Oakholme Rd . . . C1
Octagon . . . B2
Odeon . . . B5
Old St . . . B6
Orchard Square . . . B4
Orch Square Shop Ctr . B4
Oxford St . . . A2
Paradise St . . . B4
Park La . . . C2
Park Sq . . . B5
Parker's Rd . . . B1
Pearson Building (Univ) . . . C2
Penistone Rd . . . A3
Pinstone St . . . B4
Pitt St . . . B3
Police Station . . . B5
Pond Hill . . . B5
Pond St . . . B5
Ponds Forge Int Sports Ctr . . . B5
Portobello St . . . B3
Post Office . . . A2/B3/B4/B5/C1/C3/C6
Powell St . . . A2
Queen St . . . B4
Queen's Rd . . . C5
Ramsey Rd . . . B1
Red Hill . . . B3
Redcar Rd . . . B1
Regent St . . . B3
Rockingham St . . . B4
Roebuck Rd . . . A2
Royal Hallamshire Hospital . . . C2
Russell St . . . A4
Rutland Park . . . C1
St George's Cl . . . B3
St Mary's Gate . . . C3
St Mary's Rd . . . C4/C5
St Peter & St Paul Cathedral . . . B4
St Philip's Rd . . . A3
Savile St . . . A5
School Rd . . . B1
Scotland St . . . A4
Severn Rd . . . B1
Shalesmoor . . . A4
Shalesmoor . . . A3
Sheaf St . . . B5
Sheffield Hallam Univ . B5
Sheffield Ice Sports Ctr – Skate Central . . . C5
Sheffield Interchange . B5
Sheffield Parkway . . . A6
Sheffield Station . . . C5
Sheffield Sta/Sheffield Hallam Univ . . . B5
Sheffield University . . B2
Shepherd St . . . A3
Shipton St . . . A2
Shopmobility . . . B3
Shoreham St . . . C4
Showroom . . . C5
Shrewsbury Rd . . . C5
Sidney St . . . C4
Site Gallery . . . C5
Slinn St . . . A1
Smithfield . . . A4
Snig Hill . . . A5
Snow La . . . A4
Solly St . . . B3
South La . . . C4
South Street Park . . . B5
Southbourne Rd . . . C1
Spital Hill . . . A5
Spital St . . . A5
Spring Hill . . . B1
Spring Hill Rd . . . B1
Springvale Rd . . . A1
Stafford Rd . . . C6
Stafford St . . . B6
Suffolk Rd . . . C5
Summer St . . . B2
Sunny Bank . . . C3
Superstore . . . A3/C3
Surrey St . . . B4
Sussex St . . . A6
Sutton St . . . B3
Sydney Rd . . . A2
Sylvester St . . . C4
Talbot St . . . B5
Tapton Hall Conference & Banqueting Ctr . . . B1
Taptonville Rd . . . B1
Tenter St . . . B4
Town Hall . . . B4
Townend St . . . A1
Townhead St . . . B4
Trafalgar St . . . B4
Tree Root Walk . . . B2
Trinity St . . . A4
Trippet La . . . B4
Turner Mus of Glass . B3
Union St . . . B4
Univ Drama Studio . . B2
Univ of Sheffield . . . B3
Upper Allen St . . . A3
Upper Hanover St . . . B3
Upperthorpe Rd . . . A2/A3
Verdon St . . . A5
Victoria Rd . . . C2
Victoria St . . . B3
Waingate . . . B5
Watery St . . . A3
Watson Rd . . . C1
Wellesley Rd . . . B2
Wellington St . . . C3
West Bar . . . A4
West Bar Green . . . A4
West One Plaza . . . B3
West St . . . B3
West St . . . B4
Westbourne Rd . . . C1
Western Bank . . . B2
Western Rd . . . A1
Weston Park . . . B2
Weston Park Hosp . . . B2
Weston Park Mus . . . B2
Weston St . . . B2
Wharncliffe Rd . . . C3
Whitham Rd . . . B1
Wicker . . . A5
Wilkinson St . . . B2
William St . . . C3
Winter Garden . . . B4
Winter St . . . B2
York St . . . B4
Yorkshire Artspace . . C5
Young St . . . C4

Shrewsbury 342

Abbey Church . . . B3
Abbey Foregate . . . B3
Abbey Lawn Bsns Park . B3
Abbots House . . . B2
Agricultural Show Gd . A1
Albert St . . . A2
Alma St . . . B1
Ashley St . . . A3
Ashton Rd . . . C1
Avondale Dr . . . A3
Bage Way . . . C3
Barker St . . . B1
Beacall's La . . . A2
Beeches La . . . C2
Beehive La . . . C1
Belle Vue Gdns . . . C2
Belle Vue Rd . . . C2
Belmont Bank . . . C1
Berwick Ave . . . A1
Berwick Rd . . . A1
Betton St . . . C2
Bishop St . . . B3
Bradford St . . . B3
Bridge St . . . B1
Burton St . . . A3
Bus Station . . . B2
Butcher Row . . . B2
Butler Rd . . . C1
Bynner St . . . C2
Canon St . . . B3
Canonbury . . . C1
Castle Bsns Park, The . A2
Castle Foregate . . . A2
Castle Gates . . . B2
Castle Museum . . . B2
Castle St . . . B2
Cathedral (RC) . . . C1
Chester St . . . A2
Cineworld . . . C3
Claremont Bank . . . B1
Claremont Hill . . . B1
Cleveland St . . . B3
Coleham Head . . . B2
Coleham Pumping Station . . . C2
College Hill . . . B1
Corporation La . . . A1
Coton Cres . . . A1
Coton Hill . . . A2
Coton Mount . . . A1
Crescent La . . . C1
Crewe St . . . A2
Cross Hill . . . B1
Dana, The . . . B2
Darwin Centre . . . B2
Dingle, The . . . B1
Dogpole . . . B2
Draper's Hall . . . B2
English Bridge . . . B2
Fish St . . . B2
Frankwell . . . B1
Gateway Ctr, The . . . A2
Gravel Hill La . . . A1
Greyfriars Rd . . . C2
Guildhall . . . B1
Hampton Rd . . . A3
Haycock Way . . . C3
High St . . . B1
Hills La . . . B1
Holywell St . . . B3
Hunter St . . . A1
Information Ctr . . . B1
Ireland's Mansion & Bear Steps . . . B1
John St . . . A3
Kennedy Rd . . . C1
King St . . . B3
Kingsland Bridge . . . C1
Kingsland Bridge (toll) . . . C1
Kingsland Rd . . . C1
Library . . . B2
Lime St . . . C2
Longden Coleham . . . C2
Longden Rd . . . C1
Longner St . . . B1
Luciefelde Rd . . . C1
Mardol . . . B1
Marine Terr . . . C2
Market . . . B1
Monkmoor Rd . . . B3
Moreton Cr . . . C2
Mount St . . . A1
New Park Cl . . . A3
New Park Rd . . . A2
New Park St . . . A3
North St . . . A2
Oakley St . . . C1
Old Coleham . . . C2
Old Market Hall . . . B1
Old Potts Way . . . C3
Parade Centre . . . B2
Police Station . . . B1
Post Office . . . A2/B1/B2/B3
Pride Hill . . . B1
Pride Hill Centre . . . B1
Priory Rd . . . B1
Pritchard Way . . . C3
Quarry, The . . . B1
Queen St . . . A3
Raby Cr . . . C2
Rad Brook . . . C1
Rea Brook . . . C3
Riverside . . . B1
Roundhill La . . . A1
St Alkmund's . . . B2
St Chad's . . . B1
St Chad's Terr . . . B1
St John's Hill . . . B1
St Julians Friars . . . C2
St Mary's . . . B2
St Mary's St . . . B2
Salters La . . . C2
Scott St . . . C3
Severn Bank . . . A3
Severn St . . . A2
Shrewsbury . . . B2
Shrewsbury High School for Girls . . . C1
Shrewsbury Mus & Art Gall . . . B1
Shrewsbury School . . . C1
Shropshire Wildlife Trust . . . B3
Smithfield Rd . . . B1
South Hermitage . . . C1
Square, The . . . B1
Swan Hill . . . B1
Sydney Ave . . . A3
Tankerville St . . . B3
Tilbrook Dr . . . A3
Town Walls . . . C1
Trinity St . . . C2
Underdale Rd . . . B3
Victoria Ave . . . B1
Victoria Quay . . . B1
Victoria St . . . B2
Welsh Bridge . . . B1
Whitehall St . . . B3
Wood St . . . A2
Wyle Cop . . . B2

Southampton 342

Above Bar St . . . A2
Albert Rd North . . . B3
Albert Rd South . . . C3
Andersons Rd . . . B3
Argyle Rd . . . A2
Arundel Tower . . . B1
Bargate, The . . . B2
BBC Regional Centre . A1
Bedford Pl . . . A1
Belvidere Rd . . . A3
Bernard St . . . C2
Blechynden Terr . . . A1
Brinton's Rd . . . A2
Britannia Rd . . . A3
Briton St . . . C2
Brunswick Pl . . . A2
Bugle St . . . C1
Canute Rd . . . C3
Castle Way . . . C2
Catchcold Tower . . . B1
Central Bridge . . . C3
Central Rd . . . C2
Channel Way . . . C3
Chapel Rd . . . B3
City Art Gallery . . . A1
City College . . . B3
City Cruise Terminal . C1
Civic Centre . . . A1
Civic Centre Rd . . . A1
Coach Station . . . B1
Commercial Rd . . . A1
Cumberland Pl . . . A1
Cunard Rd . . . C2
Derby Rd . . . A3
Devonshire Rd . . . A1
Dock Gate 4 . . . C2
Dock Gate 8 . . . B1
East Park (Andrews Park) . . . A2
East Park Terr . . . A2
East St . . . B2
Endle St . . . B3
European Way . . . C2
Fire Station . . . A2
Floating Bridge Rd . . C3
God's House Tower . C2
Golden Gr . . . A3
Graham Rd . . . A2
Guildhall . . . A1
Hanover Bldgs . . . B2
Harbour Lights . . . C3
Harbour Pde . . . B1
Hartington Rd . . . A3
Havelock Rd . . . A1
Henstead Rd . . . A1
Herbert Walker Ave . . B1
High St . . . B2
Hoglands Park . . . B2
Holy Rood (Rems), Merchant Navy Memorial . . . B2
Houndwell Park . . . B2
Houndwell Pl . . . B2
Hythe Ferry . . . C2
Information Ctr . . . A1
Isle of Wight Ferry Terminal . . . C1
James St . . . B3
Kingsway . . . A2
Leisure World . . . B1
Library . . . A1
Lime St . . . B2
London Rd . . . A2
Marine Pde . . . B3
Marlands Shop Ctr, The . . . A1
Marsh La . . . B2
Mayflower Meml . . . C1
Mayflower Park . . . C1
Mayflower Theatre, The . . . A1
Medieval Merchant's House . . . C1
Melbourne St . . . B3
Millais . . . A2
Morris Rd . . . A1
National Oceanography Centre . . . C3
Neptune Way . . . C3
New Rd . . . A2
Nichols Rd . . . A3
North Front . . . A2
Northam Rd . . . A3
Ocean Dock . . . C2
Ocean Village Marina . C3
Ocean Way . . . C3
Odeon . . . B1
Ogle Rd . . . B1
Old Northam Rd . . . A2
Orchard La . . . B2
Oxford Ave . . . A2
Oxford St . . . C2
Palmerston Park . . . A2
Palmerston Rd . . . A2
Parsonage Rd . . . A3
Peel St . . . A3
Platform Rd . . . C2
Polygon, The . . . A1
Portland Terr . . . B1
Post Office . . . A2/A3/B2
Pound Tree Rd . . . B2
Quays Swimming & Diving Complex, The . B1
Queen's Park . . . C2
Queen's Peace Fountain . . . A2
Queen's Terr . . . C2
Queensway . . . B2
Radcliffe Rd . . . A3
Rochester St . . . A3
Royal Pier . . . C1
Royal South Hants Hospital . . . A2
St Andrew's Rd . . . A2
St Mary's . . . B3
St Mary St . . . A2
St Mary's Leisure Ctr . A2
St Mary's Pl . . . B2
St Mary's Rd . . . A2
St Mary's Stadium (Southampton FC) . . A3
St Michael's . . . C1
Sea City Mus . . . A1
Showcase Cinema de Lux . . . B3
Solent Sky . . . C3
South Front . . . B2
Southampton Central Station . . . A1
Southampton Solent University . . . A2
SS Shieldhall . . . C2
Terminus Terr . . . C2
Threefield La . . . B2
Titanic Engineers' Memorial . . . A2
Town Quay . . . C1
Town Walls . . . B2
Tudor House . . . C1
Vincent's Walk . . . B2
Westgate Hall . . . C1
West Marlands Rd . . . A1
West Park . . . A1
West Park Rd . . . A1
West Quay Rd . . . B1
West Quay Retail Park . B1
Western Esplanade . . . B1
Westquay Shop Ctr . . B1
Westquay Watermark . B1
White Star Way . . . C2
Winton St . . . A2

Southend-on-Sea 343

Adventure Island . . . C3
Albany Ave . . . A1
Albert Rd . . . C3
Alexandra Rd . . . C2
Alexandra St . . . C2
Alexandra Yacht Club . . . C2
Ashburnham Rd . . . B2
Ave Rd . . . B1
Avenue Terr . . . B1
Balmoral Rd . . . B1
Baltic Ave . . . B3
Baxter Ave . . . A2/B2
Beecroft Art Gallery . . . B2
Bircham Rd . . . A2
Boscombe Rd . . . B3
Boston Ave . . . A1/B2
Bournemouth Park Rd . A3
Browning Ave . . . A3
Bus Station . . . C3
Byron Ave . . . A3
Cambridge Rd . . . C1/C2
Canewdon Rd . . . B1
Carnarvon Rd . . . A2
Central Ave . . . A3
Chelmsford Ave . . . A1
Chichester Rd . . . B2
Church Rd . . . C3
Civic Centre . . . A2
Clarence Rd . . . C2
Clarence St . . . C2
Cliff Ave . . . B1
Cliffs Pavilion . . . C1
Clifftown Parade . . . C2
Clifftown Rd . . . C2
Colchester Rd . . . A1
Coleman St . . . B3
College Way . . . B2
County Court . . . B3
Cromer Rd . . . B3
Crowborough Rd . . . A2
Dryden Ave . . . A3
East St . . . A2
Elmer App . . . B2
Elmer Ave . . . B2
Forum, The . . . B2
Gainsborough Dr . . . A1
Gayton Rd . . . A2
Glenhurst Rd . . . A2
Gordon Pl . . . B2
Gordon Rd . . . B2
Grainger Rd . . . A2
Greyhound Way . . . A3
Grove, The . . . A3
Guildford Rd . . . B3
Hamlet Ct Rd . . . B1
Hamlet Rd . . . C1
Harcourt Ave . . . A1
Hartington Rd . . . C3
Hastings Rd . . . B3
Herbert Gr . . . C3
Heygate Ave . . . C3
High St . . . B2/C2
Information Ctr . . . C3
Kenway . . . A2
Kilworth Ave . . . B3
Lancaster Gdns . . . B3
London Rd . . . B1
Lucy Rd . . . C3
MacDonald Ave . . . A1
Magistrates' Court . . A2
Maldon Rd . . . A2
Marine Ave . . . C1
Marine Parade . . . C3
Marine Rd . . . C1
Milton Rd . . . B1
Milton St . . . B2
Napier Ave . . . B2
North Ave . . . A3
North Rd . . . A1/B1
Odeon . . . B2
Osborne Rd . . . B1
Park Cres . . . B1
Park Rd . . . B1
Park St . . . B1
Park Terr . . . B1
Pier Hill . . . C3
Pleasant Rd . . . C3
Police Station . . . A2
Post Office . . . B2/B3
Princes St . . . B2
Queens Rd . . . B2
Queensway . . . B2/B3/C3
Radio Essex . . . C2
Rayleigh Ave . . . A1
Redstock Rd . . . A2
Rochford Ave . . . A1
Royal Mews . . . C2
Royal Terr . . . C2
Royals Sh Ctr, The . . C3
Ruskin Ave . . . A3
St Ann's Rd . . . B3
St Helen's Rd . . . B1
St John's Rd . . . B1
St Leonard's Rd . . . C3
St Lukes Rd . . . A3
St Vincent's Rd . . . C1
Salisbury Ave . . . A1/B1
Scratton Rd . . . C2
Shakespeare Dr . . . A1
Shopmobility . . . B2
Short St . . . A2
South Ave . . . A3
Southchurch Rd . . . B3
Southend Central . . . B2
Southend Pier Railway . . . C3
Southend United FC . A1
Southend Victoria . . . B2
Stanfield Rd . . . A2
Stanley Rd . . . C3
Sutton Rd . . . A3/B3
Swanage Rd . . . B3
Sweyne Ave . . . A1
Sycamore Gr . . . A3
Tennyson Ave . . . A3
Tickfield Ave . . . A2
Tudor Rd . . . A1
Tunbridge Rd . . . A2
Tylers Ave . . . B3
Tyrrel Dr . . . B3
Univ of Essex . . . B2/C2
Vale Ave . . . A2
Victoria Ave . . . A2
Victoria Sh Ctr, The . . B2
Warrior Sq . . . B3
Wesley Rd . . . C3
West Rd . . . A1
West St . . . A1
Westcliff Ave . . . C1
Westcliff Parade . . . C1
Western Esplanade . . C1
Weston Rd . . . C2
Whitegate Rd . . . B3
Wilson Rd . . . C1
Wimborne Rd . . . B3
York Rd . . . C3

Stirling 343

Abbey Rd . . . A3
Abbotsford Pl . . . A3
Abercromby Pl . . . C1
Albert Halls . . . B1
Albert Pl . . . B1
Alexandra Pl . . . A3
Allan Park . . . C2
Ambulance Station . . A2
AMF Ten Pin Bowling . . . B2
Argyll Ave . . . A3
Argyll's Lodging . . . B1
Back O' Hill Ind Est . . A1
Back O' Hill Rd . . . A1
Baker St . . . B2
Ballengeich Pass . . . A1
Balmoral Pl . . . B1
Barn Rd . . . B1
Barnton St . . . B2
Bastion, The . . . C2
Bow St . . . B1
Bruce St . . . A2
Burghmuir Retail Park C2
Burghmuir Rd . . A2/B2/C2
Bus Station . . . B2
Cambuskenneth Bridge . . . A3
Castle Ct . . . B1
Causewayhead Rd . . . A2
Cemetery . . . A1
Changing Room, The . . . B1
Church of the Holy Rude . . . B1
Clarendon Pl . . . C1
Club House . . . B1
Colquhoun St . . . C3
Corn Exchange . . . B2
Council Offices . . . C2
Court . . . B2
Cowane Ctr . . . A2
Cowane St . . . A2
Cowane's Hospital . . B1
Crawford Sh Arc . . . B2
Crofthead Rd . . . A1
Dean Cres . . . A3
Douglas St . . . A2
Drip Rd . . . A1
Drummond La . . . C1
Drummond Pl . . . C1
Drummond Pl La . . . C1
Dumbarton Rd . . . C2
Eastern Access Rd . . . B2
Edward Ave . . . A3
Edward Rd . . . A2
Forrest Rd . . . A2
Fort . . . A1
Forth Cres . . . B2
Forth St . . . A2
Gladstone Pl . . . C1
Glebe Ave . . . C1
Glebe Cres . . . C1
Golf Course . . . C1
Goosecroft Rd . . . B2
Gowanhill . . . A1
Greenwood Ave . . . B1
Harvey Wynd . . . A1
Information Ctr . . . B1
Irvine Pl . . . B2
James St . . . A2
John St . . . B1
Kerse Rd . . . C3
King's Knot . . . B1
King's Park . . . C1
King's Park Rd . . . C1
Laurencecroft Rd . . . A2
Leisure Pool . . . B2
Library . . . B2
Linden Ave . . . C2
Lovers Wk . . . A2
Lower Back Walk . . . B1
Lower Bridge St . . . A2
Lower Castlehill . . . A1
Mar Pl . . . B1
Meadow Pl . . . A3
Meadowforth Rd . . . C3
Middlemuir Rd . . . C3
Millar Pl . . . A3
Morris Terr . . . B2
Mote Hill . . . A1
Murray Pl . . . B2
Nelson Pl . . . C2
Old Town Cemetery . . B1
Old Town Jail . . . B1
Park Terr . . . C1
Phoenix Industrial Est . C3
Players Rd . . . C3
Port St . . . C2
Post Office . . . B2
Princes St . . . B2
Queen St . . . B2
Queen's Rd . . . B1
Queenshaugh Dr . . . A3
Ramsay Pl . . . A2
Riverside Dr . . . A3
Ronald Pl . . . A1
Rosebery Pl . . . A2
Royal Gardens . . . B1
Royal Gdns . . . B1
St Mary's Wynd . . . B1
St Ninian's Rd . . . C2
Scott St . . . A2
Seaforth Pl . . . B2
Shore Rd . . . B2
Smith Art Gallery & Museum . . . B1
Snowdon Pl . . . C1
Snowdon Pl La . . . C1
Spittal St . . . B2
Springkerse Ind Est . . C3
Springkerse Rd . . . C3
Stirling Bsns Centre . . C2
Stirling Castle . . . A1
Stirling County Rugby Football Club . . . A3
Stirling Enterprise Pk . B3
Stirling Old Bridge . . . A2
Stirling Station . . . B2
Superstore . . . A1/A2
Sutherland Ave . . . A3
TA Centre . . . C3
Tannery La . . . A2
Thistle Industrial Est . . C3
Thistles Sh Ctr, The . . B2
Tolbooth . . . B1
Town Wall . . . B1
Union St . . . A2
Upper Back Walk . . . B1
Upper Bridge St . . . A1
Upper Castlehill . . . B1
Upper Craigs . . . C2
Victoria Pl . . . C1
Victoria Rd . . . B1
Victoria Sq . . . B1/C1
Vue . . . B2
Wallace St . . . A2
Waverley Cres . . . A3
Wellgreen Rd . . . C2
Windsor Pl . . . C1
YHA . . . B1

Stoke 343

Ashford St . . . A3
Avenue Rd . . . A3
Aynsley Rd . . . A2
Barnfield . . . C1
Bath St . . . C2
Beresford St . . . A3
Bilton St . . . C2
Boon Ave . . . C2
Booth St . . . C2
Boothen Rd . . . C2/C3
Boughey St . . . C2
Boughley Rd . . . B3
Brighton St . . . B1
Campbell Rd . . . C2
Carlton Rd . . . B3
Cauldon Rd . . . A3
Cemetery . . . A2
Cemetery Rd . . . A2
Chamberlain Ave . . . C1
Church (RC) . . . B2
Church St . . . C2
City Rd . . . C3
Civic Centre & King's Hall . . . B3
Cliff Vale Pl . . . A1
College Rd . . . A3
Convent Cl . . . B2
Copeland St . . . B2
Cornwallis St . . . C3
Corporation St . . . C2
Crowther St . . . A3
Dominic St . . . B1
Elenora St . . . B2
Elgin St . . . B2
Epworth St . . . A3
Etruscan St . . . A1
Film Theatre . . . B3
Fleming Rd . . . C2
Fletcher Rd . . . C2
Floyd St . . . B2
Foden St . . . C2
Frank St . . . C2
Franklin Rd . . . C1
Frederick Ave . . . B1
Garden St . . . C1
Garner St . . . A1
Gerrard St . . . B2
Glebe St . . . B3
Greatbach Ave . . . B1
Hanley Park . . . A3
Harris St . . . B1
Hartshill Rd . . . B1
Hayward St . . . A2
Hide St . . . B2
Higson Ave . . . B2
Hill St . . . B2
Honeywall . . . B2
Hunters Dr . . . C1
Hunters Way . . . C1
Keary St . . . C2
Kingsway . . . B2
Leek Rd . . . B3
Library . . . C2
Lime St . . . C2
Liverpool Rd . . . B2
London Rd . . . C2
Lonsdale St . . . C2
Lovatt St . . . B2
Lytton St . . . B3
Market . . . C2
Newcastle La . . . C1
Newlands St . . . A2
Norfolk St . . . A2
North St . . . A1/B2
Northcote Ave . . . B2
Oldmill St . . . C3
Oriel St . . . B1
Oxford St . . . B1
Penkhull New Rd . . . C1
Penkhull St . . . C1
Portmeirion Pottery . . . C2
Post Office . . . A3
Princes Rd . . . B1
Pump St . . . B2
Quarry Ave . . . B1
Quarry Rd . . . B1
Queen Anne St . . . A3
Queen's Rd . . . C1
Queensway . . . A1/B2/C3
Richmond St . . . B1
Richmond St Park . . . B1
Rothwell St . . . C1
St Peter's . . . B3
St Thomas Pl . . . C1
Scrivenor Rd . . . A1
Seaford St . . . A3
Selwyn St . . . C3
Shelton New Rd . . . A1
Shelton Old Rd . . . B2
Sheppard St . . . C2
Sir Stanley Matthews Sports Centre . . . B3
Spark St . . . C2
Spencer Rd . . . B3
Spode St . . . C2
Squires View . . . B3
Staffordshire Univ . . . B3
Station Rd . . . B3
Stoke Business Park . . C3
Stoke Rd . . . A2
Stoke-on-Trent College . . . A3
Stoke-on-Trent Station . . . B3
Sturgess St . . . C2
Thistley Hough . . . C1
Thornton Rd . . . B3
Tolkien Way . . . B1
Trent Valley Rd . . . C1
Vale St . . . B2
Villas, The . . . C1
Watford St . . . A3
Wellesley St . . . A3
West Ave . . . B1
Westland St . . . B1
Yeaman St . . . C2
Yoxall Ave . . . B1

Stratford-upon-Avon 343

Albany Rd . . . B1
Alcester Rd . . . B1
Ambulance Station . . B1
Arden St . . . B2
Avenue Farm . . . A1
Ave Farm Ind Est . . . A1
Avenue Rd . . . A3
Baker Ave . . . A1
Bandstand . . . C3
Benson Rd . . . A3
Birmingham Rd . . . A2

Boat Club B3
Borden Pl C1
Bridge St C2
Bridgetown Rd C3
Bridgeway B2
Broad St C2
Broad Walk C2
Brookvale Rd C1
Brunel Way C2
Bull St C2
Butterfly Farm ✦ C1
Cemetery C1
Chapel La B2
Cherry Orchard C2
Chestnut Walk C2
Children's Playground C3
Church St C2
Civic Hall B2
Clarence Rd B1
Clopton Bridge ✦ B2
Clopton Rd A2
College C2
College La C2
College St C2
Com Sports Centre B1
Council Offices
(District) B2
Courtyard, The ♨ B3
Cox's Yard ✦ B3
Cricket Ground B2
Ely Gdns B2
Ely St B2
Evesham Rd C1
Fire Station B1
Foot Ferry A2
Fordham Ave A2
Garrick Way A2
Gower Memorial ✦ B3
Great William St B2
Greenhill St B2
Greenway, The B2
Grove Rd B2
Guild St B2
Guildhall & School 🏛 B2
Hall's Croft 🏛 B2
Harvard House 🏛 B2
Henley St B1
Hertford Rd C1
High St B2
Holton St C2
Holy Trinity 🕇 B3
Information Ctr ℹ B3
Jolyffe Park Rd A2
Kipling Rd B2
Library B2
Lodge Rd A3
Maidenhead Rd A3
Mansell St B2
Masons Court A1
Masons Rd A1
Maybird Shopping Pk A2
Maybrook Retail Pk A1
Maybrook Rd A1
Mayfield Ave B2
Meer St B2
Mill La C2
Moat House Hotel B3
Narrow La C2
Nash's Ho & New Pl 🏛 B2
New St C2
Old Town C2
Orchard Way C1
Other Place, The ♨ B2
Paddock La A1
Park Rd A1
Payton St B2
Percy St B2
Police Station 🖈 B2
Post Office 🕿 B2
Recreation Ground C2
Regal Road B2
Rother St B2
Rowley Cr C1
Royal Shakespeare
Theatre ♨ B3
Ryland St C2
Saffron Meadow C2
St Andrew's Cr B1
St Gregory's ♨ A3
St Gregory's Rd A3
St Mary's Rd A2
Sanctus Dr C1
Sanctus St C1
Sandfield Rd B2
Scholars La B2
Seven Meadows Rd C2
Shakespeare Institute . C2
Shakespeare's
Birthplace ✦ B2
Sheep St B2
Shelley Rd C2
Shipston Rd C3
Shottery Rd C1
Slingates Rd A2
Southern La C2
Station Rd B1
Stratford
Healthcare 🏥 B2
Stratford Hospital 🏥 B1
Stratford Leisure Ctr B2
Stratford Sports Club B1
Stratford-upon-Avon
Station B1
Swan Theatre ♨ B3
Swan's Nest La B3
Talbot Rd C2
Tiddington Rd B3
Timothy's Bridge
Industrial Estate A1
Timothy's Bridge Rd A1
Town Hall & Council
Offices B2
Town Sq B2
Trinity Cl C2
Tyler St B2
War Memorial Gdns B3
Warwick Rd B3
Waterside B2
Welcombe Rd A3

West St C2
Western Rd A2
Wharf Rd B2
Willows North, The B1
Willows, The B1
Wood St B2

Sunderland   343

Albion Pl C2
Alliance Pl B1
Argyle St C1
Ashwood St C1
Athenaeum St C2
Azalea Terr C2
Beach St B1
Bedford St C2
Beechwood Terr C1
Belvedere Rd C2
Blandford St B2
Borough Rd B3
Bridge Cr B2
Bridge St B2
Bridges, The B2
Brooke St A2
Brougham St B2
Burdon Rd C2
Burn Park C1
Burn Park Rd C1
Burn Park Tech Park C1
Carol St B1
Charles St A3
Chester Rd C1
Chester Terr B1
Church St B1
Civic Centre C2
Cork St B3
Coronation St B3
Cowan Terr C2
Dame Dorothy St B1
Deptford Rd B1
Deptford Terr A1
Derby St C2
Derwent St C2
Dock St B1
Dundas St A2
Durham Rd C1
Easington St A1
Egerton St C3
Empire ♨ B2
Empire Theatre ♨ B2
Farringdon Row A1
Fawcett St B2
Fire Station B1
Fox St C1
Foyle St C2
Frederick St C2
Hanover Pl A1
Havelock Terr C1
Hay St B1
Headworth Sq B3
Hendon Rd C3
High St East B3
High St West B2/B3
Holmeside C2
Hylton Rd B1
Information Ctr ℹ B2
John St C2
Kier Hardie Way A1
Lambton St B2
Laura St C3
Lawrence St C3
Library & Arts Centre B3
Lily St C1
Lime St B1
Livingstone Rd B2
Low Row B2
Matamba Terr B1
Millburn St B1
Millennium Way A2
Minster ♨ B2
Monkwearmouth
Station Museum 🏛 A2
Mowbray Park C2
Mowbray Rd C3
Murton St C2
National Glass Ctr ✦ C1
New Durham Rd C1
Newcastle Rd A2
Nile St B3
Norfolk St B3
North Bridge St A2
Northern Gallery for
Contemporary Art 🏛 B3
Otto Terr C1
Park La C2
Park Lane ♒ C2
Park Rd C2
Paul's Rd C3
Peel St C3
Point, The ✦ B2
Police Station 🖈 B2
Priestly Cr A1
Queen St B2
Railway Row B1
Retail Park B1
Richmond St A2
Roker Ave A2
Royalty Theatre ♨ C1
Royalty, The C1
Ryhope Rd C2
St Mary's Way B2
St Michael's Way B2
St Peter's ♨ A3
St Peter's ♒ A2
St Peter's Way A3
St Vincent St C3
Salem Rd C3
Salem St C3
Salisbury St C3
Sans St B3
Shopmobility B2
Silksworth Row B1
Southwick Rd A1
Stadium of Light
(Sunderland AFC) A2
Stadium Way A2
Stobart St A2
Stockton Rd C1
Suffolk St C3

Sunderland ♒ B2
Sunderland
Aquatic Centre A2
Sunderland Mus 🏛 B3
Sunderland Station ≈ B2
Tatham St C3
Tavistock Pl B3
Thelma St C1
Thomas St North A2
Thornholme Rd C1
Toward Rd C3
Transport Interchange C2
Trimdon St Way B1
Tunstall Rd C2
University ♒ C1
University Library C1
University of Sunderland
(City Campus) B1
University of Sunderland
(Sir Tom Cowle at St
Peter's Campus) A3
Vaux Brewery Way A1
Villiers St B3
Villiers St South B3
Vine Pl C2
Violet St B1
Walton La B3
Waterworks Rd B1
Wearmouth Bridge A2
West Sunniside B3
West Wear St B2
Westbourne Rd C1
Western Hill C1
Wharncliffe B1
Whickham St A3
White House Rd C3
Wilson St North A1
Winter Gdns C3
Wreath Quay A1

Swansea
Abertawe   343

Adelaide St C2
Albert Row C3
Alexandra Rd B3
Argyle St C1
Baptist Well Pl A1
Beach St C1
Belle Vue Way B3
Berw Rd A1
Berwick Terr A2
Bond St C1
Brangwyn Concert
Hall C1
Bridge St B3
Brooklands Terr B1
Brunswick St C1
Bryn-Syfi Terr A2
Bryn-y-Mor Rd C1
Bullins La C1
Burrows Rd C1
Bus Station C2
Bus/Rail link B2
Cadfan Rd A1
Cadrawd Rd A1
Caer St C2
Carig Cr A1
Carlton Terr B2
Carmarthen Rd A3
Castle Square C2
Castle St B3
Catherine St C1
Cinema 🎞 C3
Civic Centre & Library . C2
Clarence St A2
Colbourne Terr A2
Constitution Hill B1
Court B3
Creidiol Rd A2
Cromwell St B2
Crown Courts C1
Duke St B1
Dunvant Pl C2
Dyfatty Park A3
Dyfatty St A3
Dyfed Ave A1
Dylan Thomas Ctr ✦ B3
Dylan Thomas
Theatre ♨ B3
Eaton Cr C1
Eigen Cr A1
Elfed Rd A1
Emlyn Rd A1
Evans Terr A3
Fairfield Terr B1
Ffynone Dr B1
Ffynone Rd B1
Fire Station B3
Firm St A2
Fleet St C1
Francis St C1
Fullers Row B2
George St B2
Glamorgan St C2
Glynn Vivian Art
Gallery 🏛 B2
Gower Coll Swansea C1
Graig Terr A3
Grand Theatre ♨ C2
Granogwen Rd A2
Guildhall C1
Guildhall Rd South C1
Gwent Rd A1
Gwynedd Ave A1
Hafod St A3
Hanover St B1
Harcourt St B2
Harries St A2
Heathfield B2
Henrietta St B1
Hewson St A2
High St A3/B3
High View A2
Hill St A2
Historic Ships
Berth C3
HM Prison B3
Information Ctr ℹ C2

Islwyn Rd A1
King Edward's Rd C1
Kingsway, The B2
LC, The C3
Long Ridge A2
Madoc St C1
Mansel St B2
Maritime Quarter C3
Market C2
Mayhill Gdns B1
Mayhill Rd B1
Milton Terr A2
Mission Gallery 🏛 C3
Montpelier Terr B1
Morfa Rd A3
Mount Pleasant B2
National Waterfront
Museum 🏛 C3
New Cut Rd A3
New St A3
Nicander Parade A2
Nicander Pl A2
Nicholl St B2
Norfolk St B2
Northampton La B2
Observatory ✦ C3
Orchard St B2
Oxford St B2
Oystermouth Rd C1
Page St B2
Pant-y-Celyn Rd C1
Parc Tawe North B3
Parc Tawe Shopping &
Leisure Centre B3
Patti Pavilion ♨ C1
Paxton St C1
Pen-y-Graig Rd A1
Penmaen Terr B1
Phillips Pde C1
Picton Terr B2
Plantasia B3
Plantasia ❀ B3
Police Station 🖈 B2
Post Office 🕿
. . . . A1/A2/C1/C2
Powys Ave A1
Primrose St B2
Princess Way C2
Promenade B2
Pryder Gdns A1
Quadrant Shop Ctr C2
Quay Park B3
Rhianfa La C1
Rhondda St B2
Richardson St C2
Rodney St C1
Rose Hill B1
Rosehill Terr B1
Russell St B1
St David's Shop Ctr C3
St Helen's Ave C1
St Helen's Cr C1
St Helen's Rd C1
St James Gdns B1
St James's Cr B1
St Mary's 🕇 B3
Sea View Terr A1
Singleton St C2
South Dock C3
Stanley Pl A2
Strand B3
Swansea Castle 🏰 B3
Swansea Metropolitan
University B1
Swansea Museum 🏛 C3
Swansea Station ≈ A3
Taliesyn Rd A2
Tan y Marian Rd A1
Tegid Rd A1
Teilo Cr A1
Tenpin Bowling ✦⛳ B3
Terrace Rd B1/B2
Tontine St B3
Townhill Rd A1
Tramshed, The 🏛 C3
Trawler Rd C3
Union St B2
Upper Strand A3
Vernon St A3
Victoria Quay C3
Victoria Rd B3
Vincent St C1
Walter Rd B1
Watkin St A2
Waun-Wen Rd A2
Wellington St C2
Westbury St C1
Western St C1
Westway C2
William St C2
Wind St B3
Woodlands Terr B1
YMCA B2
York St C3

Swindon   343

Albert St C2
Albion St C1
Alfred St A2
Alvescot Rd C3
Art Gallery & Mus 🏛 A3
Ashford Rd C1
Aylesbury St A2
Bath Rd C1
Bathampton St B1
Bathurst Rd B3
Beatrice St A2
Beckhampton St B3
Bowood Rd C1
Bristol St B1
Broad St A3
Brunel Arcade B2
Brunel Plaza B2
Brunswick St C2
Bus Station B2
Cambria Bridge Rd B1
Cambria Place B1
Canal Walk B2

Carfax St B2
Carr St A2
Cemetery C1/C3
Chandler Cl C2
Chapel C1
Chester St B1
Christ Church 🕇 C1
Church Place B1
Cirencester Way A2
Clarence St B2
Clifton St C1
Cockleberry ♒ A2
Colbourne ♒ A3
Colbourne St A3
College St B2
Commercial Rd B1
Corporation St A2
Council Offices B3
County Rd A3
Courts B2
Cricket Ground A3
Cricklade Street C3
Crombey St B1/C2
Cross St C1
Curtis St C1
Deacon St C1
Designer Outlet
(Great Western) C1
Dixon St C2
Dover St C1
Dowling St C2
Drove Rd C3
Dryden St C1
Durham St C1
East St B1
Eastcott Hill C2
Eastcott Rd B3
Edgeware Rd B2
Edmund St C2
Elmina Rd A3
Emlyn Square B1
Euclid St B2
Exeter St A1
Fairview C1
Faringdon Rd B1
Farnsby St B1
Fire Station B2
Fleet St B2
Fleming Way B2/B3
Florence St A3
Gladstone St A3
Gooch St A2
Graham St A3
Great Western WayA1/A2
Groundwell Rd B3
Hawksworth Way A1
Haydon St A2
Henry St B2
Hillside Ave C1
Holbrook Way B2
Hunt St C1
Hydro B1
Hythe Rd C2
Information Ctr ℹ B2
Joseph St C1
Kent Rd C2
King William St C2
Kingshill Rd C1
Lansdown Rd B2
Lawn, The C3
Leicester St B2
Library B2
Lincoln St B2
Little London C3
London St B1
Magic ♒ C2
Maidstone Rd A3
Manchester Rd A3
Maxwell St B1
Milford St B2
Milton Rd B1
Morse St C2
National Monuments
Record Centre B1
Newcastle St A3
Newcombe Drive A1
Newcombe
Trading Estate A1
Newhall St C2
North St C2
North Star ♒ A2
North Star Ave A2
Northampton St B3
Nurseries, The A1
Oasis Leisure Centre A1
Ocotal Way A3
Okus Rd C1
Old Town C3
Oxford St B1
Parade, The B2
Park Lane B1
Park Lane ♒ B1
Park, The C2
Pembroke St C2
Plymouth St B3
Polaris House A2
Polaris Way A2
Police Station 🖈 B2
Ponting St A2
Post Office 🕿
. . . . B1/B2/C1/C3
Poulton St A3
Princes St B2
Prospect Hill C2
Prospect Place C2
Queen St B2
Queen's Park C3
Radnor St C1
Read St C1
Reading St B1
Regent St B2
Retail Park A2/A3/B3
Rosebery St A3
St Mark's 🕇 B2
Salisbury St A3
Savernake St C2
Shelley St C1
Sheppard St B1
South St C2
Southampton St B3

Spring Gardens B3
Stafford Street C2
Stanier St C2
Station Road B2
STEAM 🏛 B1
Swindon College A2
Swindon Rd C2
Swindon Station ≈ B2
Swindon Town
Football Club A3
T A Centre B1
Tennyson St B1
Theobald St B1
Town Hall B2
Transfer Bridges ♒ A3
Union St C2
Upham Rd C3
Victoria Rd C3
Walcot Rd C3
War Memorial ✦ B2
Wells St B2
Western St C1
Westmorland Rd B3
Whalebridge ♒ B2
Whitehead St C1
Whitehouse Rd A1
William St C1
Wood St C1
Wyvern Theatre &
Arts Centre ♨🎭 B2
York Rd B3

Taunton   343

Addison Gr A1
Albemarle Rd A2
Alfred St B3
Alma St B3
Avenue, The A1
Bath Pl B2
Belvedere Rd A1
Billet St B2
Billetfield C2
Birch Gr A1
Brewhouse Theatre ♨ B2
Bridge St A1
Bridgwater &
Taunton Canal A2
Broadlands Rd C1
Burton Pl A2
Bus Station A1
Canal Rd A2
Cann St C1
Canon St B2
Castle 🏰 B1
Castle St B1
Cheddon Rd A2
Chip Lane A1
Clarence St B3
Cleveland St B1
Clifton Terr A2
Coleridge Cres C3
Compass Hill C1
Compton Cl C3
Corporation St B1
Council Offices A1
County Walk Sh Ctr C2
Courtyard B2
Cranmer Rd B2
Crescent, The C1
Critchard Way B3
Cyril St A3
Deller's Wharf B1
Duke St B2
East Reach B3
East St B2
Eastbourne Rd B3
Eastleigh Rd A3
Eaton Cres A2
Elm Gr A1
Elms Cl A2
Fons George C1
Fore St B2
Fowler St A1
French Weir Rec Grd B1
Geoffrey Farrant Wk B2
Gray's Almshouses 🏛 B2
Grays Rd B3
Greenway Ave A1
Guildford Pl A1
Hammet St B2
Haydon Rd B3
Heavitree Way A2
Herbert St A1
High St C2
Holway Ave C3
Hugo St A3
Huish's
Almshouses 🏛 B2
Hurdle Way C2
Information Ctr ℹ B2
Jubilee St A1
King's College C1
Kings Cl C3
Laburnum St B3
Lambrook Rd B3
Lansdowne Rd A1
Leslie Ave A1
Leycroft Rd B3
Library B2
Linden Gr A1
Magdalene St B1
Magistrates Court B1
Malvern Terr A2
Market House 🏛 B2
Mary St C2
Middle St B2
Midford Rd B3
Mitre Court B3
Mount Nebo B1
Mount St C2
Mount, The C2
Mountway C2
Mus of Somerset 🏛 B1
North St B2
Northern Inner
Distributor Rd A1
Northfield Ave B1
Northfield Rd B1
Northleigh Rd C3

Obridge Allotments A3
Obridge Lane A3
Obridge Rd A3
Obridge Viaduct A3
Odeon 🎞 B2
Park Lane A1
Park St C1
Paul St B2
Plais St C2
Playing Field C3
Police Station 🖈 B1
Portland St B1
Post Office 🕿 B1/B2
Priorswood Ind Est A3
Priorswood Rd A2
Priory Ave B2
Priory Bridge Rd A2
Priory Fields Retail Pk. A3
Priory Park A2
Priory Way A3
Queen St B3
Railway St A1
Records Office A1
Recreation Grd A1
Riverside Place B1
St Augustine St B2
St George's 🕇 C2
St Georges Sq C2
St James 🕇 B2
St James St B2
St John's 🕇 C1
St John's St C1
St Josephs Field C2
St Mary
Magdalene's 🕇 B2
Samuels St A1
Shire Hall & Law
Courts B1
Somerset County
Cricket Ground B2
Somerset County Hall . C1
Somerset Cricket 🏛 B2
South Rd C3
South St C2
Staplegrove Rd B1
Station Rd A1
Stephen St B2
Swimming Pool A1
Tancred St B2
Tauntfield Cl C3
Taunton Dean
Cricket Club C2
Taunton Station ≈ A1
Thomas St A1
Toneway A3
Tower St B1
Trevor Smith Pl C3
Trinity Bsns Centre C3
Trinity Rd C2
Trinity St B3
Trull Rd C1
Tudor House 🏛 B2
Upper High St C1
Venture Way A3
Victoria Gate B2
Victoria Park B3
Victoria St B3
Viney St B3
Vivary Park C2
Vivary Rd C1
War Memorial ✦ C1
Wellesley St A3
Wheatley Cres A3
Whitehall B1
Wilfred Rd B3
William St A1
Wilton Church 🕇 C1
Wilton Cl C1
Wilton Gr C1
Wilton St C1
Winchester St B2
Winters Field B2
Wood St B1
Yarde Pl B2

Torquay   344

Abbey Rd B2
Alexandra Rd A2
Alpine Rd A3
AMF Bowling C3
Ash Hill Rd A2
Babbacombe Rd B3
Bampfylde Rd B1
Barton Rd A1
Beacon Quay C2
Belgrave Rd A1/B1
Belmont Rd A3
Berea Rd A3
Braddons Hill Rd East . B3
Brewery Park A3
Bronshill Rd A2
Castle Circus A2
Castle Rd A2
Cavern Rd B3
Central ♒ B2
Chatsworth Rd A3
Chestnut Ave B1
Church St A2
Civic Offices A2
Coach Station C1
Corbyn Head C2
Croft Hill B1
Croft Rd B1
East St A1
Egerton Rd A3
Ellacombe Church Rd . A3
Ellacombe Rd A3
Falkland Rd B1
Fleet St B2
Fleet Walk Sh Ctr B2
Grafton Rd B3
Haldon Pier C2
Hatfield Rd A2
Highbury Rd A2
Higher Warberry Rd A3
Hillsdon Rd A3
Hoxton Rd A2
Hunsdon Rd B3
Information Ctr ℹ C2
Inner Harbour C2
Kenwyn Rd A3
King's Drive, The B1
Laburnum St A1
Law Courts A2
Library A2
Lime Ave B1
Living Coasts ✦ C3
Lower Warberry Rd B3
Lucius St B1
Lymington Rd A1
Magdalene Rd A1
Marina C2
Market Forum, The B2
Market St A2
Meadfoot Lane C3
Meadfoot Rd C3
Melville St B2
Middle Warberry Rd B3
Mill Lane A1
Montpellier Rd B3
Morgan Ave A1
Museum Rd B3
Newton Rd A1
Oakhill Rd A1
Outer Harbour C3
Parkhill Rd C3
Pavilion Shopping Ctr . C2
Pimlico B2
Police Station 🖈 A2
Post Office 🕿 C3
Prince of Wales Steps . C3
Princes Rd A3
Princes Rd East A3
Princes Rd West A3
Princess Gdns C2
Princess Pier C2
Princess Theatre ♨ C2
Rathmore Rd B1

Moor Rd C1
Mount Rd C1
NFU Offices B1
Odeon 🎞 A1
Park Lane A1
Police Station 🖈 A3
Priorslee Ave A3
Queen Elizabeth Ave C3
Queen Elizabeth Way . . B1
Queensway A2/B3
Rampart Way A2
Randlay Ave C3
Randlay Wood C3
Rhodes Ave B1
Royal Way B1
St Leonards Rd B2
St Quentin Gate B2
Shifnal Rd A3
Sixth Ave A2
Southwater One
(SW1) B2
Southwater Way B2
Spout Lane C1
Spout Mound C1
Spout Way C1
Stafford Court B3
Stafford Park C3
Stirchley Ave C3
Stone Row C1
Telford Bridge Ret Pk . A1
Telford Central Sta ≈ A2
Telford Forge Sh Pk A1
Telford Hornets RFC C2
Telford Int Ctr B2
Telford Way A1
Third Ave A2
Town Park C2
Town Park Visitor Ctr . B2
Walker House B2
Wellswood Ave A1
West Centre Way B1
Withywood Drive C1
Woodhouse Central C3
Yates Way A1

Telford   343

Alma St C1
Amphitheatre C2
Bowling Alley B2
Brandsfarm Way C3
Brunel Rd B1
Bus Station B2
Buxton Rd C1
Central Park A2
Civic Offices B2
Coach Central B2
Coachwell Cl B1
Colliers Way A1
Courts B2
Dale Acre Way B3
Darliston C3
Deepdale A3
Deercote B2
Dinthill C2
Doddington C3
Dodmoor Grange C3
Downemead B3
Duffryn B3
Dunsheath B3
Euston Way A3
Eyton Mound C1
Eyton Rd C1
Forgegate A2
Grange Central B2
Hall Park Way B2
Hinksay Rd C1
Hollinsworth Rd A2
Holyhead Rd C3
Housing Trust C1
Ice Rink B2
Information Ctr ℹ B2
Ironmasters Way B2
Job Centre B2
Land Registry A1
Lawn Central B2
Lawnswood C1
Library B2
Malinsgate B1
Matlock Ave C1

Recreation Grd B1
Riviera Int Ctr B1
Rock End Ave C3
Rock Rd B2
Rock Walk B2
Rosehill Rd A3
South West Coast
Path C3
St Efride's Rd A1
St John's 🕇 B3
St Luke's Rd B2
St Luke's Rd North B2
St Luke's Rd South B2
St Marychurch Rd A2
Scarborough Rd B1
Shedden Hill B1
South Pier C2
South St A1
Spanish Barn B1
Stitchill Rd B1
Strand B2
Sutherland Rd A3
Teignmouth Rd A1
Temperance St B2
Terrace, The B3
Thurlow Rd A1
Tor Bay B1
Tor Church Rd A1
Tor Hill Rd A1
Torbay Rd C2
Torquay Museum 🏛 B3
Torquay Station ≈ C1
Torre Abbey
Mansion 🏛 B1
Torre Abbey Meadows. B1
Torre Abbey Sands B1
Torwood Gdns B3
Torwood St C3
Town Hall A2
Union Square
Shopping Centre A2
Union St A1
Upton Hill A1
Upton Park A1
Upton Rd A1
Vanehill Rd C3
Vansittart Rd A1
Vaughan Parade C2
Victoria Parade C3
Victoria Rd A3
Warberry Rd West B2
Warren Rd B2
Windsor Rd A2/A3
Woodville Rd A3

Truro   344

Adelaide Ter B1
Agar Rd B3
Arch Hill C2
Arundell Pl C2
Avenue, The A3
Avondale Rd B1
Back Quay B3
Barrack La C3
Barton Meadow A1
Benson Rd A2
Bishops Cl B1
Bosvean Gdns B1
Bosvigo Gardens ❀ B1
Bosvigo La A1
Bosvigo Rd B2
Broad St A3
Burley Cl C3
Bus Station B2
Calenick St B2
Campfield Hill B2
Carclew St B2
Carew Rd A2
Carey Park C2
Carlyon Rd A2
Carvoza Rd A3
Castle St B2
Cathedral View A3
Chainwalk Dr A2
Chapel Hill B1
Charles St B2
City Hall B2
City Rd B3
Coinage Hall 🏛 B3
Comprigney Hill A1
Coosebean La A1
Copes Gdns A2
County Hall A1
Courtney Rd A2
Crescent Rd B1
Crescent Rise B1
Crescent, The B1
Daniell Court C2
Daniell Rd C2
Daniell St C2
Daubuz Cl A2
Dobbs La C1
Edward St A3
Eliot Rd A2
Elm Court A3
Enys Cl A1
Enys Rd A1
Fairmantle St B3
Falmouth Rd C1
Ferris Town B2
Fire Station B2
Frances St B2
George St B2
Green Cl C2
Green La C2
Grenville Rd B2
Hall For Cornwall ♨ B3
Hendra Rd C1
Hendra Vean A1
High Cross B3
Higher Newham La C3
Higher Trehaverne A2
Hillcrest Ave A2
Hospital 🏥 B2
Hunkin Cl A2
Hurland Rd C3
Infirmary Hill B2
James Pl B3
Kenwyn Church Rd A1

360 Wick • Winchester • Windsor • Wolverhampton • Worcester • Wrexham • York

Kenwyn Hill A1
Kenwyn Rd A2
Kenwyn St B2
Kerris Gdns A1
King St B3
Leats, The B2
Lemon Quay B3
Lemon St Gallery B3
Library B1/B3
Malpas Rd B3
Market
Memorial Gdns B3
Merrifield Close B1
Mitchell Hill A3
Moresk Cl A3
Moresk Rd A3
Morlaix Ave C3
Nancemere Rd A3
Newham Bsns Park C3
Newham Industrial Est C3
Newham Rd C3
Northfield Dr C3
Oak Way A3
Pal's Terr A3
Park View C2
Pendarves Rd A2
Plaza Cinema B3
Police Station B3
Post Office B2/B3
Prince's St B3
Pydar St A2
Quay St B3
Redannick Cres C2
Redannick La B2
Richard Lander Monument C2
Richmond Hill B1
River St B2
Rosedale Rd A2
Royal Cornwall Mus B2
St Aubyn Rd C3
St Clement St B3
St George's Rd A1
School La C2
Spires, The A2
Station Rd B1
Stokes Rd A2
Strangways Terr C3
Tabernacle St B3
Trehaverne La A2
Tremayne Rd A2
Treseder's Gdns A3
Treworder Rd B1
Treyew Rd B1
Truro Cathedral B3
Truro Harbour Office B3
Truro Station B3
Union St B2
Upper School La C2
Victoria Gdns B2
Waterfall Gdns B2

Wick 344

Ackergill Cres A2
Ackergill St A2
Albert St C2
Ambulance Station A2
Argyle Sq C2
Assembly Rooms C2
Bank Row C2
Bankhead B1
Barons Well B2
Barrogill St C2
Bay View B3
Bexley Terr C3
Bignold Park C2
Bowling Green C2
Breadalbane Terr C2
Bridge of Wick B1
Bridge St B2
Brown Pl C2
Burn St B2
Bus Station B1
Caithness General Hospital (A&E) B1
Cliff Rd B1
Coach Rd B2
Coastguard Station C3
Corner Cres B3
Coronation St C1
Council Offices B2
Court B2
Crane Rock C3
Dempster St C2
Dunnet Ave A2
Fire Station B2
Francis St C1
George St A1
Girnigoe St B2
Glamis Rd B2
Gowrie Pl B1
Grant St C2
Green Rd C2
Gunns Terr B3
Harbour Quay B2
Harbour Rd C3
Harbour Terr C2
Harrow Hill C2
Henrietta St A2/B2
Heritage Museum C2
High St B2
Hill Ave A2
Hillhead Rd B3
Hood St C1
Huddart St C2
Kenneth St C1
Kinnaird St C2
Kirk Hill B1
Langwell Cres B3
Leishman Ave B3
Leith Walk A2
Library B2
Lifeboat Station C3
Lighthouse C3
Lindsay Dr B3
Lindsay Pl B3
Loch St C2
Louisburgh St B2
Lower Dunbar St C2
Macleay La B1
Macleod Rd B3
MacRae St C2
Martha Terr B2
Miller Ave B1
Miller La B1
Moray St C2
Mowat Pl B3
Murchison St C3
Newton Ave C1
Newton Rd C1
Nicolson St C3
North Highland Coll B2
North River Pier B3
Northcote St C2
Owen Pl A2
Police Station B1
Port Dunbar B3
Post Office B2/C2
Pulteney Distillery C2
River St B2
Robert St A1
Rutherford St C2
St John's Episcopal C2
Sandigoe Rd B3
Scalesburn B3
Seaforth Ave C1
Shore La B2
Shore, The B2
Sinclair Dr B3
Sinclair Terr C2
Smith Terr C3
South Pier C3
South Quay C3
South Rd C1
South River Pier B3
Station Rd B1
Superstore A1/B1
Swimming Pool B2
Telford St B2
Thurso Rd B1
Thurso St B1
Town Hall B2
Union St B2
Upper Dunbar St C2
Vansittart St C3
Victoria Pl B2
War Memorial A1
Well of Cairndhuna C3
Wellington Ave C3
Wellington St C3
West Banks Ave C1
West Banks Terr C1
West Park C1
Whitehorse Park B2
Wick Harbour Bridge B2
Wick Industrial Estate A2
Wick Parish Church B1
Wick Station B1
Williamson St B2
Willowbank B2

Winchester 344

Andover Rd A2
Andover Rd Retail Pk A2
Archery La C2
Arthur Rd A2
Bar End Rd C3
Beaufort Rd C2
Beggar's La B3
Bereweeke Ave A1
Bereweeke Rd A1
Boscobel Rd A2
Brassey Rd A2
Broadway B3
Brooks Sh Ctr, The B3
Bus Station B3
Butter Cross B2
Canon St C2
Castle Wall C2/C3
Castle, King Arthur's Round Table B2
Cathedral C2
Cheriton Rd A1
Chesil St C3
Chesil Theatre C3
Christchurch Rd C1
City Mill B3
City Museum B2
City Rd B2
Clifton Rd B1
Clifton Terr B2
Close Wall C2/C3
Coach Park A2
Colebrook St C3
College St C2
College Walk C3
Compton Rd C2
Council Offices C3
County Council Offices B2
Cranworth Rd A2
Cromwell Rd C1
Culver Rd C2
Domum Rd C3
Durngate Pl B3
Eastgate St B3
Edgar Rd C2
Egbert Rd A2
Elm Rd B1
Everyman C2
Fairfield Rd A1
Fire Station B3
Fordington Ave B1
Fordington Rd A1
Friarsgate B3
Gordon Rd B3
Greenhill Rd B1
Guildhall B3
Hatherley Rd A1
High St B2
Hillier Way A3
HM Prison B1
Hyde Abbey (Remains) A2
Hyde Abbey Rd B2
Hyde Cl A2
Hyde St A2
Information Ctr B3
Jane Austen's Ho C2
Jewry St B2
King Alfred Pl A2
Kingsgate Arch C2
Kingsgate Park C2
Kingsgate Rd C2
Kingsgate St C2
Lankhills Rd A2
Law Courts B2
Library B2
Lower Brook St B3
Magdalen Hill B3
Market La B2
Mews La B1
Middle Brook St B3
Middle Rd B1
Military Museums B2
Milland Rd C3
Milverton Rd B1
Monks Rd A3
North Hill Cl A2
North Walls B2
North Walls Rec Gnd A3
Nuns Rd A3
Oram's Arbour B1
Owens Rd A2
Parchment St B2
Park & Ride C3
Park Ave B3
Playing Field A1
Police HQ B2
Portal Rd C3
Post Office B2/C1
Quarry Rd C3
Ranelagh Rd C1
Regiment Museum B2
River Park Leisure Ctr B3
Romans' Rd C2
Romsey Rd B1
Royal Hampshire County Hospital (A&E) B1
St Cross Rd C2
St George's St B2
St Giles Hill C3
St James Villas C2
St James' La B1
St James' Terr B1
St John's B3
St John's St B3
St Michael's Rd C2
St Paul's Hill B1
St Peter St B2
St Swithun St C2
St Thomas St C2
Saxon Rd A2
School of Art B3
Sleepers Hill Rd C1
Southgate St B2
Sparkford Rd C1
Square, The B2
Staple Gdns B2
Station Rd B2
Step Terr B1
Stockbridge Rd A1
Stuart Cres C1
Sussex St B2
Swan Lane B2
Tanner St B3
Theatre Royal B2
Tower St B2
Union St B3
Univ of Southampton (Winchester School of Art) B3
Univ of Winchester (King Alfred Campus) C1
Upper Brook St B2
Wales St B3
Water Lane B3
Weirs, The C3
West End Terr B1
Western Rd B1
Westgate B2
Wharf Hill C3
Winchester College C2
Winchester Station A2
Winnall Moors Wildlife Reserve A3
Wolvesey Castle C3
Worthy Lane A2
Worthy Rd A2

Windsor 344

Adelaide Sq C3
Albany Rd C2
Albert St B1
Alexandra Gdns B2
Alexandra Rd C2
Alma Rd B2
Ambulance Station B1
Arthur Rd B2
Bachelors Acre B3
Barry Ave B2
Beaumont Rd C2
Bexley St B1
Boat House B2
Brocas St B2
Brocas, The A2
Brook St C3
Bulkeley Ave C1
Castle Hill B3
Charles St B2
Claremont Rd C2
Clarence Cr B2
Clarence Rd B1
Clewer Court Rd B1
Coach Park B2
College Cr C1
Courts C2
Cricket Club A3
Cricket Ground C3
Dagmar Rd C2
Datchet Rd B3
Devereux Rd C2
Dorset Rd C2
Duke St B1
Elm Rd C1
Eton College A3
Eton Ct A2
Eton Sq A2
Eton Wick Rd A2
Farm Yard B3
Fire Station C2
Frances Rd C3
Frogmore Dr B3
Gloucester Pl C3
Goslar Way C1
Goswell Hill B2
Goswell Rd B2
Green La C1
Grove Rd C2
Guildhall B3
Helena Rd C2
Helston La B1
High St A2/B3
Holy Trinity C2
Home Park, The A3/C3
Hospital (Private) C2
Household Cavalry C2
Imperial Rd C1
Information Ctr B2/B3
Keats La A2
King Edward Ct B2
King Edward VII Ave A3
King Edward VII Hospital C2
King George V Meml B3
King Stable St A2
King's Rd C3
Library C2
Long Walk, The C3
Maidenhead Rd B1
Meadow La A2
Municipal Offices C3
Nell Gwynne's Ho B3
Osborne Rd C2
Oxford Rd B1
Park St B3
Peascod St B2
Police Station C2
Post Office A2
Princess Margaret Hospital C2
Queen Victoria's Walk B3
Queen's Rd C2
River St B2
Romney Island A3
Romney Lock A3
Romney Lock Rd A3
Russell St C2
St John's B3
St John's Chapel A2
St Leonards Rd C2
St Mark's Rd C2
Sheet St C3
South Meadow A2
South Meadow La A2
Springfield Rd C1
Stovell Rd B1
Sunbury Rd A2
Tangier La A2
Tangier St A3
Temple Rd C2
Thames St B3
Theatre Royal B3
Trinity Pl C2
Vansittart Rd B1/C1
Vansittart Rd Gdns C1
Victoria Barracks C2
Victoria St C2
Ward Royal B2
Westmead C1
White Lilies Island A1
William St B2
Windsor & Eton Central B2
Windsor & Eton Riverside A3
Windsor Arts Ctr C2
Windsor Bridge B3
Windsor Castle B3
Windsor Great Park C3
Windsor Leisure Ctr B1
Windsor Relief Rd A1
Windsor Royal Sh B2
York Ave C1
York Rd C1

Wolverhampton 344

Albion St B3
Alexandra St C1
Arena B2
Arts Gallery B2
Ashland St C1
Austin St A1
Badger Dr A3
Bailey St B3
Bath Ave B1
Bath Rd B1
Bell St C2
Berry St B3
Bilston Rd C3
Bilston St C3
Birmingham Canal A3
Bone Mill La A2
Brewery Rd B1
Bright St A1
Burton Cres B3
Bus Station B3
Cambridge St A3
Camp St B2
Cannock Rd A3
Castle St C2
Chapel Ash C1
Cherry St C1
Chester St A1
Church La C2
Church St C2
Civic Centre B2
Civic Hall B2
Clarence Rd B2
Cleveland St C2
Clifton St C1
Coach Station B2
Compton Rd B1
Corn Hill B3
Coven St A3
Craddock St A1
Cross St North A2
Crown & County Courts C3
Crown St A2
Culwell St B3
Dale St C1
Darlington St C1
Devon Rd A1
Drummond St B2
Dudley Rd C2
Dudley St B2
Duke St C3
Dunkley St B1
Dunstall Ave A2
Dunstall Hill A2
Dunstall Rd A1/A2
Evans St A1
Fawdry St A1
Field St B3
Fire Station C1
Fiveways A2
Fowler Playing Fields A3
Fox's La A2
Francis St A2
Fryer St B3
Gloucester St A1
Gordon St C3
Graiseley St C1
Grand B3
Granville St C3
Great Brickkiln St C1
Great Hampton St A1
Great Western St A2
Grimstone St B3
Harrow St A1
Hilton St A3
Horseley Fields C3
Humber Rd C1
Jack Hayward Way A2
Jameson St A1
Jenner St C3
Kennedy Rd B3
Kimberley St C1
King St B2
Laburnum St C1
Lansdowne Rd B1
Leicester St A1
Lever St C3
Library C3
Lichfield St B2
Light House B3
Little's La B3
Lock St A3
Lord St C1
Lowe St A1
Maltings, The B2
Mander Centre C2
Mander St C1
Market C2
Market St B2
Maxwell Rd C3
Merridale St C1
Middlecross C3
Molineux St B2
Mostyn St A1
New Hampton Rd East A1
Nine Elms La A3
North Rd A2
Oaks Cres C1
Oxley St A2
Paget St A1
Park Ave B1
Park Road East A1
Park Road West B1
Paul St C2
Pelham St C1
Penn Rd C2
Piper's Row B3
Pitt St C2
Police Station C3
Pool St C2
Poole St A3
Post Office A1/B2/B2/C2
Powlett St C3
Queen St B2
Raby St C3
Railway Dr B3
Red Hill St A2
Red Lion St B2
Retreat St C1
Ring Rd B2
Royal, The C3
Rugby St A1
Russell St C1
St Andrew's B1
St David's B3
St George's C3
St George's Parade C2
St James St C3
St John's C2
St John's C2
St John's Retail Park C2
St John's Square C2
St Mark's C1
St Marks Rd C1
St Marks St C1
St Patrick's B2
St Peter's B2
St Peter's B2
Salisbury St C1
Salop St C2
School St C2
Sherwood St A2
Smestow St A3
Snow Hill C2
Springfield Rd A3
Stafford St A2/B2
Staveley Rd A1
Steelhouse La C3
Stephenson St C1
Stewart St C2
Sun St B3
Tempest St C2
Temple St C2
Tettenhall Rd B1
Thomas St C2
Thornley St B2
Tower St C2
University B2
Upper Zoar St C1
Vicarage Rd C3
Victoria St C2
Walpole St A1
Walsall St C3
Ward St C3
Warwick St C3
Water St A3
Waterloo Rd B2
Wednesfield Rd B3
West Pk (not A&E) B1
West Park Swimming Pool B1
Wharf St C3
Whitmore Hill B2
Wolverhampton B3
Wolverhampton St George's C2
Wolverhampton Wanderers Football Gnd (Molineux) B2
Worcester St C2
Wulfrun Centre C2
Yarwell Cl A3
York St C3
Zoar St C1

Worcester 344

Albany Terr A1
Angel Pl B2
Angel St B2
Ashcroft Rd A2
Athelstan Rd C3
Avenue, The C1
Back Lane North A1
Back Lane South A1
Barbourne Rd A2
Bath Rd C2
Battenhall Rd C3
Bridge St B2
Britannia Sq A1
Broad St B2
Bromwich La C1
Bromwich Rd C1
Bromyard Rd C1
Bus Station B2
Butts, The B2
Carden St B3
Castle St A2
Cathedral C2
Cathedral Plaza B2
Charles St B3
Chequers La B1
Chestnut St A2
Chestnut Walk A2
Citizens' Advice Bureau B2
City Walls Rd B2
Cole Hill C3
College of Technology B2
College St C2
Commandery, The C3
Cripplegate Park B1
Croft Rd B1
Cromwell St B3
Cross, The B2
CrownGate Ctr B2
Deansway B2
Diglis Pde C2
Diglis Rd C2
Edgar Tower C2
Farrier St A2
Foregate St B2
Foregate Street B2
Fort Royal Hill C3
Fort Royal Park C3
Foundry St B3
Friar St C2
George St B3
Grand Stand Rd B1
Greenhill C3
Greyfriars B2
Guildhall B2
Henwick Rd B1
High St B2
Hill St B3
Hive, The B2
Huntingdon Hall B2
Hylton Rd B1
Information Ctr B2
King Charles Place Shopping Centre C1
King's School C2
King's School Playing Field C2
Kleve Walk C2
Lansdowne Cr A3
Lansdowne Rd A3
Lansdowne Walk A3
Laslett St A3
Leisure Centre A3
Little Chestnut St A2
Little London A2
London Rd C3
Lowell St A3
Lowesmoor B2
Lowesmoor Terr A3
Lowesmoor Wharf A3
Magistrates Court A2
Midland Rd B3
Mill St C2
Moors Severn Terrace, The A1
Museum & Art Gallery A2
Museum of Royal Worcester C2
New Rd C1
New St B2
Northfield St A2
Odeon B2
Padmore St B3
Park St C3
Pheasant St B3
Pitchcroft Racecourse A1
Police Station A2
Portland St C2
Post Office B2
Quay St B2
Queen St B2
Rainbow Hill A3
Recreation Ground A2
Reindeer Court B2
Rogers Hill A3
Sabrina Terr A1
St Dunstan's Cr C3
St John's C1
St Martin's Gate B3
St Martin's Quarter B3
St Oswald's Rd A2
St Paul's St B3
St Swithin's Church B2
St Wulstans Cr C3
Sansome Walk A2
Severn St C2
Shambles, The B2
Shaw St B2
Shire Hall Crown Ct A2
Shrub Hill B3
Shrub Hill Rd B3
Shrub Hill Retail Park B3
Slingpool Walk C1
South Parade B2
Southfield St A2
Sports Ground A2/C1
Stanley Rd B3
Swan, The A1
Swimming Pool A2
Tallow Hill B3
Tennis Walk A2
Tolladine Rd B3
Tudor House B2
Tybridge St B1
Tything, The A2
Univ of Worcester B2
Vincent Rd B3
Vue C2
Washington St A3
Woolhope Rd C3
Worcester Bridge B2
Worcester County Cricket Ground C1
Worcester Royal Grammar School A2
Wylds La C3

Wrexham
Wrecsam 344

Abbot St B2
Acton Rd A3
Albert St C3
Alexandra Rd C1
Aran Rd A3
Barnfield C3
Bath Rd C2
Beeches, The A3
Beechley Rd C3
Belgrave Rd C2
Belle Vue Park C2
Belle Vue Rd C2
Belvedere Dr A1
Bennion's Rd C3
Berse Rd A1
Bersham Rd C1
Birch St C3
Bodhyfryd B3
Border Retail Park B3
Bradley Rd C2
Bright St B1
Bron-y-Nant B1
Brook St C2
Bryn-y-Cabanau Rd C3
Bury St C3
Bus Station B2
Butchers Market B3
Caia Rd C3
Cambrian Ind Est C3
Caxton Pl B2
Cemetery C1
Centenary Rd C1
Chapel St C2
Charles St B3
Chester Rd A3
Chester St B3
Cilcen Gr A3
Citizens Advice Bureau B2
Cobden Rd B1
Council Offices B3
County B2
Crescent Rd B3
Crispin La A2
Croesnewyth Rd B1
Cross St A2
Cunliffe St A2
Derby Rd C3
Dolydd Rd B1
Duke St B2
Eagles Meadow C3
Earle St C2
East Ave A2
Edward St C2
Egerton St B2
Empress Rd C1
Erddig Rd C2
Fairy Rd C2
Fire Station B2
Foster Rd A3
Foxwood Dr C1
Garden Rd A2
General Market B3
Gerald St B2
Gibson St C1
Glyndŵr University Plas Coch Campus A1
Greenbank St C3
Greenfield A2
Grosvenor Rd B2
Grove Park B2
Grove Park Rd B3
Grove Rd A3
Guildhall B2
Haig Rd C2
Hampden Rd C2
Hazel Gr A3
Henblas St B3
High St B3
Hightown Rd C3
Hill St B2
Holt Rd B3
Holt St B3
Hope St B2
Huntroyde Ave C3
Information Ctr B3
Island Gn Sh Ctr B2
Job Centre B2
Jubilee Rd B2
King St B2
Kingsmills Rd C3
Lambpit St B3
Law Courts B3
Lawson Cl A3
Lawson Rd A3
Lea Rd C2
Library & Arts Centre B2
Lilac Way B1
Llys David Lord B1
Lorne St A2
Maesgwyn Rd B1
Maesydre Rd A3
Manley Rd B3
Market St B3
Mawddy Ave A2
Mayville Ave A2
Memorial Gallery B2
Memorial Hall B3
Mold Rd A1
Mount St C3
Neville Cres A3
New Rd A2
North Wales Regional Tennis Centre A1
North Wales School of Art & Design B2
Oak Dr A3
Park Ave A3
Park St A2
Peel St C1
Pen y Bryn C2
Pentre Felin C2
Penymaes Ave A3
Peoples Market B3
Percy St C2
Pines, The A3
Plas Coch Rd A1
Plas Coch Retail Park A1
Police Station B3
Poplar Rd C2
Post Office A2/B2/C2/C3
Powell Rd B3
Poyser St C2
Price's La A2
Primrose Way B1
Princess St C1
Queen St B3
Queens Sq B2
Regent St B2
Rhosddu Rd A2/B2
Rhosnesni La A3
Rivulet Rd C3
Ruabon Rd C2
Ruthin Rd C1/C2
St Giles C3
St Giles Way C3
St James Ct A2
St Mary's B2
Salisbury Rd C3
Salop Rd C3
Sontley Rd C2
Spring Rd A2
Stanley St C3
Stansty Rd A2
Station Approach B2
Studio B2
Talbot Rd C2
Techniquest Glyndŵr A2
Town Hill C2
Trevor St C2
Trinity St B2
Tuttle St C3
Vale Park A1
Vernon St B2
Vicarage Hill B2
Victoria Rd A2
Walnut St A2
War Memorial B3
Waterworld Leisure Centre B3
Watery Rd B1/B2
Wellington Rd C2
Westminster Dr A3
William Aston Hall A1
Windsor Rd A1
Wrecsam
Wrexham AFC A1
Wrexham Central B2
Wrexham General B2
Wrexham Maelor Hospital (A&E) B1
Wrexham Technology Park B1
Wynn Ave A2
Yale College B3
Yale Gr A3
Yorke St C3

York 344

Aldwark B2
Barbican Rd C3
Bar Convent Living Heritage Ctr C1
Barley Hall B2
Bishopgate St C2
Bishopthorpe Rd C2
Blossom St C1
Bootham A1
Bootham Cr A1
Bootham Terr A1
Bridge St B2
Brook St A2
Brownlow St A2
Burton Stone La A1
Castle Museum C2
Castlegate B2
Cemetery Rd C3
Cherry St C2
City Screen B2
City Wall A2/B1/C3
Clarence St A2
Clementhorpe C2
Clifford St B2
Clifford's Tower B2
Clifton A1
Coach park A2
Coney St B2
Coppergate Ctr B2
Cromwell Rd C2
Crown Court C2
Davygate B2
Deanery Gdns A2
DIG B2
Ebor Industrial Estate B3
Fairfax House B2
Fishergate C3
Foss Islands Rd B3
Foss Islands Retail Pk B3
Fossbank A3
Garden St A2
George St C3
Gillygate A2
Goodramgate B2
Grand Opera House B2
Grosvenor Terr A1
Guildhall B2
Hallfield Rd A3
Heslington Rd C3
Heworth Green A3
Holy Trinity B2
Hope St C3
Huntington Rd A3
Information Ctr B2
James St B3
Jorvik Viking Ctr B2
Kent St C3
Lawrence St C3
Layerthorpe A3
Leeman Rd B1
Lendal B2
Lendal Bridge B1
Library A2/B1
Longfield Terr A1
Lord Mayor's Walk A2
Lower Eldon St A2
Lowther St A2
Mansion House B2
Margaret St C3
Marygate A1
Melbourne St C3
Merchant Adventurers' Hall B2
Merchant Taylors' Hall B2
Micklegate B1
Micklegate Bar C1
Monkgate A2
Moss St C1
Museum Gdns B1
Museum St B1
National Railway Museum B1
Navigation Rd B3
Newton Terr C2
North Parade A1
North St B2
Nunnery La C1
Nunthorpe Rd C1
Ouse Bridge B2
Paragon St C3
Park Gr A3
Park St C1
Parliament St B2
Peasholme Green B3
Penley's Grove St A2
Piccadilly B2
Police Station B2
Post Office B1/B2/C3
Priory St B1
Purey Cust Nuffield Hospital, The A2
Queen Anne's Rd A1
Reel C1
Regimental Mus B2
Richard III Experience at Monk Bar A2
Roman Bath B2
Rowntree Park C2
St Andrewgate B2
St Benedict Rd C1
St John St A2
St Olave's Rd A1
St Peter's Gr A1
St Saviourgate B2
Scarcroft Hill C1
Scarcroft Rd C1
Shambles, The B2
Shopmobility B2
Skeldergate C2
Skeldergate Bridge C2
Station Rd B1
Stonebow, The B2
Stonegate B2
Superstore A3
Sycamore Terr A1
Terry Ave C2
Theatre Royal B2
Thorpe St C1
Toft Green B1
Tower St C2
Townend St A2
Treasurer's House A2
Trinity La B1
Undercroft Mus A2
Union Terr A2
Victor St C2
Vine St C2
Walmgate B3
War Memorial B1
Wellington St C3
York Art Gallery A1
York Barbican C3
York Brewery B1
York Dungeon, The B2
York Minster A2
York St John Uni A2
York Station B1

Abbreviations used in the index

Index to road maps of Britain

How to use the index

Example **Witham Friary** Som 45 E8
- grid square
- page number
- county or unitary authority

Aberdeen **Aberdeen City**
Aberds **Aberdeenshire**
Ald **Alderney**
Anglesey **Isle of Anglesey**
Angus **Angus**
Argyll **Argyll and Bute**
Bath **Bath and North East Somerset**
Bedford **Bedford**
Bl Gwent **Blaenau Gwent**
Blackburn **Blackburn with Darwen**
Blackpool **Blackpool**
Bmouth **Bournemouth**
Borders **Scottish Borders**
Brack **Bracknell**
Bridgend **Bridgend**
Brighton **City of Brighton and Hove**
Bristol **City and County of Bristol**
Bucks **Buckinghamshire**
C Beds **Central Bedfordshire**
Caerph **Caerphilly**
Cambs **Cambridgeshire**
Cardiff **Cardiff**
Carms **Carmarthenshire**
Ceredig **Ceredigion**
Ches E **Cheshire East**
Ches W **Cheshire West and Chester**
Clack **Clackmannanshire**
Conwy **Conwy**
Corn **Cornwall**
Cumb **Cumbria**
Darl **Darlington**
Denb **Denbighshire**
Derby **City of Derby**
Derbys **Derbyshire**
Devon **Devon**

Dorset **Dorset**
Dumfries **Dumfries and Galloway**
Dundee **Dundee City**
Durham **Durham**
E Ayrs **East Ayrshire**
E Dunb **East Dunbartonshire**
E Loth **East Lothian**
E Renf **East Renfrewshire**
E Sus **East Sussex**
E Yorks **East Riding of Yorkshire**
Edin **City of Edinburgh**
Essex **Essex**
Falk **Falkirk**
Fife **Fife**
Flint **Flintshire**
Glasgow **City of Glasgow**
Glos **Gloucestershire**
Gtr Man **Greater Manchester**
Guern **Guernsey**
Gwyn **Gwynedd**
Halton **Halton**
Hants **Hampshire**
Hereford **Herefordshire**
Herts **Hertfordshire**
Highld **Highland**
Hrtlpl **Hartlepool**
Hull **Hull**
IoM **Isle of Man**
IoW **Isle of Wight**
Invclyd **Inverclyde**
Jersey **Jersey**
Kent **Kent**
Lancs **Lancashire**
Leicester **City of Leicester**
Leics **Leicestershire**
Lincs **Lincolnshire**
London **Greater London**

Luton **Luton**
M Keynes **Milton Keynes**
M Tydf **Merthyr Tydfil**
Mbro **Middlesbrough**
Medway **Medway**
Mers **Merseyside**
Midloth **Midlothian**
Mon **Monmouthshire**
Moray **Moray**
N Ayrs **North Ayrshire**
N Lincs **North Lincolnshire**
N Lanark **North Lanarkshire**
N Som **North Somerset**
N Yorks **North Yorkshire**
NE Lincs **North East Lincolnshire**
Neath **Neath Port Talbot**
Newport **City and County of Newport**
Norf **Norfolk**
Northants **Northamptonshire**
Northumb **Northumberland**
Nottingham **City of Nottingham**
Notts **Nottinghamshire**
Orkney **Orkney**
Oxon **Oxfordshire**
Pboro **Peterborough**
Pembs **Pembrokeshire**
Perth **Perth and Kinross**

Plym **Plymouth**
Poole **Poole**
Powys **Powys**
Ptsmth **Portsmouth**
Reading **Reading**
Redcar **Redcar and Cleveland**
Renfs **Renfrewshire**
Rhondda **Rhondda Cynon Taff**
Rutland **Rutland**
S Ayrs **South Ayrshire**
S Glos **South Gloucestershire**
S Lanark **South Lanarkshire**
S Yorks **South Yorkshire**
Scilly **Scilly**
Shetland **Shetland**
Shrops **Shropshire**
Slough **Slough**
Som **Somerset**
Soton **Southampton**
Staffs **Staffordshire**
Southend **Southend-on-Sea**
Stirling **Stirling**
Stockton **Stockton-on-Tees**
Stoke **Stoke-on-Trent**
Suff **Suffolk**
Sur **Surrey**

Swansea **Swansea**
Swindon **Swindon**
T&W **Tyne and Wear**
Telford **Telford & Wrekin**
Thurrock **Thurrock**
Torbay **Torbay**
Torf **Torfaen**
V Glam **The Vale of Glamorgan**
W Berks **West Berkshire**
W Dunb **West Dunbartonshire**
W Isles **Western Isles**
W Loth **West Lothian**
W Mid **West Midlands**
W Sus **West Sussex**
W Yorks **West Yorkshire**
Warks **Warwickshire**
Warr **Warrington**
Wilts **Wiltshire**
Windsor **Windsor and Maidenhead**
Wokingham **Wokingham**
Worcs **Worcestershire**
Wrex **Wrexham**
York **City of York**

A

Aaron's Hill Sur 50 E3
Aaron's Town Cumb 240 E2
Abbas Combe Som 30 C2
Abberley Worcs 116 D5
Abberton Essex 89 B8
  Worcs 117 G9
Abberwick Northumb 264 G4
Abbess End Essex 87 C9
Abbess Roding Essex 87 C9
Abbey Devon 27 E10
Abbeycwmhir Powys 113 C11
Abbey-cwm-hir Powys 113 C11
Abbeydale Glos 80 B5
  S Yorks 186 E4
Abbeydale Park S Yorks 186 E4
Abbey Dore Hereford 97 E7
Abbey Field Essex 107 G9
Abbey Gate Kent 53 B9
Abbey Green Shrops 149 C10
  Staffs 169 D7
Abbey Hey Gtr Man 184 B5
Abbeyhill Edin 280 G5
Abbey Hulton Stoke 168 F6
Abbey Mead Sur 66 F4
Abbey St Bathans Borders 272 C5
Abbeystead Lancs 203 C7
Abbey Town Cumb 238 G5
Abbey Village Lancs 194 C6
Abbey Wood London 68 D3
Abbots Bickington Devon 24 E4
Abbots Bromley Staffs 151 E11
Abbotsbury Dorset 17 D7
Abbotsford S Yorks 36 C4
Abbotsham Devon 24 B6
Abbotskerswell Devon 9 B7
Abbotsleigh Devon 8 F6
Abbots Leigh N Som 60 E4
Abbotsley Cambs 122 F4
Abbot's Meads Ches W 166 B5
Abbots Morton Worcs 117 F10
Abbots Ripton Cambs 122 B4
Abbots Salford Warks 117 G11
Abbotstone Hants 48 G5
Abbotswood Hants 32 C5
  Sur 50 C4
Abbots Worthy Hants 48 G3
Abbotts Ann Hants 47 E10
Abcott Shrops 115 B7
Abdon Shrops 131 F11
Abdy S Yorks 186 B6
Aber Ceredig 93 B9
Aberaeron Ceredig 111 E9
Aberaman Rhondda 77 E8
Aberangell Gwyn 146 G6
Aber-Arad Carms 92 D6
Aberarder Highld 290 E6
Aberarder House Highld 300 G6
Aberarder Lodge Highld 291 E7
Aberargie Perth 286 F5
Aberarth Ceredig 111 E9
Aberavon Neath 57 C8
Aber-banc Ceredig 93 C7
Aberbargoed Caerph 77 E11
Aberbechan Powys 130 E2
Aberbeeg Bl Gwent 78 E2
Aberbran Powys 95 F9
Abercanaid M Tydf 77 F9
Abercarn Caerph 78 G2
Abercastle Pembs 91 E7
Abercegir Powys 128 C6
Aberchalder Highld 290 C5
Aberchirder Aberds 302 D6
Abercorn W Loth 279 F11
Aber Cowarth Gwyn 147 C7
Abercraf Powys 76 C4
Abercregan Neath 57 B11
Abercrombie Fife 287 G9
Abercwmboi Rhondda 77 F8
Abercych Pembs 92 C4
Abercynafon Powys 77 B9
Abercynffig / Aberkenfig Bridgend 57 E11
Abercynon Rhondda 77 F9
Aberdalgie Perth 286 E4
Aberdâr / Aberdare Rhondda 77 E7
Aberdare / Aberdâr Rhondda 77 E7

Aberdaron Gwyn 144 D3
Aberdeen Aberdeen 293 C11
Aberdesach Gwyn 162 E6
Aberdour Fife 280 D3
Aberdovey / Aberdyfi Gwyn 128 D2
Aberdulais Neath 76 E3
Ab Kettleby Leics 154 E4
Ab Lench Worcs 117 G10
Aberdyfi / Aberdovey Gwyn 128 D2
Aberedw Powys 95 B11
Abereiddy Pembs 90 E5
Abererch Gwyn 145 B7
Aberfan M Tydf 77 F9
Aberfeldy Perth 286 C2
Aberffraw Anglesey 162 B5
Aberffrwd Ceredig 112 B3
  Mon 78 D5
Aberford W Yorks 206 F4
Aberfoyle Stirling 285 G9
Abergarw Bridgend 58 C2
Abergarwed Neath 76 E4
Abergavenny Mon 78 C3
Abergele Conwy 180 F6
Aber-Giâr Carms 93 C10
Abergorlech Carms 93 E11
Abergwaun / Fishguard Pembs 91 D9
Abergwesyn Powys 113 G7
Abergwili Carms 93 G8
Abergwynant Gwyn 146 F3
Abergwyngregyn Gwyn 179 G11
Abergwynfi Neath 57 B11
Aber-gwynfi Neath 57 B11
Abergwynolwyn Gwyn 128 B3
Aber-Hirnant Gwyn 147 C9
Aberhosan Powys 128 D6
Aberkenfig / Abercynffig Bridgend 57 E11
Aberlady E Loth 281 E9
Aberlemno Angus 287 B9
Aberllefenni Gwyn 128 C5
Aberllydan / Broad Haven Pembs 72 C5
Aberllynfi / Three Cocks Powys 96 D3
Abermagwr Ceredig 112 C3
Abermaw / Barmouth Gwyn 146 F2
Abermeurig Ceredig 111 F11
Aber miwl / Abermule Powys 130 E3
Abermorddu Flint 166 D4
Abermule / Aber-miwl Powys 130 E3
Abernant Powys 148 E2
Abernant Carms 92 G6
  Powys 130 D3
Abernethy Perth 286 F5
Abernyte Perth 286 D6
Aber-oer Wrex 166 F3
Aberogwr / Ogmore by Sea V Glam 57 F11
Aberpennar / Mountain Ash Rhondda 77 F8
Aberporth Ceredig 110 G5
Aber-Rhiwlech Gwyn 147 E8
Aberriw / Berriew Powys 130 C3
Abersoch Gwyn 144 D6
Abersychan Torf 78 E3
Abertawe / Swansea Swansea 56 C6
Aberteifi / Cardigan Ceredig 92 B3
Aberthin V Glam 58 D4
Abertillery Bl Gwent 78 E2
Abertridwr Caerph 58 B6
  Powys 147 F10
Abertrinant Gwyn 128 B2
Abertysswg Caerph 77 D10
Aberuchill Castle Perth 285 E11
Aberuthven Perth 286 F3
Aberyscir Powys 95 F9
Aberystwyth Ceredig 111 A11
Abhainn Suidhe W Isles 305 H2
Abingdon-on-Thames Oxon 83 F7
Abinger Common Sur 50 D6

Abinger Hammer Sur 50 D5
Abington Northants 120 E5
  S Lanark 259 E10
Abington Pigotts Cambs 104 C6
Abington Vale Northants 120 E5
Abingworth W Sus 35 D10
Ab Lench Worcs 117 G10
Ablington Glos 81 D10
  Wilts 47 D7
Abney Derbys 185 F11
Aboyne Aberds 293 D7
Abram Gtr Man 194 G6
Abriachan Highld 300 F5
Abridge Essex 87 F7
Abronhill N Lanark 278 F5
Abshot Hants 33 F8
Abson S Glos 61 E8
Abthorpe Northants 102 B2
Abune-the-Hill Orkney 314 D2
Aby Lincs 190 F6
Acaster Malbis York 207 E7
Acaster Selby N Yorks 207 E7
Accrington Lancs 195 B9
Acha Argyll 288 D3
Achabraid Argyll 275 E9
Achachork Highld 298 E4
Achafolla Argyll 275 B8
Achagary Highld 308 D7
Achahoish Argyll 275 F8
Achalader Perth 286 C5
Achallader Argyll 285 C7
Achalone Highld 310 D5
Acha Mor W Isles 304 F5
Achanalt Highld 300 C2
Achanamara Argyll 275 E8
Achandunie Highld 300 B6
Ach'an Todhair Highld 290 F2
Achany Highld 309 J5
Achaphubuil Highld 290 F2
Acharacle Highld 289 C8
Acharn Highld 289 D9
  Perth 285 C11
Acharole Highld 310 D6
Acharossan Argyll 275 F10
Acharry Muir Highld 309 K6
Achath Aberds 293 B9
Achavanich Highld 310 E5
Achavelgin Highld 301 D9
Achavraat Highld 301 E10
Achddu Carms 74 E6
Achduart Highld 307 J5
Achentoul Highld 310 F2
Achfary Highld 306 F7
Achfrish Highld 309 H5
Achgarve Highld 307 K3
Achiemore Highld 308 C3
  Highld 310 D2
A'Chill Highld 294 E4
Achiltibuie Highld 307 J5
Achina Highld 308 C7
Achinahuagh Highld 308 C5
Achindaul Highld 290 E3
Achindown Highld 301 E8
Achinduich Highld 309 J5
Achinduin Argyll 289 F10
Achingills Highld 310 C5
Achininver Highld 308 C5
Achintee Highld 299 E9
  Highld 290 F3
Achintraid Highld 295 B10
Achlaven Argyll 289 F11
Achlean Highld 291 D10
Achleck Argyll 288 E6
Achlorachan Highld 300 D3
Achluachrach Highld 290 E4
Achlyness Highld 306 D7
Achmelvich Highld 307 G5
Achmore Highld 295 B10
  Stirling 285 D9
  W Isles 304 E5
Achnaba Argyll 275 E10
  Argyll 289 F11
Achnabat Highld 300 F5
Achnabreck Argyll 275 D9

Achnacarnin Highld 306 F5
Achnacarry Highld 290 E3
Achnacloich Argyll 289 F11
  Highld 295 E7
Achnaconeran Highld 290 B6
Achnacraig Argyll 288 E6
Achnacree Argyll 289 F11
Achnacree Bay Argyll 289 F11
Achnacroish Argyll 289 E10
Achnadrish Highld 288 D6
Achnafalnich Argyll 284 E6
Achnagarron Highld 300 C6
Achnaha Highld 288 C6
Achnahanat Highld 309 K5
Achnahannet Highld 301 G9
Achnahard Argyll 288 G5
Achnairn Highld 309 H5
Achnaluachrach Highld 309 J6
Achnandarach Highld 295 B10
Achnanellan Highld 290 E2
Achnasaul Highld 290 E3
Achnasheen Highld 299 D11
Achnashelloch Argyll 275 D9
Achnavast Highld 310 C4
Achneigie Highld 299 B10
Achormlarie Highld 309 K6
Achorn Highld 310 F5
Achosnich Highld 288 C6
Achranich Highld 289 E9
Achreamie Highld 310 C4
Achriabhach Highld 290 G3
Achriesgill Highld 306 D7
Achrimsdale Highld 311 J3
Achtoty Highld 308 C6
Achurch Northants 137 G10
Achuvoldrach Highld 308 D5
Achvaich Highld 309 K7
Achvarasdal Highld 310 C3
Ackenthwaite Cumb 211 C10
Ackergill Highld 310 D7
Acklam Mbro 225 B9
  N Yorks 216 G5
Ackleton Shrops 132 D5
Acklington Northumb 252 C6
Ackton W Yorks 197 C12
Ackworth Moor Top W Yorks 198 D2
Acle Norf 161 G8
Acock's Green W Mid 134 G2
Acol Kent 71 F10
Acomb Northumb 241 D10
  York 207 C7
Acre Gtr Man 196 F2
  Lancs 195 C9
Acrefair Wrex 166 F3
Acres Nook Staffs 168 E4
Acre Street W Sus 21 B11
Acton Ches E 167 E10
  Dorset 18 F5
  London 67 C8
  Shrops 131 G7
  Staffs 168 G4
  Suff 107 C7
  Worcs 116 D6
  Wrex 166 E4
Acton Beauchamp Hereford 116 G3
Acton Bridge Ches W 183 F9
Acton Burnell Shrops 131 C10
Acton Green Hereford 116 G3
  London 67 D8
Acton Pigott Shrops 131 C10
Acton Place Suff 107 B7
Acton Reynald Shrops 149 E10
Acton Round Shrops 132 D2
Acton Scott Shrops 131 F9
Acton Trussell Staffs 151 F8
Acton Turville S Glos 61 C10
Adabroc W Isles 304 B7
Adambrae W Loth 269 A10
Adam's Green Dorset 29 E8
Adbaston Staffs 150 D5
Adber Dorset 29 C9
Adbolton Notts 154 B2
Adderbury Oxon 101 D9
Adderley Shrops 150 B3
Adderley Green Stoke 168 G6
Adderstone Northumb 264 C4
Addiewell W Loth 269 C9
Addingham W Yorks 205 D7
Addingham Moorside W Yorks 205 D7
Addington Bucks 102 F4

Addington continued
  Corn 6 B5
  Kent 53 B7
  London 67 G11
Addinston Borders 271 E10
Addiscombe London 67 F10
Addlestone Sur 66 F5
Addlestonemoor Sur 66 F4
Addlethorpe Lincs 175 B8
Adel W Yorks 205 F11
Adeney Telford 150 F4
Adeyfield Herts 85 D9
Adfa Powys 129 C11
Adforton Hereford 115 C8
Adgestone IoW 21 D7
Adisham Kent 55 C8
Adlestrop Glos 100 F4
Adlingfleet E Yorks 199 C10
Adlington Ches E 184 E6
  Lancs 194 E6
Adlington Park Lancs 194 E5
Admaston Staffs 151 E10
  Telford 150 G2
Admington Warks 100 B4
Adpar Ceredig 92 C6
Adsborough Som 28 B3
Adscombe Som 43 F7
Adstock Bucks 102 E4
Adstone Northants 119 G11
Adswood Gtr Man 184 D5
Adversane W Sus 35 C9
Advie Highld 301 F11
Adwalton W Yorks 197 B8
Adwell Oxon 83 F11
Adwick le Street S Yorks 198 F4
Adwick upon Dearne S Yorks 198 G3
Adziel Aberds 303 D9
Ae Dumfries 247 F11
Ae Village Dumfries 247 F11
Affetside Gtr Man 195 E9
Affleck Aberds 303 G8
Affpuddle Dorset 18 D2
Affric Lodge Highld 299 G11
Afon Eitha Wrex 166 F3
Afon-wen Flint 181 G10
Afon Wen Gwyn 145 B8
Afton IoW 20 D2
Agar Nook Leics 153 G9
Agbrigg W Yorks 197 D10
Aggborough Worcs 116 B6
Agglethorpe N Yorks 213 B11
Aglionby Cumb 239 F10
Agneash IoM 192 D5
Aigburth Mers 182 D5
Aiginis W Isles 304 E6
Aike E Yorks 209 D7
Aikenway Moray 302 E2
Aikerness Orkney 314 A4
Aikers Orkney 314 G4
Aiketgate Cumb 230 B5
Aikton Cumb 239 G7
Ailby Lincs 190 F6
Ailey Hereford 96 B6
Ailstone Warks 118 G4
Ailsworth Pboro 138 D2
Ainderby Quernhow N Yorks 215 C7
Ainderby Steeple N Yorks 224 G6
Aingers Green Essex 108 G2
Ainley Top W Yorks 196 D6
Ainsdale Mers 193 E10
Ainsdale-on-Sea Mers 193 E10
Ainstable Cumb 231 C7
Ainsworth Gtr Man 195 E9
Ainthorpe N Yorks 226 D4
Aintree Mers 182 B5
Aird Argyll 275 C8
  Dumfries 236 C2
  Highld 299 B7
  Highld 298 D3
  W Isles 305 G3
  W Isles 296 F3
  W Isles 304 E7
Aird a Mhachair W Isles 297 G3
Aird a' Mhulaidh W Isles 305 G3
Aird Asaig W Isles 305 H3
Aird Dhail W Isles 304 B6

Airdens Highld 309 K6
Airdeny Argyll 289 G11
Aird Mhidhinis W Isles 297 L3
Aird Mhighe W Isles 296 C6
  W Isles 305 J3
Aird Mhòr W Isles 297 G4
Aird Mhor W Isles 297 L3
Aird of Sleat Highld 295 E7
Airdrie N Lanark 268 B5
Airds of Kells Dumfries 237 B8
Aird Thunga W Isles 304 E6
Airdtorrisdale Highld 308 C6
Aird Uig W Isles 304 E2
Aire View N Yorks 204 D5
Airedale W Yorks 198 B3
Airidh a Bhruaich W Isles 305 G4
Airieland Dumfries 237 D9
Airinis W Isles 304 E6
Airlie Angus 287 B7
Airlies Dumfries 236 D5
Airmyn E Yorks 199 B8
Airntully Perth 286 D4
Airor Highld 295 E9
Airth Falk 279 D7
Airthrey Castle Stirling 278 B6
Airton N Yorks 204 B4
Airy Hill N Yorks 227 D7
Airyligg Dumfries 236 C4
Aisby Lincs 155 B10
  Lincs 188 C5
Aisgernis W Isles 297 J3
Aish Devon 8 C3
  Devon 8 D6
Aisholt Som 43 F7
Aiskew N Yorks 214 B5
Aislaby N Yorks 226 D5
  N Yorks 227 D7
  Stockton 225 C7
Aisthorpe Lincs 188 E6
Aith Orkney 314 E2
  Shetland 312 D8
  Shetland 313 H5
Aithnen Orkney 314 E2
Aithsetter Shetland 313 K6
Aitkenhead S Ayrs 245 B8
Aitnoch Highld 301 F9
Akeld Northumb 263 D11
Akeley Bucks 102 D4
Akenham Suff 108 B3
Albany T&W 243 F7
Albaston Corn 12 G4
Alberbury Shrops 149 G7
Albert Town Pembs 72 B6
Albert Village Leics 152 F6
Albourne W Sus 36 D3
Albourne Green W Sus 36 D3
Albrighton Shrops 132 C6
  Shrops 149 F9
Alburgh Norf 142 F5
Albury Herts 105 G8
  Sur 50 D5
Albury End Herts 105 G8
Albury Heath Sur 50 D5
Alby Hill Norf 160 C3
Alcaig Highld 300 D5
Alcaston Shrops 131 F9
Alcombe Som 42 E3
  Wilts 61 F10
Alconbury Cambs 122 B3
Alconbury Weston Cambs 122 B3
Aldborough Norf 160 C3
  N Yorks 215 F8
Aldborough Hatch London 68 B3
Aldbourne Wilts 63 D9
Aldbrough E Yorks 209 F10
Aldbrough St John N Yorks 224 C4
Aldbury Herts 85 C7
Aldcliffe Lancs 211 G9
Aldclune Perth 291 G11

Aldeburgh Suff 127 F9
Aldeby Norf 143 E8
Aldenham Herts 85 F10
Alderbrook E Sus 37 B8
Alderbury Wilts 31 B11
Aldercar Derbys 170 F6
Alderford Norf 160 F2
Alder Forest Gtr Man 184 B3
Alderholt Dorset 31 E10
Alderley Glos 80 G3
Alderley Edge Ches E 184 F4
Alderman's Green W Mid 135 G2
Aldermaston W Berks 64 F5
Aldermaston Soke W Berks 64 G6
Aldermaston Wharf W Berks 64 F6
Alderminster Warks 100 B4
Aldermoor Soton 32 D5
Alder Moor Staffs 152 D4
Alderney Poole 18 C6
Alder Row Som 45 E9
Aldersbrook London 68 B2
Alder's End Hereford 98 C3
Aldersey Green Ches W 167 D7
Aldershawe Staffs 134 B2
Aldershot Hants 49 C11
Alderton Glos 99 E10
  Northants 102 B4
  Shrops 149 E9
  Suff 108 C6
  Wilts 61 C10
Alderton Fields Glos 99 E10
Alderwasley Derbys 170 E4
Aldfield N Yorks 214 F5
Aldford Ches W 166 D6
Aldgate Rutland 137 C9
Aldham Essex 107 F8
  Suff 107 B11
Aldie Highld 309 L7
Aldingbourne W Sus 22 B6
Aldingham Cumb 210 E5
Aldington Kent 54 F5
  Worcs 99 B11
Aldington Frith Kent 54 F4
Aldivalloch Moray 302 G3
Aldochlay Argyll 277 C7
Aldon Shrops 115 B8
Aldoth Cumb 229 B8
Aldourie Castle Highld 300 F6
Aldreth Cambs 123 C8
Aldridge W Mid 133 C11
Aldringham Suff 127 E8
Aldrington Brighton 36 F3
Aldsworth Glos 81 C11
  W Sus 22 B3
Aldunie Moray 302 G3
Aldwark Derbys 170 D2
  N Yorks 215 G9
Aldwarke S Yorks 186 C6
Aldwick W Sus 22 D6
Aldwincle Northants 137 G10
Aldworth W Berks 64 D5
Alehousehill Aberds 303 G10
Ale Oak Shrops 130 G4
Alexandria W Dunb 277 F7
Aley Som 43 F7
Aley Green C Beds 85 B9
Alfardisworthy Devon 24 E3
Alfington Devon 15 B8
Alfold Sur 50 F4
Alfold Bars W Sus 50 F4
Alfold Crossways Sur 50 F4
Alford Aberds 293 B7
  Lincs 191 F7
  Som 44 G6
Alfred's Well Worcs 117 C8
Alfreton Derbys 170 E6
Alfrick Worcs 116 G4
Alfrick Pound Worcs 116 G4
Algaltraig Argyll 275 F11
Algarkirk Lincs 156 B5
Alhampton Som 44 G6
Aline Lodge W Isles 305 G3
Alisary Highld 289 B9
Alkborough N Lincs 199 C11
Alkerton Glos 80 D3
  Oxon 101 C7
Alkham Kent 55 E9
Alkington Shrops 149 B10

Aar–Alm

Alkmonton Derbys 152 B3
Alkrington Garden Village Gtr Man 195 G11
Alladale Lodge Highld 309 L4
Allaleigh Devon 8 E6
Allanaquoich Aberds 292 D3
Allanbank Borders 271 F10
  N Lanark 268 D6
Allangrange Mains Highld 300 D6
Allanshaugh Borders 271 F8
Allanshaws Borders 271 G9
Allanton Borders 273 E7
  N Lanark 269 D7
  S Lanark 268 E4
Allaston Glos 79 E11
Allathasdal W Isles 297 L2
Allbrook Hants 33 C7
All Cannings Wilts 62 G5
Allendale Town Northumb 241 F8
Allen End Warks 134 D3
Allenheads Northumb 232 B3
Allensford Durham 242 G3
Allens Green Herts 87 B7
Allensmore Hereford 97 D9
Allenton Derby 153 C7
Aller Devon 27 F9
  Devon 30 G3
  Som 28 B6
Allerby Cumb 229 D7
Allerford Som 27 B11
  Som 42 D2
Allerston N Yorks 216 C6
Allerthorpe E Yorks 207 D11
Allerton Mers 182 D6
  W Yorks 205 G8
Allerton Bywater W Yorks 198 B2
Allerton Mauleverer N Yorks 206 B4
Allesley W Mid 134 G6
Allestree Derby 152 B6
Allet Corn 4 F5
Allexton Leics 136 C6
Allgreave Ches E 169 B7
Allhallows Medway 69 D10
Allhallows-on-Sea Medway 69 D10
Alligin Shuas Highld 299 D8
Allimore Green Staffs 151 F7
Allington Kent 53 B8
  Lincs 172 G5
  Wilts 47 F8
  Wilts 61 D11
  Wilts 62 G3
Allington Bar Wilts 61 E11
Allithwaite Cumb 211 D7
Alloa Clack 279 C7
Allonby Cumb 229 C7
Allostock Ches W 184 G2
Alloway S Ayrs 257 F8
Allowenshay Som 28 E5
All Saints Devon 28 G4
All Saints South Elmham Suff 142 G6
Allscot Shrops 132 D5
Allscott Telford 150 G2
All Stretton Shrops 131 D9
Allt Carms 75 E9
Alltami Flint 166 B3
Alltbeithe Highld 290 C2
Alltchaorunn Highld 284 B5
Alltforgan Powys 147 E9
Alltmawr Powys 95 B11
Alltnacaillich Highld 308 E4
Allt na h-Airbhe Highld 307 K6
Allt-nan-sùgh Highld 295 C11
Alltsigh Highld 290 B6
Alltwalis Carms 93 E8
Alltwen Neath 76 E2
Alltyblaca Ceredig 93 B10
Allt-yr-yn Newport 59 B9
Allwood Green Suff 125 C10
Alma Notts 171 E7

Almagill Dumfries 238 B3
Almeley Hereford 114 G6
Almeley Wooton
Hereford 114 G6
Almer Dorset 18 B4
Almholme S Yorks 198 F5
Almington Staffs 150 C4
Alminstone Cross Devon 24 C4
Almondbank Perth 286 E4
Almondbury W Yorks 197 D7
Almondsbury S Glos 60 C6
Almondvale W Loth 269 B11
Almshouse Green Essex 106 E5
Alne N Yorks 215 F9
Alne End Warks 118 F2
Alne Hills Warks 118 E2
Alness Highld 300 C6
Alnessferry Highld 300 C6
Alne Station N Yorks 215 F10
Alnham Northumb 263 G11
Alnmouth Northumb 264 G6
Alnwick Northumb 264 G5
Alperton London 67 C7
Alphamstone Essex 107 D7
Alpheton Suff 125 G7
Alphington Devon 14 C4
Alpington Norf 142 C5
Alport Derbys 170 C2
Powys 130 D5
Alpraham Ches E 167 D9
Alresford Essex 107 G11
Alrewas Staffs 152 F3
Alsager Ches E 168 D3
Alsagers Bank Staffs 168 F4
Alscot Bucks 84 E4
Alsop en le Dale
Derbys 169 D11
Alston Cumb 231 B10
Devon 28 G4
Alstone Glos 99 E9
Glos 99 G8
Som 43 D10
Alstonefield Staffs 169 D10
Alston Sutton Som 44 C2
Alswear Devon 26 C2
Alt Gtr Man 196 G2
Altandhu Highld 307 H4
Altanduin Highld 311 G2
Altarnun Corn 11 E10
Altass Highld 309 J4
Altbough Hereford 97 E10
Altdargue Aberds 293 C7
Alterwall Highld 310 C6
Altham Lancs 203 G11
Alt Hill Gtr Man 196 G2
Althorne Essex 88 F6
Althorpe N Lincs 199 F10
Alticane S Ayrs 244 F6
Alticry Dumfries 236 D4
Altmore Windsor 65 D11
Altnabreac Station
Highld 310 E4
Altnacealgach Hotel
Highld 307 H7
Altnacraig Argyll 289 G10
Altnafeadh Highld 284 B6
Altnaharra Highld 308 F5
Altofts W Yorks 197 C11
Alton Derbys 170 C5
Hants 49 F8
Staffs 169 G9
Wilts 47 D7
Alton Barnes Wilts 62 G6
Altonhill E Ayrs 257 B10
Alton Pancras Dorset 30 G2
Alton Priors Wilts 62 G6
Altonside Moray 302 D2
Altour Highld 290 E4
Altrincham Gtr Man 184 D3
Altrua Highld 290 E4
Altskeith Stirling 285 G8
Altyre Ho Moray 301 D10
Alum Rock W Mid 134 F2
Alva Clack 279 B7
Alvanley Ches W 183 G7
Alvaston Derby 153 C7
Alvechurch Worcs 117 C10
Alvecote Warks 134 C4
Alvediston Wilts 31 C7
Alveley Shrops 132 G5
Alverdiscott Devon 25 B8
Alverstoke Hants 21 B8
Alverstone IoW 21 D7
Alverthorpe W Yorks 197 C10
Alverton Notts 172 G3
Alves Moray 301 C11
Alvescot Oxon 82 E3
Alveston S Glos 60 B6
Warks 118 F4
Alveston Down S Glos 60 B6
Alveston Hill Warks 118 G4
Alvie Highld 291 C10
Alvingham Lincs 190 C5
Alvington Glos 79 E10
Som 29 D8
Alwalton Cambs 138 D2
Alway Newport 59 B10
Alweston Dorset 29 E11
Alwington Devon 24 C6
Alwinton Northumb 251 B10
Alwoodley W Yorks 205 E11
Alwoodley Gates
W Yorks 206 E2
Alwoodley Park
W Yorks 205 E11
Alyth Perth 286 C6
Amalebra Corn 1 B5
Amalveor Corn 1 B5
Amatnatua Highld 309 K4
Am Baile W Isles 297 K3
Ambaston Derbys 153 C8
Ambergate Derbys 170 E4
Amber Hill Lincs 174 F2
Amberley Glos 80 E5
Hereford 97 B10
W Sus 35 E8
Amble Northumb 253 C7
Amblecote W Mid 133 F7
Ambler Thorn W Yorks 196 B5
Ambleside Cumb 221 E7
Ambleston Pembs 91 F10
Ambrosden Oxon 83 B10
Am Buth Argyll 289 G10
Amcotts N Lincs 199 E11
Amen Corner Brack 65 F10
Amersham Bucks 85 F7
Amersham Common
Bucks 85 F7
Amersham Old Town
Bucks 85 F7
Amersham on the Hill
Bucks 85 F7
Amerton Staffs 151 D9
Amesbury Bath 45 B7
Wilts 47 E7
Ameysford Dorset 31 G9
Amington Staffs 134 C4
Amisfield Dumfries 247 G11
Amlwch Anglesey 178 C6
Amlwch Port Anglesey 179 C7
Ammanford / Rhydaman
Carms 75 C10
Ammerham Som 28 F5
Amod Argyll 255 D8
Amotherby N Yorks 216 E4
Ampfield Hants 32 C6
Ampleforth N Yorks 215 D11
Ampney Crucis Glos 81 E9
Ampney St Mary Glos 81 E9
Ampney St Peter Glos 81 E9
Amport Hants 47 E9
Ampthill C Beds 103 D10
Ampton Suff 125 C7
Amroth Pembs 73 D11
Amulree Perth 286 D2
Amwell Herts 85 C11
Anagach Highld 301 G10
Anaheilt Highld 289 C10
Anancaun Highld 299 C10
An Caol Highld 298 D6
Ancarraig Highld 300 G4
Ancaster Lincs 173 G7
Anchor Shrops 130 G3
Anchorage Park Ptsmth 33 G11
Anchor Corner Norf 141 D10
Anchorsholme Blackpool 202 E2
Anchor Street Norf 160 E6
An Cnoc W Isles 304 E6
Ancoats Gtr Man 184 B5
Ancroft Northumb 273 F9
Ancroft Northmoor
Northumb 273 F9
Ancrum Borders 262 E4
Ancton W Sus 35 G7
Ancumtoun Orkney 314 A7
Anderby Lincs 191 F8
Anderby Creek Lincs 191 F8
Andersea Som 43 G10
Andersfield Som 43 G8
Anderson Dorset 18 B3
Anderton Ches W 183 F10
Corn 7 E8
Lancs 194 E6
Andertons Mill Lancs 194 E4
Andover Hants 47 D11
Andover Down Hants 47 D11
Andoversford Glos 81 B8
Andreas IoM 192 C5
Andwell Hants 49 C7
Anelog Gwyn 144 D3
Anerley London 67 F10
Anfield Mers 182 C5
Angarrack Corn 2 B3
Angarrick Corn 3 B7
Angelbank Shrops 115 B11
Angersleigh Som 27 D11
Angerton Cumb 238 F6
Angle Pembs 72 E5
An Gleann Ur W Isles 304 E6
Angmering W Sus 35 G9
Angram N Yorks 206 D6
N Yorks 223 F7
Anick Northumb 241 D11
Anie Stirling 285 F9
Ankerdine Hill Worcs 116 F4
Ankerville Highld 301 B8
Anlaby E Yorks 200 B4
Anlaby Park Hull 200 B5
An Leth Meadhanach
W Isles 297 K3
Anmer Norf 158 D4
Anmore Hants 33 E11
Annan Dumfries 238 D5
Annaside Cumb 210 B1
Annat Argyll 284 E4
Highld 290 D5
Highld 299 D8
Anna Valley Hants 47 E10
Annbank S Ayrs 257 E10
Annesley Notts 171 E8
Annesley Woodhouse
Notts 171 E7
Annfield Plain Durham 242 G5
Anniesland Glasgow 267 B10
Annifirth Shetland 313 J3
Annishader Highld 298 D4
Annis Hill Suff 143 F7
Annitsford T&W 243 C7
Annscroft Shrops 131 B9
Ann's Hill Hants 33 G9
Annwell Place Derbys 152 F6
Ansdell Lancs 193 B10
Ansells End Herts 85 B11
Ansford Som 44 G6
Ansley Warks 134 E5
Ansley Common Warks 134 E6
Anslow Staffs 152 D4
Anslow Gate Staffs 152 D3
Ansteadbrook Sur 50 G2
Anstey Herts 105 E8
Leics 135 B10
Anstruther Easter Fife 287 G9
Anstruther Wester Fife 287 G9
Ansty Hants 49 E8
Warks 135 G7
Wilts 31 B7
W Sus 36 C3
Ansty Coombe Wilts 31 B7
Ansty Cross Dorset 30 G3
Anthill Common Hants 33 E10
Anthony Corn 7 E7
Anthony's Cross Glos 98 G4
Anthorn Cumb 238 F5
Antingham Norf 160 C5
An t-Ob W Isles 296 C6
Anton's Gowt Lincs 174 F3
Antonshill Falk 279 E7
Antony Corn 7 E7
Antony Passage Corn 7 D8
Antrobus Ches W 183 F10
Anvil Green Kent 54 D6
Anvilles W Berks 63 F10
Anwick Lincs 173 E10
Anwoth Dumfries 237 D7
Aonachan Highld 290 E4
Aoradh Argyll 274 G3
Apedale Staffs 168 F4
Aperfield London 52 B2
Apes Dale Worcs 117 C9
Apes Hall Cambs 139 E11
Apethorpe Northants 137 D10
Apeton Staffs 151 F7
Apley Lincs 189 F10
Apley Forge Shrops 132 D4
Apperknowle Derbys 186 F5
Apperley Glos 99 F7
Apperley Bridge
W Yorks 205 F9
Apperley Dene
Northumb 242 F3
Appersett N Yorks 223 G7
Appin Argyll 289 E11
Appin House Argyll 289 E11
Appleby N Lincs 200 E3
Appleby-in-Westmorland
Cumb 231 G9
Appleby Magna Leics 134 B6
Appleby Parva Leics 134 B6
Applecross Highld 299 E7
Applecross Ho Highld 299 E7
Appledore Devon 27 E9
Devon 40 G3
Kent 39 B7
Appledore Heath Kent 54 G3
Appleford Oxon 83 G8
Applegarthtown
Dumfries 248 G4
Applehouse Hill Windsor 65 C10
Applemore Hants 32 F5
Appleshaw Hants 47 D10
Applethwaite Cumb 229 F11
Appleton Halton 183 D8
Oxon 82 E6
Appleton-le-Moors
N Yorks 216 B4
Appleton-le-Street
N Yorks 216 E4
Appleton Park Warr 183 E10
Appleton Roebuck
N Yorks 207 E7
Appleton Thorn Warr 183 E10
Appleton Wiske N Yorks 225 E7
Appletreehall Borders 262 F2
Appletreewick
N Yorks 213 G11
Appley IoW 21 C8
Som 27 C9
Appley Bridge Lancs 194 F4
Apse Heath IoW 21 E7
Apsey Green Suff 126 E5
Apsley Herts 85 D9
Apsley End C Beds 104 E2
Apuldram W Sus 22 C4
Aqueduct Telford 132 B3
Aquhythie Aberds 293 B9
Arabella Highld 301 B8
Arbeadie Aberds 293 D8
Arberth / Narberth
Pembs 73 C10
Arbirlot Angus 287 C10
Arboll Highld 311 L2
Arborfield Wokingham 65 F9
Arborfield Cross
Wokingham 65 F9
Arborfield Garrison
Wokingham 65 F9
Arbourthorne S Yorks 186 D5
Arbroath Angus 287 C10
Arbury Cambs 123 E8
Arbuthnott Aberds 293 F9
Archavandra Muir
Highld 309 K7
Archdeacon Newton
Darl 224 B5
Archenfield Hereford 96 C5
Archiestown Moray 302 E2
Archnalea Highld 289 C10
Arclid Ches E 168 C3
Arclid Green Ches E 168 C3
Ardachu Highld 309 J6
Ardailly Argyll 255 B7
Ardalanish Argyll 274 B4
Ardallie Aberds 303 F10
Ardalum Ho Argyll 288 F6
Ardamaleish Argyll 275 G11
Ardanaiseig Argyll 284 E4
Ardaneaskan Highld 295 B10
Ardanstur Argyll 275 B9
Ardargie House Hotel
Perth 286 F4
Ardarroch Highld 295 B10
Ardban Highld 295 B9
Ardbeg Argyll 254 C5
Argyll 276 E3
Ardcharnich Highld 307 L6
Ardchiavaig Argyll 274 B4
Ardchonnell Argyll 275 B10
Ardchronie Highld 309 L6
Ardchuilk Highld 300 F2
Ardchullarie More
Stirling 285 F9
Ardchyle Stirling 285 E9
Ardclach Highld 301 E9
Ard-dhubh Highld 299 E7
Arddleen Powys 148 F5
Ardechvie Highld 290 D3
Ardeley Herts 104 F6
Ardelve Highld 295 C10
Arden Argyll 277 E7
E Renf 267 D10
Ardencaple Ho Argyll 275 B8
Ardendrain Highld 300 F5
Arden Park Gtr Man 184 C6
Ardens Grafton Warks 118 G2
Ardentallen Argyll 289 G10
Ardentinny Argyll 276 D3
Ardentraive Argyll 275 F11
Ardeonaig Stirling 285 D10
Ardersier Highld 301 D7
Ardery Highld 289 C9
Ardessie Highld 307 L5
Ardfern Argyll 275 C9
Ardfernal Argyll 274 F6
Ardgartan Argyll 284 G6
Ardgay Highld 309 K5
Ardglassie Aberds 303 C10
Ardgour Highld 290 G2
Ardgye Moray 301 C11
Ardheslaig Highld 299 D7
Ardiecow Moray 302 C5
Ardinamir Argyll 275 B8
Ardindrean Highld 307 L6
Ardingly W Sus 36 B4
Ardington Oxon 64 B2
Ardington Wick Oxon 64 B2
Ardintoul Highld 295 C10
Ardlair Aberds 302 G5
Highld 299 B9
Ardlamey Argyll 255 C7
Ardlamont Ho Argyll 275 G10
Ardlawhill Aberds 303 C8
Ardleigh Essex 107 F11
Ardleigh Green London 68 B4
Ardleigh Heath Essex 107 E10
Ardler Perth 286 C6
Ardley Oxon 101 F10
Ardley End Essex 87 C8
Ardlui Argyll 285 F7
Ardlussa Argyll 275 E7
Ardmair Highld 307 K6
Ardmay Argyll 284 G6
Ardmenish Argyll 274 F6
Ardminish Argyll 255 C7
Ardmolich Highld 289 B9
Ardmore Argyll 289 G9
Highld 306 D7
Highld 309 L7
Ardnacross Argyll 289 E7
Ardnadam Argyll 276 F3
Ardnagowan Argyll 284 G4
Ardnagrask Highld 300 E5
Ardnarff Highld 295 B10
Ardnastang Highld 289 C10
Ardnave Argyll 274 F3
Ardneil N Ayrs 266 F3
Ardno Argyll 284 G5
Ardo Aberds 303 F8
Ardoch Argyll 277 F7
Perth 286 D4
Stirling 285 F9
Ardochy House Highld 290 C4
Ardo Ho Aberds 303 G9
Ardoyne Aberds 302 G6
Ardpatrick Argyll 275 G8
Ardpatrick Ho Argyll 255 B8
Ardpeaton Argyll 276 D4
Ardradnaig Perth 285 C11
Ardrishaig Argyll 275 E9
Ardross Fife 287 G9
Highld 300 B6
Ardrossan N Ayrs 266 G4
Ardross Castle Highld 300 B6
Ardshave Highld 309 K7
Ardsheal Highld 289 D11
Ardshealach Highld 289 C8
Ardskenish Argyll 274 D4
Ardsley S Yorks 197 F11
Ardslignish Highld 289 C7
Ardtalla Argyll 254 B5
Ardtalnaig Perth 285 D11
Ardtaraig Argyll 275 E11
Ardtoe Highld 289 B8
Ardtreck Highld 294 B5
Ardtrostan Perth 285 E10
Ardtur Argyll 289 E11
Arduaine Argyll 275 B8
Ardullie Highld 300 C5
Ardvannie Highld 309 L6
Ardvar Highld 306 F6
Ardvasar Highld 295 E8
Ardveich Stirling 285 E10
Ardverikie Highld 291 E7
Ardvorlich Perth 285 E10
Ardwell Dumfries 236 E3
Moray 302 F3
S Ayrs 244 E5
Ardwell Mains Dumfries 236 E3
Ardwick Gtr Man 184 B5
Areley Kings Worcs 116 C6
Arford Hants 49 F10
Argoed Caerph 77 F11
Powys 113 E9
Powys 130 E5
Shrops 130 G6
Shrops 148 E6
Argos Hill E Sus 37 B9
Arichamish Argyll 275 C10
Arichastlich Argyll 284 D6
Aridhglas Argyll 288 G5
Arieniskill Highld 295 G9
Arileod Argyll 288 D3
Arinacrinachd Highld 299 D7
Arinagour Argyll 288 D4
Arineckaig Highld 299 E9
Arion Orkney 314 E2
Arisaig Highld 295 G8
Ariundle Highld 289 C10
Arivegaig Highld 289 C8
Arivoichallum Argyll 254 C4
Arkendale N Yorks 215 G7
Arkesden Essex 105 E9
Arkholme Lancs 211 E11
Arkleby Cumb 229 D8
Arkleton Dumfries 249 E9
Arkle Town N Yorks 223 E10
Arkley London 86 F2
Arksey S Yorks 198 F5
Arkwright Town Derbys 186 G6
Arle Glos 99 G8
Arlebrook Glos 80 D4
Arlecdon Cumb 219 B10
Arlescote Warks 101 B7
Arlesey C Beds 104 D3
Arleston Telford 150 G3
Arley Ches E 183 E11
Arley Green Ches E 183 E11
Arlingham Glos 80 C2
Arlington Devon 40 E6
E Sus 23 D8
Glos 81 D10
Arlington Beccott Devon 40 E6
Armadale Highld 308 C7
W Loth 269 B8
Armadale Castle Highld 295 E8
Armathwaite Cumb 230 B6
Armigers Essex 105 F11
Arminghall Norf 142 C5
Armitage Staffs 151 F11
Armitage Bridge
W Yorks 196 E6
Armley W Yorks 205 G11
Armscote Warks 100 C4
Armsdale Staffs 150 C5
Armshead Staffs 168 F6
Armston Northants 137 F11
Armthorpe S Yorks 198 F6
Arnabost Argyll 288 D4
Arnaby Cumb 210 C3
Arncliffe N Yorks 213 E8
Arncroach Fife 287 G9
Arndilly Ho Moray 302 E2
Arne Dorset 18 D5
Arnesby Leics 136 E2
Arngask Perth 286 F5
Arnisdale Highld 295 D10
Arnish Highld 298 E5
Arniston Midloth 270 C6
Arnol W Isles 304 D5
Arnold E Yorks 209 E8
Notts 171 F9
Arno's Vale Bristol 60 E6
Arnprior Stirling 278 C2
Arnside Cumb 211 D9
Aros Mains Argyll 289 E7
Arowry Wrex 149 B9
Arpafeelie Highld 300 D6
Arpinge Kent 55 F7
Arrad Foot Cumb 210 C6
Arram E Yorks 208 E6
Arrathorne N Yorks 224 G4
Arreton IoW 20 D6
Arrington Cambs 122 G6
Arrivain Argyll 284 D6
Arrochar Argyll 284 G6
Arrow Warks 117 F11
Arrowe Hill Mers 182 D3
Arrowfield Top Worcs 117 C10
Arrow Green Hereford 115 F8
Arrunden W Yorks 196 F6
Arscaig Highld 309 H5
Arscott Shrops 131 B8
Arthill Ches E 184 D2
Arthington W Yorks 205 E11
Arthingworth Northants 136 G5
Arthog Gwyn 146 G2
Arthrath Aberds 303 F9
Arthursdale W Yorks 206 F3
Arthurstone Perth 286 C6
Arthurville Highld 309 L7
Artington Sur 50 D3
Artrochie Aberds 303 F10
Arundel W Sus 35 F8
Arwick Orkney 314 D3
Aryhoulan Highld 290 G2
Asby Cumb 229 G7
Ascog Argyll 266 C2
Ascoil Highld 311 H2
Ascot Windsor 66 F2
Ascott Warks 100 E6
Ascott d'Oyley Oxon 82 B4
Ascott Earl Oxon 82 B3
Ascott-under-Wychwood
Oxon 82 B4
Asenby N Yorks 215 D7
Asfordby Leics 154 F4
Asfordby Hill Leics 154 F4
Asgarby Lincs 173 F10
Lincs 174 B4
Ash Devon 8 F6
Dorset 30 E5
Kent 55 B9
Kent 68 G5
Som 28 C3
Som 29 C7
Sur 49 C11
Ashaig Highld 295 C8
Ashampstead W Berks 64 D5
Ashampstead Green
W Berks 64 D5
Ashansworth Hants 48 B2
Ashbank Kent 53 C10
Ash Bank Staffs 168 F6
Ashbeer Som 42 F5
Ashbocking Suff 126 G3
Ashbourne Derbys 169 F11
Ashbrittle Som 27 C9
Ashbrook Shrops 131 E9
Ash Bullayne Devon 26 G3
Ashburnham Forge
E Sus 23 B11
Ashburton Devon 8 B5
Ashbury Devon 12 B6
Oxon 63 C9
Ashby N Lincs 200 F2
Ashby by Partney Lincs 174 B6
Ashby cum Fenby
NE Lincs 201 G9
Ashby de la Launde
Lincs 173 D9
Ashby-de-la-Zouch
Leics 153 F7
Ashby Folville Leics 154 G4
Ashby Hill NE Lincs 201 G8
Ashby Magna Leics 135 E11
Ashby Parva Leics 135 F10
Ashby Puerorum Lincs 190 G4
Ashby St Ledgers
Northants 119 D11
Ashby St Mary Norf 142 C6
Ashchurch Glos 99 E8
Ashcombe Devon 14 F4
Ashcombe Park N Som 59 G10
Ashcott Som 44 F2
Ashcott Corner Som 44 F2
Ashculme Devon 27 E10
Ashdon Essex 105 C11
Ashe Hants 48 D4
Asheldham Essex 89 E7
Ashen Essex 106 C4
Ashendon Bucks 84 C2
Asheridge Bucks 84 E6
Ashey IoW 21 D7
Ashfield Argyll 275 E8
Carms 94 F3
Hants 32 D5
Hereford 97 G11
Shrops 148 D6
Stirling 285 G11
Suff 126 E4
Ashfield Cum Thorpe
Suff 126 E4
Ashfield Green Suff 124 F5
Suff 126 C5
Ashfields Shrops 150 D4
Ashfold Crossways
W Sus 36 B2
Ashford Devon 8 F3
Devon 40 F4
Hants 31 E10
Kent 54 E4
Sur 66 E5
Ashford Bowdler
Shrops 115 C10
Ashford Carbonell
Shrops 115 C10
Ashford Common Sur 66 E5
Ashford Hill Hants 64 G5
Ashford in the Water
Derbys 185 G11
Ashgate Derbys 186 G5
Ashgill S Lanark 268 F5
Ash Green Sur 50 D2
Warks 134 F6
Ashgrove Bath 45 B8
Ash Grove Wrex 166 G5
Ash Hill Devon 14 G4
Ashiestiel Borders 261 B10
Ashill Devon 27 E9
Norf 141 C7
Som 28 D4
Ashingdon Essex 88 G5
Ashington Northumb 253 F7
Poole 18 B6
Som 29 C9
W Sus 35 D10
Ashington End Lincs 175 B8
Ashintully Castle Perth 292 G3
Ashkirk Borders 261 E11
Ashlett Hants 33 G7
Ashleworth Glos 98 F6
Ashley Cambs 124 E3
Ches E 184 E3
Devon 25 E10
Dorset 31 G10
Glos 80 G6
Hants 19 B11
Hants 47 G11
Kent 55 D10
Northants 136 E5
Staffs 150 B5
Wilts 61 F10
Ashley Dale Staffs 150 B5
Ashley Down Bristol 60 D5
Ashley Green Bucks 85 D7
Ashleyhay Derbys 170 E3
Ashley Heath Ches E 184 D3
Dorset 31 G10
Staffs 150 B4
Ashley Moor Hereford 115 D9
Ashley Park Sur 66 F6
Ash Magna Shrops 149 B11
Ashmanhaugh Norf 160 E6
Ashmansworth Hants 48 B2
Ashmansworthy Devon 24 D4
Ashmead Green Glos 80 F3
Ashmill Devon 12 B3
Ash Mill Devon 26 C3
Ash Moor Devon 26 D3
Ashmore Dorset 30 D6
Ashmore Green W Berks 64 F4
Ashmore Lake W Mid 133 D9
Ashmore Park W Mid 133 C9
Ashnashellach Lodge
Highld 299 E10
Ashopton Derbys 185 D11
Ashorne Warks 118 F6
Ashover Derbys 170 C4
Ashover Hay Derbys 170 C5
Ashow Warks 118 C6
Ash Parva Shrops 149 B11
Ashperton Hereford 98 C2
Ashprington Devon 8 D6
Ash Priors Som 27 B11
Ashreigney Devon 25 E10
Ashridge Court Devon 25 G11
Ash Street Suff 107 B10
Ashtead Sur 51 B7
Ash Thomas Devon 27 E8
Ashton Corn 2 D4
Hants 33 D9
Hereford 115 E10
Invclyd 276 F4
Northants 102 B5
Northants 137 F11
Pboro 138 B2
Som 44 D2
Ashton Common Wilts 45 B11
Ashton Gate Bristol 60 E5
Ashton Green E Sus 23 C7
Ashton Hayes Ches W 167 B8
Ashton Heath Halton 183 F9
Ashton-in-Makerfield
Gtr Man 183 B9
Ashton Keynes Wilts 81 G8
Ashton under Hill Worcs 99 D9
Ashton-under-Lyne
Gtr Man 184 B6
Ashton upon Mersey
Gtr Man 184 C3
Ashton Vale Bristol 60 E5
Ashurst Hants 32 E4
Kent 52 F4
Lancs 194 F3
W Sus 35 D11
Ashurst Bridge Hants 32 E4
Ashurst Wood W Sus 52 F2
Ashvale Bl Gwent 77 C10
Ash Vale Sur 49 C11
Ashwater Devon 12 B3
Ashwell Devon 14 G3
Herts 104 D5
Rutland 155 G7
Som 28 D5
Ashwell End Herts 104 C5
Ashwellthorpe Norf 142 D2
Ashwick Som 44 D6
Ashwicken Norf 158 F4
Ashwood Staffs 133 F7
Ashybank Borders 262 F2
Askam in Furness Cumb 210 D4
Askern S Yorks 198 E5
Askerswell Dorset 16 C6
Askerton Hill Lincs 172 F4
Askett Bucks 84 D4
Askham Cumb 230 G6
Notts 188 G2
Askham Bryan York 207 D7
Askham Richard York 206 D6
Asknish Argyll 275 D10
Askrigg N Yorks 223 G8
Askwith N Yorks 205 D9
Aslackby Lincs 155 C11
Aslacton Norf 142 E3
Aslockton Notts 154 B4
Asloun Aberds 293 B7
Asney Som 44 F3
Aspall Suff 126 D3
Aspatria Cumb 229 C8
Aspenden Herts 105 F7
Asperton Lincs 156 B5
Aspley Nottingham 171 G8
Staffs 150 C6
Aspley Guise C Beds 103 D8
Aspley Heath C Beds 103 D8
Warks 117 C11
Aspull Gtr Man 194 F6
Aspull Common
Gtr Man 183 B10
Assater Shetland 312 F4
Asselby E Yorks 199 B8
Asserby Lincs 191 F7
Asserby Turn Lincs 191 F7
Assington Suff 107 D8
Assington Green Suff 124 G5
Assynt Ho Highld 300 C5
Astbury Ches E 168 C4
Astcote Northants 120 G3
Asterby Lincs 190 F3
Asterley Shrops 131 B7
Asterton Shrops 131 E7
Asthall Oxon 82 C3
Asthall Leigh Oxon 82 C4
Astle Ches E 184 G4
Highld 309 K7
Astley Gtr Man 195 G8
Shrops 149 F10
Warks 134 F6
Worcs 116 D5
Astley Abbotts Shrops 132 D4
Astley Bridge Gtr Man 195 E8
Astley Cross Worcs 116 D6
Astley Green Gtr Man 184 B2
Astmoor Halton 183 E8
Aston Ches E 167 F10
Ches W 183 F9
Derbys 152 C3
Derbys 185 E11
Flint 166 B4
Hereford 115 C9
Hereford 115 E9
Herts 104 G5
Oxon 82 E4
Powys 130 E5
Shrops 132 E6
Shrops 149 D10
Staffs 151 E7
Staffs 168 G3
S Yorks 187 D7
Telford 132 B2
W Mid 133 F11
Wokingham 65 C9
Aston Abbotts Bucks 102 G6
Aston Bank Worcs 116 C2
Aston Botterell Shrops 132 G2
Aston-by-Stone Staffs 151 C8
Aston Cantlow Warks 118 F2
Aston Clinton Bucks 84 C5
Aston Crews Hereford 98 G3
Aston Cross Glos 99 E8
Aston End Herts 104 G5
Aston Eyre Shrops 132 E3
Aston Fields Worcs 117 D9
Aston Flamville Leics 135 E9
Aston Ingham Hereford 98 G3
Aston juxta Mondrum
Ches E 167 D11
Aston le Walls Northants 119 G9
Aston Magna Glos 100 D3
Aston Munslow Shrops 131 F10
Aston on Carrant Glos 99 E8
Aston on Clun Shrops 131 G7
Aston-on-Trent Derbys 153 D8
Aston Pigott Shrops 130 B6
Aston Rogers Shrops 130 B6
Aston Rowant Oxon 84 F2
Aston Sandford Bucks 84 D3
Aston Somerville Worcs 99 D10
Aston Square Shrops 148 D6
Aston Subedge Glos 100 C2
Aston Tirrold Oxon 64 B5
Aston Upthorpe Oxon 64 B5
Astrop Northants 101 D10
Astrope Herts 84 C5
Astwick C Beds 104 D4
Astwith Derbys 170 C6
Astwood M Keynes 103 B9
Worcs 117 D8
Worcs 117 F7
Astwood Bank Worcs 117 E10
Aswarby Lincs 173 G9
Aswardby Lincs 190 G5
Atcham Shrops 131 B10
Atch Lench Worcs 117 G10
Athelhampton Dorset 17 C11
Athelington Suff 126 C4
Athelney Som 28 B4
Athelstaneford E Loth 281 F10
Atherfield Green IoW 20 F5
Atherington Devon 25 C9
W Sus 35 G8
Athersley North
S Yorks 197 F11
Athersley South
S Yorks 197 F11
Atherstone Som 28 D5
Warks 134 D6
Atherstone on Stour
Warks 118 G4
Atherton Gtr Man 195 G7
Athnamulloch Highld 299 G11
Athron Hall Perth 286 G4
Atley Hill N Yorks 224 E5
Atlow Derbys 170 F2
Attadale Highld 295 B11
Attadale Ho Highld 295 B11
Attenborough Notts 153 B10
Atterbury M Keynes 103 D7
Atterby Lincs 189 C7
Attercliffe S Yorks 186 D5
Atterley Shrops 132 D2
Atterton Leics 135 D7
Attleborough Norf 141 D10
Warks 135 E7
Attlebridge Norf 160 F2
Attleton Green Suff 124 G4
Atwick E Yorks 209 C9
Atworth Wilts 61 F11
Auberrow Hereford 97 B9
Aubourn Lincs 172 C6
Auch Argyll 285 D7
Auchagallon N Ayrs 255 D9
Auchallater Aberds 292 E3
Auchareoch N Ayrs 255 E10
Aucharnie Aberds 302 E6
Auchattie Aberds 293 D8
Auchavan Angus 292 G3
Auchbreck Moray 302 G2
Auchenback E Renf 267 D10
Auchenbainzie Dumfries 247 D8
Auchenblae Aberds 293 F9
Auchenbrack Dumfries 247 D7
Auchenbreck Argyll 255 C8
Argyll 275 E11
Auchencairn Dumfries 237 D9
Dumfries 247 G11
N Ayrs 256 D2
Auchencairn Ho
Dumfries 237 D10
Auchencar N Ayrs 255 D9
Auchencarroch W Dunb 277 E8
Auchencrosh S Ayrs 236 B3
Auchencrow Borders 273 C7
Auchendinny Midloth 270 C5
Auchengray S Lanark 269 E9
Auchenhalrig Moray 302 C3
Auchenharvie N Ayrs 266 G5
Auchenheath S Lanark 268 G6
Auchenhew N Ayrs 256 E2
Auchenlaich Stirling 285 G10
Auchenleck Dumfries 237 D9
Auchenlochan Argyll 275 F10
Auchenmalg Dumfries 236 D4
Auchenreoch E Dunb 278 F3
Auchensoul S Ayrs 245 E7
Auchentibber S Lanark 268 E3
Auchentiber N Ayrs 267 F7
Auchertyre Highld 295 C10
Auchessan Stirling 285 E8
Auchgourish Highld 291 B11
Auchindrain Argyll 284 G4
Auchindrean Highld 307 L6
Auchininna Aberds 302 E6
Auchinleck Dumfries 236 B6
E Ayrs 258 E3
Auchinloch N Lanark 278 G3
Auchinner Perth 285 F10
Auchinraith S Lanark 268 D3
Auchinroath Moray 302 D2
Auchinstarry N Lanark 278 F4
Auchintoul Aberds 293 B7
Highld 309 K5
Auchiries Aberds 303 F10
Auchlee Aberds 293 D10
Auchleeks Ho Perth 291 G9
Auchleven Aberds 302 G6
Auchlinn Aberds 303 D7
Auchlochan S Lanark 259 B8
Auchlossan Aberds 293 C7
Auchlunachan Highld 307 L6
Auchlunies Aberds 293 D10
Auchlyne Stirling 285 E9
Auchmacoy Aberds 303 F9
Auchmair Moray 302 G3
Auchmantle Dumfries 236 C3
Auchmenzie Aberds 302 G5
Auchmillan E Ayrs 258 D2
Auchmithie Angus 287 C10
Auchmore Highld 300 D4
Auchmuirbridge Fife 286 G6
Auchmull Angus 293 F7
Auchnacraig Argyll 289 G9
Auchnacree Angus 292 G6
Auchnafree Perth 286 D2
Auchnagallin Highld 301 F10
Auchnagarron Argyll 275 E11
Auchnagatt Aberds 303 E9
Auchnaha Argyll 275 E10
Auchnahillin Highld 301 F7
Auchnarrow Moray 302 G2
Auchnashelloch Perth 285 F11
Auchnotteroch Dumfries 236 C1
Aucholzie Aberds 292 D5
Auchrannie Angus 286 B6
Auchroisk Highld 301 G10
Auchronie Angus 292 E6
Auchterarder Perth 286 F3
Auchteraw Highld 290 C5
Auchterderran Fife 280 B4
Auchterhouse Angus 287 D7
Auchtermuchty Fife 286 F6
Auchterneed Highld 300 D4
Auchtertool Fife 280 C4
Auchtertyre Moray 301 D11
Stirling 285 E7
Auchtubh Stirling 285 E9
Auckengill Highld 310 C7
Auckley S Yorks 199 G7
Audenshaw Gtr Man 184 B6
Audlem Ches E 167 G11
Audley Staffs 168 E3
Audley End Essex 105 D10
Essex 106 D6
Audley End *continued*
Norf 142 G2
Suff 125 G7
Auds Aberds 302 C6
Aughertree Cumb 229 D11
Aughton E Yorks 207 F10
Lancs 193 F11
Lancs 211 F10
S Yorks 187 D7
Wilts 47 B8
Aughton Park Lancs 194 F2
Aukside Durham 232 F4
Auldearn Highld 301 D9
Aulden Hereford 115 G9
Auldgirth Dumfries 247 F10
Auldhame E Loth 281 E11
Auldhouse S Lanark 268 E2
Auldtown of Carnoustie
Aberds 302 E6
Ault a'chruinn Highld 295 C11
Aultanrynie Highld 308 F3
Aultbea Highld 307 L3
Aultdearg Highld 300 C2
Aultgrishan Highld 307 L2
Aultguish Inn Highld 300 B3
Ault Hucknall Derbys 171 B7
Aultibea Highld 311 G4
Aultiphurst Highld 310 C2
Aultivullin Highld 310 C2
Aultmore Highld 301 G10
Moray 302 D4
Aultnagoire Highld 300 G5
Aultnamain Inn Highld 309 L6
Aultnaslat Highld 290 C3
Aulton Aberds 302 G6
Aulton of Atherb Aberds 303 E9
Aultvaich Highld 300 E5
Aunby Lincs 155 G10
Aundorach Highld 291 B11
Aunk Devon 27 G8
Aunsby Lincs 155 B10
Auquhorthies Aberds 303 G8
Aust S Glos 60 B5
Austendike Lincs 156 E5
Austen Fen Lincs 190 C5
Austenwood Bucks 66 B3
Austerfield S Yorks 187 C11
Austerlands Gtr Man 196 F3
Austhorpe W Yorks 206 G3
Austrey Warks 134 B5
Austwick N Yorks 212 F5
Authorpe Lincs 190 E6
Authorpe Row Lincs 191 G8
Avebury Wilts 62 F6
Avebury Trusloe Wilts 62 F5
Aveley Thurrock 68 C5
Avening Glos 80 F5
Avening Green S Glos 80 G2
Averham Notts 172 E3
Avernish Highld 295 C10
Avery Hill London 68 E2
Aveton Gifford Devon 8 F3
Avielochan Highld 291 B11
Aviemore Highld 291 B10
Avington Hants 48 G4
W Berks 63 F11
Avoch Highld 301 D7
Avon Hants 19 B8
Wilts 62 D3
Avonbridge Falk 279 G8
Avoncliff Wilts 45 B10
Avon Dassett Warks 101 B8
Avonmouth Bristol 60 D4
Avonwick Devon 8 D4
Awbridge Hants 32 C4
Awhirk Dumfries 236 D2
Awkley S Glos 60 B5
Awliscombe Devon 27 G10
Awre Glos 80 D2
Awsworth Notts 171 G7
Axbridge Som 44 C2
Axford Hants 48 E6
Wilts 63 F8
Axmansford Hants 64 G5
Axminster Devon 15 B11
Axmouth Devon 15 C11
Axton Flint 181 E10
Axtown Devon 7 B10
Axwell Park T&W 242 E5
Aycliff Kent 55 E10
Aycliffe Durham 233 G11
Aydon Northumb 242 D2
Aykley Heads Durham 233 C11
Aylburton Glos 79 E10
Aylburton Common
Glos 79 E10
Ayle Northumb 231 B10
Aylesbeare Devon 14 C6
Aylesbury Bucks 84 C4
Aylesby NE Lincs 201 F8
Aylesford Kent 53 B8
Aylesham Kent 55 C8
Aylestone Leicester 135 C11
Aylestone Hill Hereford 97 C10
Aylestone Park
Leicester 135 C11
Aylmerton Norf 160 B3
Aylsham Norf 160 D3
Aylton Hereford 98 D3
Aylworth Glos 100 G2
Aymestrey Hereford 115 D8
Aynho Northants 101 E10
Ayot Green Herts 86 C2
Ayot St Lawrence Herts 85 B11
Ayot St Peter Herts 86 B2
Ayr S Ayrs 257 E8
Ayre of Atler Shetland 313 G6
Ayres Shetland 313 H5
Ayres End Herts 85 C11
Ayres of Selivoe
Shetland 313 J4
Ayres Quay T&W 243 F9
Aysgarth N Yorks 213 B10
Ayshford Devon 27 D8
Ayside Cumb 211 C7
Ayston Rutland 137 C7
Aythorpe Roding Essex 87 B9
Ayton Borders 273 C8
T&W 243 F7
Ayton Castle Borders 273 C8
Aywick Shetland 312 E7
Azerley N Yorks 214 E5

B

Babbacombe Torbay 9 B8
Babbington Notts 171 G7
Babbinswood Shrops 148 C6
Babbs Green Herts 86 B5
Babcary Som 29 B9
Babel Carms 94 D6
Babel Green Suff 106 B4
Babell Flint 181 G11
Babeny Devon 13 F9
Babingley Norf 158 D3
Babraham Cambs 123 G10
Babworth Notts 187 E11
Bac W Isles 304 D6
Bachau Anglesey 178 E6
Bache Shrops 131 G9

Bacheldre Powys 130 E4
Bachelor's Bump E Sus 38 E4
Bache Mill Shrops. 131 F10
Backaland Orkney 314 C5
Backaskaill Orkney 314 A4
Backbarrow Cumb 211 C7
Backbower Gtr Man 185 C7
Backburn Aberds 293 D10
Backe Carms 74 B3
Backfolds Aberds 303 D10
Backford Ches W 182 G6
Backford Cross Ches W . . 182 G5
Backhill Aberds 303 F7
Aberds 303 F10
Backhill of Clackriach
Aberds 303 E9
Backhill of Fortree
Aberds 303 E9
Backhill of Trustach
Aberds 293 D8
Backies Highld. 311 J2
Backlass Highld 310 F6
Highld 310 E4
Back Muir Fife 279 D11
Back of Keppoch Highld. 295 G8
Back o' th' Brook Staffs. 169 E9
Back Rogerton E Ayrs . . 258 E3
Back Street Suff 124 F4
Backwell N Som. 60 F3
Backwell Common
N Som 60 F3
Backwell Green N Som . . . 60 F3
Backworth T&W 243 C8
Bacon End Essex 87 B10
Baconend Green Essex . . 87 B10
Bacon's End W Mid 134 F3
Baconsthorpe Norf 160 B2
Bacton Hereford 97 E7
Norf 160 C6
Suff 125 D11
Bacton Green Norf 160 C6
Suff 125 D10
Bacup Lancs 195 C11
Badachonacher Highld. 300 B6
Badachro Highld 299 B7
Badanloch Lodge Highld 308 F7
Badavanich Highld 299 D11
Badbea Highld 307 K5
Badbury Swindon 63 C7
Badbury Wick Swindon. . . 63 C7
Badby Northants 119 F11
Badcall Highld 306 D7
Badcaul Highld 307 K5
Baddeley Edge Stoke . . . 168 E6
Baddeley Green Stoke . . 168 E6
Baddesley Clinton
Warks 118 C4
Baddesley Ensor Warks . 134 D5
Baddidarroch Highld. . . 307 F11
Baddoch Aberds 292 E3
Baddock Highld 301 D7
Baddow Park Essex 88 E2
Badeach Moray 302 F2
Badenscallie Highld . . . 307 J5
Badenscoth Aberds 303 F7
Badentoy Park Aberds . 293 D11
Badenyon Aberds 292 B5
Badgall Corn 11 D10
Badgeney Cambs 139 D8
Badger Shrops 132 D5
Badgergate Shrops 278 B5
Badger's Hill Worcs 99 B10
Badger's Mount Kent . . . 68 G4
Badger Street Som 28 D3
Badgeworth Glos. 80 B6
Badgworth Som 43 C11
Badharlick Corn 11 D11
Badicaul Highld 295 C9
Badingham Suff 126 D6
Badintagairt Highld . . . 309 H4
Badlesmere Kent 54 C4
Badlipster Highld 310 E6
Badluarach Highld 307 K4
Badminton S Glos 61 C10
Badnaban Highld. 307 G5
Badnabay Highld. 306 E7
Badnagie Highld 310 F5
Badninish Highld 309 K7
Badrallach Highld 307 K5
Badsey Worcs 99 C11
Badshalloch W Dunb . . . 277 D9
Badshot Lea Sur 49 D11
Badsworth W Yorks 198 E3
Badwell Ash Suff 125 D9
Badwell Green Suff 125 D10
Badworthy Devon. 8 C3
Bae Cinmel / Kinmel Bay
Conwy 181 E7
Bae Colwyn / Colwyn Bay
Conwy 180 F4
Bae Penrhyn / Penrhyn Bay
Conwy 180 E4
Baffins Ptsmth. 33 G11
Bagber Dorset 30 E3
Bagby N Yorks 215 C9
Bagby Grange N Yorks . 215 C9
Bag End Lincs 190 G5
Bagendon Glos. 81 D8
Bagginswood Shrops . . . 132 G3
Baggrow Cumb 229 C9
Bagha Chaisteil W Isles . 296 D5
Bagh a Chaisteil
W Isles 297 M2
Bagham Kent 54 C5
Baghasdal W Isles 297 K3
Bagh Mor W Isles 296 F4
Bagh Shiarabhagh
W Isles 297 L3
Bagillt Flint 182 G2
Baginton Warks 118 C6
Baglan Neath 57 C8
Bagley Shrops 149 D8
Som 44 D3
W Yorks 205 F10
Bagley Green Som 27 D10
Bagley Marsh Shrops . . . 149 D7
Bagmore Hants 49 E7
Bagnall Staffs 168 E6
Bagnor W Berks 64 F2
Bagpath Glos. 80 E5
Glos 80 G4
Bagshaw Derbys 185 E9
Bagshot Sur 66 G2
Wilts 63 F10
Bagshot Heath Sur 66 G2
Bagslate Moor
Gtr Man 195 E11
Bagstone S Glos 61 B7
Bagthorpe Norf 158 C5
Notts 171 E7
Baguley Gtr Man 184 D4
Bagworth Leics 135 B8
Bagwyllydiart Hereford . 97 F8
Bagwy Llydiart Hereford . 97 F8
Bail Ard Bhuirgh
W Isles 304 C6
Bailbrook Bath 61 F9
Baildon W Yorks 205 F9

Baildon Green W Yorks . 205 F8
Baile W Isles 296 C5
Baile Ailein W Isles 304 F4
Baile a Mhanaich
W Isles 296 F3
Baile an Truiseil
W Isles 304 C5
Bailebeag Highld 291 B7
Baile Boidheach Argyll. 275 F8
Baile Gharbhaidh
W Isles 297 G3
Baile Glas W Isles 296 F4
Baile Mhartainn
W Isles 296 D3
Baile Mhic Phail
W Isles 296 D4
Baile Mor Argyll 288 G4
Baile na Creige W Isles . 297 L2
Baile nan Cailleach
W Isles 296 F3
Baile Raghaill W Isles . . 296 D3
Bailey Green Hants 33 B11
Baileyhead Cumb 240 B2
Bailiesward Aberds 302 F4
Bailiff Bridge W Yorks . 196 C6
Baillieston Glasgow 268 C3
Bail' Iochdrach W Isles . 296 F4
Bailrigg Lancs 202 B5
Bail Uachdraich
W Isles 296 E4
Bail' Ur Tholastaidh
W Isles 304 D7
Bainbridge N Yorks 223 G8
Bainsford Falk. 279 E7
Bainshole Aberds 302 F6
Bainton E Yorks 208 C5
Oxon 101 G8
Pboro 137 B11
Baintown Fife 287 G7
Baker's Cross Kent 53 F9
Bakers End Herts 86 B5
Baker's Hill Glos. 79 C9
Baker's Wood Bucks 66 B4
Bakesdown Corn 24 G2
Bakestone Moor Derbys 187 F8
Bakewell Derbys 170 B2
Bala / Y Bala Gwyn. . . . 147 B8
Balbeg Highld 300 F4
Highld 300 G4
Balbeggie Perth 286 E5
Balbegno Castle Aberds 293 F8
Balbithan Aberds 293 B9
Balbithan Ho Aberds . . 293 B10
Highld 301 C7
Highld 309 K5
Balby S Yorks 198 G5
Balcherry Highld 311 L2
Balchladich Highld. . . . 306 F5
Balchraggan Highld. . . . 300 E5
Highld 300 G5
Balchrick Highld 306 D6
Balchrystie Fife 287 G8
Balcladaich Highld 300 G2
Balcombe W Sus. 51 G10
Balcombe Lane E Sus . . . 51 G10
Balcomie Fife 287 F10
Balcraggie Lodge Highld 310 F5
Balcurvie Fife 287 G7
Baldersby N Yorks 215 D7
Baldersby St James
N Yorks 215 D7
Balderstone Gtr Man . . . 196 E2
Lancs 203 G8
Balderton Ches W 166 C5
Notts 172 E4
Baldhu Corn 4 G5
Baldingstone Gtr Man. . 195 E10
Baldinnie Fife 287 F8
Baldock Herts 104 E4
Baldon Row Oxon 83 E9
Baldoon Highld 300 B6
Baldovie Dundee 287 D8
Baldrine IoM 192 D5
Baldslow E Sus 38 E3
Baldwin IoM. 192 E2
Baldwinholme Cumb . . 239 G8
Baldwin's Gate Staffs . . 168 G3
Baldwins Hill W Sus 51 F11
Bale Norf 159 B10
Balearn Aberds 303 D10
Balemartine Argyll 288 E1
Balephuil Argyll 288 E1
Balerno Edin 270 B3
Baleromindor Argyll . . 274 D4
Balevullin Argyll 288 E1
Balfield Angus 293 G7
Balfour Orkney 314 E4
Balfour Mains Orkney . 314 E4
Balfron Stirling 277 D10
Balfron Station Stirling 277 D10
Balgaveny Aberds 302 E6
Balgavies Angus 287 B9
Balgonar Fife 279 C10
Balgove Aberds 303 F8
Balgowan Highld 291 D8
Perth 286 E3
Balgown Highld 298 C3
Balgrennie Aberds 292 C6
Balgrochan E Dunb 278 F3
Balgy Highld 299 D8
Balhaldie Stirling 286 G2
Balhalgardy Aberds . . . 303 G7
Balham London 67 E9
Balhary Perth 286 C6
Baliasta Shetland 312 C8
Baligill Highld. 310 C2
Baligortan Argyll 288 E5
Baligrundle Argyll 289 F11
Balindore Argyll 289 F11
Balinoe Argyll 288 E1
Balintore Angus 286 B6
Highld 301 B8
Balintraid Highld. 301 B7
Balintuim Aberds 292 E3
Balk N Yorks 215 C9
Balkeerie Angus 287 C7
Balkemback Angus 287 D7
Balk Field Notts 188 E2
Balkholme E Yorks 199 B9
Balkissock S Ayrs 244 G4

Ballantrae S Ayrs 244 G3
Ballaquine IoM 192 D5
Ballard's Ash Wilts 62 C5
Ballards Gore Essex 88 G5
Ballard's Green Warks . . 134 E5
Ballasalla IoM 192 C4
Highld 192 E4
Ballater Aberds 292 D5
Ballathie Perth 286 D5
Ballaugh IoM. 192 C4
Ballaveare IoM 192 E4
Highld 301 F8
Ballcorach Moray 301 G10
Ballechin Perth 286 B3
Balleich Stirling 277 B10
Balleigh Highld 309 L7
Ballencrieff E Loth 281 F9
Ballencrieff Toll
W Loth 279 G9
Ballentoul Perth 291 G10
Ball Green Stoke 168 E5
Ball Haye Green Staffs . 169 D7
Ball Hill Hants 64 G2
Ballidon Derbys 170 E2
Balliekine N Ayrs 255 D9
Balliemore Argyll 275 E11
Argyll 289 G8
Ballikinrain Stirling . . . 277 D11
Ballimeanoch Argyll . . . 284 F4
Ballimore Argyll 275 E10
Stirling 285 F9
Ballinaby Argyll. 274 G3
Ballindean Perth 286 E6
Ballingdon Essex 107 C7
Ballingdon Bottom
Herts 85 C8
Ballinger Bottom Bucks. . 84 E6
Ballinger Common Bucks . 84 E6
Ballingham Hereford . . . 97 E11
Ballingham Hill Hereford 97 E11
Ballingry Fife 280 B3
Ballinlick Perth 286 C3
Ballinluig Perth 286 B3
Ballintean Highld 291 C10
Ballintuim Perth 286 B5
Balliveolan Argyll 289 E10
Balloch Angus 287 B7
Highld 301 E7
N Lanark 278 F5
Ballochan Aberds 292 D7
Ballochearn Stirling . . . 277 D11
Ballochford Moray. 302 F3
Ballochmorrie S Ayrs . . 244 G6
Aberds 293 C8
Dumfries 236 C2
Falk 278 E4
S Lanark 269 G7
Ball's Green Glos. 80 F5
Balls Hill W Mid 133 E9
Balls Cross W Sus 35 B7
Ballygown Argyll. 288 E6
Ballygrant Argyll. 274 G4
Ballygroggan Argyll. . . 255 F7
Ballyhaugh Argyll. 288 D3
Balmacara Highld 295 C10
Balmacara Square
Highld 295 C10
Balmaclellan Dumfries . 237 B8
Balmacneil Perth 286 B3
Balmacqueen Highld . . 298 B4
Balmae Dumfries 237 E8
Balmaha Stirling 277 C8
Balmalcolm Fife 287 G7
Balmalloch N Lanark . . 278 F4
Balmeanach Highld. . . . 288 E5
Argyll 289 E8
Highld 295 B7
Highld 298 E5
Balmedie Aberds 293 B11
Balmer Heath Shrops . . 149 C8
Balmerino Fife 287 E7
Balmerlawn Hants 32 G4
Balmesh Dumfries. 236 D4
Balmichael N Ayrs 255 D10
Balminnoch Dumfries . . 236 C4
Balmirmer Angus 287 D9
Balmoral Borders 261 B11
Balmore E Dunb 278 G2
Highld 298 E2
Highld 300 E3
Highld 301 G9
Perth 286 B3
Balmule Fife 280 D4
Balmullo Fife 287 E8
Balmungie Highld. 301 D7
Balmurrie Dumfries . . . 236 C4
Balnaboth Angus 292 G5
Balnabruaich Highld . . 301 C7
Balnabruich Highld . . . 311 G5
Balnacoil Highld 311 H2
Balnacra Highld 299 E9
Balnacroft Aberds. 292 D4
Balnafoich Highld 300 F6
Balnagall Highld 311 L2
Balnagowan Highld . . . 289 C7
Balnaguard Perth 286 B3
Balnahanaid Perth 285 C10
Balnain Highld 300 F4
Balnakeil Highld 308 C3
Balnaknock Highld 298 C4
Balnamoon Aberds 303 D9
Angus 293 G7
Balnapaling Highld. . . . 301 C7
Balne N Yorks 198 D5
Balnoon Corn. 2 B2
Balochroy Argyll 255 B8
Balormock Glasgow 268 C2
Balquhanran Aberds. . . 293 G10
Balquhidder Stirling . . . 285 E9
Balquhidder Station
Stirling 285 E9
Balrownie Angus 293 G7
Balsall Common W Mid . 118 B4
Balsall Heath W Mid . . 133 G11
Balsall Street W Mid . . . 118 B4
Balsam Cambs 123 G11
Balscote Oxon 101 C7
Balsham Cambs. 123 G11
Balsporran Cottages
Highld 291 D8
Balstonia Thurrock 69 C7
Baltasound Shetland . . 312 C8
Balterley Staffs 168 E3
Balterley Green Staffs . . 168 E3

Balterley Heath Staffs . . 168 E2
Baltersan Dumfries 236 C6
Balthangie Aberds 303 D8
Balthayock Perth 286 E5
Baltonsborough Som . . . 44 G4
Balure Argyll 289 E11
Balvaird Highld 300 D5
Balvenie Moray. 302 E3
Balvicar Argyll 275 B8
Balvraid Highld 295 D10
Highld 301 F8
Balwest Corn 2 C3
Bamber Bridge Lancs . . 194 B5
Bamber's Green Essex . . 105 G11
Bamburgh Northumb . . 264 C5
Bamff Perth 286 B6
Bamford Derbys 186 E2
Gtr Man 195 E11
Bampton Cumb 221 B10
Devon 27 C7
Oxon 82 E4
Bampton Grange Cumb 221 B10
Banavie Highld. 290 F3
Banbury Oxon 101 C9
Bancffosfelen Carms . . . 75 C7
Banchor Highld 301 E9
Banchory Aberds 293 D8
Banchory-Devenick
Aberds 293 C11
Bancycapel Carms 74 B6
Banc-y-Darren Ceredig. 128 G3
Bancyfelin Carms. 74 B4
Bancyffordd Carms. 93 D8
Bandirran Perth 286 D6
Bandonhill London 67 G9
Bandrake Head Cumb . . 210 B6
Banff Aberds 302 C6
Bangor Gwyn 179 G9
Bangor is y coed / Bangor
on Dee Wrex. 166 F5
Bangor on Dee / Bangor-is-
y-coed Wrex 166 F5
Bangors Corn. 11 B10
Bangor Teifi Ceredig . . . 93 C7
Bangor's Green Lancs . . 193 E11
Banham Norf 141 F11
Bank Hants 32 F3
Bankend Dumfries 238 D2
Bank End Cumb 210 B3
Cumb 228 D6
Bank Fold Blackburn . . . 195 C8
Bank Foot Perth 286 D4
Bankfoot Perth 286 D4
Bankglen E Ayrs 258 G3
Bankhead Aberdeen . . . 293 B10
Aberds 293 C8
Dumfries 236 C2
Falk 278 E6
S Lanark 269 G7
Bank Hey Blackburn . . . 203 G8
Bank Houses Lancs 202 C4
Bankland Som 28 B4
Bank Lane Gtr Man . . . 195 D9
Bank Newton N Yorks . . 204 C4
Banknock Falk. 278 F5
Banks Cumb 240 E3
Lancs 193 C11
Orkney 314 C4
Bank's Green Worcs . . . 117 D9
Bankshill Dumfries 248 G5
Bankside Falk 279 E7
Bank Street Worcs 116 E2
Bank Top Gtr Man 195 E8
Lancs 194 F4
Staffs. 168 E5
W Yorks 196 C6
W Yorks 205 B9
Banners Gate W Mid . . 133 D11
Banningham Norf 160 D4
Bannister Ho Highld . . . 310 D5
Bannisterkirk Mains Highld 310 D5
Bannister Green Essex . . 106 G3
Bannockburn Stirling . . 278 C5
Banns Corn 4 F4
Banstead Sur 51 B8
Bantam Grove W Yorks . 197 B9
Bantaskin Highld 300 E5
Bantham Devon. 8 G4
Banton N Lanark 278 F5
Banwell N Som 43 B11
Banyard's Green Suff . . . 126 C5
Bapchild Kent 70 G2
Baptist End W Mid 133 F8
Bapton Wilts 46 F3
Barabhas W Isles. 304 D5
Barabhas Iarach
W Isles 304 D5
Barabhas Uarach
W Isles 304 C5
Barachandroman Argyll 289 B8
Baramore Highld. 289 B8
Barassie S Ayrs 257 C8
Baravullin Argyll 289 F10
Barbadoes Stirling 277 B11
Barbaraville Highld 301 B7
Barbauchlaw W Loth. . . 269 B8
Barber Booth Derbys. . . 185 E10
Barber Green Cumb 211 C7
Barber's Moor Lancs . . . 194 D3
Barbican Plym. 7 E9
Barbieston S Ayrs 257 F10
Barbon Cumb 212 C2
Barbourne Worcs 116 F6
Barbridge Ches E 167 D10
Barbrook Devon 41 D8
Barby Northants 119 C10
Barby Nortoft
Northants 119 C10
Barcaldine Argyll 289 E11
Barcelona Corn. 6 E4
Barcheston Warks 100 D5
Barclose Cumb 239 E10
Barcombe E Sus 36 D6
Barcombe Cross E Sus . . 36 D6
Barcroft W Yorks 204 F6
Bardennoch Dumfries . 246 E3
Barden N Yorks 224 G2
Barden Park Kent 52 D5
Barden Scale N Yorks . . 205 B7
Bardfield End Green
Essex 106 E2
Bardfield Saling Essex . 106 F3
Bardister Shetland 312 F5
Bardnabeinne Highld . . 309 K7
Bardney Lincs 173 B10
Bardon Leics 153 G8
Bardon Mill Northumb . 241 E7
Bardowie E Dunb 277 G11
Bardrainney Invclyd . . . 276 G6
Bardsea Cumb 210 D6
Bardsey W Yorks 206 E3
Bardsley Gtr Man 196 G2
Bardwell Suff 125 C8
Bare Lancs 211 H9
Bare Ash Som 43 E8
Bareless Northumb 263 B9

Bar End Hants 33 B7
Barepot Cumb 228 F6
Bareppa Corn. 3 D7
Barfad Argyll 275 G9
Barford Norf 142 B2
Sur. 49 E11
Warks 118 E5
Barford St John Oxon . . 101 E8
Barford St Martin Wilts. . 46 G5
Barford St Michael
Oxon 101 E8
Barfrestone Kent 55 C9
Bargaly Dumfries. 236 C6
Bargarran Renfs 277 G9
Bargate Derbys. 170 F5
Bargeddie N Lanark . . . 268 C4
Bargoed Caerph 77 F10
Bargrennan Dumfries . . 236 B5
Barham Cambs 122 B2
Kent. 55 C8
Suff 126 F2
Barharrow Dumfries . . . 237 D8
Barhill Dumfries 237 C10
Bar Hill Cambs 123 E7
Barholm Lincs 155 G11
Barkby Leics 136 B2
Barkby Thorpe Leics . . . 136 B2
Barkers Green Shrops . . 149 C10
Barkers Hill Wilts 30 B6
Barham Wokingham 65 F11
Barking London 68 C2
Suff 125 G11
Barkingside London 68 B2
Barking Tye Suff 125 G11
Barkisland W Yorks . . . 196 D5
Barkla Shop Corn. 4 E4
Barkestone-le-Vale
Leics 154 C5
Barkham Wokingham . . . 65 F11
Barkla Shop Corn 4 E4
Barkston Lincs 172 G6
N Yorks 206 F5
Barkston Ash N Yorks . . 206 F5
Barkway Herts 105 D7
Barlake Som. 45 D7
Barlanark Glasgow 268 C3
Barland Powys. 114 E5
Barland Common
Swansea 56 D5
Barlaston Staffs 151 B7
Barlavington W Sus 35 D7
Barlborough Derbys . . . 187 F7
Barlby N Yorks 207 G8
Barlestone Leics 135 B8
Barley Herts 105 D7
Lancs 204 E3
Barley End Bucks 85 C7
Barley Green Lancs 204 E2
Barley Mow T&W 243 G7
Barleythorpe Rutland . . 136 B6
Barling Essex 70 B2
Barlings Lincs 189 G9
Barlow Derbys 186 G4
N Yorks 198 B6
T&W 242 E5
Barlow Moor Gtr Man . . 184 C4
Barmby Moor E Yorks . 207 D11
Barmby on the Marsh
E Yorks 199 B7
Barmer Norf 158 C6
Barming Heath Kent 53 B8
Barmoor T&W 242 E4
Barmoor Castle
Northumb 263 B11
Barmoor Lane End
Northumb 264 B2
Barmouth / Abermaw
Gwyn. 146 F2
Barmpton Darl 224 B6
Barmston E Yorks 209 B9
T&W 243 F8
Barmulloch Glasgow . . . 268 B2
Barnacabber Argyll 276 E3
Barnacarry Argyll 275 E10
Barnacle Warks 135 G7
Barnaline Argyll 275 D7
Barnard Castle Durham . 223 B11
Barnard Gate Oxon 82 C6
Barnardiston Suff 106 B4
Barnardtown Newport . . 59 B10
Barnbarroch Dumfries . 237 D10
Barnbow Carr W Yorks . 206 F3
Barnburgh S Yorks 198 G3
Barnby Suff. 143 F9
Barnby Dun S Yorks . . . 198 F6
Barnby in the Willows
Notts. 172 E5
Barnby Moor Notts . . . 187 E11
Barnes London 67 D8
Barnes Cray London . . . 68 D4
Barnes Hall S Yorks . . . 186 B4
Barnes Street Kent 52 D6
Barnet London 86 F2
Barnetby le Wold
N Lincs 200 F5
Barnet Gate London 86 F2
Barnetby Dumfries 237 D10
Barnettbrook Worcs. . . . 117 B7
Barnett Brook Ches E . . 167 G10
Barney Norf 159 C9
Barnfield Kent 54 D2
Barnfields Hereford 97 C10
Staffs. 169 D7
Barnham Suff 125 B8
W Sus. 35 G7
Barnham Broom Norf. . 141 B11
Barnhead Angus 287 B10
Barnhill Ches W 167 E7
Dundee 287 D8
Moray 301 D11
Barnhills Dumfries 9 B4
Barningham Durham . . . 223 C11
Suff 125 B9
Barningham Green
Norf 160 C2
Barnoldby le Beck
NE Lincs 201 G8
Barnoldswick Lancs . . . 204 D3
Barns Borders 260 B6
Barnsdale Bar N Yorks . 198 E4
Barnsley Glos 81 D9
S Yorks 197 F10
Barnside W Yorks 197 F7
Barnsole Kent 55 B9
Barnstaple Devon. 40 G5
Barnston Essex 87 B11
Mers 182 E3
Barnstone Notts 154 B4
Barnt Green Worcs 117 C10
Barnton Ches W 183 F11

Barnton continued
Edin 280 F3
Barnwell Northants . . . 137 G10
Barnwell All Saints
Northants 137 G10
Barnwell St Andrew
Northants 137 F10
Barnwood Glos. 80 B5
Barochreal Argyll 289 G10
Barons Cross Hereford . 115 F9
Barr Highld 289 D8
S Ayrs 245 C7
Som 27 C11
Barra Castle Aberds . . . 303 G7
Barrachan Dumfries . . . 236 E5
Barrachnie Glasgow . . . 268 C3
Barrack Aberds 303 E8
Barrack Hill Newport . . . 59 B10
Barraer Dumfries. 236 C5
Barraglom Argyll 304 E3
Barrahormid Argyll . . . 275 E8
Barran Argyll 289 G10
Barranrioch Argyll 289 G10
Barrapol Argyll 288 E1
Barras Aberds 293 E10
Cumb 222 C6
Barrasford Northumb . . 241 C10
Barravullin Argyll 275 D9
Barregarrow IoM 192 D4
Barrhead E Renf 267 D9
Barrhill S Ayrs 244 G6
Barrington Cambs 105 B7
Som 28 D5
Barripper Corn 2 B4
Barrmill N Ayrs 267 E7
Barrock Highld 310 B6
Barrock Ho Highld 310 C6
Barrow Glos 99 G7
Lancs 203 F10
Rutland 155 F7
Shrops 132 C3
Som 45 B8
Suff 124 E5
S Yorks 186 B6
Barrow Bridge Gtr Man . 195 E7
Barroway Drove Norf . . 139 C11
Barrowburn Northumb . 263 C9
Barrowby Lincs 155 B7
Barrowcliff N Yorks . . . 217 C10
Barrowden Rutland 137 C8
Barrowford Lancs 204 F3
Barrow Green Kent 70 G3
Barrow Gurney N Som . . 60 F4
Barrow Haven N Lincs . . 200 C5
Barrow Hann N Lincs . . 200 C5
Barrowhill Kent 54 F4
Derbys 186 F6
Dorset 18 B5
Barrow-in-Furness
Cumb. 210 F4
Barrow Island Cumb . . 210 F3
Barrowmore Estate
Ches W 183 G7
Barrow Nook Lancs 194 G3
Barrows Green Ches E . . 167 D11
Cumb 211 B10
Notts 171 E7
Barrow's Green Mers . . 183 D8
Barrow Street Wilts 45 G10
Barrow upon Humber
N Lincs 200 C5
Barrow upon Soar
Leics 153 F11
Barrow upon Trent
Derbys 153 D7
Barrow Vale Bath 60 G6
Barrow Wake Glos 80 B6
Barry Angus 287 D9
V Glam 58 F6
Barry Dock V Glam 58 F6
Barry Island V Glam 58 F6
Barsby Leics. 154 G3
Barsham Suff 143 F7
Barshare E Ayrs 258 F3
Barstable Essex 69 B8
Barston W Mid 118 B4
Bartestree Hereford 97 C11
Bartholomew Green
Essex 106 G4
Barthol Chapel Aberds . 303 F8
Barthomley Ches E 168 D3
Bartington Ches W 183 F10
Bartley Hants 32 E4
Bartley Green W Mid . . 133 G10
Bartlow Cambs 105 B11
Barton Cambs 123 F8
Ches W 166 E6
Glos. 99 F11
Lancs 193 F7
Lancs 202 F6
N Som 43 B11
N Yorks 224 D4
Oxon 83 D9
Torbay 9 B8
Warks 118 G2
Barton Abbey Oxon . . . 101 G8
Barton Bendish Norf . . 140 B4
Barton Court Hereford . . 98 C4
Barton End Glos. 80 F4
Barton Gate Devon 41 E7
Staffs. 152 F3
Barton Green Staffs . . . 152 F3
Barton Hartshorn Bucks 102 E2
Barton Hill Bristol 60 E6
N Yorks 216 E3
Barton in Fabis Notts . . 153 C10
Barton in the Beans
Leics 135 B7
Barton-le-Clay C Beds . 103 E11
Barton-le-Street
N Yorks 216 E4
Barton-le-Willows
N Yorks 216 E4
Barton Mills Suff 124 C4
Barton on Sea Hants . . . 19 C10
Barton on the Heath
Warks 100 E5
Barton St David Som . . . 44 G4
Barton Seagrave
Northants 121 B7
Bartonsham Hereford . . . 97 D10
Barton Stacey Hants . . . 48 E2
Barton Town Devon 41 E7
Barton Turf Norf 160 E6
Barton Turn Staffs 152 F3
Barton-under-Needwood
Staffs 152 F3
Barton-upon-Humber
N Lincs 200 C4
Barton Waterside
N Lincs 200 C4
Barugh S Yorks 197 F10
Barugh Green S Yorks . . 197 F10

Barway Cambs 123 B10
Barwell Leics 135 D8
London 67 G7
Barwick Devon 25 C7
Herts 86 B5
Som 29 D8
Barwick in Elmet
W Yorks 206 F3
Barwinnock Dumfries . . 236 E5
Bascote Warks 119 E8
Bascote Heath Warks . . 119 E7
Base Green Suff 125 D10
Basford Shrops 131 B8
Staffs 168 F5
Basford Green Staffs . . 169 E7
Bashall Eaves Lancs . . . 203 E9
Bashley Hants 19 B10
Bashley Park Hants 19 B10
Basildon Essex 69 B8
Basingstoke Hants. 48 C6
Baslow Derbys 186 G3
Bason Bridge Som 43 D10
Bassaleg Newport 59 B9
Bassenthwaite Cumb . . 229 E10
Bassett Soton 32 D6
Bassett's Green Suff . . . 108 D3
Bassingbourn Cambs . . 104 C5
Bassingfield Notts 154 B2
Bassingham Lincs 172 C6
Bassingthorpe Lincs . . . 155 D9
Bassus Green Herts 104 F6
Basta Shetland 312 D7
Basted Kent 52 B6
Baston Lincs 156 G2
Bastonford Worcs 116 G6
Bastwick Norf 161 F8
Baswich Staffs. 151 E8
Baswick Green S Yorks . 209 D7
Batavaine Stirling 285 D8
Batch Som 43 B10
Batchcott Shrops 115 C9
Batchfields Hereford . . . 98 B3
Batchley Worcs 117 D10
Batchworth Herts 85 F9
Batchworth Heath Herts . 85 F9
Batcombe Dorset 29 G10
Som 45 F7
Bate Heath Ches E 183 F11
Bath Bath 61 F8
Bathampton Bath. 61 F9
Batheaston Bath. 61 F9
Bathford Bath 61 F9
Bathgate W Loth 269 B8
Bathley Notts 172 D3
Bathpool Corn 11 G11
Som 28 B3
Bath Side Essex 108 E5
Bath Vale Ches E 168 C5
Bathville W Loth 269 B8
Bathway Som 44 C5
Bathwick Bath. 61 F9
Batley W Yorks 197 C8
Batley Carr W Yorks . . . 197 C8
Batsford Glos. 100 E3
Batson Devon 9 G9
Batsworthy Devon 26 D4
Batten's Green Som 28 D3
Battenton Green Worcs . 116 D6
Battersby N Yorks 225 D11
Battersea London 67 D9
Battisborough Cross
Devon 7 F11
Battisford Suff 125 G10
Battisford Tye Suff 125 G10
Battle E Sus 38 D2
Powys 95 E10
Battledown Glos 99 G8
Battlefield Shrops 149 F10
Battle Hill T&W 243 D8
Battlescombe Glos 80 D6
Battlesbridge Essex 88 G3
Battlesden C Beds 103 F9
Battlesea Green Suff . . . 126 B4
Battleton Som 26 B6
Battram Leics 135 B8
Battramsley Hants. 20 B2
Battramsley Cross Hants. 20 B2
Batt's Corner Hants. . . . 49 E10
Battyeford W Yorks . . . 197 C7
Bauds of Cullen Moray . 302 C4
Baugh Argyll 288 E2
Baughton Worcs 99 C7
Baughurst Hants 48 B5
Baulking Oxon 82 G4
Baumber Lincs 190 G2
Baunton Glos. 81 E8
Baverstock Wilts 46 G4
Bawburgh Norf 142 B3
Bawdeswell Norf 159 E10
Bawdrip Som 43 F10
Bawdsey Suff 108 C6
Bawsey Norf 158 F3
Bawtry S Yorks 187 C11
Baxenden Lancs 195 B9
Baxterley Warks 134 D5
Baxter's Green Suff. . . . 124 F5
Bay Dorset 30 D2
Highld 298 D2
Baybridge Hants 33 C8
Northumb 241 G11
Baycliff Cumb 210 E5
Baydon Wilts 63 D9
Bayford Herts 86 D4
Som 30 B2
Bayles Cumb 231 C7
Bayley's Hill Kent 52 C4
Baylham Suff 126 G2
Baynard's Green Oxon . 101 F10
Baynhall Worcs 99 B7
Baysham Hereford 97 F11
Bayston Hill Shrops . . . 131 B9
Baythorne End Essex . . 106 C4
Baythorpe Lincs 174 G2
Bayton Worcs 116 C3
Bayton Common Worcs . 116 C4
Bayview Kent 70 F4
Bayworth Oxon 83 E8
Beach Highld 289 D9
S Glos 61 E8
Beachampton Bucks . . 102 D5
Beachamwell Norf 140 B5
Beachans Moray 301 E10
Beach Hay Worcs 116 C4
Beachlands E Sus 23 E11

Beachley Glos 79 G9
Beacon Corn 2 B5
Devon 27 F11
Devon 28 F2
Beacon Down E Sus 37 C9
Beacon End Essex 107 G9
Beaconhill Shrops 243 B7
Beaconhill Bath. 45 G6
Bucks. 84 G6
Cumb 210 E4
Dorset 18 C5
Essex 88 C5
Kent. 53 G10
Notts 172 E4
Suff 108 B4
Sur. 49 F11
Beacon Lough T&W . . . 243 F7
Beacon's Bottom Bucks. . 66 B2
Beaconsfield Bucks. 66 B2
Beacrabhaic W Isles . . . 305 J3
Beadlam N Yorks 216 C3
Beadlow C Beds. 104 D2
Beadnell Northumb . . . 264 D6
Beaford Devon 25 E9
Beal Northumb 273 G11
N Yorks 198 B4
Bealach Highld. 289 D11
Bealach Maim Argyll . . 275 E10
Bealbury Corn. 7 B7
Beal's Green Kent 53 G9
Bealsmill Corn. 12 F3
Beambridge Shrops . . . 131 F10
Beam Bridge Som 27 D10
Beamhurst Staffs 152 C4
Beamhurst Lane Staffs . 151 B11
Beaminster Dorset 29 G7
Beamish Durham 242 G6
Beamond End Bucks . . . 84 F6
Beamsley N Yorks 205 C7
Bean Kent 68 E5
Beanacre Wilts 62 F2
Beancross E Ayrs 279 F8
Beanhill M Keynes 103 D7
Beanley Northumb 264 F3
Beansburn E Ayrs 257 B10
Beanthwaite Cumb 210 C4
Beaquoy Orkney 314 D3
Bear Cross Bmouth. 19 B7
Beard Hill Som 44 E6
Beardly Batch Som 44 E6
Beardwood Blackburn . . 195 B8
Beare Devon 27 G7
Beare Green Sur. 51 E7
Bearley Warks 118 E3
Bearley Cross Warks . . 118 E3
Bearnus Argyll 288 E5
Bearpark Durham 233 C10
Bearsbridge Northumb . 241 F7
Bearsden E Dunb 277 G10
Bearsted Kent 53 B9
Bearstone Shrops 150 B4
Bearwood Hereford . . . 115 F7
Poole 19 B7
W Mid 133 F10
Beasley Staffs 168 F4
Beattock Dumfries 248 C3
Beauchamp Roding
Essex 87 C9
Beauchief S Yorks 186 E4
Beauclerc Northumb . . 242 F2
Beaudesert Warks 118 D3
Beaufort Castle Highld . 300 E5
Beaufort Bl Gwent. 77 C11
Beaulieu Hants 32 G5
Beaulieu Park Essex . . . 88 C2
Beaulieu Wood Dorset . . 30 F3
Beauly Highld 300 E5
Beaumaris Anglesey . . . 179 F10
Beaumont Cumb 239 F8
Essex 108 G3
Windsor 66 E4
Beaumont Hill Darl 224 B5
Beaumont Leys
Leicester 135 B11
Beausale Warks 118 C4
Beauvale Notts 171 F7
Beauworth Hants 33 B9
Beaworthy Devon 12 B5
Beazley End Essex 106 F4
Bebington Mers 182 D4
Bebside Northumb 253 G7
Beccles Suff 143 E8
Becconsall Lancs 194 C2
Beck Bottom Cumb . . . 210 C5
W Yorks 197 C10
Beckbury Shrops 132 C5
Beckces Cumb 230 F4
Beckenham London 67 F11
Beckermet Cumb 219 D10
Beckermonds N Yorks . 213 C7
Beckery Som 44 F3
Beckett End Norf 140 D5
Beckfoot Cumb 229 B7
Cumb 220 D2
Beck Foot Cumb. 222 F2
Beckford Worcs 99 D9
Beckhampton Wilts 62 F5
Beck Hole N Yorks 226 E6
Beckingham Lincs 172 D5
Notts 188 D3
Beckington Som 45 C10
Beckjay Shrops 115 B7
Beckley E Sus. 38 C5
Hants 19 B10
Oxon 83 C9
Beck Row Suff 124 B3
Beckside Cumb 212 B2
Beck Side Cumb 210 C4
Cumb 211 C7
Beckton London 68 C2
Beckwithshaw N Yorks . 205 C11
Becontree London 68 C3
Bedale N Yorks 214 B5
Bedburn Durham 233 E8
Bedchester Dorset. 30 D5
Beddau Rhondda 58 B5
Beddgelert Gwyn 163 F9
Beddingham E Sus 36 F6
Beddington London 67 G10
Beddington Corner
London 67 F9
Bedfield Suff 126 D4
Bedford Bedford 121 G11
Gtr Man 183 B11
Bedford Park London . . . 67 D8
Bedgebury Cross Kent . . 53 G8
Bedgrove Bucks 84 C4
Bedham W Sus 35 C8
Bedhampton Hants 22 B2
Bedingfield Suff 126 D3
Bedingham Green Norf . 142 E5

Bedlam N Yorks 214 G5
Som 45 D9
Bedlam Street W Sus 36 D3
Bedlar's Green Essex 105 G10
Bedlington Northumb 253 G7
Bedlington Station
Northumb 253 G7
Bedlinog M Tydf 77 E9
Bedminster Bristol 60 E5
Bedminster Down Bristol 60 F5
Bedmond Herts 85 E9
Bednall Staffs 151 F9
Bednall Head Staffs 151 F9
Bedrule Borders 262 F4
Bedstone Shrops 115 B7
Bedwas Caerph 59 B7
Bedwell Herts 104 G4
Wrex 166 F5
Bedwellty Caerph 77 E11
Bedwellty Pits Bl Gwent 77 D11
Bedwlwyn Wrex 148 B4
Bedworth Warks 135 F7
Bedworth Heath Warks 134 F6
Bedworth Woodlands
Warks 134 F6
Bed-y-coedwr Gwyn 146 D4
Beeby Leics 136 B3
Beech Hants 49 F7
Staffs 151 B7
Beechcliff Staffs 151 B7
Beechcliffe W Yorks 205 E7
Beechen Cliff Bath 61 G9
Beech Hill Gtr Man 194 F5
W Berks 65 G7
Beechingstoke Wilts 46 B5
Beech Lanes W Mid 133 F10
Beechwood Halton 183 E8
Newport 59 B10
W Mid 118 B5
W Yorks 206 F2
Beecroft C Beds 103 G10
Beedon W Berks 64 D3
Beedon Hill W Berks 64 D3
Beeford E Yorks 209 C8
Beeley Derbys 170 B3
Beelsby NE Lincs 201 G8
Beenham W Berks 64 F5
Beenham's Heath
Windsor 65 D10
Beenham Stocks
W Berks 64 F5
Beeny Corn 11 C8
Beer Devon 15 D10
Som 44 G2
Beercrocombe Som 28 C4
Beer Hackett Dorset 29 E9
Beesands Devon 8 G6
Beesby Lincs 191 E7
Beeslack Midloth 270 C4
Beeson Devon 8 G6
Beeston C Beds 104 B3
Ches W 167 D8
Norf 159 F8
Notts 153 B10
W Yorks 205 G11
Beeston Hill W Yorks 205 G11
Beeston Park Side
W Yorks 197 B9
Beeston Regis Norf 177 E11
Beeston Royds
W Yorks 205 G11
Beeston St Lawrence
Norf 160 E6
Beeswing Dumfries 237 C10
Beetham Cumb 211 D9
Som 28 E3
Beetley Norf 159 F9
Beffcote Staffs 150 F6
Began Cardiff 59 C8
Begbroke Oxon 83 C7
Begdale Cambs 139 B9
Begelly Pembs 73 D10
Beggar Hill Essex 87 E10
Beggarington Hill
W Yorks 197 C9
Beggars Ash Hereford 98 D4
Beggars Bush W Sus 35 F11
Beggar's Bush Powys 114 E5
Beggars Pound V Glam 58 F4
Beggearn Huish Som 42 F4
Beguildy Powys 114 B3
Beighton Norf 143 B7
S Yorks 186 E6
Beighton Hill Derbys 170 E3
Beili-glas Mon 78 C4
Beitearsaig W Isles 305 G1
Beith N Ayrs 266 E6
Bekesbourne Kent 55 B7
Bekesbourne Hill Kent 55 B7
Belah Cumb 239 F9
Belan Powys 130 C4
Belaugh Norf 160 F5
Belbins Hants 32 C5
Belbroughton Worcs 117 B8
Belchalwell Dorset 30 F3
Belchalwell Street Dorset 30 F3
Belchamp Otten Essex 106 C6
Belchamp St Paul Essex 106 C5
Belchamp Walter Essex 106 C6
Belcher's Bar Leics 135 B8
Belchford Lincs 190 F3
Beleybridge Fife 287 F9
Belfield Gtr Man 196 E2
Belford Northumb 264 C4
Belgrano Conwy 181 F7
Belgrave Ches W 166 C5
Leicester 135 B11
Staffs 134 C4
Belgravia London 67 D9
Belhaven E Loth 282 F3
Belhelvie Aberds 293 B11
Belhinnie Aberds 302 G4
Bellabeg Aberds 292 B5
Bellamore S Ayrs 244 F6
Bellanoch Argyll 275 D8
Bellanrigg Borders 260 B6
Bellasize E Yorks 199 B10
Bellaty Angus 286 B6
Bell Bar Herts 86 D3
Bell Busk N Yorks 204 B4
Bell Common Essex 86 E6
Belleau Lincs 190 F6
Belle Eau Park Notts 171 D11
Belle Green S Yorks 197 F11
Bellehiglash Moray 301 F11
Belle Isle W Yorks 197 B10
Bell End Worcs 117 B8
Bellerby N Yorks 224 G2
Belle Vale Mers 182 D6
W Mid 133 G9
Bellever Devon 13 F9
Bellevue Worcs 117 C9
Belle Vue Cumb 229 E8
Cumb 239 F9
Gtr Man 184 B5
Shrops 149 G9
S Yorks 198 G5
W Yorks 197 D10
Bellfield E Ayrs 257 B10
Bellfields Sur 50 C3
Bell Green London 67 E11
W Mid 135 G7
Bell Heath Worcs 117 B9
Bell Hill Hants 34 C2
Belliehill Angus 293 G7
Bellingdon Bucks 84 D6
Bellingham London 67 E11
Northumb 251 G8
Bellmount Norf 157 E10
Belloch Argyll 255 D7
Bellochantuy Argyll 255 D7
Bell o' th' Hill Ches W 167 F8
Bellsbank E Ayrs 245 C11
Bell's Close T&W 242 E5
Bell's Corner Suff 107 D9
Bellshill N Lanark 268 C4
Northumb 264 C4
Bellside N Lanark 268 D6
Bellsmyre W Dunb 277 F8
Bellspool Borders 260 B5
Bellsquarry W Loth 269 C10
Bells Yew Green E Sus 52 F6
Belluton Bath 60 G6
Bellyeoman Fife 280 D2
Belmaduthy Highld 300 D6
Belmesthorpe Rutland 155 G10
Belmont Blackburn 195 D7
Durham 234 C2
E Sus 38 E4
London 67 G9
London 85 G11
Oxon 63 B11
S Ayrs 257 E8
Shetland 312 C7
Belnacraig Aberds 292 B5
Belnagarrow Moray 302 E3
Belnie Lincs 156 C5
Belowda Corn 5 C9
Belper Derbys 170 F4
Belper Lane End Derbys 170 F4
Belph Derbys 187 F8
Belsay Northumb 242 B4
Belses Borders 262 D3
Belsford Devon 8 D5
Belsize Herts 85 E8
Belstead Suff 108 C2
Belston S Ayrs 257 E9
Belstone Devon 13 C8
Belstone Corner Devon 13 B8
Belthorn Blackburn 195 C8
Beltinge Kent 71 F7
Beltingham Northumb 241 E7
Beltoft N Lincs 199 F10
Belton Leics 153 E8
Lincs 155 B8
N Lincs 199 F9
Norf 143 C9
Belton in Rutland
Rutland 136 C6
Beltring Kent 53 D7
Belts of Collonach
Aberds 293 D8
Belvedere London 68 D3
W Loth 269 B9
Belvoir Leics 154 C6
Bembridge IoW 21 D8
Bemersyde Borders 262 C3
Bemerton Wilts 46 G6
Bemerton Heath Wilts 46 G6
Bempton E Yorks 218 E3
Benacre Suff 143 G10
Ben Alder Lodge Highld 291 F7
Ben Armine Lodge
Highld 309 H7
Benbuie Dumfries 246 D6
Ben Casgro W Isles 304 F6
Benchill Gtr Man 184 D4
Bencombe Glos 80 F3
Benderloch Argyll 289 F11
Bendish Herts 104 G3
Bendronaig Lodge
Highld 299 F10
Benenden Kent 53 G10
Benfield Dumfries 236 C5
Benfieldside Durham 242 G3
Bengal Pembs 91 E9
Bengate Norf 160 D6
Bengeo Herts 86 C4
Bengeworth Worcs 99 C10
Bengrove Glos 99 E9
Benhall Glos 99 G8
Benhall Green Suff 127 E7
Benhall Street Suff 127 E7
Benhilton London 67 F9
Benholm Aberds 293 G10
Beningbrough N Yorks 206 B6
Benington Herts 104 G5
Lincs 174 F5
Benington Sea End
Lincs 174 F6
Benllech Anglesey 179 E8
Benmore Argyll 276 E2
Stirling 285 E8
Benmore Lodge Argyll 289 F7
Highld 309 H3
Bennacott Corn 11 C11
Bennah Devon 14 E2
Bennan N Ayrs 255 E10
Bennane Lea S Ayrs 244 F3
Bennetland E Yorks 199 B10
Bennetsfield Highld 300 D6
Bennett End Bucks 84 F3
Bennetts End Herts 85 D9
Benniworth Lincs 190 E2
Benover Kent 53 D8
Ben Rhydding W Yorks 205 D8
Bensham T&W 242 E6
Benslie N Ayrs 266 G6
Benson Oxon 83 G10
Benston Shetland 313 H6
Bent Aberds 293 F8
Benter Som 44 D6
Bentfield Bury Essex 105 F9
Bentfield Green Essex 105 F10
Bentgate Gtr Man 196 E2
Bent Gate Lancs 195 C9
Benthall Northumb 264 D6
Shrops 132 C3
Bentham Glos 80 B6
Benthoul Aberdeen 293 C10
Bentilee Stoke 168 F6
Bentlass Pembs 73 E7
Bentlawnt Shrops 130 C6
Bentley Essex 87 F9
E Yorks 208 F6
Hants 49 E9
Suff 108 D2
S Yorks 198 F5
Warks 134 D5
W Mid 133 D9
Worcs 117 D9
Bentley Common Warks 134 D5
Bentley Heath Herts 86 F2
W Mid 118 B3
Bentley Rise S Yorks 198 G5
Benton Devon 41 F7
Benton Green W Mid 118 B5
Bentpath Dumfries 249 E8
Bents W Loth 269 C9
Bents Head W Yorks 205 F7
Betwichen Devon 41 G8
Bentworth Hants 49 E7
Benvie Dundee 287 D7
Benville Dorset 29 G8
Benwell T&W 242 E6
Benwick Cambs 138 E6
Beobridge Shrops 132 E5
Beoley Worcs 117 D11
Beoraidbeg Highld 295 F8
Bepton W Sus 34 D5
Berden Essex 105 F9
Bere Alston Devon 7 B8
Berechurch Essex 107 G9
Bere Ferrers Devon 7 C9
Berefold Aberds 303 F9
Berepper Corn 2 E5
Bere Regis Dorset 18 C2
Bergh Apton Norf 142 C6
Berghers Hill Bucks 66 B2
Berhill Som 44 F2
Berinsfield Oxon 83 F9
Berkeley Glos 79 F11
Berkeley Heath Glos 79 F11
Berkeley Road Glos 80 E2
Berkeley Towers
Ches E 167 E11
Berkhamsted Herts 85 D7
Berkley Som 45 D10
Berkley Down Som 45 D9
Berkley Marsh Som 45 D10
Berkswell W Mid 118 B4
Bermondsey London 67 D10
Bermuda Warks 135 F7
Bernards Heath Herts 85 D11
Bernera Highld 295 C10
Berner's Cross Devon 25 F10
Berner's Hill E Sus 53 G8
Berners Roding Essex 87 D10
Bernice Argyll 276 C2
Bernisdale Highld 298 D4
Berrick Salome Oxon 83 G10
Berriedale Highld 311 G5
Berrier Cumb 230 F3
Berriew / Aberriw
Powys 130 C3
Berrington Northumb 273 G10
Shrops 131 B10
Worcs 115 D11
Berrington Green
Worcs 115 D11
Berriowbridge Corn 11 F11
Berrow Som 43 C10
Worcs 98 E5
Berrow Green Worcs 116 F4
Berry Swansea 56 D3
Berry Brow W Yorks 196 E6
Berry Cross Devon 25 E7
Berry Down Cross Devon 40 E5
Berryfield Oxon 84 B3
Wilts 61 G11
Berrygate Hill E Yorks 201 C8
Berry Hill Glos 79 C9
Pembs 91 C11
Stoke 168 F6
Worcs 117 E7
Berryhillock Moray 302 C5
Berrylands London 67 F7
Berry Moor S Yorks 197 G9
Berrynarbor Devon 40 D5
Berry Pomeroy Devon 8 C6
Berrysbridge Devon 26 G6
Berry's Green London 52 B2
Bersham Wrex 166 F4
Berstane Orkney 314 E4
Berth-ddu Flint 166 B2
Berthengam Flint 181 F10
Berwick E Sus 23 D8
Kent 54 F6
S Glos 60 C5
Berwick Bassett Wilts 62 E5
Berwick Hill Northumb 242 B5
Berwick Hills Mbro 225 B10
Berwick St James Wilts 46 F5
Berwick St John Wilts 30 C6
Berwick St Leonard
Wilts 46 G2
Berwick-upon-Tweed
Northumb 273 E9
Berwick Wharf Shrops 149 G10
Berwyn Denb 165 G11
Bescaby Leics 154 D6
Bescar Lancs 193 E11
Bescot W Mid 133 D10
Besford Shrops 149 E11
Worcs 99 C8
Bessacarr S Yorks 198 G6
Bessels Green Kent 52 B4
Bessels Leigh Oxon 83 E7
Besses o' th' Barn
Gtr Man 195 F10
Bessingby E Yorks 218 F3
Bessingham Norf 160 B3
Best Beech Hill E Sus 52 G6
Besthorpe Norf 141 D11
Notts 172 C4
Bestwood Nottingham 171 G9
Bestwood Village Notts 171 F9
Beswick E Yorks 208 D6
Gtr Man 184 B5
Betchcott Shrops 131 D8
Betchton Heath Ches E 168 C3
Betchworth Sur 51 D8
Bethania Ceredig 111 E11
Gwyn 163 E10
Gwyn 164 F2
Bethany Corn 6 D6
Bethel Anglesey 178 G5
Corn 5 E10
Gwyn 147 B9
Gwyn 163 B8
Bethelnie Aberds 303 F7
Bethersden Kent 54 E2
Bethesda Gwyn 163 B10
Pembs 73 B9
Bethlehem Carms 94 F3
Bethnal Green London 67 C10
Betley Staffs 168 F3
Betley Common Staffs 168 F2
Betsham Kent 68 E6
Betteshanger Kent 55 C10
Bettiscombe Dorset 16 B3
Bettisfield Wrex 149 B9
Betton Shrops 130 C6
Shrops 150 B3
Betton Strange Shrops 131 B10
Bettws Bridgend 58 B2
Mon 78 B3
Newport 78 G3
Bettws Cedewain Powys 130 D2
Bettws Gwerfil Goch
Denb 165 F8
Bettws Ifan Ceredig 92 B6
Bettws Newydd Mon 78 D5
Bettws-y-crwyn Shrops 130 G4
Bettyhill Highld 308 C7
Betws Bridgend 57 D11
Carms 75 C10
Betws Bledrws Ceredig 111 G11
Betws-Garmon Gwyn 163 D8
Betws Ifan Ceredig 92 B6
Betws-y-Coed Conwy 164 D4
Betws-yn-Rhos Conwy 180 G6
Beulah Ceredig 92 B5
Powys 113 G8
Bevendean Brighton 36 F4
Bevercotes Notts 187 G11
Bevere Worcs 116 F6
Beverley E Yorks 208 F6
Beverston Glos 80 G5
Bevington Glos 79 F11
Bewaldeth Cumb 229 E10
Bewbush W Sus 51 F8
Bewcastle Cumb 240 C3
Bewdley Worcs 116 B5
Bewerley N Yorks 214 G3
Bewholme E Yorks 209 C9
Bewley Common Wilts 62 F2
Bewlie Borders 262 D3
Bewlie Mains Borders 262 D3
Bewsey Warr 183 D9
Bexfield Norf 159 D10
Bexhill E Sus 38 F2
Bexley London 68 E3
Bexleyheath London 68 D3
Bexleyhill W Sus 34 B6
Bexon Kent 53 B11
Bexwell Norf 140 C2
Beyton Suff 125 E8
Beyton Green Suff 125 E8
Bhalasaigh W Isles 304 E3
Bhaltos W Isles 304 E2
Bhatarsaigh W Isles 297 M2
Bhlàraidh Highld 290 B5
Bibstone S Glos 79 G11
Bibury Glos 81 D10
Bicester Oxon 101 G11
Bickenhall Som 28 D3
Bickenhill W Mid 134 G3
Bicker Lincs 156 B4
Bicker Bar Lincs 156 B4
Bicker Gauntlet Lincs 156 B4
Bickershaw Gtr Man 194 G6
Bickerstaffe Lancs 194 G2
Bickerton Ches E 167 E8
Devon 9 G11
N Yorks 206 C5
Bickford Staffs 151 G7
Bickham Som 42 E3
Bickingcott Devon 26 B3
Bickington Devon 13 G11
Devon 40 G4
Bickleigh Devon 7 C10
Devon 26 F6
Bickleton Devon 40 G4
Bickley Ches W 167 F8
London 68 F2
Worcs 116 C2
Bickley Moss Ches W 167 F8
Bickley Town Ches W 167 F8
Bickleywood Ches W 167 F8
Bickmarsh Warks 100 B2
Bicknacre Essex 88 E3
Bicknoller Som 42 F6
Bicknor Kent 53 B11
Bickton Hants 31 E11
Bicton Hereford 115 E9
Pembs 72 D4
Shrops 130 G5
Shrops 149 F8
Bicton Heath Shrops 149 G9
Bidborough Kent 52 E5
Bidden Hants 49 D8
Biddenden Kent 53 F11
Biddenden Green Kent 53 E11
Biddenham Bedford 103 B10
Biddestone Wilts 61 E11
Biddick T&W 243 F8
Biddick Hall T&W 243 E9
Biddisham Som 43 C11
Biddlesden Bucks 102 C2
Biddlestone Northumb 251 B11
Biddulph Staffs 168 D5
Biddulph Moor Staffs 168 D6
Bideford Devon 25 B7
Bidford-on-Avon Warks 118 G2
Bidlake Devon 12 D5
Bidston Mers 182 C3
Bidston Hill Mers 182 D3
Bidwell C Beds 103 G10
Bielby E Yorks 207 E11
Bieldside Aberdeen 293 C10
Bierley IoW 20 F6
W Yorks 205 G9
Bierton Bucks 84 B4
Bigbury Devon 8 F3
Bigbury-on-Sea Devon 8 G3
Bigby Lincs 200 F5
Bigfrith Windsor 65 C11
Biggar Cumb 210 F3
S Lanark 260 B2
Biggar Road N Lanark 268 C5
Biggin Derbys 169 D11
Derbys 170 F3
N Yorks 206 F6
Thurrock 69 D7
Biggings Shetland 313 G3
Biggin Hill London 52 B2
Biggleswade C Beds 104 C3
Bighouse Highld 310 C2
Bighton Hants 48 G6
Biglands Cumb 239 G7
Bignall End Staffs 168 E4
Big Mancot Flint 166 B4
Bignor W Sus 35 E7
Bigods Essex 106 G2
Bigram Stirling 285 G10
Bigrigg Cumb 219 C10
Big Sand Highld 299 B7
Bigswell Orkney 314 E3
Bigton Shetland 313 L5
Bilberry Corn 5 C10
Bilborough Nottingham 171 G8
Bilbrook Som 42 E4
Staffs 133 C7
Bilbrough N Yorks 206 D6
Bilbster Highld 310 D6
Bilby Notts 187 E10
Bildershaw Durham 233 G10
Bildeston Suff 107 B9
Billacombe Plym 7 E10
Billacott Corn 11 C11
Billericay Essex 87 G11
Billesdon Leics 136 C4
Billesley Warks 118 F2
W Mid 133 G11
Billesley Common
W Mid 133 G11
Billingborough Lincs 156 C2
Billinge Mers 194 G4
Billingford Norf 126 B3
Norf 159 E10
Billingham Stockton 234 G5
Billinghay Lincs 173 E11
Billingley S Yorks 198 G2
Billingshurst W Sus 35 B9
Billingsley Shrops 132 F4
Billington C Beds 103 G8
Lancs 203 F10
Staffs 151 E7
Billockby Norf 161 G8
Bill Quay T&W 243 E7
Billy Mill T&W 243 D8
Billy Row Durham 233 D9
Bilmarsh Shrops 149 D9
Bilsborrow Lancs 202 F6
Bilsby Lincs 191 F7
Bilsby Field Lincs 191 F7
Bilsdon Devon 14 C2
Bilsham W Sus 35 G7
Bilsington Kent 54 G4
Bilson Green Glos 79 C11
Bilsthorpe Notts 171 C10
Bilsthorpe Moor Notts 171 D11
Bilston Midloth 270 C5
W Mid 133 D9
Bilstone Leics 135 B7
Bilting Kent 54 D5
Bilton E Yorks 209 G9
Northumb 264 G6
N Yorks 206 B2
Warks 119 C9
Bilton Haggs N Yorks 206 D5
Bilton in Ainsty N Yorks 206 D5
Bimbister Orkney 314 E3
Binbrook Lincs 190 C2
Binchester Blocks
Durham 233 E10
Bincombe Dorset 17 E9
Som 43 F7
Bindal Highld 311 L3
Bindon Som 27 C10
Binegar Som 44 D6
Bines Green W Sus 35 D11
Binfield Brack 65 E10
Binfield Heath Oxon 65 D8
Bingfield Northumb 241 C11
Bingham Edin 280 G6
Notts 154 B4
Bingley W Yorks 205 F8
Bings Heath Shrops 149 F10
Binham Norf 159 B9
Binley Hants 48 C2
W Mid 119 B7
Binley Woods Warks 119 B7
Binnegar Dorset 18 D3
Binniehill Falk 279 G7
Binscombe Sur 50 D3
Binsey Oxon 83 D7
Binsoe N Yorks 214 D4
Binstead Hants 49 E9
IoW 21 C7
Binsted Hants 49 E9
W Sus 35 F7
Binton Warks 118 G2
Bintree Norf 159 E10
Binweston Shrops 130 C6
Birch Essex 88 B6
Gtr Man 195 F11
Birch Acre Worcs 117 C11
Birchall Hereford 98 D3
Staffs 169 E7
Bircham Newton Norf 158 C5
Bircham Tofts Norf 158 C5
Birchan Coppice Worcs 116 C6
Birchanger Essex 105 G10
Birch Berrow Worcs 116 E4
Birchburn N Ayrs 255 E10
Birch Cross Staffs 152 C2
Birchden E Sus 52 F4
Birchencliffe W Yorks 196 D6
Birchend Hereford 98 C3
Birchendale Staffs 151 B11
Bircher Hereford 115 D9
Birches Green W Mid 134 E2
Birches Head Stoke 168 F5
Birchett's Green E Sus 53 G7
Birchfield Highld 301 G9
W Mid 133 E11
Birch Green Essex 88 B6
Herts 86 C3
Lancs 194 F3
Worcs 99 B7
Birchgrove Cardiff 59 D7
E Sus 36 B6
Swansea 57 B8
Birchhall Corner Essex 107 E10
Birch Heath Ches W 167 C8
Birch Hill Brack 65 F11
Ches W 183 G8
Birchill Devon 28 G4
Birchills W Mid 133 D10
Birchington Kent 71 F9
Birchley Heath Warks 134 E5
Birchmoor Warks 134 C5
Birchmoor Green
C Beds 103 E8
Bircholt Forstal Kent 54 E5
Birchover Derbys 170 C2
Birch Vale Derbys 185 D8
Birchwood Herts 86 D2
Lincs 172 B6
Som 28 E2
Warr 183 C10
Birchy Hill Hants 19 B11
Bircotes Notts 187 C10
Birdbrook Essex 106 C4
Birdbush Wilts 30 C6
Birdfield Argyll 275 D10
Birdforth N Yorks 215 D9
Birdham W Sus 22 D4
Birdholme Derbys 170 B5
Birdingbury Warks 119 D8
Birdlip Glos 80 C6
Birdsall N Yorks 216 F6
Birds Edge W Yorks 197 F8
Birds End Suff 124 E5
Birdsgreen Shrops 132 F5
Birds Green Essex 87 D9
Birdsmoorgate Dorset 28 G5
Birdston E Dunb 278 F3
Bird Street Suff 125 G10
Birdwell S Yorks 197 G10
Birdwood Glos 80 B2
Birgham Borders 263 B7
Birichen Highld 309 K7
Birkacre Lancs 194 D5
Birkby Cumb 229 D7
N Yorks 224 E6
W Yorks 196 D6
Birkdale Mers 193 D10
Birkenbog Aberds 302 C5
Birkenhead Mers 182 D4
Birkenhills Aberds 303 E7
Birkenshaw N Lanark 268 C3
S Lanark 268 F5
W Yorks 197 B8
Birkenshaw Bottoms
W Yorks 197 B8
Birkenside Borders 271 G11
Birkett Mire Cumb 230 G2
Birkhall Aberds 292 D5
Birkhill Angus 287 D7
Borders 260 F6
Borders 271 G11
Birkholme Lincs 155 E9
Birkhouse W Yorks 197 C7
Birkin N Yorks 198 B4
Birks Cumb 222 G3
W Yorks 197 B9
Birkshaw Northumb 241 D7
Birley Hereford 115 G9
Birley Carr S Yorks 186 C4
Birley Edge S Yorks 186 C4
Birleyhay Derbys 186 E5
Birling Kent 69 G7
Northumb 252 B6
Birling Gap E Sus 23 F9
Birlingham Worcs 99 C8
Birmingham W Mid 133 F11
Birnam Perth 286 C4
Birniehill S Lanark 268 E2
Birse Aberds 293 D7
Birsemore Aberds 293 D7
Birstall Leics 135 B11
W Yorks 197 B8
Birstall Smithies
W Yorks 197 B8
Birstwith N Yorks 205 B10
Birthorpe Lincs 156 C2
Birtle Gtr Man 195 E10
Birtley Hereford 115 D7
Northumb 241 B9
Shrops 131 E9
T&W 243 F7
Birtley Green Sur 50 E4
Birtsmorton Worcs 98 D6
Birts Street Worcs 98 D5
Bisbrooke Rutland 137 D7
Biscathorpe Lincs 190 D2
Biscombe Som 27 E11
Biscot Luton 103 G11
Biscovey Corn 5 E11
Bisham Windsor 65 C10
Bishampton Worcs 117 G9
Bish Mill Devon 26 B2
Bishon Common Hereford 97 C8
Bishop Auckland
Durham 233 F10
Bishopbridge Lincs 189 C8
Bishopbriggs E Dunb 278 G2
Bishop Burton E Yorks 208 F5
Bishopdown Wilts 47 G7
Bishop Kinkell Highld 300 D5
Bishop Middleham
Durham 234 E2
Bishopmill Moray 302 C2
Bishop Monkton
N Yorks 214 F6
Bishop Norton Lincs 189 C7
Bishopsbourne Kent 55 C7
Bishops Cannings Wilts 62 G4
Bishop's Castle Shrops 130 F6
Bishop's Caundle Dorset 29 E11
Bishop's Cleeve Glos 99 F9
Bishop's Down Dorset 29 E11
Bishops Frome Hereford 98 B3
Bishopsgarth Stockton 234 G4
Bishopsgate Sur 66 E3
Bishops Green Essex 87 B10
Bishop's Green W Berks 64 G4
Bishop's Hull Som 28 C2
Bishop's Itchington
Warks 119 F7
Bishops Lydeard Som 27 B11
Bishop's Norton Glos 98 G6
Bishops Nympton Devon 26 C3
Bishop's Offley Staffs 150 D5
Bishop's Quay Corn 2 D6
Bishop's Stortford
Herts 105 G9
Bishop's Sutton Hants 48 G6
Bishop's Tachbrook
Warks 118 E6
Bishops Tawton Devon 40 G5
Bishopsteignton Devon 14 G4
Bishopstoke Hants 33 D7
Bishopston Bristol 60 D5
Swansea 56 D5
Bishopstone Bucks 84 C4
E Sus 23 E7
Hereford 97 C8
Kent 71 F8
Swindon 63 C8
Wilts 31 B9
Bishopstrow Wilts 45 E11
Bishop Sutton Bath 44 B5
Bishop's Waltham Hants 33 D9
Bishopswood Som 28 E3
Bishop's Wood Staffs 132 B6
Bishopsworth Bristol 60 F5
Bishop Thornton
N Yorks 214 G5
Bishopthorpe York 207 D7
Bishopton Darl 234 G3
Dumfries 236 E6
N Yorks 214 E5
Renfs 277 G8
Warks 118 F3
Bishopwearmouth T&W 243 F9
Bishop Wilton E Yorks 207 B11
Bishpool Newport 59 B10
Bishton Newport 59 B11
Staffs 151 E10
Bisley Glos 80 D6
Sur 50 B3
Bisley Camp Sur 50 B2
Bispham Blackpool 202 E2
Bispham Green Lancs 194 E3
Bissoe Corn 4 G5
Bissom Corn 3 C7
Bisterne Hants 31 G10
Bisterne Close Hants 32 G2
Bitchet Green Kent 52 C5
Bitchfield Lincs 155 D9
Bittadon Devon 40 E4
Bittaford Devon 8 D3
Bittering Norf 159 F8
Bitterley Shrops 115 B11
Bitterne Soton 33 E7
Bitterne Park Soton 32 E6
Bitterscote Staffs 134 C4
Bitteswell Leics 135 F10
Bittles Green Dorset 30 C5
Bitton S Glos 61 F7
Bix Oxon 65 B8
Bixter Shetland 313 H5
Blaby Leics 135 D11
Blackacre Dumfries 248 E2
Blackadder West
Borders 272 E6
Blackawton Devon 8 E6
Black Bank Cambs 139 F10
Warks 135 F7
Black Banks Darl 224 C5
Black Barn Lincs 157 D8
Blackbeck Cumb 219 D10
Blackbird Leys Oxon 83 E9
Blackborough Devon 27 F9
Norf 158 G3
Blackborough End Norf 158 G3
Black Bourton Oxon 82 E3
Blackboys E Sus 37 C8
Blackbraes Aberds 293 B10
Blackbrook Derbys 170 F4
Derbys 185 E9
Mers 183 B8
Staffs 150 B5
Sur 51 D7
Blackburn Aberds 293 B10
Aberds 302 F5
Blackburn 195 B7
S Yorks 186 C5
W Loth 269 B9
Black Callerton T&W 242 D5
Black Carr Norf 141 D11
Blackcastle Midloth 271 D8
Blackchambers Aberds 293 B9
Black Clauchrie S Ayrs 245 G7
Black Corner W Sus 51 F9
Black Corries Lodge
Highld 284 B6
Blackcraig Dumfries 246 G6
Blackcraigs Angus 293 E7
Black Crofts Argyll 289 F11
Black Cross Corn 5 C8
Black Dam Hants 48 C6
Blackden Heath Ches E 184 G3
Blackditch Oxon 82 D6
Blackdog Aberds 293 B11
Black Dog Devon 26 F4
Blackdown Dorset 28 G5
Hants 33 C8
Warks 118 D6
Blackdyke Cumb 238 G4
Blackdykes E Loth 281 E11
Blacker Hill S Yorks 197 G11
Blacketts Kent 70 F2
Blackfell T&W 243 F7
Blackfen London 68 E3
Blackfield Hants 32 G6
Blackford Cumb 239 E9
Dumfries 248 G4
Perth 286 G2
Shrops 131 G11
Som 29 B11
Som 42 D2
Som 44 D2
Blackford Bridge
Gtr Man 195 F10
Blackfordby Leics 152 F6
Blackfords Staffs 151 G9
Blackgang IoW 20 F5
Blackgate Angus 287 B8
Blackhall Aberds 293 D8
Edin 280 G4
Renfs 267 C9
Blackhall Colliery
Durham 234 D5
Blackhall Mill T&W 242 F4
Blackhall Rocks Durham 234 D5
Blackham E Sus 52 F3
Blackhaugh Borders 261 B10
Blackheath Essex 107 G10
London 67 D11
Suff 127 C8
Sur 50 D4
W Mid 133 F9
Blackheath Park London 68 D2
Black Heddon Northumb 242 B3
Blackhill Aberds 303 D10
Aberds 303 E10
Aberds 303 F10
Durham 242 G3
Hants 32 D4
Highld 298 D3
Black Hill W Yorks 204 E6
Blackhillock Moray 302 E4
Blackhills Highld 301 D9
Moray 302 D2
Swansea 56 C5
Blackhorse Devon 14 C5
S Glos 61 D7
Black Horse Drove
Cambs 139 E11
Blackjack Lincs 156 B5
Black Lake W Mid 133 E9
Blackland Wilts 62 F4
Blacklands E Sus 38 E4
Hereford 98 C2
Black Lane Gtr Man 195 F9
Blacklaw Aberds 302 D6
Blackleach Lancs 202 G5
Blackley Gtr Man 195 G11
W Yorks 196 D6
Blacklunans Perth 292 G3
Black Marsh Shrops 130 D6
Blackmarstone Hereford 97 D10
Blackmill Bridgend 58 B2
Blackminster Worcs 99 C11
Blackmoor Bath 60 G5
Gtr Man 195 G7
Hants 49 G9
N Som 60 G3
Som 27 D11
Black Moor Lancs 194 E3
W Yorks 205 F11
Blackmoorfoot W Yorks 196 E5
Blackmoor Gate Devon 41 E7
Blackmore Essex 87 E10
Shrops 130 B6
Blackmore End Essex 106 E4
Herts 85 B11
Worcs 98 C6
Black Mount Argyll 284 C6
Blackness Aberds 293 D8
E Sus 52 G4
Falk 279 F11
Blacknest Hants 49 E9
Windsor 66 F3
Blacknoll Dorset 18 D2
Black Notley Essex 106 G5
Blacko Lancs 204 E3
Blackoe Shrops 149 B10
Blackpark Dumfries 236 C5
Black Park Wrex 166 G4
Black Pill Swansea 56 C6
Blackpole Worcs 117 F7
Black Pole Lancs 202 F5
Blackpool Blackpool 202 F2
Devon 7 E11
Devon 9 F7
Devon 14 G2
Pembs 73 C9
Blackpool Gate Cumb 240 B2
Blackridge W Loth 269 B7
Blackrock Argyll 274 G4
Bath 60 F6
Mon 78 C2
Black Rock Brighton 36 G4
Corn 2 C5
Blackrod Gtr Man 194 E6
Blackshaw Dumfries 238 D2
Blackshaw Head
W Yorks 196 B3
Blackshaw Moor Staffs 169 D8
Blacksmith's Corner
Suff 108 C2
Blacksmith's Green Suff 126 D2
Blacksnape Blackburn 195 C8
Blackstone Worcs 116 C5
W Sus 36 D2
Black Street Suff 143 F10
Black Tar Pembs 73 D7
Blackthorn Oxon 83 B10
Blackthorpe Suff 125 E8
Blacktoft E Yorks 199 C10
Blacktop Aberdeen 293 C10
Black Torrington Devon 25 F7
Blacktown Newport 59 C9
Black Vein Caerph 78 G2
Blackwall Derbys 170 F3
London 67 C11
Blackwall Tunnel
London 67 C11
Blackwater Corn 4 F4
Blackwater continued
Dorset 19 B8
Hants 49 B11
IoW 20 D6
Norf 159 E11
Som 28 D3
Blackwaterfoot N Ayrs 255 E9
Blackwater Lodge
Moray 302 G3
Blackwell Cardiff 59 D7
Blackwell Cumb 239 G10
Darl 224 C5
Derbys 170 D6
Derbys 185 G10
Devon 27 B8
Warks 100 C4
Worcs 117 C9
W Sus 51 F11
Blackwood Caerph 77 F11
S Lanark 268 G5
Warr 183 C10
Blackwood Hill Staffs 168 D6
Blacon Ches W 166 B5
Bladbean Kent 55 D7
Blades N Yorks 223 F9
Bladnoch Dumfries 236 D6
Bladon Oxon 82 C6
Blaenannerch Ceredig 92 B4
Blaenau Carms 75 C10
Flint 166 D2
Blaenau Dolwyddelan
Conwy 164 E2
Blaenau Ffestiniog
Gwyn 164 F2
Blaenau-Gwent Bl Gwent 78 E2
Blaenavon Torf 78 D3
Blaenbedw Fawr
Ceredig 111 G7
Blaencaerau Bridgend 57 C11
Blaencelyn Ceredig 111 G7
Blaen-Cil-Llech Ceredig 92 C6
Blaen Clydach Rhondda 77 G7
Blaencwm Rhondda 76 F6
Blaendulais / Seven Sisters
Neath 76 D4
Blaendyryn Powys 95 D8
Blaenffos Pembs 92 D3
Blaengarw Bridgend 76 G6
Blaengwrach Neath 76 D5
Blaengwynfi Neath 57 B11
Blaen-gwynfi Neath 57 B11
Blaenllechau Rhondda 77 F8
Blaen-pant Ceredig 92 C5
Blaenpennal Ceredig 112 E2
Blaenplwyf Ceredig 111 B11
Blaenporth Ceredig 92 B5
Blaenrhondda Rhondda 76 E6
Blaenwaun Carms 92 F4
Blaen-waun Carms 92 F4
Ceredig 111 G7
Blaen-y-coed Carms 92 F6
Blaenycwm Ceredig 112 B6
Blaen-y-cwm Bl Gwent 77 C10
Denb 147 C10
Gwyn 146 E4
Powys 147 E11
Blagdon N Som 44 B4
Torbay 9 C7
Blagdon Hill Som 28 D2
Blagill Cumb 231 B10
Blaguegate Lancs 194 F3
Blaich Highld 290 F2
Blain Highld 289 C8
Blaina Bl Gwent 78 D2
Blainacraig Ho Aberds 293 D7
Blair Fife 280 C6
Blair Atholl Perth 291 G10
Blairbeg N Ayrs 256 C2
Blairburn Fife 279 D9
Blairdaff Aberds 293 B8
Blair Drummond Stirling 278 B4
Blairdryne Aberds 293 D9
Blairglas Argyll 276 D6
Blairgorm Highld 301 G10
Blairgowrie Perth 286 C5
Blairhall Fife 279 D10
Blairhill N Lanark 268 B4
Blairingone Perth 279 B9
Blairland N Ayrs 266 F6
Blairlinn N Lanark 278 G5
Blairlogie Stirling 278 B6
Blairlomond Argyll 276 B3
Blairmore Argyll 276 E3
Highld 306 D6
Blairnamarrow Moray 292 B4
Blairquhosh Stirling 277 E10
Blair's Ferry Argyll 275 G10
Blairskaith E Dunb 277 F11
Blaisdon Glos 80 B2
Blakebrook Worcs 116 B6
Blakedown Worcs 117 B7
Blake End Essex 106 G4
Blakelands M Keynes 103 C7
Blakelaw Borders 263 C7
T&W 242 D6
Blakeley Staffs 133 E7
Blakeley Lane Staffs 169 F7
Blakelow Ches E 167 E11
Blakemere Hereford 97 C7
Blakenall Heath
W Mid 133 C10
Blakeney Glos 79 D11
Norf 177 E8
Blakenhall Ches E 168 F2
W Mid 133 D8
Blakeshall Worcs 132 G6
Blakesley Northants 120 G2
Blanchland Northumb 241 G11
Blandford Camp Dorset 30 F6
Blandford Forum Dorset 30 F5
Blandford St Mary Dorset 30 F5
Bland Hill N Yorks 205 C10
Blandy Highld 308 D6
Blanefield Stirling 277 F11
Blanerne Borders 272 D6
Blank Bank Staffs 168 F4
Blankney Lincs 173 C9
Blantyre S Lanark 268 D3
Blar a'Chaorainn Highld 290 G3
Blaran Argyll 275 B9
Blarghour Argyll 275 B10
Blarmachfoldach Highld 290 G2
Blarnalearoch Highld 307 K6
Blasford Hill Essex 88 C2
Blashford Hants 31 F11
Blaston Leics 136 D6
Blatchbridge Som 45 D9
Blatherwycke Northants 137 D9
Blawith Cumb 210 B5
Blaxhall Suff 127 F7
Blaxton S Yorks 199 G7
Blaydon T&W 242 E5
Blaydon Burn T&W 242 E5
Blaydon Haughs T&W 242 E5
Bleach Green Cumb 219 B9
Suff 126 B4
Bleadney Som 44 D3
Bleadon N Som 43 B10
Bleak Acre Hereford 98 B2
Bleak Hall M Keynes 103 D7

Bleak Hey Nook
Gtr Man 196 F4
Bleak Hill Hants 31 E10
Blean Kent 70 G6
Bleasby Lincs 189 E10
Notts 172 F2
Bleasby Moor Lincs 189 E10
Bleasdale Lancs 203 D7
Bleatarn Cumb 222 C4
Blebocraigs Fife 287 F8
Bleddfa Powys 114 D4
Bledington Glos 100 G4
Bledlow Bucks 84 E3
Bledlow Ridge Bucks 84 F3
Bleet Wilts 45 B11
Blegbie E Loth 271 C9
Blegbury Devon 24 B2
Blencarn Cumb 231 E8
Blencogo Cumb 229 B9
Blendworth Hants 34 E2
Blenheim Oxon 83 D9
Oxon 83 E9
Blenheim Park Norf 158 C6
Blenkinsopp Hall
Northumb 240 E5
Blennerhasset Cumb 229 C9
Blervie Castle Moray 301 D10
Bletchingdon Oxon 83 B8
Bletchingley Sur 51 C10
Bletchley M Keynes 103 E7
Shrops 150 C2
Bletherston Pembs 91 G11
Bletsoe Bedford 121 F10
Blewbury Oxon 64 B4
Bliby Kent 54 F4
Blickling Norf 160 D3
Blidworth Notts 171 D9
Blidworth Bottoms
Notts 171 E9
Blidworth Dale Notts 171 E9
Blindburn Northumb 263 G8
Blindcrake Cumb 229 E8
Blindley Heath Sur 51 D11
Blindmoor Som 28 E3
Blingery Highld 310 E7
Blisland Corn 11 G8
Blissford Hants 31 E11
Bliss Gate Worcs 116 C4
Blisworth Northants 120 G4
Blithbury Staffs 151 E11
Blitterlees Cumb 238 G4
Blockley Glos 100 D3
Blofield Norf 142 B6
Blofield Heath Norf 160 G6
Blo' Norton Norf 125 B10
Bloodman's Corner
Suff 143 D10
Bloomfield Bath 45 B7
Bath 61 G8
Borders 262 E3
W Mid 133 E9
Bloomsbury London 67 C10
Blore Staffs 150 C4
Staffs 169 F10
Bloreheath Staffs 150 B4
Blossomfield W Mid 118 B2
Blount's Green Staffs 151 C11
Blowick Mers 193 D11
Blowinghouse Corn 4 E4
Bloxham Oxon 101 D8
Bloxholm Lincs 173 E9
Bloxwich W Mid 133 C9
Bloxworth Dorset 18 C3
Blubberhouses N Yorks 205 B9
Blue Anchor Corn 5 D8
Som 42 E4
Swansea 56 B4
Bluebell Telford 149 G11
Blue Bell Hill Kent 69 G8
Bluecairn Borders 271 G10
Blue Hill Herts 104 G5
Blue Row Essex 89 C8
Bluetown Kent 54 B2
Blue Town Kent 70 D2
Blue Vein Wilts 61 F10
Bluewater Kent 68 E5
Blughasary Highld 307 J6
Blundellsands Mers 182 B4
Blundeston Suff 143 D10
Blundies Staffs 132 F6
Blunham C Beds 122 G3
Blunsdon St Andrew
Swindon 62 B6
Bluntington Worcs 117 C7
Bluntisham Cambs 123 C7
Blunts Corn 6 C6
Blunt's Green Warks 118 D2
Blurton Stoke 168 G5
Blyborough Lincs 188 C6
Blyford Suff 127 B8
Blymhill Staffs 150 G6
Blymhill Lawns Staffs 150 G6
Blyth Borders 270 F2
Northumb 253 G8
Notts 187 D10
Blyth Bridge Borders 270 F2
Blythburgh Suff 127 B9
Blythe Borders 271 F11
Blythe Bridge Staffs 169 G7
Blythe Marsh Staffs 169 G7
Blyth End Warks 134 E4
Blythswood Renfs 267 B10
Blyton Lincs 188 C5
Boarhills Fife 287 F9
Boarhunt Hants 33 F10
Boarsgreave Lancs 195 C10
Boarshead E Sus 52 G4
Boars Hill Oxon 83 E7
Boarstall Bucks 83 C10
Boasley Cross Devon 12 C5
Boath Highld 300 B5
Boat of Garten Highld 291 B11
Bobbing Kent 69 F11
Bobbington Staffs 132 E6
Bobbingworth Essex 87 D8
Bobby Hill Suff 125 C10
Boblainy Highld 300 F4
Bocaddon Corn 6 D3
Bochastle Stirling 285 G10
Bockhanger Kent 54 E4
Bocking Essex 106 G5
Bocking Churchstreet
Essex 106 F5
Bocking's Elm Essex 89 B11
Bockleton Worcs 115 E11
Bockmer End Bucks 65 B10
Bocombe Devon 24 C5
Bodantionail Highld 299 B7
Boddam Aberds 303 E11
Shetland 313 M5
Bodden Som 44 E6
Boddington Glos 99 F7
Bodedern Anglesey 178 E4
Bodellick Corn 10 G5
Bodelva Corn 5 E11
Bodelwyddan Denb 181 F8
Bodenham Hereford 115 G10
Wilts 31 B11
Bodenham Bank Hereford 98 E2
Bodenham Moor
Hereford 115 G10
Bodermid Gwyn 144 D3
Bodewryd Anglesey 178 C5
Bodfari Denb 181 G9
Bodffordd Anglesey 178 F6
Bodham Norf 177 E10
Bodiam E Sus 38 B3
Bodicote Oxon 101 D9
Bodiechell Aberds 303 E7
Bodieve Corn 10 G5
Bodiggo Corn 5 D10
Bodilly Corn 2 C5
Bodinnick Corn 6 E2
Bodle Street Green
E Sus 23 C11
Bodley Devon 41 D7
Bodmin Corn 5 B11
Bodmiscombe Devon 27 F10
Bodney Norf 140 D6
Bodorgan Anglesey 162 B5
Bodsham Kent 54 D6
Boduan Gwyn 144 B6
Boduel Corn 6 C4
Bodwen Corn 5 C10
Bodymoor Heath Warks 134 D4
Bofarnel Corn 6 C2
Bogallan Highld 300 D6
Bogbrae Aberds 303 F10
Bogend Borders 272 F5
Notts 171 F7
S Ayrs 257 C9
Bogentory Aberds 293 C9
Boghall Midloth 270 B4
W Loth 269 B9
Boghead Aberds 293 D8
S Lanark 268 G5
Bogmoor Moray 302 C3
Bogniebrae Aberds 302 E5
Aberds 302 E6
Bognor Regis W Sus 22 D6
Bograxie Aberds 293 B9
Bogs Aberds 302 G5
Bogs Bank Borders 270 E3
Bogside N Lanark 268 E6
Bogthorn W Yorks 204 F6
Bogton Aberds 302 D6
Bogtown Aberds 302 C5
Bogue Dumfries 246 G4
Bohemia E Sus 38 E4
Wilts 32 D2
Bohenie Highld 290 E4
Bohetherick Corn 7 B8
Bohortha Corn 3 C9
Bohuntine Highld 290 E4
Bohuntinville Highld 290 E4
Boirseam W Isles 296 C6
Bojewyan Corn 1 C3
Bokiddick Corn 5 C11
Bolahaul Fm Carms 74 B6
Bolam Durham 233 G9
Northumb 252 G3
Bolam West Houses
Northumb 252 G3
Bolas Heath Telford 150 E3
Bolberry Devon 9 G8
Bold Heath Mers 183 D8
Boldmere W Mid 134 E2
Boldon T&W 243 E9
Boldon Colliery T&W 243 E8
Boldre Hants 20 B2
Boldron Durham 223 C10
Bole Notts 188 D3
Bolehall Staffs 134 C4
Bolehill Derbys 170 E3
Derbys 186 G6
S Yorks 186 E5
Bole Hill Derbys 186 G4
Bolenowe Corn 2 B5
Boleside Borders 261 C11
Boley Park Staffs 134 B2
Bolham Devon 27 E7
Notts 188 E2
Bolham Water Devon 27 E11
Bolholt Gtr Man 195 E9
Bolingey Corn 4 E5
Bolitho Corn 2 C5
Bollihope Durham 232 E6
Bollington Ches E 184 F6
Bollington Cross Ches E 184 F6
Bolney W Sus 36 C3
Bolnhurst Bedford 121 F11
Bolnore W Sus 36 C4
Bolshan Angus 287 B10
Bolsover Derbys 187 G7
Bolsterstone S Yorks 186 B3
Bolstone Hereford 97 E11
Boltby N Yorks 215 B9
Bolter End Bucks 84 G3
Bolton Cumb 231 G8
E Loth 281 G10
E Yorks 207 C11
Gtr Man 195 F8
Northumb 264 G4
W Yorks 205 F9
Bolton Abbey N Yorks 205 C7
Bolton Bridge N Yorks 205 C7
Bolton-by-Bowland
Lancs 203 D11
Boltonfellend Cumb 239 D11
Boltongate Cumb 229 C10
Bolton Green Lancs 194 D5
Bolton Houses Lancs 202 G4
Bolton-le-Sands Lancs 211 F9
Bolton Low Houses
Cumb 229 C10
Bolton New Houses
Cumb 229 C10
Bolton-on-Swale
N Yorks 224 F5
Bolton Percy N Yorks 206 E6
Bolton Town End Lancs 211 F9
Bolton upon Dearne
S Yorks 198 G3
Bolton Wood Lane
Cumb 229 C11
Bolton Woods W Yorks 205 F9
Boltshope Park Durham 232 B4
Bolventor Corn 11 F9
Bomarsund Northumb 253 G7
Bombie Dumfries 237 D9
Bomby Cumb 221 B10
Bomere Heath Shrops 149 F9
Bonaly Edin 270 B4
Bonar Bridge Highld 309 K6
Bonawe Argyll 284 D4
Bonby N Lincs 200 D4
Boncath Pembs 92 D4
Bonchester Bridge
Borders 262 G3
Bonchurch IoW 21 F7
Bondend Glos 80 B5
Bond End Staffs 152 F2
Bondleigh Devon 25 G11
Bondman Hays Leics 135 B9
Bonds Lancs 202 E5
Bondstones Devon 25 F9
Bonehill Devon 13 F10
Staffs 134 C3
Bo'ness Falk 279 E9
Bonhill W Dunb 277 F7
Boningale Shrops 132 C6
Bonjedward Borders 262 E5
Bonkle N Lanark 268 D6
Bonnavoulin Highld 289 D7
Bonning Gate Cumb 221 F9
Bonnington Borders 261 B7
Edin 270 B2
Kent 54 F5
Bonnybank Fife 287 G7
Bonnybridge Falk 278 E6
Bonnykelly Aberds 303 D8
Bonnyrigg and Lasswade
Midloth 270 B6
Bonnyton Aberds 302 F6
Angus 287 B10
Angus 287 D7
E Ayrs 257 B10
Bonsall Derbys 170 D3
Bonskeid House Perth 291 G10
Bonson Som 43 E8
Bont Mon 78 B5
Bontddu Gwyn 146 F3
Bont-Dolgadfan Powys 129 C7
Bont Fawr Carms 94 F4
Bont goch / Elerch
Ceredig 128 F3
Bonthorpe Lincs 191 G7
Bontnewydd Ceredig 112 D2
Gwyn 163 D7
Bont-newydd Conwy 181 G8
Bont Newydd Gwyn 146 E5
Gwyn 164 G2
Bontuchel Denb 165 D9
Bonvilston / Tresimwn
V Glam 58 E5
Bon-y-maen Swansea 57 B7
Boode Devon 40 F4
Booker Bucks 84 G4
Bookham Dorset 30 G2
Booleybank Shrops 149 D11
Boon Borders 271 F11
Boon Hill Staffs 168 E4
Boorley Green Hants 33 E8
Boosbeck Redcar 226 B3
Boose's Green Essex 106 E6
Boot Cumb 220 E3
Booth Staffs 151 D10
W Yorks 196 B4
Booth Bank Ches E 184 D2
Booth Bridge Lancs 204 D4
Boothby Graffoe Lincs 173 D7
Boothby Pagnell Lincs 155 C9
Boothen Stoke 168 G5
Boothferry E Yorks 199 B8
Boothgate Derbys 170 F5
Booth Green Ches E 184 E6
Boothroyd W Yorks 197 C8
Boothsdale Ches W 167 B8
Boothstown Gtr Man 195 G8
Boothtown W Yorks 196 B5
Boothville Northants 120 E5
Booth Wood W Yorks 196 D4
Bootle Cumb 210 B2
Mers 182 B4
Booton Norf 160 E2
Boots Green Ches W 184 G3
Boot Street Suff 108 B4
Booze N Yorks 223 E10
Boquhan Stirling 277 D10
Boquio Corn 2 C5
Boraston Shrops 116 D2
Boraston Dale Shrops 116 C2
Borden Kent 69 G11
W Sus 34 C4
Border Cumb 238 G5
Bordesley W Mid 133 F11
Bordesley Green W Mid 134 F2
Bordlands Borders 270 F3
Bordley N Yorks 213 G8
Bordon Hants 49 F10
Bordon Camp Hants 49 F9
Boreham Essex 88 D3
Wilts 45 E11
Boreham Street E Sus 23 C11
Borehamwood Herts 85 F11
Boreland Dumfries 236 C5
Dumfries 248 E5
Fife 280 C6
Stirling 285 D9
Boreland of Southwick
Dumfries 237 C11
Boreley Worcs 116 D6
Borestone Stirling 278 C5
Borgh W Isles 296 C5
W Isles 297 L2
Borghasdal W Isles 296 C6
Borghastan W Isles 304 D4
Borgie Highld 308 D6
Borgue Dumfries 237 E8
Highld 311 G5
Borley Essex 106 C6
Borley Green Essex 106 C6
Suff 125 E9
Bornais W Isles 297 J3
Borneskeitaig Highld 298 B3
Borness Dumfries 237 E8
Borough Scilly 1 G3
Boroughbridge N Yorks 215 F7
Borough Green Kent 52 B6
Borough Marsh
Wokingham 65 D9
Borough Park Staffs 134 B4
Borough Post Som 28 C4
Borras Wrex 166 E4
Borras Head Wrex 166 E5
Borreraig Highld 296 F7
Borrobol Lodge Highld 311 G2
Borrodale Highld 297 G7
Borrohill Aberds 303 D9
Borrowash Derbys 153 C8
Borrowby N Yorks 215 B8
N Yorks 226 B5
Borrowdale Cumb 220 C5
Borrowfield Aberds 293 D10
Borrowston Highld 310 E7
Borrowstoun Mains
Falk 279 E9
Borstal Medway 69 F8
Borthwick Midloth 271 D7
Borthwickbrae Borders 261 G10
Borthwickshiels
Borders 261 F10
Borth / Y Borth Ceredig 128 E2
Borth-y-Gest Gwyn 145 B11
Borve Highld 298 E4
Borve Lodge W Isles 305 J2
Borwick Lancs 211 E10
Borwick Rails Cumb 210 D3
Bosavern Corn 1 C3
Bosbury Hereford 98 C3
Boscadjack Corn 2 C5
Boscastle Corn 11 C8
Boscean Corn 1 C3
Boscombe Bmouth 19 C8
Wilts 47 F8
Boscomoor Staffs 151 G8
Boscoppa Corn 5 E10
Boscreege Corn 2 C3
Bosham W Sus 22 C4
Bosham Hoe W Sus 22 C4
Bosherston Pembs 73 G7
Boskednan Corn 1 C4
Boskenna Corn 1 E4
Bosleake Corn 4 G3
Bosley Ches E 168 B6
Boslowick Corn 3 C7
Boslymon Corn 5 C11
Bosoughan Corn 5 C7
Bosporthennis Corn 1 B4
Bossall N Yorks 216 G4
Bossiney Corn 11 D7
Bossingham Kent 54 D6
Bossington Hants 47 G10
Kent 55 B8
Som 41 D11
Bostadh W Isles 304 D3
Bostock Green Ches W 167 B11
Boston Lincs 174 G4
Boston Long Hedges
Lincs 174 F5
Boston Spa W Yorks 206 D4
Boston West Lincs 174 F3
Boswednack Corn 1 B4
Boswin Corn 2 C5
Boswinger Corn 5 G9
Boswyn Corn 2 B5
Botallack Corn 1 C3
Botany Bay London 86 F3
Mon 79 E8
Botcherby Cumb 239 F10
Botcheston Leics 135 B9
Botesdale Suff 125 B10
Bothal Northumb 252 F6
Bothampstead W Berks 64 D4
Bothamsall Notts 187 G11
Bothel Cumb 229 D9
Bothenhampton Dorset 16 C5
Bothwell S Lanark 268 D4
Bothy Highld 290 F4
Botley Bucks 85 E7
Hants 33 E8
Oxon 83 D7
Botloe's Green Glos 98 F4
Botolph Claydon Bucks 102 G4
Botolphs W Sus 35 F11
Bottacks Highld 300 C4
Botternell Corn 11 G11
Bottesford Leics 154 B6
N Lincs 199 F11
Bottisham Cambs 123 E10
Bottlesford Wilts 46 B6
Bottom Boat W Yorks 197 C11
Bottomcraig Fife 287 E7
Bottom House Staffs 169 E8
Bottomley W Yorks 196 D5
Bottom of Hutton Lancs 194 B3
Bottom o' th' Moor
Gtr Man 195 E7
Bottom Pond Kent 53 B11
Bottoms Corn 1 E3
Bottreaux Mill Devon 26 B4
Bottrells Close Bucks 85 G7
Botts Green Warks 134 E4
Botusfleming Corn 7 C8
Botwnnog Gwyn 144 C5
Bough Beech Kent 52 D3
Boughrood Powys 96 D2
Boughrood Brest Powys 96 D2
Boughspring Glos 79 F9
Boughton Ches W 166 B6
Lincs 173 F10
Norf 140 C3
Northants 120 D5
Notts 171 B11
Boughton Aluph Kent 54 D4
Boughton Corner Kent 54 D4
Boughton Green Kent 53 C9
Boughton Heath
Ches W 166 B6
Boughton Lees Kent 54 D4
Boughton Malherbe
Kent 53 D11
Boughton Monchelsea
Kent 53 C9
Boughton Street Kent 54 B5
Bougton End C Beds 103 D9
Boulby Redcar 226 B5
Boulden Shrops 131 F10
Boulder Clough
W Yorks 196 C4
Bouldnor IoW 20 D3
Bouldon Shrops 131 F10
Boulmer Northumb 265 G7
Boulsdon Glos 98 G4
Boulston Pembs 73 C7
Boultenstone Aberds 292 B6
Boultham Lincs 173 B7
Boultham Moor Lincs 173 B7
Boulton Derbys 153 C7
Boulton Moor Derbys 153 C7
Boundary Leics 152 F6
Staffs 169 G7
Boundstone Sur 49 E10
Bountis Thorne Devon 24 D5
Bourn Cambs 122 F6
Bournbrook W Mid 133 G10
Bourne Lincs 155 E11
N Som 44 B3
Bourne End Bedford 121 E10
Bucks 65 B11
C Beds 103 C9
Herts 85 D8
Bournemouth Bmouth 19 C7
Bournes Green Glos 80 E6
Southend 70 B2
Worcs 117 C8
Bourne Vale W Mid 133 D11
Bourne Valley Poole 19 C7
Bournheath Worcs 117 C9
Bournmoor Durham 243 G8
Bournside Glos 99 G8
Bournstream Glos 80 G2
Bournville W Mid 133 G10
Bourton Bucks 102 E4
Dorset 45 G9
N Som 59 G11
Oxon 63 B8
Shrops 131 D11
Wilts 62 G4
Bourton on Dunsmore
Warks 119 C8
Bourton-on-the-Hill
Glos 100 E3
Bourton-on-the-Water
Glos 100 G3
Bousd Argyll 288 C4
Boustead Hill Cumb 239 F7
Bouth Cumb 210 B6
Bouthwaite N Yorks 214 E2
Bouts Worcs 117 F10
Bovain Stirling 285 D9
Boveney Bucks 66 D2
Boveridge Dorset 31 E9
Boverton V Glam 58 F3
Bovey Tracey Devon 14 F2
Bovingdon Herts 85 E8
Bovingdon Green Bucks 65 B10
Herts 85 E8
Bovinger Essex 87 D8
Bovington Camp Dorset 18 D2
Bow Borders 271 G9
Bow *continued*
Devon 8 D6
Devon 26 G2
Orkney 314 G3
Oxon 82 G4
Bowbank Durham 232 G4
Bowbeck Suff 125 B8
Bow Brickhill M Keynes 103 E8
Bowbridge Glos 80 E5
Bowbrook Shrops 149 G9
Bow Broom S Yorks 187 B7
Bowburn Durham 234 D2
Bowcombe IoW 20 D5
Bow Common London 67 C11
Bowd Devon 15 C8
Bowden Borders 262 C3
Devon 8 F6
Dorset 30 C3
Bowden Hill Wilts 62 F2
Bowdens Som 28 B6
Bowderdale Cumb 222 E3
Bowdon Gtr Man 184 D3
Bower Highld 310 C6
Northumb 251 G7
Bower Ashton Bristol 60 E5
Bowerchalke Wilts 31 C8
Bower Heath Herts 85 B10
Bowerhill Wilts 62 G2
Bower Hinton Som 29 D7
Bowerhope Borders 261 E7
Bower House Tye Suff 107 C9
Bowermadden Highld 310 C6
Bowers Staffs 150 B6
Bowers Gifford Essex 69 B9
Bowershall Fife 279 C11
Bowertower Highld 310 C6
Bowes Durham 223 C9
Bowes Park London 86 G4
Bowgreave Lancs 202 E5
Bowgreen Gtr Man 184 D3
Bowhill Borders 261 D10
Fife 280 B4
Bowhouse Dumfries 238 D2
Bowhousebog or Liquo
N Lanark 269 D7
Bowing Park Mers 182 D6
Bowismiln Borders 262 E2
Bowithick Corn 11 E9
Bowker's Green Lancs 194 G2
Bowland Bridge Cumb 211 B8
Bowldown Wilts 62 D2
Bowlee Gtr Man 195 F10
Bowlees Durham 232 F4
Bowler's Town E Sus 38 C6
Bowley Hereford 115 G10
Bowley Lane Hereford 98 C3
Bowley Town Hereford 115 G10
Bowlhead Green Sur 50 F2
Bowling W Dunb 277 G9
W Yorks 205 G9
Bowling Alley Hants 49 D9
Bowling Bank Wrex 166 F5
Bowling Green Corn 5 D10
Corn 12 G3
Glos 81 E8
Hants 19 B11
Shrops 150 D2
W Mid 133 F8
Worcs 116 G6
Bowlish Som 44 E6
Bowmans Kent 68 E4
Bowmanstead Cumb 220 F6
Bowmore Argyll 254 B4
Bowness-on-Solway
Cumb 238 E6
Bowness-on-Windermere
Cumb 221 F8
Bow of Fife Fife 287 F7
Bowridge Hill Dorset 30 B4
Bowrie-fauld Angus 287 C9
Bowsden Northumb 273 G9
Bowsey Hill Windsor 65 C10
Bowshank Borders 271 G9
Bowside Lodge Highld 310 C2
Bowston Cumb 221 F9
Bow Street Ceredig 128 G2
Norf 141 D10
Bowthorpe Norf 142 B3
Bowyer's Common Hants 34 B3
Box Glos 80 E5
Wilts 61 F10
Boxbush Glos 80 C2
Glos 98 G3
Box End Bedford 103 B10
Boxford Suff 107 C9
W Berks 64 E2
Boxgrove W Sus 22 B6
Box Hill Sur 51 C7
Wilts 61 F10
Boxley Kent 53 B9
Boxmoor Herts 85 D9
Box's Shop Corn 24 G2
Boxted Essex 107 E9
Suff 124 G6
Boxted Cross Essex 107 E10
Boxted Heath Essex 107 E10
Box Trees W Mid 118 C2
Boxwell Glos 80 G4
Boxworth Cambs 122 E6
Boxworth End Cambs 123 D7
Boyatt Wood Hants 32 C6
Boyden End Suff 124 F4
Boyden Gate Kent 71 F8
Boyland Common Norf 141 G11
Boylestone Derbys 152 B3
Boylestonfield Derbys 152 B3
Boyndie Aberds 302 C6
Boyn Hill Windsor 65 C11
Boynton E Yorks 218 F2
Boysack Angus 287 C9
Angus 287 C10
Boys Hill Dorset 29 E11
Boys Village V Glam 58 F4
Boythorpe Derbys 186 G5
Boyton Corn 12 C2
Suff 109 B7
Wilts 46 F3
Boyton Cross Essex 87 D10
Boyton End Essex 106 E2
Suff 106 C4
Bozeat Northants 121 F8
Bozen Green Herts 105 F8
Braaid IoM 192 E4
Braal Castle Highld 310 C5
Brabling Green Suff 126 E5
Brabourne Kent 54 E5
Brabourne Lees Kent 54 E5
Brabster Highld 310 C7
Bracadale Highld 294 B5
Bracara Highld 295 F9
Braceborough Lincs 155 G11
Bracebridge Lincs 173 B7
Bracebridge Heath
Lincs 173 B7
Bracebridge Low Fields
Lincs 173 B7
Braceby Lincs 155 B10
Bracewell Lancs 204 D3
Bracken Bank W Yorks 204 F6
Brackenber Cumb 222 B4
Brackenbottom N Yorks 212 E6
Brackenfield Derbys 170 D5
Brackenhall W Yorks 197 D7
Bracken Hill W Yorks 197 C7
Brackenlands Cumb 229 B11
Bracken Park W Yorks 206 E3
Brackenthwaite Cumb 229 B11
Cumb 229 G9
N Yorks 205 C11
Brackla / Bragle
Bridgend 58 D2
Bracklamore Aberds 303 D8
Bracklesham W Sus 22 D4
Brackletter Highld 290 E3
Brackley Argyll 255 C8
Northants 101 D11
Brackloch Highld 307 G6
Bracknell Brack 65 F11
Braco Perth 286 G2
Bracobrae Moray 302 D5
Braco Castle Perth 286 F2
Bracon N Lincs 199 F9
Bracon Ash Norf 142 D3
Braco Park Aberds 303 C9
Bracorina Highld 295 F9
Bradaford Devon 12 C3
Bradbourne Derbys 170 E2
Bradbury Durham 234 F2
Bradda IoM 192 F2
Bradden Northants 102 B2
Braddock Corn 6 C3
Braddocks Hay Staffs 168 D5
Bradeley Stoke 168 E5
Bradeley Green Ches E 167 G8
Bradenham Bucks 84 F4
Norf 141 B8
Bradenstoke Wilts 62 D4
Brades Village W Mid 133 E9
Bradfield Devon 27 F9
Essex 108 E2
Norf 160 C5
W Berks 64 E6
Bradfield Combust Suff 125 F7
Bradfield Green
Ches E 167 D11
Bradfield Heath Essex 108 F2
Bradfield St Clare Suff 125 F8
Bradfield St George
Suff 125 E8
Bradford Corn 11 F8
Derbys 170 C2
Devon 24 F6
Gtr Man 184 B5
Northumb 264 C5
W Yorks 205 G9
Bradford Abbas Dorset 29 E9
Bradford Leigh Wilts 61 G10
Bradford-on-Avon
Wilts 61 G10
Bradford-on-Tone Som 27 C11
Bradford Peverell Dorset 17 C9
Bradgate S Yorks 186 C6
Bradiford Devon 40 G5
Brading IoW 21 D8
Bradley Derbys 170 F2
Glos 80 G3
Hants 48 E6
NE Lincs 201 F8
Staffs 151 F7
W Mid 133 D8
Wrex 166 E4
W Yorks 197 C7
Bradley Cross Som 44 C3
Bradley Fold Gtr Man 195 F9
Bradley Green Ches W 167 F8
Glos 80 G2
Som 43 F9
Warks 134 C5
Worcs 117 E9
Bradley in the Moors
Staffs 169 G9
Bradley Mills W Yorks 197 D7
Bradley Mount Ches E 184 F6
Bradley Stoke S Glos 60 C6
Bradlow Hereford 98 D4
Bradmore Notts 153 C11
W Mid 133 D7
Bradney Shrops 132 D5
Som 43 F10
Bradninch Devon 27 G8
Bradnock's Marsh
W Mid 118 B4
Bradnop Staffs 169 D8
Bradnor Green Hereford 114 F5
Bradpole Dorset 16 C5
Bradshaw Gtr Man 195 E8
Staffs 168 D6
W Yorks 196 E5
W Yorks 205 G7
Bradstone Devon 12 E3
Bradville M Keynes 102 C6
Bradwall Green Ches E 168 C3
Bradway S Yorks 186 E4
Bradwell Derbys 185 E11
Devon 40 E3
Essex 106 G6
M Keynes 102 D6
Norf 143 C10
Staffs 168 F4
Bradwell Common
M Keynes 102 D6
Bradwell Grove Oxon 82 D2
Bradwell Hills Derbys 185 E11
Bradwell on Sea Essex 89 D8
Bradwell Waterside
Essex 89 D7
Bradworthy Devon 24 E4
Bradworthy Cross Devon 24 E4
Brae Dumfries 237 B10
Highld 307 L3
Highld 309 J4
Shetland 312 G5
Braeantra Highld 300 B5
Braebuster Orkney 314 F5
Braedownie Angus 292 F4
Braeface Falk 278 E5
Braefield Highld 300 F4
Braefindon Highld 300 D6
Braegrum Perth 286 E4
Braehead Dumfries 236 D6
Orkney 314 B4
Orkney 314 F5
S Ayrs 257 E8
S Lanark 259 C8
S Lanark 267 D11
S Lanark 269 E9
Stirling 278 C6
Braehead of Lunan
Angus 287 B10
Braehoulland Shetland 312 F4
Braehour Highld 310 D4
Braehungie Highld 310 F5
Braeintra Highld 295 B10
Braelangwell Lodge
Highld 309 K5
Braemar Aberds 292 D3
Braemore Highld 299 B11
Highld 310 F4
Brae of Achnahaird
Highld 307 H5
Brae of Boquhapple
Stirling 285 G10
Braepark Edin 280 F3
Brae Roy Lodge Highld 290 D5
Braeside Invclyd 276 F4
Braes of Enzie Moray 302 D3
Braes of Ullapool Highld 307 K6
Braeswick Orkney 314 C6
Braevallich Argyll 275 C10
Braewick Shetland 312 F4
Shetland 313 H5
Brafferton Darl 233 G11
N Yorks 215 E8
Brafield-on-the-Green
Northants 120 F6
Bragar W Isles 304 D4
Bragbury End Herts 104 G5
Bragenham Bucks 103 F8
Bragle / Brackla
Bridgend 58 D2
Bragleenmore Argyll 289 G11
Braichmelyn Gwyn 163 B10
Braichyfedw Powys 129 E7
Braid Edin 280 G4
Braides Lancs 202 C4
Braidfauld Glasgow 268 C2
Braidley N Yorks 213 C10
Braids Argyll 255 C8
Braidwood S Lanark 268 F6
Braigh Chalasaigh
W Isles 296 D5
Braigo Argyll 274 G3
Brailsford Derbys 170 G3
Brailsford Green Derbys 170 G3
Braingortan Argyll 275 F11
Brain's Green Glos 79 D11
Brainshaugh Northumb 252 C6
Braintree Essex 106 G5
Braiseworth Suff 126 C2
Braishfield Hants 32 B5
Braiswick Essex 107 F9
Braithwaite Cumb 229 G10
S Yorks 198 E6
W Yorks 204 E6
Braithwell S Yorks 187 C8
Brakefield Green Norf 141 B10
Brakenhill W Yorks 198 D2
Bramber W Sus 35 E11
Bramblecombe Dorset 30 G3
Brambridge Hants 33 C7
Bramcote Notts 153 B10
Warks 135 F8
Bramcote Hills Notts 153 B10
Bramcote Mains Warks 135 F8
Bramdean Hants 33 B10
Bramerton Norf 142 C5
Bramfield Herts 86 B3
Suff 127 C7
Bramford Suff 108 B2
W Mid 133 E8
Bramhall Gtr Man 184 D5
Bramhall Moor Gtr Man 184 D6
Bramhall Park Gtr Man 184 D5
Bramham W Yorks 206 E4
Bramhope W Yorks 205 E11
Bramley Derbys 186 F6
Hants 48 B6
Sur 50 D4
S Yorks 187 C7
W Yorks 205 F10
Bramley Corner Hants 48 B6
Bramley Green Hants 49 B7
Bramley Head N Yorks 205 B8
Bramley Vale Derbys 171 B7
Bramling Kent 55 B8
Brampford Speke Devon 14 B4
Brampton Cambs 122 C4
Cumb 231 G9
Cumb 240 E2
Derbys 186 G5
Hereford 97 D8
Lincs 188 F4
Norf 160 E4
Suff 143 G8
S Yorks 198 G2
Brampton Abbotts
Hereford 98 F2
Brampton Ash Northants 136 F5
Brampton Bryan
Hereford 115 C7
Brampton en le Morthen
S Yorks 187 D7
Brampton Park Cambs 122 C4
Brampton Street Suff 143 G8
Bramshall Staffs 151 C11
Bramshaw Hants 32 D3
Bramshill Hants 65 G8
Bramshott Hants 49 G10
Bramwell Som 28 B6
Branatwatt Shetland 313 H4
Branault Highld 289 C7
Branbridges Kent 53 D7
Brancaster Norf 176 E3
Brancaster Staithe Norf 176 E3
Brancepeth Durham 233 D10
Branch End Northumb 242 E3
Branchill Moray 301 D10
Branchton Invclyd 276 F4
Brand End Lincs 174 F5
Branderburgh Moray 302 B2
Brandesburton E Yorks 209 D8
Brandeston Suff 126 E4
Brand Green Glos 98 F4
Hereford 98 C5
Brandhill Shrops 115 B8
Brandis Corner Devon 24 G6
Brandish Street Som 42 D2
Brandiston Norf 160 E2
Brandlingill Cumb 229 F8
Brandon Durham 233 D10
Lincs 172 F6
Northumb 264 F2
Suff 140 F5
Warks 119 B8
Brandon Bank Cambs 140 F2
Brandon Creek Norf 140 E2
Brandon Parva Norf 141 B11
Brandsby N Yorks 215 E11
Brands Hill Windsor 66 D4
Brandwood Shrops 149 D9
Brandwood End
W Mid 117 B11
Brandy Carr W Yorks 197 C10
Brandy Hole Essex 88 F4
Brandyquoy Orkney 314 G4
Brandy Wharf Lincs 189 B8
Brane Corn 1 D4
Bran End Essex 106 F3
Branksome Darl 224 B5
Poole 18 C6
Branksome Park Poole 19 C7
Bransbury Hants 48 E2
Bransby Lincs 188 F5
Branscombe Devon 15 D9
Bransford Worcs 116 G5
Bransgore Hants 19 B9
Branshill Clack 279 C7
Bransholme Hull 209 G8
Branson's Cross Worcs 117 C11
Branston Leics 154 D6
Lincs 173 B8
Staffs 152 E4
Branston Booths Lincs 173 B9
Branstone IoW 21 E7
Bransty Cumb 219 B9
Brant Broughton Lincs 172 E6
Brantham Suff 108 E2
Branthwaite Cumb 229 D11
Cumb 229 G7
Branthwaite Edge Cumb 229 G7
Brantingham E Yorks 200 B2
Branton Northumb 264 F2
S Yorks 198 G6
Branton Green N Yorks 215 G8
Branxholme Borders 261 G11
Branxholm Park
Borders 261 G11
Branxton Northumb 263 B9
Brascote Leics 135 C8
Brassey Green Ches W 167 C8
Brassington Derbys 170 E2
Brasted Kent 52 C3
Brasted Chart Kent 52 C3
Brathens Aberds 293 D8
Bratoft Lincs 175 B7
Brattle Kent 54 G2
Brattleby Lincs 188 E6
Bratton Som 42 D2
Telford 150 G2
Wilts 46 C2
Bratton Clovelly Devon 12 C5
Bratton Fleming Devon 40 F6
Bratton Seymour Som 29 B11
Braughing Herts 105 F7
Braughing Friars Herts 105 G8
Braulen Lodge Highld 300 F2
Braunston Northants 119 D10
Braunstone Leics 135 C11
Braunstone Town
Leicester 135 C11
Braunston-in-Rutland
Rutland 136 B6
Braunton Devon 40 F3
Brawby N Yorks 216 D4
Brawith N Yorks 225 D10
Brawl Highld 310 C2
Brawlbin Highld 310 D4
Bray Windsor 66 D2
Braybrooke Northants 136 G5
Braydon Side Wilts 62 B4
Brayford Devon 41 G7
Brayfordhill Devon 41 G7
Brays Grove Essex 87 D7
Bray Shop Corn 12 G2
Braystones Cumb 219 D10
Brayswick Worcs 98 B6
Braythorn N Yorks 205 D10
Brayton N Yorks 207 G8
Braytown Dorset 18 D2
Bray Wick Windsor 65 D11
Braywoodside Windsor 65 D11
Brazacott Corn 11 C11
Brazenhill Staffs 151 E7
Brea Corn 4 G3
Breach Bath 60 G6
Kent 69 F10
W Sus 22 B3
Breachacha Castle
Argyll 288 D3
Breachwood Green
Herts 104 G2
Breacleit W Isles 304 E3
Breaden Heath Shrops 149 B8
Breadsall Derbys 153 B7
Breadsall Hilltop Derby 153 B7
Breadstone Glos 80 E2
Bread Street Glos 80 D4
Breage Corn 2 D4
Breakachy Highld 300 E4
Brealeys Devon 25 D8
Bream Glos 79 D10
Breamore Hants 31 D11
Bream's Meend Glos 79 D9
Brean Som 43 B9
Breanais W Isles 304 F1
Brearley W Yorks 196 B4
Brearton N Yorks 214 G6
Breascleit W Isles 304 E4
Breaston Derbys 153 C9
Brechfa Carms 93 E10
Brechin Angus 293 G7
Breckan Orkney 314 F2
Breckles Norf 141 E9
Breck of Cruan Orkney 314 E3
Breckrey Highld 298 C5
Brecks S Yorks 187 C7
Brecon Powys 95 F10
Bredbury Gtr Man 184 C6
Bredbury Green
Gtr Man 184 C6
Brede E Sus 38 D4
Bredenbury Hereford 116 F2
Bredfield Suff 126 G5
Bredgar Kent 69 G11
Bredhurst Kent 69 G9
Bredicot Worcs 117 G8
Bredon Worcs 99 D8
Bredon's Hardwick
Worcs 99 D8
Bredon's Norton Worcs 99 D8
Bredwardine Hereford 96 C6
Breedon on the Hill
Leics 153 E8
Breeds Essex 87 C11
Breedy Butts Lancs 202 E2
Breibhig W Isles 297 M2
W Isles 304 E6
Breich W Loth 269 C9
Breightmet Gtr Man 195 F8
Breighton E Yorks 207 G10
Breinton Hereford 97 D9
Breinton Common
Hereford 97 C9
Breiwick Shetland 313 J6
Brelston Green Hereford 97 G11
Bremhill Wilts 62 E3
Bremhill Wick Wilts 62 E3
Bremirehoull Shetland 313 L6
Brenachoile Lodge
Stirling 285 G8
Brenchley Kent 53 E7
Brenchoillie Argyll 284 G4
Brendon Devon 24 E5
Devon 24 F5
Devon 41 D9
Brenkley T&W 242 B6
Brent Corn 6 E4
Brent Cross London 67 B8
Brent Eleigh Suff 107 B8
Brentford London 67 D7
Brentford End London 67 D7
Brentingby Leics 154 F5
Brent Knoll Som 43 C10
Brent Mill Devon 8 D3
Brent Pelham Herts 105 E8
Brentry Bristol 60 D5
Brentwood Essex 87 G9
Brenzett Kent 39 B8
Brenzett Green Kent 39 B8
Brereton Staffs 151 F11
Brereton Cross Staffs 151 F11
Brereton Green Ches E 168 C3

Brereton Heath Ches E . . 168 C4
Breretonhill Staffs . . 151 F11
Bressingham Norf . . . 141 G11
Bressingham Common
  Norf 141 G11
Bretby Derbys 152 E5
Bretford Warks 119 B8
Bretforton Worcs 99 C11
Bretherdale Head
  Cumb 221 E11
Bretherton Lancs 194 C3
Brettabister Shetland . 313 H6
Brettenham Norf 141 G8
  Suff 125 G9
Bretton Derbys 186 F2
  Flint 166 C5
  Pboro 138 C3
Brewer's End Essex . . 105 G11
Brewers Green Norf . . 142 G2
Brewer Street Sur . . . 51 C10
Brewlands Bridge
  Angus 292 G3
Brewood Staffs 133 B7
Briach Moray 301 D10
Briantspuddle Dorset . 18 C2
Briar Hill Northants . . 120 F4
Brick End Essex 105 F11
Brickendon Herts 86 D4
Bricket Wood Herts . . 85 E10
Brickfields Worcs 117 F7
Brickhill Bedford 121 G11
Brickhouses Ches E . . 168 C3
Brick Houses S Yorks . 186 E4
Brick-kiln End Notts . . 171 D9
Brickkiln Green Essex . 106 E4
Brickhampton Worcs . . 99 C9
Bride IoM 192 B5
Bridekirk Cumb 229 E8
Bridell Pembs 92 C3
Bridestowe Devon . . . 12 D6
Brideswell Aberds . . . 302 F5
Bridford Devon 14 D2
Bridfordmills Devon . . 14 D2
Bridge Corn 2 C6
  Corn 4 G3
  Kent 55 C7
  Som 28 F5
Bridge Ball Devon . . . 41 D8
Bridge End Bedford . . 121 G10
  Cumb 230 B3
  Devon 8 F3
  Durham 232 D6
  Essex 106 E3
  Flint 166 C4
  Hereford 98 B2
  Lincs 156 B2
  Northumb 241 D10
  Northumb 241 E10
  Oxon 83 G9
Bridge-End Shetland . 313 K5
Bridge End Sur 50 B5
  Warks 118 C5
  Worcs 98 E6
Bridgefoot Aberds . . . 292 C6
  Angus 287 D7
  Cumb 228 F6
Bridge Green Essex . . 105 D9
  Norf 142 G2
Bridgehampton Som . . 29 C9
Bridge Hewick N Yorks 214 E6
Bridgehill Durham . . . 242 G3
Bridge Ho Argyll 254 B4
Bridgeholm Green
  Derbys 185 E8
Bridgehouse Gate
  N Yorks 214 F3
Bridgelands Borders . 261 C11
Bridgemary Hants . . . 33 G9
Bridgemere Ches E . . . 168 F2
Bridgemont Derbys . . 185 E8
Bridgend Aberds 302 F5
  Aberds 302 F5
  Angus 293 G7
  Argyll 255 D8
  Argyll 274 G4
  Argyll 275 D7
  Corn 6 D2
  Cumb 221 C7
  Devon 7 F11
  Fife 287 F7
  Glos 80 E4
  Highld 300 D3
  Invclyd 276 F5
  Moray 302 D3
  N Lanark 278 G3
  Pembs 92 B3
  W Loth 279 F10
Bridgend of Lintrathen
  Angus 286 B6
Bridgend / Pen-y-Bont ar-
  ogwr Bridgend 58 C2
Bridgeness Falk 279 E10
Bridge of Alford
  Aberds 293 B7
Bridge of Allan Stirling . 278 B5
Bridge of Avon Moray . 301 F11
  Moray 301 G11
Bridge of Awe Argyll . 284 E4
Bridge of Balgie Perth 285 C9
Bridge of Cally Perth . 286 B5
Bridge of Canny Aberds 293 D8
Bridge of Craigisla
  Angus 286 B6
Bridge of Dee Dumfries 237 D9
Bridge of Don
  Aberdeen 293 B11
Bridge of Dun Angus . 287 B10
Bridge of Dye Aberds . 293 E8
Bridge of Earn Perth . 286 F5
Bridge of Ericht Perth . 285 B9
Bridge of Feugh Aberds 293 D9
Bridge of Forss Highld . 310 C4
Bridge of Gairn Aberds 292 D5
Bridge of Gaur Perth . 285 B9
Bridge of Lyon Perth . 285 C11
Bridge of Muchalls
  Aberds 293 D10
Bridge of Muick Aberds 292 D5
Bridge of Oich Highld . 290 C5
Bridge of Orchy Argyll 284 D6
Bridge of Waith Orkney . 314 E2
Bridge of Walls
  Shetland 313 H4
Bridge of Weir Renfs . 267 B7
Bridge Reeve Devon . 25 E11
Bridgerule Devon . . . 24 G3
Bridges Corn 5 D7
  Shrops 131 D7
Bridge Sollers Hereford 97 C8
Bridge Street Suff . . . 107 B7
Bridgetown Corn 12 D2
  Devon 8 C6
  Som 42 G2
  Staffs 133 B9
Bridge Town Warks . . 118 G4
Bridge Trafford Ches W 183 G7
Bridge Yate S Glos . . . 61 E7

Bridgham Norf 141 F9
Bridgnorth Shrops . . . 132 E4
Bridgtown Staffs 133 B9
Bridgwater Som 43 F10
Bridlington E Yorks . . 218 F3
Bridport Dorset 16 C5
Bridstow Hereford . . . 97 G11
Brierholme Carr
  S Yorks 199 E7
Brierley Glos 79 B10
  Hereford 115 F9
  S Yorks 198 E2
Brierley Hill W Mid . . 133 F8
Brierton Hrtlpl 234 E5
Briery Cumb 229 G11
Briery Hill Bl Gwent . 77 D11
Briestfield W Yorks . . 197 D8
Brigflatts Cumb 222 G2
Brigg N Lincs 200 F3
Briggate Norf 160 D6
Briggswath N Yorks . . 227 D7
Brigham Cumb 229 E7
  Cumb 229 G11
  E Yorks 209 C7
Brighouse W Yorks . . 196 C6
Brighstone IoW 20 E4
Brightgate Derbys . . . 170 D3
Brighthampton Oxon . 82 E5
Brightholmlee S Yorks 186 B3
Brightley Devon 13 B7
Brightling E Sus 37 C11
Brightlingsea Essex . . 89 B9
Brighton Brighton . . . 36 G4
  Corn 5 E8
Brighton Hill Hants . . 48 D6
Brighton le Sands Mers 182 B4
Brightons Falk 279 F8
Brightside S Yorks . . . 186 D5
Brightwalton W Berks . 64 D2
Brightwalton Green
  W Berks 64 D2
Brightwalton Holt
  W Berks 64 D2
Brightwell Suff 108 C4
Brightwell Baldwin
  Oxon 83 F11
Brightwell cum Sotwell
  Oxon 83 G9
Brigmerston Wilts . . . 47 D7
Brignall Durham 223 C11
Brig o'Turk Stirling . . 285 G9
Brigsley NE Lincs 201 G9
Brigsteer Cumb 211 B9
Brigstock Northants . . 137 F8
Brill Bucks 83 C11
  Corn 2 D6
Brilley Hereford 96 B5
Brilley Mountain Powys 114 G5
Brimaston Pembs 91 G8
Brimfield Hereford . . . 115 D10
Brimington Derbys . . . 186 G6
Brimington Common
  Derbys 186 G6
Brimley Devon 13 F11
  Devon 28 G4
Brimpsfield Glos 80 C6
Brimps Hill Glos 79 B11
Brimpton W Berks . . . 64 G5
Brimpton Common
  W Berks 64 G5
Brims Orkney 314 H2
Brims Castle Highld . . 310 B4
Brimscombe Glos 80 E5
Brimsdown London . . 86 F5
Brimstage Mers 182 E4
Brinacory Highld 295 F9
Brincliffe S Yorks . . . 186 D4
Brind E Yorks 207 G10
Brindham Som 44 E4
Brindister Shetland . . 313 H4
  Shetland 313 K6
Brindle Lancs 194 C6
Brindle Heath Gtr Man 195 G10
Brindley Ches E 167 E9
Brindley Ford Stoke . . 168 E5
Brindwoodgate Derbys 186 F4
Brineton Staffs 150 G6
Bringewood Forge
  Hereford 115 C9
Bringhurst Leics 136 E6
Bringsty Common
  Hereford 116 F4
Brington Cambs 121 B11
Brinian Orkney 314 D4
Briningham Norf 159 C10
Brinkhill Lincs 190 G5
Brinkley Cambs 124 G2
  Notts 172 E2
Brinkley Hill Hereford . 97 E11
Brinklow M Keynes . . 103 D8
  Warks 119 B8
Brinkworth Wilts 62 C4
Brinmore Highld 300 G6
Brinnington Gtr Man . 184 C6
Brinscall Lancs 194 C6
Brinsea N Som 60 G2
Brinsford Staffs 133 B8
Brinsley Notts 171 F7
Brinsop Hereford 97 C8
Brinsop Common
  Hereford 97 C8
Brinswroth S Yorks . . 186 D6
Brinsworthy Devon . . 41 G9
Brinton Norf 159 C10
Brisco Cumb 239 G10
Briscoe Cumb 219 C10
Briscoerigg N Yorks . . 205 C11
Brisley Norf 159 E8
Brislington Bristol . . . 60 E6
Brissenden Green Kent 54 F2
Bristnall Fields W Mid . 133 F9
Bristol Bristol 60 E5
Briston Norf 159 C11
Britain Bottom S Glos . 61 B9
Britannia Lancs 195 C11
Britford Wilts 31 B11
Brithdir Caerph 77 E11
  Ceredig 92 B6
  Gwyn 146 F5
Brithem Bottom Devon 27 E8
British Torf 78 E3
Briton Ferry / Llansawel
  Neath 57 C8
Britten's Bath 45 B7
Britwell Slough 66 C3
Britwell Salome Oxon . 83 G11
Brixham Torbay 9 D8
Brixton Devon 7 E10
  London 67 D10
Brixton Deverill Wilts . 45 F11
Brize Norton Oxon . . 82 D4
Broad Alley Worcs . . . 117 D7
Broad Blunsdon
  Swindon 81 G11
Broadbottom Gtr Man . 185 C7
Broadbridge Heath
  W Sus 50 G6

Broadbury Devon 12 B5
Broadbush Swindon . . 81 G11
Broad Campden Glos . 100 D3
Broad Carr W Yorks . . 196 D5
Broad Chalke Wilts . . 31 B8
Broad Clough Lancs . . 195 C11
Broadclyst Devon . . . 14 B5
Broad Colney Herts . . 85 E11
Broad Common Worcs . 117 C7
Broadfield Gtr Man . . 195 E10
  Invclyd 276 G6
  Lancs 194 C4
  Lancs 195 B8
  Pembs 73 E10
  W Sus 51 G9
Broadford Highld . . . 295 C8
  Sur 50 D3
Broad Ford Kent 53 F8
Broadford Bridge W Sus 35 C9
Broadgate Hants 32 C6
Broadgrass Green Suff 125 E9
Broad Green Cambs . . 124 F3
  C Beds 103 C9
  Essex 105 D8
  Essex 107 G2
  London 67 F10
  Mers 182 C6
  Suff 124 F5
  Suff 125 F11
  Worcs 116 F5
  Worcs 117 C9
Broadgreen Wood Herts 86 D4
Broadhalgh Gtr Man . . 195 E11
Broadham Green Sur . 51 C11
Broadhaugh Borders . 249 B10
Broadhaven Highld . . 310 D7
Broad Haven / Aberllydan
  Pembs 72 C5
Broadheath Gtr Man . 184 D3
Broad Heath Powys . . 114 F6
  Staffs 151 D7
  Worcs 116 D3
Broadhembury Devon . 27 G10
Broadhempston Devon 8 B6
Broad Hill Cambs 123 B11
Broad Hinton Wilts . . 62 D6
Broadholm Derbys . . . 170 F5
Broadholme Derbys . . 170 F5
  Lincs 188 G5
Broad Ings E Yorks . . 208 C2
Broadland Row E Sus . 38 C4
Broadlands Devon . . . 14 G3
Broadlane Corn 2 C4
Broad Lane Corn 4 G3
Broad Lanes Shrops . . 132 F5
Broadley Carms 74 D4
Broad Laying Hants . . 64 G2
Broad Layings Hants . 64 G2
Broadley Hereford . . . 96 B5
  Moray 302 C3
Broadley Common Essex 86 D6
Broadleys Aberds 303 C8
Broad Marston Worcs . 100 B2
Broadmayne Dorset . . 17 D10
Broad Meadow Staffs . 168 F4
Broadmeadows
  Borders 261 C10
Broadmere Hants 48 D6
Broadmoor Pembs . . . 73 D9
  Sur 50 D6
Broadmoor Common
  Hereford 98 D2
Broadmore Green
  Worcs 116 G6
Broadoak Dorset 16 B4
  Glos 80 C2
  Hants 33 E8
  Shrops 149 F9
  Wrex 166 D5
Broad Oak Carms . . . 93 G11
  Cumb 220 G2
  Dorset 30 E3
  E Sus 37 C10
  E Sus 38 D4
  Hants 49 F7
  Hereford 97 G9
  Kent 54 F4
  Mers 183 B8
  Shrops 132 F5
Broadoak End Herts . . 86 C4
Broadoak Park Gtr Man 195 G9
Broad Parkham Devon 24 C5
Broadplat Oxon 65 C8
Broadrashes Moray . . 302 D4
Broadrock Glos 79 F8
Broadsands Torbay . . 9 D7
Broadsea Aberds 303 C9
Broad's Green Essex . . 87 C11
  Essex 62 F3
Broadshard Som 28 E6
Broadstairs Kent 71 F11
Broadstone Kent 53 D11
  Mon 79 E8
  Poole 18 B6
  Shrops 131 F10
Broad Street E Sus . . . 38 D5
  Kent 53 B8
  Kent 54 E6
  Kent 55 E7
  Medway 69 E9
  Som 107 C9
  Wilts 46 B6
Broadstreet Common
  Newport 59 C11
Broad Street Green
  Essex 88 D5
Broad Tenterden Kent 53 G11
Broad Town Wilts . . . 62 D5
Broadwas Worcs 116 F5
Broadwater Herts . . . 104 G4
  W Sus 35 G11
Broadwater Down Kent 52 F5
Broadwaters Worcs . . 116 B6
Broadwath Cumb 239 F11
Broadway Carms 74 D3
  Carms 74 E2
  Pembs 72 C5
  Som 28 D4
  Suff 127 B7
  Worcs 99 D11
Broadway Lands
  Hereford 97 E11
Broadwell Glos 79 C9
  Glos 100 E4
  Oxon 82 E3
  Warks 119 D9
Broadwey Dorset 17 E9
Broadwindsor Dorset . 28 G6
Broadwoodkelly Devon 25 G11
Broadwoodwidger Devon 12 D4
Brobury Hereford . . . 96 C6
Brochel Highld 298 E5
Brochroy Argyll 284 D4
Brock Lancs 202 E6
Brockamin Worcs . . . 116 G5
Brockbridge Hants . . . 33 D10
Brockdish Norf 126 B4
Brockencote Worcs . . 117 C7
Brockenhurst Hants . . 32 G4
Brockfield Devon 28 F4
Brockford Green Suff . 126 D2
Brockford Street Suff . 126 D2
Brockhall Northants . . 120 E2
Brockhall Village
  Lancs 203 F10
Brockham Sur 51 D7
Brockham End Bath . . 61 F8
Brockham Park Sur . . 51 D8
Brockhampton Glos . . 99 F8
  Glos 99 F11
  Hants 22 B2
  Hereford 97 E11
Brockhampton Green
  Dorset 30 F2
Brockhill Borders . . . 261 E9
Brock Hill Essex 88 F2
Brockholes Blackburn . 195 B7
  Ches E 184 F6
  Denb 165 B9
  Lancs 211 G10
  S Yorks 187 D8
  W Yorks 196 B5
Brockhurst Derbys . . . 170 C4
  Hants 33 G10
  Warks 135 G9
Brocklebank Cumb . . . 230 C2
Brocklehirst Dumfries . 238 C3
Brocklesby Lincs 200 E6
Brockley N Som 60 F3
  Suff 124 C6
Brockley Corner Suff . 124 C6
Brockley Green Suff . . 106 B4
  Suff 124 G6
Brockleymoor Cumb . . 230 D5
Brockloch Dumfries . . 246 D2
Brockmanton Hereford 115 F10
Brockmoor W Mid . . . 133 F8
Brockscombe Devon . . 12 C5
Brock's Green Hants . . 64 G4
Brock's Watering Norf . 142 E2
Brockton Shrops 130 C6
  Shrops 130 F6
  Shrops 131 C8
  Shrops 132 C4
  Shrops 132 D6
  Staffs 150 B5
Brocton Corn 5 B10
  Staffs 151 F7
Brodick N Ayrs 256 B2
  Kent 52 D5
Brodie Moray 301 D9
Brodiesord Aberds . . . 302 C5
Brodsworth S Yorks . . 198 F4
Brogaig Highld 298 C4
Brogborough C Beds . 103 D9
Broke Hall Suff 108 C3
Brokenborough Wilts . 62 B2
Broken Cross Ches E . 184 G5
  Ches W 183 G11
Broken Green Herts . . 105 G8
Brokenwood Wilts . . . 45 C10
Brokes N Yorks 224 F3
Brombil Neath 57 D9
Bromborough Mers . . 182 E4
Bromborough Pool
  Mers 182 E4
Bromdon Shrops 132 G2
Brome Suff 126 B2
Bromeswell Suff 126 G6
Brome Street Suff . . . 126 B3
Bromfield Cumb 229 B9
  Shrops 115 B9
Bromford W Mid 134 E2
Bromham Bedford . . . 121 G10
  Wilts 62 F3
Bromley Herts 105 G8
  London 67 C11
  London 68 F2
  Shrops 132 D4
  S Yorks 186 B4
  W Mid 133 G8
Bromley Common
  London 68 F2
Bromley Cross Essex . 107 F11
  Gtr Man 195 E8
Bromley Green Kent . . 54 F3
Bromley Hall Staffs . . 150 C5
Bromley Heath S Glos . 61 D7
Bromley Park London . 67 F11
Bromley Wood Staffs . 152 E2
Bromlow Shrops 130 C6
Brompton London . . . 67 D9
  Medway 69 F9
  N Yorks 217 C8
  N Yorks 225 F7
  Shrops 131 B10
Brompton-by-Sawdon
  N Yorks 217 C8
Brompton-on-Swale
  N Yorks 224 F4
Brompton Ralph Som . 42 G5
Brompton Regis Som . 42 G3
Bromsash Hereford . . 98 G2
Bromsberrow Glos . . . 98 E4
Bromsberrow Heath
  Glos 98 E4
Bromstead Common
  Staffs 150 F6
Bromstead Heath Staffs 150 F6
Bromstone Kent 71 F11
Bromyard Hereford . . 116 G3
Bromyard Downs
  Hereford 116 F3
Bronaber Gwyn 146 C4
Broncroft Shrops 131 F10
Brondesbury London . 67 C8
Brondesbury Park
  London 67 C8
Broneirion Powys . . . 129 F10
Brongest Ceredig 92 B6
Brongwyn Ceredig . . . 92 C5
Bronington Wrex 149 B9
Bronllys Powys 96 D3
Bronnant Ceredig . . . 112 D2
Bronwydd Ceredig . . . 93 C7
Bronwydd Arms Carms 93 G8
Bronydd Powys 96 C4
Bronygarth Shrops . . 148 B5
Brook Carms 74 D3
  Devon 8 F3
  Hants 32 B4
  Hants 32 E3
  IoW 20 E3
  Kent 54 E5
  Sur 50 D5
  Sur 50 F2
Brook Bottom Gtr Man 185 D7
  Gtr Man 196 G3
  Lancs 202 E6
Brooke Norf 142 D5
  Rutland 136 B6
Brookenby Lincs 190 B2
Brookend Glos 79 E11
  Glos 80 E3
  Oxon 100 E5
Brook End Bedford . . 121 E11
  Cambs 121 C11
  C Beds 104 B3
  Herts 104 F6

Brook End continued
  M Keynes 103 C8
  Wilts 61 G10
  Worcs 99 B7
Brookfield Derbys . . . 185 B8
  Lancs 203 G7
  N Lincs 200 F3
  Renfs 267 C8
Brookfoot W Yorks . . 196 C6
Brookgreen IoW 20 E3
Brook Green London . 67 D8
Brookhampton Oxon . 83 F10
  Shrops 131 E11
  Som 29 B10
Brookhampton Green
  Dorset 30 F2
Brook Hill Hants 32 E3
  Notts 153 C11
Brookhouse Blackburn . 195 B7
  Ches E 184 F6
  Denb 165 B9
  Lancs 211 G10
  S Yorks 187 D8
  W Yorks 196 B5
Brookhouse Green
  Ches E 168 C4
Brookhouses Derbys . 185 D8
  Ches E 168 C4
  N Som 60 F3
Brookhurst Mers 182 E4
Brookland Kent 39 B7
Brooklands Dumfries . 237 B11
  Gtr Man 184 C3
  Shrops 167 G8
  Sur 66 G5
  W Yorks 206 F2
Brookleigh Devon . . . 14 B5
Brookmans Park Herts 86 E2
Brookpits W Sus 35 G8
Brook Place Sur 66 G3
Brookrow Shrops . . . 116 C2
Brooks Corn 6 C3
  Powys 130 D2
Brooksbottoms Gtr Man 195 D9
Brooksby Leics 154 F3
Brooks End Kent 71 F9
Brook Place Sur 66 G3
Brooks Green W Sus . . 35 C10
Brookside Brack 66 E2
  Telford 132 B3
Brook Street Essex . . 87 G9
  Kent 52 D5
  Kent 54 G2
  Suff 106 B5
  W Sus 36 B4
Brookthorpe Glos . . . 80 C4
Brookville Norf 140 D5
Brookwood Sur 50 B2
Broom C Beds 104 C3
  Cumb 231 G9
  Devon 28 G4
  E Renf 267 D10
  Fife 287 G7
  Pembs 73 D10
  S Yorks 186 C5
  Warks 117 G11
Broome Norf 143 E7
  Shrops 131 D10
  Shrops 132 G5
  Worcs 117 B8
Broomedge Warr 184 D2
Broome Park Northumb 264 G4
Broomer's Corner
  W Sus 35 C10
Broomershill W Sus . . 35 D9
Broomfield Aberds . . . 303 F9
  Cumb 230 B2
  Essex 88 D2
  Kent 53 C10
  Kent 71 F9
  Som 43 G8
  S Yorks 61 D11
Broomfields Shrops . . 149 F8
Broomfleet E Yorks . . 199 B11
Broom Green Norf . . . 159 E9
Broomhall Ches E . . . 167 F10
  Windsor 66 F3
Broomhall Green
  Ches E 167 F10
Broomham E Sus 23 C8
Broomhaugh Northumb 242 E2
Broomhill Bristol 60 D6
  Ches W 167 B7
  Highld 301 G9
  Kent 55 B8
  Norf 140 C2
  Northumb 252 C6
  N Yorks 171 F8
  S Yorks 186 C5
Broomhill Bank Kent . 52 E5
Broomholm Norf 160 C6
Broomhouse Glasgow . 268 C3
Broomlands N Ayrs . . 257 B8
Broomley Northumb . . 242 E2
Broompark Durham . . 233 C10
Brooms Barn Suff . . . 124 D5
Broom's Green Glos . . 98 E4
Broomsgrove E Sus . . 38 E4
Broomsthorpe Norf . . 158 D6
Broom Street Kent . . . 70 G4
Broomton Highld 301 B8
Broomy Hill Hereford . 97 D9
Broomy Lodge Hants . 32 E2
Broomyshaw Staffs . . 169 F9
Brora Highld 311 J3
Broseley Shrops 132 C3
Brotherhouse Bar Lincs 156 G5
Brotheridge Green
  Worcs 98 C6
Brotherlee Durham . . 232 D4
Brotherstone Borders . 262 B4
Brothertoft Lincs 174 F3
Brotherton N Yorks . . 198 B3
Brotton Redcar 226 B3
Broubster Highld 310 C4
Brough Cumb 222 C5
  Derbys 185 E11
  E Yorks 200 B3
  Highld 310 B6
  Notts 172 D4
  Orkney 314 H4
  Shetland 312 F7
  Shetland 312 G7
  Shetland 313 H6
  Shetland 313 J7
Brough Lodge Shetland 312 D7
Brough Sowerby Cumb 222 C5
Broughall Shrops 167 F9
Broughton Borders . . 260 B4

Broughton continued
  Bucks 84 C4
  Cambs 122 B5
  Edin 280 F5
  Flint 166 C4
  Hants 47 G10
  Lancs 202 F6
  M Keynes 103 C7
  N Lincs 200 F3
  Northants 120 B6
  N Yorks 204 C4
  N Yorks 216 E5
  Orkney 314 B4
  Oxon 101 D8
  Shrops 132 E6
  Staffs 150 C5
  V Glam 58 E2
Broughton Astley Leics 135 E10
Broughton Beck Cumb 210 C5
Broughton Common
  N Lincs 200 E3
  Wilts 61 G11
Broughton Cross Cumb 229 E7
Broughton Gifford Wilts 61 G11
Broughton Green Worcs 117 E9
Broughton Hackett
  Worcs 117 G8
Broughton in Furness
  Cumb 210 B4
Broughton Lodges Leics 154 E4
Broughton Mills Cumb 220 G4
Broughton Moor Cumb 228 E6
Broughton Park
  Gtr Man 195 G10
Broughton Poggs Oxon 82 E2
Broughtown Orkney . . 314 B6
Broughty Ferry Dundee 287 D8
Brow Edge Cumb . . . 211 C7
Browhouses Dumfries . 239 D7
Browland Shetland . . 313 H4
Brown Bank N Yorks . 205 C10
Brown Candover Hants 48 F5
Brownber Cumb 222 D4
Brownbread Street
  E Sus 23 B10
Browndown Hants . . . 33 B10
Brown Edge Lancs . . . 193 E11
  Mers 193 E11
  S Yorks 186 E5
  Staffs 168 E6
Brownheath Devon . . 27 D10
  Shrops 149 D9
Brownheath Common
  Worcs 117 E7
Brownhill Aberds 302 E6
  Aberds 303 E8
  Blackburn 203 G9
  Shrops 149 E8
Brownhills Fife 287 F9
  W Mid 133 B10
Brownieside Northumb 264 E5
Browninghill Green
  Hants 48 B5
Brown Knowl Ches W . 167 E7
Brown Lees Staffs . . . 168 D5
Brownlow Ches E . . . 168 C4
Brownlow Fold Gtr Man 195 E8
Brown Moor W Yorks . 206 G3
Brownmuir Aberds . . . 293 F9
Brown's Bank Ches E . 167 G10
Brown's End Glos . . . 98 E4
Brown's Green W Mid . 133 E10
Brownshill Glos 80 E5
Brownshill Green
  W Mid 134 G6
Brownside Lancs 204 G3
Brownsover Warks . . . 119 B10
Brownston Devon . . . 8 E3
Brown Street Suff . . . 125 D11
Browns Wood M Keynes 103 D8
Broxwood Green Norf 159 E9
Browston Green Norf . 143 D9
Browtop Cumb 229 G7
Broxa N Yorks 227 G8
Broxbourne Herts . . . 86 D5
Broxburn E Loth 282 F3
  W Loth 279 G11
Broxfield Northumb . . 264 F6
Broxholme Lincs 188 F6
Broxted Essex 105 F11
Broxton Ches W 167 E7
Broxtowe Nottingham . 171 G8
Broxwood Hereford . . 115 G7
Broyle Side E Sus . . . 23 C7
Brù W Isles 304 D5
Bruairnis W Isles 297 L3
Bruan Highld 310 F7
Bruar Lodge Perth . . . 291 F10
Brucefield E Dunb . . . 277 F7
Bruceheld Fife 280 D2
Bruche Warr 183 D10
Brucklebog Aberds . . . 293 D9
Bruckhills Aberds . . . 302 E6
Bruera Ches W 166 C6
Bruern Abbey Oxon . . 100 G5
Bruichladdich Argyll . 274 G3
Bruisyard Suff 126 D6
Brumby N Lincs 199 E11
Brunant Powys 130 B5
Brund Staffs 169 C10
Brundall Norf 142 B6
Brundish Norf 143 D7
  Suff 126 D5
Brundish Street Suff . 126 C5
Brunery Highld 289 B9
Brunnion Corn 2 B2
Brunshaw Lancs 204 G3
Brunstane Edin 280 G6
Brunstock Cumb 239 F10
Brunswick N Ayrs . . . 184 B4
Brunswick Park London 86 G3
Bruntcliffe W Yorks . . 197 B9
Bruntingthorpe Leics . 136 F2
Brunton Fife 287 E7
  Northumb 264 E6
  Wilts 47 B8
Brushes Glos 99 D11
Brushfield Derbys . . . 185 G11
Brushford Som 25 E11
  Som 26 B6
Bruton Som 45 G7
Bryanston Dorset . . . 30 F4
Bryan's Green Worcs . 117 D7
Bryans Midloth 270 C6
Bryant's Bottom Bucks 84 F4
Brydekirk Dumfries . . 238 C5
Bryher Scilly 1 F3
Brymbo Conwy 180 G4
  Wrex 166 E3
Brympton D'Evercy Som 29 D8
Bryn Caerph 77 F11

Bryn continued
  Carms 75 E8
  Ches W 183 G10
  Gtr Man 194 G5
  Gwyn 179 G9
  Neath 57 C10
  Powys 130 C3
  Rhondda 76 D6
  Shrops 130 F5
  Swansea 56 C4
Brynafon Ceredig . . . 112 C4
Brynamman Carms . . 76 C2
Brynawel Caerph 77 G11
Brynberian Pembs . . . 92 D2
Brynbryddan Neath . . 57 C9
Bryn Bwbach Gwyn . . 146 B2
Bryncae Rhondda . . . 58 C3
  Rhondda 58 C3
Bryn Celyn Anglesey . 179 F10
  Flint 181 F11
Bryncethin Bridgend . 58 C2
Bryncir Gwyn 163 G7
Bryn-coch Neath 57 B8
Bryncoch Bridgend . . 58 C3
Bryn Common Flint . . 166 D3
Bryncroes Gwyn 144 C4
Bryncrug Gwyn 128 C2
Brynderwen Powys . . 130 D3
Bryndu Anglesey 178 E4
Bryn Dulas Conwy . . . 180 F6
Bryneglwys Denb . . . 165 F10
Bryn Eglwys Gwyn . . 163 B10
Brynford Flint 181 G11
Bryn Gates Gtr Man . . 194 G5
Bryn Golau Rhondda . 58 B3
Bryngwran Anglesey . 178 F4
Bryngwyn Ceredig . . . 92 B5
  Mon 78 D5
  Powys 96 B3
Brynhenllan Pembs . . 91 D10
Bryn-henllan Pembs . . 91 D10
Brynheulog Bridgend . 57 C11
Bryniau Denb 181 E9
Bryn-Iwan Carms . . . 92 E6
Brynllywarch Powys . . 130 F3
Brynmawr Bl Gwent . . 77 C11
Bryn-mawr Gwyn . . . 144 C3
Bryn Mawr Powys . . . 148 F5
Brynmenyn Bridgend . 58 B2
Brynmill Swansea . . . 56 C6
Brynmorfudd Conwy . 164 C4
Bryn Myrddin Carms . 93 G8
Brynna Rhondda 58 C3
Bryn-nantllech Conwy 164 B6
Brynnau Gwynion
  Rhondda 58 C3
Bryn-newydd Denb . . 165 G11
Bryn Offa Wrex 166 F4
Brynore Shrops 149 B7
Bryn-penarth Powys . 130 C2
Bryn Pen-y-lan Wrex . 166 G4
Bryn Pydew Conwy . . 180 F4
Brynrefail Anglesey . . 179 D7
  Gwyn 163 C9
Bryn Rhyd-yr-Arian
  Conwy 165 B7
Bryn-rhys Conwy . . . 180 F4
Brynsadler Rhondda . 58 C4
Bryn Saith Marchog
  Denb 165 E9
Brynsiencyn Anglesey . 163 B7
Bryn Sion Gwyn 147 F7
Brynsworthy Devon . . 40 G4
Bryntanat Powys 148 E4
Brynteg Anglesey . . . 179 E7
  Ceredig 93 C9
Bryn-teg Wrex 166 E4
Bryntirion Bridgend . . 57 E11
Bryn-y-cochin Shrops . 149 B7
Bryn-y-gwenin Mon . . 78 B4
Bryn-y-maen Conwy . 180 F4
Bryn-yr-Eos Wrex . . . 166 G3
Bryn-yr-eryr Gwyn . . 162 F5
Bryn-yr-ogof Denb . . 165 D11
Buaile nam Bodach
  W Isles 297 L3
Bualintur Highld 294 C6
Bualnaluib Highld . . . 307 K3
Buarthmeini Gwyn . . 146 C6
Bubbenhall Warks . . . 119 C7
Bubbenhall Glos 80 E5
Bubnell Derbys 186 G2
Bubwith E Yorks 207 F10
Buccleuch Borders . . . 261 G8
Buchanan Smithy
  Stirling 277 D7
Buchanhaven Aberds . 303 E11
Buchan Hill W Sus . . . 51 G9
Buchanty Perth 286 E3
Buchley E Dunb 277 G11
Buchlyvie Stirling . . . 277 C11
Buckabank Cumb . . . 230 B3
Buckbury Worcs 98 E6
Buckden Cambs 122 D3
  N Yorks 213 D8
Buckenham Norf 143 B7
Buckerell Devon 27 G10
Bucket Corner Hants . 32 C6
Buckfast Devon 8 B4
Buckfastleigh Devon . 8 B4
Buckham Dorset 29 G7
Buckhaven Fife 281 B7
Buck Hill Wilts 62 E3
Buckholm Borders . . . 261 B11
Buckholt Mon 79 B8
Buckhorn Devon 12 C3
Buckhorn Weston Dorset 30 C3
Buckhurst Hill Essex . 86 G5
Buckie Moray 302 C4
Buckies Highld 310 C5
Buckingham Bucks . . 102 E3
Buckland Bucks 84 C5
  Devon 8 G4
  Glos 99 D11
  Hants 20 B2
  Herts 105 E7
  Kent 55 E10
  Oxon 82 F4
  Sur 51 D8
Buckland Brewer Devon 24 C6
Buckland Common Bucks 84 D6
Buckland Dinham Som 45 C9
Buckland Down Som . 45 C9
Buckland End W Mid . 134 F2
Buckland Filleigh Devon 24 F6
Buckland in the Moor
  Devon 13 G10
Buckland Marsh Oxon 82 F4
Buckland Monachorum
  Devon 7 B9

Buckland Newton
  Dorset 29 F11
Buckland Ripers Dorset 17 E8
Bucklands Borders . . . 262 F2
Buckland St Mary Som 28 E3
Buckland Valley Kent . 55 E10
Bucklandwharf Bucks . 84 C5
Bucklebury W Berks . . 64 E5
Bucklebury Alley
  W Berks 64 E4
Bucklegate Lincs 156 B6
Buckleigh Devon 24 B6
Buckler's Hard Hants . 20 B4
Bucklerheads Angus . 287 D8
Bucklers Hard Hants . 20 B4
Bucklesham Suff 108 C4
Buckley / Bwcle Flint . 166 C4
Buckley Green Warks . 118 C3
Buckley Hill Mers . . . 182 B4
Bucklow Hill Ches E . . 184 E2
Buckminster Leics . . . 155 E7
Bucknall Lincs 173 B11
  Stoke 168 F6
Bucknell Oxon 101 F11
  Shrops 115 C7
Buckoak Ches W 183 G8
Bucknowle Dorset . . . 18 E4
Buckover S Glos 79 G11
Buckpool Moray 302 C4
Buckridge Worcs 116 C4
Bucksburn Aberdeen . 293 C10
Bucks Green W Sus . . 50 G5
Buckshaw Village Lancs 194 C5
Bucks Hill Herts 85 E8
Bucks Horn Oak Hants 49 E10
Buckskin Hants 48 C6
Buckton E Yorks 218 E3
  Hereford 115 C7
Buckton Vale Gtr Man . 196 G3
Buckworth Cambs . . . 122 B2
Budbrooke Warks . . . 118 D5
Budby Notts 171 B10
Buddbrake Shetland . . 312 B8
Buddileigh Staffs 168 F3
Budd's Titson Corn . . 24 G2
Bude Corn 24 F2
Budge's Shop Corn . . 6 D6
Budlake Devon 14 B5
Budle Northumb 264 B5
Budleigh Som 27 D11
Budleigh Salterton Devon 15 E7
Budlett's Common E Sus 37 C7
Budock Water Corn . . 3 C7
Budworth Heath
  Ches W 183 F11
Buersil Head Gtr Man . 196 E2
Buerton Ches E 167 G11
Buffler's Holt Bucks . . 102 D3
Bufton Leics 135 B8
Bugbrooke Northants . 120 F3
Bugford Devon 40 E6
Bughtlin Edin 280 G3
Buglawton Ches E . . . 168 C5
Bugle Corn 5 D10
Bugle Gate Worcs . . . 116 D6
Bugley Dorset 30 C3
  Wilts 45 E11
Buildwas Shrops 132 C2
Builth Road Powys . . 113 G10
Builth Wells Powys . . 113 G10
Buirgh W Isles 305 J2
Bulbourne Herts 84 C6
Bulbridge Wilts 46 G5
Bulby Lincs 155 D11
Bulcote Notts 171 G11
Buldoo Highld 310 C3
Bulford Wilts 47 E7
Bulford Camp Wilts . . 47 E7
Bulkeley Ches E 167 E8
Bulkeley Hall Shrops . 168 G2
Bulkington Warks . . . 135 F7
  Wilts 46 B2
Bulkworthy Devon . . 24 E5
Bullamoor N Yorks . . 225 G7
Bull Bay / Porthllechog
  Anglesey 178 C6
Bullbridge Derbys . . . 170 E5
Bullbrook Brack 65 F11
Bulleign Kent 53 G11
Bullen's Green Herts . 86 D2
Bulley Glos 80 B3
Bullgill Cumb 229 D7
Bull Hill Hants 20 B2
Bullhurst Hill Derbys . 170 G3
Bullinghope Hereford . 97 D10
Bullington Hants 48 E3
  Lincs 189 F9
Bull's Green Herts . . . 86 C3
  Norf 143 E8
Bull's Hill Hereford . . 97 G11
Bullwood Argyll 276 F2
Bullyhole Bottom Mon 79 F7
Bulmer Essex 106 C6
  N Yorks 216 F3
Bulmer Tye Essex . . . 106 D6
Bulphan Thurrock . . . 68 B6
Bulstode Herts 85 E8
Bulthy Shrops 148 G6
Bulverhythe E Sus . . . 38 F3
Bulwark Aberds 303 E9
  Mon 79 G8
Bulwell Nottingham . . 171 F9
Bulwell Forest
  Nottingham 171 F8
Bulwick Northants . . . 137 E8
Bumble's Green Essex 86 D6
Bumwell Hill Norf . . . 142 E2
Bun Abhainn Eadarra
  W Isles 305 H3
Bunacaimb Highld . . . 295 G8
Bun a'Mhuilinn W Isles 297 K3
Bunarkaig Highld . . . 290 E3
Bunbury Ches E 167 D9
Bunbury Heath Ches E 167 D9
Bunchrew Highld 300 E6
Bundalloch Highld . . . 295 C10
Buness Shetland 312 C8
Bunessan Argyll 288 G5
Bungay Suff 142 F6
Bunkers Hill Gtr Man . 184 D6
  Oxon 83 B7
Bunker's Hill Cambs . 139 B8
  Lincs 174 E3
  Lincs 189 G7
  Norf 143 C10
Bunloit Highld 300 G5
Bun Loyne Highld . . . 290 C4

Bunnahabhain Argyll ... 274 F5
Bunny Notts ... 153 D11
Bunny Hill Notts ... 153 D11
Bunree Highld ... 290 G2
Bunroy Highld ... 290 E4
Bunsley Bank Ches E . 167 G1
Bunstead Hants ... 32 C6
Buntait Highld ... 300 F3
Bunting's Green Essex . 106 F6
Buntingford Herts ... 105 F7
Bunwell Norf ... 142 E2
Bunwell Bottom Norf . 142 D2
Buoltach Highld ... 310 F5
Burbage Derbys ... 185 G8
 Leics ... 135 E8
 Wilts ... 63 G8
Burcher Hereford ... 114 E6
Burchett's Green
 Windsor ... 65 C10
Burcombe Wilts ... 46 G5
Burcot Oxon ... 83 F9
 Worcs ... 117 C9
Burcott Bucks ... 84 B4
 Bucks ... 103 G7
 Som ... 44 D4
Burdiehouse Edin ... 270 B5
Burdon T&W ... 243 G9
Burdonshill V Glam . 58 E6
Burdrop Oxon ... 101 D7
Bures Suff ... 107 E8
Bures Green Suff ... 107 D8
Burford Ches E ... 167 G10
 Devon ... 24 C4
 Oxon ... 82 C3
 Shrops ... 115 D11
 Som ... 44 E5
Burg Argyll ... 288 E5
 Argyll ... 288 G6
Burgar Orkney ... 314 D3
Burgate Hants ... 31 D11
 Suff ... 125 B11
Burgates Hants ... 34 B3
Burgedin Powys ... 148 G4
Burge End Herts ... 104 E2
Burgess Hill W Sus . 36 D4
Burgh Suff ... 126 G4
Burgh by Sands Cumb . 239 F8
Burgh Castle Norf ... 143 B8
Burghclere Hants ... 64 G3
Burghclere Common
 Hants ... 64 G3
Burgh Common Norf . 141 E11
Burghead Moray ... 301 C11
Burghfield W Berks . 65 F7
Burghfield Common
 W Berks ... 64 F6
Burghfield Hill W Berks . 65 F7
Burgh Heath Sur ... 51 B8
Burgh Hill E Sus ... 23 C8
 E Sus ... 38 B2
Burghill Hereford ... 97 C9
Burgh le Marsh Lincs . 175 B8
Burgh Muir Aberds ... 293 B9
 Aberds ... 303 C9
Burgh next Aylsham
 Norf ... 160 D4
Burgh on Bain Lincs . 190 D2
Burgh St Margaret /
 Fleggburgh Norf ... 161 G8
Burgh St Peter Norf . 143 E9
Burghstubbs Norf ... 159 C10
Burghwallis S Yorks . 198 E4
Burgois Corn ... 10 G4
Burham Kent ... 69 G8
Burham Court Kent . 69 G8
Buriton Hants ... 34 C2
Burland Ches E ... 167 E10
Burlawn Corn ... 10 G5
Burleigh Brack ... 65 E11
 Glos ... 80 E5
Burlescombe Devon . 27 D9
Burleston Dorset ... 17 C11
Burlestone Devon ... 8 G6
Burley Hants ... 32 G2
 Rutland ... 155 G2
 Shrops ... 131 G9
 W Yorks ... 205 G11
Burley Beacon Hants . 32 G2
Burleydam Ches E ... 167 G10
Burley Gate Hereford . 97 A11
Burley in Wharfedale
 W Yorks ... 205 D9
Burley Lawn Hants ... 32 F2
Burley Lodge Hants . 32 F2
Burley Street Hants . 32 F2
Burley Woodhead
 W Yorks ... 205 E9
Burlinch Som ... 28 B3
Burlingham Green Norf . 161 G7
Burlingjobb Powys ... 114 F5
Burlish Worcs ... 116 C6
Burlorne Tregoose Corn . 5 B10
Burlow E Sus ... 23 B9
Burlton Shrops ... 149 D9
Burmantofts W Yorks . 206 G2
Burmarsh Hereford ... 97 B10
 Kent ... 54 G5
Burmington Warks ... 100 D5
Burn N Yorks ... 198 B5
Burnage Gtr Man ... 184 C5
Burnard's Ho Devon . 24 G4
Burnaston Derbys ... 152 C5
Burnbank S Lanark . 268 D4
Burn Bridge N Yorks . 206 C2
Burnby E Yorks ... 208 D2
Burncross S Yorks ... 186 B4
Burndell W Sus ... 35 G7
Burnden Gtr Man ... 195 F8
Burnedge Gtr Man ... 196 E2
Burnend Aberds ... 303 E8
Burneside Cumb ... 221 F10
Burness Orkney ... 314 B6
Burneston N Yorks . 214 B6
Burnett Bath ... 61 F7
Burnfoot Borders ... 261 G10
 Borders ... 262 F2
 Dumfries ... 239 C7
 Dumfries ... 247 E11
 E Ayrs ... 245 B10
 N Lanark ... 268 B5
 Perth ... 286 G3
Burngreave S Yorks . 186 D5
Burnham Bucks ... 66 C2
 N Lincs ... 200 D5
Burnham Deepdale
 Norf ... 176 E4
Burnham Green Herts . 86 B3
Burnham Market Norf . 176 E4
Burnham Norton
 Norf ... 176 E4
Burnham-on-Crouch
 Essex ... 88 F6
Burnham-on-Sea Som . 43 D10
Burnham Overy Staithe
 Norf ... 176 E4
Burnham Overy Town
 Norf ... 176 E4
Burnham Thorpe
 Norf ... 176 E4
Burnhead Aberds ... 293 D10
 Borders ... 262 F2
 Dumfries ... 247 D9

Burnhead continued
 Dumfries ... 247 G10
 S Ayrs ... 244 G6
Burnhervie Aberds ... 293 B9
Burnhill Green Staffs . 132 C5
Burnhope Durham ... 233 B9
Burnhouse N Ayrs ... 267 E6
Burnhouse Mains
 Borders ... 271 F8
Burniere Corn ... 10 G5
Burniestrype Moray . 302 C3
Burniston N Yorks ... 227 G10
Burnlee W Yorks ... 196 F6
Burnley Lancs ... 204 G2
Burnley Lane Lancs . 204 G2
Burnley Wood Lancs . 204 G2
Burnmouth Borders . 273 C9
Burn Naze Lancs ... 202 E2
Burn of Cambus
 Stirling ... 285 G11
Burnopfield Durham . 242 F5
Burnrigg Cumb ... 239 F11
Burnsall N Yorks ... 213 G10
Burn's Green Herts . 104 G6
Burnside Aberds ... 303 E8
 Angus ... 287 B9
 E Ayrs ... 258 G3
 Fife ... 286 G5
 Perth ... 286 E4
 Shetland ... 312 F4
 S Lanark ... 268 C2
 T&W ... 243 G8
 W Loth ... 279 G11
Burnside of Duntrune
 Angus ... 287 D8
Burnstone Devon ... 24 C4
Burnswark Dumfries . 238 B5
Burnt Ash Som ... 80 E5
Burntcommon Sur ... 50 C4
Burnt Heath Derbys . 186 F2
 Essex ... 107 F11
Burnt Hill W Berks . 64 E5
Burnthouse Corn ... 3 B7
Burnt Houses Durham . 233 G8
Burntisland Fife ... 280 D4
Burnt Mills Essex ... 88 G2
Burnt Oak London ... 86 G2
Burnton E Ayrs ... 245 B11
Burnt Tree W Mid . 133 E9
Burnturk Fife ... 287 G7
Burntwood Staffs ... 133 B11
Burntwood Green
 Staffs ... 133 B11
Burntwood Pentre Flint . 166 C3
Burnt Yates N Yorks . 214 G5
Burnworthy Som ... 27 D11
Burnwood Edin ... 270 B2
Burpham Sur ... 50 C4
 W Sus ... 35 F8
Burradon Northumb . 251 B11
 T&W ... 243 C7
Burrafirth Shetland . 312 B8
Burraland Shetland . 312 F5
 Shetland ... 313 J4
Burras Corn ... 2 C5
Burrastow Shetland . 313 J4
Burraton Corn ... 7 D8
Burraton Coombe Corn . 7 D8
Burravoe Shetland ... 312 F7
 Shetland ... 312 F7
Burray Village Orkney . 314 G4
Burreldales Aberds ... 303 F7
Burrells Cumb ... 222 B3
Burrelton Perth ... 286 D6
Burridge Devon ... 28 F4
 Devon ... 40 F5
 Hants ... 33 E8
Burrill N Yorks ... 214 B4
Burringham N Lincs . 199 F10
Burrington Devon ... 25 D10
 Hereford ... 115 C8
 N Som ... 44 B3
Burrough End Cambs . 124 F2
Burrough Green Cambs . 124 F2
Burrough on the Hill
 Leics ... 154 G5
Burroughs Grove Bucks . 65 B11
Burroughston Orkney . 314 D5
Burrow Devon ... 14 B5
 Som ... 28 C6
 Som ... 42 E2
 Gtr Man ... 196 F2
Burrowbridge Som . 43 G11
Burrow-bridge Som . 28 B5
Burrowhill Sur ... 66 G6
Burrows Cross Sur . 50 D5
Burrowsmoor Holt
 Notts ... 172 G2
Burrsville Park Essex . 89 B11
Burrswood Kent ... 52 F4
Burry Swansea ... 56 C3
Burry Green Swansea . 56 C3
Burry Port / Porth Tywyn
 Carms ... 74 E6
Burscott Devon ... 24 C4
Burscough Lancs ... 194 E2
Burscough Bridge Lancs . 194 E2
Bursdon Devon ... 24 D3
Bursea E Yorks ... 208 G2
Burshill E Yorks ... 209 D7
Bursledon Hants ... 33 F7
Burslem Stoke ... 168 F5
Burstall Suff ... 107 C11
Burstallhill Suff ... 107 B11
Burstock Dorset ... 28 G6
Burston Devon ... 26 G2
 Norf ... 142 G2
 Staffs ... 151 C8
Burstow Sur ... 51 E10
Burstwick E Yorks . 201 B8
Burtersett N Yorks . 213 B8
Burtholme Cumb ... 240 E2
Burthorpe Suff ... 124 E5
Burthwaite Cumb ... 230 B4
Burtoft Lincs ... 156 B5
Burtle Som ... 43 E11
Burtle Hill Som ... 43 E11
Burton Ches E ... 167 C8
 Ches W ... 182 G4
 Dorset ... 17 C9
 Dorset ... 19 C9
 Lincs ... 189 G7
 Northumb ... 264 C5
 Pembs ... 73 D7
 Som ... 29 E8
 Som ... 43 E7
 V Glam ... 58 F4
 Wilts ... 45 G10
 Wilts ... 61 D10
 Wrex ... 166 E5
Burton Agnes E Yorks . 218 G2
Burton Bradstock Dorset . 16 D5
Burton Corner Lincs . 174 F4
Burton Dassett Warks . 119 G7
Burton End Cambs ... 106 E2
 Essex ... 105 G2
Burton Ferry Pembs . 73 D7
Burton Fleming
 E Yorks ... 217 E11

Burton Green Essex . 106 F6
 W Mid ... 118 B5
 Wrex ... 166 E4
Burton Hastings Warks . 135 E8
Burton-in-Kendal
 Cumb ... 211 D10
Burton in Lonsdale
 N Yorks ... 212 E3
Burton Joyce Notts . 171 G10
Burton Latimer
 Northants ... 121 C8
Burton Lazars Leics . 154 F5
Burton Leonard
 N Yorks ... 214 G6
Burton Manor Staffs . 151 E8
Burton on the Wolds
 Leics ... 153 E11
Burton Overy Leics . 136 D3
Burton Pedwardine
 Lincs ... 173 G10
Burton Pidsea E Yorks . 209 G10
Burton Salmon N Yorks . 198 B3
Burton Stather N Lincs . 199 D11
Burton upon Stather
 N Lincs ... 199 D11
Burton upon Trent
 Staffs ... 152 E5
Burton Westwood
 Shrops ... 132 D2
Burtonwood Warr ... 183 C9
Burwardsley Ches W . 167 D8
Burwarton Shrops ... 132 F2
Burwash E Sus ... 37 C11
Burwash Common
 E Sus ... 37 C10
Burwash Weald E Sus . 37 C10
Burwell Cambs ... 123 D11
 Lincs ... 190 F5
Burwen Anglesey ... 178 C6
Burwick Orkney ... 314 H4
 Shetland ... 313 J5
Burwood Shrops ... 131 F9
Burwood Park Sur . 66 G6
Bury Cambs ... 138 G5
 Gtr Man ... 195 E10
 Som ... 26 B6
 W Sus ... 35 E8
Buryas Br Corn ... 1 D4
Burybank Staffs ... 151 B7
Bury End Bedford ... 121 G9
 C Beds ... 104 E2
 Worcs ... 99 D11
Bury Green Herts ... 105 G8
 Herts ... 85 G10
Bury Hollow W Sus . 35 E8
Bury Hill Som ... 43 E7
Bury Park Luton ... 103 G11
Bury St Edmunds Suff . 125 E7
Bury's Bank W Berks . 64 F3
Burythorpe N Yorks . 216 G5
Busbiehill N Ayrs ... 257 B9
Busbridge Sur ... 50 E3
Busby E Renf ... 267 D11
 Perth ... 286 E5
Buscot Oxon ... 82 F2
Bush Aberds ... 293 G9
 Corn ... 24 F2
Bushbank Hereford . 115 G9
Bush Bank Hereford . 115 G9
Bushbury W Mid ... 133 C8
Bushby Leics ... 136 C3
Bushey Dorset ... 18 E5
 Herts ... 85 G10
Bushey Ground Oxon . 82 D4
Bushey Heath Herts . 85 G11
Bushey Mead London . 67 F8
Bushfield Cumb ... 249 G11
Bush Green Norf ... 141 D10
 Norf ... 142 F4
 Suff ... 125 F8
Bush Hill Park London . 86 F4
Bushley Worcs ... 99 C7
Bushley Green Worcs . 99 E7
Bushmead Bedford . 122 E2
Bushmoor Shrops ... 131 F8
Bushton Wilts ... 62 D5
Bushy Common Norf . 159 G9
Bushy Hill Sur ... 50 C4
Busk Cumb ... 231 C8
 Gtr Man ... 196 F2
Buslingthorpe Lincs . 189 D9
Bussage Glos ... 80 E5
Bussex Som ... 43 G10
Busta Shetland ... 312 G5
Bustard Green Essex . 106 F2
Bustard's Green Norf . 142 E3
Bustatun Orkney ... 314 A4
Busveal Corn ... 4 G4
Butcher's Common Norf . 160 E6
Butcher's Cross E Sus . 37 B9
Butcombe N Som ... 60 G4
Butetown Cardiff ... 59 D7
Bute Town Caerph ... 77 D10
Butlane Head Shrops . 149 G8
Butleigh Som ... 44 G4
Butleigh Wootton Som . 44 G4
Butlersbank Shrops . 149 E11
Butlers Cross Bucks . 85 G7
 Herts ... 85 B7
Butler's End Warks . 134 G4
Butler's Hill Notts . 171 F8
Butlers Marston Warks . 118 G6
Butley Suff ... 127 G7
Butley High Corner Suff . 109 B7
Butley Low Corner Suff . 109 B7
Butley Town Ches E . 184 F6
Butlocks Heath Hants . 33 F7
Butter Bank Staffs . 151 E7
Butterburn Cumb ... 240 C5
Buttercrambe N Yorks . 207 B10
Butteriss Gate Corn . 2 D6
Butterknowle Durham . 233 F8
Butterleigh Devon . 27 F7
Butterley Derbys ... 170 E6
 Derbys ... 170 C4
Buttermere Cumb ... 220 B3
 Wilts ... 63 G10
Butterrow Glos ... 80 E5
Butters Green Staffs . 168 E4
Buttershaw W Yorks . 196 B6
Butterstone Perth ... 286 C4
Butterton Staffs ... 168 D4
 Staffs ... 169 D7
Butterwick Cumb ... 221 B10
 Durham ... 234 F3
 Lincs ... 174 F5
 N Yorks ... 216 D6
 N Yorks ... 217 E9
Butteryhaugh Northumb . 250 D4
Butt Green Ches E . 167 E11
Buttington Powys ... 130 B5
Butt Lane Staffs ... 168 E4
Buttonbridge Shrops . 116 B4
Button Haugh Green
 Suff ... 125 E10
Buttonoak Shrops ... 116 B5
Button's Green Suff . 125 G8

Butts Devon ... 14 D2
Buttsash Hants ... 32 F6
Buttsbear Cross Corn . 24 G3
Buttsbury Essex ... 87 F11
Butts Green Essex ... 105 E9
Butt's Green Hants ... 32 B4
Buttsole Kent ... 55 C10
Butt Yeats Lancs ... 211 F11
Buxhall Suff ... 125 F10
Buxley Borders ... 272 E6
Buxted E Sus ... 37 C7
Buxton Derbys ... 185 G9
 Norf ... 160 E4
Buxworth Derbys ... 185 E8
Bwcle / Buckley Flint . 166 C3
Bwlch Powys ... 96 G2
Bwlch-derwin Gwyn . 163 F7
Bwlchgwyn Wrex ... 166 E3
Bwlch-Llan Ceredig . 111 F11
Bwlchnewydd Carms . 93 G7
Bwlch-newydd Carms . 93 G7
Bwlchtocyn Gwyn ... 144 D6
Bwlch-y-cibau Powys . 148 F3
Bwlch-y-cwm Cardiff . 58 C6
Bwlchyddar Powys ... 148 E3
Bwlch-y-fadfa Ceredig . 93 B8
Bwlch-y-ffridd Powys . 129 D11
Bwlchygroes Pembs . 92 D4
Bwlch-y-Plain Powys . 114 B4
Bwlch-y-sarnau Powys . 113 C10
Bybrook Kent ... 54 E4
Bycross Hereford ... 97 C7
Byeastwood Bridgend . 58 C2
Bye Green Bucks ... 84 C5
Byerhope Northumb . 232 B3
Byermoor T&W ... 242 F5
Byers Green Durham . 233 E10
Byfield Northants ... 119 G10
Byfleet Sur ... 66 G5
Byford Hereford ... 97 C7
Byford Common Hereford . 97 C8
Bygrave Herts ... 104 D5
Byker T&W ... 243 E7
Byland Abbey N Yorks . 215 D10
Bylchau Conwy ... 165 C7
Byley Ches W ... 168 B2
Bynea Carms ... 56 B4
Byram N Yorks ... 198 B3
Byrness Northumb ... 250 C4
Bythorn Cambs ... 121 B11
Byton Hereford ... 115 E7
Byton Hand Hereford . 115 E7
Bywell Northumb ... 242 E2
Byworth W Sus ... 35 C7

C

Cabbacott Devon ... 24 C6
Cabbage Hill Brack . 65 E11
Cabharstadh W Isles . 304 F5
Cabin Shrops ... 130 F6
Cabourne Lincs ... 200 G6
Cabrach Argyll ... 274 G5
 Moray ... 302 G3
Cabrich Highld ... 300 E5
Cabus Lancs ... 202 D5
Cackle Hill Lincs ... 157 D7
Cackleshaw W Yorks . 204 F6
Cackle Street E Sus . 23 B11
 E Sus ... 37 B7
 E Sus ... 38 D4
Cadbury Devon ... 26 G6
Cadbury Barton Devon . 25 D11
Cadbury Heath S Glos . 61 E7
Caddington C Beds . 85 B9
Caddleton Argyll ... 275 B8
Caddonfoot Borders . 261 C10
Caddonlee Borders . 261 B10
Cadeby Leics ... 135 C8
 S Yorks ... 198 G4
Cadeleigh Devon ... 26 F6
Cademuir Borders ... 260 B6
Cader Denb ... 165 C8
Cade Street E Sus ... 37 C10
Cadger Path Angus . 287 B8
Cadgwith Corn ... 2 G6
Cadham Fife ... 286 G6
Cadishead Gtr Man . 184 C2
Cadle Swansea ... 56 B6
Cadley Lancs ... 202 G6
 Wilts ... 47 C8
 Wilts ... 63 F8
Cadmore End Bucks . 84 G3
Cadnam Hants ... 32 E3
Cadney N Lincs ... 200 G4
Cadney Bank Wrex . 149 C9
Cadole Flint ... 166 C2
Cadoxton V Glam ... 59 F7
Cadoxton-Juxta-Neath
 Neath ... 57 B9
Cadshaw Blackburn . 195 D8
Cadwell Herts ... 104 E3
Cadwst S Lanark ... 268 E4
Caeathro Gwyn ... 163 C7
Cae Clyd Gwyn ... 164 G2
Cae-gors Carms ... 75 E9
Caehopkin Powys ... 76 C4
Caemorgan Ceredig . 92 B3
Caenby Lincs ... 189 D8
Caenby Corner Lincs . 189 D7
Caerau Bridgend ... 57 C11
 Cardiff ... 58 D6
Caerau Park Newport . 59 B9
Cae'r-bont Powys ... 76 C4
Cae'r-bryn Carms ... 75 C9
Caerdeon Gwyn ... 146 F2
Cae'r-Lan Powys ... 76 C4
Caerleon Newport ... 78 G4
Caer Llan Mon ... 79 D7
Caermead V Glam ... 58 E3
Caermeini Pembs ... 92 D2
Caernarfon Gwyn ... 163 C7
Caerphilly / Caerffili
 Caerph ... 59 B7
Caerwedros Ceredig . 111 F7

Caerwent Mon ... 79 G7
Caerwent Brook Mon . 60 B3
Caerwych Gwyn ... 146 B2
Caerwys Flint ... 181 G10
Caethle Gwyn ... 128 D2
Cage Green Kent ... 52 D5
Caggan Highld ... 291 B10
Caggle Street Mon . 78 B5
Cailness Stirling ... 285 G7
Caim Anglesey ... 179 E10
Caio Carms ... 94 E3
Cairinis W Isles ... 296 E4
Cairisiadar W Isles . 304 E2
Cairminis W Isles ... 296 C6
Cairnbaan Argyll ... 275 D9
Cairnbanno Ho Aberds . 303 E8
Cairnborrow Aberds . 302 E4
Cairnbrogie Aberds . 303 G8
Cairnbulg Castle
 Aberds ... 303 C10
Cairncross Angus ... 292 F6
 Borders ... 273 C7
Cairndow Argyll ... 284 F5
Cairness Aberds ... 303 C10
Cairneyhill Fife ... 279 D10
Cairnfield Ho Moray . 302 C4
Cairngaan Dumfries . 236 F3
Cairngarroch Dumfries . 236 E2
Cairnhill Aberds ... 302 F6
 Aberds ... 303 D7
 N Lanark ... 268 C5
Cairnie Aberds ... 293 C10
 Aberds ... 302 E4
Cairnlea S Ayrs ... 244 G6
Cairnmuir Aberds ... 303 C9
Cairnorrie Aberds ... 303 E8
Cairnpark Aberds ... 293 C10
 Dumfries ... 247 D9
Cairnryan Dumfries . 236 C2
Cairnton Orkney ... 314 F3
Caister-on-Sea Norf . 161 G10
Caistor Lincs ... 200 G6
Caistor St Edmund Norf . 142 C4
Caistron Northumb ... 251 C11
Caitha Bowland Borders . 271 G9
Cakebole Worcs ... 117 C7
Calais Street Suff ... 107 C7
Calanais W Isles ... 304 E4
Calbost W Isles ... 305 G6
Calbourne IoW ... 20 D4
Calceby Lincs ... 190 F5
Calcoed Flint ... 181 G11
Calcot Glos ... 81 D9
 W Berks ... 65 E7
Calcot Row W Berks . 65 E7
Calcott Kent ... 71 G7
 Shrops ... 149 G8
Calcott's Green Glos . 80 B3
Calcutt N Yorks ... 206 B2
 Wilts ... 81 G10
Caldback Shetland ... 312 C8
Caldbeck Cumb ... 230 D3
Caldbergh N Yorks . 213 B11
Caldecote Cambs ... 122 F6
 Cambs ... 138 F2
 Herts ... 104 D4
 Northants ... 120 G3
Caldecote Hill Herts . 85 G11
Caldecott Northants . 121 D9
 Oxon ... 83 F7
 Rutland ... 137 E7
Calder Bridge Cumb . 219 D10
Calderbank N Lanark . 268 C5
Calderbrook Gtr Man . 196 D2
Caldercruix N Lanark . 268 B6
Calder E Dunb ... 278 G2
Calder Grove W Yorks . 197 D10
Calder Hall Cumb ... 219 D10
Calder Mains Highld . 310 D4
Caldermill S Lanark . 268 F3
Caldermoor Gtr Man . 196 D2
Calder Vale Lancs ... 202 D6
Caldervale S Lanark . 268 C6
Caldhame Angus ... 287 C8
Caldicot / Cil-y-coed
 Mon ... 60 B3
Caldmore W Mid ... 133 D10
Caldwell Derbys ... 152 F4
 N Yorks ... 224 C3
Caldy Mers ... 182 D6
Caledrhydiau Ceredig . 111 G9
Cale Green Gtr Man . 184 D5
Calenick Corn ... 4 G6
Caleys Fields Worcs . 100 C3
Calf Heath Staffs ... 133 B8
Calford Green Suff . 106 B3
Calfsound Orkney ... 314 C5
Calgary Argyll ... 288 D5
Caliach Argyll ... 288 D5
Califer Moray ... 301 D10
California Cambs ... 139 G10
 Derbys ... 152 C6
 Falk ... 279 F8
 Norf ... 161 G10
 Suff ... 108 C3
 W Mid ... 133 G10
Calke Derbys ... 153 E7
Callakille Highld ... 298 D6
Callaly Northumb ... 252 B3
Callands Warr ... 183 C9
Callaughton Shrops . 132 D2
Callendar Park Falk . 279 F7
Callert Ho Highld ... 290 G2
Callerton T&W ... 242 D5
Callerton Lane End
 T&W ... 242 D5
Callestick Corn ... 4 E5
Calligarry Highld ... 295 E8
Callingwood Staffs . 152 E3
Callington Corn ... 6 B2
Callingwood Staffs . 152 E3
Callop Highld ... 289 B11
Callow Hereford ... 97 E9
Callow End Worcs ... 98 B6
Callow Hill Mon ... 79 B8
 Som ... 44 E4
 Wilts ... 62 B4
 Worcs ... 116 C4
 Worcs ... 116 D4
Callow Marsh Hereford . 115 C11
Callows Grave Worcs . 115 D11
Calmore Hants ... 32 E5
Calmsden Glos ... 81 D8
Calne Wilts ... 62 E4
Calne Marsh Wilts ... 62 E4
Calow Derbys ... 186 G6
Calrofold Ches E ... 184 G6
Calshot Hants ... 33 G7
Calstock Corn ... 7 B8
Calstone Wellington
 Wilts ... 62 F4
Calthorpe Norf ... 160 C3

Calthorpe continued
 Oxon ... 101 D9
Calthwaite Cumb ... 230 C5
Calton Glasgow ... 268 C2
 N Yorks ... 204 B4
 Staffs ... 169 E10
Calton Lees Derbys . 170 C3
Calvadnack Corn ... 2 B5
Calveley Ches E ... 167 D9
Calver Derbys ... 186 G2
Calver Hill Hereford . 97 B7
Calverhall Shrops ... 149 B11
Calverleigh Devon ... 26 E6
Calverley W Yorks ... 205 F10
Calver Sough Derbys . 186 F2
Calvert Bucks ... 102 G3
Calverton M Keynes . 102 D5
 Notts ... 171 F10
Calvine Perth ... 291 G10
Calvo Cumb ... 238 G4
Cam Glos ... 80 F3
Camaghael Highld ... 290 F3
Camas an Staca Argyll . 274 G5
Camas-luinie Highld . 295 C11
Camasnacroise Highld . 289 D10
Camas Salach Highld . 289 C8
Camastianavaig Highld . 295 B7
Camasunary Highld . 295 D7
Camault Muir Highld . 300 E5
Camb Shetland ... 312 D7
Camber E Sus ... 39 D7
Camberley Sur ... 65 G11
Camberwell London . 67 D10
Camblesforth N Yorks . 199 B7
Cambo Northumb ... 252 F2
Cambois Northumb . 253 G8
Camborne Corn ... 4 G3
Cambourne Cambs ... 122 F6
Cambridge Borders . 271 F11
 Cambs ... 123 F9
 Glos ... 80 E3
Cambridge Batch N Som . 60 F4
Cambridge Town
 Southend ... 70 C2
Cambrose Corn ... 4 F3
Cambus Clack ... 279 C7
Cambusavie Farm
 Highld ... 309 K7
Cambusbarron Stirling . 278 C5
Cambusdrenny Stirling . 278 C5
Cambuskenneth Stirling . 278 C6
Cambuslang S Lanark . 268 C2
Cambusmore Lodge
 Highld ... 309 K7
Cambusnethan
 N Lanark ... 268 D6
Camden London ... 67 C9
Camden Hill Kent ... 53 F9
Camden Park Kent ... 52 F5
Cameley Bath ... 44 B6
Camelford Corn ... 11 E8
Camel Green Dorset . 31 E10
Camelon Falk ... 279 E7
Camelsdale Sur ... 49 G11
Camer Kent ... 69 F7
Cameron Fife ... 280 B6
Cameron Bridge Fife . 280 B6
Camerory Highld ... 301 F10
Camer's Green Worcs . 98 D5
Camerton Bath ... 45 B7
 Cumb ... 228 E6
 E Yorks ... 201 B8
Camghouran Perth ... 285 B9
Cammachmore Aberds . 293 D11
Cammeringham Lincs . 188 E6
Camnant Powys ... 113 F11
Camoquhill Stirling . 277 C9
Camore Highld ... 309 K7
Camp Corn ... 5 E8
Camp Lincs ... 172 E5
Campbeltown Argyll . 255 E8
Camp Corner Oxon . 83 E10
Camperdown T&W . 243 C7
Camp Hill N Yorks . 214 C6
 Pembs ... 73 C10
 Warks ... 135 E7
 W Yorks ... 196 C5
Campion Hills Warks . 118 D6
Campions Essex ... 87 C7
Cample Dumfries ... 247 D9
Campmuir Perth ... 286 D6
Campsall S Yorks ... 198 E4
Campsea Ashe Suff . 126 F6
Camps End Cambs ... 106 C2
Campsey Ash Suff ... 126 F6
Camps Heath Suff ... 143 E10
Campton C Beds ... 104 D2
Camptoun E Loth ... 281 F10
Camptown Borders . 262 G5
Camp Town W Yorks . 206 F2
Camquhart Argyll ... 275 D9
Camrose Pembs ... 91 G8
Camserney Perth ... 286 C2
Camster Highld ... 310 E6
Camuschoirk Highld . 289 C9
Camuscross Highld . 295 D8
Camusnagaul Highld . 290 F2
 Highld ... 307 L5
Camusrory Highld ... 295 F10
Camusteel Highld ... 299 E7
Camusterrach Highld . 299 E7
Camusurachan Perth . 285 C10
Camusvrachan Perth . 285 C10
Canada Hants ... 32 D3
 Lincs ... 200 G6
Canadia E Sus ... 38 D2
Canal Foot Cumb ... 210 D6
Canal Side S Yorks ... 199 E7
Canbus Clack ... 279 C7
Candacraig Ho Aberds . 292 B5
Candlesby Lincs ... 175 B7
Candle Street Suff ... 125 B10
Candy Mill S Lanark . 269 G11
Cane End Oxon ... 65 D7
Caneheath E Sus ... 23 D9
Canewdon Essex ... 88 G5
Canford Bottom Dorset . 31 G8
Canford Cliffs Poole . 19 D7
Canford Heath Poole . 18 B6
Canford Magna Poole . 18 B6
Cangate Norf ... 160 F6
Canham's Green Suff . 125 D10
Canholes Derbys ... 185 G8
Canisbay Highld ... 310 B7
Cann Dorset ... 30 C5
Cannalidgey Corn ... 5 B8
Cannard's Grave Som . 44 E6
Cann Common Dorset . 30 C5
Cannich Highld ... 300 F3
Cannington Som ... 43 F9
Canning Town London . 68 C2
Cannock Staffs ... 151 G9
Cannock Wood Staffs . 151 G10
Cannon's Green Essex . 87 C9
Cannop Glos ... 79 C10
Canon Bridge Hereford . 97 C8
Canonbury London ... 67 C10
Canon Frome Hereford . 98 C3
Canon Pyon Hereford . 97 B9
Canons Ashby
 Northants ... 119 G11
Canonsgrove Som ... 28 C2
Canons Park London . 85 G11
Canon's Town Corn . 2 B2
Canterbury Kent ... 54 B6
Cantley Norf ... 143 C7
 S Yorks ... 198 G6
Cantlop Shrops ... 131 B10
Canton Cardiff ... 59 D7
Cantraybruich Highld . 301 E7
Cantraydoune Highld . 301 E7
Cantraywood Highld . 301 E7
Cantsfield Lincs ... 212 E2
Canvey Island Essex . 69 C9
Canwick Lincs ... 173 B7
Canworthy Water Corn . 11 C10
Caol Highld ... 290 F3
Caolas Argyll ... 288 E2
 W Isles ... 297 M2
Caolas Fhlodaigh
 W Isles ... 296 F4
Caolas Liubharsaigh
 W Isles ... 297 G4
Caolas Scalpaigh
 W Isles ... 305 J4
Caolas Stocinis W Isles . 305 J3
Caol Ila Argyll ... 274 F5
Caolasnacon Highld . 290 G3
Capel Carms ... 75 E8
 Kent ... 52 E6
 Sur ... 51 E7
Capel Bangor Ceredig . 128 G3
Capel Betws Lleucu
 Ceredig ... 112 F2
Capel Carmel Gwyn . 144 D3
Capel Coch Anglesey . 179 E7
Capel Cross Kent ... 53 E8
Capel Curig Conwy . 164 D3
Capel Cynon Ceredig . 93 B7
Capel Dewi Carms ... 93 G9
 Ceredig ... 93 C9
 Ceredig ... 128 D3
Capel Garmon Conwy . 164 D4
Capel Green Suff ... 109 B7
Capel-gwyn Anglesey . 178 E4
Capel Gwyn Carms ... 93 G9
Capel Gwynfe Carms . 94 G4
Capel Hendre Carms . 75 C9
Capel Hermon Gwyn . 146 D4
Capel Isaac Carms ... 93 F11
Capel Iwan Carms ... 92 D5
Capel-le-Ferne Kent . 55 F8
Capel Llanilltern Cardiff . 58 C5
Capel Mawr Anglesey . 178 G6
Capel Newydd / Newchapel
 Pembs ... 92 D4
Capel Parc Anglesey . 178 D6
Capel St Andrew Suff . 109 B7
Capel St Mary Suff . 107 D11
Capel Seion Carms ... 75 C8
 Ceredig ... 112 B2
Capel Siloam Conwy . 164 E4
Capel Tygwydd Ceredig . 92 C5
Capel Uchaf Gwyn ... 162 F6
Capel-y-ffin Powys ... 96 E5
Capel-y-graig Gwyn . 163 B8
Capenhurst Ches W . 182 G5
Capernwray Lancs ... 211 E10
Capheaton Northumb . 252 G2
Capland Som ... 28 D4
Cappercleuch Borders . 260 C5
Capplegill Dumfries . 248 B4
Capstone Medway ... 69 F9
Captain Fold Gtr Man . 195 E11
Capton Devon ... 8 E6
 Som ... 42 F5
Caputh Perth ... 286 D4
Caradon Town Corn . 11 G11
Carbis Corn ... 5 D9
Carbis Bay Corn ... 2 B2
Carbost Highld ... 294 B5
 Highld ... 298 E4
Carbrain N Lanark ... 278 G5
Carbrook S Yorks ... 186 D5
Carbrooke Norf ... 141 C9
Carburton Notts ... 187 G10
Carcant Borders ... 271 E7
Carcary Angus ... 287 B10
Carclaze Corn ... 5 E10
Carclew Corn ... 3 B7
Car Colston Notts ... 172 G2
Carcroft S Yorks ... 198 E4
Cardenden Fife ... 280 C4
Cardeston Shrops ... 149 G7
Cardew Cumb ... 230 B3
Cardewlees Cumb ... 239 G8
Cardiff / Caerdydd
 Cardiff ... 59 D7
Cardigan / Aberteifi
 Ceredig ... 92 B3
Cardinal's Green Cambs . 106 C2
Cardington Bedford . 103 B11
 Shrops ... 131 D10
Cardinham Corn ... 6 B2
Cardonald Glasgow . 267 C10
Cardow Moray ... 301 E11
Cardrona Borders ... 261 B8
Cardross Argyll ... 276 F6
Cardunneth Cumb ... 230 C5
Cardurnock Cumb ... 238 F5
Careby Lincs ... 155 F10
Careston Angus ... 293 G7
Careston Castle Angus . 287 B9
Care Village Leics ... 136 D4
Carew Pembs ... 73 E8
Carew Cheriton Pembs . 73 E8
Carew Newton Pembs . 73 E8
Carey Hereford ... 97 E11
Carey Park Corn ... 6 E4
Carfin N Lanark ... 268 D5
Carfrae E Loth ... 271 B11
Carfury Corn ... 1 C4
Cargate Common Norf . 142 E2
Cargenbridge Dumfries . 237 B11
Cargill Perth ... 286 D5
Cargo Cumb ... 239 F9
Cargo Fleet Mbro ... 234 G6
Cargreen Corn ... 7 C8
Carham Northumb ... 263 B8
Carhampton Som ... 42 E4
Carharrack Corn ... 4 G4
Carie Perth ... 285 B10
 Perth ... 285 D10
Carines Corn ... 4 D5
Carisbrooke IoW ... 20 D5
Cark Cumb ... 211 D7
Carkeel Corn ... 7 C8
Carlabhagh W Isles . 304 D4
Carland Cross Corn . 5 E7
Carlbury N Yorks ... 224 B4
Carlby Lincs ... 155 G11
Carlecotes S Yorks ... 197 G7
Carleen Corn ... 2 C4
Carlenrig Borders ... 249 C9
Carlesmoor N Yorks . 214 E3
Carleton Cumb ... 219 G10
 Cumb ... 230 G6
 Lancs ... 202 F2

Carleton continued
 N Yorks ... 204 D5
Carleton Forehoe Norf . 141 B11
Carleton Hall Cumb . 219 F11
Carleton-in-Craven
 N Yorks ... 204 D5
Carleton Rode Norf . 142 E4
Carleton St Peter Norf . 142 C6
Carlidnack Corn ... 3 D7
Carlin How Redcar . 226 B4
Carlincraig Aberds . 302 E6
Carlingcott Bath ... 45 B7
Carlinghow W Yorks . 197 C8
Carlisle Cumb ... 239 F10
 Corn ... 5 E9
Carloggas Corn ... 5 E9
Carloonan Argyll ... 284 F4
Carlops Borders ... 270 D3
Carlton Bedford ... 121 F9
 Cambs ... 124 G2
 Leics ... 135 C7
 Notts ... 198 C6
 N Yorks ... 213 C11
 N Yorks ... 216 B2
 N Yorks ... 224 C5
 N Yorks ... 225 B7
 Stockton ... 234 G3
 Suff ... 127 E7
 S Yorks ... 197 E11
 W Yorks ... 197 B10
Carlton Colville Suff . 143 F10
Carlton Curlieu Leics . 136 D3
Carlton Green Cambs . 124 G2
Carlton Husthwaite
 N Yorks ... 215 D9
Carlton in Cleveland
 N Yorks ... 225 D9
Carlton in Lindrick
 Notts ... 187 E9
Carlton le Moorland
 Lincs ... 172 D6
Carlton Miniott N Yorks . 215 C8
Carlton on Trent Notts . 172 C3
Carlton Purlieus
 Northants ... 136 F6
Carlton Scroop Lincs . 172 G6
Carluddon Corn ... 5 D10
Carluke S Lanark ... 268 E6
Carlyon Bay Corn ... 5 E10
Carmarthen / Caerfyrddin
 Carms ... 93 G8
Carmel Anglesey ... 178 E5
 Carms ... 75 B9
 Flint ... 181 F11
 Gwyn ... 163 E7
 Powys ... 113 D10
Carmichael S Lanark . 259 B10
Carminow Cross Corn . 5 B11
Carmont Aberds ... 293 E10
Carmunnock Glasgow . 268 D2
Carmyle Glasgow ... 268 C2
Carmyllie Angus ... 287 C9
Carnaby E Yorks ... 218 F2
Carnach Highld ... 299 G10
 Highld ... 307 K5
 W Isles ... 305 J4
Carnachy Highld ... 308 D7
Càrnais W Isles ... 304 E2
Càrnan W Isles ... 297 G3
Carn Arthen Corn ... 2 B5
Carnbahn Perth ... 285 C10
Carnbee Fife ... 287 G9
Carnbo Perth ... 286 G4
Carnbrea Corn ... 4 G3
Carn Brea Village Corn . 4 G3
Carndu Highld ... 295 C10
Carnduff S Lanark ... 268 F3
Carnduncan Argyll ... 274 G3
Carne Corn ... 3 B10
 Corn ... 3 E7
 Corn ... 5 D9
Carnebone Corn ... 2 C6
Carnedd Powys ... 129 D10
Carnetown Rhondda . 77 G9
Carnforth Lancs ... 211 E9
Carnglas Swansea ... 56 C6
Carn-gorm Highld ... 295 C11
Carnhedryn Pembs ... 90 F5
Carnhedryn Uchaf Pembs . 90 F5
Carnhell Green Corn . 2 B4
Carnkie Corn ... 2 B5
 Corn ... 2 C6
Carnkief Corn ... 4 E5
Carno Powys ... 129 D9
Carnoch Highld ... 300 D2
 Highld ... 300 E2
Carnock Fife ... 279 D10
Carn Towan Corn ... 1 D3
Carnwadric E Renf . 267 D10
Carnwath S Lanark . 269 F9
Carnyorth Corn ... 1 C3
Caroe Corn ... 11 C9
Carol Green W Mid . 118 B5
Carpalla Corn ... 5 E9
Carpenders Park Herts . 85 G10
Carpenter's Hill Worcs . 117 C11
Carperby N Yorks ... 213 B10
Carpley Green N Yorks . 213 B9
Carr Gtr Man ... 195 D11
 S Yorks ... 187 D8
Carr Bank Cumb ... 211 D9
Carrbridge Highld ... 301 G9
Carrbrook Gtr Man ... 196 G3
Carr Cross Lancs ... 193 E11
Carreg-wen Pembs ... 92 C4
Carreg y Garth Gwyn . 163 B9
Carr Gate W Yorks ... 197 C10
Carr Green Gtr Man . 184 D2
Carr Hill T&W ... 243 E7
Carr Houses Mers ... 193 G10
Carrick Argyll ... 275 E10
 Dumfries ... 237 D7
 Fife ... 287 E8
Carrick Castle Argyll . 276 C3
Carriden Falk ... 279 E10
Carrington Gtr Man . 184 C2
 Lincs ... 174 D4
 Midloth ... 270 C6
 Nottingham ... 171 G9
Carroch Dumfries ... 246 E5
Carrog Conwy ... 164 F3
 Denb ... 165 G10
Carroglen Perth ... 285 E11

Carrol Highld 311 J2
Carron Falk 279 E7
Moray 302 E2
Carronbridge Dumfries 247 D9
Carron Bridge Stirling 278 E4
Carronshore Falk 279 E7
Carrot Angus 287 C8
Carroway Head Staffs 134 D3
Carrow Hill Mon 78 G6
Carrshield Northumb 232 B2
Carrutherstown Dumfries 238 C4
Carr Vale Derbys 171 B7
Carrville Durham 234 C2
Carry Argyll 275 G10
Carsaig Argyll 275 E8
Argyll 289 G7
Carscreugh Dumfries 236 D4
Carsegowan Dumfries 236 D6
Carse Gray Angus 287 B8
Carse Ho Argyll 275 G8
Carseriggan Dumfries 236 C5
Carsethorn Dumfries 237 D11
Carshalton London 67 G9
Carshalton Beeches London 67 G9
Carshalton on the Hill London 67 G9
Carsington Derbys 170 E3
Carskiey Argyll 255 G7
Carsluith Dumfries 236 D6
Carsphairn Dumfries 246 E3
Carstairs S Lanark 269 F8
Carstairs Junction S Lanark 269 F9
Carswell Marsh Oxon 82 F4
Cartbridge Sur 50 B4
Carterhaugh Borders 261 D10
Carter Knowle S Yorks 186 E4
Carter's Clay Hants 32 C4
Carter's Green Essex 87 C8
Carter's Hill Wokingham 65 F9
Carterspiece Glos 79 C9
Carterton Oxon 82 D3
Carterway Heads Northumb 242 G2
Carthamartha Corn 12 F3
Carthew Corn 2 B5
Corn 5 D10
Carthorpe N Yorks 214 C6
Cartington Northumb 252 C2
Cartland S Lanark 269 F7
Cartledge Derbys 186 F4
Cartmel Cumb 211 D7
Cartmel Fell Cumb 211 B8
Cartsdyke Invclyd 276 F5
Cartworth W Yorks 196 F6
Carty Port Dumfries 236 C6
Carway Carms 75 D7
Carwinley Cumb 239 C10
Carwynnen Corn 2 B5
Cary Fitzpaine Som 29 B9
Carzantic Corn 12 E3
Carzield Dumfries 247 G11
Carzise Corn 2 C3
Cascob Powys 114 D4
Cashes Green Glos 80 D4
Cashlie Perth 285 C8
Cashmoor Dorset 31 E7
Cas Mael / Puncheston Pembs 91 F10
Cassey Compton Glos 81 C9
Cassington Oxon 83 C7
Cassop Durham 234 D2
Castallack Corn 1 D5
Castell Conwy 164 B3
Denb 165 B10
Castellau Rhondda 58 B5
Castell-Howell Ceredig 93 B8
Castell nedd / Neath Neath 57 B8
Castell Newydd Emlyn / Newcastle Emlyn Carms 92 C6
Castell-y-bwch Torf 78 G3
Castell-y-rhingyll Carms 75 C9
Casterton Cumb 212 D2
Castle Devon 28 G4
Som 27 B9
Castle Acre Norf 158 F6
Castle Ashby Northants 121 F7
Castle Bolton N Yorks 223 G10
Castle Bromwich W Mid 134 F2
Castle Bytham Lincs 155 F9
Castlebythe Pembs 91 F10
Castle Caereinion Powys 130 B3
Castle Camps Cambs 106 C2
Castle Carlton Lincs 190 E5
Castle Carrock Cumb 240 F2
Castlecary N Lanark 278 F5
Castle Cary Som 44 G6
Castle Combe Wilts 61 D10
Castlecraig Highld 301 C8
Castle Craig Borders 270 G2
Castlecroft Staffs 133 D7
Castle Donington Leics 153 D8
Castle Douglas Dumfries 237 C9
Castle Eaton Swindon 81 F10
Castle Eden Durham 234 D4
Castle End Pboro 138 B2
Castlefairn Dumfries 246 F6
Castlefields Halton 183 E8
Castle Fields Shrops 149 G10
Castle Forbes Aberds 293 B8
Castleford W Yorks 198 B2
Castle Frome Hereford 98 B3
Castle Gate Corn 1 C5
Castlegreen Shrops 130 F6
Castle Green London 68 C3
Sur 66 G3
S Yorks 197 G9
Castle Gresley Derbys 152 F5
Castlehead Renfs 267 C9
Castle Heaton Northumb 273 G8
Castle Hedingham Essex 106 D5
Castlehill Argyll 254 B4
Borders 260 B6
Highld 310 C5
S Ayrs 257 E9
W Dunb 277 F7
Castle Hill E Sus 37 B9
Gtr Man 184 C6
Kent 53 E7
Suff 108 B3
Worcs 116 F5
Castle Huntly Perth 287 E7
Castle Kennedy Dumfries 236 D3
Castlemaddy Dumfries 246 F3
Castlemartin Pembs 72 F6
Castlemilk Dumfries 238 B5
Glasgow 268 D2
Castlemorris Pembs 91 E8
Castlemorton Worcs 98 D5
Castle O'er Dumfries 248 E6
Castlerigg Cumb 229 G11
Castle Rising Norf 158 E3
Castleside Durham 233 B7
Castle Street W Yorks 196 C3
Castle Stuart Highld 301 E7
Castlethorpe M Keynes 102 C6
N Lincs 200 F3
Castleton Angus 287 C7
Argyll 275 E9
Derbys 185 E11
Gtr Man 195 E11
Moray 301 G11
Newport 59 C9
N Yorks 226 D3
Castleton Village Highld 300 E6
Castle Toward Argyll 266 B2
Castletown Ches W 166 E6
Cumb 230 E6
Dorset 17 G9
Highld 301 E7
Highld 310 C5
IoM 192 F3
Staffs 151 E8
T&W 243 F9
Castle Town W Sus 36 E2
Castletump Glos 98 F4
Castle-upon-Alun V Glam 58 E2
Castle Vale W Mid 134 E2
Castleweary Borders 249 C10
Castlewigg Dumfries 236 E6
Castley N Yorks 205 D11
Castling's Heath Suff 107 C9
Caston Norf 141 D9
Castor Pboro 138 D2
Caswell Swansea 56 D5
Catacol N Ayrs 255 C10
Cat Bank Cumb 220 F6
Catbrain S Glos 60 C5
Catbrook Mon 79 E8
Catch Flint 182 G2
Catchall Corn 1 D4
Catchems Corner W Mid 118 B4
Catchems End Worcs 116 B5
Catchgate Durham 242 G5
Catchory Highld 310 D6
Catcleugh Northumb 250 C6
Catcliffe S Yorks 186 D6
Catcomb Wilts 62 D4
Catcott Som 43 F11
Caterham Sur 51 B10
Catfield Norf 161 E7
Catfirth Shetland 313 H6
Catford London 67 E11
Catforth Lancs 202 F5
Cathays Cardiff 59 D7
Cathays Park Cardiff 59 D7
Cathcart Glasgow 267 C11
Cathedine Powys 96 F2
Catherine-de-Barnes W Mid 134 G3
Catherine Slack W Yorks 196 B5
Catherington Hants 33 E11
Catherton Shrops 116 B3
Cat Hill S Yorks 197 F8
Cathiron Warks 119 B9
Catholes Cumb 222 G3
Cathpair Borders 271 F9
Catisfield Hants 33 F8
Catley Lane Head Gtr Man 195 D11
Catley Southfield Hereford 98 C3
Catlodge Highld 291 D8
Catlowdy Cumb 239 B11
Catmere End Essex 105 D9
Catmore W Berks 64 C3
Caton Devon 13 G11
Lancs 211 G10
Caton Green Lancs 211 F10
Catrine E Ayrs 258 D2
Cat's Ash Newport 78 G5
Cat's Common Norf 160 E6
Cats Edge Staffs 169 E7
Catsfield E Sus 38 E2
Catsfield Stream E Sus 38 E2
Catsgore Som 29 B8
Catsham Som 44 G5
Catshaw S Yorks 197 G8
Catshill W Mid 133 B11
Worcs 117 C9
Cat's Hill Cross Staffs 150 C6
Catslackburn Borders 261 D8
Catslip Oxon 65 B8
Catstree Shrops 132 D4
Cattadale Argyll 274 G4
Cattal N Yorks 206 C4
Cattawade Suff 108 E2
Cattedown Plym 7 E9
Catterall Lancs 202 E5
Catterick N Yorks 224 F4
Catterick Bridge N Yorks 224 F4
Catterick Garrison N Yorks 224 F3
Catterlen Cumb 230 E5
Catterline Aberds 293 F10
Catterton N Yorks 206 D6
Catteshall Sur 50 E3
Catthorpe Leics 119 B11
Cattistock Dorset 17 B7
Cattle End Northants 102 C3
Catton Northumb 241 F8
N Yorks 215 D7
Catwick E Yorks 209 D8
Catworth Cambs 121 C11
Caudle Green Glos 80 C6
Caudlesprings Norf 141 C8
Caulcott C Beds 103 C9
Oxon 101 G10
Cauld Borders 261 G11
Cauldcoats Holdings Falk 279 F10
Cauldcots Angus 287 C10
Cauldhame Stirling 278 C2
Cauldmill Borders 262 G2
Cauldon Staffs 169 F9
Cauldon Lowe Staffs 169 F9
Cauldwells Aberds 303 D7
Caulkerbush Dumfries 237 D11
Caulside Dumfries 249 G10
Caundle Marsh Dorset 29 E11
Caunsall Worcs 132 G6
Caunton Notts 172 D2
Causeway Hants 33 E11
Hants 34 C2
Mon 60 B2
Causewayend S Lanark 260 B2
Causeway End Cumb 210 C6
Cumb 211 B9
Dumfries 236 C6
Essex 87 B11
Wilts 62 C4
Causeway Foot W Yorks 197 E7
W Yorks 205 G7
Causeway Green W Mid 133 F9
Causewayhead Cumb 238 G4
Stirling 278 B6
Causewaywood Shrops 131 D10
Causey Durham 242 F6
Causeyend Aberds 293 B11
Causey Park Bridge Northumb 252 E5
Causeyton Aberds 293 B8
Caute Devon 24 E6
Cautley Cumb 222 G3
Cavendish Suff 106 B6
Cavendish Bridge Leics 153 D8
Cavenham Suff 124 D5
Cavers Carre Borders 262 D3
Caversfield Oxon 101 F11
Caversham Reading 65 E8
Caversham Heights Reading 65 D8
Caverswall Staffs 169 G7
Cavil E Yorks 207 G11
Cawdor Highld 301 D8
Cawkeld E Yorks 208 C5
Cawkwell Lincs 190 F3
Cawood N Yorks 207 F7
Cawsand Corn 7 E8
Cawston Norf 160 E2
Warks 119 C9
Cawthorne N Yorks 216 B5
S Yorks 197 F9
Cawthorpe Lincs 155 E11
Cawton N Yorks 216 D2
Caxton Cambs 122 F6
Caynham Shrops 115 C11
Caythorpe Lincs 172 F6
Notts 171 F11
Cayton N Yorks 217 C11
Ceallan W Isles 296 F4
Ceann a Bhaigh W Isles 296 E3
Ceann a Bhàigh W Isles 305 J4
Ceannacroc Lodge Highld 290 B4
Ceann a Deas Loch Baghasdail W Isles 297 K3
Ceann Shiphoirt W Isles 305 G4
Ceann Tarabhaigh W Isles 305 G4
Cearsiadair W Isles 304 F5
Ceathramh Meadhanach W Isles 296 D4
Cefn Newport 59 B9
Powys 148 G5
Cefn Berain Conwy 165 B7
Cefn-brith Conwy 164 E6
Cefn-bryn-brain Carms 76 C2
Cefn-bychan Swansea 56 B4
Wrex 166 G3
Cefncaeau Carms 56 B4
Cefn Canol Powys 148 C4
Cefn-coch Conwy 164 B5
Cefn Coch Powys 129 C10
Powys 148 D2
Cefn-coed-y-cymmer M Tydf 77 D9f
Cefn Cribbwr Bridgend 57 E11
Cefn Cross Bridgend 57 E11
Cefn-ddwysarn Gwyn 147 B9
Cefn Einion Shrops 130 F5
Cefneithin Carms 75 C9
Cefn-eurgain Flint 166 B2
Cefn Fforest Caerph 77 F11
Cefn Glas Bridgend 57 E11
Cefn Golau Bl Gwent 77 D10
Cefn-gorwydd Powys 95 B8
Cefn Hengoed Caerph 77 F10
Cefn-hengoed Swansea 57 B7
Cefn Llwyd Ceredig 128 G2
Cefn-mawr Wrex 166 G3
Cefnpennar Rhondda 77 E8
Cefn Rhigos Rhondda 76 D6
Cefn-y-bedd Flint 166 D4
Cefn-y-Crib Torf 78 F2
Cefn-y-Garth Swansea 76 E2
Cefn-y-pant Carms 92 F3
Cegidfa / Guilsfield Powys 148 G4
Cei-bach Ceredig 111 F8
Ceinewydd / New Quay Ceredig 111 F7
Ceint Anglesey 179 F7
Ceinws Powys 128 B5
Cellan Ceredig 94 B2
Cellarhead Staffs 169 F7
Cellarhill Kent 70 G3
Celyn-Mali Flint 165 B11
Cemaes Anglesey 178 C5
Cemmaes Powys 128 B6
Cemmaes Road / Glantwymyn Powys 128 C6
Cenarth Carms 92 C5
Cenin Gwyn 163 F7
Central Invclyd 276 F5
Central Milton Keynes M Keynes 102 D6
Ceos W Isles 304 F5
Ceres Fife 287 F8
Ceri / Kerry Powys 130 F2
Cerne Abbas Dorset 29 G11
Cerney Wick Glos 81 F9
Cerrigceinwen Anglesey 178 G6
Cerrig Llwydion Neath 57 C9
Cerrig-mân Anglesey 179 C7
Cerrigydrudion Conwy 165 F7
Cess Norf 161 F8
Cessford Borders 262 E6
Ceunant Gwyn 163 C8
Chaceley Glos 99 E7
Chaceley Hole Glos 98 E6
Chaceley Stock Glos 99 F7
Chacewater Corn 4 G4
Chackmore Bucks 102 D3
Chacombe Northants 101 C9
Chadbury Worcs 99 B10
Chadderton Gtr Man 196 F2
Chadderton Fold Gtr Man 195 F11
Chaddesden Derby 153 B7
Chaddesley Corbett Worcs 117 C7
Chaddlehanger Devon 12 F5
Chaddlewood Plym 7 D11
Chaddleworth W Berks 64 D2
Chadkirk Gtr Man 184 D6
Chadlington Oxon 100 G6
Chadshunt Warks 118 G6
Chadsmoor Staffs 151 G9
Chadstone Northants 121 F7
Chad Valley W Mid 133 F10
Chadwell Leics 154 E5
Shrops 150 G5
Chadwell End Bedford 121 D11
Chadwell Heath London 68 B3
Chadwell St Mary Thurrock 68 D6
Chadwick Worcs 116 D6
Chadwick End W Mid 118 C4
Chadwick Green Mers 183 B8
Chaffcombe Som 28 E5
Chafford Hundred Thurrock 68 D5
Chagford Devon 13 D10
Chailey E Sus 36 D5
Chainbridge Cambs 139 C8
Chain Bridge Lincs 174 G4
Chainhurst Kent 53 D8
Chalbury Dorset 31 F8
Chalbury Common Dorset 31 F8
Chaldon Sur 51 B10
Chaldon Herring or East Chaldon Dorset 17 E11
Chale IoW 20 F5
Chale Green IoW 20 F5
Chalfont Common Bucks 85 G8
Chalfont Grove Bucks 85 G7
Chalfont St Giles Bucks 85 G7
Chalfont St Peter Bucks 85 G8
Chalford Glos 80 E5
Oxon 84 E2
Wilts 45 C11
Chalford Hill Glos 80 E5
Chalgrave C Beds 103 F10
Chalgrove Oxon 83 F10
Chalk Kent 69 E7
Chalk End Essex 87 C10
Chalkfoot Cumb 230 B2
Chalkhill Norf 141 C7
Chalkhouse Green Oxon 65 D8
Chalkshire Bucks 84 D4
Chalksole Kent 55 E9
Chalkway Som 28 F5
Chalkwell Kent 69 G11
Southend 69 B11
Challaborough Devon 8 G3
Challacombe Devon 41 E7
Challister Shetland 312 G7
Challoch Dumfries 236 C5
Challock Kent 54 C4
Chalmington Dorset 29 G9
Chalton C Beds 103 F10
Hants 34 D2
Chalvedon Essex 69 B8
Chalvey Slough 66 D3
Chalvington E Sus 23 D8
Chambercombe Devon 40 D4
Chamber's Green Kent 54 E2
Champson Devon 26 B4
Chance Inn Fife 287 F7
Chancery / Rhydgaled Ceredig 111 B11
Chance's Pitch Hereford 98 C4
Chandler's Cross Herts 85 F9
Worcs 98 D5
Chandler's Ford Hants 32 C6
Chandlers Green Hants 49 B8
Channel's End Bedford 122 F2
Channel Tunnel Kent 55 F7
Channerwick Shetland 313 L6
Chantry Devon 25 C9
Som 45 D8
Suff 108 C2
Chapel Corn 4 C6
Cumb 229 E10
Fife 280 C5
Chapel Allerton Som 44 C2
W Yorks 206 F2
Chapel Amble Corn 10 F5
Chapel Brampton Northants 120 D4
Chapel Chorlton Staffs 150 B6
Chapel Cleeve Som 42 E4
Chapel Cross E Sus 37 C10
Chapel End Bedford 103 B11
Bedford 122 F2
Cambs 138 G2
C Beds 103 C11
Ches E 167 G11
Essex 105 G11
Northants 138 F2
Warks 134 E6
Chapel-en-le-Frith Derbys 185 E9
Chapel Field Gtr Man 195 F9
Norf 161 E7
Chapel Fields W Mid 118 B6
York 207 C7
Chapelgate Lincs 157 E8
Chapel Green Herts 104 D6
Warks 119 E9
Warks 134 F5
Chapel Haddlesey N Yorks 198 B5
Chapelhall N Lanark 268 C5
Chapel Head Cambs 138 G6
Chapelhill Dumfries 248 E3
Highld 301 B8
N Ayrs 266 G4
Perth 286 D4
Perth 286 E3
Perth 286 E6
Chapel Hill Aberds 303 F10
Glos 79 E10
Lincs 174 E2
Mon 79 F8
N Yorks 206 D2
Chapelhouse Lancs 194 F4
Chapel Knapp Wilts 61 F11
Chapelknowe Dumfries 239 C8
Chapel Lawn Shrops 114 B6
Chapel-le-Dale N Yorks 212 D4
Chapel Leigh Som 27 B10
Chapel Mains Borders 271 G11
Chapel Milton Derbys 185 E9
Chapel of Garioch Aberds 303 G7
Chapel of Stoneywood Aberdeen 293 B10
Chapel on Leader Borders 271 G11
Chapel Outon Dumfries 236 E6
Chapel Plaister Wilts 61 F10
Chapel Row Essex 88 E3
E Sus 23 C10
W Berks 64 F5
Chapels Blackburn 195 C7
Cumb 210 C4
Chapel St Leonards Lincs 191 G9
Chapel Stile Cumb 220 D6
Chapelthorpe W Yorks 197 D10
Chapelton Angus 287 C10
Devon 25 B9
Highld 291 B11
S Lanark 268 F3
Chapeltown Blackburn 195 D8
Moray 302 G2
S Yorks 186 B5
W Yorks 206 F2
Chapel Town Corn 5 D7
Chapman's Hill Worcs 117 B9
Chapmanslade Wilts 45 D10
Chapman's Town E Sus 23 B10
Chapmans Well Devon 12 C3
Chapmore End Herts 86 B4
Chappel Essex 107 F7
Charaton Cross Corn 6 B6
Charcott Kent 52 D4
Chard Som 28 F4
Chard Junction Dorset 28 G4
Chardleigh Green Som 28 E4
Chardstock Devon 28 G4
Charfield S Glos 80 G2
Charfield Green S Glos 80 G2
Charfield Hill S Glos 80 G2
Charford Worcs 117 D9
Chargrove Glos 80 B6
Charing Kent 54 D3
Charing Cross Dorset 31 E10
Charing Heath Kent 54 D2
Charing Hill Kent 54 C3
Charingworth Glos 100 D4
Charlbury Oxon 82 B5
Charlcombe Bath 61 F8
Charlcutt Wilts 62 D3
Charlecote Warks 118 F5
Charlemont W Mid 133 E10
Charles Devon 41 G7
Charles Bottom Devon 41 G7
Charlesfield Borders 262 D3
Dumfries 238 D5
Charleshill Sur 49 E11
Charleston Angus 287 C7
Renfs 267 C9
Charlestown Aberdeen 293 C11
Corn 5 E10
Derbys 185 C8
Dorset 17 F9
Fife 279 E11
Gtr Man 195 G10
Gtr Man 195 G11
Highld 299 B8
Highld 300 E6
W Yorks 196 B3
W Yorks 205 F9
Charlestown of Aberlour Moray 302 E2
Charles Tye Suff 125 G10
Charlesworth Derbys 185 C8
Charleton Devon 8 G5
Charlinch Som 43 F8
Charlottetown Fife 286 F6
Charlton Hants 47 D11
Herts 104 F3
London 68 D2
Northants 101 D10
Northumb 251 F8
Oxon 64 B2
Redcar 226 B2
Som 28 B3
Som 44 E6
Som 45 C7
Sur 66 F5
Telford 149 G11
Wilts 30 C6
Wilts 46 B6
Wilts 62 B3
Worcs 99 B10
Worcs 116 C6
W Sus 34 E5
Charlton Abbots Glos 99 G10
Charlton Adam Som 29 B8
Charlton-All-Saints Wilts 31 C11
Charltonbrook S Yorks 186 B4
Charlton Down Dorset 17 C9
Charlton Horethorne Som 29 C11
Charlton Kings Glos 99 G9
Charlton Mackrell Som 29 B8
Charlton Marshall Dorset 30 G5
Charlton Musgrove Som 30 B2
Charlton on Otmoor Oxon 83 B9
Charlton on the Hill Dorset 30 G5
Charlton Park Glos 99 G9
Charlton St Peter Wilts 46 B6
Charlwood E Sus 51 G11
Hants 49 G7
Sur 51 E8
Charlynch Som 43 F8
Charminster Bmouth 19 C8
Dorset 17 C9
Charmouth Dorset 16 C3
Charnage Wilts 45 G10
Charndon Bucks 102 G3
Charnes Staffs 150 C5
Charney Bassett Oxon 82 G5
Charnock Green Lancs 194 D5
Charnock Hall S Yorks 186 E5
Charnock Richard Lancs 194 D5
Charsfield Suff 126 F5
Chart Corner Kent 53 C9
Charter Alley Hants 48 B5
Charterhouse Som 44 B3
Chartershall Stirling 278 C6
Charterville Allotments Oxon 82 C4
Chartham Kent 54 C6
Chartham Hatch Kent 54 B6
Chart Hill Kent 53 D9
Chartridge Bucks 84 E6
Chart Sutton Kent 53 D10
Charvil Wokingham 65 D9
Charwelton Northants 119 F10
Chase Cross London 87 G8
Chase End Street Worcs 98 D5
Chase Hill S Glos 61 B8
Chase Terrace Staffs 133 B10
Chasetown Staffs 133 B10
Chastleton Oxon 100 F4
Chasty Devon 24 G4
Chatburn Lancs 203 E11
Chatcull Staffs 150 C5
Chatford Shrops 131 B9
Chatham Caerph 59 B8
Medway 69 F9
Chatham Green Essex 88 B2
Chathill Northumb 264 D5
Chat Hill W Yorks 205 G8
Chatley Worcs 117 E7
Chattenden Medway 69 E9
Chatter End Essex 105 F9
Chatteris Cambs 139 F7
Chatterley Staffs 168 E4
Chattern Hill Sur 66 E5
Chatterton Lancs 195 D9
Chattisham Suff 107 C11
Chattle Hill Warks 134 E3
Chatto Borders 263 F7
Chatton Northumb 264 D3
Chaulden Herts 85 D8
Chaul End C Beds 103 G11
Chavel Shrops 149 G8
Chavenage Green Glos 80 F5
Chavey Down Brack 65 F11
Chawleigh Devon 26 E2
Chawley Oxon 83 E7
Chawson Worcs 117 E7
Chawston Bedford 122 F3
Chawton Hants 49 F8
Chaxhill Glos 80 C2
Chazey Heath Oxon 65 D7
Cheadle Gtr Man 184 D5
Staffs 169 G8
Cheadle Heath Gtr Man 184 D5
Cheadle Hulme Gtr Man 184 D5
Cheadle Park Staffs 169 G8
Cheam London 67 G8
Cheapside Herts 105 E8
Sur 50 B4
Windsor 66 F2
Chearsley Bucks 84 C2
Chebsey Staffs 151 D7
Checkendon Oxon 65 C7
Checkley Ches E 168 F2
Hereford 97 D11
Staffs 151 B10
Checkley Green Ches E 168 F2
Chedburgh Suff 124 F5
Cheddar Som 44 C3
Cheddington Bucks 84 B6
Cheddleton Staffs 169 E7
Cheddleton Heath Staffs 169 E7
Cheddon Fitzpaine Som 28 B2
Chedglow Wilts 80 G6
Chedgrave Norf 143 D7
Chedington Dorset 29 F7
Chediston Suff 127 B7
Chediston Green Suff 127 B7
Chedworth Glos 81 C9
Chedworth Laines Glos 81 C8
Chedzoy Som 43 F10
Cheeklaw Borders 272 E5
Cheeseman's Green Kent 54 F4
Cheetam Hill Gtr Man 195 G10
Cheglinch Devon 40 E4
Chegworth Kent 53 C10
Cheldon Devon 26 E2
Chelfham Devon 40 F6
Chelford Ches E 184 G4
Chellaston Derby 153 C7
Chell Heath Stoke 168 E5
Chellington Bedford 121 F9
Chells Herts 104 F5
Chelmarsh Shrops 132 F4
Chelmer Village Essex 88 D2
Chelmick Shrops 131 E9
Chelmondiston Suff 108 D4
Chelmorton Derbys 169 B10
Chelmsford Essex 88 D2
Chelmsine Som 27 D11
Chelmsley Wood W Mid 134 F3
Chelsea London 67 D9
Chelsfield London 68 G3
Chelsham Sur 51 B11
Chelston Som 27 C11
Torbay 9 C7
Chelston Heathfield Som 27 C11
Chelsworth Suff 107 B9
Chelsworth Common Suff 107 B9
Cheltenham Glos 99 G8
Chelveston Northants 121 D9
Chelvey N Som 60 F3
Chelvey Batch N Som 60 F3
Chelwood Bath 60 G6
Chelwood Common E Sus 36 B6
Chelwood Gate E Sus 36 B6
Chelworth Wilts 81 G7
Chelworth Lower Green Wilts 81 G9
Chelworth Upper Green Wilts 81 G9
Chelynch Som 45 E7
Chemistry Shrops 167 G8
Cheney Longville Shrops 131 G8
Chenhalls Corn 2 B3
Chenies Bucks 85 F8
Cheny Longville Shrops 131 G8
Chepstow Mon 79 G8
Chequerbent Gtr Man 195 F7
Chequerfield W Yorks 198 C3
Chequers Corner Norf 139 B9
Chequertree Kent 54 F4
Cherhill Wilts 62 E4
Cherington Glos 80 F6
Warks 100 D5
Cheristow Devon 24 B3
Cheriton Devon 41 D8
Hants 33 B9
Kent 55 F7
Swansea 56 C3
Cheriton Bishop Devon 13 C11
Cheriton Cross Devon 13 C11
Cheriton Fitzpaine Devon 26 F5
Cheriton or Stackpole Elidor Pembs 73 F7
Cherrington Telford 150 E3
Cherrybank Perth 286 E5
Cherry Burton E Yorks 208 E5
Cherry Green Essex 105 F11
Herts 105 F7
Cherry Hinton Cambs 123 F9
Cherry Orchard Shrops 149 G9
Worcs 117 G7
Cherry Tree Blackburn 195 B7
Gtr Man 185 C7
Cherrytree Hill Derby 153 B7
Cherry Willingham Lincs 189 G8
Chertsey Sur 66 F4
Chertsey Meads Sur 66 F5
Cheselbourne Dorset 17 B11
Chesham Bucks 85 E7
Gtr Man 195 E10
Chesham Bois Bucks 85 F7
Cheshunt Herts 86 E5
Chesley Kent 69 G11
Cheslyn Hay Staffs 133 B9
Chessetts Wood Warks 118 C3
Chessington London 67 G7
Chessmount Bucks 85 E7
Chestall Staffs 151 G11
Chester Ches W 166 B6
Chesterblade Som 45 E7
Chesterfield Derbys 186 G5
Staffs 134 B2
Chesterhill Midloth 271 B7
Chesterhope Northumb 251 F9
Chesterknowes Borders 262 D2
Chester-le-Street Durham 243 G7
Chester Moor Durham 233 B11
Chesters Borders 262 E4
Borders 262 G4
Chesterton Cambs 123 E9
Cambs 138 D2
Glos 81 E8
Oxon 101 G11
Shrops 132 D5
Staffs 168 F4
Warks 118 F6
Chesterton Green Warks 118 F6
Chesterwood Northumb 241 D8
Chestfield Kent 70 F6
Chestnut Hill Cumb 229 G11
Chestnut Street Kent 69 G11
Cheston Devon 8 D3
Cheswardine Shrops 150 D4
Cheswell Telford 150 F4
Cheswick Northumb 273 F10
Cheswick Buildings Northumb 273 F10
Cheswick Green W Mid 118 B2
Chetnole Dorset 29 F10
Chettiscombe Devon 27 E7
Chettisham Cambs 139 G10
Chettle Dorset 31 E7
Chetton Shrops 132 E3
Chetwode Bucks 102 F2
Chetwynd Aston Telford 150 F5
Cheveley Cambs 124 E3
Chevening Kent 52 B3
Cheverell's Green Herts 85 B9
Chevin End W Yorks 205 E9
Chevington Suff 124 F5
Chevithorne Devon 27 D7
Chew Magna Bath 60 G5
Chew Moor Gtr Man 195 F7
Chew Stoke Bath 60 G5
Chewton Keynsham Bath 61 F7
Chewton Mendip Som 44 C5
Cheylesmore W Mid 118 B6
Chichacott Devon 13 B8
Chicheley M Keynes 103 B8
Chichester W Sus 22 C5
Chickenley W Yorks 197 C9
Chickerell Dorset 17 E8
Chicklade Wilts 46 G2
Chickney Essex 105 F11
Chicksands C Beds 104 D2
Chicksgrove Wilts 46 G3
Chickward Hereford 114 G5
Chidden Hants 33 D11
Chiddingfold Sur 50 F3
Chiddingly E Sus 23 C8
Chiddingstone Kent 52 D3
Chiddingstone Causeway Kent 52 D4
Chiddingstone Hoath Kent 52 E3
Chideock Dorset 16 C4
Chidgley Som 42 F4
Chidham W Sus 22 C3
Chidswell W Yorks 197 C9
Chieveley W Berks 64 E3
Chignall St James Essex 87 D11
Chignall Smealy Essex 87 C11
Chigwell Essex 86 G6
Chigwell Row Essex 87 G7
Chilbolton Hants 47 F11
Chilbolton Down Hants 48 F2
Chilbridge Dorset 31 G7
Chilcomb Hants 33 B8
Chilcombe Dorset 16 C6
Som 42 F6
Chilcompton Som 44 C6
Chilcote Leics 152 G5
Childerditch Essex 68 B6
Childerley Gate Cambs 123 F7
Childer Thornton Ches W 182 F5
Child Okeford Dorset 30 E4
Childrey Oxon 63 B11
Childsbridge Kent 52 B5
Child's Ercall Shrops 150 E3
Child's Hill London 67 B8
Childswickham Worcs 99 D11
Childwall Mers 182 D6
Childwick Bury Herts 85 C10
Childwick Green Herts 85 C10
Chilfrome Dorset 17 B7
Chilgrove W Sus 34 E4
Chilham Kent 54 C5
Chilhampton Wilts 46 G5
Chilla Devon 24 G6
Chillaton Devon 12 E4
Chillenden Kent 55 C9
Chillerton IoW 20 E5
Chillesford Suff 127 G7
Chillingham Northumb 264 D3
Chillington Devon 8 G5
Som 28 E5
Chillmill Kent 53 E7
Chilmark Wilts 46 G3
Chilmington Green Kent 54 E3
Chilsham E Sus 23 C10
Chilson Oxon 82 B4
Som 28 G4
Chilson Common Som 28 G4
Chilsworthy Corn 12 G4
Devon 24 F4
Chiltern Green C Beds 85 B10
Chilthorne Domer Som 29 D8
Chiltington E Sus 36 D5
Chilton Bucks 83 C11
Durham 233 F11
Kent 71 G11
Oxon 64 B3
Suff 107 C7
Chilton Candover Hants 48 E5
Chilton Cantelo Som 29 C9
Chilton Foliat Wilts 63 E10
Chilton Lane Durham 234 E2
Chilton Moor T&W 234 B2
Chilton Polden Som 43 F11
Chilton Street Suff 106 B5
Chilton Trinity Som 43 F9
Chilvers Coton Warks 135 E7
Chilwell Notts 153 B10
Chilworth Hants 32 D6
Sur 50 D4
Chilworth Old Village Hants 32 D6
Chimney Oxon 82 E5
Chimney-end Oxon 82 B4
Chimney Street Suff 106 B4
Chineham Hants 49 C7
Chingford London 86 G5
Chingford Green London 86 G5
Chingford Hatch London 86 G5
Chinley Derbys 185 E8
Chinley Head Derbys 185 E9
Chinnor Oxon 84 E3
Chipley Som 27 C10
Chipmans Platt Glos 80 D3
Chipnall Shrops 150 C4
Chippenhall Green Suff 126 B5
Chippenham Cambs 124 D3
Wilts 62 E2
Chipperfield Herts 85 E8
Chipping Herts 105 E7
Lancs 203 E8
Chipping Barnet London 86 F2
Chipping Campden Glos 100 D3
Chipping Hill Essex 88 B4
Chipping Norton Oxon 100 F6
Chipping Ongar Essex 87 E8
Chipping Sodbury S Glos 61 C8
Chipping Warden Northants 101 B9
Chipstable Som 27 B8
Chipstead Kent 52 B3
Sur 51 B9
Chirbury Shrops 130 D5
Chirk Bank Shrops 148 B5
Chirk Green Wrex 148 B5
Chirk / Y Waun Wrex 148 B5
Chirmorrie S Ayrs 236 B4
Chirnside Borders 273 D7
Chirnsidebridge Borders 273 D7
Chirton T&W 243 D8
Wilts 46 B5
Chisbridge Cross Bucks 65 B10
Chisbury Wilts 63 F9
Chiselborough Som 29 E7
Chiseldon Swindon 63 D7
Chiserley W Yorks 196 B4
Chislehampton Oxon 83 F9
Chislehurst London 68 E2
Chislehurst West London 68 E2
Chislet Kent 71 G8
Chislet Forstal Kent 71 G8
Chiswell Dorset 17 G9
Chiswell Green Herts 85 E10
Chiswick London 67 D8
Chiswick End Cambs 105 B7
Chisworth Derbys 185 C7
Chitcombe E Sus 38 C4
Chithurst W Sus 34 C4
Chittering Cambs 123 C9
Chitterley Devon 26 G6
Chitterne Wilts 46 E3
Chittlehamholt Devon 25 C11
Chittlehampton Devon 25 B10
Chittoe Wilts 62 F3
Chitts Hills Essex 107 F9
Chitty Kent 71 G8
Chivelstone Devon 9 G10
Chivenor Devon 40 G4
Chivery Bucks 84 D6
Chobham Sur 66 G3
Choicelee Borders 272 E4
Cholderton Wilts 47 E8
Cholesbury Bucks 84 D6
Chollerford Northumb 241 C10
Chollerton Northumb 241 C10
Cholmondeston Ches E 167 C10
Cholsey Oxon 64 B5
Cholstrey Hereford 115 F9
Cholwell Bath 44 B6
Chop Gate N Yorks 225 F11
Choppington Northumb 253 G7
Chopwell T&W 242 F4
Chorley Ches E 167 E9
Lancs 194 D5
Shrops 132 G3
Staffs 151 G11
Chorley Common W Sus 34 B4
Chorleywood Herts 85 F8
Chorleywood Bottom Herts 85 F8
Chorleywood West Herts 85 F8
Chorlton Ches E 168 E2
Chorlton-cum-Hardy Gtr Man 184 C4
Chorlton Lane Ches W 167 F7
Choulton Shrops 131 F7
Chowdene T&W 243 F7
Chowley Ches W 167 D7
Chownes Mead W Sus 36 C4
Chreagain Highld 289 C10
Chrishall Essex 105 D8
Christchurch Cambs 139 D9
Dorset 19 C9
Glos 79 C9
Newport 59 B10
Christian Malford Wilts 62 D3
Christleton Ches W 166 B6
Christmas Common Oxon 84 G2
Christon N Som 43 B11
Christon Bank Northumb 264 E6
Christow Devon 14 D2
Chryston N Lanark 278 G3
Chub Tor Devon 7 B10
Chuck Hatch E Sus 52 G3
Chudleigh Devon 14 F3
Chudleigh Knighton Devon 14 F2
Chulmleigh Devon 25 E11
Chunal Derbys 185 C8
Church Lancs 195 B8
Churcham Glos 80 B3
Church Aston Telford 150 F4
Churchbank Shrops 114 B6
Church Brampton Northants 120 D4
Churchbridge Corn 6 D4
Staffs 133 B9
Church Brough Cumb 222 C5
Church Broughton Derbys 152 C4
Church Charwelton Northants 119 F10
Church Clough Lancs 204 F3
Church Common Hants 34 B2
Church Coombe Corn 4 G3
Church Cove Corn 2 G6
Church Crookham Hants 49 C10
Churchdown Glos 80 B5
Church Eaton Staffs 150 F6
Churchend Essex 89 G8
Essex 106 G2
Glos 80 D3
Reading 65 E7
S Glos 80 G2
Church End Bedford 122 F2
Bucks 84 B6
Bucks 84 D2
Cambs 121 C11
Cambs 123 C7
Cambs 123 D7
Cambs 138 G4
Cambs 139 B7
C Beds 85 B8
C Beds 103 E9
C Beds 103 G9
C Beds 104 D3
C Beds 122 G3
Essex 88 B2
Essex 105 C11
Essex 105 F11
Essex 106 F4
E Yorks 209 C7
Glos 80 D2
Glos 99 D7
Hants 49 B7
Herts 85 C10
Herts 85 F8
Herts 104 E5
Herts 105 G8
Lincs 156 C4
Lincs 190 B6
London 67 C8
London 86 G2
Norf 157 F10
Oxon 82 D5
Oxon 100 E6
Suff 108 D4
Sur 50 B5
Warks 134 E4
Warks 134 E5
Wilts 62 D4
W Mid 119 B7
Worcs 98 C6
Church Enstone Oxon 101 G7
Churches Green E Sus 23 B10
Church Fenton N Yorks 206 F6
Churchfield Hereford 98 B4
W Mid 133 E10
Churchfields Wilts 31 B10
Churchgate Herts 86 E4
Churchgate Street Essex 87 C7
Church Green Devon 15 B9
Norf 141 E11
Church Gresley Derbys 152 F5

Church Hanborough
Oxon 82 C6
Church Hill Ches W . . . 167 C10
Pembs 73 C7
Staffs 151 G10
W Mid 133 D9
Church Houghan Kent . . 71 D11
Church Houses N Yorks 226 F3
Churchill Devon 28 G4
Devon 40 E5
N Som 44 B2
Oxon 100 G5
Worcs 117 B7
Worcs 117 G8
Churchill Green N Som . 60 G2
Churchinford Som 28 E2
Church Knowle Dorset . . 18 E4
Church Langton Leics . 136 E4
Church Lawford Warks 119 B8
Church Lawton Ches E . 151 B10
Church Leigh Staffs . . . 151 B10
Church Lench Worcs . . . 117 G10
Church Mayfield Staffs 169 G11
Church Minshull
Ches E 167 C11
Churchmoor Rough
Shrops 131 F8
Church Norton W Sus . . 22 D5
Church Oakley Hants . . 48 C5
Churchover Warks 135 G10
Church Preen Shrops . . 131 D10
Church Pulverbatch
Shrops 131 C8
Churchstanton Som . . . 27 E11
Churchstoke Powys . . . 130 E5
Churchstow Devon 8 F4
Church Stowe Northants 106 C5
Church Street Kent 69 E8
Church Stretton Shrops. 131 E9
Churchtown Corn 11 F7
Cumb 230 C3
Derbys 170 C3
Devon 24 G3
Devon 41 E7
IoM 192 C5
Lancs 202 E5
Mers 193 D11
Shrops 130 F5
Som 44 C6
Church Town Corn 4 G3
Leics 153 F7
N Lincs 199 F9
Sur 51 C11
Church Village Rhondda . 58 B5
Church Warsop Notts . . 171 B9
Church Westcote Glos . . 100 G4
Church Whitfield Kent . . 55 D10
Church Wilne Derbys . . 153 C8
Churchwood W Sus 35 D8
Churnet Grange Staffs 169 E7
Churnsike Lodge
Northumb 240 B5
Churscombe Torbay 9 C7
Churston Ferrers Torbay . 9 D8
Churt Sur 49 F11
Churton Ches W 166 D6
Churwell W Yorks 197 B9
Chute Cadley Wilts 47 C10
Chute Standen Wilts. . . 47 C10
Chwefford Conwy 180 G4
Chwilog Gwyn 145 B8
Chwitffordd / Whitford
Flint 181 F10
Chyandour Corn 1 C5
Chyanvounder Corn 2 E5
Chycoose Corn 3 B8
Chynhale Corn 2 C2
Chynoweth Corn 2 C2
Chyvarloe Corn 2 E5
Cicelyford Mon 79 E8
Cilan Uchaf Gwyn 144 E5
Cilau Pembs 91 D8
Cilcain Flint 165 B11
Cilcennin Ceredig 111 E10
Cilcewydd Powys 130 C4
Cilfor Gwyn 146 B2
Cilfrew Neath 76 E3
Cilfynydd Rhondda 77 G9
Cilgerran Pembs 92 C3
Cilgwyn Carms 94 F4
Ceredig 92 C6
Gwyn 163 E7
Pembs 91 D11
Ciliau Aeron Ceredig . . . 111 F9
Cill Amhlaidh W Isles . . 297 G3
Cill Donnain W Isles . . . 297 J3
Cill Bhrighde W Isles . . 297 K3
Cill Eighlas W Isles . . . 297 K3
Cill Pheadair W Isles . . 297 K3
Cilmaengwyn Neath 76 D2
Cilmery Powys 113 G10
Cilsan Carms 93 G11
Ciltalgarth Gwyn 164 G5
Ciltwrch Powys 96 C3
Cilybebyll Neath 76 E2
Cil y coed / Caldicot
Mon 60 B3
Cilycwm Carms 94 D5
Cimla Neath 57 C8
Cinderford Glos 79 C11
Cinderhill Derbys 170 F5
Nottingham 171 G8
Cinder Hill Gtr Man . . . 195 F9
Kent 52 D4
W Mid 133 E8
W Sus 36 B5
Cinnamon Brow Warr . . 183 C10
Cippenham Slough 66 C2
Cippyn Pembs 92 B2
Circebost W Isles 304 E3
Cirencester Glos 81 E8
Ciribhig W Isles 304 D3
City London 67 C10
Powys 130 F4
V Glam 58 D3
City Dulas Anglesey . . . 179 D7
Clabhach Argyll 288 D3
Clachaig Argyll 276 E2
Argyll 292 B2
N Ayrs 255 E10
Clachan Argyll 255 B8
Argyll 275 B8
Argyll 284 E5
Argyll 289 E10
Highld 295 B7
Highld 298 C4
Highld 307 L6
W Isles 297 G3
Clachaneasy Dumfries . . 236 B5
Clachanmore Dumfries . 236 E2
Clachan na Luib
W Isles 296 E4
Clachan of Campsie
E Dunb 278 F2
Clachan of Glendaruel
Argyll 275 E10
Clachan-Seil Argyll . . . 275 B8

Clachan Strachur Argyll 284 G4
Clachbreck Argyll 275 D11
Clachnabrain Angus . . 292 G5
Clachtoll Highld 307 G5
Clackmannan Clack . . . 279 C8
Clackmarras Moray . . . 302 D2
Clacton-on-Sea Essex . 89 B11
Cladach N Ayrs 256 B2
Cladach Chairinis
W Isles 296 F4
Cladach Chireboist
W Isles 296 E3
Claddach Argyll 254 B2
Claddach-knockline
W Isles 296 E3
Cladich Argyll 284 E4
Cladich Steading Argyll . 284 E4
Cladswell Worcs 117 F10
Claggan Highld 289 E8
Highld 290 F3
Perth 285 D11
Claigan Highld 298 D2
Claines Worcs 117 F7
Clandown Bath 45 B7
Clanfield Hants 33 D11
Oxon 82 E3
Clanking Bucks 84 D4
Clanville Hants 47 D10
Som 44 G6
Wilts 62 D2
Claonaig Argyll 255 B9
Claonel Highld 309 J5
Clapgate Dorset 31 G8
Herts 105 G8
Clapham Bedford 121 G10
Devon 14 D3
London 67 D9
N Yorks 212 F4
W Sus 35 F9
Clapham Green
Bedford 121 G10
N Yorks 205 B10
Clapham Hill Kent 70 G6
Clapham Park London . . 67 E9
Clap Hill Kent 54 F5
Clapper Corn 10 G6
Clapper Hill Kent 53 F10
Clappers Borders 273 D8
Clappersgate Cumb. . . . 221 E7
Clapphoull Shetland . . . 313 L6
Clapton Som 28 F6
Som 44 C6
W Berks 63 E11
Clapton in Gordano
N Som 60 E3
Clapton-on-the-Hill
Glos 81 B11
Clapton Park London . . 67 B11
Clapworthy Devon 25 C11
Clarach Ceredig 128 G2
Clarack Aberds 292 D6
Clara Vale T&W 242 E4
Clarbeston Pembs 91 G10
Clarbeston Road Pembs . 91 G10
Clarborough Notts. 188 E2
Clardon Highld 310 C5
Clare Oxon 83 F11
Suff 106 B5
Clarebrand Dumfries . . 237 C9
Claregate W Mid 133 C7
Clarencefield Dumfries . 238 D3
Clarence Park N Som . . . 59 G10
Clarendon Park
Leicester 135 C11
Clareston Pembs 73 C7
Clarilaw Borders 262 D3
Borders 262 F2
Clarken Green Hants. . . 48 C5
Clarksfield Gtr Man . . . 196 G2
Clark's Green Sur 51 F7
Clark's Hill Lincs 157 E7
Clarkston E Renf 267 D11
N Lanark 268 B5
Clase Swansea 57 B7
Clashandorran Highld . . 300 E5
Clashcoig Highld 309 K6
Clashgour Argyll 308 G4
Clashindarroch Aberds . 302 F4
Clashmore Highld 306 F5
Highld 309 L7
Clashnessie Highld . . . 306 F5
Clashnoir Moray 302 G2
Clate Shetland 313 G7
Clatford Wilts 63 F7
Clatford Oakcuts Hants . 47 F10
Clathy Perth 286 F3
Clatt Aberds 302 G5
Clatter Powys 129 E9
Clatterford IoW 20 D5
Clatterford End Essex . . 87 D9
Essex 87 D9
Clatterin Bridge Aberds 293 F8
Clatto Fife 287 F8
Clatworthy Som 42 G5
Clauchlands Argyll . . . 256 C2
Claughton Lancs 202 E6
Lancs 211 F11
Mers 182 D4
Clavelshay Som 43 G9
Claverdon Warks 118 E3
Claverham N Som 60 F2
Claverhambury Essex . . 86 E6
Clavering Essex 105 E9
Claverley Shrops 132 E5
Claverton Bath 61 G9
Claverton Down Bath . . 61 G9
Clawdd-côch V Glam . . . 58 D5
Clawdd-newydd Denb . . 165 E9
Clawdd Poncen Denb . . 165 G9
Clawthorpe Cumb 211 D10
Clawton Devon 12 B3
Claxby Lincs 189 C10
Lincs 191 G7
Claxby St Andrew Lincs 191 G7
Claxton Norf 142 C6
N Yorks 216 A3
Claybokie Aberds 292 D2
Clay Common Suff 143 G9
Clay Coton Northants . . 119 B11
Clay Cross Derbys. 170 C5
Claydon Glos 99 B8
Oxon 119 G9
Suff 126 G2
Clay End Herts 104 F6
Claygate Dumfries 239 B9
Kent 52 C6
Kent 53 E8
Sur 67 G7
Claygate Cross Kent . . . 52 B6
Clayhall Hants 21 B8

Clayhidon Devon 27 D11
Clayhill E Sus 38 C4
Hants 32 F4
Clay Hill Bristol 60 E6
London 86 F4
W Berks 64 E5
Clayhithe Cambs 123 E10
Clayholes Angus 287 D9
Clay Lake Lincs 156 E5
Clayland Stirling 277 D11
Clay Mills Derbys 152 D5
Clayock Highld 310 D5
Claypit Hill Cambs 123 G7
Claypits Devon 27 B7
Glos 80 D3
Kent 55 B9
Suff 140 G4
Claypole Lincs 172 F5
Clay Street Suff 125 B11
Clayton Gtr Man 184 B5
Staffs 168 G5
S Yorks 198 F3
W Sus 36 E3
W Yorks 205 G8
Clayton Brook Lancs . . 194 C5
Clayton Green Lancs . . 194 C5
Clayton Heights
W Yorks 205 G8
Clayton-le-Dale Lancs . 203 G9
Clayton-le-Moors
Lancs 203 G10
Clayton-le-Woods
Lancs 194 C5
Clayton West W Yorks . . 197 E9
Clayworth Notts 188 D2
Cleadale Highld 294 G6
Cleadon T&W 243 E9
Cleadon Park T&W 243 E9
Cleasby N Yorks 224 C5
Cleat Orkney 314 B4
Orkney 314 H4
Cleatlam Durham 224 B2
Cleator Cumb 219 B10
Cleator Moor Cumb . . . 219 B10
Cleave Devon 28 G2
Clebrig Highld 308 F5
Cleckheaton W Yorks . . 197 B7
Cleddon Mon 79 E8
Cleedownton Shrops . . . 131 G11
Cleehill Shrops 115 B11
Cleekhimin N Lanark . . 268 D5
Cleemarsh Shrops 131 G11
Clee St Margaret
Shrops 131 G11
Cleestanton Shrops . . . 115 B11
Cleethorpes NE Lincs . 201 F10
Cleeton St Mary Shrops 116 B2
Suff 125 E9
Cleeve Glos 80 C2
N Som 60 F3
Oxon 64 C6
Cleeve Hill Glos 99 F9
Cleeve Prior Worcs 99 B11
Cleghorn S Lanark 269 F8
Clegyrnant Powys 129 B8
Clehonger Hereford . . . 97 D9
Cleirwy / Clyro Powys . . 96 C4
Cleish Perth 279 B11
Cleland N Lanark 268 D5
Clements End Glos 79 D9
Clement's End C Beds . . 85 B8
Clement Street Kent . . . 68 E4
Clench Wilts 63 G7
Clench Common Wilts. . 63 F7
Clencher's Mill Hereford . 98 D3
Clenchwarton Norf . . . 157 E11
Clennell Northumb 251 B11
Clent Worcs 117 B8
Cleobury Mortimer
Shrops 116 B3
Cleobury North Shrops . 132 F2
Cleongart Argyll 255 D7
Clephanton Highld 301 D8
Clerkenwater Corn 5 B11
Clerkenwell London . . . 67 C10
Clerk Green W Yorks . . 197 C8
Clerklands Borders 262 E2
Clermiston Edin 280 G3
Clestrain Orkney 314 F3
Cleuch Head Borders . . 262 G3
Cleughbrae Dumfries . . 238 C3
Clevancy Wilts 62 D5
Clevans Renfs 267 B7
Clevedon N Som 60 E2
Cleveley Oxon 101 G7
Cleveleys Lancs 202 E2
Cleverton Wilts 62 B3
Clevis Bridgend 57 F10
Clewer Som 44 C2
Clewer Green Windsor . . 66 D2
Clewer New Town
Windsor 66 D2
Clewer Village Windsor . 66 D2
Cley next the Sea Norf . 177 E11
Cliaid W Isles 297 L2
Cliasmol W Isles 305 H2
Cliburn Cumb 231 G7
Click Mill Orkney 314 D3
Cliddesden Hants 48 D6
Cliff Derbys 185 D8
Warks 134 D4
Cliffburn Angus 287 C10
Cliffe Lancs 203 G10
Medway 69 D8
N Yorks 207 G9
N Yorks 224 B4
Cliff End E Sus 38 E5
W Sus 196 D6
Cliffe Woods Medway . . 69 E8
Clifford Devon 24 C4
Hereford 96 B4
W Yorks 206 E4
Clifford Chambers
Warks 118 G3
Clifford's Mesne Glos . . 98 G4
Cliffs End Kent 71 G10
Clifftown Southend 69 B11
Clifton Bristol 60 E5
C Beds 104 D3
Ches W 183 F8
Cumb 230 F6
Derbys 169 G11
Devon 40 E5
Gtr Man 195 G9
Lancs 202 G5
Northumb 252 G6
Nottingham 153 C11
N Yorks 205 D9
Oxon 101 E9
S Yorks 186 B6
Stirling 285 E10
S Yorks 187 B8
Worcs 98 B6
York 207 C7
Clifton Campville Staffs 152 G5
Cliftoncote Borders . . . 263 E8

Clifton Green Gtr Man . . 195 G9
Clifton Hampden Oxon . . 83 F8
Clifton Junction
Gtr Man 195 G9
Clifton Manor C Beds . . 104 D3
Clifton Maybank Dorset . 29 E9
Clifton Moor York 207 B7
Clifton Reynes
M Keynes 121 G8
Clifton upon Dunsmore
Warks 119 B10
Clifton upon Teme
Worcs 116 F4
Cliftonville Kent 71 E11
N Lanark 268 B4
Norf 160 B6
Climping W Sus 35 G8
Climpy S Lanark 269 D8
Clink Som 45 D9
Clinkham Wood Mers . . 183 B8
Clint N Yorks 205 B10
Clint Green Norf 159 G10
Clintmains Borders 262 C4
Clints N Yorks 224 E2
Cliobh W Isles 304 E2
Clipiau Gwyn 146 G6
Clippesby Norf 161 G8
Clippings Green Norf . . 159 G10
Clipsham Rutland 155 F9
Clipston Northants 136 G4
Notts 154 C2
Clipstone C Beds 103 F8
Notts 171 C9
Clitheroe Lancs 203 E10
Cliuthar W Isles 305 J3
Clive Ches W 167 C11
Shrops 149 E10
Clive Green Ches W . . . 167 C11
Clive Vale E Sus 38 E4
Clivocast Shetland 312 C8
Clixby Lincs 200 G6
Cloatley Wilts 81 G7
Cloatley End Wilts 81 G7
Clocaenog Denb 165 E9
Clochan Aberds 303 D9
Moray 302 C4
Clock Face Mers 183 C8
Clock House London . . . 67 G9
Clockmill Borders 272 E5
Clock Mills Hereford . . . 96 F5
Cloddiau Powys 130 B4
Cloddymoss Moray 301 D9
Clodock Hereford 96 F6
Cloford Som 45 E8
Cloford Common Som . . 45 E8
Cloigyn Carms 74 C6
Clola Aberds 303 E10
Clophill C Beds 103 D11
Clopton Northants 137 G11
Suff 126 G4
Clopton Corner Suff . . . 126 G4
Clopton Green Suff 124 G5
Suff 125 E9
Closeburn Dumfries . . . 247 E9
Close Clark IoM 192 E3
Close House Durham . . 233 F10
Closworth Som 29 E9
Clothall Herts 104 E5
Clothall Common Herts . 104 E5
Clotton Ches W 167 C8
Clotton Common
Ches W 167 C8
Cloudesley Bush Warks . 135 F9
Clouds Hereford 97 D11
Cloud Side Gtr Man . . . 196 D2
Clough Gtr Man 196 C2
Gtr Man 196 F2
W Yorks 196 E5
Clough Dene Durham . . 242 F5
Cloughfold Lancs 195 C10
Clough Foot W Yorks . . 196 C2
Clough Hall Staffs 168 E4
Clough Head W Yorks . . 196 C5
Cloughton N Yorks 227 G10
Cloughton Newlands
N Yorks 227 F10
Clounlaid Highld 289 D9
Clousta Shetland 313 H5
Clouston Orkney 314 E2
Clova Aberds 302 G4
Angus 292 F5
Clovelly Devon 24 C4
Clove Lodge Durham . . . 223 B8
Clovenfords Borders . . . 261 B10
Clovenstone Aberds . . . 293 B9
Cloves Moray 301 C11
Clovullin Highld 290 G2
Clowance Wood Corn . . . 2 C4
Clow Bridge Lancs 195 B10
Clows Top Worcs 116 C4
Cloy Wrex 166 G5
Cluanie Inn Highld 290 B2
Cluanie Lodge Highld . . 290 B2
Clubmoor Mers 182 C5
Clubworthy Corn 11 C11
Cluddley Telford 150 G2
Clun Shrops 130 G6
Clunbury Shrops 131 G7
Clunderwen Carms 73 B10
Clune Highld 301 D9
Highld 301 D9
Clunes Corn 4 E5
Clunes Green Suff 125 F7
Clungunford Shrops . . . 115 B7
Clunie Aberds 302 D6
Perth 286 C5
Clunton Shrops 130 G6
Cluny Fife 280 B4
Cluny Castle Aberds . . . 293 B8
Highld 291 D8
Clutton Bath 44 B6
Ches W 167 D7
Clutton Hill Bath 44 B6
Clwt-grugoer Conwy . . . 165 C7
Clwt-y-bont Gwyn 163 B10
Clwydyfagwyr M Tydf . . 77 D8
Clydach Mon 78 C2
Swansea 75 D11
Clydach Terrace Powys . 77 C11
Clydach Vale Rhondda . . 77 G7
Clydebank W Dunb 277 G9
Hereford 98 C4
Notts 172 E4
Clynder Argyll 276 E4
Clyne Neath 76 E4
Clynelish Highld 311 J2
Clynnog-fawr Gwyn . . . 162 F6
Clyro / Cleirwy Powys . . 96 C4
Clyst Honiton Devon . . . 14 C5
Clyst Hydon Devon 27 G8
Clyst St George Devon . . 14 D5
Clyst St Lawrence Devon 27 G8
Clyst St Mary Devon . . . 14 C5
Cnip W Isles 304 E2
Cnoc Amhlaigh W Isles . 304 E7
Cnoc an t-Solais
W Isles 304 D6
Cnocbreac Argyll 274 F5
Cnoc Fhionn Highld . . . 295 D10
Cnoc Màiri W Isles 304 E6
Cnoc Rolum W Isles . . . 296 F3
Cnwch-coch Ceredig . . . 112 B3
Cnwcau Pembs 92 C3
Coachford Aberds 302 E4

Coad's Green Corn 11 F11
Coal Aston Derbys 186 F5
Coal Bank Darl 234 C3
Coalbrookdale Telford . . 132 C3
Coalbrookvale Bl Gwent . 166 E3
Coalburn S Lanark 259 C8
Coalburns T&W 242 E4
Coalcleugh Northumb . . 232 B2
Coaley Glos 80 E3
Coaley Peak Glos 80 E3
Coalford Aberds 293 D10
Coalhall E Ayrs 257 F10
Coalhill Essex 88 F3
Coalmoor Telford 132 B3
Coalpit Field Warks . . . 135 F7
Coalpit Heath S Glos . . . 61 C7
Coalpit Hill Staffs 168 E4
Coal Pool W Mid 133 C10
Coalsnaughton Clack . . 279 B8
Coaltown of Balgonie
Fife 280 B5
Coaltown of Wemyss
Fife 280 B6
Coalville Leics 153 G8
Coalway Glos 79 C9
Coanwood Northumb . . . 240 F5
Coarsewell Devon 8 E4
Coat Som 29 C7
Coatbridge N Lanark . . 268 C4
Coatdyke N Lanark 268 C5
Coate Swindon 63 C7
Wilts 62 G4
Coates Cambs 138 D6
Glos 81 E7
Lancs 204 D3
Lincs 188 E6
Notts 188 E4
W Sus 35 D7
Coatham Redcar 235 F7
Coatham Mundeville
Darl 233 G11
Coatsgate Dumfries . . . 248 B3
Cobairdy Aberds 302 E5
Cobbaton Devon 25 B10
Cobbler's Corner Worcs 116 F5
Cobbler's Green Norf . . 142 E5
Cobbler's Plain Mon . . . 79 E7
Cobbs Warr 183 D10
Cobb's Cross Glos 98 E5
Cobbs Fenn Essex 106 E5
Cobby Syke N Yorks . . . 205 B9
Cobham Kent 69 F7
Sur 66 G6
Cobhall Common
Hereford 97 D9
Cobholm Island Norf . . . 143 B10
Cobleland Stirling 277 B10
Cobler's Green Essex . . 87 B11
Cobley Dorset 31 C8
Cobley Hill Worcs 117 C10
Cobnash Hereford 115 E9
Cobridge Stoke 168 F5
Cobscot Shrops 150 B3
Coburty Aberds 303 C9
Cock Alley Derbys 186 G5
Cock Bank Wrex 166 F5
Cock Bevington Warks . 117 G11
Cock Clarks Essex 88 E4
Cockden Lancs 204 G3
Cockayne N Yorks 226 F2
Cockayne Hatley C Beds 104 B5
Cock Bank Wrex 166 F5
Cock Blow Staffs 73 C10
Cockburnspath Borders . 282 C4
Cock and End Suff 124 G4
Cockenzie and Port Seton
E Loth 281 F8
Cockerham Lancs 202 C5
Cockermouth Cumb . . . 229 E8
Cockernhoe Herts 104 G2
Cockernhoe Green
Herts 104 G2
Cockersdale W Yorks . . 197 B8
Cockerton Darl 224 B5
Cockett Swansea 56 C6
Cockfield Durham 233 G8
Suff 125 G8
Cockfosters London . . . 86 F3
Cock Gate Hereford . . . 115 D9
Cock Green Essex 87 B11
Cockhill Som 44 G6
Cocking W Sus 34 D5
Cocking Causeway
W Sus 34 D5
Cockington Torbay 9 C7
Cocklake Som 44 D2
Cocklaw Northumb 241 C10
Cockleford Glos 81 C7
Cockley Beck Cumb . . . 220 E4
Cockley Cley Norf 140 C5
Cockley Hill W Yorks . . . 197 D7
Cock Marling E Sus 38 D5
Cockpole Green
Wokingham 65 C9
Cocks Corn 4 E5
Cocks Green Suff 125 F7
Cockshead Ceredig 112 F2
Cockshoot Hereford . . . 97 D11
Cockshutford Shrops . . 131 F11
Cockshutt Shrops 132 G4
Cock Street Kent 53 C9
Suff 107 D9
Cockthorpe Norf 177 E7
Cockwells Corn 2 C2
Cockwood Devon 14 E5
Cockyard Derbys 185 F8
Hereford 97 E8
Codda Corn 11 F9
Coddenham Suff 126 G2
Coddenham Green Suff . 126 G2
Coddington Ches W . . . 167 D7
Hereford 98 C4
Notts 172 E4
Codford St Mary Wilts. . 46 F3
Codford St Peter Wilts. . 46 F3
Codicote Herts 86 B2
Codicote Bottom Herts . 86 B2
Codmore Hill W Sus . . . 35 C9
Codnor Derbys 170 F6
Codnor Breach Derbys . 170 F6
Codnor Gate Derbys . . . 170 F6
Codnor Park Derbys . . . 170 F6
Codrington S Glos 61 D8
Codsall Staffs 133 B7
Codsall Wood Staffs . . . 132 B6
Codsend Som 41 F11
Coed-Cae Bl Gwent . . . 77 D11
Torf 78 F3
Coed Cwnwr Mon 78 F6
Coed Eva Torf 78 G3
Coedkernew Newport . . 59 C9

Coed Llai / Leeswood
Flint 166 D3
Coed Morgan Mon 78 C5
Coedpoeth Wrex 166 E3
Coed-Talon Flint 166 D3
Coedway Powys 148 G6
Coed-y-bryn Ceredig . . . 93 C7
Coed-y-caerau Newport . 78 G6
Coed-y-fedw Mon 78 D6
Coed y Garth Ceredig . . 128 E5
Coed-y-paen Mon 78 F4
Coed-y-parc Gwyn 163 B10
Coed-yr-ynys Powys . . . 96 G3
Coed Ystumgwern
Gwyn 145 E11
Coed-y-wlad Powys . . . 130 B4
Coelbren Powys 76 C4
Coffee Hall M Keynes . . 103 D7
Coffinswell Devon 9 B7
Cofton Devon 14 E5
Cofton Common
W Mid 117 B10
Cofton Hackett Worcs . . 117 B10
Cogan V Glam 59 E7
Cogenhoe Northants . . . 120 E6
Cogges Oxon 82 D5
Coggeshall Essex 106 G6
Coggeshall Hamlet
Essex 107 G7
Coggins End Herts 85 B7
Coignafearn Lodge
Highld 291 B9
Coignascallan Highld . . 291 B9
Coig Peighinnean
W Isles 304 C6
Coig Peighinnean Bhuirgh
W Isles 304 B7
Coilacriech Aberds 292 D5
Coilantogle Stirling 285 G9
Coileasan Argyll 284 G6
Coilleag W Isles 297 K3
Coillemore Highld 300 B6
Coillore Highld 294 B5
Coirea-chrombe Stirling 285 G9
Coireag Borders 261 B10
Coity Bridgend 58 C2
Col W Isles 304 D6
Colaboll Highld 309 H5
Colan Corn 5 C7
Colaton Raleigh Devon . . 15 D7
Colbost Highld 298 E2
Colburn N Yorks 224 F3
Colby Cumb 231 G9
IoM 192 E3
Norf 160 C5
Colchester Essex 107 F10
Colchester Green Suff . . 125 F8
Colcot V Glam 58 F6
Cold Ash W Berks 64 F4
Cold Ash Hill Hants . . . 49 G10
Cold Aston Glos 81 B10
Coldbackie Highld 308 D6
Cold and End Suff 124 G4
Coldbrook Powys 96 D3
Cold Christmas Herts . . 86 B5
Cold Cotes N Yorks 212 E4
Coldean Brighton 36 F4
Coldeast Devon 14 G2
Colden Derbys 169 D10
Cold Elm Glos 98 E6
Colden W Yorks 196 C3
Cold Hanworth Lincs . . 189 E8
Coldharbour Corn 4 F5
Devon 27 E9
Dorset 17 E9
Glos 79 E9
Kent 52 C5
London 68 D4
Sur 50 E6
Cold Harbour Dorset . . 18 E4
Herts 85 E10
Kent 69 G11
Lincs 189 E8
Oxon 64 D6
Wilts 45 D11
Cold Hatton Telford . . . 150 E2
Cold Hatton Heath
Telford 150 E2
Cold Hesledon Durham . 234 B4
Cold Hiendley W Yorks . 197 E11
Cold Higham Northants . 120 G3
Coldingham Borders . . . 273 B8
Cold Inn Pembs 73 D10
Cold Kirby N Yorks 215 C10
Coldmeece Staffs 151 C7
Cold Moss Heath
Ches E 168 C3
Cold Newton Leics 136 B4
Cold Northcott Corn . . . 11 D10
Cold Norton Essex 88 E4
Coldoch Stirling 278 B3
Cold Overton Leics 154 G5
Norf 142 B2
Cold Row Lancs 202 E3
Coldred Kent 55 D9
Coldridge Devon 25 F10
Cold Row Lancs 202 E3
Coldstream Angus 287 D7
Borders 263 B8
Coldvreath Corn 5 D9
Som 45 D7
Coldwaltham W Sus. . . . 35 D8
Cold Well Staffs 151 G11
Coldwells Aberds 303 E11
Coldwells Croft Aberds . 302 G5
Cole Som 45 G7
Colebatch Shrops 130 F6
Colebrook Devon 27 B8
Colebrooke Devon 13 B11
Coleburn Moray 302 D2
Coleby Lincs 173 C7
N Lincs 199 D11
Coleford Devon 26 G2
Glos 79 C9
Som 45 D7
Coleford Water Som . . . 42 G6
Colegate End Norf 142 F3
Cole Green Herts 86 C3
Herts 105 G8
Cole Henley Hants 48 C3

Chu-Con 369

Combe Devon 7 G10
Devon 8 B4
Devon 9 B3
E Sus 37 B10
Hereford 114 E6
Oxon 82 B6
Som 28 B6
W Berks 63 G11
Combe Almer Dorset . . . 18 B5
Combebow Devon 12 D5
Combe Common Sur . . . 50 F3
Combe Down Bath 61 G9
Combe Fishacre Devon . . . 8 C6
Combe Florey Som 43 G7
Combe Hay Bath 45 B8
Combeinteignhead
Devon 14 G4
Combe Martin Devon . . . 40 D5
Combe Moor Hereford . . 115 E7
Combe Pafford Torbay . . . 9 B8
Combe Raleigh Devon . . 27 G11
Comberbach Ches W . . . 183 F10
Comberford Staffs 134 B4
Comberton Cambs 123 F7
Hereford 115 E9
Combe St Nicholas Som . 28 E4
Combe Throop Som 30 C2
Combridge Staffs 151 B11
Combrook Warks 118 G6
Combs Derbys 185 F8
Suff 125 F10
Combs Ford Suff 125 F11
Combwich Som 43 E9
Comers Aberds 293 C8
Come-to-Good Corn 4 G6
Comeytrowe Som 28 C2
Comford Corn 2 B6
Comfort Corn 2 D6
Comhampton Worcs . . . 116 D6
Comins Coch Ceredig . . 128 G2
Comiston Edin 270 B4
Comley Shrops 131 D9
Commercial End
Cambs 123 E11
Commins Capel Betws
Ceredig 112 F2
Commins Coch Powys . . 128 C6
Commin Cefn-Ilwyn
Mon 78 G4
Commondale N Yorks . . 226 C3
Common Edge Blackpool 202 G2
Common End Cumb 228 G6
Derbys 170 C6
Common Hill Hereford . . 97 E11
Commonmoor Corn 6 B4
Common Moor Corn 6 B4
Common Platt Wilts 62 B6
Commonside Ches W . . . 183 G8
Derbys 170 G2
Notts 171 D7
Common Side Ches W . . 167 B9
Derbys 186 F4
Derbys 185 E8
Commonwood Herts . . . 85 E8
Shrops 149 D9
Wrex 166 E5
Common-y-coed Mon . . 60 B2
Comp Kent 52 B6
Compass Som 43 G9
Compstall Gtr Man 185 C7
Compton Devon 169 F11
Devon 9 C7
Hants 32 B4
Hants 33 B7
Plym 7 D9
Staffs 132 G6
Sur 49 D11
Sur 50 D3
W Berks 64 D4
W Mid 133 C7
Wilts 46 C6
W Sus 34 E3
W Yorks 206 E3
Compton Abbas Dorset . 30 D5
Compton Abdale Glos . . 81 B9
Compton Bassett Wilts . 62 E4
Oxon 63 B9
Compton Beauchamp
Oxon 63 B9
Compton Bishop Som . . 43 B11
Compton Chamberlayne
Wilts 31 B8
Compton Common Bath . 60 G6
Compton Dando Bath . . 60 G6
Compton Dundon Som . . 44 G3
Compton Durville Som . . 28 D6
Compton End Hants 33 B7
Compton Green Glos . . . 98 F4
Compton Greenfield
S Glos 60 C5
Compton Martin Bath . . 44 B4
Compton Pauncefoot
Som 29 B10
Compton Valence Dorset 17 C7
Comrie Fife 279 D10
Perth 285 E11
Comrue Dumfries 248 F3
Conaglen House Highld . 290 G2
Conanby S Yorks 187 B6
Conchra Argyll 275 E11
Highld 295 C10
Concord T&W 243 F8
Concraigie Perth 286 C5
Conder Green Lancs . . . 202 B5
Conderton Worcs 99 D9
Condicote Glos 100 F3
Condorrat N Lanark . . . 278 G4
Condover Shrops 131 B9
Coney Hall London 67 G11
Coney Hill Glos 80 B5
Coneyhurst W Sus 35 C10
Coneythorpe N Yorks . . 206 B3
Coney Weston Suff 125 B9
Conford Hants 49 G10
Congash Highld 301 G10
Congdon's Shop Corn . . 11 F11
Congeith Dumfries 237 C10
Congelow Kent 53 D7
Congerstone Leics 135 B7
Congham Norf 158 E4
Congleton Ches E 168 C5
Congleton Edge Ches E . 168 C5
Congl-y-wal Gwyn 164 G2
Congresbury N Som . . . 60 G2
Congreve Staffs 151 G8
Conham Bristol 60 E6
Conicavel Moray 301 D10
Coningsby Lincs 174 D2
Conington Cambs 122 E6
Cambs 138 F3
Conisbrough S Yorks . . 187 B6
Conisby Argyll 274 G3

Conisholme Lincs....190 B6
Coniston Cumb....220 F6
E Yorks....209 F9
Coniston Cold N Yorks....204 B4
Conistone N Yorks....213 F9
Conkwell Wilts....61 G9
Connage Moray....302 C4
Connah's Quay Flint....166 B3
Connel Argyll....289 F11
Connel Park E Ayrs....258 G4
Conniburrow M Keynes....103 D7
Connista Highld....298 B4
Connon Corn....6 C3
Connor Downs Corn....2 C4
Conock Wilts....46 B5
Conon Bridge Highld....300 D5
Conon House Highld....300 D5
Cononish Stirling....285 E7
Cononley N Yorks....204 D5
Cononley Woodside
  N Yorks....204 D5
Cononsyth Angus....287 C9
Conordan Highld....295 B7
Conquermoor Heath
  Telford....150 F3
Consall Staffs....169 F7
Consett Durham....242 G4
Constable Burton
  N Yorks....224 G3
Constable Lee Lancs....195 C10
Constantine Corn....2 D6
Constantine Bay Corn....10 G3
Contin Highld....300 D4
Contlaw Aberdeen....293 C10
Conwy Conwy....180 F3
Conyer Kent....70 G3
Conyers Green Suff....125 D7
Cooden E Sus....38 F2
Cooil IoM....192 E4
Cookbury Devon....24 F6
Cookbury Wick Devon....24 F5
Cookham Windsor....65 B11
Cookham Dean Windsor....65 C11
Cookham Rise Windsor....65 C11
Cookhill Worcs....117 F11
Cookley Suff....126 B6
  Worcs....132 G6
Cookley Green Oxon....83 G11
Cookridge W Yorks....205 E11
Cooksbridge E Sus....36 E6
Cooksey Corner Worcs....117 D7
Cooksey Green Worcs....117 D8
Cook's Green Essex....89 B11
  Suff....125 G9
Cookshill Staffs....168 G6
Cooksland Corn....5 B11
Cooksmill Green Essex....87 D10
Cooksongreen Ches W....183 G9
Coolham W Sus....35 C10
Cooling Medway....69 D9
Cooling Kent....55 F8
Cooling Street Medway....69 D9
Coombe Bucks....84 D4
  Corn....4 G2
  Corn....4 G5
  Corn....4 G6
  Corn....5 E9
  Corn....24 E2
  Devon....14 G4
  Devon....27 D8
  Glos....80 G3
  Hants....33 C11
  Kent....55 B9
  London....67 E8
  Som....28 B3
  Som....28 F6
  Wilts....30 C5
  Wilts....47 C7
Coombe Bissett Wilts....31 B10
Coombe Dingle Bristol....60 D5
Coombe Hill Glos....99 F7
Coombe Keynes Dorset....18 E2
Coombes W Sus....35 F11
Coombesdale Staffs....150 B6
Coombeswood W Mid....133 F9
Coomb Hill Kent....69 G7
Coombs End S Glos....61 C9
Coombses Som....28 F4
Coopersale Common
  Essex....87 E7
Coopersale Street Essex....87 E7
Cooper's Corner Kent....52 D3
Cooper's Green E Sus....37 C7
  Herts....85 D11
Cooper's Hill Beds....103 D10
  Sur....66 E3
Cooper Street Kent....55 B10
Cooper Turning
  Gtr Man....194 F6
Cootham W Sus....35 E9
Copcut Worcs....117 E9
Copdock Suff....108 C2
Coped Hall Wilts....62 C5
Copenhagen Denb....165 B8
Copford Essex....107 G8
Copford Green Essex....107 G8
Copgrove N Yorks....214 G6
Copister Shetland....312 F6
Cople Bedford....104 B2
Copley Durham....233 F7
  Gtr Man....185 B7
  W Yorks....196 C5
Copley Hill W Yorks....197 B8
Coplow Dale Derbys....185 F11
Copmanthorpe York....207 D7
Copmere End Staffs....150 D6
Copnor Ptsmth....33 G11
Copp Lancs....202 F4
Coppathorne Corn....24 G2
Coppenhall Ches E....168 D2
  Staffs....151 F8
Coppenhall Moss
  Ches E....168 D2
Copperhouse Corn....2 B3
Coppice Gtr Man....196 G2
Coppicegate Shrops....132 G4
Coppingford Cambs....138 G3
Coppins Corner Kent....54 D2
Coppleham Som....42 G2
Copplestone Devon....26 G3
Coppull Lancs....194 E5
Coppull Moor Lancs....194 E5
Copsale W Sus....35 C11
Copse Hill London....67 E8
Copster Green Lancs....203 G9
Copster Hill Gtr Man....196 G2
Copston Magna Warks....135 F9
Cop Street Kent....55 B9
Copt Green Warks....118 D3
Copthall Green Essex....86 E6
Copt Heath W Mid....118 B3
Copt Hewick N Yorks....214 E6
Copthill Durham....232 C3
Copthorne Ches E....167 G11
  Corn....11 C11
  Shrops....149 G9
  Sur....51 F10

Coptiviney Shrops....149 B8
Copt Oak Leics....153 G9
Copy's Green Norf....159 B8
Copythorne Hants....32 E4
Corbets Tey London....68 B5
Corbridge Northumb....241 E11
Corbriggs Derbys....170 B6
Corby Northants....137 F7
Corby Glen Lincs....155 E9
Corby Hill Cumb....239 F11
Cordon N Ayrs....256 C2
Cordwell Norf....142 E2
Coreley Shrops....116 C2
Cores End Bucks....66 B2
Corfe Som....28 D2
Corfe Castle Dorset....18 E5
Corfe Mullen Dorset....18 B5
Corfton Shrops....131 F9
Corfton Bache Shrops....131 F9
Corgarff Aberds....292 C4
Corgee Corn....5 C10
Corhampton Hants....33 C10
Corlae Dumfries....246 D5
Corlannau Neath....57 C9
Corley Warks....134 F6
Corley Ash Warks....134 F5
Corley Moor Warks....134 F5
Cornaa IoM....192 D5
Cornabus Argyll....254 C4
Cornaigbeg Argyll....288 E1
Cornaigmore Argyll....288 E1
  Argyll....288 E1
Cornard Tye Suff....107 C8
Cornbank Midloth....270 C4
Cornbrook Shrops....116 B2
Corncatterach Aberds....302 F5
Cornel Conwy....164 C2
Corner Row Lancs....202 F4
Cornett Hereford....97 B11
Corney Cumb....220 G2
Cornforth Durham....234 E2
Cornharrow Dumfries....246 C5
Cornhill Aberds....302 D5
  Powys....96 C2
  Stoke....168 B5
Cornhill-on-Tweed
  Northumb....263 B9
Cornholme W Yorks....196 B2
Cornish Hall End Essex....106 D3
Cornquoy Orkney....314 G5
Cornriggs Durham....232 C2
Cornsay Durham....233 C9
Cornsay Colliery
  Durham....233 C9
Cornton Stirling....278 B5
Cornton Highld....300 D5
Cornwell Oxon....100 F5
Cornwood Devon....8 D2
Cornworthy Devon....8 D6
Corpach Highld....290 F2
Corpusty Norf....160 C2
Corran Highld....290 G2
Corran a Chan Uachdaraich
  Highld....295 C7
Corranbuie Argyll....275 G9
Corrany IoM....192 D5
Corrichoich Highld....311 G4
Corrie N Ayrs....255 C11
Corrie Common
  Dumfries....248 F6
Corriecravie N Ayrs....255 E10
Corriecravie Moor
  N Ayrs....255 E10
Corriedoo Dumfries....246 G5
Corriegarth Lodge
  Highld....291 B7
Corriemoillie Highld....300 C3
Corriemulzie Lodge
  Highld....309 K3
Corrievarkie Lodge
  Perth....291 F7
Corrievorrie Highld....301 G7
Corrigall Orkney....314 E3
Corrimony Highld....300 F3
Corringham Lincs....188 C5
  Thurrock....69 C7
Corris Gwyn....128 B5
Corris Uchaf Gwyn....128 B4
Corrour Highld....290 G5
Corrour Shooting Lodge
  Highld....290 G6
Corrow Argyll....284 G5
Corry Highld....295 C8
Corryborough
  Highld....301 G8
Corrydon Perth....292 G3
Corryghoil Argyll....284 E5
Corrykinloch Highld....309 G3
Corrylach Argyll....255 D8
Corrymuckloch Perth....286 D2
Corrynachenchy Argyll....289 E8
Corry of Ardnagrask
  Highld....300 E5
Corsback Highld....310 B6
Corscombe Dorset....29 F8
Corse Aberds....302 E6
  Glos....98 F5
Corse Lawn Worcs....98 E6
Corse of Kinnoir Aberds....302 E5
Corsewall Dumfries....236 C2
Corsham Wilts....61 E11
Corsindae Aberds....293 C8
Corsley Wilts....45 D10
Corsley Heath Wilts....45 D10
Corsock Dumfries....237 B9
Corston Bath....61 F7
  Orkney....314 E3
  Wilts....62 C2
Corstorphine Edin....280 G3
Cors-y-Gedol Gwyn....145 E11
Cortachy Angus....287 B7
Corton Suff....143 D10
  Wilts....46 E2
Corton Denham Som....29 C10
Cortworth S Yorks....186 B6
Coruanan Lodge Highld....290 G2
Corunna W Isles....296 F4
Corvast Highld....309 K5
Corwen Denb....165 G9
Cory Devon....24 D4
Coryates Dorset....17 D8
Coryton Cardiff....58 C6
  Devon....12 E5
Cosby Leics....135 E10
Coscote Oxon....64 B4
Coseley W Mid....133 E8
Cosford Warks....119 B9
Cosgrove Northants....102 C5
Cosham Ptsmth....33 E8
Cosheston V Glam....73 E8
Cosmore Dorset....29 F11
Cossall Notts....171 G7
Cossall Marsh Notts....171 G7
Cosses S Ayrs....244 G4
Cossington Leics....154 G2
  Som....43 E11

Costa Orkney....314 D3
Costessey Norf....160 G3
Costessey Park Norf....160 G3
Costhorpe Notts....187 D9
Costislost Corn....10 G6
Costock Notts....153 D11
Coston Leics....154 E6
  Norf....141 B11
Cote Oxon....82 E4
  Som....43 E10
  W Sus....35 F10
Cotebrook Ches W....167 B9
Cotehill Cumb....239 G11
Cotes Cumb....211 B9
  Leics....153 E11
  Staffs....150 C6
Cotesbach Leics....135 G10
Cotes Heath Staffs....150 C6
Cotes Park Derbys....170 E6
Cotford St Lukes Som....27 B11
Cotgrave Notts....154 B2
Cothall Aberds....293 B10
Cotham Bristol....60 E5
  Notts....172 F3
Cothelstone Som....43 G7
Cotheridge Worcs....116 G5
Cotherstone Durham....223 B10
Cothill Oxon....83 F7
Cotland Mon....79 E8
Cotleigh Devon....28 G2
Cotmanhay Derbys....171 G7
Cotmarsh Wilts....62 D5
Cotmaton Devon....15 D11
Coton Cambs....123 F8
  Northants....120 C3
  Shrops....149 C10
  Staffs....134 B3
  Staffs....150 C6
  Staffs....150 E6
Coton Clanford Staffs....151 E7
Coton Hackett Worcs....117 C9
Coton Hill Shrops....149 G9
Coton in the Clay Staffs....152 D3
Coton in the Elms
  Derbys....152 F4
Coton Park Derbys....152 F5
Cotonwood Shrops....149 B10
  Staffs....150 D6
Cotswold Community
  Wilts....81 F8
Cott Devon....8 C5
  E Yorks....217 F9
  Lancs....202 G6
Cottam E Yorks....217 F9
Cottartown Highld....301 F10
Cottenham Cambs....123 D9
Cottenham Park London....67 F8
Cotterdale N Yorks....222 G6
Cottered Herts....104 F6
Cotterill Woods
  S Yorks....187 E9
Cotteridge W Mid....117 B10
Cotterstock Northants....137 E10
Cottesbrooke Northants....120 C4
Cottesmore Rutland....155 G8
Cotteylands Devon....26 E6
Cottingham E Yorks....208 G6
  Northants....137 F7
Cottingley W Yorks....205 F8
Cottisford Oxon....101 E11
Cotton Staffs....169 F9
  Suff....125 D11
Cotton End Bedford....103 B11
  Northants....120 F5
Cotton Stones W Yorks....196 C4
Cotton Tree Lancs....204 F4
Cottonworth Hants....47 F11
Cottown Aberds....293 B9
  Aberds....302 G5
  Aberds....303 E8
Cotts Devon....7 B8
Cottwood Devon....25 E10
Cotwall Telford....150 F2
Cotwalton Staffs....151 B8
Couch Green Hants....48 G3
Couch's Mill Corn....6 D2
Coughton Hereford....97 G11
  Warks....117 E11
Coughton Fields Warks....117 F11
Cougie Highld....300 G2
Coulaghailtop Argyll....275 G8
Coulags Highld....299 E9
Coulby Newham Mbro....225 B10
Coulderton Cumb....219 D9
Couligartan Stirling....285 G8
Coulin Highld....299 D10
Coulin Lodge Highld....299 D10
Coull Aberds....293 C7
  Argyll....274 G3
Coulmony Ho Highld....301 E9
Coulport Argyll....276 D4
Coulsdon London....51 B9
Coulshill Perth....286 G3
Coulston Wilts....46 C3
Coulter S Lanark....260 C2
Coultings Som....43 E8
Coulton N Yorks....216 E2
Coultra Fife....287 E7
Cound Shrops....131 C11
Coundlane Shrops....131 B11
Coundmoor Shrops....131 C11
Coundon Durham....233 F10
  W Mid....134 G6
Coundongate Durham....233 F10
Coundon Grange
  Durham....233 F10
Counters End Herts....85 D8
Countersett N Yorks....213 B8
Countess Wilts....47 E7
Countess Cross Essex....107 E7
Countess Wear Devon....14 C5
Countesthorpe Leics....135 D11
Countisbury Devon....41 D8
County Oak W Sus....51 F9
Coupar Angus Perth....286 C6
Coup Green Lancs....194 B5
Coupland Cumb....222 B4
  Northumb....263 C10
Cour Argyll....255 C9
Courance Dumfries....248 E3
Coursley Som....42 G6
Court-at-Street Kent....54 F5
Court Barton Devon....14 D2
Court Colman Bridgend....57 E11
Court Corner Hants....48 B6
Courteenhall Northants....120 F5
Court Henry Carms....93 G11
Courthill Perth....286 C5
Court House Green
  W Mid....135 G2
Courtsend Essex....89 G8
Courtway Som....43 G8
Cousland Midloth....271 B7
Cousley Wood E Sus....53 G7
Cousland Argyll....244 G4
Couston Argyll....275 F10
Cova Shetland....313 J5
Cove Argyll....276 E4

Cove continued
  Borders....282 G5
  Devon....27 D7
  Hants....49 B11
  Highld....307 K3
Cove Bay Aberdeen....293 C11
Cove Bottom Suff....127 B9
Covehithe Suff....143 G10
Coven Staffs....133 B8
Covender Hereford....98 C2
Coveney Cambs....139 G10
Covenham St Bartholomew
  Lincs....190 C4
Covenham St Mary
  Lincs....190 C4
Coven Heath Staffs....133 C8
Coven Lawn Staffs....133 B8
Coventry W Mid....118 B6
Coverack Corn....3 F7
Coverack Bridges Corn....2 C5
Coverham N Yorks....214 B2
Covesea Moray....301 B11
Covingham Swindon....63 B7
Covington Cambs....121 C11
  S Lanark....259 B11
Cowan Bridge Lancs....212 D2
Cow Ark Lancs....203 D9
Cowbar Redcar....226 B5
Cowbeech E Sus....23 C10
Cowbeech Hill E Sus....23 C10
Cowbit Lincs....156 F5
Cowbog Aberds....303 D8
Cowbridge Lincs....174 F4
  Som....42 E3
Cowbridge / Y Bont-Faen
  V Glam....58 E3
Cowcliffe W Yorks....196 D6
Cowdale Derbys....185 G9
Cowden Kent....52 E3
Cowdenbeath Fife....280 C2
Cowdenburn Borders....270 E4
Cowden Head Argyll....221 F9
Cowers Lane Derbys....170 F4
Cowes IoW....20 B5
Cowesby N Yorks....215 B9
Cowesfield Green Wilts....32 C3
Cowfold W Sus....36 C2
Cowgill Cumb....212 B5
Cow Green Suff....125 D11
Cowgrove Dorset....18 B5
Cowhill Derbys....170 F5
  S Glos....79 G10
Cow Hill Lancs....203 G7
Cowhorn Hill S Glos....61 E7
Cowie Aberds....293 E10
  Stirling....278 D6
Cowlands Corn....4 G6
Cowleaze Corner Oxon....82 E4
Cowley Derbys....186 F4
  Devon....14 B4
  Glos....81 C7
  London....66 C5
  Oxon....83 E8
Cowleymoor Devon....27 E7
Cowley Peachy London....66 C5
Cowling Lancs....194 D5
Cowlow Derbys....185 G8
Cowmes W Yorks....197 D7
Cowpe Lancs....195 C10
Cowpen Northumb....253 G7
Cowpen Bewley
  Stockton....234 G5
Cowplain Hants....33 E11
Cow Roast Herts....85 C7
Cowshill Durham....232 D2
Cowslip Green N Som....60 G3
Cowstrandburn Fife....279 C10
Cowthorpe N Yorks....206 C4
Coxall Hereford....115 C7
Coxbank Ches E....167 G11
Coxbench Derbys....170 G5
Coxbridge Som....44 F4
Coxford Som....42 F6
  Norf....158 D6
Coxgreen Staffs....132 F6
Cox Green Gtr Man....195 E8
  Sur....50 G5
  Windsor....65 D11
Coxheath Kent....53 C8
Coxhill Kent....55 D8
Cox Hill Corn....4 G4
Coxhoe Durham....234 D2
Coxley Som....44 E4
  W Yorks....197 D9
Coxley Wick Som....44 E4
Coxlodge T&W....242 D6
Cox Moor Notts....171 D8
Coxpark Corn....12 G4
Coxtie Green Essex....87 F9
Coxwold N Yorks....215 D9
Coychurch Bridgend....58 D2
Coylton S Ayrs....257 E11
Coylumbridge Highld....291 B11
Coynach Aberds....292 C6
Coynachie Aberds....302 F4
Coytrahen Bridgend....57 D11
Coytrahin Bridgend....57 D11
Crabadon Devon....8 E5
Crabbet Park W Sus....51 F10
Crabble Kent....55 E9
Crabbs Cross Worcs....117 E10
Crabgate Norf....159 D11
Crab Orchard Dorset....31 F9
Crabtree Plym....7 D10
  W Sus....36 B2
Crabtree Green Wrex....166 G4
Crackaig Argyll....274 G6
Crackenedge W Yorks....197 C8
Crackenthorpe Cumb....231 G9
Crackington Haven Corn....11 B8
Crackley Staffs....168 E4
  Warks....118 C5
Crackleybank Shrops....150 G5
Crackpot N Yorks....223 F9
Crackthorn Corner
  Suff....125 B10
Cracoe N Yorks....213 G9
Cracow Moss Ches E....168 F2
  Staffs....168 F3
Craddock Devon....27 E9
Cradhlastadh W Isles....304 E2
Cradle Edge W Yorks....205 F7
Cradle End Herts....105 G9
Cradley Hereford....98 B4
  W Mid....133 G8
Cradley Heath W Mid....133 F8
Crafthole Corn....7 E7
Crafton Bucks....84 B5
Cragg Bank Lancs....211 E9
Cragg Foot Lancs....211 E9
Craggan Highld....301 F10
  Highld....301 F11
  Stirling....285 E10
Cragganvallie Highld....300 F5

Craggiemore Moray....301 F11
Cragg Hill W Yorks....205 F10
Craggie Highld....301 G7
  Highld....311 H2
Cragg Vale W Yorks....196 C5
Craghead Durham....242 G6
Crahan Corn....2 C5
Crai Powys....95 G7
Craibstone Moray....302 D5
  Aberds....293 B10
Craichie Angus....287 C9
Craig Dumfries....237 B8
  Dumfries....237 C8
  Highld....299 E10
Craiganor Lodge Perth....285 B10
Craig Berthlwyd M Tydf....77 F9
Craig Castle Aberds....302 G4
Craig-cefn-parc
  Swansea....75 E11
Craigdallie Perth....286 E6
Craigdam Aberds....303 F8
Craigdarroch Dumfries....246 E6
  Highld....300 D4
Craigdhu Highld....300 E4
Craigearn Aberds....293 B9
Craigellachie Moray....302 E2
Craigencallie Ho
  Dumfries....237 B7
Craigencross Dumfries....236 C2
Craigend Borders....271 F9
  Glasgow....268 B3
  Perth....286 E5
  Perth....286 E5
  Stirling....278 D5
Craigendive Argyll....275 E11
Craigendoran Argyll....276 E6
Craigendowie Angus....293 G7
Craigends Renfs....267 B8
Craigens Argyll....274 G3
  E Ayrs....258 F3
Craigentinny Edin....280 G5
Craigerne Borders....261 B7
Craigflower Fife....286 C5
Craighall Perth....286 C5
Craighat Stirling....277 E9
Craighead Fife....287 G10
  Highld....301 C7
Craighlaw Mains
  Dumfries....236 C5
Craighouse Argyll....274 G6
Craigie Aberds....293 B11
  Dundee....287 D8
  Perth....286 C5
  Perth....286 E5
  S Ayrs....257 C10
Craigiefield Orkney....314 E4
Craigiehall Edin....280 F3
Craigielaw E Loth....281 F9
Craigierig Borders....260 E6
Craigleith Edin....280 G4
Craig Llwyn Shrops....148 D4
Craig-Ilwyn Shrops....148 D5
Craiglockhart Edin....280 G4
Craig Lodge Argyll....275 G10
Craigmalloch E Ayrs....245 E11
Craigmaud Aberds....303 D8
Craigmill Stirling....278 B6
Craigmillar Edin....280 G5
Craigmore Argyll....266 B2
Craig-moston Aberds....293 F9
Craignant Shrops....148 B5
Craigneuk N Lanark....268 D5
  N Lanark....268 D6
Craignish Castle Argyll....275 D8
Craignure Argyll....289 F9
Craigo Angus....293 G9
Craigow Perth....286 G4
Craig Penllyn V Glam....58 D3
Craigrothie Fife....287 F7
Craigroy Moray....301 D11
Craigrory Highld....300 E6
Craigruie Stirling....285 E8
Craig's End Essex....106 D4
Craigsford Mains
  Borders....262 B3
Craigshill W Loth....269 B11
Craigside Durham....233 E8
Craigston Castle Aberds....303 D7
Craigton Aberdeen....293 C10
  Angus....287 B7
  Angus....287 D9
  Glasgow....267 C10
  Highld....300 E6
  Highld....300 H6
  Highld....309 L6
Craigtown Highld....310 D2
Craig-y-don Conwy....180 E3
Craig-y-Duke Swansea....76 E2
Craig-y-nos Powys....76 B4
Craig-y-penrhyn
  Ceredig....128 E3
Craig-y-Rhacca Caerph....59 B7
Craik Borders....249 B8
Crail Fife....287 G10
Crailing Borders....262 E5
Crailinghall Borders....262 E5
Crakaig Highld....311 H3
Crakehall N Yorks....214 B5
Crakehill N Yorks....215 E8
Crakemarsh Staffs....151 B11
Crambe N Yorks....216 G4
Crambeck N Yorks....216 F4
Cramhurst Sur....50 E2
Cramlington Northumb....243 B7
Cramond Edin....280 F3
Cramond Bridge Edin....280 F3
Crampmoor Hants....32 C5
Cranage Ches E....168 B3
Cranberry Staffs....150 B6
Cranbourne Brack....66 E2
Cranbrook Devon....14 B6
  Kent....53 F9
  London....68 B3
Cranbrook Common Kent....53 F9
Crane Moor S Yorks....197 G10
Crane's Corner Norf....159 G8
Cranfield C Beds....103 C9
Cranford Devon....24 C4
  London....66 D6
Cranford St Andrew
  Northants....121 B8
Cranford St John

Crannich Argyll....289 E7
Crannoch Moray....302 D4
Cranoe Leics....136 E5
Cransford Suff....126 E6
Cranshaws Borders....272 C3
Cranstal IoM....192 B5
Cranswick E Yorks....208 C6
Crantock Corn....4 C5
Cranwell Lincs....173 F8
Cranwich Norf....140 E5
Cranworth Norf....141 C9
Craobh Haven Argyll....275 C8
Crapstone Devon....7 B10
Crarae Argyll....275 D10
Crask Highld....308 C7
Crask Inn Highld....309 G5
Craskins Aberds....293 C7
Crask of Aigas Highld....300 E4
Craster Northumb....265 F7
Craswall Hereford....96 D5
Crateford Shrops....132 F4
  Staffs....133 B8
Cratfield Suff....126 B6
Crathes Aberds....293 D9
Crathie Aberds....292 D4
  Highld....291 D7
Crathorne N Yorks....225 D8
Craven Arms Shrops....131 G8
Crawcrook T&W....242 E4
Crawford Lancs....194 G3
  S Lanark....259 E11
Crawforddyke S Lanark....269 F7
Crawfordjohn S Lanark....259 E9
Crawick Dumfries....259 G2
Crawley Devon....28 F3
  Hants....48 G2
  Oxon....82 C4
  W Sus....51 F9
Crawley Down W Sus....51 F10
Crawley End Essex....105 C9
Crawley Hill Sur....65 G11
Crawleyside Durham....232 C5
Crawshaw W Yorks....197 E8
Crawshawbooth Lancs....195 B10
Crawton Aberds....293 F10
Cray N Yorks....213 D8
  Perth....292 G3
Crayford London....68 E4
Crayke N Yorks....215 E11
Craymere Beck Norf....159 C11
Crays Hill Essex....88 G2
Cray's Pond Oxon....64 C6
Crazies Hill Wokingham....65 C9
Creacombe Devon....26 D4
Creagan Argyll....289 E11
Creag Aoil Highld....290 F3
Creag Ghoraidh
  W Isles....297 G3
Creaguaineach Lodge
  Highld....290 G5
Creaksea Essex....88 F6
Creamore Bank Shrops....149 C10
Creaton Northants....120 C4
Creca Dumfries....238 C6
Credenhill Hereford....97 C9
Crediton Devon....26 G4
Creebridge Dumfries....236 C6
Creech Dorset....18 E4
Creech Bottom Dorset....18 E4
Creech Heathfield Som....28 B3
Creech St Michael Som....28 B3
Creed Corn....5 F8
Creediknowe Shetland....312 G7
Creegbrawse Corn....4 G4
Creekmoor Poole....18 C6
Creekmouth London....68 C3
Creeksea Essex....88 F6
Creeting Bottoms Suff....126 F2
Creeting St Mary Suff....125 F11
Creeton Lincs....155 E10
Creetown Dumfries....236 D6
Creggans Argyll....284 G4
Cregneash IoM....192 F2
Cregrina Powys....114 G2
Creich Fife....287 E7
Creigau Mon....79 F7
Creighton Staffs....151 B11
Creigiau Cardiff....58 C5
Crelly Corn....2 C5
Cremyll Corn....7 E9
Crendell Dorset....31 E9
Crepkill Highld....298 E4
Creslow Bucks....102 G6
Cressage Shrops....131 C11
Cressbrook Derbys....185 G11
Cresselly Pembs....73 D9
Cressex Bucks....84 G4
Cressing Essex....106 G5
Cresswell Northumb....253 E7
  Staffs....151 B9
Cresswell Quay Pembs....73 D9
Creswell Derbys....187 G8
  Staffs....151 B8
Creswell Green Staffs....151 G11
Cretingham Suff....126 E4
Cretshengan Argyll....275 G8
Crewe Ches E....168 D2
  Ches W....166 E6
Crewe-by-Farndon
  Ches W....166 E6
Crewgarth Cumb....231 E8
Crewgreen Powys....148 F6
Crewkerne Som....28 F6
Crews Hill London....86 F4
Crew's Hole Bristol....60 E6
Crewton Derby....153 C7
Crianlarich Stirling....285 E7
Cribbs Causeway S Glos....60 C5
Cribden Side Lancs....195 C9
Cribyn Ceredig....111 G10
Crich Derbys....170 E5
Crich Carr Derbys....170 E4
Crichie Aberds....303 E9
Crichton Midloth....271 C7
Crick Mon....79 G7
  Northants....119 C11
Crickadarn Powys....95 C11
Cricket Hill Hants....65 G10
Cricket Malherbie Som....28 E5
Cricket St Thomas Som....28 F5
Crickham Som....44 D2
Crickheath Shrops....148 E5
Crickheath Wharf
  Shrops....148 E5
Crickhowell Powys....78 B2
Cricklade Wilts....81 G10
Cricklewood London....67 B8
Crickmery Shrops....150 D3
Crick's Green Hereford....116 G2
Criddlestyle Hants....31 E11
Cridling Stubbs N Yorks....198 C4
Cridmore IoW....20 E5

Crieff Perth....286 E2
Criggan Corn....5 C10
Criggion Powys....148 F5
Crigglestone W Yorks....197 D10
Crimble Gtr Man....195 E11
Crimchard Som....28 F4
Crimdon Park Durham....234 D5
Crimond Aberds....303 D10
Crimonmogate Aberds....303 D10
Crimplesham Norf....140 C3
Crimscote Warks....100 B4
Crinan Argyll....275 D8
Crinan Ferry Argyll....275 D8
Crindau Newport....59 B10
Crindledyke N Lanark....268 D6
Cringleford Norf....142 B3
Cringles W Yorks....204 D6
Cringletie Borders....270 G4
Crinow Pembs....73 C10
Cripp's Corner E Sus....38 C3
Cripplesease Corn....2 B2
Cripplestyle Dorset....31 E9
Cripp's Corner E Sus....38 C3
Crist Derbys....185 E8
Critchell's Green Hants....32 B3
Critchill Som....45 D9
Critchmere Sur....49 G11
Crit Hall Kent....53 G9
Crizeley Hereford....97 E8
Croanford Corn....10 G5
Croasdale Cumb....219 B11
Crobeag W Isles....304 F6
Crochmore Ho
  Dumfries....237 B10
Crockenhill Kent....68 F4
Crockernwell Devon....13 C11
Crockers Devon....40 F5
Crocker's Ash Hereford....79 B9
Crockerton Wilts....45 E11
Crockerton Green Wilts....45 E11
Crocketford or Ninemile Bar
  Dumfries....237 B10
Crockey Hill York....207 D8
Crockham Heath
  W Berks....64 G2
Crockham Hill Kent....52 C2
Crockhurst Street Kent....52 E6
Crockleford Heath
  Essex....107 F10
Crockleford Hill Essex....107 F10
Crockness Orkney....314 G3
Crock Street Som....28 E4
Croesau Bach Shrops....148 D4
Croeserw Neath....57 B11
Croes-goch Pembs....87 E11
Croes-Hywel Mon....78 C4
Croes-lan Ceredig....93 C7
Croesor Gwyn....163 G10
Croespenmaen Caerph....77 F11
Croes-wian Flint....181 G10
Croesyceiliog Carms....74 B6
  Torf....78 F4
Croes y pant Mon....78 E4
Croesywaun Gwyn....163 E8
Croft Hereford....115 D9
  Leics....135 D10
  Lincs....175 C8
  Pembs....92 C3
  Warr....183 C10
Croftamie Stirling....277 D9
Croftfoot S Lanark....268 C2
Crofthandy Corn....4 G4
Croftlands Cumb....210 D5
Croftmalloch W Loth....269 C8
Croftmoraig Perth....285 C11
Croft of Tillymaud
  Aberds....303 F11
Crofton Cumb....239 G8
  Wilts....63 G9
  W Yorks....197 D11
Croft-on-Tees N Yorks....224 D5
Crofts Dumfries....237 B9
Crofts Bank Gtr Man....184 B3
Crofts of Benachielt
  Highld....310 F5
Crofts of Haddo Aberds....303 F8
Crofts of Inverthernie
  Aberds....303 E7
Crofts of Meikle Ardo
  Aberds....303 E8
Croftswhannie Corn....4 E4
Croft-y-Duke Swansea....76 E2
Crofty Swansea....56 B4
Croggan Argyll....289 G9
Croglin Cumb....231 B7
Croich Highld....309 K4
Croick Argyll....288 D5
Crois Dughaill W Isles....297 J3
Cromarty Highld....301 C7
Cromasaig Highld....299 C10
Crombie Fife....279 D10
Crombie Castle Aberds....302 D5
Cromblet Aberds....303 F7
Cromdale Highld....301 G10
Cromer Herts....104 F5
  Norf....160 A4
Cromer-Hyde Herts....86 C2
Cromford Derbys....170 D3
Cromhall S Glos....79 G11
Cromhall Common
  S Glos....61 B7
Cromor W Isles....304 F6
Crompton Fold Gtr Man....196 F2
Cromra Highld....291 D7
Cromwell Notts....172 C3
Cromwell Bottom
  W Yorks....196 C6
Cronberry E Ayrs....258 E4
Crondall Hants....49 D9
Cronk-y-Voddy IoM....192 D4
Cronton Mers....183 D7
Crook Cumb....221 G9
  Durham....233 D9
Crookdake Cumb....229 C9
Crooke Gtr Man....194 F5
Crooked Billet London....67 E8
Crookedholm E Ayrs....257 B11
Crooked Soley Wilts....63 E10
Crookes S Yorks....186 D4
Crookesmoor S Yorks....186 D4
Crookfur E Renf....267 D10
Crookgate Bank Durham....242 F5
Crookhall Durham....242 G4
Crookham Northumb....263 B10
  W Berks....64 G4
Crookham Village
  Hants....49 C9
Crookhaugh Borders....260 D5
Crookhouse Borders....263 D7
Crooklands Cumb....211 C10
Crook of Devon Perth....286 G4
Crookston Glasgow....267 C10

Cropston Leics....153 G11
Cropthorne Worcs....99 C9
Cropton N Yorks....216 B5
Cropwell Bishop Notts....154 B3
Cropwell Butler Notts....154 B3
Cros W Isles....304 B7
Crosben Highld....289 D9
Crosbost W Isles....304 F5
Crosby Cumb....229 D7
  IoM....192 E4
  Mers....182 B4
  N Lincs....199 E11
Crosby Court N Yorks....225 F7
Crosby Garrett Cumb....222 D4
Crosby-on-Eden Cumb....239 F11
Crosby Ravensworth
  Cumb....222 C2
Crosby Villa Cumb....229 D7
Croscombe Som....44 E5
Crosemere Shrops....149 D8
Crosland Edge W Yorks....196 E6
Crosland Hill W Yorks....196 E6
Crosland Moor W Yorks....210 E4
Croslands Park Cumb....210 E4
  Devon....40 F3
Crossaig Argyll....255 B9
Crossal Highld....294 B6
Crossapol Argyll....288 E1
Cross Ash Mon....78 B6
Cross-at-Hand Kent....53 D9
Cross Bank Worcs....116 C4
Crossbrae Aberds....302 D6
Crossburn Falk....279 G7
Crosscanonby Cumb....229 D7
Crosscliffe N Yorks....216 B5
  4 E4
Cross End Bedford....121 F11
  Essex....107 E7
  M Keynes....103 D8
Crossens Mers....193 D11
Crossflatts W Yorks....205 E8
Crossford Fife....279 D11
  S Lanark....268 F6
Crossgate Lincs....156 D4
  Orkney....314 E4
  Staffs....151 B8
Cross Gate E Sus....35 B8
Crossgatehall E Loth....271 B7
Crossgates N Yorks....217 C11
  Fife....280 D2
  Powys....113 E11
Cross Gates W Yorks....205 F11
  W Yorks....206 G3
Crossgill Cumb....231 C10
  Lancs....211 B11
Cross Green Devon....12 D3
  Staffs....133 B8
  Suff....124 G6
  Suff....125 F7
  Suff....125 G9
  Warks....119 F7
  Worcs....116 G6
Crosshands Carms....92 G3
Cross Hands Carms....75 C9
  Pembs....73 C9
Cross Heath Staffs....168 F4
Crosshill E Ayrs....257 E11
  Fife....280 B3
  S Ayrs....245 D8
Cross Hill Corn....10 G6
  Derbys....170 F6
  Glos....79 F9
Cross Hills N Yorks....204 E6
Cross Holme N Yorks....225 F11
Crosshouse E Ayrs....257 B9
Cross Houses Shrops....131 B10
  132 E3
Cross in Hand E Sus....37 C9
  Leics....135 G10
Cross Inn Carms....74 C3
  Ceredig....111 E7
  Ceredig....111 F7
  Rhondda....58 C5
Crosskeys Caerph....78 G2
Cross Keys Sur....52 C4
  Wilts....61 E11
Crosskirk Highld....310 B4
Crosslands Cumb....210 B6
Cross Lane IoW....20 B6
Cross Lane Head Shrops....132 D4
Crosslanes Shrops....148 F6
Cross Lanes Corn....30 G3
  N Yorks....215 G10
  Oxon....65 D7
  Wrex....166 F5
Crosslee Borders....261 F8
  Renfs....267 B8
Crossley Hall W Yorks....205 G8
Cross Llyde Hereford....97 F8
Crossmichael Dumfries....237 C9
Crossmill E Renf....267 D10
Crossmoor Lancs....202 F4
Crossmount Perth....285 B11
Crossnahill Corn....79 D11
Cross Oak Powys....96 G2
Cross of Jackston
  Aberds....303 F7
Cross o' th' hands
  Derbys....170 F3
Cross o' th' Hill Ches W....167 F7
Crosspost W Sus....36 C3
Crossroads Aberds....293 D9
  E Ayrs....257 C11
  Fife....281 B7
Cross Roads Devon....12 D5
  W Yorks....204 F6
Cross Stone Aberds....303 G9
Crosston Angus....287 B9
Cross Street Suff....126 B3
Crosston Angus....287 B9
Crosstown Corn....24 D2
  V Glam....58 F4
Cross Town Ches E....184 F3
Crossual Mon....78 B6
Crossway Hereford....98 E2
Crossway Green Mon....79 G11
  Mon....79 G11
  Worcs....116 D6
Crossways Dorset....17 D11
Crosswell / Ffynnongroes
  Pembs....92 D3
Crosswood Ceredig....112 C3
Crosthwaite Cumb....221 G8
Croston Lancs....194 D3
Crostwick Norf....160 F5
Crostwight Norf....160 D6
Crothair W Isles....304 E3

Crouch Kent....52 B6
Kent....54 B5
Crouch End London....67 B9
Crouchers W Sus....22 C4
Croucheston Wilts....31 B9
Crouch Hill Dorset....30 E2
Crouch House Green
Kent....52 D2
Croughly Moray....301 G11
Croughton Northants....101 E10
Crovie Aberds....303 C8
Crow Hants....31 G11
Crowan Corn....2 C4
Crowborough E Sus....52 G4
Staffs....168 D6
Crowborough Warren
E Sus....52 G4
Crowcombe Som....42 F6
Crowcroft Worcs....116 G5
Crowden Derbys....185 B9
Devon....12 B5
Crowder Park Devon....8 D4
Crowdhill Hants....33 C7
Crowdicote Derbys....169 B10
Crowdleham Kent....52 B5
Crowdon N Yorks....227 F9
Crow Edge S Yorks....197 G7
Crowell Oxon....84 E2
Crowell Hill Oxon....84 E3
Crowfield Northants....102 C2
Suff....126 C3
Crowgate Street Norf....160 E6
Crowgreaves Shrops....132 D4
Crow Green Essex....87 F9
Crowhill Gtr Man....184 B6
M Keynes....102 D6
Crow Hill Hereford....98 F2
Crowhole Derbys....186 F4
Crowhurst E Sus....38 E3
Sur....51 D11
Crowhurst Lane End
Sur....51 D11
Crowland Lincs....156 G4
Crowlas Corn....2 C2
Crowle N Lincs....199 E9
Worcs....117 F8
Crowle Green Worcs....117 F8
Crowle Hill N Lincs....199 E9
Crowle Park N Lincs....199 E9
Crowmarsh Gifford Oxon....64 B6
Crown Corner Suff....126 C5
Crown East Worcs....116 G6
Crown Nest W Yorks....205 F8
Crownfield Bucks....84 F4
Crownhill Plym....7 D10
Crown Hills Leicester....136 C2
Crownland Suff....125 D10
Crownpits Sur....50 E3
Crownthorpe Norf....141 C11
Crown Wood Brack....65 F11
Crows-an-wra Corn....1 D3
Crow's Green Essex....106 F3
Crowshill Norf....141 B8
Crowsley Oxon....65 D8
Crowsnest Shrops....131 C7
Crow's Nest Corn....6 C2
Crowther's Pool Powys....96 B4
Crowthorne Brack....65 G10
Crowton Ches W....183 G9
Crowton Ches W....183 D8
Croxall Staffs....152 G3
Croxby Lincs....189 B11
Croxby Top Lincs....189 B11
Croxdale Durham....233 D11
Croxden Staffs....151 B11
Croxley Green Herts....85 F9
Croxteth Mers....182 B6
Croxton Cambs....122 E4
N Lincs....200 E5
Norf....141 F7
Norf....159 C9
Staffs....150 C5
Crotonbank Staffs....150 C5
Croxton Green Ches E....167 E9
Croxton Kerrial Leics....154 D6
Croy Highld....301 E7
N Lanark....278 F4
Croyde Devon....40 F2
Croyde Bay Devon....40 F2
Croydon Cambs....104 B6
London....67 F10
Crozen Hereford....97 B11
Crubenbeg Highld....291 D8
Crubenmore Lodge
Highld....291 D8
Cruckmeole Shrops....131 B8
Cruckton Shrops....149 G8
Cruden Bay Aberds....303 F10
Crudgington Telford....150 F2
Crudie Aberds....303 D7
Crudwell Wilts....81 G7
Crug Powys....114 C3
Crugmeer Corn....10 F4
Crugybar Carms....94 E3
Cruise Hill Worcs....117 E10
Crulabhig W Isles....304 E3
Crumlin Caerph....78 E2
Crumplehorn Corn....6 E4
Crumpsall Gtr Man....195 G10
Crumpsbrook Shrops....116 B2
Crumpton Hill Worcs....98 B5
Crundale Kent....54 D5
Pembs....73 B7
Cruwys Morchard Devon....26 E5
Crux Easton Hants....48 B2
Cruxton Dorset....17 B7
Crwbin Carms....75 C7
Crya Orkney....314 F3
Cryers Hill Bucks....84 F5
Crymlyn Gwyn....179 G10
Crymych Pembs....92 E3
Crynant / Creunant
Neath....76 E3
Crynfryn Ceredig....111 E11
Cuaich Highld....291 E8
Cuaig Highld....299 D7
Cuan Argyll....275 C8
Cubbington Warks....118 D6
Cubeck N Yorks....213 B9
Cubert Corn....4 D5
Cubitt Town London....67 D11
Cubley S Yorks....197 G8
Cubley Common Derbys....152 B3
Cublington Bucks....102 G6
Hereford....97 D8
Cuckfield W Sus....36 B4
Cucklington Som....30 B3
Cuckney Notts....187 G9
Cuckold's Green Suff....143 F8
Wilts....46 B3
Cuckoo Green Suff....143 D10
Cuckoo Hill Notts....188 C2
Wilts....46 B4
Cuckoo's Corner Hants....49 E8
Cuckoo's Knob Wilts....47 C7
Cuckoo Tye Suff....107 C2
Cuckron Shetland....313 H6
Cucumber Corner Norf....143 B7
Cuddesdon Oxon....83 E10
Cuddington Bucks....84 C2

Cuddington continued
Ches W....183 G10
Cuddington Heath
Ches W....167 F7
Cuddy Hill Lancs....202 F5
Cudham London....52 B2
Cudliptown Devon....12 F6
Cudworth Devon....28 E5
Sur....51 B8
S Yorks....197 F11
Cudworth Common
S Yorks....197 F11
Cuerden Green Lancs....194 C5
Cuerdley Cross Warr....183 D8
Cufaude Hants....48 B6
Cuffern Pembs....91 G7
Cuffley Herts....86 F4
Cuiashader W Isles....304 C7
Cuidhir W Isles....297 L2
Cuidhtinis W Isles....296 C6
Cuiken Midloth....270 B5
Cuilcheanna Ho Highld....290 G2
Cuin Argyll....288 D6
Culbo Highld....300 C6
Culbokie Highld....300 D6
Culburnie Highld....300 E4
Culcabock Highld....300 E6
Culcairn Highld....300 C6
Culcharry Highld....301 D8
Culcheth Warr....183 B11
Culcronchie Dumfries....237 C7
Cùl Doirlinn Highld....289 B8
Culdrain Aberds....302 F5
Culduie Highld....299 E7
Culeave Highld....309 K5
Culfordheath Suff....125 C7
Culfosie Aberds....293 C9
Culgaith Cumb....231 F8
Culham Oxon....83 F8
Culkein Highld....306 F5
Culkein Drumbeg Highld....306 F6
Culkerton Glos....80 F6
Cullachie Highld....301 G9
Cullen Moray....302 C5
Cullercoats T&W....243 C9
Cullingworth W Yorks....205 F7
Cullipool Argyll....275 B8
Cullivoe Shetland....312 C7
Culloch Perth....285 F11
Culloden Highld....301 E7
Cullompton Devon....27 F8
Culmaily Highld....311 K2
Culmazie Dumfries....236 D5
Culm Davy Devon....27 D10
Culmer Sur....50 F2
Culmers Kent....70 G5
Culmington Shrops....131 G9
Culmore Stirling....278 B3
Culmstock Devon....27 E10
Culnacraig Highld....307 J5
Culnadalloch Argyll....289 G11
Culnaightrie Dumfries....237 D9
Culnaknock Highld....298 C5
Culnamean Highld....294 C6
Culpho Suff....108 B4
Culrain Highld....309 K5
Culra Lodge Highld....291 F7
Culross Fife....279 D9
Culroy S Ayrs....257 G8
Culscadden Dumfries....236 E6
Culsh Aberds....292 D5
Aberds....303 E8
Culshabbin Dumfries....236 D5
Culswick Shetland....313 J4
Cultercullen Aberds....303 G9
Cults Aberdeen....293 C10
Aberds....302 F5
Dumfries....236 E6
Fife....287 G7
Culverlane Devon....8 C4
Culverstone Green Kent....68 G6
Culverthorpe Lincs....173 G8
Culworth Northants....101 B10
Culzie Lodge Highld....300 B5
Cumberlow Green Herts....104 E6
Cumbernauld N Lanark....278 G5
Cumbernauld Village
N Lanark....278 F5
Cumber's Bank Wrex....149 B8
Cumberworth Lincs....191 G8
Cumdivock Cumb....230 B2
Cuminestown Aberds....303 D8
Cumloden Dumfries....236 C6
Cummersdale Cumb....239 G9
Cummerton Aberds....303 C8
Cummertrees Dumfries....238 D4
Cummingston Moray....301 C11
Cumnock E Ayrs....258 E3
Cumnor Oxon....83 E7
Cumnor Hill Oxon....83 D7
Cumrew Cumb....240 G2
Cumwhinton Cumb....239 G10
Cumwhitton Cumb....240 G2
Cundall N Yorks....215 E8
Cundy Cross S Yorks....197 F11
Cundy Hos S Yorks....186 B4
Cunninghamhead
N Ayrs....267 G7
Cunnister Shetland....312 D7
Cupar Fife....287 F7
Cupar Muir Fife....287 F7
Cupernham Hants....32 C5
Cupid Green Herts....85 D9
Cupid's Hill Mon....97 F8
Curbar Derbys....186 G3
Curborough Staffs....152 G2
Curbridge Hants....33 E8
Oxon....82 D4
Curdridge Hants....33 E8
Curdworth Warks....134 E3
Curgurrell Corn....3 B9
Curin Highld....300 D3
Curland Som....28 D3
Curland Common Som....28 D3
Curlew Green Suff....127 D7
Curload Som....28 B4
Currarie S Ayrs....244 E5
Currian Vale Corn....5 D9
Curridge W Berks....64 E3
Currie Edin....270 B3
Currock Cumb....239 G10
Curry Lane Corn....11 C11
Curry Mallet Som....28 C4
Curry Rivel Som....28 B5
Cursiter Orkney....314 E3
Curtisden Green Kent....53 E11
Curtisknowle Devon....8 D5
Curtismill Green Essex....87 F8
Curry Corn....4 E4
Cusbay Orkney....314 C5
Cusgarne Corn....4 G5
Cushnie Aberds....303 C7

Cushuish Som....43 G7
Cusop Hereford....96 C4
Custards Hants....32 F3
Custom House London....68 C2
Cusveorth Coombe Corn....4 G5
Cusworth S Yorks....198 G4
Cutcloy Dumfries....236 F6
Cutcombe Som....42 F2
Cutgate Gtr Man....195 E11
Cuthill E Loth....281 G7
Cutiau Gwyn....146 F2
Cutlers Green Essex....105 E11
Cutler's Green Som....44 C5
Cutmadoc Corn....5 C11
Cutmere Corn....6 C2
Cutsyke W Yorks....198 C2
Cutsdean Glos....99 E11
Cuttiford's Door Som....28 E4
Cuttivett Corn....7 C8
Cutteslowe Oxon....83 C8
Cutthorpe Derbys....186 G4
Cuttiford's Door Som....28 E4
Cutts Shetland....313 K6
Cuttybridge Pembs....72 B6
Cuttyhill Aberds....303 D10
Cuxham Oxon....83 F11
Cuxton Medway....69 F8
Cuxwold Lincs....201 G7
Cwm Bl Gwent....77 D11
Denb....181 F9
Neath....57 C10
Powys....129 D11
Cwmafan Neath....57 C9
Cwmaman Rhondda....77 E7
Cwmann Carms....93 B11
Cwmavon Torf....78 D3
Cwmbach Carms....75 E7
Carms....92 F5
Powys....96 D3
Cwmbâch Rhondda....77 E8
Cwmbach Rhondda....77 E8
Cwmbach Llechrhyd
Powys....113 G10
Cwmbelan Powys....129 G8
Cwmbran Torf....78 G3
Cwmbrwyno Ceredig....128 G4
Cwm-byr Carms....94 E2
Cwm Capel Carms....75 E7
Cwmcarn Caerph....78 G2
Cwmcarvan Mon....79 D7
Cwm-celyn Bl Gwent....78 E2
Cwm-Cewydd Gwyn....147 G2
Cwmcoednerth Ceredig....92 B6
Cwm-cou Ceredig....92 C5
Cwmcrawnon Powys....77 B10
Cwmcych Carms....92 D5
Cwmdare Rhondda....77 E7
Cwm Dows Caerph....78 F2
Cwmdu Carms....94 E2
Cwmdu continued
Powys....96 G3
Swansea....56 C6
Cwmduad Carms....93 E7
Cwmdwr Carms....94 E4
Cwmerfyn Ceredig....128 G3
Cwmfelin Bridgend....57 E11
M Tydf....77 E9
W Yorks....205 G8
Cwmfelin Boeth Carms....73 B11
Cwmfelinfach Caerph....77 G11
Cwm-felin-fach Caerph....77 G11
Cwmfelin Mynach Carms....92 G4
Cwmffrwd Carms....74 B6
Cwm Ffrwd-oer Torf....78 E3
Cwm-Fields Torf....78 E3
Cwmgelli Caerph....77 F11
Cwmgiedd Powys....76 C3
Cwmgors Neath....76 C2
Cwmgwili Carms....75 C9
Cwmgwrach Neath....76 E5
Cwm Gwyn Swansea....56 C6
Cwm Head Shrops....131 F8
Cwm-hesgen Gwyn....146 E4
Cwmhiraeth Carms....92 D6
Cwm-hwnt Rhondda....76 D6
Cwmifor Carms....94 F3
Cwm Irfon Powys....95 B7
Cwmisfael Carms....75 C8
Cwm-Llinau Powys....128 B6
Cwm-mawr Carms....75 C8
Cwm-miles Carms....92 G3
Cwmorgan Pembs....92 E5
Cwmparc Rhondda....76 F6
Cwm-parc Rhondda....76 F6
Cwmpengraig Carms....92 D6
Cwm Penmachno Conwy....164 F3
Cwmpennar Rhondda....77 E8
Cwm Plysgog Ceredig....92 C3
Cwmrhos Powys....96 G3
Cwmrhydyceirw Swansea....57 B7
Cwmsychpant Ceredig....93 B9
Cwmsyfiog Caerph....77 E11
Cwmsymlog Ceredig....128 G4
Cwmtillery Bl Gwent....78 D2
Cwm-twrch Isaf Powys....76 C3
Cwm-twrch Uchaf Powys....76 C3
Cwmwdig Water Pembs....90 E6
Cwmwysg Powys....95 F7
Cwm-y-glo Carms....75 C9
Gwyn....163 C8
Cwmyoy Mon....96 G6
Cwmystwyth Ceredig....112 C5
Cwrt Gwyn....128 C3
Cwrt-newydd Ceredig....93 B9
Cwrt-y-cadno Carms....94 C3
Cwrt-y-gollen Powys....78 B2
Cydweli / Kidwelly
Carms....74 D6
Cyffordd Llandudno /
Llandudno Junction
Conwy....180 F3
Cyffylliog Denb....165 D9
Cyfronydd Powys....130 B2
Cymau Flint....166 D3
Cymdda Bridgend....58 C2
Cymer Neath....57 B11
Cymmer Rhondda....77 G8
Cyncoed Cardiff....59 C7
Cynghordy Carms....94 C6
Cynheidre Carms....75 D7
Cynonville Neath....57 B10
Cyntwell Cardiff....58 D6
Cynwyd Denb....165 G9
Cynwyl Elfed Carms....93 F7
Cywarch Gwyn....147 F7

D

Daccombe Devon....9 B8
Dacre Cumb....230 F5
N Yorks....214 G3
Dacre Banks N Yorks....214 G3
Daddry Shield Durham....232 D3
Dadford Bucks....102 D3
Dadlington Leics....135 D8
Dafarn Faig Gwyn....163 F7
Dafen Carms....75 E8
Daffy Green Norf....141 B9
Dagdale Staffs....151 C11
Dagenham London....68 C3
Daggons Dorset....31 E10
Daglingworth Glos....81 D7
Dagnall Bucks....85 B7
Dagtail End Worcs....117 E10
Dagworth Suff....125 E10
Dail Beag W Isles....304 D4
Dail bho Dheas W Isles....304 B6
Dail bho Thuath
W Isles....304 B6
Daill Argyll....274 G4
Dailly S Ayrs....245 C7
Dail Mor W Isles....304 D4
Dainton Devon....9 B7
Dairsie or Osnaburgh
Fife....287 F8
Daisy Green Suff....125 D10
Suff....125 D11
Daisy Hill Gtr Man....195 G7
W Yorks....205 G8
W Yorks....205 F10
Daisy Nook Gtr Man....196 G2
Dalabrog W Isles....297 J3
Dalavich Argyll....275 B10
Dalballoch Highld....291 E8
Dalbeattie Dumfries....237 C10
Dalbeg Highld....291 B8
Dalblair E Ayrs....258 F4
Dalbog Angus....293 F7
Dalbury Derbys....152 C5
Dalby IoM....192 E3
Lincs....190 G6
N Yorks....216 E2
Dalchalloch Perth....291 G10
Dalchalm Highld....311 J3
Dalchenna Argyll....284 G4
Dalchirach Moray....301 F11
Dalchonzie Perth....285 E11
Dalchork Highld....309 H5
Dalchreichart Highld....290 B4
Dalchruin Perth....285 F11
Dalderby Lincs....174 B2
Dale Cumb....230 C6
Gtr Man....196 F3
Pembs....72 D4
Shetland....312 G6
Dale Abbey Derbys....153 B8
Dalebank Derbys....170 C5
Dale Bottom Cumb....230 G3
Dale Brow Ches E....184 F6
Dale End Derbys....170 C2
N Yorks....204 D5
Dale Head Cumb....221 B8
Dale Hill E Sus....53 G7
E Sus....53 G8
Dalelia Highld....289 C9
Dale Moor Derbys....153 B8
Dale of Walls Shetland....313 H3
Dales Brow Gtr Man....195 G9
Dales Green Staffs....168 D5
Daless Highld....301 F8
Dalestie Moray....292 B3
Dalestorth Notts....171 C8
Dalfaber Highld....291 B11
Dalgarven N Ayrs....266 F5
Dalgety Bay Fife....280 E3
Dalginross Perth....285 E11
Dalguise Perth....286 C3
Dalham Suff....124 E4
Dalhenzean Perth....292 G3
Dalintober Argyll....255 E7
Dalinlongart Argyll....276 E2
Dalkeith Midloth....270 B6
Dallam Warr....183 C9
Dallas Moray....301 D11
Dallas Lodge Moray....301 D11
Dallcharn Highld....308 D6
Dalleagles E Ayrs....258 G3
Dallicott Shrops....132 E5
Dallimores IoW....20 C6
Dallinghoo Suff....126 G5
Dallington E Sus....23 B11
Northants....120 E4
Dallow N Yorks....214 E3
Dalmadilly Aberds....293 B9
Dalmally Argyll....284 E5
Dalmarnock Glasgow....268 C2
Perth....286 C3
Dalmary Stirling....277 B10
Dalmellington E Ayrs....245 B11
Dalmeny Edin....280 F2
Dalmigavie Highld....291 B9
Dalmigavie Lodge
Highld....301 G7
Dalmilling S Ayrs....257 E9
Dalmore Highld....300 C6
Dalmuir W Dunb....277 G9
Dalnabreck Highld....289 C8
Dalnacardoch Lodge
Highld....291 F9
Dalnaglar Castle Perth....292 G3
Dalnahaitnach Highld....301 G8
Dalnamein Lodge Perth....291 G9
Dalnarrow Argyll....289 F9
Dalnaspidal Lodge
Perth....291 F8
Dalnavaid Perth....292 G2
Dalnavie Highld....300 B6
Dalnaw Dumfries....236 B5
Dalnawillan Lodge
Highld....310 E4
Dalness Highld....284 B5
Dalnessie Highld....309 H6
Dalqueich Perth....286 G4
Dalreavoch Highld....309 J7
Dalriach Highld....301 F10
Dalrigh Stirling....285 E7
Dalry Edin....280 G4
N Ayrs....266 F5
Dalrymple E Ayrs....257 G9
Dalscote Northants....120 G3
Dalserf S Lanark....268 E6
Dalshannon N Lanark....278 G4
Dalston Cumb....239 G9
London....67 C10
Dalswinton Dumfries....247 F10
Datchet Common
Windsor....66 D3
Datchworth Herts....86 B3
Datchworth Green Herts....86 B3
Dauber Gtr Man....195 F8
Daugh of Kinermony
Moray....302 E2
Davenham Ches W....183 G11
Davenport Ches E....168 B4
Gtr Man....184 D5
Davenport Green
Ches E....184 F4
Dalton Cumb....211 D10
Dumfries....238 C4
Lancs....194 F3
N Yorks....224 C3
N Yorks....224 D3
Northumb....241 E10
Northumb....242 C4
S Yorks....215 D8
S Yorks....187 C7
S Lanark....268 D3
Dalton-in-Furness
Cumb....210 E4
Dalton-le-Dale Durham....234 B4
Dalton Magna S Yorks....187 C7
Dalton-on-Tees
N Yorks....224 D5

Dalton Parva S Yorks....187 C7
Dalton Piercy Hrtlpl....234 E5
Dalveich Stirling....285 E10
Dalvanie Highld....300 F6
Dalwhinnie Highld....291 E8
Dalwood Devon....28 G2
Damask Green Herts....104 F5
Damems W Yorks....204 F6
Damerham Hants....31 D10
Damery Glos....80 G2
Damgate Norf....143 B8
Norf....161 F9
Dam Green Norf....141 F11
Damhead Moray....301 D10
Damhead Holdings
Midloth....270 B5
Dam Mill Staffs....133 C7
Damnaglaur Dumfries....236 F3
Dam of Quoiggs Perth....286 F3
Damside Borders....270 F3
Dam Side Lancs....202 D4
Danaway Kent....69 G11
Danbury Essex....88 E3
Danbury Common Essex....88 E3
Danby N Yorks....226 D4
Danby Wiske N Yorks....224 F6
Dancers Hill Herts....86 F2
Dancing Green Hereford....98 G2
Dandaleith Moray....302 E2
Danderhall Midloth....270 B6
Dandy Corner Suff....125 D11
Danebank Ches E....185 E7
Dane Bank Gtr Man....184 B6
Danebridge Ches E....169 B7
Dane End Herts....104 G6
Danegate E Sus....52 G5
Danehill E Sus....36 C6
Danemoor Green Norf....141 B11
Danesbury Herts....86 B2
Danesfield Shrops....132 E4
Danesford Shrops....132 E4
Danesmoor Derbys....170 C6
Dane Street Kent....54 C5
Daneway Glos....80 E6
Dangerous Corner
Gtr Man....195 G7
Lancs....194 E4
Shrops....132 D3
Daniel's Water Kent....54 E3
Danna na Cloiche Argyll....275 F7
Dannonchapel Corn....10 E6
Danskine E Loth....271 B11
Danthorpe E Yorks....209 G10
Danygraig Caerph....78 G2
Danzey Green Warks....118 D2
Dapple Heath Staffs....151 D10
Darby End W Mid....133 F9
Darby Green Hants....65 G10
Darbys Green Worcs....116 F5
Darby's Hill W Mid....133 F9
Darcy Lever Gtr Man....195 F8
Dardy Powys....78 B2
Darenth Kent....68 E5
Daresbury Halton....183 E9
Daresbury Delph Halton....183 E9
Darfield S Yorks....198 G2
Darfoulds Notts....187 G9
Dargate Kent....70 G5
Dargate Common Kent....70 G5
Dargill Perth....286 F3
Darite Corn....6 B5
Darkland Moray....302 C2
Darland Wrex....166 D5
Darlaston W Mid....133 D9
Darlaston Green W Mid....133 D9
Darley N Yorks....205 B9
Darley Abbey Derbys....153 B7
Darley Bridge Derbys....170 C3
Darley Dale Derbys....170 C3
Darleyford Corn....11 G11
Darley Green Warks....118 C3
Darley Head N Yorks....205 B9
Darley Hillside Derbys....170 C3
Darlingscott Warks....100 C4
Darlington Darl....224 C5
Darliston Shrops....149 C11
Darlton Notts....188 G3
Darmsden Suff....125 G11
Darnall S Yorks....186 D5
Darnaway Castle Moray....301 D9
Darnford Staffs....134 B2
Darnhall Ches W....167 C10
Darnhall Mains Borders....270 F4
Darn Hill Gtr Man....195 E10
Darnick Borders....262 C2
Darowen Powys....128 C6
Darra Aberds....303 E7
Darracott Devon....24 D2
Devon....40 F3
Darras Hall Northumb....242 C5
Darrington W Yorks....198 D3
Darrow Green Norf....142 F5
Darsham Suff....127 D8
Darshill Som....44 E6
Dartford Kent....68 E4
Dartford Crossing Kent....68 D5
Dartington Devon....8 C5
Dartmeet Devon....13 G9
Dartmouth Devon....9 E7
Darton S Yorks....197 F10
Darton Park London....67 F10
Darvel E Ayrs....258 B3
Darvillshill Bucks....84 F4
Darwell Hole E Sus....23 B11
Darwen Blackburn....195 C7
Dassels Herts....105 F7
Datchet Windsor....66 D3
Davidson's Mains Edin....280 F4
Davidstow Corn....11 D9
David's Well Powys....113 C10
Davington Dumfries....248 D4
Kent....70 G4
Daviot Aberds....303 G7

Daviot continued
Highld....301 F7
Davis's Town E Sus....23 B8
Davoch of Grange
Moray....302 D4
Davo Mains Aberds....293 F9
Davyhulme Gtr Man....184 B3
Daw Cross N Yorks....205 C11
Dawdon Durham....234 B4
Daw End W Mid....133 C10
Dawesgreen Sur....51 D8
Dawker Hill N Yorks....207 F7
Dawley Telford....132 B3
Dawley Bank Telford....132 B3
Dawlish Devon....14 F5
Dawlish Warren Devon....14 F5
Dawn Conwy....180 G5
Daw's Cross Som....27 C11
Daws Heath Essex....69 B10
Dawshill Worcs....116 G6
Daw's House Corn....12 D2
Dawsmere Lincs....157 C8
Daybrook Notts....171 F9
Day Green Ches E....168 D3
Dayhills Staffs....151 C9
Dayhouse Bank Worcs....117 B9
Daylesford Glos....100 F4
Ddol Flint....181 G10
Ddôl Cownwy Powys....147 F10
Ddrydwy Anglesey....178 F4
Deacons Hill Herts....85 F11
Deadman's Cross
C Beds....104 C2
Deadman's Green
Staffs....151 B10
Deadwater Hants....49 F10
Northumb....250 D4
Deaf Hill Durham....234 D3
Deal Kent....55 C11
Deal Hall Essex....89 F8
Dean Cumb....229 F7
Devon....8 C4
Devon....40 D4
Devon....41 D8
Dorset....31 D7
Edin....280 D7
Hants....33 B7
Hants....48 G2
Oxon....100 G6
Som....45 E7
Dean Bank Durham....233 E11
Deanburnhaugh
Borders....261 G9
Dean Court Oxon....83 D7
Dean Cross Devon....40 E4
Deane Gtr Man....195 F7
Hants....48 C4
Deanend Dorset....31 D7
Deanich Lodge Highld....309 L3
Deanland Dorset....31 D7
Deanlane End W Sus....34 E2
Dean Head S Yorks....197 G9
Dean Lane Head
W Yorks....205 G7
Dean Prior Devon....8 C4
Dean Row Ches E....184 E5
Deans W Loth....269 B10
Deans Bottom Kent....69 G11
Deanscales Cumb....229 F7
Deansgreen Ches E....183 D11
Dean's Green Warks....118 D2
Deanshanger Northants....102 D5
Deanshaugh Moray....302 E3
Deanston Stirling....285 G11
Dean Street Kent....53 C8
Dearham Cumb....229 D7
Dearne S Yorks....198 G2
De Beauvoir Town
London....67 C10
Debenham Suff....126 E3
Deblin's Green Worcs....98 B6
Dechmont W Loth....279 G10
Deckham T&W....243 E7
Deddington Oxon....101 E9
Dedham Essex....107 E11
Dedham Heath Essex....107 E11
Dedridge W Loth....269 B11
Dedworth Windsor....66 D2
Deebank Aberds....293 D8
Deecastle Aberds....292 D6
Deene Northants....137 E8
Deenethorpe Northants....137 E9
Deepcar S Yorks....186 B3
Deepclough Derbys....185 B8
Deepcut Sur....50 B2
Deepdale C Beds....104 B4
Cumb....212 C4
N Yorks....213 D7
Deepdene Sur....51 D7
Deeping Gate Lincs....138 B2
Deeping St James Lincs....138 B3
Deeping St Nicholas
Lincs....156 F4
Deepthwaite Cumb....211 C10
Deepweir Mon....60 B3
Deerhill Moray....302 D4
Deerhurst Glos....99 F7
Deerhurst Walton Glos....99 F7
Deerland Pembs....73 C7
Deerness Orkney....314 F5
Deer's Green Essex....105 E9
Deerstones N Yorks....205 C7
Deerton Street Kent....70 G3
Defford Worcs....99 C8
Defynnog Powys....95 F8
Deganwy Conwy....180 F3
Degar V Glam....58 D4
Degibna Corn....2 B3
Deighton N Yorks....225 D7
W Yorks....197 D7
York....207 D8
Deiniolen Gwyn....163 C9
Deishar Highld....291 B11
Delabole Corn....11 E6
Delamere Ches W....167 B9
Delfour Highld....291 C10
Delfrigs Aberds....303 G9
Dellieture Highld....301 F10
Dell Lodge Highld....292 B2
Dell Quay W Sus....22 C4
Delly End Oxon....82 C5
Delnabo Moray....292 B3
Delnadamph Aberds....292 C4
Delnamer Angus....292 G3
Delph Gtr Man....196 F3
Delves Durham....233 B8
Delvine Perth....286 C5
Delvin End Essex....106 E5
Dembleby Lincs....155 B10
Demelza Corn....5 C9
Denaby Main S Yorks....187 B7
Denbeath Fife....281 B7
Denbigh Denb....165 B9
Denbury Devon....8 B6
Denby Derbys....170 F6
Denby Bottles Derbys....170 F6
Denby Common Derbys....170 F6
Denby Dale W Yorks....197 E8
Denchworth Oxon....82 G5
Dendron Cumb....210 E4
Denel End C Beds....103 D10
Denend Aberds....302 F6
Dene Park Kent....52 D5
Deneside Durham....234 B4
Denford Northants....121 C9
Staffs....169 E7
Dengie Essex....89 E7
Denham Bucks....66 B4
Suff....124 E5
Suff....126 C3
Denham Corner Suff....126 C3
Denham End Suff....124 E5
Denham Green Bucks....66 B4
Denham Street Suff....126 C3
Denhead Aberds....303 D9
Fife....287 F8
Denhead of Arbilot
Angus....287 C9
Denhead of Gray
Dundee....287 D7
Denholm Borders....262 F3
Denholme W Yorks....205 G7
Denholme Clough
W Yorks....205 G7
Denholme Edge
W Yorks....205 G7
Denholme Gate
W Yorks....205 G7
Denio Gwyn....145 B7
Denmead Hants....33 E11
Denmore Aberdeen....293 B11
Denmoss Aberds....302 E6
Dennington Suff....126 D5
Dennington Corner Suff....126 D5
Dennington Hall Suff....126 D5
Denny Falk....278 E6
Denny Bottom Kent....52 F5
Denny End Cambs....123 D9
Dennyloanhead Falk....278 E6
Denny Lodge Hants....32 F6
Dennystown Falk....277 F7
Denshaw Gtr Man....196 E3
Denside Aberds....293 D10
Densole Kent....55 E8
Denston Suff....124 G5
Denstone Staffs....169 G9
Denstroude Kent....70 G6
Dent Cumb....212 B4
Dent Bank Durham....232 F4
Denton Cambs....138 F2
Darl....224 B4
E Sus....23 E7
Gtr Man....184 B6
Kent....55 D8
Kent....69 E7
Lincs....155 C7
Norf....142 F5
Northants....120 F6
N Yorks....205 D8
Oxon....83 E9
Denton Burn T&W....242 D5
Denton Holme Cumb....239 G10
Denton's Green Mers....183 B8
Denver Norf....140 C2
Denvilles Hants....22 B2
Denwick Northumb....264 G6
Deopham Norf....141 C11
Deopham Green Norf....141 D10
Deopham Stalland
Norf....141 D10
Depden Suff....124 F5
Depden Green Suff....124 F5
Deppers Bridge Warks....119 F7
Deptford London....67 D11
T&W....243 F9
Wilts....46 F4
Derby Derbys....153 B7
Devon....40 G5
Derbyhaven IoM....192 F3
Derbyshire Hill Mers....183 B9
Dereham Norf....159 G9
Dergoals Dumfries....236 D4
Deri Caerph....77 E10
Derril Devon....24 G4
Derringstone Kent....55 D8
Derrington Shrops....132 E2
Staffs....151 E7
Derriton Devon....24 G4
Derry Stirling....285 E10
Derrydarroch Stirling....285 E8
Derry Downs London....68 F3
Derry Fields Wilts....81 G8
Derryguaig Argyll....288 F6
Derry Hill Wilts....62 E3
Derrythorpe N Lincs....199 F10
Dersingham Norf....158 C3
Derwen Bridgend....58 C2
Denb....165 E9
Derwenlas Powys....128 D4
Derwydd Carms....75 B10
Desborough Northants....136 G6
Desford Leics....135 C9
Deskryshiel Aberds....292 B6
Detchant Northumb....264 B3
Detling Kent....53 B9
Deuchar Angus....292 G6
Deuddwr Powys....148 F4
Deuxhill Shrops....132 F3
Devauden Mon....79 F7
Devil's Bridge /
Pontarfynach Ceredig....112 B4
Devitts Green Warks....134 E5
Devizes Wilts....62 G4
Devol Inclyd....276 G6
Devonport Plym....7 D9
Devonside Clack....279 B8
Devon Village Clack....279 B8
Devoran Corn....3 B7
Dewar Borders....271 G7
Dewartown Midloth....271 C7
Dewlands Common
Dorset....31 F9
Dewlish Dorset....17 B11
Dewsbury W Yorks....197 C8
Dewsbury Moor
W Yorks....197 C8
Dewshall Court Hereford....97 E8
Dhoon IoM....192 D5
Dhoor IoM....192 C5
Dhowin IoM....192 B5
Dhustone Shrops....115 B11

Dial Green W Sus....34 B6
Dial Post W Sus....35 D11
Dibberford Dorset....29 G7
Dibden Hants....32 F6
Dibden Purlieu Hants....32 G6
Dickens Heath W Mid....118 B2
Dickleburgh Norf....142 G3
Dickleburgh Moor Norf....142 G3
Dickon Hills Lincs....174 D6
Didbrook Glos....99 E11
Didcot Oxon....64 B4
Diddington Cambs....122 D3
Diddlebury Shrops....131 F10
Diddywell Devon....25 B7
Didley Hereford....97 E9
Didling W Sus....34 D4
Didlington Norf....140 D5
Didmarton Glos....61 B10
Didsbury Gtr Man....184 C4
Didworthy Devon....8 C3
Diebidale Highld....309 L4
Digbeth W Mid....133 F11
Digg Highld....298 C4
Diggle Gtr Man....196 F4
Diglis Worcs....116 G6
Digmoor Lancs....194 F3
Digswell Herts....86 B3
Digswell Park Herts....86 C2
Digswell Water Herts....86 C3
Dihewyd Ceredig....111 F9
Dilham Norf....160 D6
Dilhorne Staffs....169 G7
Dillarburn S Lanark....268 G6
Dill Hall Lancs....195 B8
Dillington Cambs....122 D2
Dilston Northumb....241 E10
Dilton Marsh Wilts....45 D11
Dilwyn Hereford....115 G8
Dimlands V Glam....58 F3
Dimmer Som....44 G6
Dimple Derbys....170 C3
Gtr Man....195 D8
Dimsdale Staffs....168 F4
Dimson Corn....12 G4
Dinas Carms....92 E5
Corn....10 G4
Gwyn....144 B5
Gwyn....163 D7
Dinas Cross Pembs....91 D10
Dinas Dinlle Gwyn....162 D6
Dinas Mawddwy Gwyn....147 G2
Dinas Mawr Conwy....164 E4
Dinas Powys V Glam....59 E7
Dinbych / Denbigh
Denb....165 B9
Dinbych-y-Pysgod / Tenby
Pembs....73 E10
Dinckley Lancs....203 F9
Dinder Som....44 E5
Dinedor Hereford....97 D10
Dinedor Cross Hereford....97 D10
Dines Green Worcs....116 F6
Dingestow Mon....79 C7
Dingle Mers....182 D5
Dingleden Kent....53 G11
Dingley Northants....136 F5
Dingwall Highld....300 D5
Dinlabyre Borders....250 E2
Dinmael Conwy....165 G8
Dinnet Aberds....292 D6
Dinnington Som....28 E6
S Yorks....187 D8
T&W....242 C6
Dinorwic Gwyn....163 C9
Dinton Bucks....84 C3
Wilts....46 G4
Dinwoodie Mains
Dumfries....248 E4
Dinworthy Devon....24 D4
Dipford Som....28 C2
Dipley Hants....49 B8
Dippenhall Sur....49 D10
Dippertown Devon....12 E4
Dippin N Ayrs....256 E2
Dipple Moray....302 D3
S Ayrs....244 C6
Diptford Devon....8 D4
Dipton Durham....242 G5
Diptonmill Northumb....241 E9
Dirdhu Highld....301 G10
Direcleit W Isles....305 J3
Dirleton E Loth....281 E11
Dirt Pot Northumb....232 B3
Discoed Powys....114 E5
Discove Som....45 G7
Diseworth Leics....153 E9
Dishes Orkney....314 D6
Dishforth N Yorks....215 E7
Dishley Leics....153 E10
Disley Ches E....185 E7
Diss Norf....126 B2
Disserth Powys....113 F10
Distington Cumb....228 G6
Ditchampton Wilts....46 G5
Ditcheat Som....44 F6
Ditchfield Bucks....84 G4
Ditchford Hill Worcs....100 D4
Ditchingham Norf....142 E6
Ditchling E Sus....36 D4
Ditherington Shrops....149 G10
Ditteridge Wilts....61 F10
Dittisham Devon....9 E7
Ditton Halton....183 D7
Kent....53 B8
Ditton Green Cambs....124 F3
Ditton Priors Shrops....132 F2
Dittons E Sus....23 E10
Divach Highld....300 G4
Divlyn Carms....94 D5
Dixton Glos....99 E9
Mon....79 C8
Dizzard Corn....11 B9
Dobcross Gtr Man....196 F3
Dobs Hill Flint....166 C4
Dobson's Bridge Shrops....149 C9
Dobwalls Corn....6 C4
Doccombe Devon....13 D11
Dochamroch Highld....300 F6
Dochgarroch Highld....300 F6
Docker Lancs....211 E11
Docking Norf....158 B5
Docklow Hereford....115 F11
Dockray Cumb....230 G4
Cumb....239 G7
Dockroyd W Yorks....204 F6
Doc Penfro / Pembroke
Dock Pembs....73 E7
Docton Devon....24 C2
Dodbrooke Devon....8 G4
Dodburn Borders....249 B11
Doddenham Worcs....116 F5
Doddinghurst Essex....87 F9
Doddington Cambs....139 E7
Kent....54 B2
Lincs....188 G6

Doddington continued
Northumb 263 C11
Shrops 116 B2
Doddiscombsleigh Devon 14 D3
Doddshill Norf 158 C3
Doddycross Corn 6 C6
Dodford Northants 120 E2
Worcs 117 C8
Dodington S Glos 61 C9
Som 43 E7
Dodleston Ches W 166 C5
Dodmarsh Hereford 97 C11
Dodscott Devon 25 D8
Dods Leigh Staffs 151 C10
Dodworth S Yorks 197 F10
Dodworth Bottom
S Yorks 197 G10
Dodworth Green
S Yorks 197 G10
Doe Bank W Mid 134 D2
Doe Green Warr 183 D9
Doehole Derbys 170 D5
Doe Lea Derbys 171 B7
Doffcocker Gtr Man 195 E7
Dogdyke Lincs 174 D2
Dog & Gun Mers 182 B5
Dog Hill Gtr Man 196 F3
Dogingtree Estate
Staffs 151 G9
Dogley Lane W Yorks 197 E7
Dogmersfield Hants 49 C9
Dogridge Wilts 62 B5
Dogsthorpe Pboro 138 C3
Dog Village Devon 14 B5
Doirlinn Highld 289 D8
Dolanog Powys 147 G11
Dolau Powys 114 D2
Rhondda 58 C3
Dolbenmaen Gwyn 163 G8
Dole Ceredig 128 F2
Dolemeads Bath 61 G9
Doley Staffs 150 D4
Dolfach Powys 129 C8
Dol-ffanog Gwyn 146 G4
Dolfor Powys 130 F2
Dol-fôr Powys 128 B6
Dolgarrog Conwy 164 B3
Dolgellau Gwyn 146 F4
Dolgerdd Ceredig 111 G8
Dolgoch Gwyn 128 C3
Dolgran Carms 93 E8
Dolhelfa Powys 113 C8
Dolhendre Gwyn 147 C7
Doll Highld 311 J2
Dollar Clack 279 B9
Dolley Green Powys 114 D5
Dollis Hill London 67 B8
Dollwen Ceredig 128 G3
Dolphin Flint 181 G11
Dolphingstone E Loth 281 G7
Dolphinholme Lancs 202 C6
Dolphinston Borders 262 F5
Dolphinton S Lanark 270 F2
Dolton Devon 25 E9
Dolwen Conwy 180 G5
Powys 129 B9
Dolwyd Conwy 180 F4
Dolwyddelan Conwy 164 E2
Dôl-y-Bont Ceredig 128 F2
Dol-y-cannau Powys 96 B3
Dolydd Gwyn 163 D7
Dolyhir Powys 114 F4
Dolymelinau Powys 129 D11
Dolywern Wrex 148 B4
Domewood Sur 51 E10
Domgay Powys 148 F5
Dommett Som 28 E3
Doncaster S Yorks 198 G5
Doncaster Common
S Yorks 198 G6
Dones Green Ches W 183 F10
Donhead St Andrew
Wilts 30 C6
Donhead St Mary Wilts 30 C6
Donibristle Fife 280 D3
Doniford Som 42 E5
Donington Lincs 156 B4
Shrops 132 C6
Donington Eaudike
Lincs 156 B4
Donington le Heath
Leics 153 G8
Donington on Bain
Lincs 190 E2
Donington South Ing
Lincs 156 C4
Donisthorpe Leics 152 G6
Don Johns Essex 106 F6
Donkey Street Kent 54 G6
Donkey Town Sur 66 G2
Donna Nook Lincs 190 B6
Donnington Glos 100 F3
Hereford 98 E4
Shrops 131 B11
Telford 150 G4
W Berks 64 F3
W Sus 22 C5
Donnington Wood
Telford 150 G4
Donwell T&W 243 F7
Donyatt Som 28 E4
Doomsday Green
W Sus 35 B11
Doonfoot S Ayrs 257 F8
Dora's Green Hants 49 D10
Dorback Lodge Highld 292 B2
Dorcan Swindon 63 C7
Dorchester Dorset 17 C9
Oxon 83 G9
Dordale Worcs 117 C8
Dordon Warks 134 C5
Dore S Yorks 186 E4
Dores Highld 300 F5
Dorking Sur 51 D7
Dorking Tye Suff 107 D8
Dorley's Corner Suff 127 D7
Dormansland Sur 52 E2
Dormans Park Sur 51 E11
Dormanstown Redcar 235 G7
Dormer's Wells London 66 C6
Dormington Hereford 97 C11
Dormston Worcs 117 F9
Dorn Glos 100 E4
Dornal S Ayrs 236 B4
Dorney Bucks 66 D2
Dorney Reach Bucks 66 D2
Dorn Hill Worcs 100 E3
Dornie Highld 295 C10
Dornoch Highld 309 L7
Dornock Dumfries 238 D6
Dorrery Highld 310 D4
Dorridge W Mid 118 B3
Dorrington Lincs 173 E9
Shrops 131 C9
Dorsington Warks 100 B2
Dorstone Hereford 96 C6
Dorton Bucks 83 C11
Dorusduain Highld 295 C11
Doseley Telford 132 B3
Dosmuckeran Highld 300 C2
Dosthill Staffs 134 C4
Staffs 134 D4
Dothan Anglesey 178 G5
Dothill Telford 150 G2
Dottery Dorset 16 B5
Doublebois Corn 6 C3
Double Hill Bath 45 B8
Dougarie N Ayrs 255 D9
Doughton Glos 80 G5
Norf 159 D7
Douglas IoM 192 E4
S Lanark 259 C8
Douglas & Angus
Dundee 287 D8
Douglastown Angus 287 C8
Douglas Water S Lanark 259 B9
Douglas West S Lanark 259 C8
Doulting Som 44 E6
Dounby Orkney 314 D2
Doune Highld 291 C10
Highld 309 J4
Stirling 285 G11
Doune Park Aberds 303 C7
Douneside Aberds 292 C6
Dounie Argyll 275 D8
Highld 309 K5
Highld 309 L6
Dounreay Highld 310 C3
Doura N Ayrs 266 G6
Dousland Devon 7 B10
Dovaston Shrops 149 E7
Dovecot Mers 182 C6
Dovecothall Glasgow 267 D10
Dove Green Notts 171 E7
Dove Holes Derbys 185 F9
Dovenby Cumb 229 E7
Dovendale Lincs 190 E4
Dove Point Mers 182 C2
Dover Gtr Man 194 G6
Kent 55 E10
Dovercourt Essex 108 E5
Doverdale Worcs 117 D7
Doverhay Som 41 D11
Doveridge Derbys 152 C2
Doversgreen Sur 51 D9
Dowally Perth 286 C4
Dowanhill Glasgow 267 B11
Dowbridge Lancs 202 G4
Dowdeswell Glos 81 B7
Dowe Hill Norf 161 F10
Dowlais M Tydf 77 D10
Dowlais Top M Tydf 77 D9
Dowland Devon 25 E9
Dowles Worcs 116 B5
Dowlesgreen Wokingham 65 F10
Dowlish Ford Som 28 E5
Dowlish Wake Som 28 E5
Downall Green Gtr Man 194 G5
Down Ampney Glos 81 F10
Downan Moray 301 F11
S Ayrs 244 G3
Downcraig Ferry
N Ayrs 266 D3
Downderry Corn 6 E6
Downe London 68 G2
Downend Glos 80 F4
IoW 20 D6
S Glos 60 D6
W Berks 64 D3
Down End Som 43 E10
Downfield Dundee 287 D7
Down Field Cambs 124 C2
Downgate Corn 11 G11
Corn 12 G3
Down Hall Cumb 239 G7
Downham Essex 88 F2
Lancs 203 E11
London 67 E11
Northumb 263 C9
Downham Market Norf 140 C2
Down Hatherley Glos 99 G7
Downhead Som 29 B9
Som 45 D7
Downhead Park
M Keynes 103 C7
Downhill Corn 5 B7
Perth 286 D4
T&W 243 F9
Downholland Cross
Lancs 193 F11
Downholme N Yorks 224 F2
Downicary Devon 12 C3
Downies Aberds 293 D11
Downinney Corn 11 C10
Downley Bucks 84 G4
Down Park W Sus 51 F10
Downside C Beds 103 G10
E Sus 23 E9
N Som 60 F3
Som 44 D6
Sur 50 B6
Sur 51 B7
Down Street E Sus 36 C6
Down Thomas Devon 7 E10
Downton Hants 19 C11
Powys 114 E4
Shrops 149 G10
Wilts 31 C11
Downton on the Rock
Hereford 115 C8
Dowsby Lincs 156 D2
Dowsdale Lincs 156 G5
Dowslands Som 28 C2
Dowthwaitehead Cumb 230 G3
Doxey Staffs 151 E8
Doxford Park T&W 243 G9
Doynton S Glos 61 E8
Drabblegate Norf 160 D4
Draethen Newport 59 B8
Draffan S Lanark 268 F5
Dragley Beck Cumb 210 D5
Dragonby N Lincs 200 E2
Dragons Green W Sus 35 C10
Drakehouse S Yorks 186 E6
Drakeland Corner Devon 7 D11
Drakelow Worcs 132 G6
Drakemyre Aberds 303 F9
N Ayrs 266 E5
Drake's Broughton Worcs 99 B8
Drakes Cross Worcs 117 B11
Drakestone Green Suff 107 B9
Drakewalls Corn 12 G4
Draughton Northants 120 B5
N Yorks 204 C6
Drawbridge Corn 6 B3
Drax N Yorks 199 B7
Draycot Oxon 83 D10
Draycot Cerne Wilts 62 D2
Draycote Warks 119 C8
Draycot Fitz Payne Wilts 62 G6
Draycot Foliat Swindon 63 D7
Draycott Derbys 153 C8
Glos 80 E2
Glos 100 D3
Shrops 132 E6
Som 29 C8
Som 44 C3
Worcs 99 B7
Draycott in the Clay
Staffs 152 D3
Draycott in the Moors
Staffs 169 G7
Drayford Devon 26 E3
Drayton Leics 136 E6
Lincs 156 B4
Norf 160 G3
Northants 119 E11
Oxon 83 G7
Oxon 101 C8
Ptsmth 33 F11
Som 28 C6
Som 29 D7
Warks 118 F3
Worcs 117 B8
Drayton Bassett Staffs 134 C3
Drayton Beauchamp
Bucks 84 C6
Drayton Parslow Bucks 102 F6
Drayton St Leonard
Oxon 83 F10
Drebley N Yorks 205 B7
Dreemskerry IoM 192 C5
Dreenhill Pembs 72 C6
Drefach Carms 75 C8
Carms 92 G5
Carms 93 D7
Dre-fach Carms 75 B11
Ceredig 93 B10
Drefelin Carms 93 D7
Dreggie Highld 301 G10
Dreghorn Edin 270 B4
N Ayrs 257 B9
Dre-gôch Denb 165 B10
Drellingore Kent 55 E8
Drem E Loth 281 F10
Dresden Stoke 168 G6
Dreumasdal W Isles 297 H3
Drewsteignton Devon 13 C10
Driby Lincs 190 G5
Driffield E Yorks 208 B6
Glos 81 F9
Drift Corn 1 D4
Drigg Cumb 219 F11
Drighlington W Yorks 197 B8
Drimnin Highld 289 D7
Drimnin Ho Highld 289 D7
Drimpton Dorset 28 F6
Drimsynie Argyll 284 G5
Dringhoe E Yorks 209 C9
Dringhouses York 207 D7
Drinisiadar W Isles 305 J3
Drinkstone Suff 125 E9
Drinkstone Green Suff 125 E9
Drishaig Argyll 284 F5
Drissaig Argyll 275 B10
Drive End Dorset 29 F9
Driver's End Herts 86 B2
Drochedlie Aberds 302 C5
Drochil Borders 270 G3
Drointon Staffs 151 D10
Droitwich Spa Worcs 117 E7
Droman Highld 306 D6
Dromore Dumfries 237 C7
Dron Perth 286 F5
Dronfield Derbys 186 F5
Dronfield Woodhouse
Derbys 186 F4
Drongan E Ayrs 257 F10
Dronley Angus 287 D7
Droop Dorset 30 F3
Drope Cardiff 58 D6
Dropping Well S Yorks 186 C5
Droughduil Dumfries 236 D3
Droxford Hants 33 D10
Droylsden Gtr Man 184 B6
Drub W Yorks 197 B7
Druggers End Worcs 98 D5
Druid Denb 165 G8
Druidston Pembs 72 B5
Druim Highld 301 D9
Druimarbin Highld 290 F2
Druimavuic Argyll 284 C4
Druimdrishaig Argyll 275 F8
Druimindarroch Highld 295 G8
Druimkinnerras Highld 300 F4
Druimnacroish Argyll 288 E6
Druimsornaig Argyll 289 F9
Druimyeon More Argyll 255 B7
Drum Argyll 275 F10
Edin 270 B6
Perth 286 G4
Drumardoch Stirling 285 F10
Drumbeg Highld 306 F6
Drumblade Aberds 302 E5
Drumblair Aberds 302 E6
Drumbuie Dumfries 246 G3
Highld 295 B9
Drumburgh Cumb 239 F7
Drumburn Dumfries 237 C11
Drumchapel Glasgow 277 G10
Drumchardine Highld 300 E5
Drumchork Highld 307 L3
Drumclog S Lanark 258 B4
Drumdelgie Aberds 302 E4
Drumderfit Highld 300 D6
Drumdollo Aberds 302 F6
Drumeldrie Fife 287 G8
Drumelzier Borders 260 C4
Drumfearn Highld 295 D8
Drumgask Highld 291 D8
Drumgelloch N Lanark 268 B5
Drumgley Angus 287 B8
Drumgreen Angus 292 F6
Drumguish Highld 291 D9
Drumhead Aberds 293 B11
Drumin Moray 301 F11
Drumindorsair Highld 300 E4
Drumlasie Aberds 293 C8
Drumlean Stirling 285 G8
Drumlemble Argyll 255 F7
Drumliah Highld 309 K6
Drumligair Aberds 293 B11
Drumlithie Aberds 293 E9
Drumloist Stirling 285 G10
Drummersdale Lancs 193 E11
Drummick Perth 286 E3
Drummoddie Dumfries 236 E5
Drummond Highld 300 C6
Drummore Dumfries 236 F3
Drummuir Moray 302 E3
Drummuir Castle Moray 302 E3
Drumnadrochit Highld 300 G5
Drumnagorrach Moray 302 D5
Drumness Perth 286 F2
Drumoak Aberds 293 D9
Drumore Argyll 255 E8
Drumpark Dumfries 247 G9
Drumpellier N Lanark 268 B4
Drumphail Dumfries 236 C4
Drumrash Dumfries 237 B8
Drumrunie Highld 307 J6
Drumry W Dunb 277 G10
Drums Aberds 303 G9
Drumsallie Highld 289 B11
Drumsmittal Highld 300 E6
Drumstinchall
Dumfries 237 D10
Drumsturdy Angus 287 D8
Drumtochty Castle
Aberds 293 F8
Drumtroddan Dumfries 236 E5
Drumuie Highld 298 E4
Drumuillie Highld 301 G9
Drumvaich Stirling 285 G10
Drumwalt Dumfries 236 D5
Drumwhindle Aberds 303 F9
Drunkendub Angus 287 C10
Drury Flint 166 C3
Drurylane Norf 141 C8
Drury Lane Wrex 167 G7
Drury Square Norf 159 F8
Drybeck Cumb 222 B3
Drybridge Moray 302 C4
N Ayrs 257 B9
Drybrook Glos 79 B10
Dryburgh Borders 262 C3
Dryden Borders 261 E11
Dry Doddington Lincs 172 F4
Dry Drayton Cambs 123 E7
Dryhill Kent 52 B3
Dry Hill Hants 49 F7
Dryhope Borders 261 E7
Drylaw Edin 280 F4
Drym Corn 2 C4
Drymen Stirling 277 D9
Drymere Norf 140 B5
Drymuir Aberds 303 E9
Drynachan Lodge Highld 301 F8
Drynain Argyll 276 D3
Drynham Wilts 45 B11
Dryne Park Highld 300 D5
Drynoch Highld 294 B6
Dry Sandford Oxon 83 E7
Dryslwyn Carms 93 G11
Dry Street Essex 69 B7
Dryton Shrops 131 B11
Drywells Aberds 302 D6
Duag Bridge Highld 309 K3
Duartbeg Highld 306 F6
Duartmore Bridge
Highld 306 F6
Dubbs Cross Devon 12 C3
Dubford Aberds 303 C8
Dubhchladach Argyll 275 G9
Dublin Suff 126 D3
Dubton Angus 287 B9
Dubwath Cumb 229 E9
Duchally Highld 309 H3
Duchlage Argyll 276 D6
Duchrae Dumfries 246 G5
Duck Corner Suff 109 C7
Duck End Bedford 103 C11
Bedford 121 G9
Bucks 102 F5
Cambs 122 E4
Essex 105 G10
Essex 106 E3
Essex 106 F3
Duckend Green Essex 106 G4
Duckhole S Glos 79 G10
Duckington Ches W 167 E7
Ducklington Oxon 82 D5
Duckmanton Derbys 186 G6
Duck's Cross Bedford 122 F2
Ducks Island London 86 F2
Duckswich Worcs 98 D6
Dudbridge Glos 80 E4
Dudden Hill London 67 B8
Duddenhoe End Essex 105 D9
Duddingston Edin 280 G5
Duddington Northants 137 C9
Duddlestone Som 28 C2
Duddleswell E Sus 37 B7
Duddlewick Shrops 132 G3
Duddo Northumb 273 G8
Duddon Ches W 167 C8
Duddon Bridge Cumb 210 B3
Duddon Common
Ches W 167 B8
Dudleston Shrops 148 B6
Dudleston Grove Shrops 149 B7
Dudleston Heath (Criftins)
Shrops 149 B7
Dudley T&W 243 C7
W Mid 133 E8
Dudley Hill W Yorks 205 G9
Dudley Port W Mid 133 E9
Dudley's Fields W Mid 133 C9
Dudley Wood W Mid 133 F8
Dudlows Green Warr 183 E10
Dudsbury Dorset 19 B7
Dudswell Herts 85 D7
Dudwells Pembs 91 G8
Duerdon Devon 24 D4
Duffield Derbys 170 G4
Duffieldbank Derbys 170 G5
Duffryn Neath 57 B10
Newport 59 B9
Shrops 130 G4
Dufftown Moray 302 F3
Duffus Moray 301 C11
Dufton Cumb 231 F9
Duggleby N Yorks 217 F7
Duich Argyll 254 B4
Duiletter Argyll 284 D5
Duinish Perth 291 G8
Duirinish Highld 295 B9
Duisdalebeg Highld 295 D8
Duisdalemore Highld 295 D9
Duisky Highld 290 F2
Duke End Warks 134 F4
Dukesfield Northumb 241 F10
Dukestown Bl Gwent 77 C10
Dukinfield Gtr Man 184 B6
Dulas Anglesey 179 D7
Dulcote Som 44 E5
Dulford Devon 27 F9
Dull Perth 286 C2
Dullatur N Lanark 278 F4
Dullingham Cambs 124 F2
Dullingham Ley Cambs 124 F2
Dulnain Bridge Highld 301 G9
Duloch Fife 280 D2
Duloe Bedford 122 E3
Corn 6 D4
Dulsie Highld 301 E9
Dulverton Som 26 B6
Dulwich London 67 E10
Dulwich Village London 67 E10
Dumbarton W Dunb 277 F7
Dumbleton Glos 99 D10
Dumcrieff Dumfries 248 C4
Dumfries Dumfries 237 B11
Dumgoyne Stirling 277 E10
Dummer Hants 48 D5
Dumpford W Sus 34 C4
Dumpinghill Devon 24 F6
Dumpling Green Norf 159 G10
Dumplington Gtr Man 184 B3
Dumpton Kent 71 F11
Dun Angus 287 B10
Dunach Argyll 289 G10
Dunadd Argyll 275 D9
Dunain Ho Highld 300 E6
Dunalastair Perth 285 B11
Dunan Highld 295 C7
Dunans Argyll 275 D9
Argyll 275 D11
Dunball Som 43 E10
Dunbar E Loth 282 F3
Dunbeath Highld 311 G5
Dunbeg Argyll 289 F10
Dunblane Stirling 285 G11
Dunbog Fife 286 F6
Dunbridge Hants 32 B4
Duncansclett Shetland 313 K5
Duncanston Highld 300 D5
Duncanstone Aberds 302 G5
Dun Charlabhaigh
W Isles 304 D3
Dunchideock Devon 14 D3
Dunchurch Warks 119 C9
Duncombe Lancs 202 F6
Duncote Northants 120 G3
Duncow Dumfries 247 G11
Duncraggan Stirling 285 G9
Duncrievie Perth 286 G5
Duncroisk Stirling 285 D9
Duncton W Sus 35 D7
Dundas Ho Orkney 314 H4
Dundee Dundee 287 D8
Dundeugh Dumfries 246 F3
Dundon Som 44 G3
Dundonald Fife 280 C4
S Ayrs 257 C9
Dundon Hayes Som 44 G3
Dundonnell Highld 307 L5
Dundonnell Hotel Highld 307 L5
Dundonnell House
Highld 307 L6
Dundraw Cumb 229 B10
Dundreggan Highld 290 B5
Dundreggan Lodge
Highld 290 B5
Dundrennan Dumfries 237 E9
Dundridge Hants 33 D9
Dundry N Som 60 F5
Dundurn Perth 285 E11
Dundyvan N Lanark 268 C4
Dunecht Aberds 293 C9
Dunfermline Fife 279 D11
Dunfield Glos 81 F10
Dunford Bridge S Yorks 197 G7
Dungate Kent 54 B2
Dunge Wilts 45 C11
Dungeness Kent 39 D9
Dungworth S Yorks 186 D3
Dunham Notts 188 G4
Dunham-on-the-Hill
Ches W 183 G7
Dunham on Trent Notts 188 G4
Dunhampstead Worcs 117 E8
Dunhampton Worcs 116 D6
Dunham Town Gtr Man 184 D2
Dunham Woodhouses
Gtr Man 184 D2
Dunholme Lincs 189 F8
Dunino Fife 287 F9
Dunipace Falk 278 E6
Dunira Perth 285 E11
Dunkeld Perth 286 C4
Dunkerton Bath 45 B8
Dunkeswell Devon 27 F10
Dunkeswick N Yorks 206 D2
Dunkirk Cambs 139 F10
Ches W 182 G5
Kent 54 B5
Norf 160 D4
Nottingham 153 B11
S Glos 61 B9
Staffs 168 E4
Wilts 62 G3
Dunk's Green Kent 52 C6
Dunlappie Angus 293 G7
Dunley Hants 48 C3
Worcs 116 D5
Dunlichity Lodge Highld 300 F6
Dunlop E Ayrs 267 F8
Dunmaglass Lodge
Highld 300 G5
Dunmere Corn 5 B10
Dunmore Argyll 275 G8
Falk 279 D7
Highld 300 E5
Dunnerholme Cumb 210 D4
Dunnet Highld 310 B6
Dunnichen Angus 287 C9
Dunnikier Fife 280 C5
Dunninald Angus 287 B11
Dunning Perth 286 F4
Dunnington E Yorks 209 C9
Warks 117 G11
York 207 C9
Dunningwell Cumb 210 C3
Dunnockshaw Lancs 195 B10
Dunnose IoW 21 F7
Dunnsheath Shrops 149 F9
Dunn Street Kent 54 D3
Kent 69 G9
Dunollie Argyll 289 F10
Dunoon Argyll 276 F3
Dunragit Dumfries 236 D3
Dunrobin Mains Highld 311 J2
Dunrostan Argyll 275 E8
Duns Borders 272 E5
Dunsa Derbys 186 G2
Dunsby Lincs 156 D2
Dunscar Gtr Man 195 E8
Dunscore Dumfries 247 G9
Dunscroft S Yorks 199 F7
Dunsdale Redcar 226 B2
Dunsden Green Oxon 65 D8
Dunsfold Sur 50 F4
Dunsfold Common Sur 50 F4
Dunsfold Green Sur 50 F4
Dunsford Devon 14 D2
Sur 50 F4
Dunshalt Fife 286 F6
Dunshillock Aberds 303 E9
Dunsill Notts 171 C7
Dunsinnan Perth 286 D5
Dunskey Ho Dumfries 236 D2
Dunslea Corn 11 G11
Dunsley N Yorks 227 C7
Staffs 133 G7
Dunsmore Bucks 84 D5
Warks 119 B10
Dunsop Bridge Lancs 203 C9
Dunstable C Beds 103 G10
Dunstal Staffs 151 D11
Dunstall Staffs 152 E3
Dunstall Common Worcs 99 C7
Dunstall Green Suff 124 E4
Dunstall Hill W Mid 133 C8
Dunstan Northumb 265 F7
Dunstan Steads
Northumb 264 E6
Dunster Som 42 E3
Duns Tew Oxon 101 F9
Dunston Derbys 186 G5
Lincs 173 C9
Norf 142 C4
Staffs 151 F8
T&W 242 E6
Dunstone Devon 7 E11
Devon 8 G5
Dunston Heath Staffs 151 F8
Dunston Hill T&W 242 E6
Dunsville S Yorks 198 F6
Dunswell E Yorks 209 F7
Dunsyre S Lanark 269 F11
Dunterton Devon 12 F3
Dunthrop Oxon 101 F7
Duntisbourne Abbots
Glos 81 D7
Duntisbourne Leer Glos 81 D7
Duntisbourne Rouse
Glos 81 D7
Duntish Dorset 29 F11
Duntocher W Dunb 277 G9
Dunton Bucks 102 G6
C Beds 104 C4
Norf 159 C7
Dunton Bassett Leics 135 E10
Dunton Green Kent 52 B4
Dunton Patch Norf 159 C7
Dunton Wayletts Essex 87 G11
Duntrune Castle Argyll 275 D8
Duntulm Highld 298 B4
Dunure S Ayrs 257 F7
Dunvant / Dynfant
Swansea 56 C5
Dunvegan Highld 298 E2
Dunveth Corn 10 G5
Dunwear Som 43 F10
Dunwich Suff 127 C9
Dunwood Staffs 168 D6
Dupplin Castle Perth 286 F4
Durdar Cumb 239 G10
Durgan Corn 3 D7
Durgates E Sus 52 G6
Durham Durham 233 C11
Durisdeer Dumfries 247 C9
Durisdeermill Dumfries 247 C9
Durkar W Yorks 197 D10
Durleigh Som 43 F9
Durleighmarsh W Sus 34 C3
Durley Hants 33 D8
Wilts 63 G8
Durley Street Hants 33 D8
Durlock Kent 55 B9
Durlow Common
Hereford 98 D2
Durn Gtr Man 196 D2
Durnamuck Highld 307 K5
Durness Highld 308 C4
Durnfield Som 29 C7
Durno Aberds 303 G7
Durns Town Hants 19 B11
Duror Highld 289 D11
Durran Argyll 275 C10
Highld 310 C5
Durrant Green Kent 53 F11
Durrants Hants 22 B2
Durrington Wilts 47 E7
W Sus 35 F10
Durrisdale Orkney 314 D3
Dursley Glos 80 F3
Wilts 45 C11
Dursley Cross Glos 98 G3
Durston Som 28 B3
Durweston Dorset 30 F5
Dury Shetland 313 G6
Duryard Devon 14 C4
Duston Northants 120 E4
Dutch Village Essex 69 C9
Duthil Highld 301 G9
Dutlas Powys 114 B4
Duton Hill Essex 106 F2
Dutson Corn 12 D2
Dutton Ches W 183 F9
Duxford Cambs 105 B9
Oxon 82 F5
Duxmoor Shrops 115 B8
Dwygyfylchi Conwy 180 F2
Dwyran Anglesey 162 B6
Dwyrhiw Powys 129 C11
Dyce Aberdeen 293 B10
Dyche Som 43 E7
Dye House Northumb 241 F10
Dyer's Common S Glos 60 C5
Dyer's Green Cambs 105 B7
Dyffryn Bridgend 57 C11
Carms 92 G6
Ceredig 110 G5
Pembs 91 D8
Dyffryn Ardudwy Gwyn 145 E11
Dyffryn-bern Ceredig 110 G5
Dyffryn Castell Ceredig 128 G5
Dyffryn Ceidrych Carms 94 F4
Dyffryn Cellwen Neath 76 D5
Dyke Lincs 156 E2
Moray 301 D9
Dykehead Angus 292 G5
N Lanark 269 D7
Stirling 277 B11
Dykelands Aberds 293 G9
Dykends Angus 286 B6
Dykeside Aberds 303 E7
Dykesmains N Ayrs 266 G5
Dylife Powys 129 E7
Dymchurch Kent 39 B9
Dymock Glos 98 E4
Dynfant / Dunvant
Swansea 56 C5
Dyrham S Glos 61 D8
Dysart Fife 280 C6
Dyserth Denb 181 F9

E

Eabost Highld 294 B5
Eabost West Highld 298 E3
Each End Kent 55 B10
Eachway Worcs 117 B9
Eachwick Northumb 242 C4
Eadar Dha Fhadhail
W Isles 304 E2
Eagland Hill Lancs 202 D4
Eagle Lincs 172 B5
Eagle Barnsdale Lincs 172 B5
Eagle Moor Lincs 172 B5
Eaglesfield Cumb 229 F7
Dumfries 238 C6
Eaglesham E Renf 267 E11
Eaglestone M Keynes 103 D7
Eaglethorpe Northants 137 E11
Eagle Tor Derbys 170 C2
Eagley Gtr Man 195 E8
Eairy IoM 192 E3
Eakley Lanes M Keynes 120 G6
Eakring Notts 171 C11
Ealand N Lincs 199 E9
Ealing London 67 C7
Eals Northumb 240 F5
Eamont Bridge Cumb 230 F6
Earby Lancs 204 D3
Earcroft Blackburn 195 C7
Eardington Shrops 132 E4
Eardisland Hereford 115 F8
Eardisley Hereford 96 B6
Eardiston Shrops 149 D7
Worcs 116 D3
Earith Cambs 123 C7
Earle Northumb 263 D11
Earlestown Mers 183 B9
Earley Wokingham 65 E9
Earlham Norf 142 B4
Earlish Highld 298 C3
Earls Barton Northants 121 E7
Earls Colne Essex 107 F7
Earl's Common Worcs 117 F9
Earl's Court London 67 D9
Earl's Croome Worcs 99 C7
Earlsdon W Mid 118 B6
Earl's Down E Sus 23 B10
Earlsferry Fife 281 B9
Earlsfield Lincs 155 B8
London 67 E9
Earlsford Aberds 303 F8
Earl's Green Suff 125 D10
Earlsheaton W Yorks 197 C9
Earl Shilton Leics 135 D9
Earlsmill Moray 301 D9
Earl Soham Suff 126 E4
Earl Sterndale Derbys 169 B9
Earlston Borders 262 B3
E Ayrs 257 B10
Earlstone Common
Hants 64 G3
Earl Stoneham Suff 126 F2
Earl Stonham Suff 126 F2
Earlstoun Dumfries 246 G4
Earlswood Mon 79 F7
Sur 51 D9
Warks 118 C2
Earnley W Sus 22 D4
Earnock S Lanark 268 E3
Earnshaw Bridge Lancs 194 C4
Earsairidh W Isles 297 M3
Earsdon T&W 243 C8
Earsham Norf 142 F6
Earsham Street Suff 126 B4
Earswick York 207 B8
Eartham W Sus 22 B6
Earthcott Green S Glos 61 B7
Easby N Yorks 224 E3
N Yorks 225 D11
Easdale Argyll 275 B8
Easebourne W Sus 34 C5
Easenhall Warks 119 B9
Eashing Sur 50 E2
Easington Bucks 83 C11
Durham 234 C4
E Yorks 201 D11
Lancs 203 C10
Northumb 264 C4
Oxon 83 F11
Oxon 101 D9
Redcar 226 B4
Easington Colliery
Durham 234 C4
Easington Lane T&W 234 B3
Easingwold N Yorks 215 F10
Easole Street Kent 55 C9
Eason's Green E Sus 23 B8
Eassie Angus 287 C7
East Aberthaw V Glam 58 F4
Eastacombe Devon 25 B8
Devon 25 C9
Eastacott Devon 25 C10
East Acton London 67 C8
East Adderbury Oxon 101 D9
East Allington Devon 8 F5
East Amat Highld 309 K4
East Anstey Devon 26 B5
East Anton Hants 47 D11
East Appleton N Yorks 224 F4
East Ardsley W Yorks 197 B10
East Ashling W Sus 22 B4
East Aston Hants 48 D2
East Auchronie Aberds 293 C10
East Ayton N Yorks 217 B9
East Bank Bl Gwent 78 D2
East Barkwith Lincs 189 E11
East Barming Kent 53 C8
East Barnby N Yorks 226 C6
East Barnet London 86 F3
East Barns E Loth 282 F4
East Barsham Norf 159 C8
East Barton Suff 125 D8
East Beach W Sus 22 E5
East Beckham Norf 177 E11
East Bedfont London 66 E5
East Bergholt Suff 107 D11
East Bierley W Yorks 197 B7
East Bilney Norf 159 F9
East Blackdene Durham 232 D3
East Blatchington E Sus 23 E7
East Bloxworth Dorset 18 C3
East Boldon T&W 243 E9
East Boldre Hants 32 G5
East Bonhard Perth 286 E5
Eastbourne Darl 224 C6
E Sus 23 F10
East Bower Som 43 F10
East Brent Som 43 C11
Eastbridge Suff 127 D9
East Bridgford Notts 171 G11
East Briscoe Durham 223 B9
Eastbrook Som 28 C2
V Glam 59 E7
East Buckland Devon 41 G7
East Budleigh Devon 15 E7
Eastburn E Yorks 208 B5
W Yorks 204 E6
Eastburn Br W Yorks 204 E6
East Burnham Bucks 66 C3
East Burrafirth Shetland 313 H5
East Burton Dorset 18 D2
Eastbury London 85 G9
W Berks 63 D10
East Butsfield Durham 233 B8
East Butterleigh Devon 27 F7
East Butterwick
N Lincs 199 F10
Eastby N Yorks 204 C6
East Cairnbeg Aberds 293 F9
East Calder W Loth 269 B11
East Carleton Norf 142 C3
East Carlton Northants 136 F6
W Yorks 205 E10
East Chaldon or Chaldon
Herring Dorset 17 E11
East Challow Oxon 63 B11
East Charleton Devon 8 G5
East Chelborough Dorset 29 F9
East Chiltington E Sus 36 D5
East Chinnock Som 29 E7
East Chisenbury Wilts 46 C6
East Cholderton Hants 47 D9
Eastchurch Kent 70 E3
East Clandon Sur 50 C5
East Claydon Bucks 102 F4
East Clevedon N Som 60 E2
East Clyne Highld 311 J3
East Clyth Highld 310 F7
East Coker Som 29 E8
Eastcombe Glos 80 E5
East Combe Som 43 G7
East Common N Yorks 207 G8
East Compton Dorset 30 D5
Som 44 E6
East Cornworthy Devon 8 D6
Eastcote London 66 B6
Northants 120 G3
W Mid 118 B3
Eastcote Village London 66 B6
Eastcott Corn 24 D3
Wilts 46 B4
East Cottingwith
E Yorks 207 E10
Eastcotts Bedford 103 B11
Eastcourt Wilts 63 G8
Wilts 81 G7
East Cowes IoW 20 B6
East Cowick E Yorks 199 C7
East Cowton N Yorks 224 E6
East Cramlington
Northumb 243 B7
East Cranmore Som 45 E7
East Creech Dorset 18 E4
East Croachy Highld 300 G6
East Croftmore Highld 291 B11
East Curthwaite Cumb 230 B2
East Dean E Sus 23 F9
Glos 98 G3
Hants 32 B3
W Sus 34 E6
East Dene S Yorks 186 C6
East Denton T&W 242 D6
East Didsbury Gtr Man 184 C5
Eastdon Devon 14 F5
Eastdown Devon 8 F6
East Down Devon 40 E6
East Drayton Notts 188 F3
East Dulwich London 67 E10
East Dundry N Som 60 F5
East Ella Hull 200 B5
Eastend Essex 86 C6
Oxon 100 G6
East End Bedford 122 F2
Bucks 84 B4
C Beds 103 C9
Dorset 18 B5
Essex 89 D8
E Yorks 201 B9
E Yorks 209 B9
E Yorks 209 G9
Glos 81 E11
Hants 20 B3
Hants 33 C11
Hants 64 G2
Herts 105 F9
Kent 53 E11
Kent 53 F10
Kent 70 E3
M Keynes 103 C8
N Som 60 E3
Oxon 82 C5
Oxon 101 D9
Oxon 101 E7
S Glos 61 E9
Som 29 B10
Som 44 C5
Som 45 D7
Suff 108 E2
Suff 126 F3
East End Green Herts 86 C3
Easter Aberchalder
Highld 291 B7
Easter Ardross Highld 300 B6
Easter Balgedie Perth 286 G5
Easter Balmoral Aberds 292 D4
Easter Boleskine Highld 300 G5
Easter Brackland
Stirling 285 G10
Easter Brae Highld 300 C6
Easter Cardno Aberds 303 C9
Easter Compton S Glos 60 C5
Easter Cringate Stirling 278 D4
Easter Culfosie Aberds 293 C9
Easter Davoch Aberds 292 C6
Easter Earshaig
Dumfries 248 C2
Easter Ellister Argyll 254 B3
Easter Fearn Highld 309 L6
Easter Galcantray
Highld 301 E8
Eastergate W Sus 22 B6
Easterhouse Glasgow 268 B3
Easter Housebyres
Borders 262 B2
Easter Howgate Midloth 270 C4
Easter Howlaws Borders 272 G4
Easter Kinkell Highld 300 D5
Easter Knox Angus 287 D9
Easter Langlee Borders 262 B2
Easter Lednathie Angus 292 G5
Easter Milton Highld 301 D9
Easter Moniack Highld 300 E5
Eastern Green W Mid 134 G5
Easter Ord Aberdeen 293 C10
Easter Quarff Shetland 313 K6
Easter Rhynd Perth 286 F5
Easter Row Stirling 278 B5
Easterside Mbro 225 B10
Easter Silverford Aberds 303 C7
Easter Skeld Shetland 313 J5
Easter Softlaw Borders 263 C7
Easterton Wilts 46 C4
Easterton of Lenabo
Aberds 303 E10
Easterton Sands Wilts 46 B4
Eastertown Som 43 C10
Eastertown of Auchleuchries
Aberds 303 F10
Easter Tulloch Highld 291 B11
Easter Whyntie Aberds 302 C6
East Everleigh Wilts 47 C8
East Ewell Sur 67 G8
East Farleigh Kent 53 C8
East Farndon Northants 136 F4
East Fen Common
Cambs 124 C2
East Ferry Lincs 188 B4
Eastfield Borders 262 D2
Bristol 60 D5
N Lanark 269 C7
N Lanark 278 G4
Northumb 243 B7
N Yorks 217 C10
Pboro 138 D4
S Lanark 268 C2
S Yorks 197 G9
Eastfield Hall Northumb 252 B6
East Fields W Berks 64 F3
East Finchley London 67 B9
East Finglassie Fife 280 B5
East Firsby Lincs 189 D8
East Fleet Dorset 17 E8
East Fortune E Loth 281 F10
East Garforth W Yorks 206 G4
East Garston W Berks 63 D11
Eastgate Durham 232 D5
Norf 160 E2
Pboro 138 D4
East Gateshead T&W 243 E7
East Ginge Oxon 64 B2
East Gores Essex 107 G7
East Goscote Leics 154 G2
East Grafton Wilts 63 G9
East Grange Moray 301 C10
East Green Hants 49 E9
Suff 124 G3
Suff 127 D8
East Grimstead Wilts 32 B2
East Grinstead W Sus 51 F11
East Guldeford E Sus 38 C6
East Haddon Northants 120 D3
East Hagbourne Oxon 64 B4

Easthall Herts . . . 104 G3
East Halton N Lincs . . . 200 D6
Eastham Mers . . . 182 E5
— Worcs . . . 116 D3
East Ham London . . . 68 C2
Eastham Ferry Mers . . . 182 E5
Easthampstead Brack . . . 65 F11
Easthampton Hereford . . . 115 E8
East Hanney Oxon . . . 82 G6
East Hanningfield Essex . . . 88 E3
East Hardwick W Yorks . . . 198 D3
East Harling Norf . . . 141 F9
East Harlsey N Yorks . . . 225 F8
East Harnham Wilts . . . 31 B10
East Harptree Bath . . . 44 A5
East Hartford Northumb . . . 243 B7
East Harting W Sus . . . 34 D3
East Hatch Wilts . . . 30 B6
East Hatley Cambs . . . 122 G5
Easthaugh Norf . . . 159 F11
East Hauxwell N Yorks . . . 224 G3
East Haven Angus . . . 287 D9
Eastheath Wokingham . . . 65 F11
East Heckington Lincs . . . 173 G11
East Hedleyhope
Durham . . . 233 C11
East Helmsdale Highld . . . 311 H4
East Hendred Oxon . . . 64 B3
East Herringthorpe
S Yorks . . . 187 C7
East Herrington T&W . . . 243 G9
East Heslerton N Yorks . . . 217 D8
East Hewish N Som . . . 59 G11
East Hill Kent . . . 68 G5
East Hoathly E Sus . . . 23 B8
East Hogaland Shetland . . . 313 K5
East Holme Dorset . . . 18 D3
East Holton Dorset . . . 18 C5
Easthope Shrops . . . 131 D11
Easthopewood Shrops . . . 131 D11
East Horndon Essex . . . 68 B6
— Leics . . . 154 B6
— Notts . . . 172 E2
East Horrington Som . . . 44 D5
East Horsley Sur . . . 50 C5
East Horton Northumb . . . 264 C2
Easthouse Shetland . . . 313 J6
Easthouses Midloth . . . 270 B6
East Howdon T&W . . . 243 D8
East Howe Bmouth . . . 19 B7
East Huntspill Som . . . 43 E10
East Hyde C Beds . . . 85 B10
East Ilkerton Devon . . . 41 D8
East Ilsley W Berks . . . 64 C3
Easting Orkney . . . 314 A7
Eastington Devon . . . 26 F2
— Glos . . . 80 D3
— Glos . . . 81 D10
East Keal Lincs . . . 174 C5
East Kennett Wilts . . . 62 F6
East Keswick W Yorks . . . 206 E3
East Kilbride S Lanark . . . 268 C2
East Kimber Devon . . . 12 B5
East Kingston W Sus . . . 35 G9
East Kirkby Lincs . . . 174 C4
East Knapton N Yorks . . . 217 D7
East Knighton Dorset . . . 18 D2
East Knowstone Devon . . . 26 C4
East Knoyle Wilts . . . 45 G11
East Kyloe Northumb . . . 264 B3
East Kyo Durham . . . 242 G5
East Lambrook Som . . . 28 D6
East Lamington Highld . . . 301 B7
Eastland Gate Hants . . . 33 E11
East Langdon Kent . . . 55 D10
East Langton Leics . . . 136 E4
East Langwell Highld . . . 309 J7
East Lavant W Sus . . . 22 B5
East Lavington W Sus . . . 34 D6
East Layton N Yorks . . . 224 D3
Eastleach Martin Glos . . . 82 D2
Eastleach Turville Glos . . . 81 D11
East Leake Notts . . . 153 D11
East Learmouth
Northumb . . . 263 B9
Eastleigh Devon . . . 25 B7
— Hants . . . 32 D6
East Leigh Devon . . . 8 E3
— Devon . . . 25 H11
East Lexham Norf . . . 159 F7
East Lilburn Northumb . . . 264 E2
Eastling Kent . . . 54 B3
East Linton E Loth . . . 281 F11
East Liss Hants . . . 34 B3
East Lockinge Oxon . . . 64 B2
East Loftus Redcar . . . 226 B4
East Looe Corn . . . 6 E5
East Lound N Lincs . . . 199 G10
East Lulworth Dorset . . . 18 E3
East Lutton N Yorks . . . 217 F8
East Lydeard Som . . . 27 B11
East Lydford Som . . . 44 G5
East Lyng Som . . . 28 B4
East Mains Aberds . . . 293 D8
— Borders . . . 271 F11
— S Lanark . . . 268 E2
East Malling Kent . . . 53 B8
East Malling Heath Kent . . . 53 B7
East March Angus . . . 287 D8
East Marden W Sus . . . 34 E4
East Markham Notts . . . 188 G2
East Marsh NE Lincs . . . 201 E9
East Martin Hants . . . 31 D9
East Marton N Yorks . . . 204 C4
East Melbury Dorset . . . 30 C5
East Meon Hants . . . 33 C11
East Mere Devon . . . 27 D7
East Mersea Essex . . . 89 C9
East Mey Highld . . . 310 B7
East Molesey Sur . . . 67 F7
Eastmoor Derbys . . . 186 G4
— Norf . . . 140 C4
East Moors Cardiff . . . 59 D8
East Morden Dorset . . . 18 B4
East Morton W Yorks . . . 205 E7
East Moulsecoomb
Brighton . . . 36 F4
East Ness N Yorks . . . 216 D3
East Newton E Yorks . . . 209 F11
— N Yorks . . . 216 D2
Eastney Ptsmth . . . 21 B9
Eastnor Hereford . . . 98 D4
East Norton Leics . . . 136 C5
East Nynehead Som . . . 27 C11
East Oakley Hants . . . 48 C5
Eastoft N Lincs . . . 199 D10
East Ogwell Devon . . . 14 G2
Eastoke Hants . . . 21 B10
Easton Bristol . . . 60 E6
— Cambs . . . 122 C2
— Cumb . . . 239 C10
— Cumb . . . 239 F7
— Devon . . . 13 D10
— Dorset . . . 17 G9
— Hants . . . 48 G4

Easton continued
— IoW . . . 20 D2
— Lincs . . . 155 D8
— Norf . . . 160 G2
— Som . . . 44 D4
— Suff . . . 126 F5
— W Berks . . . 64 E2
— Wilts . . . 61 E11
Easton Grey Wilts . . . 61 E11
Easton in Gordano
N Som . . . 60 D4
Easton Maudit Northants . . . 121 F7
Easton on the Hill
Northants . . . 137 C10
Easton Royal Wilts . . . 63 G8
Easton Town Som . . . 44 G5
— Wilts . . . 61 B11
East Orchard Dorset . . . 30 D4
East Ord Northumb . . . 273 E9
Eastover Som . . . 43 F10
East Panson Devon . . . 12 C3
East Parley Dorset . . . 19 B8
East Peckham Kent . . . 53 D7
East Pennard Som . . . 44 F5
East Perry Cambs . . . 122 C3
East Portholland Corn . . . 5 G9
East Portlemouth Devon . . . 6 G6
East Prawle Devon . . . 9 G10
East Preston W Sus . . . 35 G9
East Pulham Dorset . . . 30 F2
East Putford Devon . . . 24 D5
East Quantoxhead Som . . . 42 E6
East Rainton T&W . . . 234 B2
East Ravendale NE Lincs . . . 201 G8
East Raynham Norf . . . 159 D7
Eastrea Cambs . . . 138 D5
East Rhidorroch Lodge
Highld . . . 307 K7
East Rigton W Yorks . . . 206 E3
Eastriggs Dumfries . . . 238 D6
Eastrington E Yorks . . . 199 B9
Eastrip Wilts . . . 61 E10
East Rolstone N Som . . . 59 G11
East Rounton N Yorks . . . 225 E8
East Row N Yorks . . . 227 C7
East Rudham Norf . . . 158 D6
East Runton Norf . . . 177 E11
East Ruston Norf . . . 160 D6
Eastry Kent . . . 55 C10
East Saltoun E Loth . . . 271 B9
East Sheen London . . . 67 D8
East Skelston Dumfries . . . 247 F8
East Sleekburn
Northumb . . . 253 G7
East Somerton Norf . . . 161 F9
East Stanley Durham . . . 242 G6
East Stockwith Lincs . . . 188 C3
East Stoke Dorset . . . 18 D3
— Notts . . . 172 F3
— Som . . . 29 D7
East Stour Dorset . . . 30 C4
East Stour Common
Dorset . . . 30 C4
East Stourmouth Kent . . . 71 G9
East Stowford Devon . . . 25 B10
East Stratton Hants . . . 48 F4
East Street Kent . . . 55 B10
— Som . . . 44 F4
East Studdal Kent . . . 55 D10
East Taphouse Corn . . . 6 C3
East-the-Water Devon . . . 25 B7
East Third Borders . . . 262 B4
East Thirston Northumb . . . 252 D5
East Tilbury Thurrock . . . 69 D7
East Tisted Hants . . . 49 F8
East Torrington Lincs . . . 189 E10
East Town Dorset . . . 30 C4
— Som . . . 44 E6
— Wilts . . . 45 B11
East Trewent Pembs . . . 73 F8
East Tuddenham Norf . . . 159 G11
East Tuelmenna Corn . . . 6 B4
East Tytherley Hants . . . 32 C4
East Tytherton Wilts . . . 62 E3
East Village Devon . . . 26 F4
— V Glam . . . 58 E3
Eastville Bristol . . . 60 E6
— Lincs . . . 174 D6
East Wall Shrops . . . 131 E10
East Walton Norf . . . 158 F4
East Water Som . . . 44 C4
East Week Devon . . . 13 C9
Eastwell Leics . . . 154 D5
East Wellow Hants . . . 32 C4
East Wemyss Fife . . . 280 B6
East Whitburn W Loth . . . 269 B9
Eastwick Herts . . . 86 C6
— Shetland . . . 312 F5
East Wickham London . . . 68 D3
East Williamston Pembs . . . 73 E8
East Winch Norf . . . 158 F3
East Winterslow Wilts . . . 47 G8
East Wittering W Sus . . . 21 B11
East Witton N Yorks . . . 214 B2
Eastwood Hereford . . . 98 C2
— Notts . . . 171 F7
— Southend . . . 69 B10
— S Yorks . . . 186 C6
— W Yorks . . . 196 B3
East Woodburn
Northumb . . . 251 F10
Eastwood End Cambs . . . 139 E8
Eastwood Hall Notts . . . 171 F7
East Woodhay Hants . . . 64 G2
East Woodlands Som . . . 45 E9
East Worldham Hants . . . 49 F8
East Worlington Devon . . . 26 D2
East Worthing W Sus . . . 35 G11
East Wretham Norf . . . 141 E8
East Youlstone Devon . . . 24 D3
Eathorpe Warks . . . 119 D7
Eaton Ches E . . . 168 B5
— Ches W . . . 167 D10
— Hereford . . . 115 F10
— Leics . . . 154 D4
— Norf . . . 142 B4
— Notts . . . 188 F2
— Oxon . . . 82 E6
— Shrops . . . 131 F7
— Shrops . . . 131 F10
Eaton Bishop Hereford . . . 97 D8
Eaton Bray C Beds . . . 103 G9
Eaton Constantine
Shrops . . . 131 B11
Eaton Ford Cambs . . . 122 F3
Eaton Green C Beds . . . 103 G9
Eaton Hastings Oxon . . . 82 F3
Eaton Mascott Shrops . . . 131 B10
Eaton on Tern Shrops . . . 150 E3
Eaton Socon Cambs . . . 122 F3
Eaton upon Tern Shrops . . . 150 E3
Eau Withington
Hereford . . . 97 C10
Eaves Green W Mid . . . 134 G5
Eavestone N Yorks . . . 214 F4
Ebberly Hill Devon . . . 25 D7

Ebberston N Yorks . . . 217 C7
Ebbesbourne Wake Wilts . . . 31 C7
Ebblake Hants . . . 31 F10
Ebbw Vale Bl Gwent . . . 77 D11
Ebchester Durham . . . 242 F4
Ebdon N Som . . . 59 G11
Ebford Devon . . . 14 D5
Ebley Glos . . . 80 D4
Ebnal Ches W . . . 167 F7
Ebnall Hereford . . . 115 F9
Ebreywood Shrops . . . 149 F10
Ebrington Glos . . . 100 C3
Ecchinswell Hants . . . 48 A4
Ecclaw Borders . . . 272 B5
Ecclefechan Dumfries . . . 238 C5
Eccles Borders . . . 272 G5
— Gtr Man . . . 184 B3
— Kent . . . 69 G8
Ecclesall S Yorks . . . 186 E4
Ecclesfield S Yorks . . . 186 C5
Ecclesgreig Aberds . . . 293 G9
Eccleshall Staffs . . . 150 D6
Eccleshill W Yorks . . . 205 F9
Ecclesmachan W Loth . . . 279 G11
Eccles on Sea Norf . . . 161 D8
Eccles Road Norf . . . 141 E10
Eccleston Ches W . . . 166 C6
— Lancs . . . 194 D4
— Mers . . . 183 B7
Eccleston Park Mers . . . 183 C7
Eccup W Yorks . . . 205 E11
Echt Aberds . . . 293 C9
Eckford Borders . . . 262 D6
Eckfordmoss Borders . . . 262 D6
Eckington Derbys . . . 186 F6
— Worcs . . . 99 C8
Eckington Corner E Sus . . . 23 D8
Ecklands S Yorks . . . 197 G8
Eckworthy Devon . . . 24 D6
Ecton Devon . . . 120 E6
— Staffs . . . 169 D9
Ecton Brook Northants . . . 120 E6
Edale Derbys . . . 185 D11
Edale End Derbys . . . 185 D11
Edbrook Som . . . 43 E8
Edburton W Sus . . . 36 E2
Edderside Cumb . . . 229 B7
Edderton Highld . . . 309 L7
Eddington Kent . . . 71 F7
— W Berks . . . 63 F11
Eddistone Devon . . . 24 C3
Eddleston Borders . . . 270 F4
Eddlewood S Lanark . . . 268 E4
Edenbridge Kent . . . 52 D2
Edenfield Lancs . . . 195 D9
Edenhall Cumb . . . 231 E7
Edenham Lincs . . . 155 E11
Eden Mount Cumb . . . 211 D8
Eden Park London . . . 67 F11
Edensor Derbys . . . 170 B2
Edentaggart Argyll . . . 276 C6
Edenthorpe S Yorks . . . 198 F6
Edentown Cumb . . . 239 F9
Eden Vale Durham . . . 234 D4
Ederline Argyll . . . 275 C9
Edern Gwyn . . . 144 B5
Edgarley Som . . . 44 F4
Edgbaston W Mid . . . 133 G11
Edgcote Northants . . . 101 B10
Edgcott Bucks . . . 102 G3
— Som . . . 41 F10
Edge Glos . . . 80 D4
— Shrops . . . 131 B7
Edgebolton Shrops . . . 149 E11
Edge End Glos . . . 79 C9
— Lancs . . . 203 G10
Edgefield Norf . . . 159 C11
Edgefield Street Norf . . . 159 C11
Edge Fold Blackburn . . . 195 F8
— Gtr Man . . . 195 F8
Edge Green Ches W . . . 167 E7
— Gtr Man . . . 183 B9
— Norf . . . 141 F10
Edgehill Warks . . . 101 B7
Edge Hill Mers . . . 182 C5
— Warks . . . 134 C4
Edgeley Gtr Man . . . 184 D5
— Shrops . . . 167 F8
Edgerston Borders . . . 262 G5
Edgerton W Yorks . . . 196 D6
Edgeside Lancs . . . 195 C10
Edgeworth Glos . . . 80 D6
Edgeworthy Devon . . . 26 E4
Edgiock Worcs . . . 117 E10
Edgmond Telford . . . 150 F4
Edgmond Marsh Telford . . . 150 E4
Edgton Shrops . . . 131 F7
Edgware London . . . 85 G11
Edgworth Blackburn . . . 195 D8
Edham Borders . . . 262 B6
Edial Staffs . . . 133 B11
Edinample Stirling . . . 285 E9
Edinbane Highld . . . 298 D3
Edinburgh Edin . . . 280 G5
Edinchip Stirling . . . 285 E9
Edingale Staffs . . . 152 G4
Edingight Ho Moray . . . 302 D5
Edinglassie Ho Aberds . . . 292 B5
Edingley Notts . . . 171 D11
Edingthorpe Norf . . . 160 C6
Edingthorpe Green Norf . . . 160 C6
Edington Som . . . 43 E11
— Wilts . . . 46 D2
Edingworth Som . . . 43 D11
Edintore Moray . . . 302 E4
Edistone Devon . . . 24 C2
Edithmead Som . . . 43 D10
Edith Weston Rutland . . . 137 B8
Edlaston Derbys . . . 169 G11
Edlesborough Bucks . . . 85 B7
Edlingham Northumb . . . 252 B5
Edlington Lincs . . . 190 G2
Edmondsham Dorset . . . 31 F8
Edmondsley Durham . . . 233 B10
Edmondstown Rhondda . . . 77 G8
Edmondthorpe Leics . . . 155 F7
Edmonston S Lanark . . . 269 G10
Edmonstone Orkney . . . 314 D5
Edmonton Corn . . . 10 G5
— London . . . 86 G4
Edmundbyers Durham . . . 242 G2
Ednam Borders . . . 262 B6
Ednaston Derbys . . . 170 G2
Edney Common Essex . . . 87 E11
Edradynate Perth . . . 286 B2
Edrom Borders . . . 272 D6
Edstaston Shrops . . . 149 C10
Edstone Warks . . . 118 E3
Edvin Loach Hereford . . . 116 F3
Edwalton Notts . . . 154 B2
Edwardstone Suff . . . 107 C8
Edwardsville M Tydf . . . 77 F9
Edwinsford Carms . . . 94 E2

Edwinstowe Notts . . . 171 B10
Edworth C Beds . . . 104 C4
Edwyn Ralph Hereford . . . 116 F2
Edzell Angus . . . 293 G7
Efail-fôch Neath . . . 57 B9
Efail Isaf Rhondda . . . 58 C5
Efailnewydd Gwyn . . . 145 B7
Efailwen Carms . . . 92 F2
Efenechtyd Denb . . . 165 D10
Effingham Sur . . . 50 C5
Effirth Shetland . . . 313 H5
Effledge Borders . . . 262 F1
Efflinch Staffs . . . 152 E4
Efford Devon . . . 26 G5
— Plym . . . 7 D10
Egbury Hants . . . 48 C2
Egdon Worcs . . . 117 G8
Egerton Gtr Man . . . 195 E8
— Kent . . . 54 D2
Egerton Forstal Kent . . . 53 D11
Egerton Green Ches E . . . 167 E8
Egford Som . . . 45 D9
Eggbeare Corn . . . 12 D2
Eggborough N Yorks . . . 198 C5
Eggbuckland Plym . . . 7 D10
Eggesford Station
Devon . . . 25 E11
Eggington C Beds . . . 103 F9
Egginton Derbys . . . 152 D5
Egginton Common
Derbys . . . 152 D5
Egglesburn Durham . . . 232 G5
Egglescliffe Stockton . . . 225 C8
Eggleston Durham . . . 232 G5
Egham Sur . . . 66 E4
Egham Hythe Sur . . . 66 E4
Egham Wick Sur . . . 66 E3
Egleton Rutland . . . 137 B7
Eglingham Northumb . . . 264 F4
Egloshayle Corn . . . 10 G5
Egloskerry Corn . . . 11 D11
Eglwysbach Conwy . . . 180 G4
Eglwys-Brewis V Glam . . . 58 F4
Eglwys Cross Wrex . . . 167 G7
Eglwys Fach Ceredig . . . 128 D3
Eglwyswen Pembs . . . 92 D3
Eglwyswrw Pembs . . . 92 D2
Egmanton Notts . . . 172 B2
Egmere Norf . . . 159 B8
Egremont Cumb . . . 219 C10
— Mers . . . 182 C4
Egton N Yorks . . . 226 D6
Egton Bridge N Yorks . . . 226 D6
Egypt Bucks . . . 66 B3
— Hants . . . 48 E3
— W Berks . . . 64 E4
Eiden Highld . . . 309 J7
Eight Ash Green Essex . . . 107 F8
Eighton Banks T&W . . . 243 F7
Eignaig Highld . . . 289 E9
Eign Hill Hereford . . . 97 D10
Eil Highld . . . 291 B10
Eilanreach Highld . . . 295 D10
Eilean Anabaich
W Isles . . . 305 H4
Eilean Darach Highld . . . 307 L6
Eilean Shona Ho Highld . . . 289 B8
Eisgean W Isles . . . 305 G5
Eisingrug Gwyn . . . 146 C2
Eland Green Northumb . . . 242 C5
Elan Village Powys . . . 113 D8
Elberton S Glos . . . 60 B6
Elborough N Som . . . 43 B11
Elbridge W Sus . . . 22 B6
Elburton Plym . . . 7 E10
Elcho Perth . . . 286 E5
Elcombe Swindon . . . 62 C6
Elcot W Berks . . . 63 F11
Eldene Swindon . . . 63 C7
Eldernell Cambs . . . 138 D6
Eldersfield Worcs . . . 98 E6
Elderslie Renfs . . . 267 C8
Elder Street Essex . . . 105 E11
Eldon Durham . . . 233 F10
Eldon Lane Durham . . . 233 F10
Eldrick S Ayrs . . . 245 G2
Eldroth N Yorks . . . 212 F5
Eldwick W Yorks . . . 205 E8
Elemore Vale T&W . . . 234 B3
Elerch / Bont-goch
Ceredig . . . 128 F3
Elfhowe Cumb . . . 221 F9
Elford Northumb . . . 264 C5
— Staffs . . . 152 F3
Elford Closes Cambs . . . 123 C10
Elgin Moray . . . 302 C2
Elgol Highld . . . 295 D7
Elham Kent . . . 55 E7
Elilaw Northumb . . . 264 D2
Elim Anglesey . . . 178 D5
Eling Hants . . . 32 E5
— W Berks . . . 64 D4
Eliock Dumfries . . . 247 G9
Elishader Highld . . . 298 C5
Elishaw Northumb . . . 251 D9
Elizafield Dumfries . . . 238 C2
Elkesley Notts . . . 187 F11
Elkington Northants . . . 120 B2
Elkins Green Essex . . . 87 E10
Elkstone Glos . . . 81 C7
Ellacombe Torbay . . . 9 C8
Elland W Yorks . . . 196 C6
Elland Lower Edge
W Yorks . . . 196 C6
Elland Upper Edge
W Yorks . . . 196 C6
Ellary Argyll . . . 275 F7
Ellastone Staffs . . . 169 G10
Ellel Lancs . . . 202 B5
Ellemford Borders . . . 272 C4
Ellenabeich Argyll . . . 275 B8
Ellenborough Cumb . . . 228 D6
Ellenbrook Herts . . . 86 D2
— IoM . . . 192 E4
Ellenglaze Corn . . . 4 D5
Ellenhall Staffs . . . 150 D6
Ellen's Green Sur . . . 50 F5
Ellerbeck N Yorks . . . 225 F8
Ellerburn N Yorks . . . 217 C8
Ellerby N Yorks . . . 226 C5
Ellerdine Telford . . . 150 E2
Ellerdine Heath Telford . . . 150 E2
Elleric Argyll . . . 284 C4
Ellerker E Yorks . . . 200 B2
Ellerton E Yorks . . . 207 F10
— N Yorks . . . 224 F4
— Shrops . . . 150 D4
Ellesborough Bucks . . . 84 D4
Ellesmere Shrops . . . 149 C8
Ellesmere Park Gtr Man . . . 184 B3
Ellesmere Port Ches W . . . 182 F6

Ellicombe Som . . . 42 E3
Ellingham Hants . . . 31 F10
— Norf . . . 143 E7
— Northumb . . . 264 D5
Ellingstring N Yorks . . . 214 C3
Ellington Cambs . . . 122 C3
— Northumb . . . 253 E7
Ellington Thorpe Cambs . . . 122 C3
Elliot Angus . . . 287 D10
Elliots Green Som . . . 45 D9
Elliot's Town Caerph . . . 77 E10
Ellisfield Hants . . . 48 D6
Ellistown Leics . . . 153 G8
Elliston Borders . . . 262 D3
Ellonby Cumb . . . 230 D4
Ellough Suff . . . 143 F8
Elloughton E Yorks . . . 200 B2
Ellwood Glos . . . 79 D9
Elm Cambs . . . 139 B9
Elm Corner Sur . . . 50 B5
Elm Cross Wilts . . . 62 D6
Elmdon Essex . . . 105 D9
— W Mid . . . 134 G3
Elmdon Heath W Mid . . . 134 G3
Elmer W Sus . . . 35 G7
Elmer's End London . . . 67 F11
Elmers Green Lancs . . . 194 F3
Elmesthorpe Leics . . . 135 E9
Elm Hill Dorset . . . 30 B4
Elmhurst Staffs . . . 152 G2
Elmley Castle Worcs . . . 99 C9
Elmley Lovett Worcs . . . 117 D7
Elmore Glos . . . 80 B3
Elmore Back Glos . . . 80 B3
Elm Park London . . . 68 B4
Elmscott Devon . . . 24 C3
Elmsett Suff . . . 107 B11
Elms Green Hereford . . . 115 D10
— Worcs . . . 116 D4
Elmslack Lancs . . . 211 D9
Elmstead Essex . . . 107 F11
Elmstead Heath Essex . . . 107 G11
Elmstead Market
Essex . . . 107 G11
Elmsted Kent . . . 54 E6
Elmsthorpe Leics . . . 135 D9
Elmstone Kent . . . 71 G9
Elmstone Hardwicke
Glos . . . 99 F8
Elmswell E Yorks . . . 208 C5
— Suff . . . 125 E9
Elmton Derbys . . . 187 G8
Elness Orkney . . . 314 C6
Elphin Highld . . . 307 H7
Elphinstone E Loth . . . 281 G7
Elrick Aberds . . . 293 C10
Elrig Dumfries . . . 236 E5
Elrington Northumb . . . 241 E9
Elsdon Hereford . . . 114 G6
— Northumb . . . 251 E10
Elsecar S Yorks . . . 186 B5
Elsenham Essex . . . 105 F10
Elsenham Sta Essex . . . 105 F10
Elsfield Oxon . . . 83 C8
Elsham N Lincs . . . 200 E4
Elsing Norf . . . 159 F11
Elslack N Yorks . . . 204 D4
Elson Hants . . . 33 G10
— Shrops . . . 149 B7
Elsrickle S Lanark . . . 269 G11
Elstead Sur . . . 50 E2
Elsted W Sus . . . 34 D4
Elsthorpe Lincs . . . 155 E11
Elston Devon . . . 26 G3
— Lancs . . . 203 G7
— Notts . . . 172 F3
— Wilts . . . 46 E5
Elstone Devon . . . 25 D11
Elstow Bedford . . . 103 B11
Elstree Herts . . . 85 F11
Elstronwick E Yorks . . . 209 G10
Elswick Lancs . . . 202 F4
— T&W . . . 242 E6
Elswick Leys Lancs . . . 202 F4
Elsworth Cambs . . . 122 E6
Elterwater Cumb . . . 220 E6
Eltham London . . . 68 D2
Eltisley Cambs . . . 122 F5
Elton Cambs . . . 137 E11
— Ches W . . . 183 G7
— Derbys . . . 170 C2
— Glos . . . 80 C2
— Gtr Man . . . 195 E9
— Hereford . . . 115 C9
— Notts . . . 154 B4
— Stockton . . . 225 B9
Elton Green Ches W . . . 183 G7
Elton's Marsh Hereford . . . 97 C9
Eltringham Northumb . . . 242 E3
Elvanfoot S Lanark . . . 259 F11
Elvaston Derbys . . . 153 C8
Elveden Suff . . . 124 G6
Elvet Hill Durham . . . 233 C11
Elvingston E Loth . . . 281 G9
Elvington Kent . . . 55 C9
— York . . . 207 D9
Elwell Devon . . . 25 D11
— Dorset . . . 17 E9
Elwick Hrtlpl . . . 234 E5
— Northumb . . . 264 B4
Elworth Ches E . . . 168 C2
Elworthy Som . . . 42 G5
Ely Cambs . . . 139 G10
— Cardiff . . . 58 D6
Emberton M Keynes . . . 103 B7
Embleton Cumb . . . 229 E9
— Durham . . . 234 F4
— Northumb . . . 264 E6
Embo Highld . . . 311 K2
Emborough Som . . . 44 C6
Embo Street Highld . . . 311 K2
Embsay N Yorks . . . 204 C6
Emersons Green S Glos . . . 61 D7
Emerson Park London . . . 68 B4
Emerson's Green S Glos . . . 61 D7
Emerson Valley
M Keynes . . . 102 D6
Emery Down Hants . . . 32 F3
Emley W Yorks . . . 197 E8
Emley Moor W Yorks . . . 197 E8
Emmbrook Wokingham . . . 65 F9
Emmer Green Reading . . . 65 D8
Emmett Carr Derbys . . . 187 F7
Emmington Oxon . . . 84 E2
Emneth Norf . . . 139 B9
Emneth Hungate Norf . . . 139 B10
Empingham Rutland . . . 137 B8
Empshott Hants . . . 49 F8
Empshott Green Hants . . . 49 G8
Emstrey Shrops . . . 149 G10
Emsworth Hants . . . 22 B2

Enborne W Berks . . . 64 F2
Enborne Row W Berks . . . 64 F2
Enchmarsh Shrops . . . 131 D10
Enderby Leics . . . 135 D10
Endmoor Cumb . . . 211 C10
Endon Staffs . . . 168 E6
Endon Bank Staffs . . . 168 E6
Energlyn Caerph . . . 58 B6
Enfield London . . . 86 F4
— Worcs . . . 117 D10
Enfield Highway London . . . 86 F5
Enfield Lock London . . . 86 F5
Enfield Town London . . . 86 F4
Enfield Wash London . . . 86 F5
Enford Wilts . . . 46 D6
Engamoor Shetland . . . 313 H4
Engedi Anglesey . . . 178 F5
Engine Common S Glos . . . 61 C7
Englefield W Berks . . . 64 E6
Englefield Green Sur . . . 66 E3
Englesea-brook Ches E . . . 168 E3
English Bicknor Glos . . . 79 B9
Englishcombe Bath . . . 61 G8
English Frankton
Shrops . . . 149 D9
Engollan Corn . . . 10 G3
Enham Alamein Hants . . . 47 D11
Enmore Som . . . 43 G8
Enmore Field Hereford . . . 115 E9
Enmore Green Dorset . . . 30 C5
Ennerdale Bridge
Cumb . . . 219 B11
Enniscaven Corn . . . 5 D9
Enoch Dumfries . . . 247 C9
Enochdhu Perth . . . 292 G2
Ensay Argyll . . . 288 E5
Ensbury Bmouth . . . 19 B7
Ensbury Park Bmouth . . . 19 C7
Ensdon Shrops . . . 149 F8
Ensis Devon . . . 25 B9
Enslow Oxon . . . 83 B7
Enstone Oxon . . . 101 G7
Enterkinfoot Dumfries . . . 247 C9
Enterpen N Yorks . . . 225 D9
Enton Green Sur . . . 50 E3
Enville Staffs . . . 132 F6
Eolaigearraidh W Isles . . . 297 L3
Eòrabus Argyll . . . 288 G5
Eòropaidh W Isles . . . 304 B7
Epney Glos . . . 80 C3
Epperstone Notts . . . 171 F11
Epping Essex . . . 87 E7
Epping Green Essex . . . 86 D6
— Herts . . . 86 D3
Epping Upland Essex . . . 86 E6
Eppleby N Yorks . . . 224 C3
Eppleworth E Yorks . . . 208 G6
Epsom Sur . . . 67 G8
Epwell Oxon . . . 101 C7
Epworth N Lincs . . . 199 G9
Epworth Turbary
N Lincs . . . 199 G9
Erbistock Wrex . . . 166 G5
Erbusaig Highld . . . 295 C9
Erchless Castle Highld . . . 300 E4
Erdington W Mid . . . 134 E2
Eredine Highld . . . 275 C10
Eriboll Highld . . . 308 D4
Ericstane Dumfries . . . 260 C3
Eridge Green E Sus . . . 52 F5
Erines Argyll . . . 275 F9
Eriswell Suff . . . 124 B4
Erith London . . . 68 D4
Erlestoke Wilts . . . 46 D3
Ermine Lincs . . . 189 G7
Ermington Plym . . . 8 E2
Ernesettle Plym . . . 7 D8
Erpingham Norf . . . 160 C3
Erriottwood Kent . . . 54 B2
Errogie Highld . . . 300 G5
Errol Perth . . . 286 E6
Errol Station Perth . . . 286 E6
Erskine Renfs . . . 277 G9
Erskine Bridge Renfs . . . 277 G9
Ervie Dumfries . . . 236 C2
Erwarton Suff . . . 108 E4
Erwood Powys . . . 95 C11
Eryholme N Yorks . . . 224 D6
Eryrys Denb . . . 166 D2
Escomb Durham . . . 233 E9
Escott Som . . . 42 F5
Escrick N Yorks . . . 207 E8
Esgairdawe Carms . . . 94 C2
Esgairgeiliog Powys . . . 128 B5
Esgyryn Conwy . . . 180 F4
Esh Durham . . . 233 C9
Esher Sur . . . 66 G6
Eshiels Borders . . . 261 B7
Esholt W Yorks . . . 205 E9
Eshott Northumb . . . 252 D6
Eshton N Yorks . . . 204 B4
Esh Winning Durham . . . 233 C9
Eskadale Highld . . . 300 F4
Eskbank Midloth . . . 270 B6
Eskdale Green Cumb . . . 220 E2
Eskdalemuir Dumfries . . . 249 D7
Eske E Yorks . . . 209 E7
Eskham Lincs . . . 190 B5
Eskholme S Yorks . . . 198 D6
Esknish Argyll . . . 274 G4
Esperley Lane Ends
Durham . . . 233 G8
Esprick Lancs . . . 202 F4
Essendine Rutland . . . 155 G10
Essendon Herts . . . 86 D3
Essich Highld . . . 300 F6
Essington Staffs . . . 133 C9
Esslemont Aberds . . . 303 G9
Eston Redcar . . . 225 B11
Estover Plym . . . 7 D10
Eswick Shetland . . . 313 H6
Etal Northumb . . . 263 B10
Etchilhampton Wilts . . . 62 G4
Etchingham E Sus . . . 38 G2
Etchinghill Kent . . . 55 F7
— Staffs . . . 151 F11
Etchingwood E Sus . . . 37 C8
Etherley Dene Durham . . . 233 F9
Ethie Mains Angus . . . 287 C10
Etling Green Norf . . . 159 F10
Etloe Glos . . . 79 D11
Eton Windsor . . . 66 D3
Eton Wick Windsor . . . 66 D3
Etruria Stoke . . . 168 F5
Etsell Shrops . . . 131 C7
Etteridge Highld . . . 291 D8
Ettersgill Durham . . . 232 F3
Ettiley Heath Ches E . . . 168 C2
Ettingshall W Mid . . . 133 D8
Ettingshall Park W Mid . . . 133 D8
Ettington Warks . . . 100 B5
Etton E Yorks . . . 208 E5
— Pboro . . . 138 B2
Ettrick Borders . . . 261 G7
Ettrickbridge Borders . . . 261 E10
Ettrickdale Argyll . . . 275 G11
Ettrickhill Borders . . . 261 G7
Etwall Derbys . . . 152 C5
Etwall Common Derbys . . . 152 C5
Eudon Burnell Shrops . . . 132 F3
Eudon George Shrops . . . 132 F3
Euston Suff . . . 125 B7
Euximoor Drove Cambs . . . 139 D9
Euxton Lancs . . . 194 D5
Evancoyd Powys . . . 114 F5
Evanstown Bridgend . . . 58 B3
Evanton Highld . . . 300 C6
Evedon Lincs . . . 173 F9
Evelix Highld . . . 309 K7
Evendine Hereford . . . 98 C5
Evenjobb / Einsiob
Powys . . . 114 E5
Evenley Northants . . . 101 E11
Evenlode Glos . . . 100 F4
Even Pits Hereford . . . 97 D11
Even Swindon Swindon . . . 62 B6
Evenwood Durham . . . 233 G9
Evenwood Gate Durham . . . 233 G9
Everbay Orkney . . . 314 D6
Evercreech Som . . . 44 F6
Everdon Northants . . . 119 F11
Everingham E Yorks . . . 208 E2
Everland Shetland . . . 312 D8
Everleigh Wilts . . . 47 C8
Everley N Yorks . . . 217 B9
Eversholt C Beds . . . 103 D9
Evershot Dorset . . . 29 G9
Eversley Hants . . . 65 G9
Eversley Centre Hants . . . 65 G9
Eversley Cross Hants . . . 65 G9
Everthorpe E Yorks . . . 208 G4
Everton C Beds . . . 122 G4
— Hants . . . 19 C11
— Mers . . . 182 C5
— Notts . . . 187 C11
Evertown Dumfries . . . 239 B9
Evesbatch Hereford . . . 98 B3
Evesham Worcs . . . 99 C10
Evington Kent . . . 54 D6
— Leicester . . . 136 C2
Ewanrigg Cumb . . . 228 D6
Ewden Village S Yorks . . . 186 B3
Ewell Sur . . . 67 G8
Ewell Minnis Kent . . . 55 E9
Ewelme Oxon . . . 83 G10
Ewen Glos . . . 81 F7
Ewenny V Glam . . . 58 D2
Ewerby Lincs . . . 173 F10
Ewerby Thorpe Lincs . . . 173 F10
Ewes Dumfries . . . 249 E9
Ewesley Northumb . . . 252 E4
Ewhurst Sur . . . 50 E5
Ewhurst Green E Sus . . . 38 G3
— Sur . . . 50 F5
Ewloe Flint . . . 166 B4
Ewloe Green Flint . . . 166 B3
Ewood Blackburn . . . 195 B8
Ewood Bridge Lancs . . . 195 C9
Eworthy Devon . . . 12 C5
Ewshot Hants . . . 49 C10
Ewyas Harold Hereford . . . 97 F7
Exbourne Devon . . . 25 G10
Exbury Hants . . . 20 B4
Exceat E Sus . . . 23 F8
Exebridge Devon . . . 26 C6
Exelby N Yorks . . . 214 B5
Exeter Devon . . . 14 C4
Exford Som . . . 41 F10
Exfords Green Shrops . . . 131 B9
Exhall Warks . . . 118 F2
— Warks . . . 135 F7
Exlade Street Oxon . . . 65 C7
Exley W Yorks . . . 196 C5
Exley Head W Yorks . . . 204 F6
Exminster Devon . . . 14 D4
Exmouth Devon . . . 14 E5
Exnaboe Shetland . . . 313 M5
Exning Suff . . . 124 D2
Exted Kent . . . 55 E7
Exton Devon . . . 14 D5
— Hants . . . 33 C10
— Rutland . . . 155 G8
— Som . . . 42 F3
Exwick Devon . . . 14 C4
Eyam Derbys . . . 186 F2
Eydon Northants . . . 119 G10
Eye Hereford . . . 115 E9
— Pboro . . . 138 C3
— Suff . . . 126 C2
Eye Green Pboro . . . 138 C3
Eyemouth Borders . . . 273 C8
Eyeworth C Beds . . . 104 B4
Eyhorne Street Kent . . . 53 C10
Eyke Suff . . . 126 G6
Eynesbury Cambs . . . 122 F3
Eynort Highld . . . 294 C5
Eynsford Kent . . . 68 F4
Eynsham Oxon . . . 82 D6
Eype Dorset . . . 16 C5
Eyre Highld . . . 295 B7
— Highld . . . 298 D4
Eyres Monsell
Leicester . . . 135 D11
Eythorne Kent . . . 55 D9
Eyton Hereford . . . 115 E9
— Shrops . . . 131 F7
— Shrops . . . 149 G7
— Wrex . . . 166 G5
Eyton on Severn
Shrops . . . 131 B11
Eyton upon the Weald
Moors Telford . . . 150 G3

F

Faberstown Wilts . . . 47 C9
Faccombe Hants . . . 47 B11
Faceby N Yorks . . . 225 D9
Fachell Gwyn . . . 163 B8
Fachwen Gwyn . . . 163 C9
Facit Lancs . . . 195 D11
Fackley Notts . . . 171 C7
Faddiley Ches E . . . 167 E9
Faddonch Highld . . . 295 D11
Fadmoor N Yorks . . . 216 B3
Faerdre Swansea . . . 75 E11
Fagley W Yorks . . . 205 G9
Fagwyr Swansea . . . 75 E11
Faichem Highld . . . 290 C4
Faifley W Dunb . . . 277 G10
Failand N Som . . . 60 E4
Failford S Ayrs . . . 257 D11
Failsworth Gtr Man . . . 195 G11
Fairbourne Gwyn . . . 146 G2
Fairbourne Heath Kent . . . 53 C11
Fairburn N Yorks . . . 198 B3
Fairfield Clack . . . 279 C7
— Derbys . . . 185 G9

Fairfield continued
— Gtr Man . . . 184 B6
— Gtr Man . . . 195 E10
— Kent . . . 39 B7
— Mers . . . 182 C5
— Stockton . . . 225 B8
— Worcs . . . 99 C10
— Worcs . . . 117 B8
Fairfield Park Bath . . . 61 F9
Fairfields Glos . . . 98 E4
Fairford Glos . . . 81 E11
Fairford Park Glos . . . 81 E11
Fairgirth Dumfries . . . 237 D10
Fairhaven N Ayrs . . . 255 C10
— Lancs . . . 193 B10
Fairhill S Lanark . . . 268 E4
Fair Hill Cumb . . . 230 E6
Fairlands Sur . . . 50 C3
Fairlie N Ayrs . . . 266 D4
Fairlight E Sus . . . 38 E5
Fairlight Cove E Sus . . . 38 E5
Fairmile Devon . . . 15 B7
— Sur . . . 66 G6
Fairmilehead Edin . . . 270 B4
Fair Moor Northumb . . . 252 E6
Fairoak Caerph . . . 77 F11
— Staffs . . . 150 B5
Fair Oak Hants . . . 33 D7
— Hants . . . 64 G5
Fair Oak Green Hants . . . 65 G7
Fairseat Kent . . . 68 G6
Fairstead Essex . . . 88 B3
— Norf . . . 158 F2
Fairview Glos . . . 99 G9
Fairwarp E Sus . . . 37 B7
Fairwater Cardiff . . . 58 D6
— Torf . . . 78 G3
Fairwood Wilts . . . 45 C10
Fairy Cottage IoM . . . 192 D5
Fairy Cross Devon . . . 24 C6
Fakenham Norf . . . 159 D8
Fakenham Magna Suff . . . 125 B8
Fala Midloth . . . 271 C8
Fala Dam Midloth . . . 271 C8
Falahill Borders . . . 271 D7
Falcon Hereford . . . 98 E2
Falcon Lodge W Mid . . . 134 D2
Falconwood London . . . 68 D3
Falcutt Northants . . . 101 C11
Faldingworth Lincs . . . 189 E9
Falfield Borders . . . 262 C2
— S Glos . . . 79 G11
Falkenham Suff . . . 108 E5
Falkenham Sink Suff . . . 108 E5
Falkland Fife . . . 286 G6
Falla Borders . . . 262 G6
Fallgate Derbys . . . 170 C5
Fallin Stirling . . . 278 C6
Fallings Heath W Mid . . . 133 D9
Fallowfield Gtr Man . . . 184 C5
Fallside N Lanark . . . 268 C4
Falmer E Sus . . . 36 F5
Falmouth Corn . . . 3 C8
Falsgrave N Yorks . . . 217 B10
Falside W Loth . . . 269 B9
Falsidehill Borders . . . 272 G5
Falstone Northumb . . . 250 F6
Fanagmore Highld . . . 306 E6
Fancott C Beds . . . 103 F10
Fangdale Beck
N Yorks . . . 225 G10
Fangfoss E Yorks . . . 207 C11
Fanich Highld . . . 311 J2
Fankerton Falk . . . 278 E5
Fanmore Argyll . . . 288 E6
Fanner's Green Essex . . . 87 C11
Fannich Lodge Highld . . . 300 C2
Fans Borders . . . 272 F2
Far Arnside Cumb . . . 211 D8
Far Bank S Yorks . . . 198 E6
Far Banks Lancs . . . 194 C2
Far Bletchley M Keynes . . . 103 E7
Farcet Cambs . . . 138 E4
Far Coton Leics . . . 135 C7
Far Cotton Northants . . . 120 F4
Farden Shrops . . . 115 B11
Fareham Hants . . . 33 F9
Far End Cumb . . . 220 F6
Farewell Staffs . . . 151 G11
Far Forest Worcs . . . 116 C4
Farforth Lincs . . . 190 F4
Far Green Glos . . . 80 E3
Farhill Derbys . . . 170 C5
Far Hoarcross Staffs . . . 152 E2
Faringdon Oxon . . . 82 F3
Farington Moss Lancs . . . 194 C4
Far Laund Derbys . . . 170 F5
Farlam Cumb . . . 240 F3
Farlands Booth Derbys . . . 185 D9
Farlary Highld . . . 309 J7
Far Ley Staffs . . . 132 B2
Farleigh N Som . . . 60 F3
— Sur . . . 67 G11
Farleigh Court Sur . . . 67 G11
Farleigh Green Kent . . . 53 C8
Farleigh Hungerford
Som . . . 45 B10
Farleigh Wallop Hants . . . 48 D6
Farleigh Wick Wilts . . . 61 G11
Farlesthorpe Lincs . . . 191 G7
Farleton Cumb . . . 211 C11
— Lancs . . . 211 F11
Farley Bristol . . . 60 E2
— Derbys . . . 170 C3
— Shrops . . . 131 B7
— Shrops . . . 132 C2
— Staffs . . . 169 G9
— Wilts . . . 32 B2
Farley Green Suff . . . 124 G4
— Sur . . . 50 D5
Farley Hill Luton . . . 103 D11
— Wokingham . . . 65 G8
Farleys End Glos . . . 80 B3
Farlington N Yorks . . . 216 F2
— Ptsmth . . . 33 F11
Farlow Shrops . . . 132 G2
Farmborough Bath . . . 61 G7
Farmbridge End Essex . . . 87 C10
Farmcote Glos . . . 99 F11
— Shrops . . . 132 D5
Farmington Glos . . . 81 B10
Farmoor Oxon . . . 82 D6
Farms Common Corn . . . 2 C5
Farmtown Moray . . . 302 D5
Far Moor Gtr Man . . . 194 G4
Farnah Green Derbys . . . 170 F4
Farnborough Hants . . . 49 C11

Farnborough *continued*
London......68 G2
Warks......101 B8
W Berks......64 C2
Farnborough Green Hants......49 B11
Farnborough Park Hants......49 B11
Farnborough Street Hants......49 B11
Farncombe Sur......50 E3
Farndish Bedford......121 E8
Farndon Ches W......166 E6
Notts......172 E3
Farnell Angus......287 B10
Farnham Dorset......31 D7
Essex......105 G9
N Yorks......215 G7
Suff......127 E7
Sur......49 G8
Farnham Common Bucks......66 C3
Farnham Green Essex......105 F9
Farnham Park Bucks......66 C3
Farnham Royal Bucks......66 C3
Farnhill N Yorks......204 D6
Farningham Kent......68 F4
Farnley N Yorks......205 D10
W Yorks......205 G11
Farnley Bank W Yorks......197 E7
Farnley Tyas W Yorks......197 E7
Farnsfield Notts......171 D10
Farnworth Gtr Man......195 F8
Halton......183 D8
Far Oakridge Glos......80 E6
Farr Highld......291 C10
Highld......300 F6
Highld......308 C7
Farraline Highld......300 G5
Farr House Highld......300 F6
Farringdon Devon......14 C6
T&W......243 D9
Farrington Dorset......30 D4
Farrington Gurney Bath......44 B6
Far Royds W Yorks......205 G11
Far Sawrey Cumb......221 F7
Farsley W Yorks......205 F10
Farsley Beck Bottom W Yorks......205 F10
Farther Howegreen Essex......88 E4
Farthing Corner Medway......69 G10
Farthing Green Kent......53 D10
Farthinghoe Northants......101 D10
Farthingloe Kent......55 E9
Farthingstone Northants 120 F2
Far Thrupp Glos......80 E5
Fartown W Yorks......196 D6
Farway Devon......15 B9
Farway Marsh Devon......28 G4
Fasach Highld......297 G2
Fascadale Highld......289 B7
Faslane Port Argyll......276 D4
Fasnacloich Argyll......284 C4
Fasnakyle Ho Highld......300 G3
Fassfern Highld......290 F2
Fatfield T&W......243 G8
Fattahead Aberds......302 D6
Faucheldean W Loth......279 G11
Faugh Cumb......240 G2
Faughill Borders......262 C2
Fauld Staffs......152 D3
Fauldhouse W Loth......269 C8
Fauldiehill Angus......287 D9
Fauldshope Borders......261 D10
Faulkbourne Essex......88 B3
Faulkland Som......45 C8
Fauls Shrops......149 C11
Faverdale Darl......224 B5
Faversham Kent......70 G4
Favillar Moray......302 F2
Fawdington N Yorks......215 E8
Fawdon Northumb......264 F2
T&W......242 D6
Fawfieldhead Staffs......169 C9
Fawkham Green Kent......68 F5
Fawler Oxon......63 B10
Oxon......82 B5
Fawley Bucks......65 B11
Hants......33 G7
W Berks......63 C11
Fawley Bottom Bucks......65 B8
Fawley Chapel Hereford. 97 F11
FaxFleet E Yorks......199 C11
Faygate W Sus......51 G8
Fazakerley Mers......182 B5
Fazeley Staffs......134 C4
Feagour Highld......291 D7
Fearby N Yorks......214 C3
Fearn Highld......301 B8
Fearnan Highld......285 C11
Fearnbeg Highld......299 D7
Fearnhead Warr......183 C10
Fearn Lodge Highld......309 L6
Fearnmore Highld......299 C7
Fearn Station Highld......301 B8
Fearnville W Yorks......206 F2
Featherstone Staffs......133 B8
W Yorks......198 C2
Featherwood Northumb 251 C8
Feckenham Worcs......117 E10
Fedw Fawr Anglesey......179 E10
Feering Essex......107 G7
Feetham N Yorks......223 F9
Fegg Hayes Stoke......168 E5
Fèith Mhor Highld......301 G8
Feizor N Yorks......212 F5
Felbridge Sur......51 F11
Felbrigg Norf......160 B4
Felcourt Sur......51 E11
Felden Herts......85 E8
Felderland Kent......55 B10
Feldy Ches E......183 F11
Felhampton Shrops......131 F8
Felin-Crai Powys......95 G7
Felindre Carms......75 C7
Carms......93 D7
Carms......93 G11
Carms......94 E3
Carms......94 F4
Ceredig......111 F10
Powys......96 B3
Powys......96 G3
Powys......130 D3
Powys......130 G3
Rhondda......58 C3
Swansea......75 E8
Felindre Farchog Pembs. 92 D2
Felinfach Ceredig......111 F10
Powys......95 E11
Felinfoel Carms......75 E8
Felingwmisaf Carms......93 G10
Felingwmuchaf Carms......93 G10
Felin Newydd Powys......94 D3
Felin-newydd Powys......96 G2
Felin Newydd / New Mills Powys......129 C11
Felin Puleston Wrex......166 F4

Felin-Wnda Ceredig......92 B6
Felinwynt Ceredig......110 G4
Felixkirk N Yorks......215 C9
Felixstowe Suff......108 E5
Felixstowe Ferry Suff. 108 D6
Felkirk W Yorks......197 E11
Felldyke Cumb......219 B11
Fell End Cumb......222 F4
Fellgate T&W......243 E7
Felling T&W......243 E7
Felling Shore T&W......243 E7
Fell Lane W Yorks......204 E6
Fellside T&W......242 E5
Fell Side Cumb......230 D2
Felmersham Bedford....121 F9
Felmingham Norf......160 D5
Felmore......69 B8
Felpham W Sus......35 H7
Felsham Suff......125 F8
Felsted Essex......106 G3
Feltham London......66 E6
Som......28 D2
Felthamhill London......66 E5
Felthorpe Norf......160 F3
Felton Hereford......97 B11
Northumb......252 C5
N Som......60 F4
Felton Butler Shrops....149 F7
Feltwell Norf......140 E4
Fenay Bridge W Yorks. 197 D7
Fence Lancs......204 F2
Fence Houses T&W....243 G8
Fencott Oxon......83 B9
Fen Ditton Cambs......123 E9
Fen Drayton Cambs....122 D6
Fen End Lincs......156 E4
W Mid......118 B4
Fengate Norf......160 E3
Pboro......138 D4
Fenham Northumb......273 G11
T&W......242 E6
Fenhouses Lincs......174 G3
Feniscliffe Blackburn. 195 B7
Feniscowles Blackburn. 194 B6
Feniton Devon......15 B8
Fenlake Bedford......103 B11
Fenn Green Shrops......132 G5
Fennington Som......27 B11
Fenn's Bank Wrex......149 B10
Fenn Street Medway....69 D9
Fenny Bentley Derbys. 169 E11
Fenny Bridges Devon...15 B8
Fenny Castle Som......44 E4
Fenny Compton Warks. 119 G8
Fenny Drayton Leics....134 D6
Fenny Stratford M Keynes......103 E7
Fenrother Northumb....252 E5
Fen Side Lincs......174 D4
Fenstanton Cambs......122 D6
Fenstead End Suff......124 G6
Fen Street Norf......141 G11
Suff......125 B9
Suff......125 B11
Fenton Cambs......122 B6
Cumb......240 F2
Lincs......172 E5
Lincs......188 G4
Northumb......263 C11
Stoke......168 G5
S Yorks......198 D5
Fenton Barns E Loth....281 E10
Fenton Low Stoke......168 F5
Fenton Pits Corn......5 C11
Fenton Town Northumb. 263 C11
Fenwick E Ayrs......267 G9
Northumb......242 C3
Northumb......273 G11
S Yorks......198 D5
Feochaig Argyll......255 F8
Feock Corn......3 B8
Feolin Ferry Argyll......274 G5
Fergushie Park Renfs.. 267 C9
Ferindonald Highld......295 E8
Feriniquarrie Highld....296 G2
Ferlochan Argyll......289 E11
Fern Angus......292 G6
Fern Bank Gtr Man......185 B7
Ferndale Kent......52 E5
Rhondda......77 F7
Ferndown Dorset......31 G9
Ferness Highld......301 E10
Ferne Wilts......30 C6
Ferney Green Cumb....221 F8
Fernham Oxon......82 G3
Fernhill Gtr Man......195 E10
Rhondda......77 F8
W Sus......51 E10
Fern Hill Suff......106 B6
Fernhill Gate Gtr Man. 195 F7
Fernhill Heath Worcs...117 F7
Fernhurst W Sus......34 B5
Fernie Fife......287 F7
Ferniebrae Aberds......303 D9
Ferniegair S Lanark....268 E4
Ferniehirst Borders....271 G8
Fernilea Highld......294 B5
Fernilee Derbys......185 F8
Fernsplatt Corn......4 G5
Ferrensby N Yorks......215 G7
Ferrers W Sus......35 G9
Ferry Hill Cambs......139 G7
Ferrybridge W Yorks... 198 C3
Ferryden Angus......287 B11
Ferryhill Aberdeen....293 C11
Durham......233 E11
Ferryhill Station Durham 234 E2
Ferry Point Highld......309 L7
Ferryside / Glan-y-Ffer Carms......74 C5
Fersfield Norf......141 G11
Fersit Highld......290 F5
Ferwig Ceredig......92 B3

Ffos-y-go Wrex......166 E4
Ffridd Powys......130 D3
Ffrith Wrex......166 D3
Ffrwd Gwyn......163 D7
Ffwl y mwn / Fonmon V Glam......58 F4
Ffynnon Carms......74 B5
Ffynnon ddrain Carms... 93 G8
Ffynnongroes / Crosswell Pembs......92 D2
Ffynnon Gron Pembs....91 F8
Ffynnongroyw Flint....181 E10
Ffynnon Gynydd Powys... 96 C3
Ffynnon-oer Ceredig...111 G10
Fickleshole Sur......67 G11
Fidden Argyll......288 G5
Fiddes Aberds......293 E10
Fiddington Glos......99 E8
Som......43 E8
Fiddington Sands Wilts... 46 C4
Fiddleford Dorset......30 E4
Fiddler' Green Norf....141 D10
Fiddler's Green Glos....99 G8
Hereford......97 B11
Fiddlers Hamlet Essex... 87 E7
Field Hereford......116 G2
Som......44 E6
Staffs......151 D10
Field Assarts Oxon......82 C4
Field Broughton Cumb. 211 C7
Field Common Sur......66 F6
Field Dalling Norf......159 B10
Field Green Kent......38 B3
Field Head Leics......135 B9
Fields End Herts......85 D8
Field's Place Hereford. 115 G8
Fife Keith Moray......302 D4
Fifehead Magdalen Dorset......30 C3
Fifehead Neville Dorset... 30 E3
Fifehead St Quintin Dorset......30 E3
Fife Moray......302 D4
Fifield Oxon......82 B2
Wilts......46 C6
Windsor......66 D2
Fifield Bavant Wilts......31 B8
Figheldean Wilts......47 D7
Filands Wilts......62 B2
Filby Norf......161 G9
Filby Heath Norf......161 G9
Filchampstead Oxon......83 D7
Filey N Yorks......218 C2
Filgrave M Keynes......103 B7
Filham Devon......8 D2
Filkins Oxon......82 E2
Filleigh Devon......25 B11
Devon......26 E2
Fillingham Lincs......188 D6
Fillongley Warks......134 F5
Filmore Hill Hants......33 B11
Filton S Glos......60 D6
Filwood Park Bristol....60 F5
Fimber E Yorks......217 G2
Finavon Angus......287 B8
Finberry Kent......54 F4
Fincastle Ho Perth.....291 G10
Finchairn Argyll......275 C10
Fincham Mers......182 C6
Norf......140 B3
Finchampstead Wokingham......65 G9
Finchdean Hants......34 E2
Finchingfield Essex.....106 E3
Finchley London......86 G3
Findern Derbys......152 C6
Findhorn Moray......301 C10
Findhorn Bridge Highld. 301 G8
Findochty Moray......302 C4
Findo Gask Perth......286 E4
Findon Aberds......293 D11
W Sus......35 F10
Findon Mains Highld....300 C6
Findon Valley W Sus....35 F10
Findrack Ho Aberds....293 C8
Finedon Northants......121 C8
Fineglen Argyll......275 B10
Fine Street Hereford....96 D6
Fingal Street Suff......126 D4
Fingask Aberds......303 G7
Fingerpost Worcs......116 C4
Fingest Bucks......84 G3
Finghall N Yorks......214 B3
Fingland Cumb......239 F7
Dumfries......259 F7
Dumfries......247 G9
Fingleton Gtr Man......55 C10
Fingringhoe Essex......107 G10
Finham W Mid......118 B6
Finkle Street S Yorks....186 B4
Finlarig Stirling......285 D9
Finmere Oxon......102 E2
Finnart Perth......285 B9
Finney Green Ches E... 184 E5
Staffs......168 F3
Finningham Suff......125 D11
Finningley S Yorks......187 B11
Finnygaud Aberds......302 D5
Finsbury London......67 C10
Finsbury Park London... 67 B10
Finstall Worcs......117 D9
Finsthwaite Cumb......211 B7
Finstock Oxon......82 B5
Finstown Orkney......314 E3
Fintry Aberds......303 D7
Dundee......287 D8
Stirling......278 D2
Finwood Warks......118 D3
Finzean Aberds......293 D8
Fionnphort Argyll......288 G5
Fionnsbhagh W Isles....296 C6
Fir Bank Cumb......222 G2
Firbeck S Yorks......187 D9
Firby N Yorks......216 F4
N Yorks......214 B4
Firgrove Gtr Man......196 E2
Firkin Argyll......285 G7
Firle E Sus......23 D7
Firsby Lincs......175 C7
Firsdown Wilts......47 G8
Firs Lane Gtr Man......194 G6
First Coast Highld......307 K4
Firswood Gtr Man......184 B4
Firth Borders......262 G5
Firth Moor Darl......224 C6
Firth Park S Yorks......186 C5
Fir Toll Kent......54 E2
Fir Tree Durham......233 E8
Fir Vale S Yorks......186 C5
Firwood Fold Gtr Man.. 195 F8
Fishbourne IoW......21 C7
W Sus......22 C4
Fishburn Durham......234 E3
Fishcross Clack......279 B7
Fisherford Aberds......302 F6
Fishermead M Keynes.. 103 D7
Fisher Place Cumb......220 B6
Fisherrow E Loth......280 G6
Fishersgate Brighton....36 F3

Fishers Green Herts....104 F4
Fisher's Pond Hants......33 C7
Fisherstreet W Sus......50 G3
Fisherton Highld......301 D7
S Ayrs......257 F7
Fisherton de la Mere Wilts......46 F4
Fisherwick Staffs......134 B3
Fishery Windsor......65 C11
Fishguard / Abergwaun Pembs......91 D9
Fishlake S Yorks......199 E7
Fishleigh Devon......25 F8
Fishleigh Castle Devon... 25 F8
Fishley Norf......161 G8
W Mid......133 C10
Fishmere End Lincs....156 B5
Fishponds Bristol......60 D6
Fishpool Glos......98 F3
Gtr Man......195 F10
N Yorks......205 D10
Fishpools Powys......114 D3
Fishtoft Lincs......174 G5
Fishtoft Drove Lincs....174 F4
Fishtown of Usan Angus......287 B11
Fishwick Borders......273 E8
Lancs......194 B5
Fiskavaig Highld......294 B5
Fiskerton Lincs......189 G8
Notts......172 E2
Fitling E Yorks......209 G11
Fittleton Wilts......46 D6
Fittleworth W Sus......35 D8
Fitton End Cambs......157 G8
Fitton Hill Gtr Man......196 G2
Fitz Shrops......149 F8
Fitzhead Som......27 B10
Fitzwilliam W Yorks....198 D2
Fiunary Highld......289 E8
Five Acres Glos......79 C9
Five Ash Down E Sus....37 C7
Five Ashes E Sus......37 C9
Five Bells Som......42 E5
Five Bridges Hereford...98 B3
Fivecrosses Ches W....183 F8
Fivehead Som......28 C5
Five Houses IoW......20 D4
Five Lane Ends Lancs...202 C6
Five Lanes Mon......78 G6
Five Oak Green Kent....52 E6
Five Oaks W Sus......35 B9
Five Roads Carms......75 D7
Five Ways Warks......118 D4
Five Wents Kent......53 D11
Fixby W Yorks......196 C6
Flackley Ash E Sus......38 C5
Flack's Green Essex......88 B3
Flackwell Heath Bucks... 65 B11
Fladbury Worcs......99 B9
Fladbury Cross Worcs...99 B9
Fladda Shetland......312 E6
Fladdabister Shetland... 313 K6
Flagg Derbys......169 B10
Flaggoners Green Hereford......116 G2
Flamborough E Yorks...218 E4
Flamstead Herts......85 C10
Flamstead End Herts....86 E4
Flansham W Sus......35 G7
Flanshaw W Yorks......197 C10
Flappit Spring W Yorks. 205 F7
Flasby N Yorks......204 B4
Flash Staffs......169 B8
Flashader Highld......298 D3
Flask Inn N Yorks......227 E8
Flathurst W Sus......35 C7
Flaunden Herts......85 E8
Flawborough Notts....172 G3
Flawith N Yorks......215 F9
Flax Bourton N Som......60 F4
Flaxby N Yorks......206 B3
Flaxholme Derbys......170 G5
Flaxlands Norf......142 E2
Flaxley Glos......79 B11
Flaxley Green Staffs....151 F11
Flaxmere Ches W......183 G8
Flax Moss Lancs......195 C9
Flaxpool Som......42 F6
Flaxton N Yorks......216 G3
Fleckney Leics......136 E2
Flecknoe Warks......119 D10
Fledborough Notts......188 G4
Fleet Dorset......17 E8
Hants......22 C2
Hants......49 C10
Lincs......157 E7
Fleet Downs Kent......68 E5
Fleetend Hants......33 F8
Fleet Hargate Lincs....157 E7
Fleetlands Hants......33 G9
Fleets N Yorks......213 G9
Fleetville Herts......85 D11
Fleetwood Lancs......202 D2
Fleggburgh / Burgh St Margaret Norf......161 G8
Fleisirin W Isles......304 E7
Flemingston V Glam......58 E4
Flemington S Lanark....268 D3
S Lanark......268 G4
Flemmington Highld....301 D8
Flempton Suff......124 D6
Fleoideabhagh W Isles. 296 C6
Fletchersbridge Corn....6 B2
Fletcher's Green Kent....52 C4
Fletchertown Cumb....229 C10
Fletching E Sus......36 C6
Fletching Common E Sus......36 C6
Fleuchary Highld......309 K7
Fleur-de-lis Caerph......77 F11
Flexbury Corn......24 F2
Flexford Hants......32 C6
Sur......50 D2
Flimby Cumb......228 E6
Flimwell E Sus......53 G8
Flint Flint......182 G2
Flint Cross Cambs......105 C8
Flintham Notts......172 F2
Flint Hill Durham......242 G5
Flint Mountain / Mynydd Fflint Flint......182 G2
Flinton E Yorks......209 F10
Flint's Green W Mid....134 G5
Flintsham Hereford....114 F6
Flishinghurst Kent......53 F9
Flitcham Norf......158 D4
Flitton C Beds......103 D11
Flitwick C Beds......103 D10
Flixborough N Lincs....199 E11
Flixborough Stather N Lincs......199 E11
Flixton Gtr Man......184 C2
N Yorks......217 D10
Suff......142 G6
Flockton W Yorks......197 E8
Flockton Green W Yorks......197 E8
Flockton Moor W Yorks. 197 E8

Flodaigh W Isles......296 F4
Flodden Northumb......263 B10
Flodigarry Highld......298 B4
Floodgates Hereford....114 F5
Flood's Ferry Cambs....139 E7
Flood Street Hants......31 D10
Flookburgh Cumb......211 D7
Flordon Norf......142 D3
Flore Northants......120 E2
Florence Stoke......168 G6
Flotterton Northumb...251 C11
Flowers Bottom Bucks... 84 F4
Flowers Green E Sus....23 C10
Flowery Field Gtr Man.. 184 B6
Flowton Suff......107 B11
Flugarth Shetland......313 G6
Flush House W Yorks....196 F6
Flushdyke W Yorks....197 C9
Flushing Aberds......303 E10
Corn......3 C8
Corn......3 D7
Flyford Flavell Worcs... 117 G9
Foals Green Suff......126 C5
Fobbing Thurrock......69 C8
Fochabers Moray......302 D3
Fochriw Caerph......77 D10
Fockerby N Lincs......199 D10
Fodderletter Moray......301 G11
Fodderstone Gap Norf. 140 B3
Fodderty Highld......300 D5
Foddington Som......29 B9
Foel Powys......147 G9
Foel-gastell Carms......75 C8
Foffarty Angus......287 C8
Foggathorpe E Yorks...207 F11
Foggbrook Gtr Man......184 D6
Fogo Borders......272 F5
Fogorig Borders......272 F5
Fogrigarth Shetland....313 H4
Fogwatt Moray......302 D2
Foindle Highld......306 E6
Folda Angus......292 G3
Fold Head Lancs......195 D11
Fold Hill Lincs......175 E7
Foldrings S Yorks......186 C3
Fole Staffs......151 B10
Foleshill W Mid......135 G7
Foley Park Worcs......116 B6
Folke Dorset......29 E11
Folkestone Kent......55 F8
Folkingham Lincs......155 C11
Folkington E Sus......23 E9
Folksworth Cambs......138 F2
Folkton N Yorks......217 D11
Folla Rule Aberds......303 F7
Folley Shrops......132 D5
Follifoot N Yorks......206 C2
Folly Dorset......18 D3
Pembs......91 G8
Folly Cross Devon......25 F7
Folly Gate Devon......13 B7
Folly Green Essex......106 F6
Fonmon / Ffwl-y-mwn V Glam......58 F4
Fonston Corn......11 C10
Fonthill Bishop Wilts....46 F2
Fonthill Gifford Wilts....46 G2
Fontmell Magna Dorset. 30 E4
Fontmell Parva Dorset... 30 E4
Fontwell W Sus......35 F7
Font-y-gary / Ffont-y-gari V Glam......58 F5
Foodieash Fife......287 F7
Foolow Derbys......185 F11
Footbridge Glos......99 F10
Footherley Staffs......134 C2
Footrid Worcs......116 C3
Foots Cray London......68 E3
Forbestown Aberds....292 B5
Force Forge Cumb......220 G6
Force Green Kent......52 B2
Force Mills Cumb......220 G6
Forcett N Yorks......224 C3
Ford Argyll......275 C9
Bucks......84 D3
Derbys......186 D6
Devon......8 G5
Devon......8 G2
Devon......13 D7
Glos......99 F11
Hants......49 C10
Hereford......115 F10
Kent......71 F8
Mers......182 B4
Northumb......263 B10
Pembs......91 F9
Plym......7 D9
Shrops......149 G8
Som......27 B9
Som......44 C5
Staffs......169 E8
Wilts......47 G9
Wilts......61 E10
W Sus......35 G7
Forda Devon......12 C6
Devon......40 F3
Fordbridge W Mid......134 F3
Fordcombe Kent......52 E4
Fordell Fife......280 D3
Forden / Ffodun Powys. 130 C4
Forder Corn......7 D8
Forder Green Devon......8 B5
Ford Forge Northumb... 263 B10
Fordgate Som......43 G10
Ford Green Lancs......202 D5
Fordham Cambs......124 C2
Essex......107 F8
Norf......140 D2
Fordham Heath Essex.. 107 F8
Ford Heath Shrops......149 G8
Ford Hill Northumb......263 B11
Fordhouses W Mid......133 C8
Fordingbridge Hants....31 E11
Fordley T&W......243 C7
Fordon E Yorks......217 D10
Fordoun Aberds......293 F9
Ford's Green E Sus......36 B6
Suff......125 D11
Ford Street Essex......107 F8
Som......27 D11
Fordton Devon......14 B2
Fordwater Devon......28 G4
Fordwells Oxon......82 C4
Fordwich Kent......55 B7
Fordyce Aberds......302 C5
Forebridge Staffs......151 E8
Foredale N Yorks......212 F6
Forehill S Ayrs......257 E8
Foreland Fields IoW......21 D9
Foreland Ho Argyll......274 G3
Foremark Derbys......152 D6
Forest N Yorks......225 B11
Forest Becks Lancs......203 C11
Forestburn Gate Northumb......252 D3
Forest Coal Pit Mon......96 G6

Forestdale London......67 G11
Foresterseat Moray....301 D11
Forest Gate Hants......33 E10
London......68 C2
Forest Green Glos......80 E4
Sur......50 E6
Forest Hall Cumb......221 E10
T&W......243 D7
Forest Head Cumb......240 F3
Forest Hill London......67 E11
Oxon......83 D9
W Sus......63 E8
Forest Holme Lancs....195 B10
Forest-in-Teesdale Durham......232 F3
Forest Lane Head N Yorks......206 B2
Forest Lodge Argyll....284 C6
Highld......292 B2
Perth......291 K12
Forest Mill Clack......279 C9
Forest Moor N Yorks....206 B2
Forestreet Devon......24 E5
Forest Row E Sus......52 G2
Forestside W Sus......34 E3
Forest Side IoW......20 D5
Forest Town Notts......171 C9
Forewoods Common Wilts......61 G10
Forfar Angus......287 B8
Forgandenny Perth....286 F4
Forge Corn......4 F3
Powys......128 D5
Forge Hammer Torf......78 F3
Forge Side Torf......78 D2
Forgewood N Lanark....268 D4
Forgie Moray......302 D3
Forglen Ho Aberds......302 D6
Forhill Worcs......117 B11
Forncett End Norf......142 E3
Forncett St Mary Norf.. 142 E3
Forncett St Peter Norf. 142 E3
Forneth Perth......286 C4
Fornham All Saints Suff 124 D6
Fornham St Genevieve Suff......124 D6
Fornham St Martin Suff. 125 D7
Fornighty Highld......301 D9
Forrabury Corn......11 C7
Forres Moray......301 D10
Forrestfield N Lanark... 269 B7
Forrest Lodge Dumfries. 246 F3
Forry's Green Essex.... 106 E5
Forsbrook Staffs......169 G7
Forse Highld......310 F6
Forse Ho Highld......310 F6
Forshaw Heath Worcs. 117 C11
Forsinain Highld......310 E3
Forsinard Highld......310 E2
Forsinard Station Highld 310 E2
Forstal Kent......53 B8
Forston Dorset......17 B9
Fort Augustus Highld...290 C5
Forteviot Perth......286 F4
Fort George Highld......301 D7
Perth S Lanark......269 E8
Forthampton Glos......99 E7
Forthay Glos......80 F2
Fort Hommet Guern....17 C11
Fortingall Perth......285 C11
Fortis Green London....67 B9
Fort Matilda Invclyd... 276 F5
Forton Hants......33 G10
Lancs......202 C5
Shrops......149 F8
Som......28 E4
Staffs......150 E5
Forton Heath Shrops...149 F8
Fortrie Aberds......302 E6
Aberds......303 D7
Fortrose Highld......301 D7
Fortuneswell Dorset.....17 G9
Fort William / An Gearasdan Highld......290 F3
Forty Green Bucks......84 G6
Bucks......84 G6
Forty Hill London......86 F4
Forward Green Suff.... 125 F11
Forwood Glos......80 E5
Fosbury Wilts......47 B10
Foscot Oxon......100 G4
Foscote Bucks......102 D4
Northants......102 B3
Wilts......61 D11
Fosdyke Lincs......156 C6
Fosdyke Bridge Lincs...156 C6
Foss Perth......285 B11
Foss Cross Glos......81 D9
Fossebridge Glos......81 C9
Fostall Kent......70 G5
Foster Green Kent......53 F10
Foster Street Essex......87 D7
Foston Derbys......152 C3
Leics......136 E2
Lincs......172 G5
N Yorks......216 F3
Foston on the Wolds E Yorks......209 B8
Fotherby Lincs......190 C4
Fothergill Cumb......228 E6
Fotheringhay Northants 137 E11
Foubister Orkney......314 F5
Foul Anchor Cambs....157 E9
Foulbridge Cumb......230 B4
Foulby W Yorks......197 D11
Foulden Borders......273 D8
Norf......140 D4
Foul End Warks......134 E4
Foulford Hants......31 F11
Foulis Castle Highld....300 C5
Foul Mile E Sus......23 B10
Foulridge Lancs......204 E3
Foulsham Norf......159 E10
Fountain Hereford......97 B10
Foundry Corn......2 C3
Hill......97 F11
Foundry Hill Norf......159 D11
Fountain Bridgend......57 E11
Fountainhall Borders...271 F8
Four Ashes Bucks......84 F5
Staffs......132 G6
Staffs......133 B8
Suff......125 C11
W Mid......118 B3
Four Crosses Powys....148 G5
Staffs......133 B9
Wrex......166 E3
Four Elms Devon......28 D3
Kent......52 D3
Four Foot Som......44 G5
Four Forks Som......43 F8
Four Gates Gtr Man......194 F6
Four Gotes Cambs......157 F9
Four Houses Corner W Berks......64 F6

Four Lane End S Yorks.. 197 G9
Fourlane Ends Derbys.. 170 D5
Four Lane Ends Blackburn......195 B7
Ches W......167 C9
Gtr Man......195 E9
N Yorks......205 G8
Four Lanes Corn......2 B5
Fourlanes End Ches E.. 168 D4
Four Marks Hants......49 G7
Four Mile Bridge Anglesey......178 F3
Four Mile Elm Glos......80 C4
Four Oaks E Sus......38 C5
Glos......98 F3
Kent......70 G3
W Mid......134 C4
W Mid......134 D4
Four Oaks Park W Mid. 134 C4
Fourpenny Highld......311 K2
Four Points W Berks......64 D5
Four Pools Worcs......99 C10
Four Roads Carms......74 D6
IoM......192 F3
Fourstones Northumb.. 241 D10
Four Throws Kent......38 B3
Four Wants Kent......53 F9
Four Wents Kent......53 F9
Fovant Wilts......31 B8
Foveran Aberds......303 G9
Fowey Corn......6 E2
Fowler's Plot Som......43 F10
Fowley Common Warr. 183 B11
Fowlis Angus......287 D8
Fowlis Wester Perth....286 E3
Fowlmere Cambs......105 C8
Fownhope Hereford......97 E11
Foxash Estate Essex....107 E11
Foxbar Renfs......267 C9
Foxbury London......68 E2
Foxcombe Hill Oxon......83 E8
Foxcote Glos......81 B8
Som......45 B8
Foxcote Hereford......97 B10
Foxdale IoM......192 E3
Foxdown Hants......48 C4
Foxearth Essex......106 C6
Foxendown Kent......69 F7
Foxfield Cumb......210 B4
Foxford W Mid......135 G7
Foxham Wilts......62 D3
Fox Hatch Essex......87 F9
Fox Hill Bath......61 G9
Hereford......98 B3
Foxhills Hants......32 E4
Foxhole Corn......5 E9
Norf......142 D4
Swansea......57 C7
Fox Hole Swansea......56 D5
Foxholes N Yorks......217 E10
Fox Holes Wilts......45 E11
Foxhunt Green E Sus....23 B8
Fox Lane Hants......49 B11
Foxley Hereford......97 B8
Norf......159 E10
Staffs......168 E3
Wilts......61 B11
Foxlydiate Worcs......117 D10
Fox Royd W Yorks......197 D8
Fox Street Essex......107 F10
Foxt Staffs......169 F8
Foxton Cambs......105 B8
Durham......234 F3
Leics......136 F4
N Yorks......225 F8
Foxup N Yorks......213 D7
Foxwist Green Ches W. 167 B10
Foxwood Shrops......116 B2
Foy Hereford......97 F11
Foyers Highld......300 G4
Foynesfield Highld......301 D8
Fraddam Corn......2 C3
Fraddon Corn......5 D8
Fradley Staffs......152 G3
Fradley Junction Staffs. 152 G3
Fradswell Staffs......151 C9
Fraisthorpe E Yorks....218 G3
Framfield E Sus......37 C7
Framingham Earl Norf.. 142 C5
Framingham Pigot Norf. 142 C5
Framlingham Suff......126 E5
Frampton Dorset......17 B8
Lincs......156 B6
Frampton Cotterell S Glos......61 C7
Frampton Court Glos.... 99 E10
Frampton End S Glos.... 61 C7
Frampton Mansell Glos. 80 E6
Frampton on Severn Glos......80 D2
Frampton West End Lincs......174 G3
Framsden Suff......126 F3
Framwellgate Moor Durham......233 C11
France Lynch Glos......80 E6
Franche Worcs......116 B6
Frandley Ches W......183 F10
Frankby Mers......182 D2
Frankfort Norf......160 E6
Franklands Gate Hereford......97 B10
Frankley Worcs......133 G9
Frankley Green Worcs. 133 G9
Frankley Hill Worcs....117 B9
Frank's Bridge Powys.. 114 F2
Frankton Warks......119 C8
Frankwell Shrops......149 G9
Frans Green Norf......160 G2
Frant E Sus......52 F5
Fraserburgh Aberds....303 C9
Frating Essex......107 G11
Frating Green Essex....107 G11
Fratton Ptsmth......21 B9
Freasley Warks......134 D4
Freathy Corn......7 E8
Frecheville S Yorks......186 E6
Freckenham Suff......124 C3
Freckleton Lancs......194 B2
Freebirch Derbys......170 B5
Freeby Leics......154 E6
Freefolk Hants......48 D3
Freehay Staffs......169 G8
Freeland Oxon......82 C6
Renfs......267 B9
Freeland Corner Norf.. 160 F3
Freester Shetland......313 H6
Freethorpe Norf......143 B8
Free Town Gtr Man......195 E10
Freezy Water London....86 F5
Freiston Lincs......174 G5
Freiston Shore Lincs....174 G5
Fremington Devon......40 G4
N Yorks......223 F10
Frenchay S Glos......60 D6
Frenchbeer Devon......13 D9
Frenches Green Essex.. 106 G4

Frenchmoor Hants......32 B3
French Street Kent......52 C3
Frenchwood Lancs......194 B4
Frensham Sur......49 E10
Frenze Norf......142 G3
Fresgoe Highld......310 C3
Freshbrook Swindon....62 C6
Freshfield Mers......193 F9
Freshford Bath......61 G9
Freshwater IoW......20 D2
Freshwater Bay IoW....20 D2
Freshwater East Pembs. 73 F8
Fressingfield Suff......126 B5
Freston Suff......108 D3
Freswick Highld......310 C7
Fretherne Glos......80 D2
Frettenham Norf......160 F4
Freuchie Fife......286 G6
Freuchies Angus......292 G4
Freystrop Pembs......73 C7
Friar Park W Mid......133 E10
Friars Cliff Dorset......19 C9
Friar's Gate E Sus......52 G3
Friarn Som......43 F7
Friar Park W Mid......133 E10
Friar Waddon Dorset....17 E8
Friday Bridge Cambs....139 C9
Friday Hill London......86 G5
Friday Street E Sus......23 E10
Suff......126 G6
Suff......127 E7
Sur......50 D6
Fridaythorpe E Yorks... 208 B3
Friendly W Yorks......196 C5
Friern Barnet London... 86 G3
Friesland Argyll......288 D3
Friesthorpe Lincs......189 E9
Frieston Lincs......172 F6
Frieth Bucks......84 G3
Friezeland Notts......171 E7
Frilford Oxon......82 F6
Frilford Heath Oxon......82 F6
Frilsham W Berks......64 E4
Frimley Sur......49 B11
Frimley Green Sur......49 B11
Frimley Ridge Sur......49 B11
Frindsbury Medway......69 E8
Fring Norf......158 C4
Fringford Oxon......102 F2
Friningham Kent......53 B10
Frinkle Green Essex....106 C4
Frinsted Kent......53 B11
Frinton-on-Sea Essex.. 108 G4
Friockheim Angus......287 C9
Friog Gwyn......146 G2
Frisby Lincs......136 C5
Frisby on the Wreake Leics......154 F3
Friskney Lincs......175 D7
Friskney Eaudyke Lincs. 175 D7
Friskney Tofts Lincs....175 E7
Friston E Sus......23 F8
Suff......127 E8
Fritchley Derbys......170 E5
Frith Kent......54 B2
Fritham Hants......32 E2
Frith Bank Lincs......174 F4
Frith Common Worcs... 116 D3
Frithelstock Devon......25 D7
Frithelstock Stone Devon 25 D7
Frithend Hants......49 E10
Frith Hill Sur......50 E3
Frithsden Herts......85 D8
Frithville Lincs......174 E4
Frittenden Kent......53 E10
Frithville Herts......85 B8
Frittiscombe Devon......8 G6
Fritton Norf......142 E4
Norf......143 C9
Norf......161 E8
Fritwell Oxon......101 F10
Frizinghall W Yorks....205 F8
Frizington Cumb......219 B10
Frizzeler's Green Suff.. 124 E5
Frocester Glos......80 E3
Frochas Powys......148 G5
Frodesley Shrops......131 D10
Frodesley Lane Shrops. 131 D10
Frodingham N Lincs.... 199 E11
Frodsham Ches W......183 F8
Frogden Borders......263 D7
Frog End Cambs......123 G8
Cambs......123 G8
Froggatt Derbys......186 F2
Froghall Staffs......169 F8
Frogham Hants......31 E11
Kent......55 C9
Froghole Kent......52 C2
Frogland Cross S Glos... 60 C6
Frogmore Devon......8 G5
Hants......49 B11
Herts......85 D11
Frognall Lincs......156 G3
Frogpool Corn......4 G5
Frogs' Green Essex......105 D11
Frogshall Norf......160 B5
Frogwell Corn......6 B6
Frolesworth Leics......135 E10
Fromebridge Glos......80 D3
Fromefield Som......45 D9
Frome St Quintin Dorset. 29 G9
Fromes Hill Hereford.... 97 B10
Fron Denb......165 B9
Gwyn......145 B7
Gwyn......163 D8
Gwyn......163 G7
Powys......113 G11
Powys......129 C8
Powys......130 C4
Powys......130 D3
Powys......148 G5
Shrops......148 B5
Fron-Bache Denb......166 G2
Froncysyllte Wrex......166 G3
Fron-deg Wrex......166 F3
Frongoch Gwyn......147 B8
Fron Isaf Wrex......166 G3
Frost Devon......26 F3
Frostenden Suff......143 G8
Frostenden Corner Suff 143 G8
Frosterley Durham......232 E6
Frost Hill N Som......60 G3
Frostlane Hants......32 F6
Frost Row Norf......141 C10
Frotoft Orkney......314 D4
Froxfield C Beds......103 D8
Wilts......63 F9
Froxfield Green Hants... 34 B2
Froyle Hants......49 E9
Fryerning Essex......87 E10
Fryerns Essex......69 B8
Fryton N Yorks......216 E3

Fugglestone St Peter
Wilts 46 G6
Fulbeck Lincs 172 E6
Northumb 252 F5
Fulbourn Cambs 123 F10
Fulbrook Oxon 82 C3
Fulflood Hants 33 B7
Fulford Som 28 B2
Staffs 151 B9
York 207 D8
Fulham London 67 D8
Fulking W Sus 36 E2
Fullabrook Devon 40 E4
Fullarton Glasgow 268 C2
N Ayrs 257 B8
Fuller's End Essex 105 F10
Fuller's Moor Ches W 167 E7
Fuller Street Essex 88 B2
Fullerton Hants 47 F11
Fulletby Lincs 190 G3
Fullshaw S Yorks 197 G8
Full Sutton E Yorks 207 B10
Fullwell Cross London 86 G6
Fullwood E Ayrs 267 E8
Gtr Man 196 F2
Fulmer Bucks 66 B3
Fulmodestone Norf 159 C9
Fulneck W Yorks 205 G10
Fulnetby Lincs 189 F9
Fulney Lincs 156 E5
Fulready Warks 100 B5
Fulshaw Park Ches E 184 E4
Fulstone W Yorks 197 F7
Fulstow Lincs 190 B4
Fulthorpe Stockton 234 G4
Fulwell Oxon 101 G7
T&W 243 F9
Fulwood Lancs 202 G6
Som 28 C2
S Yorks 186 D4
Fundenhall Norf 142 D3
Fundenhall Street Norf . . . 142 D2
Funtington W Sus 22 B3
Funtley Hants 33 F9
Funtullich Perth 285 E11
Funzie Shetland 312 D8
Furley Devon 28 G3
Furnace Argyll 284 G4
Carms 74 E6
Carms 75 E8
Ceredig 128 D3
Highld 299 B9
Furnace End Warks 134 E4
Furnace Green W Sus 51 F9
Furnace Wood W Sus 51 F11
Furneaux Pelham Herts . . . 105 F8
Furner's Green E Sus 36 B6
Furness Vale Derbys 185 E8
Furneux Pelham Herts . . . 105 F8
Furnham Som 28 F4
Further Ford End Essex . . 105 E9
Further Quarter Kent 53 F11
Furtho Northants 102 C5
Furze Devon 25 B10
Furzebrook Dorset 18 E4
Furzedown Hants 32 B5
London 67 E9
Furzehill Devon 41 D8
Dorset 31 G8
Furze Hill Hants 31 E11
Furzeley Corner Hants . . . 33 E11
Furze Platt Windsor 65 C11
Furzey Lodge Hants 32 G5
Furzley Hants 32 D3
Furzton M Keynes 102 D6
Fyfett Som 28 E2
Fyfield Essex 87 D9
Glos 82 E2
Hants 47 D9
Oxon 82 F6
Wilts 63 F7
Wilts 63 G7
Fylingthorpe N Yorks 227 D8
Fyning W Sus 34 C4
Fyvie Aberds 303 F7

G

Gabalfa Cardiff 59 D7
Gabhsann bho Dheas
W Isles 304 C6
Gabhsann bho Thuath
W Isles 304 C6
Gable Head Hants 21 B10
Gablon Highld 309 K7
Gabroc Hill E Ayrs 267 E9
Gadbrook Sur 51 D8
Gaddesby Leics 154 G3
Gadebridge Herts 85 D8
Gadfa Anglesey 179 D7
Gadfield Elm Worcs 98 E5
Gadlas Shrops 149 B7
Gadlys Rhondda 77 E7
Gadshill Kent 69 E8
Gaer Newport 59 B9
Powys 96 G3
Gaer-fawr Mon 78 F6
Gaerllwyd Mon 78 F6
Gaerwen Anglesey 179 G7
Gagingwell Oxon 101 F8
Gaick Lodge Highld 291 E9
Gailey Staffs 151 G8
Gailey Wharf Staffs 151 G8
Gainfield Oxon 82 F4
Gainford Durham 224 B3
Gain Hill Kent 53 D8
Gainsborough Lincs 188 C4
Suff 108 C3
Gainsford End Essex 106 D4
Gairletter Argyll 276 E3
Gairloch Highld 299 B8
Gairlochy Highld 290 E3
Gairney Bank Perth 280 B2
Gairnshiel Lodge
Aberds 292 C4
Gaisgill Cumb 222 D2
Gaitsgill Cumb 230 B3
Galadean Borders 271 G11
Galashiels Borders 261 B11
Galdlys Flint 182 G2
Gale Gtr Man 196 D2
Galgate Lancs 202 B5
Galhampton Som 29 B10
Gallaberry Dumfries 247 G11
Gallachoille Argyll 275 E8
Gallanach Argyll 288 C4
Argyll 289 G10
Highld 294 G6
Gallantry Bank Ches E 167 E8
Gallatown Fife 280 C5
Galley Common Warks . . . 134 E6
Galleyend Essex 88 E2
Galley Hill Cambs 122 D6
Lincs 190 F6
Galleywood Essex 88 E2
Gallgill Cumb 231 B11
Gallin Perth 285 C9
Gallovie Highld 291 E7
Gallowfauld Angus 287 C8
Gallowhill Glasgow 267 D11
Gallowhill continued
Renfs 267 B9
Gallowhills Aberds 303 D10
Gallows Corner London . . 87 G8
Gallowsgreen Torf 78 D3
Gallows Green Essex 106 F2
Essex 107 F8
Staffs 169 G9
Worcs 117 E8
Gallows Inn Derbys 171 G7
Gallowstree Common
Oxon 65 C7
Galltair Highld 295 C10
Galltegfa Denb 165 D10
Gallt Melyd / Meliden
Denb 181 E9
Gallt-y-foel Gwyn 163 C9
Gallypot Street E Sus 52 F3
Galmington Som 28 C2
Galmisdale Highld 294 G6
Galmpton Devon 8 G3
Torbay 9 D7
Galon Uchaf M Tydf 77 D9
Galphay N Yorks 214 E5
Galston E Ayrs 258 B2
Galtrigill Highld 296 F7
Gam Corn 11 F7
Gamble Hill W Yorks 205 G11
Gamblesby Cumb 231 D8
Gamble's Green Essex 88 C3
Gamelsby Cumb 239 G7
Gamesley Derbys 185 C8
Gamlingay Cambs 122 G4
Gamlingay Cinques
Cambs 122 G4
Gamlingay Great Heath
Cambs 122 G4
Gammaton Devon 25 B7
Gammaton Moor Devon . . 25 C7
Gammersgill N Yorks 213 C11
Gamston Notts 154 B2
Notts 188 F2
Ganarew Hereford 79 B8
Ganavan Argyll 289 F10
Ganders Green Glos 98 G4
Gang Corn 6 B6
Ganllwyd Gwyn 146 E4
Gannetts Dorset 30 D3
Gannochy Angus 293 F7
Perth 286 E5
Gansclet Highld 310 E7
Ganstead E Yorks 209 G9
Ganthorpe N Yorks 216 E3
Ganton N Yorks 217 D9
Gants Hill London 68 B2
Ganwick Corner Herts 86 F3
Gaodhail Argyll 289 F8
Gappah Devon 14 F3
Garafad Highld 298 C4
Garamor Highld 295 F8
Garbat Highld 300 C4
Garbhallt Argyll 275 D11
Garboldisham Norf 141 G10
Garbole Highld 301 G7
Garden City Bl Gwent 77 D11
Flint 166 B4
Gardeners Green
Wokingham 65 F10
Gardenstown Aberds 303 C7
Garden Village Swansea . . 56 B5
S Yorks 186 B3
Wrex 166 E4
W Yorks 206 G4
Garderhouse Shetland 313 J5
Gardham E Yorks 208 E5
Gardie Shetland 312 D7
Gardin Shetland 312 G6
Gare Hill Som 45 E9
Garelochhead Argyll 276 C4
Garford Oxon 82 F6
Garforth W Yorks 206 G4
Gargrave N Yorks 204 C4
Gargunnock Stirling 278 C4
Garizim Conwy 179 F11
Garker Corn 5 E10
Garlandhayes Devon 27 D11
Garlands Cumb 239 G10
Garleffin S Ayrs 244 G3
Garlic Street Norf 142 G4
Garlieston Dumfries 236 E6
Garlinge Kent 71 F10
Garlinge Green Kent 54 C6
Garlogie Aberds 293 C9
Garmelow Staffs 150 D5
Garmond Aberds 303 D8
Garmondsway Durham . . . 234 E2
Garmony Argyll 289 E8
Garmouth Moray 302 C3
Garmston Shrops 132 B2
Garn Powys 130 G2
Garnant Carms 75 C11
Garndiffaith Torf 78 E3
Garndolbenmaen Gwyn . 163 G7
Garnedd Conwy 164 E2
Garnett Bridge Cumb . . . 221 F10
Garnetts Essex 87 B10
Garnfadryn Gwyn 144 C5
Garnkirk N Lanark 268 B3
Garnlydan Bl Gwent 77 C11
Garnsgate Lincs 157 E8
Garnswllt Swansea 75 D10
Garn-swllt Swansea 75 D10
Garn-yr-erw Torf 78 C2
Garrabost W Isles 304 E7
Garrachra Argyll 275 E11
Garra Eallabus Argyll 274 F3
Garralburn Moray 302 D4
Garraron Argyll 275 C9
Garras Corn 2 E6
Garreg Flint 181 F10
Gwyn 163 G10
Garrets Green W Mid 134 F2
Garrick Perth 286 F2
Garrigill Cumb 231 C10
Garrison Stirling 285 G7
Garriston N Yorks 224 G3
Garroch Dumfries 246 G3
Garrogie Lodge Highld . . . 291 B7
Garros Highld 298 C4
Garrow Perth 286 C2
Garrowhill Glasgow 268 C3
Garrygualach Highld 290 C3
Garryhorn Dumfries 246 E2
Garsdale Cumb 212 B4
Garsdale Head Cumb 222 G5
Garsdon Wilts 62 B3
Garshall Green Staffs 151 C9
Garsington Oxon 83 E9
Garstang Lancs 202 D5
Garston Herts 85 F10
Mers 182 E6
Garswood Mers 183 B9
Gartachoil Stirling 277 C10
Gartbreck Argyll 254 B3
Gartcosh N Lanark 268 B3
Garth Bridgend 57 C11
Ceredig 128 G2
Flint 181 E10
Gwyn 179 G9
Newport 59 B9
Garth continued
Newport 78 G4
Perth 285 B11
Powys 95 B9
Powys 114 C5
Shetland 313 H4
Shetland 313 H6
Wrex 166 G3
Garthamlock Glasgow . . . 268 B3
Garthbeg Highld 291 B7
Garthbrengy Powys 95 E10
Garthdee Aberdeen 293 C11
Gartheli Ceredig 111 F11
Garthmyl Powys 130 D3
Garthorpe Leics 154 E6
N Lincs 199 D11
Garth Owen Powys 130 E2
Garth Row Cumb 221 F10
Garth Trevor Wrex 166 G3
Gartlea N Lanark 268 C5
Gartloch Glasgow 268 B3
Gartly Aberds 302 F5
Gartmore Stirling 277 B10
Gartmore Ho Stirling 277 B10
Gartnagrenach Argyll 255 B8
Gartness N Lanark 268 C5
Stirling 277 D10
Gartocharn W Dunb 277 D8
Garton E Yorks 209 F11
Garton-on-the-Wolds
E Yorks 208 B5
Gartsherrie N Lanark 268 B4
Gartur Stirling 277 B11
Gartymore Highld 311 H4
Garvald E Loth 281 G11
Garvamore Highld 291 D7
Garvard Argyll 274 D4
Garvault Hotel Highld . . . 308 F7
Garve Highld 300 C3
Garvestone Norf 141 B10
Garvock Aberds 293 F9
Invclyd 276 G5
Garvock Hill Fife 280 D2
Garway Hereford 97 G9
Garway Hill Hereford 97 F8
Gaskan Highld 289 B9
Gasper Wilts 45 G9
Gastard Wilts 61 F11
Gasthorpe Norf 141 G9
Gaston Green Essex 87 B7
Gatacre Park Shrops 132 F5
Gatcombe IoW 20 D5
Gateacre Mers 182 D6
Gatebeck Cumb 211 B10
Gate Burton Lincs 188 E4
Gateford Notts 187 E9
Gateford Common
Notts 187 E9
Gateforth N Yorks 198 B5
Gatehead E Ayrs 257 B9
Gate Helmsley N Yorks . . 207 B9
Gatehouse Northumb 251 F7
Gatehouse of Fleet
Dumfries 237 D8
Gatelawbridge
Dumfries 247 D10
Gateley Norf 159 E9
Gatenby N Yorks 214 B6
Gatesgarth Cumb 220 B3
Gateshead T&W 243 E7
Gatesheath Ches W 167 C7
Gateside Aberds 293 B8
Angus 287 C8
Dumfries 248 E4
E Renf 267 D9
Fife 286 G5
N Ayrs 267 E7
Shetland 312 F4
Gatewen Wrex 166 E4
Gatherley Devon 12 E3
Gathurst Gtr Man 194 F4
Gatlas Newport 78 G4
Gatley End Cambs 104 C5
Gtr Man 184 D4
Gatton Sur 51 C9
Gattonside Borders 262 B2
Gatwick Glos 80 C2
Gatwick Airport W Sus 51 E9
Gaufron Powys 113 D9
Gaulby Leics 136 C3
Gauldry Fife 287 E7
Gauntons Bank Ches E . . . 167 F9
Gaunt's Common Dorset . . 31 F8
Gaunt's Earthcott S Glos . 60 C6
Gaunt's End Essex 105 F10
Gautby Lincs 189 G11
Gavinton Borders 272 E5
Gawber S Yorks 197 F10
Gawcott Bucks 102 E3
Gawsworth Ches E 168 B5
Gawthorpe W Yorks 197 C9
W Yorks 197 D7
Gawthrop Cumb 212 B3
Gawthwaite Cumb 210 C5
Gay Bowers Essex 88 E3
Gaydon Warks 119 G7
Gayfield Orkney 314 A4
Gayhurst M Keynes 103 B7
Gayle N Yorks 213 B7
Gayles N Yorks 224 D2
Gay Street W Sus 35 C9
Gayton Mers 182 E3
Norf 158 F4
Northants 120 G4
Staffs 151 D9
Gayton Engine Lincs 191 D7
Gayton le Marsh Lincs . . . 190 E6
Gayton le Wold Lincs 190 D2
Gayton Thorpe Norf 158 F4
Gaywood Norf 158 E2
Gaza Shetland 312 F5
Gazeley Suff 124 E4
Geanies House Highld . . . 301 B8
Gearraidh Bhailteas
W Isles 297 J3
Gearraidh Bhaird
W Isles 304 F5
Gearraidh Dubh W Isles . 296 F4
Gearraidh na h-Aibhne
W Isles 304 E4
Gearraidh na Monadh
W Isles 297 K3
Geàrraidh Sheilidh
W Isles 297 J3
Geary Highld 298 C2
Geat Wolford Warks 100 E4
Geddes House Highld 301 D8
Gedding Suff 125 F9
Geddington Northants . . . 137 G7
Gedgrave Hall Suff 109 B8
Gedintailor Highld 295 B7
Gedling Notts 171 G10
Gedney Lincs 157 E8
Gedney Broadgate Lincs 157 E8
Gedney Drove End
Lincs 157 D9
Gedney Dyke Lincs 157 D8
Gedney Hill Lincs 156 G6
Gee Cross Gtr Man 185 C7
Geeston Rutland 137 C9
Gegin Wrex 166 E3
Geilston Argyll 276 F6
Geinas Denb 165 B9
Geirinis W Isles 297 G3
Geise Highld 310 C5
Geisiadar W Isles 304 E3
Geldeston Norf 143 E7
Gell Conwy 164 B5
Gelli Pembs 73 B9
Rhondda 77 G7
Gellideg M Tydf 77 D8
Gellifor Denb 165 C10
Gelligaer Caerph 77 F10
Gelli-gaer Neath 57 C9
Gelligroes Caerph 77 G11
Gelli-hôf Caerph 77 F11
Gellilydan Gwyn 146 B3
Gellinud Neath 76 E2
Gellinudd Neath 76 E2
Gellyburn Perth 286 D4
Gellygron Neath 76 E2
Gellywen Carms 92 G5
Gelsmoor Leics 153 F8
Gelston Dumfries 237 D9
Lincs 172 G6
Gembling E Yorks 209 B8
Gemini Warr 183 C9
Gendros Swansea 56 B6
Genesis Green Suff 124 F4
Gentleshaw Staffs 151 G11
Geocrab W Isles 305 J3
Georgefield Dumfries 249 E7
George Green Bucks 66 C4
Georgeham Devon 40 F3
George Nympton Devon . . 26 C2
Georgetown Bl Gwent 77 D10
Georgia Corn 1 B5
Gergask Highld 291 D8
Gerlan Gwyn 163 B10
Germansweek Devon 12 C4
Germiston Glasgow 268 B2
Germoe Corn 2 D3
Gernon Bushes Essex 87 E7
Gerrans Corn 3 B9
Gerrard's Bromley
Staffs 150 C5
Gerrards Cross Bucks 66 B4
Gerrick Redcar 226 C4
Geseilfa Powys 129 E8
Gestingthorpe Essex 106 D6
Gesto Ho Highld 294 B5
Geuffordd Powys 148 G4
Geufron Denb 166 G2
Gibbet Hill Warks 135 G10
W Mid 118 C6
Gibb Hill Ches W 183 F10
Gibbshill Dumfries 237 B9
Gib Heath W Mid 133 F11
Gibraltar Bedford 103 B10
Bucks 84 C3
Kent 55 F8
Gibralter Oxon 83 B7
Gibshill Invclyd 276 G6
Gibsmere Notts 172 F2
Giddeahall Wilts 61 E11
Giddy Green Dorset 18 D2
Gidea Park London 68 B4
Gidleigh Devon 13 D9
Giffard Park M Keynes . . . 103 C7
Giffnock E Renf 267 D11
Gifford E Loth 271 B10
Giffordland N Ayrs 266 F5
Giffordtown Fife 286 F6
Gigg Gtr Man 195 F10
Giggetty Staffs 133 E7
Giggleswick N Yorks 212 G6
Giggshill Sur 67 F7
Gignog Pembs 91 G7
Gilberdyke E Yorks 199 B10
Gilbert's Coombe Corn . . . 4 G3
Gilbert's End Worcs 98 C6
Gilbert's Green Warks . . . 118 C2
Gilbertstone W Mid 134 G2
Gilbert Street Hants 49 G7
Gilchriston E Loth 271 B9
Gilcrux Cumb 229 D8
Gildersome W Yorks 197 B8
Gildersome Street
W Yorks 197 B8
Gildingwells S Yorks 187 D9
Gilesgate Durham 233 C11
Gilesgate Moor
Durham 233 C11
Gileston V Glam 58 F4
Gilfach Caerph 77 F11
Hereford 96 E6
Gilfach Goch Rhondda 58 B3
Gilfachrheda Ceredig 111 F8
Gilgarran Cumb 228 G6
Gill N Yorks 204 E5
Gillamoor N Yorks 216 B3
Gillan Corn 3 E7
Gillar's Green Mers 183 B7
Gillbank Cumb 221 F7
Gillbent Gtr Man 184 E5
Gillen Highld 298 D2
Gillesbie Dumfries 248 E5
Gilling East N Yorks 216 D2
Gillingham Dorset 30 B4
Medway 69 F9
Norf 143 E8
Gilling West N Yorks 224 D3
Gillmoss Mers 182 B6
Gillock Highld 310 D6
Gillow Heath Staffs 168 D5
Gills Highld 310 B7
Gill's Green Kent 53 G9
Gillway Staffs 134 C4
Gilmanscleuch Borders . . 261 E8
Gilmerton Edin 270 B5
Perth 286 E2
Gilmonby Durham 223 C9
Gilmorton Leics 135 F11
Gilmourton S Lanark 268 G3
Gilnow Gtr Man 195 F8
Gilroyd S Yorks 197 G10
Gilsland Northumb 240 D4
Gilsland Spa Cumb 240 D4
Gilson Warks 134 E3
Gilstead W Yorks 205 F8
Gilston Borders 271 D8
Herts 86 C6
Gilston Park Herts 86 C6
Giltbrook Notts 171 F7
Gilver's Lane Worcs 98 C6
Gilwell Park Essex 86 F5
Gilwern Mon 78 C2
Gimingham Norf 160 B5
Ginclough Ches E 185 F7
Ginger's Green E Sus 23 C10
Giosla W Isles 304 F3
Gipping Suff 125 E11
Gipsey Bridge Lincs 174 F3
Gipsy Row Suff 107 D11
Gipsyville Hull 200 B5
Gipton W Yorks 206 F2
Gipton Wood W Yorks 206 F2
Girdle Toll N Ayrs 266 G6
Girlington W Yorks 205 G8
Girlsta Shetland 313 H6
Girsby Lincs 190 D2
N Yorks 225 D7
Girt Som 29 C10
Girtford C Beds 104 B3
C Beds 122 G3
Girthon Dumfries 237 D8
Girton Cambs 123 E8
Notts 172 B4
Girvan S Ayrs 244 D5
Gisburn Lancs 204 D2
Gisleham Suff 143 F10
Gislingham Suff 125 C11
Gissing Norf 142 F2
Gittisham Devon 15 B8
Givons Grove Sur 51 C7
Glachavoil Argyll 275 F11
Glackmore Highld 300 D6
Glack of Midthird Moray 302 E3
Gladestry Powys 114 F4
Gladsmuir E Loth 281 G9
Glaichbea Highld 300 F5
Glais Swansea 76 E2
Glaisdale N Yorks 226 D5
Glame Highld 298 E5
Glamis Angus 287 C7
Glan Adda Gwyn 179 G9
Glanafon Pembs 73 B7
Glanaman Carms 75 C11
Glan-Conwy Conwy 164 E4
Glandford Norf 177 E8
Glan-Duar Carms 93 C10
Glandwr Caerph 78 E2
Pembs 92 F3
Glan-Dwyfach Gwyn 163 G7
Glandy Cross Carms 92 F2
Glandyfi Ceredig 128 D3
Glan Gors Anglesey 179 F7
Glangrwyney Powys 78 B2
Glanhanog Powys 129 D8
Glanmule Powys 130 E3
Glanrafon Ceredig 128 G2
Glanrhyd Gwyn 144 B5
Pembs 92 C2
Glan-rhyd Gwyn 163 D7
Powys 76 D3
Glantlees Northumb 252 B4
Glanton Northumb 264 G3
Glanton Pike Northumb . . 264 G3
Glan-traeth Anglesey 178 F3
Glanvilles Wootton
Dorset 29 F11
Glanwern Ceredig 128 F2
Glanwydden Conwy 180 E4
Glan-y-don Flint 181 F11
Glan y Ffer / Ferryside
Carms 74 C5
Glan-y-llyn Rhondda 58 C6
Glan-y-môr Carms 74 C4
Glan-y-nant Caerph 77 F10
Powys 129 G8
Glan-yr-afon Anglesey . 179 E10
Flint 181 E10
Gwyn 165 G6
Gwyn 165 G8
Shrops 148 E4
Glan-y-wern Gwyn 146 C2
Glapthorn Northants 137 E10
Glapwell Derbys 171 B7
Glas-allt Shiel Aberds . . . 292 E4
Glasbury Powys 96 D3
Glaschoil Highld 301 F10
Glascoed Denb 181 G7
Mon 78 E4
Powys 129 F11
Powys 148 G2
Wrex 166 E3
Glascorrie Aberds 292 D5
Perth 286 E2
Glascote Staffs 134 C4
Glascwm Powys 114 G3
Glasdir Flint 181 E10
Glasdrum Argyll 284 C4
Glasfryn Conwy 164 E6
Glasgoed Ceredig 92 B6
Glasgoforest Aberds 293 B10
Glasgow Glasgow 267 B11
Glashvin Highld 298 C4
Glasinfryn Gwyn 163 B9
Glasllwch Newport 59 B9
Glasnacardoch Highld . . . 295 F8
Glasnakille Highld 295 D7
Glasphein Highld 297 G7
Glaspwll Powys 128 D4
Glassburn Highld 300 F3
Glassenbury Kent 53 F8
Glasserton Dumfries 236 F6
Glassford S Lanark 268 F4
Glassgreen Moray 302 C2
Glass Houghton
W Yorks 198 C2
Glasshouse Glos 98 G4
Glasshouse Hill Glos 98 G4
Glasshouses N Yorks 214 G3
Glasslie Fife 286 G6
Glasson Cumb 228 D6
Cumb 239 E7
Lancs 202 B4
Glassonby Cumb 231 D7
Glasterlaw Angus 287 B9
Glaston Rutland 137 C7
Glastonbury Som 44 F4
Glatton Cambs 138 F3
Glazebrook Warr 183 C11
Glazebury Warr 183 B11
Glazeley Shrops 132 F4
Gleadless S Yorks 186 E5
Gleadless Valley
S Yorks 186 E5
Gleadmoss Ches E 168 B4
Gleadsmoss Ches E 168 B4
Gleanhead Dumfries 245 G10
Gleann Tholàstaidh
W Isles 304 D7
Gleaston Cumb 210 E5
Glebe Hants 33 D9
Shetland 313 J6
T&W 243 F8
Glecknabae Argyll 275 G11
Gledhow W Yorks 206 F2
Gledrid Shrops 148 B5
Gleiniant Powys 129 E9
Glemsford Suff 106 B6
Glen Dumfries 237 B10
Dumfries 237 D7
Glenallachie Moray 302 E2
Glenalmond College
Perth 286 E3
Glenalmond Ho Perth . . . 286 E3
Glenamachrie Argyll 289 G11
Glenample Stirling 285 E9
Glenancross Highld 295 F8
Glenapp Castle S Ayrs . . . 244 G3
Glenaros Ho Argyll 289 E7
Glen Auldyn IoM 192 C5
Glenbarr Argyll 255 D7
Glenbeg Highld 289 C7
Highld 301 G10
Glen Bernisdale Highld . . 298 E4
Glenbervie Aberds 293 E9
Glenboig N Lanark 268 B4
Glenborrodale Highld . . . 289 C8
Glenbranter Argyll 276 B2
Glenbreck Borders 260 E3
Glenbrein Lodge Highld . 290 B6
Glenbrittle House
Highld 294 C6
Glenbrook Edin 270 B2
Glenbuchat Castle
Aberds 292 B5
Glenbuchat Lodge
Aberds 292 B5
Glenbuck E Ayrs 259 D7
Glenburn Renfs 267 C9
Glenbyre Argyll 289 G7
Glencalvie Lodge Highld 309 L4
Glencanisp Lodge
Highld 307 G6
Glencaple Dumfries 237 C11
Glencarron Lodge
Highld 299 D10
Glencarse Perth 286 E5
Glencassley Castle
Highld 309 J4
Glencat Aberds 293 D7
Glenceitlein Highld 284 C5
Glencoe Highld 284 B4
Glencraig Fife 280 B3
Glencripesdale Highld . . . 289 D8
Glencrosh Dumfries 247 F7
Glendavan Ho Aberds 292 C6
Glendearg Borders 262 B2
Glendevon Perth 286 G3
Glendoebeg Highld 290 C6
Glendoe Lodge Highld . . . 290 C6
Glendoick Perth 286 E6
Glendoll Lodge Angus . . . 292 F4
Glendoune S Ayrs 244 D5
Glenduckie Fife 286 F6
Glendye Lodge Aberds . . . 293 E8
Gleneagles Hotel Perth . . 286 F3
Gleneagles House Perth 286 G3
Glenearn Perth 286 F5
Glenegedale Argyll 254 B4
Glenelg Highld 295 D10
Glenernie Moray 301 E10
Glenfarg Perth 286 F5
Glenfarquhar Lodge
Aberds 293 E9
Glenferness House
Highld 301 E9
Glenfeshie Lodge
Highld 291 D10
Glenfiddich Lodge
Moray 302 F3
Glenfield Leics 135 B10
Glenfinnan Highld 295 G10
Glenfinnan Lodge
Highld 295 G11
Glenfintaig Ho Highld . . . 290 E4
Glenfoot Perth 286 F5
Glenfyne Lodge Argyll . . . 284 F6
Glengap Dumfries 237 D8
Glengarnock N Ayrs 266 E6
Glengolly Highld 310 C5
Glengorm Castle Argyll . . 288 D6
Glengoulandie Perth 285 B11
Glengrasco Highld 298 E4
Glenhead Farm Angus . . . 292 G4
Glen Ho Borders 261 C7
Glenholt Plym 7 C10
Glenhoul Dumfries 246 F4
Glenhurich Highld 289 C10
Glenkerry Borders 261 G7
Glenkiln Dumfries 237 B10
Glenkindie Aberds 292 B6
Glenlair Dumfries 237 B9
Glenlatterach Moray 301 D11
Glenlee Dumfries 246 G4
Glenleigh Park E Sus 38 F2
Glenleraig Highld 306 F6
Glenlichorn Perth 285 F11
Glenlicht Ho Highld 290 B2
Glenlivet Moray 301 G11
Glenlochar Dumfries 237 C9
Glenlochsie Perth 292 F2
Glenlocksie Lodge
Perth 292 F2
Glenloig N Ayrs 255 D10
Glenlomond Perth 286 G5
Glenluce Dumfries 236 D4
Glenlussa Ho Argyll 255 E8
Glenmallan Argyll 276 B5
Glenmark Angus 292 E6
Glenmarkie Lodge
Angus 292 G4
Glenmarksie Highld 300 D3
Glenmavis N Lanark 268 B4
W Loth 269 B9
Glenmaye IoM 192 E3
Glenmayne Borders 261 C11
Glenmeanie Highld 300 D2
Glenmidge Dumfries 247 F9
Glenmoidart Ho Highld . . 289 B9
Glen Mona IoM 192 D5
Glen Mor Highld 295 B10
Glenmore Argyll 275 B9
Argyll 275 G11
Highld 298 E4
Glenmore Lodge
Highld 291 C11
Glenmoy Angus 292 G6
Glen Nevis House Highld 290 F3
Glennoe Argyll 284 D4
Glen of Newmill Moray . . 302 D4
Glenogil Angus 292 G6
Glenowen Pembs 73 D7
Glen Parva Leics 135 D11
Glenprosen Lodge
Angus 292 G4
Glenprosen Village
Angus 292 G5
Glenquaich Lodge
Perth 286 D2
Glenquiech Angus 292 G6
Glenquithlie Aberds 303 C8
Glenrath Borders 260 C6
Glenrazie Dumfries 236 C5
Glenreasdell Mains
Argyll 255 B9
Glenree N Ayrs 255 E10
Glenridding Cumb 221 B7
Glenrosa N Ayrs 256 B2
Glenrossal Highld 309 J4
Glenrothes Fife 286 G6
Glensanda Highld 289 E10
Glensaugh Aberds 293 F8
Glensburgh Falk 279 E8
Glenshero Lodge Highld 291 D7
Glenshoe Lodge Perth . . . 292 G3
Glen Sluain Argyll 275 D11
Glenstockadale
Dumfries 236 C2
Glenstriven Argyll 275 F11
Glentaggart S Lanark 259 D8
Glen Tanar House
Aberds 292 D6
Glentarkie Perth 286 F5
Glenternie Borders 260 B6
Glentham Lincs 189 C8
Glentirranmuir Stirling . . 278 C3
Glenton Aberds 302 G6
Glentress Borders 261 B7
Glentromie Lodge
Highld 291 D9
Glen Trool Lodge
Dumfries 245 G10
Glentrool Village
Dumfries 236 B5
Glentruan IoM 192 B5
Glentruim House Highld 291 D8
Glentworth Lincs 188 D6
Glenuaig Lodge Highld . 299 E11
Glenuig Highld 289 B8
Glenure Argyll 284 C4
Glenurquhart Highld 301 C7
Glen Vic Askil Highld 298 E3
Glenview Argyll 284 E5
Glen Village Falk 279 F7
Glen Vine IoM 192 E4
Glespin S Lanark 259 D8
Gletness Shetland 313 H6
Glewstone Hereford 97 G11
Glinton Pboro 138 B3
Globe Town London 67 C11
Glodwick Gtr Man 196 G2
Glogue Pembs 92 E4
Glooston Leics 136 D4
Glororum Northumb 264 C5
Glossop Derbys 185 C8
Gloster Hill Northumb . . . 253 C7
Gloucester Glos 80 B4
Gloup Shetland 312 C7
Gloweth Corn 4 G5
Glusburn N Yorks 204 E6
Glutt Lodge Highld 310 F3
Glutton Bridge Staffs 169 B9
Gluvian Corn 5 C8
Glympton Oxon 101 G8
Glyn Mon 79 F7
Powys 129 F8
Glynarthen Ceredig 92 B6
Glynbrochan Powys 129 G8
Glyn Castle Neath 76 E4
Glyn-Ceiriog Wrex 148 B4
Glyncoch Rhondda 77 G9
Glyncoed Bl Gwent 77 C11
Glyncorrwg Neath 57 B11
Glyn-cywarch Gwyn 146 C2
Glynde E Sus 23 D7
Glyndebourne E Sus 23 C7
Glyndyfrdwy Denb 165 G10
Glynedd / Glyn neath
Neath 76 D5
Glyne Gap E Sus 38 F3
Glyn Etwy Bl Gwent 77 D11
Glynhafren Powys 129 G7
Glynllan Bridgend 58 B2
Glynmorlas Shrops 148 B6
Glyn-neath / Glynedd
Neath 76 D5
Glynogwr Bridgend 58 B3
Glyntaff Rhondda 58 B5
Glyntawe Powys 76 B4
Gnosall Staffs 150 E6
Gnosall Heath Staffs 150 E6
Goadby Leics 136 D4
Goadby Marwood Leics . . 154 D5
Goatacre Wilts 62 D4
Goatham Green E Sus 38 C4
Goathill Dorset 29 D11
Goathland N Yorks 226 E6
Goathurst Som 43 G9
Goathurst Common Kent 52 C3
Goat Lees Kent 54 D4
Gobernuisgach Lodge
Highld 308 E4
Gobernuisgeach Highld . 310 F3
Gobhaig W Isles 305 H2
Gobley Hole Hants 48 D6
Gobowen Shrops 148 C6
Godalming Sur 50 E3
Goddards Bucks 84 G3
Goddard's Corner Suff . . 126 D5
Goddard's Green Kent . . . 53 G10
W Berks 65 F7
Goddards' Green W Sus . . 36 C3
Godden Green Kent 52 B5
Goddington London 68 F3
Godley Gtr Man 185 B7
Godleybrook Staffs 169 G7
Godley Hill Gtr Man 185 C7
Godleys Green E Sus 36 D5
Godmanchester Cambs . 122 C4
Godmanstone Dorset 17 B9
Godmersham Kent 54 C5
Godney Som 44 E3
Godolphin Cross Corn 2 C4
Godre'r-graig Neath 76 D3
God's Blessing Green
Dorset 31 G8
Godshill Hants 31 E11
IoW 20 E6
Godstone Sur 51 C10
Godswinscroft Hants 19 B9
Godwell Devon 8 D2
Godwick Norf 159 E8
Godwinscroft Hants 19 B9
Goetre Mon 78 D4
Goferydd Anglesey 178 E2
Goff's Oak Herts 86 E4
Gogar Edin 280 G3
Goginan Ceredig 128 G3
Goirtean a'Chladaich
Highld 290 F2
Golan Gwyn 163 G8
Golant Corn 6 E2
Golberdon Corn 12 G2
Golborne Gtr Man 183 B10
Golcar W Yorks 196 D6
Golch Flint 181 F11
Goldcliff Newport 59 C11
Golden Balls Oxon 83 F9
Golden Cross E Sus 23 C8
E Sus 23 C10
Golden Green Kent 52 D6
Golden Grove Carms 75 B9
Goldenhill Stoke 168 E5
Golden Hill Bristol 60 D5
Hants 19 B11
Pembs 73 E7
Pembs 91 G9
Golden Park Devon 24 C2
Golden Pot Hants 49 E8
Golden Valley Derbys . . . 170 E6
Glos 99 G8
Hereford 98 B3
Golder Field Hereford . . 115 E11
Golders Green London . . . 67 B9
Goldfinch Bottom
W Berks 64 G4
Goldhanger Essex 88 D6
Gold Hill Dorset 30 E4
Norf 139 E10
Golding Shrops 131 C10
Goldington Bedford 121 G11
Goldsborough N Yorks . . 206 B3
N Yorks 226 C6
Gold's Cross Bath 60 G5
Golds Green W Mid 133 E9
Goldsithney Corn 2 C2
Goldstone Shrops 150 D4
Goldthorn Park W Mid . . 133 D8
Goldthorpe S Yorks 198 G3
Goldworthy Devon 24 C5
Golford Kent 53 F9
Golftyn Flint 182 G3
Golgotha Kent 55 D9
Gollanfield Highld 301 D8
Gollawater Corn 4 E5
Gollinglith Foot
N Yorks 214 C3
Golly Wrex 166 D4
Golsoncott Som 42 F4
Golspie Highld 311 J2
Golval Highld 310 C2
Golynos Torf 78 E3
Gomeldon Wilts 47 F7
Gomersal W Yorks 197 B8
Gometra Ho Argyll 288 E5
Gomshall Sur 50 D5
Gonalston Notts 171 F11
Gonamena Corn 11 G11
Gonerby Hill Foot Lincs . 155 B8
Gonfirth Shetland 313 G5
Good Easter Essex 87 C10
Gooderstone Norf 140 C5
Goodleigh Devon 40 G6
Goodley Stock Kent 52 C2
Goodmanham E Yorks . . 208 E3
Goodmayes London 68 B3
Goodnestone Kent 55 C9
Kent 70 G4
Goodrich Hereford 79 B9
Goodrington Torbay 9 D7
Good's Green Worcs 132 G5
Goodshaw Lancs 195 B10
Goodshaw Chapel
Lancs 195 B10
Goodshaw Fold Lancs . . 195 B10
Goodstone Devon 13 G11
Goodwick / Wdig Pembs . 91 D8
Goodworth Clatford
Hants 47 E11
Goodyers End Warks 134 F6
Goodyhills Cumb 229 B8
Goole E Yorks 199 C8
Goom's Hill Worcs 117 G10
Goonabarn Corn 5 E9
Goonbell Corn 4 F4
Goon Gumpas Corn 4 G4
Goonhavern Corn 4 E5
Goonhusband Corn 2 D5
Goonlaze Corn 2 B6
Goonown Corn 4 E4
Goonpiper Corn 3 B8
Goonvrea Corn 4 F4
Gooseberry Green Essex 87 F11
Goose Eye W Yorks 204 E6
Gooseford Devon 13 C9
Goose Green Cumb 211 C10
Essex 108 F2
Gtr Man 194 G5
Hants 32 F4
Herts 86 D5
Kent 52 C6
Kent 53 F10
Lancs 194 C3
Norf 142 F2
S Glos 61 C8
W Sus 34 C3
W Sus 35 D10
Gooseham Mill Devon 24 D2
Goosehill W Yorks 197 C11
Goose Hill Hants 64 G4
Goosehill Green Worcs . . 117 E8
Goosemoor Staffs 150 F6
Goosemoor Green
Staffs 151 G11
Goosenford Som 28 B2
Goose Pool Hereford 97 D9
Goosewell Devon 40 D5
Goosey Oxon 82 G5
Goosnargh Lancs 203 F7
Goostrey Ches E 184 G3
Gorbals Glasgow 267 C11
Gorcott Hill Warks 117 D11
Gord Shetland 313 L6
Gorddinog Conwy 179 G11
Gordon Borders 272 G2
Gordonbush Highld 311 J2
Gordonsburgh Moray . . . 302 C4
Gordonstoun Moray 301 C11
Gordonstown Aberds . . . 302 D5
Aberds 303 F7
Gore Dorset 29 D9
Kent 55 B10
Gorebridge Midloth 270 C6
Gore Cross Wilts 46 C4
Gore End Hants 64 G2
Gorefield Cambs 157 G8
Gorehill W Sus 35 C7
Gore Pit Essex 88 B5
Gore Street Kent 71 F9
Gorgie Edin 280 G4
Gorhambury Herts 85 D10
Goring Oxon 64 C6
Goring-by-Sea W Sus . . . 35 G10
Goring Heath Oxon 65 D7
Gorleston-on-Sea
Norf 143 C10
Gornalwood W Mid 133 E8
Gorrachie Aberds 303 D7
Gorran Churchtown Corn . 5 G9
Gorran Haven Corn 5 G10
Gorran High Lanes Corn . . 5 G9
Gorrenberry Borders 249 D11
Gorrig Ceredig 93 C8
Gorse Covert Warr 183 C11
Gorsedd Flint 181 F11
Gorse Hill Gtr Man 184 B4
Swindon 63 B7
Gorseinon Swansea 56 B5
Gorseness Orkney 314 E4
Gorsethorpe Notts 171 B9
Gorseybank Derbys 170 E3
Gorsgoch Ceredig 111 G9
Gorslas Carms 75 C9
Gorsley Glos 98 F3
Gorsley Common
Hereford 98 F3
Gorsley Ley Staffs 133 B11
Gorstage Ches W 183 G10
Gorstan Highld 300 C3
Gorstanvorran Highld . . 289 B10
Gorstella Ches W 166 C5
Gorsteyhill Ches E 168 E2
Gorst Hill Worcs 116 C4
Gorstyhill Staffs 168 E2
Gorsty Hill Staffs 151 D11
Gortan Argyll 274 G3
Gortantaoid Argyll 274 F4
Gortenacullish Highld . . . 295 G8
Gorteneorn Highld 289 C8
Gortenfern Highld 289 C8
Gortinanane Argyll 255 C8
Gorton Gtr Man 184 B5
Gortonallister N Ayrs . . . 256 D2
Gosbeck Suff 126 F3
Gosberton Lincs 156 C4
Gosberton Cheal Lincs . . 156 D4
Gosberton Clough Lincs 156 D3
Goscote W Mid 133 C10

Goseley Dale Derbys 152 E6
Gosfield Essex 106 F5
Gosford Hereford 115 D10
Oxon 83 C7
Gosford Green W Mid 118 B6
Gosforth Cumb 219 E11
T&W 242 D6
Gosforth Valley Derbys 186 F4
Gosland Green Suff 124 G5
Gosling Green Suff 107 C9
Gosmere Kent 54 B4
Gosmore Herts 104 F3
Gospel Ash Staffs 132 E6
Gospel End Village
Staffs 133 E7
Gospel Green W Sus 50 G2
Gospel Oak London 67 B9
Gosport Hants 21 B8
Hants 32 C5
Gossabrough Shetland 312 E7
Gossard's Green C Beds 103 C9
Gossington Glos 80 E2
Gossops Green W Sus 51 F9
Goswick Northumb 273 F11
Gotham Dorset 31 E9
E Sus 38 F2
Notts 153 C10
Gothelney Green Som 43 F9
Gotherington Glos 99 F9
Gothers Corn 5 D9
Gott Argyll 288 E2
Shetland 313 J6
Gotton Som 28 B2
Goudhurst Kent 53 F8
Goukstone Moray 302 D4
Goulceby Lincs 190 F3
Goulton N Yorks 225 E9
Gourdas Aberds 303 E7
Gourdon Aberds 293 F10
Gourock Invclyd 276 F4
Govan Glasgow 267 B11
Govanhill Glasgow 267 C11
Gover Hill Kent 52 C6
Goverton Notts 172 E2
Goveton Devon 8 F5
Govilon Mon 78 C3
Gowanhill Aberds 303 C10
Gowanwell Aberds 303 E8
Gowdall E Yorks 198 C6
Gowerton / Tre-Gwyr
Swansea 56 B5
Gowhole Derbys 185 E8
Gowkhall Fife 279 D11
Gowkthrapple N Lanark 268 E5
Gowthorpe E Yorks 207 C11
Goxhill E Yorks 209 E9
N Lincs 200 C6
Goxhill Haven N Lincs 200 B6
Goybre Neath 57 D9
Goytre Neath 57 D9
Gozzard's Ford Oxon 82 F7
Grabhair W Isles 305 G5
Graby Lincs 155 D11
Gracca Corn 5 D10
Gracemount Edin 270 B5
Grade Corn 2 G6
Graffham W Sus 34 D6
Grafham Cambs 122 D3
Sur 50 E4
Grafton Hereford 97 D9
N Yorks 215 G8
Oxon 82 E3
Shrops 149 F8
Worcs 99 D9
Worcs 115 E11
Grafton Flyford Worcs 117 F9
Grafton Regis Northants 102 B5
Grafton Underwood
Northants 137 G8
Grafty Green Kent 53 D11
Grahamston Falk 279 E7
Graianrhyd Denb 166 D2
Graig Carms 74 E6
Conwy 180 G4
Denb 181 G9
Rhondda 58 B5
Wrex 148 B4
Graig-Fawr Swansea 75 E10
Graig-fechan Denb 165 E10
Graig Felen Swansea 75 E11
Graig Penllyn V Glam 58 D3
Graig Trewyddfa Swansea 57 B7
Grain Medway 69 D11
Grains Bar Gtr Man 196 F3
Grainsby Lincs 190 B3
Grainthorpe Lincs 190 B5
Grainthorpe Fen Lincs 190 B5
Graiselound N Lincs 188 B3
Grampound Corn 5 F8
Grampound Road Corn 5 E8
Gramsdal W Isles 296 F4
Granborough Bucks 102 F5
Granby Notts 154 B5
Grandborough Warks 119 D9
Grandpont Oxon 83 D8
Grandtully Perth 286 B3
Grange Cumb 220 B5
Dorset 31 G8
E Ayrs 257 B10
Fife 287 G8
Halton 183 E8
Lancs 203 G7
Medway 69 F9
Mers 182 D2
NE Lincs 201 F9
N Yorks 223 G8
Perth 286 E6
Warr 183 C10
Grange Crossroads
Moray 302 D4
Grange Estate Dorset 31 G10
Grange Hall Moray 301 C10
Grange Hill Durham 233 F10
Essex 86 G6
Grangemill Derbys 170 D2
Grange Moor W Yorks 197 D8
Grangemouth Falk 279 E8
Grangemuir Fife 287 G9
Grange of Cree
Dumfries 236 D6
Grange of Lindores Fife 286 F6
Grange-over-Sands
Cumb 211 D8
Grangepans Falk 279 E10
Grange Park London 86 F4
Mers 183 C7
Northants 120 F5
Swindon 62 C6
Grangetown Cardiff 59 E7
Redcar 235 G7
T&W 243 G10
Grange Villa Durham 242 G6
Grange Village Glos 79 C11
Granish Highld 291 B11
Gransmoor E Yorks 209 B8
Gransmore Green Essex 106 G3
Granston / Treopert
Pembs 91 E7
Grantchester Cambs 123 F8
Grantham Lincs 155 B8
Grantley N Yorks 214 F4
Grantley Hall N Yorks 214 F4
Grantlodge Aberds 293 B9
Granton Dumfries 248 B3
Edin 280 F4
Grantown Aberds 302 D5
Grantown-on-Spey
Highld 301 G10
Grantsfield Hereford 115 E10
Grantshouse Borders 272 B6
Grant Thorold NE Lincs 201 F9
Graplin Dumfries 237 E8
Grappenhall Warr 183 D10
Grasby Lincs 200 G5
Grasmere Cumb 220 D6
Grasscroft Gtr Man 196 G3
Grassendale Mers 182 D5
Grassgarth Cumb 221 F8
Cumb 230 C2
Grass Green Essex 106 D4
Grassholme Durham 232 G4
Grassington N Yorks 213 G10
Grassmoor Derbys 170 B6
Grassthorpe Notts 172 B3
Grasswell T&W 243 G8
Grateley Hants 47 E9
Gratton Devon 24 E5
Gratwich Staffs 151 C10
Gravel Ches W 167 B11
Gravel Castle Kent 55 D8
Graveley Cambs 122 E4
Herts 104 F4
Gravelhill Shrops 149 G9
Gravel Hill Bucks 85 G8
Gravel Hole Gtr Man 196 F2
Shrops 149 B7
Gravelly Hill W Mid 134 E2
Gravels Shrops 130 D6
Gravelsbank Shrops 130 C6
Graven Shetland 312 F6
Graveney Kent 70 G5
Gravenhunger Moss
Shrops 168 G2
Gravesend Herts 105 F8
Kent 68 E6
Grayingham Lincs 188 B6
Grayrigg Cumb 221 F11
Grays Thurrock 68 D6
Grayshott Hants 49 F11
Grayson Green Cumb 228 F5
Grayswood Sur 50 G2
Graythorp Hrtlpl 234 F6
Grazeley Wokingham 65 F7
Grazeley Green W Berks 65 F7
Greagdhubh Lodge
Highld 291 D8
Greamchary Highld 310 F2
Greasbrough S Yorks 186 B6
Greasby Mers 182 D3
Greasley Notts 171 F7
Great Abington Cambs 105 B10
Great Addington
Northants 121 B9
Great Alne Warks 118 F2
Great Altcar Lancs 193 F10
Great Amwell Herts 86 C5
Great Asby Cumb 222 C3
Great Ashfield Suff 125 D9
Great Ashley Wilts 61 G10
Great Ayton N Yorks 225 C11
Great Baddow Essex 88 E2
Great Bardfield Essex 106 E3
Great Barford Bedford 122 G2
Great Barrington Glos 82 C2
Great Barrow Ches W 167 B7
Great Barton Suff 125 D7
Great Barugh N Yorks 216 D4
Great Bavington
Northumb 251 G11
Great Bealings Suff 108 B4
Great Bedwyn Wilts 63 G9
Great Bentley Essex 108 G2
Great Berry Essex 69 B7
Great Billing Northants 120 E6
Great Bircham Norf 158 C5
Great Blakenham Suff 126 G2
Great Blencow Cumb 230 E5
Great Bolas Telford 150 E2
Great Bookham Sur 50 C6
Great Bosullow Corn 1 C4
Great Bourton Oxon 101 B9
Great Bowden Leics 136 F4
Great Bower Kent 54 C4
Great Bradley Suff 124 G3
Great Braxted Essex 88 C5
Great Bricett Suff 125 G10
Great Brickhill Bucks 103 E8
Great Bridge W Mid 133 E9
Great Bridgeford Staffs 151 D7
Great Brington
Northants 120 D3
Great Bromley Essex 107 F11
Great Broughton Cumb 229 E7
N Yorks 225 D10
Great Buckland Kent 69 G7
Great Budworth
Ches W 183 F11
Great Burdon Darl 224 B6
Great Burgh Sur 51 B8
Great Burstead Essex 87 G11
Great Busby N Yorks 225 D10
Great Canfield Essex 87 B9
Great Carlton Lincs 190 D6
Great Casterton Rutland 137 B9
Rutland 137 B10
Great Cellws Powys 113 E11
Great Chalfield Wilts 61 G11
Great Chart Kent 54 E3
Great Chatwell Staffs 150 G5
Great Chell Stoke 168 E5
Great Chesterford
Essex 105 C10
Great Cheveney Kent 53 E8
Great Cheverell Wilts 46 C3
Great Chilton Durham 233 E11
Great Chishill Cambs 105 D8
Great Clacton Essex 89 B11
Great Claydons Essex 88 E3
Great Cliff W Yorks 197 D10
Great Clifton Cumb 228 F6
Great Coates NE Lincs 201 F8
Great Comberton Worcs 99 C9
Great Common Suff 143 F7
W Sus 35 B8
Great Corby Cumb 239 G11
Great Cornard Suff 107 C7
Great Cowden E Yorks 209 E10
Great Coxwell Oxon 82 G3
Great Crakehall
N Yorks 224 G4
Great Cransley
Northants 120 B6
Great Cressingham
Norf 141 C7
Great Crosby Mers 182 B4
Great Crosthwaite
Cumb 229 G11
Great Cubley Derbys 152 B3
Great Dalby Leics 154 G4
Great Denham Bedford 103 B10
Great Doddington
Northants 121 E7
Great Doward Hereford 79 B9
Great Dunham Norf 159 G7
Great Dunmow Essex 106 G2
Great Durnford Wilts 46 F6
Great Easton Essex 106 F2
Leics 136 E6
Great Eccleston Lancs 202 E4
Great Edstone N Yorks 216 C4
Great Ellingham Norf 141 D10
Great Elm Som 45 D8
Great Eppleton T&W 234 B3
Greater Doward Hereford 79 B9
Great Eversden Cambs 123 G7
Great Fencote N Yorks 224 G5
Greatfield Wilts 62 B5
Great Finborough Suff 125 F10
Greatford Lincs 155 G11
Great Fransham Norf 159 G7
Great Gaddesden Herts 85 C8
Greatgap Bucks 84 B6
Greatgate Staffs 169 G9
Great Gate Staffs 169 G9
Great Gidding Cambs 138 G2
Great Givendale
E Yorks 208 C2
Great Glemham Suff 126 E6
Great Glen Leics 136 D3
Great Gonerby Lincs 155 B7
Great Gransden Cambs 122 F5
Great Green Cambs 104 C5
Norf 142 F5
Suff 125 B11
Suff 125 F8
Suff 126 B2
Great Habton N Yorks 216 D5
Great Hale Lincs 173 G10
Great Hallingbury Essex 87 B8
Greatham Hants 49 G9
Hrtlpl 234 F5
W Sus 35 D8
Great Hampden Bucks 84 E4
Great Harrowden
Northants 121 C7
Great Harwood Lancs 203 G10
Great Haseley Oxon 83 E10
Great Hatfield E Yorks 209 E9
Great Haywood Staffs 151 E9
Staffs 151 E10
Great Heath W Mid 134 G6
Great Heck N Yorks 198 C5
Great Henny Essex 107 D7
Great Hinton Wilts 46 B2
Great Hivings Bucks 85 E7
Great Hockham Norf 141 E9
Great Holcombe Oxon 83 F10
Great Holland Essex 89 B12
Great Hollands Brack 65 F11
Great Holm M Keynes 102 D6
Great Honeyborough
Pembs 73 D7
Great Horkesley Essex 107 E9
Great Hormead Herts 105 F7
Great Horton W Yorks 205 G8
Great Horwood Bucks 102 E5
Great Houghton
Northants 120 F5
S Yorks 198 F2
Great Howarth Gtr Man 196 D2
Great Hucklow Derbys 185 F11
Great Job's Cross Kent 38 B4
Great Kelk E Yorks 209 B8
Great Kendale E Yorks 217 G10
Great Kimble Bucks 84 D4
Great Kingshill Bucks 84 F5
Great Langton N Yorks 224 F5
Great Lea Common
Reading 65 F8
Great Leighs Essex 88 B2
Great Lever Gtr Man 195 F8
Great Limber Lincs 200 F6
Great Linford M Keynes 103 C7
Great Livermere Suff 125 C7
Great Longstone Derbys 186 G2
Great Lumley Durham 233 B11
Great Lyth Shrops 131 B9
Great Malgraves Thurrock 69 C7
Great Malvern Worcs 98 B5
Great Maplestead Essex 106 E6
Great Marton Blackpool 202 F2
Great Marton Moss
Blackpool 202 G2
Great Massingham Norf 158 E5
Great Melton Norf 142 B2
Great Milton Oxon 83 E10
Great Missenden Bucks 84 E5
Great Mitton Lancs 203 F10
Great Mongeham Kent 55 C10
Greatmoor Bucks 102 G4
Great Moor Gtr Man 184 D6
Staffs 132 D6
Great Moulton Norf 142 E3
Great Munden Herts 105 G7
Great Musgrave Cumb 222 C5
Greatness Kent 52 B4
Great Ness Shrops 149 F7
Great Notley Essex 106 G4
Great Oak Mon 78 D5
Great Oakley Essex 108 F3
Northants 137 F7
Great Offley Herts 104 F2
Great Ormside Cumb 222 B4
Great Orton Cumb 239 G8
Great Ouseburn
N Yorks 215 G8
Great Oxendon
Northants 136 G4
Great Oxney Green
Essex 87 D11
Great Palgrave Norf 158 G6
Great Parndon Essex 86 D6
Great Pattenden Kent 53 E8
Great Paxton Cambs 122 E4
Great Plumpton Lancs 202 G3
Great Plumstead Norf 160 G6
Great Ponton Lincs 155 C8
Great Preston W Yorks 198 B2
Great Purston
Northants 101 D10
Great Raveley Cambs 138 G5
Great Rissington Glos 81 B11
Great Rollright Oxon 100 E6
Great Ryburgh Norf 159 D9
Great Ryle Northumb 264 G2
Great Ryton Shrops 131 C9
Great Saling Essex 106 F4
Great Salkeld Cumb 231 D7
Great Sampford Essex 106 D2
Great Sankey Warr 183 D9
Great Saredon Staffs 133 B9
Great Saxham Suff 124 E5
Great Shefford W Berks 63 E11
Great Shelford Cambs 123 G9
Great Shoddesden Hants 47 D9
Great Smeaton N Yorks 224 E6
Great Snoring Norf 159 C8
Great Somerford Wilts 62 C3
Great Stainton Darl 234 G2
Great Stambridge Essex 88 G5
Great Staughton Cambs 122 E2
Great Steeping Lincs 174 C6
Great Stoke S Glos 60 C6
Great Stonar Kent 55 B10
Greatstone-on-Sea Kent 39 C9
Great Stretton Leics 136 C3
Great Strickland Cumb 231 G7
Great Stukeley Cambs 122 C4
Great Sturton Lincs 190 F2
Great Sutton Ches W 182 F5
Shrops 131 G10
Great Swinburne
Northumb 241 B10
Great Tew Oxon 101 F7
Great Tey Essex 107 F7
Great Thirkleby N Yorks 215 D9
Great Thurlow Suff 124 G3
Great Torrington Devon 25 D7
Great Tosson Northumb 252 C2
Great Totham Essex 88 C5
Great Tows Lincs 190 C2
Great Tree Corn 6 D5
Great Urswick Cumb 210 E5
Great Wakering Essex 70 B2
Great Waldingfield Suff 107 C8
Great Walsingham Norf 159 B8
Great Waltham Essex 87 C11
Great Warley Essex 87 G9
Great Washbourne Glos 99 E9
Great Weeke Devon 13 D10
Great Weldon Northants 137 F8
Great Welnetham Suff 125 F7
Great Wenham Suff 107 D11
Great Whittington
Northumb 242 C2
Great Wigborough Essex 89 C7
Great Wilbraham
Cambs 123 F10
Great Wilne Derbys 153 C8
Great Wishford Wilts 46 F5
Great Witchingham
Norf 160 E2
Great Witcombe Glos 80 C6
Great Witley Worcs 116 D5
Great Wolford Warks 100 E4
Greatworth Northants 101 C11
Great Wratting Suff 106 B3
Great Wymondley Herts 104 F4
Great Wyrley Staffs 133 B9
Great Wytheford
Shrops 149 F11
Great Yarmouth Norf 143 B10
Great Yeldham Essex 106 D5
Greave Gtr Man 184 C6
Lancs 195 C11
Grebby Lincs 174 B6
Greeba IoM 192 D4
Green Denb 165 B9
Pembs 73 E7
Powys 130 E5
Greenacres Gtr Man 196 F2
Greenan Argyll 275 G11
Greenbank Ches W 183 G10
Falk 279 F7
Shetland 312 C7
Green Bank Cumb 211 C7
Green Bottom Corn 4 F5
Glos 79 B11
Greenburn W Loth 269 C8
Green Close N Yorks 212 F4
Green Clough W Yorks 205 G7
Green Crize Hereford 97 D10
Greencroft Durham 242 G5
Green Cross Sur 49 F11
Greendale Ches E 184 F5
Greendikes Northumb 264 D3
Greendown Som 44 C5
Green Down Devon 28 G3
Greendykes Northumb 264 D3
Greenend N Lanark 268 C4
Oxon 100 G6
Green End Bedford 103 B10
Bedford 121 E11
Bedford 122 E2
Bedford 122 G2
Bucks 84 F4
Bucks 103 E8
Cambs 122 C4
Cambs 123 F7
C Beds 103 C10
Herts 85 D8
Herts 104 E5
Herts 104 E6
Herts 104 G6
Herts 105 F7
Lancs 204 D4
N Yorks 226 E6
Warks 134 F5
Greenfaulds N Lanark 278 G5
Greenfield C Beds 103 E11
Glasgow 268 C2
Gtr Man 196 G3
Highld 289 D11
Highld 290 C4
Oxon 84 G2
Greenfield / Maes-Glas
Flint 181 F11
Greenfoot N Lanark 268 B4
Greenford London 66 C6
Greengairs N Lanark 278 G5
Greengarth Hall Cumb 219 E11
Greengate Gtr Man 196 D2
Norf 159 F10
Green Gate Devon 27 D8
Greengates W Yorks 205 F9
Greengill Cumb 229 D8
Green Hailey Bucks 84 E4
Greenhalgh Lancs 202 F4
Greenhall S Lanark 268 D3
Greenham Dorset 28 G6
Som 27 C9
W Berks 64 F3
Green Hammerton
N Yorks 206 B5
Greenhaugh Northumb 251 F7
Green Haworth Lancs 195 B9
Greenhead Borders 261 D11
Dumfries 247 D9
N Lanark 268 E6
Northumb 240 D5
Staffs 169 F7
Greenheath Staffs 151 G9
Green Head Cumb 230 B3
Green Heath Staffs 151 G9
Greenheys Gtr Man 195 G8
Greenhill Dumfries 238 B4
Durham 234 B3
Falk 278 F6
Hereford 98 B4
Kent 71 F7
Leics 153 G8
London 67 B7
S Yorks 186 E4
Worcs 99 B10
Worcs 116 B6
Green Hill Kent 53 C9
Lincs 155 B8
Wilts 62 B5
W Yorks 206 F4
Greenhill Bank Shrops 149 B7
Greenhillocks Derbys 170 F6
Greenhills N Ayrs 267 E7
S Lanark 268 E2
Greenhithe Kent 68 E5
Greenholm E Ayrs 258 B2
Greenholme Cumb 221 D11
Greenhouse Borders 262 E3
Greenhow N Yorks 214 G2
Greenhow Hill N Yorks 214 G2
Greenigoe Orkney 314 F4
Greenland Highld 310 C6
S Yorks 186 D5
Greenland Mains Highld 310 C6
Greenlands Bucks 65 B9
Worcs 117 D11
Green Lane Devon 13 F11
Hereford 98 B2
Powys 130 D3
Warks 117 E11
Warks 118 B6
Greenlaw Aberds 302 D6
Borders 272 F4
Greenlaw Mains Midloth 270 C4
Greenlea Dumfries 238 B2
Greenley M Keynes 102 C6
Greenloaning Perth 286 G2
Greenlooms Ches W 167 C7
Greenman's Lane Wilts 62 C3
Greenmeadow Swindon 62 B6
Torf 78 F3
Green Moor S Yorks 186 B3
Greenmount Gtr Man 195 E9
Greenmow Shetland 313 L6
Greenoak E Yorks 199 B10
Greenock Invclyd 276 F5
Greenock West Invclyd 276 F5
Greenodd Cumb 210 C6
Green Ore Som 44 C5
Green Parlour Bath 45 C8
Green Quarter Cumb 221 E9
Greenrigg W Loth 269 C8
Greenrow Cumb 238 G4
Greens Borders 249 F11
Green St Green London 68 G3
Greensforge Staffs 133 F7
Greensgate Norf 160 F2
Greenside Cumb 222 E4
Derbys 186 F5
Gtr Man 184 B6
T&W 242 E4
W Yorks 197 D7
Green Side W Yorks 197 E7
W Yorks 205 G11
Greensidehill Northumb 263 F11
Greens Norton
Northants 102 B3
Greensplat Corn 5 D9
Greenstead Essex 107 F10
Greenstead Green Essex 106 F6
Greensted Essex 87 E8
Greensted Green Essex 87 E8
Green Street Essex 87 F10
E Sus 38 E3
Glos 80 B5
Glos 80 E3
Herts 85 F11
Herts 105 G9
Worcs 99 B7
Worcs 99 C7
W Sus 35 C10
Greenstreet Green
Suff 107 B10
Green Street Green Kent 68 E5
London 68 G3
Green Tye Herts 86 B6
Greenway Hereford 98 E4
Pembs 91 E11
Som 27 B11
V Glam 58 E5
Worcs 116 C4
Greenwell Cumb 240 F2
Greenwells Borders 262 C3
Greenwich London 67 D11
Suff 108 C3
Wilts 46 G2
Greenwith Common Corn 4 G5
Greenwoods Essex 87 F11
Greeny Orkney 314 D2
Greep Highld 298 E2
Greet Glos 99 E10
Kent 54 B2
Greete Shrops 115 C11
Greetham Lincs 190 G4
Rutland 155 G8
Greetland W Yorks 196 C5
Greetland Wall Nook
W Yorks 196 C5
Greetwell N Lincs 200 G2
Gregg Hall Cumb 221 G9
Gregson Lane Lancs 194 B5
Gregynog Powys 129 D11
Grèin W Isles 297 L2
Greinetobht W Isles 296 D4
Greinton Som 44 F2
Gremista Shetland 313 J6
Grenaby IoM 192 E3
Grendon Northants 121 E7
Warks 134 C5
Grendon Bishop
Hereford 115 F11
Grendon Common
Warks 134 D5
Grendon Green
Hereford 115 F11
Grendon Underwood
Bucks 102 G3
Grenofen Devon 12 G5
Grenoside S Yorks 186 C4
Greosabhagh W Isles 305 J3
Gresford Wrex 166 E5
Gresham Norf 160 B3
Greshornish Highld 298 D3
Gressenhall Norf 159 F9
Gressingham Lancs 211 F11
Gresty Green Ches E 168 E2
Greta Bridge Durham 223 C11
Gretna Dumfries 239 D8
Gretna Green Dumfries 239 D8
Gretton Glos 99 E10
Northants 137 E7
Shrops 131 D10
Gretton Fields Glos 99 E10
Grewelthorpe N Yorks 214 D4
Greyfield Bath 44 B6
Greygarth N Yorks 214 E3
Grey Green N Lincs 199 F9
Greylake Som 43 G11
Greylake Fosse Som 44 F2
Greynor Carms 75 D9
Greynor-isaf Carms 75 D9
Greyrigg Dumfries 248 F3
Greys Green Oxon 65 C8
Greysouthen Cumb 229 F7
Greystead Northumb 251 F7
Greystoke Cumb 230 E4
Greystoke Gill Cumb 230 F4
Greystone Aberds 292 D6
Aberds 302 F6
Angus 287 C9
Cumb 211 D10
Dumfries 237 B11
Greystonegill N Yorks 212 F3
Greystones S Yorks 186 D4
Warks 99 B11
Greytree Hereford 97 F11
Greywell Hants 49 C8
Griais W Isles 304 D6
Grianan W Isles 304 E6
Gribb Dorset 28 G5
Gribthorpe E Yorks 207 F11
Gridley Corner Devon 12 C3
Griff Warks 135 F7
Griffins Hill W Mid 133 G10
Griffithstown Torf 78 F3
Griffydam Leics 153 F8
Grigg Kent 53 E11
Griggs Green Hants 49 G10
Grillis Corn 2 B5
Grilstone Devon 26 C2
Grimbister Orkney 314 E3
Grimblethorpe Lincs 190 D2
Grimeford Village Lancs 194 E6
Grimes Hill Worcs 117 B11
Grimesthorpe S Yorks 186 C5
Grimethorpe S Yorks 198 F2
Griminis W Isles 296 D3
W Isles 296 F3
Grimister Shetland 312 D6
Grimley Worcs 116 E6
Grimness Orkney 314 G4
Grimoldby Lincs 190 D5
Grimpo Shrops 149 D7
Grimsargh Lancs 203 G7
Grimsbury Oxon 101 C9
Grimsby NE Lincs 201 E9
Grimscote Northants 120 G3
Grimscott Corn 24 F3
Grimshaw Blackburn 195 C8
Grimshaw Green Lancs 194 E3
Grimsthorpe Lincs 155 E10
Grimston E Yorks 209 F11
Leics 154 E3
Norf 158 E4
York 207 C8
Grimstone Dorset 17 C8
Grimstone End Suff 125 D8
Grinacombe Moor Devon 12 C4
Grindale E Yorks 218 E2
Grindigar Orkney 314 F5
Grindiscol Shetland 313 K6
Grindle Shrops 132 C5
Grindleford Derbys 186 F2
Grindleton Lancs 203 D11
Grindley Staffs 151 D10
Grindley Brook Shrops 167 G8
Grindlow Derbys 185 F11
Grindon Northumb 273 G8
Staffs 169 E9
Stockton 234 F3
T&W 243 G9
Grindonmoor Gate
Staffs 169 E9
Grindsbrook Booth
Derbys 185 D10
Gringley on the Hill
Notts 188 C2
Grinsdale Cumb 239 F9
Grinshill Shrops 149 E10
Grinstead Hill Suff 125 G11
Grinton N Yorks 223 F10
Griomasaigh W Isles 297 G4
Griomsidar W Isles 304 F5
Grisdale Cumb 222 G5
Grishipoll Argyll 288 D3
Grisling Common E Sus 36 C6
Gristhorpe N Yorks 217 C11
Griston Norf 141 D8
Gritley Orkney 314 F5
Grittenham Wilts 62 C4
Grittlesend Hereford 98 B4
Grittleton Wilts 61 C11
Grizebeck Cumb 210 C4
Grizedale Cumb 220 G6
Groam Highld 300 E5
Grobister Orkney 314 D6
Grobsness Shetland 313 G5
Groby Leics 135 B10
Groes Conwy 165 C8
Neath 57 D9
Groes Efa Denb 165 B10
Groes-faen Rhondda 58 C5
Groes-fawr Denb 165 B10
Groesffordd Gwyn 144 B5
Powys 95 F11
Groesffordd Marli Denb 181 G8
Groeslon Gwyn 163 C8
Gwyn 163 D7
Groes-lwyd Mon 96 G6
Powys 148 G4
Groespluan Powys 130 B4
Groes-wen Caerph 58 B6
Grogport Argyll 255 C9
Gromford Suff 127 F7
Gronant Flint 181 E9
Gronwen Shrops 148 D5
Groombridge E Sus 52 F4
Grosmont Mon 97 G8
N Yorks 226 D6
Gross Green Warks 119 F7
Grotaig Highld 300 G4
Groton Suff 107 C9
Grotton Gtr Man 196 G3
Grougfoot Falk 279 F10
Grove Bucks 103 G8
Dorset 17 G10
Hereford 98 C2
Kent 71 G8
Notts 188 F2
Oxon 82 G6
Pembs 73 E7
Grove End Kent 69 G11
Warks 100 D6
Warks 134 D3
Grove Green Kent 53 B9
Grovehill E Yorks 208 F6
Herts 85 D9
Grove Hill E Sus 23 C10
Kent 71 G8
Grove Park London 67 D8
London 68 E2
Groves Kent 55 B9
Grovesend Swansea 75 E9
Grove Town W Yorks 198 C3
Grove Vale W Mid 133 E10
Grubb Street Kent 68 F5
Grub Street Staffs 150 D5
Grudie Highld 300 C3
Gruids Highld 309 J5
Gruinard House Highld 307 K4
Gruinards Highld 309 K5
Grula Highld 294 C5
Gruline Argyll 289 E7
Gruline Ho Argyll 289 F7
Grumbeg Highld 308 F6
Grumbla Corn 1 D4
Grunasound Shetland 313 K5
Grundisburgh Suff 126 G4
Grunsagill Lancs 203 C11
Gruting Shetland 313 J4
Grutness Shetland 313 N6
Gryn Goch Gwyn 162 F6
Gualachulain Highld 284 C5
Gualin Ho Highld 308 D3
Guardbridge Fife 287 F8
Guard House W Yorks 204 E6
Guarlford Worcs 98 B6
Guay Perth 286 C4
Gubbion's Green Essex 88 B2
Gubblecote Herts 84 C6
Guesachan Highld 289 B10
Guestling Green E Sus 38 E5
Guestling Thorn E Sus 38 D4
Guestwick Norf 159 D11
Guestwick Green Norf 159 D11
Guide Blackburn 195 B8
Guide Bridge Gtr Man 184 B6
Guide Post Northumb 253 F7
Guilden Morden Cambs 104 C5
Guilden Sutton Ches W 166 B6
Guildford Sur 50 D3
Guildford Park Sur 50 D3
Guildiehaugh W Loth 269 B9
Guildtown Perth 286 D5
Guilford Pembs 73 D7
Guilsborough Northants 120 C3
Guilsfield / Cegidfa
Powys 148 G4
Guilthwaite S Yorks 187 D7
Guilton Kent 55 B9
Guineaford Devon 40 F5
Guisachan Highld 300 G3
Guisborough Redcar 226 B2
Guiseley W Yorks 205 E9
Guist Norf 159 D9
Guith Orkney 314 C5
Guiting Power Glos 99 G11
Gulberwick Shetland 313 K6
Gullane E Loth 281 E9
Guller's End Worcs 99 D7
Gulling Green Suff 124 F6
Gullom Holme Cumb 231 F9
Gulval Corn 1 C5
Gulworthy Devon 12 G4
Gumfreston Pembs 73 E10
Gumley Leics 136 E3
Gummow's Shop Corn 5 D7
Gunby E Yorks 207 F10
Lincs 155 E8
Lincs 175 B7
Gundenham Som 27 C10
Gundleton Hants 48 G6
Gun Green Kent 53 G9
Gun Hill E Sus 23 C9
Gunn Devon 40 G6
Gunnersbury London 67 D7
Gunnerside N Yorks 223 F9
Gunnerton Northumb 241 C10
Gunness N Lincs 199 E10
Gunnislake Corn 12 G4
Gunnista Shetland 313 J7
Gunstone Staffs 133 C7
Guns Village W Mid 133 E9
Gunter's Bridge W Sus 35 C7
Gunthorpe Lincs 188 B4
Norf 159 C10
Notts 171 G11
Pboro 138 C3
Rutland 137 B7
Gunton Suff 143 D10
Gunville IoW 20 D5
Gunwalloe Corn 2 E5
Gunwalloe Fishing Cove
Corn 2 E5
Gupworthy Som 42 F3
Gurnard IoW 20 B5
Gurnett Ches E 184 G6
Gurney Slade Som 44 D6
Gurnos M Tydf 77 D8
Powys 76 D3
Gushmere Kent 54 B4
Gussage All Saints Dorset 31 E8
Gussage St Andrew
Dorset 31 E7
Gussage St Michael
Dorset 31 E7
Gustard Wood Herts 85 B11
Guston Kent 55 E10
Gutcher Shetland 312 D7
Guthram Gowt Lincs 156 E3
Guthrie Angus 287 B9
Guyhirn Cambs 139 C7
Guyhirn Gull Cambs 139 C7
Guy's Cliffe Warks 118 D5
Guy's Head Lincs 157 D9
Guy's Marsh Dorset 30 C4
Guyzance Northumb 252 C6
Gwaelod-y-garth Cardiff 58 C6
Gwaenysgor Flint 181 E9
Gwalchmai Anglesey 178 F5
Gwalchmai Uchaf
Anglesey 178 F5
Gwallon Corn 2 C2
Gwastad Pembs 91 G10
Gwastadgoed Gwyn 145 G11
Gwastadnant Gwyn 163 D10
Gwaun-Cae-Gurwen
Neath 76 C2
Gwaun-Leision Neath 76 C2
Gwavas Corn 2 D5
Corn 2 G6
Gwbert Ceredig 92 B3
Gwedna Corn 2 C4
Gweek Corn 2 D6
Gwehelog Mon 78 E5
Gwenddwr Powys 95 C11
Gwennap Corn 2 B6
Gwenter Corn 2 F6
Gwernaffield-y-Waun
Flint 166 C2
Gwernafon Powys 129 E8
Gwerneirin Powys 129 F10
Powys 130 G3
Gwernesney Mon 78 E6
Gwernogle Carms 93 E10
Gwernol Denb 166 E2
Gwern y brenin Shrops 148 D6
Gwernydd Powys 129 C11
Gwernymynydd Flint 166 C2
Gwern-y-Steeple V Glam 58 D5
Gwersyllt Wrex 166 E4
Gwespyr Flint 181 E10
Gwills Corn 4 D6
Gwinear Corn 2 B3
Gwinear Downs Corn 2 C4
Gwithian Corn 2 A3
Gwredog Anglesey 178 D6
Gwrhay Caerph 77 F11
Gwyddelwern Denb 165 F9
Gwyddgrug Carms 93 D9
Gwynfryn Wrex 166 E3
Gwystre Powys 113 D11
Gwytherin Conwy 164 C5
Gyfelia Wrex 166 F4
Gyffin Conwy 180 F3
Gylen Park Argyll 289 G10
Gyre Orkney 314 F3
Gyrn Denb 165 D11
Gyrn-goch Gwyn 162 F6

H

Habberley Shrops 131 C7
Worcs 116 B6
Habergham Lancs 204 G2
Habertoft Lincs 175 B8
Habin W Sus 34 C4
Habrough NE Lincs 200 E6
Haccombe Devon 14 G3
Haceby Lincs 155 B10
Hacheston Suff 126 F6
Hackbridge London 67 F9
Hackenthorpe S Yorks 186 E6
Hackford Norf 141 C11
Hackforth N Yorks 224 G4
Hack Green Ches E 167 F10
Hackland Orkney 314 D3
Hackleton Northants 120 F6
Hacklinge Kent 55 C10
Hackman's Gate Worcs 117 B7
Hackness N Yorks 227 G9
Orkney 314 G3
Som 43 D10
Hackney London 67 C10
Hackney Wick London 67 C11
Hackthorn Lincs 189 E7
Wilts 47 D7
Hackthorpe Cumb 230 G6
Haclait W Isles 297 G4
Haconby Lincs 156 D2
Hacton London 68 B4
Haddacott Devon 25 C8
Hadden Borders 263 B7
Haddenham Bucks 84 D2
Cambs 123 B9
Haddenham End Field
Cambs 123 B9
Haddington E Loth 281 G10
Lincs 172 C6
Haddiscoe Norf 143 D8
Haddoch Aberds 302 E5
Haddon Cambs 138 E2
Ches E 169 B7
Hade Edge W Yorks 196 F6
Hademore Staffs 134 B3
Haden Cross W Mid 133 F9
Hadfield Derbys 185 B8
Hadham Cross Herts 86 B6
Hadham Ford Herts 105 G8
Hadleigh Essex 69 B10
Suff 107 C10
Hadleigh Heath Suff 107 C9
Hadley London 86 F2
Telford 150 G3
Worcs 117 E7
Hadley Castle Telford 150 G3
Hadley End Staffs 152 E2
Hadley Wood London 86 F3
Hadlow Kent 52 D6
Hadlow Down E Sus 37 C8
Hadlow Stair Kent 52 D6
Hadnall Shrops 149 F10
Hadspen Som 45 G7
Hadstock Essex 105 C11
Hadston Northumb 253 D7
Hady Derbys 186 G5
Hadzor Worcs 117 E8
Haffenden Quarter Kent 53 E11
Hafod Swansea 57 C7
Hafod-Dinbych Conwy 164 E5
Hafod Grove Pembs 92 C2
Hafodiwan Ceredig 111 G7
Hafod-lom Conwy 180 G5
Hafod-y-Green Denb 181 G8
Hafodyrynys Bl Gwent 78 F2
Hag Fold Gtr Man 195 G7
Haggate Gtr Man 196 F2
Lancs 204 F3
Haggbeck Cumb 239 C11
Haggersta Shetland 313 J5
Haggerston London 67 C10
Northumb 273 G10
Hagginton Hill Devon 40 D5
Haggrister Shetland 312 F5
Haggs Falk 278 F5
Haghill Glasgow 268 B2
Hagley Hereford 97 C11
Worcs 133 G8
Hagloe Glos 79 D11
Hagmore Green Suff 107 D9
Hagnaby Lincs 174 C4
Lincs 191 F7
Hagnaby Lock Lincs 174 D4
Hague Bar Derbys 185 D7
Hagworthingham Lincs 174 B4
Haigh Gtr Man 194 F6
S Yorks 197 E9
Haigh Moor W Yorks 197 C9
Haighton Green Lancs 203 G7
Haighton Top Lancs 203 G7
Haile Cumb 219 D10
Hailes Glos 99 E10
Hailey Herts 86 C5
Oxon 64 B6
Oxon 82 C5
Hailsham E Sus 23 D9
Hailstone Hill Wilts 81 G9
Hail Weston Cambs 122 E3
Haimer Highld 310 C5
Haimwood Powys 148 F6
Hainault London 87 G7
Haine Kent 71 F11
Hainford Norf 160 F4
Hains Dorset 30 D3
Hainton Lincs 189 E11
Hainworth W Yorks 205 F7
Hainworth Shaw
W Yorks 205 F7
Hairmyres S Lanark 268 E2
Haisthorpe E Yorks 218 G2
Hakeford Devon 40 F6
Hakin Pembs 72 D5
Halabezack Corn 2 C6
Halam Notts 171 E11
Halamanning Corn 2 C3
Halbeath Fife 280 D2
Halberton Devon 27 E8
Halcon Som 28 B2
Halcro Highld 310 C6
Haldens Herts 86 C2
Hale Cumb 211 D10
Gtr Man 184 D3
Halton 183 E7
Hants 31 D11
Kent 71 F9
Medway 69 F9
Som 30 B3
Sur 49 D10
Hale Bank Halton 183 E7
Hale Barns Gtr Man 184 D3
Halecommon W Sus 34 C4
Hale Coombe N Som 44 B2
Hale End London 86 G5
Hale Green E Sus 23 C9
Hale Mills Corn 4 G5
Hale Nook Lancs 202 E3
Hales Norf 143 D7
Staffs 150 C4
Hales Bank Hereford 116 G2
Halesfield Telford 132 C4
Halesgate Lincs 156 D6
Hales Green Derbys 169 G11
Norf 143 D7
Halesowen W Mid 133 G9
Hales Park Worcs 116 B5
Hales Place Kent 54 B6
Hales Street Norf 142 F3

Hale Street Kent 53 D7
Hales Wood Hereford 98 E2
Halesworth Suff 127 B7
Halewood Mers. 183 D7
Half Moon Village Devon . . 14 B3
Halford Shrops 131 G8
　Warks 100 B5
Halfpenny Cumb 211 B10
Halfpenny Furze Carms . . . 74 C3
Halfpenny Green Staffs . . . 132 E6
Halfway Carms 75 E8
　Carms 94 E4
　Carms 94 E6
　S Yorks 186 E6
　W Berks 64 F2
　Wilts 45 D11
Halfway Bridge W Sus. . . . 34 C6
Halfway House Shrops . . . 148 G6
Halfway Houses
　Gtr Man 195 F9
　Kent 70 E2
Halfway Street Kent 55 D9
Halgabron Corn 11 D7
Halifax W Yorks 196 B5
Halkburn Borders 271 G9
Halket E Ayrs 267 E8
Halkirk Highld 310 D5
Halkyn / Helygain Flint . . 182 G2
Halkyn Mountain Flint . . . 182 G2
Halland E Sus 23 B8
Hallaton Leics 136 D5
Hallatrow Bath 44 B6
Hallbankgate Cumb. 240 F3
Hall Bower W Yorks 196 E6
Hall Broom S Yorks. 186 D3
Hall Cross Lancs 202 G4
Hall Dunnerdale Cumb . . . 220 F4
Halleaths Dumfries. 248 G3
Hallen S Glos. 60 C5
Halland Warks 118 D2
Hall End Bedford 103 B10
　C Beds 103 D11
　Lincs 174 E6
　S Glos 61 B8
　Warks 134 C5
Hallew Corn 5 D10
Hallfield Gate Derbys 170 D5
Hall Flat Worcs 117 C9
Hallgarth Durham 234 C2
Hallglen Falk 279 F7
Hall Garth York 207 C9
Hallin Highld 298 D2
Halling Medway 69 G8
Hallingbury Street Essex . 87 B8
Hallington Lincs 190 D4
　Northumb 241 B11
Halliwell Gtr Man. 195 E8
Hall of Clestrain Orkney. . 314 F2
Hall of Tankerness
　Orkney 314 F5
Hall of the Forest
　Shrops 130 G4
Hallon Shrops 132 D5
Halloughton Notts 171 E11
Hallow Worcs 116 F6
Hallowes Derbys 186 F5
Hallow Heath Worcs 116 F6
Hallowsgate Ches W 167 B8
Hallrule Borders 262 G3
Halls E Loth 282 G3
Hallsands Devon 9 G11
Hall Santon Cumb 220 E2
Hall's Cross E Sus 23 D11
Hallsford Bridge Essex . . . 87 E9
Halls Green Essex 86 C6
　Kent 52 D4
Hall's Green Herts 104 F5
Hallspill Devon 25 C7
Hallthwaites Cumb. 210 B3
Hall Waberthwaite
　Cumb. 220 F2
Hallwood Green Glos. 98 E3
Hallworthy Corn 11 D9
Hallyards Borders 260 B6
Hallyburton House
　Perth 286 D6
Hallyne Borders 270 G3
Halmer End Staffs 168 F3
Halmond's Frome
　Hereford 98 B3
Halmore Glos 79 E11
Halmyre Mains Borders . . 270 F3
Halnaker W Sus. 22 B6
Halsall Lancs 193 E11
Halse Northants 101 C11
　Som 27 B10
Halsetown Corn 2 B2
Halsfordwood Devon 14 C3
Halsham E Yorks 201 B9
Halsinger Devon 40 F4
Halstead Essex 106 E6
　Kent 68 G3
　Leics 136 B4
Halstock Dorset 29 E8
Halsway Som 42 F6
Haltcliff Bridge Cumb. . . . 230 D3
Halterworth Hants. 32 C5
Haltham Lincs 174 C2
Haltoft End Lincs 174 F5
Halton Bucks 84 C5
　Halton 183 E8
　Lancs 211 G10
　Northumb 241 D11
　Wrex 148 B6
　W Yorks 206 G2
Halton Barton Corn. 7 B8
Halton Brook Halton 183 E8
Halton East N Yorks 204 C6
Halton Fenside Lincs 174 C6
Halton Gill N Yorks 213 D7
Halton Green Lancs 211 F10
Halton Holegate Lincs 174 B6
Halton Lea Gate
　Northumb 240 F5
Halton Moor W Yorks 206 G2
Halton Shields
　Northumb 242 D4
Halton View Halton 183 D8
Halton West N Yorks 204 C2
Haltwhistle Northumb. . . . 240 E6
Halvergate Norf 143 B8
Halvosso Corn 2 C6
Halwell Devon 8 E5
Halwill Devon 12 B4
Halwill Junction Devon . . . 24 G6
Halwin Corn 2 C5

Ham Devon 28 G2
　Glos 79 F11
　Glos 99 G9
　Highld 310 B6
　Kent 55 C10
　London 67 E7
　Plym. 7 D9
　Shetland 313 K1
　Som 27 C11
　Som 28 B3
　Som 28 E3
　Som 45 D7
　Wilts 63 G10
Ham Common Dorset 30 B4
Hameringham Lincs 174 B4
Hamerton Cambs 122 B2
Hametoun Shetland 313 K1
Ham Green Bucks 83 B11
　Hants. 48 G2
　Hereford 98 C4
　Kent 38 B5
　Kent 69 F10
　N Som 60 D4
　Wilts 61 G11
Ham Hill Kent 69 G8
Hamilton S Lanark 268 D3
Hamister Shetland 313 G7
Hamlet Dorset 29 F9
　Dorset 30 E4
Hammer W Sus 49 G11
Hammer Bottom Hants . . . 49 G11
Hammerfield Herts. 85 D8
Hammermoor W Sus 35 F9
Hammersmith Derbys 170 E5
　London 67 D8
Hammerwich Staffs 133 B11
Hammerwood E Sus 52 F2
Hammill Kent 55 B9
Hammond Street Herts . . . 86 E5
Hammoor Dorset 30 E4
Ham Moor Sur. 66 G5
Hamnavoe Shetland 312 E4
　Shetland 312 E6
　Shetland 312 F6
　Shetland 313 K5
Hamnish Clifford
　Hereford 115 F10
Hamp Som 43 G10
Hampden Park E Sus 23 E10
Hampen Glos 81 B9
Hamperden End Essex . . . 105 E11
Hamperley Shrops 131 F8
Hampers Green W Sus . . . 35 C7
Hampeth Northumb 252 B5
Hampnett Glos 81 B10
Hampole S Yorks 198 E4
Hampreston Dorset 19 B7
Hampsfield Cumb 211 C8
Hampson Green Lancs . . . 202 C5
Hampstead London 67 B9
Hampstead Garden Suburb
　London 67 B9
Hampstead Norreys
　W Berks 64 D4
Hampsthwaite N Yorks . . 205 B11
Hampton Kent 71 F7
　London 66 F6
　Shrops 132 F4
　Swindon 81 G11
　Worcs 99 C10
Hampton Bank Shrops . . . 149 C9
Hampton Beech Shrops . . 130 B6
Hampton Bishop
　Hereford 97 D11
Hampton Fields Glos 80 F5
Hampton Gay Oxon 83 B7
Hampton Green Ches W. . 167 F8
　Glos 80 E5
Hampton Hargate Pboro . 138 E3
Hampton Heath Ches W. . 167 F7
Hampton Hill London. . . . 66 E6
Hampton in Arden
　W Mid 134 G4
Hampton Loade Shrops . . 132 F5
Hampton Lovett Worcs . . 117 D7
Hampton Lucy Warks 118 F5
Hampton Magna Warks . . 118 D5
Hampton on the Hill
　Warks 118 D5
Hampton Park Hereford . . 97 D10
　Soton 32 D6
Hampton Poyle Oxon 83 B8
Hamptons Kent 52 C6
Hampton Wick London . . . 67 F7
Hamptworth Wilts. 32 D3
Hamrow Norf. 159 E8
Hamsey E Sus 36 E6
Hamsey Green London . . . 51 B10
Hamshill Glos 80 E3
Hamstall Ridware Staffs . 152 F2
Hamstead IoW 20 C4
　W Mid 133 E10
Hamstead Marshall
　W Berks 64 F2
Hamsterley Durham 233 E8
　Durham 242 F4
Hamstreet Kent 54 G4
Ham Street Som 44 G5
Hamworthy Poole 18 C5
Hanbury Staffs 152 D3
　Worcs 117 E9
Hanbury Woodend
　Staffs 152 D3
Hanby Lincs 155 C10
Hanchett Village Suff 106 B3
Hanchurch Staffs 168 G4
Handbridge Ches W. 166 B6
Handcross W Sus 36 B3
Handforth Ches E 184 E5
Hand Green Ches W 167 C8
Handless Shrops 131 F7
Handley Ches W 167 D7
　Derbys 170 C5
Handley Green Essex 87 E11
Handsacre Staffs 151 F11
Handside Herts 86 C2
Handsworth S Yorks. 186 D6
　W Mid 133 E11
Handsworth Wood
　W Mid 133 E11
Handy Cross Bucks 84 G5
　Devon 24 B6
Hanford Dorset 30 E4
　Stoke 168 G5
Hangersley Hants 31 F11

Hanging Bank Kent 52 C3
Hanging Heaton
　W Yorks 197 C9
Hanging Houghton
　Northants 120 C5
Hanging Langford Wilts . . 46 F4
Hangingshaw Borders . . . 261 G9
　Dumfries 248 F11
Hangleton Brighton 36 F3
　W Sus. 35 G9
Hangsman Hill S Yorks . . 199 E7
Hanham S Glos 60 E6
Hanham Green S Glos. . . . 60 E6
Hankelow Ches E. 167 F11
Hankerton Wilts 81 G7
Hankham E Sus 23 D10
Hanley Stoke 168 F5
Hanley Castle Worcs 98 C6
Hanley Child Worcs 116 E3
Hanley Swan Worcs 98 C6
Hanley William Worcs . . . 116 D3
Hanlith N Yorks 213 G8
Hanmer Wrex. 149 B9
Hannaford Devon 25 B10
Hannah Lincs 191 F8
Hannington Hants 48 B4
　Northants 120 C6
　Swindon 81 G11
Hannington Wick
　Swindon 81 F11
Hanscombe End C Beds . . 104 E2
Hansel Devon 8 F6
Hansel Village S Ayrs 257 C9
Hansley Cross Staffs 169 G9
Hanslope M Keynes. 102 B6
Hanthorpe Lincs 155 E11
Hanwell London 67 C7
　Oxon 101 C8
Hanwood Shrops 131 B8
Hanwood Bank Shrops . . . 149 G8
Hanworth Brack 65 F11
　London 66 E6
　Norf 160 B3
Happendon S Lanark 259 C9
Happisburgh Norf. 161 C7
Happisburgh Common
　Norf. 161 D7
Hapsford Ches W 183 G7
　Som 45 D9
Hapton Lancs 203 G11
　Norf 142 D3
Haraden / Penarlȇg
　Flint 166 B4
Harberton Devon 8 E5
Harbertonford Devon 8 E5
Harbledown Kent. 54 B6
Harborne W Mid 133 G10
Harborough Magna
　Warks 119 B9
Harborough Parva
　Warks 119 B9
Harbottle Northumb 251 C10
Harbour Heights E Sus . . . 36 G4
Harbourland Kent 53 B9
Harbourneford Devon 8 C4
Harbours Hill Worcs 117 D9
Harbour Village Pembs . . 91 D8
Harbridge Hants 31 E10
Harbridge Green Hants . . 31 E10
Harburn W Loth 269 C10
Harbury Warks 119 F7
Harby Leics 154 C4
　Notts 188 G5
Harcombe Devon 14 E3
　Devon 15 C9
Harcourt Corn 3 B8
Harcourt Hill Oxon. 83 E7
Hardeicke Glos 80 C4
Harden S Yorks 197 G7
　W Yorks 205 F7
Hardendale Cumb 221 C11
Hardenhuish Wilts. 62 E2
Harden Park Ches E 184 F4
Hardgate Aberds 293 C9
　Dumfries 237 C10
　N Yorks. 214 G5
　W Dunb 277 G10
Hardham W Sus 35 D8
Hardhorn Lancs 202 F3
Hardingham Norf 141 C10
Hardingstone
　Northants 120 F5
Hardings Booth Staffs . . . 169 C9
Hardingstone Wood
　Staffs 168 E4
Hardington Mandeville
　Som 29 E8
Hardington Marsh
　Som 29 E8
Hardington Moor
　Som 29 E8
Hardiston Perth 279 B11
Hardisworthy Devon 24 C2
Hardley Hants 32 G6
Hardley Street Norf. 143 C7
Hardmead M Keynes. 103 B8
Hardrow N Yorks. 223 G7
Hardstoft Derbys 170 C6
Hardstoft Common
　Derbys 170 C6
Hardway Hants 33 G10
　Som 45 G8
Hardwick Bucks 84 B4
　Cambs 123 F7
　Norf 142 F4
　Northants 121 D7
　Oxon 82 B5
　Oxon 101 C11
　Shrops 131 E7
　Stockton 234 G4
　S Yorks 187 D7
　W Mid 133 D11
Hardwicke Glos 80 C3
　Glos 99 F8
　Hereford 96 C5
Hardwick Green Worcs . . 98 E6
Hardwick Village Notts . . 187 G8
Hardy's Green Essex 107 G7
Hare Som. 28 D3
Hare Appletree Lancs 202 B6
Hareby Lincs 174 B4
Harecroft W Yorks 205 F7
Hareden Lancs 203 C8
Hare Edge Derbys 186 G4
Harefield London 85 G9
　Soton 33 D7
Harefield Grove London . . 85 G9
Haregate Staffs 169 D7
Hare Green Essex 107 G11
Harehill Derbys 152 B3
Harehills W Yorks 206 G2
Harehope Borders 270 G4
　Northumb 264 D3
Harelaw Durham 242 G5
Hareleeshill S Lanark . . . 268 E5

Hareplain Kent 53 F10
Haresceugh Cumb 231 C8
Harescombe Glos 80 C4
Haresfinch Mers. 183 B8
Harestock Hants 48 G3
Hare Street Essex 86 D6
　Herts 104 F6
　Herts 105 F7
Harewood W Yorks 206 D2
Harewood End Hereford . . 97 F10
Harewood Hill N Yorks . . . 204 F6
Harford Carms 94 C2
　Devon 8 D2
　Devon 40 G6
Hargate Norf 142 E2
Hargate Hill Derbys 185 C8
Hargatewall Derbys 185 F10
Hargrave Ches W 167 C7
　Northants 121 C10
　Suff 124 F5
Harker Cumb 239 E9
Harker Marsh Cumb. 229 E7
Harkland Shetland. 312 E6
Harkstead Suff 108 E3
Harlaston Staffs 152 G4
Harlaw Ho Aberds 303 G7
Harlaxton Lincs 155 C7
Harle Syke Lancs 204 F3
Harlech Gwyn 145 C11
Harlescott Shrops 149 F10
Harlesden London 67 C8
Harleston Devon 8 F5
　Norf 142 G4
　Suff 125 F10
Harlestone Northants 120 E4
Harle Syke Lancs 204 F3
Harley Shrops 131 C11
　S Yorks. 186 B5
Harleyholm S Lanark 259 B10
Harley Shute E Sus. 38 F3
Harleywood Glos 80 F4
Harling Road Norf 141 F9
Harlington C Beds 103 D11
　London 66 D5
　S Yorks 198 G3
Harlosh Highld 298 E2
Harlow Essex 86 C6
Harlow Carr N Yorks. 205 C11
Harlow Green T&W 243 F7
Harlow Hill Northumb . . . 242 D3
　N Yorks. 205 C11
Harlthorpe E Yorks 207 F10
Harlton Cambs 123 G7
Harlyn Corn 10 F3
Harman's Corner Kent . . . 69 G11
Harman's Cross Dorset . . . 18 E5
Harmans Water Brack . . . 65 F11
Harmby N Yorks 214 B2
Harmer Green Herts 86 C3
Harmer Hill Shrops 149 E9
Harmondsworth London . . 66 D5
Harmston Lincs 173 C7
Harnage Shrops 131 C11
Harnham Northumb 242 B3
　Wilts 31 B10
Harnhill Glos 81 E9
Harold Hill London 87 G8
Harold Park London 87 G9
Haroldston West Pembs . . 72 C5
Haroldswick Shetland. . . . 312 B8
Harome N Yorks 216 C2
Harpenden Herts. 85 C11
Harperley Durham 242 G5
Harper's Green Norf. 159 E8
Harpford Devon 15 C7
Harpham E Yorks 217 G11
Harpley Norf 158 D5
　Worcs 116 E3
Harpole Northants 120 E3
Harpsdale Highld 310 D5
Harpsden Oxon 65 C9
Harpsden Bottom Oxon . . 65 C9
Harpswell Lincs 188 D6
Harpton Powys 114 F4
Harpurhey Gtr Man. 195 G11
Harpur Hill Derbys 185 G9
Harraby Cumb 239 G10
Harracott Devon 25 B9
Harrapool Highld 295 C8
Harras Cumb. 219 B9
Harraton T&W 243 G7
Harrier Shetland 313 J1
Harrietfield Perth 286 E3
Harrietsham Kent 53 C11
Harringay London 67 B10
Harrington Cumb 228 F5
　Lincs 190 G5
　Northants 136 G5
Harringworth
　Northants 137 D8
Harris Highld 294 F5
Harriseahead Staffs 168 D5
Harriston Cumb 229 C9
Harrogate N Yorks 206 C2
Harrold Bedford 121 F8
Harrop Dale Gtr Man 196 F4
Harrovian Bedford 234 C3
Harrow Highld 310 B6
　London 66 B7
Harrowbarrow Corn. 7 B7
Harrowbeer Devon. 7 B10
Harrowby Lincs 155 B8
Harrowden Bedford 103 B10
Harrowgate Hill Darl 224 B5
Harrowgate Village
　Darl. 224 B5
Harrow Green Suff 125 G7
Harrow Hill Glos 79 B10
Harrow on the Hill
　London 67 B7
Harrow Street Suff 107 D9
Harrow Weald London . . . 85 G11
Harston Cambs 123 G8
　Leics 154 C6
Harswell E Yorks 208 E2
Hart Hrtlpl 234 E5
Hartburn Northumb 252 F3
　Stockton 225 B8
Hart Common Gtr Man . . . 194 F6
Hartest Suff 124 G6
Hartest Hill Suff 124 G6
Hartfield E Sus 52 F2
　Highld 299 E7
Hartford Cambs 122 C5
　Ches W. 183 G10
Som 27 B8

Hartfordbeach
　Ches W 183 G10
Hatford Oxon 82 G4
Harthill Ches W 167 D8
　N Lanark 269 C8
　S Yorks. 187 E7
Hart Hill Luton 104 G2
Hartington Derbys 169 C10
Hartland Devon 24 C3
Hartle Worcs 117 B8
Hartlebury Shrops 132 D4
　Worcs 116 C6
Hartlebury Common
　Worcs 116 C6
Hartlepool Hrtlpl 234 E6
Hartley Cumb 222 D5
　Kent 53 G9
　Kent 68 F6
　Northumb 243 B8
　Plym. 7 D9
Hartley Green Kent 68 F6
　Staffs 151 D9
Hartley Mauditt Hants . . . 49 F8
Hartley Westpall Hants . . 49 B7
Hartley Wintney Hants . . 49 B9
Hartlington N Yorks 213 G10
Hartlip Kent 69 G10
Hartmoor Dorset 30 C3
Hartmount Highld 301 B7
Hartoft End N Yorks 226 G5
Harton N Yorks 216 G4
　Shrops 131 F9
　T&W 243 E9
Hartpury Glos 98 F5
Hartsgreen Shrops. 132 G5
Hart's Green Suff. 125 F7
Hartshead W Yorks 197 C7
Hartshead Green
　Gtr Man 196 G3
Hartshead Moor Side
　W Yorks. 197 C7
Hartshead Moor Top
　W Yorks. 197 B7
Hartshead Pike
　Gtr Man 196 G3
Hartshill Stoke 168 F5
　Warks 134 E6
Hartshill Green Warks . . . 134 E6
Hartshorne Derbys 152 E6
Hartsop Cumb 221 C8
Hart Station Hrtlpl. 234 D5
Hartswell Som 27 B9
Hartwell Northants 120 G5
　Staffs. 151 B8
Hartwith N Yorks 214 G4
Hartwood N Lanark 269 D7
　N Lanark 268 D6
Hartwoodburn Borders . . 261 D11
Harvel Kent 68 G6
Harvest Hill W Mid 134 G5
Harvieston Stirling 277 D11
Harvills Hawthorn
　W Mid 133 E9
Harvington Worcs 99 B11
　Worcs 117 C7
Harvington Cross Worcs . 99 B11
Harvington Hill Worcs . . . 99 B11
Harwell Notts 187 C11
　Oxon 64 B3
Harwich Essex 108 E3
Harwood Durham 232 E2
　Gtr Man 195 E8
Harwood Dale N Yorks . . . 227 F9
Harwood Lee Gtr Man . . . 195 E8
Harwood Wood Norf 87 G8
Harwood on Teviot
　Borders 249 B10
Harworth Notts 187 C10
Hasbury W Mid 133 G9
Hascombe Sur. 50 E3
Haselbech Northants 120 B4
Haselbury Plucknett Som . 29 E7
Haseley Warks 118 D4
Haseley Green Warks 118 D4
Haseley Knob Warks 118 C4
Haselor Warks 118 F2
Hasfield Glos 98 F6
Hasguard Pembs 72 D5
Haskayne Lancs 193 F11
Hasketon Suff 126 G4
Hasland Derbys 170 B5
Haslemere Sur 50 G2
Haslingbourne W Sus 35 C7
Haslingden Lancs 195 C9
Haslingden Grane Lancs . 195 C8
Haslingfield Cambs 123 G8
Haslington Ches E. 168 D2
Hasluck's Green W Mid . . 118 B2
Hassall Ches E 168 D3
Hassall Green Ches E 168 D3
Hassell Street Kent 54 D5
Hassendean Borders 262 E2
Hassingham Norf 143 C7
Hassness Cumb 220 B3
Hassocks W Sus 36 D4
Hassop Derbys 186 G2
Haster Highld 310 D7
Hasthorpe Lincs 175 B7
Hasting Hill T&W 243 G9
Hastingleigh Kent 54 E5
Hastings E Sus 38 F4
　Som 28 D4
Hastingwood Essex 87 D7
Hastoe Herts 84 D6
Haston Shrops 149 E10
Haswell Durham 234 C3
Haswell Moor Durham . . . 234 C3
Haswell Plough Durham . 234 C3
Haswellsykes Borders. . . . 260 B6
Hatch C Beds 104 B3
　Devon 8 F4
　Hants 49 C7
　Wilts 30 B6
Hatch Beauchamp Som . . . 28 C4
Hatch Bottom Hants 33 E7
Hatch End Bedford 121 E11
　London 85 G11
Hatch Farm Hill W Sus . . 34 B6
Hatchet Gate Hants 32 G5
Hatching Green Herts . . . 85 C10
Hatchmere Ches W 183 G9
Hatch Warren Hants 48 D6
Hateley Heath W Mid 133 E10
Hatfield Hereford 115 F10
　Herts 86 D2
　S Yorks 199 F7
　Worcs 117 G7
Hatfield Broad Oak Essex . 87 B8
Hatfield Chase S Yorks . . . 199 E8
Hatfield Garden Village
　Herts 86 D2
Hatfield Heath Essex 87 B8
Hatfield Hyde Herts 86 C2
Hatfield Peverel Essex . . . 88 C3

Hatfield Woodhouse
　S Yorks 199 F7
Hatford Oxon 82 G4
Hatherden Hants 47 C10
Hatherleigh Devon 25 G8
Hatherley Glos 99 G8
Hathern Leics 153 E9
Hatherop Glos 81 D11
Hathersage Derbys 186 E2
Hathersage Booths
　Derbys 186 E2
Hathershaw Gtr Man 196 G2
Hatherton Ches W 167 F11
　Staffs. 151 G9
Hatley St George Cambs . 122 G5
Hatston Orkney 314 E4
Hatt Corn 7 C7
Hatterseat Aberds 303 G9
Hattersley Gtr Man 185 C7
Hatt Hill Hants 32 B4
Hattingley Hants 48 F6
Hatton Aberds 303 F10
　Angus 287 D9
　Derbys. 152 D4
　Lincs 189 F11
　London 66 D5
　Moray 301 D11
　Shrops 131 E9
　Warr 183 E9
Hatton Castle Aberds 303 E7
Hattoncrook Aberds 303 G8
Hatton Grange Shrops . . . 132 C5
Hatton Heath Ches W 167 C7
Hatton Hill Sur 66 G2
Hattonknowe Borders. . . . 270 F4
Hatton of Fintray
　Aberds 293 B10
Hatton Park Northants . . . 121 D7
Haugh E Ayrs 257 D11
　Gtr Man 196 E2
　Lincs 190 F6
Haugham Lincs 190 E4
Haugh-head Borders 261 B8
Haugh Head Northumb . . . 264 D2
Haughland Orkney 314 E5
Haughley Suff 125 E10
Haughley Green Suff 125 E10
Haughley New Street
　Suff. 125 E10
Haugh of Glass Moray . . . 302 F4
Haugh of Kilmaichlie
　Moray 301 F11
Haugh of Urr Dumfries . . 237 C10
Haughs of Clinterty
　Aberdeen 293 B10
Haughton Ches E. 167 D9
　Notts 187 G11
　Powys 148 F6
　Shrops 132 D3
　Shrops 132 D3
　Shrops 149 F11
　Staffs 151 E7
Haughton Castle
　Northumb 241 C10
Haughton Green
　Gtr Man 184 C6
Haughton Le Skerne
　Darl. 224 B6
Haultwick Herts 104 G6
Haunn Argyll 288 E5
　W Isles 297 K3
Haunton Staffs 152 G4
Hauxley Northumb 253 C7
Hauxton Cambs 123 G8
Havannah Ches E 168 C5
Havant Hants 22 B2
Haven Hereford 97 B11
Haven Bank Lincs 174 E2
Haven Side E Yorks 201 B7
Havenstreet IoW 21 C7
Havercroft W Yorks 197 E11
Haverfordwest / Hwlffordd
　Pembs. 73 B7
Haverhill Suff 106 B3
Havering Cumb 210 D3
Havering-atte-Bower
　London 87 G8
Haveringland Norf. 160 E3
Haversham M Keynes. . . . 102 C6
Haverthwaite Cumb 210 C6
Haverton Hill Stockton . . 234 G5
Haviker Street Kent 53 D8
Havyatt Som 44 F4
Havyatt Green N Som . . . 60 G3
Hawarden / Penarlȃg
　Flint 166 B4
Hawbridge Worcs 99 B8
Hawbush Green Essex . . . 106 G5
Hawcoat Cumb 210 E4
Hawcross Glos 98 E5
Hawddamor Gwyn 146 F3
Hawen Ceredig 92 B6
Hawes N Yorks 213 B7
Hawes' Green Norf 142 D4
Hawes Side Blackpool . . . 202 G2
Hawford Worcs 116 E6
Hawgreen Shrops 150 D2
Hawick Borders 262 F2
Hawkchurch Devon. 28 G4
Hawkcombe Som 41 D11
Hawkedon Suff 124 G5
Hawkenbury Kent 52 E6
　Kent 53 F11
Hawkeridge Wilts 45 C11
Hawkerland Devon. 15 D7
Hawkersland Cross
　Hereford 97 B10
Hawkesbury S Glos 61 B9
　Warks 135 G7
Hawkesbury Upton
　S Glos 61 B9
Hawkes End W Mid 134 G6
Hawkesley W Mid 117 B10
Hawk Green Gtr Man 185 D7
Hawkhill Northumb 264 F6
Hawkhurst Kent 53 G9
Hawkhurst Common
　E Sus. 23 B8
Hawkinge Kent 55 F8
Hawkin's Hill Essex 106 E3
Hawkley Hants 34 B2
　Gtr Man. 194 G5
Hawkridge Som 41 G11
Hawksdale Cumb 230 B3
Hawkshaw Blackburn. . . . 195 D9
Hawkshead Cumb. 221 F7
Hawkshead Hill Cumb. . . . 220 F6
Hawk's Hill Bucks 66 B2
Hawk's Hill Sur 51 B7
Hawksland S Lanark 259 B8
Hawkspur Green Essex . . . 106 E3
Hawks Stones W Yorks . . 196 B2
Hawkswick N Yorks 213 E9

Hawksworth Notts. 172 G3
　W Yorks. 205 E9
Hawkwell Essex 88 G4
　Kent 68 E4
Hawley Bottom Devon . . . 28 G2
Hawley Lane Hants 49 B11
　Kent 68 E4
Hawley Bottom Devon . . . 28 G2
Hawling Glos 99 G11
Hawn Orkney 314 B2
Hawnby N Yorks 215 B10
Haworth W Yorks. 204 F6
Haws Bank Cumb 220 F6
Hawstead Suff 125 F7
Hawstead Green Suff. . . . 125 F7
Hawthorn Durham 234 B4
　Hants 49 G7
　Rhondda 58 B6
　Wilts 61 F11
Hawthorn Corner Kent . . . 71 F8
Hawthorn Hill Brack 65 E11
　Lincs 174 D2
Hawthorns Staffs 168 F4
Hawthorpe Lincs 155 D10
Hawton Notts 172 E3
Haxby York 207 B8
Haxey N Lincs 199 G9
Haxey Carr N Lincs 199 G9
Haxted Sur 52 D2
Haxton Wilts 46 D6
Hay Corn 10 G5
Haybridge Shrops. 116 C3
　Som 44 D4
　Telford 150 G3
Hayden Glos 99 G8
Haydock Mers. 183 B9
Haydon Bath 45 C7
　Dorset 29 D11
　Som 28 C3
　Som 44 D5
　Swindon 62 B6
Haydon Bridge
　Northumb 241 E8
Haydon Wick Swindon . . . 62 B6
Haye Corn. 7 B7
Haye Fm Corn 6 B6
Hayes London 66 C5
　London 68 F2
　Staffs 169 G8
Hayes End London 66 C5
Hayes Knoll Wilts 81 G10
Hayes Town London 66 C6
Hayfield Derbys 185 D8
Hay Field S Yorks 187 B11
Hayfield Green
　S Yorks 187 B11
Haygate Telford 150 G2
Haygrass Som 28 C2
Hay Green Essex 87 G10
　Herts 104 D6
　Norf 157 F10
Hayhill E Ayrs 257 F11
Hayhillock Angus 287 C9
Haylands IoW 21 C7
Hayle Corn 2 B3
Hayley Green W Mid 133 G8
Hay Mills W Mid 134 G2
Haymoor End Som 28 B4
Haymoor Green
　Ches E 167 E11
Hayne Devon. 26 F5
Haynes C Beds 103 C11
Haynes Church End
　C Beds 103 C11
Haynes West End
　C Beds 103 C11
Hay-on-Wye Powys 96 C4
Hayscastle Pembs 91 F7
Hayscastle Cross Pembs . 91 G8
Haysford Pembs 91 G8
Hayshead Angus 287 C10
Hayston E Dunb 278 G2
Hayton Borders 261 B7
　Cumb 229 B7
　Cumb 240 F2
　E Yorks 208 E2
　Notts 188 E2
Hayton's Bent Shrops . . . 131 G11
Haytor Vale Devon 13 F11
Haytown Devon 24 E5
Haywards Heath W Sus . . 36 C4
Haywood S Lanark 269 E9
Haywood Oaks Notts 171 D10
Hazard's Green E Sus 23 C11
Hazelbank S Lanark 268 F6
Hazelbeach Pembs 72 E6
Hazelbury Bryan Dorset . . 30 F2
Hazeleigh Essex 88 E4
Hazel End Essex 105 G9
Hazeley Hants 49 B8
Hazeley Bottom Hants . . . 49 B8
Hazeley Heath Hants. . . . 49 B8
Hazel Grove Gtr Man 184 D6
Hazelgrove Notts 171 F8
Hazel Grove Gtr Man 184 D6
Hazelhead Gtr Man 195 D9
　S Yorks 197 G8
Hazelslack Cumb 211 D9
Hazelslade Staffs 151 G10
Hazel Street Kent 53 B11
Hazel Stub Suff 106 C3
Hazelton Glos 81 B9
Hazelton Walls Fife 287 E7
Hazelwood Derbys 170 F4
　Devon 8 E4
　London 68 G2
Hazlehead S Yorks 197 G7
Hazlemere Bucks 84 F5
Hazler Shrops 131 E9
Hazlerigg T&W 242 C6
Hazles Staffs 169 F8
Hazlescross Staffs 169 F8
Hazleton Glos 81 B9
Hazlewood N Yorks 205 C8
Hazon Northumb 252 C5
Heacham Norf 158 B3
Headbourne Worthy
　Hants 48 G3
Headbrook Hereford 114 F6
Headcorn Kent 53 E10
Headingley W Yorks 205 F11
Headington Oxon 83 D8
Headington Hill Oxon . . . 83 D8
Headlam Durham 224 B3
Headland Devon 41 G7
Headless Cross Cumb . . . 211 D7
　Worcs 117 D10
Headley Hants 49 G10
　Hants 64 G4
　Sur. 51 C8
Headley Down Hants 49 G10
Headley Heath Worcs . . . 117 B10
Headley Park Bristol. . . . 60 F5

Head of Muir Falk. 278 E6
Headon Devon 24 G5
　Notts 188 F2
Heads S Lanark. 268 F4
Headshaw Borders 261 E11
Headstone London 66 B6
Headwell Fife 279 D11
Heady Hill Gtr Man 195 E10
Heage Derbys 170 E5
Healaugh N Yorks 206 D5
　N Yorks 223 F11
Heald Green Gtr Man 184 D5
Heale Devon 40 D6
　Som 28 B5
　Som 28 D2
　Som 45 E7
Healey Gtr Man. 195 D11
　N Yorks 242 F6
　N Yorks 214 C3
　W Yorks 197 C8
　W Yorks 197 D9
Healey Cote Northumb . . 252 C4
Healeyfield Durham. 233 B7
Healey Hall Northumb . . . 242 F2
Healey NE Lincs 201 E8
Healing NE Lincs 201 E8
Heamoor Corn 1 C5
Heaning Cumb 221 F8
Heanish Argyll 288 E2
Heanor Derbys 170 F6
Heanor Gate Derbys 170 F6
Heanton Punchardon
　Devon 40 F4
Heap Bridge Gtr Man 195 E10
Heapham Lincs 188 D5
Hearn Hants 49 F10
Hearnden Green Kent. . . . 53 D10
Hearthstane Borders 260 D4
Hearthstone Derbys 170 D4
Hearts Delight Kent. 69 G11
Heasley Mill Devon 41 G8
Heast Highld 295 D8
Heath Cardiff 59 D7
　Derbys 170 B6
　Lincs 183 B10
Heath and Reach
　C Beds 103 F8
Heath Charnock Lancs . . . 194 E6
Heath Common W Sus . . . 35 D10
Heathcote Derbys 169 C10
　Shrops 150 D3
　Warks 118 E6
Heath Cross Devon. 13 B10
　Som 14 C2
Heathcote Derbys 169 C10
Heath End Hants 64 F5
　Bucks. 85 D7
　Derbys 153 E7
　Hants 64 G5
　Sur. 49 D10
　Sur. 50 D4
　Warks 118 A4
　W Mid 133 C10
　Wilts 45 D7
Heather Leics 153 G7
Heathercombe Devon 13 E10
Heatherfield Highld. 298 E4
Heather Row Hants 49 C8
Heatherside Sur 50 B2
Heatherwood Park
　Highld 311 K2
Heatherybanks Aberds . . . 303 E7
Heathfield Cambs. 105 B9
　Devon 14 F2
　E Sus 37 C9
　Glos 80 F2
　Lincs 189 C10
　N Yorks 214 F2
　S Ayrs 257 E9
　Som 27 B11
　Sur. 50 D4
　Warr 118 A4
Heathfield Village Oxon . 83 B8
Heath Green Hants 117 C11
Heath Hall Dumfries 237 B11
Heath Hayes Staffs 151 G10
Heath Hill Shrops. 150 G5
Heath House Som 44 D2
Heathlands Wokingham . . 65 F10
Heath Lanes Telford 150 E2
Heath Park London 68 B4
Heathrow Airport London 66 D5
Heath Side Kent 68 E4
Heathstock Devon. 28 G2
Heathton Shrops 132 E6
Heath Town W Mid 133 D8
Heathwaite Cumb 221 F8
　N Yorks 225 E9
Heatley Staffs 151 D11
　Warr 184 D2
Heaton Gtr Man 195 F7
　Lancs 211 G8
　Staffs 169 C7
　T&W 243 D7
Heaton Chapel Gtr Man. . 184 C5
Heaton Mersey Gtr Man . 184 C5
Heaton Moor Gtr Man . . . 184 C5
Heaton Norris Gtr Man . . 184 C5
Heaton Royds W Yorks . . 205 F8
Heaton's Bridge Lancs. . . 194 E2
Heaton Shay W Yorks . . . 205 F8
Heaven's Door Som 29 C10
Heaverham Kent 52 B5
Heaviley Gtr Man. 184 D6
Heavitree Devon 14 C4
Hebburn T&W 243 D8
Hebburn Colliery T&W . . 243 D8
Hebburn New Town
　T&W 243 D8
Hebden N Yorks 213 G10
Hebden Bridge W Yorks . . 196 B3
Hebden Green Ches W . . . 167 B10
Hebing End Herts 104 G6
Hebron Anglesey 179 E7
　Carms. 92 F3
　Northumb 252 F5
Heck Dumfries. 248 G3
Heck N Lincs 188 B3
Heckfield Hants 65 G8
Heckfield Green Suff 126 B3
Heckfordbridge Essex . . . 107 G8
Heckingham Norf 143 E7
Heckington Lincs 173 G10
Heckmondwike
　W Yorks 197 C8
Heddington Wilts 62 F3
Heddington Wick Wilts . . 62 F3
Heddle Orkney 314 E3
Heddon Devon 25 B11
Heddon-on-the-Wall
　Northumb 242 D4
Hedenham Norf 142 E6
Hedge End Dorset 30 F4

Hedge End *continued*
Hants 33 E7
Hedgehog Bridge Lincs 174 F3
Hedgerley Bucks 66 B3
Hedgerley Green Bucks 66 B3
Hedgerley Hill Bucks 66 B3
Hedging Som 28 B4
Hedley Hill Durham 233 C9
Hedley on the Hill
Northumb 242 F3
Hednesford Staffs 151 G9
Hedon E Yorks 201 B7
Hedsor Bucks 66 B2
Hedworth T&W 243 E8
Heelands M Keynes 102 D6
Heeley S Yorks 186 E5
Hegdon Hill Hereford 115 G11
Heggerscales Cumb 222 C6
Heggle Lane Cumb 230 D3
Heglibister Shetland 313 H5
Heighington Darl 233 G11
Lincs 173 B8
Heighley Staffs 168 F3
Height End Lancs 195 C9
Heightington Worcs 116 C5
Heights Gtr Man 196 F3
Heights of Brae Highld 300 C5
Heights of Kinlochewe
Highld 299 C10
Heilam Highld 308 C4
Heiton Borders 262 C6
Helbeck Cumb 222 B5
Hele Devon 12 C2
Devon 13 G10
Devon 27 G7
Devon 40 D4
Som 27 C11
Torbay 9 B8
Helebridge Corn 24 G2
Helensburgh Argyll 276 E5
Helford Corn 3 D7
Helford Passage Corn 3 D7
Helham Green Herts 86 B5
Helhoughton Norf 159 D7
Helions Bumpstead
Essex 106 C3
Hellaby S Yorks 187 C8
Helland Corn 11 G7
Som 28 C4
Hellandbridge Corn 11 G7
Hell Corner W Berks 63 G11
Hellesdon Norf 160 G4
Hellesveor Corn 2 A2
Hellidon Northants 119 F10
Hellifield N Yorks 204 B3
Hellifield Green
N Yorks 204 B3
Hellingly E Sus 23 C9
Hellington Norf 142 C6
Hellister Shetland 313 J5
Hellman's Cross Essex 87 B9
Helm Northumb 252 D5
N Yorks 223 G8
Helmburn Borders 261 E9
Helmdon Northants 101 C11
Helme W Yorks 196 E5
Helmingham Suff 126 F3
Helmington Row
Durham 233 D9
Helmsdale Highld 311 H4
Helmshore Lancs 195 C9
Helmside Cumb 212 B3
Helmsley N Yorks 216 C2
Helperby N Yorks 215 F8
Helperthorpe N Yorks 217 E9
Helpringham Lincs 173 G10
Helpston Pboro 138 B2
Helsby Ches W 183 F7
Helscott Corn 24 G2
Helsey Lincs 191 G8
Helston Corn 2 D5
Helstone Corn 11 E7
Helston Water Corn 4 G5
Helton Cumb 230 G6
Helwith Bridge N Yorks 212 F6
Helygain / Halkyn Flint 182 G2
Hemblington Norf 160 G6
Hemblington Corner
Norf 160 G6
Hembridge Som 44 F5
Hemel Hempstead Herts 85 D9
Hemerdon Devon 7 D11
Hemford Shrops 130 C6
Hem Heath Stoke 168 G5
Hemingbrough N Yorks 207 G9
Hemingby Lincs 190 G2
Hemingfield S Yorks 197 G11
Hemingford Abbots
Cambs 122 C5
Hemingford Grey
Cambs 122 C5
Hemingstone Suff 126 G3
Hemington Leics 153 D9
Northants 137 F11
Som 45 C8
Hemley Suff 108 C5
Hemlington Mbro 225 C10
Hemp Green Suff 127 D7
Hempholme E Yorks 209 C7
Hempnall Norf 142 E4
Hempnall Green Norf 142 E4
Hempriggs House
Highld 310 E7
Hemp's Green Essex 107 F8
Hempshill Vale Notts 171 G8
Hempstead Essex 106 D2
Medway 69 G9
Norf 160 B2
Norf 161 D8
Hempsted Glos 80 B4
Hempton Norf 159 D8
Oxon 101 E8
Hempton Wainhill Oxon 84 E3
Hemsby Norf 161 F9
Hemsted Kent 54 E6
Hemswell Lincs 188 C6
Hemswell Cliff Lincs 188 D6
Hemsworth Dorset 31 F7
S Yorks 186 E5
W Yorks 198 E2
Hemyock Devon 27 E10
Henaford Devon 24 D2
Hen Bentref Llandegfan
Anglesey 179 G9
Henbrook Worcs 117 D8
Henbury Bristol 60 D5
Ches E 184 G5
Dorset 18 B5
Hendomen Powys 130 D4
Hendon London 67 B8
T&W 243 F10
Hendra Corn 2 B6
Corn 2 C5
Corn 2 D3
Corn 2 F6
Corn 5 C9
Corn 5 D9
Corn 11 E7
Hendrabridge Corn 6 B5
Hendraburnick Corn 11 D8
Hendra Croft Corn 4 D5
Hendre Flint 165 B11
Gwyn 110 B2
Powys 129 D9
Hendre-ddu Conwy 164 B5
Hendredenny Park
Caerph 58 B6
Hendreforgan Rhondda 58 B3
Hendrerwydd Denb 165 C10
Hendrewen Swansea 75 D10
Hendy Carms 75 E9
Hendy-Gwyn Carms 74 B2
Hendy Gwyn / Whitland
Carms 73 B11
Hên-efail Denb 165 C9
Heneglwys Anglesey 178 F6
Hen-feddau fawr Pembs 92 E4
Henfield S Glos 61 D7
W Sus 36 D2
Henford Devon 12 C3
Henfords Marsh Wilts 45 E11
Henghurst Kent 54 F3
Hengoed Caerph 77 F10
Denb 165 D9
Powys 114 G4
Shrops 148 C5
Hengrave Norf 160 F2
Suff 124 D6
Hengrove Bristol 60 F6
Hengrove Park Bristol 60 F5
Henham Essex 105 F10
Heniarth Powys 130 B2
Henlade Som 28 C3
Henleaze Bristol 60 D5
Henley Dorset 29 G11
Glos 80 B6
Shrops 115 B10
Shrops 131 F9
Som 44 G2
Suff 126 G3
Wilts 47 B10
Wilts 61 F10
W Sus 34 B5
Henley Common W Sus 34 B5
Henley Green W Mid 135 G7
Henley-in-Arden Warks 118 D3
Henley-on-Thames Oxon 65 C9
Henley's Down E Sus 38 E2
Henley Street Kent 69 F7
Henllan Ceredig 93 C7
Denb 165 B8
Henllan Amgoed Carms 92 G3
Henlle Shrops 148 C6
Henllys Torf 78 G3
Henllys Vale Torf 78 G3
Henlow C Beds 104 D3
Hennock Devon 14 E2
Henny Street Essex 107 D7
Henryd Conwy 180 G3
Henry's Moat Pembs 91 F10
Hensall N Yorks 198 C5
Henshaw Northumb 241 E7
W Yorks 205 E10
Hensingham Cumb 219 B9
Hensington Oxon 83 B7
Henstead Suff 143 F9
Hensting Hants 33 C7
Henstridge Devon 40 E5
Som 30 D2
Henstridge Ash Som 30 C2
Henstridge Bowden
Som 29 C11
Henstridge Marsh Som 30 C2
Henton Oxon 84 E3
Som 44 D3
Henwood Corn 11 G11
Oxon 83 E7
Henwood Green Kent 52 E6
Heogan Shetland 313 J6
Heol-ddu Carms 75 E7
Swansea 56 B6
Heolgerrig M Tydf 77 D8
Heol-laethog Bridgend 58 C2
Heol-las Bridgend 58 C2
Swansea 57 B7
Heol Senni Powys 95 G8
Heol-y-gaer Powys 96 D3
Heol-y-mynydd V Glam 57 G11
Hepburn Northumb 264 E3
Hepple Northumb 251 C11
Hepscott Northumb 252 G6
Hepthorne Lane Derbys 170 C6
Heptonstall W Yorks 196 B3
Hepworth Suff 125 C9
W Yorks 197 F7
Herbrandston Pembs 72 D5
Hereford Hereford 97 C10
Heribusta Highld 298 B4
Heriot Borders 271 E7
Hermiston Edin 280 G3
Hermitage Borders 250 D2
Dorset 29 F10
W Berks 64 E4
W Sus 22 B3
Hermitage Green Mers 183 C10
Hermit Hill S Yorks 197 G10
Hermit Hole W Yorks 205 F7
Hermon Anglesey 162 B5
Carms 93 E7
Carms 94 F3
Pembs 92 E4
Herne Kent 71 F7
Herne Bay Kent 71 F7
Herne Common Kent 71 F7
Herne Hill London 67 E10
Herne Pound Kent 53 C7
Herner Devon 25 B9
Hernhill Kent 70 G5
Herniss Corn 2 C6
Herodsfoot Corn 6 C4
Heron Cross Stoke 168 G5
Heronden Kent 55 C9
Herongate Essex 87 G10
Heronsford S Ayrs 244 G4
Heronsgate Herts 85 G8
Heron's Ghyll E Sus 37 B7
Herons Green Bath 44 B5
Heronston Bridgend 58 D2
Herra Shetland 312 D8
Herriard Hants 49 D7
Herringfleet Suff 143 D9
Herring's Green
Bedford 103 C11
Herringswell Suff 124 C4
Herringthorpe S Yorks 186 C6
Hersden Kent 71 G8
Hersham Corn 24 F3
Sur 66 G6
Herstmonceux E Sus 23 C10
Herston Dorset 18 F6
Orkney 314 G4
Hertford Herts 86 C4
Hertford Heath Herts 86 C4
Hertingfordbury Herts 86 C4
Hesketh Bank Lancs 194 C2
Hesketh Lane Lancs 203 E8
Hesketh Moss Lancs 194 C2
Hesket Newmarket
Cumb 230 D2
Heskin Green Lancs 194 D4
Hesleden Durham 234 D4
Hesleyside Northumb 251 G8
Heslington York 207 C8
Hessay York 206 C6
Hessenford Corn 6 D6
Hessett Suff 125 E8
Hessle E Yorks 200 B4
W Yorks 198 D2
Hest Bank Lancs 211 F9
Hester's Way Glos 99 G8
Hestinsetter Shetland 313 J4
Heston London 66 D6
Hestwall Orkney 314 E2
Heswall Mers 182 E3
Hethe Oxon 101 F11
Hethel Norf 142 C3
Hethelpit Cross Glos 98 F5
Hethersett Norf 142 C3
Hethersgill Cumb 239 D11
Hetherside Cumb 239 D10
Hetherson Green
Ches W 167 F8
Hethpool Northumb 263 D9
Hett Durham 233 D11
Hetton N Yorks 204 B5
Hetton Downs T&W 234 B3
Hetton-le-Hill T&W 234 B3
Hetton-le-Hole T&W 234 B3
Hetton Steads Northumb 264 B2
Heugh Northumb 242 C3
Heugh-head Aberds 292 B5
Heveningham Suff 126 C6
Hever Kent 52 E3
Heversham Cumb 211 C9
Hevingham Norf 160 E3
Hewas Water Corn 5 F9
Hewelsfield Glos 79 E9
Hewelsfield Common
Glos 79 E8
Hewer Hill Cumb 230 D3
Hew Green N Yorks 205 B10
Hewish N Som 60 G2
Som 28 F6
Hewood Dorset 28 G5
Heworth T&W 243 E7
York 207 C8
Hexham Northumb 241 E10
Hextable Kent 68 E4
Hexthorpe S Yorks 198 G5
Hexton Herts 104 E2
Hexworthy Devon 13 G9
Hey Lancs 204 E3
Heybridge Essex 87 F10
Essex 88 D5
Heybridge Basin Essex 88 D5
Heybrook Bay Devon 7 F10
Heydon Cambs 105 C8
Norf 160 D2
Heydour Lincs 155 B10
Hey Green W Yorks 196 E4
Heyheads Gtr Man 196 G3
Hey Houses Lancs 193 B10
Heylipol Argyll 288 E1
Heylor Shetland 312 E4
Heyope Powys 114 C4
Heyrod Gtr Man 185 B7
Heysham Lancs 211 G8
Heyshaw N Yorks 214 G3
Heyshott W Sus 34 D5
Heyshott Green W Sus 34 D5
Heyside Gtr Man 196 F2
Heytesbury Wilts 46 E2
Heythrop Oxon 101 F7
Heywood Gtr Man 195 E11
Wilts 45 C11
Hibaldstow N Lincs 200 G3
Hibb's Green Suff 125 G7
Hickford Hill Essex 106 C5
Hickleton S Yorks 198 F3
Hickling Norf 161 E8
Notts 154 D3
Hickling Green Norf 161 E8
Hickling Heath Norf 161 E8
Hickling Pastures Notts 154 D3
Hickmans Green Kent 54 B5
Hicks Forstal Kent 71 G7
Hicks Gate Bath 60 F6
Hick's Mill Corn 4 G5
Hickstead W Sus 36 C3
Hidcote Bartrim Glos 100 C3
Hidcote Boyce Glos 100 C3
Hifnal Shrops 132 D4
Higginshaw Gtr Man 196 F2
High Ackworth W Yorks 198 D2
Higham Derbys 170 D5
Fife 286 F6
Kent 69 E8
Lancs 204 F2
Suff 107 D10
Suff 124 E4
S Yorks 197 F10
Higham Common
S Yorks 197 F10
Higham Dykes Northumb 242 B4
Higham Ferrers
Northants 121 D9
Higham Gobion C Beds 104 E2
Higham Hill London 86 G5
Higham on the Hill
Leics 135 D7
Highampton Devon 25 G7
Highams Park London 86 G5
Higham Wood Kent 52 D5
High Angerton Northumb 252 F3
High Bankhill Cumb 231 C7
High Banton N Lanark 278 E4
High Barn Lincs 174 C5
High Barnes T&W 243 F9
High Barnet London 86 F2
High Beach Essex 86 F6
High Bentham N Yorks 212 F3
High Bickington Devon 25 C10
High Biggins Cumb 212 D2
High Birkwith N Yorks 212 D5
High Birstwith N Yorks 205 B10
High Blantyre S Lanark 268 D3
High Bonnybridge Falk 278 F6
High Bradfield S Yorks 186 C3
High Bradley N Yorks 204 D6
High Bray Devon 41 G7
Highbridge Cumb 230 C3
Hants 33 C7
Highld 290 E3
Som 43 D10
W Mid 133 C10
Highbrook W Sus 51 G11
High Brooms Kent 52 E5
High Brotheridge Glos 80 C5
High Bullen Devon 25 C8
Highburton W Yorks 197 E7
Highbury London 67 B10
Ptsmth 33 G11
Som 45 D7
Highbury Vale
Nottingham 171 G8
High Buston Northumb 252 B6
High Callerton
Northumb 242 C5
High Cark Cumb 211 C7
High Casterton Cumb 212 D2
High Catton E Yorks 207 C10
High Church Northumb 252 F5
Highclere Hants 64 G2
Highcliffe Derbys 186 F2
Dorset 19 C10
High Cogges Oxon 82 D5
High Common Norf 141 B9
High Coniscliffe Darl 224 B4
High Crompton Gtr Man 196 F2
High Cross Cambs 123 F8
Corn 2 D6
E Sus 37 B9
Hants 34 B2
Herts 85 F10
Herts 86 B5
Newport 59 B9
Warks 118 D3
W Sus 36 D2
High Crosshill S Lanark 268 C2
High Cunsey Cumb 221 G7
High Dubmire T&W 234 B2
High Dyke Durham 232 F5
High Easter Essex 87 C10
High Eggborough
N Yorks 198 C5
High Eldrig Dumfries 236 C4
High Ellington N Yorks 214 C3
Higher Alham Som 45 E7
Higher Ansty Dorset 30 G3
Higher Ashton Devon 14 E3
Higher Audley Blackburn 195 B7
Higher Bal Corn 4 E4
Higher Ballam Lancs 202 G3
Higher Bartle Lancs 202 G6
Higher Bebington Mers 182 D4
Higher Berry End
C Beds 103 E9
Higher Blackley
Gtr Man 195 G10
Higher Boarshaw
Gtr Man 195 F11
Higher Bockhampton
Dorset 17 C10
Higher Bojewyan Corn 1 C3
Higher Boscaswell Corn 1 C3
Higher Brixham Torbay 9 D8
Higher Broughton
Gtr Man 195 G10
Higher Burrow Som 28 C6
Higher Burwardsley
Ches W 167 D8
High Ercall Telford 149 F11
Higher Chalmington
Dorset 29 G9
Higher Cheriton Devon 27 G10
Higher Chillington Som 28 E5
Higher Chisworth
Derbys 185 C7
Highercliff Corn 6 D4
Higher Clovelly Devon 24 C4
Higher Condurrow Corn 2 B5
Higher Crackington Corn 11 B9
Higher Cransworth Corn 5 B9
Higher Croft Blackburn 195 B7
Higher Denham Bucks 66 B4
Higher Dinting Derbys 185 C8
Higher Disley Ches E 185 E7
Higher Downs Corn 2 C3
Higher Durston Som 28 B3
Higher End Gtr Man 194 G4
Higher Folds Gtr Man 195 G7
Higherford Lancs 204 E3
Higher Gabwell Torbay 9 B8
Higher Green Gtr Man 195 G8
Higher Halstock Leigh
Dorset 29 F8
Higher Heysham Lancs 211 G8
Higher Hogshead
Lancs 195 C11
Higher Holton Som 29 B11
Higher Hurdsfield
Ches E 184 G6
Higher Kingcombe
Dorset 16 B6
Higher Kinnerton Flint 166 C4
Higher Land Corn 12 G3
Higher Marsh Som 30 C2
Higher Melcombe Dorset 30 G2
Higher Menadew Corn 5 D10
Higher Molland Devon 41 G8
Higher Muddiford Devon 40 F5
Higher Nyland Dorset 30 C2
Higher Penwortham
Lancs 194 B4
Higher Pertwood Wilts 45 F11
Higher Porthpean Corn 5 E10
Higher Poynton Ches E 184 E6
Higher Prestacott Devon 12 B3
Higher Rads End
C Beds 103 E9
Higher Ridge Shrops 149 C7
Higher Rocombe Barton
Devon 9 B8
Higher Row Dorset 31 G8
Higher Runcorn Halton 183 E8
Higher Sandford Dorset 29 C10
Higher Shotton Flint 166 B4
Higher Shurlach
Ches W 183 G11
Higher Slade Devon 40 D4
Higher Street Som 42 E6
Higher Tale Devon 27 G9
Higher Tolcarne Corn 5 B7
Higher Totnell Dorset 29 F10
Highertown Corn 4 G6
Corn 11 E8
Higher Town Corn 5 C10
Scilly 1 F4
Som 42 D3
Higher Tremarcoombe
Corn 6 B5
Higher Vexford Som 42 F6
Higher Walreddon Devon 12 G5
Higher Walton Lancs 194 B5
Warr 183 D9
Higher Wambrook Som 28 F3
Higher Warcombe Devon 40 D3
Higher Weaver Devon 27 G9
Higher Whatcombe
Dorset 30 G4
Higher Wheelton Lancs 194 C6
Higher Whitley
Ches W 183 E10
Higher Wincham
Ches W 183 F11
Higher Woodsford
Dorset 17 D11
Higher Wraxall Dorset 29 G9
Higher Wych Ches W 167 G7
High Etherley Durham 233 F9
High Ferry Lincs 174 F5
Highfield E Yorks 207 F10
Glos 79 E10
Gtr Man 194 G5
Gtr Man 195 F8
Herts 85 D9
N Ayrs 266 E6
Oxon 101 G11
Soton 32 E6
S Yorks 186 D5
T&W 242 F4
High Field Lancs 203 C10
Highfields Cambs 123 F7
Derbys 170 B6
Essex 88 B5
Glos 80 F3
Leicester 136 C2
Northumb 273 E9
Staffs 151 E8
S Yorks 198 F4
High Flatts W Yorks 197 F8
High Forge Durham 242 G6
High Friarside Durham 242 F5
High Gallowhill E Dunb 278 G2
High Garrett Essex 106 F5
Highgate E Sus 52 G2
Kent 53 G9
London 67 B9
Powys 130 D2
S Yorks 198 G3
W Mid 133 F11
High Grange Durham 233 E9
High Grantley N Yorks 214 F4
High Green Cumb 221 E8
Norf 141 B8
Norf 142 B2
Norf 159 G8
Shrops 132 G4
Suff 125 E7
S Yorks 186 B4
Worcs 99 B7
W Yorks 197 E7
High Halden Kent 53 F11
High Halstow Medway 69 D9
High Ham Som 44 G2
High Handenhold
Durham 242 G6
High Harrington Cumb 228 F6
High Harrogate N Yorks 206 B2
High Haswell Durham 234 C3
High Hatton Shrops 150 E2
High Hauxley Northumb 253 C7
High Hawsker N Yorks 227 D8
High Heath Shrops 150 D3
W Mid 133 C10
High Hesket Cumb 230 C5
High Hesleden Durham 234 D5
High Hill Cumb 229 G11
High Houses Essex 87 C11
High Hoyland S Yorks 197 E9
High Hunsley E Yorks 208 F4
High Hurstwood E Sus 37 B7
High Hutton N Yorks 216 F5
High Ireby Cumb 229 D10
High Kelling Norf 177 E10
High Kilburn N Yorks 215 D10
High Lands Durham 233 F8
Highlane Ches E 168 B5
Derbys 186 E6
High Lane Gtr Man 185 D7
Worcs 116 E3
Highlanes Corn 10 G4
Staffs 150 C5
High Lanes Corn 2 B3
High Laver Essex 87 D8
Highlaws Cumb 229 B8
Highleadon Glos 98 G5
High Legh Ches E 184 E2
Highleigh W Sus 22 D4
High Leven Stockton 225 C8
Highley Shrops 132 G4
High Littleton Bath 44 B6
High Longthwaite
Cumb 229 B11
High Lorton Cumb 229 F9
High Marishes N Yorks 216 D6
High Marnham Notts 188 G4
High Melton S Yorks 198 G4
High Mickley Northumb 242 E3
High Mindork Dumfries 236 D5
Highmoor Cumb 229 B11
Oxon 65 B8
High Moor Derbys 187 E7
Lancs 194 E4
Highmoor Cross Oxon 65 C8
Highmoor Hill Mon 60 B3
High Moorsley T&W 234 B2
Highnam Glos 80 B3
Highnam Green Glos 98 G5
High Nash Glos 79 C9
High Newton Cumb 211 C8
High Newton-by-the-Sea
Northumb 264 D6
High Nibthwaite Cumb 210 B5
Highoak Norf 141 C11
High Oaks Cumb 222 G2
High Offley Staffs 150 D5
High Ongar Essex 87 E9
High Onn Staffs 150 F6
High Onn Wharf Staffs 150 F6
High Park Cumb 221 G10
Mers 193 D11
Highridge Bristol 60 F5
High Risby N Lincs 200 E2
Highroad Well Moor
W Yorks 196 B5
High Roding Essex 87 B10
High Rougham Suff 125 E8
High Row Cumb 230 D3
Cumb 230 G3
High Salvington W Sus 35 F10
High Scales Cumb 229 B9
High Sellafield Cumb 219 E10
High Shaw N Yorks 223 G7
High Shields T&W 243 D9
High Shincliffe Durham 233 C11
High Side Cumb 229 E10
High Southwick T&W 243 F9
High Spen T&W 242 F4
High Stakesby N Yorks 227 C7
Highstead Kent 71 F8
Highsted Kent 70 G2
High Stoop Durham 233 C8
Highstreet Kent 70 G5
High Street Corn 5 E9
Kent 53 G8
Pembs 73 B11
Suff 107 B7
Suff 127 C8
Suff 127 F8
Suff 143 G7
Highstreet Green Essex 106 E5
Sur 50 F3
High Street Green Suff 125 F10
High Sunderland
Borders 261 C11
Hightae Dumfries 238 B3
Highter's Heath W Mid 117 B11
High Throston Hrtlpl 234 E5
High Tirfergus Argyll 255 F7
Hightown Ches E 168 C5
Hants 31 G11
Mers 193 G10
Soton 33 E7
Wrex 166 F4
W Yorks 197 C7
High Town Luton 103 G11
Shrops 132 E4
Staffs 151 G9
Hightown Green Suff 125 F9
Hightown Heights
W Yorks 197 C7
High Toynton Lincs 174 B3
High Trewhitt Northumb 252 B2
High Urpeth Durham 242 G6
High Valleyfield Fife 279 D10
High Walton Cumb 219 C9
High Warden Northumb 241 D10
High Water Head Cumb 220 F6
Highway Corn 4 G4
Hereford 97 B9
Som 29 C7
Wilts 62 E4
Windsor 65 C11
Highweek Devon 14 G2
High Westwood Durham 242 F4
High Whinnow Cumb 239 G8
Highwood Devon 27 F10
Dorset 18 D3
Essex 87 E10
Hants 31 F11
Worcs 116 D3
Highwood Hill London 86 G2
High Woolaston Glos 79 F9
High Worsall N Yorks 225 D7
Highworth Swindon 82 G2
Highworthy Devon 24 F6
High Wray Cumb 221 F7
High Wych Herts 87 C7
High Wycombe Bucks 84 G5
Hilborough Norf 140 C6
Hilborough Ho Norf 140 C6
Hilcot Glos 81 B7
Hilcote Derbys 171 D7
Hilcot End Glos 81 E9
Hilcott Wilts 46 B6
Hildenborough Kent 52 D5
Hilden Park Kent 52 D5
Hildersham Cambs 105 B10
Hildersley Hereford 98 G2
Hilderstone Staffs 151 C8
Hilderthorpe E Yorks 218 F3
Hilfield Dorset 29 F10
Hilgay Norf 140 D2
Hill S Glos 79 G10
Warks 119 D9
W Mid 134 D2
Hillam N Yorks 198 B4
Hillbeck Cumb 222 B5
Hillblock Pembs 73 B8
Hillborough Kent 71 F8
Hill Bottom Oxon 64 D6
Hillbourne Poole 18 C6
Hillbrae Aberds 302 E6
Aberds 303 G7
Hill Brow W Sus 34 B3
Hillbutts Dorset 31 G7
Hill Chorlton Staffs 150 B5
Hillcliffe Warr 183 D10
Hillcliffane Derbys 170 F3
Hillcommon Som 27 B11
Hill Common Norf 161 E8
Hill Corner Som 45 D10
Hill Croome Worcs 99 C7
Hillcross Derbys 152 C6
Hill Dale Lancs 194 E3
Hill Deverill Wilts 45 E11
Hilldyke Lincs 174 F4
Hill Dyke Lincs 174 F4
Hillend Fife 280 E2
N Lanark 268 B6
N Som 43 B11
Shrops 132 E6
Swansea 56 C2
Hill End Durham 232 D6
Fife 279 B10
Glos 99 D8
London 85 G8
N Yorks 205 C7
Som 29 E8
Worcs 117 E8
Hillend Green Glos 98 F4
Hillersland Glos 79 C9
Hillerton Devon 13 B10
Hillesden Bucks 102 F3
Hillesden Hamlet Bucks 102 E3
Hillesley Glos 61 B9
Hillfarance Som 27 C11
Hillfarrance Som 27 C11
Hillfield Devon 8 E6
W Mid 118 B2
Hillfields S Glos 60 D6
W Mid 118 B6
Hillfoot Aberds 303 D9
W Yorks 205 G10
Hillfoot End C Beds 104 E2
Hill Furze Worcs 99 B9
Hill Gate Hereford 97 F9
Hillgreen W Berks 64 D3
Hill Green Essex 105 E9
Kent 69 G10
Hillgrove W Sus 34 B6
Hillhampton Hereford 97 B11
Hillhead Aberds 302 F5
Aberds 303 G8
Corn 5 C11
Devon 9 E8
E Ayrs 257 B10
S Ayrs 257 F10
Hill Head Hants 33 G8
Northumb 241 D10
Hillhead of Auchentumb
Aberds 303 D9
Hillhead of Blairy
Aberds 302 D6
Hillhead of Cocklaw
Aberds 303 E10
Hill Hoath Kent 52 E3
Hill Hook W Mid 134 C2
Hillhouse Borders 271 D10
Hill Houses Shrops 116 B2
Hilliard's Cross Staffs 152 G3
Hilliclay Highld 310 C5
Hillingdon London 66 C5
Hillingdon Heath London 66 C5
Hillington Glasgow 267 C10
Norf 158 D4
Hillis Corner IoW 20 C5
Hillmoor Devon 27 E10
Hillmorton Warks 119 C10
Hill Mountain Pembs 73 D7
Hillockhead Aberds 292 B6
Aberds 292 C5
Hillock Vale Lancs 195 B9
Hill of Beath Fife 280 C3
Hill of Drip Stirling 278 B5
Hill of Fearn Highld 301 B8
Hill of Keillor Angus 286 C6
Hill of Mountblairy
Aberds 302 D6
Hill of Overbrae Aberds 303 C8
Hill Park Hants 33 F9
Kent 52 B2
Hillpool Worcs 117 B7
Hillpound Hants 33 D9
Hill Ridware Staffs 151 F11
Hillsborough S Yorks 186 C4
Hillside Aberds 293 D11
Angus 293 G9
Devon 8 C4
Devon 27 F11
Hants 49 C9
Mers 193 E10
Orkney 314 D3
Hillside *continued*
Orkney 314 G4
Shetland 313 G6
Shrops 131 F11
Wilts 81 G9
Hill Side Hants 34 B3
S Yorks 197 G8
Worcs 116 E5
W Yorks 197 D7
Hill Somersal Derbys 152 C2
Hills Town Derbys 171 B7
Hillstreet Hants 32 D4
Hill Street Kent 54 D6
Hillswick Shetland 312 F4
Hilltop Bl Gwent 77 D11
Bucks 85 E7
Derbys 170 C4
Hill Top Derbys 186 F5
Durham 232 G5
Durham 233 C10
Durham 242 G5
Gtr Man 195 G8
Hants 32 G6
Notts 171 F7
N Yorks 214 G3
N Yorks 214 G5
Staffs 133 B7
S Yorks 186 C5
S Yorks 186 D3
S Yorks 187 B7
S Yorks 197 F9
Warks 134 E5
Warks 135 E7
W Mid 133 E9
W Sus 34 C5
W Yorks 196 E5
W Yorks 197 D10
W Yorks 205 G7
W Yorks 205 G11
Hillview T&W 243 G9
Hill View Dorset 18 B5
Hillway IoW 21 D8
Hillwell Shetland 313 M5
Hill Wood W Mid 134 C2
Hill Wootton Warks 118 D6
Hillyfields Hants 32 D5
Hilmarton Wilts 62 D4
Hilperton Wilts 45 B11
Hilperton Marsh Wilts 45 B11
Hilsea Ptsmth 33 G11
Hilston E Yorks 209 G11
Hiltingbury Hants 32 C6
Hilton Aberds 303 F9
Borders 273 E7
Cambs 122 D5
Cumb 231 G10
Derbys 152 C4
Dorset 30 G3
Durham 233 G9
Highld 309 L7
Highld 311 L3
Shrops 132 D5
Staffs 133 B11
Stockton 225 C9
Hilton House Gtr Man 194 F6
Hilton Lodge Highld 300 G2
Hilton of Cadboll Highld 301 B8
Hilton Park Gtr Man 195 G10
Himbleton Worcs 117 F8
Himley Staffs 133 E7
Hincaster Cumb 211 C10
Hinchley Wood Sur 67 F7
Hinchliffe Mill W Yorks 196 F6
Hinchwick Glos 100 E2
Hinckley Leics 135 E8
Hinderclay Suff 125 B10
Hinderton Ches W 182 F4
Hinderwell N Yorks 226 B5
Hindford Shrops 148 C6
Hindhead Sur 49 F11
Hindle Fold Lancs 203 G10
Hindley Gtr Man 194 G6
Northumb 242 F2
Hindley Green Gtr Man 194 G6
Hindlip Worcs 117 F7
Hindolveston Norf 159 D10
Hindon Wilts 46 G2
Hindpool Cumb 210 F3
Hindringham Norf 159 B9
Hindsford Gtr Man 195 G7
Hingham Norf 141 C10
Hinstock Shrops 150 D3
Hintlesham Suff 107 C11
Hinton Glos 79 E11
Hants 19 B10
Hereford 96 D6
Northants 119 G10
S Glos 61 D8
Shrops 131 B8
Som 29 C9
Hinton Ampner Hants 33 B9
Hinton Blewett Bath 44 B5
Hinton Charterhouse
Bath 45 B9
Hinton Cross Worcs 99 C10
Hinton-in-the-Hedges
Northants 101 D11
Hinton Martell Dorset 31 F8
Hinton on the Green
Worcs 99 C10
Hinton Parva Dorset 31 G7
Swindon 63 C8
Hinton St George Som 28 E6
Hinton St Mary Dorset 30 D3
Hinton Waldrist Oxon 82 F5
Hints Shrops 116 C2
Staffs 134 C3
Hinwick Bedford 121 E8
Hinwood Shrops 131 B7
Hinxhill Kent 54 E5
Hinxton Cambs 105 B9
Hinxworth Herts 104 C4
Hipperholme W Yorks 196 B6
Hipplecote Worcs 116 F4
Hipsburn Northumb 264 G6
Hipswell N Yorks 224 F3
Hirael Gwyn 179 G9
Hiraeth Carms 92 G3
Hirn Aberds 293 C9
Hirnant Powys 147 E11
Hirst N Lanark 269 C7
Northumb 253 F7
Hirst Courtney N Yorks 198 C6
Hirwaen Denb 165 C10
Hirwaun Rhondda 77 D7
Hirwaun Common
Bridgend 58 C2
Hiscott Devon 25 B8
Hislop Borders 249 C9
Hisomley Wilts 45 D11
Histon Cambs 123 E8
Hitcham Suff 125 G9
Hitchill Dumfries 238 D4
Hitchin Herts 104 F3
Hitchin Hill Herts 104 F3
Hitcombe Bottom Wilts 45 E10
Hither Green London 67 E11
Hittisleigh Devon 13 C10
Hittisleigh Barton Devon 13 B10
Hive E Yorks 208 G2
Hixon Staffs 151 D10
Hoaden Kent 55 B9
Hoar Cross Staffs 152 E2
Hoarwithy Hereford 97 F10
Hoath Kent 71 G8
Hoath Corner Kent 52 E3
Hobarris Shrops 114 B6
Hobbister Orkney 314 F3
Hobble End Staffs 133 B10
Hobbles Green Suff 124 G4
Hobbs Cross Essex 87 C7
Essex 87 F7
Hobbs Wall Bath 61 G7
Hob Hill Ches W 167 E7
Hobkirk Borders 262 G3
Hobroyd Derbys 185 C8
Hobson Durham 242 F5
Hoby Leics 154 F3
Hoccombe Som 27 B10
Hockenden London 68 F3
Hockerill Herts 105 G9
Hockering Norf 159 G11
Hockering Heath Norf 159 G11
Hockerton Notts 172 D2
Hockholler Som 27 C11
Hockholler Green Som 27 C11
Hockley Ches E 184 E6
Essex 88 G4
Kent 54 B3
Staffs 134 C4
W Mid 118 B5
Hockley Heath W Mid 118 C3
Hockliffe C Beds 103 F9
Hockwold cum Wilton
Norf 140 F4
Hockworthy Devon 27 D8
Hocombe Hants 32 C6
Hoddesdon Herts 86 D5
Hoddlesden Blackburn 195 C8
Hoddomcross Dumfries 238 C5
Hoddom Mains Dumfries 238 C5
Hoden Worcs 99 B11
Hodgefield Staffs 168 E6
Hodgehill Ches E 168 B4
W Mid 134 F2
Hodgeston Pembs 73 F8
Hodley Powys 130 E3
Hodnet Shrops 150 D2
Hodnetheath Shrops 150 D2
Hodsock Notts 187 D10
Hodsoll Street Kent 68 G6
Hodson Swindon 63 C7
Hodthorpe Derbys 187 F8
Hoe Hants 33 D9
Norf 159 F9
Sur 50 D5
Hoe Benham W Berks 64 F2
Hoe Gate Hants 33 E10
Hoff Cumb 222 B3
Hoffleet Stow Lincs 156 B4
Hogaland Shetland 312 F5
Hogben's Hill Kent 54 B4
Hogganfield Glasgow 268 B2
Hoggard's Green Suff 125 F7
Hoggeston Bucks 102 G6
Hoggington Wilts 45 B10
Hoggrill's End Warks 134 E4
Hogha Gearraidh
W Isles 296 D3
Hog Hatch Sur 49 D10
Hoghton Lancs 194 B6
Hoghton Bottoms Lancs 194 B6
Hogley Green W Yorks 196 F6
Hognaston Derbys 170 E2
Hogpits Bottom Herts 85 E8
Hogsthorpe Lincs 191 G8
Hogstock Dorset 31 F7
Holbeach Lincs 157 E7
Holbeach Bank Lincs 157 D7
Holbeach Clough Lincs 156 D6
Holbeach Drove Lincs 156 G6
Holbeache Worcs 116 B5
Holbeach Hurn Lincs 157 D7
Holbeach St Johns
Lincs 156 F6
Holbeach St Marks
Lincs 157 C7
Holbeach St Matthew
Lincs 157 C8
Holbeck Notts 187 G8
W Yorks 205 G11
Holbeck Woodhouse
Notts 187 G8
Holberrow Green
Worcs 117 F10
Holbeton Devon 8 E2
Holborn London 67 C10
Holborough Kent 69 G8
Holbrook Derbys 170 G5
Suff 108 D3
S Yorks 186 E6
Holbrook Common
S Glos 61 E7
Holbrook Moor Derbys 170 F5
Holbrooks W Mid 134 G6
Holburn Northumb 264 B2
Holbury Hants 32 G6
Holcombe Devon 14 G5
Gtr Man 195 D9
Som 45 D7
Holcombe Brook
Gtr Man 195 E9
Holcombe Rogus Devon 27 D9
Holcot Northants 120 D5
Holdbrook London 86 F5
Holden Lancs 203 D11
Holdenby Northants 120 D3
Holden Fold Gtr Man 196 F2
Holdenhurst Bmouth 19 B8
Holder's Green Essex 106 F2
Holders Hill London 86 G2
Holdfast Worcs 99 D7
Holdgate Shrops 131 F11
Holdingham Lincs 173 F9
Holditch Dorset 28 G4
Holdsworth W Yorks 196 B5
Holdworth S Yorks 186 C3
Hole Devon 24 D4
W Yorks 204 F6
Hole Bottom W Yorks 196 C2
Holefield Borders 263 C8
Holehills N Lanark 268 B5
Holehouse Derbys 185 C8
Holehouses Ches E 184 F2
Hole-in-the-Wall
Hereford 98 F2
Holemill Aberdeen 293 C10
Holemoor Devon 24 F6
Hole's Hole Devon 7 B8
Holestane Dumfries 247 D9
Holestone Derbys 170 C4
Hole Street W Sus 35 E10
Holewater Devon 41 F8
Holford Som 43 E7
Holgate York 207 C7
Holker Cumb 211 D7
Holkham Norf 176 E5
Hollacombe Devon 24 G5
Devon 26 G4
Hollacombe Hill Devon 7 E10
Holland Orkney 314 A4
Orkney 314 D6

Holland continued

Sur....52 C2
Holland Fen Lincs....174 F2
Holland Lees Lancs....194 F4
Holland-on-Sea Essex..89 B12
Hollands Som....29 D9
Hollandstoun Orkney..314 A7
Hollee Dumfries....239 D7
Hollesley Suff....109 C7
Hollicombe Torbay....9 C2
Hollies Common Staffs..150 E6
Hollinfare Warr....183 C11
Hollingbourne Kent....53 B10
Hollingbury Brighton....36 F4
Hollingdean Brighton....36 F4
Hollingrove E Sus....37 C11
Hollingthorpe W Yorks..197 D10
Hollington Derbys....152 B4
E Sus....38 E3
Hants....48 B2
Staffs....151 B11
Hollington Cross Hants..48 C2
Hollington Grove
Derbys....152 B4
Hollingwood Derbys....186 G6
Hollingworth Gtr Man..185 B8
Hollin Hall W Yorks....204 F4
Hollin Park W Yorks....206 F2
Hollins Cumb....222 G3
Derbys....186 G4
Gtr Man....195 F8
Gtr Man....195 F10
Gtr Man....195 F11
Staffs....168 G6
Staffs....168 E4
Staffs....169 F7
Hollinsclough Staffs..169 B9
Hollins End S Yorks....186 E5
Hollinsgreen Ches E....168 C2
Hollins Green Warr....183 C11
Hollins Lane Lancs....202 C5
Shrops....149 B10
Hollinswood Telford....132 B4
Hollinthorpe W Yorks..206 F3
Hollinwood Gtr Man....196 G2
Shrops....149 B10
Hollis Green Devon....27 F9
Hollis Head Devon....27 G7
Hollocombe Devon....25 E10
Hollocombe Town
Devon....25 E10
Wilts....45 G11
Windsor....65 C10
Holloway Derbys....170 D4
Wilts....45 G11
Windsor....65 C10
Holloway Hill Sur....50 E3
Hollow Brook Bath....60 G5
Hollowell Northants....120 C3
Hollow Meadows
S Yorks....186 D2
Hollowmoor Heath
Ches W....167 B7
Hollow Oak Dorset....18 C2
Hollows Dumfries....239 B9
Hollow Street Kent....71 G8
Holly Bank W Mid....133 C11
Hollyberry End W Mid..134 G5
Holly Brook Som....44 D4
Hollybush Caerph....77 E11
E Ayrs....244 D2
Stoke....168 G5
Torf....78 G3
Worcs....98 D5
Holly Bush Wrex....166 F4
Hollybush Corner Bucks..66 B3
Suff....125 F8
Hollybushes Kent....54 B2
Hollybush Hill Bucks....66 C3
Essex....89 B10
Hollycroft Leics....135 E8
Holly End Norf....139 B9
Holly Green Bucks....84 F3
Worcs....99 C7
Holly Hill N Yorks....224 E3
Hollyhurst Shrops....131 D9
Warks....135 F7
Hollym E Yorks....201 B10
Hollywaste Shrops....116 B2
Hollywater Hants....49 G10
Hollywood Worcs....117 B11
Holmacott Devon....25 B8
Holman Clavel Som....28 D2
Holmbridge W Yorks....196 F6
Holmbury St Mary Sur..50 E6
Holmbush Corn....5 E10
Dorset....28 G5
Holmcroft Staffs....151 D8
Holme Cambs....138 F3
CBeds....104 C3
Cumb....211 D10
N Lincs....200 F2
Notts....172 D4
N Yorks....215 C2
W Yorks....196 F6
W Yorks....205 G9
Holmebridge Dorset....18 D3
Holme Chapel Lancs....195 B11
Holme Green CBeds....104 C3
N Yorks....207 E2
Wokingham....65 F10
Holme Hale Norf....141 B7
Holme Hill NE Lincs....201 G8
Holme Lacy Hereford....97 D11
Holme Lane Notts....154 B2
Holme Marsh Hereford..114 G6
Holme Mills Cumb....211 D10
Holme next the Sea
Norf....176 G2
Holme-on-Spalding-Moor
E Yorks....208 F2
Holme on the Wolds
E Yorks....208 D5
Holme Pierrepont Notts..154 B2
Holmer Hereford....97 C10
Holmer Green Bucks....84 F6
Holmes Lancs....194 D2
Holme St Cuthbert
Cumb....229 B8
Holmes Chapel Ches E..168 B3
Holmesdale Derbys....186 F5
Holme Slack Lancs....203 G7
Holmes's Hill E Sus....23 C8
Holmeswood Lancs....194 D2
Holmethorpe Sur....51 C9
Holmewood Derbys....170 B6
Holme Wood W Yorks..205 G9
Holmfield W Yorks....196 B5
Holmfirth W Yorks....196 F6
Holmhead Angus....293 F7
Dumfries....246 F6
E Ayrs....258 E3
Holmhill Dumfries....247 D9
Holmisdale Highld....297 G7
Holmley Common
Derbys....186 F5
Holmpton E Yorks....201 C11
Holmrook Cumb....219 F11
Holmsgarth Shetland....313 J6
Holmside Durham....233 B10

Holmsleigh Green Devon..28 G2
Holmston S Ayrs....257 E9
Holmwood Corner Sur....51 E7
Holmwrangle Cumb....230 B6
Holne Devon....8 B3
Holnest Dorset....29 E11
Holsworthy Devon....24 G4
Holsworthy Beacon
Devon....24 G5
Holt Dorset....31 G8
Hants....49 C8
Mers....183 C7
Norf....159 B11
Wilts....61 G11
Worcs....116 E6
Wrex....166 E6
Holtby York....207 C9
Holt End Hants....49 F7
Worcs....117 D11
Holt Fleet Worcs....116 E6
Holt Green Lancs....193 G11
Holt Head W Yorks....196 F5
Holt Heath Dorset....31 G9
Worcs....116 E6
Holt Hill Kent....53 B8
Staffs....152 D2
Holton Oxon....83 D10
Som....29 B11
Suff....127 B7
Holton cum Beckering
Lincs....189 E10
Holton Heath Dorset....18 D4
Holton le Clay Lincs....201 G9
Holton le Moor Lincs....189 B9
Holton St Mary Suff....107 D11
Holtspur Bucks....84 G6
Holt Wood Dorset....31 F8
Holtye E Sus....52 F3
Holway Dorset....28 G5
Dorset....29 C10
Flint....181 F11
Som....28 C2
Holwell Dorset....30 E2
Herts....104 E3
Leics....154 E4
Oxon....82 D2
Som....45 D8
Holwellbury CBeds....104 E3
Holwick Durham....232 F4
Holworth Dorset....17 E11
Holybourne Hants....49 E8
Holy City Devon....28 G3
Holy Cross T&W....243 D8
Worcs....117 B8
Holyfield Essex....86 E5
Holygate Hereford....98 B2
Holyhead / Caergybi
Anglesey....178 E2
Holy Island Northumb....273 B11
Holylee Borders....261 B9
Holymoorside Derbys....170 B4
Holyport Windsor....65 D11
Holystone Northumb....251 C11
Holytown N Lanark....268 C5
Holy Vale Scilly....1 G4
Holywell Cambs....122 C6
CBeds....85 B8
Corn....4 D5
Dorset....29 G9
E Sus....23 F9
Glos....80 G3
Hereford....97 C7
Herts....85 F9
Northumb....243 C8
Som....29 E8
Warks....118 D3
Holywell Green
W Yorks....196 D5
Holywell Lake Som....27 C10
Holywell Row Suff....124 B4
Holywell / Treffynnon
Flint....181 F11
Holywood Derbys....247 G10
Homedowns Glos....99 E8
Homer Shrops....132 C2
Homer Green Mers....193 G10
Homersfield Suff....142 F5
Homerton London....67 C11
Hom Green Hereford....97 G11
Homington Wilts....31 B10
Honeyborough Pembs....72 D6
Honeybourne Worcs....100 C2
Honeychurch Devon....25 G9
Honeydon Bedford....122 F2
Honey Hall N Som....60 G2
Honeyhill Wokingham....65 F10
Honey Hill Kent....70 G6
Honeystreet Wilts....62 G6
Honey Street Wilts....62 G6
Honey Tye Suff....107 D9
Honeywick CBeds....103 G9
Honicknowle Plym....7 D9
Honiley Warks....118 C4
Honing Norf....160 D6
Honingham Norf....160 G2
Honington Lincs....172 G6
Suff....125 C8
Warks....100 C5
Honiton Devon....27 G11
Honkley Wrex....166 D4
Honley W Yorks....196 E6
Honley Moor W Yorks..196 E6
Honnington Telford....150 F4
Honor Oak London....67 E11
Honor Oak Park London..67 E11
Honresfeld Gtr Man....196 D2
Hoo Kent....71 G9
Hoober S Yorks....186 B6
Hoobrook Worcs....116 C6
Hood Green S Yorks....197 G10
Hood Hill S Yorks....186 B5
Hood Manor Warr....183 D9
Hooe E Sus....23 D11
Plym....7 E10
Hooe Common E Sus....23 C11
Hoo End Herts....85 B11
Hoofield Ches E....167 C8
Hoogh Blackpool....202 F2
Hoo Hole W Yorks....196 B4
Hook Cambs....139 E8
Devon....28 F4
E Yorks....199 B9
Hants....33 F8
Hants....49 C8
London....67 G7
Pembs....73 C7
Wilts....62 C5
Hook-a-gate Shrops....131 B9
Hook Bank Worcs....98 C6
Hooke Dorset....16 B6
Hook End Essex....87 F9
Oxon....65 C7
Hooker Gate T&W....242 F4
Hookgate Staffs....150 B4
Hook Green Kent....53 F7
Kent....68 F6
Hook Heath Sur....50 B3

Hook Norton Oxon....101 E7
Hook Park Hants....33 G7
Hook's Cross Herts....104 G5
Hants....47 G10
Hook Street Glos....79 F11
Wilts....62 C5
Hooksway W Sus....34 D4
Hookway Devon....14 B3
Hookwood Sur....51 E9
Hoole Ches W....166 B6
Hoole Bank Ches W....166 B6
Hooley Sur....51 B9
Hooley Bridge Gtr Man..195 E11
Hooley Brow Gtr Man....195 E11
Hooley Hill Gtr Man....184 B6
Hoo Meavy Devon....7 B10
Hoop Mon....79 D8
Hoopers Pool Wilts....45 C10
Hoops Devon....24 C5
Hoo St Werburgh
Medway....69 E9
Hereford....114 C6
Norf....161 E9
Powys....130 B5
Shrops....130 C6
Staffs....169 D10
Hope Bagot Shrops....115 C11
Hopebeck Cumb....229 G9
Hope Bowdler Shrops....131 E9
Hopedale Staffs....169 D9
Hope End Green Essex..105 G11
Hope Green Ches E....184 E6
Hopeman Moray....301 C11
Hope Mansell Hereford..79 B10
Hope Park Shrops....130 C6
Hopesay Shrops....131 G7
Hopesgate Shrops....130 C6
Hope's Green Essex....69 B9
Hope's Rough Hereford..98 B2
Hopetown W Yorks....197 C11
Hope under Dinmore
Hereford....115 G10
Hope / Yr Hôb Flint....166 D4
Hopgoods Green
W Berks....64 F4
Hopkinstown Rhondda....77 G9
Hopley's Green Hereford..114 G6
Hopperton N Yorks....206 B4
Hop Pole Lincs....156 G3
Hopsford Warks....135 G8
Hopstone Shrops....132 E5
Hopton Derbys....170 E3
Shrops....149 D11
Shrops....149 E7
Staffs....151 D8
Staffs....125 B9
Hopton Cangeford
Shrops....131 G10
Hopton Castle Shrops....115 B7
Hoptongate Shrops....131 G10
Hoptonheath Shrops....115 B7
Hopton Heath Staffs....151 D9
Hopton on Sea Norf....143 D10
Hopton Wafers Shrops..116 B2
Hopwas Staffs....134 B3
Hopwood Gtr Man....195 F11
Worcs....117 B10
Hopworthy Devon....24 G4
Horam E Sus....23 B9
Horbling Lincs....156 B2
Horbury W Yorks....197 D9
Horbury Bridge
W Yorks....197 D9
Horbury Junction
W Yorks....197 D9
Horcott Glos....81 E11
Horden Durham....234 C4
Horderley Shrops....131 F8
Hordle Hants....19 B11
Hordley Shrops....149 C7
Horeb Carms....75 D7
Carms....93 F10
Ceredig....93 C7
Flint....166 D3
Horfield Bristol....60 D6
Horgabost W Isles....305 J2
Horham Suff....126 C4
Horkesley Heath Essex..107 F9
Horkstow N Lincs....200 D3
Horkstow Wolds
N Lincs....200 D3
Horley Oxon....101 C8
Sur....51 E9
Horn Ash Dorset....28 G5
Hornblotton Som....44 G5
Hornblotton Green Som..44 G5
Hornby Lancs....211 E11
N Yorks....224 G4
N Yorks....225 D7
Horncastle Lincs....174 B3
Hornchurch London....68 B4
Horncliffe Northumb....273 F7
Horndean Borders....273 F7
Hants....34 E2
Horndon Devon....12 F6
Horndon on the Hill
Thurrock....69 C7
Horne Sur....51 E10
Horner Som....41 D11
Horner Row Devon....88 E3
Horner's Green Suff....107 C9
Hornestreet Essex....107 E10
Horney Common E Sus....37 B7
Horn Hill Som....43 E8
Hornick Corn....5 E9
Horniehaugh Angus....292 G6
Horning Norf....160 F6
Horninghold Leics....136 D6
Horninglow Staffs....152 D4
Horningsea Cambs....123 E9
Horningsham Wilts....45 E10
Horningtoft Norf....159 E8
Horningtops Corn....6 C5
Hornsbury Som....28 D3
Hornsby Cumb....240 G2
Hornsbygate Cumb....240 G2
Horns Corner Kent....38 B2
Horns Cross Devon....24 C5
E Sus....38 C4
Hornsea E Yorks....209 D10
Hornsea Bridge
E Yorks....209 D10
Hornsea Burton
E Yorks....209 D10
Hornsey London....67 B10
Hornsey Vale London....67 B10
Horns Green Kent....52 C2
Horn Street Kent....55 F7
Kent....69 G7
Hornton Oxon....101 B7
Horpit Swindon....63 C8
Horrabridge Devon....7 B10
Horringer Suff....124 E6
Horringford IoW....20 D6
Horrocks Fold Gtr Man..195 E8
Horrocksford Lancs....203 E10

Horsalls Kent....53 C11
Horsebridge Devon....12 G4
Hants....47 G10
Shrops....131 B7
Horse Bridge Staffs....169 E7
Horsebrook Devon....8 D4
Staffs....151 G7
Horsecastle N Som....60 F2
Horsedown Wilts....61 D11
Horsedowns Corn....2 C4
Horsehay Telford....132 B3
Horseheath Cambs....106 B2
Horsehouse N Yorks....213 C11
Horseley Heath W Mid..133 E10
Horsell Sur....50 B3
Horsell Birch Sur....50 B3
Horseman's Green
Wrex....166 G6
Horseman Side Essex....87 F8
Horsemere Green W Sus..35 G8
Horsenden Bucks....84 E3
Horsepools Glos....80 C4
Horseway Cambs....139 F8
Horseway Head
Hereford....114 C6
Horsey Norf....161 E9
Horsey Corner Norf....161 E9
Horsey Down Wilts....81 G9
Horsford Norf....160 F3
Horsforth W Yorks....205 F10
Horsforth Woodside
W Yorks....205 F10
Horsham Worcs....116 F4
W Sus....51 G7
Horsham St Faith Norf..160 F4
Horshoe Green Kent....52 E3
Horsington Lincs....173 B11
Som....30 C2
Horsley Derbys....170 G5
Glos....80 F4
Northumb....242 D3
Northumb....251 B10
Horsley Cross Essex....108 F2
Horsleycross Street
Essex....108 F2
Horsleyhill Borders....262 F2
Horsley Hill T&W....243 D9
Horsleyhope Durham....233 B7
Horsleys Green Bucks....84 F3
Horsley Woodhouse
Derbys....170 G5
Horsmonden Kent....53 E7
Horspath Oxon....83 E9
Horstead Norf....160 F5
Horsted Green E Sus....23 B7
Horsted Keynes W Sus..36 B5
Horton Bucks....84 B6
Dorset....31 F8
Kent....54 B6
Lancs....204 C3
Northants....120 G6
S Glos....61 C9
Shrops....149 D9
Som....28 D3
Staffs....168 D6
Swansea....56 D3
Telford....150 G3
Wilts....62 G5
Windsor....66 D4
Horton Common Dorset..31 F9
Horton Cross Som....28 D4
Horton-cum-Studley
Oxon....83 C9
Horton Green Ches W....167 F7
Horton Heath Dorset....31 F9
Hants....33 D7
Horton in Ribblesdale
N Yorks....212 E5
Horton Kirby Kent....68 F5
Hortonlane Shrops....149 G8
Horton Wharf Bucks....84 B6
Hortonwood Telford....150 G3
Horwich Gtr Man....194 E6
Horwich End Derbys....185 E8
Horwood Devon....25 B8
Horwood Riding S Glos....61 B8
Hoscar Lancs....194 E3
Hose Leics....154 D4
Hoselaw Borders....263 C8
Hoseham Surrey....204 G6
Hosey Hill Kent....52 C3
Hosh Perth....286 E2
Hoswick Shetland....313 L6
Hotham E Yorks....208 G3
Hothfield Kent....54 D3
Hotley Bottom Bucks....84 E5
Hoton Leics....153 E11
Hotwells Bristol....60 E5
Houbans Shetland....312 F5
Houbie Shetland....312 D8
Houdston S Ayrs....244 G5
Hough Argyll....288 E1
Ches E....168 E2
Ches E....184 F5
Hougham Lincs....172 G5
Hough Green Halton....183 D7
Hough-on-the-Hill
Lincs....172 F6
Hough Side W Yorks....205 G10
Houghton Cambs....122 C5
Cumb....239 F10
Hants....47 G10
Pembs....73 D7
W Sus....35 E8
Houghton Bank Darl....233 G10
Houghton Conquest
CBeds....103 C10
Houghton Green E Sus....38 C6
Warr....183 C10
Houghton-le-Side
Darl....233 G10
Houghton-le-Spring
T&W....234 B2
Houghton on the Hill
Leics....136 C3
Houghton Regis
CBeds....103 F10
Houghton St Giles Norf..159 B8
Houlland Shetland....312 F5
Shetland....313 H5
Shetland....313 J6
Houlsyke N Yorks....226 D4
Hound Hants....33 G7
Hound Green Hants....49 B8
Houndmills Hants....48 C6
Houndscroft Glos....80 E5
Houndslow Borders....272 F2
Houndsmoor Som....27 B10
Houndstone Som....29 D8
Houndwood Borders....272 C6
Hounsdown Hants....32 E5
Hounsley Batch N Som....60 G4
Hounslow London....66 D6

Hounslow Green Essex..87 B11
Hounslow West London..66 D6
Hourston Orkney....314 E2
Housabister Shetland....313 H6
Housay Shetland....312 F8
Househill Highld....301 D8
House of Daviot Highld..301 E7
House of Glenmuick
Aberds....292 D5
Houses Hill W Yorks....197 D7
Housetter Shetland....312 E5
Housham Tye Essex....87 C8
Houss Shetland....313 K5
Houston Renfs....267 B8
Houstry Highld....310 F5
Houton Orkney....314 F3
Hove Brighton....36 G3
Hove Edge W Yorks....196 C6
Hoveringham Notts....171 F11
Hoveton Norf....160 F6
Hovingham N Yorks....216 D3
How Cumb....240 F2
Howbeck Bank Ches E....167 F11
Howbrook S Yorks....186 B4
How Caple Hereford....98 E2
Howden Borders....262 E5
E Loth....269 B11
E Yorks....199 B8
Howden Clough
W Yorks....197 B8
Howden-le-Wear
Durham....233 E9
Howden T&W....243 D8
Howden Pans T&W....243 D8
Howe Highld....310 C7
Norf....142 C5
N Yorks....214 C6
How End CBeds....103 C10
Howe Green Essex....88 E4
Essex....87 B8
Warks....134 F6
Howegreen Essex....88 E2
Howell Lincs....173 F10
How End CBeds....103 C10
Howe of Teuchar
Aberds....303 E7
Howe Street Essex....87 C11
Essex....106 F3
Howey Powys....113 F11
Howford Borders....261 E9
Borders....261 E9
Howgate Cumb....228 G5
Midloth....270 D4
Howgill Cumb....222 F2
Lancs....204 D2
N Yorks....205 B7
Howick Cross Lancs....194 B4
Northumb....265 F7
Howle Durham....233 F7
Telford....150 E3
Howleigh Som....28 D2
Howlett End Essex....105 E11
Howley Glos....80 G2
Som....28 F3
Warr....183 D10
Hownam Borders....263 F7
Hownam Mains Borders..263 E7
Howpasley Borders....249 B8
Howsham N Lincs....200 G4
N Yorks....216 G3
Howslack Dumfries....248 B3
Howtel Northumb....263 C9
Howt Green Kent....69 F11
Howton Hereford....97 F8
Howtown Cumb....221 B8
Howwood Renfs....267 C7
How Wood Herts....85 E10
Hoxne Suff....126 B3
Hoxton London....67 C10
Hoy Orkney....314 F2
Hoylake Mers....182 D2
Hoyland S Yorks....197 G11
Hoyland Common
S Yorks....197 G11
Hoylandswaine S Yorks..197 G9
Hoyle W Sus....34 D6
Hoyle Mill W Yorks....197 F11
Hubbard's Hill Kent....52 C4
Hubberholme N Yorks....213 D8
Hubberston Pembs....72 D5
Hubbersty Head Cumb....221 G8
Hubberton Green
W Yorks....196 C4
Hubbert's Bridge Lincs..174 G3
Huby N Yorks....205 D11
N Yorks....215 F11
Hucclecote Glos....80 B5
Hucking Kent....53 B10
Hucknall Notts....171 F8
Huddersfield W Yorks....197 D7
Huddington Worcs....117 F8
Huddisford Devon....24 D4
Huddlesford Staffs....134 B3
Hud Hey Lancs....195 C9
Hudnall Herts....85 C8
Hudnalls Glos....79 E8
Hudswell N Yorks....224 E3
Wilts....61 F11
Huggate E Yorks....208 B3
Hugglepit Devon....24 C4
Hugglescote Leics....153 G8
Hughenden Valley Bucks..84 F5
Hughley Shrops....131 D11
Hugh Mill Lancs....195 C10
Hugh Town Scilly....1 G4
Hugus Corn....4 G5
Huish Devon....25 E8
Devon....25 E8
Wilts....62 G6
Huish Champflower Som..27 B9
Huish Episcopi Som....28 B6
Huisinis W Isles....305 G1
Hulcote CBeds....103 D8
Northants....102 B4
Northants....102 B4
Hulcott Bucks....84 B5
Hulham Devon....14 E6
Hull Hull E Yorks....185 E9
Hulland Derbys....170 F3
Hulland Moss Derbys....170 F3
Hulland Ward Derbys....170 F3
Hullavington Wilts....61 C11
Hull Bridge E Yorks....209 E7
Hullwood Mers....194 G4
Hulme Gtr Man....184 B4
Staffs....168 G6
Staffs....169 G7
Warr....183 C10
Hulme End Staffs....169 D10
Hulme Walfield Ches E....168 B4
Hulseheath Ches E....184 E2
Hulver Street Suff....143 F9
Norf....14 G3
Humber Devon....14 G3
Hereford....115 F11
Humber Bridge N Lincs..200 C4
Humberston NE Lincs....201 F10
Humberstone Leicester..136 B2
Humberston Fitties
NE Lincs....201 F10
Humbie E Loth....271 C9

Humbledon T&W....243 F9
Humble Green Suff....107 B8
Humbleton E Yorks....209 G10
Northumb....263 D11
Humby Lincs....155 C10
Hume Borders....272 G4
Hummersknott Darl....224 C5
Humshaugh Northumb....241 C10
Huna Highld....310 B7
Huncoat Lancs....203 G11
Huncote Leics....135 D10
Hundalee Borders....262 F4
Hundall Derbys....186 F5
Hunderthwaite Durham..232 G5
Hunderton Hereford....97 D9
Hundle Houses Lincs....174 E3
Hundleshope Borders....260 B6
Hundleton Pembs....73 E7
Hundon Suff....106 B4
Hundred Acres Hants....33 E9
Hundred End Lancs....194 C3
Hundred House Powys....114 G2
Hungarton Leics....136 B3
Hungate N Yorks....197 B11
Hungerford Hants....31 E11
Shrops....131 F11
Som....42 E4
W Berks....63 F10
Windsor....65 D10
Hungerford Green
W Berks....64 D5
Hungerford Newtown
W Berks....63 E11
Hunger Hill Gtr Man....195 F7
Lancs....194 E4
Hungershall Park Kent....52 F5
Hungerstone Hereford....97 D8
Hungerton Lincs....155 D7
Hungladder Highld....298 B3
Hungreyhatton Shrops..150 D3
Hunmanby N Yorks....217 D11
Hunmanby Moor
N Yorks....218 D2
Hunningham Warks....119 D7
Hunningham Hill Warks..119 D7
Hunnington Worcs....133 G9
Hunny Hill IoW....20 D5
Hunsdon Herts....86 C6
Hunsdonbury Herts....86 C6
Hunsingore N Yorks....206 C4
Hunslet W Yorks....206 G2
Hunslet Carr W Yorks....206 G2
Hunsonby Cumb....231 D7
Hunspow Highld....310 B6
Hunstanton Norf....175 G11
Hunstanworth Durham..232 B5
Hunsterson Ches E....167 F11
Hunston Suff....125 D9
W Sus....22 C5
Hunston Green Suff....125 D9
Hunstrete Bath....60 G6
Hunt End Worcs....117 E10
Huntenhull Green Wilts..45 D10
Huntercombe End Oxon..65 B7
Hunters Forstal Kent....71 F7
Hunter's Quay Argyll....276 F3
Huntham Som....28 B4
Hunthill Lodge Angus....292 F6
Huntingdon Cambs....122 C4
Huntingfield Suff....127 C7
Huntingford Dorset....45 G10
S Glos....80 G2
Huntington Ches W....166 C6
E Loth....281 F9
Hereford....97 C9
Hereford....115 G7
Staffs....151 G9
Telford....132 B3
York....207 B8
Huntingtower Perth....286 E4
Huntley Glos....80 B2
Staffs....169 G8
Huntly Aberds....302 F5
Huntlywood Borders....272 G2
Hunton Hants....48 F3
Kent....53 D8
N Yorks....224 G3
Hunton Bridge Herts....85 E9
Hunt's Corner Norf....141 F11
Huntscott Som....42 E2
Hunt's Cross Mers....182 D6
Hunts Green Warks....134 D3
Hunt's Green Bucks....84 E6
W Berks....64 E2
Huntsham Devon....27 C8
Huntshaw Devon....25 C8
Huntshaw Water Devon..25 C8
Hunt's Hill Bucks....84 F4
Hunt's Lane Leics....135 C9
Huntspill Som....43 D10
Huntstile Som....43 G9
Huntworth Som....43 G9
Hunwick Durham....233 E9
Hunworth Norf....159 B11
Hurcott Som....28 D5
Som....29 B8
Worcs....116 B7
Hurdcott Wilts....47 G7
Hurdley Powys....130 E5
Hurdsfield Ches E....184 G6
Hurgill N Yorks....224 E3
Hurlet Glasgow....267 C10
Hurley Warks....134 D4
Windsor....65 C10
Hurley Bottom Windsor..65 C10
Hurley Common Warks..134 D4
Hurlford E Ayrs....257 B11
Hurliness Orkney....314 H2
Hurlston Lancs....194 E3
Hurlston Green Lancs....193 E11
Hurn Dorset....19 B8
E Yorks....208 B6
Hurn's End Lincs....174 F6
Hursey Dorset....28 G6
Hursley Hants....32 B6
Hurst Cumb....230 C4
Dorset....17 C11
Gtr Man....196 G2
N Yorks....223 E11
Som....29 D7
Wokingham....65 E9
Hurstbourne Priors
Hants....48 D2
Hurstbourne Tarrant
Hants....47 C11
Hurst Green Essex....89 B8
E Sus....38 B2
Lancs....203 F9
Surrey....51 C11
W Mid....133 F9
Hurst Hill W Mid....133 E8
Hurstley Hereford....97 B7
Hurst Park Sur....66 F6
Hurstpierpoint W Sus....36 D3
Hurst Wickham W Sus....36 D3
Hurstwood Lancs....204 G3
Hurtmore Sur....50 E3
Hurworth-on-Tees Darl..224 C6
Hurworth Place Darl....224 C5
Hury Durham....223 B9
Husabost Highld....298 D2
Husbands Bosworth
Leics....136 G2
Husbandtown Angus....287 D8
Husborne Crawley
CBeds....103 D9
Husthwaite N Yorks....215 D10
Hutcherleigh Devon....8 E5
Hutchesontown
Glasgow....267 C11
Hutchwns Bridgend....57 F10
Hut Green N Yorks....198 C5
Huthwaite Notts....171 D7
Hutlerburn Borders....261 E10
Huttock Top Lancs....195 C11
Huttoft Lincs....191 F8
Hutton Borders....273 E9
Cumb....230 F4
Essex....87 F10
E Yorks....208 C6
Lancs....194 B3
Hutton Bonville N Yorks..224 E6
Hutton Buscel N Yorks..217 C9
Hutton Conyers N Yorks..214 E6
Hutton Cranswick
E Yorks....208 C6
Hutton End Cumb....230 D4
Hutton Gate Redcar....225 B11
Hutton Hang N Yorks....214 B3
Hutton Henry Durham....234 D4
Hutton-le-Hole
N Yorks....226 G4
Hutton Magna Durham..224 C2
Hutton Mount Essex....87 G10
Hutton Roof Cumb....211 D11
Cumb....230 E3
Hutton Rudby N Yorks....225 D9
Huttons Ambo N Yorks..216 F5
Hutton Sessay N Yorks..215 D9
Hutton Village Redcar....225 B11
Hutton Wandesley
N Yorks....206 C6
Huxham Devon....14 B4
Huxham Green Som....44 F5
Huxley Ches E....167 C8
Huxter Shetland....313 C11
Shetland....313 H3
Huyton Mers....182 C6
Huyton Park Mers....182 C6
Huyton Quarry Mers....182 C6
Hwlffordd / Haverfordwest
Pembs....73 B7
Hycemoor Cumb....210 B1
Hyde Glos....99 F11
Gtr Man....184 B6
Hants....31 E11
Hants....48 G3
Hereford....115 F9
Hyde Chase Essex....88 E4
Hyde End W Berks....64 G5
Hyde Heath Bucks....84 E6
Hyde Lea Staffs....151 E8
Hyde Park S Yorks....198 G5
Hydestile Sur....50 E3
Hylton Castle T&W....243 F9
Hylton Red House T&W..243 F9
Hyltons Crossways Norf..160 D4
Lancs....203 G10
Hyndford Bridge
S Lanark....269 G8
Hyndhope Borders....261 E9
Hynish Argyll....288 F1
Hyssington Powys....130 E6
Hystfield Glos....79 F11
Hythe Hants....32 F6
Kent....55 G7
Som....44 C2
Sur....66 E4
Hythe End Windsor....66 E4
Hythie Aberds....303 D10
Hyton Cumb....210 B1

I

Iarsiadar W Isles....304 E3
Ibberton Dorset....30 F3
Ible Derbys....170 D2
Ibrox Glasgow....267 C10
Ibsley Hants....31 F11
Ibstock Leics....153 G8
Ibstone Bucks....84 G3
Ibthorpe Hants....47 C11
Iburndale N Yorks....227 D7
Ibworth Hants....48 C5
Icelton N Som....59 F11
Ichrachan Argyll....284 D4
Ickburgh Norf....140 D6
Ickenham London....66 B5
Ickenthwaite Cumb....210 B6
Ickford Bucks....83 D11
Ickham Kent....55 B8
Ickleford Herts....104 E3
Icklesham E Sus....38 D5
Ickleton Cambs....105 C9
Icklingham Suff....124 C5
Ickornshaw N Yorks....204 E5
Ickwell CBeds....104 B3
Ickwell Green CBeds....104 B3
Icomb Glos....100 G4
Icy Park Devon....8 F3
Idbury Oxon....82 B2
Iddesleigh Devon....25 F9
Ide Devon....14 C3
Ideford Devon....14 F3
Ide Hill Kent....52 C3
Iden E Sus....38 C5
Iden Green Kent....53 E10
Kent....53 F10
Idle W Yorks....205 F9
Idless Corn....4 F6
Idlicote Warks....100 C5
Idmiston Wilts....47 F7
Idole Carms....74 B6
Idridgehay Derbys....170 F3
Idridgehay Green
Derbys....170 F3
Idrigill Highld....298 C3
Idstone Oxon....63 C9
Idvies Angus....287 C9
Iet-y-bwlch Carms....92 F3
Iffley Oxon....83 E8
Ifield W Sus....51 F9
Ifield Green W Sus....51 F9
Ifieldwood W Sus....51 F9
Ifold W Sus....50 G4
Iford Bmouth....19 C8
E Sus....36 F6
Ifton Heath Shrops....148 B6
Ightfield Shrops....149 B11
Ightfield Heath Shrops..149 B11
Ightham Kent....52 B5
Igtham Common Kent....52 B5
Iken Suff....127 F8
Ilam Staffs....169 E10

Ilchester Som....29 C8
Ilchester Mead Som....29 C8
Ilderton Northumb....264 E2
Ileden Kent....55 C8
Ilford London....68 B2
Som....28 D5
Ilfracombe Devon....40 D4
Ilkeston Derbys....171 G7
Ilketshall St Andrew
Suff....143 F7
Ilketshall St Lawrence
Suff....143 G7
Ilketshall St Margaret
Suff....142 F6
Ilkley W Yorks....205 E8
Illand Corn....11 E11
Illey W Mid....133 G9
Illidge Green Ches E....168 C3
Illington Norf....141 F8
Illingworth W Yorks....196 B5
Illogan Corn....4 G3
Illogan Highway Corn....4 G3
Illshaw Heath W Mid....118 C2
Ilmer Bucks....84 D3
Ilmington Warks....100 C4
Ilminster Som....28 E5
Ilsington Devon....13 F11
Dorset....17 C11
Ilston Swansea....56 C5
Ilton N Yorks....214 D3
Som....28 D5
Imachar N Ayrs....255 C9
Imber Wilts....46 D3
Immeravoulin Stirling....285 F9
Immervoulin Stirling....285 F9
Impington Cambs....123 E8
Ince Ches W....183 F7
Ince Blundell Mers....193 G10
Ince in Makerfield
Gtr Man....194 G5
Inchbae Lodge Highld....300 C4
Inchbare Angus....293 G8
Inchberry Moray....302 D3
Inchbraoch Angus....287 B11
Inchbrook Glos....80 E4
Inchcape Highld....309 J6
Incheril Highld....299 C10
Inchgrundle Angus....292 F6
Inchina Highld....307 K4
Inchinnan Renfs....267 B9
Inchkinloch Highld....308 E5
Inchlaggan Highld....290 C3
Inchlumpie Highld....300 B5
Inchmore Highld....300 E3
Highld....300 E5
Inchnacardoch Hotel
Highld....290 B5
Inchnadamph Highld....307 G2
Inchock Angus....287 C10
Inch of Arnhall Aberds..293 F8
Inchree Highld....290 G2
Inchrory Moray....292 C3
Inchture Perth....286 E6
Inchyra Perth....286 E5
Indian Queens Corn....5 D8
Inerval Argyll....254 C4
Ingatestone Essex....87 F11
Ingbirchworth S Yorks....197 F8
Ingerthorpe N Yorks....214 F5
Ingestre Staffs....151 E9
Ingham Lincs....188 E6
Norf....161 D7
Suff....125 C7
Ingham Corner Norf....161 D7
Ingleborough Norf....157 F9
Ingleby Derbys....152 D6
Lincs....188 F5
Ingleby Arncliffe
N Yorks....225 E8
Ingleby Barwick
Stockton....225 C9
Ingleby Cross N Yorks....225 E8
Ingleby Greenhow
N Yorks....225 D11
Ingleigh Green Devon....25 F10
Inglemire Hull....209 G7
Inglesbatch Bath....61 G8
Inglesham Swindon....82 F2
Ingleton Durham....233 G9
N Yorks....212 E3
Inglewhite Lancs....202 E6
Ingmanthorpe N Yorks..206 C4
Ingoe Northumb....242 C2
Ingol Lancs....202 G6
Ingoldisthorpe Norf....158 C3
Ingoldmells Lincs....175 B9
Ingoldsby Lincs....155 C10
Ingon Warks....118 F4
Ingram Northumb....264 F2
Ingrams Green W Sus....34 C4
Ingrave Essex....87 G10
Ingrow W Yorks....205 F7
Ings Cumb....221 F8
S Lincs....60 E5
Ingst S Glos....60 B5
Ingthorpe Rutland....137 B9
Ingworth Norf....160 D3
Inham's End Cambs....138 D5
Inhurst Hants....64 G5
Inkberrow Worcs....117 F10
Inkerman Durham....233 D8
Inkersall Derbys....186 G6
Inkersall Green Derbys..186 G6
Inkford Worcs....117 C11
Inkpen W Berks....63 G11
Inkpen Common
W Berks....63 G11
Inkstack Highld....310 B6
Inlands W Sus....22 B3
Inmarsh Wilts....62 G2
Inn Cumb....221 D8
Innellan Argyll....276 G3
Inner Hope Devon....9 G8
Innerleithen Borders....261 B8
Innerleven Fife....287 G7
Innermessan Dumfries..236 C2
Innerwick E Loth....282 F4
Perth....285 C9
Innie Argyll....275 D9
Inninbeg Highld....289 E8
Innis Chonain Argyll....284 E5
Innistrynich Argyll....284 E5
Innox Hill Som....45 D9
Innsworth Glos....99 G7
Insch Aberds....302 G6
Insh Highld....291 C10
Inshegra Highld....306 D7
Inshore Highld....308 C3
Inskip Lancs....202 F5
Inskip Moss Side Lancs..202 F5
Instoneville S Yorks....198 E5
Instow Devon....40 G3
Intack Blackburn....195 B8
Intake S Yorks....186 E6
S Yorks....198 G5
Intanke N Yorks....205 F10
Interfield Worcs....98 B5

Intwood Norf 142 C3
Inver Aberds 292 D4
Highld 311 L2
Perth 286 C4
Inverailort Highld 295 G9
Inveraldie Angus 287 D8
Inveralivaig Highld 298 E4
Inveralligin Highld 299 D8
Inverallochy Aberds 303 C10
Inveran Highld 299 B8
Highld 309 K5
Inveraray Argyll 284 G4
Inverarish Highld 295 B7
Inverarity Angus 287 C8
Inverarnan Stirling 285 F7
Inverasdale Highld 307 L3
Inverawe Ho Argyll 284 D4
Inverbeg Argyll 276 B6
Inverbervie Aberds 293 F10
Inverboyndie Aberds 302 C6
Inverbroom Highld 307 L6
Invercarron Mains
Highld 309 K5
Invercassley Highld 309 J4
Invercauld House
Aberds 292 D3
Inverchaolain Argyll 275 F11
Invercharnan Highld 284 C5
Inverchoran Highld 300 D2
Invercreran Argyll 284 C4
Inverdruie Highld 291 B11
Inverebrie Aberds 303 F9
Invereck Argyll 276 E2
Inverernan Ho Aberds 292 B5
Invereshie House
Highld 291 C10
Inveresk E Loth 280 G6
Inverey Aberds 292 E2
Inverfarigaig Highld 300 G5
Invergarry Highld 290 C5
Invergelder Aberds 292 D4
Invergeldie Perth 285 E11
Invergordon Highld 301 C7
Invergowrie Perth 287 D7
Inverguseran Highld 295 E9
Inverhadden Perth 285 B10
Inverhaggernie Stirling 285 E7
Inverharroch Moray 302 F3
Inverherive Stirling 285 E7
Inverie Highld 295 F9
Inverinan Argyll 275 B10
Inverinate Highld 295 C11
Inverkeilor Angus 287 C10
Inverkeithing Fife 280 E2
Inverkeithny Aberds 302 E6
Inverkip Invclyd 276 G4
Inverkirkaig Highld 307 H5
Inverlael Highld 307 L6
Inverleith Edin 280 F4
Inverliever Lodge Argyll 275 C9
Inverliver Argyll 284 D4
Inverlochlarig Stirling 285 F8
Inverlochy Argyll 284 E5
Highld 290 F3
Moray 301 G11
Inverlounin Argyll 276 B4
Inverlussa Argyll 275 E7
Inver Mallie Highld 290 E3
Invermark Lodge Angus 292 E6
Invermoidart Highld 289 B8
Invermoriston Highld 290 B6
Invernaver Highld 308 C7
Inverneill Argyll 275 E9
Inverness Highld 300 E6
Invernettie Aberds 303 E11
Invernoaden Argyll 276 B2
Inveronich Argyll 284 G6
Inveroran Hotel Argyll 284 C6
Inverpolly Lodge Highld 307 H5
Inverquharity Angus 287 B8
Inverquhomery Aberds 303 E10
Inverroy Highld 290 E4
Inversanda Highld 289 D11
Invershiel Highld 295 D11
Invershin Highld 309 K5
Invershore Highld 310 F6
Inversnaid Hotel Stirling 285 G7
Invertrossachs Stirling 285 G9
Inverugie Aberds 303 E11
Inveruglas Argyll 285 G7
Inveruglass Highld 291 C10
Inverurie Aberds 303 G7
Invervar Perth 285 C10
Inverythan Aberds 303 E7
Inwardleigh Devon 13 B7
Inwood Shrops 131 D9
Inworth Essex 88 B5
Iochdar W Isles 297 G3
Iping W Sus 34 C5
Ipplepen Devon 8 B6
Ipsden Oxon 64 B6
Ipsley Worcs 117 D11
Ipstones Staffs 169 F8
Ipswich Suff 108 C3
Irby Mers 182 E3
Irby in the Marsh Lincs 175 C7
Irby upon Humber
NE Lincs 201 G7
Irchester Northants 121 D8
Ireby Cumb 229 D10
Lancs 212 D3
Ireland C Beds 104 C2
Orkney 314 F3
Shetland 313 L5
Wilts 45 C10
Ireland's Cross Shrops 168 G2
Ireland Wood W Yorks 205 F11
Ireleth Cumb 210 D4
Ireshopeburn Durham 232 D3
Ireton Wood Derbys 170 F3
Irlam Gtr Man 184 C2
Irlams o' th' Height
Gtr Man 195 G9
Irnham Lincs 155 D10
Iron Acton S Glos 61 C7
Ironbridge Telford 132 C3
Iron Bridge Cambs 139 D9
Iron Cross Warks 117 G11
Irongray Dumfries 237 B11
Iron Lo Highld 299 G10
Ironmacannie Dumfries 237 B8
Irons Bottom Sur 51 D9
Ironside Aberds 303 D8
Ironville Derbys 170 E6
Irstead Norf 161 E7
Irstead Street Norf 161 F7
Irthington Cumb 239 E11
Irthlingborough
Northants 121 C8
Irton N Yorks 217 C10
Irvine N Ayrs 257 B8
Irwell Vale Lancs 195 C9
Isabella Pit Northumb 253 G8
Isallt Bach Anglesey 178 F3
Isauld Highld 310 C3
Isbister Orkney 314 D2
Orkney 314 E3
Shetland 312 D5
Shetland 313 G7
Isel Cumb 229 E9
Isfield E Sus 36 D6
Isham Northants 121 C7
Ishriff Argyll 289 F8
Isington Hants 49 E9
Island Carr N Lincs 200 F3
Islands Common Cambs 122 E3
Islay Ho Argyll 274 G4
Isle Abbotts Som 28 C5
Isle Brewers Som 28 C5
Isleham Cambs 124 C2
Isle of Axholme N Lincs 199 F9
Isle of Dogs London 67 D11
Isle of Man Dumfries 238 B2
Isle of Whithorn
Dumfries 236 F6
Isleornsay Highld 295 D9
Islesburgh Shetland 312 G5
Islesteps Dumfries 237 B11
Isleworth London 67 D7
Isley Walton Leics 153 D8
Islibhig W Isles 304 F1
Islington London 67 C10
Telford 150 E4
Islip Northants 121 B9
Oxon 83 C8
Isombridge Telford 150 G2
Istead Rise Kent 68 F6
Isycoed Wrex 166 E6
Itchen Soton 32 E6
Itchen Abbas Hants 48 G4
Itchen Stoke Hants 48 G5
Itchingfield W Sus 35 B10
Itchington S Glos 61 B7
Itteringham Norf 160 C2
Itteringham Common
Norf 160 D3
Itton Devon 13 B9
Mon 79 F7
Itton Common Mon 79 F7
Ivegill Cumb 230 C4
Ivelet N Yorks 223 F8
Iver Bucks 66 C4
Iver Heath Bucks 66 C4
Iverley Staffs 133 G7
Iveston Durham 242 G4
Ivinghoe Bucks 84 B6
Ivinghoe Aston Bucks 85 B7
Ivington Hereford 115 F9
Ivington Green Hereford 115 F9
Ivybridge Devon 8 D2
Ivy Chimneys Essex 86 E6
Ivychurch Kent 39 B8
Ivy Cross Dorset 30 C5
Ivy Hatch Kent 52 C5
Ivy Todd Norf 141 B7
Iwade Kent 69 F11
Iwerne Courtney or Shroton
Dorset 30 E5
Iwerne Minster Dorset 30 E5
Ixworth Suff 125 C8
Ixworth Thorpe Suff 125 C8

J

Jackfield Telford 132 C3
Jack Green Lancs 194 B5
Jack Hayes Staffs 168 F6
Jack Hill N Yorks 205 C10
Jack in the Green Devon 14 B6
Jacksdale Notts 170 E6
Jack's Green Essex 105 G11
Glos 80 D5
Jack's Hatch Essex 86 D6
Jackson Bridge
W Yorks 197 F7
Jackstown Aberds 303 F7
Jacobstow Corn 11 B9
Jacobstowe Devon 25 G9
Jacobs Well Sur 50 C3
Jagger Green W Yorks 196 D5
Jameston Pembs 73 F9
Jamestown Dumfries 249 D8
Highld 300 D4
W Dunb 277 E7
Jamphlars Fife 280 B4
Janetstown Highld 310 C4
Janke's Green Essex 107 F8
Jarrow T&W 243 D8
Jarvis Brook E Sus 37 B8
Jasper's Green Essex 106 F4
Java Argyll 289 F9
Jawcraig Falk 278 F6
Jaw Hill W Yorks 197 C9
Jaywick Essex 89 C11
Jealott's Hill Brack 65 E11
Jeanfield Borders 271 G10
Jedburgh Borders 262 E5
Jedurgh Borders 262 F5
Jeffreyston Pembs 73 D9
Jellyhill E Dunb 278 G2
Jemimaville Highld 301 C7
Jennetts Hill W Berks 64 E5
Jennyfield N Yorks 205 B11
Jericho Gtr Man 195 E10
Jersey Farm Herts 85 D11
Jersey Marine Neath 57 C8
Jerviswood S Lanark 269 F7
Jesmond T&W 243 D7
Jevington E Sus 23 E9
Jewell's Cross Corn 24 G3
Jingle Street Mon 79 C7
Jockey End Herts 85 C8
Jodrell Bank Ches E 184 G3
Johnby Cumb 230 E4
John O'Gaunt Leics 136 B4
John O'Gaunts
W Yorks 197 B11
John o'Groats Highld 310 B7
John's Cross E Sus 38 C2
Johnshaven Aberds 293 G9
Johnson Fold Gtr Man 195 E7
Johnson's Hillock Lancs 194 C5
Johnson Street Norf 161 F7
Johnston Pembs 72 C6
Johnstone Renfs 267 C8
Johnstonebridge
Dumfries 248 E3
Johnstone Mains
Aberds 293 F9
Johnstown Carms 74 B6
Wrex 166 F4
Jolly's Bottom Corn 4 F5
Joppa Corn 2 B3
Edin 280 G6
S Ayrs 257 F10
Jordan Green Norf 159 E11
Jordanhill Glasgow 267 B10
Jordans Bucks 85 G7
Jordanston Pembs 91 E8
Jordanthorpe S Yorks 186 E5
Jordon S Yorks 186 C6
Joyford Glos 79 C9
Joy's Green Glos 79 B10
Jubilee Gtr Man 196 E2
Notts 170 E6
Jugbank Staffs 150 B5
Jump S Yorks 197 G11
Jumpers Common Dorset 19 C8
Jumpers Green Dorset 19 C8
Jumper's Town E Sus 52 G3
Junction N Yorks 204 D6
Juniper Northumb 241 F10
Juniper Green Edin 270 B3
Jurby East IoM 192 C4
Jurby West IoM 192 C4
Jurston Devon 13 E9
Jury's Gap E Sus 39 D7

K

Kaber Cumb 222 C5
Kaimend S Lanark 269 F9
Kaimes Edin 270 B5
Kaimrig End Borders 269 G11
Kalemouth Borders 262 D6
Kame Fife 287 G7
Kames Argyll 275 B9
Argyll 275 F10
E Ayrs 258 D5
Kates Hill W Mid 133 E9
Kea Corn 4 G6
Keadby N Lincs 199 E10
Keal Cotes Lincs 174 C5
Kearby Town End
N Yorks 206 D2
Kearnsey Kent 55 E9
Kearsley Gtr Man 195 F9
Kearstwick Cumb 212 C2
Kearton N Yorks 223 F9
Kearvaig Highld 306 B7
Keasden N Yorks 212 F4
Kebroyd W Yorks 196 C4
Keckwick Halton 183 E9
Keddington Lincs 190 D4
Keddington Corner
Lincs 190 D5
Kedington Suff 106 B4
Kedleston Derbys 170 G4
Kedslie Borders 271 G11
Keekle Cumb 219 B10
Keelars Tye Essex 107 G11
Keelby Lincs 201 E7
Keele Staffs 168 F4
Keeley Green Bedford 103 B10
Keelham W Yorks 205 G7
Keenley Northumb 241 F7
Keenthorne Som 43 F8
Keeres Green Essex 87 C9
Keeston Pembs 72 B6
Keevil Wilts 46 B2
Kegworth Leics 153 D9
Kehelland Corn 4 G2
Keig Aberds 293 B8
Keighley W Yorks 205 E7
Keil Highld 289 D11
Keilarsbrae Clack 279 C7
Keilhill Aberds 303 D7
Keillmore Argyll 275 E7
Keillor Perth 286 C6
Keillour Perth 286 E3
Keills Argyll 274 G5
Keils Argyll 274 G6
Keinton Mandeville Som 44 G4
Keir Mill Dumfries 247 E9
Keisby Lincs 155 D10
Keiss Highld 310 C7
Keistle Highld 298 D4
Keith Moray 302 D4
Keith Hall Aberds 303 G7
Keith Inch Aberds 303 E11
Keithock Angus 293 G8
Kelbrook Lancs 204 E4
Kelby Lincs 173 G8
Kelcliffe W Yorks 205 E9
Keld Cumb 221 C11
N Yorks 223 E7
Keldholme N Yorks 216 B4
Keld Houses N Yorks 214 G2
Kelfield N Lincs 199 G10
N Yorks 207 F7
Kelham Notts 172 D3
Kelhurn Argyll 276 F6
Kellacott Devon 12 D4
Kellamergh Lancs 194 B2
Kellan Argyll 289 E7
Kellas Angus 287 D8
Moray 301 D11
Kellaton Devon 9 G11
Kellaways Wilts 62 D3
Kelleth Cumb 222 D3
Kelleythorpe E Yorks 208 B5
E Yorks 208 B6
Kelling Norf 177 E9
Kellingley N Yorks 198 C4
Kellington N Yorks 198 C5
Kelloe Durham 234 D2
Kelloholm Dumfries 258 G6
Kells Cumb 219 B9
Kelly Corn 10 G6
Devon 12 E3
Kelly Bray Corn 12 G3
Kelmarsh Northants 120 B4
Kelmscott Oxon 82 F3
Kelsale Suff 127 D7
Kelsall Ches W 167 B8
Kelsall Hill Ches W 167 B8
Kelsay Argyll 254 B2
Kelshall Herts 104 D6
Kelsick Cumb 238 G5
Kelso Borders 262 C6
Kelstedge Derbys 170 C4
Kelstern Lincs 190 C3
Kelsterton Flint 182 G3
Kelston Bath 61 F8
Keltneyburn Perth 285 C11
Kelton Dumfries 237 B11
Durham 232 G4
Kelty Fife 280 C2
Keltybridge Fife 280 B2
Kelvedon Essex 88 B5
Kelvedon Hatch Essex 87 F9
Kelvin S Lanark 268 E2
Kelvindale Glasgow 267 B11
Kelvinside Glasgow 267 B11
Kelynack Corn 1 D3
Kemacott Devon 41 D7
Kemback Fife 287 F8
Kemberton Shrops 132 C4
Kemble Glos 81 F7
Kemble Wick Glos 81 F7
Kemerton Worcs 99 D8
Kemeys Commander
Mon 78 E4
Kemincham Ches E 168 B4
Kemnay Aberds 293 B9
Kempe's Corner Kent 54 D4
Kempie Highld 308 D4
Kempley Glos 98 F3
Kempley Green Glos 98 F3
Kempsey Worcs 99 B7
Kempsford Glos 81 F11
Kemps Green Warks 118 C2
Kempshott Hants 48 C6
Kempston Bedford 103 B10
Kempston Church End
Bedford 103 B10
Kempston Hardwick
Bedford 103 B10
Kempston West End
Bedford 103 B9
Kempton Shrops 131 G7
Kemp Town Brighton 36 G4
Kemsing Kent 52 B4
Kemsley Kent 70 F2
Kemsley Street Kent 69 G10
Kenardington Kent 54 G3
Kenchester Hereford 97 C8
Kencot Oxon 82 E3
Kendal Cumb 221 G10
Kendal End Worcs 117 C10
Kendleshire S Glos 61 D7
Kendon Caerph 77 F11
Kendoon Dumfries 246 F4
Kendray S Yorks 197 F11
Kenfig Bridgend 57 E10
Kenfig Hill Bridgend 57 E10
Kengharair Argyll 288 E6
Kenilworth Warks 118 C5
Kenknock Stirling 285 D8
Kenley London 51 B10
Shrops 131 C11
Kenmore Argyll 284 G4
Highld 299 D7
Perth 285 C11
Kenmure Dumfries 237 B8
Kenn Devon 14 D4
N Som 60 F2
Kennacley W Isles 305 J3
Kennacraig Argyll 275 G9
Kennards House Corn 11 E11
Kenneggy Corn 2 D3
Kenneggy Downs Corn 2 D3
Kennerleigh Devon 26 F4
Kennet Clack 279 C8
Kennet End Suff 124 D4
Kennethmont Aberds 302 G5
Kennett Cambs 124 D3
Kennford Devon 14 D4
Kenninghall Norf 141 F10
Kenninghall Heath
Norf 141 G10
Kennington Kent 54 E4
London 67 D10
Oxon 83 E8
Kenn Moor Gate N Som 60 F2
Kennoway Fife 287 G7
Kenny Som 28 D4
Kenny Hill Suff 124 B3
Kennythorpe N Yorks 216 F5
Kenovay Argyll 288 E1
Kensaleyre Highld 298 D4
Kensal Green London 67 C8
Kensal Rise London 67 C8
Kensal Town London 67 C8
Kensary Highld 310 E6
Kensington London 67 D9
Mers 182 C5
Kensworth C Beds 85 B8
Kentallen Highld 284 B4
Kentchurch Hereford 97 F8
Kentford Suff 124 D4
Kentisbeare Devon 27 F9
Kentisbury Devon 40 E6
Kentisbury Ford Devon 40 E6
Kentish Town London 67 C9
Kentmere Cumb 221 E9
Kenton Devon 14 E5
London 67 B7
Suff 126 D3
T&W 242 D6
Kenton Bankfoot T&W 242 D6
Kenton Bar T&W 242 D6
Kenton Corner Suff 126 D4
Kenton Green Glos 80 C3
Kentra Highld 289 C8
Kentrigg Cumb 221 G10
Kents Corn 11 B9
Kents Bank Cumb 211 D7
Kent's Green Glos 98 G4
Kents Hill M Keynes 103 D7
Kent's Oak Hants 32 C4
Kent Street E Sus 38 D3
Kent 53 C7
W Sus 36 C2
Kenwick Shrops 149 C8
Kenwick Park Shrops 149 D8
Kenwyn Corn 4 F6
Kenyon Warr 183 B10
Keoldale Highld 308 C3
Keonchulish Ho Highld 307 K6
Kepdowrie Stirling 277 C11
Kepnal Wilts 63 G7
Keppanach Highld 290 G2
Keppoch Highld 295 C11
Keprigan Argyll 255 F7
Kepwick N Yorks 225 G9
Kerchesters Borders 263 B7
Kerdiston Norf 159 E11
Keresforth Hill S Yorks 197 F10
Keresley W Mid 134 G6
Keresley Newlands
Warks 134 G6
Kerfield Borders 270 G5
Kerley Downs Corn 4 G5
Kernborough Devon 8 G5
Kerne Bridge Hereford 79 B9
Kernsary Highld 299 B8
Kerridge Ches E 184 F6
Kerridge-end Ches E 184 F6
Kerris Corn 1 D4
Kerry / Ceri Powys 130 F2
Kerrycroy Argyll 266 C2
Kerry Hill Staffs 168 F6
Kerrysdale Highld 299 B8
Kerry's Gate Hereford 97 E7
Kersal Gtr Man 195 G10
Kersall Notts 172 C2
Kersbrook Cross Corn 12 F2
Kerscott Devon 25 B10
Kersey Suff 107 C9
Kersey Tye Suff 107 C9
Kersey Upland Suff 107 C9
Kershopefoot Cumb 249 G11
Kersoe Worcs 99 D9
Kerswell Devon 27 F9
Kerswell Green Worcs 99 B7
Kerthen Wood Corn 2 C3
Kesgrave Suff 108 B4
Kessingland Suff 143 F10
Kessingland Beach
Suff 143 F10
Kessington E Dunb 277 G11
Kestle Corn 5 F9
Kestle Mill Corn 5 D7
Keston London 68 G2
Keston Mark London 68 F2
Keswick Cumb 229 G11
Norf 142 C4
Norf 161 C7
Kete Pembs 72 E4
Ketford Glos 98 E4
Ketley Telford 150 G3
Ketley Bank Telford 150 G3
Ketsby Lincs 190 F5
Kettering Northants 121 B7
Ketteringham Norf 142 C3
Kettins Perth 286 D6
Kettlebaston Suff 125 G9
Kettlebridge Fife 287 G7
Kettlebrook Staffs 134 C4
Kettleburgh Suff 126 E5
Kettle Corner Kent 53 C8
Kettle Green Herts 86 B6
Kettlehill Fife 287 G7
Kettleholm Dumfries 238 B4
Kettleness N Yorks 226 B6
Kettleshulme Ches E 185 F7
Kettleshume Ches E 185 F7
Kettlesing N Yorks 205 B10
Kettlesing Bottom
N Yorks 205 B10
Kettlesing Head
N Yorks 205 B10
Kettlestone Norf 159 C9
Kettlethorpe Lincs 188 F4
W Yorks 197 D10
Kettletoft Orkney 314 C6
Kettlewell N Yorks 213 E9
Ketton Rutland 137 C9
Kevingtown London 68 F3
Kew London 67 D7
Keward Som 44 E4
Kew Bridge London 67 D7
Kewstoke N Som 59 G10
Kexbrough S Yorks 197 F9
Kexby Lincs 188 D5
York 207 C10
Keybridge Corn 11 G7
Keycol Kent 69 G11
Keyford Som 45 D9
Key Green Ches E 168 C5
N Yorks 226 E6
Keyham Leics 136 B3
Keyhaven Hants 20 C2
Keyingham E Yorks 201 B8
Keymer W Sus 36 D4
Keynsham Bath 61 F7
Keysers Estate Essex 86 D5
Key's Green Kent 53 F7
Keysoe Bedford 121 E11
Keysoe Row Bedford 121 E11
Keyston Cambs 121 B10
Key Street Kent 69 G11
Keyworth Notts 154 C2
Khantore Aberds 292 D4
Kibbear Som 28 C2
Kibblesworth T&W 242 F6
Kibworth Beauchamp
Leics 136 E3
Kibworth Harcourt
Leics 136 E3
Kidbrooke London 68 D2
Kidburngill Cumb 229 G7
Kiddal Lane End
W Yorks 206 F4
Kiddemore Green Staffs 133 B7
Kidderminster Worcs 116 B6
Kiddington Oxon 101 G8
Kidd's Moor Norf 142 C2
Kidlington Oxon 83 C7
Kidmore End Oxon 65 D7
Kidnal Ches W 167 F7
Kidsdale Dumfries 236 F6
Kidsgrove Staffs 168 E4
Kidstones N Yorks 213 C9
Kidwelly / Cydweli
Carms 74 D6
Kiel Crofts Argyll 289 F11
Kielder Northumb 250 E4
Kierfiold Ho Orkney 314 E2
Kiff Green W Berks 64 F5
Kilbagie Fife 279 D8
Kilbarchan Renfs 267 C8
Kilbeg Highld 295 E8
Kilberry Argyll 275 G8
Kilbirnie N Ayrs 266 E6
Kilbowie W Dunb 277 G10
Kilbraur Highld 311 H2
Kilbride Argyll 254 C4
Argyll 275 D9
Argyll 289 G10
Argyll 289 G11
Highld 295 C7
Kilbridemore Argyll 275 D11
Kilbryde Castle Stirling 285 G11
Kilburn Angus 292 G5
Derbys 170 F5
London 67 C9
N Yorks 215 D10
Kilby Leics 136 D2
Kilby Bridge Leics 136 D2
Kilchamaig Argyll 275 G9
Kilchattan Argyll 274 D4
Kilchattan Bay Argyll 266 E2
Kilchenzie Argyll 255 E7
Kilcheran Argyll 289 F10
Kilchiaran Argyll 274 G3
Kilchoan Argyll 275 B8
Highld 288 C6
Kilchoman Argyll 274 G3
Kilchrenan Argyll 284 E4
Kilconquhar Fife 287 G8
Kilcot Glos 98 F3
Kilcoy Highld 300 D5
Kilcreggan Argyll 276 E4
Kildale N Yorks 226 D2
Kildalloig Argyll 255 F8
Kildary Highld 301 B7
Kildaton Ho Argyll 254 C5
Kildavanan Argyll 275 G11
Kildermorie Lodge
Highld 300 B5
Kildonan Dumfries 236 D2
Highld 298 D3
N Ayrs 256 E2
Kildonan Lodge Highld 311 G3
Kildonnan Highld 294 G6
Kildrum N Lanark 278 F5
Kildrummy Aberds 292 B6
Kildwick N Yorks 204 D6
Kilfinan Argyll 275 F10
Kilfinnan Highld 290 D4
Kilgetty Pembs 73 D10
Kilgour Fife 286 G6
Kilgrammie S Ayrs 245 C7
Kilgwrrwg Common Mon 79 F7
Kilhallon Corn 5 E11
Kilham E Yorks 217 G11
Northumb 263 C9
Kilkeddan Argyll 255 E8
Kilkenneth Argyll 288 E1
Kilkenny Glos 81 B8
Kilkerran Argyll 255 F8
Kilkhampton Corn 24 E3
Killamarsh Derbys 187 E7
Killaworgey Corn 5 C8
Killay Swansea 56 C6
Killbeg Argyll 289 E8
Killean Argyll 255 C7
Killearn Stirling 277 D10
Killegruer Argyll 255 D7
Killen Highld 300 D6
Killerby Darl 224 B3
Killichonan Perth 285 B9
Killiechoinich Argyll 289 G10
Killiechonate Highld 290 E4
Killiechronan Argyll 289 E7
Killiecrankie Perth 291 G11
Killiemor Argyll 288 F6
Killiemore House Argyll 288 G6
Killilan Highld 295 B11
Killimster Highld 310 D7
Killin Stirling 285 D9
Killinallan Argyll 274 F4
Killingbeck W Yorks 206 G2
Killinghall N Yorks 205 B11
Killington Cumb 212 B2
Devon 41 D7
Killingworth T&W 243 C7
Killingworth Moor T&W 243 C7
Killingworth Village
T&W 243 C7
Killin Lodge Highld 291 C7
Killivose Corn 2 B4
Killmahumaig Argyll 275 D8
Killochyett Borders 271 F9
Killocraw Argyll 255 D7
Killundine Highld 289 E7
Killylung Dumfries 247 G11
Kilmacolm Invclyd 267 B7
Kilmaha Argyll 275 C10
Kilmahog Stirling 285 G10
Kilmalieu Highld 289 D10
Kilmaluag Highld 298 B4
Kilmany Fife 287 E7
Kilmarie Highld 295 D7
Kilmarnock E Ayrs 257 B10
Kilmaron Castle Fife 287 F7
Kilmartin Argyll 275 D9
Kilmaurs E Ayrs 267 G8
Kilmelford Argyll 275 B9
Kilmeny Argyll 274 G4
Kilmersdon Som 45 C7
Kilmeston Hants 33 B9
Kilmichael Argyll 255 E7
Argyll 275 F10
Kilmichael Glassary
Argyll 275 D9
Kilmichael of Inverlussa
Argyll 275 E8
Kilmington Devon 15 B11
Wilts 45 F9
Kilmington Common
Wilts 45 F9
Kilmoluaig Argyll 288 E1
Kilmonivaig Highld 290 E3
Kilmorack Highld 300 E4
Kilmore Argyll 289 G10
Highld 295 E8
Kilmory Argyll 275 F8
Highld 289 B7
Highld 294 E5
N Ayrs 255 E10
Kilmory Lodge Argyll 275 C8
Kilmote Highld 311 H3
Kilmuir Highld 298 B3
Highld 298 E2
Highld 300 E6
Highld 301 B7
Kilmun Argyll 275 B10
Argyll 276 E3
Kilnave Argyll 274 F3
Kilncadzow S Lanark 269 F7
Kilndown Kent 53 G8
Kiln Green Hereford 79 B10
Wokingham 65 D10
Kilnhill Cumb 229 E10
Kilnhurst S Yorks 187 B7
Kilninian Argyll 288 E5
Kilninver Argyll 289 G10
Kiln Pit Hill Northumb 242 G2
Kilnsea E Yorks 201 D12
Kilnsey N Yorks 213 F9
Kilnwick E Yorks 208 D5
Kilnwick Percy E Yorks 208 C2
Kilnwood Vale W Sus 51 G8
Kiloran Argyll 274 D4
Kilpatrick N Ayrs 255 E10
Kilpeck Hereford 97 E8
Kilphedir Highld 311 H3
Kilpin E Yorks 199 B9
Kilpin Pike E Yorks 199 B9
Kilrenny Fife 287 G9
Kilsby Northants 119 C11
Kilspindie Perth 286 E6
Kilsyth N Lanark 278 F4
Kiltarlity Highld 300 E5
Kilton Notts 187 F9
Redcar 226 B4
Som 43 E7
Kilton Thorpe Redcar 226 B3
Kiltyrie Perth 285 D10
Kilvaxter Highld 298 C3
Kilve Som 43 E7
Kilvington Notts 172 G3
Kilwinning N Ayrs 266 G6
Kimberley Norf 141 C11
Notts 171 G8
Kimberworth S Yorks 186 C6
Kimberworth Park
S Yorks 186 C6
Kimblesworth Durham 233 B11
Kimble Wick Bucks 84 D4
Kimbolton Cambs 121 D11
Hereford 115 E10
Kimbridge Hants 32 B4
Kimcote Leics 135 F11
Kimmeridge Dorset 18 F4
Kimmerston Northumb 263 B11
Kimpton Hants 47 D9
Herts 85 B11
Kimworthy Devon 24 E4
Kinabus Argyll 254 C3
Kinbeachie Highld 300 C6
Kinbrace Highld 310 F2
Kinbuck Stirling 285 G11
Kincaidston S Ayrs 257 F9
Kincaple Fife 287 F8
Kincardine Fife 279 D8
Highld 309 L6
Kincardine Bridge Falk 279 D8
Kincardine O'Neil
Aberds 293 D7
Kinclaven Perth 286 D5
Kincorth Aberdeen 293 C11
Kincorth Ho Moray 301 C10
Kincraig Highld 291 C10
Kincraigie Perth 286 C3
Kindallachan Perth 286 C3
Kine Moor S Yorks 197 G9
Kineton Glos 99 F11
Warks 118 G6
Kineton Green W Mid 134 G2
Kinfauns Perth 286 E5
Kingairloch Highld 289 D10
Kingarth Argyll 255 B11
Kingates IoW 20 F6
Kingbeare Corn 11 G11
Kingcoed Mon 78 D6
Kingdown N Som 60 G4
King Edward Aberds 303 D7
Kingerby Lincs 189 C9
Kingfield Sur 50 B4
Kingford Devon 24 F3
Devon 25 D10
Kingham Oxon 100 G5
Kinghay Wilts 30 B5
Kingholm Quay
Dumfries 237 B11
Kinghorn Fife 280 D5
Kingie Highld 290 C3
Kinglassie Fife 280 B4
Kingledores Borders 260 D4
Kingoodie Perth 287 E7
King's Acre Hereford 97 C9
Kingsand Corn 7 E8
Kingsash Bucks 84 D5
Kingsbarns Fife 287 F9
Kingsbridge Devon 8 G4
Som 42 F3
King's Bromley Staffs 152 F2
Kingsburgh Highld 298 D3
Kingsbury London 67 B8
Warks 134 D4
Kingsbury Episcopi Som 28 C6
Kingsbury Regis Som 29 D11
King's Caple Hereford 97 F11
Kingscauseway Highld 301 B7
Kingscavil W Loth 279 F10
Kingsclere Hants 48 B4
Kingsclere Woodlands
Hants 64 G4
King's Cliffe Northants 137 D10
Kings Clipstone Notts 171 C10
Kingscote Glos 80 F4
Kingscott Devon 25 D8
King's Coughton Warks 117 F11
Kingscourt Glos 80 E4
Kingscross N Ayrs 256 D2
Kingsditch Glos 99 G8
Kingsdon Som 29 B8
Kingsdown Kent 54 B2
Kent 55 D11
Swindon 63 B7
Wilts 61 F10
King's Dyke Cambs 138 D4
Kingseat Fife 280 C2
Kingseathill Fife 280 D2
King's End Worcs 116 G6
Kingsett Devon 12 E6
Kingsey Bucks 84 D2
Kingsfield Hereford 97 B10
Kingsfold Lancs 194 B4
W Sus 51 F7
Kingsford Aberds 293 B7
E Ayrs 267 F8
Worcs 132 G6
Kingsforth N Lincs 200 D4
King's Furlong Hants 48 C6
Kingsgate Kent 71 E11
King's Green Glos 98 E5
Worcs 116 E5
Kingshall Green Suff 125 E8
Kingshall Street Suff 125 E8
Kingsheanton Devon 40 F5
King's Heath Northants 120 E4
W Mid 133 G11
Kings Hedges Cambs 123 E9
Kingshill Glos 80 F3
Swindon 62 C6
Kings Hill Glos 81 E8
King's Hill Kent 53 C7
W Mid 133 D9
Kingsholm Glos 80 B4
Kingshouse Hotel
Highld 284 B6
Kingshurst W Mid 134 F3
Kingside Hill Cumb 238 G5
Kingskerswell Devon 9 B7
Kingskettle Fife 287 G7
Kingsknowe Edin 280 G4
Kingsland Anglesey 178 E2
Hereford 115 E8
London 67 C10
Shrops 149 G9
Kings Langley Herts 85 E9
Kingsley Ches W 183 G9
Hants 49 F9
Staffs 169 F8
Kingsley Green W Sus 49 G11
Kingsley Holt Staffs 169 F8
Kingsley Moor Staffs 169 F7
Kingsley Park Northants 120 E5
Kingslow Shrops 132 D5
King's Lynn Norf 158 E2
King's Meaburn Cumb 231 G8
Kingsmead Hants 33 E9
Kingsmere Oxon 101 G11
King's Mills Derbys 153 D8
Wrex 166 F4
Kingsmoor Essex 86 D6
Kings Moss Mers 194 G4
Kingsmuir Angus 287 C8
Fife 287 G9
Kings Muir Borders 261 B7
King's Newnham Warks 119 B9
King's Newton Derbys 153 D7
Kingsnordley Shrops 132 F5
Kingsnorth Kent 54 F4
King's Norton Leics 136 C3
W Mid 117 B11
King's Nympton Devon 25 D11
King's Pyon Hereford 115 G8
Kings Ripton Cambs 122 B5
King's Somborne Hants 47 G11
King's Stag Dorset 30 E2
King's Stanley Glos 80 E4
King's Sutton Northants 101 D9
King's Tamerton Plym 7 D9
Kingstanding W Mid 133 E11
Kingsteignton Devon 14 G3
Kingsteps Highld 301 D9
King Sterndale Derbys 185 G9
King's Thorn Hereford 97 E10
Kingsthorpe Northants 120 E5
Kingsthorpe Hollow
Northants 120 E5
Kingston Cambs 122 F6
Devon 8 F2
Devon 9 E8
Dorset 18 F5
Dorset 30 F3
E Loth 281 E10
Gtr Man 184 B6
Hants 31 G11
IoW 20 E5
Kent 55 C7
M Keynes 103 D8
Moray 302 C3
Ptsmth 33 G11
Suff 108 B5
Kingston Bagpuize Oxon 82 F6
Kingston Blount Oxon 84 F2
Kingston by Sea W Sus 36 G2
Kingston Deverill Wilts 45 F10
Kingstone Hereford 97 D8
Hereford 98 F2
Som 28 E5
Staffs 151 D11
S Yorks 197 F10
Kingstone Winslow Oxon 63 B9
Kingston Gorse W Sus 35 G9
Kingston Lisle Oxon 63 B10
Kingston Maurward
Dorset 17 C10
Kingston near Lewes
E Sus 36 F5
Kingston on Soar
Notts 153 D10
Kingston Park T&W 242 D6
Kingston Russell Dorset 17 C7
Kingston St Mary Som 28 B2
Kingston Seymour
N Som 60 F2
Kingston Stert Oxon 84 E2
Kingston upon Hull Hull 200 B5
Kingston upon Thames
London 67 F7
Kingston Vale London 67 E8
Kingstown Cumb 239 F9
King Street Essex 87 E9
King's Walden Herts 104 G3
Kingsway Bath 61 G8
Halton 183 D8
Kingswear Devon 9 E7
Kingswells Aberdeen 293 C10
Kingswinford W Mid 133 F7
Kingswood Bucks 83 B11
Essex 69 B8
Glos 80 G2
Hereford 114 G5
Herts 85 E10
Kent 53 C10
Powys 130 C4
S Glos 60 E6
Som 42 F6
Sur 51 B8
Warks 118 C3
Warr 183 C9
Kingswood Brook
Warks 118 C3
Kingswood Common
Staffs 132 C6
Worcs 116 D4
Kings Worthy Hants 48 G3
Kingthorpe Lincs 189 F10
Kington Hereford 114 F5
S Glos 79 G10
Worcs 117 F9
Kington Langley Wilts 62 D2
Kington Magna Dorset 30 C3
Kington St Michael Wilts 62 D2
Kingussie Highld 291 C9
Kingweston Som 44 G4
Kinhrive Highld 301 B7
Kininvie Ho Moray 302 E3
Kinkell Bridge Perth 286 F3
Kinknockie Aberds 303 E10
Aberds 303 G9
Kinkry Hill Cumb 240 B2
Kinlet Shrops 132 G4
Kinloch Fife 286 F6
Highld 289 D8
Highld 294 F5
Highld 295 D8
Highld 308 F3
Perth 286 C5
Perth 286 C6
Kinlochan Highld 289 C10
Kinlochard Stirling 285 G8
Kinlochbeoraid Highld 295 G10
Kinlochbervie Highld 306 D7
Kinloch Damph Highld 299 E8
Kinlocheil Highld 289 B11
Kinlochewe Highld 299 C10
Kinloch Hourn Highld 295 E11
Kinloch Laggan Highld 291 E7
Kinlochleven Highld 290 G3
Kinloch Lodge Highld 308 D5
Kinlochmoidart Highld 289 B9
Kinlochmorar Highld 295 F10
Kinlochmore Highld 290 G3
Kinloch Rannoch Perth 285 B10
Kinlochspelve Argyll 289 G8
Kinloid Highld 295 G8
Kinloss Moray 301 C10
Kinmel Bay / Bae Cinmel
Conwy 181 E7
Kinmuck Aberds 293 B10
Kinmundy Aberds 293 B10
Kinnadie Aberds 303 E9
Kinnaird Perth 286 B3
Perth 286 E6
Kinnaird Castle Angus 287 B10
Kinnauld Highld 309 J7
Kinneff Aberds 293 F10
Kinneil Falk 279 E9
Kinnelhead Dumfries 248 C2
Kinnell Angus 287 B10
Kinnerley Shrops 148 E6
Kinnersley Hereford 96 B6
Worcs 99 C7
Kinnerton Powys 114 E4
Kinnerton Green Flint 166 C4
Kinnesswood Perth 286 G5
Kinninvie Durham 233 G7
Kinnordy Angus 287 B7
Kinoulton Notts 154 C3
Kinross Perth 286 G5
Kinrossie Perth 286 D5
Kinsbourne Green Herts 85 B10
Kinsey Heath Ches E 167 G11
Kinsham Hereford 115 E7
Worcs 99 D8
Kinsley W Yorks 198 E2
Kinson Bmouth 19 B7
Kintallan Argyll 275 E8
Kintbury W Berks 63 F11
Kintessack Moray 301 C9
Kintillo Perth 286 F5
Kintocher Aberds 293 C7
Kinton Hereford 115 C8
Shrops 149 F7
Kintore Aberds 293 B9
Kintour Argyll 254 B5
Kintra Argyll 254 C4
Argyll 288 G5
Kintradwell Highld 311 J3
Kintraw Argyll 275 C9
Kinuachdrachd Argyll 275 D8
Kinveachy Highld 291 B11
Kinver Staffs 132 G6
Kinwalsey Warks 134 F5
Kip Hill Durham 242 G6
Kiplin N Yorks 224 F5
Kippax W Yorks 206 G4
Kippen Stirling 278 C3
Kippford or Scaur
Dumfries 237 D10
Kippilaw Borders 262 D2
Kippilaw Mains Borders 262 D2
Kipping's Cross Kent 52 F6
Kippington Kent 52 C4
Kirbister Orkney 314 D6
Orkney 314 E2
Orkney 314 F3
Kirbuster Orkney 314 D2
Kirby Bedon Norf 142 B5
Kirby Bellars Leics 154 F4
Kirby Cane Norf 143 E7
Kirby Corner W Mid 118 B5
Kirby Cross Essex 108 G4
Kirby Fields Leics 135 C10
Kirby Green Norf 143 E7
Kirby Grindalythe
N Yorks 217 F8
Kirby Hill N Yorks 215 F7
N Yorks 224 D2
Kirby Knowle N Yorks 215 B9
Kirby-le-Soken Essex 108 G4
Kirby Misperton
N Yorks 216 D5
Kirby Moor Cumb 240 E2

Kirby Muxloe Leics. 135 C10
Kirby Row Norf 143 E7
Kirby Sigston N Yorks . . 225 G8
Kirby Underdale
 E Yorks 208 B2
Kirby Wiske N Yorks . . 215 C7
Kirdford W Sus 35 B8
Kirk Highld. 310 D6
Kirkabister Shetland . 312 G6
 Shetland 313 K6
Kirkandrews N Yorks . 237 E8
Kirkandrews-on-Eden
 Cumb. 239 F9
Kirkapol Argyll. 288 E2
Kirkbampton Cumb. . . 239 F8
Kirkbean Dumfries . . . 237 D11
Kirkborough Cumb . . . 229 D7
Kirkbrae Angus 314 B4
Kirk Bramwith S Yorks . 198 E6
Kirkbride Cumb. 238 F6
Kirkbuddo Angus 287 C9
Kirkburn Borders 261 B7
 E Yorks 208 B5
Kirkburton W Yorks . . 197 E7
Kirkby Lincs 189 C9
 Mers 182 B6
 N Yorks. 225 D10
Kirkby Fenside Lincs . 174 C4
Kirkby Fleetham
 N Yorks 224 G5
Kirkby Green Lincs . . . 173 F10
Kirkby Hill N Yorks . . . 213 B7
 N Yorks 214 B5
Kirkby in Ashfield Notts 171 D8
Kirkby-in-Furness
 Cumb. 210 C4
Kirkby la Thorpe Lincs 173 F10
Kirkby Lonsdale Cumb . 212 D2
Kirkby Malham N Yorks 213 G2
Kirkby Mallory Leics . 135 C9
Kirkby Malzeard
 N Yorks 214 E4
Kirkby Mills N Yorks . . 216 B4
Kirkbymoorside
 N Yorks 216 B3
Kirkby on Bain Lincs . 174 C2
Kirkby Overblow
 N Yorks 206 D2
Kirkby Stephen Cumb . 222 D5
Kirkby Thore Cumb . . 231 F8
Kirkby Underwood
 Lincs 155 D11
Kirkby Wharfe N Yorks . 206 E6
Kirkby Woodhouse
 Notts. 171 E7
Kirkcaldy Fife 280 C5
Kirkcambeck Cumb . . 240 D2
Kirkcarswell Dumfries 237 E9
Kirkcolm Dumfries . . . 236 C1
Kirkconnel Dumfries . 258 G6
Kirkconnell Dumfries . 237 C11
Kirkcowan Dumfries . 236 C5
Kirkcudbright Dumfries 237 D8
Kirkdale Mers 182 C4
Kirk Deighton N Yorks . 206 C3
Kirk Ella E Yorks 200 B4
Kirkfieldbank S Lanark . 269 G7
Kirkforthar Feus Fife . 286 G6
Kirkgunzeon Dumfries 237 C10
Kirk Hallam Derbys . . 171 E7
Kirkham Lancs 202 G4
 N Yorks 216 F4
Kirkhamgate W Yorks . 197 C9
Kirk Hammerton
 N Yorks 206 B5
Kirkhams Gtr Man . . . 195 F10
Kirkharle Northumb . . 252 F3
Kirkheaton Northumb . 242 B2
 W Yorks 197 D7
Kirkhill Angus 293 G8
 E Renf. 267 D11
 Highld. 300 E5
 Midloth 270 C4
 Moray 302 F2
 W Loth 279 G11
Kirkholt Gtr Man 195 E11
Kirkhope Borders 261 E9
Kirkhouse Borders . . . 261 C8
 Cumb 240 F3
Kirkiboll Highld. 308 D5
Kirkibost Highld 295 D7
Kirkinch Angus 287 C7
Kirkinner Dumfries . . 236 D6
Kirkintilloch E Dunb . . 278 G3
Kirk Ireton Derbys . . . 170 E3
Kirkland Cumb. 219 B11
 Cumb 229 B11
 Cumb 231 E8
 Dumfries 247 E8
 Dumfries 258 C6
 S Ayrs. 244 E6
Kirkland Guards Cumb 229 C9
Kirk Langley Derbys . 152 B5
Kirkleatham Redcar . . 235 G7
Kirklees Gtr Man 195 E9
Kirklevington Stockton 225 D8
Kirkley Suff. 143 E10
Kirklington Notts 171 D11
 N Yorks 214 C6
Kirklinton Cumb 239 D10
Kirkliston Edin. 280 G2
Kirkmaiden Dumfries . 236 F3
Kirk Merrington
 Durham 233 E11
Kirkmichael Perth . . . 286 B4
 S Ayrs. 245 B8
Kirk Michael IoM 192 C4
Kirkmichael Mains
 Dumfries 248 F2
Kirkmuirhill S Lanark . 268 G5
Kirknewton Northumb. 263 C10
 W Loth 270 B2
Kirkney Aberds 302 F5
Kirk of Shotts N Lanark 268 C6
Kirkoswald Cumb 231 C7
 S Ayrs 244 B6
Kirkpatrick Durham
 Dumfries 247 E10
Kirkpatrick Durham
 Dumfries 237 B9
Kirkpatrick-Fleming
 Dumfries 239 C7
Kirk Sandall S Yorks . 198 F6
Kirksanton Cumb 210 C2
Kirkshaw N Lanark . . . 268 C4
Kirk Smeaton N Yorks . 198 D4
Kirkstall W Yorks. 205 F11
Kirkstead Borders . . . 261 E7
 Lincs 173 C11
Kirkstile Aberds 302 F5
Kirkstyle Highld. 310 B7
Kirkthorpe W Yorks . . 197 C11
Kirkton Aberds 302 G6
 Aberds 286 C8
 Angus 287 C8
 Angus 287 D8
 Argyll 275 C8
 Borders 262 G2
 Dumfries 247 G11
 Fife 280 D4
 Fife 287 F11

Kirkton continued
 Highld. 295 C10
 Highld 299 E9
 Highld 301 D7
 Highld 309 K7
 Perth 286 F5
 S Lanark 259 G11
 Stirling 285 G9
 W Dunb 277 E8
Kirktonhill Borders . . 271 E9
 W Dunb 277 F6
Kirkton Manor Borders. 260 B6
Kirkton of Airlie Angus. 287 B7
Kirkton of Auchterhouse
 Angus. 287 D7
Kirkton of Auchterless
 Aberds 303 E7
Kirkton of Barevan
 Highld. 301 E8
Kirkton of Bourtie
 Aberds 303 G8
Kirkton of Collace
 Perth. 286 D5
Kirkton of Craig Angus . 287 B11
Kirkton of Culsalmond
 Aberds 302 F6
Kirkton of Durris
 Aberds 293 D9
Kirkton of Glenbuchat
 Aberds 292 B5
Kirkton of Glenisla
 Angus 292 G4
Kirkton of Kingoldrum
 Angus 287 B7
Kirkton of Largo Fife . 287 G8
Kirkton of Lethendy
 Perth. 286 C5
Kirkton of Logie Buchan
 Aberds 303 G9
Kirkton of Maryculter
 Aberds 293 D10
Kirkton of Menmuir
 Angus 293 G7
Kirkton of Monikie
 Angus 287 D9
Kirkton of Oyne Aberds . 302 G6
Kirkton of Rayne
 Aberds 302 G6
Kirkton of Skene
 Aberds 293 C10
Kirkton of Tough
 Aberds 293 B8
Kirktoun E Ayrs 267 G8
Kirktown Aberds. 303 D10
Kirktown of Alvah
 Aberds 302 C6
Kirktown of Deskford
 Moray 302 C5
Kirktown of Fetteresso
 Aberds 293 E10
Kirktown of Mortlach
 Aberds 302 F3
Kirktown of Slains
 Aberds 303 G10
Kirkurd Borders 270 G2
Kirkwall Orkney. 314 E4
Kirkwhelpington
 Northumb 251 G11
Kirkwood Dumfries . . 238 B4
 N Lanark 268 C4
Kirk Yetholm Borders . 263 D8
Kirmington N Lincs . . . 200 E6
Kirmond le Mire Lincs . 189 C11
Kirn Argyll. 276 F3
Kirriemuir Angus 287 B7
Kirstead Green Norf . 142 D5
Kirtlebridge Dumfries . 238 C5
Kirtleton Dumfries . . 249 G7
Kirtling Cambs 124 F3
Kirtling Green Cambs . 124 F3
Kirtlington Oxon. 83 B7
Kirtomy Highld. 308 C7
Kirton Lincs 156 B6
 Notts 171 B11
 Suff. 108 D5
Kirton Campus W Loth . 269 B10
Kirton End Lincs 174 G3
Kirton Holme Lincs . . 174 G3
Kirton in Lindsey
 N Lincs. 188 B6
Kiskin Highld. 210 B1
Kislingbury Northants . 120 F3
Kitbridge Devon 28 F4
Kitchenroyd W Yorks . 197 F8
Kitebrook Warks 100 E4
Knotting Green
 Bedford. 121 E10
Knottingley W Yorks . 198 C4
Knott Lanes Gtr Man . 196 G2
Knott Oak Som 28 E5
Knotts Cumb. 230 G4
 Lancs 203 C11
Knotty Ash Mers 182 C6
Knotty Corner Devon . 24 B6
Knotty Green Bucks . . 84 G6
Knowbury Shrops . . . 115 C11
Knowe Dumfries 236 B5
 Shetland 313 G5
Knowefield Cumb . . . 239 F10
Knowehead Aberds . . 293 C7
 Aberds 302 D5
 Dumfries 246 E4
 E Loth 282 F2
Knowes E Loth 282 F2
Knowesgate Northumb. 251 F11
Knowes of Elrick
 Aberds 302 D6
Knoweton N Lanark . . 268 D5
Knowetop N Lanark . . 268 D5
Knowhead Aberds . . . 303 D9
 Aberds 302 C5
Knowl Bank Staffs . . . 168 F3
Knowle Bristol. 60 E6
 Devon 15 E7
 Devon 26 G3
 Devon 27 F8
 Devon 40 F3
 Hants 33 F9
 Shrops 115 C11
 Som 43 F10
 Wilts 31 B8
Knowle Fields Worcs . 117 F10
Knowlegate Shrops . . 115 C11
Knowle Green Lancs . 203 F8
 Sur. 66 E4
Knowle Grove W Mid . 118 B3
Knowle Hill Sur. 66 F4
Knowle Park W Yorks . 205 E7
Knowlesands Shrops . 132 E4
Knowle St Giles Som . 28 E4
Knowles Hill Devon . . 14 G3
Knowl Green Essex . . 106 C5
Knowl Hill Windsor . . 65 D10
Knowlton Dorset 31 E8
 Kent. 55 C9
Knowl Wall Staffs . . . 151 B7
Knowl Wood W Yorks . 196 C2
Knowsley Mers 182 B6
Knowstone Devon . . . 26 C4
Knox Bridge Kent . . . 53 E9
Knucklas Powys 114 C5
Knuston Northants . . 121 D8
Knutsford Ches E 184 F3
Knutton Staffs 168 F4
Knuzden Brook Lancs . 195 B8
Knypersley Staffs . . . 168 D5
Kraiknish Highld. 294 C5
Krumlin W Yorks 196 D5
Kuggar Corn. 2 F6
Kyleakin Highld. 295 C9
Kyle of Lochalsh Highld . 295 C9
Kylepark N Lanark . . . 268 C3
Kylerhea Highld. 295 C9
Kylesknoydart Highld . 295 F10
Kylesku Highld. 306 F7
Kylesmorar Highld . . . 295 F10
Kylestrome Highld . . . 306 F7
Kyllachy House Highld . 301 G7
Kymin Hereford 97 B11
 Mon 79 C8
Kynaston Hereford . . 97 F11
 Shrops 149 E7
Kynnersley Telford . . 150 F3
Kyre Worcs 116 E2
Kyre Green Worcs . . . 116 E2
Kyre Magna Worcs . . . 116 E2
Kyre Park Worcs 116 E2
Kyrewood Worcs. 116 D2

L

Labost W Isles 304 D4
Lacasaidh W Isles . . . 304 F5
Lacasdal W Isles. 304 E6
Laceby NE Lincs 201 F8
Laceby Acres NE Lincs . 201 F8
Lacey Green Bucks . . . 84 F4
Lach Dennis Ches W . . 184 G2
Lache Ches W 166 C5
Lackenby Redcar 225 B11
Lackford Suff. 124 C5
Lacock Wilts 62 F2
Ladbroke Warks 119 F8
Laddenvean Corn. . . . 2 G3
Laddingford Kent. . . . 53 D7
Lade Kent 39 C9
Lade Bank Lincs 174 E5
Ladies Riggs N Yorks . 214 F2
Ladmanlow Derbys . . 185 G8
Ladock Corn. 5 E7
Lady Orkney 314 B6
Ladybank Fife 287 F7
Ladyburn Inverclyd . . 276 F6
Ladycross Corn. 12 D2
Ladyes Hill Warks . . . 118 C5
Lady Green Mers 193 G10
Lady Hall Cumb 210 C3
Lady Halton Shrops . . 115 B9
Lady House Gtr Man . . 196 F2
Ladykirk Borders 273 F7
Ladyoak Shrops 131 C7
Lady Park T&W 242 F6
Ladyridge Hereford . . 97 E11
Ladysford Aberds . . . 303 C9
Lady's Green Suff. . . . 124 F5
Ladywell London 67 E11
 Shrops 149 C9
 W Loth 269 B10
Lady Wood W Mid . . . 133 F11
Laffak Mers 183 B8
Laga Highld 289 C8
Lagafater Lodge
 Dumfries 236 B3
Lagalochan Argyll . . . 275 B9
Lagavulin Argyll 254 C5
Lagg Argyll 274 F6
 N Ayrs 255 E10
Laggan Argyll. 254 B3
 Highld 289 B9
 Highld 290 D4
 Highld 291 D8
 S Ayrs. 245 G7
Lagganlia Highld 291 C10
Laggan Lodge Argyll . 289 G8
Lagganmullan Dumfries 237 D7
Lagganulva Argyll . . . 288 E6
Lagness W Sus 22 C5
Laide Highld 307 K3
Laig Highld 294 G6
Laigh Carnduff S Lanark 268 F3
Laigh Fenwick E Ayrs . 267 G9
Laigh Glengall S Ayrs . 257 F8
Laighmuir E Ayrs 267 F9
Laighstonehall S Lanark 268 E4
Laindon Essex 69 B7
Lair Highld. 299 E10
 Perth. 292 G3
Laira Devon 7 D10
Lairg Highld 309 J5
Lairg Lodge Highld . . 309 J5
Lairgmore Highld . . . 300 F5
Lairg Muir Highld . . . 309 J5
Laisterdyke W Yorks . 205 G9
Laithes Cumb 230 E5
Laithkirk Durham. . . . 232 G5
Laity Moor Corn 4 F3
Lake Devon 12 D6
 Devon 24 F6
 Devon 40 G5
 IoW 21 E7
 Poole 18 C5
 Wilts 46 D6
Lake End Bucks 66 D2
Lakenham Norf. 142 B4
Lakenheath Suff 140 G4
Laker's Green Sur . . . 50 F4
Lakesend Norf. 139 D10
Lakeside Cumb 211 B7
 Thurrock 68 D5
 Worcs 117 D11
Laleham Sur. 66 F5
Laleston / Trelales
 Bridgend. 57 F11
Lamanva Corn 3 C7
Lamarsh Essex 107 D7
Lamas Norf 160 E4
Lamb Corner Essex . . 107 E10
Lambden Borders . . . 272 G4
Lamberden Kent. 38 B4
Lamberhead Green
 Gtr Man 194 G4
Lamberhurst Kent . . . 53 F7
Lamberhurst Quarter
 Kent. 53 F7
Lamberton Borders . . 273 D9
 Devon 14 B4
 Essex 88 D4
 Notts 172 D7
Lambfair Green Suff . 124 G4
Lambfoot Cumb. 229 E8
Lambhill Glasgow . . . 267 B11
Lambley Northumb . . 240 F5
 Notts. 171 F10
Lambourn W Berks . . 63 D10
Lambourne End
 Essex 87 G7

Knighton continued
 Dorset 29 E10
 Leicester 135 C11
 Oxon 63 B9
 Poole 18 B6
 Som 43 E7
 Staffs 150 D4
 Staffs 168 G2
 Wilts 63 D9
 Worcs 117 F10
Knighton Fields
 Leicester. 135 C11
Knighton on Teme
 Worcs 116 C2
Knighton / Tref-y-Clawdd
 Powys 114 C5
Knightor Corn 5 D10
Knightsbridge Glos. . . 99 F7
 London. 67 D9
Knight's End Cambs . . 139 E8
Knight's Enham Hants . 47 D11
Knight's End W London . 67 E10
Knightsmill Corn 11 E7
Knightsridge W Loth . 269 B10
Knightswood Glasgow . 267 B10
Knightwick Worcs . . . 116 F4
Knill Hereford 114 E5
Knipe Fold Cumb. . . . 220 F6
Knipton Leics 154 C6
Knitsley Durham 233 B8
Kniveton Derbys 170 E2
Knock Argyll. 289 F7
 Cumb 231 F9
 Moray 302 D5
Knockally Highld. 311 G5
Knockan Highld. 307 H7
Knockando Moray . . . 301 E11
Knockando Ho Moray . 302 E2
Knockbain Highld. . . . 301 D7
Knockbreck Highld . . 298 C2
Knockbrex Dumfries . 237 E7
Knockcarrach Highld . 290 B6
Knockdee Highld. 310 C5
Knockdolian S Ayrs . . 244 F4
Knockdown Wilts 61 B10
Knockenbaird Aberds . 302 G6
Knockenkelly N Ayrs . 256 D2
Knockentiber E Ayrs . 257 B9
Knockerdown Derbys . 170 E2
Knockespock Ho Aberds 302 G5
Knockfarrel Highld . . 300 D5
Knockglass Dumfries . 236 D2
Knockhall Kent 68 E5
Knockholt Kent. 52 B3
Knockholt Pound Kent. 52 B3
Knockie Lodge Highld. 290 B6
Knockin Shrops 148 E6
Knockin Heath Shrops . 149 E7
Knockinlaw E Ayrs . . . 257 B10
Knockinnon Highld . . 310 F5
Knocklaw Northumb . . 252 C3
Knocklearn Dumfries . 237 B9
Knocklearoch Argyll . 274 G4
Knockmill Kent. 68 G5
Knocknaha Argyll . . . 255 F7
Knocknain Dumfries . 236 C1
Knocknalling Dumfries 246 F4
Knockothie Aberds . . 303 F9
Knockrome Argyll . . . 274 F6
Knocksharry IoM 192 D3
Knockstapplemore
 Argyll 255 F7
Knockvologan Argyll . 274 B4
Knodishall Suff. 127 E8
Knokan Argyll 288 G6
Knole Som 29 B7
Knollbury Mon 60 B2
Knoll Green Som 43 F8
Knoll Top N Yorks . . . 214 F3
Knolls Green Ches E . 184 F4
Knolton Wrex. 149 B7
Knolton Bryn Wrex . . 149 B7
Knook Wilts. 46 E2
Knossington Leics . . . 136 B5
Knotbury Staffs. 169 B8
Knott End-on-Sea
 Lancs. 202 D3
Knotting Bedford . . . 121 E10

Lambourn Woodlands
 W Berks 63 D10
Lambridge Bath 61 F9
Lamb's Cross Kent . . . 53 D9
Lambs Green W Sus. . 51 F8
Lambston Pembs 72 B6
Lambton T&W 243 G7
Lamellion Corn 6 C4
Lamerton Devon 12 F5
Lamesley T&W 243 F7
Laminess Orkney . . . 314 C6
Lamington Highld. . . . 301 B7
 S Lanark 259 C11
Lamlash N Ayrs 256 C2
Lamledra Corn 5 G10
Lamloch Dumfries . . . 246 D2
Lammack Blackburn . 195 B7
Lamonby Cumb 230 D4
Lamorick Corn. 5 C10
Lamorna Corn 1 E4
Lamorran Corn 5 F7
Lampardbrook Suff. . 126 E5
Lampeter / Llanbedr Pont
 Steffan Ceredig . . 93 B11
Lampeter Velfrey Pembs 73 C11
Lamphey Pembs 73 E8
Lamplugh Cumb 229 G7
Lamport Northants . . 120 C5
Lamyatt Som 45 E7
Lana Devon 24 F4
 Devon 24 E5
Lanark S Lanark 269 F7
Lancaster Lancs 211 G9
Lanchester Durham . 233 B9
Lancing W Sus 35 G11
Landbeach Cambs . . 123 D9
Landcross Devon 25 C7
Landerberry Aberds . 293 C9
Landewednack Corn. . 2 H6
Landford Wilts 32 D3
Landford Manor Wilts . 32 C3
Landfordwood Wilts . 32 C3
Land Gate Gtr Man . . 194 G5
Landguard Manor IoW . 21 E7
Landhill Devon 12 B4
Landican Mers 182 D3
Landimore Swansea . 56 C3
Landkey Devon 40 G5
Landkey Newland Devon 40 G5
Landore Swansea . . . 57 B7
Landport E Sus 36 E6
 Ptsmth 33 G10
Landrake Corn. 7 C7
Landscove Devon . . . 8 C5
Land Side Lancs 195 C9
Landshipping Pembs . 73 C8
Landshipping Quay
 Pembs 73 C8
Landslow Green
 Gtr Man 185 B7
Landulph Corn. 7 C8
Landwade Suff 124 D2
Landywood Staffs . . . 133 B9
Lane Corn 4 C6
Laneast Corn 11 E10
Lane Bottom Lancs . . 204 F3
Lane End Bucks 84 G4
 Corn 5 B10
 Cumb 220 G2
 Derbys 170 C6
 Dorset 18 C3
 Hants 33 B9
 IoW 21 D9
 Lancs 204 D3
 Sur. 49 E10
 Wilts 45 D10
 W Yorks 204 F6
Lane Ends Ches E . . . 168 D2
 Derbys 152 D5
 Gtr Man 185 C7
 Lancs 194 D6
 Lancs 203 C11
 Lancs 203 D11
 N Yorks. 204 F6
Lane Green Staffs . . . 133 C7
Lane Head Derbys . . . 185 F11
 Durham 224 C3
 Gtr Man 183 B10
 W Mid 133 C9
 W Yorks 197 F7
Lanehouse Dorset. . . 17 F9
Laneshaw Bridge Lancs 204 E4
Lanercost Cumb 240 E3
Lanescot Corn 5 D11
Lane's End Shrops . . . 132 E4
Lanesfield W Mid . . . 133 D9
Laneshaw Bridge Lancs 204 E4
Laney Green Staffs . . 133 B9
Langaford Devon. . . . 12 B4
Langage Devon 7 E11
Langal Highld 289 C9
Langaller Som. 28 B3
Langar Notts 154 C4
Langbank Renfs 277 G7
Langbar N Yorks 205 C7
Langbaurgh N Yorks . 225 C11
Langburnshiels Borders 250 G2
Langcliffe N Yorks . . . 212 G6
Langdale End N Yorks . 227 G8
Langdale Staffs 168 G6
Langdon Corn 12 E2
 Corn 12 D2
Langdon Beck Durham 232 E3
Langdon Hills Essex . 69 B7
Langdown Hants. . . . 32 G6
Langdyke Borders . . . 272 G6
 Fife. 287 G7
Langenhoe Essex . . . 89 B8
Langford C Beds 104 C3
 Devon 14 B4
 Essex 88 D4
 N Som 44 B2
 Notts 172 D4
 Oxon 82 E2
Langford Budville Som 27 C10
Langford Green Devon 27 F8
 N Som 44 B2
Langham Dorset. 30 B3
 Essex 107 E10
 Norf 177 E8
 Rutland 154 G4

Langham continued
 Som 28 E4
 Suff 125 C9
Langhaugh Borders . 260 C6
Langho Lancs 203 G10
Langholm Dumfries . . 249 G9
Langholme N Lincs . . 188 B3
Langhope Borders . . 261 E10
Langland Swansea . . 56 D6
Langlee Borders 262 B2
Langlee Mains Borders. 262 B2
Langlees Falk 279 E7
Langley Ches E 184 G6
 Derbys 170 F6
 Essex 105 E8
 Glos 99 F10
 Gtr Man 195 F11
 Hants 32 G6
 Herts 104 G4
 Kent 53 C10
 Northum 241 B9
 Oxon 82 B4
 Slough 66 D4
 Som 27 B9
 Warks 118 E3
 W Mid 133 F9
Langley Burrell Wilts . 62 D2
Langleybury Herts. . . 85 E9
Langley Common
 Derbys. 152 B5
 Wokingham 65 F11
Langley Corner Bucks . 66 C4
Langley Green Derbys . 152 B5
 Essex 107 G7
 Warks 118 E3
 W Mid 133 F9
Langley Heath Kent . . 53 C10
Langley Marsh Som . . 27 B9
Langley Mill Derbys . 170 F6
Langley Moor Durham 233 C11
Langley Park Durham . 233 C10
Langley Street Norf . . 143 C7
Langley Vale Sur 51 B8
Langloan N Lanark . . 268 C4
Langney E Sus 23 E10
Langold Notts 187 D9
Langore Corn. 12 D2
Langport Som 28 B6
Langrick Lincs 174 F3
Langrick Bridge Lincs . 174 F3
Langridge Bath 61 F8
Langridge Ford Devon 25 C9
Langrigg Cumb 229 B9
Langrish Hants 34 C2
Langsett S Yorks 197 G8
Langshaw Borders . . 262 B2
Langside Glasgow . . . 267 C11
 Perth 285 F11
Langskaill Orkney . . . 314 B4
Langstone Devon . . . 13 E10
 Hants 22 C2
 Newport. 78 G5
Langthorne N Yorks . 224 G5
Langthorpe N Yorks . 215 F7
Langthwaite N Yorks . 223 E10
Langtoft E Yorks 217 F10
 Lincs 156 G2
Langton Durham 224 B3
 Lincs 174 B2
 Lincs 190 G5
 N Yorks. 216 F5
Langton by Wragby
 Lincs 189 F11
Langton Green Kent . 52 F4
 Suff 126 C2
Langton Herring Dorset. 17 E8
Langton Long Blandford
 Dorset. 30 F5
Langton Matravers
 Dorset. 18 E6
Langtree Devon 25 D7
Langtree Week Devon . 25 D7
Langwathby Cumb . . 231 E7
Langwell Ho Highld. . 311 F5
Langwell Lodge Highld . 307 J6
Langwith Derbys 171 B8
Langwith Junction
 Derbys 171 B8
Langworth Lincs 189 F9
Lanham Green Essex . 106 G5
Lanivet Corn 5 C9
Lanjeth Corn 5 E9
Lanjew Corn 5 C9
Lank Corn 11 F7
Lanlivery Corn 6 D1
Lanner Corn 2 B6
Lanreath Corn 6 D3
Lansallos Corn 6 E3
Lansbury Park Caerph . 59 B7
Lansdown Bath 61 F8
 Glos 99 G9
Lanstephan Corn . . . 12 D2
Lanteglos Corn 11 E7
Lanteglos Highway Corn . 6 E3
Lanton Borders 262 E4
 Northumb 263 C10
Lantuel Corn 5 B9
Lantyan Corn 6 D2
Lapal W Mid 133 G9
Lapford Devon 26 F2
Lapford Cross Devon . 26 F2
Laphroaig Argyll 254 C4
Lapley Staffs 151 G7
Lapworth Warks 118 C3
Larachbeg Highld . . . 289 E8
Larbert Falk 279 E7
Larbreck Lancs 202 E4
Larches Lancs 202 G6
Larden Green Ches E . 167 E9
Larg Aberds 302 F6
Largie Aberds 302 F6
Largiebaan Argyll . . . 255 F7
Largiemore Argyll . . . 275 E10
Largoward Fife 287 G8
Largs N Ayrs 266 D4
Largue Aberds 302 E6
Largybeg N Ayrs 256 E2
Largymeanoch N Ayrs . 256 E2
Largymore N Ayrs . . . 256 E2
Larkfield Involyd 276 F4
 Kent. 53 B8
 W Yorks 205 F10
Larkhall Bath 61 F9
 S Lanark 268 E5
Larkhill Wilts 46 E6
Larkhill Gtr Man 195 C7
Larking Norf 141 F9
Larport Hereford 97 D11
Larrick Corn. 12 E2
Larriston Borders . . . 250 F2
Lartington Durham . . 223 B10
Lary Aberds 292 C5
Lasborough Glos 80 G4
Lasham Hants 49 E7

Lashenden Kent 53 E10
Lask Edge Staffs 168 D6
Lassington Glos 98 G5
Lassodie Fife 280 C2
Lastingham N Yorks . 226 G4
Latcham Som. 44 D2
Latchbrook Corn 7 D8
Latchford Herts 105 G7
 Oxon 83 E11
 Warr 183 D10
Latchingdon Essex . . 88 E5
Latchley Corn 12 G4
Latchmere Green
 Hants 64 G6
Latchmore Bank Essex. 87 B7
Latchmore Bank Essex. 87 B7
Lately Common Warr . 183 B11
Lathallan Mill Fife . . . 287 G8
Lathbury M Keynes . . 103 B7
Latheron Highld 310 F5
Latheronwheel Highld . 310 F5
Latheronwheel Ho
 Highld 310 F5
Lathom Lancs 194 E3
Lathones Fife 287 G8
Latimer Bucks. 85 F8
Latteridge S Glos . . . 61 C7
Lattiford Som 29 B11
Lattinford Hill Suff. . 107 D11
Latton London 81 F9
Latton Bush Essex . . . 87 D7
Launcells Corn 24 F2
Launcells Cross Corn . 24 F3
Launceston Corn 12 D2
Launcherley Som. . . . 44 E4
Laund Lancs 195 C10
Launton Oxon 102 G2
Laurencekirk Aberds . 293 F8
Laurieston Dumfries . 237 C8
 Falk 279 F8
Lavendon M Keynes . 121 G8
Lavenham Suff 107 B8
Laverackloch Moray . 301 C11
Laverhay Dumfries . . 248 D4
Laverlaw Borders . . . 261 B7
Laverley Som. 44 F5
Lavernock V Glam . . . 59 F7
Laversdale Cumb . . . 239 E11
Laverstock Wilts 47 G7
Laverstoke Hants . . . 48 D3
Laverton Glos 99 D11
 N Yorks. 214 E4
 Som 45 C9
Lavister Wrex. 166 D5
Lavrean Corn 5 D10
Lawers Perth 285 D11
 Perth. 285 E11
Lawford Essex 107 E11
 Som 42 F6
Lawford Heath Warks . 119 C9
Lawhill Perth 286 F3
Lawhitton Corn 12 E3
Lawkland Green
 N Yorks 212 F5
Lawley Telford 132 B3
Lawn Swindon 63 C7
Lawnhead Staffs. . . . 150 D6
Lawns W Yorks 197 C10
Lawnswood W Yorks . 205 F11
Lawnt Denb 165 B8
Lawrence Hill Newport. 59 B7
Lawrenny Pembs 73 D8
Lawrenny Quay Pembs 73 D8
Lawshall Suff 125 G7
Lawshall Green Suff . 125 G7
Lawton Hereford 115 F8
 Shrops 131 G10
Lawton-gate Ches E . 168 D4
Lawton Heath End
 Ches E 168 D4
Laxey IoM 192 D5
 Staffs 126 C5
Laxfield Suff 126 C5
Laxfirth Shetland . . . 313 H6
 Shetland 313 J6
Laxford Bridge Highld. 306 E7
Laxo Shetland 313 G6
Laxobigging Shetland 312 F6
Laxton E Yorks 199 B9
 Northants 137 D8
 Notts 172 B2
Laycock W Yorks 204 E6
Layer Breton Essex . . 88 B6
Layer de la Haye Essex 89 B7
Layer Marney Essex . 88 B6
Layerthorpe York . . . 207 C8
Layham Suff 107 C10
Laylands Green
 W Berks 64 D2
Laymore Dorset 28 G5
Layof Moor IoW 21 C7
Layters Green Bucks . 85 G7
Laytham E Yorks 207 F10
Layton Blackpool . . . 202 F2
Lazenby Redcar 225 B11
Lazonby Cumb 230 D6
Lea Derbys 170 D4
 Hereford 98 G3
 Lincs 188 D4
 Shrops 131 B8
 Shrops 131 F7
 Wilts 62 B3
Lea Bridge London . . 67 B11
Lea by Backford
 Ches W 182 G5
Leac a Li W Isles 305 J3
Leacainn W Isles. 304 F5
Leachkin Highld. 300 E6
Leadburn Midloth . . . 270 D4
Leadendale Staffs . . . 151 B8
Leadenham Lincs . . . 173 D7
Leaden Roding Essex . 87 C9
Leadgate Cumb 231 C10
 Durham 242 G4
 T&W 242 F4
Leadhills S Lanark . . 259 G9
Leadingcross Green
 Kent. 53 C11
Leadmill Derbys. 186 E2
 Flint 166 C2
Lea End Worcs 117 B10
Leafield Oxon 82 B4
Lea Forge Ches E 168 F2
Leagrave Luton 103 G10
Leagreen Hants 19 C11
Lea Green Mers 183 C8
Lea Hall W Mid 134 F2
Lea Heath Staffs 151 D10
Leake Lincs 174 F6
 N Yorks 225 G8
Leake Commonside
 Lincs 174 E5
Leake Fold Hill Lincs . 174 E6
Lealholm N Yorks . . . 226 D5
Lealholm Side N Yorks 226 D5
Lea Line Hereford . . . 98 G3
Lealt Argyll 275 D7
 Highld 298 C5
Leam Derbys 186 F2
Lea Marston Warks . . 134 E4
Leamington Hastings
 Warks 119 D8
Leamoor Common
 Shrops 131 F8
Leamore W Mid 133 C9
Leamside Durham. . . 234 B2
Leanach Argyll 275 D11
Leanachan Highld . . . 290 F4
Leanaig Highld. 300 D5
Leapgate Worcs 116 C6
Leargybreck Argyll . . 274 F6
Lease Rigg N Yorks . . 226 E6
Leasey Bridge Herts . 85 C11
Leasgill Cumb 211 C9
Leasingham Lincs . . . 173 F9
Leasingthorne Durham. 233 F11
Leason Swansea 56 C3
Leasowe Mers 182 C3
Leatherhead Sur 51 B7
Leatherhead Common
 Sur. 51 B7
Leathern Bottle Glos . 80 E2
Leathley N Yorks 205 D10
Leaths Dumfries 237 C9
Leaton Shrops 149 F9
 Telford 150 G2
Leaton Heath Shrops . 149 F9
Lea Town Lancs 202 G5
Lea Valley Herts 85 B11
Leavedon Essex 54 C4
Leavenheath Suff. . . . 107 D9
Leavening N Yorks . . 216 G5
Leaves Green London . 68 G2
Lea Yeat Cumb 212 B5
Leazes Durham 242 F5
Lebberston N Yorks . 217 C11
Leburnick Corn 12 E3
Lechlade-on-Thames
 Glos. 82 F2
Leck Lancs 212 D2
Leckford Hants 47 F11
Leckfurin Highld. . . . 308 D7
Leckgruinart Argyll . . 274 G3
Leckhampstead Bucks. 102 D4
 W Berks 64 D2
Leckhampstead Thicket
 W Berks 64 D2
Leckhampton Glos . . 80 B6
Leckie Highld 299 C10
Leckmelm Highld . . . 307 K6
Leckuary Argyll 275 D9
Leckwith V Glam 59 F7
Leconfield E Yorks . . 208 D6
Ledaig Argyll 289 F11
Ledburn Bucks. 103 G8
Ledbury Hereford . . . 98 D4
Ledcharrie Stirling . . 285 E9
Leddington Glos. 98 E3
Ledgemoor Hereford . 115 G8
Ledgowan Highld . . . 299 C10
Ledicot Hereford 115 E8
Ledmore Angus 293 G7
 Highld 307 H7
Lednagullin Highld. . . 308 C7
Ledsham Ches W . . . 182 G5
 W Yorks 198 B3
Ledston W Yorks 198 B2
Ledston Luck W Yorks . 206 G4
Ledwell Oxon 101 F8
Lee Argyll 288 G6
 Devon 40 D3
 Devon 40 D5
 Hants 32 D5
 Lancs 203 B7
 London 67 E11
 Northumb 241 F10
 Shrops 149 C8
Leebotwood Shrops . 131 E9
Lee Bank W Mid 133 F11
Leece Cumb 210 F4
Lee Chapel Essex . . . 69 B7
Leechpool Mon 60 B4
Lee Clump Bucks . . . 84 E6
Leeds Kent 53 C10
 W Yorks 205 G11
Leedstown Corn 2 C4
Leeford Devon 41 D9
Lee Gate Bucks 84 D5
Leegomery Telford . . 150 G3
Lee Ground Hants . . . 33 F8
Lee Head Derbys . . . 185 C8
Leek Staffs 169 D7
Leekbrook Staffs . . . 169 E7
Leek Wootton Warks . 118 D5
Lee Mill Devon 8 D2
Leeming N Yorks 214 B5
 W Yorks 204 G6
Leeming Bar N Yorks . 224 G5
Leemings Lancs 203 D10
Lee Moor Devon 7 C11
 W Yorks 197 B10
Lee-on-the-Solent
 Hants 33 G9
Lee-over-Sands Essex . 89 C10
Lees Derbys 152 B5
 Gtr Man 196 G3
 W Yorks 204 F6
Leesthorpe Leics . . . 154 G5
Leeswood / Coed-Llai
 Flint 166 D3
Leetown Perth 286 E6
Leftwich Ches W. 183 G11
Legar Powys 78 B2
Legbourne Lincs 190 E5
Legerwood Borders . 271 G11
Leggatt Hill W Sus . . 34 C6
Legsby Lincs 189 D10
Leicester Leicester . . 135 C10
Leicester Forest East
 Leics 135 C10
Leicester Grange Warks 135 E8
Leigh Devon 26 E2
 Dorset 18 B6

Leigh continued
Dorset 29 F10
Dorset 30 F3
Glos 99 F7
Gtr Man 195 G2
Kent 52 D4
Shrops 130 C6
Sur 51 D8
Wilts 81 G9
Worcs 116 G5
Leigham Plym 7 D10
Leigh Beck Essex 69 C10
Leigh Common Som 30 B2
Leigh Delamere Wilts 61 D11
Leigh Green Kent 54 G2
Leighland Chapel Som 42 F4
Leigh-on-Sea Southend 69 B10
Leigh Park Hants 22 B2
Leigh Sinton Worcs 116 G5
Leighswood W Mid 133 C11
Leighterton Glos 80 G4
Leighton N Yorks 214 D3
Shrops 132 B2
Som 45 E8
Leighton Bromswold
Cambs 122 B2
Leighton Buzzard
C Beds 103 F8
Leighton / Tre'r llai
Powys 130 B4
Leigh upon Mendip Som 45 D7
Leigh Woods N Som 60 E5
Leinthall Earls Hereford 115 D8
Leinthall Starkes
Hereford 115 D8
Leintwardine Hereford 115 C8
Leire Leics 135 E10
Leirinmore Highld 308 C4
Leiston Suff 127 E8
Leitfie Perth 286 C6
Leith Edin 280 F5
Leithenhall Dumfries 248 D4
Leitholm Borders 272 G5
Lelant Corn 2 B2
Lelant Downs Corn 2 B2
Lelley E Yorks 209 G11
Lem Hill Worcs 116 C4
Lemington T&W 242 E5
Lemmington Hall
Northumb 264 G4
Lempitlaw Borders 263 C7
Lemsford Herts 86 C2
Lenacre Cumb 212 B3
Lenborough Bucks 102 E3
Lenchwick Worcs 99 B10
Lendalfoot S Ayrs 244 F4
Lendrick Lodge Stirling 285 G9
Lenham Kent 53 C11
Lenham Heath Kent 54 D2
Lennel Borders 272 F5
Lennoxtown E Dunb 278 F2
Lent Bucks 66 C2
Lenten Pool Denb 165 B8
Lenton Lincs 155 C10
Nottingham 153 B11
Lenton Abbey
Nottingham 153 B11
Lentran Highld 300 E5
Lent Rise Bucks 66 C2
Lenwade Norf 159 F11
Leny Ho Stirling 285 G10
Lenzie E Dunb 278 G3
Lenziemill N Lanark 278 G5
Leoch Angus 287 D7
Leochel-Cushnie
Aberds 293 B7
Leomansley Staffs 134 B2
Leominster Hereford 115 F9
Leomonsley Staffs 134 B2
Leonard Stanley Glos 80 E4
Leonardston Pembs 72 D6
Leorin Argyll 254 C4
Lepe Hants 20 B5
Lephin Highld 297 G7
Lephinchapel Argyll 275 D10
Lephinmore Argyll 275 D10
Leppington N Yorks 216 G5
Lepton W Yorks 197 D8
Lepton Edge W Yorks 197 D8
Lerigoigan Argyll 275 C9
Lerrocks Stirling 285 G11
Lerryn Corn 6 D2
Lerwick Shetland 313 J6
Lesbury Northumb 264 G6
Leschangie Aberds 293 B9
Le Skerne Haughton
Darl 224 B6
Leslie Aberds 302 G5
Fife 286 G6
Lesmahagow S Lanark 259 B8
Lesnewth Corn 11 C8
Lessendrum Aberds 302 E5
Lessingham Norf 161 D7
Lessness Heath London 68 D3
Lessonhall Cumb 238 G6
Leswalt Dumfries 236 C2
Letchmore Heath Herts 85 F11
Letchworth Herts 104 E4
Letcombe Bassett Oxon 63 B11
Letcombe Regis Oxon 63 B11
Letham Angus 287 C9
Falk 279 D7
Fife 287 F7
Perth 286 D6
Letham Grange Angus 287 C10
Lethem Borders 250 B5
Lethem Ho Highld 301 D9
Lethenty Aberds 303 E8
Aberds 303 G7
Letheringham Suff 126 F5
Letheringsett Norf 159 B11
Lettaford Devon 13 E10
Lettan Orkney 314 B7
Letter Aberds 293 B9
Letterewe Highld 299 B9
Letterfearn Highld 295 C10
Letterfinlay Highld 290 D4
Lettermay Argyll 284 G5
Lettermorar Argyll 295 G9
Lettermore Argyll 288 G3
Letters Highld 307 L6
Letterston / Treletert
Pembs 91 F8
Lettoch Highld 292 B2
Highld 301 F10
Moray 301 G11
Perth 291 G11
Letton Hereford 96 B6
Hereford 115 C7
Lett's Green Kent 52 B3
Letty Brongu Bridgend 57 D11
Letty Green Herts 86 C3
Letwell S Yorks 187 D9
Leuchars Fife 287 E8
Leuchars Ho Moray 302 C2
Leumrabhagh W Isles 305 G5
Levalsa Meor Corn 5 F10
Levan Inclyd 276 F4

Levaneap Shetland 313 G6
Levedale Staffs 151 F7
Level of Mendalgief
Newport 59 B10
Leven's Green Essex 105 G9
Leven E Yorks 209 D8
Fife 287 G8
Levencorroch N Ayrs 256 E2
Levenhall E Loth 281 G7
Levens Cumb 211 B9
Levens Seat W Loth 269 D8
Levens Green Herts 105 G9
Levenshulme Gtr Man 184 C5
Leventhorpe W Yorks 205 G8
Leverburgh W Isles 305 J2
Leverington Cambs 157 G8
Leverington Common
Cambs 157 G8
Leverstock Green Herts 85 D9
Leverton Lincs 174 F6
W Berks 63 E10
Leverton Highgate Lincs 174 F6
Leverton Lucasgate
Lincs 174 F6
Leverton Outgate Lincs 174 F6
Levington Suff 108 D4
Levisham N Yorks 226 G6
Levishie Highld 290 B6
Lew Oxon 82 D4
Lewannick Corn 11 E11
Lewcombe Dorset 29 F9
Lewdown Devon 12 D4
Lewes E Sus 36 E6
Leweston Pembs 91 G8
Lewisham London 67 D11
Lewiston Highld 300 G5
Lewistown Bridgend 58 B2
Lewknor Oxon 84 F2
Leworthy Devon 24 G4
Devon 41 F7
Lewson Street Kent 70 G3
Lewth Lancs 202 F5
Lewthorn Cross Devon 13 F11
Lewtrenchard Devon 12 D5
Lexden Essex 107 G9
Ley Aberds 293 B7
Corn 6 B3
Corn 41 F10
Leybourne Kent 53 B7
Leyburn N Yorks 224 G2
Leycett Staffs 168 F3
Leyfields Staffs 134 B4
Ley Green Herts 104 G3
Ley Hey Park Gtr Man 185 D7
Leyhill Bucks 85 E7
S Glos 79 G11
Ley Hill W Mid 134 D2
Leyland Lancs 194 C4
Leylodge Aberds 293 B9
Leymoor W Yorks 196 D6
Leys Aberds 292 C6
Aberds 303 D10
Cumb 219 B11
Perth 286 D6
Staffs 169 F8
Leys Castle Highld 300 E6
Leys of Cossans Angus 287 C7
Leysdown-on-Sea Kent 70 E4
Leys Hill Hereford 79 B9
Leysmill Angus 287 C10
Leysters Hereford 115 E11
Leysters Pole Hereford 115 E11
Leyton London 67 B11
Leytonstone London 67 B11
Lezant Corn 12 F2
Lezerea Corn 2 C5
Leziate Norf 158 F3
Lhanbryde Moray 302 C2
Liatrie Highld 300 F2
Libanus Powys 95 F9
Libberton S Lanark 269 G9
Libbery Worcs 117 F9
Liberton Edin 270 B5
Liceasto W Isles 305 J3
Lichfield Staffs 134 B2
Lick Perth 286 B2
Lickey Worcs 117 B9
Lickey End Worcs 117 C9
Lickfold W Sus 34 B6
Lickhill Worcs 116 C6
Lickleyhead Castle
Aberds 302 G6
Liddaton Devon 12 E5
Liddel Orkney 314 H4
Liddesdale Highld 289 D7
Liddington Swindon 63 C8
Liden Swindon 63 C7
Lidgate Suff 124 F4
Lidget S Yorks 199 G7
Lidget Green W Yorks 205 G8
Lidgett Notts 171 B10
Lidham Hill E Sus 38 D4
Lidlington C Beds 103 D9
Lidsey W Sus 22 C6
Lidsing Kent 69 G9
Lidstone Oxon 101 G7
Lieth Angus 287 C8
Liff Angus 287 D7
Lifton Devon 12 D3
Liftondown Devon 12 D3
Lightcliffe W Yorks 196 B6
Lightfoot Green Lancs 202 G6
Lighthazles W Yorks 196 C3
Lighthorne Warks 118 F6
Lighthorne Heath Warks 119 F7
Lighthorne Rough
Warks 118 F6
Lightmoor Telford 132 B3
Light Oaks Staffs 168 E6
Lightpill Glos 80 E4
Lightwater Sur 66 G2
Lightwood Shrops 132 E2
Shrops 150 D3
Staffs 169 G8
Stoke 168 G6
S Yorks 186 E5
Lightwood Green
Ches E 167 G10
Wrex 166 G5
Lilbourne Northants 119 B11
Lilburn Tower Northumb 264 D2
Lilleshall Telford 150 F4
Lilley Herts 104 F2
W Berks 64 D2
Lilliesleaf Borders 262 E2
Lillingstone Dayrell
Bucks 102 D4
Lillingstone Lovell
Bucks 102 C4
Lillington Dorset 29 E10
Warks 118 D6
Lilliput Poole 18 C6
Lilstock Som 43 E7
Lilybank Inclyd 276 G6

Lilyhurst Shrops 150 G4
Lilyvale Kent 54 F5
Limbrick Lancs 194 D6
Limbury Luton 103 G11
Limebrook Hereford 115 D7
Limefield Gtr Man 195 E10
Limehouse London 67 C11
Limehurst Gtr Man 196 G2
Limekiln Field Derbys 187 G7
Limekilns Fife 279 E11
Limerigg Falk 279 G7
Limerstone IoW 20 E4
Lime Side Gtr Man 196 G2
Limestone Brae
Northumb 231 B11
Lime Street Worcs 98 E6
Lime Tree Park W Mid 118 B5
Limington Som 29 C8
Limpenhoe Norf 143 C7
Limpenhoe Hill Norf 143 C6
Limpers Hill Wilts 45 G10
Limpley Stoke Wilts 61 G9
Limpsfield Sur 52 C2
Limpsfield Chart Sur 52 C2
Limpsfield Common Sur 52 C2
Linbriggs Northumb 251 B9
Linburn W Loth 270 B2
Linby Notts 171 E8
Linchmere W Sus 49 G11
Lincluden Dumfries 237 B11
Lincoln Lincs 189 G7
Lincomb Worcs 116 D6
Lincombe Devon 8 D4
Devon 40 D3
Lindale Cumb 211 C8
Lindal in Furness Cumb 210 D5
Lindean Borders 261 C11
Linden Glos 80 B4
Lindfield W Sus 36 B4
Lindford Hants 49 F10
Lindifferon Fife 287 F7
Lindley N Yorks 205 D10
W Yorks 196 D6
Lindley Green N Yorks 205 D10
Lindores Fife 287 F7
Lindow End Ches E 184 F4
Lindridge Worcs 116 D3
Lindsell Essex 106 F2
Lindsey Suff 107 C9
Lindsey Tye Suff 107 B9
Lindwell W Yorks 196 C5
Lineholt Common
Worcs 116 D6
Liney Som 43 F11
Linfitts Gtr Man 196 F3
Linford Hants 31 F11
Thurrock 69 D7
Lingague IoM 192 E3
Lingards Wood W Yorks 196 E5
Lingbob W Yorks 205 F7
Lingdale Redcar 226 B3
Lingen Hereford 115 D7
Lingfield Darl 224 C6
Sur 51 E11
Lingfield Common Sur 51 E11
Lingley Green Warr 183 D10
Lingley Mere Warr 183 D10
Lingreabhagh W Isles 296 C6
Lingwood Norf 143 B7
Linhope Borders 249 C10
Northumb 263 F11
Linicro Highld 298 C3
Linkend Worcs 98 E6
Linkenholt Hants 47 B11
Linkhill Kent 38 B4
Linkinhorne Corn 12 G2
Linklater Orkney 314 H4
Linklet Orkney 314 A7
Linksness Orkney 314 E5
Orkney 314 G3
Linktown Fife 280 C5
Linley Shrops 131 E7
Shrops 132 D3
Linley Brook Shrops 132 D3
Linleygreen Shrops 132 D3
Linley Green Hereford 116 G3
Linlithgow W Loth 279 F10
Linlithgow Bridge
W Loth 279 F9
Linndhu Ho Argyll 289 D7
Linneraineach Highld 307 J6
Linns Angus 292 F3
Linnyshaw Gtr Man 195 G8
Linshiels Northumb 251 B9
Linsiadar W Isles 304 E4
Linsidemore Highld 309 K5
Linslade C Beds 103 F8
Linstead Parva Suff 126 B6
Linstock Cumb 239 F10
Linthurst Worcs 117 C9
Linthwaite W Yorks 196 E6
Lintlaw Borders 272 E6
Lintmill Moray 302 C5
Linton Borders 263 D7
Cambs 105 B11
Derbys 152 F5
Hereford 98 F3
Kent 53 D9
Northumb 253 E7
N Yorks 213 G9
W Yorks 206 D3
Linton Heath Derbys 152 F5
Linton Hill Hereford 98 G3
Linton-on-Ouse
N Yorks 215 G9
Lintridge Glos 98 E4
Lintz Durham 242 F5
Lintzford T&W 242 F4
Lintzgarth Durham 232 C4
Linwood Hants 31 F11
Lincs 189 D10
Renfs 267 C9
Lionacleit W Isles 297 G3
Lional W Isles 304 B7
Lions Green E Sus 23 B9
Liphook Hants 49 G10
Lipley Shrops 150 C4
Lippitts Hill Essex 86 F5
Liquo or Bowhousebog
N Lanark 269 D7
Liscard Mers 182 C4
Liscombe Som 41 G11
Liskeard Corn 6 C5
Liss Hants 34 B3
Liss Forest Hants 34 B3
Lissett E Yorks 209 B8
Lissington Lincs 189 E10
Lisson Grove London 67 C9
Lisvane Cardiff 59 C7
Liswerry Newport 59 B10
Litcham Norf 159 F7

Litchard Bridgend 58 C2
Litchborough Northants 120 G2
Litchfield Hants 48 C3
Litchurch Derbys 153 B7
Litherland Mers 182 B4
Litlington Cambs 104 C6
E Sus 23 E8
Litmarsh Hereford 97 B10
Little Abington Cambs 105 B10
Little Addington
Northants 121 C9
Little Airmyn E Yorks 199 B8
Little Almshoe Herts 104 F3
Little Alne Warks 118 E2
Little Altcar Mers 193 F10
Little Ann Hants 47 E11
Little Arowry Wrex 167 G7
Little Asby Cumb 222 D3
Little Ashley Wilts 61 G10
Little Assynt Highld 307 G6
Little Aston Staffs 133 C11
Little Atherfield IoW 20 E5
Little Ayre Orkney 314 G3
Little-ayre Shetland 313 G5
Little Ayton N Yorks 225 C11
Little Baddow Essex 88 D3
Little Badminton S Glos 61 C10
Little Ballinluig Perth 286 B3
Little Bampton Cumb 239 F7
Little Bardfield Essex 106 E3
Little Barford Bedford 122 F3
Little Barningham Norf 160 C2
Little Barrington Glos 82 C2
Little Barrow Ches W 183 G7
Little Barugh N Yorks 216 D5
Little Bavington
Northumb 241 B11
Little Bayham E Sus 52 F6
Little Bealings Suff 108 B4
Littlebeck N Yorks 227 D7
Little Beckford Glos 99 E9
Little Bedwyn Wilts 63 F9
Little Bentley Essex 108 F2
Little Berkhamsted Herts 86 D3
Little Billing Northants 120 E6
Little Billington C Beds 103 G8
Little Birch Hereford 97 E10
Little Bispham Blackpool 202 E2
Little Blakenham Suff 108 B2
Little Blencow Cumb 230 E5
Little Bloxwich W Mid 133 C10
Little Bognor W Sus 35 C8
Little Bolehill Derbys 170 E3
Little Bollington Ches E 184 D2
Little Bolton Gtr Man 184 B3
Little Bookham Sur 50 C6
Littleborough Devon 26 E4
Gtr Man 196 D2
Notts 188 E4
Littlebourne Kent 55 B8
Little Bourton Oxon 101 C9
Little Bowden Leics 136 F4
Little Boys Heath Bucks 84 F6
Little Bradley Suff 124 G3
Little Braithwaite
Cumb 229 G10
Little Brampton Shrops 131 G7
Little Braxted Essex 88 C4
Little Bray Devon 41 F7
Little Brechin Angus 293 G7
Littlebredy Dorset 17 D7
Little Brickhill
M Keynes 103 E8
Little Bridgeford Staffs 151 D7
Little Brington Northants 120 E3
Little Bristol S Glos 80 G2
Little Britain Warks 118 G2
Little Bromley Essex 107 F11
Little Bromwich W Mid 134 F2
Little Broughton Cumb 229 E7
Little Budworth Ches W 167 B9
Little Burstead Essex 87 G11
Little Burton E Yorks 209 D7
Littlebury Essex 105 D10
Littlebury Green Essex 105 D9
Little Bytham Lincs 155 F10
Little Cambridge Essex 106 F2
Little Canfield Essex 105 G11
Little Canford Poole 18 B6
Little Carleton Lancs 202 F2
Little Carlton Lincs 190 D5
Notts 172 D3
Little Casterton
Rutland 137 B10
Little Catwick E Yorks 209 E8
Little Catworth Cambs 122 C2
Little Cawthorpe Lincs 190 E5
Little Chalfield Wilts 61 G11
Little Chalfont Bucks 85 F7
Little Chart Kent 54 D2
Little Chart Forstal Kent 54 D3
Little Chell Stoke 168 E5
Little Chester Derby 153 B7
Little Chesterford Essex 105 C10
Little Cheverell Wilts 46 C3
Little Chishill Cambs 105 D8
Little Clacton Essex 89 B11
Little Clanfield Oxon 82 E3
Little Clegg Gtr Man 196 E2
Little Clifton Cumb 229 F7
Little Coates NE Lincs 201 F8
Little Colp Aberds 303 E7
Little Comberton Worcs 99 C9
Little Comfort Corn 12 E2
Little Common E Sus 38 F2
Lincs 156 D6
Shrops 149 C10
Little Compton Warks 100 E5
Little Corby Cumb 239 F11
Little Cornard Suff 107 D7
Littlecote Bucks 102 G6
Littlecott Wilts 46 C6
Little Cowarne Hereford 116 G2
Little Coxwell Oxon 82 G3
Little Crakehall N Yorks 224 G4
Little Cransley Northants 120 C6
Little Crawley M Keynes 103 B8
Little Creaton Northants 120 C4
Little Creich Highld 309 L6
Little Cressingham Norf 141 D7
Little Crosby Mers 193 G10
Little Cubley Derbys 152 B3
Little Dalby Leics 154 F4
Little Dawley Telford 132 B3
Littledean Glos 79 C11
Littledean Hill Glos 79 C11
Little Dens Aberds 303 E10
Little Dewchurch
Hereford 97 E10
Little Ditton Cambs 124 F3
Little Doward Hereford 79 B8
Littledown Bmouth 19 C8
Little Down Hants 47 B11
Little Downham Cambs 139 G10
Little Drayton Shrops 150 C3
Little Driffield E Yorks 208 B6
Little Dunham Norf 159 G7
Little Dunkeld Perth 286 C4
Little Dunmow Essex 106 G3
Little Durnford Wilts 46 G6
Little Eastbury Worcs 116 F6
Little Easton Essex 106 G2
Little Eaton Derbys 170 G5
Little Eccleston Lancs 202 F4
Little Ellingham Norf 141 D10
Little End Cambs 122 F3
Essex 87 E8
Little Everdon
Northants 119 F11
Wilts 45 B11
Little Eversden Cambs 123 G7
Little Faringdon Oxon 82 E2
Little Fencote N Yorks 224 G5
Little Fenton N Yorks 206 F6
Little Finborough Suff 125 G10
Little Fransham Norf 159 G8
Little Frith Kent 54 B2
Little Gaddesden Herts 85 C7
Littlegain Shrops 132 D5
Little Gidding Cambs 138 G2
Little Glemham Suff 126 F6
Little Glenshee Perth 286 D3
Little Gorsley Glos 98 F3
Little Gransden Cambs 122 F5
Little Green Cambs 104 B5
Lancs 203 E10
Notts 172 G2
Som 45 D8
Wrex 125 C11
Little Grimsby Lincs 190 C5
Little Gringley Notts 188 E2
Little Gruinard Highld 307 L4
Little Habton N Yorks 216 D4
Little Hadham Herts 105 G8
Little Hale Lincs 173 G10
Norf 141 B8
Little Hallam Derbys 171 G7
Little Hallingbury Essex 87 B7
Littleham Devon 14 E6
Littleham Devon 24 C6
Little Hampden Bucks 84 E5
Littlehampton W Sus 35 G8
Little Haresfield Glos 80 D4
Little Harrowden
Northants 121 C7
Little Harwood
Blackburn 195 B8
Little Haseley Oxon 83 E10
Little Hatfield E Yorks 209 E8
Little Hautbois Norf 160 E5
Little Haven Pembs 72 C5
W Sus 51 G7
Little Hay Staffs 134 C2
Little Hayfield Derbys 185 D8
Little Haywood Staffs 151 E10
Little Heath Ches E 167 E11
Derby 170 G5
London 68 B3
Oxon 82 F4
Staffs 151 B8
Staffs 168 D3
Warks 135 G7
W Berks 65 E7
W Mid 134 G6
Little Heck N Yorks 198 C5
Littlehempston Devon 8 C6
Little Henham Essex 105 E10
Little Henny Essex 107 D7
Little Herbert's Glos 81 B7
Little Hereford
Hereford 115 D11
Little Hill Hereford 97 F9
Little Horkesley Essex 107 E9
Little Hormead Herts 105 F8
Little Horsted E Sus 23 B7
Little Horton Wilts 46 B4
W Yorks 205 G9
Little Horwood Bucks 102 E5
Little Houghton
Northants 120 F6
S Yorks 198 G2
Littlehoughton
Northumb 264 F6
Little Hucklow Derbys 185 F11
Little Hulton Gtr Man 195 G8
Little Humber E Yorks 201 B8
Little Hungerford
W Berks 64 E4
Little Irchester
Northants 121 D8
Little Keyford Som 45 D9
Little Kimble Bucks 84 D4
Little Kineton Warks 118 G6
Little Kingshill Bucks 84 F5
Little Knowles Green
Suff 124 F5
Little Langdale Cumb 220 E6
Little Langford Wilts 46 F4
Little Laver Essex 87 D8
Little Lawford Warks 119 B9
Little Leigh Ches W 183 F10
Little Leighs Essex 88 B2
Little Leighton W Yorks 197 E8
Little Lever Gtr Man 195 F8
Little Limber Lincs 200 E6
Little Linford M Keynes 102 C6
Little London Bucks 83 C10
Bucks 84 D5
E Sus 23 B9
Essex 105 E10
Essex 106 E3
Glos 80 B2
Hants 47 D11
Hants 48 C6
Lincs 156 E6
Lincs 157 E8
Lincs 189 D10
Lincs 157 D7
Norf 140 D5
Norf 160 C5
Norf 160 F5
Powys 114 B2
Suff 125 E10
W Yorks 205 F11
Little Longstone
Derbys 185 G11
Little Lynturk Aberds 293 B7
Little Lyth Shrops 131 B9
Little Madeley Staffs 168 F3
Little Malvern Worcs 98 C5
Little Mancot Flint 166 B4
Little Maplestead Essex 106 E6
Little Marcle Hereford 98 D3
Little Marlow Bucks 65 B11
Little Marsden Lancs 204 F3
Little Marsh Bucks 102 G3
Norf 159 B10
Wilts 45 B11
Little Massingham Norf 158 E5
Little Melton Norf 142 B3
Little Mill Mon 78 E4
Little Milton Newport 59 B11
Oxon 83 E10
Little Minster Oxon 82 C4
Little Missenden Bucks 84 F6
Little Mongeham Kent 55 C10
Littlemoor Derbys 170 C5
Dorset 17 E9
Little Moor Gtr Man 184 D6
Lancs 203 F10
Little Moor End Lancs 195 B8
Littlemore Oxon 83 E8
Little Morrell Warks 118 F6
Littlemoss Gtr Man 184 B6
Little Mountain Flint 166 C3
Little Musgrave Cumb 222 C5
Little Ness Shrops 149 F8
Little Neston Ches W 182 F3
Little Newcastle Pembs 91 F9
Little Newsham Durham 224 B2
Little Norlington E Sus 23 C7
Little Norton Som 29 D7
Staffs 133 B11
Little Oakley Essex 108 F4
Northants 137 F7
Little Odell Bedford 121 F9
Little Offley Herts 104 F2
Little Onn Staffs 150 F6
Little Ormside Cumb 222 B4
Little Orton Cumb 239 F9
Leics 134 B6
Little Ouse Cambs 140 G2
Little Ouseburn N Yorks 215 G8
Littleover Derby 152 C6
Little Overton Wrex 166 G5
Little Oxney Green
Essex 87 D11
Little Packington Warks 134 G4
Little Parndon Essex 86 C6
Little Paxton Cambs 122 E3
Little Petherick Corn 10 G4
Little Pitlurg Moray 302 E4
Little Plumpton Lancs 202 G3
Little Plumstead Norf 160 G6
Little Ponton Lincs 155 C8
Littleport Cambs 139 F11
Little Posbrook Hants 33 G7
Little Poulton Lancs 202 F3
Little Preston Kent 53 B8
W Yorks 206 G3
Little Raveley Cambs 122 B5
Little Reedness
E Yorks 199 C10
Little Reynoldston
Swansea 56 D3
Little Ribston N Yorks 206 C3
Little Rissington Glos 81 B11
Little Rogart Highld 309 J7
Little Rollright Oxon 100 E5
Little Ryburgh Norf 159 D9
Little Ryle Northumb 264 G2
Little Ryton Shrops 131 C9
Little Salkeld Cumb 231 D7
Little Sampford Essex 106 E3
Little Sandhurst Brack 65 G10
Little Saredon Staffs 133 B8
Little Saxham Suff 124 E6
Little Scatwell Highld 300 D3
Little Scotland Gtr Man 194 E6
Little Sessay N Yorks 215 D9
Little Shelford Cambs 123 G9
Little Shoddesden Hants 47 D9
Little Shrewley Warks 118 D4
Little Shurdington Glos 80 B6
Little Silver Devon 26 F6
Devon 40 E4
Little Singleton Lancs 202 F3
Little Skillymarno
Aberds 303 D9
Little Smeaton N Yorks 198 D4
N Yorks 224 F6
Little Snoring Norf 159 C9
Little Sodbury S Glos 61 C9
Little Sodbury End
S Glos 61 C8
Little Somborne Hants 47 G11
Little Somerford Wilts 62 C3
Little Soudley Shrops 150 D4
Little Stainforth
N Yorks 212 F6
Little Stainton Darl 234 G2
Little Stanmore London 85 G11
Little Stanney Ches W 183 F7
Little Staughton Bedford 122 E2
Littlestead Green Oxon 65 D8
Little Steeping Lincs 174 C6
Staffs 133 B11
Littlestone-on-Sea Kent 39 C9
Little Stoke S Glos 60 C6
Staffs 151 C8
Little Stonham Suff 126 E2
Little Stretton Leics 136 C3
Shrops 131 E9
Little Strickland Cumb 221 B11
Little Studley N Yorks 214 E6
Little Stukeley Cambs 122 B4
Little Sugnall Staffs 150 C6
Little Sutton Ches W 182 F5
Lincs 157 E9
Shrops 131 G10
Little Swinburne
Northumb 241 B10
Little Tarrington Hereford 98 C2
Little Tew Oxon 101 F7
Little Tey Essex 107 G7
Little Thetford Cambs 123 B10
Little Thirkleby N Yorks 215 D9
Little Thornage Norf 159 B11
Little Thornton Lancs 202 E3
Little Thorpe Durham 234 C4
W Yorks 197 C7
Little Thorpe Leics 135 C10
Little Thurlow Suff 124 G3

Little Thurlow Green
Suff 124 G3
Little Thurrock Thurrock 68 D6
Littleton Bath 60 G5
Ches W 166 B6
Dorset 30 G5
Hants 48 G3
Perth 286 D6
Som 44 G3
Sur 50 D3
Sur 66 F5
Wilts 62 G2
Littleton Common Sur 66 E5
Littleton Drew Wilts 61 D10
Littleton-on-Severn
S Glos 79 G9
Littleton Pannel Wilts 46 C4
Littleton-upon-Severn
S Glos 79 G9
Little Torboll Highld 309 K7
Little Torrington Devon 25 D7
Little Totham Essex 88 C5
Little Toux Aberds 302 D5
Littletown Durham 234 C2
IoW 20 C6
W Yorks 197 C8
Little Town Cumb 220 B4
Lancs 203 F10
Warr 183 C10
Little Tring Herts 84 C6
Little Twycross Leics 134 B6
Little Tyrie Aberds 303 C8
Little Urswick Cumb 210 E5
Little Vantage W Loth 270 C2
Little Wakering Essex 70 B2
Little Walden Essex 105 C10
Little Waldingfield Suff 107 C8
Little Walsingham Norf 159 B8
Little Waltham Essex 88 C2
Little Warley Essex 87 G10
Little Warton Warks 134 C5
Little Washbourne Glos 99 E9
Little Weighton E Yorks 208 G5
Little Weldon Northants 137 F8
Little Welland Worcs 98 D6
Little Welnetham Suff 125 E7
Little Welton Lincs 190 D4
Little Wenham Suff 107 D11
Little Wenlock Telford 132 B2
Little Weston Som 29 B10
Little Whitehouse IoW 20 C5
Little Whittingham Green
Suff 126 B5
Littlewick Green
Windsor 65 D10
Little Wigborough Essex 89 B7
Little Wilbraham
Cambs 123 F10
Littlewindsor Dorset 28 G6
Little Wisbeach Lincs 156 C2
Little Wishford Wilts 46 F5
Little Witcombe Glos 80 B6
Little Witley Worcs 116 E5
Little Wittenham Oxon 83 G9
Little Wolford Warks 100 D5
Littleworth Bedford 103 C9
Glos 80 E4
Glos 100 D2
Oxon 82 F4
Oxon 83 D9
Staffs 151 E8
S Yorks 187 B10
Wilts 63 G7
Worcs 117 G7
W Sus 35 C11
Littleworth Common
Bucks 66 B2
Glos 80 E4
Oxon 82 F4
Staffs 151 F8
S Yorks 187 B10
Little Worthen Shrops 130 B6
Littleworth End
Cambs 123 C7
Little Wratting Suff 106 B3
Little Wymington
Bedford 121 D9
Little Wymondley Herts 104 F4
Little Wyrley Staffs 133 B10
Little Wytheford
Shrops 149 F11
Little Yeldham Essex 106 D5
Littley Green Essex 87 B11
Litton Derbys 185 G11
N Yorks 213 E8
Som 44 C5
Litton Cheney Dorset 17 C7
Litton Mill Derbys 185 G11
Liurbost W Isles 304 F5
Liverpool Mers 182 C4
Liverpool Airport Mers 182 E6
Liversedge W Yorks 197 C8
Liverton Devon 14 F2
Redcar 226 B4
Liverton Mines Redcar 226 B4
Liverton Street Kent 53 C11
Livesey Street Kent 53 C8
Livingshayes Devon 27 G7
Livingston W Loth 269 B11
Livingston Village
W Loth 269 B11
Lix Toll Stirling 285 D9
Lixwm Flint 181 G10
Lizard Corn 2 G6
Llaingoch Anglesey 178 E2
Llaithddu Powys 129 G11
Llampha V Glam 58 D2
Llan Powys 129 C7
Llanaber Gwyn 146 F2
Llanaelhaearn Gwyn 162 G5
Llanafan Ceredig 112 C3
Llanafan-fawr Powys 113 F9
Llanallgo Anglesey 179 D7
Llananno Powys 113 C11
Llanarmon Gwyn 145 B8
Llanarmon Dyffryn Ceiriog
Wrex 148 C3
Llanarmon Mynydd-mawr
Powys 148 D2
Llanarmon-yn-Ial
Denb 165 D10
Llanarth Ceredig 111 F8
Mon 78 C4
Llanarthne Carms 93 G10
Llanasa Flint 181 E10
Llanbabo Anglesey 178 D5
Llanbad Rhondda 58 C3
Llanbadarn Fawr
Ceredig 128 G2
Llanbadarn Fynydd
Powys 114 B2
Llanbadarn-y-Garreg
Powys 96 B2
Llanbadoc Mon 78 E5

Llanbadrig Anglesey 178 C5
Llanbeder Newport 78 G5
Llanbedr Gwyn 145 D12
Powys 96 B2
Powys 96 G4
Llanbedr-Dyffryn-Clwyd
Denb 165 D10
Llanbedrgoch Anglesey 179 D8
Llanbedr Pont Steffan /
Lampeter Ceredig 93 B11
Llanbedr-y-cennin
Conwy 164 B3
Llanberis Gwyn 163 D9
Llanbethery V Glam 58 E4
Llanbister Powys 114 C2
Llanblethian /
Llanfleiddan
V Glam 58 E3
Llanboidy Carms 92 G4
Llanbradach Caerph 77 G10
Llanbrynmair Powys 129 C7
Llancadle / Llancatal
V Glam 58 F4
Llancaiach Caerph 77 F10
Llancarfan V Glam 58 E4
Llancatal / Llancadle
V Glam 58 F4
Llancayo Mon 78 E5
Llancloudy Hereford 97 G9
Llancowrid Powys 130 E3
Llancynfelyn Ceredig 128 E2
Llan-dafal Bl Gwent 77 E11
Llandaff Cardiff 59 D7
Llandaff North Cardiff 59 D7
Llandanwg Gwyn 145 D11
Llandarcy Neath 57 B8
Llandawke Carms 74 C2
Llanddaniel Fab
Anglesey 179 G7
Llanddarog Carms 75 D8
Llanddeiniol Ceredig 111 C11
Llanddeiniolen Gwyn 163 B8
Llandderfel Gwyn 147 B9
Llanddeusant Anglesey 178 D4
Carms 94 G5
Llanddew Powys 95 E11
Llanddewi Swansea 56 D3
Llanddewi-Brefi Ceredig 112 F3
Llanddewi Fach Mon 78 F4
Llanddewi'r Cwm Powys 95 B10
Llanddewi Rhydderch
Mon 78 C5
Llanddewi Skirrid Mon 78 B4
Llanddewi Velfrey
Pembs 73 B10
Llanddewi Ystradenni
Powys 114 D2
Llanddoged Conwy 164 C4
Llanddona Anglesey 179 F9
Llanddowror Carms 74 D3
Llanddulas Conwy 180 F6
Llanddwywe Gwyn 145 E11
Llanddyfnan Anglesey 179 F8
Llandecwyn Gwyn 146 B2
Llandefaelog Fach
Powys 95 E10
Llandefaelog-tre'r-graig
Powys 96 F2
Llandefalle Powys 96 E2
Llandegai Gwyn 179 G9
Llandegfan Anglesey 179 G9
Llandegla Denb 165 E11
Llandegley Powys 114 E2
Llandegveth Mon 78 F4
Llandegwning Gwyn 144 C5
Llandeilo Carms 94 G3
Llandeilo Graban Powys 95 C11
Llandeilo'r Fan Powys 95 E7
Llandeloy Pembs 91 F7
Llandenny Mon 78 E5
Llandenny Walks Mon 78 E5
Llandevaud Newport 78 G5
Llandevenny Mon 60 D2
Llandewednock Corn 2 G6
Llandewi Ystradenny
Powys 114 D2
Llandilo Pembs 92 F2
Llandinabo Hereford 97 F10
Llandinam Powys 129 F10
Llandissilio Pembs 92 G2
Llandogo Mon 79 E8
Llandough V Glam 58 D3
V Glam 59 E7
Llandovery / Llanymddyfri
Carms 94 E4
Llandow / Llandw
V Glam 58 E2
Llandre Carms 94 C3
Ceredig 128 F2
Llandrillo Denb 147 B10
Llandrillo-yn-Rhôs
Conwy 180 E4
Llandrindod Wells
Powys 113 E11
Llandrinio Powys 148 F5
Llandruidion Pembs 90 G5
Llandsadwrn Conwy 180 E3
Llandudno Conwy 180 D3
Llandudno Junction /
Cyffordd Llandudno
Conwy 180 F3
Llandudoch / St Dogmaels
Pembs 92 B3
Llandw / Llandow
V Glam 58 E2
Llandwrog Gwyn 163 D7
Llandybie Carms 75 C10
Llandyfaelog Carms 74 C6
Llandyfan Carms 75 C10
Llandyfriog Ceredig 92 C6
Llandyfrydog Anglesey 178 D6
Llandygai Gwyn 179 G9
Llandygwydd Ceredig 92 C4
Llandynan Denb 165 G11
Llandyrnog Denb 165 C10
Llandysilio Powys 148 F5
Llandyssil Powys 130 D3
Llandysul Ceredig 93 C8
Llanedeyrn Cardiff 59 C8
Llanedi Carms 75 D9
Llanedwen Anglesey 163 B8
Llaneglwys Powys 95 D11
Llanegryn Gwyn 110 B2
Llanegwad Carms 93 G10
Llaneilian Anglesey 179 C7
Llanelian-yn-Rhôs
Conwy 180 F5
Llanelidan Denb 165 E10
Llanelieu Powys 96 E3
Llanellen Mon 78 C4
Llanelli Carms 56 B4
Llanelltyd Gwyn 146 F4
Llanelly Mon 78 C2
Llanelly Hill Mon 78 C2
Llanelwedd Powys 113 G10
Llanelwy / St Asaph
Denb 181 G8
Llanenddwyn Gwyn 145 E11
Llanengan Gwyn 144 D5
Llanerch Powys 130 E6
Llanerch Emrys Powys 148 E4

Llanerchymedd Anglesey 178 E6
Llanerfyl Powys 129 B10
Llaneuddog Anglesey 179 D7
Llan eurgain / Northop
Flint 166 B2
Llanfabon Caerph 77 G10
Llanfachraeth Anglesey . . . 178 E4
Llanfachreth Gwyn 146 E5
Llanfaelog Anglesey 178 G4
Llanfaelrhys Gwyn 144 D4
Llanfaenor Mon 78 B6
Llanfaes Anglesey 179 F10
Powys 95 F10
Llanfaethlu Anglesey 178 D4
Llanfaglan Gwyn 163 C7
Llanfair Gwyn 145 D11
Llanfair Caereinion
Powys 130 B2
Llanfair Clydogau
Ceredig 112 G2
Llanfair-Dyffryn-Clwyd
Denb 165 D10
Llanfairfechan Conwy . . . 179 F11
Llanfair Kilgeddin Mon . . 78 C4
Llanfair Kilgheddin Mon . . 78 C4
Pembs 72 D8
Llanfairpwll-gwyngyll
Anglesey 179 E10
Llanfair Talhaiarn
Conwy 180 G6
Llanfair Waterdine
Shrops 114 B4
Llanfairyneubwll
Anglesey 178 F3
Llanfairynghornwy
Anglesey 178 C4
Llanfallteg Carms 73 C11
Llanfallteg West Carms . . 73 B10
Llanfaredd Ceredig 113 G11
Llanfechain Powys 148 E3
Llanfechell Anglesey . . . 113 C9
Llanfechell Anglesey . . . 178 C5
Llanferres Denb 165 C11
Llan Ffestiniog Gwyn . . . 164 G2
Llanfflewyn Anglesey . . . 178 D5
Llanfigael Anglesey 178 E4
Llanfihangel-ar-arth
Carms 93 D9
Llanfihangel-Crucorney
Mon 96 G6
Llanfihangel Glyn Myfyr
Conwy 165 F7
Llanfihangel-helygen
Powys 113 E10
Llanfihangel Nant Bran
Powys 95 E8
Llanfihangel-nant-Melan
Powys 114 F3
Llanfihangel Rhydithon
Powys 114 D3
Llanfihangel Rogiet Mon . 60 D2
Llanfihangel Tal-y-llyn
Powys 96 F2
Llanfihangel Tor y Mynydd
Mon 79 E7
Llanfihangel-uwch-Gwili
Carms 93 G9
Llanfihangel-y-Creuddyn
Ceredig 112 B3
Llanfihangel-yng-Ngwynfa
Powys 147 F11
Llanfihangel yn Nhowyn
Anglesey 178 F4
Llanfihangel-y-pennant
Gwyn 128 B3
Gwyn 163 F8
Llanfilo Powys 96 E2
Llanfleiddan / Llanblethian
V Glam 58 E3
Llanfoist Mon 78 C3
Llanfor Gwyn 147 B8
Llanfrechfa Torf 78 G4
Llanfrothen Gwyn 163 G10
Llanfrynach Powys 95 F11
Llanfwrog Anglesey 178 E3
Denb 165 D10
Llanfynydd Carms 93 F11
Flint 166 B3
Llanfyrnach Pembs 92 C4
Llangadfan Powys 147 G10
Llangadog Carms 74 D6
Carms 94 F4
Llangadwaladr Anglesey . . 148 B5
Powys 148 B5
Llangaffo Anglesey 162 B6
Llangain Carms 74 B5
Llangammarch Wells
Powys 95 B8
Llangan V Glam 58 D3
Llangarron Hereford 79 C8
Llangasty Talyllyn Powys . 96 F2
Llangathen Carms 93 G11
Llangattock Powys 78 B2
Llangattock Lingoed
Mon 97 G7
Llangattock nigh Usk
Mon 78 D4
Llangattock-Vibon-Avel
Mon 79 B7
Llangedwyn Powys 148 E3
Llangefni Anglesey 179 E7
Llangeinor Bridgend 58 B2
Llangeitho Ceredig 112 F2
Llangeler Carms 93 D7
Llangendeirne Carms . . . 75 C7
Llangennech Carms 75 E9
Llangennith Swansea . . . 56 C2
Llangenny Powys 78 B2
Llangernyw Conwy 164 B5
Llangeview Mon 78 E5
Llangewydd Court
Bridgend 57 E11
Llangian Gwyn 144 D5
Llangloffan Pembs 91 E8
Llanglydwen Carms 92 F3
Llangoed Anglesey 179 F10
Llangoedmor Ceredig . . . 92 B3
Llangollen Denb 166 G2
Llangolman Pembs 92 F2
Llangors Powys 96 F2
Llangorwen Ceredig 128 G2
Llangovan Mon 79 D7
Llangower Gwyn 147 C8
Llangrannog Ceredig . . . 110 G6
Llangristiolus Anglesey . . 178 G6
Llangrove Hereford 79 B8
Llangua Mon 97 F7
Llangunllo Powys 114 C4
Llangunnor Carms 74 B6
Llangurig Powys 113 B8
Llangwm Conwy 165 G8
Mon 78 E6
Pembs 73 D7
Llangwnnadl Gwyn 144 C4
Llangwyfan Denb 165 B10
Llangwyfan-isaf
Anglesey 162 B4

Llangwyllog Anglesey 178 F6
Llangwyryfon Ceredig . . . 111 C11
Llangybi Ceredig 112 G2
Gwyn 162 G6
Mon 78 G5
Llangyfelach Swansea . . . 56 B6
Llangynderyn Carms 75 C7
Llangynhafal Denb 165 C10
Llangynidr Powys 77 B11
Llangyniew Powys 130 B2
Llangynin Carms 74 B2
Llangynog Carms 74 B4
Powys 147 D11
Llangynwyd Bridgend . . . 57 D11
Llanhamlach Powys 95 F11
Llanharan Rhondda 58 C4
Llanharry Rhondda 58 C4
Llanhennock Mon 78 G5
Llanhilleth Bl Gwent 78 E2
Llanhowel Pembs 90 F6
Llanidloes Powys 129 G9
Llaniestyn Gwyn 144 C5
Llanifyny Powys 129 G7
Llanigon Powys 96 D4
Llanilar Ceredig 112 C2
Ceredig 148 C4
Llanilid Rhondda 58 C3
Llanilltud Fawr / Llantwit
Major V Glam 58 F3
Llanio Ceredig 112 F2
Llanion Pembs 73 E7
Llanishen Cardiff 59 C7
Mon 79 E7
Llanllawddog Carms 93 F9
Llanllechid Gwyn 163 B10
Llanllowell Mon 78 F5
Llanllugan Powys 129 C11
Llanllwch Carms 74 B5
Llanllwchaiarn Powys . . . 130 E2
Llanllwni Carms 93 D9
Llanllwyd Shrops 130 G3
Llanllyfni Gwyn 163 E7
Llanmadoc Swansea 56 C2
Llanmaes Cardiff 58 F3
V Glam 58 F3
Llanmartin Newport 59 B11
Llanmerwig Powys 130 E3
Llanmihangel V Glam . . . 58 E3
Llan-mill Pembs 73 C10
Llanmiloe Carms 74 D3
Llanmorlais Swansea 56 C4
Llannefydd Conwy 181 G7
Llannerch-y-môr Flint . . . 181 F11
Llannon Carms 75 D8
Llan-non / Llanon
Ceredig 111 D10
Llannor Gwyn 145 B7
Llanon Pembs 90 E6
Llanon / Llan-non
Ceredig 111 D10
Llanover Mon 78 D4
Llanpumsaint Carms 93 F8
Llanreath Pembs 73 E7
Llanreithan Pembs 91 F7
Llanrhaeadr Denb 165 C9
Llanrhaeadr-ym-Mochnant
Powys 148 D2
Llanrhian Pembs 90 E6
Llanrhidian Swansea 56 C3
Llanrhos Conwy 180 E3
Llanrhyddlad Anglesey . . . 178 D4
Llanrhystud Ceredig 111 D10
Llanrosser Hereford 96 D5
Llanrothal Hereford 79 B7
Llanrug Gwyn 163 C8
Llanrumney Cardiff 59 C8
Llanrwst Conwy 164 C4
Llansadurnen Carms 74 C3
Llansadwrn Anglesey . . . 179 F9
Carms 94 E3
Llansaint Carms 74 D5
Llansamlet Swansea 57 B7
Llansanffraid Glan Conwy
Conwy 180 G4
Llansannan Conwy 164 B6
Llansannor V Glam 58 D3
Llansantffraed Ceredig . . 111 D10
Powys 96 F2
Llansantffraed Cwmdeuddwr
Powys 113 D9
Llansantffraed-in-Elwel
Powys 113 G11
Llansantffraid-ym-Mechain
Powys 148 E3
Llansawel Carms 94 D2
Neath 57 C8
Llansawel / Briton Ferry
Neath 57 C8
Llansilin Powys 148 D4
Llansoy Mon 78 E6
Llanspyddid Powys 95 F10
Llanstadwell Pembs 72 D6
Llansteffan Carms 74 C5
Llanstephan Powys 96 C2
Llanstephan Torf 78 G4
Llanteems Mon 78 F5
Llanteg Pembs 73 C11
Llanthony Mon 96 F5
Llantilio Crossenny Mon . . 78 C5
Llantilio Pertholey Mon . . 78 B4
Llantood Pembs 92 C3
Llantrisant Anglesey 178 E5
Mon 78 F5
Rhondda 58 C4
Llantrithyd V Glam 58 E4
Llantwit Neath 57 B9
Llantwit Fardre Rhondda . . 58 B5
Llantwit Major / Llanilltud
Fawr V Glam 58 F3
Llanuwchllyn Gwyn 147 C7
Llanvaches Newport 78 G6
Llanvair Discoed Mon . . . 78 G6
Llanvapley Mon 78 C5
Llanvetherine Mon 78 B5
Llanveynoe Hereford 96 E6
Llanvihangel Crucorney
Mon 96 G6
Llanvihangel Gobion
Mon 78 D5
Llanvihangel-Ystern-
Llewern Mon 78 C6
Llanwarne Hereford 97 F10
Llanwddyn Powys 147 F10
Llanwenarth Mon 78 C3
Llanwenog Ceredig 93 B9
Llanwern Newport 59 B11
Llanwinio Carms 92 F5
Llanwnda Gwyn 163 D7
Pembs 91 D8
Llanwnnen Ceredig 93 B10
Llanwnog Powys 129 E10
Llanwrda Carms 94 E4
Llanwrin Powys 128 C5
Llanwrthwl Powys 113 E9
Llanwrtud / Llanwrtyd Wells
Powys 95 B7
Llanwrtyd Wells / Llanwrtud
Powys 95 B7
Llanwyddelan Powys . . . 129 C11
Llanyblodwel Shrops 148 E4
Llanybri Carms 74 C4
Llanybydder Carms 93 C10
Llanycefn Pembs 91 G11

Llanychaer Pembs 91 D9
Llanycil Gwyn 147 C8
Llanycrwys Carms 94 B2
Llanymawddwy Gwyn . . . 147 F8
Llanymddyfri / Llandovery
Carms 94 E4
Llanymynech Powys 148 E5
Llanynghenedl Anglesey . . 178 E4
Llanynys Denb 165 C10
Llan-y-pwll Wrex 166 E5
Llanyrafon Torf 78 G4
Llanyre Powys 113 E10
Llanystumdwy Gwyn . . . 145 B9
Llanywern Powys 96 F2
Llawhaden Pembs 73 B9
Llawnt Shrops 148 C5
Llawr Dref Belfaf Gwyn . . 144 D5
Llawr-y-glyn Powys 129 E8
Llechcynfarwy Anglesey . . 178 E5
Llecheiddior Gwyn 163 G7
Llechfaen Powys 95 F11
Llechfraith Gwyn 146 F3
Llechryd Caerph 77 D10
Ceredig 92 C4
Llechrydau Wrex 148 C4
Lledrod Ceredig 112 C2
Llenmerewig Powys 130 E3
Llethrid Swansea 56 C4
Llettyrerchen Carms 75 E7
Llidiad Nenog Carms 93 D10
Llidiardau Gwyn 147 B9
Llidiart-y-parc Denb 165 G10
Llithfaen Gwyn 162 G5
Lloc Flint 181 F10
Llong Flint 166 C3
Llowes Powys 96 C3
Lloyney Powys 114 B4
Llugwy Powys 128 C3
Llundain-fach Ceredig . . . 111 F10
Llwydcoed Rhondda 77 E7
Llwydiarth Powys 147 F11
Llwyn Powys 114 B6
Shrops 130 G5
Llwyncelyn Ceredig 111 F8
Llwyndafydd Ceredig 111 F7
Llwynderw Powys 130 C4
Llwyn-derw Powys 129 G8
Llwyn-du Mon 78 B3
Llwynduris Ceredig 92 C4
Llwyndyrys Gwyn 162 G5
Llwyneinion Wrex 166 F3
Llwyngwril Gwyn 110 B2
Llwynhendy Carms 56 B4
Llwyn-hendy Carms 56 B4
Llwynmawr Wrex 148 B4
Llwyn-on Village M Tydf . . 77 C8
Llwyn-Têg Carms 75 D9
Llwyn-y-brain Carms 73 C11
Llwyn-y-go Shrops 148 E6
Llwynypia Rhondda 129 E7
Llwyn-yr-groes Ceredig . . 111 F11
Llwyn-yr-hwrdd Pembs . . 92 E4
Llynclys Shrops 148 E5
Llynfaes Anglesey 178 F6
Llysfaen Conwy 180 F5
Llyswen Powys 96 D2
Llysworney V Glam 58 E3
Llys-y-frân Pembs 91 G10
Llywel Powys 95 F7
Llywernog Ceredig 128 G4
Load Brook S Yorks 186 D3
Lôn Falk 279 F9
Loandhu Highld 301 B8
Loanend Northumb 273 E8
Loanhead Aberds 302 D6
Midloth 270 B5
Perth 286 D5
Loans S Ayrs 257 C8
Loansdean Northumb . . . 252 G5
Loans of Tullich Highld . . 301 B8
Lobb Devon 40 F3
Lobhillcross Devon 12 D5
Lobley Hill T&W 242 E6
Lobthorpe Lincs 155 E9
Loch a Charnain
W Isles 297 G4
Loch a' Ghainmhich
W Isles 304 F3
Lochailort Highld 295 G9
Lochaline Highld 289 E8
Lochanhully Highld 301 G9
Lochans Dumfries 236 D2
Locharbriggs Dumfries . . 247 G11
London Apprentice Corn. . 5 E10
London Beach Kent 53 F11
London Colney Herts . . . 85 E11
Londonderry N Yorks . . . 214 B6
London End Cambs 122 G6
London Fields W Mid . . . 133 E8
London Minstead Hants . . 32 E4
Londonthorpe Lincs 155 C8
Londubh Highld 307 L3
Lonemore Highld 299 B7
Highld 309 L2
Long Ashton N Som 60 E5
Long Bank Worcs 116 C5
Longbar N Ayrs 266 E6
Longbar Warr 183 C10
Long Bennington Lincs . . 172 G4
Longbenton T&W 243 D7
Longborough Glos 100 F3
Long Bredy Dorset 17 C7
Longbridge Plym 7 D10
Warks 118 E5
W Mid 117 B10
Longbridge Deverill
Wilts 45 E11
Longbridge Hayes Stoke . 168 E5
Longbridgemuir
Dumfries 238 D3
Long Buckby Northants . . 120 D2
Long Buckby Wharf
Northants 120 D2
Longburgh Cumb 239 F8
Longburton Dorset 29 E11
Longcause Devon 8 C5
Longcliffe Derbys 170 D2
Long Clawson Leics 154 D4
Long Common Hants . . . 33 E8
Long Compton Staffs . . . 151 E7
Warks 100 E5
Longcot Oxon 38 E2
Long Crendon Bucks . . . 83 D11
Long Crichel Dorset 31 E7
Longcroft Cumb 238 F6
Falk 278 F5
Longcross Devon 12 F4
Sur 66 F3
Long Cross Wilts 45 G9
Longden Shrops 131 B8
Longden Common
Shrops 131 B8
Long Dean Wilts 61 D11
Longden Shrops 131 B8
Long Ditton Sur 67 F7
Longdon Staffs 151 F11
Worcs 99 D7

Loch nam Madadh
W Isles 296 E5
Lochboisdale / Loch Baghasdail
W Isles 296 E5
Lochore Fife 280 B3
Lochпортain W Isles 296 D5
Lochran Perth 280 B2
Lochranza N Ayrs 255 B10
Lochs Crofts Moray 302 C3
Loch Sgioport W Isles . . . 297 H4
Lochside Aberds 293 G9
Highld 301 D8
Highld 308 D4
Highld 309 J5
Lochslin Highld 311 L2
Lochstack Lodge Highld . . 306 E7
Lochton Aberds 293 D9
Lochty Angus 293 G7
Fife 287 G9
Perth 286 E5
Lochuisge Highld 289 D9
Lochurr Dumfries 247 F11
Lochwinnoch Renfs 267 D7
Lochwood Dumfries 248 D3
Glasgow 268 B3
Lochyside Highld 290 F3
Lockengate Corn 5 C10
Lockerbie Dumfries 248 G4
Lockeridge Wilts 63 F7
Lockeridge Dene Wilts . . 62 F6
Lockerley Hants 32 B3
Lockhills Cumb 230 B6
Locking N Som 43 B11
Lockinge Oxon 64 B2
Locking Stumps Warr. . . 183 C10
Lockington E Yorks 208 D5
Leics 153 D9
Lockleywood Shrops . . . 150 D3
Locksbottom London . . . 68 F2
Locksbrook Bath 61 G8
Locksgreen IoW 20 C4
Locks Heath Hants 33 F8
Lockton N Yorks 226 G6
Lockwood N Yorks 196 D6
Loddington Leics 136 C5
Northants 120 B6
Loddiswell Devon 8 F4
Loddon Norf 143 D7
Loddon Ingloss Norf 142 D6
Lode Cambs 123 E10
Lode Heath W Mid 134 G3
Loders Dorset 16 C5
Lodge Bank Shrops 149 D11
Lodge Green N Yorks . . . 223 F9
W Mid 134 G5
Lodge Hill Corn 6 C4
W Yorks 197 C9
Lodge Lees Kent 55 D8
Lodge Moor S Yorks 186 D3
Lodge Park Worcs 117 D10
Lodsworth W Sus 34 C6
Lodsworth Common
W Sus 34 C6
Lodway Bristol 60 D4
Lofthouse N Yorks 214 E2
W Yorks 197 B10
Lofthouse Gate
W Yorks 197 C10
Loftus Redcar 226 B4
Logan E Ayrs 258 E3
Loganlea W Loth 269 C9
Logan Mains Dumfries. . . 236 E2
Loggerheads Denb 165 C11
Staffs 150 B4
Logie Angus 293 G8
Fife 287 E7
Moray 301 D10
Logiealmond Lodge
Perth 286 D3
Logie Coldstone Aberds . . 292 C6
Logie Hill Highld 301 B7
Logie Newton Aberds . . . 302 E6
Logie Pert Angus 293 G8
Logierait Perth 286 B3
Login Carms 92 G3
Logmore Green Sur 50 D6
Lolworth Cambs 123 E7
Lomeshaye Lancs 204 F2
Lôn Gwyn 147 C7
Lonbain Highld 298 D6
Londesborough E Yorks . . 208 D3
London 67 C10
Londonderry N Yorks . . . 214 B6
London End Lincs 155 C8
Londonthorpe Lincs 155 C8
Lôn-las Swansea 57 B8

London continued
Worcs 98 D6
London Green Staffs . . . 151 F11
London Heath Worcs 98 D6
London on Tern
Telford 150 F2
Londesborough Devon . . . 14 C3
Longdowns Corn 2 C6
Long Drax N Yorks 199 B7
Longdrum Angus 292 G4
Long Duckmanton
Derbys 186 G6
Long Eaton Derbys 153 C9
Longfield Kent 68 F6
Shetland 313 M5
Longfield Hill Kent 68 F6
Longfleet Poole 18 C6
Longford Derbys 152 B4
Glos 98 G6
Kent 52 B4
London 66 D4
Shrops 150 C2
Telford 150 F4
Warr 183 C10
W Mid 135 G7
Longforgan Perth 287 E7
Longformacus Borders . . . 272 D3
Longframlington
Northumb 252 C4
Long Gardens Essex 106 D6
Long Green Ches W 183 G7
Suff 125 B11
Worcs 98 E6
Longham Dorset 19 B7
Norf 159 F8
Long Hanborough Oxon. . 82 C6
Longhaven Aberds 303 F11
Longhedge Wilts 45 E10
Longhill Aberds 303 D9
Longhirst Northumb 252 F6
Longhope Glos 79 B11
Orkney 314 G3
Longhorsley Northumb . . 252 E4
Longhoughton
Northumb 264 G6
Long Itchington Warks . . 119 D8
Long John's Hill Norf . . . 142 B4
Longlands Cumb 229 D11
London 68 E2
Longlane Derbys 152 B5
W Berks 64 E3
Long Lane Telford 150 F2
Long Lawford Warks . . . 119 B9
Longlevens Glos 99 G7
Longley W Yorks 196 E6
W Yorks 197 C9
Longley Estate S Yorks . . 186 C5
Longley Green Worcs . . . 116 G4
Longleys Perth 286 C6
Longmanhill Aberds 303 C7
Long Marston Herts 84 B5
N Yorks 206 C6
Warks 100 B3
Long Marton Cumb 231 G9
Long Meadow Cambs . . 123 E10
Long Meadowend
Shrops 131 G8
Long Melford Suff 107 B7
Longmoor Camp Hants . . 49 F7
Longmorn Moray 302 D2
Longmoss Ches E 184 G5
Long Newnton Glos 80 G6
Long Newton Borders . . . 262 D3
Stockton 225 B7
Long Newton E Loth 271 C10
Longney Glos 80 C3
Longniddry E Loth 281 F9
Longnor Shrops 131 B9
Staffs 151 G7
Longnor Park Shrops . . . 131 C9
Long Oak Shrops 149 E7
Longparish Hants 48 E2
Longpark Corn 2 C6
Cumb 239 E10
Long Park S Yorks 48 G2
Longport Stoke 168 F5
Long Preston N Yorks . . . 204 B2
Longridge Lancs 203 F8
Staffs 151 F8
W Loth 269 C9
Long Riston E Yorks 209 E8
Longrock Corn 1 C5
Long Sandall S Yorks . . . 198 F6
Longscales N Yorks 205 B10
Longsdon Staffs 169 E7
Longshaw Gtr Man 194 G4
Longside Aberds 303 E10
Longsight Gtr Man 184 B5
Long Sight Gtr Man 196 F2
Longslow Shrops 150 B3
Longsowerby Cumb 239 G9
Longstanton Cambs 123 D7
Longstock Hants 47 F11
Longstone Corn 11 G7
Pembs 73 D10
Longstowe Cambs 122 G6
Long Stratton Norf 142 E3
Longstreet Wilts 46 D6
Long Street M Keynes . . . 102 B5
Long Sutton Hants 49 D8
Lincs 157 E8
Som 29 C7
Longthorpe Pboro 138 D3
Long Thurlow Suff 125 D10
Longthwaite Cumb 230 G4
Longton Lancs 194 B3
Stoke 168 G6
Longtown Cumb 239 D10
Hereford 96 F6
Longview Mers 182 C6
Longville in the Dale
Shrops 131 D11
Long Whatton Leics 153 E9
Longwick Bucks 84 E3
Long Wittenham Oxon . . 83 G8
Longwitton Northumb . . . 252 F3
Longwood Shrops 132 B2
Longwood Edge
W Yorks 196 D6
Longworth Oxon 82 F5
Longyester E Loth 271 B10

Lonmay Aberds 303 D10
Lonmore Highld 298 E2
Looe Corn 6 E5
Looe Mills Corn 6 C5
Loose Kent 53 C9
Loose Hill Kent 53 C9
Loosegate Lincs 156 D6
Loosley Row Bucks 84 E4
Lopcombe Corner Wilts . . 47 F9
Lopen Som 28 E6
Loppergarth Cumb 210 D5
Loppington Shrops 149 D9
Lopwell Devon 7 C9
Lorbottle Northumb 264 G2
Lorbottle Hall Northumb . . 252 B2
Lordsbridge Norf 157 G11
Lord's Hill Soton 32 D5
Lordshill Common Sur. . . 50 E4
Lordswood Soton 32 D6
Lords Wood Medway 69 G9
Lornty Perth 286 C5
Loscoe Derbys 170 F6
W Yorks 198 C2
Loscombe Dorset 16 B6
Losgaintir W Isles 305 J2
Lossiemouth Moray 302 B2
Lossit Argyll 254 B2
Lossit Lodge Argyll 274 G5
Lostock Gtr Man 195 F7
Lostock Gralam
Ches W 183 F11
Lostock Green Ches W . . 183 G11
Lostock Hall Lancs 194 B4
Lostock Junction
Gtr Man 195 F7
Lostwithiel Corn 6 D2
Loth Orkney 314 C6
Lothbeg Highld 311 H3
Lothersdale N Yorks 204 D5
Lothianbridge Midloth . . 270 C6
Lothmore Highld 311 H3
Lottisham Som 44 G5
Loudwater Bucks 85 F9
Loughborough Leics . . . 153 F10
Loughor Swansea 56 B5
Loughton Essex 86 F6
M Keynes 102 D6
Shrops 132 G2
Lound Lincs 155 F11
Notts 187 D11
Suff 143 D10
Loundsley Green Derbys . 186 G5
Lount Leics 153 F7
Lour Angus 287 C8
Louth Lincs 190 D4
Lovat Highld 300 E5
Lovaton Devon 7 B10
Love Clough Lancs 195 B10
Lovedean Hants 33 E11
Love Green Bucks 66 C4
Lover Wilts 32 C2
Loversall S Yorks 187 B9
Loves Green Essex 87 E10
Lovesome Hill N Yorks . . 225 F7
Loveston Pembs 73 D9
Lovington Som 44 G5
Low Ackworth W Yorks . . 198 D3
Low Alwinton
Northumb 251 B10
Low Angerton Northumb . 252 G3
Lowbands Glos 98 E5
Low Barlings Lincs 189 F7
Low Barugh S Yorks . . . 197 F10
Low Bentham N Yorks . . 212 F2
Low Biggins Cumb 212 D2
Low Blantyre S Lanark . . 268 D3
Low Borrowbridge
Cumb 222 E2
Low Bradfield S Yorks . . 186 C3
Low Bradley N Yorks . . . 204 D6
Low Braithwaite Cumb . . 230 C4
Low Bridge Wilts 62 E3
Low Brunton Northumb . . 241 C10
Low Burnham N Lincs . . . 199 G9
Low Burton N Yorks 214 C4
Low Buston Northumb . . . 252 B6
Lowca Cumb 228 G5
Low Catton E Yorks 207 C10
Low Clanfield Oxon 82 E2
Low Common Norf 142 E2
Low Compton Gtr Man . . 196 F2
Low Coniscliffe Darl 224 C5
Low Cotehill Cumb 239 G11
Low Coylton S Ayrs 257 F8
Low Crosby Cumb 239 F10
Lowcross Hill Ches W . . . 167 E7
Low Dalby N Yorks 217 B7
Lowdham Notts 171 F11
Low Dinsdale Darl 224 C6
Low Ellington N Yorks . . . 214 C4

Lower Bodham Norf 160 B2
Lower Bodinnar Corn 1 C4
Lower Boscaswell Corn. . . 1 C4
Lower Bordean Hants . . . 33 C11
Lower Bourne Sur 49 E10
Lower Bradley W Mid . . . 133 D9
Lower Brailes Warks . . . 100 D5
Lower Breakish Highld . . 295 C8
Lower Breinton Hereford . 97 D9
Lower Broadheath
Worcs 116 F6
Lower Broughton
Gtr Man 184 B4
Lower Brynamman Neath . 76 C2
Lower Brynn Corn 5 C9
Lower Buckenhill
Hereford 98 D2
Lower Buckland Hants . . . 20 B2
Lower Burgate Hants . . . 31 D11
Lower Burrow Som 28 C6
Lower Burton Hereford . . 115 F8
Lower Bush Medway 69 F7
Lower Cadsden Bucks . . . 84 E4
Lower Caldecote
C Beds 104 B3
Lower Cam Glos 80 E2
Lower Canada N Som . . . 43 B11
Lower Carden Ches W . . 167 E7
Lower Catesby
Northants 119 F10
Lower Chapel Powys 95 D10
Lower Chedworth Glos . . 81 C9
Lower Cheriton Devon . . . 27 G10
Lower Chicksgrove Wilts . 46 G3
Lower Chute Wilts 47 C11
Lower Clapton London . . 67 B11
Lower Clent Worcs 117 B8
Lower Clicker Corn 6 C5
Lower Clopton Warks . . . 118 F3
Lower Common
Hants 65 G9
Mon 78 B2
Shrops 131 B8
Lower Coppthurst Lancs . 194 C5
Lower Cotburn Aberds . . 303 D7
Lower Cousley Wood
E Sus 53 G7
Lower Coxhead Lancs . . . 69 G10
Lower Cragabus Argyll . . 254 C4
Lower Creedy Devon . . . 26 G4
Lower Cumberworth
W Yorks 197 F8
Lower Cwm-twrch Powys . 76 C3
Lower Daggons Hants . . . 31 E9
Lower Darwen Blackburn . 195 B7
Lower Dean Bedford . . . 121 D11
Devon 8 C4
Lower Dell Highld 292 B2
Lower Denby W Yorks . . 197 F8
Lower Denzell Corn 5 B7
Lower Deuchries
Aberds 302 D6
Lower Diabaig Highld . . . 299 C7
Lower Dicker E Sus 23 C9
Lower Dinchope Shrops . 131 G9
Lower Dowdeswell Glos . 81 B8
Lower Down Shrops 130 G6
Lower Drift Corn 1 D4
Lower Dunsforth
N Yorks 215 G8
Lower Durston Som 28 B3
Lower Earley Wokingham . 65 E9
Lower East Carleton
Norf 142 C3
Lower Eastern Green
W Mid 118 B5
Lower Edmonton London . 86 G4
Lower Egleton Hereford . . 98 B2
Lower Elkstone Staffs . . . 169 D9
Lower Ellastone Staffs . . 169 G10
Lower End Bucks 83 D11
Bucks 102 C4
C Beds 103 G8
Glos 81 E7
Northants 120 G6
M Keynes 120 G5
Northants 121 F7
Oxon 82 B4
Lower Everleigh Wilts . . . 47 C7
Lower Eythorne Kent 55 D9
Lower Failand N Som . . . 60 E4
Lower Faintree Shrops . . . 132 F3
Lower Falkenham Suff . . . 108 D5
Lower Farringdon Hants . . 49 F8
Lower Feltham London . . 66 E5
Lower Fittleworth W Sus . 35 D8
Lower Foxdale IoM 192 E3
Lower Frankton Shrops . . 149 C7
Lower Freystrop Pembs . . 73 C7
Lower Froyle Hants 49 E9
Lower Gabwell Devon . . . 9 B8
Lower Gledfield Highld . . 309 K5
Lower Godney Som 44 E3
Lower Goldstone Kent . . . 71 G9
Lower Gornal W Mid . . . 133 E8
Lower Grange W Yorks . . 205 G8
Lower Gravenhurst
C Beds 104 D2
Lower Green Essex 88 E2
Essex 105 E8
Essex 106 E4
Herts 104 E6
Kent 52 E5
Kent 52 E6
Norf 159 B9
Staffs 133 C7
Suff 124 D4
W Berks 63 E11
Lower Green Bank
Lancs 202 B6
Lower Grove Common
Hereford 97 F11
Lower Hacheston Suff . . . 126 F6
Lower Halistra Highld . . . 298 D2
Lower Halford Sur 66 F5
Lower Halstock Leigh
Dorset 29 F8
Lower Halstow Kent 69 F11
Lower Hamworth Poole . . 18 C6
Lower Hardres Kent 55 C7
Lower Hardwick
Hereford 115 F8

Lower Hartlip Kent 69 G10
Lower Hartshay Derbys . . 170 E5
Lower Hartwell Bucks . . . 84 C3
Lower Hatton Staffs 150 B6
Lower Hawthwaite
Cumb 210 B4
Lower Haysden Kent 52 D5
Lower Hayton Shrops . . . 131 G10
Lower Hazel S Glos 60 B6
Lower Heath Ches E 168 C5
Lower Hempriggs
Moray 301 C11
Lower Heppington Kent . . 54 C6
Lower Hergest Hereford . . 114 F5
Lower Herne Kent 71 F7
Lower Heyford Oxon 101 G9
Lower Heysham Lancs . . . 211 G8
Lower Higham Kent 69 E8
Lower Highmoor Oxon . . . 65 B8
Lower Holbrook Suff 108 E3
Lower Holditch Dorset . . . 28 G4
Lower Hook Worcs 98 C6
Lower Hookner Devon . . . 13 E10
Lower Hopton Shrops . . . 149 E7
W Yorks 197 D7
Lower Hordley Shrops . . . 149 D7
Lower Horncroft W Sus . . 35 D8
Lower Horsebridge
E Sus 23 C9
Lowerhouse Ches E 184 F6
Lancs 204 G2
Lower House Halton 183 D8
Lower Houses W Yorks . . 197 D7
Lower Howsell Worcs . . . 98 B5
Lower Illey W Mid 133 G9
Lower Island Kent 71 F7
Lower Kersal Gtr Man . . . 195 G10
Lower Kilburn Derbys . . . 170 F5
Lower Kilcott Glos 61 B9
Lower Killeyan Argyll . . . 254 C3
Lower Kingcombe Dorset .17 B7
Lower Kingswood Sur . . . 51 D8
Lower Kinnerton
Ches W 166 C4
Lower Kinsham
Hereford 115 E7
Lower Knapp Som 28 B3
Lower Knightley Staffs . . 150 E6
Lower Knowle Bristol . . . 60 E5
Lower Langford N Som . . 60 G3
Lower Largo Fife 287 G8
Lower Layham Suff 107 C10
Lower Ledwyche
Shrops 115 C10
Lower Leigh Staffs 151 B10
Lower Lemington Glos . . 100 E4
Lower Lenie Highld 300 G5
Lower Lode Glos 99 E7
Lower Lovacott Devon . . . 25 B8
Lower Loxhore Devon . . . 40 F6
Lower Lydbrook Glos . . . 79 B9
Lower Lye Hereford 115 D8
Lower Machen Newport . . 59 B8
Lower Maes-coed
Hereford 96 E6
Lower Mains Clack 279 B9
Lower Mannington
Dorset 31 F9
Lower Marsh Som 30 C2
Lower Marston Som 45 E9
Lower Meend Glos 79 E8
Lower Menadue Corn . . . 5 D10
Lower Merridge Som . . . 43 G8
Lower Mickletown
W Yorks 198 B2
Lower Middleton Cheney
Northants 101 C10
Lower Midway Derbys . . . 152 E6
Lower Mill Corn 3 B10
Lower Milovaig Highld . . . 296 F7
Lower Milton Som 44 D4
Lower Moor Wilts 81 G8
Worcs 99 B9
Lower Morton S Glos . . . 79 G10
Lower Mountain Flint . . . 166 D5
Lower Nazeing Essex . . . 86 D5
Lower Netchwood
Shrops 132 E2
Lower Netherton Devon . . 14 G3
Lower New Inn Torf 78 F4
Lower Ninnes Corn 1 C5
Lower Nobut Staffs 151 C10
Lower North Dean 84 F5
Lower Nyland Dorset . . . 30 C2
Lower Ochrwyth Caerph . 59 B8
Lower Odcombe Som . . . 29 D8
Lower Oddington Glos . . 100 F4
Lower Ollach Highld 295 B7
Lower Padworth W Berks . 64 F6
Lower Penarth V Glam . . . 59 E7
Lower Penn Staffs 133 D7
Lower Pennington
Hants 20 C2
Lower Penwortham
Lancs 194 B4
Lower Peover Ches E . . . 184 G2
Lower Pexhill Ches E . . . 184 G5
Lower Pilsley Derbys . . . 170 C6
Lower Pitkerrie Highld . . 311 L2
Lower Place Gtr Man . . . 196 F2
London 67 C8
Lower Pollicot Bucks . . . 84 C2
Lower Porthkerry V Glam . 58 F5
Lower Porthpean Corn. . . 5 E11
Lower Quinton Warks . . . 100 B3
Lower Rabber Hereford . . 114 G5
Lower Race Torf 78 E3
Lower Radley Oxon 83 F8
Lower Rainham Medway . 69 F10
Lower Ratley Hants 32 C4
Lower Rea Glos 80 B4
Lower Ridge Devon 28 G4
Shrops 132 F3
Lower Roadwater Som . . .42 F4
Lower Rochford Worcs . . 116 D2
Lower Rose Corn 4 E5
Lower Row Dorset 31 G8
Lower Sapey Worcs 116 E3
Lower Seagry Wilts 62 C3
Lower Sheering Essex . . . 87 C7
Lower Shelton C Beds . . . 103 C9
Lower Shiplake Oxon . . . 65 D9
Lower Shuckburgh
Warks 119 E9
Lower Sketty Swansea . . . 56 C6
Lower Slackstead Hants . . 32 C5
Lower Slade Devon 40 D4
Lower Slaughter Glos . . . 100 G3
Lower Solva Pembs 87 G11
Lower Soothill W Yorks . . 197 C9
Lower Soudley Glos 79 D11
Lower Southfield
Hereford 98 C3
Lower Stanton St Quintin
Wilts 62 C2

Lower Stoke Medway . . . 69 D10
W Mid 119 B7
Lower Stondon C Beds . . 104 D3
Lower Stone Glos. 79 G11
Lower Stonnall Staffs . 133 C11
Lower Stow Bedon Norf 141 E9
Lower Stratton Som 28 D6
Swindon 63 B7
Lower Street E Sus. 38 E2
Norf 160 B5
Norf 160 C3
Norf 160 F6
Suff 108 E3
Suff 124 G5
Lower Stresham Worcs . . 99 C8
Lower Stretton Warr . 183 E10
Lower Studley Wilts 45 B11
Lower Sundon C Beds . . 103 F10
Lower Swainswick Bath . . 61 F9
Lower Swanwick Hants . . 19 B7
Lower Swell Glos 100 F3
Lower Sydenham
London 67 E11
Lower Tadmarton Oxon . 101 D8
Lower Tale Devon 27 G9
Lower Tasburgh Norf . . 142 D3
Lower Tean Staffs 151 B10
Lower Thorpe
Northants 101 B10
Lower Threapwood
Wrex 166 G6
Lower Thurlton Norf . . 143 D8
Lower Thurnham Lancs . 202 C5
Lower Thurvaston
Derbys 152 B4
Lower Todding Hereford 115 B8
Lower Tote Highld 298 C5
Lowertown
Corn 5 C11
Devon 12 E5
Lower Town Devon 27 G8
Hereford 98 C2
Pembs 91 D9
Worcs 117 F7
W Yorks 204 G6
Lower Trebullett Corn . . 12 F2
Lower Tregunnon Corn . 11 E10
Lower Treworrick Corn . . 6 B4
Lower Tuffley Glos. 80 C4
Lower Turmer Hants. . . . 31 F10
Lower Twitchen Devon . 24 D5
Lower Tysoe Warks . . . 100 B6
Lower Upham Hants 33 D8
Lower Upnor Medway . . . 69 E9
Lower Vexford Som 42 F6
Lower Wainhill Oxon. . . . 84 E3
Lower Walton Warr . . . 183 D10
Lower Wanborough
Swindon 63 C8
Lower Weacombe Som . . 42 E6
Lower Weald M Keynes . 102 D5
Lower Wear Devon 14 D4
Lower Weare Som 44 C2
Lower Weedon
Northants 120 F2
Lower Welson Hereford . 114 G5
Lower Westholme Som . . 44 E5
Lower Westhouse
N Yorks 212 E3
Lower Westmancote
Worcs 99 D8
Lower Weston Bath 61 F8
Lower Whatcombe
Dorset 30 G4
Lower Whatley Som 45 D8
Lower Whitley Ches W . 183 F10
Lower Wick Glos 80 F2
Worcs 116 G6
Lower Wield Hants 48 E6
Lower Willingdon E Sus . . 23 E9
Lower Winchendon or
Nether Winchendon
Bucks 84 C2
Lower Withington
Ches E 168 B4
Lower Wolverton Worcs 117 G8
Lower Woodend Aberds 293 B8
Bucks 65 B10
Lower Woodford Wilts . . 46 G6
Lower Woodley Corn 5 B8
Lower Woodside Herts . . 86 D2
Lower Woolston Som . . . 29 B11
Lower Woon Corn. 5 C10
Lower Wraxall Dorset . . 29 G9
Som 44 F6
Wilts 61 G10
Lower Wyche Worcs . . . 98 C5
Lower Wyke W Yorks . . 197 B7
Lower Yelland Devon . . . 40 G3
Lower Zeals Wilts 45 G9
Lowes Barn Durham . . 233 C11
Lowesby Leics 136 B4
Lowestoft Suff 143 E10
Loweswater Cumb 229 G8
Low Etherley Durham . 233 F9
Low Fell T & W 243 F7
Lowfield S Yorks 186 D5
Lowfield Heath W Sus. . . . 51 E19
Low Fold W Yorks 205 F8
Lowford Hants 33 E7
Low Fulney Lincs 156 E5
Low Garth N Yorks 226 D4
Low Gate Northumb . . 241 E10
N Yorks 214 F5
Low Geltbridge Cumb . 240 F2
Lowgill Cumb 222 F2
Lancs 212 G3
Low Grantley N Yorks . 214 E4
Low Green N Yorks . . . 205 B10
Suff 125 F1
W Yorks 205 F10
Low Greenside T & W . 242 E4
Low Habberley Worcs . 116 B6
Low Ham Som 28 B6
Low Hawsker Northumb 253 C7
Low Hawsker N Yorks . 227 D8
Low Hesket Cumb 230 B5
Low Hesleyhurst
Northumb 252 D3
Low Hill W Mid 133 C8
Low Hutton N Yorks . . 216 F5
Lowick Cumb 210 B5
Northants 137 G9
Northumb 264 B2
Lowick Bridge Cumb . . 210 B5
Lowick Green Cumb . . 210 B5
Low Knipe Cumb 230 G6
Low Laithe N Yorks . . . 214 G3
Low Laithes S Yorks . . 197 G11
Lowlands Torf 78 G3
Low Leighton Derbys. . . 185 D8
Low Lorton Cumb 229 F9
Low Marishes N Yorks . 216 D6
Low Marnham Notts . . 172 B4
Low Mill N Yorks 226 F3
Low Moor Lancs 203 E10
W Yorks 197 B8

Lowmoor Row Cumb . . 231 F8
Low Moorsley T & W . . 234 B2
Low Moresby Cumb . . . 228 G5
Lowna N Yorks 226 G3
Low Newton Corn. 11 C8
Low Newton-by-the-Sea
Northumb 264 E6
Lownie Moor Angus . . . 287 C8
Lowood Borders 262 B2
Low Prudhoe Northumb 242 E4
Low Risby N Lincs 200 E2
Low Row Cumb 229 C9
Cumb 240 E3
N Yorks 223 F9
Low Salchrie Dumfries . 236 C2
Low Smerby Argyll 255 E8
Low Snaygill N Yorks . . 204 D5
Lowsonford Warks. 118 D3
Low Street Norf 141 B10
Thurrock 69 D7
Low Tharston Norf. 142 D3
Lowther Cumb 230 G6
Lowthertown Dumfries. 238 D6
Lowther N Yorks 214 F5
Lowthorpe E Yorks 217 G11
Lowton Gtr Man 183 B10
Lowton Common
Gtr Man. 183 B10
Lowton Heath Gtr Man . 183 B10
Lowton St Mary's
Gtr Man 183 B10
Low Torry Fife 279 D10
Low Town Shrops 132 E4
Low Toynton Lincs 190 G3
Low Valley S Yorks 198 G2
Low Valleyfield Fife . . . 279 D10
Low Walton Cumb 219 C9
Low Waters S Lanark . . 268 E4
Low Westwood Durham . 242 F4
Low Whinnow Cumb . . 239 G8
Low Whita N Yorks . . . 223 F10
Low Wood Cumb 210 C6
Low Worsall N Yorks . . 225 C7
Low Wray Cumb 221 E7
Loxbeare Devon 26 D6
Loxford London 68 B2
Loxhill Sur 50 E4
Loxhore Devon. 40 F6
Loxhore Cott Devon 40 F6
Loxley S Yorks. 186 D4
Warks 118 G5
Loxley Green Staffs . . . 151 C11
Loxton Hereford 98 C4
Loxton N Som 43 B11
Loxwood W Sus 50 G4
Loyter's Green Essex . . . 87 C8
Loyterton Kent 70 G3
Lozells W Mid 133 F11
Lubachlaggan Highld . . 300 B3
Lubachoinnich Highld. . 309 K4
Lubberland Shrops 116 B2
Lubcroy Highld. 309 J3
Lubenham Leics 136 F4
Lubinvullin Highld 308 C5
Lucas End Herts 86 E4
Lucasgate Lincs 174 E5
Lucas Green Lancs. 194 C5
Luccombe Som 42 E3
Luccombe Village IoW . . . 21 F7
Lucker Northumb. 264 C5
Luckett Corn 12 G3
Lucking Street Essex . . 106 E6
Luckington Wilts 61 C10
Lucklawhill Fife 287 E8
Luckwell Bridge Som . . . 42 F2
Lucton Hereford 115 E8
Ludag W Isles 297 K3
Ludborough Lincs 190 B3
Ludbrook Devon 8 E3
Ludchurch Pembs 73 C10
Luddenden W Yorks . . . 196 B4
Luddenden Foot
W Yorks 196 C4
Luddenham Cumb 221 G8
Luddesdown Kent 69 F7
Luddington N Lincs . . . 199 D10
Luddington Warks 118 G3
Luddington in the Brook
Northants 138 G2
Lude House Perth. 291 G10
Ludford Lincs 190 D2
Shrops 115 C10
Ludgershall Bucks 83 B11
Wilts 47 C9
Ludgvan Corn. 2 C2
Ludham Norf 161 F7
Ludlow Shrops 115 C10
Ludney Lincs 190 B5
Som 28 E5
Ludstock Hereford 98 D3
Ludstone Shrops 132 E6
Ludwell Wilts. 30 C6
Ludworth Durham 234 C3
Luffenhall Herts 104 F5
Luffincott Devon 12 C2
Lufton Som. 29 D8
Lugar E Ayrs 258 F3
Lugate Borders 271 G8
Lugg Green Hereford . . 115 E9
Luggiebank N Lanark . . 278 G5
Lugsdale Halton 183 D8
Lugton E Ayrs 267 E8
Lugwardine Hereford . . 97 C11
Luib Highld 295 C7
Luibeilt Highld 290 G4
Lulham Hereford 97 C8
Lullenden Sur. 52 E2
Lullington Derbys. 152 G5
Som 45 C9
Sur. 66 F4
Lulsgate Bottom N Som . .60 F4
Lulsley Worcs. 116 F4
Lulworth Camp Dorset . . 18 E2
Lumb Lancs 195 C10
Lancs 195 D9
W Yorks 196 C4
W Yorks 197 E7
Lumb Foot W Yorks . . . 204 F6
Lumburn Devon. 12 G5
Lumbutts W Yorks 196 C3
Lumby N Yorks 206 G5
Lumley W Sus. 22 B5
Lumley Thicks Durham . 243 G8
Lumloch E Dunb. 268 B2
Lumphanan Aberds . . . 293 C7
Lumphinnans Fife 280 C3
Lumsdaine Borders . . . 273 B7
Lumsden Aberds 302 G4
Lunan Angus 287 B10
Lunanhead Angus 287 B8
Luncarty Perth 286 E4
Lund E Yorks 208 D5
N Yorks 207 G7
Shetland 312 C7
Lundal W Isles. 304 E3
Lundavra Highld 290 G2
Lunderton Aberds 303 E11
Lundie Angus 286 D6
Highld 290 B4

Lundin Links Fife 287 G8
Lundwood S Yorks 197 F11
Lundy Green Norf. 142 E4
Lunga Argyll 275 C8
Lunna Shetland 312 G6
Lunning Shetland 312 G7
Lunnon Swansea 56 D4
Lunsford Kent 53 B7
Lunsford's Cross E Sus . . 38 E2
Lunt Mers 193 G10
Luntley Hereford 115 F7
Lunts Heath Halton . . . 183 D8
Lupin Staffs 152 F2
Luppitt Devon. 27 F11
Lupridge Devon. 8 D4
Lupset W Yorks 197 D10
Lupton Cumb. 211 C11
Lurg Aberds 293 C8
Lurgashall W Sus. 34 D6
Lurignich Argyll 289 D11
Lurley Devon 26 E6
Lusby Lincs 174 B4
Luscombe Devon 8 F2
Luson Devon 8 F3
Luss Argyll. 277 C7
Lussagiven Argyll. 275 E7
Lusta Highld 298 D2
Lustleigh Devon 13 E11
Lustleigh Cleave Devon . 13 E11
Luston Hereford. 115 E9
Lusty Som 45 G7
Luthermuir Aberds . . . 293 G8
Luthrie Fife 287 F7
Lutley W Mid 133 G8
Luton Devon 14 F4
Devon 27 G9
Luton 103 G11
Medway 69 F9
Lutsford Devon 24 D3
Lutterworth Leics 135 G10
Lutton Devon 7 D11
Devon 8 C3
Lincs 157 D8
Northants 138 F2
Lutton Gowts Lincs . . . 157 E8
Lutworthy Devon 26 E3
Luxborough Som 42 F3
Luxley Glos. 98 G3
Luxted London 68 G2
Luxton Devon 28 E2
Luxulyan Corn 5 D11
Luzley Gtr Man 196 G3
Luzley Brook Gtr Man . . 196 F2
Lyatts Som 29 E8
Lybster Highld 310 F6
Lydbury North Shrops . 131 F7
Lydcott Devon. 41 F7
Lydd Kent 39 C8
Kent. 71 F11
Lydden Kent 55 D9
Kent. 71 F11
Lyddington Rutland . . . 137 D7
Lydd on Sea Kent 39 C9
Lyde Orkney 314 E3
Shrops 130 C6
Lydeard St Lawrence
Som 42 G6
Lyde Cross Hereford . . 97 C10
Lyde Green Hants. 49 B8
S Glos. 61 D7
Lydford Devon 12 E6
Lydford Fair Place Som . 44 G5
Lydford-on-Fosse Som . 44 G5
Lydgate Gtr Man. 186 F4
Gtr Man 196 G3
W Yorks 196 B2
Lydham Shrops 130 E6
Lydiard Green Wilts. . . . 62 B5
Lydiard Millicent Wilts. . 62 B5
Lydiard Plain Wilts. 62 B5
Lydiard Tregoze Swindon 62 C6
Lydiate Mers 193 G11
Lydiate Ash Worcs 117 B9
Lydlinch Dorset 30 E2
Lydmarsh Som. 28 E5
Lydney Glos 79 E10
Lydstep Pembs 73 F9
Lye W Mid 133 G8
Lye Cross N Som 60 G3
Lye Green Bucks 85 E7
E Sus 52 G4
Warks 118 D3
Wilts 45 B10
Lye Head Worcs 116 C5
Lye Hole N Som 60 G4
Lyewood Common E Sus . 52 F4
Lyford Oxon 82 G5
Lymbridge Green Kent . . 54 E6
Lyme Green Ches E . . . 184 G6
Lyme Regis Dorset 16 C2
Lymiecleuch Borders . . 249 C9
Lyminge Kent. 55 E7
Lymington Hants 20 B2
Lyminster W Sus. 35 G8
Lymm Warr 183 D11
Lymore Hants. 19 C11
Lympne Kent 54 F6
Lympsham Som. 43 C10
Lympstone Devon. 14 E5
Lynbridge Devon. 41 E7
Lynch Hants 48 D4
Som 42 D2
Lynchat Highld. 291 C9
Lynchgate Shrops. 131 F7
Lynch Hill Hants 48 D3
Slough 66 C2
Lyndale Ho Highld 298 D3
Lyndhurst Hants 32 F4
Lyndon Rutland 137 C8
Lyndon Green W Mid . . 134 F2
Lyne Borders 270 G4
Sur. 66 F4
Lyneal Shrops. 149 C8
Lyneal Mill Shrops. . . . 149 C9
Lyneal Wood Shrops . . 149 C9
Lyne Down Hereford . . . 98 E2
Lyneham Oxon. 100 G5
Wilts 62 D4
Lynemore Highld. 301 G10
Lynemouth Northumb . 253 E7
Lyne of Gorthleck
Highld 300 G5
Lyne of Skene Aberds . 293 B9
Lyness Orkney 314 G3
Lyng Station Borders . . 260 B6
Lynford Norf. 140 E6
Lyng Norf. 159 F11
Som 28 B4
Lyngate Norf 160 C5
Norf 160 D6
Lynmore Highld. 301 F10
Lynmouth Devon. 41 D8
Lynnouth Northumb . . 253 E7
Lyne of Gorthleck
Highld 300 G5
Lynn Staffs 133 C11
Telford 150 F5
Lynsted Kent 70 G2
Lynstone Corn 24 F2
Lynton Devon 41 D8
Lynwilg Highld 291 B10
Highld 290 B4
Lynworth Glos 99 G9

Lyons T & W 234 B3
Lyon's Gate Dorset. 29 F11
Lyons Green Norf 159 G8
Lyonshall Hereford . . . 114 F6
Lyons Hall Essex. 88 B2
Lypiatt Glos. 80 D6
Lyrabus Argyll 274 G3
Lytchett Matravers
Dorset 18 B4
Lytchett Minster Dorset . 18 C5
Lyth Highld 310 C6
Lythbank Shrops. 131 B9
Lythe N Yorks 226 C6
Lythes Orkney 314 H4
Lythmore Highld 310 C4

M

Maam Argyll 284 F5
Mabe Burnthouse Corn . . 3 C7
Mabie Dumfries. 237 B11
Mablethorpe Lincs 191 D8
Macclesfield Ches E. . . 184 G6
Macclesfield Forest
Ches E. 185 G7
Macduff Aberds. 303 C7
Mace Green Suff. 108 C2
Machan S Lanark. 268 E5
Macharioch Argyll. 255 G8
Machen Caerph 59 B8
Machrie N Ayrs. 255 D9
Machrie Hotel Argyll. . . 254 C4
Machrihanish Argyll. . . 255 E7
Machroes Gwyn 144 D6
Machynlleth Powys . . . 128 C4
Machynys Carms 56 B4
Mackerel's Common
W Sus 35 B8
Mackerye End Herts . . . 85 B11
Mackham Devon 27 F11
Mackney Oxon. 64 B5
Mackside Borders. 262 G4
Mackworth Derbys. . . . 152 B6
Macmerry E Loth. 281 G8
Madderty Perth. 286 E3
Maddington Wilts. 46 E5
Maddiston Falk 279 F8
Maddox Moor Pembs . . 73 C7
Madehurst W Sus. 35 E7
Madeley Staffs 168 G3
Telford 132 C3
Madeley Heath Staffs. . 168 F3
Worcs 117 B9
Madeley Park Staffs . . . 168 G3
Madeleywood Telford. . 132 C3
Maders Corn 12 G2
Madford Devon 27 E10
Madingley Cambs. 123 E7
Madjeston Dorset. 30 B4
Madley Hereford 97 D8
Madresfield Worcs 98 B6
Madron Corn 1 C4
Maenaddwyn Anglesey . 179 E7
Maenclochog Pembs. . . . 91 F11
Maendy V Glam. 58 D4
Maenporth Corn. 3 D7
Maentwrog Gwyn. 163 G11
Maen-y-groes Ceredig . . 111 F7
Maer Corn. 24 F2
Staffs 150 B5
Maerdy Carms. 94 G2
Conwy 165 G8
Rhondda. 77 F7
Maerdy Newport 78 G4
W Berks 64 E6
Maes-bangor Ceredig . 128 G3
Maesbrook Shrops 148 E5
Maesbury Shrops 148 D6
Maesbury Marsh Shrops 148 D6
Maesgeirchen Gwyn . . 179 G9
Maes-glas / Greenfield
Flint 181 F11
Maesgwyn-Isaf Powys . 148 G3
Maeshafn Denb 166 C2
Maesllyn Ceredig 93 C7
Maesmynis Powys 95 B10
Maes Pennant Flint . . . 181 F11
Maesteg Bridgend. 57 C10
Maes-Treylow Powys . . 114 D5
Maesybont Carms 75 B9
Maesycoed Rhondda. . . 58 B5
Maescrugiau Carms . . . 93 C9
Maesycwmmer Caerph . 77 G11
Maes-y-dre Flint 166 C2
Maesygwartha Mon . . . 77 D8
Maesymeillion Ceredig . 93 B8
Maespyandy Powys . . . 129 D9
Maesyrhandir Powys . . 129 E11
Magdalen Laver Essex . 87 D8
Maggieknockater Moray 302 E3
Maggots End Essex. . . . 105 F9
Magham Down E Sus . . 23 C10
Maghull Mers 193 G11
Magor Mon. 60 B2
Magpie Green Suff 125 B11
Maida Vale London 67 C9
Maidenbower W Sus . . . 51 F9
Maiden Bradley Wilts . . 45 F10
Maidencombe Torbay . . 9 B8
Maidenhall Suff 108 C3
Maidenhead Windsor . . 65 C11
Maiden Head N Som . . . 60 F5
Maidenhead Court
Windsor 66 C2
Maiden Law Durham . . 233 B9
Maiden Newton Dorset . 17 B7
Maidenpark Falk 279 E9
Maidens S Ayrs 244 B6
Maiden's Green Brack . . 65 E11
Maidensgrove Oxon. . . 65 B8
Maiden's Hall Northumb 252 D6
Maidenwell Corn 11 F7
Lincs 190 F4
Maiden Wells Pembs . . . 73 F7
Maidford Northants . . . 120 G2
Maids Moreton Bucks. . 102 D4
Maidstone Kent. 53 B9
Maidwell Northants . . . 120 B5
Mail Shetland 313 L6
Mailand Shetland 312 C8
Mailingsland Borders . . 270 G4
Main Powys 148 F3
Maindee Newport 59 B10
Maindy Cardiff 59 D7

Lyons T & W 234 B3

Mainland Ardcanny
Aberds 303 E9
Mains of Ardestie
Angus 287 D9

Mains of Arnage Aberds. 303 F9
E Sus 37 C7
London 68 B2
Notts 153 C11
Slough 66 C3
S Yorks 186 D5
Mains of Auchoynanie
Moray 302 E4
Mains of Baldoon
Dumfries. 236 D6
Mains of Balhall Angus. 293 G8
Mains of Ballindarg
Angus 287 B8
Mains of Balnakettle
Aberds 293 F8
Mains of Birness Aberds 303 F9
Mains of Blackhall
Aberds 303 G7
Mains of Burgie Moray. 301 D10
Mains of Cairnbrogie
Aberds 303 G8
Mains of Cairnty Moray. 302 D3
Mains of Clunas Moray . 301 E7
Mains of Crichie Aberds. 303 E9
Mains of Daltulich
Highld 301 E7
Mains of Dalvey Highld 301 F11
Mains of Dellavaird
Aberds 293 E9
Mains of Drum Aberds . 293 D10
Mains of Edingight
Moray 302 D5
Mains of Fedderate
Aberds 303 E8
Mains of Flichity Highld 300 G6
Mains of Hatton Aberds 303 D9
Aberds 303 E9
Mains of Inkhorn Aberds 303 F9
Mains of Innerpeffray
Perth. 286 F3
Mains of Kirktonhill
Aberds 293 G9
Mains of Laithers
Aberds 302 E6
Mains of Mayen Moray . 302 E5
Mains of Melgund
Angus 287 B9
Mains of Taymouth
Perth. 285 C11
Mains of Thornton
Aberds 293 F8
Mains of Towie Aberds . 303 F8
Mains of Ulbster Highld 310 E7
Mains of Watten Highld . 310 D6
Mainsriddle Dumfries . 237 D11
Mainstone Shrops 130 F5
Maisemore Glos. 98 G6
Maitland Park London . . 67 C9
Major's Green W Mid. . . 118 B2
Makeney Derbys 170 G5
Makerstoun Borders . . . 262 C5
Malacleit W Isles 296 C3
Malborough Devon 9 G9
Malcoff Derbys 185 E9
Malden Rushett London . 67 G7
Maldon Essex 88 D5
Malham N Yorks 213 G8
Maligar Highld 298 C4
Malinbridge S Yorks . . 186 D4
Malinslee Telford 132 B3
Malkin's Bank Ches E . . 168 D3
Mallaig Highld 295 F8
Mallaig Bheag Highld . . 295 F8
Malldraeth Anglesey . . 162 B6
Malleny Mills Edin 270 B3
Malling Stirling 285 G9
Mallows Green Essex . . 105 F9
Maltby Lincs 190 E4
Stockton 225 C9
S Yorks 187 C8
Maltby le Marsh Lincs . 191 E7
Malting End Suff. 124 G4
Malting Green Essex . . 107 G9
Maltings Angus 293 G9
Maltman's Hill Kent. . . . 54 E2
Malton N Yorks 216 E5
Malvern Common Worcs 98 C5
Malvern Link Worcs. . . . 98 B5
Malvern Wells Worcs . . 98 C5
Mamble Worcs 116 C3
Mambeg Argyll 276 D4
Mamhilad Mon. 78 E4
Manaccan Corn 3 E7
Manafon Powys 130 C2
Manais W Isles. 296 C7
Manar Ho Aberds 303 G7
Manaton Devon 13 E11
Manby Lincs. 190 D5
Mancetter Warks 134 D6
Manchester Airport
Gtr Man. 184 D4
Mancot Flint 166 B4
Mancot Royal Flint . . . 166 B4
Mandally Highld 290 C4
Mandances Cambs 139 F9
Maney W Mid 134 D2
Manfield N Yorks. 224 C4
Mangaster Shetland. . . 312 F5
Mangotsfield S Glos. . . . 61 D7
Mangrove Green Herts . 104 G2
Mangurstadh W Isles . . 304 E2
Manhay Corn 2 C5
Manian-fawr Pembs. . . . 92 B3
Manian-glas Pembs. . . . 92 B3
Mankinholes W Yorks . . 196 C3
Manley Ches W 183 G8
Devon 27 E7
Manley Common
Ches W 183 G8
Manmoel Caerph 77 E11
Man-moel Caerph 77 E11
Mannal Argyll. 288 E1
Mannamead Plym 7 D9
Mannerston W Loth . . . 279 F10
Manningford Bohune
Wilts 46 B6
Manningford Bruce Wilts 46 B6
Manningham W Yorks . . 205 G9
Mannings Heath W Sus . 36 B2
Mannington Dorset . . . 31 F9
Manningtree Essex . . . 107 E11
Mannofield Aberdeen . . 293 C11
Manor London 68 B2
Manor Bourne Devon . . . 7 F9
Manordeilo Carms 94 F3
Manor Estate S Yorks . . 186 D5
Manorhill Borders 262 C5
Manor Hill Corner Lincs 157 F7
Manor House W Mid . . . 135 G7
Manorowen Pembs. . . . 91 D8
Manor Park Pembs 84 C4
 Ches W. 167 B11

Manor Park continued
E Sus 37 C7
London 68 B2
Notts 153 C11
Slough 66 C3
S Yorks 186 D5
Manor Parsley Corn 4 E4
Manor Royal W Sus 51 F9
Man's Cross Essex 106 D5
Mansegate Dumfries . . 247 G9
Mansell Gamage
Hereford 97 C7
Manselton Swansea . . . 56 B5
Mansell Lacy Hereford . 97 B8
Mansell Gamage
Hereford 97 C7
Mansergh Cumb 212 C2
Mansfield E Ayrs 258 G4
Notts 171 C8
Mansfield Woodhouse
Notts 171 C8
Manson Green Norf. . . . 141 C10
Mansriggs Cumb. 210 C5
Manston Dorset 30 D4
Kent 71 F10
W Yorks 206 F3
Manswood Dorset 31 F7
Manthorpe Lincs 155 B8
Lincs 155 F11
Manton N Lincs 200 G3
Notts 187 F9
Rutland 137 C7
Wilts 63 F7
Manton Warren N Lincs . 200 F2
Manuden Essex 105 F9
Manwood Green Essex . 87 C8
Manywells Height
W Yorks 205 F7
Maperton Som 29 B11
Maplebeck Notts 172 C2
Maple Cross Herts 85 G8
Mapledurham Oxon. . . . 65 D7
Mapledurwell Hants . . . 49 C7
Maple End Essex 105 D11
Maplehurst W Sus 35 C11
Maplescombe Kent 68 G5
Mapleton Derbys 169 F11
Nottingham 171 G9
Mapperley Derbys 170 G6
Nottingham 171 G9
Mapperley Park
Nottingham 171 G9
Mapperton Dorset. 16 B6
Dorset 18 B4
Mappleborough Green
Warks 117 D11
Mappleton E Yorks 209 D10
Mappowder Dorset 30 F2
Mapperley Park
Nottingham 171 G9
Mappowell S Yorks . . . 197 F10
Marazanvose Corn. 4 E4
Marazion Corn 2 C2
Marbhig W Isles 305 G6
Marbrack Dumfries . . . 246 E3
Marbury Ches E 167 F9
March Cambs. 139 D8
S Lanark 259 G11
Marcham Oxon 83 F7
Marchamley Shrops. . . 149 D11
Marchamley Wood
Shrops 149 D11
Marchington Staffs. . . . 152 C2
Marchington Woodlands
Staffs 152 D2
Marchroes Gwyn. 144 D6
Marchwiel Wrex 166 F5
Marchwood Hants. 32 E5
Marcross V Glam. 58 F2
Marden Hereford. 97 B10
Kent. 53 E8
T & W 243 C9
Wilts 46 B5
Marden Ash Essex 87 E9
Marden Beech Kent. . . . 53 E8
Marden's Hill E Sus 52 G3
Marden's Hill E Sus 52 G3
Marden Thorn Kent. . . . 53 E9
Mardleybury Herts 86 B3
Mardu Shrops 130 G5
Mardy Mon 78 B4
Shrops 148 C5
Marefield Leics 136 B4
Mareham le Fen Lincs . 174 C3
Mareham on the Hill
Lincs 174 B3
Marehay Derbys 170 F5
Marehill W Sus 35 D9
Maresfield E Sus 37 C7
Maresfield Park E Sus . . 37 C7
Marfleet Hull 200 B6
Marford Wrex 166 D5
Margam Neath 57 D9
Margaret Marsh Dorset . 30 D4
Margaret Roding Essex . 87 C9
Margaretting Essex . . . 87 E11
Margaretting Tye Essex. 87 E11
Margate Kent. 71 E11
Hereford 115 F7
Margery Sur 51 D9
Margnaheglish N Ayrs . 256 C2
Margreig Dumfries . . . 237 B10
Margrove Park Redcar . 226 B3
Marham Norf 140 B3
Marhamchurch Corn . . 24 G2
Marholm Pboro 138 C2
Marian Flint 181 F9
Marian Cwm Denb 181 F9
Mariandyrys Anglesey . 179 E10
Marianglas Anglesey . . 179 E8
Mariansleigh Devon . . . 26 C2
Marian y de / South Beach
Gwyn. 145 C2
Marian y mor / West End
Gwyn. 145 C2
Marine Town Kent 70 E2
Marionburgh Aberds. . . 293 C9
Marishader Highld 298 C4
Marjoriebanks Dumfries 248 G3
Mark Dumfries 236 D3
Dumfries 237 C7
S Ayrs 236 B2
Markbeech Kent 52 E3
Markby Lincs 191 F7
Mark Causeway Som. . . 43 D11
Mark Cross E Sus 52 G5
E Sus 23 C8
Markeaton Derbys 152 B6
Market Bosworth Leics . 135 C8
Market Deeping Lincs . 138 B2
Market Drayton Shrops . 150 C3
Market Harborough
Leics 136 F4
Markethill Perth. 286 D6
Market Lavington Wilts . 46 C4
Market Overton Rutland . 155 F7
Market Rasen Lincs . . . 189 D10
Market Stainton Lincs . 190 E3
Market Warsop Notts . . 171 B9
Market Weighton
E Yorks 208 E3

Market Weston Suff . . . 125 B9
Markfield Leics 153 G9
Mark Hall North Essex . 87 C7
Mark Hall South Essex . 87 C7
Markham Caerph 77 E11
Markham Moor Notts . . 188 G2
Markinch Fife 286 G6
Markington N Yorks . . . 214 F5
Markland Hill Gtr Man. 195 F7
Markle E Loth 281 F11
Marksbury Bath 61 G7
Mark's Corner IoW 20 C5
Marks Gate London 87 G7
Marks Tey Essex. 107 G8
Markyate Herts 85 B9
Marland Gtr Man 195 E11
Marlas Hereford. 97 F8
Marl Bank Worcs 98 C5
Marlborough Wilts 63 F7
Marlbrook Hereford. . . 115 G10
Worcs 117 C9
Marlcliff Warks 117 G11
Marldon Devon 9 C7
Marle Green E Sus 23 B9
Marle Hill Glos. 99 G9
Marlesford Suff 126 F6
Marley Kent 55 C7
Kent. 55 C10
Marley Green Ches E . . 167 F9
Marley Heights W Sus . . 49 G11
Marley Hill T & W 242 F6
Marley Pots T & W 243 F9
Marlingford Norf 142 B2
Mar Lodge Aberds 292 D2
Marloes Pembs 72 D3
Marlow Bucks 65 B10
Hereford 115 B8
Marlow Bottom Bucks . 65 B10
Marlow Common Bucks . 65 B10
Marlpit Hill Kent. 52 E2
Marlpool Derbys 170 F6
Marnhull Dorset 30 D3
Marnock N Lanark 268 B4
Marple Gtr Man 185 D7
Marple Bridge Ches E . 185 D7
Marr S Yorks 198 F4
Marrel Highld 311 H4
Marrick N Yorks 223 F11
Marridge Hill Wilts 63 F11
Marros Carms 74 D2
Marsden T & W. 243 E9
W Yorks 196 E4
Marsden Height Lancs . 204 F3
Marsett N Yorks 213 B8
Marsh Bucks. 84 D4
Devon 28 E3
W Yorks 204 F6
Marshall Meadows
Northumb 273 D9
Marshall's Cross Mers . 183 C8
Marshall's Elm Som . . . 44 G3
Marshall's Heath Herts . 85 B11
Marshalsea Dorset 28 G5
Marshalswick Herts . . . 85 D11
Marsham Norf. 160 E3
Marshaw Lancs 203 C7
Marsh Baldon Oxon . . . 83 F9
Marsh Benham W Berks . 64 F2
Marshborough Kent . . . 55 B10
Marshbrook Shrops . . . 131 F8
Marshchapel Lincs . . . 190 B5
Marsh Common S Glos . 60 C5
Marsh End Worcs 98 D6
Marshfield Newport . . . 59 C9
S Glos 61 D9
Marshfield Bank
Ches E 167 D11
Marshgate Corn 11 C3
Marsh Gate W Berks. . . 63 F10
Marsh Gibbon Bucks . . 102 G2
Marsh Green Devon . . . 14 C6
Gtr Man 194 F5
Kent. 52 E2
Staffs 168 D5
Telford 150 G2
Marsh Houses Lancs . . 202 C5
Marshland St James
Norf. 139 B10
Marsh Lane Derbys . . . 186 F6
Glos 79 D9
Marsh Mills Som 43 F7
Marshmoor Herts 86 D2
Marshside Kent 71 F8
Mers 193 D11
Marsh Side Norf 176 E3
Marsh Street Som 42 E3
Marshwood Dorset 16 B3
Marske N Yorks 224 E2
Marske-by-the-Sea
Redcar 235 G8
Marston Ches W 183 F11
Hereford 115 F7
Lincs 172 G5
Oxon 83 D8
Staffs 150 G6
Staffs 151 D8
Warks 134 E4
Wilts 46 B3
Marston Bigot Som . . . 45 D8
Marston Doles Warks . . 119 F9
Marston Gate Som. 45 D9
Marston Green W Mid . 134 F3
Marston Hill Glos. 81 F9
Marston Jabbett Warks. 135 F7
Marston Magna Som . . 29 C9
Marston Meysey Wilts . 81 F10
Marston Montgomery
Derbys 152 B2
Marston Moretaine
C Beds 103 C9
Marston on Dove
Derbys 152 D4
Marston St Lawrence
Northants 101 C10
Marston Stannett
Hereford 115 F11
Marston Trussell
Northants 136 F3
Marstow Hereford. 79 B9
Marsworth Bucks 84 C6
Marten Wilts 47 B9
Marthall Ches E 184 F4
Martham Norf 161 F9
Marthwaite Cumb. 222 G3
Martin Hants 31 E9
Kent. 55 D10
Lincs 173 D10
Lincs 174 B2
Martin Dales Lincs . . . 173 C11
Martin Drove End Hants . 31 C9
Martinhoe Devon 41 D7
Martinhoe Cross Devon . 41 D7

Martin Hussingtree
Worcs 117 E7
Martin Mill Kent 55 D10
Martin Moor Lincs 174 C2
Martinscroft Warr 183 D11
Martinstown or
Winterbourne St Martin
Dorset 17 D8
Martlesham Suff 108 B4
Martlesham Heath Suff. 108 B4
Martletwy Pembs. 73 C8
Martley Worcs 116 E5
Martock Som 29 D7
Marton Ches E 168 B5
Ches W. 167 B8
Cumb 210 D4
E Yorks 209 F9
Lincs 188 E4
Mbro 225 B10
N Yorks 215 G8
N Yorks 216 C4
Shrops 130 C5
Shrops 149 D8
Warks 119 D8
Marton Green Ches W . 167 B10
Marton Grove Mbro. . . . 225 B9
Marton-in-the-Forest
N Yorks 215 F11
Marton-le-Moor
N Yorks 215 E7
Marton Moor Warks . . . 119 D8
Marton Moss Side
Blackpool 202 G2
Martyr's Green Sur. 50 B5
Martyr Worthy Hants . . 48 G4
Marwick Orkney 314 D2
Marwood Devon 40 F4
Marybank Highld 300 D4
Highld 301 B7
Maryburgh Highld 300 D5
Maryfield Aberds 293 D7
Corn 7 D8
Maryhill Glasgow 267 B11
Marykirk Aberds 293 G8
Maryland Mon 79 D8
Marylebone Gtr Man . . 194 F5
Marypark Moray 301 F11
Maryport Cumb 228 D2
Dumfries 236 F3
Mary Tavy Devon 12 F6
Maryton Angus 287 B10
Angus 287 B10
Marywell Aberds 293 D7
Aberds 293 D10
Angus 287 C10
Masbrough S Yorks . . . 186 C6
Mascle Bridge Pembs . . 73 D7
Masham N Yorks 214 C4
Mashbury Essex 87 C11
Masongill N Yorks 212 D3
Masonhill S Ayrs 257 E9
Mastin Moor Derbys . . 187 F7
Mastrick Aberdeen . . . 293 C10
Matchborough Worcs. . 117 D11
Matching Essex 87 C8
Matching Green Essex . 87 C8
Matching Tye Essex . . . 87 C8
Matfen Northumb 242 C2
Matfield Kent 53 E7
Mathern Mon. 79 G8
Mathon Hereford 98 B4
Mathry Pembs 91 E7
Matlaske Norf 160 C3
Matley Gtr Man 185 B7
Matlock Derbys 170 C3
Matlock Bank Derbys . . 170 C3
Matlock Bath Derbys . . 170 D3
Matlock Bridge Derbys . 170 C3
Matlock Cliff Derbys . . 170 C3
Matlock Dale Derbys . . 170 D3
Matshead Lancs 202 E6
Matson Glos 80 B4
Matterdale End Cumb . 230 G3
Mattersey Notts 187 D11
Mattersey Thorpe
Notts 187 D11
Matthewsgreen
Wokingham 65 F11
Mattingley Hants 49 B8
Mattishall Norf 159 G11
Mattishall Burgh Norf . 159 G11
Mauchline E Ayrs 257 D11
Maud Aberds 303 E9
Maudlin Corn. 5 C11
Dorset 28 F5
W Sus 22 B5
Maudlin Cross Dorset. . 28 F5
Maugersbury Glos. 100 F4
Maughold IoM 192 C5
Mauld Highld 300 F4
Maulden C Beds 103 D11
Maulds Meaburn Cumb . 222 B2
Maunby N Yorks 215 B9
Maund Bryan Hereford . 115 G11
Maundown Som 27 B9
Mauricewood Midloth . . 270 C4
Mautby Norf 161 G9
Mavesyn Ridware
Staffs 151 F11
Mavis Enderby Lincs . . 174 B5
Maviston Highld 301 D9
Mawbray Cumb 229 B7
Mawdesley Lancs 194 E3
Mawdlam Bridgend. . . . 57 E10
Mawgan Corn 2 D6
Mawgan Porth Corn 5 B7
Maw Green Ches E. . . . 168 D2
Mawla Corn. 4 F4
Mawnan Corn 3 D7
Mawnan Smith Corn 3 D7
Mawsley Northants. . . . 120 B6
Mawson Green S Yorks . 198 D6
Mawthorpe Lincs 191 G7
Maxey Pboro. 138 B2
Maxstoke Warks 134 F4
Maxted Street Kent 54 E6
Maxton Borders 262 C4
Kent. 55 E10
Maxwellheugh Borders . 262 C6
Maxwelltown Dumfries . 237 B11
Mayals Swansea 56 C6
May Bank Staffs 168 F5
Maybole S Ayrs 257 G9
Maybury Sur. 50 B4
Maybush Soton 32 E5
Mayer's Green W Mid . 133 E10
Mayes Green Sur 50 F6
Mayeston Pembs. 73 E8
Mayfair London 67 C9
Mayfield E Sus. 37 C9
Midloth 271 C7
Northumb 243 F11
Staffs 169 F11
W Loth 269 B8
Mayford Sur 50 B3
Mayhill Swansea 56 B6
May Hill Mon 79 C8
Glos 98 G4
May Hill Village Glos. . . 98 G4

Mayland Essex 88 E6
Maylandsea Essex 88 E6
Maynard's Green E Sus . . .23 B9
Mayne Ho Moray 302 C2
Mayon Corn 1 D3
Maypole Kent 68 E4
Kent 71 G4
London 68 G3
Mon 79 B7
Scilly 1 G4
Maypole Green Essex . . .107 G4
Norf 143 D8
Suff 125 F8
Suff 126 B5
Mays Green Oxon 65 C8
May's Green N Som 59 G11
Sur 50 B5
Mayshill S Glos 61 C7
Maythorn S Yorks 197 F7
Maythorne Notts 171 D11
Maywick Shetland 313 L5
Mead Devon 13 G11
Devon 24 D2
Mead End Hants 19 B11
Hants 33 C8
Meadgate Bath 45 B7
Meadle Bucks 84 D4
Meadowbank Ches W .167 B11
Edin 280 G5
Meadowend Essex 106 C4
Meadowfield Durham . .233 D10
Meadowfoot N Ayrs 266 F4
Meadow Green Hereford 116 F4
Meadow Hall S Yorks . . .186 C5
Meadowley Shrops 132 E3
Meadowmill E Loth 281 G8
Meadows Nottingham . .153 B11
Meadowtown Shrops . . .130 C6
Meads E Sus 23 F10
Meadside Oxon 83 F9
Mead Vale Sur 51 D9
Meadwell Devon 12 E4
Meaford Staffs 151 B7
Meagill N Yorks 205 B9
Mealabost W Isles 304 E6
Mealabost Bhuirgh
    W Isles 304 C6
Mealasta W Isles 304 F11
Meal Bank Cumb 221 F10
Meal Hill W Yorks 197 F7
Mealrigg Cumb 229 B8
Mealsgate Cumb 229 C10
Meanwood W Yorks 205 F11
Mearbeck N Yorks 212 G6
Meare Som 44 E3
Som 28 C3
Meare Green Som 28 B4
Som 28 C3
Mearns Bath 45 B7
E Renf 267 D10
Mears Ashby Northants .120 D6
Measborough Dike
    S Yorks 197 F11
Measham Leics 152 G6
Meath Green Sur 51 E9
Meathop Cumb 211 C8
Meaux E Yorks 209 F7
Meaver Corn 2 G5
Meavy Devon 7 B10
Medbourne Leics 136 E5
M Keynes 102 D6
Medburn Northumb 242 C4
Meddon Devon 24 D3
Meden Vale Notts 171 B9
Medhurst Row Kent 52 D3
Medlam Lincs 174 D4
Medlar Lancs 202 F4
Medlicott Shrops 131 E8
Medlyn Corn 2 C6
Medmenham Bucks 65 C10
Medomsley Durham 242 G4
Medstead Hants 49 F7
Meerbrook Staffs 169 C7
Meer End W Mid 118 C4
Meerhay Dorset 29 G7
Meers Bridge Lincs 191 D7
Meersbrook S Yorks . . .186 E5
Meesden Herts 105 E8
Meeson Telford 150 E3
Meeson Heath Telford . .150 E3
Meeth Devon 25 E8
Meethe Devon 25 C11
Meeting Green Suff 124 G4
Meeting House Hill
    Norf 160 D6
Meggernie Castle Perth 285 C9
Meggethead Borders . . .260 E5
Meidrim Carms 92 G5
Meifod Denb 165 D7
Powys 148 G3
Meigle N Ayrs 266 B3
Perth 286 C6
Meikle Earnock
    S Lanark 268 E4
Meikle Ferry Highld 309 L7
Meikle Forter Angus . . .292 G3
Meikle Gluich Highld . . .309 L6
Meikleour Perth 286 D5
Meikleour Perth 286 D5
Meikle Obney Perth 286 D4
Meikle Pinkerton
    E Loth 282 F4
Meikle Strath Aberds . .293 F8
Meikle Tarty Aberds . . .303 G9
Meikle Wartle Aberds . .303 F7
Meinciau Carms 75 C8
Meir Stoke 168 G6
Meir Heath Staffs 168 G6
Melbourn Cambs 105 C7
Melbourne Derbys 153 D7
E Yorks 207 E11
S Lanark 269 G11
Melbury Abbas Dorset . .30 D5
Melbury Bubb Dorset . . .29 F9
Melbury Osmond Dorset .29 F9
Melbury Sampford
    Dorset 29 F9
Melby Shetland 313 H3
Melchbourne Bedford . .121 D10
Melcombe Som 43 G9
Melcombe Bingham
    Dorset 30 G3
Melcombe Regis Dorset .17 E9
Meldon Devon 13 C7
Northumb 252 G4
Meldreth Cambs 105 B7
Meldrum Ho Aberds 303 G8
Melfort Argyll 275 B9
Melgarve Highld 290 D6
Meliden / Gallt Melyd
    Denb 181 E9
Melinbyrhedyn Powys . .128 D6
Melin Caiach Caerph 77 F10
Melincourt Neath 76 D4
Melincryddan Neath 57 B8
Melinsey Corn 3 B10
Melin-y-coed Conwy . . .164 C4
Melin-y-ddol Powys 129 B11
Melin-y-grug Powys 129 B11
Melin-y-Wig Denb 165 F8

Melkington Northumb . .273 G7
Melkinthorpe Cumb 231 F7
Melkridge Northumb 240 E6
Melksham Wilts 62 G2
Melksham Forest Wilts .62 G2
Mellangain Highld 307 L3
Mellangoose Corn 2 D5
Mell Green W Berks 64 D3
Melling Lancs 211 E11
Mers 193 G11
Melling Mount Mers 194 G2
Mellis Suff 126 C2
Mellis Green Suff 126 C2
Mellon Charles Highld . .307 K3
Mellon Udrigle Highld . .307 K3
Mellor Gtr Man 185 D7
Lancs 203 G9
Mellor Brook Lancs 203 G8
Mells Som 45 D8
Suff 127 B8
Mells Green Som 45 D8
Melmerby Cumb 231 D8
N Yorks 213 B1
N Yorks 214 D6
Melon Green Suff 124 F6
Melplash Dorset 16 B5
Melrose Borders 262 C2
Melsetter Orkney 314 H2
Melsonby N Yorks 224 D3
Meltham W Yorks 196 E6
Meltham Mills W Yorks .196 E6
Melton E Yorks 200 B3
Suff 126 G5
Meltonby E Yorks 207 C11
Melton Constable Norf 159 C10
Melton Mowbray Leics . .154 F5
Melton Ross N Lincs 200 E5
Melvaig Highld 307 L2
Melverley Shrops 148 F6
Melverley Green Shrops 148 F6
Melvich Highld 310 C2
Membland Devon 7 F11
Membury Devon 28 G3
Memsie Aberds 303 C9
Memus Angus 287 B8
Mena Corn 5 C10
Menabilly Corn 5 E11
Menadarva Corn 4 G2
Menagissey Corn 4 F2
Menai Bridge / Porthaethwy
    Anglesey 179 G9
Mendham Suff 142 G5
Mendlesham Suff 126 D2
Mendlesham Green
    Suff 125 E11
Menethorpe N Yorks . . .216 F5
Mengham Hants 21 B10
Menheniot Corn 6 C5
Menherion Corn 2 B6
Menithwood Worcs 116 D4
Menna Corn 5 E8
Mennock Dumfries 247 B8
Menston W Yorks 205 E9
Menstrie Clack 278 B6
Mentmore Bucks 84 B6
Menzion Borders 260 E3
Meoble Highld 295 G9
Meole Brace Shrops 149 G9
Meols Mers 182 C2
Meon Hants 33 G8
Meonstoke Hants 33 D10
Meopham Kent 68 F6
Meopham Green Kent . . .68 F6
Meopham Station Kent . .68 F6
Mepal Cambs 139 G8
Meppershall C Beds 104 D2
Merbach Hereford 96 B6
Mercaton Derbys 170 G3
Merchiston Edin 280 G4
Mere Ches E 184 E2
Wilts 45 G10
Mere Brow Lancs 194 D2
Mereclough Lancs 204 G3
Mere Green W Mid 134 D2
Worcs 117 E9
Merehead Wrex 149 B9
Mere Heath Ches W 183 G11
Meresborough Medway . .69 G10
Mereside Blackpool 202 G2
Meretown Staffs 150 E5
Mereworth Kent 53 C7
Mergie Aberds 293 E9
Meriden W Mid 134 G4
Meriden Herts 85 F10
Merkadale Highld 294 B5
Merkland Dumfries 237 B9
    N Ayrs 256 B2
    S Ayrs 244 E6
Merkland Lodge Highld .309 G4
Merley Poole 18 B6
Merlin's Bridge Pembs . .72 C6
Merlin's Cross Pembs . . .73 E7
Merridale W Mid 133 D7
Merridge Som 43 G8
Merrie Gardens IoW 21 E7
Merrifield Devon 8 G6
    Devon 24 G3
Merrington Shrops 149 E9
Merrion Pembs 72 F6
Merriott Som 28 E6
    Devon 28 C6
Merriottsford Som 28 E6
Merrivale Devon 12 F6
    Hereford 98 G2
Merrow Sur 50 C4
Merrybent Darl 224 C4
Merry Field Hill Dorset . .31 G8
Merry Hill Herts 85 G10
    W Mid 133 D7
Merryhill Green
    Wokingham 65 E9
Merrylee E Renf 267 D11
Merry Lees Leics 135 B9
Merrymeet Corn 6 B5
Merry Meeting Corn 11 G7
Merry Oak Soton 32 E6
Mersham Kent 54 F5
Merstham Sur 51 C9
Merston W Sus 22 C5
Merstone IoW 20 E6
Merther Corn 5 G7
Merther Lane Corn 5 G7
Merthyr Carms 93 G7
Merthyr Cynog Powys . . .95 D9
Merthyr-Dyfan V Glam . .58 F6
Merthyr Mawr Bridgend .57 F11
Merthyr Tydfil M Tydf . . .77 D8
Merthyr Vale M Tydf 77 F9
Merton Devon 25 E8
    London 67 F9
    Norf 141 D8
    Oxon 83 B9
Merton Park London 67 F9
Mervinslaw Borders 262 G5

Meshaw Devon 26 D3
Messing Essex 88 B5
Messingham N Lincs 199 G11
Mesty Croft W Mid 133 E9
Mesur-y-dorth Pembs . . .87 E11
Metal Bridge Durham . . .233 E11
Metcombe Devon 15 C7
Metfield Suff 142 G5
Metherell Corn 7 B8
Metheringham Lincs 173 C9
Methersgate Suff 108 B5
Methil Fife 281 B7
Methilhill Fife 281 B7
Methlem Gwyn 144 C3
Methley W Yorks 197 B11
Methley Junction
    W Yorks 197 B11
Methley Lanes
    W Yorks 197 B11
Methlick Aberds 303 F8
Methven Perth 286 E4
Methwold Norf 140 E4
Methwold Hythe Norf . .140 E4
Mettingham Suff 143 F7
Metton Norf 160 B3
Mevagissey Corn 5 G10
Mewith Head N Yorks . .212 F4
Mexborough S Yorks . . .187 B7
Meyrick Park Bmouth . . .19 C7
Meysey Hampton Glos . .81 F10
Miabhag W Isles 305 H2
    W Isles 305 J3
Miabhig W Isles 304 E2
Mial Highld 299 B7
Michaelchurch
    Hereford 97 F10
Michaelchurch Escley
    Hereford 96 E6
Michaelchurch on Arrow
    Powys 114 G4
Michaelston-le-Pit
    V Glam 59 E7
Michaelston-y-Fedw
    Newport 59 C8
Michaelstow Corn 11 F7
Michealston-super-Ely
    Cardiff 58 D6
Michelcombe Devon 8 B3
Micheldever Hants 48 F4
Michelmersh Hants 32 B4
Mickfield Suff 126 E2
Micklebring S Yorks . . .187 C8
Mickleby N Yorks 226 C5
Micklefield Bucks 84 G5
    W Yorks 206 G4
Micklefield Green Herts .85 F8
Mickleham Sur 51 C7
Micklehurst Gtr Man . . .196 G3
Micklejohn . . . .
Mickleover Derbys 152 C6
Micklethwaite Cumb . . .239 G7
    W Yorks 205 E8
Mickleton Durham 232 G5
    Glos 100 C3
Mickletown W Yorks . . .197 B11
Mickle Trafford Ches W .166 B6
Mickley Derbys 186 F4
    N Yorks 214 D5
    Shrops 150 C2
Mickley Green Suff 124 F6
Mickley Square
    Northumb 242 E3
Midanbury Hants 33 E7
Mid Ardlaw Aberds 303 C9
Mid Auchinleck Inverclyd .276 G6
Midbea Orkney 314 B4
Mid Beltie Aberds 293 C8
Mid Calder W Loth 269 B11
Middle Aston Oxon 101 G9
Middle Balnald Perth . . .286 B4
Middle Barton Oxon 101 F8
Middlebie Dumfries 238 B6
Middle Bickenhill
    W Mid 134 G4
Middle Bockhampton
    Dorset 19 B9
Middle Bourne Sur 49 E10
Middle Bridge N Som . . .60 D3
Middle Burnham Som . . .43 D10
Middle Cairncake
    Aberds 303 E8
Middlecave N Yorks 216 E5
Middle Chinnock Som . . .29 E7
Middle Claydon Bucks . .102 F4
Middlecliffe S Yorks . . .198 F2
Middlecott Devon 13 D10
    Devon 24 F6
Middle Crackington
    Corn 11 B3
Middlecroft Derbys 186 G6
Middle Drums Angus . . .287 B9
Middle Duntisbourne
    Glos 81 D7
Middlefield Falk 279 E7
Middleforth Green
    Lancs 194 B4
Middle Green Bucks 66 C4
    Som 27 D10
    Suff 124 D4
Middleham N Yorks 214 B2
Middle Handley Derbys .186 F6
Middle Harling Norf 141 F9
Middle Herrington T&W 243 G9
Middlehill Corn 6 B5
    Wilts 61 F10
Middle Hill Pembs 73 C7
    Staffs 133 B9
Middlehope Shrops 131 F9
Middle Kames Argyll . . .275 E10
Middle Littleton Worcs . .99 B11
Middle Luxton Devon . . .28 E2
Middle Madeley Staffs . .168 F3
Middle Maes-coed
    Hereford 96 E6
Middlemarsh Dorset 29 F11
Middle Marwood Devon . .40 F4
Middle Mayfield Staffs .169 G10
Middle Mill Pembs 87 F11
Middlemoor Devon 12 G5
Middlemuir Aberds 303 D9
    Aberds 303 D8
    Aberds 303 E9
Middle Quarter Kent 53 F11
Middle Rainton T&W . . .234 B2
Middle Rasen Lincs 189 D9
Middle Rigg Perth 286 G4
Middle Rocombe Devon . .9 B8
Middlesbrough Mbro . . .234 G4
Middlesceugh Cumb 230 C4
Middleshaw Cumb 211 B11
Middle Side Durham 232 F4
Middlesmoor N Yorks . .213 E11
Middlestoford Devon 28 C6
Middle Stoke Devon 13 G9
    Medway 69 D10
    Suff 108 D3
    W Mid 119 B7

Middlestone Durham . . .233 E11
Middlestone Moor
    Durham 233 E10
Middlestown W Yorks . .197 D9
Middle Strath W Loth . . .279 G8
Middle Street Glos 80 E3
Middle Taphouse Corn . . .6 C3
Middlethird Borders 272 G3
Middlethorpe York 207 D7
    Argyll 288 E1
    Cumb 212 B2
    Derbys 169 C11
    Derbys 170 D3
    Essex 107 F9
    Gtr Man 195 F11
    Hants 48 E2
    Hereford 115 D10
    Hrtlpl 234 E6
    IoW 20 D7
    Lancs 202 B4
    Midloth 271 D7
    Norf 158 F3
    Northants 136 F6
    Northumb 252 F3
    Northumb 264 B4
    N Yorks 204 E5
    N Yorks 225 D8
    N Yorks 216 B5
    Perth 286 C5
    Perth 286 F2
    Perth 286 G5
    Shrops 115 B10
    Shrops 130 D5
    Shrops 148 D6
    Staffs 127 D8
    Sur 50 E2
    Swansea 56 D2
    W Mid 134 D3
    W Yorks 197 B10
Middleton Baggot
    Shrops 132 E2
Middleton Cheney
    Northants 101 C9
Middleton Green Staffs .151 B9
Middleton Hall
    Northumb 263 D11
Middleton-in-Teesdale
    Durham 232 F4
Middleton Junction
    Gtr Man 195 G11
Middleton Moor Suff . . .127 D8
Middleton of Rora
    Aberds 303 E10
Middleton One Row
    Darl 225 C7
Middleton-on-Leven
    N Yorks 225 D9
Middleton-on-Sea
    W Sus 35 G7
Middleton-on-the-Wolds
    E Yorks 208 D4
Middleton Place Cumb . .219 G11
Middleton Priors Shrops 132 E2
Middleton Quernhow
    N Yorks 214 D6
Middleton Scriven
    Shrops 132 F3
Middleton St George
    Darl 224 C6
Middleton Stoney
    Oxon 101 G10
Middleton Tyas N Yorks 224 D4
Middletown Cumb 219 D9
    N Som 60 E3
    Powys 148 G6
    Warks 117 C11
Middle Town Scilly 1 F4
Middle Tysoe Warks 100 C5
Middle Wallop Hants 47 F9
Middle Weald M Keynes .102 D5
Middlewich Ches E 167 B11
Middlewick Wilts 61 C11
Middle Winterslow Wilts 47 G8
Middlewood Ches E 184 E6
    Corn 11 F11
    S Yorks 186 C4
Middle Woodford Wilts . .46 F6
Middlewood Green
    Suff 125 E11
Middleyard Glos 80 E4
    Herts 86 B2
Middlezoy Som 43 G11
Middridge Durham 233 F11
Midelney Som 28 C6
Midfield Highld 308 C5
Midford Bath 61 G9
Midgard Borders 262 F3
Mid Garrary Dumfries . .237 B7
Midge Hall Lancs 194 C4
Midgeholme Cumb 240 F4
Midgham W Berks 64 F5
Midgham Green W Berks .64 F5
Midgley W Yorks 196 B4
    W Yorks 197 E9
Mid Holmwood Sur 51 D7
Midhopestones S Yorks .186 B2
Midhurst W Sus 34 C5
Mid Lambrook Som 28 D6
Midland Orkney 314 F3
Mid Lavant W Sus 22 B5
Midlem Borders 262 E3
Midley Kent 39 C7
Midlock S Lanark 259 E11
Midloe Grange Cambs . .122 D3
Mid Main Highld 300 F4
Midmar Aberds 293 C8
Midmuir Argyll 289 G11
Midpark Argyll 255 F11
Midplaugh Aberds 302 E6
Midsomer Norton Bath . .45 C7
Midton Inverclyd 276 F4
Midtown Highld 307 L3
    Highld 308 C5
Midtown of Buchromb
    Moray 302 E3
Midtown of Glass
    Aberds 302 E4
Mid Urchany Highld 301 E8
Mid Walls Shetland 313 H4
Midway Ches E 184 E6
    Derbys 153 F7
Mid Yell Shetland 312 D7
Miekle Toux Aberds 302 D5
Migdale Highld 309 K6
Migvie Aberds 292 C6
Milarrochy Stirling 277 C8
Milber Devon 9 B7
Milborne Port Som 29 D11
Milborne St Andrew
    Dorset 18 B2
Milborne Wick Som 29 C11
Milbourne Northumb . . .242 B4
    Wilts 62 B2
Milburn Cumb 231 E9
Milbury Heath S Glos . . .79 G11

Milby N Yorks 215 F8
Milch Hill Essex 106 G4
Milcombe Corn 6 D4
    Oxon 101 E8
Milden Suff 107 B9
Mildenhall Suff 124 C4
    Wilts 63 F8
Milebrook Powys 114 C6
Milebush Kent 53 D9
Mile Cross Norf 160 G4
Mile Elm Wilts 62 F3
Mile End Cambs 140 G2
    Devon 14 G2
    Essex 107 F9
    Glos 79 C9
    London 67 C11
    Suff 124 G6
Mileham Norf 159 F7
Mile Oak Brighton 36 F2
    Kent 53 E7
    Shrops 148 B6
    Staffs 134 C3
Miles Green Staffs 168 F4
    Sur 50 B3
Miles Hill W Yorks 205 F11
Milesmark Fife 279 D11
Miles Platting Gtr Man . .184 B5
Miley's Green W Berks . .64 F4
Mile Town Kent 70 E2
Milfield Northumb 263 D10
Milford Derbys 170 F5
    Devon 24 C2
    Powys 129 D11
    Shrops 149 E8
    Staffs 151 E9
    Sur 50 E2
    Wilts 31 B11
Milford Haven Pembs . . .72 D6
Milford on Sea Hants . . .19 C11
Milkhall Midloth 270 C4
Milkieston Borders 270 G4
Milkwall Glos 79 D9
Milkwell Wilts 30 C6
Milland W Sus 34 B4
Milland Marsh W Sus . . .34 B4
Millarston Renfs 267 C9
Millbank Aberds 303 E11
    Highld 310 C5
Millbeck Cumb 229 F11
Millbounds Orkney 314 C5
Millbreck Aberds 303 E10
Millbridge Sur 49 E10
Millbrook C Beds 103 D10
    Corn 7 E8
    Devon 27 D11
    Gtr Man 185 B7
    Soton 32 E5
Mill Brow Gtr Man 185 D7
Millburn S Ayrs 257 D10
Millcombe Devon 8 F6
Mill Common Norf 142 G6
    Suff 143 G8
Mill Corner E Sus 38 C4
Milldale Staffs 169 E10
Mill Dam N Yorks 212 F3
Millden Lodge Angus . . .293 F7
Milldens Angus 287 B9
Millend Glos 80 D3
    Glos 80 F3
Mill End Bucks 65 C9
    Cambs 124 F2
    Glos 81 D10
    Herts 85 G8
    Herts 104 E6
Mill End Green Essex . . .106 F2
Millendreath Corn 6 E5
    Pembs 73 E8
    Powys 114 G4
Millerhill Midloth 270 B6
Miller's Dale Derbys 185 G10
Miller's Green Derbys . .170 E3
Millersneuk E Dunb 278 A3
Millerston Glasgow 268 B2
Mill Farm Aberds 303 C8
Millfield Pboro 138 C3
    T&W 243 F9
Millgate Lancs 195 D11
    Norf 160 D3
Millgillhead Cumb 229 G3
Mill Green Cambs 106 B2
    Essex 87 E10
    Herts 86 D2
    Norf 142 G2
    Shrops 150 D3
    Suff 107 C9
    Suff 125 F9
    Suff 126 F2
    W Mid 133 D11
Millhalf Hereford 96 B5
Millhayes Devon 27 F10
    Devon 28 E2
Millhead Lancs 211 E9
Millheugh S Lanark 268 E5
Mill Hill Blackburn 195 B7
    London 86 G2
    M Keynes 103 D7
Milton Keynes Village
    M Keynes 103 D7
Milton Lilbourne Wilts . .63 G7
Milton Malsor Northants 120 F4
Milton Morenish Perth . .285 D10
Milton of Auchinhove
    Aberds 293 C7
Milton of Balgonie Fife .287 G7
Milton of Buchanan
    Stirling 277 C8
Milton of Campfield
    Aberds 293 C8
Milton of Campsie
    E Dunb 278 F3
Milton of Corsindae
    Aberds 293 C8
Milton of Cullerlie
    Aberds 293 C9
Milton of Cultoquhey
    Perth 286 E2
Milton of Cushnie
    Aberds 293 B7
Milton of Dalcapon
    Perth 286 B3
Milton of Drimmie
    Perth 286 B5
Milton of Edradour
    Perth 286 B3
Milton of Gollanfield
    Highld 301 D7
Milton of Lesmore
    Aberds 302 G4
Milton of Logie Aberds .292 C6
Milton of Machany
    Perth 286 F3
Milton of Mathers
    Aberds 293 G9
Milton of Murtle
    Aberdeen 293 C10
Milton of Noth Aberds . .302 G5
Milton of Tullich Aberds 292 D5
Milton on Stour Dorset . .30 B3

Mill Place N Lincs 200 F2
Millpool Corn 2 C3
    Corn 11 G8
Millport N Ayrs 266 E3
Millquarter Dumfries . . .246 G4
Mill Shaw W Yorks 205 G11
Mill Side Cumb 211 C8
Mill Street Kent 53 B7
    Norf 159 F11
    Suff 107 D9
Millthorpe Derbys 186 F4
    Lincs 156 C2
Mill Throop Bmouth 19 B8
Millthrop Cumb 222 G3
Milltimber Aberdeen . . .293 C10
Milltown Aberds 6 D2
    Corn 6 D2
    Derbys 170 C5
    Devon 40 F5
    Dumfries 239 C8
Milltown of Aberdalgie
    Perth 286 E4
Milltown of Auchindoun
    Moray 302 E3
Milltown of Craigston
    Aberds 303 D7
Milltown of Edinvillie
    Moray 302 E2
Milltown of Kildrummy
    Aberds 292 B6
Milltown of Rothiemay
    Moray 302 E5
Milltown of Towie
    Aberds 292 B6
Millwall London 67 D11
Milnathort Perth 286 G5
Milner's Heath Ches W . .167 C7
Milngavie E Dunb 277 G11
Milnquarter Falk 278 F6
Milnrow Gtr Man 196 E2
Milnsbridge W Yorks . . .196 D6
Milnshaw Lancs 195 B9
Milnthorpe Cumb 211 C9
    W Yorks 197 D10
Milnwood N Lanark 268 D4
Milo Carms 75 B9
Milson Shrops 116 C2
Milstead Kent 54 B2
Milston Wilts 47 D7
Milthorpe Northants 101 B11
Milton Angus 287 C7
    Angus 292 E6
    Cambs 123 E9
    Cumb 211 C10
    Cumb 240 E2
    Derbys 152 D6
    Dumfries 236 D4
    Dumfries 237 B10
    Dumfries 247 G8
    Fife 287 F8
    Glasgow 267 B11
    Highld 299 E7
    Highld 300 D5
    Highld 300 E5
    Highld 301 D7
    Moray 302 C5
    Notts 188 G2
    N Som 59 G10
    Oxon 83 G7
    Oxon 101 B8
    Pembs 73 D8
    Perth 286 F3
    Ptsmth 21 B9
    Som 29 C7
    Stirling 285 G9
    Stoke 168 F6
    S Yorks 197 G11
    W Dunb 277 F7
    W Dunb 45 B11
Milton Abbas Dorset 30 G4
Milton Abbot Devon 12 F4
Milton Bridge Midloth . .270 C4
Milton Bryan C Beds 103 E9
Milton Clevedon Som . . .45 F7
Milton Coldwells Aberds 303 F9
Milton Combe Devon 7 B9
Milton Common Oxon . . .83 E11
Milton Coombe Devon . . .7 B9
Milton Damerel Devon . .24 E5
Miltonduff Moray 301 C11
Milton End Glos 80 C2
    Glos 81 E10
Milton Ernest Bedford . .121 G10
Milton Green Ches W . . .167 D7
Milton Heights Oxon 83 G7
Miltonhill Moray 301 C10
Milton Hill Devon 14 F4
    Oxon 83 G7
Miltonise Dumfries 236 B3
Milton Keynes
    M Keynes 103 D7

Milton Regis Kent 70 F2
Milton Street E Sus 23 E7
Milton under Wychwood
    Oxon 82 B3
Milverton Som 27 B10
    Warks 118 D6
Milwich Staffs 151 C9
Milwr Flint 181 G11
Mimbridge Sur 66 G3
Minard Argyll 275 D10
Minard Castle Argyll . . .275 D10
Minchington Dorset 31 E7
Minchinhampton Glos . . .80 E5
Mindrum Northumb 263 D8
Minehead Som 42 D3
Minera Wrex 166 E3
Minety Wilts 81 G8
Minffordd Gwyn 145 B11
    Gwyn 146 G4
    Gwyn 179 G9
Mingarrypark Highld . . .289 C8
Mingoose Corn 4 F4
Miningsby Lincs 174 C4
Minions Corn 11 G11
Minishant S Ayrs 257 G8
Minllyn Gwyn 147 G2
Minnes Aberds 303 G9
Minngearraidh W Isles .297 J3
Minnigaff Dumfries 236 C6
Minnonie Aberds 303 C7
Minnow End Essex 88 C2
Minnygap Dumfries 248 D2
Minshull Vernon
    Ches E 167 C11
Minskip N Yorks 215 G7
Minstead Hants 32 E3
Minsted W Sus 34 C5
Minster Kent 70 E4
    Kent 71 G11
Minsterley Shrops 131 C7
Minster Lovell Oxon 82 C4
Minsterworth Glos 80 B3
Minterne Magna Dorset .29 G11
Minterne Parva Dorset . .29 G11
Minting Lincs 189 G11
Mintlaw Aberds 303 E10
Minto Borders 262 E3
Minto Kames Borders . .262 E3
Mintsfeet Cumb 221 G10
Minwear Pembs 73 C8
Minworth W Mid 134 E3
Mirbister Orkney 314 E2
Mirehouse Cumb 219 B9
Mireland Highld 310 C7
Mirfield W Yorks 197 D8
Miserden Glos 80 D6
Misery Corner Norf 142 F5
Miskin Rhondda 58 C4
    Rhondda 77 F8
Misselfore Wilts 31 C8
Misson Notts 188 C3
Misterton Leics 135 G11
    Notts 188 C3
    Som 29 F7
Misterton Soss Notts . . .188 B3
Mistley Essex 108 E2
Mistley Heath Essex 108 E2
Mitcham London 67 F9
Mitchel Troy Mon 79 C7
Mitcheldean Glos 79 B11
Mitchell Corn 5 E7
Mitchell Hill Borders . . .260 C3
Mitchellslacks
    Dumfries 247 G11
Mitcheltroy Common
    Mon 79 D7
Mitford Northumb 252 F5
Mithian Corn 4 E4
Mithian Downs Corn 4 F4
Mitton Staffs 151 F7
    Worcs 99 C8
Mixbury Oxon 102 E2
Mixenden W Yorks 196 B5
Mixtow Corn 6 E2
Moat Cumb 239 C10
Moats Tye Suff 125 F10
Mobberley Ches E 184 F3
    Staffs 169 G8
Moblake Ches E 167 G11
Mobwell Bucks 84 E5
Moccas Hereford 97 C7
Mochdre Conwy 180 F4
    Powys 129 F11
Mochrum Dumfries 236 E5
Mockbeggar Hants 31 F11
    Kent 54 E6
    Medway 69 E8
Mockerkin Cumb 229 G2
Moclett Orkney 314 B4
Modbury Devon 8 E3
Moddershall Staffs 151 B8
Model Village Derbys . . .187 G8
Modest Corner Kent 52 E5
Moelfre Anglesey 179 D8
    Conwy 181 G7
    Powys 148 D3
Moel Tryfan Gwyn 163 D8
Moel-y-crio Flint 165 B11
Moffat Dumfries 248 B3
Moffat Mills N Lanark . . .268 B5
Mogador Sur 51 C8
Mogerhanger C Beds . . .104 B2
Mogworthy Devon 26 D5
Moira Leics 152 F6
Moity Powys 96 C3
Molash Kent 54 C4
Mol-chlach Highld 294 D6
Mold Flint 166 C2
Moldgreen W Yorks 197 D7
Molehill Green Essex . . .105 G11
    Essex 106 G4
Molescroft E Yorks 208 E6
Molesden Northumb 252 G4
Molesworth Cambs 121 B11
Molinnis Corn 5 D10
Moll Highld 295 B7
Molland Devon 26 B4
Mollington Ches W 182 G5
    Oxon 101 B8
Mollinsburn N Lanark . . .278 G4
Monachty Ceredig 111 E10
Monachylemore Stirling 285 E9
Monar Lodge Highld 300 E2
Monaughty Powys 114 D4
Monboddo House
    Aberds 293 F9

Moneyrow Green
    Windsor 65 D11
Moneystone Staffs 169 F9
Mongleath Corn 3 C7
Moniaive Dumfries 247 E2
Monifieth Angus 287 D8
Monikie Angus 287 D8
Monimail Fife 286 F6
Monington Pembs 92 C2
Monk Bretton S Yorks . .197 F11
Monk Fryston N Yorks . .198 B4
Monken Hadley London . .86 F3
Monkerton Devon 14 C5
Monk Hesleden Durham .234 D5
Monkhide Hereford 98 C2
Monkhill Cumb 239 F8
    W Yorks 198 C3
Monkhopton Shrops 132 E2
Monkland Hereford 115 F9
Monkleigh Devon 25 C7
Monkmoor Shrops 149 G10
Monknash V Glam 58 E2
Monkokehampton Devon .25 F9
Monkscross Corn 12 G3
Monkseaton T&W 243 C8
Monks Eleigh Suff 107 B9
Monk's Gate W Sus 36 B2
Monks Heath Ches E . . .184 G4
Monk Sherborne Hants . .48 B6
Monkshill Aberds 303 E7
Monks Hill Kent 53 E11
Monksilver Som 42 F5
Monks Kirby Warks 135 G9
Monk Soham Suff 126 D4
Monk's Orchard London . .67 F11
Monk's Park Wilts 61 F11
Monkspath W Mid 118 B2
Monks Risborough Bucks .84 E4
Monksthorpe Lincs 174 B6
Monkston Park
    M Keynes 103 D7
Monk Street Essex 106 F2
Monkswood Mon 78 E4
    Monmouth 78 F4
    W Yorks 206 F2
Monkton Devon 27 G11
    Kent 71 G9
    Pembs 73 E7
    S Ayrs 257 D9
    T&W 243 E8
    V Glam 58 E2
Monkton Combe Bath . . .61 G9
Monkton Deverill Wilts . .45 F11
Monkton Farleigh Wilts .61 F10
Monkton Heathfield Som 28 B3
Monkton Up Wimborne
    Dorset 31 E8
Monkwearmouth T&W . .243 F9
Monkwood Green
    Worcs 116 E6
Monmarsh Hereford 97 B10
Monmore Green W Mid .133 D8
Monmouth Cap Mon 97 F7
Monmouth / Trefynwy
    Mon 79 C8
Monnington on Wye
    Hereford 97 C7
Monreith Dumfries 236 E5
Monreith Mains
    Dumfries 236 E5
Montacute Som 29 D7
Montcliffe Gtr Man 195 E7
Montcoffer Ho Aberds . .302 C6
Montford Argyll 266 C2
    Shrops 149 G8
Montford Bridge Shrops 149 F8
Montgarrie Aberds 293 B7
Montgomery Powys 130 D4
Montgomery Lines
    Hants 49 C11
Monton Gtr Man 184 B3
Montpelier Bristol 60 D5
Montrave Fife 287 G7
Montrose Angus 287 B11
Montsale Essex 89 F8
Monwode Lea Warks . . .134 E5
Monxton Hants 47 E10
Monyash Derbys 169 B11
Monymusk Aberds 293 B8
Monzie Perth 286 E2
Monzie Castle Perth 286 E2
Moodiesburn N Lanark . .278 G3
Moolham Som 28 E5
Moon's Green Kent 38 B5
Moonzie Fife 287 F7
Moor Som 28 D6
Mooradale Shetland 312 F6
Moor Allerton W Yorks . .205 F11
Mooray Wilts 46 G3
Moorby Lincs 174 C3
Moorclose Cumb 228 F5
    Gtr Man 195 F11
Moor Common Bucks . . .84 G4
Moorcot Hereford 115 F7
Moor Crichel Dorset 31 F7
Moor Cross Devon 8 D2
Moordown Bmouth 19 C7
Moore Halton 183 E9
Moor Edge W Yorks 205 F8
Moorend Cumb 239 G8
    Glos 170 F2
    Glos 80 E2
    Glos 80 E3
    Gtr Man 185 D7
    S Glos 61 D7
Moor End Bucks 84 G4
    Cambs 105 B7
    C Beds 103 G9
    Durham 234 C2
    E Yorks 208 F2
    Glos 99 G9
    Lancs 202 B4
    N Yorks 207 F7
    W Yorks 196 B5
    W Yorks 206 G3
Moor End Field N Yorks .215 F8
Moorends S Yorks 199 D7
Moorgate Norf 160 C3
    S Yorks 186 C5
Moorgreen Hants 33 D7
    Notts 171 F7
Moor Green Herts 104 F6
    Staffs 169 G7
    W Mid 133 G11
Moorhaigh Notts 171 C7
Moorhall Derbys 186 G4
Moor Hall W Mid 134 D2

Moorhampton Hereford 97 B7
Moorhaven Village Devon. .8 D3
Moorhayne Devon 28 F2
Moorhead W Yorks 205 F8
Moor Head W Yorks 197 B8
W Yorks 197 E8
Moorhey Gtr Man 196 G2
Moorhole S Yorks 186 E6
Moorhouse Cumb 239 F8
Cumb 239 G7
Notts 172 B3
S Yorks 198 E3
Moorhouse Bank Sur 52 C2
Moorhouses Lincs 174 D3
Moorland or Northmoor
  Green Som 43 G10
Moorledge Bath 60 G5
Moorlinch Som 43 F11
Moor Monkton N Yorks 206 B6
Moor Monkton Moor
  N Yorks 206 B6
Moor of Balvack Aberds . . .293 B8
Moor of Granary
  Moray 301 D10
Moor of Ravenstone
  Dumfries 236 E5
Moor Park Cumb 229 D7
  Hereford 97 C9
  Herts 85 G9
  Sur 49 D11
Moor Row Cumb 219 C10
  Cumb 229 B10
Moorsholm Redcar 226 C3
Moorside Ches W 182 F3
  Dorset 30 D3
  Durham 233 B7
  Gtr Man 195 G9
  Gtr Man 196 F3
  W Yorks 197 B7
  W Yorks 205 F10
Moor Side Lancs 202 F5
  Lancs 202 G4
  Lincs 174 D3
  W Yorks 197 B7
  W Yorks 204 F6
Moorstock Kent 54 F6
Moorswater Corn 6 C4
Moorthorpe W Yorks 198 E3
Moor Top W Yorks 197 C7
Moortown Devon 12 B2
  Devon 12 G6
  Hants 31 G11
  IoW 20 E4
  Lincs 189 B9
  Telford 150 F2
  W Yorks 206 F2
Morangie Highld 309 L7
Morar Highld 295 F8
Moravian Settlement
  Derbys 153 B8
Môrawelon Anglesey 178 E3
Morayhill Highld 301 E7
Morborne Cambs 138 E2
Morchard Bishop Devon . . .26 F3
Morchard Road Devon 26 G3
Morcombelake Dorset 16 C4
Morcott Rutland 137 C8
Morda Shrops 148 D5
Morden Dorset 18 B4
  London 67 F9
Morden Green Cambs 104 C5
Morden Park London 67 F8
Mordiford Hereford 97 D11
Mordington Holdings
  Borders 273 D8
Mordon Durham 234 F2
More Shrops 130 E6
Morebath Devon 27 C7
Morebattle Borders 263 E7
Morecambe Lancs 211 G8
Moor Crichel Dorset 31 F8
Moredon Swindon 62 B6
Moredun Edin 270 B5
Morefield Highld 307 K6
Morehall Kent 55 F8
Morelaggan Argyll 284 G6
Moreleigh Devon 8 E5
Morenish Perth 285 D9
Moresby Cumb 228 G5
Moresby Parks Cumb 219 B9
Morestead Hants 33 B8
Moreton Dorset 18 D2
  Essex 87 D8
  Hereford 115 E10
  Mers 182 C3
  Oxon 83 E11
  Staffs 150 F5
  Staffs 152 D2
Moreton Corbet
  Shrops 149 E11
Moretonhampstead
  Devon 13 D11
Moreton-in-Marsh Glos .100 E4
Moreton Jeffries
  Hereford 98 B2
Moreton Morrell Warks . . .118 F6
Moreton on Lugg
  Hereford 97 B10
Moreton Paddox Warks . . .118 G6
Moreton Pinkney
  Northants 101 B11
Moreton Say Shrops 150 C2
Moreton Valence Glos 80 D3
Moretonwood Shrops 150 C2
Morfa Carms 56 B4
  Carms 75 C9
  Ceredig 110 G6
  Gwyn 144 C3
Morfa Bach Carms 74 C5
Morfa Bychan Gwyn 145 B10
Morfa Dinlle Gwyn 162 D6
Morfa Glas Neath 76 D5
Morfa Nefyn Gwyn 162 G3
Morfydd Denb 165 F10
Morganstown Cardiff 58 C6
Morgan's Vale Wilts 31 C11
Moriah Ceredig 112 B2
Mork Glos 79 D9
Morland Cumb 231 G7
Morley Ches E 184 E4
  Derbys 170 G5
  Durham 233 F8
  W Yorks 197 B9
Morley Green Ches E 184 E4
Morleymoor Derbys 170 G5
Morley Park Derbys 170 F5
Morley St Botolph
  Norf 141 D11
Morley Smithy Derbys 170 G5
Mornick Corn 12 G2
Morningside Edin 280 G3
  N Lanark 268 D6
Morningthorpe Norf 142 E4
Morpeth Northumb 252 F6
Morphie Aberds 293 G9
Morrey Staffs 152 F2

Morridge Side Staffs 169 E8
Morrilow Heath Staffs 151 B9
Morris Green Essex 106 E4
Morriston / Treforys
  Swansea 57 B7
Morriston V Glam 59 E7
Morston Norf 177 E8
Mortehoe Devon 40 D3
Morthen S Yorks 187 D7
Mortimer W Berks 65 G7
Mortimer's Cross
  Hereford 115 E8
Mortlake London 67 D8
Mortomley S Yorks 186 B4
Morton Cumb 230 D4
  Cumb 239 G9
  Derbys 170 C6
  IoW 21 D8
  Lincs 155 E11
  Lincs 172 C5
  Lincs 188 C4
  Norf 160 F2
  Notts 172 E2
  S Glos 79 G10
  Shrops 148 E5
Morton Bagot Warks 118 E2
Morton Common Shrops . . .148 E5
Morton Mains Dumfries . . .247 D9
Morton Mill Shrops 149 E11
Morton-on-Swale
  N Yorks 224 G6
Morton Spirit Warks 117 G10
Morton Tinmouth
  Durham 233 G9
Morton Underhill
  Worcs 117 F10
Morvah Corn 1 B4
Morval Corn 6 D5
Morven Lodge Aberds 292 C5
Morvich Highld 295 C11
  Highld 309 J7
Morville Shrops 132 E3
Morville Heath Shrops 132 E3
Morwellham Quay Devon . . .7 B8
Morwenstow Corn 24 C3
Mosborough S Yorks 186 E6
Moscow E Ayrs 267 G9
Mose Shrops 132 E5
Mosedale Cumb 230 E3
Moseley W Mid 133 D8
  W Mid 133 G11
  Worcs 116 F6
Moses Gate Gtr Man 195 F8
Mosley Common
  Gtr Man 195 G8
Moss Argyll 288 E1
  Highld 289 C8
  S Yorks 198 E5
  Wrex 166 E4
Mossbay Cumb 228 F5
Mossbank Shetland 312 F6
Moss Bank Halton 183 D8
  Mers 183 B8
Mossblown S Ayrs 257 E10
Mossbrow Gtr Man 184 D2
Mossburnford Borders 262 F5
Mossdale Dumfries 237 B8
Mossedge Cumb 239 D11
Moss Edge Lancs 202 E4
Mossend N Lanark 268 C4
Moss End Brack 65 E11
  Ches E 183 F11
Mosser Mains Cumb 229 F8
Mossfield Highld 300 B6
Mossgate Staffs 151 B8
Mosshouses Borders 262 B2
Moss Houses Ches E 184 G5
Mosside Aberds 287 B8
Moss Lane Ches E 184 G6
Mossley Ches E 168 C5
  Gtr Man 196 G3
Mossley Brow Gtr Man 196 G3
Mossley Hill Mers 182 D5
Moss Nook Gtr Man 184 D5
  Mers 183 C8
Moss of Barmuckity
  Moray 302 C2
Moss of Meft Moray 302 C2
Mosspark Glasgow 267 C10
Moss Pit Staffs 151 E8
Moss Side Cumb 238 G5
  Gtr Man 184 B4
Moss-side Highld 301 D8
Moss Side Lancs 193 G11
  Lancs 194 C4
  Lancs 202 G3
  Mers 182 B6
Moss-side Moray 302 D5
Mosstodloch Moray 302 D3
Mossy Lea Lancs 194 E4
Mosterton Dorset 29 F7
Moston Ches E 168 C2
  Ches M 182 G6
  Gtr Man 195 G11
  Shrops 149 D11
Moston Green Ches E 168 C2
Mostyn Flint 181 E11
Mostyn Quay Flint 181 E11
Motcombe Dorset 30 B5
Mothecombe Devon 8 F2
Motherby Cumb 230 F4
Motherwell N Lanark 268 D5
Mottingham London 68 F7
Mottisfont Hants 32 B4
Mottistone IoW 20 E4
Mottram in Longdendale
  Gtr Man 185 B7
Mottram Rise Gtr Man 185 B7
Mottram St Andrew
  Ches E 184 F5
Mott's Green Essex 87 B8
Mott's Mill E Sus 52 F4
Mouldsworth Ches W 183 G8
Moulin Perth 286 B3
Moulsecoomb Brighton . . .36 F4
Moulsford Oxon 64 C5
Moulsham Essex 88 D2
Moulsoe M Keynes 103 C8
Moultavie Highld 300 B6
Moulton Ches W 167 B11
  Lincs 156 E6
  Northants 120 D5
  N Yorks 224 E4
  Suff 124 E3
  V Glam 58 E5
Moulton Chapel Lincs 156 F5
Moulton Eaugate Lincs 156 F6
Moulton Park Northants . . .120 E5
Moulton Seas End Lincs . .156 D6
Moulzie Angus 292 F4
Mounie Castle Aberds 303 G7
Mount Corn 4 D5

Mount continued
  Corn 6 B2
  Highld 301 E10
  W Yorks 196 D5
Mountain Anglesey 178 E2
  W Yorks 205 G7
Mountain Air Bl Gwent 77 D11
Mountain Ash / Aberpennar
  Rhondda 77 F8
Mountain Bower Wilts 61 F10
Mountain Cross Borders . .270 F2
Mountain Street Kent 54 C5
Mountain Water Pembs 91 G8
Mount Ambrose Corn 4 G4
Mount Ballan Mon 60 B3
Mount Batten Plym 7 E9
Mountbenger Borders 261 D8
Mountbengerburn
  Borders 261 D8
Mountblow W Dunb 277 G9
Mount Bovers Essex 88 G4
Mount Bures Essex 107 E8
Mount Canisp Highld 301 B7
Mount Charles Corn 5 E10
  Corn 5 D10
Mount Cowdown Wilts 47 C9
Mount End Essex 87 E7
Mount Ephraim E Sus 37 B7
Mounters Dorset 30 D3
Mountfield E Sus 38 C2
Mountgerald Highld 300 C5
Mount Gould Plym 7 D9
Mount Hawke Corn 4 F4
Mount Hermon Corn 2 F6
  Sur 50 B4
Mount Hill S Glos 61 E7
Mountjoy Corn 5 C7
Mount Lane Devon 12 B3
Mountnessing Essex 87 F10
Mounton Mon 79 G8
Mount Pleasant Bucks 84 F5
  Ches E 168 D4
  Corn 5 C10
  Derbys 152 D6
  Derbys 152 F5
  Devon 27 G11
  Durham 233 E11
  E Sus 23 E7
  E Sus 36 D6
  Flint 182 G2
  Hants 33 E11
  Kent 71 F10
  London 85 G8
  M Tydf. 77 F7
  Neath 57 B9
  Norf 141 E9
  Pembs 73 D8
  Shrops 149 G9
  Stockton 234 B4
  Suff 106 B4
  T&W 243 E7
  Warks 135 F7
  Worcs 99 D10
  Worcs 117 E10
  W Yorks 197 C8
Mount Sion Wrex 166 E3
Mount Skippett Oxon 82 B5
Mountsolie Aberds 303 D9
Mountsorrel Leics 153 F11
Mount Sorrel Wilts 31 C8
Mount Tabor W Yorks 196 B5
Mount Vernon Glasgow . . .268 C3
Mount Wise Corn 7 E9
Mousehill Sur 50 E2
Mousehole Corn 1 D5
Mousen Northumb 264 C4
Mousley End Warks 118 D4
Mouswald Dumfries 238 C3
Mouth Mill Devon 24 B3
Mowbreck Lancs 202 G4
Mow Cop Ches E 168 D5
Mowden Darl 224 B5
  Essex 88 C3
Mowhaugh Borders 263 E8
Mowmacre Hill
  Leicester 135 B11
Mowshurst Kent 52 D3
Mowsley Leics 136 F2
Moxby N Yorks 215 F11
Moxley W Mid 133 D9
Moy Argyll 255 E8
  Highld 290 E6
  Highld 301 F7
Moy Hall Highld 301 F7
Moy Ho Moray 301 C10
Moyles Court Hants 31 F11
Moylgrove / Trewyddel
  Pembs 92 C2
Moy Lodge Highld 290 E6
Muasdale Argyll 255 C7
Muchalls Aberds 293 D11
Much Birch Hereford 97 E10
Much Cowarne Hereford . . .98 B2
Much Cowarne Hereford . . .98 B2
Much Dewchurch
  Hereford 97 E9
Muchelney Som 28 C6
Muchelney Ham Som 28 C6
Much Hadham Herts 86 B5
Much Hoole Lancs 194 C3
Much Hoole Moss Houses
  Lancs 194 C3
Much Hoole Town
  Lancs 194 C3
Muchlarnick Corn 6 D4
Much Marcle Hereford 98 E3
Muchrachd Highld 300 F2
Much Wenlock Shrops 132 C2
Muckairn Argyll 289 F11
Muckernich Highld 300 D5
Mucking Thurrock 69 C7
Muckle Breck Shetland . . .312 G6
Muckleford Dorset 17 C8
Mucklestone Staffs 150 B4
Muckleton Norf 158 B6
  Shrops 149 E11
Muckletown Aberds 302 G5
Muckley Shrops 132 D2
Muckley Corner Staffs 133 B11
Muckley Cross Shrops 132 D2
Muckton Lincs 190 E5
Muckton Bottom Lincs . . .190 E5
Mudale Highld 308 F5
Mudd Gtr Man 185 C7
Muddiford Devon 40 F5
Muddlebridge Devon 40 G4
Muddles Green E Sus 23 C8
Mudeford Dorset 19 C9
Mudford Som 29 D9
Mudgley Som 44 D2
Mugdock Stirling 277 F11
Mugeary Highld 294 B6
Muggington Derbys 170 G3
Muggintonlane End
  Derbys 170 G3
Muggleswick Durham 232 B6
Mugswell Sur 51 C7
Muie Highld 309 J6

Muir Aberds 292 E2
Muircleugh Borders 271 F10
Muirden Aberds 303 D7
Muirdrum Angus 287 D9
Muiredge Fife 281 B7
Muirhead Angus 287 D7
  Fife 286 G6
  Fife 287 F8
  N Lanark 268 B3
Muirhouse Edin 280 F4
  N Lanark 268 D5
Muirhouselaw Borders 262 D4
Muirhouses Falk 279 E10
Muirkirk E Ayrs 258 D5
Muirmill Stirling 278 E4
Muir of Alford Aberds 293 B7
Muir of Fairburn Highld . . .300 D3
Muir of Fowlis Aberds 293 B7
Muir of Kinellar
  Aberds 293 B10
Muir of Miltonduff
  Moray 301 D11
Muir of Ord Highld 300 D5
Muir of Pert Angus 287 D8
Muirshearlich Highld 290 E3
Muirskie Aberds 293 D10
Muirtack Aberds 303 F9
  Aberds 303 E8
Muirton Aberds 303 E9
  Highld 301 C7
  Perth 286 E5
  Perth 286 F3
Muirton Mains Highld 300 D4
Muirton of Ardblair
  Perth 286 C5
Muirton of Ballochy
  Angus 293 G8
Muiryfold Aberds 303 D7
Muker N Yorks 223 F8
Mulbarton Norf 142 C3
Mulben Moray 302 D3
Mulberry Corn 5 B9
Mulfra Corn 1 C5
Mulindry Argyll 254 B4
Mulla Shetland 313 G6
Mullardoch House
  Highld 300 F2
Mullenspond Hants 47 D9
Mullion Corn 2 E5
Mullion Cove Corn 2 F5
Mumbles Hill Swansea 56 D6
Mumby Lincs 191 G8
Mumps Gtr Man 196 F2
Mundale Moray 301 D10
Munderfield Row
  Hereford 116 G2
Munderfield Stocks
  Hereford 116 G2
Mundesley Norf 160 B6
Mundford Norf 140 E6
Mundham Norf 142 D6
Mundon Essex 88 E5
Mundurno Aberdeen 293 B11
Mundy Bois Kent 54 D2
Munerigie Highld 290 C4
Muness Shetland 312 C8
Mungasdale Highld 307 K4
Mungrisdale Cumb 230 E3
Munlochy Highld 300 D6
Munsary Cottage Highld . .310 E6
Munsley Hereford 98 C3
Munslow Shrops 131 F11
  Hereford 97 C10
Murch V Glam 59 E7
Murchington Devon 13 D9
Murcot Worcs 99 C11
Murcott Oxon 83 B9
  Wilts 81 G7
Murdieston Stirling 278 B3
Murdishaw Halton 183 E9
Murieston W Loth 269 C11
Murkle Highld 310 C5
Murlaggan Highld 290 D2
  Highld 290 E6
Murra Orkney 314 F2
Murrayfield Edin 280 G4
Murrayshall Perth 286 E5
Murraythwaite Dumfries . .238 C4
Murrell Green Hants 49 B8
Murrell's End Glos 98 E4
  Glos 98 G5
Murrion Shetland 312 F4
Murrow Cambs 139 B7
Mursley Bucks 102 F6
Murston Kent 70 G2
Murthill Angus 287 B8
Murthly Perth 286 D4
Murton Cumb 231 G10
  Durham 234 B3
  Northumb 273 F9
  Swansea 56 D5
  T&W 243 G8
  York 207 C8
Murton Grange
  N Yorks 215 B10
Murtwell Devon 8 D5
Musbury Devon 15 C11
Muscliff Bmouth 19 B7
Muscoates N Yorks 216 C3
Muscott Northants 120 E2
Musdale Argyll 289 G11
Mushroom Green
  W Mid 133 F8
Musselburgh E Loth 280 G6
Musselwick Pembs 72 D4
Mustard Hyrn Norf 161 F8
Muston Leics 154 B6
  N Yorks 217 D11
Mustow Green Worcs 117 C7
Muswell Hill London 86 G3
Mutehill Dumfries 237 E8
Mutford Suff 143 F9
Muthill Perth 286 F2
Mutley Plym 7 D9
Mutterton Devon 27 G8
Mutton Hall E Sus 37 C9
Mwdwl-eithin Flint 181 F11
Mynydd Flint 165 B11
Mybster Highld 310 D5
Myddfai Carms 94 F5
Myddle Shrops 149 E9
Myddlewood Shrops 149 E9
Myddyn-fych Carms 75 C10
Mydroilyn Ceredig 111 F9
Myerscough Lancs 202 F5
Myerscough Smithy
  Lancs 203 G8
Mylor Bridge Corn 3 C8
Mylor Churchtown Corn 3 B8
Mynachdy Cardiff 59 D7
Mynachlog-ddu Pembs 92 C2
Mynd Shrops 115 C7
Mynydd Bach Ceredig 112 B4
Mynydd-bach Mon 79 G7
Mynydd-bach
  Swansea 57 B7

Mynydd-bach-y-glo
  Swansea 56 B6
Mynydd Bodafon
  Anglesey 179 D7
Mynydd Ffllint / Flint
  Mountain Flint 182 G2
Mynydd Gilan Gwyn 144 E5
Mynydd-isa Flint 166 C3
Mynyddislwyn Caerph. 77 G11
Mynydd-llan Flint 181 G11
Mynydd Marian Conwy . . .180 F5
Mynydd Mechell
  Anglesey 178 D5
Mynyddygarreg Carms 74 D6
Mynytho Gwyn 144 C6
Myrebird Aberds 293 D9
Myreside Perth 286 E6
Myrtle Hill Carms 94 E5
Mytchett Sur 49 B11
Mytchett Place Sur 49 C11
Mytholm W Yorks 196 B3
Mytholmes W Yorks 204 F6
Mytholmroyd W Yorks 196 B4
Mythop Lancs 202 G3
Myton-le-Hall N Yorks 215 A8
Myton Hall N Yorks 215 A8
Myton-on-Swale
  N Yorks 215 F8
Mytton Shrops 149 F8

N

Naast Highld 307 L3
Nab Hill W Yorks 197 D7
Nab's Head Lancs 194 B6
Naburn York 207 D7
Na Buirgh W Isles 305 J2
Naccolt Kent 54 E4
Nackington Kent 55 C7
Nacton Suff 108 C4
Nadderwater Devon 14 C3
Nafferton E Yorks 209 B7
Na Gearrannan W Isles . . .304 D3
Nag's Head Glos 80 F5
Naid-y-march Flint 181 F11
Nailbridge Glos 79 B10
Nailsbourne Som 28 B2
Nailsea N Som 60 D3
Nailstone Leics 135 B8
Nailsworth Glos 80 F5
Nailwell Bath 61 G8
Nairn Highld 301 D8
Nalderswood Sur 51 D8
Nance Corn 4 G3
Nanceddan Corn 2 C2
Nancegollan Corn 2 C4
Nancemellin Corn 4 G2
Nancenoy Corn 3 D7
Nancledra Corn 1 B5
Nangreaves Lancs 195 D10
Nanhoron Gwyn 144 C5
Nanhyfer / Nevern
  Pembs 91 D11
Nannau Gwyn 146 E4
Nannerch Flint 165 B11
Nanpantan Leics 153 F10
Nanpean Corn 5 D9
Nanquidno Corn 1 D3
Nanstallon Corn 5 C10
Nant Carms 74 B6
  Denb 165 D11
Nant Alyn Flint 165 B11
Nant-ddu Powys 77 B8
Nanternis Ceredig 111 F7
Nant Uchaf Denb 165 D9
Nantgaredig Carms 93 G9
Nantgarw Rhondda 58 B6
Nant-glas Powys 113 C9
Nantglyn Denb 165 C8
Nantgwyn Powys 113 B9
Nant Peris / Old Llanberis
  Gwyn 163 D10
Nantserth Powys 113 C9
Nant-y-Bai Carms 94 C5
Nant-y-Bwch Bl Gwent 77 C11
Nant-y-cafn Neath 76 D4
Nantycaws Carms 75 B7
Nant y Caws Shrops 148 D5
Nant-y-ceisiad Caerph. 59 B8
Nant-y-derry Mon 78 D4
Nant-y-felin Conwy 179 G11
Nant-y-ffin Carms 93 E11
Nantyffyllon Bridgend. 57 C11
Nantyglo Bl Gwent 77 C11
Nant-y-gollen Shrops 148 D4
Nant-y-moel Bridgend 76 G6
Nant-y-pandy Conwy 179 G11
Nant-y-Rhiw Conwy 164 C4
Nantyronen Station
  Ceredig 112 B3
Napchester Kent 55 D10
Naphill Bucks 84 F4
Napleton Worcs 99 B7
Napley Staffs 150 B4
Napley Heath Staffs 150 B4
Nappa N Yorks 204 B3
Nappa Scar N Yorks 223 G8
Napton on the Hill
  Warks 119 E9
Narberth / Arberth
  Pembs 73 C10
Narberth Bridge Pembs . . .73 C10
Narborough Leics 135 D10
  Norf 158 G4
Narkurs Corn 6 D6
Narracott Devon 24 D5
Narrowgate Corner
  Norf 161 F8
Nasareth Gwyn 163 E7
Naseby Northants 120 B3
Nash Bucks 102 D5
  Hereford 114 E6
  Kent 55 B9
  London 68 G2
  Newport 59 C10
  Shrops 116 C2
  Som 29 B8
Nash End Worcs 132 G5
Nashend Glos 80 D5
Nashes Green Hants 49 D7
Nash Hill Wilts 61 G11
Nash Mills Herts 85 D9
Nash Street E Sus 23 C8
  Kent 68 F6
Nassington Northants 137 D11
Nasty Herts 86 B4
Natcott Devon 24 C3
Nateby Cumb 222 D5

Nateby continued
  Lancs 202 E5
Nately Scures Hants 49 C8
Natland Cumb 211 B10
Natton Glos 99 E8
Naughton Suff 107 B10
Naunton Glos 100 G2
  Worcs 99 D7
Naunton Beauchamp
  Worcs 117 G9
Navant Hill W Sus 34 B6
Navenby Lincs 173 D7
Navestock Essex 87 F8
Navestock Side Essex 87 F9
Navidale Highld 311 H4
Navity Highld 301 C7
Nawton N Yorks 216 C3
Nayland Suff 107 E9
Nazeing Essex 86 D6
Nazeing Gate Essex 86 D6
Nazeing Long Green
  Essex 86 E6
Neacroft Hants 19 B9
Nealhouse Cumb 239 G8
Neal's Green Warks 134 G6
Neames Forstal Kent 54 B5
Neap Shetland 313 H7
Near Hardcastle
  N orks 214 F2
Near Sawrey Cumb 221 F7
Nearton End Bucks 102 F6
Neasham Darl 224 C6
Neat Enstone Oxon 101 G7
Neath / Castell-nedd
  Neath 57 B8
Neath Abbey Neath 57 B8
Neatham Hants 49 E8
Neatishead Norf 160 E6
Neat Marsh E Yorks 209 G9
Neaton Norf 141 C8
Nebo Anglesey 179 C7
  Ceredig 111 D10
  Conwy 164 D4
  Gwyn 163 E7
Nebsworth Warks 100 C4
Nechells W Mid 133 F11
Necton Norf 141 B7
Nedd Highld 306 F6
Nedderton Northumb 252 G6
Nedge Hill Som 44 C5
Nedging Tye Suff 107 B10
Needham Norf 142 G4
Needham Green Essex 87 B9
Needham Market Suff 125 G11
Needham Street Suff 124 D4
Needingworth Cambs 122 C6
Needwood Staffs 152 E3
Neen Savage Shrops 116 B3
Neen Sollars Shrops 116 C3
Neenton Shrops 132 F2
Nefod Shrops 148 B6
Nefyn Gwyn 162 G4
Neighbourne Som 44 D6
Neight Hill Worcs 117 F8
Neilston E Renf 267 D9
Neithrop Oxon 101 C8
Nelly Andrews Green
  Powys 130 B5
Nelson Caerph 77 F10
  Lancs 204 F3
Nelson Village Northumb . .243 B7
Nemphlar S Lanark 269 G7
Nempnett Thrubwell
  N Som 60 G4
Nene Terrace Lincs 138 B5
Nenthall Cumb 231 B11
Nenthead Cumb 231 C11
Nenthorn Borders 262 B5
Nepcote W Sus 35 F10
Nepgill Cumb 229 F7
Nep Town W Sus 36 E2
Nerabus Argyll. 254 B3
Nercwys Flint 166 C2
Nerston S Lanark 268 D2
Nesbit Northumb 263 C11
Ness Ches W 182 F4
  Orkney 314 F4
Nesscliffe Shrops 149 F7
Nessholt Ches W 182 F4
Nesstoun Orkney 314 A7
Neston Ches W 182 F3
  Wilts 61 F11
Nethchells Green
  W Mid 133 F11
Netham Bristol 60 E6
Netheranven Wilts 47 D7
Nether Alderley Ches E . . .184 F4
Netheravon Wilts 46 D6
Nether Blainslie
  Borders 271 G10
Nether Booth Derbys 185 D10
Netherbrae Aberds 303 D7
Netherbrough Orkney 314 E3
Nether Broughton Leics . .154 D3
Netherburn S Lanark 268 F6
Nether Burrow Lancs 212 D2
Nether Burrows Derbys . . .152 B5
Netherbury Dorset 16 B5
Netherby Cumb 239 C9
  N Yorks 206 D2
Nether Cassock
  Dumfries 248 C6
Nether Cerne Dorset 17 B9
Nether Chanderhill
  Derbys 186 G4
Netherclay Som 28 C3
Nether Compton Dorset . . .29 D9
Nethercote Oxon 101 C9
  Warks 119 E10
Nethercott Devon 12 B3
  Devon 40 F3
  Oxon 101 G9
  Oxon 83 F8
Nether Crimond Aberds . . .303 G8
Netherdale Shetland 313 H3
Nether Dalgliesh
  Borders 249 B7
Nether Dallachy Moray . . .302 C3
Nether Edge S Yorks 186 E4
Netherend Glos 79 E9
Nether End Derbys 186 G3
  Leics 154 G4
  W Yorks 197 F8
Nether Exe Devon 26 G6
Netherfield E Sus 23 B11
  M Keynes 103 D7
  Notts 171 G10
Nethergate Norf 159 D11
Nether Glasslaw Aberds . .303 D8
Nether Hall Leicester 136 B2
Netherhampton Wilts 31 B10
Nether Handley Derbys . . .186 F6
Nether Handwick Angus . .287 C7
Nether Haugh S Yorks 186 B6

Nether Headon Notts 188 F2
Nether Heage Derbys 170 E5
Nether Heyford
  Northants 120 F3
Nether Hindhope
  Borders 263 G7
Nether Horsburgh
  Borders 261 B8
Nether Howecleuch
  S Lanark 260 G2
Nether Kellet Lancs 211 F10
Nether Kidston Borders . . .270 G4
Nether Kinmundy
  Aberds 303 E10
Nether Kirton E Renf 267 D9
Netherland Green Staffs . .152 C2
Nether Langwith Notts . . .187 G8
Netherlaw Dumfries 237 E9
Netherlay Dorset 28 F6
Nether Leask Aberds 303 F10
Netherlee E Renf 267 D11
Nether Lenshie Aberds . . .302 E6
Nazeing Mead Essex 86 D5
Neacroft Hants 19 B9
Netherley Aberds 293 D10
  Mers 182 D6
Nether Loads Derbys 170 B4
Nethermill Dumfries 248 F2
Nethermills Moray 302 D5
Nether Monynut
  Borders 272 C4
Nether Moor Derbys 170 B5
Nethermuir Aberds 303 E9
Netherne-on-the-Hill
  Sur 51 B9
Netheroyd Hill W Yorks . . .196 D6
Nether Padley Derbys 186 F3
Nether Park Aberds 303 D10
Netherplace E Renf 267 D10
Nether Poppleton York . . .207 C7
Netherrow Aberds 262 E3
Netherseal Derbys 152 F6
Nethershields E Renf 268 F2
Nether Silton N Yorks 225 G9
Nether Skyborry Shrops . .114 C5
Netherstoke Dorset 29 F8
Nether Stowe Staffs 152 G2
Nether Stowey Som 43 F7
Nether Street Essex 87 C9
  Herts 86 B6
Netherthird E Ayrs 258 F3
Netherthong W Yorks 196 F6
Netherthorpe Derbys 186 F6
  S Yorks 187 E8
Netherton Aberds 303 E8
  Angus 287 B9
  Ches W 183 F8
  Corn 11 G5
  Devon 14 G3
  Glos 81 G11
  Hants 47 B10
  Hereford 97 F10
  Mers 193 G11
  N Lanark 268 E5
  Northumb 251 B11
  Oxon 82 E6
  Perth 286 B5
  Shrops 132 G4
  W Mid 133 F8
  Worcs 99 C9
  W Yorks 196 E5
  W Yorks 197 E7
Netherton of Lonmay
  Aberds 303 C10
Nethertown Cumb 219 D9
  Highld 310 B7
  Lancs 203 F10
  Staffs 152 F2
Nether Urquhart Fife 286 G5
Nether Wallop Hants 47 F10
Nether Warden
  Northumb 241 D10
Nether Wasdale Cumb 220 E2
Nether Welton Cumb 230 D3
Nether Whitacre Warks . . .134 E4
Nether Winchendon or
  Lower Winchendon
  Bucks 84 C2
Netherwitton Northumb . . .252 E4
Netherwood E Ayrs 258 D5
Nether Worton Oxon 101 E8
Nether Yeadon
  W Yorks 205 E10
Netley Bridge Highld 301 G10
Netley Hants 33 F7
Netley Hill Soton 33 E7
Netley Marsh Hants 32 E4
Nettacott Devon 14 B4
Netteswell Essex 87 C7
Nettlebed Oxon 65 B8
Nettlebridge Som 44 D6
Nettlecombe Dorset 16 B6
  IoW 20 F6
Nettleden Herts 85 C8
Nettleham Lincs 189 F8
Nettlestead Kent 53 C7
  Suff 107 B11
Nettlestead Green Kent . . .53 C7
Nettlestone IoW 21 C8
Nettlesworth Durham 233 B11
Nettleton Lincs 189 C9
  Wilts 61 D10
Nettleton Green Wilts 61 D10
Nettleton Hill W Yorks 196 D5
Nettleton Shrub Wilts 61 D10
Nettleton Top Lincs 189 B10
Netton Wilts 46 F6
Neuadd Carms 94 G3
Nevendon Essex 88 G2
Nevern / Nanhyfer
  Pembs 91 D11
Nevilles Cross Durham . . .233 C11
Nevill Holt Leics 136 E6
New Abbey Dumfries 237 C11
New Aberdour Aberds 303 C8
New Addington London . . .51 B11
New Allas Kent 52 B6
Newall W Yorks 205 D10
Newall Green Gtr Man 184 D4
New Alresford Hants 48 G5
New Alyth Perth 286 C6
Newark Orkney 314 B7
  Pboro 138 C4
Newark-on-Trent Notts . . .172 E3
New Arley Warks 134 F4
New Arram E Yorks 208 E6
Newarthill N Lanark 268 D5
New Ash Green Kent 68 F6
New Balderton Notts 172 E4
Newball Lincs 189 F9
Newbarn Kent 55 F7
  Oxon 68 H6
New Barn Kent 68 F6
New Barnet London 86 F3
New Barnetby N Lincs 200 E5
New Barton Northants 121 D7
New Basford Nottingham . .171 G9

Newbattle Midloth 270 B6
New Beaupre V Glam 58 E4
New Beckenham London . .67 E11
New Bewick Northumb 264 E3
Newbie Dumfries 238 D5
Newbiggin Cumb 210 E5
  Cumb 211 D11
  Cumb 219 G11
  Cumb 230 E5
  Cumb 231 B8
  Cumb 231 G7
  Durham 232 F4
  Durham 233 E7
  N Yorks 213 B9
  N Yorks 223 G9
Newbiggin-by-the-Sea
  Northumb 253 F8
Newbiggin Aberds 303 G7
  Angus 287 D8
  Borders 262 F6
  Borders 280 E2
  S Lanark 269 F10
New-bigging Cumb 286 C6
Newbigging Orkney 314 B6
Newbigging Hall Estate
  Cumb 242 D6
Newbiggin-on-Lune
  Cumb 222 D4
New Bilton Warks 119 B9
New Bolingbroke Lincs . . .174 D4
New Bolsover Derbys 187 G7
New Boston Mers 183 B9
New Botley Oxon 83 D7
New Boultham Lincs 189 G7
New Bradwell M Keynes . . .102 C6
New Brancepeth
  Durham 233 C10
Newbridge Bath 61 F8
  Caerph. 78 F2
  Ceredig 111 F10
  Corn 1 C4
  Corn 4 G5
  Dumfries 237 B11
  Edin 280 G2
  E Sus 52 G3
  Hants 32 D3
  IoW 20 D4
  N Lanark 204 F3
  Pembs 91 B8
  Shrops 148 G6
  W Mid 133 D7
  Wrex 166 G3
New Bridge Wrex 166 G3
Newbridge Green Worcs . . .98 D6
New Brighton Flint 166 B3
  Flint 182 C4
  Mers 182 C4
  Wrex 166 E3
  W Yorks 197 B7
  W Yorks 205 F8
New Brimington Derbys . . .186 G6
New Brinsley Notts 171 E7
New Brotton Redcar 235 G9
Newbrough Northumb 241 D9
New Broughton Wrex 166 E4
New Buckenham Norf 141 E11
Newbuildings Devon 26 G3
New Buildings Bath 45 B7
  Dorset 18 C5
New Burgh Aberds 303 G9
  Aberds 303 G9
  Borders 261 F8
  Fife 286 E6
  Lancs 194 E3
Newburn T&W 242 D5
Newbury Kent 54 B6
  W Berks 64 F3
  Wilts 45 D10
New Bury Gtr Man 195 F8
Newbury Park London 68 B2
Newby Cumb 231 F7
  Lancs 204 C2
  N Yorks 205 D11
  N Yorks 212 E5
  N Yorks 215 F7
  N Yorks 225 C10
  N Yorks 227 G10
Newby Bridge Cumb 211 B7
Newby Cote N Yorks 212 E4
Newby East Cumb 239 F11
Newby Head Cumb 231 F7
New Byth Aberds 303 D8
Newby West Cumb 239 G9
Newby Wiske N Yorks 215 B7
Newcastle Bridgend. 58 D2
  Mon 78 B6
  Shrops 130 F5
Newcastle Emlyn / Castell
  Newydd Emlyn Carms. . . .92 C6
Newcastleton or Copshaw
  Holm Borders 249 F11
Newcastle-under-Lyme
  Staffs 168 F4
Newcastle upon Tyne
  T&W 242 D6
New Catton Norf. 160 G4
Newchapel Powys 129 G9
  Pembs 92 D4
  Staffs 168 E5
  Sur 51 E11
Newchapel / Capel Newydd
  Pembs 92 D4
New Charlton London 68 D2
New Cheriton Hants 33 B9
Newchurch Bl Gwent 77 G11
  Carms 93 G7
  Hereford 115 G7
  IoW 21 D7
  Kent 54 G5
  Lancs 195 C11
  Mon 79 F7
  Powys 114 G4
  Staffs 152 E3
Newchurch in Pendle
  Lancs 204 F2
New Clipstone Notts 171 C9
New Costessey Norf 160 G3

Newcott Devon .28 F2
New Coundon Durham . 233 E10
New Cowper Cumb 229 B8
Newcraighall Edin 280 G6
New Crofton W Yorks 197 D11
New Cross Ceredig 112 B2
　London 67 D11
　Oxon 65 D9
New Cross Gate London 67 D7
New Cumnock E Ayrs 258 G4
New Deer Aberds 303 E8
New Delaval Northumb 243 B7
New Delph Gtr Man 196 F3
New Denham Bucks 66 C4
Newdigate Sur 51 E7
New Downs Corn 1 C3
　Corn 4 E4
New Duston Northants 120 E4
New Earswick York 207 B8
New Eastwood Notts 171 F7
New Edlington S Yorks 187 B8
New Elgin Moray 302 C2
New Ellerby E Yorks 209 F9
Newell Green Brack 65 E11
New Eltham London 68 E2
New End Lincs 174 E3
　Warks 118 E2
　Worcs 117 F11
Newenden Kent 38 B4
New England Essex 106 C4
　Lincs 175 D8
　Pboro 138 C3
　Som 28 E4
Newent Glos 98 F4
Newerne Glos 79 E10
New Farnley W Yorks 205 G10
New Ferry Mers 182 D4
Newfield Durham 233 E10
　Durham 242 F6
　Highld 301 B7
　Stoke 168 E6
New Fletton Pboro 138 D3
Newford Scilly 1 G4
Newfound Hants 48 C5
New Fryston W Yorks 198 B3
Newgale Pembs 90 G6
New Galloway Dumfries 237 D8
Newgarth Orkney 314 E2
Newgate Lancs 194 F4
　Norf 177 E9
Newgate Corner Norf 161 G8
Newgate Street Herts 86 D4
New Gilston Fife 287 G8
New Greens Herts 85 D10
New Grimsby Scilly 85 C7
New Ground Herts 85 C7
Newgrounds Hants 31 E11
Newhailes Edin 280 G6
New Hainford Norf 160 F4
Newhall Ches E 167 F10
　Derbys 152 E5
Newhall Green Warks 134 F5
New Hall Hey Lancs 195 C10
Newhall House Highld 300 C6
Newhall Point Highld 301 C7
Newham Lincs 174 E3
　Northumb 264 D5
New Hartley Northumb 243 B8
Newhaven Derbys 169 C11
　Devon 24 C5
　Edin 280 F5
　E Sus 36 G6
New Haw Sur 66 G5
Newhay N Yorks 207 G9
New Headington Oxon 83 D8
New Heaton Northumb 273 G7
New Hedges Pembs 73 E10
Newhey Gtr Man 196 E2
New Herrington T&W 243 G8
Newhey Gtr Man 196 E2
Newhill Fife 286 F6
　Perth 286 G5
　S Yorks 186 B6
Newhills Aberdeen 293 C10
New Hinksey Oxon 83 E8
New Holkham Norf 159 B7
New Holland N Lincs 200 C5
　W Yorks 205 F7
Newholm N Yorks 227 C7
New Horwich Derbys 185 E8
New Houghton Derbys 171 B7
　Norf 158 D5
Newhouse Borders 262 D5
　N Lanark 268 C5
　Shetland 313 G6
New House Kent 68 G6
Newhouses Borders 271 G10
New Houses Gtr Man 194 G5
　N Yorks 212 E6
New Humberstone Leicester 136 B2
New Hunwick Durham 233 E9
New Hutton Cumb 221 G11
New Hythe Kent 53 B8
Newick E Sus 36 C6
Newingreen Kent 54 F6
Newington Edin 280 G5
　Kent 55 F7
　Kent 69 G11
　Kent 71 F11
　London 67 D10
　Notts 187 C11
　Oxon 83 F10
　Shrops 131 G8
Newington Bagpath Glos 80 G4
New Inn Carms 93 D9
　Devon 24 F6
　Mon 79 E7
　Pembs 91 E11
　Torf 78 F4
New Invention Shrops 114 B5
　W Mid 133 C9
New Kelso Highld 299 E9
New Kingston Notts 153 D10
New Kyo Durham 242 G5
New Ladykirk Borders 273 F7
New Lanark S Lanark 269 G7
Newland Cumb 210 D6
　E Yorks 199 B10
　Glos 79 D9
　Hull 209 G7
　N Yorks 197 C7
　Oxon 98 B5
Newland Bottom Cumb 210 D6
Newland Common Worcs 117 E8
Newland Green Kent 54 D2
Newlandrig Midloth 271 C7
Newlands Borders 250 E1
　Borders 262 E2
　Cumb 229 G10
　Cumb 230 D2
　Derbys 170 F6
　Dumfries 247 F11
　Glasgow 267 C11
　Highld 301 D7
　Moray 302 D3
　Northumb 242 F6
　Notts 171 C9

Newlands continued
　Staffs 151 E11
Newlands Corner Sur 50 D4
Newlandsmuir S Lanark 268 E2
Newlands of Geise Highld 310 C4
Newlands of Tynet Moray 302 C3
Newlands Park Anglesey 178 E3
New Lane Lancs 194 E2
New Lane End Warr 183 B10
New Langholm Dumfries 249 G9
New Leake Lincs 174 D6
New Leeds Aberds 303 D9
New Lodge S Yorks 197 F10
New Longton Lancs 194 B4
Newlot Orkney 314 E5
New Luce Dumfries 236 C3
Newlyn Corn 1 D5
Newmachar Aberds 293 B10
New Malden London 67 F8
Newman's End Essex 87 C8
Newman's Green Suff 107 C7
Newman's Place Hereford 96 B5
Newmarket Glos 80 F4
　Suff 124 E2
　W Isles 304 E6
New Marske Redcar 235 G8
New Marston Oxon 83 D8
New Marton Shrops 148 C6
New Micklefield W Yorks 206 G4
Newmill Borders 261 G11
　Corn 1 C5
　Moray 302 D4
New Mill Aberds 293 E9
　Borders 262 G2
　Corn 1 C5
　Corn 4 C5
　Cumb 219 E11
　Herts 84 C6
　Wilts 63 G7
　W Yorks 197 F7
Newmillerdam W Yorks 197 D10
Newmill of Inshewan Angus 292 G6
Newmills Corn 11 D11
　Fife 279 D10
　Highld 300 C6
New Mills Borders 271 F10
　Ches E 184 E3
　Corn 5 E7
　Derbys 185 D7
　Glos 79 E10
　Hereford 98 D4
New Mills / Felin Newydd Powys 129 C11
Newmills of Boyne Aberds 302 D5
Newmiln Perth 286 D5
Newmilns E Ayrs 258 B2
New Milton Hants 19 B10
New Mistley Essex 108 E2
New Moat Pembs 91 F11
Newmore Highld 300 B6
　Highld 300 C6
New Moston Gtr Man 195 G11
Newnes Shrops 149 C7
Newney Green Essex 87 D11
Newnham Cambs 123 E8
　Glos 79 C11
　Hants 49 C8
　Herts 104 D4
　Kent 54 B3
　Northants 119 F11
　Warks 118 E3
Newnham Bridge Worcs 116 D2
New Ollerton Notts 171 B11
New Oscott W Mid 133 E11
New Pale Ches W 183 G8
Newpark Fife 287 F8
New Park N Yorks 205 B11
New Parks Leicester 135 B11
New Passage S Glos 60 B4
New Pitsligo Aberds 303 D8
New Polzeath Corn 10 F4
Newpool Staffs 168 D5
Newport Corn 12 D2
　Devon 40 G5
　Dorset 18 C3
　Essex 105 D10
　E Yorks 208 G3
　Glos 79 F11
　Highld 311 G5
　IoW 20 D6
　Newport 59 B10
　Norf 161 F10
　Som 28 C4
　Telford 150 F4
Newport-on-Tay Fife 287 E8
Newport Pagnell M Keynes 103 C7
Newport / Trefdraeth Pembs 91 D11
Newpound Common W Sus 35 B9
Newquay Corn 4 C6
New Quay / Ceinewydd Ceredig 111 F7
New Rackheath Norf 160 G5
New Radnor Powys 114 E4
New Rent Cumb 230 D5
New Ridley Northumb 242 F3
New Road Side N Yorks 204 E5
　W Yorks 197 B7
New Romney Kent 39 C9
New Rossington S Yorks 187 B10
New Row Ceredig 112 C4
　Lancs 203 F8
　N Yorks 226 C2
Newsam Green W Yorks 206 G3
New Sarum Wilts 46 G6
New Sawley Derbys 153 C9
Newsbank Ches E 168 B4
New Scarbro W Yorks 205 G10
Newseat Aberds 303 F10
　Aberds 303 F7
Newsells Herts 105 D7
Newsham N Yorks 202 F6
　N Yorks 223 B8
　N Yorks 215 C2
　N Yorks 224 C2
Newsholme E Yorks 199 B8
　Lancs 204 C2
　W Yorks 204 F6
New Silksworth T&W 243 G9
New Skelton Redcar 226 B3
New Smithy Derbys 185 E8
Newsome W Yorks 196 E6
New Southgate London 86 G3
New Springs Gtr Man 194 F6
New Sprowston Norf 160 G4
New Stanton Derbys 153 B9

Newstead Borders 262 C3
　Northumb 264 D5
　Notts 171 E8
　Staffs 168 G5
　W Yorks 197 E11
New Stevenston N Lanark 268 D5
New Street Kent 68 G6
　Staffs 169 E9
Newstreet Lane Shrops 150 B2
New Swanage Dorset 18 E6
New Swannington Leics 153 F8
Newtake Devon 14 G3
Newton Argyll 275 D11
　Borders 262 E3
　Borders 262 E2
　Bridgend 57 F10
　Cambs 105 B8
　Cambs 121 C11
　Cardiff 59 D8
　Ches W 184 E6
　Ches W 183 F8
　Ches W 166 B6
　Ches W 167 D8
　Corn 5 C11
　Corn 11 F11
　Cumb 229 B7
　Cumb 239 F9
　Cumb 240 E2
　Derbys 185 E7
　Dorset 30 E3
　Dorset 29 G7
　Dumfries 239 C7
　Dumfries 248 E4
　Gtr Man 185 B7
　Hereford 96 C5
　Hereford 96 E6
　Hereford 115 D7
　Hereford 115 G10
　Highld 301 C7
　Highld 301 E7
　Highld 306 C7
　Highld 310 E7
　Highld 197 F7
　Lancs 202 F2
　Lancs 202 G4
　Lancs 203 C9
　Lancs 211 C11
　Lincs 155 B10
　Mers 182 D2
　Moray 301 C11
　Norf 143 B10
　Northants 137 G7
　Northumb 242 E2
　Northumb 171 G11
　Northumb 263 D11
　Northumb 264 D2
　Oxon 65 C9
　Perth 286 D5
　Poole 18 C6
　S Lanark 259 C10
　S Lanark 268 C3
　Som 42 F6
　Staffs 151 D10
　Suff 107 C8
　Swansea 56 D6
　Warks 119 B10
　Wilts 32 C2
　W Loth 279 B11
　W Mid 133 D10
　W Loth 279 E11
　W Mid 133 E11
Newton Abbot Devon 14 G3
Newtonairds Dumfries 247 G9
Newton Arlosh Cumb 238 F5
Newton Aycliffe Durham 233 G11
Newton Bewley Hrtlpl 234 F5
Newton Blossomville M Keynes 121 G8
Newton Bromswold Northants 121 D9
Newton Burgoland Leics 135 B7
Newton by Toft Lincs 189 D9
Newton Cross Pembs 91 F11
Newton Ferrers Devon 7 E11
Newton Flotman Norf 142 D4
Newtongrange Midloth 270 C6
Newton Green Mon 79 G8
Newton Hall Durham 233 B11
　Northumb 242 D2
Newton Harcourt Leics 136 D2
Newton Heath Gtr Man 195 G11
Newtonhill Aberds 293 D11
　Highld 300 E5
Newton Hill N Yorks 197 C10
Newton Ho Aberds 302 G6
Newton Hurst Staffs 151 D11
Newtonia Ches E 167 B11
Newton Ketton Darl 234 G2
Newton Kyme N Yorks 206 E5
Newton-le-Willows Mers 183 B9
　N Yorks 214 B4
Newton Longville Bucks 102 E6
Newton Mearns E Renf 267 D10
Newtonmill Angus 293 G8
Newtonmore Highld 291 D9
Newton Morrell N Yorks 224 D4
　Oxon 102 F2
Newton Mulgrave N Yorks 226 B6
Newton of Ardtoe Highld 289 B8
Newton of Balcanquhal Perth 286 F6
Newton of Balcormo Fife 287 G8
Newton of Falkland Fife 286 F6
Newton of Mountblairy Aberds 302 D6
Newton of Pitcairns Perth 286 F4
Newton on Ayr S Ayrs 257 E8
Newton on Ouse N Yorks 206 B6
Newton-on-Rawcliffe N Yorks 226 G5
Newton on the Hill Shrops 149 E8
Newton on the Moor Northumb 252 B5
Newton on Trent Lincs 188 G4
Newton Park Argyll 266 C2
Newton Peveril Dorset 18 B4
Newton Poppleford Devon 15 D7
Newton Purcell Oxon 102 E2
Newton Regis Warks 134 B5
Newton Reigny Cumb 230 E5
Newton Rigg Cumb 230 E5
Newton St Boswells Borders 262 C3

Newton St Cyres Devon 14 B3
Newton St Faith Norf 160 F4
Newton St Loe Bath 61 G8
Newton St Petrock Devon 24 C6
Newton Solney Derbys 152 D5
Newton Stacey Hants 48 C2
Newton Stewart Dumfries 236 C6
Newton Tony Wilts 47 E8
Newton Tracey Devon 25 B8
Newton under Roseberry Redcar 225 C11
Newton Underwood Northumb 252 F4
Newton upon Derwent E Yorks 207 D10
Newton Valence Hants 49 G8
Newton with Scales Lancs 202 G4
Newton Wood Norf 184 B6
New Totley S Yorks 186 F4
Newtown Argyll 284 G4
　Bl Gwent 77 C11
　Bucks 85 E7
　Caerph 78 G2
　Cambs 121 D11
　Cardiff 59 D8
　Ches E 184 E6
　Ches W 183 F8
　Ches W 166 B6
　Ches W 167 D8
　Corn 5 C11
　Corn 11 F11
　Cumb 229 B7
　Cumb 239 F9
　Cumb 240 E2
　Derbys 185 E7
　Devon 26 B3
　Dorset 29 G7
　Falk 279 E9
　Glos 79 D11
　Glos 80 D3
　Glos 96 C5
　Gtr Man 194 F5
　Gtr Man 195 G9
　Hants 21 B8
　Hants 32 C4
　Hants 32 E3
　Hants 33 D8
　Hants 33 F7
　Hants 49 B8
　Hants 49 G10
　Hants 64 G3
　Hereford 97 C10
　Hereford 98 C2
　Highld 290 C5
　IoM 192 C4
　IoW 20 D6
　Lancs 202 F2
　Lancs 202 G4
　Lancs 203 C9
　Lancs 211 C11
　Lincs 155 B10
　Mers 182 D2
　Moray 301 C11
　Norf 143 B10
　Northumb 252 C2
　Northumb 263 D11
　Northumb 264 D2
　Oxon 65 C9
　Poole 18 C6
　Powys 130 E2
　Rhondda 77 F9
　Shrops 132 C2
　Shrops 149 C9
　Shrops 149 E8
　Som 43 E9
　Staffs 151 D10
　Suff 107 C8
　Swansea 56 D6
　Warks 119 B10
　Wilts 32 C2
　W Loth 279 B11
　W Mid 133 D10
　Wilts 30 B6
　Wilts 63 G10
　Wilts 133 F11
　Worcs 116 F5
　Worcs 117 E7
New Town Bath 45 B9
　Bath 60 G5
　Dorset 30 C3
　Dorset 30 D6
　Dorset 31 D7
　Dorset 31 F8
　E Sus 23 D11
　E Sus 37 C7
　Edin 280 G4
　Edin 281 G8
　E Loth 281 G11
　Kent 53 B7
　Kent 68 E4
　Lancs 203 D8
　Luton 103 G11
　Medway 69 G8
　Northumb 273 F8
　Oxon 100 F5
　Reading 65 E8
　Shetland 312 E6
　Som 29 D11
　Som 44 D3
　Soton 33 E7
　Swindon 63 C7
　T&W 234 B2
　T&W 243 E8
　W Berks 64 D4
　Wilts 46 C6
　Wilts 63 E9
　W Mid 133 B10
　W Mid 133 E9
　W Sus 35 B11
　W Yorks 198 C3
Newtown-in-St Martin Corn 2 E6
Newtown Linford Leics 135 B10
Newtown St Boswells Borders 262 C3
Newtown Unthank Leics 135 B8
New Tredegar Caerph 77 E10
New Trows S Lanark 259 B8
Newtyle Angus 286 C6
New Ulva Argyll 275 E8
New Village E Yorks 209 G7
　S Yorks 198 F5
New Walsoken Cambs 139 B9
New Waltham NE Lincs 201 G9
New Well Powys 113 B11
New Wells Powys 130 D3
New Whittington Derbys 186 F5
New Wimpole Cambs 104 B6
New Winton E Loth 281 G8
New Woodhouses Shrops 167 G9
New Works Telford 132 B3
New Wortley W Yorks 205 G11
New Yatt Oxon 82 C5
Newyears Green London 66 B5
New York Lincs 174 D2
　N Yorks 214 G3
　T&W 243 C8
New Zealand Wilts 62 D4
Nextend Hereford 114 F6
Neyland Pembs 73 D7
Niarbyl IoM 192 E3
Nib Heath Shrops 149 F8
Nibley Glos 79 C11
　S Glos 61 C7
Nibley Green Glos 80 F2
Nibon Shetland 312 F5
Nicholashayne Devon 27 D10
Nicholaston Swansea 56 D4
Nidd N Yorks 214 G6

Niddrie Edin 280 G5
Nigg Aberdeen 293 C11
　Highld 301 B8
Nigg Ferry Highld 301 C7
Nimble Nook Gtr Man 196 G2
Nimlet S Glos 61 E8
Nine Ashes Essex 87 E9
Ninebanks Northumb 241 G7
Nine Elms Swindon 62 B6
　Swindon 63 C7
Nine Mile Burn Midloth 270 D3
Ninewells Glos 79 C9
Nine Wells Pembs 90 G5
Ninfield E Sus 38 E2
Ningwood IoW 20 D3
Ningwood Common IoW 20 D3
Ninnes Bridge Corn 2 B2
Nisbet Borders 262 D5
　Borders 273 B8
Nisthouse Orkney 314 E3
　Shetland 313 G7
Niton IoW 20 F6
Nitshill Glasgow 267 C10
Nithbank Dumfries 247 D9
Noah's Arks Kent 52 B5
Noah's Green Worcs 117 E10
Noak Bridge Essex 87 G11
Noak Hill Essex 87 G11
　London 87 G8
Nob End Gtr Man 195 F9
Nobland Green Herts 86 B5
Noblethorpe S Yorks 197 F9
Nobold Shrops 149 G9
Nobottle Northants 120 E3
Nob's Crook Hants 33 C7
Nocton Lincs 173 C9
Nocturnum Mers 182 D3
Nodmore W Berks 64 D2
Noel Park London 86 G4
Nogdam End Norf 143 C7
Nog Tow Lancs 202 G6
Noke Oxon 83 C8
Noke Street Medway 69 E8
Nolton Pembs 72 B5
Nolton Haven Pembs 72 B5
No Man's Heath Ches W 167 F8
　Warks 134 B5
No Man's Land Corn 5 D11
Nomansland Devon 26 E4
　Herts 85 C11
　Wilts 32 D3
Noneley Shrops 149 D9
Noness Shetland 313 L6
Nonikiln Highld 300 B6
Nonington Kent 55 C9
Nook Cumb 211 C10
　Cumb 219 E11
Noon Nick W Yorks 205 F8
Noonsbrough Shetland 313 H4
Noonsun Ches E 184 F4
Noonvares Corn 2 C3
Noranside Angus 292 G6
Norbiton London 67 F7
Norbreck Blackpool 202 E2
Norbridge Hereford 98 C4
Norbury Ches E 167 F9
　Derbys 169 G10
　London 67 F10
　Shrops 131 E7
　Staffs 150 E5
Norbury Common Ches E 167 F9
Norbury Junction Staffs 150 E5
Norbury Moor Gtr Man 184 D6
Norby N Yorks 215 C8
　Shetland 313 H3
Norchard Worcs 116 D6
Norcote Glos 81 E8
Norcott Brook Ches W 183 E10
Norcross Blackpool 202 E2
Nordelph Norf 139 C11
Nordelph Corner Norf 141 C11
Norden Dorset 18 E4
Norden Heath Dorset 18 E4
Nordley Shrops 132 D3
Norham Northumb 273 F8
Norham West Mains Northumb 273 F8
Nork Sur 51 B8
Norland Town W Yorks 196 C5
Norleaze Wilts 45 C11
Norley Ches W 183 G9
Norley Common Sur 50 E4
Norleywood Hants 20 B3
Norlington E Sus 36 E6
Normacot Stoke 168 G6
Normanby N Lincs 199 D11
　N Yorks 216 C4
　Redcar 225 B10
Normanby-by-Spital Lincs 189 D7
Normanby by Stow Lincs 188 E5
Normanby le Wold Lincs 189 B10
Norman Cross Cambs 138 E3
Normandy Sur 50 C2
Norman's Bay E Sus 23 D11
Norman's Green Devon 27 G9
Normanston Suff 143 D10
Normanton Derby 152 C6
　Leics 172 G4
　Lincs 172 G5
　Lincs 172 E2
　Notts 172 D2
　Rutland 137 B8
　Wilts 46 E6
　W Yorks 197 C11
Normanton le Heath Leics 153 G7
Normanton on Soar Notts 153 E10
Normanton-on-the-Wolds Notts 154 C2
Normanton on Trent Notts 172 B3
Normanton Spring S Yorks 186 E6
Normanton Turville Leics 135 D9
Normoss Lancs 202 F2
Norney Sur 50 E2
Norrington Common Wilts 61 G11
Norris Green Corn 7 B8
　Mers 182 C5
Norris Hill Leics 152 F6
Norristhorpe W Yorks 197 C8
Norseman Moray 302 D4
Northacre Norf 141 D9
North Acton London 67 C8
North Aston Bucks 103 G9
North Anston S Yorks 187 E8

North Hall Green Norf 159 G9
Northam Devon 24 B6
　Soton 32 E6
Northampton Northants 120 E5
North Anston S Yorks 187 E8
North Ascot Brack 66 E2
North Aston Oxon 101 F9
Northaw Herts 86 E3
Northay Devon 28 E3
　Som 28 E3
North Ayre Shetland 312 F6
North Baddesley Hants 32 D5
North Ballachulish Highld 290 C2
North Barrow Som 29 B10
North Barsham Norf 159 C7
North Batsom Som 41 G10
Northbeck Lincs 173 G9
North Beer Corn 12 C2
North Benfleet Essex 69 B9
North Bersted W Sus 22 C6
North Berwick E Loth 281 D11
North Bitchburn Durham 233 E9
North Blyth Northumb 253 F8
North Boarhunt Hants 33 E10
North Bockhampton Dorset 19 B9
Northborough Pboro 138 B3
Northbourne Bmouth 19 B8
　Kent 55 C10
North Bovey Devon 13 D11
North Bradley Wilts 45 C11
North Brentor Devon 12 E5
North Brewham Som 45 F8
Northbridge Street E Sus 38 C2
Northbrook Dorset 17 C11
　Hants 33 D9
　Oxon 101 G9
North Brook End Cambs 104 C5
North Broomage Falk 279 E7
North Buckland Devon 40 E3
North Burlingham Norf 161 G7
North Cadbury Som 29 B10
North Cairn Dumfries 236 B1
North Camp Hants 49 C11
North Carlton Lincs 188 F6
　Notts 187 E9
North Carrine Argyll 255 G7
North Cave E Yorks 208 G4
North Cerney Glos 81 D8
North Chailey E Sus 36 C5
Northchapel W Sus 35 B7
North Charford Wilts 31 D11
North Charlton Northumb 264 D5
North Cheam London 67 G9
North Cheriton Som 29 B11
Northchurch Herts 85 D7
North Cliff E Yorks 209 D11
North Cliffe E Yorks 208 F3
North Clifton Notts 188 G4
North Close Durham 233 E11
North Cockerington Lincs 190 C5
North Coker Som 29 E8
North Collafirth Shetland 312 E5
North Common S Glos 61 E7
　Suff 125 B9
North Connel Argyll 289 F11
North Cornelly Bridgend 57 E10
North Corner Corn 3 F7
　S Glos 61 C7
North Corriegills N Ayrs 256 C2
North Corry Highld 289 D10
Northcote Devon 27 G11
North Cotes Lincs 201 G11
Northcott Corn 24 F2
　Corn 12 C2
　Devon 27 E11
North Country Corn 4 G3
Northcourt Oxon 83 F8
North Court Som 41 F11
North Cove Suff 143 F9
North Cowton N Yorks 224 E5
North Craig E Ayrs 258 B4
North Craigo Angus 293 G8
North Crawley M Keynes 103 C8
North Cray London 68 E3
North Creake Norf 159 B7
North Curry Som 28 B4
North Dalton E Yorks 208 C4
North Darley Corn 11 G11
North Dawn Orkney 314 F4
North Deighton N Yorks 206 C3
North Denes Norf 161 G10
North Dronley Angus 287 D10
North Drumachter Lodge Highld 291 F8
North Duffield N Yorks 207 F9
Northdyke Orkney 314 D2
North Dykes Cumb 230 D6
North Eastling Kent 54 B3
Northedge Derbys 170 B5
North Elham Kent 55 E7
North Elkington Lincs 190 C4
North Elmham Norf 159 E9
North Elmsall W Yorks 198 E2
North Emsall W Yorks 198 E2
North Elphinstone E Loth 281 G8
Northend Bath 61 F9
　Bucks 84 G2
　Essex 89 E7
　Warks 119 G7
North End Bath 60 G6
　Bedford 103 B9
　Bedford 121 F10
　Bucks 102 F4
　Cumb 239 F8
　Dorset 30 B4
　Durham 233 C11
　Essex 87 B11
　Essex 106 C5
　E Yorks 209 G9
　E Yorks 209 G11
　Hants 31 D10
　Hants 33 F11
　Leics 153 F11
　Lincs 174 F3
　Lincs 189 B8
　Lincs 201 G10
　Lincs 201 G11
　N Som 59 G10
　Powys 114 D6

North End continued
　N Som 60 F2
　Ptsmth 33 G11
　Som 28 B3
　Wilts 81 G8
North Erradale Highld 307 L2
North Evington Leicester 136 C2
North Ewster N Lincs 199 G11
North Fambridge Essex 88 F5
North Fearns Highld 295 B8
North Featherstone W Yorks 198 C2
North Feltham London 66 E6
North Feorline N Ayrs 255 E10
North Ferriby E Yorks 200 B3
Northfield Aberdeen 293 C11
　Borders 262 D3
　Borders 273 B8
　Edin 280 G5
　E Yorks 200 B4
　Hants 33 B7
　Som 43 F9
　W Mid 117 B10
Northfields Hants 33 B7
　Lincs 137 B10
North Finchley London 86 G3
Northfleet Kent 68 E6
Northfleet Green Kent 68 E6
North Flobbets Aberds 303 F7
North Frodingham E Yorks 209 C8
Northgate Lincs 156 D3
　W Sus 51 F9
North Gluss Shetland 312 F5
North Gorley Hants 31 E11
North Green Norf 141 B10
　Norf 142 F4
　Suff 126 B6
　Suff 126 E6
　Suff 127 D7
North Greetwell Lincs 189 G8
North Grimston N Yorks 216 F6
North Halley Orkney 314 F5
North Halling Medway 69 F8
North Harrow London 66 B6
North Hayling Hants 22 C2
North Hazelrigg Northumb 264 C3
North Heasley Devon 41 G8
North Heath W Berks 64 E3
　W Sus 35 C9
North Hill Corn 11 F11
North Hillingdon London 66 C5
North Hinksey Village Oxon 83 D7
North Ho Shetland 313 J5
North Holmwood Sur 51 D7
North Houghton Hants 47 G10
Northhouse Borders 249 B10
North Howden E Yorks 207 G11
North Huish Devon 8 D4
North Hyde London 66 D6
North Hykeham Lincs 172 B6
North Hylton T&W 243 F8
Northiam E Sus 38 B4
Northill C Beds 104 B2
Northington Glos 80 D2
　Hants 48 F5
North Kelsey Lincs 200 G4
North Kelsey Moor Lincs 200 G5
North Kensington London 67 C9
North Kessock Highld 300 E6
North Killingholme Lincs 200 D6
North Kilvington N Yorks 215 B8
North Kilworth Leics 136 G2
North Kingston Hants 31 G11
North Kirkton Aberds 303 D11
North Kiscadale N Ayrs 256 D2
North Kyme Lincs 173 E11
North Laggan Highld 290 D4
North Lancing W Sus 35 F11
North Landing E Yorks 218 E2
Northlands Lincs 174 E4
North Lee Bucks 84 D4
North Lees N Yorks 214 E6
Northleigh Devon 15 G9
　Devon 40 G6
　Som 27 B10
North Leigh Kent 54 D6
　Oxon 82 C5
North Leverton with Habblesthorpe Notts 188 E3
Northlew Devon 12 B6
North Littleton Worcs 99 B11
North Lopham Norf 141 G10
North Luffenham Rutland 137 C8
North Marden W Sus 34 D4
North Marston Bucks 102 G5
North Middleton Midloth 271 D7
　Northumb 264 E2
North Millbrex Aberds 303 E8
North Milmain Dumfries 236 D2
North Molton Devon 26 B2
Northmoor Oxon 82 E6
North Moor Som 43 G10
Northmoor Corner Som 43 G10
Northmoor Green or Moorland Som 43 G10
North Moreton Oxon 64 B5
North Mosstown Aberds 303 D10
North Motherwell N Lanark 268 D4
North Moulsecoomb Brighton 36 F4
Northmuir Angus 287 B7
North Mundham W Sus 22 C5
North Muskham Notts 172 D3
North Newbald E Yorks 208 F4
North Newington Oxon 101 C8
North Newnton Wilts 46 B6
North Newton Som 43 G9
Northney Hants 22 C2
North Nibley Glos 80 F2
North Oakley Hants 48 C5
North Ockendon London 68 C5
Northolt London 66 C6
North Ormesby Mbro 234 G6
North Ormsby Lincs 190 C3
Northorpe Lincs 155 F11
　Lincs 156 C5
　Lincs 188 C5

Northorpe continued
　W Yorks 197 C8
Northover Som 29 C8
　Som 44 F3
North Owersby Lincs 189 C9
Northowram W Yorks 196 B6
Northpark Argyll 275 G11
North Perrott Som 29 F7
North Petherton Som 43 G9
North Petherwin Corn 11 E11
North Pickenham Norf 141 B7
North Piddle Worcs 117 G9
North Poorton Dorset 16 B6
Northport Dorset 18 D4
North Port Argyll 284 E4
North Poulner Hants 31 F11
North Queensferry Fife 280 E2
North Radworthy Devon 41 G9
North Rauceby Lincs 173 F8
North Reddish Gtr Man 184 C5
Northrepps Norf 160 B4
North Reston Lincs 190 E5
North Rigton N Yorks 205 D11
North Ripley Hants 19 B9
North Rode Ches E 168 B5
North Roe Shetland 312 E5
North Row Cumb 229 E10
North Runcton Norf 158 F2
North Sandwick Shetland 312 D7
North Scale Cumb 210 F3
North Scarle Lincs 172 B5
North Seaton Northumb 253 F7
North Seaton Colliery Northumb 253 F7
North Sheen London 67 D7
North Shian Argyll 289 E11
North Shields T&W 243 D9
North Shoebury Southend 70 B2
North Shore Blackpool 202 F2
North Side Aberds 303 D8
　Cumb 228 F6
　Pboro 138 D5
North Skelmanae Aberds 303 D9
North Skelton Redcar 226 B3
North Somercotes Lincs 190 B6
North Stainley N Yorks 214 D5
North Stainmore Cumb 222 B6
North Stifford Thurrock 68 C6
North Stoke Bath 61 F8
　Oxon 64 B6
　W Sus 35 E8
North Stoneham Hants 32 D6
Northstowe Cambs 123 D8
North Street Hants 31 D11
　Hants 48 G5
　Kent 54 B4
　Medway 69 E10
　W Berks 64 E6
North Sunderland Northumb 264 C6
North Synton Borders 261 E11
North Tamerton Corn 11 B11
North Tawton Devon 25 G11
North Thoresby Lincs 190 B3
North Tidworth Wilts 47 D8
North Togston Northumb 252 C6
Northton Aberds 293 C9
　Borders 262 E2
North Town Devon 25 F8
　Hants 49 C11
　Som 44 A5
　W & M 65 C11
North Tuddenham Norf 159 G10
Northumberland Heath London 68 D4
Northville Torf 78 F3
North Walbottle T&W 242 D5
North Walney Cumb 210 F3
North Walsham Norf 160 C5
North Waltham Hants 48 D5
North Warnborough Hants 49 C8
North Water Bridge Angus 293 G8
North Watergate Devon 8 C4
North Watford Herts 85 F10
North Watten Highld 310 D6
Northway Devon 24 C5
　Glos 99 E8
　Som 27 B10
　Swansea 56 D5
North Weald Bassett Essex 87 E7
North Weirs Hants 32 G3
North Wembley London 67 B7
North Weston N Som 60 D3
　Oxon 83 D11
North Wheatley Notts 188 E3
North Whilborough Devon 9 B7
North Whiteley Moray 302 E4
Northwich Ches W 183 G11
　S Glos 43 D11
　Som 43 D11
North Wick Bath 60 F5
North Widcombe Bath 44 B5
North Willingham Lincs 189 D11
North Wingfield Derbys 170 B6
North Witham Lincs 155 E8
Northwold Norf 140 D5
Northwood Derbys 170 C3
　IoW 20 C5
　Kent 71 F11
　London 85 G9
　Mers 182 B6
　Shrops 149 C9
　Staffs 168 G5
　Stoke 168 F5
Northwood Green Glos 80 B2
Northwood Hills London 85 G9
North Woolwich London 68 D2
North Wootton Dorset 29 E11
　Norf 158 E2
　Som 44 E5
North Wraxall Wilts 61 D10
North Wroughton Swindon 63 C7
Norton Devon 9 E7
　E Sus 23 E7
　Glos 99 G7
　Halton 183 E9
　Herts 104 E4
　IoW 20 D2
　Mon 78 B6
　Northants 120 E2
　Notts 187 G9
　Powys 114 D6

Norton continued
Shrops ... 131 B11
Shrops ... 131 G9
Shrops ... 132 C4
Stockton ... 234 G4
Suff ... 125 D9
Swansea ... 56 D3
Swansea ... 56 D6
S Yorks ... 186 E5
S Yorks ... 198 D4
Wilts ... 61 C11
W Mid ... 118 C3
Worcs ... 99 B10
Worcs ... 117 G2
W Sus ... 22 B6
Poole ... 18 C6
N Yorks ... 205 B11
Norton Ash Kent ... 70 G3
Norton Bavant Wilts ... 46 E2
Norton Bridge Staffs ... 151 C7
Norton Canes Staffs ... 133 B10
Norton Canon Hereford ... 97 B7
Norton Corner Norf ... 159 D11
Norton Disney Lincs ... 172 D11
Norton East Kent ... 133 B10
Norton Ferris Wilts ... 45 F9
Norton Fitzwarren Som ... 27 B11
Norton Green Herts ... 104 G4
IoW ... 20 D2
Staffs ... 168 E6
W Mid ... 118 C3
Norton Hawkfield Bath ... 60 G5
Norton Heath Essex ... 87 E10
Norton in Hales Shrops ... 150 B4
Norton-in-the-Moors
Stoke ... 168 E5
Norton-Juxta-Twycross
Leics ... 134 B6
Norton-le-Clay N Yorks ... 215 E8
Norton Lindsey Warks ... 118 E4
Norton Little Green
Suff ... 125 D9
Norton Malreward Bath ... 60 F6
Norton Mandeville Essex ... 87 E7
Norton-on-Derwent
N Yorks ... 216 E5
Norton St Philip Som ... 45 B9
Norton Subcourse Norf ... 143 D8
Norton sub Hamdon Som ... 29 D7
Norton's Wood N Som ... 60 E2
Norton Woodseats
S Yorks ... 186 E5
Norwell Notts ... 172 C3
Norwell Woodhouse
Notts ... 172 C2
Norwich Norf ... 142 B4
Norwick Shetland ... 312 B8
Norwood Derbys ... 187 E7
Dorset ... 29 F8
Norwood End Essex ... 87 E2
Norwood Green London ... 66 D6
W Yorks ... 196 B6
Norwood Hill Sur ... 51 E8
Norwood New Town
London ... 67 E10
Norwoodside Cambs ... 139 D8
Noseley Leics ... 136 D4
Noss Highld ... 310 D7
Shetland ... 313 M5
Noss Mayo Devon ... 7 F11
Nosterfield N Yorks ... 214 C5
Nosterfield End Cambs ... 106 C2
Nostie Highld ... 295 C10
Notgrove Glos ... 100 G2
Nottage Bridgend ... 57 F10
Notter Corn ... 7 C7
Nottingham Nottingham ... 153 B11
Notting Hill London ... 67 C8
Nottington Dorset ... 17 E9
Notton Wilts ... 62 F2
W Yorks ... 197 E10
Nounsley Essex ... 88 C3
Noutard's Green Worcs ... 116 D5
Nova House Highld ... 300 C6
Nova Scotia Bristol ... 60 E5
Novers Park Bristol ... 60 F5
Noverton Glos ... 99 G9
Nowton Suff ... 125 E7
Nox Shrops ... 149 G8
Noyadd Trefawr Ceredig ... 92 B5
Noyadd Wilym Ceredig ... 92 C4
Nuffield Oxon ... 65 B7
Nun Appleton N Yorks ... 207 F7
Nunburnholme E Yorks ... 208 D2
Nuncargate Notts ... 171 E8
Nunclose Cumb ... 230 B5
Nuneaton Warks ... 135 F7
Nuneham Courtenay
Oxon ... 83 F9
Nuney Green Oxon ... 65 D7
Nunhead London ... 67 D11
Nun Hills Lancs ... 195 C11
Nun Monkton N Yorks ... 206 B6
Nunney Som ... 45 D8
Nunney Catch Som ... 45 E8
Nunnington N Yorks ... 216 D3
Nunnykirk Northumb ... 252 E3
Nunsthorpe NE Lincs ... 201 F9
Nunthorpe Mbro ... 225 C10
York ... 207 C8
Nunton Wilts ... 31 B11
Nunwick N Yorks ... 214 E6
Nupdown S Glos ... 79 F10
Nupend Glos ... 80 D3
Glos ... 80 F4
Nup End Bucks ... 84 B5
Herts ... 86 B2
Nuper's Hatch Essex ... 87 G8
Nuppend Glos ... 79 E10
Nuptown Brack ... 65 E11
Nursling Hants ... 32 D5
Nursted Hants ... 34 C3
Nurston V Glam ... 58 F5
Nurton Staffs ... 132 D6
Nurton Hill Staffs ... 132 D6
Nutbourne W Sus ... 22 B3
W Sus ... 35 D9
Nutbourne Common
W Sus ... 35 D9
Nutburn Hants ... 32 C5
Nutcombe Sur ... 49 G11
Nutfield Sur ... 51 C10
Nut Grove Mers ... 183 C7
Nuthall Notts ... 171 G8
Nuthampstead Herts ... 105 E8
Nuthurst Warks ... 118 C3
W Sus ... 35 B11
Nutley E Sus ... 36 B6
Hants ... 48 E6
Nuttall Gtr Man ... 195 D9
Nutwell S Yorks ... 198 G6
Nybster Highld ... 310 C7
Nye N Som ... 60 G2
Nyetimber W Sus ... 22 D5
Nyewood W Sus ... 34 C4
Nyland Som ... 44 D3
Nymet Rowland Devon ... 26 F2
Nymet Tracey Devon ... 26 F2
Nympsfield Glos ... 80 E4
Nynehead Som ... 27 C10
Nythe Som ... 44 G2
Swindon ... 63 B7
Nyton W Sus ... 22 B6

O
Oadby Leics ... 136 C2
Oad Street Kent ... 69 G11
Oakall Green Worcs ... 116 E6
Oakamoor Staffs ... 169 G9
Oakbank W Loth ... 269 B11
Oak Bank Gtr Man ... 195 F10
Oak Cross Devon ... 12 B6
Oakdale Caerph ... 77 F11
N Yorks ... 205 B11
Poole ... 18 C6
Oake Som ... 27 C11
Oak Green Som ... 27 B11
Oaken Staffs ... 133 C7
Oakenclough Lancs ... 202 D6
Oakengates Telford ... 150 G4
Oakenholt Flint ... 182 G3
Oakenshaw Durham ... 233 D10
Lancs ... 203 G10
Oakerthorpe Derbys ... 170 E5
Oakes W Yorks ... 196 D6
Oakfield Herts ... 104 F3
IoW ... 21 C7
Torf ... 78 G4
Oakford Ceredig ... 111 F9
Devon ... 26 C6
Oakfordbridge Devon ... 26 C6
Oakgrove Ches E ... 168 B6
M Keynes ... 103 D7
Oakham Rutland ... 137 B7
Oakhanger Ches E ... 168 E3
Hants ... 49 F9
Oakhill Som ... 44 D6
Som ... 51 G7
Oak Hill Stoke ... 168 G5
Suff ... 109 B7
Oakhurst Kent ... 52 C4
Oaklands Cambs ... 123 E8
Carms ... 74 B6
Herts ... 86 B2
Oakle Street Glos ... 80 B3
Oakley Bedford ... 121 G10
Bucks ... 83 C10
Fife ... 279 D10
Oxon ... 84 E3
Poole ... 18 B6
Staffs ... 150 B4
Suff ... 126 B3
Oakley Court Oxon ... 64 B6
Oakley Green Windsor ... 66 D2
Oakley Park Powys ... 129 F9
Suff ... 126 B3
Oakley Wood Oxon ... 64 B6
Oakmere Ches W ... 167 B9
Oakridge Glos ... 80 E6
Hants ... 48 C6
Oakridge Lynch Glos ... 80 E6
Oaks Shrops ... 131 C8
Oaksey Wilts ... 81 G7
Oaks Green Derbys ... 152 C3
Oakshaw Ford Cumb ... 240 B2
Oakshott Hants ... 34 B2
Oaks in Charnwood
Leics ... 153 F9
Oakthorpe Leics ... 152 G6
Oak Tree Darl ... 225 C7
Oakwell W Yorks ... 197 B8
Oakwood Derby ... 153 B7
London ... 86 F3
Northumb ... 241 D10
Warr ... 183 C11
W Yorks ... 206 F2
Oakwoodhill Sur ... 50 F6
Oakworth W Yorks ... 204 F6
Oape Highld ... 309 J4
Oare Devon ... 41 D8
Kent ... 70 G4
Som ... 41 D11
W Berks ... 64 E4
Wilts ... 63 G7
Oareford Devon ... 41 D10
Oasby Lincs ... 155 B10
Oath Som ... 28 B5
Oathill Dorset ... 28 F6
Oathlaw Angus ... 287 B8
Oatlands Glasgow ... 267 C11
N Yorks ... 205 C11
Oatlands Park Sur ... 66 G5
Oban Argyll ... 289 G10
Highld ... 295 G10
W Isles ... 305 H3
Obley Shrops ... 114 B6
Oborne Dorset ... 29 D11
Obthorpe Lincs ... 156 F2
Obthorpe Lodge Lincs ... 156 F2
Occlestone Green
Ches W ... 167 C11
Occold Suff ... 126 C3
Occumster Highld ... 310 F6
Ocean Village Soton ... 32 E6
Ochiltree S Ayrs ... 258 E2
Ochr-y-foel Denb ... 181 F9
Ochtermuthill Perth ... 286 F2
Ochtertyre Perth ... 286 E2
Ochtow Highld ... 309 J4
Ockbrook Derbys ... 153 B8
Ocker Hill W Mid ... 133 E9
Ockeridge Worcs ... 116 E5
Ockford Ridge Sur ... 50 E3
Ockham Sur ... 50 B5
Ockle Highld ... 289 B7
Ockley Sur ... 50 F6
Ocle Pychard Hereford ... 97 B11
Octon E Yorks ... 217 F10
Octon Cross Roads
E Yorks ... 217 F10
Odam Barton Devon ... 26 E2
Odcombe Som ... 29 D8
Odd Down Bath ... 61 G8
Oddendale Cumb ... 221 C11
Odder Lincs ... 188 G6
Oddingley Worcs ... 117 F8
Oddington Glos ... 100 F4
Oxon ... 83 C9
Odell Bedford ... 121 F9
Odham Devon ... 25 G7
Odie Orkney ... 314 D6
Odiham Hants ... 49 C8
Odsal W Yorks ... 197 B7
Odsey Cambs ... 104 D5
Odstock Wilts ... 31 B10
Odstone Leics ... 135 B7
Offchurch Warks ... 119 D7
Offenham Worcs ... 99 B11
Offenham Cross Worcs ... 99 B11
T&W ... 243 F8
Offerton Gtr Man ... 184 D6
Offerton Green Gtr Man ... 36 E5
E Sus ... 36 E5
Kent ... 53 B7

Offham continued
W Sus ... 35 F8
Offleyhay Staffs ... 150 D5
Offleymarsh Staffs ... 150 D5
Offleyrock Staffs ... 150 D5
Offord Cluny Cambs ... 122 D4
Offord D'Arcy Cambs ... 122 D4
Offton Suff ... 107 B11
Offwell Devon ... 15 B9
Ogbourne Maizey Wilts ... 63 E7
Ogbourne St Andrew
Wilts ... 63 E7
Ogbourne St George
Wilts ... 63 E8
Ogden W Yorks ... 205 G7
Ogdens Hants ... 31 E11
Ogil Angus ... 292 G6
Ogle Northumb ... 242 B4
Ogmore V Glam ... 57 F11
Ogmore-by-Sea / Aberogwr
V Glam ... 57 F11
Ogmore Vale Bridgend ... 76 G6
Okeford Fitzpaine Dorset ... 30 E4
Okehampton Devon ... 13 B7
Okehampton Camp
Devon ... 13 C7
Oker Derbys ... 170 C3
Okewood Hill Sur ... 50 F6
Okle Green Glos ... 98 F5
Okraquoy Shetland ... 313 K6
Okus Swindon ... 62 C6
Olchard Devon ... 14 F3
Old Northants ... 120 C5
Old Aberdeen
Aberdeen ... 293 C11
Old Alresford Hants ... 48 G5
Oldany Highld ... 306 F6
Old Arley Warks ... 134 E5
Old Basford Nottingham ... 171 G8
Old Basing Hants ... 49 C7
Old Belses Borders ... 262 E3
Oldberrow Warks ... 118 D2
Old Bewick Northumb ... 264 E3
Old Bexley London ... 68 E3
Old Blair Perth ... 291 G10
Old Bolingbroke Lincs ... 174 B4
Oldborough Devon ... 26 F3
Old Boston Mers ... 183 B9
Old Bramhope
W Yorks ... 205 E10
Old Brampton Derbys ... 186 G4
Old Bridge of Tilt
Perth ... 291 G10
Old Bridge of Urr
Dumfries ... 237 C9
Oldbury Kent ... 52 B5
Shrops ... 132 E4
Warks ... 134 E6
W Mid ... 133 F9
Oldbury-on-Severn
S Glos ... 79 G10
Oldbury on the Hill Glos ... 61 B10
Old Byland N Yorks ... 215 B11
Old Cambus Borders ... 272 B6
Old Cardinham Castle
Corn ... 6 B2
Old Carlisle Cumb ... 229 B11
Old Cassop Durham ... 234 D2
Oldcastle Mon ... 96 G6
Oldcastle Heath Ches W ... 167 F7
Old Castleton Borders ... 250 E2
Old Catton Norf ... 160 G4
Old Chalford Oxon ... 100 F6
Old Church Stoke
Powys ... 130 E5
Old Clee NE Lincs ... 201 F9
Old Cleeve Som ... 42 E4
Old Clipstone Notts ... 171 C10
Old Colwyn Conwy ... 180 F5
Old Coppice Shrops ... 131 B9
Old Trafford Gtr Man ... 184 B4
Oldcotes Notts ... 187 D9
Old Coulsdon London ... 51 B10
Old Country Hereford ... 98 C4
Old Craig Aberds ... 303 G9
Angus ... 292 C4
Oldcroft Glos ... 79 D10
Old Crombie Aberds ... 302 D5
Old Cryals Kent ... 53 E7
Old Cullen Moray ... 302 C5
Old Dailly S Ayrs ... 244 D6
Old Dalby Leics ... 154 E3
Old Dam Derbys ... 185 F10
Old Deer Aberds ... 303 E9
Old Denaby S Yorks ... 187 B7
Old Ditch Som ... 44 D4
Old Dolphin W Yorks ... 205 G8
Old Down S Glos ... 60 B6
Old Duffus Moray ... 301 C11
Old Edlington S Yorks ... 187 B8
Old Eldon Durham ... 233 F10
Old Ellerby E Yorks ... 209 F9
Oldend Glos ... 80 D4
Old Fallings W Mid ... 133 C8
Oldfallow Staffs ... 151 G8
Old Farm Park
M Keynes ... 103 D8
Old Felixstowe Suff ... 108 D6
Oldfield Cumb ... 229 F7
Shrops ... 132 F3
Worcs ... 116 E6
W Yorks ... 196 B6
W Yorks ... 204 F6
Old Field Shrops ... 115 B9
Oldfield Brow Gtr Man ... 184 D3
Oldfield Park Bath ... 61 G8
Old Fletton Pboro ... 138 D3
Old Fold T&W ... 243 E7
Oldford Som ... 45 C9
Old Ford London ... 67 C11
Old Forge Hereford ... 79 B9
Oldfurnace Staffs ... 169 G8
Old Furnace Torf ... 78 E3
Old Gate Lincs ... 157 E8
Old Glossop Derbys ... 185 C8
Old Goginan Ceredig ... 128 G3
Old Goole E Yorks ... 199 C8
Old Gore Hereford ... 98 F2
Old Graitney Dumfries ... 239 D8
Old Grimsby Scilly ... 1 F3
Oldhall Renfs ... 267 C10
Old Hall Powys ... 129 G8
Oldhall Green Suff ... 125 F7
Old Hall Green Herts ... 105 G7
Oldhall Street Norf ... 160 C6
Oldham Gtr Man ... 196 F2
Oldham Edge Gtr Man ... 196 F2
Oldhamstocks E Loth ... 282 G4
Old Harlow Essex ... 87 C7
Old Heath Essex ... 107 G10
Old Heathfield E Sus ... 37 C9
Old Hill W Mid ... 133 F9
Old Hills Worcs ... 98 B6
Old Hunstanton Norf ... 175 G11
Oldhurst Cambs ... 122 B6
Old Hutton Cumb ... 211 B11
Old Idlington Shrops ... 132 C4
Old Kea Corn ... 4 G6
Old Kilpatrick W Dunb ... 277 G9
Old Kinnernie Aberds ... 293 C9
Old Knebworth Herts ... 104 G4
Oldland S Glos ... 61 E7
Old Langho Lancs ... 203 F10
Old Laxey IoM ... 192 D5
Old Leake Lincs ... 174 E6
Old Leckie Stirling ... 278 C3
Old Lindley W Yorks ... 196 D5
Old Linslade C Beds ... 103 F8
Old Malden London ... 67 F8
Old Malton N Yorks ... 216 E5
Old Marton Shrops ... 148 C6
Old Mead Essex ... 105 F10
Old Micklefield
W Yorks ... 206 G4
Old Mill Corn ... 12 G3
Old Milton Hants ... 19 C10
Old Milverton Warks ... 118 D5
Oldmixon N Som ... 43 B10
Old Monkland N Lanark ... 268 C4
Old Nenthorn Borders ... 262 B5
Old Netley Hants ... 33 F7
Old Neuadd Powys ... 129 F11
Old Newton Suff ... 125 E11
Old Oak Common London ... 67 C8
Old Park Corn ... 6 B4
Telford ... 132 B3
Old Passage S Glos ... 60 B5
Old Perton Staffs ... 133 D7
Old Philpstoun W Loth ... 279 F11
Old Portsmouth Ptsmth ... 21 B8
Old Quarrington
Durham ... 234 D2
Old Radnor Powys ... 114 F5
Old Rattray Aberds ... 303 D10
Old Rayne Aberds ... 302 G6
Old Romney Kent ... 39 B8
Old Shirley Soton ... 32 E5
Oldshore Beg Highld ... 306 D6
Oldshoremore Highld ... 306 D7
Old Snydale W Yorks ... 198 C2
Old Sodbury S Glos ... 61 C9
Old Somerby Lincs ... 155 C9
Oldstead N Yorks ... 215 C10
Old Stillington Stockton ... 234 G2
Old Storridge Common
Worcs ... 116 G4
Old Stratford Northants ... 102 C5
Old Struan Perth ... 291 G10
Old Swan Mers ... 182 C5
Old Swarland Northumb ... 252 C5
Old Swinford W Mid ... 133 G8
Old Tame Gtr Man ... 196 F3
Old Tebay Cumb ... 222 D2
Old Thirsk N Yorks ... 215 C8
Old Tinnis Borders ... 261 D9
Old Toll S Ayrs ... 257 E9
Oldtown Aberds ... 293 C7
Aberds ... 302 G5
Highld ... 309 L5
Old Town Corn ... 11 C11
Cumb ... 230 C5
Edin ... 280 G5
E Sus ... 23 E7
E Sus ... 38 F2
E Yorks ... 218 F3
Herts ... 104 F4
Scilly ... 1 G4
Swindon ... 63 C7
W Yorks ... 196 B3
Oldtown of Ord Aberds ... 302 D6
Old Trafford Gtr Man ... 184 B4
Old Tree Kent ... 71 G7
Old Tupton Derbys ... 170 B5
Oldwalls Swansea ... 56 C3
Old Warden C Beds ... 104 C2
Old Warren Flint ... 166 C4
Oldway Swansea ... 56 D5
Torbay ... 9 C7
Old Way Som ... 28 B5
Oldways End Devon ... 26 B6
Old Weston Cambs ... 121 B11
Old Wharf Hereford ... 98 D4
Oldwhat Aberds ... 303 D8
Old Whittington Derbys ... 186 G5
Oldwich Lane W Mid ... 118 C5
Old Wick Highld ... 310 D7
Old Wimpole Cambs ... 122 G6
Old Windsor Windsor ... 66 E3
Old Wingate Durham ... 234 D3
Old Wives Lees Kent ... 54 C5
Old Woking Sur ... 50 B4
Old Wolverton
M Keynes ... 102 C6
Oldwood Worcs ... 115 D11
Old Woodhall Lincs ... 174 B2
Old Woodhouses
Shrops ... 167 G9
Old Woodstock Oxon ... 82 B6
Olgrinmore Highld ... 310 D4
Oliver's Battery Hants ... 33 B7
Ollaberry Shetland ... 312 E5
Ollag W Isles ... 297 G3
Ollerbrook Booth
Derbys ... 185 D10
Ollerton Ches E ... 184 F3
Notts ... 171 B11
Shrops ... 150 D2
Ollerton Fold Lancs ... 194 C6
Ollerton Lane Shrops ... 150 D3
Olmarch Ceredig ... 112 F2
Olmstead Green Essex ... 106 C2
Olney M Keynes ... 121 G7
Olrig Ho Highld ... 310 C5
Olton W Mid ... 134 G2
Olveston S Glos ... 60 B6
Olwen Ceredig ... 93 B11
Ombersley Worcs ... 116 E6
Ompton Notts ... 171 B11
Omunsgarth Shetland ... 313 J5
Onchan IoM ... 192 E4
Onecote Staffs ... 169 D9
Onehouse Suff ... 125 F10
Onen Mon ... 78 C6
Ones Acre S Yorks ... 186 D4
Ongar Hill Norf ... 157 E11
Ongar Street Hereford ... 115 D7
Onibury Shrops ... 115 B9
Onich Highld ... 290 G2
Onllwyn Neath ... 76 C4
Onneley Staffs ... 168 G3
Onslow Village Sur ... 50 C3
Onthank E Ayrs ... 267 G8
Openwoodgate Derbys ... 170 F5
Opinan Highld ... 299 B7
Highld ... 307 K3
Orange Lane Borders ... 272 G5
Orange Row Norf ... 157 E10
Orasaigh W Isles ... 305 G5
Orbliston Moray ... 302 D3
Orbost Highld ... 298 E2
Orby Lincs ... 175 B7
Orchard Hill Devon ... 24 B6
Orchard Leigh Bucks ... 85 E7
Orchard Portman Som ... 28 C2
Orcheston Wilts ... 46 D5
Orcop Hereford ... 97 F9
Orcop Hill Hereford ... 97 F9
Ord Highld ... 295 D8
Ordale Shetland ... 312 C8
Ordhead Aberds ... 293 B8
Ordie Aberds ... 292 C6
Ordiequish Moray ... 302 D3
Ordighill Aberds ... 302 D5
Ordsall Gtr Man ... 184 B4
Notts ... 187 E11
Ore E Sus ... 38 E4
Oreston Plym ... 7 E10
Oreton Shrops ... 132 G3
Orford Suff ... 109 B8
Warr ... 183 C10
Organford Dorset ... 18 C4
Orgreave Staffs ... 152 F3
Oridge Street Glos ... 98 F5
Orlandon Pembs ... 72 D4
Orleton Worcs ... 115 D10
Orleton Common
Hereford ... 115 D9
Orlingbury Northants ... 121 C7
Ormacleit W Isles ... 297 H3
Ormathwaite Cumb ... 229 F11
Ormesby Redcar ... 225 C10
Ormesby St Margaret
Norf ... 161 G9
Ormesby St Michael
Norf ... 161 G9
Ormiclate Castle
W Isles ... 297 H3
Ormiston E Loth ... 271 B8
Ormsaigbeg Highld ... 288 C6
Ormsaigmore Highld ... 288 C6
Ormsary Argyll ... 275 E8
Ormskirk Lancs ... 194 F2
Ornsby Hill Durham ... 233 B9
Orpington London ... 68 F3
Orrell Gtr Man ... 194 F4
Mers ... 182 B4
Warks ... 134 G4
Orrell Post Gtr Man ... 194 G4
Orrisdale IoM ... 192 C4
Orrock Fife ... 280 D4
Orroland Dumfries ... 237 E9
Orsett Thurrock ... 68 C6
Orsett Heath Thurrock ... 68 C6
Orslow Staffs ... 150 F6
Orston Notts ... 172 G3
Ortner Lancs ... 202 C6
Orton Cumb ... 222 D2
Northants ... 120 B6
Staffs ... 133 D7
Orton Brimbles Pboro ... 138 D3
Orton Goldhay Pboro ... 138 D3
Orton Longueville
Pboro ... 138 D3
Orton-on-the-Hill Leics ... 134 C6
Orton Rigg Cumb ... 239 G9
Orton Southgate Pboro ... 138 E2
Orton Waterville Pboro ... 138 D2
Orton Wistow Pboro ... 138 D2
Orwell Cambs ... 123 G7
Osbaldeston Lancs ... 203 G8
Osbaldeston Green
Lancs ... 203 G8
Osbaldwick York ... 207 C8
Osbaston Leics ... 135 C8
Shrops ... 148 E6
Telford ... 149 F11
Osbaston Hollow Leics ... 135 B8
Osbournby Lincs ... 155 B11
Oscroft Ches W ... 167 B8
Ose Highld ... 298 E3
Osea Island Essex ... 88 D6
Osehill Green Dorset ... 29 F11
Osgathorpe Leics ... 153 F8
Osgodby Lincs ... 189 C9
N Yorks ... 207 G8
N Yorks ... 217 C11
Osgodby Common
N Yorks ... 207 F8
Osidge London ... 86 G3
Oskaig Highld ... 295 B7
Oskamull Argyll ... 288 E6
Osleston Derbys ... 152 B4
Osmaston Derby ... 153 C7
Derbys ... 170 G2
Osmington Dorset ... 17 E10
Osmington Mills Dorset ... 17 E10
Osmondthorpe W Yorks ... 206 G2
Osmotherley N Yorks ... 225 F9
Osney Oxon ... 83 D8
Ospisdale Highld ... 309 L7
Ospringe Kent ... 70 G4
Ossaborough Devon ... 40 E3
Ossemsley Hants ... 19 B10
Ossett W Yorks ... 197 D9
Ossett Spa W Yorks ... 197 D9
Ossett Street Side
W Yorks ... 197 D9
Ossington Notts ... 172 C3
Ostend Essex ... 88 F6
Norf ... 160 C6
Osterley London ... 66 D6
Oswaldkirk N Yorks ... 216 D2
Oswaldtwistle Lancs ... 195 B8
Oswestry Shrops ... 148 D5
Otby Lincs ... 189 C10
Oteley Shrops ... 149 C8
Otford Kent ... 52 B4
Otham Kent ... 53 C9
Otham Hole Kent ... 53 C10
Otherton Staffs ... 151 G8
Othery Som ... 43 G11
Otley Suff ... 126 F4
W Yorks ... 205 D10
Otterbourne Hants ... 33 C7
Otterburn Northumb ... 251 E9
N Yorks ... 204 B3
Otterburn Camp
Northumb ... 251 D9
Otterden Place Kent ... 54 C2
Otter Ferry Argyll ... 275 E10
Otterham Corn ... 11 C9
Otterhampton Som ... 43 E8
Otterham Quay Kent ... 69 F10
Otterham Station Corn ... 11 D9
Ottershaw Sur ... 66 G4
Otterspool Mers ... 182 D5
Otterswick Shetland ... 312 E7
Otterton Devon ... 15 D7
Otterwood Hants ... 32 G6
Ottery St Mary Devon ... 15 B8
Ottinge Kent ... 55 E7
Ottringham E Yorks ... 201 C9
Oughterby Cumb ... 239 F8
Oughtershaw N Yorks ... 213 C7
Oughterside Cumb ... 229 C8
Oughtibridge S Yorks ... 186 C4
Oughtrington Warr ... 183 D11
Oulston N Yorks ... 215 D10
Oulton Cumb ... 238 G6
Norf ... 160 D2
Staffs ... 150 D5
Staffs ... 151 B8
Suff ... 143 D10
W Yorks ... 197 B11
Oulton Broad Suff ... 143 E10
Oulton Grange Staffs ... 151 B8
Oulton Heath Staffs ... 151 B8
Oulton Street Norf ... 160 D3
Oundle Northants ... 137 F10
Ousdale Highld ... 311 G4
Ousden Suff ... 124 F4
Ousefleet E Yorks ... 199 C10
Ouston Durham ... 243 G7
Northumb ... 241 C10
Northumb ... 242 C3
Outcast Cumb ... 210 D6
Out Elmstead Kent ... 55 C8
Outer Hope Devon ... 8 G3
Outertown Orkney ... 314 E2
Outgate Cumb ... 221 F7
Outhgill Cumb ... 222 E5
Outhill Warks ... 118 D2
Outhills Aberds ... 303 D10
Outlands Staffs ... 150 C5
Outlane W Yorks ... 196 D5
Outlane Moor W Yorks ... 196 D5
Outlet Village Ches W ... 182 G6
Outmarsh Wilts ... 61 G11
Out Newton E Yorks ... 201 C11
Out Rawcliffe Lancs ... 202 E4
Outwell Norf ... 139 C10
Outwick Hants ... 31 D10
Outwood Gtr Man ... 195 F9
Som ... 28 B4
Sur ... 51 D10
W Yorks ... 197 C10
Warks ... 134 G4
Outwoods Leics ... 153 F8
Staffs ... 150 F5
Warks ... 134 G4
Ouzlewell Green
W Yorks ... 197 B11
Ovenden W Yorks ... 196 B5
Ovenscloss Borders ... 261 C11
Over Cambs ... 123 C7
Ches W ... 167 B10
Glos ... 80 B4
S Glos ... 60 C5
Overbister Orkney ... 314 B6
Over Burrows Derbys ... 152 B5
Over Compton Dorset ... 29 D9
Over End Cambs ... 137 E11
Derbys ... 186 G3
Overgreen Derbys ... 186 G4
Over Green W Mid ... 134 E3
Over Haddon Derbys ... 170 B2
Over Hulton Gtr Man ... 195 F7
Over Kellet Lancs ... 211 E10
Over Kiddington Oxon ... 101 G8
Over Knutsford Ches E ... 184 F3
Over Langshaw
Borders ... 271 G10
Overleigh Som ... 44 F3
Overley Staffs ... 152 F2
Overley Green Warks ... 117 F11
Over Monnow Mon ... 79 C8
Over Norton Oxon ... 100 F6
Over Peover Ches E ... 184 G3
Overpool Ches W ... 182 F5
Overscaig Hotel Highld ... 309 G4
Overseal Derbys ... 152 F5
Oversland Kent ... 54 B5
Oversley Green Warks ... 117 F11
Overstone Northants ... 120 D6
Over Stowey Som ... 43 F7
Over Stratton Som ... 28 D6
Over Tabley Ches E ... 184 E2
Overthorpe Northants ... 101 C9
W Yorks ... 197 D8
Overton Aberdeen ... 293 B10
Aberds ... 293 B9
Ches W ... 183 F8
Dumfries ... 237 C11
Glos ... 80 C2
Hants ... 48 D4
Lancs ... 202 B4
N Yorks ... 207 B7
Shrops ... 115 C10
Staffs ... 151 B10
Swansea ... 56 D3
W Yorks ... 197 D9
Overton / Owrtyn Wrex ... 166 G5
Overton Bridge Wrex ... 166 G5
Overtown Lancs ... 212 D2
N Lanark ... 268 E6
Swindon ... 63 D7
W Yorks ... 197 D11
Over Town Lancs ... 195 B11
Over Wallop Hants ... 47 F9
Over Whitacre Warks ... 134 E5
Over Worton Oxon ... 101 F8
Oving Bucks ... 102 G5
W Sus ... 22 C6
Ovingdean Brighton ... 36 G5
Ovingham Northumb ... 242 E3
Ovington Durham ... 224 C2
Essex ... 106 C5
Hants ... 48 G5
Norf ... 141 C8
Northumb ... 242 E3
Ower Hants ... 32 D4
Hants ... 32 G5
Owermoigne Dorset ... 17 E11
Owlbury Shrops ... 130 E6
Owler Bar Derbys ... 186 F3
Owlerton S Yorks ... 186 D4
Owlet W Yorks ... 205 F9
Owlpen Glos ... 80 F4
Owl's Green Suff ... 126 D5
Owlsmoor Brack ... 65 G11
Owlswick Bucks ... 84 D3
Owlthorpe S Yorks ... 186 E6
Owmby Lincs ... 200 G5
Owmby-by-Spital Lincs ... 189 D8
Ownham W Berks ... 64 E2
Owrtyn / Overton Wrex ... 166 G5
Owslebury Hants ... 33 C8
Owston Leics ... 136 B5
S Yorks ... 198 E4
Owston Ferry N Lincs ... 199 G10
Owstwick E Yorks ... 209 G11
Owthorne E Yorks ... 201 B10
Owthorpe Notts ... 154 C3
Oxborough Norf ... 140 C4
Oxclose T&W ... 243 F7
Oxcombe Lincs ... 190 F4
Oxcroft Derbys ... 187 G7
Oxcroft Estate Derbys ... 187 G7
Oxen End Essex ... 106 F3
Oxenhall Glos ... 98 F4
Oxenholme Cumb ... 211 B10
Oxenhope W Yorks ... 204 F6
Oxen Park Cumb ... 210 B6
Oxenpill Som ... 44 E2
Oxenton Glos ... 99 E9
Oxenwood Wilts ... 47 B10
Oxford Oxon ... 83 D8
Stoke ... 168 E5
Oxgang E Dunb ... 278 G3
Oxgangs Edin ... 270 B4
Oxhey Herts ... 85 F10
Oxhill Durham ... 242 G5
Warks ... 100 B6
Oxlease Herts ... 86 D2
Oxley W Mid ... 133 C8
Oxley Green Essex ... 88 C6
Oxley's Green E Sus ... 37 C11
Oxlode Cambs ... 139 F9
Oxnam Borders ... 262 F5
Oxnead Norf ... 160 E4
Oxshott Sur ... 66 G6
Oxspring S Yorks ... 197 G9
Oxted Sur ... 51 C11
Oxton Borders ... 271 E9
Mers ... 182 D3
N Yorks ... 206 E6
Notts ... 171 E10
Oxton Rakes Derbys ... 186 G4
Oxwich Swansea ... 56 D3
Oxwich Green Swansea ... 56 D3
Oxwick Norf ... 159 D8
Oykel Bridge Highld ... 309 J3
Oyne Aberds ... 302 G6
Oystermouth Swansea ... 56 D6
Ozleworth Glos ... 80 G3

P
Pabail Iarach W Isles ... 304 E7
Pabail Uarach W Isles ... 304 E7
Pabo Conwy ... 180 F4
Pace Gate N Yorks ... 205 C8
Packers Hill Dorset ... 30 E2
Packington Leics ... 153 G7
Packmoor Staffs ... 168 E5
Packmores Warks ... 118 D5
Packwood W Mid ... 118 C3
Packwood Gullet
W Mid ... 118 C3
Padanaram Angus ... 287 B8
Padbury Bucks ... 102 E4
Paddington London ... 67 C9
Warr ... 183 D10
Paddlesworth Kent ... 55 F7
Kent ... 69 G7
Paddock Kent ... 54 C3
W Yorks ... 196 D6
Paddockhaugh Moray ... 302 D2
Paddockhill Ches E ... 184 F4
Paddock Wood Kent ... 53 E7
Paddolgreen Shrops ... 149 C10
Padfield Derbys ... 185 B8
Padgate Warr ... 183 D10
Padham's Green Essex ... 87 F10
Padiham Lancs ... 203 G11
Padney Cambs ... 123 C10
Padog Conwy ... 164 E4
Padside N Yorks ... 205 B9
Padside Green N Yorks ... 205 B9
Padson Devon ... 13 B7
Padstow Corn ... 10 F4
Padworth W Berks ... 64 F6
Padworth Common
Berks ... 64 G6
Page Bank Durham ... 233 D10
Page Moss Mers ... 182 C6
Page's Green Suff ... 126 D2
Pagham W Sus ... 22 D5
Paglesham Churchend
Essex ... 88 G6
Paglesham Eastend
Essex ... 88 G6
Paibeil W Isles ... 296 E3
Paible W Isles ... 305 J2
Paignton Torbay ... 9 C7
Pailton Warks ... 135 G9
Painleyhill Staffs ... 151 C10
Painscastle Powys ... 96 B3
Painshawfield Northumb ... 242 E3
Pains Hill Sur ... 52 C2
Painsthorpe E Yorks ... 208 B2
Painswick Glos ... 80 D5
Painter's Forstal Kent ... 54 B3
Painter's Green Wrex ... 167 G8
Painthorpe W Yorks ... 197 D10
Paintmoor Som ... 28 E4
Pairc Shiaboist W Isles ... 304 D4
Paisley Renfs ... 267 C9
Pakefield Suff ... 143 E10
Pakenham Suff ... 125 D8
Pale Gwyn ... 147 B9
Pale Green Essex ... 106 C3
Palehouse Common
E Sus ... 23 B7
Palestine Hants ... 47 E9
Paley Street Windsor ... 65 D11
Palfrey W Mid ... 133 D10
Palgowan Dumfries ... 245 G9
Palgrave Suff ... 126 B2
Pallaflat Cumb ... 219 C9
Pallington Dorset ... 17 C11
Pallion T&W ... 243 F9
Pallister Mbro ... 225 B10
Palmarsh Kent ... 54 G6
Palmer Moor Derbys ... 152 C2
Palmers Cross W Sus ... 50 G4
Sur ... 50 E4
Palmer's Flat Glos ... 79 D9
Palmers Green London ... 86 G4
Palmer's Green Kent ... 53 E7
Palmerstown V Glam ... 58 F6
Palmersville T&W ... 243 C7
Palmstead Kent ... 55 C7
Palnackie Dumfries ... 237 D10
Palnure Dumfries ... 236 C6
Palterton Derbys ... 171 B7
Pamber End Hants ... 48 B6
Pamber Green Hants ... 48 B6
Pamber Heath Hants ... 64 G5
Pamington Glos ... 99 E8
Pamphill Dorset ... 31 G7
Pampisford Cambs ... 123 G10
Orkney ... 314 G3
Panbride Angus ... 287 D9
Pancakehill Glos ... 81 C9
Pancrasweek Devon ... 24 F3
Pancross V Glam ... 58 F4
Pandy Gwyn ... 128 C2
Gwyn ... 146 F4
Gwyn ... 147 D7
Mon ... 96 G6
Powys ... 129 C8
Wrex ... 148 B3
Pandy'r Capel Denb ... 165 E9
Pandy Tudur Conwy ... 164 C5
Panfield Essex ... 106 F4
Pangbourne W Berks ... 64 D6
Panhall Fife ... 280 C6
Panks Bridge Hereford ... 98 B2
Pannal N Yorks ... 206 C2
Pannal Ash N Yorks ... 205 C11
Pannel's Ash Essex ... 106 C5
Panpunton Powys ... 114 C5
Panshanger Herts ... 86 C3
Pant Denb ... 166 E2
Gwyn ... 146 F4
Flint ... 181 G10
Gwyn ... 144 C4
MTydf ... 77 D9
Powys ... 129 C8
Shrops ... 148 E5
Wrex ... 166 D5
Wrex ... 166 F3
Pantasaph Flint ... 181 F11
Pantdu Neath ... 57 C9
Panteg Ceredig ... 111 E9
Torf ... 78 F4
Pantersbridge Corn ... 6 B3
Pant-glas Gwyn ... 163 F7
Pant-glâs Powys ... 128 D5
Pant-glas Shrops ... 148 C5
Pantgwyn Carms ... 93 F11
Ceredig ... 92 B4
Pant-lasau Swansea ... 57 B7
Pantmawr Cardiff ... 58 C6
Pant Mawr Powys ... 129 G7
Panton Lincs ... 189 F11
Pant-pastynog Denb ... 165 C8
Pantperthog Gwyn ... 128 C4
Pantside Caerph ... 78 F2
Pant-teg Carms ... 93 F9
Pant-y-Caws Carms ... 92 F3
Pant-y-crûg Ceredig ... 112 B3
Pant-y-dwr Powys ... 113 B9
Powys ... 113 C9
Pantyffynnon Carms ... 75 C10
Pantygasseg Torf ... 78 F3
Pantymwyn Flint ... 165 C11
Pant-y-pyllau Bridgend ... 58 C2
Pant-yr-awel Bridgend ... 58 B2
Pant-y-Wacco Flint ... 181 F10
Panxworth Norf ... 161 G7
Papcastle Cumb ... 229 E8
Papermill Bank Shrops ... 149 D11
Papigoe Highld ... 310 D7
Papil Shetland ... 313 K5
Papley Northants ... 138 F2
Orkney ... 314 G4
Papple E Loth ... 281 G11
Papplewick Notts ... 171 E8
Papworth Everard
Cambs ... 122 D5
Papworth St Agnes
Cambs ... 122 D5
Papworth Village Settlement
Cambs ... 122 E5
Par Corn ... 5 E11
Paradise Glos ... 80 C5
Paradise Green Hereford ... 97 B10
Paramoor Corn ... 5 F9
Paramour Street Kent ... 71 G9
Parbold Lancs ... 194 E3
Parbrook Som ... 44 F5
W Sus ... 35 C9
Parc Gwyn ... 147 C7
Parc Erissey Corn ... 4 G3
Parc-hendy Swansea ... 56 B4
Parciau Anglesey ... 179 E7
Parcllyn Ceredig ... 110 F5
Parc Mawr Caerph ... 77 G10
Parc-Seymour Newport ... 78 G6
Parc-y-rhôs Carms ... 93 B11
Pardown Hants ... 48 D5
Pardshaw Cumb ... 229 F7
Pardshaw Hall Cumb ... 229 F8
Parham Suff ... 126 E6
Park Corn ... 10 G6
Devon ... 14 B2
Dumfries ... 247 G10
Som ... 44 G3
Swindon ... 63 C7
Park Barn Sur ... 50 C3
Park Bottom Corn ... 4 G3
Park Bridge Gtr Man ... 196 G2
Park Close Lancs ... 204 E3
Park Corner Bath ... 45 B8
E Sus ... 23 C8
E Sus ... 52 F4
Oxon ... 65 B7
Windsor ... 65 C11
Parkend Glos ... 79 D10
Glos ... 80 C3
Park End Bedford ... 121 G9
Cambs ... 123 E11
Mbro ... 225 B10
Northumb ... 241 D9
Som ... 43 G7
Staffs ... 168 E3
Worcs ... 116 C5
Parkeston Essex ... 108 E2
Parkfield Corn ... 6 B4
S Glos ... 61 D7
W Mid ... 133 D8
Parkfoot Falk ... 278 F6
Parkgate Ches E ... 184 G6
Ches W ... 182 F3
Cumb ... 229 B10
Dumfries ... 248 G2
Essex ... 87 B11
Kent ... 53 E9
Sur ... 51 E8

Parkgate *continued*
S Yorks 186 B6
Park Gate Dorset 30 F2
Hants 33 F8
Kent 55 D7
Suff 124 F4
Worcs 117 C8
W Yorks 197 E8
Park Green Essex 105 F9
Parkhall W Dunb 277 G9
Park Hall Shrops 148 C6
Parkham Devon 24 C5
Parkham Ash Devon 24 C5
Parkhead Cumb 230 C2
Glasgow 268 C2
S Yorks 186 E4
Park Head Cumb 231 C7
Derbys 170 E5
W Yorks 197 F7
Parkhill Aberds 303 E10
Invclyd 277 G7
Park Hill Glos 79 F9
Kent 54 G3
Mers 194 G3
Notts 171 E11
N Yorks 214 F6
S Yorks 186 D5
Parkhill Ho Aberds 293 B10
Parkhouse Mon 79 E7
Parkhouse Green
Derbys 170 C6
Parkhurst IoW 20 C5
Parklands W Yorks 206 F3
Park Lane Staffs 133 B7
Wrex 149 B8
Park Langley London 67 F11
Park Mains Renfs 277 G9
Parkmill Swansea 56 D4
Park Mill W Yorks 197 E9
Parkneuk Aberds 293 F9
Fife 279 D11
Park Royal London 67 C7
Parkside C Beds 103 G10
Cumb 219 B10
Durham 234 B4
N Lanark 268 D6
Staffs 151 D8
Wrex 166 D5
Parkstone Poole 18 C6
Park Street Herts 85 E10
W Sus 50 G6
Park Town Luton 103 G11
Oxon 83 D8
Park Village Northumb 240 E5
W Mid 133 C8
Park Villas W Yorks 206 F2
Parkway Hereford 98 D4
Som 29 C9
Park Wood Kent 53 C9
Medway 69 G10
Parkwood Springs
S Yorks 186 D4
Parley Cross Dorset 19 B7
Parley Green Dorset 19 B7
Parliament Heath Suff 107 C9
Parlington W Yorks 206 F4
Parmoor Bucks 65 B9
Parnacott Devon 24 F4
Parney Heath Essex 107 E10
Parr Mers 183 C8
Parracombe Devon 41 E7
Parr Brow Gtr Man 195 G8
Parrog Pembs 91 D10
Parsley Hay Derbys 169 C10
Parslow's Hillock Bucks 84 E4
Parsonage Green Essex 88 D2
Parsonby Cumb 229 D8
Parson Cross S Yorks 186 C5
Parson Drove Cambs 139 B7
Parsons Green London 67 D9
Parson's Heath Essex 107 F10
Partick Glasgow 267 B11
Partington Gtr Man 184 C2
Partney Lincs 174 B6
Parton Cumb 228 G5
Cumb 239 G7
Dumfries 237 B8
Glos 99 G7
Hereford 96 B6
Partridge Green W Sus 35 D11
Partrishow Powys 96 G5
Parwich Derbys 169 E11
Pasford Staffs 132 D6
Passenham Northants 102 D5
Passfield Hants 49 G10
Passingford Bridge Essex 87 F8
Passmores Essex 86 D6
Paston Norf 160 C6
Pboro 138 C3
Paston Green Norf 160 C6
Pasturefields Staffs 151 D9
Patchacott Devon 12 B5
Patcham Brighton 36 F4
Patchetts Green Herts 85 F10
Patching W Sus 35 F9
Patchole Devon 40 E6
Patchway S Glos 60 C6
Pategill Cumb 230 F6
Pateley Bridge N Yorks 214 F3
Paternoster Heath Essex 88 C6
Pathe Som 43 G11
Pather N Lanark 268 E5
Pathfinder Village Devon 14 C2
Pathhead Aberds 293 G9
E Ayrs 258 G4
Fife 280 C5
Midloth 271 C7
Path Head T&W 242 E5
Pathlow Warks 118 F3
Path of Condie Perth 286 F4
Pathstruie Perth 286 F4
Patient End Herts 105 F8
Patmore Heath Herts 105 F8
Patna E Ayrs 257 G10
Patney Wilts 46 B5
Patrick IoM 192 D3
Patrick Brompton
N Yorks 224 G4
Patricroft Gtr Man 184 B3
Patrington E Yorks 201 C10
Patrington Haven
E Yorks 201 C10
Patrixbourne Kent 55 B7
Patsford Devon 40 F4
Patterdale Cumb 221 B7
Pattiesmuir Fife 279 E11
Pattingham Staffs 132 D6
Pattishall Northants 120 G3
Pattiswick Essex 106 G6
Patton Shrops 131 E11
Patton Bridge Cumb 221 F11
Paul Corn 1 D5
Paulerspury Northants 102 B4
Paull E Yorks 201 B7
Paul's Green Corn 2 C4
Paulsgrove Ptsmth 33 F10
Paulton Bath 45 B7
Paulville W Loth 269 B9
Pave Lane Telford 150 F5
Pavenham Bedford 121 F9
Pawlett Som 43 E10
Pawlett Hill Som 43 E9
Pawston Northumb 263 C9
Paxford Glos 100 D3
Paxton Borders 273 E8
Payden Street Kent 54 C2
Payhembury Devon 27 G9
Paynes Green Sur 50 F6
Paynter's Cross Corn 7 C7
Paynter's Lane End Corn 4 G3
Paythorne Lancs 204 C2
Payton Som 27 C10
Peacehaven E Sus 36 G6
Peacehaven Heights
E Sus 36 G6
Peacemarsh Dorset 30 B4
Peak Dale Derbys 185 F9
Peak Forest Derbys 185 F10
Peak Hill Lincs 156 F5
Peakirk Pboro 138 B3
Pean Hill Kent 70 G6
Pear Ash Som 45 G9
Pearsie Angus 287 B7
Pearson's Green Kent 53 E7
Peartree Herts 86 C2
Pear Tree Derby 153 C7
Peartree Green Essex 87 F9
Hereford 97 E11
Soton 32 E6
Sur 50 F3
Peas Acre W Yorks 205 E8
Peasedown St John Bath 45 B8
Peasehill Derbys 170 F6
Peaseland Green Norf 159 F11
Peasemore W Berks 64 D3
Peasenhall Suff 127 D7
Pease Pottage W Sus 51 G9
Peas Hill Cambs 139 D8
Peaslake Sur 50 E5
Peasley Cross Mers 183 C8
Peasmarsh E Sus 38 C5
Som 28 E4
Sur 50 D3
Peaston E Loth 271 B8
Peastonbank E Loth 271 B8
Peathill Aberds 303 C9
Peat Inn Fife 287 G8
Peatling Magna Leics 135 E11
Peatling Parva Leics 135 F11
Peaton Shrops 131 G10
Peatonstrand Shrops 131 G10
Peats Corner Suff 126 E3
Pebmarsh Essex 107 E7
Pebsham E Sus 38 F3
Pebworth Worcs 100 B2
Pecket Well W Yorks 196 B3
Peckforton Ches E 167 D8
Peckham London 67 D10
Peckham Bush Kent 53 D7
Peckingell Wilts 62 E2
Pecking Mill Som 44 F6
Peckleton Leics 135 C9
Pedair-ffordd Powys 148 E2
Pedham Norf 160 G6
Pedlars End Essex 87 D8
Pedlar's Rest Shrops 131 G9
Pedlinge Kent 54 F6
Pedmore W Mid 133 G8
Pednor Bottom Bucks 84 E6
Pednormead End Bucks 85 E7
Pedwell Som 44 F2
Peebles Borders 270 G5
Peel Borders 261 B10
IoM 192 D3
Lancs 202 G3
Peel Common Hants 33 G9
Peel Green Gtr Man 184 B2
Peel Hall Gtr Man 184 D4
Peel Hill Lancs 202 G3
Peel Park S Lanark 268 E2
Peene Kent 55 F7
Peening Quarter Kent 38 B5
Peggs Green Leics 153 F8
Pegsdon C Beds 104 E2
Pegswood Northumb 252 F6
Pegwell Kent 71 G11
Peinaha Highld 298 D4
Peinchorran Highld 295 B7
Peingown Highld 298 B4
Peinlich Highld 298 D4
Peinmore Highld 298 E4
Pelaw T&W 243 E7
Pelcomb Pembs 72 B6
Pelcomb Bridge Pembs 72 B6
Pelcomb Cross Pembs 72 B6
Peldon Essex 89 B7
Pelhamfield IoW 21 C7
Pell Green E Sus 52 G6
Pellon W Yorks 196 B5
Pelsall W Mid 133 C10
Pelsall Wood W Mid 133 C10
Pelton Durham 243 G7
Pelton Fell Durham 243 G7
Pelutho Cumb 229 B8
Pelynt Corn 6 D4
Pemberton Carms 75 E8
Gtr Man 194 G5
Pembles Cross Kent 53 D11
Pembre / Pembrey
Carms 74 E6
Pembrey / Pembre
Carms 74 E6
Pembridge Hereford 115 F7
Pembroke Pembs 73 E7
Pembroke Dock / Doc
Penfro Pembs 73 E7
Pembroke Ferry Pembs 73 E7
Pembury Kent 52 E6
Pempwell Corn 12 F3
Penallt Mon 79 C8
Pen-allt Hereford 97 F11
Penally / Penalun
Pembs 73 F10
Penalt Hereford 97 F11
Penalun / Penally
Pembs 73 F10
Penare Corn 5 G9
Penarlâg / Hawarden
Flint 166 B4
Penarron Powys 130 F2
Penarth V Glam 59 E7
Penarth Moors Cardiff 59 E7
Penbeagle Corn 2 B2
Penbedw Flint 165 B11
Pen-bedw Pembs 92 D4
Penberth Corn 1 E4
Penbidwal Mon 96 G6
Penbodlas Gwyn 144 C5
Pen-bont Rhydybeddau
Ceredig 128 G3
Penboyr Carms 93 D7
Penbryn Ceredig 110 G5
Pencader Carms 93 D8
Pencaenewydd Gwyn 162 G6
Pencaerau Neath 57 B8
Pen-caer-fenny Swansea 56 B4
Pencaitland E Loth 271 B8
Pencarnisiog Anglesey 178 G5
Pencarreg Carms 93 B10
Pencarrow Corn 11 E8
Penceiliogi Carms 75 E8
Pencelli Powys 95 F11
Pen-clawdd Swansea 56 B4
Pencoed Bridgend 58 C3
Pencombe Hereford 115 G11
Pen-common Powys 76 D6
Pencoyd Hereford 97 F10
Pencoys Corn 2 B5
Pencraig Anglesey 179 F7
Hereford 97 G11
Powys 147 D10
Pencroesoped Mon 78 D4
Pencuke Corn 11 C9
Pendas Fields W Yorks 206 F3
Pendeen Corn 1 C3
Pendeford W Mid 133 C7
Penderyn Rhondda 77 D7
Pendine / Pentwyn
Carms 74 D2
Pendlebury Gtr Man 195 G9
Pendleton Gtr Man 184 B4
Lancs 203 F11
Pendock Worcs 98 E5
Pendoggett Corn 10 F6
Pendomer Som 29 E8
Pendoylan V Glam 58 D5
Pendre Bridgend 58 C2
Gwyn 110 C2
Powys 95 F10
Pendrift Corn 11 G8
Penegoes Powys 128 C5
Penelewey Corn 4 G6
Penenden Heath Kent 53 B9
Penffordd Pembs 91 G11
Penffordd Lâs / Staylittle
Powys 129 E7
Pengam Caerph 77 F11
Penge London 67 E11
Pengegon Corn 2 B5
Pengelly Corn 11 E7
Pengenffordd Powys 96 E3
Pengersick Corn 2 D3
Pen-gilfach Gwyn 163 C9
Pengold Corn 11 C8
Pengorffwysfa Anglesey 179 C7
Pengover Green Corn 6 B5
Pen-groes-oped Mon 78 D4
Penguithal Hereford 97 G10
Pengwern Denb 181 F8
Penhale Corn 2 F5
Corn 5 D8
Penhale Jakes Corn 2 D4
Penhallick Corn 3 F7
Corn 4 G3
Penhallow Corn 4 E5
Penhalurick Corn 2 B6
Penhalvean Corn 2 B6
Penhelig Gwyn 128 D2
Penhill Devon 40 G4
Swindon 63 B7
Penhow Newport 78 G6
Penhurst E Sus 23 B11
Peniarth Gwyn 128 B2
Penicuik Midloth 270 C4
Peniel Carms 93 G8
Denb 165 C8
Penifiler Highld 298 E4
Peninver Argyll 255 E8
Penisa'r Waun Gwyn 163 C9
Penistone S Yorks 197 G8
Penjerrick Corn 3 C7
Penketh Warr 183 D9
Penkhull Stoke 168 G5
Penkill S Ayrs 244 D6
Penknap Wilts 45 D11
Penkridge Staffs 151 G8
Pen-lan Swansea 56 B6
Pen-Lan-mabws Pembs 91 F7
Penleigh Wilts 45 C11
Penley Wrex 149 B8
Penllech Gwyn 144 C4
Penllergaer Swansea 56 B6
Penllwyn Caerph 77 F11
Ceredig 128 G3
Penllyn V Glam 58 D3
Pen-llyn Anglesey 178 E4
Pen-lon Anglesey 162 B6
Penmachno Conwy 164 E3
Penmaen Caerph 77 F11
Swansea 56 D4
Penmaenan Conwy 180 F2
Penmaenmawr Conwy 180 F2
Penmaenpool Gwyn 146 F3
Penmaen Rhôs Conwy 180 F5
Penmark V Glam 58 F5
Penmarth Corn 2 B6
Penmayne Corn 10 F4
Pen Mill Som 29 D9
Penmon Anglesey 179 E10
Penmore Mill Argyll 288 D6
Penmorfa Ceredig 110 G6
Gwyn 163 G8
Penmynydd Anglesey 179 G8
Penn Bucks 84 G6
W Mid 133 D7
Pennal Gwyn 128 C4
Pennan Aberds 303 C8
Pennance Corn 4 G4
Pennant Ceredig 111 E10
Conwy 164 D5
Denb 147 C10
Denb 165 E8
Powys 129 D7
Pennant Melangell
Powys 147 D10
Pennar Pembs 73 E7
Pennard Swansea 56 D5
Pennar Park Pembs 72 E6
Penn Bottom Bucks 84 G6
Pennerley Shrops 131 D7
Pennington Cumb 210 D5
Gtr Man 183 B11
Hants 20 C2
Pennington Green
Gtr Man 194 F6
Pennorth Powys 96 F2
Penn Street Bucks 84 F6
Pennsylvania Devon 14 C4
S Glos 61 E8
Penny Bridge Cumb 210 C6
Pennycross Argyll 289 G7
Plym 7 D9
Pennygate Norf 160 E6
Pennygown Argyll 289 E7
Penny Green Derbys 187 F8
Penny Hill Lincs 157 D7
W Yorks 196 D5
Pennylands Lancs 194 F3
Pennymoor Devon 26 E5
Pennypot Kent 54 G6
Penny's Green Norf 142 D3
Pennytinney Corn 10 F6
Pennywell T&W 243 F9
Pen-onn V Glam 58 F5
Penparc Ceredig 92 B4
Pembs 91 E7
Penparcau Ceredig 111 B11
Penpedairheol Caerph 77 F10
Mon 78 E4
Penpergym Mon 78 C4
Penperlleni Mon 78 E4
Penpethy Corn 11 D7
Penpillick Corn 5 D11
Penplas Carms 74 B5
Penpol Corn 3 B8
Penpoll Corn 6 E2
Penponds Corn 2 B4
Penpont Corn 11 G7
Dumfries 247 E8
Powys 95 F9
Penprysg Bridgend 58 C3
Penquit Devon 8 E2
Penrallt Gwyn 145 B7
Powys 129 F9
Penrherber Carms 92 D5
Penrhiw Caerph 78 G2
Penrhiwceiber Rhondda 77 F8
Pen-Rhiw-fawr Neath 76 C2
Penrhiwgarreg Bl Gwent 78 E2
Penrhiw-llan Ceredig 93 C7
Penrhiw-pal Ceredig 92 B6
Penrhiwtyn Neath 57 B8
Penrhos Anglesey 178 E3
Gwyn 144 C6
Hereford 114 F6
Mon 78 C6
Penrhôs Mon 78 C6
Penrhos Powys 76 C3
Pen-rhos Wrex 166 E3
Penrhosfeilw Anglesey 178 E2
Penrhos-garnedd Gwyn 179 G9
Penrhyd Lastra Anglesey 178 C6
Penrhyn Bay / Bae-Penrhyn
Conwy 180 E4
Penrhyn Castle Pembs 92 B2
Penrhyn-coch Ceredig 128 G2
Penrhyndeudraeth
Gwyn 146 B2
Penrhynside Conwy 180 E4
Penrhyn side Conwy 180 E4
Penrhys Rhondda 77 F8
Penrice Swansea 56 D3
Penrith Cumb 230 E6
Penrose Corn 10 G3
Corn 11 F7
Penrose Hill Corn 2 D4
Penruddock Cumb 230 F4
Penryn Corn 3 C7
Pensarn Carms 74 B6
Conwy 181 F7
Pen-sarn Gwyn 145 D11
Gwyn 162 G6
Pensax Worcs 116 D4
Pensby Mers 182 E3
Penselwood Som 45 G9
Pensford Bath 60 G6
Pensham Worcs 99 C8
Penshaw T&W 243 G8
Penshurst Kent 52 E4
Pensilva Corn 6 B5
Pensnett W Mid 133 F8
Penston E Loth 281 G8
Penstone Devon 26 G3
Penstraze Corn 4 F5
Pentewan Corn 5 F10
Pentiken Shrops 130 G4
Pentir Gwyn 163 B9
Pentire Corn 4 C5
Pentirvin Shrops 130 C6
Pentlepoir Pembs 73 D10
Pentlow Essex 106 B6
Pentlow Street Essex 106 B6
Pentney Norf 158 G4
Penton Corner Hants 47 D10
Penton Grafton Hants 47 D10
Penton Mewsey Hants 47 D10
Pentonville London 67 C10
Pentowin Carms 74 B3
Pentraeth Anglesey 179 F8
Pentrapeod Caerph 77 E11
Pentre Carms 75 C8
Denb 165 D10
Flint 165 C11
Flint 166 B4
Flint 166 C2
Flint 166 D2
Powys 129 F11
Powys 130 B4
Powys 130 E5
Powys 147 D11
Powys 148 G3
Rhondda 77 F7
Shrops 148 D4
Shrops 149 F7
Wrex 148 B2
Wrex 166 G3
Pentrebach Carms 94 E6
M Tydf 77 E9
Rhondda 58 B5
Swansea 75 D10
Pentre-bâch Ceredig 93 B11
Pentre-bach Powys 95 E8
Pentrebane Cardiff 58 D6
Pentrebeirdd Powys 148 G3
Pentre Berw Anglesey 179 G7
Pentre-bont Conwy 164 E2
Pentre Broughton Wrex 166 E4
Pentre Bychan Wrex 166 F4
Pentrecagal Carms 92 C6
Pentre-cefn Shrops 148 D4
Pentre-celyn Denb 165 E11
Powys 129 B7
Pentre-chwyth Swansea 57 B7
Pentre Cilgwyn Wrex 148 B4
Pentre-clawdd Shrops 148 C5
Pentre-coed Shrops 149 B7
Pentre-cwrt Carms 93 D7
Pentre Dolau-Honddu
Powys 95 C9
Pentredwr Denb 165 F11
Pentre-dwr Swansea 57 B7
Pentrefelin Anglesey 178 C6
Carms 93 G11
Ceredig 94 B2
Conwy 180 G4
Denb 166 G2
Gwyn 145 B10
Pentre-Ffwrndan Flint 182 G3
Pentrefoelas Conwy 164 E5
Pentref-y-groes Caerph 77 F11
Pentre-galar Pembs 92 E3
Pentregat Ceredig 111 G7
Pentre-Gwenlais Carms 75 B10
Pentre Gwynfryn Gwyn 145 D11
Pentre Halkyn Flint 182 G2
Pentreheyling Shrops 130 E4
Pentre Hodre Shrops 114 B6
Pentre Isaf Conwy 164 B5
Pentre Llanrhaeadr
Denb 165 C9
Pentre Llifior Powys 130 D2
Pentrellwyn Ceredig 93 C8
Pentre-llwyn-llwyd
Powys 113 G9
Pentre-llyn Ceredig 112 C2
Pentre-llyn cymmer
Conwy 165 E7
Pentre Maelor Wrex 166 F5
Pentre Meyrick V Glam 58 D3
Pentre-newydd Shrops 148 B5
Pentre-Piod Torf 78 E3
Pentre-Poeth Carms 75 E8
Newport 59 B9
Pentre'r beirdd Powys 148 G3
Pentre'r Felin Conwy 164 B4
Pentre'r-felin Denb 165 B10
Powys 95 E8
Pentre-rhew Ceredig 112 G3
Pentre-tafarn-y-fedw
Conwy 164 C4
Pentre-ty-gwyn Carms 94 D6
Pentreuchaf Gwyn 145 B7
Pentre-uchaf Conwy 180 F5
Pentrich Derbys 170 E5
Pentridge Dorset 31 D8
Pentrisil Pembs 91 E11
Pentwyn Caerph 77 E10
Cardiff 59 C8
Pen-twyn Caerph 78 E2
Carms 75 C9
Mon 79 D8
Torf 78 E3
Pentwyn Berthlwyd
Caerph 77 F10
Pentwyn-mawr Caerph 77 F11
Pentwyn / Pendine
Carms 74 D2
Pentyrch Cardiff 58 C6
Penuchadre V Glam 57 G11
Pen-Uchar Plwyf Flint 181 G11
Penuwch Ceredig 111 E11
Penwartha Corn 4 E5
Penwartha Coombe Corn 4 E5
Penweathers Corn 4 G6
Penwithick Corn 5 D10
Penwood Hants 64 G2
Penwortham Lane
Lancs 194 B4
Penwyllt Powys 76 B5
Pen-y-Ball Top Flint 181 F11
Penybanc Carms 75 C10
Pen-y-banc Carms 93 G8
Carms 94 G2
Pen-y-bank Caerph 77 E10
Penybedd Carms 74 E6
Penybont Ceredig 128 F2
Powys 114 E2
Pen-y-Bont Bl Gwent 78 D2
Carms 92 F6
Gwyn 128 C4
Gwyn 146 D2
Powys 148 E4
Pen y Bont ar ogwr /
Bridgend Bridgend 58 C2
Penybontfawr Powys 147 E11
Penybryn Caerph 77 F10
Pen-y-Bryn Gwyn 145 B9
Gwyn 146 F3
Pembs 92 C3
Powys 130 C3
Shrops 148 B6
Wrex 166 G3
Penycae Wrex 166 F3
Pen-y-cae Bridgend 58 C2
Neath 57 D9
Powys 76 C4
Pen-y-cae-mawr Mon 78 F6
Penycaerau Gwyn 144 D3
Pen-y-cefn Flint 181 F10
Pen-y-clawdd Mon 79 D7
Pen-y-coed Shrops 148 E5
Pen-y-coedcae Rhondda 58 B5
Penycwm Pembs 90 G6
Pen-y-Darren M Tydf 77 D9
Penydre Swansea 75 E11
Pen-y-fai Bridgend 57 E11
Carms 75 E7
Pen-y-fan Carms 56 B4
Mon 79 D8
Penyfeidr Pembs 91 F7
Pen-y-felin Flint 165 B11
Penyffordd Flint 166 C4
Pen-y-ffordd Denb 181 F8
Flint 181 E10
Penyffridd Gwyn 163 D8
Pen y Foel Shrops 148 E5
Penygarn Torf 78 E3
Pen-y-garn Carms 93 E11
Ceredig 128 F2
Penygarnedd Powys 148 E2
Pen-y-garnedd
Anglesey 179 F8
Penygelli Powys 130 E2
Pen-y-gop Conwy 164 G6
Penygraig Rhondda 77 G7
Pen-y-graig Gwyn 144 C3
Penygraigwen Anglesey 178 D6
Penygroes Gwyn 163 E7
Pembs 92 D3
Pen-y-groes Carms 75 C9
Pen-y-groeslon Gwyn 144 C4
Pen-y-Gwryd Hotel
Gwyn 163 D11
Pen-y-lan Cardiff 59 D7
Newport 59 B9
V Glam 58 D3
Pen-y-maes Flint 181 F11
Pen-y-Myndd Carms 75 E7
Penymynydd Flint 166 C4
Pen-y-Park Hereford 96 C5
Penyraber Pembs 91 D9
Pen-yr-englyn Rhondda 76 F6
Penyrheol Caerph 58 B6
Swansea 56 B5
Torf 78 F3
Pen-yr-heol Bridgend 58 C2
Mon 78 C6
Pen-yr-Heolgerrig
M Tydf 77 D8
Pen-y-rhiw Rhondda 58 B5
Penysarn Anglesey 179 C7
Pen-y-stryt Denb 165 E11
Penywaun Rhondda 77 E7
Pen-y-wern Shrops 114 B6
Penzance Corn 1 C5
Peopleton Worcs 117 G8
Peover Heath Ches E 184 G3
Peper Harow Sur 50 E2
Peppercombe Devon 24 C5
Pepper Hill Som 43 F7
W Yorks 196 B6
Peppermoor Northumb 264 F6
Pepper's Green Essex 87 C10
Pepperstock C Beds 85 B9
Perceton N Ayrs 267 G7
Percie Aberds 293 D7
Percuil Corn 3 C9
Percyhorner Aberds 303 C9
Percy Main T&W 243 D8
Per-ffordd-llan Flint 181 F10
Perham Down Wilts 47 D9
Periton Som 42 D3
Perivale London 67 C7
Perkhill Aberds 293 C7
Perkinsville Durham 243 G7
Perlethorpe Notts 187 G11
Perranarworthal Corn 3 B7
Perrancoombe Corn 4 E5
Perran Downs Corn 2 C3
Perranporth Corn 4 E5
Perranuthnoe Corn 2 D2
Perranwell Corn 3 B7
Corn 4 E5
Perranwell Station Corn 3 B7
Perran Wharf Corn 3 B7
Perranzabuloe Corn 4 E5
Perrott's Brook Glos 81 D8
Perry Devon 26 F5
Kent 55 B9
W Mid 133 E11
Perry Barr W Mid 133 E11
Perry Beeches W Mid 133 E11
Perry Common W Mid 133 E11
Perry Crofts Staffs 134 C4
Perryfields Worcs 117 C8
Perryfoot Derbys 185 E10
Perry Green Essex 106 G6
Herts 86 B6
Som 43 F9
Wilts 62 B3
Perrymead Bath 61 G9
Perrystone Hill Hereford 98 F2
Perry Street Kent 68 E6
Som 28 F4
Perrywood Kent 54 B4
Pershall Staffs 150 C6
Pershore Worcs 99 B8
Pert Angus 293 G8
Pertenhall Bedford 121 D11
Perth Perth 286 E5
Perthcelyn Rhondda 77 F9
Perthy Shrops 149 C7
Perton Hereford 97 C11
Staffs 133 D7
Pertwood Wilts 45 F11
Pested Kent 54 C4
Peterborough Pboro 138 D3
Peterburn Highld 307 L2
Peterchurch Hereford 96 D6
Peterculter Aberdeen 293 C10
Peterhead Aberds 303 E11
Peterlee Durham 234 C4
Petersburn N Lanark 268 C5
Petersfield Hants 34 C2
Peter's Finger Devon 12 D3
Peter's Green Herts 85 B10
Petersham London 67 E7
Peters Marland Devon 25 E7
Peterstone Wentlooge
Newport 59 C9
Peterston-super-Ely
V Glam 58 D5
Peterstow Hereford 97 G11
Peter Tavy Devon 12 F6
Petertown Orkney 314 F3
Peterville Corn 4 E4
Petham Kent 54 C6
Petherwin Gate Corn 11 D11
Petrockstow Devon 25 F8
Petsoe End M Keynes 103 B7
Pett E Sus 38 E5
Pettaugh Suff 126 F3
Pett Bottom Kent 55 C7
Kent 55 C7
Petteridge Kent 53 E7
Pettinain S Lanark 269 G9
Pettings Kent 68 G6
Pettistree Suff 126 G5
Pett Level E Sus 38 E5
Petton Devon 27 C8
Shrops 149 D8
Petts Wood London 68 F2
Petty Aberds 303 F7
Pettycur Fife 280 D5
Petty France S Glos 61 B9
Pettymuick Aberds 303 G9
Pettywell Norf 159 E11
Petworth W Sus 35 C7
Pevensey E Sus 23 E10
Pevensey Bay E Sus 23 E11
Peverell Plym 7 D9
Pewsey Wilts 63 G7
Pewsey Wharf Wilts 63 G7
Pewterspear Warr 183 E10
Phantassie E Loth 281 F11
Pharisee Green Essex 106 G2
Pheasants Bucks 65 B9
Pheasant's Hill Bucks 65 B9
Pheasey W Mid 133 D11
Pheonix Green Hants 49 B9
Phepson Worcs 117 F8
Philadelphia T&W 243 G8
Philham Devon 24 C3
Philiphaugh Borders 261 D10
Phillack Corn 2 B3
Philleigh Corn 3 B9
Phillip's Town Caerph 77 E10
Philpot End Essex 87 B10
Philpstoun W Loth 279 F10
Phocle Green Hereford 98 F2
Phoenix Green Hants 49 B9
Phoenix Row Durham 233 F9
Phorp Moray 301 D10
Pibsbury Som 28 B6
Pibwrlwyd Carms 74 B6
Pica Cumb 228 G6
Piccadilly S Yorks 187 B7
Warks 134 D4
Piccadilly Corner Norf 142 F5
Piccotts End Herts 85 D9
Pickburn S Yorks 198 F4
Picken End Worcs 98 C6
Pickering N Yorks 216 C5
Pickering Nook Durham 242 F5
Picket Hill Hants 31 F11
Picket Piece Hants 47 D11
Picket Post Hants 31 F11
Pickford W Mid 134 G5
Pickford Green W Mid 134 G5
Pickhill N Yorks 214 C6
Picklenash Glos 98 F4
Picklescott Shrops 131 D8
Pickles Hill W Yorks 204 F6
Pickletillem Fife 287 E8
Pickley Green Gtr Man 195 G7
Pickmere Ches E 183 F11
Pickney Som 27 B11
Pickstock Telford 150 E4
Pickup Bank Blackburn 195 C8
Pickwell Devon 40 E3
Leics 154 G5
Pickwick Wilts 61 E11
Pickwood Scar W Yorks 196 C5
Pickworth Lincs 155 C10
Rutland 155 G9
Picton Ches W 182 G6
Flint 181 E10
N Yorks 225 D8
Pict's Hill Som 28 B6
Piddinghoe E Sus 36 G6
Piddington Bucks 84 G4
Northants 120 G6
Oxon 83 B10
Piddlehinton Dorset 17 B10
Piddletrenthide Dorset 17 B10
Pidley Cambs 122 B6
Pidney Dorset 30 F2
Piece Corn 2 B5
Piercebridge Darl 224 B4
Piercing Hill Essex 86 F6
Pierowall Orkney 314 B4
Piff's Elm Glos 99 F8
Pigdon Northumb 252 F5
Pightley Som 43 F8
Pig Oak Dorset 31 G8
Pigstye Green Essex 87 D10
Pike End W Yorks 196 D4
Pikehall Derbys 169 D11
Pike Hill Lancs 204 G3
Pike Law W Yorks 196 D4
Pikeshill Hants 32 F3
Pikestye Hereford 97 B10
Pilford Dorset 31 G8
Pilgrims Hatch Essex 87 F9
Pilham Lincs 188 C5
Pilhough Derbys 170 C3
Pill N Som 60 D4
Pembs 72 D6
Pillaton Corn 7 C7
Staffs 151 G8
Pillerton Hersey Warks 100 B6
Pillerton Priors Warks 100 B5
Pilleth Powys 114 D5
Pilley Glos 81 B7
Hants 20 B2
S Yorks 197 G10
Pilley Bailey Hants 20 B2
Pillgwenlly Newport 59 B10
Pilling Lancs 202 D4
Pilling Lane Lancs 202 D3
Pillmouth Devon 25 C7
Pillowell Glos 79 D10
Pillows Green Glos 98 F5
Pillwell Dorset 30 D3
Pilmuir Borders 261 G11
Pilning S Glos 60 B5
Pilrig Edin 280 F5
Pilsbury Derbys 169 C10
Pilsdon Dorset 16 B4
Pilsgate Pboro 137 B11
Pilsley Derbys 170 C6
Derbys 186 G2
Pilsley Green Derbys 170 C6
Pilson Green Norf 161 G7
Piltdown E Sus 36 C6
Pilton Devon 40 G5
Edin 280 F4
Northants 137 G10
Rutland 137 C8
Som 44 E5
Pilton Green Swansea 56 D2
Piltown Som 44 F5
Pimhole Gtr Man 195 E10
Pimlico Herts 85 D9
Lancs 203 E10
London 67 D9
Northants 102 C2
Pimperne Dorset 29 F9
Dorset 30 F6
Pinchbeck Lincs 156 D4
Pinchbeck Bars Lincs 156 D3
Pinchbeck West Lincs 156 E4
Pincheon Green
S Yorks 199 D7
Pinckney Green Wilts 61 G10
Pincock Lancs 194 D5
Pineham Kent 55 D10
M Keynes 103 C7
Pinehurst Swindon 63 B7
Pinfarthings Glos 80 E5
Pinfold Lancs 193 E11
Pinfold Hill S Yorks 197 G9
Pinfoldpond C Beds 103 E8
Pinford End Suff 124 F6
Pinged Carms 74 E6
Pingewood W Berks 65 F7
Pin Green Herts 104 F4
Pinhoe Devon 14 C5
Pinkett's Booth W Mid 134 G5
Pink Green Worcs 117 D11
Pinkie Braes E Loth 281 G7
Pinkney Wilts 61 B11
Pinkneys Green Windsor 65 C11
Pinksmoor Som 27 D10
Pinley W Mid 119 B7
Pinley Green Warks 118 D4
Pin Mill Suff 108 D4
Pinminnoch Dumfries 236 D2
S Ayrs 244 E5
Pinmore S Ayrs 244 E6
Pinmore Mains S Ayrs 244 E6
Pinnacles Essex 86 D6
Pinner London 66 B6
Pinner Green London 85 G10
Pinnerwood Park
London 85 G10
Pin's Green Worcs 98 B6
Pinsley Green Ches E 167 F9
Pinstones Shrops 131 F9
Pinvin Worcs 99 B9
Pinwall Leics 134 C6
Pinwherry S Ayrs 244 F5
Pinxton Derbys 171 E7
Pipe and Lyde Hereford 97 C10
Pipe Aston Hereford 115 C9
Pipe Gate Shrops 168 G2
Pipehill Staffs 133 B11
Piperhall Argyll 266 D2
Piperhill Highld 301 D8
Pipe Ridware Staffs 151 F11
Piper's Ash Ches W 166 B6
Piper's End Worcs 98 E6
Piper's Hill Worcs 117 D9
Piper's Pool Corn 11 E11
Pipewell Northants 136 F6
Pippacott Devon 40 F4
Pippin Street Lancs 194 C5
Pipps Hill Essex 69 B7
Pipsden Kent 53 G9
Pipton Powys 96 D3
Pirbright Sur 50 B2
Pirbright Camp Sur 50 B2
Pirnmill N Ayrs 255 C9
Pirton Herts 104 E2
Worcs 99 B7
Pisgah Ceredig 112 B3
Stirling 285 G11
Pishill Oxon 65 B8
Pishill Bank Oxon 84 G2
Pismire Hill S Yorks 186 C5
Pistyll Gwyn 162 G4
Pit Mon 78 D5
Pitagowan Perth 291 G10
Pitblae Aberds 303 C9
Pitcairngreen Perth 286 E4
Pitcalnie Highld 301 B8
Pitcaple Aberds 303 G7
Pitchcombe Glos 80 D5
Pitchcott Bucks 102 G5
Pitcher's Green Suff 125 F8
Pitchford Shrops 131 C10
Pitch Green Bucks 84 E3
Pitch Place Sur 49 F11
Sur 50 C3
Pitcombe Som 45 G7
Pitcorthie Fife 280 D2
Fife 287 G9
Pitcot Som 45 D7
V Glam 57 G11
Pitcox E Loth 282 F2
Pitcur Perth 286 D6
Pitfancy Aberds 302 E5
Pitfichie Aberds 293 B8
Pitforthie Aberds 293 F10
Pitgair Aberds 303 D7
Pitgrudy Highld 309 K7
Pithmaduthy Highld 301 B7
Pitkennedy Angus 287 B9
Pitkevy Fife 286 G6
Pitkierie Fife 287 G9
Pitlessie Fife 287 G7
Pitlochry Perth 286 B3
Pitmachie Aberds 302 G6
Pitmain Highld 291 C9
Pitmedden Aberds 303 G8
Pitminster Som 28 D2
Pitmuies Angus 287 C9
Pitmunie Aberds 293 B8
Pitney Som 29 B7
Pitrocknie Perth 286 C6
Pitscottie Fife 287 F8
Pitsea Essex 69 B8
Pitses Gtr Man 196 G2
Pitsford Northants 120 D5
Pitsford Hill Som 42 G6
Pitsmoor S Yorks 186 D5
Pitstone Bucks 84 B6
Pitstone Green Bucks 84 B6
Pitstone Hill Bucks 85 C7
Pitt Hants 33 B7
Pittachar Perth 286 E2
Pitt Court Glos 80 F3
Pittendreich Moray 301 C11
Pittentrail Highld 309 J7
Pittenweem Fife 287 G9
Pitteuchar Fife 280 B5
Pittington Durham 234 C2
Pittodrie Aberds 302 G6
Pitton Swansea 56 D2
Wilts 47 G8
Pitts Hill Stoke 168 E5
Pittswood Kent 52 D6
Pittulie Aberds 303 C9
Pittville Glos 99 G9
Pityme Corn 10 F5
Pity Me Durham 233 B11
Pityoulish Highld 291 B11
Pixey Green Suff 126 B4
Pixham Sur 51 C7
Worcs 98 B6
Pixley Hereford 98 D3
Shrops 150 D3
Pizien Well Kent 53 C7
Place Newton N Yorks 217 E7
Plaidy Aberds 303 D7
Corn 6 E5
Plain-an-Gwarry Corn 4 G3
Plain Dealings Pembs 73 B9
Plains N Lanark 268 B5
Plainsfield Som 43 F7
Plain Spot Notts 171 E7
Plain Street Corn 10 F5
Plaish Shrops 131 D10
Plaistow London 68 C2
London 68 E2
W Sus 50 G4
Plaistow Green Essex 106 F6
Plaitford Wilts 32 D3
Plaitford Green Hants 32 C3
Plank Lane Gtr Man 194 G6
Plans Dumfries 238 D3
Plantation Bridge Cumb 221 F9
Plantationfoot Dumfries 248 E4
Plardiwick Staffs 150 E6
Plasau Shrops 149 E7
Plâs Berwyn Denb 165 G11
Plas-canol Gwyn 145 F11
Plas Coch Wrex 166 E4
Plas Dinam Powys 129 F10
Plas Gogerddan Ceredig 128 G2
Plashet London 68 C2
Plashett Carms 74 D3
Plasiolyn Powys 129 C11
Plas Llwyngwern Powys 128 C5
Plas Meredydd Powys 130 D3
Plas Nantyr Wrex 148 B3
Plasnewydd Powys 129 D9
Plaster's Green Bath 60 G4
Plastow Green Hants 64 G4
Plas-yn-Cefn Denb 181 G8
Platt Kent 52 B6
Platt Bridge Gtr Man 194 G6
Platt Lane Shrops 149 B10
Platts Common
S Yorks 197 G11
Platt's Heath Kent 53 C11
Plawsworth Durham 233 B11
Plaxtol Kent 52 C6
Playden E Sus 38 C6
Playford Suff 108 B4
Play Hatch Oxon 65 D8
Playing Place Corn 4 G6
Playley Green Glos 98 E5
Plealey Shrops 131 B8
Pleamore Cross Som 27 D10
Plean Stirling 278 D6
Pleasant Valley Pembs 73 D10
Pleasington Blackburn 194 B6
Pleasley Derbys 171 C8
Pleasleyhill Notts 171 C8
Pleck Dorset 30 D3
Dorset 30 E2
W Mid 133 D9
Pleckgate Blackburn 203 G9
Pleck or Little Ansty
Dorset 30 G3
Pledgdon Green Essex 105 F11
Pledwick W Yorks 197 D10
Plemstall Ches W 183 G7
Plenmeller Northumb 240 E6
Pleshey Essex 87 C11
Plockton Highld 295 B10
Plocrapol W Isles 305 J3
Plot Gate Som 44 G4
Plot Street Som 44 F5
Ploughfield Hereford 97 C7
Plough Hill Warks 134 E6
Plowden Shrops 131 F7
Ploxgreen Shrops 131 C7
Pluckley Kent 54 D2
Pluckley Thorne Kent 54 E2
Plucks Gutter Kent 71 G9
Plumbland Cumb 229 D9
Plumbley S Yorks 186 E6
Plumford Kent 54 B4
Plumley Ches E 184 F2
Plump Hill Glos 79 B11
Plumpton Cumb 230 D5
E Sus 36 E5
Northants 101 B11
Plumpton End Northants 102 B4
Plumpton Foot Cumb 230 D5
Plumpton Green E Sus 36 D5
Plumpton Head Cumb 230 E6
Plumstead London 68 D3
Norf 160 C2
Plumstead Common
London 68 D3
Plumstead Green Norf 160 C2
Plumtree Notts 154 C2
Plumtree Green Kent 53 D10
Plumtree Park Notts 154 C2
Plungar Leics 154 C5
Plush Dorset 30 G2
Plusha Corn 11 E11

Plushabridge Corn 12 G2
Plusterwine Glos 79 F9
Plwmp Ceredig 111 G7
Plymouth Plym 7 E9
Plympton Plym 7 D10
Plymstock Plym 7 E10
Plymtree Devon 27 G9
Pobgreen Gtr Man 196 F4
Pochin Houses Caerph 77 E11
Pocket Nook Gtr Man 183 B10
Pockley N Yorks 216 B2
Pocklington E Yorks 208 D2
Pockthorpe Norf 141 D8
Norf 158 D6
Norf 159 E10
Norf 159 F11
Pode Hole Lincs 156 E4
Podimore Som 29 C8
Podington Bedford 121 E8
Podmoor Worcs 117 C7
Podmore Norf 159 G9
Staffs 150 B5
Podsmead Glos 80 B4
Poffley End Oxon 82 C5
Pogmoor S Yorks 197 F10
Point Corn 3 B8
Point Clear Essex 89 C9
Pointon Lincs 156 C2
Pokesdown Bmouth 19 C8
Pol a Charra W Isles 297 K3
Polbae Dumfries 236 B4
Polbain Highld 307 H4
Polbathic Corn 7 D7
Polbeth W Loth 269 C10
Polborder Corn 7 C7
Polbrock Corn 5 B10
Polchar Highld 291 C10
Polebrook Northants 137 F11
Pole Elm Worcs 98 B6
Polegate E Sus 23 D9
Pole Moor W Yorks 196 D5
Poles Highld 309 K7
Polesden Lacey Sur 50 C6
Poleshill Som 27 C9
Pole's Hole Wilts 45 C10
Polesworth Warks 134 C5
Polgear Corn 2 B5
Polgigga Corn 1 E3
Polglass Highld 307 J5
Polgooth Corn 5 E9
Poling W Sus 35 G8
Poling Corner W Sus 35 F8
Polkerris Corn 5 E11
Polla Highld 308 D3
Polladras Corn 2 C4
Pollard Street Norf 160 C6
Pollhill Kent 53 C11
Poll Hill Mers 182 E3
Pollie Highld 309 H7
Pollington E Yorks 198 D6
Polliwilline Argyll 255 G8
Polloch Highld 289 C9
Pollok Glasgow 267 C10
Pollokshields Glasgow 267 C11
Polmadie Glasgow 267 C11
Polmarth Corn 2 B6
Polmassick Corn 5 F9
Polmear Corn 5 E11
Polmont Falk 279 F8
Polmorla Corn 10 G5
Polnessan E Ayrs 257 G10
Polnish Highld 295 G9
Polopit Northants 121 B10
Polpenwith Corn 2 D6
Polpeor Corn 2 B2
Polperro Corn 6 E4
Polruan Corn 6 E2
Polsham Som 44 E4
Polsloe Devon 14 C4
Polstead Suff 107 D9
Polstead Heath Suff 107 C9
Poltalloch Argyll 275 D9
Poltesco Corn 2 F6
Poltimore Devon 14 B5
Polton Midloth 270 C5
Polwarth Borders 272 E4
Polwheveral Corn 2 D6
Polyphant Corn 11 E11
Polzeath Corn 10 F4
Pomeroy Derbys 169 B10
Pomphlett Plym 7 E10
Ponciau Wrex 166 F3
Pond Close Som 27 B10
Ponde Powys 96 D2
Pondersbridge Cambs 138 E5
Ponders End London 86 F5
Pond Park Bucks 85 E7
Pond Street Essex 105 D9
Pondtail Hants 49 C10
Pondwell IoW 21 C8
Poniou Corn 1 B4
Ponjeravah Corn 2 D6
Ponsanooth Corn 3 B7
Ponsford Devon 27 F8
Ponsonby Cumb 219 D11
Ponsongath Corn 3 F7
Ponsworthy Devon 13 G10
Pont Corn 6 E2
Pont Aber Carms 94 G4
Pont Aber-Geirw Gwyn 146 D5
Pontamman Carms 75 C10
Pontantwn Carms 74 C6
Pontardawe Neath 76 E2
Pontarddulais Swansea 75 E9
Pontarfynach / Devils Bridge Ceredig 112 B4
Pont-ar-gothi Carms 93 G10
Pont ar Hydfer Powys 95 F7
Pont-ar-llechau Carms 94 G4
Pontarsais Carms 93 F8
Pontblyddyn Flint 166 C3
Pontbren Araeth Carms 94 G3
Pontbren Llwyd Rhondda 76 D6
Pontcanna Cardiff 59 D7
Pont Cyfyng Conwy 164 D2
Pont Cysyllte Wrex 166 G3
Pontdolgoch Powys 129 E10
Pont Dolydd Prysor Gwyn 146 B4
Pontefract W Yorks 198 C3
Ponteland Northumb 242 C5
Ponterwyd Ceredig 128 G4
Pontesbury Shrops 131 B7
Pontesbury Hill Shrops 131 B7
Pontesford Shrops 131 B8
Pontfadog Wrex 148 B4
Pontfaen Pembs 91 E10
Pont-faen Powys 95 E9
Shrops 148 B5
Pont Fronwydd Gwyn 146 E6
Pont-gareg Pembs 92 C2
Pontgarreg Ceredig 110 G6
Ponthen Shrops 148 F6
Pont-Henri Carms 75 D7
Ponthir Torf 78 G4
Ponthirwaun Ceredig 92 B5
Pont Hwfa Anglesey 178 E2
Pontiago Pembs 91 D8
Pont iets / Pontyates Carms 75 D7
Pontithel Powys 96 D3
Pontllanfraith Caerph 77 F11
Pontlliw Swansea 75 E10
Pont-Llogel Powys 147 F10
Pontllyfni Gwyn 162 E6
Pontlottyn Caerph 77 D10
Pontneddfechan Powys 76 D6
Pontnewydd Torf 78 F3
Pont-newydd Carms 74 D6
Flint 165 B11
Pontnewynydd Torf 78 E3
Pont Pen-y-benglog Gwyn 163 C10
Pontrhydfendigaid Ceredig 112 D4
Pont Rhydgaled Powys 128 G6
Pont Rhyd-goch Conwy 163 C11
Pont-Rhyd-sarn Gwyn 147 D7
Pont Rhyd-y-berry Powys 95 D9
Pont Rhyd-y-cyff Bridgend 57 D11
Pontrhydyfen Neath 57 C9
Pont-rhyd-y-groes Ceredig 112 C4
Pontrhydyrun Torf 78 F3
Pont-Rhythallt Gwyn 163 C8
Pontrilas Hereford 97 F7
Pontrobert Powys 148 G2
Pont-rug Gwyn 163 C8
Pont Senni / Sennybridge Powys 95 F8
Ponts Green E Sus 23 B11
Pontshill Hereford 98 G2
Pont-siôn Ceredig 93 B8
Pont Siôn Norton Rhondda 77 G9
Pontsticill M Tydf 77 C9
Pont-Walby Neath 76 D5
Pontwgan Conwy 180 G3
Pontyates / Pont-iets Carms 75 D7
Pontyberem Carms 75 C8
Pont-y-blew Shrops 148 B6
Pontyclun Rhondda 58 C4
Pontycymer Bridgend 76 G6
Pontyglasier Pembs 92 D2
Pont-y-gwaith Rhondda 77 G8
Pontymister Caerph 78 G2
Pontymoel Torf 78 E3
Pont-y-pant Conwy 164 E3
Pont y Pennant Gwyn 147 E8
Pontypool Torf 78 E3
Pontypridd Rhondda 58 B5
Pont yr Afon-Gam Gwyn 164 G2
Pont-yr-hafod Pembs 91 F8
Pont-y-rhyl Bridgend 58 B2
Pont-Ystrad Denb 165 C9
Pont-y-wal Powys 96 D2
Pontywaun Caerph 78 G2
Pooksgreen Hants 32 E5
Pool Corn 4 G3
W Yorks 205 D10
Poolbrook Worcs 98 C5
Poole N Yorks 198 B3
Poole 18 C6
Som 27 C10
Poole Keynes Glos 81 F8
Poolend Staffs 169 D7
Poolestown Dorset 30 D2
Poolewe Highld 307 L3
Pooley Bridge Cumb 230 G5
Pooley Street Norf 141 G11
Poolfold Staffs 168 D5
Poolhead Shrops 149 C9
Pool Head Hereford 115 G11
Pool Hey Lancs 193 D11
Poolhill Glos 98 F4
Poolmill Hereford 97 G11
Pool o' Muckhart Clack 286 G4
Pool Quay Powys 148 G5
Poolsbrook Derbys 186 G6
Poolside Moray 302 E4
Poolstock Gtr Man 194 G5
Pooltown Som 42 F3
Pootings Kent 52 D3
Pope Hill Pembs 72 C6
Pope's Hill Glos 79 C11
Popeswood Brack 65 F10
Popham Devon 41 G8
Hants 48 E5
Poplar London 67 C11
Poplar Grove Lincs 190 B6
Poplars Herts 104 G5
Popley Hants 48 C6
Porchester Nottingham 171 G9
Porchfield IoW 20 C4
Porin Highld 300 D3
Poringland Norf 142 C5
Porkellis Corn 2 C5
Porlock Som 41 D11
Porlockford Som 41 D11
Porlock Weir Som 41 D11
Portachoillan Argyll 255 B8
Port Allen Perth 286 E6
Port Ann Argyll 275 E10
Port Appin Argyll 289 E11
Port Arthur Shetland 313 K5
Portash Wilts 46 G3
Port Askaig Argyll 274 G5
Portavadie Argyll 275 G10
Port Bannatyne Argyll 275 G11
Port Brae Fife 280 C5
Port Bridge Devon 9 D7
Portbury N Som 60 D4
Port Carlisle Cumb 238 E6
Port Charlotte Argyll 254 B3
Portchester Hants 33 F10
Portclair Highld 290 B6
Port Clarence Stockton 234 G5
Port Dinorwic / Y Felinheli Gwyn 163 B8
Port Driseach Argyll 275 F10
Port Dundas Glasgow 267 B11
Porteath Corn 10 F5
Port Edgar Edin 280 F2
Port Ellen Argyll 254 C4
Port Elphinstone Aberds 293 B9
Portencalzie Dumfries 236 B2
Portencross N Ayrs 266 F3
Porterfield Renfs 267 B9
Port Erin IoM 192 F2
Port Erroll Aberds 303 F10
Porter's End Herts 85 B11
Portesham Dorset 17 D8
Portessie Moray 302 C4
Port e Vullen IoM 192 C5
Port-Eynon Swansea 56 D3
Portfield Argyll 289 G9
Som 28 B6
W Sus 22 B5
Portfield Gate Pembs 72 B6
Portgate Devon 12 D4
Port Gaverne Corn 10 E6
Port Glasgow Invclyd 276 G6
Portgordon Moray 302 C3
Portgower Highld 311 H4
Porth Corn 4 C6
Rhondda 77 G8
Porthallow Corn 3 E7
Corn 6 E4
Porthcawl Bridgend 57 F10
Porth Colmon Gwyn 144 C3
Porthcothan Corn 10 G3
Porthcurno Corn 1 E3
Portheiddy Pembs 90 E6
Port Henderson Highld 299 B7
Porthgain Pembs 90 E6
Porthgwarra Corn 1 E3
Porthhallow Corn 3 E7
Porthill Shrops 149 G9
Staffs 168 F5
Port Hill Oxon 65 B7
Porthilly Corn 10 F4
Porth Kea Corn 4 G6
Porthkerry V Glam 58 F5
Porthleven Corn 2 D4
Porthllechog / Bull Bay Anglesey 178 C6
Porthloo Scilly 1 G4
Porthmadog Gwyn 145 B11
Porthmeor Corn 1 B4
Porth Navas Corn 3 D7
Porthoustock Corn 3 E8
Porthpean Corn 5 E10
Porthtowan Corn 4 F3
Porth Tywyn / Burry Port Carms 74 E6
Porth-y-felin Anglesey 178 E2
Porthyrhyd Carms 75 B8
Carms 94 D4
Porth-y-waen Shrops 148 E5
Portico Mers 183 C7
Portincaple Argyll 276 C4
Portington Devon 12 F4
E Yorks 207 G11
Portinnisherrich Argyll 275 B10
Portinscale Cumb 229 G11
Port Isaac Corn 10 E5
Portishead N Som 60 D3
Portkil Argyll 276 E5
Portknockie Moray 302 C4
Port Lamont Argyll 275 F11
Portland Som 44 F3
Portlethen Aberds 293 D11
Portlethen Village Aberds 293 D11
Portlevorchy Highld 306 D7
Portling Dumfries 237 D10
Port Lion Pembs 73 D7
Portloe Corn 3 B10
Port Logan Dumfries 236 E2
Portlooe Corn 6 E4
Portmahomack Highld 311 L3
Port Mead Swansea 56 B6
Portmeirion Gwyn 145 B11
Portmellon Corn 5 G10
Port Mholair W Isles 304 E7
Port Mor Highld 288 B6
Portmore Hants 20 B2
Port Mulgrave N Yorks 226 B5
Portnacroish Argyll 289 E11
Portnahaven Argyll 254 B2
Portnalong Highld 294 B5
Portnaluchaig Highld 295 G8
Portnancon Highld 308 C4
Port Nan Giùran W Isles 304 E7
Port nan Long W Isles 296 D4
Portnellan Stirling 285 E8
Stirling 285 F8
Port Nis W Isles 304 B7
Portobello Edin 280 G6
T&W 243 F7
W Mid 133 D9
W Yorks 197 D10
Port of Menteith Stirling 285 G9
Porton Wilts 47 F7
Portpatrick Dumfries 236 D2
Port Quin Corn 10 E5
Portrack Stockton 225 B9
Port Ramsay Argyll 289 E10
Portreath Corn 4 F3
Portree Highld 298 E4
Port St Mary IoM 192 F3
Portscatho Corn 3 B9
Portsea Ptsmth 33 G10
Portsea Island Ptsmth 33 G11
Portskerra Highld 310 C2
Portskewett Mon 60 B4
Portslade Brighton 36 F3
Portslade-by-Sea Brighton 36 G3
Portslade Village Brighton 36 F3
Portsmouth Ptsmth 21 B9
W Yorks 196 B2
Port Solent Ptsmth 33 F10
Portsonachan Argyll 284 E4
Portsoy Aberds 302 C5
Port Sunlight Mers 182 E4
Port Sutton Bridge Lincs 157 E9
Portswood Soton 32 E6
Port Talbot Neath 57 D9
Porttanachy Moray 302 C3
Port Tennant Swansea 57 C7
Portuairk Highld 288 C6
Portvasgo Highld 308 C5
Portway Dorset 18 D2
Glos 98 E5
Hereford 97 B9
Hereford 97 D9
Som 28 B6
Som 44 F3
W Mid 133 F9
Worcs 117 C11
Port Wemyss Argyll 254 B2
Port William Dumfries 236 E5
Portwood Gtr Man 184 C6
Portwrinkle Corn 7 E7
Posenhall Shrops 132 C3
Poslingford Suff 106 B5
Posso Borders 260 C6
Postbridge Devon 13 F9
Postcombe Oxon 84 F2
Post Green Dorset 18 C5
Postling Kent 54 F6
Postlip Glos 99 F10
Post Mawr / Synod Inn Ceredig 111 G8
Postwick Norf 142 B5
Potarch Aberds 293 D8
Potash Suff 108 D2
Potbridge Hants 49 C8
Pot Common Sur 50 E2
Potholm Dumfries 249 F9
Potmaily Highld 300 F4
Potman's Heath Kent 38 B5
Potsgrove C Beds 103 F9
Potten End Herts 85 D8
Potten Street Kent 71 F9
Potter Brompton N Yorks 217 D9
Pottergate Street Norf 142 E3
Potterhanworth Lincs 173 B9
Potterhanworth Booths Lincs 173 B9
Potter Heigham Norf 161 F8
Potter Hill Leics 154 E4
S Yorks 186 B4
Potterne Wilts 46 B3
Potterne Wick Wilts 46 B4
Potternewton W Yorks 206 F2
Potters Bar Herts 86 E3
Potters Brook Lancs 202 C5
Potters Corner Kent 54 E3
Potter's Cross Staffs 132 G6
Potters Crouch Herts 85 D10
Potter's Forstal Kent 53 D11
Potter's Green E Sus 37 C8
W Mid 135 G7
Pottersheath Herts 86 B2
Potters Hill N Som 60 F4
Potters Marston Leics 135 D9
Potter Somersal Derbys 152 B2
Potterspury Northants 102 C5
Potter Street Essex 87 D7
Potterton Aberds 293 B11
W Yorks 206 F4
Pottery Field W Yorks 206 G2
Potthorpe Norf 159 E8
Pottington Devon 40 G5
Potto N Yorks 225 E9
Potton C Beds 104 B4
Pott Row Norf 158 E4
Pott Shrigley Ches E 184 F6
Pouchen End Herts 85 D8
Poughill Corn 24 F2
Devon 26 F5
Poulner Hants 31 F11
Poulshot Wilts 46 B3
Poulton Ches W 166 D5
Glos 81 E10
Mers 182 C4
Mers 182 E4
Poulton-le-Fylde Lancs 202 F2
Pound Som 28 D6
Pound Bank Worcs 98 B5
Worcs 116 C4
Poundbury Dorset 17 C9
Poundffald Swansea 56 C5
Poundfield E Sus 52 G4
Poundford E Sus 37 C9
Poundgate E Sus 37 B7
Poundgreen Wokingham 65 F7
Pound Green E Sus 37 C8
Hants 48 B5
IoW 20 D2
Suff 124 G4
Worcs 116 B5
Pound Hill W Sus 51 F9
Poundland S Ayrs 244 F5
Poundon Bucks 102 F2
Poundsbridge Kent 52 E4
Poundsgate Devon 13 G10
Poundstock Corn 11 B10
Pound Street Hants 64 G3
Pounsley E Sus 37 C8
Poverest London 68 F3
Povey Cross Sur 51 E9
Powburn Northumb 264 F3
Powderham Devon 14 E5
Powder Mills Kent 52 D5
Powers Hall End Essex 88 B4
Powerstock Dorset 16 B6
Powfoot Dumfries 238 D4
Pow Green Hereford 98 C4
Powhill Cumb 238 F6
Powick Worcs 116 G6
Powler's Piece Devon 24 D5
Powmill Perth 279 B10
Pownall Park Ches E 184 E4
Powntley Copse Hants 49 E8
Poxwell Dorset 17 E10
Poyle Slough 66 D4
Poynings W Sus 36 E3
Poyntington Dorset 29 D11
Poynton Ches E 184 E6
Telford 149 F11
Poynton Green Telford 149 F11
Poyntzfield Highld 301 C7
Poyston Pembs 73 B7
Poyston Cross Pembs 73 B7
Poystreet Green Suff 125 F9
Praa Sands Corn 2 D3
Pratling Street Kent 53 B8
Pratt's Bottom London 68 G3
Praze Corn 2 B3
Praze-an-Beeble Corn 2 B4
Predannack Wollas Corn 2 F5
Prees Shrops 149 C11
Preesall Lancs 202 D3
Preesall Park Lancs 202 D3
Prees Green Shrops 149 C11
Preesgweene Shrops 148 B5
Prees Heath Shrops 149 B11
Preeshenlle Shrops 148 C6
Prees Higher Heath Shrops 149 B11
Prees Lower Heath Shrops 149 C11
Prees Wood Shrops 149 C11
Prenbrigog Flint 166 C3
Prendergast Pembs 73 B7
Pembs 90 G6
Prenderguest Borders 273 D8
Prendwick Northumb 264 G2
Pren-gwyn Ceredig 93 C8
Prenteg Gwyn 163 G9
Prenton Mers 182 D4
Prescot Mers 183 C7
Prescott Devon 27 E9
Glos 99 F9
Shrops 132 G3
Shrops 149 E8
Presdales Herts 86 C5
Preshome Moray 302 C4
Press Derbys 170 B5
Pressen Northumb 263 B8
Prestatyn Denb 181 E9
Prestbury Ches E 184 F6
Glos 99 G9
Presteigne Powys 114 E6
Presthope Shrops 131 D11
Prestleigh Som 44 E6
Prestolee Gtr Man 195 F9
Preston Borders 272 D5
Brighton 36 F4
Devon 14 G3
Dorset 17 E10
E Loth 281 F11
E Loth 281 G7
E Yorks 209 G9
Glos 81 E8
Glos 98 E3
Herts 104 G3
Kent 70 G4
Kent 71 G8
Lancs 194 B4
London 67 B7
Northumb 264 D5
Rutland 137 C7
Shrops 149 G10
Torbay 9 C7
T&W 243 D8
Wilts 62 D4
Wilts 63 E9
Preston Bagot Warks 118 D3
Preston Bissett Bucks 102 F3
Preston Bowyer Som 27 B10
Preston Brockhurst Shrops 149 E10
Preston Brook Halton 183 E9
Preston Candover Hants 48 E6
Preston Capes Northants 119 G11
Preston Crowmarsh Oxon 83 G10
Preston Deanery Northants 120 F5
Prestonfield Edin 280 G5
Preston Fields Warks 118 D3
Preston Grange T&W 243 C8
Preston Green Warks 118 D3
Preston Gubbals Shrops 149 F9
Preston-le-Skerne Durham 234 G2
Preston Marsh Hereford 97 B11
Prestonmill Dumfries 237 D11
Preston Montford Shrops 149 G8
Preston on Stour Warks 118 G4
Preston-on-Tees Stockton 225 B8
Preston on the Hill Halton 183 E9
Preston on Wye Hereford 97 C7
Prestonpans E Loth 281 G7
Preston Pastures Worcs 100 B3
Preston Plucknett Som 29 D8
Preston St Mary Suff 125 G8
Preston-under-Scar N Yorks 223 G11
Preston upon the Weald Moors Telford 150 F3
Preston Wynne Hereford 97 B11
Prestwich Gtr Man 195 G10
Prestwick Northumb 242 C5
S Ayrs 257 D9
Prestwold Leics 153 E11
Prestwood Bucks 84 E5
Staffs 133 F7
Staffs 169 G10
Prey Heath Sur 50 B3
Price Town Bridgend 76 G6
Prickwillow Cambs 139 G11
Priddy Som 44 C4
Pride Park Derbys 153 B7
Priestacott Devon 24 F6
Priestcliffe Derbys 185 G10
Priestcliffe Ditch Derbys 185 G10
Priest Down Bath 60 G6
Priestfield W Mid 133 D8
Worcs 98 C6
Priesthaugh Borders 249 C11
Priesthill Glasgow 267 C10
Priesthorpe W Yorks 205 F10
Priest Hutton Lancs 211 E10
Priestley Green W Yorks 196 B6
Prieston Borders 262 D2
Priestside Dumfries 238 D4
Priestthorpe W Yorks 205 F8
Priest Weston Shrops 130 D5
Priestwood Brack 65 F11
Kent 69 G7
Priestwood Green Kent 69 G7
Primethorpe Leics 135 E10
Primrose T&W 243 E8
Primrose Corner Norf 160 G6
Primrose Green Norf 159 F11
Primrosehill Herts 85 E9
Primrose Hill Bath 61 F8
Lancs 193 F11
London 67 C9
W Mid 133 F8
Primrose Valley N Yorks 218 D2
Primsland Worcs 117 E8
Prince Hill Ches E 168 G2
Prince Royd W Yorks 196 D6
Princes End W Mid 133 E9
Princes Gate Pembs 73 C10
Prince's Marsh Hants 34 B3
Princes Park Mers 182 D5
Princes Risborough Bucks 84 E4
Princethorpe Warks 119 C8
Princetown Caerph 77 C10
Devon 13 G7
Prinsted W Sus 22 B3
Printstile Kent 52 E5
Prion Denb 165 C9
Prior Muir Fife 287 F9
Prior Park Northumb 273 E9
Prior Rigg Cumb 239 D11
Priors Frome Hereford 97 D11
Priors Halton Shrops 115 B9
Priors Hardwick Warks 119 F9
Priorslee Telford 150 G4
Priors Marston Warks 119 F9
Prior's Norton Glos 99 G7
Priors Park Glos 99 E7
Priorswood Som 28 B2
Priory Pembs 72 D6
Priory Green Suff 107 C8
Priory Heath Suff 108 C3
Priory Wood Hereford 96 B5
Prisk V Glam 58 D4
Pristacott Devon 25 B8
Priston Bath 61 G7
Pristow Green Norf 142 F2
Prittlewell Southend 69 B11
Privett Hants 21 B7
Hants 33 B11
Prixford Devon 40 F4
Probus Corn 5 F7
Proncy Highld 309 K7
Prospect Cumb 229 C8
Prospect Village Staffs 151 G10
Prospidnick Corn 2 C4
Provanmill Glasgow 268 B2
Prowse Devon 26 F4
Prudhoe Northumb 242 E3
Prussia Cove Corn 2 D3
Ptarmigan Lodge Stirling 285 G7
Pubil Perth 285 C8
Publow Bath 60 G6
Puckeridge Herts 105 G7
Puckington Som 28 D5
Pucklechurch S Glos 61 D7
Pucknall Hants 32 B5
Puckrup Glos 99 D7
Puckshole Glos 80 D4
Puddaven Devon 8 C5
Puddinglake Ches W 168 B2
Pudding Pie Nook Lancs 202 F6
Puddington Ches W 182 G4
Devon 26 E4
Puddle Corn 5 D11
Puddlebridge Som 28 E4
Puddledock Kent 52 C3
Kent 68 E4
Norf 141 E11
Puddletown Dorset 17 C11
Pudleigh Som 28 E4
Pudleston Hereford 115 F11
Pudsey W Yorks 196 B2
W Yorks 205 G10
Pulborough W Sus 35 D8
Pulcree Dumfries 237 D7
Pule Hill W Yorks 196 B5
Puleston Telford 150 E4
Pulford Ches W 166 D5
Pulham Dorset 30 F2
Pulham Market Norf 142 F3
Pulham St Mary Norf 142 F4
Pullens Green S Glos 79 G10
Pulley Shrops 131 B9
Pullington Kent 53 G10
Pulloxhill C Beds 103 E11
Pulverbatch Shrops 131 C8
Pumpherston W Loth 269 B11
Pumsaint Carms 94 C3
Puncheston / Cas-Mael Pembs 91 F10
Puncknowle Dorset 16 D6
Punnett's Town E Sus 37 C10
Purbrook Hants 33 F11
Purewell Dorset 19 C9
Purfleet Thurrock 68 D5
Puriton Som 43 E10
Purleigh Essex 88 E4
Purley London 67 G10
Purley on Thames W Berks 65 D7
Purlogue Shrops 114 B5
Purlpit Wilts 61 F11
Purls Bridge Cambs 139 F9
Purn N Som 43 B10
Purse Caundle Dorset 29 D11
Purslow Shrops 131 G7
Purston Jaglin W Yorks 198 D2
Purtington Som 28 F5
Purton Glos 79 E11
W Berks 64 D3
Wilts 62 B5
Purton Common Wilts 62 B5
Purton Stoke Wilts 81 G9
Purwell Herts 104 F4
Pury End Northants 102 B4
Pusey Oxon 82 F5
Putley Hereford 98 D2
Putley Common Hereford 98 D2
Putley Green Hereford 98 D3
Putloe Glos 80 D3
Putney London 67 D8
Putney Heath London 67 E8
Putney Vale London 67 E8
Putnoe Bedford 121 G11
Putsborough Devon 40 E3
Putson Hereford 97 D10
Puttenham Herts 84 C5
Sur 50 D2
Puttock End Essex 106 C6
Puttock's End Essex 87 B9
Putton Dorset 17 E9
Puxey Dorset 30 E3
Puxley Northants 102 C5
Puxton N Som 60 G2
Pwll Carms 75 E7
Powys 130 C3
Pwll-clai Flint 181 G11
Pwllcrochan Pembs 72 E6
Pwll-glas Denb 165 E10
Pwllgloyw Powys 95 E10
Pwllheli Gwyn 145 B7
Pwll-Mawr Cardiff 59 D8
Pwll-melyn Flint 181 G11
Pwllmeyric Mon 79 G8
Pwll-trap Carms 74 B3
Pwll-y-glaw Neath 57 C9
Pwllypant Caerph 59 B7
Pye Bridge Derbys 170 E6
Pyecombe W Sus 36 E3
Pye Corner Devon 14 B4
Kent 53 D11
Newport 59 B9
S Glos 60 D6
Pye Green Staffs 151 G9
Pye Hill Notts 170 E6
Pyewipe NE Lincs 201 E9
Pyle IoW 20 F5
Swansea 56 D5
Pylehill Hants 33 D7
Pyle Hill Sur 50 B3
Pyleigh Som 42 G6
Pyle / Y Pîl Bridgend 57 E10
Pylle Som 44 F6
Pymore or Pymoor Cambs 139 F9
Pype Hayes W Mid 134 E2
Pyrford Sur 50 B4
Pyrford Green Sur 50 B4
Pyrford Village Sur 50 B4
Pyrland Som 28 B2
Pyrton Oxon 83 F11
Pytchley Northants 121 C7
Pyworthy Devon 24 G4

Q

Quabbs Shrops 130 G4
Quabrook E Sus 52 G2
Quadring Lincs 156 C4
Quadring Eaudike Lincs 156 C4
Quags Corner W Sus 34 C5
Quainton Bucks 84 B2
Quaker's Yard M Tydf 77 F9
Quaking Houses Durham 242 G5
Quality Corner Cumb 219 B9
Quarhouse Glos 80 E5
Quarley Hants 47 E9
Quarmby W Yorks 196 D6
Quarndon Derbys 170 G4
Quarndon Common Derbys 170 G4
Quarrelton Renfs 267 C8
Quarrendon Bucks 84 B4
Quarr Hill IoW 21 C7
Quarriers Village Invclyd 267 B7
Quarrington Lincs 173 G9
Quarrington Hill Durham 234 D2
Quarrybank Ches W 167 B8
Quarry Bank W Mid 133 F8
Quarryford E Loth 271 B11
Quarryhead Aberds 303 C9
Quarry Heath Staffs 151 G8
Quarryhill Highld 309 L7
Quarry Hill Staffs 134 C4
Quarrywood Moray 301 C11
Quarter S Lanark 268 E4
Quartley Devon 27 B7
Quatford Shrops 132 E4
Quatquoy Orkney 314 E3
Quatt Shrops 132 F5
Quebec Durham 233 C9
W Sus 34 C3
Quedgeley Glos 80 C4
Queen Adelaide Cambs 139 G11
Queenborough Kent 70 E2
Queen Camel Som 29 C9
Queen Charlton Bath 60 F6
Queen Dart Devon 26 D4
Queenhill Worcs 99 D7
Queen Oak Dorset 45 G9
Queen's Bower IoW 21 E7
Queensbury London 67 B7
W Yorks 205 G8
Queen's Corner W Sus 34 B5
Queensferry Edin 280 F2
Flint 166 B4
Queen's Head Shrops 148 D6
Queenslie Glasgow 268 B3
Queen's Park Bedford 103 B10
Blackburn 195 B7
Ches W 166 B6
Essex 87 F11
Northants 120 E5
Queenstown Blackpool 202 F2
Queen Street Kent 53 D7
Wilts 62 B4
Queensville Staffs 151 E8
Queenzieburn N Lanark 278 F3
Quemerford Wilts 62 F4
Quendale Shetland 313 M5
Quendon Essex 105 E10
Queniborough Leics 154 G2
Quenington Glos 81 E10
Quernmore Lancs 202 B6
Queslett W Mid 133 E11
Quethiock Corn 6 C6
Quhamm Shetland 312 G6
Quholm Orkney 314 E2
Quick Gtr Man 196 G3
Quick Edge Gtr Man 196 G3
Quicks Green W Berks 64 D5
Quidenham Norf 141 F10
Quidhampton Hants 48 C4
Wilts 46 G6
Quilquox Aberds 303 F9
Quina Brook Shrops 149 C10
Quinbury End Northants 120 G2
Quindry Orkney 314 G4
Quinton Northants 120 G5
W Mid 133 G9
Quintrell Downs Corn 5 C7
Quixhill Staffs 169 G10
Quoditch Devon 12 B4
Quoig Perth 286 E2
Quoisley Ches E 167 F8
Quoit Corn 5 C8
Quorndon or Quorn Leics 153 F11
Quothquan S Lanark 259 B11
Quoyloo Orkney 314 D2
Quoynee Highld 310 D6
Quoyness Orkney 314 F2
Quoys Shetland 312 B8
Shetland 313 G6

R

Raasay Ho Highld 295 B7
Rabbit's Cross Kent 53 D9
Rableyheath Herts 86 B2
Raby Cumb 238 G5
Mers 182 F4
Racecourse Suff 108 C3
Racedown Hants 47 E9
Rachan Mill Borders 260 C4
Rachub Gwyn 163 B10
Rack End Oxon 82 E6
Rackenford Devon 26 D5
Rackham W Sus 35 E9
Rackheath Norf 160 G5
Rackley Som 43 C11
Racks Dumfries 238 C2
Rackwick Orkney 314 B4
Orkney 314 G2
Radbourne Derbys 152 B5
Radcliffe Gtr Man 195 F9
Northumb 253 C7
Radcliffe on Trent Notts 154 B2
Radclive Bucks 102 E3
Radcot Oxon 82 F3
Raddery Highld 301 D7
Raddington Som 27 B8
Raddon Devon 26 G6
Radernie Fife 287 G8
Radfall Kent 70 G6
Radfield Kent 70 G2
Radford Bath 45 B7
Nottingham 171 G9
Oxon 101 G8
W Mid 134 G6
Worcs 117 F10
Radfordbridge Oxon 101 G8
Radford Semele Warks 118 E6
Radipole Dorset 17 E9
Radlet Som 43 F8
Radlett Herts 85 F11
Radley Oxon 83 F8
Radley Green Essex 87 D10
Radley Park Oxon 83 F8
Radlith Shrops 131 B8
Radmanthwaite Notts 171 C8
Radmoor Shrops 150 E2
Radmore Green Ches E 167 D9
Radmore Wood Staffs 151 D11
Radnage Bucks 84 F3
Radnor Corn 4 G4
Radnor Park W Dunb 277 G9
Radstock Bath 45 C7
Radstone Northants 101 C11
Radway Warks 101 B7
Radway Green Ches E 168 E3
Radwell Bedford 121 F10
Herts 104 D4
Radwinter Essex 106 D2
Radwinter End Essex 106 D2
Radyr Cardiff 58 C6
Raehills Dumfries 248 E3
Raera Argyll 289 G10
Rafborough Hants 49 B11
Rafford Moray 301 D10
Raga Shetland 312 D6
Ragdale Leics 154 F3
Ragdon Shrops 131 E9
Raggalds W Yorks 205 G7
Ragged Appleshaw Hants 47 D10
Raginnis Corn 1 D5
Raglan Mon 78 D6
Ragmere Norf 141 E11
Ragnal Wilts 63 E10
Ragnall Notts 188 G4
Rahane Argyll 276 D4
Rahoy Highld 289 D8
Raigbeg Highld 301 G8
Rails S Yorks 186 D3
Rainbow Hill Worcs 117 F7
Rainford Mers 194 G3
Rainford Junction Mers 194 G3
Rainham London 68 C4
Medway 69 F10
Rainhill Mers 183 C7
Rainhill Stoops Mers 183 C8
Rainow Ches E 185 F7
Rainowlow Ches E 185 F7
Rain Shore Gtr Man 195 D11
Rainsough Gtr Man 195 G10
Rainton Dumfries 237 D8
N Yorks 215 D7
Rainton Bridge T&W 234 B2
Rainton Gate Durham 234 B2
Rainworth Notts 171 D9
Raisbeck Cumb 222 D2
Raise Cumb 231 B10
Rait Perth 286 E6
Raithby Lincs 190 E4
Raithby by Spilsby Lincs 174 B5
Rake W Sus 34 B4
Rake Common Hants 34 B3
Rake End Staffs 151 F11
Rake Head Lancs 195 C10
Rakes Dale Staffs 169 G9
Rakeway Staffs 169 G8
Rakewood Gtr Man 196 E2
Raleigh Devon 40 G5
Ralia Lodge Highld 291 D9
Rallt Swansea 56 C4
Ram Carms 93 B11
Ram Alley Wilts 63 G8
Ramasaig Highld 297 G7
Rame Corn 2 C6
Corn 7 F8
Rameldry Mill Bank Fife 287 G7
Ram Hill S Glos 61 D7
Ram Lane Kent 54 D3
Ramnageo Shetland 312 C8
Rampisham Dorset 29 G9
Rampside Cumb 210 F4
Rampton Cambs 123 D8
Notts 188 F3
Ramsbottom Gtr Man 195 D9
Ramsburn Moray 302 D5
Ramsbury Wilts 63 E9
Ramscraigs Highld 311 G5
Ramsdean Hants 34 C2
Ramsdell Hants 48 B5
Ramsden London 68 F3
Oxon 82 B5
Worcs 99 B8
Ramsden Bellhouse Essex 88 G2
Ramsden Heath Essex 88 F2
Ramsden Wood W Yorks 196 C2
Ramsey Cambs 138 F5
Essex 108 E4
IoM 192 C5
Ramseycleuch Borders 261 G7
Ramsey Forty Foot Cambs 138 F6
Ramsey Heights Cambs 138 F5
Ramsey Island Essex 89 D7
Ramsey Mereside Cambs 138 F5
Ramsey St Mary's Cambs 138 F5
Ramsgate Kent 71 G11
Ramsgill N Yorks 214 E2
Ramshaw Durham 232 B5
Durham 233 F8
Ramsholt Suff 108 C6
Ramshorn Staffs 169 F9
Ramsley Devon 13 C8
Ramslye Kent 52 F5
Ramsnest Common Sur 50 G2
Ranais W Isles 304 F6
Ranby Lincs 190 F2
Notts 187 E11
Rand Lincs 189 F10
Randwick Glos 80 D4
Ranfurly Renfs 267 C7
Rangag Highld 310 E5
Rangemore Staffs 152 E3
Rangeworthy S Glos 61 B7
Rankinston E Ayrs 257 G11
Rank's Green Essex 88 B3
Ranmoor S Yorks 186 D4
Ranmore Common Sur 50 C6
Rannerdale Cumb 220 B3
Rannoch Lodge Perth 285 B9
Rannoch Station Perth 285 B8
Ranochan Highld 295 G10
Ranskill Notts 187 D11
Ranton Staffs 151 E7
Ranton Green Staffs 150 E6
Ranworth Norf 161 G7
Rapkyns W Sus 50 G6
Raploch Stirling 278 C5
Rapness Orkney 314 B5
Rapps Som 28 D4
Rascal Moor E Yorks 208 F2
Rascarrel Dumfries 237 E9
Rashielee Renfs 277 G9
Rashiereive Aberds 303 G9
Rashwood Worcs 117 D8
Raskelf N Yorks 215 E9
Rassal Highld 299 E8
Rassau Bl Gwent 77 C11
Rastrick W Yorks 196 C6
Ratagan Highld 295 D11
Ratby Leics 135 B10
Ratcliff London 67 C11
Ratcliffe Culey Leics 134 D6
Ratcliffe on Soar Leics 153 D9
Ratcliffe on the Wreake Leics 154 G2
Ratford Wilts 62 E3
Ratfyn Wilts 47 E7
Rathen Aberds 303 C10
Rathillet Fife 287 E7
Rathmell N Yorks 204 B2
Ratho Edin 280 G2
Ratho Station Edin 280 G2
Rathven Moray 302 C4
Ratlake Hants 32 C6
Ratley Warks 101 B7
Ratling Kent 55 C8
Ratlinghope Shrops 131 D8
Ratsloe Devon 14 B5
Rattar Highld 310 B6
Ratten Row Cumb 230 B3
Cumb 230 C2
Lancs 202 E4
Norf 157 G10
Rattery Devon 8 C4
Rattlesden Suff 125 F9
Rattray Perth 286 C5
Raughton Cumb 230 B3
Raughton Head Cumb 230 B3
Raunds Northants 121 C9
Ravelston Edin 280 G4
Ravenfield S Yorks 187 B7
Ravenglass Cumb 219 F11
Ravenhead Mers 183 C8
Ravenhills Green Worcs 116 G4
Raveningham Norf 143 D7
Ravenscar N Yorks 227 E9
Ravenscliffe Stoke 168 E4
W Yorks 205 F9
Ravenscraig Invclyd 276 F5
Ravensdale IoM 192 C4
Ravensden Bedford 121 G11
Ravenseat N Yorks 223 E7
Raven's Green Essex 108 G2
Ravenshall Staffs 168 F3
Ravenshead Notts 171 E9
Ravensmoor Ches E 167 E10
Ravensthorpe Northants 120 C3
Pboro 138 C3

Ravensthorpe continued
W Yorks 197 C8
Ravenstone Leics 153 G8
M Keynes 120 G6
Ravenstonedale Cumb . . 222 E4
Ravenstown Cumb 211 D7
Ravenstruther S Lanark . 269 F8
Ravenswood Village
Settlement Wokingham . 65 G10
Ravensworth N Yorks . . 224 D2
Raw N Yorks 227 D8
Rawcliffe E Yorks 199 C7
York 207 C7
Rawcliffe Bridge
E Yorks 199 C7
Rawdon W Yorks 205 F10
Rawdon Carrs W Yorks . 205 F10
Rawfolds W Yorks 197 C7
Rawgreen Northumb . . . 241 F10
Raw Green S Yorks 197 F9
Rawmarsh S Yorks 186 B6
Rawnsley Staffs 151 G10
Rawreth Essex 88 G3
Rawreth Shot Essex 88 G3
Rawridge Devon 28 F2
Rawyards N Lanark 268 B5
Raxton Aberds 303 F8
Raydon Suff 107 D11
Raygill N Yorks 204 D4
Raylees Northumb 251 E10
Rayleigh Essex 88 G4
Rayne Essex 106 G4
Rayners Lane London 66 B6
Raynes Park London 67 F8
Reabrook Shrops 131 C7
Reach Cambs 123 D11
Read Lancs 203 G11
Reader's Corner Essex . . 88 E2
Reading Reading 65 E8
Readings Glos 79 B10
Reading Street Kent 54 G2
Kent 71 F11
Readymoney Corn 6 E2
Ready Token Glos 81 E10
Reagill Cumb 222 B2
Rearquhar Highld 309 K7
Rearsby Leics 154 G3
Reasby Lincs 189 F9
Rease Heath Ches E . . . 167 E10
Reaster Highld 310 C6
Reaulay Highld 299 D7
Reawick Shetland 313 J5
Reawla Corn 2 B4
Reay Highld 310 C3
Rechullin Highld 299 D8
Reculver Kent 71 F8
Red Ball Devon 27 D9
Redberth Pembs 73 E9
Redbourn Herts 85 C10
Redbournbury Herts 85 C10
Redbourne N Lincs 189 B7
N Lincs 200 G3
Redbridge Dorset 17 D11
London 68 B2
Soton 32 E5
Red Bridge Lancs 211 D9
Red Bull Ches E 168 D4
Staffs 150 B4
Redburn Highld 301 E9
Highld 301 E9
Northumb 241 E7
Redcar Redcar 235 G8
Redcastle Angus 287 B10
Highld 300 E5
Redcliff Bay N Som 60 D2
Redcroft Dumfries 237 B9
Redcross Worcs 117 C7
Red Dial Cumb 229 B11
Reddicap Heath W Mid . 134 D2
Redding Falk 279 F8
Reddingmuirhead Falk . 279 F8
Reddish Gtr Man 184 C5
Warr 183 D11
Redditch Worcs 117 D10
Rede Suff 124 F6
Redenhall Norf 142 G5
Redenham Hants 47 D10
Redesdale Camp
Northumb 251 D8
Redesmouth Northumb . 251 G10
Redford Aberds 293 F9
Angus 287 C9
Dorset 29 F10
Durham 233 E7
W Sus 34 B5
Redfordgreen Borders . . 261 F9
Redgorton Perth 286 E4
Redgrave Suff 125 B10
Redheugh Angus 292 G6
Redhill Aberds 293 C9
Aberds 302 F6
Herts 104 E6
Notts 171 F9
N Som 60 G4
Shrops 131 B9
Shrops 150 G4
Staffs 150 D6
Sur 51 C9
Telford 150 G4
Red Hill Bmouth 19 B7
Hants 34 E2
Hereford 97 D10
Kent 135 D10
Leics 135 D10
Pembs 72 B6
Warks 118 F2
Worcs 117 G7
W Yorks 198 B2
Redhills Cumb 230 F6
Devon 14 C4
Redhouse Argyll 275 G9
Red House Common
E Sus 36 C5
Redhouses Argyll 274 G4
Redisham Suff 143 G8
Red Lake Telford 150 G3
Redland Bristol 60 D5
Orkney 314 D3
Redland End Bucks 84 E4
Redlands Dorset 17 E9
Som 44 G3
Swindon 81 G11
Redlane Som 28 E2
Redlingfield Suff 126 C3
Red Lodge Suff 124 C3
Red Lumb Gtr Man 195 D10
Redlynch Som 45 G8
Wilts 32 C2
Redmain Cumb 229 E8
Redmarley D'Abitot Glos . 98 E5
Redmarshall Stockton . . 234 G3
Redmile Leics 154 B5
Redmire N Yorks 223 G10
Redmonsford Devon 24 D4
Redmoss Aberds 303 F8

Rednal Shrops 149 D7
W Mid 117 B10
Redpath Borders 262 B3
Red Pits Norf 159 D11
Redpoint Highld 299 C7
Red Post Corn 24 F3
Red Rail Hereford 97 F10
Red Rice Hants 47 E10
Red Rock Gtr Man 194 F5
Red Roses Carms 74 C2
Red Scar Lancs 203 G7
Redscarhead Borders . . 270 G4
Redstocks Wilts 62 G2
Red Street Staffs 168 E4
Redtye Corn 5 C10
Redvales Gtr Man 195 F10
Red Wharf Bay Anglesey 179 E8
Redwick Newport 60 B4
S Glos 60 B4
Redwith Shrops 148 E6
Redworth Darl 233 G10
Reed Herts 105 D7
Reed End Herts 104 D6
Reedham Lincs 174 D2
Norf 143 C8
Reedley Lancs 204 F2
Reedness E Yorks 199 C9
Reed Point Lincs 174 E2
Reeds Beck Lincs 174 B2
Reedsford Northumb . . 263 C9
Reeds Holme Lancs . . . 195 C10
Reedy Devon 14 D2
Reen Manor Corn 4 E5
Reepham Lincs 189 G8
Norf 159 E11
Reeth N Yorks 223 F10
Reeves Green W Mid . . . 118 B5
Refail Powys 130 C3
Regaby IoM 192 C5
Regil N Som 60 G4
Regoul Highld 301 D8
Reiff Highld 307 H4
Reigate Sur 51 C9
Reigate Heath Sur 51 C8
Reighton N Yorks 218 D2
Reighton Gap N Yorks . 218 D2
Reinigeadal W Isles . . . 305 H4
Reisque Aberds 293 B10
Reiss Highld 310 D7
Rejerrah Corn 4 D5
Releath Corn 2 C5
Relubbus Corn 2 C3
Relugas Moray 301 E9
Remenham Wokingham . . 65 C9
Remenham Hill
Wokingham 65 C9
Remony Perth 285 C11
Rempstone Notts 153 E11
Remusaig Highld 309 J7
Rendcomb Glos 81 D8
Rendham Suff 126 E6
Rendlesham Suff 126 G6
Renfrew Renfs 267 B10
Renhold Bedford 121 G11
Renishaw Derbys 186 F6
Renmure Angus 287 B10
Rennington Northumb . 264 F6
Renton W Dunb 277 F7
Renwick Cumb 231 C7
Repps Norf 161 F8
Repton Derbys 152 D6
Reraig Highld 295 C10
Reraig Cot Highld 295 B10
Rerwick Shetland 313 M5
Rescassa Corn 5 G9
Rescobie Angus 287 B9
Rescorla Corn 5 D10
Resipole Highld 289 C9
Reskadinnick Corn 4 G2
Resolfen / Resolven
Neath 76 E4
Resolis Highld 300 C6
Resolven / Resolfen
Neath 76 E4
Cumb 221 F9
Restalrig Edin 280 G4
Reston Borders 273 C7
Cumb 221 F9
Restronguet Passage Corn 3 B8
Restrop Wilts 62 B5
Resugga Green Corn 5 D10
Reswallie Angus 287 B9
Retallack Corn 5 B8
Retew Corn 5 D8
Retford Notts 188 E2
Retire Corn 5 C10
Rettendon Essex 88 F3
Rettendon Place Essex . . 88 F3
Revesby Lincs 174 C3
Revesby Bridge Lincs . . 195 B7
Revidge Blackburn 195 B7
Rew Devon 9 G9
Devon 13 G11
Dorset 29 F11
Rewe Devon 14 B4
Rew Street IoW 20 C5
Rexon Devon 12 D4
Rexon Cross Devon 12 D4
Reybridge Wilts 62 F2
Reydon Suff 127 B9
Reydon Smear Suff 127 B9
Reymerston Norf 141 B10
Reynalton Pembs 73 D9
Reynoldston Swansea . . 56 C3
Rezare Corn 12 F3
Rhadyr Mon 78 E5
Rhaeadr Gwy / Rhayader
Powys 113 D9
Rhandir Conwy 180 G4
Rhandirmwyn Carms . . 94 C5
Rhayader / Rhaeadr Gwy
Powys 113 D9
Rhedyn Gwyn 144 C5
Rhegreanoch Highld . . 307 H5
Rhemore Highld 289 D7
Rhencullen IoM 192 C4
Rhenetra Highld 298 D4
Rhes-y-cae Flint 181 G11
Rhewl Denb 165 C10
Denb 165 F11
Shrops 148 C6
Wrex 149 B7
Rhewl-fawr Flint 181 E10
Rhewl-Mostyn Flint . . . 181 E11
Rhian Highld 309 H5
Rhicarn Highld 307 G5
Rhiconich Highld 306 D7
Rhiculfen IoM 300 B6
Rhidorroch Ho Highld . 307 K6
Rhiews Highld 150 B2
Rhifail Highld 308 E7
Rhigolter Highld 308 D3
Rhigos Rhondda 76 D6
Rhilochan Highld 309 J7
Rhippinllwyd Ceredig . . 92 C5
Ceredig 110 G6
Rhiroy Highld 307 L6
Rhitongue Highld 308 D6
Rhivichie Highld 306 D7

Rhiw Gwyn 144 D4
Rhiwabon / Ruabon
Wrex 166 G4
Rhiwbebyll Denb 165 B10
Rhiwbina Cardiff 59 C7
Rhiwbryfdir Gwyn 163 F11
Rhiwceiliog Bridgend . . 58 C3
Rhiwen Gwyn 163 C9
Rhiwderin Newport 59 B9
Rhiwinder Rhondda 58 B4
Rhiwlas Gwyn 147 B8
Gwyn 163 B9
Powys 148 C3
Rhodes Gtr Man 195 F11
Rhodes Minnis Kent 55 E7
Rhodiad Pembs 90 F5
Rhonadale Argyll 255 D8
Rhondda Rhondda 77 F7
Rhonehouse or Kelton Hill
Dumfries 237 D9
Rhoose V Glam 58 F5
Rhos Carms 93 D7
Rhôs Denb 165 C10
Neath 76 E2
Rhos Powys 148 F5
Rhosaman Carms 76 C2
Rhosbeirio Anglesey . . 178 C5
Rhoscefnhir Anglesey . 179 F8
Rhoscolyn Anglesey . . 178 F3
Rhôs Common Powys . . 148 F5
Rhoscrowther Pembs . . 72 E6
Rhosddu Wrex 166 E4
Rhos-ddû Gwyn 144 B5
Rhosdylluan Gwyn 147 D7
Rhosesmor Flint 166 B2
Rhosfach Pembs 92 F2
Rhos-fawr Gwyn 145 B7
Rhosgadfan Gwyn 163 D8
Rhosgoch Anglesey . . . 178 D6
Powys 96 B3
Rhos-goch Powys 96 B3
Rhosgyll Gwyn 163 D8
Rhos Haminiog Ceredig 111 E10
Rhos-hill Pembs 92 C3
Rhoshirwaun Gwyn . . . 144 D3
Rhos Isaf Gwyn 163 D7
Rhoslan Gwyn 163 G7
Rhoslefain Gwyn 110 B2
Rhosllanerchrugog
Wrex 166 F3
Rhôs Lligwy Anglesey . 179 D7
Rhosmaen Carms 94 G2
Rhosmeirch Anglesey . 179 F7
Rhosneigr Anglesey . . 178 G4
Rhosnesni Wrex 166 E5
Rhôs-on-Sea Conwy . . 180 E4
Rhosrobin Wrex 166 E4
Rhossili Swansea 56 D2
Rhosson Pembs 90 F4
Rhostrehwfa Anglesey . 178 G6
Rhostryfan Gwyn 163 D7
Rhostyllen Wrex 166 F4
Rhoswiel Shrops 148 B5
Rhosybol Anglesey . . . 178 D6
Rhos-y-brithdir Powys . 148 E2
Rhos-y-caerau Pembs . . 91 D8
Rhosygadfa Shrops . . . 148 C6
Rhos-y-garth Ceredig . 112 C2
Rhosygwaliau Gwyn . . 147 C8
Rhosy-gwaliau Gwyn . . 147 C8
Rhos-y-llan Gwyn 144 B4
Rhos-y-Madoc Wrex . . 166 G4
Rhosymedre Wrex 166 G3
Rhos-y-meirch Powys . 114 D5
Rhosyn-coch Carms . . . 92 G5
Rhu Argyll 276 E5
Argyll 276 E5
Rhuallt Denb 181 F9
Rhubodach Argyll 275 F11
Rhuddall Heath Ches W . 167 C9
Rhuddlan Ceredig 93 C9
Denb 181 F8
Rhue Highld 307 K5
Rhulen Powys 96 B2
Rhunahaorine Argyll . . 255 C8
Rhyd Ceredig 92 C5
Gwyn 163 G10
Powys 129 C9
Rhydaman / Ammanford
Carms 75 C10
Rhydargaeau Carms . . . 93 F8
Rhydcymerau Carms . . 93 D11
Rhydd Worcs 98 B6
Rhyd-Ddu Gwyn 163 E9
Rhyd Green Worcs 98 B6
Rhydding Neath 57 B8
Rhydfudr Ceredig 111 E11
Rhydgaled Conwy 165 C9
Rhydgaled / Chancery
Ceredig 111 B11
Rhydlewis Ceredig 92 B6
Rhydlios Ceredig 144 C3
Rhydlydan Conwy 164 E5
Powys 129 C11
Rhydmoelddu Powys . . 113 B11
Rhydness Powys 96 C2
Rhydowen Carms 92 F3
Ceredig 93 B8
Rhyd-Rosser Ceredig . . 111 E11
Rhydspence Hereford . . 96 B4
Rhydtalog Flint 166 D2
Rhyd-uchaf Gwyn 147 B8
Rhyd-wen Gwyn 146 F4
Rhydwyn Anglesey . . . 178 D4
Rhyd-y-meirch Mon . . 78 D4
Rhyd-y-meudwy Denb . 165 D10
Sur 50 B5
Rhyd-y-Brown Pembs . . 91 G11
Rhyd-y-clafdy Gwyn . . 144 B6
Rhydycroesau Shrops . . 148 C4
Rhyd-y-cwm Shrops . . 130 G3
Northants 121 B9
Rhydyfelin Carms 92 D5
Ceredig 111 B11
Powys 129 G11
Rhondda 58 B5
Rhyd-y-foel Conwy . . . 180 F6
Rhyd-y-fro Neath 76 D2
Rhydygwin Swansea . . . 75 E11
Rhyd-y-gwystl Gwyn . . 145 B8
Rhydymain Gwyn 146 E6
Rhyd-y-meudwy Denb . 165 D10
Rhydymwyn Flint 166 B2
Rhyd-yr-onen Gwyn . . 128 C2
Rhyd-y-sarn Gwyn . . . 163 G11
Rhydwrach Carms 73 B11
Rhyl Denb 181 E8
Rhymney Caerph 77 D7
Rhyn Wrex 148 B6
Rhynd Fife 287 E8
Perth 286 E5
Rhynie Aberds 302 G4
Highld 301 B8
Ribbesford Worcs 116 C5
Ribblehead N Yorks . . . 212 D5
Ribbleton Lancs 203 G7

Ribbleton Lancs 203 G7
Ribby Lancs 202 G4
Ribchester Lancs 203 F8
Riber Derbys 170 D4
Ribigill Highld 308 D5
Riby Lincs 201 F7
Riby Cross Roads Lincs 201 F7
Riccall N Yorks 207 F8
Riccarton E Ayrs 257 B10
Richards Castle
Hereford 115 D9
Richborough Port Kent . 71 G10
Richings Park Bucks . . . 66 D4
Richmond London 67 E7
N Yorks 224 E3
S Yorks 186 D6
Richmond Hill W Yorks 206 G2
Richmond's Green
Essex 106 F2
Rich's Holford Som 42 G6
Rickard's Down Devon . 24 B6
Rickarton Aberds 293 E10
Rickerby Cumb 239 F10
Rickerscote Staffs 151 E8
Rickford N Som 44 B3
Rickinghall Suff 125 B10
Rickleton T&W 243 G7
Rickling Essex 105 E9
Rickling Green Essex . . 105 F9
Rickmansworth Herts . . 85 G9
Rickney E Sus 23 D10
Riddell Borders 262 E2
Riddings Derbys 170 E6
Riddlecombe Devon . . . 25 E10
Riddlesden W Yorks . . . 205 E7
Riddrie Glasgow 268 B2
Ridgacre W Mid 133 G10
Ridge Bath 44 B5
Dorset 18 D4
Hants 32 D4
Herts 86 E2
Lancs 211 D9
Som 28 F3
Wilts 46 E3
Ridgebourne Powys . . . 113 E11
Ridge Common Hants . . 34 C2
Ridge Green Sur 51 D10
Ridgehill N Som 60 G4
Ridge Hill Gtr Man . . . 185 B7
Ridge Lane Warks 134 E5
Ridgemarsh Herts 85 G8
Ridge Row Kent 55 E8
Ridgeway Bristol 60 D6
Derbys 170 E5
Derbys 186 E6
Kent 54 E5
Newport 59 B9
Pembs 73 D10
Staffs 168 E5
Ridgeway Cross Hereford 98 B5
Ridgeway Moor Derbys 186 E6
Ridgewell Essex 106 C4
Ridgewood E Sus 23 B7
Ridgmont C Beds 103 D9
Ridgway Shrops 131 F7
Sur 50 B4
Riding Gate Som 30 B2
Riding Mill Northumb . 242 E2
Ridley Kent 68 G6
Northumb 241 E7
Ridley Stokoe Northumb 250 F6
Ridleywood Wrex 166 D5
Ridlington Norf 160 C6
Rutland 136 C5
Ridlington Street Norf . 160 C6
Ridsdale Northumb . . . 251 G10
Riechip Perth 286 C4
Riemore Perth 286 C4
Rienachait Highld 306 F5
Rievaulx N Yorks 215 B11
Riff Orkney 314 E4
Riffin Aberds 303 E7
Rifle Green Torf 78 D3
Rift House Hrtlpl 234 E5
Rigg Dumfries 239 D7
Riggend N Lanark 268 B5
Riggindale Cumb 221 C9
Rigsby Lincs 190 F6
Rigside S Lanark 259 B9
Riley Green Lancs 194 B6
Rileyhill Staffs 152 F2
Rilla Mill Corn 11 G11
Rillaton Corn 11 G11
Rillington N Yorks . . . 217 E7
Rimac Lincs 191 C7
Rimington Lancs 204 D2
Rimpton Som 29 C10
Rimswell E Yorks 201 B10
Rimswell Valley
E Yorks 201 B10
Rinaston Pembs 91 F9
Rindleford Shrops 132 D4
Ringasta Shetland 313 M5
Ringford Dumfries . . . 237 D8
Ringing Hill Leics 153 F9
Ringinglow S Yorks . . . 186 E3
Ringland Newport 59 B10
Norf 160 G2
Ringles Cross E Sus . . . 37 C7
Ringlestone Kent 53 B9
Kent 53 B11
Ringley Gtr Man 195 F9
Ringmer E Sus 36 E6
Ringmore Devon 8 F3
Devon 14 G6
Ring o' Bells Lancs . . . 194 E3
Ringorm Moray 302 E2
King's End Cambs 41 D9
Ringshall Suff 125 G10
Ringshall Herts 85 C7
Ringshall Stocks Suff . . 125 G10
Ringstead Norf 176 E2
Northants 121 B9
Ringtail Green Essex . . 87 B11
Ringwood Hants 31 F11
Ringwould Kent 55 D11
Rinmore Aberds 292 B6
Rinnigill Orkney 314 G3
Rinsey Corn 2 D3
Rinsey Croft Corn 2 D4
Riof W Isles 304 E3
Ripe E Sus 23 C8
Ripley Derbys 170 E5
Hants 19 B9
N Yorks 214 G5
Sur 50 B5
Riplingham E Yorks . . . 208 G5
Ripon N Yorks 214 E6
Rippingale Lincs 155 D11
Ripple Kent 55 D11
Worcs 99 D7
Ripponden W Yorks . . 196 D4
Rireavach Highld 307 K5
Risabus Argyll 254 C4
Risbury Hereford 115 G10
Risby E Yorks 208 G6
Lincs 189 C10
N Yorks 207 G7
Suff 124 D5
Risca Caerph 78 G2

Rise E Yorks 209 E9
Rise Carr Darl 224 B5
Riseden E Sus 52 G6
Kent 53 F8
Rise End Derbys 170 D3
Risegate Lincs 156 D4
Riseholme Lincs 189 F7
Risehow Cumb 228 E6
Riseley Bedford 121 E10
Wokingham 65 G8
Rise Park London 87 G8
Rishangles Suff 126 D3
Rishton Lancs 203 G10
Rishworth W Yorks . . . 196 D4
Rising Bridge Lancs . . 195 B9
Risinghurst Oxon 83 D9
Rising Sun Corn 12 G3
Risley Derbys 153 B9
Warr 183 C10
Risplith N Yorks 214 F4
Rispond Highld 308 C4
Rivar Wilts 63 G10
Rivenhall Essex 88 B4
Rivenhall End Essex . . . 88 B4
River Kent 55 E9
W Sus 34 C6
River Bank Cambs . . . 123 D10
Riverhead Kent 52 B4
Rivers' Corner Dorset . . 30 E3
Riverside Cardiff 59 D7
Plym 7 D8
Stirling 278 C6
Riverside Docklands
Lincs 194 B4
Riverton Devon 40 G6
Riverview Park Kent . . . 69 E7
Rivington Lancs 194 E6
Rixon Dorset 30 E3
Rixton Warr 183 C11
Roa Island Cumb 210 G4
Roach Bridge Lancs . . 194 B5
Roachill Devon 26 C4
Roade Northants 120 G5
Roadend Corn 240 C2
Roadhead Cumb 240 C2
Roadmeetings S Lanark 269 F7
Roadside Highld 310 C5
Roadside of Catterline
Aberds 293 F10
Roadside of Kinneff
Aberds 293 F10
Roadwater Som 42 F4
Roag Highld 298 E2
Roa Island Cumb 210 G4
Roast Green Essex 105 E9
Roath Cardiff 59 D7
Roath Park Cardiff 59 D7
Rob Roy's House Argyll 284 F5
Robroyston Glasgow . . 268 B2
Roberton Borders 261 G10
S Lanark 259 D10
Robertsbridge E Sus . . . 38 C2
Robertstown Moray . . 302 E2
Rhondda 77 E8
Roberttown W Yorks . . 197 C7
Robeston Back Pembs . . 73 B9
Robeston Cross Pembs . 72 D5
Robeston Wathen Pembs 73 C9
Robeston West Pembs . . 72 D5
Robin Hood Lancs . . . 194 E4
Derbys 186 G3
W Yorks 197 C10
Robin Hood's Bay
N Yorks 227 D9
Robinhood End Essex . 106 D4
Robins W Sus 34 C4
Robinson's End Warks . 134 E6
Roborough Devon 7 C10
Devon 25 D9
Roby Mers 182 C6
Roby Mill Lancs 194 F4
Rocester Staffs 152 B2
Roch Pembs 91 G7
Rochdale Gtr Man 195 E11
Roche Corn 5 C9
Roche Grange Staffs . . 169 C7
Rochester Medway 69 F7
Northumb 251 D8
Rochford Essex 88 G5
Worcs 116 D2
Rock Caerph 77 F11
Corn 10 F4
Devon 28 G3
Neath 57 C9
Northumb 264 E6
Som 28 C4
W Sus 35 E10
Worcs 116 C4
Rock End Staffs 168 D5
Rockbeare Devon 14 C6
Rockbourne Hants 31 D10
Rockcliffe Cumb 239 E9
Dumfries 237 D10
Lancs 195 C11
Rockcliffe Cross Cumb . 239 E8
Rock End Staffs 168 D5
Rock Ferry Mers 182 D4
Rockfield Highld 311 L3
Mon 79 C7
Rockford Devon 41 D9
Hants 31 F11
Rockgreen Shrops 115 B10
Rockhampton S Glos . . 79 G11
Rockhead Corn 11 E7
Rockhill Shrops 114 B5
Rockingham Northants . 137 E7
Rockland All Saints
Norf 141 E9
Rockland St Mary Norf . 142 C6
Rockland St Peter Norf 141 E9
Rockley Notts 188 G2
Wilts 63 D7
Rockley Ford Som 45 C8
Rockness Glos 80 F4
Rockrobin E Sus 52 G6
Rocksavage Halton . . . 183 E8
Rocks Park E Sus 37 C7
Rockstowes Glos 80 F3
Rockville Argyll 276 D4
Rockwell End Bucks . . . 65 B9
Rockwell Green Som . . 27 D11
Rocky Hill Scilly 1 G4
Rodbaston Staffs 151 G8
Rodborough Glos 80 E4
Rodbourne Swindon . . . 62 C6
Wilts 62 B2
Rodbourne Bottom Wilts 62 C2
Rodbourne Cheney
Swindon 62 B6
Rodbridge Corner
Suff 107 C7
Rodd Hereford 114 E6
Roddam Northumb . . . 264 E2
Rodden Dorset 17 E8

Rodd Hurst Hereford . . 114 E6
Roddymoor Durham . . 233 D9
Rode Som 45 C10
Rodeheath Ches E 168 B5
Rode Heath Ches E . . . 168 D3
Rode Hill Som 45 C10
Roden Telford 149 F11
Rodford S Glos 61 C7
Rodgrove Som 30 C2
Rodhuish Som 42 F4
Rodington Telford 149 F11
Rodington Heath
Telford 149 G11
Rodley Glos 80 C2
W Yorks 205 F10
Rodmarton Glos 80 F6
Rodmell E Sus 36 F6
Rodmer Clough
W Yorks 196 B3
Rodmersham Kent 70 G2
Rodmersham Green Kent 70 G2
Rodney Stoke Som 44 C3
Rodsley Derbys 170 G2
Rodway Som 43 F9
Telford 150 F3
Rodwell Dorset 17 F9
Roe Cross Gtr Man . . . 185 B7
Roedean Brighton 36 G4
Roe End Herts 85 B8
Roe Green Herts 104 E6
Herts 86 F2
London 67 B8
Roffey W Sus 51 G7
Rogart Highld 309 J7
Rogart Station Highld . 309 J7
Rogate W Sus 34 C4
Roger Ground Cumb . . 221 F7
Rogerstone Newport . . . 59 B9
Rogerton S Lanark . . . 268 D2
Rogiet Mon 60 B3
Rogue's Alley Cambs . . 139 B7
Roke Oxon 83 G10
Rokemarsh Oxon 83 G10
Roker T&W 243 F10
Rollesby Norf 161 F8
Rolleston Leics 136 C4
Notts 172 E2
Rolleston S Yorks 186 E5
Wilts 46 E5
Rolleston Camp Wilts . . 46 E5
Rolleston-on-Dove
Staffs 152 D4
Rolston E Yorks 209 E10
Rolstone N Som 59 G11
Rolvenden Kent 53 G10
Rolvenden Layne Kent . 53 G11
Romaldkirk Durham . . 232 G5
Romanby N Yorks 225 G7
Roman Hill Suff 143 E10
Romannobridge Borders 270 F3
Romansleigh Devon . . . 26 C2
Romesdal Highld 298 D4
Romford Dorset 31 F9
London 68 B4
Romiley Gtr Man 184 C6
Romney Street Kent . . . 68 G4
Rompa Shetland 313 L6
Romsey Hants 32 C5
Romsey Town Cambs . . 123 F9
Romsley Shrops 132 G5
Worcs 117 B9
Ronachan Ho Argyll . . 255 B8
Ronague IoM 192 E3
Rondlay Telford 132 B4
Ronkswood Worcs 117 G7
Rood End W Mid 133 F10
Rookby Cumb 222 C5
Rooke Essex 105 E11
Rookhope Durham . . . 232 C4
Rooking Cumb 221 B8
Rookley IoW 20 E6
Rookley Green IoW 20 E6
Rooks Bridge Som 43 C11
Rooksey Green Suff . . . 125 G8
Rooks Hill Kent 52 C5
Rook's Nest Som 42 G5
Rook Street Som 45 G10
Rookwith N Yorks 214 B4
Rookwood W Sus 21 B11
Roos E Yorks 209 G11
Roosebeck Cumb 210 F5
Roosecote Cumb 210 F5
Roost End Essex 106 C4
Rootham's Green
Bedford 122 F2
Rooting Street Kent . . . 54 D3
Rootpark S Lanark . . . 269 E9
Ropley Hants 48 G6
Ropley Dean Hants 48 G6
Ropley Soke Hants 49 G7
Ropsley Lincs 155 C9
Rora Aberds 303 D10
Rorandle Aberds 293 B8
Rorrington Shrops . . . 130 C5
Rosarie Moray 302 E3
Roscroggan Corn 4 G3
Rose Corn 4 E5
Roseacre Kent 53 B9
Lancs 202 F4
Rose-an-Grouse Corn . . . 2 B4
Rose Ash Devon 26 C3
Rosebank S Lanark . . . 268 F6
Rosebery Midloth 270 C6
Rosebrae Moray 301 C11
Rosebush Pembs 91 F11
Rosecare Corn 11 B9
Rosecliston Corn 4 D6
Rosedale Abbey
N Yorks 226 F4
Roseden Northumb . . . 264 E2
Rosedinnick Corn 5 B8
Rosedown Devon 24 C3
Rosefield Highld 301 D8
Rose Green Essex 107 F8
Essex 107 D7
Suff 107 D8
W Sus 22 D5
Rose Grove Lancs 204 G3
Rosehall Highld 309 J4
N Lanark 268 C4
Rosehaugh Mains
Highld 300 D6
Rosehearty Aberds . . . 303 C9
Rosehill Blackburn . . . 195 C8
Corn 4 C5
Corn 5 C10
Rodden Dorset 17 E8

Rosehill continued
Gtr Man 184 D3
London 67 F9
Pembs 72 B5
Shrops 150 C3
T&W 243 D8
Rose Hill Bucks 66 C2
Derbys 153 B8
E Sus 23 B7
Gtr Man 195 E8
Lancs 204 G2
Oxon 83 E8
Suff 108 C3
Sur 51 B7
Roseisle Moray 301 C11
Roseland Corn 6 E6
Roselands E Sus 23 E10
Rosemarket Pembs 73 D7
Rosemarkie Highld . . . 301 D7
Rosemary Lane Devon . 27 E11
Rosemelling Corn 5 D10
Rosemergy Corn 1 B4
Rosemount Perth 286 C5
Rosenannon Corn 5 B9
Rosenithon Corn 3 E8
Roser's Cross E Sus . . . 37 C9
Rose Valley Pembs 73 E8
Rosevean Corn 5 D10
Rosevear Corn 2 E5
Roseville W Mid 133 E8
Rosewarne Corn 2 B5
Corn 4 G2
Rosewell Midloth 270 C5
Roseworth Stockton . . 234 G4
Roseworthy Corn 2 B4
Roseworthy Barton Corn . 2 B4
Rosgill Cumb 221 B10
Rosherville Kent 68 E6
Roshven Highld 289 B9
Roskear Croft Corn 4 G3
Roskhill Highld 298 E2
Roskill House Highld . 300 D6
Roskorwell Corn 3 E7
Rosley Cumb 230 B2
Roslin Midloth 270 C5
Rosliston Derbys 152 F4
Rosneath Argyll 276 E5
Ross Borders 273 C9
Dumfries 237 E8
Northumb 264 B4
Perth 285 E11
Rossett Wrex 166 D5
Rossett Green N Yorks . 206 C2
Ross Green Worcs 116 E5
Rossie Ochill Perth . . . 286 F4
Rossie Priory Perth . . . 286 D6
Rossington S Yorks . . . 187 B10
Rosskeen Highld 300 C6
Rossland Renfs 277 G8
Ross-on-Wye Hereford . 98 G2
Roster Highld 310 F6
Rostherne Ches E 184 E2
Rostholme S Yorks . . . 198 F5
Rosthwaite Cumb 220 C5
Cumb 220 G4
Roston Derbys 169 G10
Rosudgeon Corn 2 D3
Rosyth Fife 280 E2
Rotchfords Essex 107 E8
Rotcombe Bath 44 B6
Rothbury Northumb . . 252 C2
Rotherbridge W Sus . . . 35 C7
Rotherby Leics 154 F3
Rotherfield E Sus 37 B9
Rotherfield Greys
Oxon 65 C8
Rotherfield Peppard
Oxon 65 C8
Rotherham S Yorks . . . 186 C6
Rotherhithe London . . . 67 D11
Rothersthorpe Northants 120 F4
Rotherwas Hereford . . . 97 D10
Rotherwick Hants 49 B8
Rothes Moray 302 E2
Rothesay Argyll 275 G11
Rothiebrisbane Aberds . 303 F7
Rothiemay Crossroads
Moray 302 E5
Rothiemurchus Lodge
Highld 291 C11
Rothienorman Aberds . 303 F7
Rothiesholm Orkney . . 314 D6
Rothley Leics 153 G11
Northumb 252 F2
Rothley Plain Leics . . . 153 G11
Rothley Shield East
Northumb 252 C2
Rothmaise Aberds 302 F6
Rothwell Lincs 189 B11
Northants 136 G6
W Yorks 197 B10
Rothwell Haigh
W Yorks 197 B10
Rotsea E Yorks 209 C7
Rottal Angus 292 G5
Rotten End Suff 127 E7
Suff 127 D7
Rotten Green Hants . . . 49 B9
Rotten Row W Berks . . . 64 E5
W Mid 118 B3
S Yorks 197 E11
Rottingdean Brighton . . 36 G5
Rottington Cumb 219 C9
Rotton Park W Mid . . . 133 F11
Rotton Row W Mid . . . 133 F8
Roud IoW 20 E6
Rougham Norf 158 E6
Suff 125 E8
Rougham Green Suff . . 125 E8
Rough Bank Gtr Man . . 196 E2
Roughbirchworth
S Yorks 197 G9
Roughburn Highld . . . 290 E6
Rough Close Staffs . . . 151 B8
Rough Common Kent . . 54 B6
Rough Haugh Highld . . 308 E7
Rough Hay Staffs 152 E4
Roughlee Lancs 204 E2
Roughley W Mid 134 D2
Roughmoor S Lanark . . 278 G4
Roughsike Cumb 240 B2
Roughton Lincs 174 C2
Norf 160 B4
Shrops 132 D5
Roughton Moor Lincs . 174 C2
Roughway Kent 52 C6
Roundbush Essex 88 E5
Round Bush Herts 85 F10
Roundbush Green Essex 87 C9
Round Green Luton . . . 103 G11
Roundham Som 28 F6
Roundhay W Yorks . . . 206 F2
Round Maple Suff 107 C8
Round Oak Shrops . . . 131 G7
W Mid 133 F8
Round's Green W Mid . 133 F9
Roundshaw London . . . 67 G10

Round Spinney
Northants 120 D5
Roundstonefoot
Dumfries 248 B4
Round Street Kent 69 F7
Roundswell Devon 40 G4
Roundthorn Gtr Man . . 184 D4
Roundthwaite Cumb . . 222 E2
Roundway Wilts 62 G4
Roundyhill Angus 287 B7
Rousdon Devon 15 C11
Rousham Oxon 101 G9
Rous Lench Worcs 117 G9
Routenburn N Ayrs . . . 266 C3
Routh E Yorks 209 E7
Rout's Green Bucks 84 F3
Row Corn 11 F7
Cumb 211 B8
Cumb 231 E8
Rowanburn Dumfries . 239 B10
Rowanfield Glos 99 G8
Rowardennan Stirling . 277 B7
Rowarth Derbys 185 D8
Row Ash Hants 33 E8
Rowbarton Som 28 B2
Rowberrow Som 44 B3
Row Brow Cumb 229 D7
Rowde Wilts 62 G3
Rowden N Yorks 205 B11
Row Head N Yorks 210 D5
Rowen Conwy 180 G3
Rowfoot Northumb . . . 240 E5
Rowford Som 28 B2
Row Green Essex 106 G4
Row Heath Essex 89 B10
Rowhedge Essex 107 G10
Rowhill Sur 66 G4
Rowhook W Sus 50 G6
Rowington Warks 118 D4
Rowington Green
Warks 118 D4
Rowland Derbys 186 G2
Rowlands Castle Hants . 34 E2
Rowlands Gill T&W . . . 242 F5
Rowland's Green
Hereford 98 D3
Rowledge Sur 49 E10
Rowley E Yorks 208 G5
Shrops 130 B6
Rowley Green London . . 86 F2
Rowley Hill W Yorks . . 197 E7
Rowley Park Staffs . . . 151 E8
Rowley Regis W Mid . . 133 F9
Rowley's Green W Mid . 134 G6
Rowling Kent 55 C9
Rowly Sur 50 E4
Rownall Staffs 169 F7
Rowner Hants 33 G9
Rowney Green Worcs . . 117 C10
Rownhams Hants 32 D5
Row-of-trees Ches E . . 184 F4
Rowrah Cumb 219 B11
Rowsham Bucks 84 B4
Rowsley Derbys 170 C2
Rowstock Oxon 64 B4
Rowston Lincs 173 D9
Rowthorne Derbys . . . 170 C6
Rowton Ches W 166 C6
Shrops 149 G7
Telford 150 F2
Rowton Moor Ches W . 166 C6
Row Town Sur 66 G5
Roxburgh Borders . . . 262 C5
Roxburgh Mains
Borders 262 D5
Roxby N Lincs 200 D2
N Yorks 226 B5
Roxeth London 66 B6
Roxton Bedford 122 G3
Roxwell Essex 87 D10
Royal British Legion Village
Kent 53 B8
Royal Leamington Spa
Warks 118 D6
Royal Oak Darl 233 G10
Lancs 194 G3
N Yorks 218 D2
Royal Tunbridge Wells /
Tunbridge Wells Kent . 52 F5
Royal Wootton Bassett
Wilts 62 C5
Roybridge Highld 290 E4
Royd S Yorks 197 G8
Roydhouse W Yorks . . 197 E8
Royd Moor S Yorks . . . 197 G8
Roydon Essex 86 D6
Norf 141 G11
Norf 158 E4
Roydon Hamlet Essex . . 86 D6
Royds Green W Yorks . 197 B11
Royston Glasgow 268 B2
Herts 105 C7
S Yorks 197 E11
Royston Water Som . . . 28 E2
Royton Gtr Man 196 F2
Ruabon / Rhiwabon
Wrex 166 G4
Ruaig Argyll 288 E2
Ruan High Lanes Corn . . 3 B10
Ruan Lanihorne Corn . . 5 G7
Ruan Major Corn 2 F6
Ruan Minor Corn 2 F6
Ruarach Highld 295 C11
Ruardean Glos 79 B10
Ruardean Hill Glos . . . 79 B10
Ruardean Woodside
Glos 79 B10
Rubery Worcs 117 B9
Rubha Ghaisinis
W Isles 297 G4
Rubha Stoer Highld . . 306 F5
Ruchazie Glasgow 268 B3
Ruchill Glasgow 267 B11
Ruckcroft Cumb 230 C6
Ruckhall Hereford 97 D9
Ruckinge Kent 54 G4
Ruckland Lincs 190 F4
Ruckley Shrops 131 C10
Rudbaxton Pembs 91 G9
Rudby N Yorks 225 D9
Ruddington Notts 153 C11
Ruddle Glos 79 C11
Rudford Glos 98 G5
Rudge Shrops 132 D6
Som 45 C10
Rudge Heath Shrops . . 132 D5
Rudgeway S Glos 60 B6
Rudgwick W Sus 50 G5
Rudhall Hereford 98 F2
Rudheath Ches W 183 G11
Rudheath Woods
Ches W 184 G2

Rudhja Garbh Argyll...289 E11
Rudley Green Essex...88 E4
Rudloe Wilts...61 E10
Rudry Caerph...59 B7
Rudston E Yorks...217 F11
Rudyard Staffs...169 D7
Ruewood Shrops...149 D9
Rufford Lancs...194 D3
Rufforth York...206 C6
Ruffs Notts...171 F8
Rugby Warks...119 B10
Rugeley Staffs...151 F10
Rugeley Bridge Perth 279 B10
Ruggin Som...27 D11
Ruglen S Ayrs...245 C7
Rugley Northumb...264 G5
Ruilick Highld...300 E5
Ruishton Som...28 C3
Ruisigearraidh W Isles...66 K3
Ruislip London...66 B5
Ruislip Common London...66 B5
Ruislip Gardens London...66 B5
Ruislip Manor London...66 B6
Ruiton W Mid...133 E8
Ruloe Ches W...183 G9
Rumach Highld...295 G8
Rumbling Bridge Perth 279 B10
Rumbow Cottages
  Worcs...117 B8
Rumburgh Suff...142 G6
Rumbush W Mid...118 B2
Rumer Hill Staffs...133 B9
Rumford Corn...10 G3
  Falk...279 F8
Rumney Cardiff...59 D8
Rumsam Devon...40 G5
Rumwell Som...27 C11
Runcorn Halton...183 E8
Runcton W Sus...22 C5
Runcton Holme Norf...140 B2
Rundlestone Devon...13 G6
Runfold Sur...49 D11
Runhall Norf...141 B11
Runham Norf...143 B10
  Norf...161 G9
Runham Vauxhall Norf. 143 B10
Running Hill Head
  Gtr Man...196 F4
Runnington Som...27 C10
Running Waters Durham 234 C2
Runsell Green Essex...88 D3
Runshaw Moor Lancs...194 D4
Runswick Bay N Yorks...226 B6
Runwell Essex...88 G2
Ruscombe Glos...80 D4
  Wokingham...65 D9
Ruscoe Oxon...101 C8
Rushall Hereford...98 E2
  Norf...142 G3
  Wilts...46 B6
  W Mid...133 C10
Rushbrooke Suff...125 E7
Rushbury Shrops...131 E10
Rushcombe Bottom
  Poole...18 B5
Rushden Herts...104 E6
  Northants...121 D9
Rushenden Kent...70 E2
Rusher's Cross E Sus...37 B10
Rushey Mead Leicester...136 B2
Rushford Devon...12 G4
  Norf...141 G8
Rushgreen Warr...183 D11
Rush Green Essex...89 B11
  Herts...86 C5
  Herts...104 G4
  London...68 B4
  Norf...141 B11
Rush-head Aberds...303 E8
Rush Hill Bath...61 G8
Rushington Hants...32 E5
Rushlake Green E Sus...23 B10
Rushland Green Cumb...210 B6
Rushley Green Essex...106 D5
Rushmere C Beds...103 F8
  Suff...143 F9
Rushmere St Andrew
  Suff...108 B4
Rushmere Street Suff...108 B4
Rushmoor Sur...49 E11
  Telford...150 G2
Rushmore Hants...33 E11
Rushmore Hill London...68 G3
Rushock Hereford...114 F6
  Worcs...117 C7
Rusholme Gtr Man...184 B5
Rushton Ches W...167 C9
  Dorset...18 D3
  Northants...136 G6
  N Yorks...217 C9
  Shrops...132 B2
Rushton Spencer Staffs. 168 C6
Rushwick Worcs...116 G6
Rushyford Durham...233 F11
Rushy Green E Sus...23 C7
Ruskie Stirling...285 G10
Ruskington Lincs...173 E9
Rusland Cumb...210 B6
Rusling End Herts...104 G4
Rusper W Sus...51 F8
Ruspidge Glos...79 C11
Russell Hill London...67 G10
Russell's Green E Sus...38 E2
Russell's Hall W Mid...133 F8
Russell's Water Oxon...65 B8
Russel's Green Suff...126 C5
Russ Hill Sur...51 E8
Rusthall Kent...52 F5
Rustington W Sus...35 G9
Ruston N Yorks...217 C9
Ruston Parva E Yorks...217 G11
Ruswarp N Yorks...227 D7
Ruthall Shrops...131 F11
Rutherford Borders...262 C4
Rutherglen S Lanark...268 C2
Ruthernbridge Corn...5 B10
Ruthin Denb...165 D10
  V Glam...58 D3
Ruthrieston Aberdeen...293 C11
Ruthven Aberds...302 E5
  Angus...286 C6
  Highld...291 D9
  Highld...301 F8
Ruthven House Angus...287 C7
Ruthvoes Corn...5 C8
Ruthwaite Cumb...229 D10
Ruthwell Dumfries...238 D3
Ruxley London...68 E3
Ruxton Hereford...97 F11
Ruxton Green N Yorks 97 B8
Ruyton-XI-Towns
  Shrops...149 E7
Ryal Northumb...242 C2
Ryal Fold Blackburn...195 C7
Ryall Dorset...16 C4
  Worcs...99 C7
Ryarsh Kent...53 B7
Rychraggan Highld...300 F4
Rydal Cumb...221 D7

Ryde IoW...21 C7
Rydens Sur...66 F6
Rydeshill Sur...50 C3
Rydon Devon...14 G3
Rye E Sus...38 C6
Ryebank Shrops...149 C10
Rye Common Hants...49 C9
Ryecroft S Yorks...186 B6
  W Yorks...205 F7
Ryecroft Gate Staffs...168 C6
Ryeford Glos...80 E4
Rye Foreign E Sus...38 C5
Rye Harbour E Sus...38 D6
Ryehill E Yorks...201 B8
Ryeish Green Wokingham...65 F8
Ryelands Hereford...115 F9
Rye Park Herts...86 C5
Rye Street Worcs...98 D5
Ryeworth Glos...99 G9
Ryhall Rutland...155 G10
Ryhill W Yorks...197 E11
Ryhope T&W...243 G10
Rylah Derbys...171 B7
Rylands Notts...153 B10
Rylstone N Yorks...204 B5
Ryme Intrinseca Dorset...29 E9
Ryther N Yorks...207 F7
Ryton Glos...98 E4
  N Yorks...216 D5
  Shrops...132 C5
  T&W...242 E5
  Warks...135 F7
Ryton-on-Dunsmore
  Warks...119 C7
Ryton Woodside T&W...242 E4

S

Sabden Lancs...203 F11
Sabine's Green Essex...87 F8
Sackers Green Suff...107 D8
Sacombe Herts...86 B4
Sacombe Green Herts...86 B4
Sacriston Durham...233 B10
Sadberge Darl...224 B6
Saddell Argyll...255 D8
Saddell Ho Argyll...255 D8
Saddington Leics...136 E3
Saddle Bow Norf...158 F2
Saddlescombe W Sus...36 E3
Saddle Street Dorset...28 G5
Sadgill Cumb...221 D9
Saffron's Cross
  Hereford...115 G10
Saffron Walden Essex...105 D10
Sageston Pembs...73 E9
Saham Hills Norf...141 C8
Saham Toney Norf...141 C8
Saighdinis W Isles...296 E4
Saighton Ches W...166 C6
Sain Dunwyd / St Donats
  V Glam...58 F2
St Abbs Borders...273 B8
St Abb's Haven Borders...273 B8
St Agnes Corn...4 E4
  Scilly...1 H3
St Albans Herts...85 D10
St Allen Corn...4 E6
St Andrews Fife...287 F9
St Andrew's Major
  V Glam...58 E6
St Andrew's Wood Devon...27 F9
St Annes Lancs...193 B10
St Anne's Park Bristol...60 E6
St Ann's Dumfries...248 E3
  Nottingham...171 G9
St Ann's Chapel Corn...12 G4
  Devon...8 F3
St Anthony Corn...3 C7
St Anthony-in-Meneage
  Corn...3 D7
St Anthony's T&W...243 E7
St Anthony's Hill E Sus...23 E10
St Arvans Mon...79 F8
St Asaph / Llanelwy
  Denb...181 G8
St Athan / Sain Tathon
  V Glam...58 F4
Sain Tathon / St Athan
  V Glam...58 F4
St Augustine's Kent...54 C6
St Austell Corn...5 E10
St Austins Hants...20 B2
St Bees Cumb...219 C9
St Blazey Corn...5 E11
St Blazey Gate Corn...5 E11
St Boswells Borders...262 C3
St Breock Corn...10 G5
St Breward Corn...11 F7
St Briavels Glos...79 E9
St Briavels Common Glos. 79 E8
St Bride's Pembs...72 C4
St Brides Major / Saint-y-
  Brid V Glam...57 G11
St Bride's Netherwent
  Mon...60 B2
St Brides-super-Ely
  V Glam...58 D5
St Brides Wentlooge
  Newport...59 D9
Saintbridge Glos...80 B5
St Budeaux Plym...7 D8
Saintbury Glos...100 D2
St Buryan Corn...1 D4
St Catherine Bath...61 E9
St Catherine's Argyll...284 G5
St Catherine's Hill Dorset. 19 B8
St Chloe Glos...80 E4
St Clears / Sancler
  Carms...74 B3
St Cleer Corn...6 B5
St Clement Corn...4 F6
St Clether Corn...11 E10
St Colmac Argyll...275 G11
St Columb Major Corn...5 C8
St Columb Minor Corn...4 C6
St Columb Road Corn...5 D8
St Combs Aberds...303 C10
St Cross South Elmham
  Suff...142 G5
St Cyrus Aberds...293 G9
St David's Perth...286 E3
St David's / Tyddewi
  Pembs...90 F5
St Day Corn...4 G4
St Decumans Som...42 E5
St Dennis Corn...5 D9
St Denys Soton...32 E6
St Devereux Hereford...97 E8
St Dogmaels / Llandudoch
  Pembs...92 B3
St Dominick Corn...7 B7
St Donat's / Sain Dunwyd
  V Glam...58 F2
St Edith's Wilts...62 G3
St Endellion Corn...10 F5
St Enoder Corn...5 D7
St Erme Corn...4 E6

St Erney Corn...7 D7
St Erth Corn...2 B3
St Erth Praze Corn...2 B3
St Ervan Corn...10 G3
St Eval Corn...5 B7
St Ewe Corn...5 F9
St Fagans Cardiff...58 D6
St Fergus Aberds...303 D10
St Fillans Perth...285 E10
St Florence Pembs...73 E9
St Gennys Corn...11 B8
St George Bristol...60 E6
St George in the East
  London...67 C10
St Georges N Som...59 G11
St George's Gtr Man...184 B4
  Telford...150 G4
  V Glam...58 D5
St George's Hill Sur...66 G5
St George's Well Devon...27 F8
St Germans Corn...7 D7
St Giles Lincs...189 G7
  London...67 C10
St Giles in the Wood
  Devon...25 D8
St Giles on the Heath
  Devon...12 C3
St Giles's Hill Hants...33 B7
St Gluvias Corn...3 C7
St Godwalds Worcs...117 D9
St Harmon Powys...113 C9
St Helena Warks...134 C5
St Helen Auckland
  Durham...233 F9
St Helens Cumb...228 E6
  IoW...21 D8
  Mers...183 B8
St Helen's E Sus...38 E4
  S Yorks...197 F11
St Helen's Wood E Sus...38 E4
St Helier London...67 F9
St Hilary Corn...2 F6
  V Glam...58 E4
Saint Hill Devon...27 F9
  W Sus...51 F11
St Ibbs Herts...104 F3
St Illtyd Bl Gwent...78 E2
St Ippollytts Herts...104 F3
St Ishmael's Pembs...72 D4
St Issey Corn...10 G4
St Ive Corn...6 B6
St Ive Cross Corn...6 B6
St Ives Cambs...122 C5
  Corn...2 A2
  Dorset...31 G10
St James Dorset...30 C5
  London...67 C9
  Norf...160 E5
St James's End
  Northants...120 E4
St James South Elmham
  Suff...142 G6
St Jidgey Corn...5 B8
St John Corn...7 E8
St Johns London...67 D11
St John's E Sus...52 G4
  IoM...192 D3
  Kent...52 B4
  Sur...50 B3
  Worcs...116 G5
  W Yorks...206 F4
St John's Chapel Devon...25 B8
  Durham...232 D3
St John's Fen End
  Norf...157 G10
St John's Highway
  Norf...157 G10
St John's Park IoW...21 C8
St John's Town of Dalry
  Dumfries...246 G4
St John's Wells Aberds...303 F7
St John's Wood London...67 C9
St Judes IoM...192 C4
St Julians Herts...85 D10
  Newport...59 B10
St Just Corn...1 C3
St Justinian Pembs...90 F4
St Just in Roseland Corn...3 B9
St Katharines Wilts...63 G9
St Katherine's Aberds...303 F7
St Keverne Corn...3 E7
St Kew Corn...10 F6
St Kew Highway Corn...10 F6
St Keyne Corn...6 C4
St Lawrence Corn...5 B10
  E Sus...89 G7
  IoW...21 E6
  Kent...71 F11
St Leonards Dorset...31 G10
  E Sus...38 F3
  S Lanark...268 E2
St Leonard's Bucks...84 D6
St Leonard's Street Kent...53 B7
St Levan Corn...1 E3
St Luke's Derby...152 B6
  London...67 C10
St Lythans V Glam...58 E6
St Mabyn Corn...10 G6
St Madoes Perth...286 E5
St Margarets Herts...86 C5
  London...67 E7
St Margaret's Hereford...97 E7
St Margaret's at Cliffe
  Kent...55 E11
St Margaret's Hope
  Orkney...314 G4
St Margaret South Elmham
  Suff...142 G6
St Mark's Glos...99 G8
  IoM...192 E3
St Martin Corn...2 E6
  Corn...6 D5
St Martins Perth...286 D5
St Martin's Shrops...148 B6
St Martin's Moor Shrops 148 B6
St Mary Bourne Hants...48 D2
St Marychurch Torbay...9 B8
St Mary Church V Glam...58 D3
St Mary Cray London...68 F3
St Mary Hill V Glam...58 D3
St Mary Hoo Medway...69 D10
St Mary in the Marsh
  Kent...39 B9
St Mary's Orkney...314 F4
St Mary's Bay Kent...39 B9
St Maughans Mon...79 B7
St Maughans Green Mon. 79 B7
St Mawes Corn...3 C8
St Mawgan Corn...5 C7
St Mellion Corn...7 B7
St Mellons Cardiff...59 C8
St Merryn Corn...10 G3
St Mewan Corn...5 E9
St Michael Caerhays Corn...5 G9
St Michael Church Som. 43 G10
St Michael Penkevil Corn...5 G7
St Michaels Kent...53 F11
  Torbay...9 C7

St Michaels continued
  Worcs...115 D11
St Michael's Hamlet
  Mers...182 D5
St Michael's on Wyre
  Lancs...202 E5
St Michael South Elmham
  Suff...142 G6
St Minver Corn...10 F5
St Monans Fife...287 G9
St Neot Corn...6 B3
St Neots Cambs...122 E3
St Newlyn East Corn...4 D6
St Nicholas Herts...104 F5
  Pembs...91 D7
  V Glam...58 E5
St Nicholas at Wade Kent...71 F9
St Nicholas Park Warks...135 E7
St Nicholas South Elmham
  Suff...142 G6
St Nicolas Park Warks...135 E7
St Ninians Stirling...278 C5
St Olaves Norf...143 D9
St Osyth Essex...89 B10
St Osyth Heath Essex...89 B10
St Owens Cross
  Hereford...97 G10
St Pancras London...67 C9
St Paul's Glos...80 B4
St Paul's Cray London...68 F3
St Paul's Walden Herts...104 G3
St Peters Kent...71 F11
St Peter's Glos...99 G8
  T&W...243 E9
St Peter South Elmham
  Suff...142 G6
St Peter The Great
  Worcs...117 G7
St Petrox Pembs...73 F7
St Pinnock Corn...6 C4
St Quivox S Ayrs...257 E9
St Ruan Corn...2 F6
Saint's Hill Kent...52 E4
St Stephen Corn...5 E8
St Stephens Corn...7 D8
  Herts...85 D10
St Stephen's Corn...12 D2
St Teath Corn...11 F7
St Thomas Devon...14 C4
  Swansea...57 C7
St Tudy Corn...11 F7
St Twynnells Pembs...73 F7
St Veep Corn...6 E2
St Vigeans Angus...287 C10
St Vincent's Hamlet
  Essex...87 G9
St Wenn Corn...5 C9
St Weonards Hereford...97 G9
St Winnow Corn...6 D2
Saint y Brid / St Brides
  Major V Glam...57 G11
St y-Nyll V Glam...58 D5
Saith ffynnon Flint...181 F11
Salcombe Devon...9 G9
Salcombe Regis Devon...15 D9
Salcott-cum-Virley
  Essex...88 C6
Salden Bucks...102 F6
Sale Gtr Man...184 C3
Saleby Lincs...191 F7
Sale Green Worcs...117 F8
Salehurst E Sus...38 C2
Salem Carms...94 F2
  Ceredig...128 G3
  Corn...4 G4
Salen Argyll...289 G7
  Highld...289 C8
Salendine Nook
  W Yorks...196 D6
Salenside Borders...261 E11
Salesbury Lancs...203 G9
Saleway Worcs...117 F8
Salford C Beds...103 D8
  Gtr Man...184 B4
  Oxon...100 F5
Salford Ford S Beds...184 B4
Salford Priors Warks...117 G11
Salfords Sur...51 D9
Salhouse Norf...160 G6
Saligo Argyll...274 G3
Salisbury Wilts...31 B11
Salkeld Dykes Cumb...230 D6
Sallachan Highld...289 C11
Sallachy Highld...295 B11
  Highld...309 J5
Salle Norf...160 E2
Salmans Kent...52 E4
Salmonby Lincs...190 G4
Salmond's Muir Angus...287 D9
Salmonhutch Devon...14 B2
Salperton Glos...81 B9
Salperton Park Glos...81 B9
Salph End Bedford...121 G11
Salsburgh N Lanark...268 C6
Salt Staffs...151 D9
Salta Cumb...229 B7
Saltaire W Yorks...205 F8
Saltash Corn...7 D8
Saltburn Highld...301 C7
Saltburn-by-the-Sea
  Redcar...235 G9
Saltby Leics...155 D7
Salt Coates Cumb...228 B6
Saltcoats Cumb...219 F11
  E Loth...281 E9
  N Ayrs...266 G4
Saltcotes Lancs...193 B11
Saltdean Brighton...36 G5
Salt End E Yorks...201 B7
Salter Lancs...212 G2
Salterbeck Cumb...228 F5
Salterforth Lancs...204 D3
Salters Heath Hants...48 B6
Salters Lode Norf...139 C11
Salter Street W Mid...118 C2
Salterswall Ches W...167 B10
Salterton Wilts...46 F6
Saltfleet Lincs...191 C7
Saltfleetby All Saints
  Lincs...191 C7
Saltfleetby St Clement
  Lincs...191 C7
Saltfleetby St Peter
  Lincs...190 D6
Saltford Bath...61 F7
Salt Hill Slough...66 C3
Salthouse Norf...177 E7
Saltley W Mid...133 F11
Saltmarsh Newport...59 C11
Saltmarshe E Yorks...199 C9
Saltness Orkney...314 G2
Saltness Shetland...313 J4
Saltney Flint...166 B5
Salton N Yorks...216 D4
Saltrens Devon...25 C7
Saltwell T&W...243 E7
Saltwick Northumb...242 B5
Saltwood Kent...55 F7
Salum Argyll...288 E2
Salvington W Sus...35 F10

Salwarpe Worcs...117 E7
Salwayash Dorset...16 B5
Sambourne Warks...117 E11
  Wilts...45 E11
Sambrook Telford...150 E4
Samhla W Isles...296 E3
Samlesbury Lancs...203 G7
Samlesbury Bottoms
  Lancs...194 B6
Sampford Arundel Som. 27 D10
Sampford Brett Som...42 E5
Sampford Chapple
  Devon...25 G10
Sampford Courtenay
  Devon...25 G10
Sampford Moor Som...27 D10
Sampford Peverell Devon 27 E8
Sampford Spiney Devon 12 G6
Sanaigmore Argyll...274 F3
Sancler / St Clears
  Carms...74 B3
Sancreed Corn...1 D4
Sancton E Yorks...208 F4
Sand Highld...307 K4
  Shetland...313 J5
  Som...44 D2
Sandaig Highld...295 E9
Sandale Cumb...229 C10
Sandal Magna
  W Yorks...197 D10
Sandavore Highld...294 G6
Sandbach Ches E...168 C3
Sandbach Heath Ches E. 168 C3
Sandbank Argyll...276 E3
Sandbanks Poole...18 D6
Sandborough Staffs...152 F2
Sandend Aberds...302 C5
Sanderstead London...67 G10
Sandfields Glos...99 G8
  Neath...57 C8
Sandford Cumb...222 B4
  Devon...26 G4
  Dorset...18 D4
  Hants...31 G11
  IoW...21 E6
  N Som...44 B2
  Shrops...149 C11
  Shrops...149 E8
  S Lanark...268 G4
  Worcs...99 B7
Sandford Batch N Som...44 B2
Sandfordhill Aberds...303 E11
Sandford Hill Stoke...168 G6
Sandford on Thames
  Oxon...83 E8
Sandford Orcas Dorset...29 C10
Sandford St Martin
  Oxon...101 F8
Sandgate Kent...55 G7
Sand Gate Cumb...211 D7
Sandgreen Dumfries...237 D7
Sandhaven Aberds...303 C9
Sandhead Dumfries...236 E2
Sandhill Bucks...102 F4
  Cambs...139 F11
  S Yorks...198 F2
Sandhills Dorset...29 E9
  Dorset...29 G9
  Mers...182 C4
  Oxon...83 D9
  Sur...50 F2
  W Sus...50 F3
Sandholme E Yorks...208 G2
  Lincs...156 B6
Sandhurst Brack...65 G10
  Glos...98 G6
  Kent...38 B3
Sandhutton N Yorks...215 C7
Sand Hutton N Yorks...207 B9
Sandiacre Derbys...153 B9
Sandilands Lincs...191 E8
  S Lanark...259 B9
Sandleheath Hants...31 E10
Sandling Kent...53 B9
Sandlow Green Ches E...168 B3
Sandness Shetland...313 H3
Sandon Essex...88 E2
  Herts...104 E6
  Staffs...151 C8
Sandonbank Staffs...151 C8
Sandon Bank Staffs...151 C8
Sandown IoW...21 E7
Sandown Park Kent...52 E6
Sandpit Dorset...28 G6
Sandpits Glos...98 F6
Sandplace Corn...6 D5
Sandridge Herts...85 C11
  Wilts...62 F2
Sandringham Norf...158 D3
Sands Bucks...84 G4
Sandsend N Yorks...227 D7
Sands End London...67 D9
Sandside Cumb...211 D7
  Cumb...211 C9
  Orkney...314 F2
Sandside Ho Highld...310 C3
Sandsound Shetland...313 J5
Sandtoft N Lincs...199 F8
Sandvoe Shetland...312 D5
Sandway Kent...53 C11
Sandwell W Mid...133 F10
Sandwich Kent...55 B10
Sandwich Bay Estate
  Kent...55 B11
Sandwick Cumb...221 B8
  Orkney...314 H4
  Shetland...313 L6
Sandwith Cumb...219 C9
Sandy Carms...75 D7
  C Beds...104 B3
Sandy Bank Lincs...174 D3
Sandy Carrs Durham...234 C3
Sandycroft Flint...166 B4
Sandy Cross E Sus...37 C9
Sandy Down Hants...20 B2
Sandyford Dumfries...248 E6
  Stoke...168 E5
Sandygate Devon...14 G3
  IoM...192 C4
Sandy Gate Devon...14 C5

Sandy Haven Pembs...72 D5
Sandyhills Dumfries...237 D10
Sandylake Corn...6 C2
Sandylands Lancs...211 G8
  Som...27 C10
Sandylane Swansea...56 D5
Sandy Lane Wilts...62 F3
  Wrex...166 G5
  W Yorks...205 F8
Sandypark Devon...13 D10
Sandysike Cumb...239 D9
Sandy Way IoW...20 E5
Sangobeg Highld...308 C4
Sangomore Highld...308 C4
Sanham Green W Berks...63 F10
Sankey Bridges Warr...183 D9
Sankyns Green Worcs...116 E5
Sanna Highld...288 C6
Sanndabhaig W Isles...297 G4
  W Isles...304 E6
Sannox N Ayrs...255 C11
Sanquhar Dumfries...247 B7
Sansaw Heath Shrops...149 E10
Santon Cumb...220 E2
  N Lincs...200 E2
Santon Bridge Cumb...220 E3
Santon Downham Suff...140 F6
Sapcote Leics...135 E9
Sapey Bridge Worcs...116 F4
Sapey Common
  Hereford...116 E4
Sapiston Suff...125 C8
Sapley Cambs...122 C4
Sapperton Derbys...152 C3
  Glos...80 E6
  Lincs...155 C10
Saracen's Head Lincs...156 D6
Sarclet Highld...310 E7
Sardis Carms...75 D9
  Pembs...73 D10
Sarisbury Hants...33 F8
Sarn Bridgend...58 C2
  Powys...130 E4
Sarnau Carms...74 B4
  Ceredig...110 G6
  Gwyn...147 B9
  Powys...130 F4
  Powys...148 F4
Sarn Bach Gwyn...144 D6
Sarnesfield Hereford...115 G7
Sarn Meyllteyrn Gwyn...144 C4
Saron Carms...75 C10
  Carms...93 D7
  Denb...165 C8
  Gwyn...163 D7
  Gwyn...163 D9
Sarratt Herts...85 F8
Sarratt Bottom Herts...85 F8
Sarre Kent...71 G9
Sarsden Oxon...100 G5
Sarsden Halt Oxon...100 G5
Sarsgrum Highld...308 C3
Satley Durham...233 C8
Satmar Kent...55 F9
Satron N Yorks...223 F8
Satterleigh Devon...25 C11
Satterthwaite Cumb...220 B6
Satwell Oxon...65 C8
Sauchen Aberds...293 B8
Saucher Perth...286 D5
Sauchie Clack...279 C7
Sauchieburn Aberds...293 G8
Saughall Ches W...182 G5
Saughall Massie Mers...182 D3
Saughton Edin...280 G4
Saughtree Borders...250 D3
Saul Glos...80 E2
Saundby Notts...188 D3
Saundersfoot Pembs...73 E10
Saunderton Bucks...84 E3
Saunderton Lee Bucks...84 F4
Saunton Devon...40 F3
Sausthorpe Lincs...174 B5
Saval Highld...309 J5
Savary Highld...289 E8
Saveock Corn...4 F5
Saverley Green Staffs...151 B9
Savile Park W Yorks...196 C5
Savile Town W Yorks...197 C8
Sawbridge Warks...119 D10
Sawbridgeworth Herts...87 B7
Sawdon N Yorks...217 B8
Sawley Derbys...153 C9
  Lancs...203 D11
  N Yorks...214 F4
Sawood W Yorks...205 B9
Sawston Cambs...105 B9
Sawtry Cambs...138 G3
Sawyers Hill Wilts...81 G8
Sawyer's Hill Som...27 C11
Saxby Leics...154 F6
  Lincs...189 D8
  N Sus...35 G7
Saxby All Saints N Lincs...200 E3
Saxelbye Leics...154 E4
Saxham Street Suff...125 E11
Saxilby Lincs...188 F5
Saxlingham Norf...177 E10
Saxlingham Green Norf. 142 D4
Saxlingham Nethergate
  Norf...142 D4
Saxlingham Thorpe
  Norf...142 D4
Saxmundham Suff...127 E7
Saxondale Notts...154 B3
Saxon Street Cambs...124 F3
Saxtead Suff...126 E5
Saxtead Green Suff...126 E5
Saxtead Little Green
  Suff...126 D5
Saxthorpe Norf...160 C2
Saxton N Yorks...206 F5
Scackleton N Yorks...216 E2
Scadabhagh W Isles...305 J3
Scaftworth Notts...187 C11
Scagglethorpe N Yorks...216 F6
Scaitcliffe Lancs...195 B9
Scaladal W Isles...305 G3
Scalan Moray...292 B4
Scalasaig Argyll...274 D4
Scalby E Yorks...199 B10
  N Yorks...227 G10
Scald End Bedford...121 F10
Scaldwell Northants...120 C5
Scaleby Cumb...239 E11
Scalebyhill Cumb...239 E11
Scale Hall Lancs...211 G9
Scale Houses Cumb...231 B7
Scales Cumb...210 E5
  Cumb...230 F2
  Cumb...231 C7
  Lancs...202 E6
  N Yorks...206 F5
Scalford Leics...154 E5
Scaliscro W Isles...304 F3

Scallastle Argyll...289 F8
Scalloway Shetland...313 K6
Scalpaigh Lancs...202 D4
Scalpay W Isles...305 J4
Scalpay Ho Highld...295 C8
Scalpsie Argyll...255 B11
Scamadale Highld...295 F9
Scamblesby Lincs...190 F3
Scamland E Yorks...207 E11
Scamodale Highld...289 B9
Scampston N Yorks...217 D7
Scampton Lincs...189 F7
Scapa Orkney...314 F4
Scapegoat Hill W Yorks...196 D5
Scar Orkney...314 B6
Scarborough N Yorks...217 B10
Scarcewater Corn...5 E8
Scarcliffe Derbys...171 B7
Scarcroft W Yorks...206 E3
Scarcroft Hill W Yorks...206 E3
Scardroy Highld...300 D2
Scarff Shetland...312 E4
Scarfskerry Highld...310 B6
Scargill Durham...223 C11
Scarinish Argyll...288 E2
Scarisbrick Lancs...193 E11
Scarness Cumb...229 E10
Scarning Norf...159 G9
Scarrington Notts...172 G2
Scarth Hill Lancs...194 F2
Scarthingwell N Yorks...206 F5
Scartho NE Lincs...201 F9
Scarvister Shetland...313 J5
Scarwell Orkney...314 D2
Scatness Shetland...313 M5
Scatraig Highld...301 F7
Scawby N Lincs...200 F3
Scawby Brook N Lincs...200 F3
Scawsby S Yorks...198 F4
Scawton N Yorks...215 C10
Scayne's Hill W Sus...36 C5
Scethrog Powys...96 F2
Scholar Green Ches E...168 D4
Scholemoor W Yorks...205 G8
Scholes Gtr Man...194 F5
  S Yorks...186 B5
  W Yorks...197 B7
  W Yorks...197 D7
  W Yorks...204 F6
  W Yorks...206 F3
Scholey Hill W Yorks...197 B11
School Aycliffe
  Durham...233 G11
Schoolgreen Wokingham...65 F8
School Green Ches W...167 C10
  Essex...106 E4
  IoW...20 D2
  Norf...159 E11
School House Oxon...28 G5
Schoolhill Aberds...293 D11
Sciberscross Highld...309 H7
Scilly Bank Cumb...219 B9
Scissett W Yorks...197 E8
Scleddau Pembs...91 E8
Scofton Notts...187 E10
Scole Norf...126 B2
Scole Common Norf...142 G2
Scolpaig W Isles...296 D3
Sconser Highld...295 B7
Scoonie Fife...287 G7
Scoor Argyll...274 B5
Scopwick Lincs...173 D9
Scoraig Highld...307 K5
Scorborough E Yorks...208 D6
Scorrier Corn...4 G4
Scorriton Devon...8 B4
Scorton Lancs...202 D6
  N Yorks...224 E5
Sco Ruston Norf...160 E5
Scotbheinn W Isles...296 G4
Scotby Cumb...239 G10
Scotch Corner N Yorks...224 E4
  Som...43 B7
Scotches Derbys...170 E6
Scotforth Lancs...202 B5
Scotgate W Yorks...196 E6
Scot Hay Staffs...168 F4
Scothern Lincs...189 F8
Scotland Leics...136 D3
  Lincs...155 C10
  W Berks...64 F5
Scotland End Oxon...100 E6
Scotland Gate Northumb 253 G6
Scotlands W Mid...133 C8
Scotland Street Suff...107 D9
Scotlandwell Perth...286 G5
Scot Lane End Gtr Man...194 F6
Scotsburn Highld...301 B7
Scotscalder Station
  Highld...310 D4
Scotscraig Fife...287 E8
Scot's Gap Northumb...252 F2
Scotston Aberds...293 F9
  Perth...286 C3
Scotstoun Glasgow...267 B10
Scotstown Highld...289 C10
Scotswood T&W...242 E5
  Windsor...66 F2
Scottas Highld...295 E9
Scotter Lincs...199 G11
Scotterthorpe Lincs...199 G11
Scottlethorpe Lincs...155 E11
Scotton Lincs...188 B5
  N Yorks...206 B2
  N Yorks...224 F3
Scottow Norf...160 E5
Scott Willoughby Lincs 155 B11
Scoughall E Loth...282 E2
Scoulag Argyll...266 D2
Scoulton Norf...141 C9
Scounslow Green
  Staffs...151 D11
Scourie Highld...306 E6
Scourie More Highld...306 E6
Scousburgh Shetland...313 M5
Scout Dike S Yorks...197 G8
Scout Green Cumb...221 D11
Scouthead Gtr Man...196 F3
Scowles Glos...79 C9
Scrabster Highld...310 B4
Scrafield Lincs...174 B4
Scragged Oak Kent...69 G10
Scrainwood Northumb...251 B11
Scrane End Lincs...174 F5
Scrapsgate Kent...70 E2
Scrapton Som...28 E3
Scratby Norf...161 F10
Scrayingham N Yorks...216 G4
Scredda Corn...5 E10
Scredington Lincs...173 G10
Scremby Lincs...174 B6
Scremerston Northumb 273 F11
Screveton Notts...172 G2
Scrivelsby Lincs...174 B3

Scriven N Yorks...206 B2
Scronkey Lancs...202 D4
Scrooby Notts...187 C11
Scropton Derbys...152 C3
Scrub Hill Lincs...174 D2
Scruton N Yorks...224 G5
Scugdale N Yorks...225 E10
Scurlage Swansea...56 D3
Sculcoates Hull...209 G7
Sculthorpe Norf...159 C7
Scunthorpe N Lincs...199 E11
Sea Som...28 E4
Seaborough Dorset...28 F5
Seabridge Staffs...168 G4
Seabrook Kent...55 G7
Seacombe Mers...182 C4
Seacox Heath Kent...53 G8
Seacroft Lincs...175 C9
  W Yorks...206 F3
Seadyke Lincs...156 B6
Seafar N Lanark...278 G5
Seafield Highld...311 L3
  Midloth...270 C5
  S Ayrs...257 E8
  W Loth...269 B10
Seaford E Sus...23 F7
Seaforth Mers...182 B4
Seagrave Leics...154 F2
Seagry Heath Wilts...62 C3
Seaham Durham...234 B4
Seahouses Northumb...264 C6
Seal Kent...52 B4
Sealand Flint...166 B5
Seale Sur...49 D11
Seamer N Yorks...217 C10
  N Yorks...225 C9
Seamill N Ayrs...266 F4
Sea Mills Bristol...60 D5
Sea Palling Norf...161 D8
Searby Lincs...200 F5
Seasalter Kent...70 F5
Seascale Cumb...219 E10
Seathorne Lincs...175 B9
Seathwaite Cumb...220 C4
  Cumb...220 F4
Seatle Cumb...211 C7
Seatoller Cumb...220 C4
Seaton Corn...6 E6
  Cumb...228 E6
  Devon...15 C10
  Durham...243 G9
  E Yorks...209 D9
  Kent...55 B8
  Northumb...243 B8
  Rutland...137 D8
Seaton Burn T&W...242 C6
Seaton Carew Hrtlpl...234 F6
Seaton Delaval
  Northumb...243 B8
Seaton Ross E Yorks...207 D11
Seaton Sluice Northumb. 243 B8
Seatown Aberds...302 C5
  Aberds...303 C9
  Dorset...16 C4
Seaureaugh Moor Corn...2 B6
Seave Green N Yorks...225 E11
Seaview IoW...21 C8
Seaville Cumb...238 G5
Seavington St Mary Som...28 E6
Seavington St Michael
  Som...28 D6
Seawick Essex...89 C10
Sebastopol Torf...78 F3
Sebay Orkney...314 F5
Sebergham Cumb...230 D3
Seckington Warks...134 B5
Second Coast Highld...307 K4
Second Drove Cambs...139 F10
Sedbergh Cumb...222 G3
Sedbury Glos...79 G8
Sedbusk N Yorks...223 G7
Seddington C Beds...104 B3
Sedgeberrow Worcs...99 D10
Sedgebrook Lincs...155 B7
Sedgefield Durham...234 F3
Sedgeford Norf...158 B4
Sedgehill Wilts...30 B5
Sedgemere W Mid...118 B4
Sedgley Staffs...133 E8
Sedgley Park Gtr Man...195 G10
Sedgwick Cumb...211 B10
Sedlescombe E Sus...38 D3
Sedlescombe Street
  E Sus...38 D3
Seed Kent...54 C2
Seed Lee Lancs...194 C5
Seedley Gtr Man...184 B4
Seend Wilts...62 G2
Seend Cleeve Wilts...62 G2
Seend Head Wilts...62 G2
Seer Green Bucks...85 G7
Seething Norf...142 D6
Seething Wells London...67 F7
Sefton Mers...193 G11
Segensworth Hants...33 F8
Seggat Aberds...303 E7
Seghill Northumb...243 C7
Seifton Shrops...131 G9
Seighford Staffs...151 D7
Seilebost W Isles...305 J2
Seion Gwyn...163 B8
Seisdon Staffs...132 E6
Seisiadar W Isles...304 E7
Selattyn Shrops...148 C5
Selborne Hants...49 G8
Selby N Yorks...207 G8
Selgrove Kent...54 C4
Selham W Sus...34 C6
Selhurst London...67 F10
Selkirk Borders...261 D11
Sellack Hereford...97 F11
Sellack Boat Hereford...97 F11
Sellafirth Shetland...312 D7
Sellan Corn...1 C4
Sellibister Orkney...314 B7
Sellick's Green Som...28 D2
Sellindge Kent...54 F5
Selling Kent...54 B4
Sells Green Wilts...62 G3
Selly Hill N Yorks...227 D7
Selly Oak W Mid...133 G10
Selly Park W Mid...133 G11
Selmeston E Sus...23 D8
Selsdon London...67 G10
Selsey Glos...80 E4
Selsey W Sus...22 E5
Selsfield Common
  W Sus...51 G10
Selside Cumb...221 G10
  N Yorks...212 D5
Selsley Glos...80 E4
Selsmore Hants...21 B10
Selson Kent...55 B10
Selsted Kent...55 E8
Selston Notts...171 E7

Selston Common Notts . 171 E7
Selston Green Notts . . 171 E7
Selwick Orkney 314 F2
Selworthy Som 42 D2
Semblister Shetland . . . 313 H15
Semer Suff 107 B9
Sem Hill Wilts 30 B5
Semington Wilts 61 G11
Semley Wilts 30 B5
Send Sur 50 B4
Send Grove Sur 50 B4
Send Marsh Sur 50 B4
Sennen Corn 1 D3
Sennen Cove Corn 1 D3
Sennybridge / Pont Senni
  Powys 95 F8
Serlby Notts 187 D10
Serrington Wilts 46 F5
Sessay N Yorks 215 D9
Setchey Norf 158 G2
Setley Hants 32 G4
Seton E Loth 281 G8
Seton Mains E Loth . . . 281 F8
Setter Shetland 312 E6
  Shetland 313 H5
  Shetland 313 J7
  Shetland 313 L6
Settiscarth Orkney . . . 314 E3
Settle N Yorks 212 G6
Settrington N Yorks . . 216 E6
Seven Ash Som 43 G7
Sevenhampton Glos . . 99 G10
  Swindon 82 G2
Seven Kings London . . . 68 B3
Sevenoaks Kent 52 C4
Sevenoaks Common
  Kent 52 C4
Sevenoaks Weald Kent . 52 C4
Seven Sisters / Blaendulais
  Neath 76 D4
Seven Springs Glos . . . 81 B7
Seven Star Green Essex 107 F8
Severn Beach S Glos . . 60 B4
Severnhampton Swindon 82 G2
Severn Stoke Worcs . . 99 C7
Sevick End Bedford . . 121 G11
Sevington Kent 54 E4
Sewards End Essex . . . 105 D11
Sewardstone Essex 86 F5
Sewardstonebury Essex .86 F5
Sewell C Beds 103 G9
Sewerby E Yorks 218 F3
Seworgan Corn 2 C6
Sewstern Leics 155 E7
Sexhow N Yorks 225 D9
Sezincote Glos 100 E3
Sgarasta Mhor W Isles . 305 J2
Sgiogarstaigh W Isles . 304 B7
Sgiwen / Skewen Neath . 57 B7
Shabbington Bucks . . . 83 D11
Shab Hill Glos 80 B6
Shackerley Shrops . . . 132 B6
Shackerstone Leics . . . 135 B7
Shacklecross Derbys . . 153 C8
Shackleford Sur 50 D2
Shackleton W Yorks . . 196 B3
Shacklewell London 67 B10
Shacklford Sur 50 D2
Shade W Yorks 196 C2
Shadforth Durham . . . 234 C2
Shadingfield Suff 143 G8
Shadoxhurst Kent 54 F4
Shadsworth Blackburn 195 B8
Shadwell Glos 80 F3
  London 67 C11
  Norf 141 G8
  W Yorks 206 F2
Shaftalong Staffs 169 E7
Shaftenhoe End Herts . 105 D8
Shaftesbury Dorset . . . 30 C5
Shafton S Yorks 197 E11
Shafton Two Gates
  S Yorks 197 E11
Shaggs Dorset 18 E3
Shakeford Shrops 150 D3
Shakerley Gtr Man . . . 195 G7
Shakesfield Glos 98 E3
Shalbourne Wilts 63 G11
Shalcombe IoW 20 D3
Shalden Hants 49 E7
Shalden Green Hants . . 49 E7
Shaldon Devon 14 G4
Shalfleet IoW 20 D4
Shalford Essex 106 F4
  Som 45 G8
  Sur 50 D4
Shalford Green Essex . 106 F4
Shallochmore Moray . . 302 D3
Shallowford Devon . . . 25 B11
  Devon 41 E8
  Staffs 151 D7
Shalmsford Street Kent. 54 C5
Shalstone Bucks 102 D2
Shamley Green Sur . . . 50 E4
Shandon Argyll 276 D5
Shandwick Highld 301 B8
Shangton Leics 136 D4
Shankhouse Northumb 243 B7
Shanklin IoW 21 E7
Shannochie N Ayrs . . . 255 E10
Shannochill Stirling . . 277 B10
Shanquhar Aberds . . . 302 F5
Shanwell Fife 287 E8
Shanzie Perth 286 B6
Shap Cumb 221 B11
Shapridge Glos 79 B11
Shapwick Dorset 30 G6
  Som 44 F6
Sharcott Wilts 46 C6
Shard End W Mid 134 F3
Shardlow Derbys 153 C8
Shareshill Staffs 133 B8
Sharlston W Yorks . . . 197 D11
Sharlston Common
  W Yorks 197 D11
Sharmans Cross W Mid. 118 B2
Sharnal Street Medway .69 E10
Sharnbrook Bedford . . 121 F9
Sharneyford Lancs . . . 195 C11
Sharnford Leics 135 E9
Sharnhill Green Dorset . 30 F2
Sharoe Green Lancs . . 202 G6
Sharow N Yorks 214 E6
Sharpenhoe C Beds . . 103 E11
Sharperton Northumb . 251 C11
Sharpley Gtr Man 195 E8
Sharpley Heath Staffs . 151 E8
Sharpness Glos 79 E11
Sharpsbridge E Sus . . . 36 C6
Sharp's Corner E Sus . . 23 A7
Sharpstone Bath 45 B9
Sharp Street Norf 161 E7
Sharpthorne W Sus . . . 51 G11
Sharpway Gate Worcs . 117 D9
Sharptor Corn 11 G11
Sharrington Norf 159 B10
Sharrow S Yorks 186 D4
Shatton Gtr Man 184 D4
Shatterford Worcs 132 G5

Shatterling Kent 55 B9
Shatton Derbys 185 E11
Shaugh Prior Devon 7 C10
Shavington Ches E . . . 168 E2
Shaw Gtr Man 196 F2
  Swindon 62 B6
  W Berks 64 F3
  Wilts 61 F11
  W Yorks 204 F6
Shawbank Shrops 131 G9
Shawbirch Telford . . . 150 G2
Shawbury Shrops 149 E11
Shawclough Gtr Man . 195 E11
Shaw Common Glos . . . 98 F3
Shawdon Hall Northumb 264 G3
Shawell Leics 135 G10
Shawfield Gtr Man . . . 195 E11
  Staffs 169 D7
Shawfield Head
  N Yorks 205 C11
Shawford Hants 33 C7
  Som 45 C9
Shawforth Lancs 195 C11
Shaw Green Herts 104 E5
  Lancs 194 D4
  N Yorks 205 C11
Shawhead Dumfries . . . 237 B10
  N Lanark 268 C4
Shaw Heath Ches E . . . 184 F3
  Gtr Man 184 D5
Shawhill Dumfries 238 D6
Shawlands Glasgow . . 267 C11
Shaw Lands S Yorks . . 197 F10
Shaw Mills N Yorks . . 214 G5
Shawsburn S Lanark . . 268 E5
Shaw Side Gtr Man . . . 196 F2
Shawton S Lanark . . . 268 F3
Shawtonhill S Lanark . 268 F3
Shay Gate W Yorks . . . 205 F8
Sheandow Moray 302 F2
Shear Cross Wilts 45 E11
Shearington Dumfries . 238 D2
Shearsby Leics 136 E2
Shearston Som 43 G9
Shebbear Devon 24 F6
Shebdon Staffs 150 D5
Shebster Highld 310 C4
Sheddens E Renf 267 D11
Shedfield Hants 33 E9
Sheen Staffs 169 C10
Sheepbridge Derbys . . 186 G5
Sheepdrove W Berks . . 63 D10
Sheep Hill Durham . . . 242 F5
Sheeplane C Beds 103 E8
Sheepridge Bucks 65 B11
  W Yorks 197 D7
Sheepscar W Yorks . . 206 G2
Sheepscombe Glos . . . 80 C5
Sheepstor Devon 7 B11
Sheepwash Devon 25 F7
  Northumb 253 F7
Sheepway N Som 60 D3
Sheepy Magna Leics . . 134 C6
Sheepy Parva Leics . . 134 C6
Sheering Essex 87 C8
Sheerness Kent 70 E2
Sheerwater Sur 66 G4
Sheet Hants 34 C3
  Shrops 115 C10
Sheets Heath Sur 50 B2
Sheffield Corn 1 D5
  S Yorks 186 D5
Sheffield Bottom
  W Berks 65 F7
Sheffield Green E Sus . . 36 C6
Sheffield Park W Yorks 196 B5
Shefford C Beds 104 D2
Shefford Woodlands
  W Berks 63 E11
Sheigra Highld 306 C6
Sheinton Shrops 132 C2
Shelderton Shrops . . . 115 B8
Sheldon Derbys 169 B11
  Devon 27 F10
  W Mid 134 G3
Sheldwich Kent 54 B4
Sheldwich Lees Kent . . 54 B4
Shelf Bridgend 58 C2
  W Yorks 196 B6
Shelfanger Norf 142 G2
Shelfield Warks 118 E2
  W Mid 133 C10
Shelfield Green Warks. 118 E2
Shelfleys Northants . . 120 F4
Shelford Notts 171 G11
  Warks 135 F8
Shell Worcs 117 F9
Shelland Suff 125 E10
Shellbrook Leics 152 F6
Shelley Essex 87 E9
  Suff 107 D10
  W Yorks 197 E8
Shelley Woodhouse
  W Yorks 197 E8
Shell Green Halton . . . 183 D8
Shellingford Oxon 82 G4
Shellow Bowells Essex . 87 D10
Shellwood Cross Sur . . 51 D8
Shelsley Beauchamp
  Worcs 116 E4
Shelsley Walsh Worcs . 116 E4
Shelthorpe Leics 153 F10
Shelton Bedford 121 D10
  Norf 142 E4
  Notts 172 G3
  Shrops 149 G9
  Stoke 168 F5
Shelton Green Norf . . . 142 E4
Shelton Lock Derby . . 153 C7
Shelton under Harley
  Staffs 150 B6
Shelve Shrops 130 D6
Shelvin Devon 27 G11
Shelvingford Kent 71 F8
Shelwick Hereford . . . 97 C10
Shelwick Green
  Hereford 97 C10
Shenfield Essex 87 G10
Shenington Oxon 101 C7
Shenley Herts 85 E11
Shenley Brook End
  M Keynes 102 D6
Shenleybury Herts . . . 85 E11
Shenley Church End
  M Keynes 102 D6
Shenley Fields W Mid . 133 G10
Shenley Lodge
  M Keynes 102 D6
Shenley Wood
  M Keynes 102 D6
Shenmore Hereford . . 97 D7
Shennanton Dumfries . 236 C5
Shennanton Ho
  Dumfries 236 C5
Shenstone Staffs 134 C2
  Worcs 117 C7
Shenstone Woodend
  Staffs 134 C2
Shenton Leics 134 C6
Shenval Highld 300 A4

Shenval continued
  Moray 302 G2
Shenvault Moray 301 G10
Shepeau Stow Lincs . . 156 G6
Shephall Herts 104 G5
Shepherd Hill W Yorks 197 C10
Shepherd's Bush London 67 C8
Shepherd's Green Oxon 65 C8
Shepherd's Gate Norf . 157 F11
Shepherd's Hill Sur . . . 50 G2
Shepherd's Patch Glos .80 E2
Shepherd's Port Norf . 158 C3
Shepherdswell or
  Sibertswold Kent 55 D9
Shepley W Yorks 197 F7
Shepperdine S Glos . . . 79 F10
Shepperton Sur 66 F5
Shepperton Green Sur .66 F5
Shepreth Cambs 105 B7
Shepshed Leics 153 F9
Shepton Beauchamp
  Som 28 D6
Shepton Mallet Som . . 44 E6
Shepton Montague Som 45 G7
Shepway Kent 53 C9
Sheraton Durham . . . 234 D4
Sherberton Devon 13 G8
Sherborne Bath 44 B5
  Dorset 29 D10
  Glos 81 C11
Sherborne St John . . . 48 B6
  Hants 48 B6
Sherbourne Warks . . . 118 E5
Sherbourne Street Suff 107 C9
Sherburn Durham . . . 234 C2
  N Yorks 217 D9
Sherburn Grange
  Durham 234 C2
Sherburn Hill Durham . 234 C2
Sherburn in Elmet
  N Yorks 206 G5
Sherfield English Hants. 32 C3
Sherfield on Loddon
  Hants 49 B7
Sherfin Lancs 195 B9
Sherford Devon 8 G5
  Dorset 18 C4
  Som 28 C2
Sheriffhales Shrops . . . 150 G5
Sheriff Hill T&W 243 E7
Sheriff Hutton N Yorks 216 F2
Sheriff's Lench Worcs . 99 B10
Sheringham Norf 177 E11
Sherington M Keynes . 103 B7
Sheringwood Norf 177 E11
Shermanbury W Sus . . 36 D2
Shernal Green Worcs . 117 E8
Shernborne Norf 158 C4
Sherrard's Green Worcs 98 B5
Sherrardspark Herts . . 86 C2
Sherrington Wilts 46 F3
Sherston Wilts 61 B11
Sherwood Nottingham . 171 G9
Sherwood Green Devon 25 C9
Sherwood Park Kent . . 52 E6
Shettleston Glasgow . 268 C2
Shevington Gtr Man . . 194 F4
Shevington Moor
  Gtr Man 194 E4
Shevington Vale
  Gtr Man 194 F4
Sheviock Corn 7 D7
Shewalton Corn 257 B8
Shewsmoor Devon . . . 27 G10
Shibden Head W Yorks 196 B5
Shide IoW 20 D5
Shiel Bridge Highld . . 295 D11
Shieldaig Highld 299 B8
  Highld 299 D8
Shieldhall S Lanark . . 267 B10
Shieldhill Dumfries . . . 248 F2
  Falk 279 F7
  S Lanark 269 G10
Shield Row Durham . . 242 G6
Shielfoot Highld 289 C8
Shielhill Angus 287 B8
  Involyd 276 G4
Shifford Oxon 82 E5
Shifnal Shrops 132 B4
Shilbottle Northumb . . 252 B5
Shilbottle Grange
  Northumb 252 B6
Shildon Durham 233 F10
Shillford E Renf 267 D8
Shillingford Devon . . . 27 C7
  Oxon 83 G9
Shillingford Abbot Devon 14 D4
Shillingford St George
  Devon 14 D4
Shillingstone Dorset . . 30 E4
Shillington C Beds . . . 104 E2
Shillmoor Northumb . . 251 B9
Shilton Oxon 82 D3
  Warks 135 G8
Shilvington Northumb . 252 G5
Shimpling Norf 142 G3
  Suff 125 G7
Shimpling Street Suff . 125 G7
Shincliffe Durham . . . 233 C11
Shiney Row T&W 243 G8
Shinfield Wokingham . . 65 F8
Shingay Cambs 104 B6
Shingham Norf 140 C5
Shingle Street Suff . . . 109 C7
Shinness Highld 309 H5
Shipbourne Kent 52 C5
Shipbrookhill Ches W . 183 G11
Shipham Som 44 B2
Shiphay Torbay 9 B7
Shiplake Oxon 65 D9
Shiplake Bottom Oxon . 65 B8
Shiplake Row Oxon . . . 65 D9
Shiplate N Som 43 B11
Shiplaw Borders 270 F4
Shipley Derbys 170 G6
  Northumb 264 F5
  Shrops 132 D6
  W Sus 35 C10
  W Yorks 205 F8
Shipley Bridge Sur . . . 51 E10
Shipley Common
  Derbys 171 G7
Shipley Shiels Northumb 251 E8
Shipmeadow Suff 143 F7
Shipping Pembs 73 D10
Shippon Oxon 83 F7
Shipston-on-Stour
  Warks 100 C5
Shipton Bucks 102 F5
  Glos 81 B8
  N Yorks 207 B7
  Shrops 131 E11
Shipton Bellinger Hants 47 D8
Shipton Gorge Dorset . 16 C5
Shipton Green W Sus . 22 C4
Shipton Lee Bucks . . . 102 G4
Shipton Moyne Glos . . 61 B11

Shipton Oliffe Glos 81 B8
Shipton on Cherwell
  Oxon 83 B7
Shipton Solers Glos . . . 81 B8
Shiptonthorpe E Yorks 208 E2
Shipton-under-Wychwood
  Oxon 82 B3
Shirburn Oxon 83 F11
Shirdley Hill Lancs . . . 193 E11
Shirdley Green Oxon . . 65 C8
Shirecliffe S Yorks . . . 186 C4
Shiregreen S Yorks . . . 186 C5
Shirehampton Bristol . 60 D4
Shiremoor T&W 243 C8
Shirenewton Mon 79 G7
Shire Oak W Mid 133 C11
Shireoaks Notts 187 F9
Shires Mill Fife 279 D10
Shirkoak Kent 54 F2
Shirland Derbys 170 D6
Shirlett Shrops 132 D3
Shirley Derbys 170 G2
  Hants 19 B9
  London 67 F11
  Soton 32 E6
  W Mid 118 B2
Shirley Heath W Mid . . 118 B2
Shirley holms Hants . . 20 B2
Shirley Warren Soton . 32 E5
Shirl Heath Hereford . 115 F8
Shirrell Heath Hants . . 33 D9
Shirwell Devon 40 F5
Shirwell Cross Devon . 40 F5
Shiskine N Ayrs 255 E10
Shobdon Hereford . . . 115 E8
Shobley Hants 31 F11
Shobnall Staffs 152 E4
Shobrooke Devon 26 G5
Shoby Leics 154 F3
Shocklach Ches W . . . 166 F6
Shocklach Green
  Ches W 166 F6
Shoeburyness Southend 70 C2
Sholden Kent 55 C11
Sholing Soton 32 E6
Sholing Common Soton 33 E7
Sholver Gtr Man 196 F3
Shooters Hill London . . 68 D2
Shootersway Herts . . . 85 D7
Shoot Hill Shrops 149 G8
Shop Corn 10 G3
  Corn 24 E2
  Devon 24 E5
Shop Corner Suff 108 E4
Shopford Cumb 240 C3
Shopnoller Som 43 G7
Shoppil Mill S Yorks . . 34 B6
Shopwyke W Sus 22 B5
Shore Gtr Man 196 B2
  W Yorks 196 B2
Shore Bottom Devon . . 28 G2
Shoreditch London . . . 67 C10
  Som 28 C2
Shoregill Cumb 222 E5
Shoreham Kent 68 G4
Shoreham Beach W Sus 36 G3
Shoreham-by-Sea
  W Sus 36 G2
Shore Mill Highld 301 C7
Shoresdean Northumb 273 F9
Shores Green Oxon . . . 82 D5
Shoreside Shetland . . . 313 J4
Shoreswood Northumb 273 F8
Shoreton Highld 300 C6
Shorley Hants 33 B9
Shorncliffe Camp Kent. 55 F7
Shorncote Glos 81 F8
Shorne Kent 69 E7
Shorne Ridgeway Kent. 69 E7
Shorne West Kent 69 E7
Shortacombe Devon . . 12 D6
Shortacross Corn 6 D5
Shortbridge E Sus 37 C7
Short Cross W Mid . . . 133 G9
Shortfield Common Sur 49 E10
Short Green Norf 141 F11
Short Heath Derbys . . 152 F6
  W Mid 133 C9
  W Mid 133 D11
Shorthill Shrops 131 B8
Shortlands London . . . 67 F11
Shortlanesend Corn . . .4 F6
Shortlees E Ayrs 257 B10
Shortmoor Devon 28 G2
Shorton Torbay 9 C7
Shortroods Renfs 267 B9
Shortstanding Glos . . . 79 C9
Shortstown Bedford . . 103 B11
Short Street Wilts 45 C11
Shortwood Bristol 61 D7
  S Glos 61 D7
Shorwell IoW 20 E5
Shoscombe Bath 45 B8
Shoscombe Vale Bath . 45 B8
Shotatton Shrops 149 E7
Shotesham Norf 142 D5
Shotgate Essex 88 G3
Shotley Northants . . . 137 D8
  Suff 108 D4
Shotley Bridge Durham 242 G3
Shotleyfield Northumb 242 G3
Shotley Gate Suff 108 E4
Shottenden Kent 54 C4
Shottermill Sur 49 G11
Shottery Warks 118 G3
Shotteswell Warks . . . 101 B8
Shottisham Suff 108 C6
Shottle Derbys 170 F4
Shottlegate Derbys . . 170 F4
Shotton Durham 234 D4
  Durham 234 F3
  Flint 166 B4
  Northumb 242 B6
  Northumb 263 C8
Shotton Colliery
  Durham 234 C3
Shotwick Ches W 182 G4
Shouldham Norf 140 B3
Shouldham Thorpe Norf 140 B3
Shoulton Worcs 116 F6
Shover's Green E Sus . 53 G7
Shraleybrook Staffs . . 168 F3
Shrawardine Shrops . . 149 F8
Shrawley Worcs 116 E6
Shreding Green Bucks . 66 C4
Shrewley Warks 118 D4
Shrewley Common
  Warks 118 D4
Shrewsbury Shrops . . 149 G9
Shrewton Wilts 46 E5
Shripney W Sus 22 C6
Shrivenham Oxon 63 B8

Shropham Norf 141 E9
Shroton or Iwerne Courtney
  Dorset 30 E5
Shrub End Essex 107 G9
Shrubs Hill Sur 66 F3
Shrutherhill S Lanark . 268 F5
Shucknall Hereford . . . 97 C11
Shudy Camps Cambs . 106 C2
Shulishadermor Highld 298 E4
Shulista Highld 298 B4
Shuna Ho Argyll 275 C8
Shurdington Glos 80 B6
Shurlock Row Windsor . 65 E10
Shurnock Worcs 117 E10
Shurrery Highld 310 D4
Shurrery Lodge Highld 310 D4
Shurton Som 43 E8
Shustoke Warks 134 E4
Shute Devon 15 B11
  Devon 26 G5
Shute End Wilts 31 B11
Shutford Oxon 101 C7
Shut Heath Staffs . . . 151 E7
Shuthonger Glos 99 D7
Shutlanger Northants . 120 G4
Shutta Corn 6 E5
Shutt Green Staffs . . . 133 C7
Shuttington Warks . . . 134 B5
Shuttlesfield Kent 55 E7
Shuttlewood Derbys . . 187 G7
Shuttleworth Gtr Man . 195 D10
Siabost bho Dheas
  W Isles 304 D4
Siabost bho Thuath
  W Isles 304 D4
Siadar W Isles 304 C5
Siadar Iarach W Isles . 304 C5
Siadar Uarach W Isles . 304 C5
Sibbaldbie Dumfries . . 248 F4
Sibbertoft Northants . 136 G3
Sibdon Carwood Shrops 131 G8
Sibford Ferris Oxon . . 101 D7
Sibford Gower Oxon . . 101 D7
Sible Hedingham Essex 106 E5
Sibley's Green Essex . . 106 F2
Sibsey Lincs 174 E4
Sibsey Fen Side Lincs . 174 E4
Sibson Cambs 137 D11
  Leics 135 C7
Sibster Highld 310 D7
Sibthorpe Notts 172 F3
Sibton Suff 127 D7
Sibton Green Suff . . . 127 C7
Sicklesmere Suff 125 E7
Sicklinghall N Yorks . . 206 D3
Sid Devon 15 D8
Sidbrook Som 28 B3
Sidbury Devon 15 C8
  Shrops 132 F3
Sidcot N Som 44 B2
Sidcup London 68 E3
Siddal W Yorks 196 C6
Siddick Cumb 228 E6
Siddington Ches E . . . 184 G4
  Glos 81 F8
Sidemoor Worcs 117 C9
Side of the Moor
  Gtr Man 195 E8
Sidestrand Norf 160 B5
Sideway Stoke 168 G5
Sidford Devon 15 C8
Sidlesham W Sus 22 D5
Sidlesham Common
  W Sus 22 C5
Sidley E Sus 38 F2
Sidlow Sur 51 D9
Sidmouth Devon 15 D8
Sidway Staffs 150 B5
Sigford Devon 13 G11
Sigglesthorne E Yorks 209 E8
Sighthill Edin 280 G3
Signingstone / Tresigin
  V Glam 58 E3
Signet Oxon 82 C2
Sigwells Som 29 C10
Silchester Hants 64 F6
Sildinis W Isles 305 G4
Sileby Leics 153 F11
Silecroft Cumb 210 C2
Silfield Norf 142 D2
Silford Devon 24 B6
Silian Ceredig 111 G11
Silk Willoughby Lincs . 173 G9
Silloth Cumb 238 G4
Sills Northumb 251 C8
Sillyearn Moray 302 D5
Siloh Carms 94 E4
Silpho N Yorks 227 G9
Silsden W Yorks 204 D6
Silsoe C Beds 103 D11
Silton Dorset 30 B3
Silverburn Midloth . . . 270 C4
Silverdale Lancs 211 E9
  Staffs 168 F4
Silverdale Green Lancs 211 E9
Silver End Essex 88 B4
  W Mid 133 F8
Silver Green Norf 142 E5
Silverhill E Sus 38 E3
Silverhill Park E Sus . . 38 E4
Silver Hill E Sus 38 B3
Silverknowes Edin . . . 280 F4
Silverley's Green Suff . 126 B5
Silvermuir S Lanark . . 269 F8
Silverstone Glos 80 E3
  Northants 102 C3
  Som 27 C11
  Som 44 G4
  Worcs 117 D11
Silverton Devon 27 G7
  W Dunb 277 F8
Silvertonhill S Lanark . 268 E4
Silvington Shrops 116 B2
Silwick Shetland 313 J4
Simister Gtr Man 195 F10
Simmondley Derbys . . 185 C8
Simm's Cross Halton . 183 D8
Simm's Lane End Mers. 194 G4
Simonburn Northumb . 241 C9
Simonsbath Som 41 F9
Simonsburrow Devon . 27 D10
Simonside T&W 243 E8
Simonstone Lancs . . . 203 G11
  N Yorks 223 G7
Simprim Borders 272 F6

Simpson M Keynes . . . 103 D7
  Pembs 72 B5
Simpson Cross Pembs . 72 B5
Simpson Green W Yorks 205 F9
Sinclair's Hill Borders . 272 E6
Sinclairston E Ayrs . . . 257 F11
Sinclairtown Fife 280 C5
Sinderby N Yorks 214 C6
Sinderhope Northumb . 241 G8
Sinderland Green
  Gtr Man 184 C2
Sindlesham Wokingham . 65 F9
Sinfin Derby 152 C6
Sinfin Moor Derby . . . 153 C7
Singdean Borders 250 C3
Singleborough Bucks . 102 E5
Single Hill Bath 45 B8
Singleton Lancs 202 F3
  W Sus 34 E5
Singlewell Kent 69 E7
Singret Wrex 166 D4
Sinkhurst Green Kent . . 53 E11
Sinnahard Aberds . . . 292 B6
Sinnington N Yorks . . . 216 B4
Sinton Worcs 116 E6
Sinton Green Worcs . . 116 E6
Sion Hill Bath 61 F8
Sipson London 66 D5
Sirhowy Bl Gwent 77 C11
Sisland Norf 142 D6
Sissinghurst Kent 53 F9
Sisterpath Borders . . . 272 F5
Siston S Glos 61 D7
Sithney Corn 2 D4
Sithney Common Corn . .2 D4
Sithney Green Corn 2 D4
Sittingbourne Kent . . . 70 G2
Siulaisiadar W Isles . . 304 E7
Six Ashes Staffs 132 F5
Six Bells Bl Gwent 78 E2
Sixhills Lincs 189 D11
Six Hills Leics 154 E2
Sixmile Kent 54 E6
Six Mile Bottom Cambs 123 F11
Sixpenny Handley Dorset 31 D7
Sizewell Suff 127 E9
Skaigh Devon 13 C8
Skail Highld 308 E7
Skaill Orkney 314 C4
  Orkney 314 E2
Skares E Ayrs 258 F2
Skateraw E Loth 282 F4
Skaw Shetland 312 B8
  Shetland 312 G7
Skeabost Highld 298 E4
Skeabrae Orkney 314 D2
Skeeby N Yorks 224 E4
Skeete Kent 54 E6
Skeffington Leics 136 C4
Skeffling E Yorks 201 D11
Skegby Notts 171 C7
  Notts 188 G3
Skegness Lincs 175 C9
Skelberry Shetland . . . 313 G6
  Shetland 313 M5
Skelbo Highld 309 K7
Skelbo Street Highld . 309 K7
Skelbrooke S Yorks . . 198 E4
Skeldyke Lincs 156 B6
Skelfhill Borders 249 C11
Skellingthorpe Lincs . . 188 G6
Skellister Shetland . . . 313 H6
Skellorn Green Ches E . 184 E6
Skellow S Yorks 198 E4
Skelmanthorpe W Yorks 197 E8
Skelmersdale Lancs . . 194 G3
Skelmonae Aberds . . . 303 F8
Skelmorlie N Ayrs . . . 266 B3
Skelmuir Aberds 303 E9
Skelpick Highld 308 D7
Skelton Cumb 230 D4
  E Yorks 199 B9
  N Yorks 223 E11
  Redcar 226 B3
  York 207 B7
Skelton-on-Ure
  N Yorks 215 F7
Skelwick Orkney 314 B4
Skelwith Bridge Cumb . 220 E6
Skendleby Lincs 174 B6
Skendleby Psalter Lincs 190 G6
Skene Ho Aberds 293 C9
Skenfrith Mon 97 G9
Skerne E Yorks 208 B6
Skerne Park Darl 224 C5
Skeroblingarry Argyll . 255 E8
Skerray Highld 308 C6
Skerricha Highld 306 D7
Skerryford Pembs 72 C6
Skerton Lancs 211 G9
Sketchley Leics 135 E8
Sketty Swansea 56 C6
Skewen / Sgiwen Neath .57 B8
Skewes Corn 4 F4
Skewsby N Yorks 216 E2
Skeyton Norf 160 D5
Skeyton Corner Norf . . 160 D5
Skiag Bridge Highld . . 307 G7
Skibo Castle Highld . . 309 L7
Skidbrooke Lincs 190 C6
Skidbrooke North End
  Lincs 190 B6
Skidby E Yorks 208 G6
Skilgate Som 27 B7
Skillington Lincs 155 D7
Skinburness Cumb . . . 238 F5
Skinflats Falk 279 E8
Skinidin Highld 298 E2
Skinner's Bottom Corn . 4 F4
Skinners Green W Berks 64 F2
Skinnet Highld 308 C5
Skinningrove Redcar . . 226 B4
Skipness Argyll 255 B9
Skippool Lancs 202 E3
Skiprigg Cumb 230 B3
Skipsea E Yorks 209 B9
Skipsea Brough E Yorks 209 C9
Skipton N Yorks 204 C5
Skipton-on-Swale
  N Yorks 215 D7
Skipwith N Yorks 207 F9
Skirbeck Lincs 174 G4
Skirbeck Quarter Lincs 174 G4
Skirethorns N Yorks . . 213 G9
Skirlaugh E Yorks 209 F8
Skirling Borders 260 B3
Skirmett Bucks 65 B9
Skirpenbeck E Yorks . . 207 B10
Skirwith Cumb 231 E8
  N Yorks 212 C4
Skirza Highld 310 C7
Skitby Cumb 239 D10
Skitham Lancs 202 E4
Skittle Green Bucks . . .84 E3
Skulamus Highld 295 C8
Skullomie Highld 308 C6
Skyborry Green Shrops 114 C5
Skye Green Essex 107 G7
Skye of Curr Highld . . 301 G9
Skyfog Pembs 90 F6
Skyreholme N Yorks . . 213 G11
Slack Derbys 170 C4

Slack continued
  W Isles 196 B3
  W Yorks 196 B5
Slackcote Gtr Man . . . 196 F3
Slackhall Derbys 185 E9
Slackhead Moray 302 C4
Slack Head Cumb 211 D9
Slackholme End Lincs . 191 G8
Slacks of Cairnbanno
  Aberds 303 E8
Slad Glos 80 D5
Sladbrook Glos 98 F5
Slade Devon 27 E9
  Devon 40 D4
  Kent 54 C2
  Pembs 72 B6
  Swansea 56 E3
Slade End Oxon 83 G9
Slade Green London . . 68 D5
Slade Heath Staffs . . . 133 B8
Slade Hooton S Yorks . 187 D8
Sladen Green Hants . . 48 C2
Sladesbridge Corn . . . 10 G6
Slades Green Worcs . . 99 E7
  Gtr Man 184 D5
Slaggyford Northumb . 240 G5
Slaidburn Lancs 203 C10
Slaithwaite W Yorks . . 196 E5
Slaley Derbys 170 D3
  Northumb 241 F10
Slamannan Falk 279 G7
Slape Cross Som 43 G9
Slapewath Redcar . . . 226 B2
Slapton Bucks 103 G8
  Devon 8 G6
  Northants 102 B2
Slateford Edin 280 G4
Slate Haugh Moray . . 302 C4
Slatepit Dale Derbys . 170 B4
Slattocks Gtr Man . . . 195 F11
Slaugham W Sus 36 B3
Slaughterbridge Corn . 11 D8
Slaughterford Wilts . . 61 E10
Slaughter Hill Ches E . 168 D2
Slawston Leics 136 E5
Slay Pits S Yorks 199 F7
Sleaford Hants 49 F10
  Lincs 173 G9
Sleagill Cumb 221 B11
Sleapford Telford 150 F2
Sleapshyde Herts 86 D2
Sleastary Highld 309 K6
Slebech Pembs 73 B8
Sledge Green Worcs . . .98 E6
Sledmere E Yorks 217 G8
Sleetbeck Cumb 240 B2
Sleet Moor Derbys . . . 170 E6
Sleight Dorset 18 B5
Sleightholme Durham . 223 C8
Sleights N Yorks 227 D7
Slepe Dorset 18 C4
Sliabh-na-Airde
  W Isles 296 F3
Slickly Highld 310 C6
Sliddery N Ayrs 255 E10
Slideslow Worcs 117 C9
Sligachan Hotel Highld. 294 C6
Sligneach Argyll 288 G4
Sligrachan Argyll 276 C3
Slimbridge Glos 80 E2
Slindon Staffs 150 C6
  W Sus 35 F7
Slinfold W Sus 35 B9
Sling Glos 79 D9
  Gwyn 163 B10
Slingsby N Yorks 216 E3
Slioch Aberds 302 F5
Slip End C Beds 85 B9
  Herts 104 D5
Slipper Chapel Norf . . 159 C7
Slippery Ford W Yorks . 204 E6
Slipton Northants 121 B9
Slitting Mill Staffs . . . 151 F10
Slochd Highld 301 G8
Slochnacraig Perth . . 292 G3
Slockavullin Argyll . . . 275 D9
Slogan Moray 302 E3
Sloley Norf 160 E5
Sloncombe Devon . . . 13 D10
Sloothby Lincs 191 G7
Slop Madam Wilts . . . 62 G4
Slough Slough 66 C3
  Som 28 D3
Slough Green Som . . . 28 C2
  W Sus 36 B3
Slough Hill Suff 125 F7
Sluggan Highld 301 G8
Sluggans Highld 298 E4
Slumbay Highld 295 B10
Sly Corner Kent 54 G3
Slyfield Sur 50 C3
Slyne Lancs 211 F9
Smailholm Borders . . 262 B4
Smallbridge Gtr Man . 196 E2
Smallbrook Devon . . . 14 B3
  Glos 79 D9
Smallburgh Norf 160 E6
Smallburn Aberds . . . 303 E10
  E Ayrs 258 C5
Smalldale Derbys 185 F11
  Derbys 185 G10
Small Dole W Sus 36 E2
Small End Lincs 174 D5
Smalley Derbys 170 G6
Smalley Common
  Derbys 170 G6
Smalley Green Derbys . 170 G6
Smallfield Sur 51 E10
Smallford Herts 85 D11
Small Heath W Mid . . . 134 F2
Smallholm Dumfries . . 238 B4
Small Hythe Kent 53 G11
Smallmarsh Devon . . . 25 C10
Smallrice Staffs 151 C9
Smallridge Devon 28 G4
Smallthorne Stoke . . . 168 E5
Small Way Som 44 G6
Smallwood Ches E . . . 168 C4
  Worcs 117 D7
Smallwood Green Suff . 125 E8
Smallworth Norf 141 G10
Smannell Hants 47 D11
Smardale Cumb 222 D4
Smarden Kent 53 E11
Smarden Bell Kent . . . 53 E11
Smart's Hill Kent 52 E4
Smeatharpe Devon . . . 27 E11
Smeaton Fife 280 C5
Smeeth Kent 54 F5
Smeeton Westerby
  Leics 136 E2
Smelthouses N Yorks . 214 G3
Smercleit W Isles 297 K3
Smerral Highld 310 F5
Smestow Staffs 133 E7
Smethcott Shrops . . . 131 D9
Smethwick W Mid . . . 133 F10
Smethwick Green
  Ches E 168 C4
Sminary Highld 289 B8
Smisby Derbys 152 F6
Smith End Green Worcs 116 G5
Smith Hill Worcs 117 F7

Smithaleigh Devon 7 D11
Smith's End Lincs 34 C6
Smithfield Cumb 239 D10
Smith Green Lancs . . . 202 C5
Smithies S Yorks 197 F11
Smithincott Devon . . . 27 E9
Smithley S Yorks 197 G11
Smith's End Herts . . . 105 D8
Smiths Green Ches E . 184 G4
  Essex 105 G11
  Essex 106 G3
Smithston Aberds . . . 302 G5
Smithstown Highld . . . 299 B7
Smithton Highld 301 E7
Smithwood Green Suff 125 G8
Smithy Bridge Gtr Man 196 D2
Smithy Gate Flint 181 F11
Smithy Green Ches E . 184 G2
  Gtr Man 184 D5
Smithy Houses Derbys 170 F5
Smithy Lane Ends Lancs 194 E3
Smock Alley W Sus . . . 35 D9
Smockington Leics . . . 135 F9
Smoky Row Bucks 84 D4
Smoogro Orkney 314 F3
Smug Oak Herts 85 E10
Smyrton S Ayrs 244 G4
Smythe's Green Essex . 88 B6
Snagshall E Sus 38 C3
Snaigow House Perth . 286 C4
Snailbeach Shrops . . . 131 C7
Snails Hill Som 29 E7
Snailswell Herts 104 E3
Snainton N Yorks 217 C8
Snaisgill Durham 232 F5
Snaith E Yorks 198 C6
Snape N Yorks 214 C5
  Suff 127 F7
Snape Green Lancs . . . 193 E11
Snape Hill Derbys 186 F5
  S Yorks 197 G11
Snapper Devon 40 G5
Snaresbrook London . . 67 B11
Snarestone Leics 134 B6
Snarford Lincs 189 E9
Snargate Kent 39 B7
Snarraness Shetland . . 313 H4
Snatchwood Torf 78 E3
Snave Kent 39 B8
Sneachill Worcs 117 G8
Snead Powys 130 E6
Snead Common Worcs . 116 D4
Sneads Green Worcs . . 117 D7
Sneath Common Norf . 142 F3
Sneaton N Yorks 227 D7
Sneatonthorpe N Yorks 227 D8
Snedshill Telford 132 B4
Sneinton Nottingham . 153 B11
Snelland Lincs 189 E9
Snelston Derbys 169 G11
Snetterton Norf 141 E9
Snettisham Norf 158 C3
Sneyd Green Stoke . . . 168 F5
Sneyd Park Bristol 60 D5
Snibston Leics 153 G8
Snig's End Glos 98 F5
Snipeshill Kent 70 G2
Sniseabhal W Isles . . . 297 H3
Snitter Northumb 252 C2
Snitterby Lincs 189 C7
Snitterfield Warks . . . 118 F4
Snitterton Derbys . . . 170 C3
Snitton Shrops 115 B11
Snittongate Shrops . . 115 B11
Snodhill Hereford 96 C6
Snodland Kent 69 G7
Snods Edge Northumb . 242 G3
Snowden Hill S Yorks . 197 G9
Snowdown Kent 55 C9
Snow End Herts 105 E8
Snow Hill W Yorks . . . 167 E10
  W Yorks 197 C10
Snow Lea W Yorks . . . 196 D5
Snowshill Glos 99 E11
Snow Street Norf 141 G11
Snydale W Yorks 198 D2
Soake Hants 33 E10
Soar Anglesey 178 G5
  Carms 94 F2
  Devon 9 G9
  Gwyn 146 B2
  Powys 95 G9
Soar-y-Mynydd Ceredig 112 G5
Soberton Hants 33 D10
Soberton Heath Hants . 33 E10
Sockbridge Cumb 230 F6
Sockburn Darl 224 D6
Sodom Denb 181 G9
  Shetland 313 G7
Sodylt Bank Shrops . . 148 B6
Soham Cambs 123 C11
Soham Cotes Cambs . . 123 B11
Soho London 67 C9
  Som 45 B7
  W Mid 133 F10
Solas W Isles 296 D4
Soldon Cross Devon . . 24 E4
Soldridge Hants 49 G7
Sole Street Kent 54 E5
  Kent 69 F7
Solfach / Solva Pembs . 90 G5
Solihull W Mid 118 B2
Solihull Lodge W Mid . 117 B11
Sollers Dilwyn Hereford 115 F8
Sollers Hope Hereford . 98 E2
Sollom Lancs 194 D3
Solva / Solfach Pembs . 90 G5
Somerby Leics 154 F5
  Lincs 200 G4
Somercotes Derbys . . 170 E6
Somerford Ches E . . . 168 C4
  Dorset 19 C9
Somerford Keynes Glos 81 F8
Somerley W Sus 22 D4
Somerleyton Suff 143 D9
Somersal Herbert
  Derbys 152 B2
Somersby Lincs 190 G4
Somersham Cambs . . 123 B8
  Suff 107 B11
Somers Town London . 67 C9
  Ptsmth 21 B8
Somerton Newport . . . 59 B10
  Oxon 101 F9
  Som 29 B7
  Suff 124 G6
Somerton Hill Som . . . 29 B7
Somerwood Shrops . . 149 G11
Sompting W Sus 35 G11
Sompting Abbotts
  W Sus 35 F11
Sonning Wokingham . . 65 D9

Sonning Common Oxon. . . 65 C8
Sonning Eye Oxon 65 D9
Sontley Wrex. . . . 166 F4
Sookholme Notts. . . . 171 B8
Sopley Hants. . . . 19 B9
Sopwell Herts. . . . 85 D11
Sopworth Wilts. . . . 61 B10
Sorbie Dumfries. . . . 236 E6
Sordale Highld. . . . 310 C5
Sorisdale Argyll. . . . 288 C4
Sorley Devon. . . . 8 F4
Sorn E Ayrs. . . . 258 D3
Sornhill E Ayrs. . . . 258 C2
Sortat Highld. . . . 310 C6
Sotby Lincs. . . . 190 F2
Sothall S Yorks. . . . 186 E6
Sots Hole Lincs. . . . 173 C10
Sotterley Suff. . . . 143 G9
Soudley Shrops. . . . 131 E9
  Shrops. . . . 150 D4
Soughley S Yorks. . . . 197 G7
Soughton / Sychdyn
  Flint. . . . 166 B2
Soulbury Bucks. . . . 103 F7
Soulby Cumb. . . . 222 C4
  Cumb. . . . 230 D4
Souldern Oxon. . . . 101 E10
Souldrop Bedford. . . . 121 E9
Sound Ches E. . . . 167 F10
  Shetland. . . . 313 H5
  Shetland. . . . 313 J6
Sound Heath Ches E. . . . 167 F10
Soundwell S Glos. . . . 60 D6
Sourhope Borders. . . . 263 E8
Sourin Orkney. . . . 314 C4
Sourlie N Ayrs. . . . 266 G6
Sour Nook Cumb. . . . 230 C3
Soutergate Cumb. . . . 210 C4
South Acre Norf. . . . 158 G6
South Acton London. . . . 67 D7
South Alkham Kent. . . . 55 E8
Southall London. . . . 66 C6
South Allington Devon. . . . 9 G10
South Alloa Falk. . . . 279 C10
Southam Cumb. . . . 219 C9
  Glos. . . . 99 F9
  Warks. . . . 119 E8
South Ambersham
  W Sus. . . . 34 C6
Southampton Soton. . . . 32 E6
South Anston S Yorks. . . . 187 E8
South Ascot Windsor. . . . 66 F2
South Ashford Kent. . . . 54 E4
South Auchmachar
  Aberds. . . . 303 E9
Southay Som. . . . 28 D6
South Baddesley Hants. . . . 20 B3
South Ballachulish
  Highld. . . . 284 B4
South Balloch S Ayrs. . . . 245 D8
South Bank Redcar. . . . 234 G6
  York. . . . 207 C7
South Barrow Som. . . . 29 B10
South Beach Northumb. . . . 243 B8
South Beach / Marian-y-de
  Gwyn. . . . 145 C7
South Beddington
  London. . . . 67 G9
South Benfleet Essex. . . . 69 B9
South Bents T&W. . . . 243 E10
South Bersted W Sus. . . . 22 C6
South Blainslie
  Borders. . . . 271 G10
South Bockhampton
  Dorset. . . . 19 B9
Southborough Kent. . . . 52 E5
  London. . . . 67 F7
  London. . . . 68 F2
Southbourne Bmouth. . . . 19 C8
  W Sus. . . . 22 B3
South Bramwith
  S Yorks. . . . 198 E6
South Brent Devon. . . . 8 D3
South Brewham Som. . . . 45 F8
South Bromley London. . . . 67 C11
Southbrook Wilts. . . . 45 G10
South Broomage Falk. . . . 279 E7
South Broomhill
  Northumb. . . . 252 D6
Southburgh Norf. . . . 141 C9
South Burlingham Norf. . . . 143 B7
Southburn E Yorks. . . . 208 C5
South Cadbury Som. . . . 29 B10
South Cairn Dumfries. . . . 236 C1
South Carlton Lincs. . . . 189 F7
  Notts. . . . 187 E9
South Carne Corn. . . . 11 E10
South Cave E Yorks. . . . 208 G4
South Cerney Glos. . . . 81 F8
South Chailey E Sus. . . . 36 D5
South Chard Som. . . . 28 F4
South Charlton
  Northumb. . . . 264 E5
South Cheriton Som. . . . 29 C11
Southchurch Southend. . . . 70 B2
South Church Durham. . . . 233 F10
South Cliffe E Yorks. . . . 208 F3
South Clifton Notts. . . . 188 G4
South Clunes Highld. . . . 300 E5
South Cockerington
  Lincs. . . . 190 D5
South Common Devon. . . . 28 G4
Southcoombe Oxon. . . . 100 F6
South Corriegills
  N Ayrs. . . . 256 C2
South Corrielaw
  Dumfries. . . . 248 G3
Southcote Reading. . . . 65 E7
Southcott Corn. . . . 11 B9
  Devon. . . . 24 D6
  Wilts. . . . 47 B7
Southcourt Bucks. . . . 84 C4
South Cove Suff. . . . 143 G9
South Creagan Argyll. . . . 289 E11
South Creake Norf. . . . 159 B7
Southcrest Worcs. . . . 117 D10
South Crosland
  W Yorks. . . . 196 E6
South Croxton Leics. . . . 154 G3
South Croydon London. . . . 67 G10
South Cuil Highld. . . . 298 C3
South Dalton E Yorks. . . . 208 D5
South Darenth Kent. . . . 68 F5
Southdean Borders. . . . 250 B4
Southdene Mers. . . . 182 B6
South Denes Norf. . . . 143 C10
Southdown Bath. . . . 61 G8
  Corn. . . . 7 E8
South Down Hants. . . . 33 C7
  Som. . . . 28 E2
South Duffield N Yorks. . . . 207 G9
South Dunn Highld. . . . 310 D5
South Earlswood Sur. . . . 51 E9
Southease E Sus. . . . 36 F6
South Elkington Lincs. . . . 190 D3
South Elmsall W Yorks. . . . 198 E3

South Elphinstone
  E Loth. . . . 281 G7
Southend Argyll. . . . 255 G7
  Bucks. . . . 65 B9
  Glos. . . . 80 F2
  London. . . . 67 E11
  Oxon. . . . 83 E9
  W Berks. . . . 64 D2
  W Berks. . . . 64 E5
  Wilts. . . . 63 E7
South-end Bedford. . . . 103 B10
  Bucks. . . . 103 F7
  Cumb. . . . 210 G4
  Hants. . . . 31 D10
South-end Herts. . . . 86 B6
South End N Lincs. . . . 200 C6
  Norf. . . . 141 E9
Southend-on-Sea
  Southend. . . . 69 B11
Southerhouse Shetland. . . . 313 K5
Southerly Devon. . . . 12 D6
Southernby Cumb. . . . 230 D3
Southern Cross Brighton. . . . 36 F3
Southenden Kent. . . . 53 D11
Southerndown V Glam. . . . 57 G11
Southerness Dumfries. . . . 237 D11
Southern Green Herts. . . . 104 E6
South Erradale Highld. . . . 299 B7
Southery Norf. . . . 140 E2
Southey Green Essex. . . . 106 E5
South Fambridge Essex. . . . 88 F5
South Farnborough
  Hants. . . . 49 C11
South Fawley W Berks. . . . 63 C11
South Ferriby N Lincs. . . . 200 C3
Southfield Northumb. . . . 243 B7
South Field E Yorks. . . . 200 B4
  Windsor. . . . 66 D3
Southfields London. . . . 67 E9
  Thurrock. . . . 69 C7
South Flobbets Aberds. . . . 303 F7
Southford Devon. . . . 20 F6
South Garth Shetland. . . . 312 D7
South Garvan Highld. . . . 289 B11
Southgate Ceredig. . . . 111 A11
  London. . . . 86 G3
  Norf. . . . 159 C7
  Norf. . . . 160 E2
  Swansea. . . . 56 D5
South Glendale W Isles. . . . 297 K3
South Gluss Shetland. . . . 312 F5
South Godstone Sur. . . . 51 D11
South Gorley Hants. . . . 31 E11
South Gosforth T&W. . . . 242 D6
South Green Essex. . . . 87 G11
  Essex. . . . 89 B8
  Kent. . . . 69 G11
  Norf. . . . 157 F10
  Norf. . . . 159 G11
  Suff. . . . 126 B3
South Gyle Edin. . . . 280 G3
South-haa Shetland. . . . 312 E5
South Hackney London. . . . 67 C11
South Ham Hants. . . . 48 C6
South Hampstead London. . . . 67 C9
South Hanningfield Essex. . . . 88 F2
South Harefield London. . . . 66 B5
South Harrow London. . . . 66 B6
South Harting W Sus. . . . 34 D3
South Hatfield Herts. . . . 86 D2
South Hayling Hants. . . . 21 B10
South Hazelrigg
  Northumb. . . . 264 C3
South Heath Bucks. . . . 84 E6
  Essex. . . . 89 B10
South Heighton E Sus. . . . 23 E7
South-heog Shetland. . . . 312 E6
South Hetton Durham. . . . 234 B3
South Hiendley
  S Yorks. . . . 197 E11
  N Som. . . . 42 F5
South Hill Corn. . . . 12 G2
South Hinksey Oxon. . . . 83 E8
South Hole Devon. . . . 24 C2
South Holme N Yorks. . . . 216 D3
South Holmwood Sur. . . . 51 D7
South Hornchurch
  London. . . . 68 C4
South Huish Devon. . . . 8 G3
South Hykeham Lincs. . . . 172 C6
South Hylton T&W. . . . 243 F9
Southill C Beds. . . . 104 C3
  Dorset. . . . 17 E9
Southington Hants. . . . 48 D4
South Kelsey Lincs. . . . 189 B8
South Kensington London. . . . 67 D9
South Kessock Highld. . . . 300 E6
South Killingholme
  N Lincs. . . . 201 D7
South Kilvington
  N Yorks. . . . 215 C8
South Kilworth Leics. . . . 136 G2
South Kirkby W Yorks. . . . 198 E3
South Kirkton Aberds. . . . 293 C9
South Kiscadale N Ayrs. . . . 256 D2
South Knighton Devon. . . . 14 G2
  Leicester. . . . 136 C2
South Kyme Lincs. . . . 173 F11
South Lambeth London. . . . 67 D10
South Lancing W Sus. . . . 35 G11
Southlands Dorset. . . . 15 C10
South Lane S Yorks. . . . 197 F9
Southleigh Devon. . . . 15 C11
South Leigh Oxon. . . . 82 D5
South Leverton Notts. . . . 188 E3
South Littleton Worcs. . . . 99 B11
South Lopham Norf. . . . 141 G10
South Luffenham
  Rutland. . . . 137 C8
South Malling E Sus. . . . 36 E6
Southmarsh Som. . . . 45 G8
South Marston Swindon. . . . 63 B7
Southmead Bristol. . . . 60 D5
South Merstham Sur. . . . 51 C9
South Middleton
  Northumb. . . . 263 E11
South Milford N Yorks. . . . 206 G5
South Millbrex Aberds. . . . 303 E8
South Milton Devon. . . . 8 G4
South Mimms Herts. . . . 86 E2
Southminster Essex. . . . 89 F7
South Molton Devon. . . . 26 C2
Southmoor Oxon. . . . 82 F5
South Moor Durham. . . . 242 G5
South Moreton Oxon. . . . 64 B5
South Mundham W Sus. . . . 22 C5
South Muskham Notts. . . . 172 D3
South Newbald E Yorks. . . . 208 F4
South Newbarns Cumb. . . . 210 F3
South Newington Oxon. . . . 101 E8
South Newsham
  Northumb. . . . 243 B8
South Newton Wilts. . . . 46 G5
South Normanton
  Derbys. . . . 170 D6
South Norwood London. . . . 67 F10
South Nutfield Sur. . . . 51 D10

South Ockendon Thurrock. . . . 68 C5
Southoe Cambs. . . . 122 E3
Southolt Suff. . . . 126 D3
South Ormsby Lincs. . . . 190 F5
Southorpe Pboro. . . . 137 C11
South Ossett W Yorks. . . . 197 D9
South Otterington
  N Yorks. . . . 215 B7
Southover Dorset. . . . 17 C8
  E Sus. . . . 36 F6
  E Sus. . . . 37 B11
South Owersby Lincs. . . . 189 C9
Southowram W Yorks. . . . 196 C6
South Oxhey Herts. . . . 85 G10
South Park Sur. . . . 51 D8
South Pelaw Durham. . . . 243 G7
South Perrott Dorset. . . . 29 F7
South Petherton Som. . . . 28 D6
South Petherwin Corn. . . . 12 E2
South Pickenham Norf. . . . 141 C7
South Pill Corn. . . . 7 D7
South Pool Devon. . . . 8 G5
South Poorton Dorset. . . . 16 B6
Southport Mers. . . . 193 D10
South Port Argyll. . . . 284 E4
Southpunds Shetland. . . . 313 L6
South Quilquox Aberds. . . . 303 F8
South Radworthy Devon. . . . 41 G9
South Rauceby Lincs. . . . 173 F8
South Raynham Norf. . . . 159 E7
Southrepps Norf. . . . 160 B5
South Reston Lincs. . . . 190 E6
Southrey Lincs. . . . 173 B10
Southrop Glos. . . . 81 E11
  Oxon. . . . 101 E7
South Runcton Norf. . . . 140 B2
South Scarle Notts. . . . 172 C4
Southsea Ptsmth. . . . 21 B8
  Wrex. . . . 166 E4
South Shian Argyll. . . . 289 E11
South Shields T&W. . . . 243 D9
South Shore Blackpool. . . . 202 G2
South Side Durham. . . . 233 F8
  Orkney. . . . 314 D5
South Somercotes Lincs. . . . 190 C6
South Stainley N Yorks. . . . 214 G6
South Stainmore Cumb. . . . 222 C6
South Stanley Durham. . . . 242 G5
South Stifford Thurrock. . . . 68 D6
Southstoke Bath. . . . 61 G8
South Stoke Oxon. . . . 64 C6
  W Sus. . . . 35 F8
South Stour E Sus. . . . 54 F4
South Street E Sus. . . . 36 D5
  Kent. . . . 68 G6
  Kent. . . . 69 G10
  Kent. . . . 70 F6
  London. . . . 52 B2
South Tawton Devon. . . . 13 C9
South Tehidy Corn. . . . 4 G3
South Thoresby Lincs. . . . 190 F6
South Tidworth Wilts. . . . 47 D8
South Tottenham
  London. . . . 67 B10
Southtown Norf. . . . 143 B10
  Orkney. . . . 314 G4
  Som. . . . 28 D4
  Torf. . . . 78 F3
South Town Devon. . . . 14 E5
  Hants. . . . 49 F7
South Twerton Bath. . . . 61 G8
South Ulverston Cumb. . . . 210 D6
South View Hants. . . . 48 C6
Southville Devon. . . . 8 G4
South Voxter Shetland. . . . 313 G5
Southwaite Cumb. . . . 230 C4
South Walsham Norf. . . . 161 G7
Southwark London. . . . 67 D10
South Warnborough
  Hants. . . . 49 D8
Southwater W Sus. . . . 35 B11
Southwater Street
  W Sus. . . . 35 B11
Southway Plym. . . . 7 C9
  Som. . . . 44 E4
South Weald Essex. . . . 87 G9
South Weirs Hants. . . . 32 G3
Southwell Dorset. . . . 17 G9
  Notts. . . . 172 E2
South Weston Oxon. . . . 84 F2
South Wheatley Corn. . . . 11 C10
  Notts. . . . 188 D3
South Whiteness
  Shetland. . . . 313 J5
Southwick Hants. . . . 33 F10
  Northants. . . . 137 E10
  Som. . . . 43 D11
  T&W. . . . 243 F9
  Wilts. . . . 45 B10
  W Sus. . . . 36 F2
South Widcombe Bath. . . . 44 B5
South Wigston Leics. . . . 135 D11
South Willesborough
  Kent. . . . 54 E4
South Willingham
  Lincs. . . . 189 E11
South Wimbledon London. . . . 67 E9
South Wingate Durham. . . . 234 E4
South Wingfield Derbys. . . . 170 D5
South Witham Lincs. . . . 155 F8
Southwold Suff. . . . 127 B10
South Wonford Devon. . . . 24 F5
South Wonston Hants. . . . 48 F3
Southwood Derbys. . . . 153 E12
  Hants. . . . 49 B10
  Norf. . . . 143 B7
  Som. . . . 44 G5
  Worcs. . . . 116 A4
South Woodford London. . . . 86 G6
South Woodham Ferrers
  Essex. . . . 88 F4
South Wootton Norf. . . . 158 E2
South Wraxall Wilts. . . . 61 G10
South Yardley W Mid. . . . 134 G2
South Yarrows Highld. . . . 310 E7
South Yeo Devon. . . . 25 G8
South Zeal Devon. . . . 13 C9
Soval Lodge W Isles. . . . 304 F5
Sowber Gate N Yorks. . . . 215 B7
Sowerby N Yorks. . . . 215 C8
  W Yorks. . . . 196 C4
Sowerby Bridge
  W Yorks. . . . 196 C5
Sowerby Row Cumb. . . . 230 D3
Sower Carr Lancs. . . . 202 E3
Sowley Green Suff. . . . 124 G4
Sowood W Yorks. . . . 196 D5
Sowood Green W Yorks. . . . 196 D5
Sowton Devon. . . . 14 C5
Sowton Barton Devon. . . . 14 D2
Soyal Highld. . . . 309 K5
Soyland Town W Yorks. . . . 196 C4
Spacey Houses N Yorks. . . . 206 C2
Spa Common Norf. . . . 160 C5
Spalding Lincs. . . . 156 E4
Spaldington E Yorks. . . . 207 G11

Spaldwick Cambs. . . . 122 C2
Spalford Notts. . . . 172 B4
Spanby Lincs. . . . 155 B11
Spango Invclyd. . . . 276 G4
Spanish Green Hants. . . . 49 B7
Sparham Norf. . . . 159 F11
Sparhamhill Norf. . . . 159 F11
Spark Bridge Cumb. . . . 210 C6
Sparkbrook W Mid. . . . 133 G11
Sparkford Som. . . . 29 B10
Sparkhill W Mid. . . . 133 G11
Sparkwell Devon. . . . 7 D11
  Norf. . . . 216 C2
Sparl Shetland. . . . 312 G5
Sparnon Gate Corn. . . . 4 G3
Sparrow Green Norf. . . . 159 G9
Sparrow Hill Som. . . . 44 C2
Sparrowpit Derbys. . . . 185 E9
Sparrow's Green E Sus. . . . 52 G6
Sparsholt Hants. . . . 48 G2
  Oxon. . . . 63 B10
Spartylea Northumb. . . . 232 B3
Spath Staffs. . . . 151 B11
Spaunton N Yorks. . . . 226 G4
Spaxton Som. . . . 43 F8
Spean Bridge Highld. . . . 290 E4
Spear Hill W Sus. . . . 35 D11
Spearywell Hants. . . . 32 B4
Speckington Som. . . . 29 C8
Speed Gate Kent. . . . 68 F5
Speedwell Bristol. . . . 60 E6
Speen Bucks. . . . 84 F4
  W Berks. . . . 64 F3
Speeton N Yorks. . . . 218 E2
Speke Mers. . . . 182 E6
Speldhurst Kent. . . . 52 E5
Spellbrook Herts. . . . 87 B7
Spelsbury Oxon. . . . 101 G7
Spelter Bridgend. . . . 57 C11
Spen W Yorks. . . . 197 B7
Spencers Wood
  Wokingham. . . . 65 F8
Spen Green Ches E. . . . 168 C4
Spennells Worcs. . . . 116 C6
Spennithorne N Yorks. . . . 214 B2
Spennymoor Durham. . . . 233 E11
Spernall Warks. . . . 117 E11
Spetchley Worcs. . . . 117 G7
Spetisbury Dorset. . . . 30 G6
Spexhall Suff. . . . 143 G7
Speybank Highld. . . . 291 C10
Spey Bay Moray. . . . 302 C3
Speybridge Highld. . . . 301 G10
Speyview Moray. . . . 302 E2
Spillardsford Aberds. . . . 303 D10
Spilsby Lincs. . . . 174 B6
Spindlestone Northumb. . . . 264 C5
Spinkhill Derbys. . . . 187 F7
Spinney Hill Northants. . . . 120 E5
Spinney Hills Leicester. . . . 136 C2
Spinningdale Highld. . . . 309 L6
Spion Kop Notts. . . . 171 B9
Spirthill Wilts. . . . 62 D3
Spital Mers. . . . 182 E4
  Windsor. . . . 66 D3
Spitalbrook Herts. . . . 86 D5
Spitalfields London. . . . 67 C10
Spithill Derbys. . . . 169 F11
Spital Hill S Yorks. . . . 187 C10
Spital in the Street
  Lincs. . . . 189 D7
Spital Tongues T&W. . . . 242 D6
Spithurst E Sus. . . . 36 D6
Spittal Dumfries. . . . 236 D5
  E Loth. . . . 281 F9
  E Yorks. . . . 207 C11
  Highld. . . . 310 D5
  Lincs. . . . 190 G4
  Northumb. . . . 273 E9
  Pembs. . . . 91 G9
  Stirling. . . . 277 D10
Spittalfield Perth. . . . 286 C5
Spittal Houses S Yorks. . . . 186 B5
Spittal of Glenmuick
  Aberds. . . . 292 E5
Spittal of Glenshee
  Perth. . . . 292 F3
Spittlegate Lincs. . . . 155 C8
Spixworth Norf. . . . 160 F4
Splatt Corn. . . . 10 F4
  Corn. . . . 11 D10
  Devon. . . . 25 F10
  Som. . . . 43 F8
Splayne's Green E Sus. . . . 36 C6
Splott Cardiff. . . . 59 D7
Spofforth N Yorks. . . . 206 C3
Spon End W Mid. . . . 118 B6
Spooner Row Norf. . . . 141 D11
Spon Green Flint. . . . 166 C3
Spondon Derby. . . . 153 B8
Spoole Norf. . . . 158 G6
Spotland Bridge
  Gtr Man. . . . 195 E11
Spott E Loth. . . . 282 F3
Spratton Northants. . . . 120 C4
Spreakley Sur. . . . 49 E10
Spreyton Devon. . . . 13 B9
Spriddlestone Devon. . . . 7 E10
Spridlington Lincs. . . . 189 E8
Sprig's Alley Oxon. . . . 84 F3
Springbank Glos. . . . 99 G8
Spring Bank Cumb. . . . 229 G10
Springbok Glasgow. . . . 268 D2
Springbourne Bmouth. . . . 19 C8
Springburn Glasgow. . . . 268 B2
Spring Cottage Leics. . . . 152 F6
Spring End N Yorks. . . . 223 F9
Springfield Argyll. . . . 275 F11
  Caerph. . . . 77 F11
  Dumfries. . . . 239 D8
  Essex. . . . 88 D2
  Fife. . . . 287 F7
  Gtr Man. . . . 194 F5
  Highld. . . . 300 C6
  M Keynes. . . . 103 D7
  Moray. . . . 301 D10
  W Mid. . . . 133 G8
  W Mid. . . . 133 G11
Springfields Stoke. . . . 168 G5
Spring Gardens Som. . . . 45 D9
Spring Green Lancs. . . . 204 E4
Spring Grove London. . . . 67 D7
Springhead Gtr Man. . . . 196 G3
Springhill A Renf. . . . 267 D10
  IoW. . . . 20 B6
  N Lanark. . . . 269 D7
  Staffs. . . . 133 B11
  Staffs. . . . 133 C9
Spring Hill Gtr Man. . . . 196 F2
  Lancs. . . . 195 B8
Springholm Dumfries. . . . 237 C10
Springkell Dumfries. . . . 238 B6
Spring Park London. . . . 67 G11
Springthorpe Lincs. . . . 188 D5
Spring Vale S Yorks. . . . 197 G9
Spring Valley IoM. . . . 192 E4
Springwell Essex. . . . 105 C10
  T&W. . . . 243 F7

Springwell continued
  T&W. . . . 243 F9
Springwells Dumfries. . . . 248 G3
Sproatley E Yorks. . . . 209 G9
Sproston Green Ches W. . . . 168 B3
Sprotbrough S Yorks. . . . 198 G4
Sproughton Suff. . . . 108 C2
Sprouston Borders. . . . 263 B7
Sprowston Norf. . . . 160 G4
Sproxton Leics. . . . 155 E7
  N Yorks. . . . 216 C2
Sprunston Cumb. . . . 230 B3
Spurhill Shrops. . . . 149 C8
Spurlands End Bucks. . . . 84 F5
Spurstow Ches E. . . . 167 D9
Spurtree Shrops. . . . 116 D2
Spyway Dorset. . . . 16 C6
Square and Compass
  Pembs. . . . 91 E7
Squires Gate Blackpool. . . . 202 G2
Sraid Ruadh Argyll. . . . 288 E1
Sranda W Isles. . . . 296 C6
Sronphadruig Lodge
  Perth. . . . 291 F9
Stableford Shrops. . . . 132 D5
  Staffs. . . . 150 B6
Stacey Bank S Yorks. . . . 186 C3
Stackhouse N Yorks. . . . 212 F6
Stackpole Pembs. . . . 73 F7
Stackpole Quay Pembs. . . . 73 F7
Stacksford Norf. . . . 141 E11
Stacksteads Lancs. . . . 195 C10
Stackyard Green Suff. . . . 107 B9
Staddiscombe Plym. . . . 7 E10
Staddlethorpe E Yorks. . . . 199 B10
Staddon Devon. . . . 24 G5
Staden Derbys. . . . 185 G9
Stadhampton Oxon. . . . 83 F10
Stadmorslow Staffs. . . . 168 D5
Staffield Cumb. . . . 230 C6
Staffin Highld. . . . 298 C4
Stafford Staffs. . . . 151 E8
Stafford Park Telford. . . . 132 B4
Stafford's Corner Essex. . . . 89 B7
Stafford's Green Dorset. . . . 29 C10
Stagden Cross Essex. . . . 87 C10
Stagehall Borders. . . . 271 G9
Stagsden Bedford. . . . 103 B9
Stagsden West End
  Bedford. . . . 103 B9
Stag's Head Devon. . . . 25 B11
Stainburn Cumb. . . . 228 F6
  N Yorks. . . . 205 D10
Stainby Lincs. . . . 155 E8
Staincliffe W Yorks. . . . 197 C8
Staincross S Yorks. . . . 197 E10
Staindrop Durham. . . . 233 G8
Staines Green Herts. . . . 86 C3
Staines-upon-Thames
  Sur. . . . 66 E4
Stainfield Lincs. . . . 155 D11
  Lincs. . . . 189 G10
Stainforth N Yorks. . . . 212 F6
  S Yorks. . . . 198 E6
Staining Lancs. . . . 202 F3
Stainland W Yorks. . . . 196 D5
Stainsacre N Yorks. . . . 227 D8
Stainsby Derbys. . . . 170 B6
  Lincs. . . . 190 G4
Stainton Cumb. . . . 211 B10
  Cumb. . . . 230 F5
  Cumb. . . . 239 F9
  Durham. . . . 223 B11
  Mbro. . . . 225 C9
  N Yorks. . . . 224 F2
  S Yorks. . . . 187 D10
Stainton by Langworth
  Lincs. . . . 189 F9
Stainton le Vale Lincs. . . . 189 C11
Stainton with Adgarley
  Cumb. . . . 210 E5
Stair Cumb. . . . 229 G10
  E Ayrs. . . . 257 E10
Stairhaven Dumfries. . . . 236 D4
Staithes N Yorks. . . . 226 B5
Stakeford Northumb. . . . 253 F7
Stake Hill Gtr Man. . . . 195 F11
Stakenbridge Worcs. . . . 117 B7
Stake Pool Lancs. . . . 202 D4
Stalbridge Dorset. . . . 30 D2
Stalbridge Weston
  Dorset. . . . 30 D2
Stalham Norf. . . . 161 D7
Stalham Green Norf. . . . 161 D7
Stalisfield Green Kent. . . . 54 C3
Stallen Dorset. . . . 29 D10
Stallingborough
  NE Lincs. . . . 201 E7
Stalling Busk N Yorks. . . . 213 B8
Stallington Staffs. . . . 151 B8
Stalmine Lancs. . . . 202 D3
Stalmine Moss Side
  Lancs. . . . 202 D3
Stalybridge Gtr Man. . . . 185 B7
Stambermill W Mid. . . . 133 G8
Stambourne Essex. . . . 106 D4
Stambourne Green
  Essex. . . . 106 D4
Stamford Lincs. . . . 137 B10
  Northumb. . . . 264 F6
Stamford Bridge
  Ches W. . . . 167 B7
  E Yorks. . . . 207 B10
Stamfordham Northumb. . . . 242 C3
Stamford Hill London. . . . 67 B10
Stamperland E Renf. . . . 267 D10
Stamshaw Ptsmth. . . . 33 G10
Stanah Cumb. . . . 220 B6
  Lancs. . . . 202 E3
Stanborough Herts. . . . 86 C2
Stanbridge C Beds. . . . 103 G9
  Dorset. . . . 31 G8
Stanbridgeford C Beds. . . . 103 G9
Stanbrook Essex. . . . 106 F2
  Worcs. . . . 98 B6
Stanbury W Yorks. . . . 204 F6
Stand Gtr Man. . . . 195 F9
  N Lanark. . . . 268 B5
Standburn Falk. . . . 279 G8
Standeford Staffs. . . . 133 B8
Standen Kent. . . . 53 E11
  Lancs. . . . 203 E10
Standen Hall Lancs. . . . 203 E10
Standen Street Kent. . . . 53 G11
Standford Hants. . . . 49 G10
Standingstone Cumb. . . . 229 B7
Standish Glos. . . . 80 D4
  Gtr Man. . . . 194 E5
Standish Lower Ground
  Gtr Man. . . . 194 F5

Stapleford continued
  Herts. . . . 86 B4
  Leics. . . . 154 F6
  Lincs. . . . 172 D5
  Notts. . . . 153 B9
  Wilts. . . . 46 F5
Stapleford Abbotts Essex. . . . 87 G8
Stapleford Tawney Essex. . . . 87 F8
Staplegrove Som. . . . 28 B2
Staplehay Som. . . . 28 C2
Staple Hill S Glos. . . . 61 D7
  Worcs. . . . 117 C9
Staplehurst Kent. . . . 53 E9
Staplers IoW. . . . 20 D6
Staple Lawns Som. . . . 28 D3
Staplestreet Kent. . . . 70 G5
Stapleton Bristol. . . . 60 D6
  Cumb. . . . 240 C2
  Hereford. . . . 114 D6
  Leics. . . . 135 D8
  N Yorks. . . . 198 A5
  N Yorks. . . . 224 C5
  Shrops. . . . 131 C9
  Som. . . . 29 C7
Staplow Hereford. . . . 98 C3
Stapness Shetland. . . . 313 J4
Star Anglesey. . . . 179 G8
  Fife. . . . 287 G7
  Pembs. . . . 92 E4
  Som. . . . 44 B2
Stara Orkney. . . . 314 D2
Starbeck N Yorks. . . . 206 B2
Starbotton N Yorks. . . . 213 E9
Starcross Devon. . . . 14 E5
Stareton Warks. . . . 118 C6
Stargate T&W. . . . 242 E5
Star Hill Mon. . . . 79 E7
Starkholmes Derbys. . . . 170 D3
Starling Gtr Man. . . . 195 E9
Starlings Green Essex. . . . 105 E9
Starr's Green E Sus. . . . 38 D3
Starston Norf. . . . 142 G4
Start Devon. . . . 8 G6
Startforth Durham. . . . 223 B10
Start Hill Essex. . . . 105 G10
Startley Wilts. . . . 62 C2
Startop's End Bucks. . . . 84 C6
Starveall S Glos. . . . 61 B9
Starvecrow Kent. . . . 52 D5
Statenborough Kent. . . . 55 B10
Statford St Andrew Suff. . . . 127 E7
Statham Warr. . . . 183 D11
Stathe Som. . . . 28 B4
Stathern Leics. . . . 154 C5
Station Hill Cumb. . . . 229 B11
Station Town Durham. . . . 234 D4
Statland Common
  Norf. . . . 141 D10
Staughton Green Cambs. . . . 122 D2
Staughton Highway
  Cambs. . . . 122 E2
Staughton Moor Cambs. . . . 122 E2
Staunton Glos. . . . 79 C8
  Glos. . . . 98 F5
Staunton in the Vale
  Notts. . . . 172 G4
Staunton on Arrow
  Hereford. . . . 115 E7
Staunton on Wye
  Hereford. . . . 97 B7
Staupes N Yorks. . . . 205 B10
Staveley Cumb. . . . 211 B7
  Cumb. . . . 221 F9
  Derbys. . . . 186 G6
  N Yorks. . . . 215 G7
Staveley-in-Cartmel
  Cumb. . . . 211 B7
Staverton Devon. . . . 8 C5
  Glos. . . . 99 G7
  Northants. . . . 119 E10
  Wilts. . . . 61 G11
Staverton Bridge Glos. . . . 99 G7
Stawell Som. . . . 43 F11
Stawley Som. . . . 27 C9
Staxigoe Highld. . . . 310 D7
Staxton N Yorks. . . . 217 D10
Staylittle Ceredig. . . . 128 F2
Staylittle / Penffordd-Lâs
  Powys. . . . 129 E7
Staynall Lancs. . . . 202 E3
Staythorpe Notts. . . . 172 E3
Stead W Yorks. . . . 205 D8
Steam Mills Glos. . . . 79 B10
Stean N Yorks. . . . 213 E11
Steanbow Som. . . . 44 F5
Stearsby N Yorks. . . . 216 E2
Steart Som. . . . 43 D9
  Som. . . . 43 D9
Stebbing Essex. . . . 106 G2
Stebbing Green Essex. . . . 106 G3
Stechford W Mid. . . . 134 F2
Stede Quarter Kent. . . . 53 F11
Stedham W Sus. . . . 34 C5
Steel Northumb. . . . 241 F10
  Northumb. . . . 251 G9
Steel Bank S Yorks. . . . 186 D4
Steel Cross E Sus. . . . 52 G4
Steelend Fife. . . . 279 C10
Steele Road Borders. . . . 250 E2
Steel Green Cumb. . . . 210 D3
Steel Heath Shrops. . . . 149 B10
Steen's Bridge
  Hereford. . . . 115 F10
Steep Hants. . . . 34 B2
Steephill IoW. . . . 21 E7
Steep Lane W Yorks. . . . 196 C4
Steeple Dorset. . . . 18 E4
  Essex. . . . 88 E6
Steeple Ashton Wilts. . . . 46 B2
Steeple Aston Oxon. . . . 101 F9
Steeple Bumpstead
  Essex. . . . 106 C3
Steeple Claydon Bucks. . . . 102 F3
Steeple Gidding Cambs. . . . 138 G2
Steeple Langford Wilts. . . . 46 F4
Steeple Morden Cambs. . . . 104 C5
Steeton W Yorks. . . . 204 E6
Steeraway Telford. . . . 132 B3
Stein Highld. . . . 298 D2
Steinmanhill Aberds. . . . 303 E7
Stella T&W. . . . 242 E5
Stelling Minnis Kent. . . . 54 E6
Stelvio Newport. . . . 59 B9
Stembridge Som. . . . 28 C6
  Swansea. . . . 56 C3
Stemster Highld. . . . 310 C5
Stemster Ho Highld. . . . 310 C5
Stenalees Corn. . . . 5 D10
Stenaquoy Orkney. . . . 314 C5
Stencoose Corn. . . . 4 F4
Stenhill Devon. . . . 27 E9
Stenhouse Dumfries. . . . 247 G8
  Edin. . . . 280 G4
Stenhousemuir Falk. . . . 279 E7
Stenigot Lincs. . . . 190 E3

Stennack Corn. . . . 2 B5
Stenness Shetland. . . . 312 F4
Stenscholl Highld. . . . 298 C4
Stenso Orkney. . . . 314 D3
Stenson Derbys. . . . 152 D6
Stenton E Loth. . . . 282 G2
  Fife. . . . 280 B5
Stentwood Devon. . . . 27 F10
Stenwith Lincs. . . . 154 B6
Stepaside Corn. . . . 73 D10
  Pembs. . . . 73 D10
  Powys. . . . 129 F11
Stepping Hill Gtr Man. . . . 184 D6
Steppingley C Beds. . . . 103 D10
Stepps N Lanark. . . . 268 B3
Sterndale Moor Derbys. . . . 169 B10
Sternfield Suff. . . . 127 E7
Sterridge Devon. . . . 40 D5
Stert Wilts. . . . 46 B4
Sterte Poole. . . . 18 C6
Stetchworth Cambs. . . . 124 F2
Stevenage Herts. . . . 104 G4
Steven's Crouch E Sus. . . . 38 D2
Stevenston N Ayrs. . . . 266 G5
Stevenstone Devon. . . . 25 D8
Steventon Hants. . . . 48 D4
  Oxon. . . . 83 G7
Stevington Bedford. . . . 121 F9
Stewards Essex. . . . 87 D7
Steward's Green Essex. . . . 87 E7
Stewartby Bedford. . . . 103 C10
Stewarton Argyll. . . . 255 F7
  E Ayrs. . . . 267 F8
Stewkley Bucks. . . . 103 F7
Stewkley Dean Bucks. . . . 102 F6
Stewley Som. . . . 28 D4
Stewton Lincs. . . . 190 D5
Steyne Cross IoW. . . . 21 D8
Steyning W Sus. . . . 35 E11
Steynton Pembs. . . . 72 D6
Stibb Corn. . . . 24 E2
Stibbard Norf. . . . 159 D9
Stibb Cross Devon. . . . 24 E6
Stibb Green Wilts. . . . 63 G8
Stibbington Cambs. . . . 137 D11
Stichill Borders. . . . 262 B6
Sticker Corn. . . . 5 E9
Stickford Lincs. . . . 174 D5
Stick Hill Kent. . . . 52 E3
Sticklepath Devon. . . . 13 C8
  Som. . . . 28 A4
  Som. . . . 42 F4
Sticklinch Som. . . . 44 F5
Stickling Green Essex. . . . 105 E9
Stickney Lincs. . . . 174 D4
Stiffkey Norf. . . . 177 E7
Stifford's Bridge Hereford. . . . 98 B4
Stileway Som. . . . 44 E3
Stillingfleet N Yorks. . . . 207 E7
Stillington N Yorks. . . . 215 F11
  Stockton. . . . 234 G3
Stilton Cambs. . . . 138 F3
Stinchcombe Glos. . . . 80 F2
Stinsford Dorset. . . . 17 C10
Stiperstones Shrops. . . . 131 C7
Stirchley Telford. . . . 132 B4
  W Mid. . . . 133 G11
Stirkoke Ho Highld. . . . 310 D7
Stirling Aberds. . . . 303 E11
  Stirling. . . . 278 C5
Stirtloe Cambs. . . . 122 D3
Stirton N Yorks. . . . 204 C5
Stisted Essex. . . . 106 G5
Stitchcombe Wilts. . . . 63 F8
Stitchin's Hill Worcs. . . . 116 G5
Stithians Corn. . . . 2 B6
Stittenham Highld. . . . 300 B6
Stivichall W Mid. . . . 118 B6
Stixwould Lincs. . . . 173 B11
Stoak Ches W. . . . 182 G6
Stobhill Northumb. . . . 252 F6
Stobieside S Lanark. . . . 258 B4
Stobo Borders. . . . 260 B5
Stoborough Dorset. . . . 18 D4
Stoborough Green
  Dorset. . . . 18 D4
Stobs Castle Borders. . . . 250 B2
Stobshiel E Loth. . . . 271 C9
Stobswood Northumb. . . . 252 D6
Stock Essex. . . . 87 F11
  Lancs. . . . 204 D3
  N Som. . . . 60 G3
Stockbridge Hants. . . . 47 G11
  S Yorks. . . . 198 F5
  W Sus. . . . 22 C5
  W Yorks. . . . 205 E7
Stockbridge Village
  Mers. . . . 182 C6
Stockbury Kent. . . . 69 G10
Stockcross W Berks. . . . 64 F2
Stockend Glos. . . . 80 D4
Stocker's Head Kent. . . . 54 C3
Stockerston Leics. . . . 136 E6
Stockfield W Mid. . . . 134 G2
Stock Green Worcs. . . . 117 F9
Stockheath Hants. . . . 22 B2
Stock Hill Suff. . . . 125 B10
Stockholes Turbary
  N Lincs. . . . 199 F10
Stockiemuir Stirling. . . . 277 E10
Stocking Hereford. . . . 98 E2
Stockingford Warks. . . . 134 E6
Stocking Green Essex. . . . 105 D11
Stocking Pelham Herts. . . . 105 F9
Stockland Devon. . . . 28 G2
Stockland Bristol Som. . . . 43 E8
Stockland Green Kent. . . . 52 E5
  W Mid. . . . 134 E2
Stockleigh English Devon. . . . 26 F5
Stockleigh Pomeroy
  Devon. . . . 26 G5
Stockley Wilts. . . . 62 F4
Stocklinch Som. . . . 28 D5
Stockport Gtr Man. . . . 184 C5
Stocksbridge S Yorks. . . . 186 B3
Stocksfield Northumb. . . . 242 E3
Stocks Green Kent. . . . 52 E5
Stockstreet Essex. . . . 106 G6
Stockton Hereford. . . . 115 E10
  Norf. . . . 143 E7
  Shrops. . . . 130 C6
  Shrops. . . . 132 D5
  Telford. . . . 150 F5
  Warks. . . . 119 E8
Stockton Brook Staffs. . . . 168 E6
Stockton Heath Warr. . . . 183 D10
Stockton-on-Tees
  Stockton. . . . 225 B8
Stockton on Teme
  Worcs. . . . 116 D4
Stockton on the Forest
  York. . . . 207 B8
Stocktonwood Shrops. . . . 130 C5
Stockwell Devon. . . . 27 G7
  Glos. . . . 80 C6

Stockwell continued
London.........................67 D10
Stockwell End W Mid.......133 C7
Stockwell Heath 151 E11
Stockwitch Cross Som.......29 C9
Stockwood Bristol...........60 F6
Dorset.........................29 F9
Stock Wood Worcs.........117 F10
Stockwood Vale Bath........60 F6
Stodday Lancs..............202 B5
Stodmarsh Kent............71 G8
Stody Norf................159 C11
Stoer Highld..............307 G5
Stoford Som...............29 E9
Wilts.........................46 F5
Stoford Water Devon........27 F9
Stogumber Som.............43 E8
Stogursey Som.............43 E8
Stoke Devon...............24 C2
Hants.........................22 C2
Hants.........................48 C2
Medway.......................69 D10
Plym...........................7 D9
Suff..........................108 C3
W Mid..........................119 B7
Stoke Abbott Dorset........29 G7
Stoke Albany Northants...136 F6
Stoke Aldermoor
W Mid.......................119 B7
Stoke Ash Suff.............126 C2
Stoke Bardolph Notts.....171 G10
Stoke Bishop Bristol.......60 D5
Stoke Bliss Worcs.........116 E3
Stoke Bruerne Northants...102 B4
Stoke by Clare Suff.......106 C4
Stoke-by-Nayland Suff....107 D9
Stoke Canon Devon.........14 B4
Stoke Charity Hants........48 F3
Stoke Climsland Corn.......12 G3
Stoke Common Hants........33 C7
Stoke Cross Hereford.......98 C2
Stoke D'Abernon Sur........50 B6
Stoke Doyle Northants.....137 F10
Stoke Dry Rutland.........137 D7
Stoke Edith Hereford.......98 C2
Stoke End Warks...........134 D3
Stoke Farthing Wilts.......31 B9
Stoke Ferry Norf..........140 D4
Stoke Fleming Devon........9 F7
Stokeford Dorset...........18 D3
Stoke Gabriel Devon........8 D6
Stoke Gifford S Glos.......60 D6
Stoke Golding Leics.......135 D7
Stoke Goldington
M Keynes....................102 B6
Stokegorse Shrops.........131 G11
Stoke Green Bucks..........66 C3
Stokeham Notts............188 G2
Stoke Hammond Bucks......103 F7
Stoke Heath Shrops........150 D3
W Mid..........................135 G7
Worcs.........................117 D8
Stoke Hill Devon...........14 B4
Hereford.......................98 B2
Stoke Holy Cross Norf....142 C4
Stokeinteignhead Devon....14 G4
Stoke Lacy Hereford........98 B2
Stoke Lane Hereford.......116 G2
Stoke Lyne Oxon..........101 F9
Stoke Mandeville Bucks....84 C4
Stokenchurch Bucks.......84 F3
Stoke Newington
London.......................67 B10
Stokenham Devon...........8 G6
Stoke on Tern Shrops.....150 D2
Stoke-on-Trent Stoke.....168 F5
Stoke Orchard Glos........99 F8
Stoke Park Suff...........108 C3
Stoke Poges Bucks.........66 C3
Stoke Pound Worcs.......117 D9
Stoke Prior Hereford.....115 F10
Worcs.........................117 D8
Stoke Rivers Devon........40 F6
Stoke Rochford Lincs.....155 D8
Stoke Row Oxon............65 C7
Stoke St Gregory Som......28 B3
Stoke St Mary Som.........28 C2
Stoke St Michael Som......45 D7
Stoke St Milborough
Shrops......................131 G11
Stokesay Shrops...........131 G8
Stokesby Norf.............161 G8
Stokesley N Yorks........225 D10
Stoke sub Hamdon Som.....29 D7
Stoke Talmage Oxon........83 F11
Stoke Trister Som..........30 B2
Stoke Wake Dorset..........30 F3
Stoke Water Dorset........29 G7
Stoke Wharf Worcs.......117 D9
Stokoe Northumb..........250 F6
Stolford Som...............43 D8
Stondon Massey Essex......87 E9
Stone Bucks................84 C3
Glos..........................79 F11
Kent..........................38 B6
Kent..........................68 E5
Som...........................44 G5
Staffs.......................151 C8
S Yorks......................187 D9
Worcs.......................117 B7
Stonea Cambs.............139 E9
Stoneacton Shrops........131 E10
Ston Easton Som...........44 C6
Stonebow Worcs............99 B8
Stonebridge Essex.........70 B2
London.......................67 C8
Norf..........................141 E8
N Som........................43 B11
Sur............................51 D7
W Mid.........................134 G4
Stone Bridge Corner
Pboro.......................138 C5
Stonebridge Green Kent....54 D2
Stonebroom Derbys........170 D6
Stonebyres Holdings
S Lanark....................268 G6
Stone Chair W Yorks.......196 B6
Stoneclough Gtr Man.....195 F9
Stonecombe Devon..........40 E6
Stone Cross E Sus..........23 E10
E Sus..........................37 B8
E Sus..........................52 G6
Kent..........................52 F4
Kent..........................54 F4
Kent..........................55 B10
W Mid.........................133 E10
Stonecrouch Kent..........53 G7
Stonedge Borders.........250 B3
Stone-edge Batch
N Som........................60 E3
Stoneferry Hull...........209 G8
Stonefield Argyll........289 F11
S Lanark....................268 D3
Staffs......................151 C7
Stonefield Castle Hotel
Argyll......................275 F9
Stonegate E Sus...........37 B11
N Yorks.....................226 D5
Stonegravels Derbys......186 G5

Stonehall Kent............55 D9
Worcs.........................99 B7
Stonehaugh Northumb.....241 B7
Stonehaven Aberds.......293 E10
Stone Head N Yorks.......204 E4
Stone Heath Staffs.......151 B9
Stonehill Sur..............66 G4
Stone Hill Kent............54 D2
Kent..........................54 F5
S Glos.........................60 E6
S Yorks......................199 F1
Stonehills Hants..........33 G7
Stonehouse Aberds.......303 F8
Glos..........................80 D4
Northumb....................240 F5
Plym...........................7 E9
Stone House Cumb.........212 B5
Stonehouses Staffs.......169 G7
Stone in Oxney Kent.......38 B6
Stoneleigh London.........67 G8
Warks.........................118 D6
Stoneley Green Ches E...167 E10
Stonely Cambs............122 D2
Stonepits Worcs..........117 F10
Stonequarry W Sus.........52 F2
Stone Raise Cumb..........230 B4
Stonesby Leics...........154 E6
Stonesfield Oxon...........82 B5
Stones Green Essex........108 F3
Stone Street Kent..........52 C5
Suff..........................143 G7
Stonestreet Green Kent....54 F5
Stonethwaite Cumb........220 C5
Stoneton Warks...........119 G9
Stonewells Moray.........302 C2
Stonewood Kent............68 E5
Stoneyard Green
Hereford......................98 C4
Stoneybank E Loth........280 G6
Stoneybreck Shetland.....313 N2
Stoneyburn W Loth.......269 C9
Stoneycombe Devon.........9 B7
Stoneycroft Mers.........182 C5
Stoney Cross Hants........32 E3
Stoneyfield Gtr Man.....195 F10
Stoney Gate W Mid........133 F11
Leicester.....................136 C2
Stoney Hill Worcs.........117 C9
Stoneyhills Essex.........88 F6
Stoneykirk Dumfries......236 D2
Stoneylane Shrops.......115 B11
Stoney Middleton
Derbys......................186 F2
Stoney Royd W Yorks.....196 C5
Stoney Stanton Leics.....135 E9
Stoney Stoke Som..........45 G8
Stoney Stratton Som.......45 F7
Stoney Stretton Shrops...131 B7
Stoneywood Aberdeen....293 B10
Falk..........................278 E5
Stongaress Shetland......312 C7
Stonham Aspal Suff.......126 F2
Stonnall Staffs..........133 C11
Stonor Oxon................65 B8
Stonton Wyville Leics...136 D4
Stony Batter Hants........32 B3
Stony Cross Devon..........25 B8
Hereford......................98 B4
Hereford.....................115 C10
Stony Dale Notts.........172 G2
Stonyfield Hants..........32 D4
Stony Green Bucks.........84 F5
Stony Heap Durham.......242 G4
Stony Heath Hants.........48 B5
Stony Houghton Derbys...171 B7
Stony Knaps Dorset.......28 G5
Stonyland Devon...........25 B8
Stonymarsh Hants.........32 B4
Stony Stratford
M Keynes....................102 C5
Stoodleigh Devon.........26 B6
Stop-and-Call Pembs......91 D8
Stopes S Yorks...........186 D3
Stopgate Devon............28 F2
Stopham W Sus.............35 D8
Stopper Lane Lancs.......204 D2
Stopsley Luton...........104 G2
Stoptide Corn...............10 F4
Stores Corner Suff.......109 B7
Storeton Mers.............182 E4
Storiths N Yorks.........205 C7
Stormontfield Perth......286 E5
Stormore Wilts............45 D10
Stornoway W Isles........304 E6
Storridge Hereford........98 B4
Storrington W Sus.........35 E9
Storrs Cumb...............221 G7
S Yorks......................186 D3
Storth Cumb...............211 C9
Storwood E Yorks........207 E10
Stotfield Moray..........302 B2
Stotfold C Beds..........104 D4
Stottesdon Shrops.......132 G3
Stoughton Leics..........136 C2
Sur............................50 C3
W Sus..........................34 E4
Stoughton Cross Som......44 D2
Stoul Highld.............295 F9
Stoulton Worcs............99 B8
Stourbridge W Mid.......133 G8
Stourpaine Dorset.........30 F5
Stourport on Severn
Worcs........................116 C6
Stour Provost Dorset......30 C3
Stour Row Dorset..........30 C4
Stourton Staffs..........133 F7
Warks.........................100 D5
Wilts.........................45 G9
W Yorks......................206 G3
Stourton Caundle Dorset..30 D3
Stourton Hill Warks......100 D5
Stout Som....................44 G2
Stove Orkney.............314 C6
Shetland....................313 L6
Stoven Suff................143 G8
Stow Borders.............271 G9
Lincs.........................155 B11
Lincs.........................188 E5
Stow Bardolph Norf......140 B2
Stow Bedon Norf..........141 D9
Stowbridge Norf..........140 B2
Stow cum Quy Cambs......123 E9
Stowe Glos..................79 D9
Hereford......................96 B5
Lincs.........................156 G2
Shrops.......................114 C6
Staffs.......................152 G2
Stowe-by-Chartley
Staffs.......................151 D10
Stowe Green Glos.........79 D9
Stowell Glos...............81 C9

Stowey Bath...............44 B4
Stowford Hereford.........79 B9
Devon.........................12 B4
Devon.........................12 G4
Devon.........................25 B10
Devon.........................41 E7
Stowgate Lincs...........156 B3
Stowlangtoft Suff.......125 D9
Stow Lawn W Mid.........133 D8
Stow Longa Cambs.........122 C2
Stow Maries Essex.........88 F4
Stowmarket Suff.........125 F10
Stow-on-the-Wold
Glos..........................100 F3
Stow Park Newport........59 B10
Stowting Kent.............54 E6
Stowting Common Kent....54 E6
Stowting Court Kent......54 E6
Stowupland Suff.........125 F11
Stow-on-the-Fosse
Warks.........................100 D3
Straad W Isles...........275 G11
Strachan Aberds.........293 D8
Strachurmore Argyll.....284 G5
Stradbroke Suff..........126 C4
Stradishall Suff.........124 G4
Stradsett Norf...........140 C3
Stragglethorpe Lincs.....172 E6
Straid S Ayrs.............244 E4
Straight Soley Wilts......63 E10
Straith Dumfries.........247 F8
Straiton Edin.............270 B5
S Ayrs.........................245 C9
Straloch Aberds..........303 G8
Perth.........................292 G4
Stramshall Staffs........151 B11
Strand Glos.................80 C2
London.........................67 C10
Strands Cumb.............210 C3
Strang IoM.................192 E4
Strangeways Gtr Man....184 B4
Strangford Hereford.......97 F11
Stranghow Redcar........226 B3
Strangways Wilts..........46 G5
Stranog Aberds...........293 D10
Stranraer Dumfries.......236 C2
Strata Florida Ceredig...112 D4
Stratfield Mortimer
W Berks......................65 G7
Stratfield Saye Hants.....65 G7
Stratfield Turgis Hants...49 B7
Stratford C Beds.........104 B3
Glos............................99 D9
London.........................67 C11
Stratford Marsh London...67 C11
Stratford New Town
London.........................67 C11
Stratford St Andrew
Suff..........................127 E7
Stratford St Mary Suff...107 E10
Stratford Sub Castle
Wilts..........................46 G6
Stratford Tony Wilts......31 B9
Stratford-upon-Avon
Warks.........................118 F3
Strath Highld............299 B7
Highld.......................310 D6
Strathallan Castle Perth..286 F3
Strathan Highld..........295 F11
Highld.......................307 G5
Highld.......................308 C7
Strathan Skerray Highld..308 C6
Strathaven S Lanark......268 F4
Strathavon Lo Moray.....301 G11
Strathblane Stirling.....277 F11
Strathcanaird Highld....307 J6
Strathcarron Highld......299 E9
Strathcoil Argyll.........289 F8
Strathcona Highld........310 D5
Strathdon Aberds........292 B5
Strathellie Aberds.......303 C10
Strathgarve Lodge
Highld.......................300 C4
Strathkinness Fife.......287 F8
Strathmashie House
Highld.......................291 D7
Strathmiglo Fife.........286 F6
Strathmore Lodge
Highld.......................310 E5
Strathpeffer Highld......300 D4
Strathrannoch Highld....300 B3
Strathtay Perth..........286 B3
Strathvaich Lodge
Highld.......................300 B3
Strathwhillan N Ayrs....256 B2
Strathy Highld...........310 C2
Strathyre Stirling.......285 F9
Stratton Corn..............24 F2
Dorset.........................17 C9
Glos............................81 E8
Stratton Audley Oxon....102 F2
Stratton Chase Bucks.....85 G7
Stratton-on-the-Fosse
Som...........................45 C7
Stratton St Margaret
Swindon.......................63 B7
Stratton St Michael
Norf..........................142 E4
Stratton Strawless Norf..160 E4
Stravithie Fife...........287 F9
Strawberry Bank Cumb....211 B8
Strawberry Hill E Sus.....52 F5
London.........................67 E7
Strawberry Hill
London.........................67 E7
W Sus..........................34 E4
Streat E Sus................36 D5
Streatham London..........67 E10
Streatham Hill London....67 E10
Streatham Park London....67 E9
Streatham Vale London....67 E9
Streatley C Beds.........103 F11
W Berks......................64 C5
Street Cumb...............222 D2
Lancs........................202 C6
N Yorks......................226 E4
Som...........................28 E3
Som...........................44 E3
Street Ash Som............28 E3
Street Ashton Warks.....135 G9
Street Dinas Shrops.....148 B6
Street End Hants..........33 D9
Kent...........................54 C6
W Sus..........................22 D5
Street Gate T&W.........242 F6
Streethay Staffs.........152 G2
Streethouse W Yorks....197 C11
Street Houses N Yorks...206 D6
Streetlam N Yorks.......224 F6
Street Lane Derbys.......170 F5
Streetly W Mid...........133 D11
Streetly End Cambs.......106 B2
Street Lydan Wrex........149 B8
Streetly Ash Som..........28 E3
Streetly End Cambs.......106 B2
Street of Kincardine
Highld.......................291 B11
Street on the Fosse Som..45 F7
Strefford Shrops.........131 F8
Strelley Notts...........171 G8
Strensall York...........216 G2
Strensham Worcs...........99 C8
Stretcholt Som.............43 E11
Strete Devon.................8 F6

Stretford Gtr Man........184 C4
Hereford.....................115 F10
Stretford Court Hereford 115 F10
Strethall Essex..........105 D9
Stretham Cambs..........123 C10
Strettington W Sus........22 C5
Stretton Ches W..........166 E6
Derbys.......................170 C5
Rutland......................155 F8
Staffs........................151 C7
Staffs.......................152 D5
Warr..........................183 E10
Stretton en le Field
Leics........................152 G6
Stretton Grandison
Hereford......................98 C2
Stretton-on-Dunsmore
Warks.........................119 C8
Stretton-on-Fosse
Warks.........................100 D3
Stretton Sugwas
Hereford......................97 C9
Stretton under Fosse
Warks.........................135 G8
Stretton Westwood
Shrops......................131 D11
Strichen Aberds..........303 D9
Strines Gtr Man..........185 D7
Stringston Som............43 E7
Strixton Northants.......121 E8
Stroat Glos..................79 F9
Stromeferry Highld......295 B10
Stromemore Highld.......295 B10
Stromness Orkney........314 F2
Stronaba Highld..........290 E4
Stronachlachar Stirling..285 E8
Stronachullin Lodge
Argyll.......................275 F9
Argyll.......................276 E3
Argyll.......................290 E3
Stronchreggan Highld....290 F2
Stronchrubie Highld.....307 H7
Strone Argyll.............255 F7
Argyll.......................274 G5
Argyll.......................276 E3
Highld.......................290 E3
Highld.......................291 D9
Invclyd......................276 G5
Stronelairg Lodge
Highld.......................291 C7
Stroneskar Argyll........275 C9
Stronmachair Stirling...285 G8
Stronmilchan Argyll.....284 E5
Stronord Dumfries.......237 C7
Stronsaul Argyll.........276 F2
Strontian Highld.........289 C10
Stronvar Stirling........285 E9
Strood Kent.................53 G11
Medway.........................69 F8
Strood Green Sur..........51 D8
Sur............................35 C8
W Sus..........................50 G6
Strothers Dale
Northumb....................241 F11
Stroud Glos.................80 D4
Hants.........................34 C2
Sur............................50 F2
Stroude Sur..................66 F4
Stroud Green Essex........88 G5
Glos............................80 D4
London.........................67 B10
Stroul Argyll.............276 E4
Stroupster Highld........310 C7
Stroxton Lincs............155 D8
Stroxworthy Devon........24 D4
Struan Highld.............294 B5
Perth.........................291 G10
Strubby Lincs..............191 E7
Lincs.........................190 F4
Structon's Heath Worcs..116 D4
Strugg's Hill Lincs.......156 B5
Strumpshaw Norf.........142 B6
Strutherhill S Lanark....268 F5
Struthers Fife...........287 G7
Struy Highld..............300 F3
Stryd Anglesey...........178 G2
Stryd y Facsen Anglesey..178 E4
Stryt-issa Wrex..........166 F3
Stuartfield Aberds.......303 E9
Stubb Norf.................161 E8
Stubbermere W Sus........22 C3
Stubber's Green
W Mid.........................133 C10
Stubbings Windsor.........65 C10
Stubbing's Green Suff...125 C11
Stubbington Hants.........33 G9
Stubbins Lancs............195 D9
Lancs.........................202 E6
Stubble Green Cumb......219 F11
Stubbles W Berks..........64 D5
Stubbs Cross Kent.........54 F3
Stubb's Green Norf.......143 D7
Stubb's Green Norf.......142 D5
Stubhampton Dorset.......30 E6
Stub Place Cumb..........219 G1
Stubshaw Cross
Gtr Man......................194 G5
Stubton Lincs.............172 F5
Stuckgowan Argyll.......285 G7
Stuckton Hants............31 E11
Studdal Kent................55 D10
Studd Hill Kent...........71 F7
Studfold N Yorks.........212 E6
Stud Green Ches E........168 C2
Windsor.......................65 D11
Studham C Beds............85 B8
Studland Dorset...........18 E6
Studley Warks............117 E11
Wilts.........................62 E3
Studley Green
Studley Green Bucks.......84 F3
Studley Roger N Yorks...214 E5
Studley Royal N Yorks...214 E5
Stump Cross Essex.......105 C10
Stuntney Cambs..........123 B11
Stunts Green E Sus........23 C10
Sturbridge Staffs.........150 C6
Sturford Wilts.............45 E10
Sturgate Lincs............188 D5
Sturmer Essex...........106 C3
Sturminster Common
Dorset.........................30 E3
Sturminster Marshall
Dorset.........................31 G7
Sturminster Newton
Dorset.........................30 E3
Sturry Kent.................71 G7
Sturton N Lincs..........200 G3
Sturton by Stow Lincs...188 E5
Sturton le Steeple Notts.188 E2
Stuston Suff..............126 B2
Stutton N Yorks..........206 E5
Suff..........................108 E3
Styal Ches E...............184 E4
Styants Bottom Kent......52 B5
Stydd Lancs................203 F9
Styrrup Notts.............187 C11

Suainebost W Isles......304 B7
Suardail W Isles.........304 E6
Succoth Aberds...........302 F4
Argyll.......................284 G6
Suckley Worcs.............116 G4
Suckley Green Worcs......116 G4
Suckley Knowl Worcs.....116 G4
Suckquoy Orkney.........314 H4
Sudborough Northants...137 G9
Sudbourne Suff...........127 G8
Sudbrook Lincs...........173 G7
Mon............................60 B4
Sudbrooke Lincs.........189 F8
Sudbury Derbys...........152 C3
London.........................67 C7
Suddie Highld.............300 D6
Sudgrove Glos..............80 D6
Suffield Norf.............160 C4
N Yorks......................227 G9
Sugnall Staffs...........150 C5
Sugwas Pool Hereford.....97 C9
Suisnish Highld..........295 C7
Sulaisiadar W Isles......304 E7
Sulby IoM..................192 C4
Sulgrave Northants......101 B11
Sulham W Berks............64 F6
Sulhamstead W Berks.....64 F6
Sulhamstead Abbots
W Berks......................64 F6
Sulhamstead Bannister
Upper End W Berks.........64 F6
Sulland Orkney...........314 B5
Sullington W Sus..........35 E9
Sullington Warren
W Sus..........................35 E9
Sullom Shetland..........312 F5
Sullom Voe Oil Terminal
Shetland....................312 F5
Sully V Glam................59 F7
Sumburgh Shetland.......313 N6
Summer Bridge N Yorks..214 G4
Summercourt Corn...........5 D7
Summerfield Norf........158 B5
Worcs.........................116 C6
Summerfield Park
W Mid.........................133 F10
Summergangs Hull........209 G8
Summer Heath Bucks......84 G2
Summerhill Newport.......59 B10
Pembs..........................73 D11
Staffs........................133 B11
Telford......................150 F4
Summerhouse Darl........224 B4
Summerlands Cumb.......211 B10
Summerleaze Mon..........60 C2
Summerley Derbys........186 F5
Summerscales N Yorks...205 C7
Summerseat Gtr Man.....195 E9
Summersgill Lancs.......211 F11
Summerston Glasgow....277 G11
Summerstown Bucks.......67 E9
London.........................67 E9
Summertown Oxon..........83 D8
Summit Gtr Man..........195 E10
Gtr Man......................196 D2
Gtr Man......................196 F2
Sunbrick Cumb...........210 E5
Sunbury Common Sur.......66 F4
Sunbury-on-Thames Sur..66 F6
Sundaywell Dumfries.....247 G8
Sunderland Argyll.......274 G3
Cumb..........................229 D9
Lancs.........................202 B4
T&W...........................243 F9
Sunderland Bridge
Durham......................233 D11
Sundhope Borders.........261 D8
Sundon Park Luton.......103 F11
Sundridge Kent............52 B3
London.........................68 E2
Sun Green Gtr Man........185 B7
Sunhill Glos................81 D10
Sunipol Argyll............288 D5
Sunk Marsh Essex..........69 C10
Sunk Island E Yorks......201 D9
Sunningdale Windsor......66 F3
Sunninghill Windsor......66 F2
Sunningwell Oxon..........83 E8
Sunniside Durham.........233 D8
T&W...........................242 F6
Sunny Bank Gtr Man.....195 F10
Sunny Bower Lancs.......203 G10
Sunnybrow Durham.......233 E9
Sunnyfields S Yorks.....198 F4
Sunny Hill Derby.........152 C6
Sunnyhurst Blackb.......195 C7
Sunnylaw Stirling.......278 B5
Sunnymead Oxon...........83 D8
Sunnymeads Windsor......66 D4
Sunnymede S Yorks.......187 C7
Sunnyside S Yorks.......187 C7
W Sus..........................51 F11
Sunset Hereford..........114 F6
Sunton Wilts...............47 C8
Sunton London..............67 F7
Sun IoM.....................192 E3
Surfleet Lincs...........156 D5
Surfleet Seas End Lincs.156 D5
Surlingham Norf.........142 B6
Surrex Essex.............107 G7
Suspension Bridge
Norf..........................139 E10
Sustead Norf.............160 B3
Susworth Lincs..........199 G10
Sutcombe Devon............24 E4
Sutcombemill Devon.......24 E4
Suton Norf.................142 D2
Sutors of Cromarty
Highld.......................301 C8
Sutterby Lincs...........190 G5
Sutterton Lincs..........156 B5
Sutterton Dowdyke
Lincs.........................156 C5
Sutton Bucks...............66 D4
Cambs.........................123 B8
C Beds.......................104 B4
Devon...........................8 G4
E Sus..........................23 E7
Kent...........................55 D10
London.........................67 G9
Mers..........................183 B11
Norf..........................161 E7

Sutton continued
Notts.........................154 B5
Notts.........................187 E11
N Yorks......................198 B3
Oxon..........................83 F8
Pboro........................137 D11
Shrops........................72 B6
Shrops........................132 F4
Shrops........................149 D7
Shrops........................149 G10
Som............................44 G6
Staffs........................150 B5
Suff...........................108 B6
Sur............................50 D5
S Yorks......................198 E5
Sutton Abinger Sur........50 D6
Sutton at Hone Kent......68 E5
Sutton Bassett
Northants....................136 E5
Sutton Benger Wilts......62 D2
Sutton Bingham Som.......29 E8
Sutton Bonington
Notts.........................153 E10
Sutton Bridge Lincs.....157 E9
Sutton Cheney Leics.....135 C8
Sutton Coldfield W Mid..134 D2
Sutton Corner Lincs.....157 D8
Sutton Courtenay Oxon...83 G8
Sutton Crosses Lincs....157 E8
Sutton Cum Lound
Notts.........................187 E11
Sutton End W Sus..........35 D7
Sutton Forest Side
Notts.........................171 D8
Sutton Gault Lincs.......123 B8
Sutton Green Ches W.....182 F5
Sur............................50 C4
Wrex..........................166 F6
Sutton Hall Warks........132 C4
Sutton Heath Mers.......183 C8
Sutton Hill Telford......132 C4
Sutton Holms Dorset......31 F9
Sutton Howgrave
N Yorks......................214 D6
Sutton Ings Hull.........209 G8
Sutton in the Elms
Leics........................135 E10
Sutton in Ashfield Notts.171 D7
Sutton-in-Craven
N Yorks......................204 E6
Sutton Lakes Hereford....97 B10
Sutton Lane Ends
Ches E.......................184 G6
Sutton Leach Mers........183 C8
Sutton Maddock Shrops..132 C4
Sutton Mallet Som........43 G11
Sutton Mandeville Wilts..31 B7
Sutton Manor Mers.......183 C8
Sutton Marsh Hereford....97 C10
Sutton Mill N Yorks......204 E6
Sutton Montis Som........29 C10
Sutton on Hull Hull.....209 G8
Sutton on Sea Lincs.....191 E8
Sutton-on-the-Forest
N Yorks......................215 G11
Sutton on the Hill
Derbys.......................152 C4
Sutton on Trent Notts...172 B3
Sutton Poyntz Dorset.....17 E10
Sutton Row Wilts..........31 B7
Sutton St Edmund Lincs..157 G7
Sutton St James Lincs...157 F7
Sutton St Michael
Hereford......................97 B10
Sutton St Nicholas
Hereford......................97 B10
Sutton Scarsdale
Derbys.......................170 B6
Sutton Scotney Hants.....48 F3
Sutton Street Suff.......108 C6
Sutton under Brailes
Warks.........................100 D5
Sutton-under-
Whitestonecliffe
N Yorks......................215 C9
Sutton upon Derwent
E Yorks......................207 D10
Sutton Valence Kent.......53 D10
Sutton Veny Wilts.........45 E11
Sutton Waldron Dorset....30 E5
Sutton Weaver Ches W....183 F8
Sutton Wick Bath.........44 B5
Oxon..........................83 G7
Swaby Lincs...............190 F5
Swadlincote Derbys.......152 F6
Swaffham Norf............140 B6
Swaffham Bulbeck
Cambs.........................123 E11
Swaffham Prior Cambs...123 E11
Swafield Norf............160 C5
Swainby N Yorks.........225 E9
Swainbost W Isles.......304 B7
Swainby N Yorks.........214 D5
Swainshill Hereford......97 C9
Swainsthorpe Norf.......142 C4
Swainswick Bath..........61 F9
Swaithe S Yorks..........197 G11
Swalcliffe Oxon..........101 D7
Swalecliffe Kent..........70 F6
Swallow Lincs............201 G2
Swallow Beck Lincs......173 B7
Swallowcliffe Wilts......31 B7
Swallowfield Wokingham..65 G8
Swallowfields Dorset.....8 C4
Swallowhurst Cumb......220 G2
Swallow's Cross Essex....87 F10
Swallownest S Yorks.....187 D7
Swalwell T&W............242 E6
Swampton Hants...........48 C2
Swanage Dorset............18 F6
Swan Bottom Bucks.......84 D6
Swanbourne Bucks........102 F6
Swanbridge V Glam........59 F7
Swan Green Ches W........184 G2
Suff..........................126 C5
Swanland E Yorks........200 B3
Swanley Kent...............68 F4
Swanley Bar Herts.........86 E3
Swanley Village Kent.....68 F4
Swanmore Hants............33 D9
IoW............................21 C7
Swannay Orkney..........314 D2
Swannington Leics.......153 F8
Norf..........................160 F2
Swanpool Lincs..........189 G7
Swanscombe Kent.........68 E6
Swansea / Abertawe
Swansea.......................56 C6
Swanside Mers............182 C6
Swanston Edin...........270 B4
Swanton Abbott Norf.....160 D5
Swanton Hill Norf.......160 D5
Swanton Morley Norf....159 F10
Swanton Novers Norf.....159 C10

Swanton Street Kent......53 D10
Swan Village W Mid......133 E9
Swanwick Derbys.........170 E6
Hants.........................33 F8
Swanwick Green Ches E..167 F9
Swarby Lincs..............173 G8
Swarcliffe W Yorks......206 F3
Swardeston Norf.........142 C4
Swarister Shetland......312 E7
Swarkestone Derbys......153 D7
Swarland Northumb.......252 C5
Swarraton Hants...........48 F5
Swartha W Yorks..........205 D7
Swarthmoor Cumb........210 D5
Swathwick Derbys.........170 B5
Swati on Hants............35 E4
Swavesey Cambs..........123 D7
Sway Hants.................19 B11
Swayfield Lincs..........155 E9
Swaythling Soton.........32 D6
Sweet Green Worcs.......116 E2
Sweetham Devon...........14 B3
Sweethaws E Sus..........37 B8
Sweethay Som...............28 C2
Sweetholme Cumb........221 B11
Sweets Corn.................11 B9
Sweetshouse Corn..........5 C11
Sweffling Suff...........126 E6
Swelling Hill Hants.......48 G5
Swepstone Leics.........153 G7
Swerford Oxon...........101 E7
Swettenham Ches E.......168 B4
Swetton N Yorks.........214 E3
Swffryd Caerph............78 F2
Swffryd Caerph............78 F2
Swiftsden E Sus...........38 G2
Swilland Suff............126 F3
Swillbrook Lancs.........202 G5
Swillington W Yorks.....206 G3
Swimbridge Devon..........40 G6
Swimbridge Newland
Devon..........................40 G6
Swincliffe N Yorks......205 B10
W Yorks......................197 B8
Swincombe Devon..........41 E7
Highld.......................310 C6
Swinden N Yorks..........204 C3
Swinderby Lincs.........172 C5
Swindon Glos...............99 G8
Staffs........................133 E7
Swindon.......................63 C7
Swine E Yorks.............209 F8
Swinefleet E Yorks......199 C9
Swineford S Glos..........61 F7
Swineshead Bedford......121 D11
Lincs.........................174 G2
Swineshead Bridge
Lincs.........................174 G2
Swinethorpe Lincs.......172 B5
Swiney Highld............310 F6
Swinford Leics..........119 B11
Oxon..........................82 D6
Swingate Notts..........171 G8
Swingbrow Cambs.........139 F7
Swingfield Minnis Kent...55 E8
Swingfield Street Kent...55 E8
Swingleton Green Suff...107 B9
Swinhoe Northumb........264 D6
Swinhope Lincs...........190 C2
Swinister Shetland......312 E5
Shetland....................313 L6
Swinithwaite N Yorks....213 B10
Swinmore Common
Hereford......................98 C3
Swinnie Borders.........262 F4
Swinnow Moor
W Yorks......................205 G10
Swinscoe Staffs.........169 F10
Swinside Cumb...........229 G10
Swinside Townfoot
Borders......................262 F4
Swinstead Lincs.........155 E10
Swinton Borders.........272 F6
Gtr Man......................195 G9
N Yorks......................214 E4
N Yorks......................216 E5
S Yorks......................186 B6
Swinton Bridge S Yorks..187 B7
Swinton Hill Borders....272 F6
Swintonmill Borders....272 F6
Swinton Park Gtr Man...195 G9
Swiss Valley Carms.......75 E8
Swithland Leics.........153 G10
Swordale Highld.........300 C5
Swordland Highld........295 F9
Swordly Highld..........308 C7
Sworton Heath Ches E...183 E11
Swydd-ffynnon Ceredig..112 D3
Swynnerton Staffs.......151 B7
Swyre Dorset...............16 D6
Sycamore Devon............28 E3
Sychdyn / Soughton
Flint.........................166 B2
Sychnant Powys..........129 B9
Sychtyn Powys............129 B9
Sydallt Wrex..............166 D4
Syde Glos....................81 C7
Sydenham London..........67 E10
Oxon..........................84 E2
Sur............................43 F10
Sydenham Damerel
Devon..........................12 F4
Syderstone Norf.........158 C6
Sydling St Nicholas
Dorset.........................17 B8
Sydmonton Hants.........48 B3
Sydney Ches E............168 D2
Syerston Notts..........172 F2
Syke Gtr Man.............195 D11
Sykehouse S Yorks.......198 D6
Sykes Lancs...............203 C8
Syleham Suff.............126 B4
Sylen Carms................75 D8
Sylfaen Powys............130 B2
Symbister Shetland......313 G7
Symington Borders......271 F8
S Ayrs.........................257 C9
S Lanark....................259 G11
Symondsbury Dorset.......16 C4
Symonds Green Herts....104 F4
Symonds Yat Hereford....79 B9
Synod Inn / Post Mawr
Ceredig......................111 G8
Synton Borders...........261 E11
Synton Mains Borders....261 E11
Synwell Glos...............80 G3
Syre Highld...............308 E6
Syreford Glos..............99 G10
Syresham Northants......102 C2
Syston Leics.............153 G11
Lincs.........................173 G7
Sytch Ho Green Shrops...132 E5

Swanton Street Kent......53 D10
Swan Village W Mid......133 C7
Sytch Lane Telford......150 E2
Sywell Northants........120 D6

T

Taagan Highld...........299 C10
Tabley Hill Ches E.......184 F2
Tabor Gwyn...............146 F5
Tàbost W Isles..........304 B7
Tàbost W Isles..........305 G5
Tachbrook Mallory
Warks.........................118 E6
Tacker Street Som........42 F4
Tackley Oxon.............101 G9
Tacleit W Isles..........304 E3
Tacolneston Norf........142 D2
Tadcaster N Yorks.......206 E5
Tadden Dorset............31 G7
Taddington Derbys.......185 G10
Glos............................99 E11
Taddiport Devon...........25 D7
Tadhill Som................45 D7
Tadley Hants..............64 G6
Oxon..........................64 B4
Tadlow Cambs............104 B5
C Beds.......................104 B5
Tadmarton Oxon.........101 D7
Tadnoll Dorset............17 D11
Tadwick Bath..............61 E8
Tadworth Sur..............51 B8
Tafarnau-bach
Bl Gwent......................77 C10
Tafarn-y-bwlch Pembs....91 E11
Tafarn-y-gelyn Denb.....165 C11
Taff Merthyr Garden Village
M Tydf.........................77 F10
Taff's Well Rhondda.......58 C6
Tafolwern Powys..........129 C7
Tai Conwy.................164 C3
Taibach Neath.............57 D9
Tai-bach Powys...........148 D3
Taigh a Ghearraidh
W Isles......................296 D3
Taigh Bhalaigh W Isles..296 D3
Tai-mawr Conwy..........165 G7
Tai-morfa Gwyn...........144 D5
Tain Highld...............309 L7
Highld.......................310 C6
Tai-nant Wrex............166 F3
Tainlon Gwyn.............162 E6
Tairbeart W Isles........305 H3
Tai'r-Bull Powys..........95 F7
Tairgwaith Neath..........76 C2
Tai'r-heol Caerph.........77 G10
Tai'r-ysgol Swansea......57 B7
Tai-Ucha Denb............165 D8
Takeley Essex............105 G11
Takeley Street Essex....105 G11
Talacharn / Laugharne
Carms.........................74 C4
Talachddu Powys..........95 E11
Talacre Flint.............181 E10
Talardd Gwyn.............147 D7
Talaton Devon.............15 B7
Talbenny Pembs...........72 C4
Talbot Green Rhondda.....58 C4
Talbot Heath Poole.......19 C7
Talbot Village Poole......19 C7
Talbot Woods Bmouth.....19 C7
Taleford Devon............15 B7
Talerddig Powys..........129 C8
Talgarreg Ceredig.......111 G8
Talgarth Powys...........96 E3
Talgarth's Well Swansea..56 D2
Talisker Highld..........294 B5
Talke Staffs..............168 E4
Talke Pits Staffs........168 E4
Talkin Cumb...............240 F3
Talladale Highld.........299 B9
Talla Linnfoots Borders.260 E4
Tallaminnoch S Ayrs.....245 D10
Tallarn Green Wrex......166 G6
Tallentire Cumb.........229 D8
Talley Carms..............94 E2
Tallington Lincs........137 B11
Talmine Highld..........308 C5
Talog Carms...............92 F6
Talsarn Carms.............94 F5
Tal-sarn Ceredig........111 F10
Talsarnau Gwyn...........146 B2
Talskiddy Corn.............5 B8
Talwrn Anglesey.........179 F7
Wrex..........................166 F3
Tal-y-bont Ceredig......128 F3
Conwy........................164 B3
Talybont-on-Usk Powys...96 G2
Tal-y-cafn Conwy.........180 G3
Tal-y-coed Mon............78 B6
Talygarn Rhondda.........58 C4
Talyllyn Powys............96 F2
Tal-y-llyn Gwyn...........128 B4
Talysarn Gwyn............163 E7
Tal-y-waenydd Gwyn.....163 F11
Talywain Powys...........78 E3
Tal-y-wern Powys........128 C6
Tamanabhagh W Isles....304 F2
Tamerton Foliot Plym......7 C9
Tame Water Gtr Man.....196 F3
Tamfourhill Falk........279 E7
Tamworth Staffs.........134 C4
Tamworth Green Ches S..174 G5
Tancred N Yorks.........206 B5
Tan Gwent................197 D7
Tanden Kent................54 F2
Tandlehill Renfs........267 C8
Tandridge Sur.............51 C11
Tanerdy Carms............93 G8
Tanfield Durham.........242 F5
Tanfield Lea Durham....242 F5
Tang N Yorks.............205 B10
Tang Hall York............207 C8
Tanglwst Carms............92 E6
Tangley Hants.............47 C10
Tanglwst Carms............92 E6
Tangmere W Sus...........22 B6
Tangwick Shetland.......312 F4
Tangy Argyll..............255 E7
Tan Hills Durham.........233 B11
Tan Hinon Powys.........129 F7
Tanhouse Lancs..........194 F3
Tanis Wilts................47 F8
Tankersley S Yorks.......197 G10
Tankerton Kent............70 F6
Tan-lan Gwyn.............163 F8
Tan-lan Conwy...........164 C2
Tanlan Banks Flint.......181 E10
Tannach Highld..........310 E7
Tannachie Aberds.......293 E9
Tannadice Angus.........287 B8

Tanner's Green Worcs ...117 C11
Tannington Suff ...126 D4
Tannington Place Suff ...126 D4
Tannochside N Lanark ...268 C4
Tan Office Suff ...124 F5
Tan Office Green Suff ...124 F5
Tansley Derbys ...170 D4
Tansley Hill W Mid ...133 F9
Tansley Knoll Derbys ...170 C4
Tansor Northants ...137 E11
Tanterton Lancs ...202 G6
Tantobie Durham ...242 G5
Tanton N Yorks ...225 C10
Tanwood Worcs ...117 C8
Tanworth-in-Arden
　Warks ...118 C2
Tan-y-bwlch Gwyn ...163 G11
Tanyfron Wrex ...166 E3
Tan-y-fron Conwy ...165 C7
Tan-y-graig Anglesey ...179 F8
　Gwyn ...144 B6
Tangrisiau Gwyn ...163 F11
Tan-y-groes Ceredig ...92 B5
Tan-y-mynydd Gwyn ...144 C6
Tan-y-pistyll Powys ...147 D11
Tan-yr-allt Denb ...181 E9
　Gwyn ...163 E7
Tanyrhydiau Ceredig ...112 D4
Tanysgafell Gwyn ...163 B10
Taobh a Chaolais
　W Isles ...297 K3
Taobh a' Ghlinne
　W Isles ...305 G5
Taobh a Thuath Loch
　Aineort W Isles ...297 J3
Taobh a Tuath Loch
　Baghasdail W Isles ...297 J3
Taobh Siar W Isles ...305 H3
Taobh Tuath W Isles ...296 C5
Taplow Bucks ...66 C2
Tapnage Hants ...33 E9
Tapton Derbys ...186 G5
Tapton Hill S Yorks ...186 D4
Tarbat Ho Highld ...301 B7
Tarbert Argyll ...6
　Argyll ...275 E7
　Argyll ...275 G9
Tarbert Argyll ...285 G7
　Highld ...295 F9
　Highld ...306 E6
Tarbock Green Mers ...183 D7
Tarbolton S Ayrs ...257 D10
Tarbrax S Lanark ...269 D10
Tardebigge Worcs ...117 D10
Tardy Gate Lancs ...194 B4
Tarfside Angus ...292 F6
Tarland Aberds ...292 C6
Tarleton Lancs ...194 C3
Tarleton Moss Lancs ...194 C3
Tarlogie Highld ...309 L7
Tarlscough Lancs ...194 E2
Tarlton Glos ...81 F7
Tarn W Yorks ...205 F9
Tarnbrook Lancs ...203 B7
Tarnock Som ...43 C11
Tarns Cumb ...229 B8
Tarnside Cumb ...221 G8
Tarporley Ches W ...167 C9
Tarpots Essex ...69 B9
Tarr Som ...42 G6
Tarraby Cumb ...239 F10
Tarrant Crawford Dorset ...30 G6
Tarrant Gunville Dorset ...30 E6
Tarrant Hinton Dorset ...30 E6
Tarrant Keyneston
　Dorset ...30 G6
Tarrant Launceston
　Dorset ...30 F6
Tarrant Monkton Dorset ...30 F6
Tarrant Rawston Dorset ...30 G6
Tarrant Rushton Dorset ...30 G6
Tarrel Highld ...311 L2
Tarring Neville E Sus ...36 G6
Tarrington Hereford ...98 C2
Tarrington Common
　Hereford ...98 C2
Tarryblake Ho Moray ...302 D5
Tarsappie Perth ...286 E5
Tarskavaig Highld ...295 E7
Tarts Hill Shrops ...149 B8
Tarves Aberds ...303 F8
Tarvie Highld ...300 D4
　Perth ...292 G2
Tarvin Ches W ...167 B7
Tarvin Sands Ches W ...167 B7
Tasburgh Norf ...142 D4
Tasley Shrops ...132 E3
Taston Oxon ...101 G7
Tat Bank W Mid ...133 F9
Tatenhill Staffs ...152 E4
Tatenhill Common
　Staffs ...152 E3
Tathall End M Keynes ...102 B6
Tatham Lancs ...212 F2
Tathwell Lincs ...190 E4
Tatling End Bucks ...66 B4
Tatsfield Sur ...52 B2
Tattenhall Ches W ...167 D7
Tattenhoe M Keynes ...102 E6
Tatterford Norf ...159 D7
Tattersett Norf ...158 C6
Tattershall Norf ...174 D2
Tattershall Bridge
　Lincs ...173 D11
Tattershall Thorpe
　Lincs ...174 D2
Tattingstone Suff ...108 D2
Tattingstone White Horse
　Suff ...108 D2
Tattle Bank Warks ...118 E3
Tatton Dale Ches E ...184 E2
Tatworth Som ...28 F4
Taunton Gtr Man ...196 G2
　Som ...28 C2
Taverham Norf ...160 G3
Taverners Green Essex ...87 B9
Tavernspite Pembs ...73 C11
Tavistock Devon ...12 G5
Taw Green Devon ...13 B9
Tawstock Devon ...25 B9
Taxal Derbys ...185 F8
Tay Bridge Dundee ...287 E8
Tayinloan Argyll ...255 C7
Taynuilt Argyll ...284 D4
Tayport Fife ...287 E8
Tayvallich Argyll ...275 E8
Taynton Glos ...98 G4
　Oxon ...82 C2
Tayvallich Argyll ...275 E8
Tea Green Herts ...104 G2
Tealby Lincs ...189 C11
Tealing Angus ...287 D8
Teams T&W ...242 E6
Team Valley T&W ...242 E6
Teanford Staffs ...169 G8
Teangue Highld ...295 E8
Teanna Mhachair
　W Isles ...296 E3

Teasley Mead E Sus ...52 F4
Tebay Cumb ...222 E2
Tebworth C Beds ...103 F9
Tedburn St Mary Devon ...14 C2
Teddington Glos ...99 E9
　London ...67 E7
Teddington Hands Worcs ...99 B9
Tedsmore Shrops ...149 D7
Tedstone Delamere
　Hereford ...116 F3
Tedstone Wafer
　Hereford ...116 F3
Teesville Redcar ...225 B10
Teeton Northants ...120 C3
Teffont Evias Wilts ...46 G3
Teffont Magna Wilts ...46 G3
Tegryn Pembs ...92 E4
Teigh Rutland ...155 F7
Teigncombe Devon ...13 D9
Teigngrace Devon ...14 G4
Teignmouth Devon ...14 G4
Teign Village Devon ...14 E2
Telford Telford ...132 B3
Telham E Sus ...38 E3
Tellisford Som ...45 B10
Telscombe E Sus ...36 G6
Telscombe Cliffs E Sus ...36 G5
Templand Dumfries ...248 F3
Temple Corn ...11 G8
　Glasgow ...267 B10
　Midloth ...270 D6
　Windsor ...65 C10
Temple Balsall W Mid ...118 B4
Temple Bar Carms ...75 B9
　Ceredig ...111 G10
Temple Cloud Bath ...44 B6
Templecombe Som ...30 C2
Temple Cowley Oxon ...83 E8
Temple End Essex ...106 C6
　Suff ...124 G3
Temple Ewell Kent ...55 E9
Temple Fields Essex ...87 C7
Temple Grafton Warks ...118 G2
Temple Guiting Glos ...99 F11
Templehall Fife ...280 C5
Temple Herdewyke
　Warks ...119 G7
Temple Hill Kent ...68 D5
Temple Hirst N Yorks ...198 C6
Templeman's Ash Dorset ...28 G6
Temple Normanton
　Derbys ...170 C6
Temple Sowerby Cumb. ...231 F8
Templeton Devon ...26 E5
　Pembs ...73 C10
Templeton Bridge Devon ...26 E5
Templetown Durham ...242 G4
Tempsford C Beds ...122 G3
Ten Acres W Mid ...133 G11
Tenandry Perth ...291 G11
Tenbury Wells Worcs ...115 D11
Tenby / Dinbych-y-Pysgod
　Pembs ...73 D10
Tencreek Corn ...6 E4
Tendring Essex ...108 G3
Tendring Green Essex ...108 F3
Tendring Heath Essex ...108 F2
Ten Mile Bank Norf ...140 D2
Tenston Orkney ...314 E2
Tenterden Kent ...53 G11
Terfyn Conwy ...181 G7
　Gwyn ...163 C9
Terhill Som ...43 G7
Terling Essex ...88 B3
Ternhill Shrops ...150 C2
Terpersie Castle Aberds ...302 G5
Terras Corn ...5 E8
Terregles Banks
　Dumfries ...237 B11
Terrible Down E Sus ...23 B7
Terrick Bucks ...84 D4
Terriers Bucks ...84 G5
Terrington N Yorks ...216 E3
Terrington St Clement
　Norf ...157 E10
Terrington St John
　Norf ...157 G10
Terryhorn Aberds ...302 F4
Terry's Green Warks ...118 C3
Terwick Common W Sus ...34 C4
Teston Kent ...53 C8
Testwood Hants ...32 E5
Tetbury Glos ...80 G5
Tetbury Upton Glos ...80 F5
Tetchill Shrops ...149 C7
Tetchwick Bucks ...83 B11
Tetcott Devon ...12 B2
Tetford Lincs ...190 G4
Tetney Lincs ...201 G10
Tetney Lock Lincs ...201 G10
Tetsworth Oxon ...83 E11
Tettenhall W Mid ...133 D7
Tettenhall Wood W Mid ...133 D7
Tetworth Cambs ...122 G4
Teuchan Aberds ...303 F10
Teversham Cambs ...123 F9
Teviothead Borders ...249 B10
Tewel Aberds ...293 E10
Tewin Herts ...86 C3
Tewin Wood Herts ...86 B3
Tewitfield Lancs ...211 E10
Tewkesbury Glos ...99 E7
Teynham Kent ...70 G3
Teynham Street Kent ...70 G3
Thackley W Yorks ...205 F9
Thackley End W Yorks ...205 F9
Thackthwaite Cumb ...229 G8
Thainston Aberds ...293 F8
Thakeham W Sus ...35 D10
Thame Oxon ...84 D2
Thames Ditton Sur ...67 F7
Thames Haven Thurrock ...69 C8
Thames Head Glos ...81 E7
Thamesmead London ...68 C3
Thanington Kent ...54 B6
Thankerton S Lanark ...259 B11
Tharston Norf ...142 E3
Thatcham W Berks ...64 F4
Thatto Heath Mers ...183 C8
Thaxted Essex ...106 E2
　The Aird Highld ...298 D4
Theakston N Yorks ...214 B6
Thealby N Lincs ...199 D11
Theale Som ...44 D3
　W Berks ...64 E6
Thearne E Yorks ...209 F7
Theberton Suff ...127 D8
Theddingworth Leics ...136 F3
Theddlethorpe All Saints
　Lincs ...191 D7
Theddlethorpe St Helen
　Lincs ...191 D7
The Dell Suff ...143 D9
The Delves W Mid ...133 D10
The Den N Ayrs ...266 E6
The Den Durham ...242 G4
The Down Kent ...53 F7
　Shrops ...132 E3
The Downs Sur ...50 F3
The Dunks Wrex ...166 E4
The Eals Northumb ...251 F7
The Eaves Glos ...79 D10
The Fall W Yorks ...197 B10
The Fence Glos ...79 D8
The Flat Glos ...80 B3
The Flatt Cumb ...240 B3
The Flourish Derbys ...153 B8
The Folly Herts ...85 C11
　S Glos ...61 B8
The Fording Hereford ...98 F3
The Forge Hereford ...114 F6
The Forstal Kent ...54 F4
The Forties Derbys ...152 F6
The Four Alls Shrops ...150 C3
The Fox Wilts ...62 B6
The Foxholes Shrops ...132 G2
The Frenches Hants ...32 C4
The Frythe Herts ...86 C2
The Garths Shetland ...312 B8
The Gibb Wilts ...61 D10
The Glack Borders ...260 B6
The Gore Wilts ...131 G11
The Grange Norf ...160 E2
　N Yorks ...225 F11
The Green Cambs ...122 D5
　C Beds ...85 B8
　Cumb ...210 C3
　Cumb ...211 D7
　Essex ...88 B3
　Hants ...32 B3
　M Keynes ...103 C7
　Norf ...141 C11
　Norf ...159 E9
　Northants ...102 C5
　Oxon ...101 F9
　Shrops ...130 G6
　S Yorks ...197 G8
　Warks ...118 F4
　Wilts ...45 G11
The Grove Dumfries ...237 B11
　Durham ...242 G3
　Herts ...85 F9
　Shrops ...131 B7
　Wilts ...131 G8
　Worcs ...99 C7
The Gutter Derbys ...170 F5
　Shrops ...117 B9
The Hacket S Glos ...61 B7
The Hague Derbys ...185 C8
The Hall Shetland ...312 D8
The Hallands N Lincs ...200 C5
The Ham Wilts ...45 C11
The Handfords Staffs ...151 E7
The Harbour Kent ...53 D10
The Haven W Sus ...50 G5
The Headland Hrtlpl ...234 E6
The Heath Norf ...159 D8
　Norf ...160 E4
　Staffs ...151 C11
　Suff ...108 D2
The Hem Shrops ...132 B4
The Hendre Mon ...79 C7
The Herberts V Glam ...58 E3
The Hermitage Cambs ...123 D7
The High Essex ...86 C6
The Highlands W Sus ...34 C5
The Hill Cumb ...210 C3
The Hobbins Shrops ...132 E4
The Hollands Staffs ...168 D6
The Hollies Lincs ...155 B11
The Holmes Derbys ...153 B7
The Holt Wokingham ...65 D11
The Hook Worcs ...98 C6
The Hope Shrops ...115 B8
The Howe Cumb ...211 B9
　IoM ...192 F3
The Hundred Hereford ...115 E10
The Hyde London ...67 B8

The Hyde continued
　Worcs ...98 C6
The Hythe Essex ...107 G10
The Inch Edin ...280 G5
Theydon Bois Essex ...86 F6
Theydon Garnon Essex ...87 F7
Theydon Mount Essex ...87 F7
The Yeld Shrops ...131 G11
Thicket Mead Bath ...45 B7
Thick Hollins W Yorks ...196 E6
Thickthorn Hall Norf ...142 B3
Thickwood Wilts ...61 E10
Thimbleby Lincs ...190 G2
　N Yorks ...225 F9
Thimble End W Mid ...134 E2
Thingley Wilts ...62 E11
Thingwall Mers ...182 E3
Thirdpart N Ayrs ...266 F3
Thirlby N Yorks ...215 C9
Thirlestane Borders ...271 F11
Thirn N Yorks ...214 B4
Thirsk N Yorks ...215 C8
Thirtleby E Yorks ...209 G9
Thistleton Lancs ...202 F4
　Rutland ...155 F8
Thistley Green Essex ...88 B2
　Suff ...124 B3
Thixendale N Yorks ...216 G6
The Lunt W Mid ...133 D9
Thockrington Northumb ...241 B11
Tholomas Drove Cambs ...139 B7
Tholthorpe N Yorks ...215 F9
Thomas Chapel Pembs ...73 D10
Thomas Close Cumb ...230 E4
Thomastown Aberds ...302 F5
　Rhondda ...58 B4
Thompson Norf ...141 D8
Thomshill Moray ...302 D2
Thong Kent ...69 E7
Thongsbridge W Yorks ...196 F6
Thoralby N Yorks ...213 B10
Thoresby Notts ...187 G10
Thoresthorpe Lincs ...191 F7
Thoresway Lincs ...189 B11
Thorganby Lincs ...190 B2
　N Yorks ...207 E9
Thorgill N Yorks ...226 F4
Thorington Suff ...127 C8
Thorington Street Suff ...107 D10
Thorlby N Yorks ...204 C5
Thorley Herts ...87 B7
　IoW ...20 D3
Thorley Houses Herts ...105 G9
Thorley Street Herts ...87 B7
　IoW ...20 D3
Thormanby N Yorks ...215 E9
The Node Herts ...104 G4
Thornaby on Tees
　Stockton ...225 B9
Thornage Norf ...159 B11
Thornborough Bucks ...102 E4
　N Yorks ...214 D5
Thornbury Devon ...24 E6
　Hereford ...116 F2
　S Glos ...79 G10
　W Yorks ...205 G9
Thornby Cumb ...239 G7
　Northants ...120 B3
Thorncliff Staffs ...169 D8
Thorncliffe Staffs ...169 D8
Thorncombe Dorset ...28 G5
　Dorset ...30 G5
Thorncombe Street Sur ...50 E4
Thorncote Green
　C Beds ...104 B3
Thorncross IoW ...20 E4
Thorndon Suff ...126 D2
Thorndon Cross Devon ...12 B6
Thorne Corn ...24 G2
Thorne S Yorks ...199 E7
Thorne Coffin Som ...29 D8
Thornehillhead Devon ...24 D6
Thorner Moor Devon ...12 D3
Thorner W Yorks ...206 E3
Thornes Staffs ...133 C11
　W Yorks ...197 D10
Thorne St Margaret Som ...27 C9
Thorney Bucks ...66 D4
　Notts ...188 G5
　Pboro ...138 C6
　Som ...28 C6
Thorney Crofts E Yorks ...201 C8
Thorney Green Suff ...125 E11
Thorney Hill Hants ...19 B9
Thorney Island W Sus ...22 C3
Thorney Toll Pboro ...138 C6
Thornfalcon Som ...28 C3
Thorngrafton Northumb ...241 D7
Thorngrove Som ...43 G11
Thorngumbald E Yorks ...201 B8
Thornham Norf ...176 E2
Thornham Fold
　Gtr Man ...195 F11
Thornham Magna Suff ...126 C2
Thornham Parva Suff ...126 C2
Thornhaugh Pboro ...137 C11
Thornhill Cardiff ...59 C7
　Cumb ...219 D10
　Derbys ...185 E11
　Dumfries ...247 D9
　Soton ...33 E7
　Stirling ...278 B3
　Torf ...78 F3
　Wilts ...62 D5
　W Yorks ...197 D9
Thornhill Edge W Yorks ...197 D8
Thornhill Lees W Yorks ...197 D8
Thornhill Park Hants ...33 E7
Thornhills W Yorks ...197 C7
Thornholme E Yorks ...218 G2
Thornicombe Dorset ...30 G5
Thornielee Borders ...261 B10
Thornley Durham ...233 D8
　Durham ...234 D3
Thorn Ley W Mid ...133 G10
Thornliebank E Renf ...267 D10
Thornly Park Renfs ...267 C9
Thornroan Aberds ...303 F8
Thorns N Yorks ...223 E7
　Suff ...124 F4
Thornseat S Yorks ...186 C2
Thornsett Derbys ...185 D8
Thorns Green Ches E ...184 E3
Thornthwaite Cumb ...229 G10
　N Yorks ...205 B9
Thornton Angus ...287 C7
　Bucks ...102 D5
　E Yorks ...207 D11
　Fife ...280 B5
　Lancs ...202 E2
　Leics ...135 B9
　Lincs ...174 B2
　Mbro ...225 C10
　Mers ...193 G10
　Northumb ...273 H6
　Pembs ...72 B6
　W Yorks ...205 G8
Thornton Curtis N Lincs ...200 D5
Thornton Hall N Lanark ...267 D11
Thornton Heath London ...67 F10
Thornton Hough Mers ...182 E4
Thornton in Craven
　N Yorks ...204 D4
Thornton in Lonsdale
　N Yorks ...212 E3
Thornton-le-Beans
　N Yorks ...225 G7
Thornton-le-Clay
　N Yorks ...216 F3
Thornton-le-Dale
　N Yorks ...216 C6
Thornton le Moor Lincs ...189 B9
Thornton-le-Moor
　N Yorks ...215 B7
Thornton-le-Moors
　Ches W ...182 G6
Thornton-le-Street
　N Yorks ...215 B8
Thorntonloch E Loth ...282 G4
Thornton Park Northumb ...273 H6
Thornton Rust N Yorks ...213 B9
Thornton Steward
　N Yorks ...214 B3
Thornton Watlass
　N Yorks ...214 B3
Thornwood Common
　Essex ...87 D7
Thornydykes Borders ...272 F2
Thoroton Notts ...172 G3
Thorp Gtr Man ...196 F2
Thorp Arch W Yorks ...206 D4
Thorpe Cumb ...230 F5
　Derbys ...169 E11
　E Yorks ...208 D5
　Lincs ...191 E7
　Norf ...143 D8
　Notts ...172 F3
　N Yorks ...213 G10
　Sur ...66 F4
Thorpe Abbotts Norf ...126 B3
Thorpe Acre Leics ...153 E10
Thorpe Arnold Leics ...154 E5
Thorpe Audlin W Yorks ...198 D3
Thorpe Bassett N Yorks ...217 E7
Thorpe Bay Southend ...70 B2
Thorpe by Water
　Rutland ...137 D7
Thorpe Common Suff ...108 D5
Thorpe Constantine
　Staffs ...134 B5
Thorpe Culvert Lincs ...175 C7
Thorpe Edge W Yorks ...205 F9
Thorpe End Norf ...160 G5
Thorpe Fendykes Lincs ...175 C7
Thorpe Green Essex ...108 G3
　Lancs ...194 C5
　Suff ...125 G8
Thorpe Hall N Yorks ...66 F4
Thorpe Hamlet Norf ...142 B4
Thorpe Hesley S Yorks ...186 B5
Thorpe in Balne
　S Yorks ...198 E5
Thorpe in the Fallows
　Lincs ...188 E6
Thorpe Langton Leics ...136 E4
Thorpe Larches Durham ...234 F3
Thorpe Latimer Lincs ...156 B2
Thorpe Lea Sur ...66 F4
Thorpe-le-Soken Essex ...108 G3
Thorpe le Street
　E Yorks ...208 E2
Thorpe le Vale Lincs ...190 C3
Thorpe Malsor
　Northants ...136 G6
Thorpe Mandeville
　Northants ...101 B10
Thorpe Market Norf ...160 B4
Thorpe Marriot Norf ...160 F3
Thorpe Morieux Suff ...125 G8
Thorpeness Suff ...127 F9
Thorpe on the Hill Lincs ...172 B6
　W Yorks ...197 B10
Thorpe Row Norf ...141 B9
Thorpe St Andrew Norf ...142 B5
Thorpe St Peter Lincs ...175 C7
Thorpe Salvin S Yorks ...187 E8
Thorpe Satchville Leics ...154 G4
Thorpe Street Lincs ...125 B10
Thorpe Thewles
　Stockton ...234 G4
Thorpe Tilney Lincs ...173 D10
Thorpe Underwood
　Northants ...136 G5
　N Yorks ...206 B6
Thorpe Waterville
　Northants ...137 G10
Thorpe Willoughby
　N Yorks ...198 B5
Thorpe Wood N Yorks ...207 G7
Thorrington Essex ...89 B9
Thorverton Devon ...26 G6
Thrandeston Suff ...126 B2
Thrapston Northants ...121 B9
Thrashbush N Lanark ...268 B5
Threapland Cumb ...229 D9
　N Yorks ...213 G9
Threapwood Ches W ...166 F6
　Staffs ...169 G8
Three Ashes Hants ...64 G6
　Hereford ...97 G10
　Shrops ...115 B7
　Som ...45 D7
Three Bridges Argyll ...284 F4
　Lincs ...190 D6
　W Sus ...51 F9
Three Burrows Corn ...4 F4
Three Chimneys Kent ...53 F10
Three Cocked Hat Norf ...143 D8
Three Cocks / Aberllynfi
　Powys ...96 D3
Three Crosses Swansea ...56 C5
Three Cups Corner
　E Sus ...37 C10
Three Fingers Wrex ...166 F6
Three Gates Dorset ...29 F10
Threehammer Common
　Norf ...160 E6
Three Hammers Corn ...11 D10
Three Holes Norf ...139 C10
ThreehS Cross Corn ...10 G6
Threekingham Lincs ...155 B11
Three Leg Cross E Sus ...53 G7
Three Legged Cross
　Dorset ...31 F9
　E Sus ...37 C10
Threelows Staffs ...169 F8
Three Maypoles W Mid ...118 B2
Threemile Cross
　Wokingham ...65 F8
Three Mile Cross
　Wokingham ...65 F8
Threemiletown W Loth ...279 F11
Three Oaks E Sus ...38 E4
Threepwood Borders ...271 G10
Threewaters Corn ...5 B10

The Wrythe London ...67 F9
The Wyke Shrops ...132 B4
The Wymm Hereford ...97 B10
Thicket Mead Bath ...45 B7
Thimble End W Mid ...134 E2
Thornton Curtis N Lincs ...200 D5
...

The Barony continued
　Orkney ...314 D2
The Barton Wilts ...62 D5
The Batch S Glos ...61 E7
The Beeches Glos ...81 E8
The Bell Gtr Man ...194 F4
The Bents Staffs ...151 C10
The Berton Suff ...127 D8
The Blythe Staffs ...151 D10
The Bog Shrops ...131 D7
The Borough Dorset ...30 E2
　London ...67 D10
　Worcs ...117 F9
The Bourne Sur ...49 E10
The Bows Stirling ...285 G11
The Braes Highld ...295 B7
The Brampton Staffs ...168 F4
The Brand Leics ...153 G10
The Brents Kent ...70 G4
The Breck Orkney ...314 F3
The Bridge Dorset ...30 E3
The Broad Hereford ...115 E9
The Brook Suff ...125 B11
The Brushes Derbys ...186 F5
The Bryn Mon ...78 D4
The Burf Worcs ...116 D6
The Butts Hants ...49 F8
　Som ...45 D9
The Camp Glos ...80 D6
　Herts ...85 D11
The Cape Warks ...118 D5
The Chart Kent ...52 C3
The Chequer Wrex ...167 G7
The Chuckery W Mid ...133 D10
The City Bucks ...84 F3
The Cleaver Hereford ...97 F10
The Close W Sus ...22 C5
The Colony Oxon ...100 D6
The Common Bath ...60 G4
　Bucks ...102 E5
　Dorset ...30 E3
　Shrops ...150 D3
　Suff ...108 B2
　Swansea ...56 C4
　Wilts ...47 G8
　Wilts ...61 C11
　W Sus ...62 C4
　W Sus ...51 G7
The Corner Kent ...53 E8
　Shrops ...131 F8
The Cot Wrex ...79 F8
The Craigs Highld ...309 K4
The Crofts E Yorks ...218 E4
The Cronk IoM ...192 C4
The Cross Hands Leics ...134 C6
The Cwm Wrex ...79 G7
The Common Shrops ...150 D3
Theddingworth Leics ...136 F3
Theobald's Green Wilts ...62 F4
The Oval Bath ...61 G8
The Park Glos ...99 G8
The Parks S Yorks ...198 F6
The Pitts Wilts ...31 B9
The Platt Oxon ...83 E9
The Pludds Glos ...79 B10
The Point Devon ...14 E5
The Pole of Itlaw
　Aberds ...302 D6
The Port of Felixstowe
　Suff ...108 E5
The Potteries Stoke ...168 F5
The Pound Glos ...98 E4
The Quarry Glos ...80 F2
　Shrops ...149 G9
The Quarter Kent ...53 E11
　Kent ...53 G11
The Rampings Worcs ...99 E7
The Rectory Lincs ...156 G2
The Reddings Glos ...99 G8
　Staffs ...199 E7
Therfield Herts ...104 D6
The Rhos Pembs ...73 C8
The Rhydd Hereford ...97 E9
The Riddle Hereford ...115 E9
The Ridge Wilts ...61 F11
The Ridges Wokingham ...65 G10
The Ridgeway Herts ...86 E3
The Riding Northumb ...241 D10
The Riggs Borders ...261 C8
The Rink Borders ...261 C11
The Rise Windsor ...66 F2
The Rock Telford ...132 B3
The Rocks Kent ...53 B8
　S Glos ...61 C8
The Roe Denb ...181 G8
The Rookery Herts ...85 G10
　Staffs ...168 D5
The Row Lancs ...211 D9
The Rowe Staffs ...150 B6
The Ryde Herts ...86 D2
The Sands Sur ...49 D11
The Scarr Glos ...98 F4
The Shoe Wilts ...61 E10
The Shruggs Staffs ...151 C8
The Slack Durham ...233 F8
The Slade W Berks ...64 F4
The Smeeth Norf ...157 G10
The Smithies Shrops ...132 D3
The Spa Wilts ...62 G2
The Spring Warks ...118 C5
The Square Torf ...78 F3
The Stocks Kent ...38 B6
　Wilts ...62 G2
The Straits Hants ...49 F9
　Derbys ...185 D11
　Dumfries ...247 D9
The Strand Wilts ...46 B2
The Swillett Herts ...85 F8
The Sydnall Shrops ...150 C3
Thetford Lincs ...156 F2
　Norf ...141 G7
　W Yorks ...197 B9
The Thrift Herts ...104 D6
The Throat Wokingham ...65 F10
The Toft Staffs ...151 F8
The Towans Corn ...2 B3
The Town Scilly ...1 F3
The Twittocks Glos ...99 D7
The Tynings Glos ...80 B6
The Vale W Mid ...133 G10
　Glam ...34 D4
Thornley Durham ...233 D8
The Valley Ches E ...167 D11
　Kent ...54 C3
　Leics ...154 F4
　Pembs ...73 D10
The Vauld Hereford ...97 B10
The Village Newport ...78 G4
　Windsor ...66 E3
　W Mid ...133 F7
The Walshes Worcs ...117 C7
The Weaven Hereford ...97 F10
The Wells Sur ...67 G7
The Willows NE Lincs ...201 F8
The Wood Shrops ...148 E6
　Shrops ...149 D9
The Woodlands Leics ...136 D9
　Mbro ...225 C10
The Woods Worcs ...98 B6
The Wrangle N Yorks ...72 G6
　Bath ...44 B4

Threlkeld Cumb ...230 F2
Threshers Bush Essex ...87 D7
Threshfield N Yorks ...213 G9
Thrigby Norf ...161 G8
Thringarth Durham ...232 G4
Thringstone Leics ...153 F8
Thrintoft N Yorks ...224 G6
Thriplow Cambs ...105 B8
Throapham S Yorks ...187 D8
Throckenholt Lincs ...139 B7
Throcking Herts ...104 E6
Throckley T&W ...242 D5
Throckmorton Worcs ...99 B9
Throop Dorset ...18 C2
Throophill Northumb ...252 F5
Thropton Northumb ...252 C2
Throsk Stirling ...279 C7
Througham Glos ...80 D6
Throughgate Dumfries ...247 G9
Throwleigh Devon ...13 C9
Throwley Kent ...54 C3
Throwley Forstal Kent ...54 C3
Throxenby N Yorks ...217 B10
Thrumpton Notts ...153 C10
　Notts ...188 E2
Thrumster Highld ...310 E7
Thrunton Northumb ...264 G3
Thrupe Som ...44 D6
Thrupp Glos ...80 E5
　Oxon ...82 F3
　Oxon ...83 B7
Thruscross N Yorks ...205 B8
Thrushelton Devon ...12 D4
Thrussington Leics ...154 F2
Thruxton Hants ...47 D9
　Hereford ...97 E9
Thrybergh S Yorks ...187 B7
Thulston Derbys ...153 C8
Thundergay N Ayrs ...255 C9
Thunder Bridge
　W Yorks ...197 E7
Thundersley Essex ...69 B9
Thundridge Herts ...86 B5
Thurcaston Leics ...153 G11
Thurcroft S Yorks ...187 D7
Thurdon Corn ...24 E3
Thurgarton Norf ...160 C3
　Notts ...171 F11
Thurgoland S Yorks ...197 G9
Thurlaston Leics ...135 D10
　Warks ...119 C9
Thurlbear Som ...28 C3
Thurlby Lincs ...156 F2
　Lincs ...172 C6
　Lincs ...191 F7
Thurleigh Bedford ...121 F11
Thurlestone Devon ...8 G5
Thurloxton Som ...43 G9
Thurlstone S Yorks ...197 G8
Thurlton Norf ...143 D8
Thurlwood Ches E ...168 D4
Thurmaston Leics ...136 B2
Thurnby Leics ...136 C2
Thurne Norf ...161 F8
Thurnham Kent ...53 B10
　Lancs ...202 C5
Thurning Norf ...159 D11
　Northants ...137 G11
Thurnscoe S Yorks ...198 F3
Thurnscoe East S Yorks ...198 F3
Thursby Cumb ...239 G8
Thursford Norf ...159 C9
Thursford Green Norf ...159 C9
Thurso Highld ...310 C5
Thurso East Highld ...310 C5
Thurstaston Mers ...182 E2
Thurston Suff ...125 D8
Thurston Clough
　Gtr Man ...196 F3
Thurston End Suff ...124 G5
Thurstonfield Cumb ...239 F8
Thurstonland W Yorks ...197 E7
Thurton Norf ...142 C6
Thurvaston Derbys ...152 B2
　Derbys ...152 B4
Thuxton Norf ...141 B10
Thwaite Suff ...126 D2
Thwaite N Yorks ...223 F7
Thwaite Flat Cumb ...210 E4
Thwaite Head Cumb ...220 G6
Thwaites W Yorks ...205 E7
Thwaite St Mary Norf ...142 E6
Thwaites Brow W Yorks ...205 F7
Thwing E Yorks ...217 E11
Tibberton Glos ...98 G5
　Telford ...150 E3
　Worcs ...117 F8
Tibbermore Perth ...286 E4
Tibberton Glos ...98 G5
Tibenham Norf ...142 F2
Tibshelf Derbys ...170 C6
Tibshelf Wharf Notts ...171 C7
Tibthorpe E Yorks ...208 B5
Ticehurst E Sus ...53 G7
Tichborne Hants ...48 G5
Tickencote Rutland ...137 B9
Tickenham N Som ...60 E3
Ticket Wood Devon ...8 G4
Tickford End M Keynes ...103 C7
Tickhill S Yorks ...187 C9
Ticklerton Shrops ...131 E9
Tickleback Row Brack ...65 E11
Ticklerton Shrops ...131 E9
Tickmorend Glos ...80 F4
Tickton E Yorks ...209 E7
Tidbury Green W Mid ...117 B11
Tidcombe Wilts ...47 B8
Tiddington Oxon ...83 E11
　Warks ...118 F4
Tidebrook E Sus ...37 B10
Tideford Corn ...6 D6
Tideford Cross Corn ...6 C6
Tidenham Glos ...79 F9
Tidenham Chase Glos ...79 E9
Tideswell Derbys ...185 F11
Tidmarsh W Berks ...64 E6
Tidmington Warks ...100 D5
Tidnor Hereford ...97 D11
Tidpit Hants ...31 D9
Tidworth Wilts ...47 D8
Tiers Cross Pembs ...72 C6
Tiffield Northants ...120 G3
Tifty Aberds ...303 E7
Tigerton Angus ...293 G7
Tigh-na-Blair Perth ...285 F11
Tighnabruaich Argyll ...275 F10
Tighnacachla Argyll ...274 G3
Tighnafiline Highld ...307 L3
Tighness Argyll ...284 G6
Tigley Devon ...8 C5
Tilbrook Cambs ...121 D11
Tilbury Thurrock ...68 D6
Tilbury Green Essex ...106 C4
Tilbury Juxta Clare
　Essex ...106 C4
Tile Cross W Mid ...134 F3
Tile Hill W Mid ...118 B5

Tilehouse Green W Mid ...118 B3
Tilekiln Green Essex ...105 G10
Tilehurst Reading ...65 E7
Tilford Sur ...49 E11
Tilford Common Sur ...49 E11
Tilford Reeds Sur ...49 E11
Tilgate W Sus ...51 G9
Tilgate Forest Row
　W Sus ...51 G9
Tilkey Essex ...106 G6
Tilland Corn ...6 C6
Tillathrowie Aberds ...302 F4
Tillers' Green Glos ...98 E3
Tilley Shrops ...149 D10
Tilley Green Shrops ...149 D10
Tilleycombe Clack ...279 B7
Tillicoultry Clack ...279 B7
Tillietudlem S Lanark ...268 F6
Tillingham Essex ...89 E7
Tillington Hereford ...97 B9
　Staffs ...151 E8
　W Sus ...35 C7
Tillington Common
　Hereford ...97 B9
Tillislow Devon ...12 C3
Tillworth Devon ...28 G4
Tillyarblet Angus ...293 G7
Tillycorthie Aberds ...303 G8
Tilly Down Hants ...47 D10
Tillydrine Aberds ...293 D7
Tillyfour Aberds ...293 B7
Tillyfourie Aberds ...293 B8
Tillygarmond Aberds ...293 D8
Tillygreig Aberds ...303 G8
Tillykerie Aberds ...303 G8
Tilly Loss N Yorks ...293 C7
Tillynaught Aberds ...302 C5
Tilmanstone Kent ...55 C10
Tilney All Saints Norf ...157 F11
Tilney cum Islington
　Norf ...157 G11
Tilney Fen End Norf ...157 G10
Tilney High End Norf ...157 F11
Tilney St Lawrence
　Norf ...157 G10
Tilsdown Glos ...80 F2
Tilshead Wilts ...46 D4
Tilsmore E Sus ...37 C9
Tilsop Shrops ...116 C2
Tilstock Shrops ...149 B10
Tilston Ches W ...167 E7
Tilstone Bank Ches W ...167 D9
Tilstone Fearnall
　Ches W ...167 C9
Tilsworth C Beds ...103 F9
Tilton on the Hill Leics ...136 B4
Tilts S Yorks ...198 F5
Tiltups End Glos ...80 F4
Tilty Essex ...105 F11
Timberden Bottom Kent ...68 G4
Timberhonger Worcs ...117 C7
Timberland Lincs ...173 D10
Timbersbrook Ches E ...168 C5
Timberscombe Som ...42 E3
Timble N Yorks ...205 C9
Timbold Hill Kent ...54 B2
Timbrelham Corn ...12 E3
Timperley Gtr Man ...184 D3
Timsbury Bath ...45 B7
　Hants ...32 C4
Timsgearraidh W Isles ...304 E2
Timworth Suff ...125 D7
Timworth Green Suff ...125 D7
Tincleton Dorset ...17 C11
Tindale Cumb ...240 F4
Tindale Crescent
　Durham ...233 F9
Tindon End Essex ...106 E2
Tingewick Bucks ...102 E3
Tingley W Yorks ...197 B9
Tingon Shetland ...312 E4
Tingrith C Beds ...103 E10
Tingwall Orkney ...314 D3
Tinhay Devon ...12 E3
Tinkers End Bucks ...102 F5
Tinshill W Yorks ...205 F11
Tinsley S Yorks ...186 C6
Tinsley Green W Sus ...51 F9
Tintagel Corn ...11 D7
Tintern Parva Mon ...79 E8
Tintinhull Som ...29 D8
Tintwistle Derbys ...185 B8
Tinwald Dumfries ...248 G2
Tinwell Rutland ...137 B10
Tipner Ptsmth ...33 G10
Tippacott Devon ...41 D9
Tipper's Hill Warks ...134 F5
Tipperty Aberds ...302 C6
　Aberds ...303 G9
Tipple Cross Devon ...12 D3
Tipps End Norf ...139 D10
Tip's Cross Essex ...87 E9
Tiptoe Hants ...19 B11
Tipton W Mid ...133 E8
Tipton Green W Mid ...133 E9
Tipton St John Devon ...15 C7
Tiptree Essex ...88 B6
Tiptree Heath Essex ...88 B5
Tirabad Powys ...95 C7
Tiraghoil Argyll ...288 G5
Tircanol Swansea ...57 B7
Tirdeunaw Swansea ...57 B7
Tirinie Perth ...291 G10
Tirley Glos ...98 F5
Tirley Knowle Glos ...98 F6
Tiroran Argyll ...288 G6
Tirphil Caerph ...77 E10
Tirril Cumb ...230 F7
Tirryside Highld ...309 H5
Tir-y-berth Caerph ...77 F11
Tir-y-dail Carms ...75 C10
Tisbury Wilts ...30 C6
Tisman's Common
　W Sus ...50 G5
Tissington Derbys ...169 E11
Titchberry Devon ...24 B2
Titchfield Hants ...33 F8
Titchfield Common Hants ...33 F8
Titchfield Park Hants ...33 F8
Titchmarsh Northants ...121 B10
Titchwell Norf ...176 E3
Tithby Notts ...154 B3
Tithebarn Staffs ...169 F8
Tithe Barn Hillock Mers ...183 B8
Titley Hereford ...114 F6
Titlington Northumb ...264 F4
Titmore Green Herts ...104 F4
Titsey Sur ...52 C2
Tittensor Staffs ...151 B7
Tittenhurst Windsor ...66 F3
Titterhill Shrops ...131 G10
Tittle Row Windsor ...65 C11
Tittleshall Norf ...159 E7
Titton Worcs ...116 D6
Titty Hill W Sus ...34 B5
Tiverton Ches W ...167 C9
　Devon ...27 E7

Tivetshall St Margaret Norf... 142 F3
Tivetshall St Mary Norf 142 F3
Tividale W Mid... 133 E9
Tivington Som... 42 E2
Tivington Knowle Som... 42 E2
Tivoli Cumb... 228 G5
Tivy Dale S Yorks... 197 F9
Tixall Staffs... 151 E9
Tixover Rutland... 137 C9
Toab Orkney... 314 F5
Shetland... 313 M5
Toadmoor Derbys... 170 E4
Toad Row Suff... 143 F10
Tobermory Argyll... 289 D7
Toberonochy Argyll... 275 C8
Tobha Beag W Isles... 296 D5
Tobha Mor W Isles... 297 H3
Tobhtarol W Isles... 304 E3
Tobson W Isles... 304 E3
Toby's Hill Lincs... 191 C7
Tocher Aberds... 302 F6
Tockenham Wilts... 62 C4
Tockenham Wick Wilts... 62 C4
Tockholes Blackburn... 195 C7
Tockington S Glos... 60 B6
Tockwith N Yorks... 206 C5
Todber Dorset... 30 C4
Todding Hereford... 115 B8
Toddington C Beds... 103 F10
Glos... 99 E10
W Sus... 35 G8
Toddlehills Aberds... 303 E10
Todenham Glos... 100 D4
Todhill Angus... 287 D8
Todhills Cumb... 239 E9
Durham... 233 E10
Todlachie Aberds... 293 B8
Todmorden W Yorks... 196 C2
Todpool Corn... 4 G4
Todrig Borders... 261 F10
Todwick S Yorks... 187 E7
Toft Cambs... 123 F7
Lincs... 155 F11
Shetland... 312 F6
Warks... 119 C9
Toft Hill Durham... 233 F9
Lincs... 174 C2
Toft Monks Norf... 143 E8
Toft next Newton Lincs... 189 D8
Toftrees Norf... 159 D7
Tofts Highld... 310 C7
Toftshaw W Yorks... 197 B7
Toftwood Norf... 159 G9
Togston Northumb... 252 C6
Tokavaig Highld... 295 D8
Tokers Green Oxon... 65 D8
Tokyngton London... 67 C7
Tolastadh a Chaolais W Isles... 304 E3
Tolastadh bho Thuath W Isles... 304 D7
Tolborough Corn... 11 F9
Tolcarne Corn... 2 B5
Corn... 2 C5
Tolcarne Wartha Corn... 2 B5
Toldish Corn... 5 D8
Tolgus Mount Corn... 4 G3
Tolhurst E Sus... 53 G7
Tolladine Worcs... 117 F7
Tolland Som... 42 G6
Tollard Farnham Dorset... 30 D6
Tollard Royal Wilts... 30 D6
Toll Bar Mers... 183 C7
Rutland... 137 B10
S Yorks... 198 F5
Tollbar End W Mid... 119 B7
Toll End W Mid... 133 E9
Tollerford Dorset... 17 B7
Toller Fratrum Dorset... 17 B7
Toller Porcorum Dorset... 17 B7
Tollerton Notts... 154 C2
N Yorks... 215 G10
Toller Whelme Dorset... 29 G8
Tollesbury Essex... 89 C7
Tollesby Mbro... 225 B10
Tolleshunt D'Arcy Essex... 88 C6
Tolleshunt Knights Essex... 88 C6
Tolleshunt Major Essex... 88 C5
Tollie Highld... 300 D5
Tollie Farm Highld... 299 C8
Tolm W Isles... 304 E6
Tolmers Herts... 86 E4
Tolpuddle Dorset... 17 C11
Tolvaddon Downs Corn... 4 G3
Tolvah Highld... 291 D10
Tolworth London... 67 F7
Tomaknock Perth... 286 E2
Tom an Fhuadain W Isles... 305 G5
Tomatin Highld... 301 G8
Tombreck Highld... 300 F6
Tombui Perth... 286 B2
Tomchrasky Highld... 290 B4
Tomdoun Highld... 290 C3
Tomich Highld... 300 B6
Highld... 300 G3
Tomich House Highld... 300 E5
Tomintoul Aberds... 292 D3
Moray... 292 B3
Tomlow Warks... 119 E9
Tomnaven Moray... 302 F4
Tomnavoulin Moray... 302 G2
Tomperrow Corn... 4 G5
Tompkin Staffs... 168 E6
Tompset's Bank E Sus... 52 G2
Tomsleibhe Argyll... 289 F8
Tomthorn Derbys... 185 F9
Ton Mon... 78 F5
Ton Breigam V Glam... 58 D3
Tonbridge Kent... 52 D5
Tonderghie Dumfries... 236 F6
Tondu Bridgend... 57 E11
Tone Som... 27 C10
Tonedale Som... 27 C10
Tone Green Som... 27 C11
Tong Kent... 53 D10
Shrops... 132 B5
W Yorks... 205 G10
Tong Corner Kent... 70 F2
Tonge Leics... 153 E8
Tonge Corner Kent... 70 F2
Tonge Fold Gtr Man... 195 F8
Tonge Moor Gtr Man... 195 E8
Tong Forge Shrops... 132 B5
Tong Green Kent... 54 C3
Tongham Sur... 49 D11
Tong Norton Shrops... 132 B5
Tongland Dumfries... 237 D8
Tong Park W Yorks... 205 F9
Tong Street W Yorks... 205 G9
Tongue Highld... 308 D5
Tongue End Lincs... 156 F3
Tongwynlais Cardiff... 58 C6
Tonmawr Neath... 57 B10
Tonna / Tonnau Neath... 57 B9
Ton-Pentre Rhondda... 77 F7
Ton-teg Rhondda... 58 B5

Tontine Lancs... 194 G4
Tonwell Herts... 86 B4
Tonypandy Rhondda... 77 G8
Ton-y-pistyll Caerph... 77 F11
Tonyrefail Rhondda... 58 B4
Toot Baldon Oxon... 83 E9
Toothill Hants... 32 D5
Swindon... 62 C6
W Yorks... 196 C6
Toot Hill Essex... 87 E8
Staffs... 169 G9
Topcliffe N Yorks... 215 D8
Topcroft Norf... 142 E5
Topcroft Street Norf... 142 E5
Top End Bedford... 121 E10
Topham S Yorks... 198 D6
Top Green Notts... 172 F3
Topleigh W Sus... 34 C6
Top Lock Gtr Man... 194 F6
Top of Hebers Gtr Man... 195 F11
Top o' th' Lane Lancs... 194 C5
Top o' th' Meadows Gtr Man... 196 F3
Toppesfield Essex... 106 D4
Toppings Gtr Man... 195 E8
Toprow Norf... 142 D3
Topsham Devon... 14 D5
Torbeg N Ayrs... 255 E10
Torboll Farm Highld... 309 K7
Torbothie N Lanark... 269 D7
Torbreck Highld... 309 J7
Torbryan Devon... 8 B6
Torbush N Lanark... 268 D6
Torcross Devon... 8 G6
Torcroy Highld... 291 D9
Tore Highld... 300 D6
Torfrey Corn... 6 E2
Torgyle Highld... 290 B5
Torinturk Argyll... 275 G9
Torksey Lincs... 188 F4
Torlum W Isles... 296 F3
Torlundy Highld... 290 F3
Tormarton S Glos... 61 D9
Tormisdale Argyll... 254 B2
Tormitchell S Ayrs... 244 E6
Tormore Highld... 295 C8
Lancs... 194 F2
Ayrs... 255 D9
Tornagrain Highld... 301 E7
Tornahaish Aberds... 292 C4
Tornapress Aberds... 299 E8
Tornaveen Aberds... 293 C8
Torness Highld... 300 G5
Toronto Durham... 233 E9
Torpenhow Cumb... 229 D10
Torphichen W Loth... 279 G9
Torphin Edin... 270 B4
Torphins Aberds... 293 C8
Torpoint Corn... 7 E8
Torquay Torbay... 9 C8
Torr Devon... 7 E11
Devon... 8 C2
Torra Argyll... 254 B4
Torran Argyll... 275 C9
Highld... 298 E5
Highld... 301 B7
Derbys... 185 F11
Torrance E Dunb... 278 G2
Torrans Argyll... 288 G6
Torranyard N Ayrs... 267 G7
Torre Som... 42 E4
Torbay... 9 C8
Torridon Highld... 299 D9
Torridon Ho Highld... 299 D8
Torries Aberds... 293 B8
Torrin Highld... 295 C7
Torrisdale Highld... 308 C6
Torrisdale Castle Argyll... 255 D8
Torrisdale-Square Argyll... 255 D8
Torrish Highld... 311 H3
Torrisholme Lancs... 211 G9
Torroble Highld... 309 J5
Torroy Highld... 309 K5
Torrpark Corn... 11 D10
Torry Aberdeen... 293 C11
Aberds... 302 F4
Torryburn Fife... 279 D10
Torsonce Borders... 271 F8
Torsonce Mains Borders... 271 G9
Torterston Aberds... 303 E10
Torthorwald Dumfries... 238 B2
Tortington W Sus... 35 F8
Torton Worcs... 116 C6
Tortworth S Glos... 80 G2
Torvaig Highld... 298 E4
Torver Cumb... 220 G5
Torwood Falk... 278 E6
Torwoodlee Mains Borders... 261 B10
Torworth Notts... 187 D11
Tosberry Devon... 24 C3
Toscaig Highld... 295 B9
Toseland Cambs... 122 E4
Tosside N Yorks... 203 B11
Tostock Suff... 125 E9
Totaig Highld... 295 C10
Highld... 298 D2
Totardor Highld... 294 B5
Totegan Highld... 310 C2
Tote Hill W Sus... 34 C4
Hants... 48 F5
Totford Hants... 48 F5
Totham Hill Essex... 88 C5
Totham Plains Essex... 88 C5
Tothill Lincs... 190 E6
Tot Hill Hants... 64 G3
Totland IoW... 20 D2
Totley S Yorks... 186 F4
Totley Brook S Yorks... 186 E4
Totley Rise S Yorks... 186 E4
Totmonslow Staffs... 151 B9
Totnell Dorset... 29 F10
Totnes Devon... 8 C6
Totnor Hereford... 97 E11
Toton Notts... 153 C10
Totronald Argyll... 288 D3
Totscore Highld... 298 C3
Tottenham London
Tottenham Hale London... 67 B10
Tottenhill Norf... 158 G2
Tottenhill Row Norf... 158 G2
Totteridge Bucks... 84 G2
London... 86 G2
Totternhoe C Beds... 103 G9
Totterton Shrops... 131 F7
Totties W Yorks... 197 F7
Tottington Gtr Man... 195 E9
Norf... 141 D7
Tottleworth Lancs... 203 G10
Totton Hants... 32 E5
Touchen End Windsor... 65 D11
Toulston N Yorks... 206 E5
Toulton Som... 43 G7

Toulvaddie Highld... 311 L2
Tournaig Highld... 307 L3
Toux Aberds... 303 D9
Tovil Kent... 53 C9
Towan Corn... 10 G3
Towan Cross Corn... 4 F4
Toward Argyll... 266 B2
Towcester Northants... 102 B3
Towednack Corn... 1 B3
Towerage Bucks... 84 G4
Tower End Norf... 158 F3
Tower Hamlets Kent... 55 E10
T N Som... 44 B2
Towerhead N Som... 44 B2
Tower Hill Ches E... 184 F6
Devon... 12 C3
Essex... 108 E5
Herts... 85 E8
Mers... 194 G2
Sur... 51 D7
W Sus... 35 E11
Towersey Oxon... 84 D2
Tow Law Durham... 233 D8
Towie Aberds... 292 B6
Aberds... 302 G5
Aberds... 303 C8
Towiemore Moray... 302 E3
Town Law Durham... 233 D8
Town Barton Devon... 14 C2
Townend Derbys... 185 E9
Staffs... 151 B9
W Dunb... 277 F8
Town End Bucks... 84 F3
Cambs... 139 D8
Cumb... 211 B7
Cumb... 211 C8
Cumb... 212 C2
Cumb... 220 D6
Cumb... 221 E8
Cumb... 221 F7
Cumb... 231 F8
Derbys... 185 F11
E Yorks... 207 C10
Mers... 183 D7
W Yorks... 196 D5
Townfield Durham... 232 B5
Town Fields Ches W... 167 B10
Towngate Cumb... 230 B6
Lincs... 156 G2
Town Green Gtr Man... 183 B9
Lancs... 194 F2
Townhead Argyll... 275 G11
Cumb... 229 D7
Cumb... 230 D6
Cumb... 231 B8
Cumb... 231 E8
Dumfries... 237 D8
N Lanark... 268 A4
Northumb... 251 E9
S Ayrs... 244 G6
S Yorks... 197 G7
Town Head Cumb... 220 D6
Cumb... 221 E8
Cumb... 222 C2
Cumb... 222 C3
Cumb... 231 F7
Cumb... 231 G8
N Yorks... 204 B2
N Yorks... 212 F5
Staffs... 169 F8
W Yorks... 204 D6
Townhead of Greenlaw Dumfries... 237 C9
Townhill Fife... 280 D2
Swansea... 56 C6
Townhill Park Hants... 33 E7
Town Kelloe Durham... 234 D3
Townlake Devon... 12 G4
Town Littleworth E Sus... 36 D6
Townland Green Kent... 54 G2
Town Lane Gtr Man... 183 B11
Town Littleworth E Sus... 36 D6
Town of Lowton Mers... 183 B10
Town Park Telford... 132 B3
Town Row E Sus... 52 G5
Townsend Bath... 44 B5
Bucks... 84 D2
Devon... 8 F3
Herts... 85 D10
Oxon... 63 B11
Pembs... 72 D4
Som... 45 G7
Town's End Bucks... 102 G2
Dorset... 18 B3
Dorset... 18 E5
Dorset... 29 F9
Som... 45 D7
Townsend Fold Lancs... 195 C10
Townshend Corn... 2 C4
Town Street Glos... 98 F6
Townwell S Glos... 79 G11
Town Yetholm Borders... 263 D8
Towthorpe E Yorks... 217 G8
York... 207 B8
Towton N Yorks... 206 F5
Towyn Conwy... 181 F7
Toxteth Mers... 182 D5
Toynton All Saints Lincs... 174 C5
Toynton Fen Side Lincs... 174 C5
Toynton St Peter Lincs... 174 C6
Toy's Hill Kent... 52 C3
Trabboch E Ayrs... 257 E10
Traboe Corn... 2 E6
Trabrown Borders... 271 F10
Tracebridge Som... 27 C9
Tradespark Highld... 301 D8
Orkney... 314 F4
Trafford Park Gtr Man... 184 B3
Traigh Ho Highld... 295 F8
Trallong Powys... 95 F9
Trallwn Rhondda... 58 B7
Swansea... 57 B7
Tramagenna Corn... 11 E7
Tram Inn Hereford... 97 E9
Tranch Torf... 78 E3
Tranent E Loth... 281 G8
Tranmere Mers... 182 D4
Trantlebeg Highld... 310 D2
Trantlemore Highld... 310 D2
Tranwell Northumb... 252 G5
Trapp Carms... 75 B11
Traprain E Loth... 281 F11
Trap's Green Warks... 118 D3
Trapshill W Berks... 63 G11
Traquair Borders... 261 B10
Trash Green W Berks... 65 F7
Travellers' Rest Carms... 74 B5
Travellers Rest Devon... 26 F6
Trawden Lancs... 204 F3
Trawscoed Powys... 95 E11
Trawsfynydd Gwyn... 146 B4
Trawsnant Ceredig... 111 D11
Treadam Mon... 78 B5
Treaddow Hereford... 97 G10

Treal Corn... 2 F6
Trealaw Rhondda... 77 G8
Treales Lancs... 202 G4
Trearddur Anglesey... 178 F3
Treaslane Highld... 298 D3
Treath Corn... 3 D7
Treator Corn... 10 F4
Tre-Aubrey V Glam... 58 E4
Trebanog Rhondda... 77 G8
Trebanos Neath... 76 E2
Trebarber Corn... 5 C7
Trebartha Corn... 11 F11
Trebarvah Corn... 2 C5
Trebarwith Corn... 11 D7
Trebarwith Strand Corn... 10 D6
Trebeath Corn... 11 D11
Tre-Beferad V Glam... 58 F3
Trebell Green Corn... 5 C11
Treberfydd Powys... 96 F2
Trebetherick Corn... 10 F4
Treble's Holford Som... 43 G7
Trebudannon Corn... 5 C7
Trebullett Corn... 12 F2
Treburgett Corn... 11 F7
Treburick Corn... 10 G3
Treburley Corn... 12 F3
Treburrick Corn... 10 G3
Trebyan Corn... 5 C11
Trecastle Powys... 95 F7
Trecenydd Caerph... 58 B6
Trecott Devon... 25 G10
Trecwn Pembs... 91 E9
Trecynon Rhondda... 77 E7
Tredannick Corn... 10 G6
Tredaule Corn... 11 E10
Tredavoe Corn... 1 D5
Treddiog Pembs... 91 F7
Tredegar Bl Gwent... 77 D10
Trederwen Powys... 148 F5
Tre-derwen Powys... 148 F4
Tredethy Corn... 11 G7
Tredington Glos... 99 F8
Warks... 100 C5
Tredinnick Corn... 1 C4
Corn... 5 D10
Corn... 6 C4
Corn... 6 D4
Corn... 10 G4
Corn... 11 E10
Corn... 11 F11
Tredogan V Glam... 58 F5
Tredomen Caerph... 77 G10
Powys... 96 E2
Tredown Devon... 24 D2
Tredrizzick Corn... 10 F5
Tredunnock Mon... 78 G5
Tredustan Powys... 96 E2
Tredworth Glos... 80 B4
Treen Corn... 1 E4
Corn... 1 E3
Treesmill Corn... 5 D11
Treeton S Yorks... 186 D6
Trefaes Corn... 144 C5
Trefanny Hill Corn... 6 D4
Trefasser Pembs... 91 D7
Trefdraeth Anglesey... 178 G6
Trefdraeth / Newport Pembs... 91 D11
Trefecca Powys... 96 E2
Trefechan Ceredig... 111 A11
M Tydf... 77 D8
Wrex... 166 F3
Trefeglwys Powys... 129 E9
Trefeitha Powys... 96 E2
Trefenter Ceredig... 112 D2
Treffgarne Pembs... 91 G9
Treffynnon / Holywell Flint... 181 F11
Treffynnon Pembs... 91 F7
Trefil Bl Gwent... 77 C10
Trefilan Ceredig... 111 F11
Trefin / Trevine Pembs... 90 E6
Treflach Shrops... 148 E5
Trefnanney Powys... 148 F4
Trefnant Denb... 181 G9
Trefonen Shrops... 148 D5
Trefor Anglesey... 178 E5
Gwyn... 162 F5
Treforda Corn... 11 E7
Treforest Rhondda... 58 B5
Treforgan Ceredig... 92 B4
Tre-Forgan Neath... 76 D3
Treforys / Morriston Swansea... 57 B7
Trefrew Conwy... 164 C3
Trefriw Conwy... 164 C3
Trefrize Corn... 12 F2
Tref y Clawdd / Knighton Powys... 114 C5
Trefynwy / Monmouth Mon... 79 C8
Tregada Corn... 12 E2
Tregadgwith Corn... 1 D4
Tregadillett Corn... 12 E2
Tre-gagle Mon... 79 D8
Tregaian Anglesey... 178 F6
Tregajorran Corn... 4 G3
Tregamere Corn... 5 C8
Tregardock Corn... 10 E6
Tregare Mon... 78 C6
Tregarland Corn... 6 D4
Tregarlandbridge Corn... 6 D4
Tregarne Corn... 3 E7
Tregaron Ceredig... 112 F3
Tregarth Gwyn... 163 B10
Tregaswith Corn... 5 C7
Tregatta Corn... 11 D7
Tregavarah Corn... 1 D4
Tregear Corn... 5 D8
Tregeare Corn... 11 D10
Tregeiriog Wrex... 148 C3
Tregele Anglesey... 178 C5
Tregeseal Corn... 1 C3
Tregew Corn... 3 B8
Tre-Gibbon Rhondda... 77 E7
Tregidden Corn... 3 E7
Treginnis Pembs... 90 G4
Treglemais Pembs... 90 F6
Tregole Corn... 11 C7
Tregolls Corn... 2 B6
Tregolwyn / Colwinston V Glam... 58 D2
Tregonce Corn... 10 G4
Tregonetha Corn... 5 C9
Tregonna Corn... 10 G4
Tregonning Corn... 5 C7
Tregony Corn... 5 F9
Tregoodwell Corn... 11 E8
Tregorden Corn... 10 G6
Tregorrick Corn... 5 E10
Tregoss Corn... 5 C9
Tregowris Corn... 3 E7
Tregoyd Powys... 96 E3
Tregoyd Mill Powys... 96 E3
Tregreenwell Corn... 11 E7
Tregrehan Mills Corn... 5 E10
Tre-groes Ceredig... 93 C8
Tregullon Corn... 5 C11

Tregunna Corn... 10 G5
Tregurrian Corn... 5 B7
Tregurtha Downs Corn... 2 C2
Tre Gwyr / Gowerton Swansea... 56 B5
Tregynon Powys... 129 D11
Tre-gynwr Carms... 74 B6
Trehafod Rhondda... 77 G8
Trehafren Powys... 129 E11
Trehan Corn... 7 D8
Treharris M Tydf... 77 F9
Trehemborne Corn... 10 G3
Treherbert Rhondda... 76 F6
Tre-hill V Glam... 58 E5
Tre-Ifor Rhondda... 77 D7
Trekeivesteps Corn... 11 G10
Trekenner Corn... 12 F2
Trekenning Corn... 5 C8
Treknow Corn... 11 D7
Trelales / Laleston Bridgend... 57 F11
Trelan Corn... 2 F6
Tre-Tan Flint... 165 B11
Trelash Corn... 11 C9
Trelassick Corn... 5 E7
Trelawnyd Flint... 181 F9
Trelech Carms... 92 E5
Treleddyd-fawr Pembs... 90 F5
Treleigh Corn... 4 G4
Trellech Mon... 79 E7
Treleaver Corn... 3 E7
Trelewis M Tydf... 77 F10
Treligga Corn... 11 E7
Trelights Corn... 10 F5
Trelill Corn... 10 F6
Trelion Corn... 5 E8
Treliske Corn... 4 F6
Trelissick Corn... 3 B8
Treliver Corn... 5 B9
Trelleck Mon... 79 E7
Trelleck Grange Mon... 79 E7
Trelogan Flint... 181 E10
Trelowia Corn... 6 D5
Trelowth Corn... 5 E9
Trelystan Powys... 130 C5
Tremadog Gwyn... 163 G9
Tremail Corn... 11 D9
Tremain Ceredig... 92 B4
Tremaine Corn... 11 D10
Tremains Bridgend... 58 D2
Tremar Corn... 6 B5
Trematon Corn... 7 D7
Trematon Castle Corn... 7 D8
Tremayne Corn... 2 B4
Trembraze Corn... 6 B5
Tremedda Corn... 1 B5
Tremeirchion Denb... 181 G9
Tremethick Cross Corn... 1 C4
Tremollett Corn... 11 G11
Tremore Corn... 5 C10
Tremorebridge Corn... 5 C10
Tremorfa Cardiff... 59 D8
Tre-Mostyn Flint... 181 F10
Trenance Corn... 4 C6
Corn... 5 B7
Corn... 5 C9
Corn... 10 G4
Trenant Corn... 6 B4
Trenarren Corn... 5 F10
Trenay Corn... 6 B4
Trench Telford... 150 G3
Trench Green Oxon... 65 D7
Trench Wood Worcs... 52 D5
Trencreek Corn... 4 C6
Corn... 11 E10
Trencrom Corn... 2 B2
Trendeal Corn... 5 E7
Trenear Corn... 2 C5
Treneglos Corn... 11 D10
Trenerth Corn... 2 B4
Trenewan Corn... 6 E3
Trengune Corn... 11 C8
Trenhorne Corn... 11 F11
Treningle Corn... 5 C10
Treninnick Corn... 4 C6
Trenoon Corn... 2 F6
Trenoweth Corn... 3 C7
Trent Dorset... 29 D9
Trentham Stoke... 168 G5
Trentishoe Devon... 40 D6
Trentlock Derbys... 153 C9
Trent Vale Stoke... 168 G5
Trenwheal Corn... 2 C4
Treoes V Glam... 58 D2
Treopert / Granston Pembs... 91 E7
Treorchy / Treorci Rhondda... 77 F7
Treorci / Treorchy Rhondda... 77 F7
Trewennack Corn... 2 D5
Trewern Powys... 148 G5
Trewetha Corn... 10 E6
Trewethern Corn... 10 F6
Trewidland Corn... 6 D5
Trewint Corn... 11 B9
Corn... 11 F11
Trewithian Corn... 3 B9
Trewithick Corn... 2 D5
Trewollock Corn... 5 G10
Trewoodloe Corn... 12 G2
Trewoofe Corn... 1 D4
Trewoon Corn... 2 E5
Corn... 5 E9
Treworga Corn... 5 F7
Treworgan Common Mon... 78 D6
Treworlas Corn... 3 B9
Treworld Corn... 11 C8
Treworrick Corn... 10 G5
Treworthal Corn... 3 B9
Trewyddel / Moylgrove Pembs... 92 C2
Trewyn Devon... 24 G4
Tre-wyn Mon... 96 G6
Treyarnon Corn... 10 G3
Treyford W Sus... 34 D4
Trezaise Corn... 5 D9
Trezelah Corn... 1 C5
Triangle Glos... 79 E11
Staffs... 133 B11
W Yorks... 196 C4
Trickett's Cross Dorset... 31 G9
Triffleton Pembs... 91 G9
Trillacott Corn... 11 D11
Trimdon Durham... 234 E3
Trimdon Colliery Durham... 234 D3
Trimdon Grange Durham... 234 D3
Trimingham Norf... 160 B5
Trimley Lower Street Suff... 108 D5
Trimley St Martin Suff... 108 D5
Trimley St Mary Suff... 108 D5
Trimpley Worcs... 116 B5
Trimsaran Carms... 75 E7
Trims Green Herts... 87 B7
Trimstone Devon... 40 E3
Trinafour Perth... 291 G9
Trinant Caerph... 78 E2
Tring Herts... 84 C6
Tringford Herts... 84 C6
Tring Wharf Herts... 84 C6
Trinity Angus... 293 G8
Edin... 280 F4
Trinity Fields Staffs... 151 B8
Trisant Ceredig... 112 B4
Triscombe Som... 43 F7
Som... 42 G6
Trislaig Highld... 290 F2
Trispen Corn... 4 E6
Tritlington Northumb... 252 E6
Troan Corn... 5 D8
Trochry Perth... 286 C3

Troedrhiwfuwch Caerph... 77 E10
Troedyraur Ceredig... 92 B5
Troedyrhiw M Tydf... 77 E9
Trofarth Conwy... 180 G5
Trolliloes E Sus... 23 C10
Tromode IoM... 192 E4
Trondavoe Shetland... 312 F5
Troon Corn... 2 B5
S Ayrs... 257 C8
Trooper's Inn Pembs... 73 C7
Trosaraidh W Isles... 297 K3
Trossachs Hotel Stirling... 285 G9
Troston Suff... 125 C7
Trostre Carms... 56 B4
Trostrey Common Mon... 78 E5
Troswell Corn... 11 C11
Trotshill Worcs... 117 F7
Trotten Marsh W Sus... 34 C4
Trottiscliffe Kent... 68 G6
Trotton W Sus... 34 C4
Trough Gate Lancs... 195 C11
Troutbeck Cumb... 221 E8
Cumb... 230 F3
Troutbeck Bridge Cumb... 221 F8
Troway Derbys... 186 F5
Trowbridge Cardiff... 59 C8
Wilts... 45 B11
Trowell Notts... 153 B9
Trow Green Glos... 79 D9
Trowle Common Wilts... 45 B10
Trowley Bottom Herts... 85 C9
Trows Borders... 262 C5
Trowse Newton Norf... 142 B4
Troydale W Yorks... 205 G10
Troy Town Kent... 52 D2
Kent... 54 E5
Medway... 69 F8
Truas Corn... 11 D7
Trub Gtr Man... 195 F11
Trudoxhill Som... 45 E8
Trueman's Heath Worcs... 117 B11
True Street Devon... 8 C6
Trull Som... 28 C2
Trumaisgearraidh W Isles... 296 D4
Trumfleet S Yorks... 198 E5
Trumpan Highld... 298 C2
Trumpet Hereford... 98 D3
Trumpington Cambs... 123 F8
Trumpsgreen Sur... 66 F3
Trunch Norf... 160 C5
Trunnah Lancs... 202 E3
Truro Corn... 4 G6
Truscott Corn... 12 D2
Trusham Devon... 14 E3
Trusley Derbys... 152 B5
Trussall Corn... 2 D5
Trussell Corn... 11 D10
Trusthorpe Lincs... 191 E8
Truthan Corn... 4 E6
Truthwall Corn... 2 C2
Tryfil Anglesey... 178 E6
Trysull Staffs... 133 E7
Trythogga Corn... 1 C5
Tubbs Mill Corn... 5 G9
Tubney Oxon... 82 F6
Tubslake Kent... 53 G9
Tuckenhay Devon... 8 D6
Tuckermarsh Devon... 7 B8
Tuckerton Som... 28 B3
Tuckhill Shrops... 132 F5
Tuckingmill Corn... 4 G3
Corn... 11 F7
Wilts... 30 B6
Tucking Mill Bath... 61 G8
Tuckton Bmouth... 19 C8
Tuddenham Suff... 124 C4
Tuddenham St Martin Suff... 108 B3
Tudeley Kent... 52 D6
Tudeley Hale Kent... 52 D6
Tudhay Devon... 28 G4
Tudhoe Durham... 233 D11
Tudhoe Grange Durham... 233 E11
Tudor Hill W Mid... 134 D2
Tudorville Hereford... 97 G11
Tudweiliog Gwyn... 144 B4
Tuebrook Mers... 182 C5
Tuesley Sur... 50 E3
Tuesnoad Kent... 54 E2
Tuffley Glos... 80 C4
Tufnell Park London... 67 C9
Tufton Hants... 48 D3
Pembs... 91 F10
Tugby Leics... 136 C5
Tugford Shrops... 131 F11
Tughall Northumb... 264 D6
Tulchan Lodge Angus... 292 F3
Tullecombe W Sus... 34 B4
Tullibardine Perth... 286 F3
Tullibody Clack... 279 B7
Tullich Argyll... 284 F4
Highld... 299 E9
Highld... 300 G6
Tullich Muir Highld... 301 B7
Tulliemet Perth... 286 B3
Tulloch Aberds... 293 F9
Aberds... 303 F8
Highld... 290 E6
Perth... 286 E4
Tulloch Castle Highld... 300 C5
Tullochgorm Argyll... 275 D10
Tulloch-gribban Highld... 301 G9
Tullochroisk Perth... 285 B11
Tullochvenus Aberds... 293 C7
Tulloes Angus... 287 C9
Tullybannocher Perth... 285 E11
Tullybelton Perth... 286 D4
Tullyfergus Perth... 286 C6
Tullymurdoch Perth... 286 B5
Tullynessle Aberds... 293 B7
Tulse Hill London... 67 E10
Tumble / Y Tymbl Carms... 75 C8
Tumbler's Green Essex... 106 G6
Tumby Lincs... 174 D2
Tumby Woodside Lincs... 174 D3
Tummel Bridge Perth... 285 B11
Tumpy Green Glos... 80 D2
Tumpy Lakes Hereford... 97 B10
Tunbridge Hill Medway... 69 E10
Tunbridge Wells Royal... 52 F5
Tunga W Isles... 304 E6
Tungate Norf... 160 D5
Tunley Bath... 45 B7
Glos... 80 E6
Tunnel Hill Worcs... 98 C6
Tunnel Pits N Lincs... 199 G8
Tunshill Gtr Man... 196 F2
Tunstall E Yorks... 209 G12
Kent... 69 G11
Lancs... 212 E2
N Yorks... 224 F4
Norf... 143 B8
Staffs... 150 D5
Stoke... 168 E5

Tunstall continued
Suff... 127 G7
T&W... 243 G9
Tunstead Derbys... 185 G10
Gtr Man... 196 C4
Norf... 160 E5
Tunworth Hants... 49 D7
Tupsley Hereford... 97 C10
Tupton Derbys... 170 B5
Turbary Common Poole... 19 C7
Turfdown Corn... 5 B11
Turf Hill Mers... 196 E2
Turfholm S Lanark... 259 B8
Turfmoor Devon... 28 G3
Shrops... 149 F7
Turgis Green Hants... 49 B7
Turin Angus... 287 B9
Turkdean Glos... 81 B10
Turkey Island Hants... 33 E9
Som... 34 D3
Turkey Tump Hereford... 97 F10
Turleigh Wilts... 136 E4
Turleygreen Shrops... 132 F5
Turlin Moor Poole... 18 C5
Turmer Hants... 31 F10
Turn Lancs... 195 D10
Turnalt Argyll... 275 C9
Turnastone Hereford... 97 D7
Turnberry S Ayrs... 244 B6
Turnchapel Plym... 7 E9
Turnditch Derbys... 170 F3
Turner Green Lancs... 203 G8
Turner's Green E Sus... 23 B10
E Sus... 52 G6
Warks... 118 D3
W Berks... 64 F4
Turners Hill W Sus... 51 F10
Turners Puddle Dorset... 18 C2
Turnerwood S Yorks... 187 E8
Turnford Herts... 86 E5
Turnhouse Edin... 280 G3
Turnhurst Stoke... 168 E5
Turnstead Milton Derbys... 185 E8
Turnworth Dorset... 30 F4
Turrerich Perth... 286 D2
Turriff Aberds... 303 D7
Tursdale Durham... 234 D2
Turton Bottoms Blackburn... 195 D8
Turves Cambs... 138 D6
Turves Green W Mid... 117 B10
Turvey Bedford... 121 G8
Turville Bucks... 84 G3
Turville Heath Bucks... 84 G3
Turweston Bucks... 102 D2
Tushielaw Borders... 261 F8
Tutbury Staffs... 152 D4
Tutnall Worcs... 117 C9
Tutshill Glos... 79 G10
Tutts Clump W Berks... 64 E5
Tuttington Norf... 160 D4
Tutts Clump W Berks... 64 E5
Tutwell Corn... 12 F2
Tuxford Notts... 188 G2
Twatt Orkney... 314 D2
Shetland... 313 H5
Twechar E Dunb... 278 F4
Tweedale Telford... 132 C4
Tweeddalebumn Borders... 270 E3
Tweedmouth Northumb... 273 E9
Tweedsmuir Borders... 260 E3
Twelve Heads Corn... 4 G5
Twelve Oaks E Sus... 37 C11
Twelvewoods Corn... 6 B4
Twemlow Green Ches E... 168 B3
Twenties Kent... 71 F10
Twenty Lincs... 156 E3
Twerton Bath... 61 G8
Twickenham London... 67 E7
Twigworth Glos... 98 G6
Twineham W Sus... 36 D3
Twineham Green W Sus... 36 D3
Twinhoe Bath... 45 B8
Twinstead Essex... 106 D6
Twinstead Green Essex... 106 D6
Twiss Green Warr... 183 B11
Twist Devon... 28 G3
Twiston Lancs... 204 E2
Twitchen Devon... 41 G9
Shrops... 115 B7
Twitchen Mill Devon... 41 G9
Twitham Kent... 55 B9
Twitton Kent... 52 B4
Two Bridges Devon... 13 G8
Glos... 79 D11
Two Burrows Corn... 4 F4
Two Dales Derbys... 170 C3
Two Gates Staffs... 134 C4
Two Mile Ash M Keynes... 102 D6
W Sus... 35 B10
Two Mile Hill Bristol... 60 E6
Two Mile Oak Cross Devon... 8 B6
Two Mills Ches W... 182 G5
Two Pots Devon... 40 E4
Two Waters Herts... 85 D8
Twr Anglesey... 178 E2
Twycross Leics... 134 C6
Twydall Medway... 69 F9
Twyford Bucks... 102 F3
Derbys... 152 D6
Dorset... 30 D5
Hants... 33 C7
Leics... 154 G4
Lincs... 155 E8
Norf... 159 E10
Oxon... 101 D9
Shrops... 148 D6
Wokingham... 65 D9
Worcs... 99 B10
Twyford Common Hereford... 97 D10
Twyn-Allws Mon... 78 C3
Twynholm Dumfries... 237 D8
Twyning Glos... 99 D7
Twyning Green Glos... 99 D7
Twynllanan Carms... 94 G5
Twynmynydd Carms... 75 C10
Twyn Shôn-Ifan Caerph... 77 G11
Twynyrodyn M Tydf... 77 E9
Twyn-yr-odyn V Glam... 58 E6
Twyn-y-Sheriff Mon... 78 E6
Twywell Northants... 121 B9
Tyberton Hereford... 97 D7
Tyburn W Mid... 134 E2
Tycroes Carms... 75 C10
Tycrwyn Powys... 148 F2
Tyddewi / St Davids Pembs... 90 F5
Tydd Gote Lincs... 157 F9
Tydd St Giles Cambs... 157 F8
Tydd St Mary Lincs... 157 F8
Tyddyn Angharad Denb... 165 F9
Tyddyn Dai Anglesey... 178 C6

Tyddyn-mawr Gwyn ...163 G9
Ty-draw Conwy ...164 D5
  Swansea ...57 C7
Tye Hants ...22 C2
Tye Common Essex ...87 G11
Tyegate Green Norf ...161 G7
Tye Green Essex ...87 G7
  Essex ...87 F11
  Essex ...105 D11
  Essex ...105 G10
  Essex ...106 G5
Tyersal W Yorks ...205 G9
Ty-fry Mon ...78 F6
Tyganol V Glam ...58 E4
Ty-hen Carms ...92 G6
  Gwyn ...144 C3
Ty-isaf Carms ...56 B4
Tyla Mon ...78 C2
Tylagwyn Bridgend ...58 B2
Tyldesley Gtr Man ...195 G7
Tyle Carms ...75 D8
Tyle-garw Rhondda ...58 C4
Tyler Hill Kent ...70 G6
Tylers Causeway Herts ...86 D3
Tylers Green Bucks ...84 G6
Tyler's Green Essex ...87 D8
  Sur ...51 C11
Tyler's Hill Bucks ...85 E7
Ty Llwyn Bl Gwent ...77 D11
Tylorstown Rhondda ...77 F8
Tylwch Powys ...129 G9
Ty Mawr Anglesey ...179 D7
Ty-mawr Carms ...181 F7
Ty Mawr Conwy ...164 F6
Tynant Rhondda ...58 B5
Ty-nant Conwy ...165 G7
  Gwyn ...147 D8
Tyncelyn Ceredig ...112 E2
Tyndrum Stirling ...285 D7
Tyne Dock T&W ...243 D9
Tyneham Dorset ...18 E3
Tynehead Midloth ...271 D7
Tynemouth T&W ...243 D8
Tyne Tunnel T&W ...243 D8
Tynewydd Ceredig ...92 B4
  Neath ...76 D4
  Rhondda ...76 F6
Ty-Newydd Ceredig ...111 D10
Tyning Bath ...45 B7
Tyningham E Loth ...282 F2
Tyn-lon Gwyn ...163 D7
Tynron Dumfries ...247 E8
Tyntesfield N Som ...60 E4
Tyn-y-bryn Rhondda ...58 B4
Tyn-y-celyn Wrex ...148 B3
Tyn-y-coed Shrops ...148 E4
Ty'n-y-coedcae Caerph ...59 B7
Tyn-y-fedw Swansea ...75 E10
Tynyfedw Conwy ...165 B7
Tyn-y-fedwen Powys ...148 C2
Tyn-y-ffordd Denb ...181 G8
Ty'n-y-garn Bridgend ...57 E11
Tyn-y-graig Powys ...113 G10
Ty'n-y-groes Conwy ...180 G3
Tyn-y-maes Gwyn ...163 C10
Tyn-y-pwll Anglesey ...178 D6
Tyn-yr-eithin Ceredig ...112 E3
Tynyrwtra Powys ...129 F7
Tyrells End C Beds ...103 E9
Tyrell's Wood Sur ...51 B7
Ty~r-felin-isaf Conwy ...164 C5
Ty Rhiw Rhondda ...58 C6
Tyringham M Keynes ...103 C7
Tyseley W Mid ...134 G2
Ty-Sign Caerph ...78 G2
Tythecott Devon ...24 D6
Tythegston Bridgend ...57 F11
Tytherington Ches E ...184 F6
  S Glos ...61 B7
  Som ...45 D9
  Wilts ...46 E2
Tytherleigh Devon ...28 G4
Tytherton Lucas Wilts ...62 E2
Tyttenhanger Herts ...85 D11
Ty-uchaf Powys ...147 E10
Tywardreath Corn ...5 E11
Tywardreath Highway
  Corn ...5 D11
Tywyn Conwy ...180 F3
  Gwyn ...110 C2

U

Uachdar W Isles ...296 F3
Uags Highld ...295 B9
Ubberley Stoke ...168 F6
Ubbeston Green Suff ...126 C6
Ubley Bath ...44 B4
Uckerby N Yorks ...224 E4
Uckfield E Sus ...37 C7
Uckinghall Worcs ...99 D7
Uckington Glos ...99 G8
  Shrops ...131 B11
Uddingston S Lanark ...268 C3
Uddington S Lanark ...259 C10
Udimore E Sus ...38 D5
Udley N Som ...60 G3
Udny Green Aberds ...303 G8
Udny Station Aberds ...303 G9
Udston S Lanark ...268 D3
Udstonhead S Lanark ...268 F4
Uffcott Wilts ...62 D6
Uffculme Devon ...27 E9
Uffington Lincs ...137 B11
  Oxon ...63 B10
  Shrops ...149 G10
Ufford Pboro ...137 C11
  Suff ...126 G5
Ufton Warks ...119 E7
Ufton Green W Berks ...64 F6
Ufton Nervet W Berks ...64 F6
Ugadale Argyll ...255 E8
Ugborough Devon ...8 D3
Ugford Wilts ...46 G5
Uggeshall Suff ...143 G8
Ugglebarnby N Yorks ...227 D7
Ughill S Yorks ...186 C3
Ugley Essex ...105 F10
Ugley Green Essex ...105 F10
Ugthorpe N Yorks ...226 C5
Uidh W Isles ...297 M2
Uig Argyll ...276 E2
  Argyll ...288 D3
  Highld ...296 F7
  Highld ...298 C3
Uigen W Isles ...304 E2
Uigshader Highld ...298 E4
Uisken Argyll ...274 B4
Ulaw Aberds ...303 G9
Ulbster Highld ...310 E7
Ulcat Row Cumb ...230 G4

Ulceby Lincs ...190 G6
  N Lincs ...200 E6
Ulceby Skitter N Lincs ...200 E6
Ulcombe Kent ...53 D10
Uldale Cumb ...229 D10
Uley Glos ...80 F3
Ulgham Northumb ...252 E6
Ullapool Highld ...307 K6
Ullcombe Devon ...28 F2
Ullenhall Warks ...118 D2
Ullenwood Glos ...80 B6
Ulleskelf N Yorks ...206 E6
Ullesthorpe Leics ...135 F10
Ulley S Yorks ...187 D7
Ullingswick Hereford ...97 B11
Ullington Worcs ...100 B3
Ullinish Highld ...294 B5
Ullock Cumb ...229 G7
  Cumb ...229 G10
Ulnes Walton Lancs ...194 D4
Ulpha Cumb ...220 G3
Ulrome E Yorks ...209 B9
Ulshaw N Yorks ...214 B2
Ulsta Shetland ...312 E6
Ulva House Argyll ...288 F6
Ulverley Green W Mid ...134 G2
Ulverston Cumb ...210 D5
Ulwell Dorset ...18 E6
Umberleigh Devon ...25 C10
Unapool Highld ...306 F7
Unasary W Isles ...297 J3
Under Bank W Yorks ...196 F6
Underbarrow Cumb ...221 G9
Undercliffe W Yorks ...205 G9
Underdale Shrops ...149 G10
Underdown Devon ...14 D3
Underhill London ...86 F2
Underhoull Shetland ...312 C7
Underling Green Kent ...53 D9
Underriver Kent ...52 C5
Underriver Ho Kent ...52 C5
Under the Wood Kent ...71 F8
Under Tofts S Yorks ...186 D4
Underton Shrops ...132 E3
Underwood Newport ...59 B11
  Notts ...171 E7
  Plym ...7 D10
Undley Suff ...140 G3
Undy Mon ...60 B2
Ungisiadar W Isles ...304 F3
Unifirth Shetland ...313 H4
Union Cottage Aberds ...293 D10
Union Mills IoM ...192 E4
Union Street E Sus ...53 G8
United Downs Corn ...4 G4
Unstone Derbys ...186 F5
Unstone Green Derbys ...186 F5
Unsworth Gtr Man ...195 F10
Unthank Cumb ...230 B3
  Cumb ...230 D5
  Cumb ...231 C8
  Derbys ...186 F4
Unthank End Cumb ...230 D5
Upavon Wilts ...46 C6
Up Cerne Dorset ...29 G11
Upchurch Kent ...69 G11
Upcott Devon ...24 D2
  Devon ...25 F9
  Devon ...25 F11
  Devon ...40 F3
  Hereford ...97 D11
Upend Cambs ...124 F3
Up End M Keynes ...103 B8
Up Exe Devon ...26 G6
Upgate Norf ...160 F2
Upgate Street Norf ...141 E11
  Norf ...142 E5
Up Green W Berks ...65 G9
Upgreen Hants ...49 C9
Uphall Dorset ...29 G9
  W Loth ...279 G11
Uphall Station W Loth ...279 G11
Upham Devon ...26 F5
  Hants ...33 C8
Uphampton Hereford ...115 E7
  Worcs ...116 E6
Up Hatherley Glos ...99 G8
Uphempston Devon ...8 C6
Uphill N Som ...43 B10
Uphill Manor N Som ...43 B10
Up Holland Lancs ...194 F4
Uplands Glos ...80 D5
  Swansea ...56 C6
Uplawmoor E Renf ...267 D8
Upleadon Glos ...98 F5
Upleadon Court Glos ...98 F5
Upleatham Redcar ...226 B2
Uplees Kent ...70 G3
Uploders Dorset ...16 C6
Uplowman Devon ...27 D8
Uplyme Devon ...16 C2
Up Marden W Sus ...34 E3
Upminster London ...68 B5
Up Mudford Som ...29 D9
Up Nately Hants ...49 C7
Upnor Medway ...69 E9
Uppottery Devon ...28 F2
Uppacott Devon ...25 B9
Uppat Highld ...311 J2
Uppend Essex ...105 F9
Upper Affcot Shrops ...131 F8
Upper Ardchronie
  Highld ...309 L6
Upper Ardgrain Aberds ...303 F9
Upper Ardroscadale
  Argyll ...275 G11
Upper Arley Worcs ...132 G5
Upper Armley W Yorks ...205 G11
Upper Arncott Oxon ...83 B10
Upper Astley Shrops ...149 F10
Upper Aston Shrops ...132 E6
Upper Astrop
  Northants ...101 D10
Upper Badcall Highld ...306 E6
Upper Bangor Gwyn ...179 G9
Upper Basildon W Berks ...64 E6
Upper Batley W Yorks ...197 B8
Upper Battlefield
  Shrops ...149 F10
Upper Beeding W Sus ...35 E11
Upper Benefield
  Northants ...137 F9
Upper Bentley Worcs ...117 D9
Upper Bighouse Highld ...310 D2
Upper Birchwood
  Derbys ...170 E6
Upper Blainslie
  Borders ...271 G10
Upper Boat Rhondda ...58 B6
Upper Boddam Aberds ...302 F6
Upper Boddington
  Northants ...119 G9
Upper Bogrow Highld ...309 L7
Upper Bogside Moray ...302 D2
Upper Booth Derbys ...185 D10
Upper Borth Ceredig ...128 E2
Upper Boyndlie Aberds ...303 C9
Upper Brailes Warks ...100 D4

Upper Brandon Parva
  Norf ...141 B10
Upper Breakish Highld ...295 C8
Upper Breinton Hereford ...97 C9
Upper Broadheath
  Worcs ...116 F6
Upper Brockholes
  W Yorks ...196 B5
Upper Broughton Notts ...154 D3
Upper Broxwood
  Hereford ...115 G7
Upper Bruntingthorpe
  Leics ...136 F2
Upper Brynamman
  Carms ...76 C2
Upper Buckenhill
  Hereford ...97 E11
Upper Bucklebury
  W Berks ...64 F4
Upper Bullington Hants ...48 E3
Upper Burgate Hants ...31 D11
Upper Burnhaugh
  Aberds ...293 D10
Upper Bush Medway ...69 F7
Upperby Cumb ...239 G10
Upper Caldecote
  C Beds ...104 B3
Upper Cam Glos ...80 F3
Upper Canada N Som ...43 B11
Upper Canterton Hants ...32 E3
Upper Catesby
  Northants ...119 F10
Upper Catshill Worcs ...117 C9
Upper Chapel Powys ...95 C10
Upper Cheddon Som ...28 B2
Upper Chicksgrove Wilts ...31 B7
Upper Church Village
  Rhondda ...58 B5
Upper Chute Wilts ...47 C9
Upper Clapton London ...67 B10
Upper Clatford Hants ...47 E11
Upper Coberley Glos ...81 B7
Upper College Shrops ...149 C11
Upper Colwall Hereford ...98 C5
Upper Common Hants ...48 D6
Upper Cotburn Aberds ...303 D7
Upper Cotton Staffs ...169 F9
Upper Coullie Aberds ...293 B9
Upper Cound Shrops ...131 C11
Upper Coxley Som ...44 E4
Upper Cudworth
  S Yorks ...197 F11
Upper Culphin Aberds ...302 D6
Upper Cumberworth
  W Yorks ...197 F8
Upper Cwmbran Torf ...78 F3
Upper Cwm-twrch Powys ...76 C3
Upperdale Derbys ...185 G11
Upper Dallachy Moray ...302 C3
Upper Deal Kent ...55 C11
Upper Dean Bedford ...121 D10
  Devon ...8 C4
Upper Denby W Yorks ...197 G8
  W Yorks ...197 F8
Upper Denton Cumb ...240 D4
Upper Derraid Highld ...301 G10
Upper Dicker E Sus ...23 D9
Upper Dinchope Shrops ...131 G9
Upper Dormington
  Hereford ...97 D11
Upper Dounreay Highld ...310 C4
Upper Dovercourt Essex ...108 E4
Upper Dowdeswell Glos ...81 B8
Upper Druimfin Argyll ...289 D7
Upper Dunsforth
  N Yorks ...215 G8
Upper Dunsley Herts ...84 C6
Upper Eashing Sur ...50 E3
Upper Eastern Green
  W Mid ...134 G5
Upper Eathie Highld ...301 C7
Upper Edmonton London ...86 G4
Upper Egleton Hereford ...98 C2
Upper Elkstone Staffs ...169 D9
Upper Ellastone Staffs ...169 G9
Upper Elmers End
  London ...67 F11
Upper End Derbys ...185 F9
  Glos ...81 C10
  Glos ...81 D8
  Leics ...154 G4
Upper Enham Hants ...47 D11
Upper Farmcote Shrops ...132 E5
Upper Farringdon Hants ...49 F8
Upper Feorlig Highld ...298 E2
Upper Fivehead Som ...28 C4
Upper Forge Shrops ...132 F4
Upper Framilode Glos ...80 C3
Upper Froyle Hants ...49 E9
Upper Gambolds Worcs ...117 D9
Upper Gills Highld ...310 B7
Upper Glenfintaig
  Highld ...290 E4
Upper Godney Som ...44 E3
Upper Goldstone Kent ...71 G9
Upper Gornal W Mid ...133 E8
Upper Gravenhurst
  C Beds ...104 D2
Upper Green Essex ...105 E8
  Mon ...78 B5
  Suff ...124 E4
  W Berks ...63 G11
  W Yorks ...197 B9
Upper Grove Common
  Hereford ...97 F11
Upper Guist Norf ...159 D10
Upper Hackney Derbys ...170 C3
Upper Hale Sur ...49 D10
Upper Halistra Highld ...298 D2
Upper Halliford Sur ...66 F5
Upper Halling Medway ...69 G7
Upper Ham Worcs ...99 D7
Upper Hambleton
  Rutland ...137 B8
Upper Hamnish
  Hereford ...115 F10
Upper Harbledown Kent ...54 B6
Upper Hardres Court
  Kent ...55 C7
Upper Hardwick
  Hereford ...115 F8
Upper Hartfield E Sus ...52 G3
Upper Hartshay Derbys ...170 E5
Upper Haselor Worcs ...99 C10
Upper Hatton Staffs ...150 B6
Upper Haugh S Yorks ...186 B6
Upper Hawkhillan
  Aberds ...303 F10
Upper Hayesden Kent ...52 E5
Upper Hayton Shrops ...131 G10
Upper Heath Shrops ...131 F11
Upper Heaton W Yorks ...197 D7
Upper Helmsley
  N Yorks ...207 B9
Upper Hengoed Shrops ...148 C5
Upper Hergest Hereford ...114 G5
Upper Heyford
  Northants ...120 F3
  Oxon ...101 F9
  Northumb ...241 C9

Upper Hill Glos ...79 F11
  Hereford ...115 G9
Upper Hindhope
  Borders ...251 B7
Upper Holloway London ...67 B9
Upper Holton Suff ...127 B8
Upper Hopton W Yorks ...197 D7
Upper Horsebridge
  E Sus ...23 C9
Upper Howsell Worcs ...98 B5
Upper Hoyland
  S Yorks ...197 G11
Upper Hulme Staffs ...169 C8
Upper Hyde IoW ...21 E7
Upper Ifold Sur ...50 G4
Upper Inglesham Swindon ...82 F2
Upper Inverbrough
  Highld ...301 F10
Upper Kergord Shetland ...313 H6
Upper Kidston Borders ...270 G4
Upper Kilcott Glos ...61 B9
Upper Killay Swansea ...56 C5
Upper Killeyan Argyll ...254 C3
Upper Kinsham
  Hereford ...115 D7
Upper Knockando
  Moray ...301 E11
Upper Lambourn
  W Berks ...63 C10
Upper Landywood
  Staffs ...133 B9
Upper Langford N Som ...44 B3
Upper Langwith Derbys ...171 B8
Upper Layham Suff ...107 C12
Upper Leigh Staffs ...151 B10
Upper Lenie Highld ...300 G5
Upper Littleton N Som ...60 F5
Upper Loads Derbys ...170 B4
Upper Lochton Aberds ...293 D8
Upper Lode Worcs ...99 E7
Upper Longdon Staffs ...151 G11
Upper Longwood
  Shrops ...132 B2
Upper Ludstone Shrops ...132 D6
Upper Lybster Highld ...310 F6
Upper Lydbrook Glos ...79 B10
Upper Lyde Hereford ...97 C9
Upper Lye Hereford ...115 D7
Upper Maes-coed
  Hereford ...96 D6
Upper Marsh W Yorks ...204 F6
Upper Midhope S Yorks ...186 B2
Upper Midway Derbys ...152 E5
Uppermill Gtr Man ...196 F3
Upper Milovaig Highld ...297 G7
Upper Milton Oxon ...82 B3
  Som ...44 D4
Upper Minety Wilts ...81 G8
Upper Mitton Worcs ...116 C6
Upper Moor Worcs ...99 B9
Upper Moor Side
  W Yorks ...205 G10
Upper Morton S Glos ...79 G11
Upper Nash Pembs ...73 E8
Upper Netchwood
  Shrops ...132 E2
Upper Newbold Derbys ...186 G5
Upper Nobut Staffs ...151 B10
Upper North Dean Bucks ...84 F4
Upper Norwood London ...67 F10
  W Sus ...34 D6
Upper Obney Perth ...286 D4
Upper Ochrwyth Caerph ...59 B8
Upper Oddington Glos ...100 F4
Upper Ollach Highld ...295 B7
Upper Padley Derbys ...186 F2
Upper Pickwick Wilts ...61 E11
Upper Pollicott Bucks ...84 C2
Upper Poppleton York ...207 C7
Upper Port Highld ...301 G10
Upper Postern Kent ...52 D6
Upper Quinton Warks ...100 B3
Upper Race Torf ...78 E3
Upper Ratley Hants ...32 C4
Upper Ridinghill
  Aberds ...303 D10
Upper Rissington Glos ...82 B2
Upper Rochford Worcs ...116 D2
Upper Rodmersham Kent ...70 G2
Upper Sandaig Highld ...295 D9
Upper Sanday Orkney ...314 F5
Upper Sapey Hereford ...116 E3
Upper Saxondale Notts ...154 B3
Upper Seagry Wilts ...62 C2
Upper Shelton C Beds ...103 C9
Upper Sheringham
  Norf ...177 E10
Upper Shirley London ...67 G11
  Soton ...32 E6
Upper Siddington Glos ...81 F8
Upper Skelmorlie
  N Ayrs ...266 B4
Upper Slackstead Hants ...32 B5
Upper Slaughter Glos ...100 G3
Upper Solva Pembs ...90 G5
Upper Soudley Glos ...79 C11
Uppersound Shetland ...313 J6
Upper Stanton Drew
  Bath ...60 G6
Upper Staploe Bedford ...122 F2
Upper Stoke Norf ...142 C5
  W Mid ...135 G7
Upper Stondon C Beds ...104 D2
Upper Stowe Northants ...120 F2
Upper Stratton Swindon ...63 B7
Upper Street Norf ...31 D11
  Norf ...142 G3
  Norf ...160 B5
  Norf ...160 F6
  Norf ...161 F7
  Suff ...108 E2
  Suff ...124 G5
  Suff ...126 G2
Upper Strensham Worcs ...99 D8
Upper Studley Wilts ...45 B11
Upper Sundon C Beds ...103 F10
Upper Swainswick Bath ...61 F9
Upper Swanmore Hants ...33 D9
Upper Swell Glos ...100 F3
Upper Sydenham
  London ...67 E10
Upper Tankersley
  S Yorks ...186 B4
Upper Tean Staffs ...151 B10
Upper Threapwood
  Ches W ...166 F6
Upper Tillyrie Perth ...286 G5
Upperton E Sus ...23 E10
  Oxon ...83 E11
  W Sus ...35 C7
Upper Tooting London ...67 E9
Upper Tote Highld ...298 D5
Uppertown Derbys ...170 C4
  Highld ...300 F4
  Highld ...310 B7
  Northumb ...241 C9

Uppertown continued
  Orkney ...314 G4
Upper Town Derbys ...170 D3
  Derbys ...170 E2
  Durham ...233 D7
  Hereford ...97 B11
  N Som ...60 E4
  Suff ...125 D8
  Wilts ...62 D3
  Worcs ...204 G6
Upper Treverward
  Shrops ...114 B5
Upper Tysoe Warks ...100 C6
Upper Up Glos ...81 F8
Upper Upham Wilts ...63 D8
Upper Upnor Medway ...69 E9
Upper Vobster Som ...45 D8
Upper Walthamstow
  London ...67 B11
Upper Wardington Oxon ...101 B9
Upper Wardley W Sus ...34 B4
Upper Weald M Keynes ...102 D6
Upper Weedon
  Northants ...120 F2
Upper Welland Worcs ...98 C5
Upper Wellingham E Sus ...36 E6
Upper Welson Hereford ...114 G5
Upper Westholme Som ...44 E5
Upper Weston Bath ...61 F8
Upper Weybread Suff ...126 B4
Upper Whiston S Yorks ...187 D7
Upper Wick Glos ...80 F2
  Worcs ...116 G6
Upper Wield Hants ...48 F6
Upper Wigginton
  Shrops ...148 B6
Upper Winchendon
  Bucks ...84 C2
Upper Witton W Mid ...133 E11
Upper Wolvercote Oxon ...83 D7
Upper Wolverton Worcs ...117 G8
Upperwood Derbys ...170 D3
Upper Woodend Aberds ...293 B8
Upper Woodford Wilts ...46 F6
Upper Woolhampton
  W Berks ...64 F5
Upper Wootton Hants ...48 C5
Upper Wraxall Wilts ...61 E10
Upper Wyche Hereford ...98 C5
Uppincott Devon ...26 G5
Uppingham Rutland ...137 D7
Uppington Dorset ...31 F8
  Shrops ...132 B2
Upsall N Yorks ...215 B9
Upshire Essex ...86 E6
Up Somborne Hants ...47 G11
Upstreet Kent ...71 G8
Up Sydling Dorset ...29 G10
Upthorpe Glos ...80 E3
  Suff ...125 C9
Upton Bucks ...84 C3
  Cambs ...122 B3
  Cambs ...138 F2
  Ches W ...166 B6
  Corn ...11 G11
  Corn ...24 G2
  Cumb ...230 D2
  Devon ...8 F4
  Devon ...27 G9
  Dorset ...17 D10
  Dorset ...18 C5
  E Yorks ...209 C8
  Hants ...32 D5
  Hants ...47 B11
  IoW ...21 C7
  Kent ...71 F11
  Leics ...135 D7
  Lincs ...188 D5
  London ...68 C2
  Mers ...182 D3
  Mers ...183 D7
  Norf ...161 G7
  Norf ...142 D4
  Notts ...172 E2
  Notts ...188 F7
  Oxon ...64 B4
  Oxon ...82 C2
  Pboro ...138 C2
  Slough ...66 D3
  Som ...27 B7
  Som ...29 B9
  Warks ...118 F2
  Wilts ...45 G11
  W Sus ...198 G3
Upton Bishop Hereford ...98 F2
Upton Cheyney S Glos ...61 F8
Upton Cressett Shrops ...132 E3
Upton Crews Hereford ...98 F2
Upton Cross Corn ...11 G11
Upton End C Beds ...104 E2
Upton Field Notts ...172 E2
Upton Green Norf ...161 G7
Upton Grey Hants ...49 D7
Upton Heath Ches W ...166 B6
Upton Hellions Devon ...26 G4
Upton Lea Bucks ...66 C3
Upton Lovell Wilts ...46 E2
Upton Magna Shrops ...149 G11
Upton Noble Som ...45 F8
Upton Park London ...68 C2
Upton Pyne Devon ...14 B4
Upton Rocks Halton ...183 D8
Upton St Leonards Glos ...80 C5
Upton Scudamore Wilts ...45 D11
Upton Snodsbury Worcs ...117 G8
Upton upon Severn
  Worcs ...99 C7
Upton Warren Worcs ...117 D8
Upwaltham W Sus ...34 E6
Upware Cambs ...123 C10
Upwell Norf ...139 C9
Upwey Dorset ...17 E9
Upwick Green Herts ...105 G9
Upwood Cambs ...138 G5
Uradale Shetland ...313 K6
Urafirth Shetland ...312 F5
Uragaig Argyll ...274 D4
Urchany Highld ...301 E8
Urchfont Wilts ...46 B4
Urdimarsh Hereford ...97 B10
Ure Shetland ...312 F4
Ure Bank N Yorks ...214 E6
Urgashay Som ...29 C9
Urgha W Isles ...305 J3
Urgha Beag W Isles ...305 H3
Urishay Common
  Hereford ...96 D6
Urlar Perth ...286 C2
Urlay Nook Stockton ...225 C7
Urmston Gtr Man ...184 C3
Urpeth Durham ...242 G6
Urquhart Highld ...300 D5
  Moray ...302 C2
Urra N Yorks ...225 E11
Urray Highld ...300 D5
Ushaw Moor Durham ...233 C10
Usk Mon ...78 E5
Usselby Lincs ...189 C9
Usworth T&W ...243 F8
Utkinton Ches W ...167 C8
Utley W Yorks ...204 E6
Uton Devon ...14 B2

Utterby Lincs ...190 C4
Uttoxeter Staffs ...151 C11
Uwchmynydd Gwyn ...144 D3
Uxbridge London ...66 C5
Uxbridge Moor London ...66 C5
Uyea Shetland ...312 D5
Uyeasound Shetland ...312 C7
Uzmaston Pembs ...73 C7

V

Vachelich Pembs ...90 F5
Vadlure Shetland ...313 J4
Vagg Som ...29 D8
Vaila Hall Shetland ...313 J4
Vaivoe Shetland ...312 G7
Vale Glam ...196 B2
Vale Down Devon ...12 D6
Vale of Health London ...67 B9
Valeswood Shrops ...149 F7
Valleyfield Dumfries ...237 D8
Valley Park Hants ...32 C6
Valley Truckle Corn ...11 E7
Valley / Y Fali Anglesey ...178 F3
Valsgarth Shetland ...312 B8
Valtos Highld ...298 C5
Van Caerph ...59 B7
  Powys ...129 F9
Vange Essex ...69 B8
Vanlop Shetland ...313 M5
Varchoel Powys ...148 G3
Varfell Corn ...2 C2
Varteg Torf ...78 D3
Vassa Shetland ...313 H6
Vastern Wilts ...62 C5
Vatsetter Shetland ...312 E7
  Shetland ...313 L5
Vatten Highld ...298 E2
Vaul Argyll ...288 E2
Vauxhall London ...67 D10
  Mers ...182 C4
  W Mid ...133 F11
Vaynol Hall Gwyn ...163 B8
Vaynor M Tydf ...77 C8
Veensgarth Shetland ...313 J6
Velator Devon ...40 F3
Veldo Hereford ...97 C11
Velindre Powys ...96 D3
Vellanoweth Corn ...2 C2
Vellow Som ...42 F5
Velly Devon ...24 C3
Veness Orkney ...314 D5
Venn Devon ...8 F4
Venngreen Devon ...24 E5
Venn Green Devon ...24 E5
Vennington Shrops ...130 B6
Venn Ottery Devon ...15 C7
Venn's Green Hereford ...97 B10
Venterdon Corn ...12 G3
Vention Devon ...40 E3
Ventnor IoW ...21 F7
Venton Devon ...7 D11
Ventongimps Corn ...4 E5
Ventonleague Corn ...2 B3
Venus Hill Herts ...85 E8
Veraby Devon ...26 B3
Vermentry Shetland ...313 H5
Vernham Bank Hants ...47 B10
Vernham Dean Hants ...47 B10
Vernham Row Hants ...47 B10
Vernham Street Hants ...47 B11
Vernolds Common
  Shrops ...131 G9
Verwood Dorset ...31 F9
Veryan Corn ...3 B10
Veryan Green Corn ...5 G8
Vicarage Devon ...15 D10
Vicarscross Ches W ...166 B6
Vickerstown Cumb ...210 F3
Victoria Corn ...5 C9
  S Yorks ...197 F7
Victoria Dock Village
  Hull ...200 B6
Victoria Park Bucks ...84 C4
Victory Gardens Renfs ...267 B10
Vidlin Shetland ...312 G6
Vigo W Mid ...133 C10
Vigo Village Kent ...68 G6
Vinegar Hill Mon ...60 B2
Vinehall Street E Sus ...38 C3
Vines Cross E Sus ...23 B9
Viney Hill Glos ...79 D11
Virginia Green S Glos ...60 D7
Virginia Water Sur ...66 F3
Virginstow Devon ...12 C3
Viscar Corn ...2 C6
Vobster Som ...45 D8
Voe Shetland ...312 E5
  Shetland ...313 G6
Vogue Corn ...4 G4
Vowchurch Hereford ...97 D7
Vowchurch Common
  Hereford ...97 D7
Voxmoor Som ...27 D10
Voxter Shetland ...312 F5
Vron Gate Shrops ...130 B6
Vulcan Village Mers ...183 C9

W

Waberthwaite Cumb ...220 G2
Wackerfield Durham ...233 G9
Wacton Hereford ...116 F2
  Norf ...142 E3
Wacton Common Norf ...142 E3
Wadbister Shetland ...313 J6
Wadborough Worcs ...99 B8
Wadbrook Devon ...28 G4
Waddesdon Bucks ...84 B2
Waddicar Mers ...182 B5
Waddicombe Devon ...26 C3
Waddingham Lincs ...189 B7
Waddington Lancs ...203 E10
  Lincs ...173 C7
Waddingworth Lincs ...189 G11
Waddon Devon ...14 F3
  London ...67 G10
Wadebridge Corn ...10 G5
Wadeford Som ...28 E4
Wade Hall Lancs ...194 C4
Wadenhoe Northants ...137 G10
Wades Green Ches E ...167 C11
Wadesmill Herts ...86 B5
Wadhurst E Sus ...52 G6
Wadshelf Derbys ...186 G4
Wadsley S Yorks ...186 C4
Wadsley Bridge S Yorks ...186 C4
Wadswick Wilts ...61 E10
Wadwick Hants ...48 C2
Wadworth S Yorks ...187 B9
Waen Denb ...165 B10
  Denb ...165 C8
  Flint ...181 G11
  Powys ...129 E9

Waen Aberwheeler
  Denb ...165 B9
Waen-fâch Powys ...148 F4
Waen Goleugoed Denb ...181 G9
Waen-pentir Gwyn ...163 B9
Waen-wen Gwyn ...163 B9
Wag Highld ...311 G4
Wagbeach Shrops ...131 C7
Wagg Som ...28 B6
Waggersley Staffs ...151 B7
Waggs Plot Devon ...28 G4
Wainfelin Torf ...78 E3
Wainfleet All Saints
  Lincs ...175 D7
Wainfleet Bank Lincs ...175 D7
Wainfleet St Mary Lincs ...175 D8
Wainfleet Tofts Lincs ...175 D7
Wainford Norf ...142 F6
Waingroves Derbys ...170 F6
Wainhouse Corner Corn ...11 B8
Wain Lee Staffs ...168 D5
Wainscott Medway ...69 E8
Waitby Cumb ...222 D5
Waithe Lincs ...201 G9
Wakefield W Yorks ...197 D10
Wake Green W Mid ...133 G11
Wake Hill N Yorks ...214 E3
Wake Lady Green
  N Yorks ...226 F3
Wakeley Herts ...104 F6
Wakerley Northants ...137 D9
Wakes Colne Essex ...107 F7
Wakes Colne Green
  Essex ...107 E7
Walberswick Suff ...127 C9
Walberton W Sus ...35 F7
Walbottle T&W ...242 D5
Walby Cumb ...239 G10
Walcombe Som ...44 D5
Walcot Bath ...61 F9
  Lincs ...155 B11
  N Lincs ...199 C11
  Oxon ...82 B4
  Shrops ...130 F6
  Telford ...149 G11
  Worcs ...99 B8
Walcote Leics ...135 G11
  Warks ...118 F2
Walcot Green Norf ...142 G2
Walcott Lincs ...173 D10
  Norf ...161 C7
Walden N Yorks ...213 C10
Walden Head N Yorks ...213 C9
Walden Stubbs N Yorks ...198 D5
Waldersey Cambs ...139 C8
Waldershaigh S Yorks ...186 B3
Waldershare Kent ...55 C9
Walderslade Medway ...69 G9
Walderton W Sus ...34 E3
Walditch Dorset ...16 C5
Waldley Derbys ...152 B2
Waldridge Durham ...243 G7
Waldringfield Suff ...108 C5
Waldringfield Heath
  Suff ...108 B5
Waldron E Sus ...23 B8
Wales Som ...29 C9
  S Yorks ...187 E7
Wales Bar S Yorks ...187 E7
Walesby Lincs ...189 C10
  Notts ...187 G11
Wales End Suff ...106 B5
Waleswood S Yorks ...187 E7
Walford Hereford ...97 G11
  Hereford ...115 C7
  Shrops ...149 E8
  Staffs ...150 C6
Walford Heath Shrops ...149 F8
Walgherton Ches E ...167 F11
Walgrave Northants ...120 C6
Walhampton Hants ...20 B2
Walkden Gtr Man ...195 G8
Walker T&W ...243 E7
Walker Barn Ches E ...185 G7
Walkerburn Borders ...261 B9
Walker Fold Lancs ...203 E9
Walkeringham Notts ...188 C3
Walkerith Notts ...188 C3
Walkern Herts ...104 F5
Walker's Green Hereford ...97 B10
Walker's Heath W Mid ...117 B11
Walkerville N Yorks ...224 F4
Walkford Dorset ...19 C10
Walkhampton Devon ...7 B10
Walkingham Hill
  N Yorks ...206 B4
Walkington E Yorks ...208 F5
Walkley S Yorks ...186 D4
Walkmill Shrops ...131 F7
Walk Mill Lancs ...204 G3
Walkmills Shrops ...131 D9
Wall Corn ...2 C4
  Northumb ...241 D10
  Staffs ...133 C11
Wallaceton Falk ...279 F8
Wallacestone Falk ...279 F8
Wallacetown Dumfries ...247 F8
  S Ayrs ...245 C7
  S Ayrs ...257 E8
  Shetland ...313 H5
Wallands Park E Sus ...36 E6
Wallasey Mers ...182 C4
Wallbank Lancs ...195 D11
Wallbrook W Mid ...133 E8
Wallcrouch E Sus ...53 G7
Wallend London ...68 C2
Wall End Cumb ...210 C4
  Kent ...71 D8
Waller's Green Hereford ...98 D3
Walley's Green Ches E ...167 C11
Wall Hill Gtr Man ...196 F3
Wallingford Oxon ...64 B6
Wallington Hants ...33 F9
  Herts ...104 E5
  London ...67 G9
  W Mid ...133 C10
Wallingwells Notts ...187 E9
Wallis Pembs ...91 F10
Wallisdown Poole ...19 C7
Wall Mead Bath ...45 B7
Wall Nook Durham ...233 B10
Wallow Green Glos ...80 F4
Walls Shetland ...313 J4
Wallsend T&W ...243 D7
Wallston V Glam ...58 E6
Wallsuches Gtr Man ...195 E7
Wallsworth Glos ...98 G6
Wall under Heywood
  Shrops ...131 D10
Walmer Kent ...55 C11
Walmer Bridge Lancs ...194 C3
  Gtr Man ...196 D6

Walmgate Stray York ...207 C8
Walmley W Mid ...134 E2
Walmsgate Lincs ...190 F5
Walnut Grove Perth ...286 E5
Walnut Tree Kent ...103 D7
Walnuttree Green Herts ...105 G9
Walpole Som ...43 E10
  Suff ...127 C7
Walpole Cross Keys
  Norf ...157 F10
Walpole Highway Norf ...157 G10
Walpole Marsh Norf ...157 F9
Walpole St Andrew
  Norf ...157 F10
Walpole St Peter Norf ...157 F10
Walrow Som ...43 D10
Walsal End W Mid ...118 B4
Walsall W Mid ...133 D10
Walsall Wood W Mid ...133 C11
Walsden W Yorks ...196 C2
Walsgrave on Sowe
  W Mid ...135 G7
Walsham le Willows
  Suff ...125 C9
Walshaw Gtr Man ...195 E9
Walshford N Yorks ...206 C4
Walsoken Norf ...157 G9
Walston S Lanark ...269 F11
Walsworth Herts ...104 E4
Walters Ash Bucks ...84 F4
Walter's Green Kent ...52 E4
Walterston V Glam ...58 E5
Walterstone Hereford ...96 F6
Waltham Kent ...54 D6
  NE Lincs ...201 G9
Waltham Abbey Essex ...86 E5
Waltham Chase Hants ...33 D9
Waltham Cross Herts ...86 E5
Waltham on the Wolds
  Leics ...154 E6
Waltham St Lawrence
  Windsor ...65 D10
Waltham's Cross Essex ...106 E3
Walthamstow London ...67 B11
Walton Bucks ...84 C4
  Cumb ...240 E2
  Derbys ...170 B5
  Leics ...135 F11
  Mers ...182 C5
  M Keynes ...103 D8
  Pboro ...138 C3
  Powys ...114 F5
  Shrops ...115 B9
  Som ...44 F3
  Staffs ...151 C7
  Staffs ...151 D7
  Suff ...108 D5
  Telford ...149 F11
  Warks ...118 G5
  W Yorks ...197 D11
  W Yorks ...206 D4
Walton Cardiff Glos ...99 E8
Walton Court Bucks ...84 C4
Walton East Pembs ...91 G10
Walton Elm Dorset ...30 D3
Walton Grounds
  Northants ...101 E10
Walton Heath Hants ...33 F10
Walton Highway Norf ...157 G9
Walton in Gordano
  N Som ...60 E2
Walton-le-Dale Lancs ...194 B5
Walton Manor Oxon ...83 D8
Walton-on-Thames Sur ...66 F6
Walton on the Hill
  Staffs ...151 E9
  Sur ...51 C7
Walton-on-the-Naze
  Essex ...108 G5
Walton on the Wolds
  Leics ...153 F11
Walton Pool W Mid ...117 B8
Walton St Mary N Som ...60 E2
Walton Summit Lancs ...194 B5
Walton Warren Norf ...158 F4
Walton West Pembs ...72 C5
Walwen Flint ...181 F10
  Flint ...181 G11
  Flint ...182 F5
Walwick Northumb ...241 C10
Walworth Darl ...224 B4
  London ...67 D10
Walworth Gate Darl ...233 G10
Walwyn's Castle Pembs ...72 C5
Wambrook Som ...28 F3
Wampool Cumb ...238 G6
Wanborough Sur ...50 D2
  Swindon ...63 C8
Wandel Dyke S Lanark ...259 D11
Wandle Park London ...67 F10
Wandon End Herts ...104 G3
Wandsworth London ...67 E9
Wangford Suff ...127 B9
  Suff ...140 G2
Wanlip Leics ...154 G2
Wanlockhead Dumfries ...259 G9
Wannock E Sus ...23 E9
Wansbeck Corn ...137 D11
Wanshurst Green Kent ...53 D9
Wanson Corn ...24 G2
Wanstead London ...68 B2
Wanstrow Som ...45 E8
Wanswell Glos ...79 D11
Wantage Oxon ...63 B11
Wants Green Worcs ...116 F5
Wapley S Glos ...61 D8
Wappenbury Warks ...119 D7
Wappenham Northants ...102 B2
Wapping London ...67 C10
Warbleton E Sus ...23 B10
Warblington Hants ...22 B2
Warborough Oxon ...83 G9
Warboys Cambs ...138 G6
Warbreck Blackpool ...202 F2
Warbstow Corn ...11 C10
Warbstow Cross Corn ...11 C10
Warburton Gtr Man ...184 D2
Warcop Cumb ...222 B4
Warden Kent ...70 E4
  Northumb ...241 D10
  Powys ...114 C6
Warden Hill Glos ...99 G8
Warden Street C Beds ...104 C2
Warden Point IoW ...20 D2
Ward End W Mid ...134 F2
Ward Green Suff ...125 E10
  S Yorks ...197 G10
Ward Green Cross
  Lancs ...203 F8
Wardhedges C Beds ...103 D11
Wardington Oxon ...101 B9
Wardlaw Borders ...261 F7
Wardle Ches E ...167 D10
  Gtr Man ...196 D6
Wardle Bank Ches E ...167 D10

Wardley Gtr Man 195 G9
Rutland 136 C6
T&W 243 E7
W Sus 34 B4
Wardlow Derbys 185 G11
Wardour Wilts 30 B6
Wardpark N Lanark 278 F5
Wardrobes Bucks 84 E4
Wardsend Ches E 184 E6
Wardy Hill Cambs 139 G9
Ware Herts 86 C5
Kent 71 G9
Wareham Dorset 18 D4
Warehorne Kent 54 G3
Warenford Northumb 264 D4
Waren Mill Northumb 264 C4
Warenton Northumb 264 C4
Wareside Herts 86 B5
Waresley Cambs 122 G4
Worcs 116 C6
Ware Street Kent 53 B9
Warfield Brack 65 E11
Warfleet Devon 9 E7
Wargate Lincs 156 C4
Wargrave Mers 183 C9
Wokingham 65 D9
Warham Hereford 97 D9
Norf 176 E6
Warhill Gtr Man 185 B7
Waring's Green W Mid 118 C2
Wark Northumb 241 B9
Northumb 263 B8
Wark Common
Northumb 263 B8
Warkleigh Devon 25 C10
Warkton Northants 121 B7
Warkworth Northants 101 C9
Northumb 252 B6
Warlaby N Yorks 224 G6
Warland W Yorks 196 C2
Warleggan Corn 6 B3
Warleigh Bath 61 G9
Warley Essex 87 G9
Warley Town W Yorks 196 B5
Warley Woods W Mid 133 F10
Warlingham Sur 51 B11
Warmbrook Derbys 170 E3
Warmfield W Yorks 197 C11
Warmingham Ches E 168 C2
Warminghurst W Sus 35 D10
Warmington Northants 137 E11
Warks 101 B8
Warminster Wilts 45 D11
Warminster Common
Wilts 45 E11
Warmlake Kent 53 C10
Warmley S Glos 61 E7
Warmley Hill S Glos 61 E7
Warmley Tower S Glos 61 E7
Warmonds Hill
Northants 121 D9
Warmsworth S Yorks 198 G4
Warmwell Dorset 17 D11
Warnborough Green
Hants 49 C8
Warndon Worcs 117 F7
Warners End Herts 85 D8
Warnford Hants 33 C10
Warnham W Sus 51 G7
Warningcamp W Sus 35 F8
Warninglid W Sus 36 B2
Warpsgrove Oxon 83 F10
Warren Ches E 184 G5
Dorset 18 C3
Pembs 72 F6
S Yorks 186 B5
Warrenby Redcar 235 F7
Warren Corner Hants 34 B2
Hants 49 D10
Warren Heath Suff 108 C4
Warren Row Windsor 65 C10
Warren's Green Herts 104 F5
Warren Street Kent 54 C2
Warrington M Keynes 121 G7
Warr 183 D10
Warriston Edin 280 F5
Warsash Hants 33 F7
Warsill N Yorks 214 F4
Warslow Staffs 169 D9
Warsop Vale Notts 171 B8
Warstock W Mid 117 B11
Warstone Staffs 133 B9
Warter E Yorks 208 C3
Warthermarske N Yorks 214 D4
Warthill N Yorks 207 B9
Wartle Aberds 293 C7
Wartling E Sus 23 D11
Wartnaby Leics 154 E4
Warton Lancs 194 B2
Lancs 211 E9
Northumb 252 C2
Warks 134 C5
Warton Bank Lancs 194 B2
Warwick Warks 118 E5
Warwick Bridge Cumb 239 F11
Warwick on Eden
Cumb 239 F11
Warwicksland Cumb 239 B10
Warwick Wold Sur 51 C10
Wasbister Orkney 314 C3
Wasdale Head Cumb 220 D3
Wash Derbys 185 E9
Washall Green Herts 105 E8
Washaway Corn 5 B10
Washbourne Devon 8 E5
Washbrook Som 44 C2
Suff 108 C2
Washbrook Street Suff 108 C2
Wash Common W Berks 64 G3
Wash Dyke Norf 157 F10
Washerwall Staffs 168 F6
Washfield Devon 26 D6
Washfold N Yorks 223 E11
Washford Som 42 E5
Worcs 117 D11
Washford Pyne Devon 26 E4
Washingborough Lincs 189 G8
Washingley Cambs 138 F2
Washington T&W 243 F8
W Sus 35 E10
Washington Village
T&W 243 F8
Washmere Green Suff 107 B8
Washpit W Yorks 196 F6
Wash Water W Berks 64 G3
Washwood Heath
W Mid 134 F2
Wasing W Berks 64 G5
Waskerley Durham 233 B7
Wasperton Warks 118 F5
Wasp Green Sur 51 D10
Wasps Nest Lincs 173 C9
Wass N Yorks 215 D11
Waste Green Warks 118 D4
Wastor Devon 8 F2
Watchet Som 42 E5
Watchfield Oxon 63 B8
Som 43 D10
Watchgate Cumb 221 F10
Watchhill Cumb 229 C9
Watch House Green
Essex 106 G3
Watchill Dumfries 238 D6
Dumfries 248 G3
Watcombe Torbay 9 B8
Watendlath Cumb 220 B5
Water Devon 13 E11
Lancs 195 B10
Waterbeach Cambs 123 D9
W Sus 22 B5
Waterbeck Dumfries 238 B6
Waterdale Herts 85 E10
Waterden Norf 159 B7
Waterditch Hants 19 B9
Water Eaton M Keynes 103 E7
Oxon 83 C8
Waterend Bucks 84 F3
Cumb 229 G8
Glos 80 C3
Herts 86 C2
Water End Bedford 104 B2
C Beds 103 D11
C Beds 104 B5
Essex 105 C11
E Yorks 207 F11
Hants 49 C7
Herts 85 C8
Herts 86 E2
Waterfall Staffs 169 E9
Waterfoot Argyll 255 D9
Cumb 230 G5
E Renf 267 D11
Lancs 195 C10
Waterford Hants 20 B2
Herts 86 C4
Water Fryston W Yorks 198 B3
Water Garth Nook Cumb 210 F3
Watergate Corn 6 E4
Corn 11 E8
Watergore Som 28 D6
Waterhales Essex 87 F8
Waterham Kent 70 G5
Waterhay Wilts 81 G9
Waterhead Angus 292 F6
Cumb 221 E7
Devon 8 F3
Dumfries 248 E5
Waterhead on Minnoch
S Ayrs 245 E9
Waterheads Borders 270 E4
Waterheath Norf 143 E8
Waterhouses Durham 233 C9
Staffs 169 E9
Water Houses N Yorks 213 F7
Wateringbury Kent 53 C7
Waterlane Glos 80 E6
Waterlip Som 45 E7
Waterloo Blackburn 195 B7
Corn 11 G8
Derbys 170 C6
Gtr Man 196 G2
Highld 295 C8
Mers 182 B4
N Lanark 268 E6
Norf 126 B2
Norf 143 E8
Norf 160 F4
Pembs 73 E7
Perth 286 D4
Poole 18 C6
Shrops 149 C9
Waterloo Park Mers 182 B4
Waterloo Port Gwyn 163 C7
Waterlooville Hants 33 F11
Waterman Quarter Kent 53 E10
Watermead Glos 80 B5
Watermeetings
S Lanark 259 G11
Watermill E Sus 38 E2
Watermillock Cumb 230 G4
Watermoor Glos 81 E8
Water Newton Cambs 138 D2
Water Orton Warks 134 E3
Waterperry Oxon 83 D10
Waterrow Som 27 B9
Watersfield W Sus 35 D8
Watersheddings
Gtr Man 196 F2
Waterside Aberds 292 B5
Aberds 303 G10
Blackburn 195 C8
Bucks 85 E7
Cumb 229 B10
Derbys 185 E8
E Ayrs 245 B10
E Ayrs 267 G9
E Dunb 278 G3
E Renf 267 D10
Sur 51 D11
S Yorks 199 E7
Telford 150 F2
Waterslack Lancs 211 D9
Water's Nook Gtr Man 195 F7
Waterstein Highld 297 G7
Waterstock Oxon 83 D10
Waterston Pembs 72 D6
Water Stratford Bucks 102 E3
Waters Upton Telford 150 F2
Waterthorpe S Yorks 186 E6
Waterton Aberds 303 F9
Bridgend 58 D2
Water Yeat Cumb 210 B5
Watford Herts 85 F10
Northants 120 D2
Watford Gap Staffs 134 C2
Watford Heath Herts 85 G10
Watford Park Caerph 58 B6
Wath Cumb 222 D3
N Yorks 214 D6
N Yorks 214 F2
N Yorks 216 D3
Wath Brow Cumb 219 C10
Watherston Borders 271 F8
Wath upon Dearne
S Yorks 198 G2
Watledge Glos 80 E4
Watley's End S Glos 61 C7
Watlington Norf 158 G2
Oxon 83 G11
Watnall Notts 171 F8
Watsness Shetland 313 H3
Watten Highld 310 D6
Wattisfield Suff 125 C10
Wattisham Suff 125 G10
Wattisham Stone Suff 125 G10
Wattlefield Norf 142 D2
Wattlesborough Heath
Shrops 149 G7
Watton E Yorks 208 C6
Norf 141 C8
Watton at Stone Herts 86 B4
Watton Green Norf 141 C8
Watton's Green Essex 87 F8
Wattston N Lanark 268 B5
Wattstown Rhondda 77 G8
Wattsville Caerph 78 G2
Wauchan Highld 295 G11
Waulkmill Lodge Orkney 314 F3
Waun Gwyn 163 C9
Powys 148 F4
Waunarlwydd Swansea 56 B6
Waun Beddau Pembs 90 F5
Wauncluda Carms 94 E3
Waunfawr Gwyn 163 D8
Waun Fawr Ceredig 128 G2
Waungilwen Carms 92 D6
Waungron Swansea 75 E9
Waunlwyd Bl Gwent 77 D11
Waun-Lwyd Bl Gwent 77 D11
Waun-y-clyn Carms 75 E7
Waun y Gilfach Bridgend 57 D10
Wavendon M Keynes 103 D8
Wavendon Gate
M Keynes 103 D8
Waverbridge Cumb 229 B10
Waverton Ches W 167 C7
Cumb 229 B10
Wavertree Mers 182 D5
Wawcott W Berks 63 F11
Wawne E Yorks 209 F7
Waxham Norf 161 D8
Waxholme E Yorks 201 B10
Way Kent 71 F10
Waye Devon 13 G11
Wayend Street Hereford 98 D4
Wayfield Medway 69 F9
Wayford Som 28 F6
Waymills Shrops 167 G9
Wayne Green Mon 78 B6
Way's Green Ches W 167 B10
Waytown Devon 24 C5
Devon 40 G5
Way Village Devon 26 E5
Way Wick N Som 59 G11
Wdig / Goodwick Pembs 91 D8
Weachyburn Aberds 302 D6
Weacombe Som 42 E6
Weald Oxon 82 E4
Wealdstone London 67 B7
Wearde Corn 7 D8
Weardley W Yorks 205 E11
Weare Som 44 C2
Weare Giffard Devon 25 C7
Wearhead Durham 232 D3
Wearne Som 28 B6
Weasdale Cumb 222 E3
Weasenham All Saints
Norf 158 E6
Weasenham St Peter
Norf 159 E7
Weaste Gtr Man 184 B4
Weatherhill Sur 51 E10
Weatheroak Hill Worcs 117 C11
Weaverham Ches W 183 G10
Weavering Street Kent 53 B9
Weaverslake Staffs 152 F2
Weaverthorpe N Yorks 217 E9
Webbington Som 43 B11
Webheath Worcs 117 D10
Webscott Shrops 149 E9
Wecock Hants 33 E11
Wedderlairs Aberds 303 F8
Wedderlie Borders 272 E2
Weddington Kent 55 B9
Warks 135 E7
Wedhampton Wilts 46 B5
Wedmore Som 44 D2
Wednesbury W Mid 133 D9
Wednesbury Oak
W Mid 133 E9
Wednesfield W Mid 133 C8
Weecar Notts 172 B4
Weedon Bucks 84 B4
Weedon Bec Northants 120 F2
Weedon Lois Northants 102 B2
Weeford Staffs 134 C2
Week Devon 8 C5
Devon 12 E5
Devon 25 B9
Devon 26 D2
Weeke Devon 26 F3
Hants 48 G3
Week Green Corn 11 B10
Weekley Northants 137 G7
Weekmoor Som 27 B10
Weeks IoW 21 C7
Week St Mary Corn 11 B10
Weel E Yorks 209 F7
Weeley Essex 108 G2
Weeley Heath Essex 108 G3
Weelsby NE Lincs 201 F9
Weem Perth 286 C2
Weeping Cross Staffs 151 E8
Weethley Warks 117 F11
Weethley Bank Warks 117 G11
Weethley Gate Warks 117 G11
Weeting Norf 140 F5
Weeton E Yorks 201 C11
Lancs 202 G3
N Yorks 205 D11
Weetwood W Yorks 205 F11
Weetwood Common
Ches W 167 B8
Weetwood Hall
Northumb 264 D2
Weir Essex 69 B10
Lancs 195 B11
Weirbrook Shrops 148 E6
Weir Quay Devon 7 C8
Welborne Norf 159 G11
Welborne Common
Norf 141 B11
Welbourn Lincs 173 E7
Welburn N Yorks 216 C3
N Yorks 216 F4
Welbury N Yorks 225 E7
Welby Lincs 155 B9
Welches Dam Cambs 139 F9
Welcombe Devon 24 D2
Weld Bank Lancs 194 D5
Weldon Northants 137 F8
Northumb 252 D4
Welford Northants 136 G2
W Berks 64 E2
Welford-on-Avon
Warks 118 G3
Welham Leics 136 E5
Notts 188 E2
Som 45 G7
Welhambridge
E Yorks 207 G11
Welham Green Herts 86 D2
Well Hants 49 D9
Lincs 190 G6
N Yorks 214 C5
Welland Worcs 98 C5
Welland Stone Worcs 98 D6
Wellbank Angus 287 D8
Well Bottom Dorset 30 D6
Wellbrook E Sus 37 B9
Welldale Dumfries 238 D5
Well End Bucks 65 B11
Herts 86 F2
Weller's Town Kent 52 E4
Wellesbourne Warks 118 F5
Well Green Gtr Man 184 D3
Wellheads Aberds 302 F4
Well Heads W Yorks 205 G7
Well Hill Kent 68 G3
Wellhouse W Berks 64 E4
W Yorks 196 E5
Welling London 68 D3
Wellingborough
Northants 121 D7
Wellingham Norf 159 E7
Wellingore Lincs 173 D7
Wellington Cumb 219 E11
Hereford 97 B9
Som 27 C10
Telford 150 G3
Wellington Heath
Hereford 98 C4
Wellington Hill W Yorks 206 F2
Wellisford Som 27 C9
Wellow Bath 45 B8
IoW 20 D3
NE Lincs 201 F9
Notts 171 B11
Wellow Wood Hants 32 C3
Well Place Oxon 65 B7
Wellpond Green Herts 105 G8
Wellroyd W Yorks 205 F10
Wells Som 44 D5
Wellsborough Leics 135 C7
Wells Green Ches E 167 E11
Wells-next-the-Sea
Norf 176 E6
Wellsprings Som 28 B2
Well Street Kent 53 B7
Wellstye Green Essex 87 B10
Wellswood Torbay 9 C8
Welltown Corn 6 B2
Well Town Devon 26 F6
Wellwood Fife 279 D11
Welney Norf 139 E10
Welsford Devon 24 C3
Welshampton Shrops 149 B8
Welsh Bicknor Hereford 79 B9
Welsh End Shrops 149 B10
Welsh Frankton Shrops 149 C7
Welsh Harp London 67 B8
Welsh Hook Pembs 91 F8
Welsh Newton Hereford 79 B7
Welsh Newton Common
Hereford 79 B8
Welshpool Powys 130 B4
Welsh St Donats V Glam 58 D4
Welshwood Park Essex 107 F10
Welstor Devon 13 G10
Welton Bath 45 C7
Cumb 230 C3
E Ayrs 258 D2
E Yorks 200 B3
Lincs 189 F8
Northants 119 D11
Welton Hill Lincs 189 E8
Welton le Marsh Lincs 175 B7
Welton le Wold Lincs 190 D3
Welwick E Yorks 201 C10
Welwyn Herts 86 B2
Welwyn Garden City
Herts 86 C2
Wem Shrops 149 D10
Wembdon Som 43 F9
Wembley London 67 B7
Wembley Park London 67 B7
Wembury Devon 7 F10
Wembworthy Devon 25 F11
Wemyss Bay Invclyd 266 B3
Wenallt Ceredig 112 C3
Gwyn 146 F4
Gwyn 165 G7
Wendens Ambo Essex 105 D10
Wendlebury Oxon 83 B9
Wendling Norf 159 G8
Wendover Bucks 84 D5
Wendover Dean Bucks 84 E5
Wendron Corn 2 C5
Wendy Cambs 104 B6
Wenfordbridge Corn 11 F7
Wenhaston Suff 127 B8
Wenhaston Black Heath
Suff 127 C8
Wennington Cambs 122 B4
Lancs 212 E2
London 68 C4
Wensley Derbys 170 C3
N Yorks 213 B11
Wentbridge W Yorks 198 D3
Wentnor Shrops 131 E7
Wentworth Cambs 123 B9
S Yorks 186 B5
Wenvoe V Glam 58 E6
Weobley Hereford 115 G8
Weobley Marsh
Hereford 115 G8
Weoley Castle W Mid 133 G10
Wepham W Sus 35 F8
Wepre Flint 166 B3
Wereham Norf 140 C3
Wereham Row Norf 140 C3
Wereton Staffs 168 E3
Wergs W Mid 133 C7
Wern Gwyn 145 B10
Powys 77 B10
Powys 147 G9
Powys 148 E5
Powys 148 G5
Shrops 148 C5
Swansea 56 C4
Wern ddu Shrops 148 D4
Werneth Gtr Man 196 G2
Werneth Low Gtr Man 185 C7
Wernffrwd Swansea 56 C4
Wern-Gifford Mon 96 G6
Wernlas Shrops 148 E6
Wern-olau Swansea 56 B5
Wernrheolydd Mon 78 C5
Wern Tarw Bridgend 58 C3
Wern-y-cwrt Mon 78 D5
Wern-y-gaer Flint 166 B2
Wernyrheolydd Mon 78 C5
Werrington Corn 12 D2
Pboro 138 C3
Staffs 168 F6
Wervin Ches W 182 G6
Wescoe Hill N Yorks 205 D11
Wesham Lancs 202 G4
Wessington Derbys 170 D5
West Aberthaw V Glam 58 F4
Westacott Devon 40 G5
West Acre Norf 158 F5
West Acton London 67 C7
West Adderbury Oxon 101 D9
West Allerdean
Northumb 273 F9
West Allotment T&W 243 C8
West Alvington Devon 8 G4
West Amesbury Wilts 46 E6
West Anstey Devon 26 B5
West Appleton N Yorks 224 G4
West Ardhu Argyll 288 D6
West Ardsley W Yorks 197 B9
West Ardwell Dumfries 236 E2
West Arthurlie E Renf 267 D9
West Ashby Lincs 190 G3
West Ashford Devon 40 F4
West Ashling W Sus 22 B4
West Ashton Wilts 45 B11
West Auckland Durham 233 F9
West Ayton N Yorks 217 C9
West Bagborough Som 43 G7
West Bank Bl Gwent 78 D2
West Bank *continued*
Halton 183 E8
West Barkwith Lincs 189 E11
West Barnby N Yorks 226 C6
West Barnes London 67 F8
West Barns E Loth 282 F3
West Barsham Norf 159 C8
West Bay Dorset 16 C5
West Beckham Norf 160 B2
West Bedfont Sur 66 E5
West Benhar N Lanark 269 C7
Westbere Kent 71 G7
West Bergholt Essex 107 F9
West Bexington Dorset 16 D6
West Bilney Norf 158 F4
West Blackdene Durham 232 D3
West Blackdown Devon 12 E5
West Blatchington
Brighton 36 F3
West Bold Borders 261 B9
West Boldon T&W 243 E9
Westborough Lincs 172 G5
Westbourne Bmouth 19 C7
Suff 108 B2
W Sus 22 B3
Westbourne Green
London 67 C9
West Bourton Dorset 30 B3
West Bowling W Yorks 205 G9
West Bradford Lancs 203 E10
West Bradley Som 44 F5
West Bretton W Yorks 197 E9
West Bridgford Notts 153 B11
West Brompton London 67 D9
West Bromwich
W Mid 133 E10
Westbrook Hereford 96 C5
Kent 71 E10
Sur 50 E3
Warr 183 C9
W Berks 64 E2
Wilts 62 F3
Westbrook Green Norf 142 G2
Westbrook Hay Herts 85 D8
West Broughton Derbys 152 C2
West Buckland Devon 41 G7
Som 27 C11
Westburn S Lanark 268 C3
West Burnside Aberds 293 F8
West Burrafirth
Shetland 313 H4
West Burton N Yorks 213 B10
W Sus 35 E7
Westbury Bucks 102 D2
Shrops 131 B7
Wilts 45 C11
Westbury Leigh Wilts 45 C11
Westbury-on-Severn
Glos 80 C2
Westbury on Trym Bristol 60 D5
Westbury Park Bristol 60 D5
Westbury-sub-Mendip
Som 44 D4
West Butsfield Durham 233 C8
West Butterwick
N Lincs 199 F10
Westby Lancs 202 G3
Lincs 155 D9
West Byfleet Sur 66 G4
West Caister Norf 161 G10
West Calder W Loth 269 C10
West Camel Som 29 C9
West Carlton W Yorks 205 E10
West Carr Hull 209 G7
N Lincs 199 F8
West Chadsmoor Staffs 151 G9
West Challow Oxon 63 B11
West Charleton Devon 8 G5
West Chelborough Dorset 29 F8
West Chevington
Northumb 252 D6
West Chiltington W Sus 35 D9
West Chiltington Common
W Sus 35 D9
West Chinnock Som 29 E7
West Chirton T&W 243 D8
West Chisenbury Wilts 46 C6
West Clandon Sur 50 C4
West Cliff Bmouth 19 C7
N Yorks 227 C7
West Cliffe Kent 55 E10
Westcliff-on-Sea
Southend 69 B11
West Clyne Highld 311 J2
Highld 311 J2
West Clyth Highld 310 F6
Highld 310 F6
West Coker Som 29 E8
Westcombe Som 29 B7
Som 45 F7
West Common Hants 32 G6
West Compton Dorset 17 C7
Som 44 E5
West Cornforth Durham 234 E2
Westcot Oxon 63 B10
Westcote Glos 100 G4
Westcotes Leicester 135 C11
Westcott Bucks 84 B2
Devon 27 G8
Shrops 131 C8
Sur 50 D6
Westcott Barton Oxon 101 F8
Westcourt Wilts 63 G8
West Cowick E Yorks 199 C7
West Cranmore Som 45 E7
Westcroft M Keynes 102 E6
W Mid 133 C8
West Cross Kent 53 G10
Swansea 56 D6
West Crudwell Wilts 80 G6
West Cullery Aberds 293 C9
West Curry Corn 11 C11
West Curthwaite Cumb 230 B2
West Darlochan Argyll 255 E7
Westdean E Sus 23 F8
West Dean Wilts 32 B3
W Sus 34 E5
West Deeping Lincs 138 B2
West Denant Pembs 72 C6
Westdene Brighton 36 F3
West Denton T&W 242 D5
West Derby Mers 182 C5
West Dereham Norf 140 C3
West Didsbury Gtr Man 184 C4
West Down Devon 40 E4
Hants 47 F11
Westdown Camp Wilts 46 D4
Westdowns Corn 11 E7
West Downs Corn 5 C10
West Drayton London 66 D5
Notts 188 G2
West Dulwich London 67 E10
West Ealing London 67 C7
West Edge Derbys 170 C4
West Ella E Yorks 200 B4
Westend Oxon 100 G6
S Glos 79 G10
West End Bedford 121 E11
Bedford 121 G9
Brack 65 E11
Brack 66 G2
West End *continued*
Caerph 78 F2
Cumb 239 F8
Dorset 30 G6
E Yorks 201 B9
E Yorks 208 G4
E Yorks 209 B9
E Yorks 209 G9
E Yorks 217 G11
Glos 80 F5
Hants 33 E7
Hants 33 F9
Hants 48 F6
Herts 86 D3
Kent 54 B2
Kent 71 F7
Lancs 195 B8
Lancs 211 G8
Leics 153 F8
Lincs 174 F5
Lincs 190 B5
Mon 78 F6
Norf 141 B8
Norf 161 G10
N Som 60 F3
N Yorks 205 B8
N Yorks 206 E6
N Yorks 207 F7
Oxon 64 B5
Oxon 82 E6
S Glos 61 B8
S Lanark 269 F9
Som 44 C5
Som 45 G7
Suff 143 G9
Sur 49 E10
Sur 66 G6
S Yorks 199 F7
Wilts 30 C6
Wilts 31 C7
Wilts 62 D3
Windsor 65 D10
Worcs 99 D11
W Sus 36 D2
W Yorks 197 B7
W Yorks 205 F10
West End Green Hants 65 G7
West End / Marian-y-mor
Gwyn 145 C7
Westend Town
Northumb 241 D7
West-end Town V Glam 58 F3
Westenhanger Kent 54 F6
Wester Aberchalder
Highld 300 G5
Wester Arboll Highld 311 L2
Wester Auchinloch
N Lanark 278 G3
Wester Auchnagallin
Highld 301 F10
Wester Balgedie Perth 286 G5
Wester Brae Highld 300 C6
Wester Broomhouse
E Loth 282 F3
Wester Craiglands
Highld 301 D7
Wester Culbeuchly
Aberds 302 C6
Westerdale Highld 310 D5
N Yorks 226 D3
Wester Dalvoult Highld 291 B11
Wester Dechmont
W Loth 269 B10
Wester Deloraine
Borders 261 E8
Wester Denoon Angus 287 C7
Wester Ellister Argyll 254 B2
Wester Essendy Perth 286 C5
Wester Essenside
Borders 261 E10
Wester Feddal Perth 286 G2
Westerfield Shetland 313 H5
Suff 108 B3
Wester Fintray Aberds 293 B10
Westerfolds Moray 301 C11
Wester Galgantray
Highld 301 E8
Westergate W Sus 22 C6
Wester Gospetry Fife 286 G5
Wester Gruinards
Highld 309 K5
Wester Hailes Edin 270 B4
Westerham Kent 52 C2
Westerhope T&W 242 D5
Wester Housebyres
Borders 262 B2
Wester Kershope
Borders 261 D9
Wester Lealty Highld 300 B6
Westerleigh S Glos 61 D8
Westerleigh Hill S Glos 61 D8
Wester Lix Stirling 285 E9
Wester Milton Highld 301 D9
Wester Mosshead
Aberds 302 F5
Western Bank Cumb 229 B10
Western Downs Staffs 151 E8
Wester Newburn Fife 287 G8
Western Heights Kent 55 E10
Western Hill Durham 233 C11
Western Park Leicester 135 C11
Wester Ord Aberds 293 C10
Wester Parkgate
Dumfries 248 F2
Wester Quarff Shetland 313 K6
Wester Skeld Shetland 313 J4
Wester Strath Highld 300 D6
Westerton Aberds 293 B9
Aberds 302 E5
Angus 287 B10
Durham 233 E10
Moray 302 D3
W Sus 22 B5
Westertown Aberds 303 F7
Wester Watten Highld 310 D6
Westerwick Shetland 313 J4
West Ewell Sur 67 G8
West Farleigh Kent 53 C8
West Farndon
Northants 119 G10
West Felton Shrops 148 D6
West Fenton E Loth 281 E9
West Ferry Dundee 287 D8
Westfield Bath 45 C7
Cumb 228 F5
E Sus 38 D4
Hants 21 B10
Hereford 98 B4
Highld 310 C4
N Lanark 278 G4
Norf 141 B9
Redcar 235 G7
Sur 50 B4
S Yorks 186 E6
W Loth 279 G8
W Yorks 197 C8
W Yorks 205 E9
West Field N Lincs 200 D6
York 207 C7
Westfields Dorset 30 F2
Hereford 97 C9
West Fields W Berks 64 F3
Westfields of Rattray
Perth 286 C5
Westfield Sole Kent 69 G9
West Firle E Sus 23 D7
West Fleetham
Northumb 264 D5
West Flodden
Northumb 263 C10
Westford Som 27 C10
West Garforth W Yorks 206 G3
Westgate Durham 232 D4
N Lincs 199 F9
Norf 176 E4
Norf 177 E7
Westgate Hill W Yorks 197 B8
Westgate on Sea Kent 71 E10
Westgate Street Norf 160 E3
West Ginge Oxon 64 B2
West Gorton Gtr Man 184 B5
West Grafton Wilts 63 G8
West Green Hants 49 B8
London 67 B10
S Yorks 197 F11
W Sus 51 F9
West Greenskares
Aberds 303 C7
West Grimstead Wilts 32 B2
West Grinstead W Sus 35 C11
West Haddlesey
N Yorks 198 B5
West Haddon Northants 120 C2
West Hagbourne Oxon 64 B4
West Hagley Worcs 133 G8
Westhall Aberds 302 G6
Suff 143 G8
West Hall Cumb 240 D3
West Hallam Derbys 170 G6
Westhall Hill Oxon 82 C3
West Halton N Lincs 200 C2
Westham Dorset 17 F9
E Sus 23 E10
Som 44 D2
West Ham Hants 48 C6
London 68 C2
Westhampnett W Sus 22 B5
West Hampstead London 67 B9
West Handley Derbys 186 F5
West Hanney Oxon 82 G6
West Hanningfield Essex 88 F2
West Hardwick
W Yorks 198 D2
West Harling Norf 141 G9
West Harlsey N Yorks 225 F8
West Harnham Wilts 31 B10
West Harptree Bath 44 B5
West Harrow London 66 B6
West Harting W Sus 34 C3
West Harton T&W 243 E9
West Hatch Som 28 C3
Wilts 30 B6
Westhay Som 44 E2
Westhead Lancs 194 F2
West Head Norf 139 B11
West Heath Ches E 168 C4
Hants 48 B5
Hants 49 B11
London 68 D3
W Mid 117 B10
West Helmsdale Highld 311 H4
West Hendon London 67 B8
West Hendred Oxon 64 B2
West Herrington T&W 243 G8
West Heslerton N Yorks 217 D8
West Hewish N Som 59 G11
Westhide Hereford 97 C11
Westhill Aberds 293 C10
E Yorks 209 F10
Highld 301 E7
West Hill Devon 15 C7
E Sus 38 E4
E Yorks 218 F3
London 67 E8
N Som 60 D3
Som 28 C3
Staffs 151 G9
Wilts 61 F11
W Sus 51 G10
West Hoathly W Sus 51 G11
West Holme Dorset 18 D3
Westholme Som 44 E5
West Holywell T&W 243 C8
Westhope Hereford 115 G9
Shrops 131 F9
West Horndon Essex 68 B6
Westhorp Northants 119 G10
Westhorpe Lincs 156 C4
Notts 171 E11
Suff 125 D10
West Horrington Som 44 D5
West Horsley Sur 50 C5
West Horton Northumb 264 C2
West Hougham Kent 55 E9
Westhoughton Gtr Man 195 F7
West Houlland Shetland 313 H4
Westhouse N Yorks 212 E3
Westhouses Derbys 170 D6
West Houses Lincs 174 E4
West Howe Bmouth 19 B7
West Howetown Som 42 G2
Westhumble Sur 51 C7
West Huntington York 207 B8
West Huntspill Som 43 E10
West Hurn Dorset 19 B8
West Hyde Herts 85 G8
West Hynish Argyll 288 F1
West Hythe Kent 54 G6
West Ilkerton Devon 41 D8
West Ilsley W Berks 64 C3
Westing Shetland 312 C7
Westington Glos 100 D2
West Itchenor W Sus 22 C3
West Jesmond T&W 243 D7
West Keal Lincs 174 C5
West Kennett Wilts 62 F6
West Kensington London 67 D8
West Kilbride N Ayrs 266 F4
West Kilburn London 67 C8
West Kingsdown Kent 68 G5
West Kingston W Sus 35 G9
West Kington Wilts 61 D10
West Kington Wick
Wilts 61 D10
West Kinharrachie
Aberds 303 F9
West Kirby Mers 182 D2
West Kirkby Mers 182 D2
West Knapton N Yorks 217 D7
West Knighton Dorset 17 D10
West Knoyle Wilts 45 G11
West Kyloe Northumb 273 G11
West Kyo Durham 242 G5
Westlake Devon 8 E2
West Lambrook Som 28 D6
Westland Argyll 275 G11
Westland Green Herts 105 G8
Westlands Staffs 168 G4
Worcs 117 E7
West Langdon Kent 55 D10
West Langwell Highld 309 J6
West Lavington Wilts 46 C4
W Sus 34 C5
West Layton N Yorks 224 D2
Westlea Northumb 252 G6
Swindon 62 C6
West Lea Durham 234 B4
West Leake Notts 153 D10
West Learmouth
Northumb 263 B9
Westleigh Devon 25 B7
Devon 27 D9
Gtr Man 194 G6
West Leigh Devon 25 F11
Hants 22 B2
Som 42 G6
Westleton Suff 127 D8
West Lexham Norf 158 F6
Westley Shrops 131 B7
Suff 124 E6
Westley Heights Essex 69 B7
Westley Waterless
Cambs 124 F2
West Lilling N Yorks 216 F2
Westlington Bucks 84 C3
Westlinton Cumb 239 E9
West Linton Borders 270 E2
West Liss Hants 34 B3
West Littleton S Glos 61 D9
West Lockinge Oxon 64 B2
West Looe Corn 6 E5
West Luccombe Som 41 D11
West Lulworth Dorset 18 E2
West Lutton N Yorks 217 F8
West Lydford Som 44 G5
West Lydiatt Hereford 97 C11
West Lyn Devon 41 D8
West Lyng Som 28 B4
West Lynn Norf 158 E2
West Mains Borders 271 F11
S Lanark 268 E2
West Malling Kent 53 B7
West Malvern Worcs 98 B5
Westmancote Worcs 99 D8
West Marden W Sus 34 E3
West Marina E Sus 38 F3
West Markham Notts 188 G2
Westmarsh Kent 71 G9
West Marsh NE Lincs 201 E9
West Marton N Yorks 204 C3
West Mathers Aberds 293 G9
West Melbury Dorset 30 C5
West Melton S Yorks 198 G2
West Meon Hants 33 C10
West Meon Woodlands
Hants 33 B10
West Merkland Highld 308 F3
West Mersea Essex 89 C8
Westmeston E Sus 36 E4
Westmill Herts 104 E3
Herts 105 F7
West Milton Dorset 16 B6
Westminster London 67 D10
West Minster Kent 70 E2
West Molesey Sur 66 F6
West Monkseaton T&W 243 C8
West Monkton Som 28 B3
West Moor T&W 243 C7
Westmoor End Cumb 229 D8
West Moors Dorset 31 G9
West Morden Dorset 18 B4
West Morriston Borders 272 G2
West Morton W Yorks 205 E7
West Mudford Som 29 C9
Westmuir Angus 287 B7
West Muir Angus 293 G7
West Myreriggs Perth 286 C6
Westness Orkney 314 D3
West Ness N Yorks 216 D3
West Newham Northumb 242 B3
Westnewton Cumb 229 C8
Northumb 263 C10
West Newton E Yorks 209 F9
Norf 158 D3
Som 28 B3
West Norwood London 67 E10
Westoe T&W 243 D9
West Ogwell Devon 14 G2
Weston Bath 61 F8
Ches E 168 E2
Ches E 184 G5
Devon 15 D9
Devon 27 G10
Dorset 17 G9
Dorset 29 F8
Halton 183 E8
Hants 34 C2
Hereford 115 F7
Herts 104 E5
Lincs 156 D5
Northants 101 B11
Notts 172 B3
N Yorks 205 D9
Pembs 73 C8
Shrops 114 C6
Shrops 131 E11
Shrops 148 D5
Shrops 149 D11
S Lanark 269 F10
Soton 32 E6
Staffs 151 D9
Suff 143 F8
W Berks 63 E11
Weston Bampfylde Som 29 C10
Weston Beggard
Hereford 97 C11
Westonbirt Glos 61 B11
Weston by Welland
Northants 136 E5
Weston Colley Hants 48 F4
Weston Colville Cambs 124 G2
Westoncommon Shrops 149 D8
Weston Common Soton 33 E7
Weston Corbett Hants 49 D7
Weston Coyney Stoke 168 G6
Weston Ditch Suff 124 B3
Weston Favell Northants 120 E5
Weston Green Cambs 124 G2
Norf 160 G2
Sur 67 F7
Weston Heath Shrops 150 G5
Weston Hills Lincs 156 E5
Weston in Arden Warks 135 F7
Westoning C Beds 103 E10
Weston-in-Gordano
N Som 60 E2
Weston Jones Staffs 150 E5
Weston Longville Norf 160 F2
Weston Lullingfields
Shrops 149 E8
Weston Manor IoW 20 D2
Weston Mill Plym 7 D9
Weston-on-Avon
Warks 118 G3
Weston-on-the-Green
Oxon 83 B8
Weston-on-Trent
Derbys 15
Weston Park Bath
Weston Patrick Hants.
Weston Point Halton
Weston Rhyn Shrop

Weston-sub-Edge Glos. 100 C2
Weston-super-Mare
  N Som 59 G10
Weston Town Som 45 E8
Weston Turville Bucks 84 C5
Weston under Lizard
  Staffs 150 G6
Weston under Penyard
  Hereford 98 G2
Weston under Wetherley
  Warks 119 D7
Weston Underwood
  Derbys 170 G3
  M Keynes 121 G2
Westonwharf Shrops 149 D8
Westonzoyland Som 43 G11
West Orchard Dorset 30 D4
West Overton Wilts 62 F6
Westow N Yorks 216 F5
Westowe Som 42 G6
Westown Devon 27 E10
  Perth 286 E6
West Panson Devon 12 C2
West Park Hrtlpl 234 E5
  Hull 200 B5
  Mers 183 B7
  T&W 243 D9
  W Yorks 205 F11
West Parley Dorset 19 B7
West Pasture Durham 232 G4
West Peckham Kent 52 C6
West Pelton Durham 242 G6
West Pennard Som 44 F4
West Pentire Corn 4 C5
West Perry Cambs 122 D2
West Pontnewydd Torf 78 F3
West Poringland Norf 142 C5
West Porlock Som 41 D11
Westport Argyll 255 E7
  Som 28 D5
West Portholland Corn 5 G9
West Porton Wilts 277 G8
West Pulham Dorset 30 F2
West Putford Devon 24 D4
West Quantoxhead Som 42 E6
Westquarter Falk 279 F8
Westra V Glam 58 E6
West Rainton Durham 234 B2
West Rasen Lincs 189 D9
West Ravendale
  NE Lincs 190 B2
West Raynham Norf 159 D7
West Retford Notts 187 E11
Westridge Green
  W Berks 64 D5
Westrigg W Loth 269 B8
Westrip Glos 80 D4
Westrop Wilts 61 E11
Westrop Green W Berks 64 E4
West Rounton N Yorks 225 E8
West Row Suff 124 B3
West Royd W Yorks 205 F9
West Rudham Norf 158 D6
West Runton Norf 177 E11
Westruther Borders 272 F2
Westry Cambs 139 D7
West Saltoun E Loth 271 B9
West Sandford Devon 26 G4
West Sandwick Shetland 312 E6
West Scholes W Yorks 205 G7
West Scrafton N Yorks 213 C11
West Shepton Som 44 E6
West Side Bl Gwent 77 D11
  Orkney 314 C5
West Skelston Dumfries 247 F8
West Sleekburn
  Northumb 253 G7
West Somerton Norf 161 F9
West Southbourne
  Bmouth 19 C8
West Stafford Dorset 17 D10
West Stockwith Notts 188 C3
West Stoke Devon 13 G9
  Som 29 D7
  W Sus 22 B4
West Stonesdale
  N Yorks 223 E7
West Stoughton Som 44 D2
West Stour Dorset 30 C3
West Stourmouth Kent 71 G9
West Stow Suff 124 C6
West Stowell Wilts 62 G6
West Stratton Hants 48 E4
West Street Kent 54 C2
  Kent 55 C10
  Medway 69 D8
  Suff 125 C9
West Tanfield N Yorks 214 D5
West Taphouse Corn 6 C3
West Tarbert Argyll 275 G9
West Tarring W Sus 35 G10
West Third Borders 262 B4
West Thirston Northumb 252 D5
West Thorney W Sus 22 C3
Westthorpe Derbys 187 F7
West Thurrock Thurrock 68 D5
West Tilbury Thurrock 69 D7
West Tisted Hants 33 B11
West Tofts Norf 140 E6
  Perth 286 D6
West Tolgus Corn 4 G3
West Torrington Lincs 189 E10
West Town Bath 60 G4
  Devon 14 B3
  Devon 24 C4
  Hants 21 B10
  Hereford 115 E8
  N Som 60 F3
  Som 44 F4
  Som 36 D3
West Tytherley Hants 32 B3
West Tytherton Wilts 62 E2
Westvale Mers 182 B6
West Vale W Yorks 196 C5
West View Hrtlpl 234 D5
West Village V Glam 58 E3
Westville Devon 14 B5
  Notts 171 F8
West Walton Norf 157 G9
West Walton Highway
  Norf 157 G10
Westward Cumb 229 C11
Westward Ho! Devon 24 C6
West Watergate Corn 6 E4
  85 F10

West Wickham Cambs 106 B2
  London 67 F11
Westwick Row Herts 85 D9
West Williamston Pembs 73 D8
West Willoughby Lincs 173 G7
West Winch Norf 158 F2
West Winterslow Wilts 47 G8
West Wittering W Sus 21 B11
West Witton N Yorks 213 B11
Westwood Devon 14 B6
  Devon 14 E5
  Kent 55 D7
  Kent 71 F11
  Notts 171 E7
  Pboro 138 D3
  S Lanark 268 E2
  Wilts 45 B10
  Wilts 46 G6
West Woodburn
  Northumb 251 F9
West Woodhay W Berks 63 G11
Westwood Heath
  W Mid 118 B5
West Woodlands Som 45 E9
Westwood Park Essex 107 E9
West Worldham Hants 49 F8
Westwoodside N Lincs 188 B3
West Worlington Devon 26 E3
West Worthing W Sus 35 G10
West Wratting Cambs 124 G2
West Wycombe Bucks 84 G4
West Wylam Northumb 242 E4
West Yatton Wilts 61 E11
West Yell Shetland 312 E6
West Yeo Som 43 G10
West Yoke Kent 68 F5
West Youlstone Corn 24 D3
Wetham Green Kent 69 F10
Wetheral Cumb 239 G11
Wetheral Plain Cumb 239 G11
Wetherby W Yorks 206 D4
Wetherden Suff 125 D10
Wetherden Upper Town
  Suff 125 D10
Wetheringsett Suff 126 D2
Wethersfield Essex 106 E4
Wethersta Shetland 312 G5
Wetherup Street Suff 126 E2
Wetley Rocks Staffs 169 F7
Wetmore Staffs 152 E5
Wettenhall Ches E 167 C10
Wettenhall Green
  Ches E 167 C10
Wettles Shrops 131 F8
Wetton Staffs 169 D10
Wetwang E Yorks 208 B4
Wetwood Staffs 150 C5
Wexcombe Wilts 47 B9
Wexham Street Bucks 66 C3
Weybourne Norf 177 E10
  Sur 49 D11
Weybread Suff 142 G4
Weybridge Sur 66 G5
Weycroft Devon 16 B2
Weydale Highld 310 C5
Weyhill Hants 47 D10
Weymouth Dorset 17 F9
Weythel Powys 114 F4
Whaddon Bucks 102 E6
  Cambs 104 B6
  Glos 80 C4
  Glos 99 G9
  Wilts 31 B11
  Wilts 46 B6
Whaddon Gap Cambs 104 B6
Whale Cumb 230 G6
Whaley Derbys 187 G8
Whaley Bridge Derbys 185 E8
Whaley Thorns Derbys 187 G8
Whaligoe Highld 310 E7
Whalley Lancs 203 F10
Whalley Banks Lancs 203 F10
Whalley Range Gtr Man 184 C4
Whalleys W Yorks 194 F3
Whalton Northumb 252 G4
Wham N Yorks 212 G5
Whaplode Lincs 156 E6
Whaplode Drove Lincs 156 G6
Whaplode St Catherine
  Lincs 156 E6
Wharf Warks 119 G8
Wharfe N Yorks 212 F5
Wharles Lancs 202 F4
Wharley End C Beds 103 C8
Wharncliffe Side
  S Yorks 186 C3
Wharram le Street
  N Yorks 217 F7
Wharram Percy
  N Yorks 217 G7
Wharton Ches W 167 B11
  Hereford 115 F10
  Lincs 188 C4
Wharton Green
  Ches W 167 B11
Whashton N Yorks 224 D3
Whatcombe Dorset 30 G4
Whatcote Warks 100 C6
Whatcroft Ches W 167 B11
Whateley Staffs 134 D4
Whatfield Suff 107 B10
Whatley Som 28 F5
  Som 45 D8
Whatlington E Sus 38 D3
Whatmore Shrops 116 C2
Whatsole Street Kent 54 E6
Whatstandwell Derbys 170 E4
Whatton Notts 154 B4
Whauphill Dumfries 236 E6
Whaw N Yorks 223 E9
Wheal Alfred Corn 2 B3
Wheal Baddon Corn 4 G5
Wheal Busy Corn 4 G4
Wheal Frances Corn 4 E5
Wheal Kitty Corn 4 E4
Wheal Rose Corn 4 G4
Wheatacre Norf 143 E9
Wheatcroft Derbys 170 D5
Wheatenhurst Glos 80 D3
Wheathall Shrops 131 C9
Wheathampstead Herts 85 C11
Wheathill Shrops 132 G2
  Som 44 G5
Wheat Hold Hants 64 G5
Wheatley Devon 14 C4
  Hants 49 E9
  Oxon 83 D9
  W Yorks 196 B5
  W Yorks 205 G7
Wheatley Hill Durham 234 D3
Wheatley Hills S Yorks 198 G6
Wheatley Lane Lancs 204 F2
Wheatley Park W Yorks 198 F5
Wheaton Aston Staffs 151 G7
Wheddon Cross Som 42 F3
Wheedlemont Aberds 302 G4
Wheelbarrow Town Kent 55 D7

Wheeler End Bucks 84 G4
Wheelerstreet Sur 50 E2
Wheelock Ches E 168 D3
Wheelock Heath
  Ches E 168 D2
Wheelton Lancs 194 C6
Wheen Angus 292 F5
Wheldale W Yorks 198 B3
Wheldrake York 207 D9
Whelford Glos 81 F11
Whelley Gtr Man 194 F5
Whelpley Hill Herts 85 E7
Whelpo Cumb 230 D2
Whelp Street Suff 107 B8
Whelston Flint 182 F2
Whempstead Herts 104 G6
Whenby N Yorks 216 F2
Whepstead Suff 124 F6
Wherry Town Corn 1 D5
Wherstead Suff 108 C3
Wherwell Hants 47 E11
Wheston Derbys 185 F10
Whetley Cross Dorset 29 G7
Whetsted Kent 53 D7
Whetstone Leics 135 D11
  London 86 G3
Whettleton Shrops 131 G8
Whicham Cumb 210 C2
Whichford Warks 100 E6
Whickham T&W 242 E6
Whickham Fell T&W 242 F6
Whiddon Devon 40 F5
Whiddon Down Devon 13 C9
Whifflet N Lanark 268 C4
Whigstreet Angus 287 C8
Whilton Northants 120 E2
Whilton Locks Northants 120 E2
Whimble Devon 24 G5
Whim Farm Borders 270 E4
Whimple Devon 14 B6
Whimpwell Green Norf 161 D7
Whinburgh Norf 141 B10
Whinfield Darl 224 B6
Whinhall N Lanark 268 B5
Whin Lane End Lancs 202 E3
Whinmoor W Yorks 206 F3
Whinney Hill Stockton 225 B7
  S Yorks 187 C7
Whinnieliggate
  Dumfries 237 D9
Whinnyfold Aberds 303 F10
Whinny Heights
  Blackburn 195 B7
Whins of Milton Stirling 278 C5
Whins Wood W Yorks 205 F7
Whipcott Devon 27 D9
Whippendell Botton
  Herts 85 E9
Whippingham IoW 20 C6
Whipsiderry Corn 4 C6
Whipsnade C Beds 85 B8
Whipton Devon 14 C5
Whirley Grove Ches E 184 F5
Whirlow S Yorks 186 E4
Whisby Lincs 172 B6
Whissendine Rutland 154 G6
Whissonsett Norf 159 E8
Whisterfield Ches E 184 G4
Whistlefield Argyll 276 C2
  Argyll 276 C4
Whistley Green
  Wokingham 65 E9
Whistlow Oxon 101 F9
Whiston Mers 183 C7
  Northants 120 E6
  Staffs 151 E7
  Staffs 169 F8
  S Yorks 186 D6
Whiston Cross Mers 183 C7
  Shrops 132 C5
Whitacre Heath Warks 134 E4
Whitbarrow Village
  Cumb 230 F4
Whitbeck Cumb 210 C2
Whitbourne Hereford 116 F4
Whitbourne Moor Wilts 45 D10
Whitburn T&W 243 E10
  W Loth 269 C8
Whitburn Colliery
  T&W 243 E10
Whitby Ches W 182 F5
  N Yorks 227 C7
Whitbyheath Ches W 182 F5
Whitchurch Bath 60 F6
  Bucks 102 G5
  Cardiff 59 C7
  Devon 12 G5
  Hants 48 D3
  Hereford 79 B9
  Pembs 90 F5
  Shrops 167 G8
  Som 30 C2
Whitchurch Canonicorum
  Dorset 16 B3
Whitchurch Hill Oxon 64 D6
Whitchurch-on-Thames
  Oxon 64 D6
Whitcombe Dorset 17 D10
  Som 29 C10
Whitcot Shrops 131 E7
Whitcott Keysett Shrops 130 G5
Whiteacen Moray 302 E2
Whiteacre Kent 54 D6
Whiteacre Heath Warks 134 E4
Whiteash Green Essex 106 E5
White Ball Som 27 D9
Whitebirk Blackburn 195 B8
Whitebog Highld 301 C7
Whitebridge Highld 290 B6
Whitebrook Mon 79 D7
Whiteburn Borders 271 F11
Whitebushes Sur 51 D9
Whitecairns Aberds 293 B11
Whitecastle S Lanark 269 G10
Whitechapel Lancs 203 E7
  London 67 C10
Whitchurch Maund
  Hereford 97 B11
Whitecleat Orkney 314 F5
Whitecliff Glos 79 C9
Whiteclosegate Cumb 239 F10
White Colne Essex 107 F7
Whitecote W Yorks 205 F10
Whitecraig E Loth 281 G7
Whitecraigs E Renf 267 D11
Whitecroft Glos 79 D10
Whitecross Corn 4 B5
  Corn 2 C2
  Corn 10 G5
  Falk 279 F9
  Som 28 C6
  Staffs 151 E7
White Cross Bath 44 B5
  Bath 44 B6
  continued

White Cross continued
  Corn 5 D7
  Hereford 97 C9
  Som 43 D10
  Wilts 45 G9
White Cross Hill Som 123 B9
White End Worcs 98 E5
Whiteface Highld 309 L7
White End N Yorks 255 C9
Whitefarland N Ayrs 255 C9
Whitefaulds S Ayrs 245 B7
Whitefield Aberds 303 G7
  Dorset 18 C4
  Gtr Man 195 F10
  Perth 286 D5
  Som 27 B9
Whitefield Lane End
  Mers 183 D7
Whiteflat E Ayrs 258 D2
Whiteford Aberds 303 G7
Whitegate Gtr Man 195 G11
White Gate Gtr Man 195 G11
Whitehall Blackburn 195 C7
  Bristol 60 E6
  Devon 27 E10
  Devon 40 F4
  Hants 49 C8
  Hants 49 E9
  Kent 54 B4
  Kent 71 F11
  Kent 104 E6
  W Sus 35 C10
  W Sus 104 G5
Whitehall Village
  Orkney 314 D6
Whitehawk Brighton 36 G4
Whiteheath Gate W Mid 133 F9
Whitehill E Sus 37 B8
  Hants 49 C9
  Kent 54 B4
  Leics 135 A9
  Midloth 271 B7
  Moray 302 D5
  S Lanark 268 D4
  Staffs 168 G4
Whitehills Aberds 302 C6
  S Lanark 268 D2
  T&W 243 E7
White Hills Northants 120 E4
Whiteholme Blackpool 202 E2
Whitehough Derbys 185 E8
Whitehouse Aberds 293 C9
  Argyll 275 G9
White House Suff 108 B2
Whitehouse Common
  W Mid 134 D2
Whitehouse Green
  W Berks 65 F7
White Houses Notts 188 F2
Whiteinch Glasgow 267 B10
Whitekirk E Loth 281 E10
Whiteknights Reading 65 E9
Whiteknowes Aberds 293 C7
Whitelackington Som 28 D5
White Lackington
  Dorset 17 B10
White Ladies Aston
  Worcs 117 G8
Whitelaw S Lanark 268 G2
Whiteleaf Bucks 84 E4
Whiteleas T&W 243 E9
Whiteleaved Oak Glos 98 D5
Whitelee Borders 262 C3
Whitelees Northumb 250 B6
White Lee W Yorks 197 B8
Whiteley Bank IoW 21 E7
Whiteley Green Ches E 184 F6
Whiteley Village Sur 66 G5
White Lund Lancs 211 G9
Whiteley W Yorks 79 B8
Whitemans Green W Sus 36 B4
White Mill Carms 93 G9
Whitemire Moray 301 D9
Whitemoor Corn 5 D9
  Nottingham 171 G8
  Warks 118 C5
White Moor Derbys 170 F5
Whitemore Staffs 168 C5
Whitenap Hants 32 C5
White Ness Shetland 313 J5
White Notley Essex 88 B3
White Oak Kent 68 E4
White Ox Mead Bath 45 B8
Whiteparish Wilts 32 C2
White Pit Lincs 190 F5
Whitepits Wilts 45 F10
White Post Kent 52 E4
  Notts 171 D10
Whiterashes Aberds 303 G8
Whiteriggs Borders 262 C5
Whiterock Bridgend 58 D2
White Rocks Hereford 97 G8
White Roding or White
  Roothing Essex 87 C9
Whiteleafe Sur 51 B10
White's Green W Sus 34 B6
Whiteshill Glos 80 D4
  S Glos 60 C6
Whiteside Northumb 240 D6
  W Loth 269 B9
Whitesmith E Sus 23 C8
Whitestaunton Som 28 E3
Whitestone Aberds 293 D8
  Devon 14 C3
  Devon 40 D3
  Warks 135 F7
White Stone Hereford 97 C11
Whitestones Aberds 303 D8
Whitestreet Green Suff 107 D9
Whitewall Corner
  N Yorks 216 F5
White Waltham Windsor 65 D10
Whiteway Bath 61 G8
  Glos 80 C6
  Glos 80 F4
Whitewell Aberds 303 C9
  Lancs 203 D9
  Wrex 167 G7
Whitewell Bottom
  Lancs 195 C10
Whiteworks Devon 13 G8
Whitfield Kent 55 D10
  Northants 102 D2
  Northumb 241 F7
  S Glos 79 G11
Whitfield Court Sur 50 B3
Whitford Devon 15 B10
Whitford / Chwitffordd
  Flint 181 F10

Whitgift E Yorks 199 C10
Whitgreave Staffs 151 D7
Whithaugh Borders 249 F11
Whitehebeir Orkney 314 C5
Whiting Bay N Ayrs 256 D2
Whitington Norf 140 D4
Whitkirk W Yorks 206 G3
Whitland / Hendy-Gwyn
  Carms 73 D11
Whitlaw Borders 271 F9
Whitleigh Plym 7 C9
Whitletts S Ayrs 257 E9
Whitley Gtr Man 194 F5
  Reading 65 E8
  S Yorks 186 C4
  Wilts 61 F11
  W Mid 119 B7
Whitley Bay T&W 243 C9
Whitley Bridge N Yorks 198 C5
Whitley Chapel
  Northumb 241 F10
Whitley Head W Yorks 204 E6
Whitley Heath Staffs 150 D6
Whitley Lower W Yorks 197 D8
Whitley Reed Ches W 183 E10
Whitley Row Kent 52 C3
Whitley Sands T&W 243 C9
Whitley Thorpe N Yorks 198 C5
Whitley Wood Reading 65 F8
Whitlock's End W Mid 118 B2
Whitminster Glos 80 D3
Whitmoor Devon 27 E9
Whitmore Dorset 31 F9
  Staffs 168 G4
Whitmore Park W Mid 119 B7
Whitnage Devon 27 D8
Whitnash Warks 118 E6
Whitnell Som 43 F8
Whitney Bottom Som 28 E4
Whitney-on-Wye
  Hereford 96 B5
Whitrigg Cumb 229 D10
  Cumb 238 F6
Whitriggs Borders 262 F3
Whitsbury Hants 31 D10
Whitshiels Aberds 302 C6
S Lanark 268 D2
  T&W 243 E7
White Hills Northants 120 E4
Whitsome Borders 273 E7
Whitsomehill Borders 273 F7
Whitson Newport 59 C11
Whitstable Kent 70 E6
Whitstone Corn 11 B11
Whittingham Northumb 264 G3
Whittingslow Shrops 131 F8
Whittington Glos 99 G10
  Lancs 212 D2
  Norf 140 D4
  Shrops 148 C6
  Staffs 133 C6
  Staffs 134 B5
  Staffs 150 C5
  Warks 134 D5
  Worcs 117 G7
Whittington Moor
  Derbys 186 G5
Whittlebury Northants 102 C3
Whittleford Warks 134 C6
Whittle-le-Woods
  Lancs 194 C5
Whittlesey Cambs 138 D5
Whittlesford Cambs 105 B9
Whittlestone Head
  Blackburn 195 D8
Whitton Borders 263 E7
  Hereford 115 C9
  London 66 E6
  N Lincs 200 C2
  Northumb 252 C3
  Powys 114 D5
  Shrops 115 C11
  Stockton 234 G3
  Suff 108 B2
Whittonditch Wilts 63 E9
Whittonstall Northumb 242 F3
Whittytree Shrops 115 B8
Whitway Hants 48 B3
Whitwell Derbys 187 F8
  Herts 104 G3
  IoW 20 F6
  N Yorks 224 F5
  Rutland 137 B8
Whitwell-on-the-Hill
  N Yorks 216 F4
Whitwell Street Norf 160 E2
Whitwick Leics 153 F8
Whitwood W Yorks 198 C2
Whitworth Lancs 195 D11
Whixall Shrops 149 C11
Whixley N Yorks 206 B4
Whoberley W Mid 118 B6
Whole Orkney 314 G3
Wholeflats Falk 279 E8
Whorlton Durham 224 C2
  N Yorks 225 E9
Whydown E Sus 38 E2
  Worcs 116 C6
Whygate Northumb 241 B7
Whyle Hereford 115 E11
Whyteleafe Sur 51 B10
Wibdon Glos 79 E10
Wibsey W Yorks 205 G8
Wibtoft Leics 135 F9
Wichenford Worcs 116 E5
Wichling Kent 54 B2
Wick Bmouth 19 C8
  Devon 27 G11
  Highld 310 D7
  S Glos 61 E8
  Som 43 G10
  Som 28 B6
  Som 43 C10
  V Glam 58 E2
  Wilts 31 C11
  Worcs 99 B8
  W Sus 35 G8
Wick Episcopi Worcs 116 G6
Wickersley S Yorks 187 C7
Wick Hill Brack 65 F11
  Kent 53 E10
  Wokingham 65 G9
Wickham Hants 33 E9
Wickham Heath W Berks 64 F2
Wickham Market Suff 126 F6
Wickhampton Norf 143 B8
Wickham St Paul Essex 106 D6
Wickham's Cross Som 44 G3

Wickham Skeith Suff 125 D11
Wickham Street Suff 124 G5
  Suff 125 D11
Wick St Lawrence
  N Som 59 G11
Wickstreet E Sus 23 D8
Wick Street Glos 80 D5
Wickwar S Glos 61 B8
Widbrook Wilts 45 B10
Widcombe Bath 61 G9
Widdington Essex 105 E10
Widdrington Northumb 253 D7
Widdrington Station
  Northumb 252 E6
Widecombe in the Moor
  Devon 13 G10
Widegates Corn 6 D5
Widemarsh Hereford 97 C10
Widemouth Bay Corn 24 G2
Wideopen T&W 242 C6
Widewall Orkney 314 G4
Widford Essex 87 D11
  Herts 86 B6
Widgham Green Cambs 124 F3
Widham Wilts 62 B5
Widley Hants 33 F11
Widmer End Bucks 84 F5
Widmerpool Notts 154 D2
Widmoor Bucks 66 B2
Widmore London 68 F2
Widnes Halton 183 D8
Wierton Kent 53 D9
Wigan Gtr Man 194 F5
Wiganthorpe N Yorks 216 E3
Wigbeth Dorset 31 F8
Wigborough Som 28 D6
Wig Fach Bridgend 57 F10
Wiggaton Devon 15 C8
Wiggenhall St Germans
  Norf 157 G11
Wiggenhall St Mary
  Magdalen Norf 157 G11
Wiggenhall St Mary the
  Virgin Norf 157 G11
Wiggenhall St Peter
  Norf 158 G2
Wiggens Green Essex 106 C3
Wigginton Herts 84 C6
  Oxon 101 E7
  Shrops 148 B6
  Staffs 134 B4
  York 207 B7
Wigginton Bottom Herts 84 D6
Wigglesworth N Yorks 204 B2
Wiggonby Cumb 239 G2
Wiggonholt W Sus 35 D9
Wighton Norf 159 B8
Wightwick Manor Staffs 133 D7
Wigley Derbys 186 G4
  Hants 32 D4
Wigmarsh Shrops 149 D7
Wigmore Hereford 115 D8
  Medway 69 G10
Wigsley Notts 188 G5
Wigsthorpe Northants 137 G10
Wigston Leics 136 D2
Wigston Magna Leics 136 D2
Wigston Parva Leics 135 F9
Wigthorpe Notts 187 E9
Wigtoft Lincs 156 B5
Wigton Cumb 229 B11
Wigtown Dumfries 236 D6
Wigtwizzle S Yorks 186 B2
Wike W Yorks 206 E2
Wike Well End S Yorks 199 E7
Wilbarston Northants 136 F6
Wilberfoss E Yorks 207 C10
Wilburton Cambs 123 C9
Wilby Norf 141 F10
  Northants 121 D7
  Suff 126 C4
Wilcot Wilts 62 G6
Wilcott Shrops 149 F7
Wilcott Marsh Shrops 149 F7
Wilcove Corn 7 D8
Wilcrick Newport 60 B2
Wilday Green Derbys 186 G4
Wildboarclough Ches E 169 B7
Wilden Bedford 121 F11
  Worcs 116 C6
Wildern Hants 33 E7
Wildernesse Kent 52 B4
Wilderspool Warr 183 D10
Wilde Street Suff 124 C4
Wildhern Hants 47 C11
Wildhill Herts 86 D2
Wildmanbridge
  S Lanark 268 E6
Wild Mill Bridgend 58 C2
Wildmoor Hants 49 B7
  Oxon 83 F7
  Worcs 117 B9
Wildridings Brack 65 F11
Wildsworth Lincs 188 C4
Wildwood Staffs 151 E8
Wilford Nottingham 153 B11
Wilgate Green Kent 54 B3
Wilkesley Ches E 167 G10
Wilkhaven Highld 311 L3
Wilkieston W Loth 270 B2
Wilkin Throop Som 29 C11
Wilksby Lincs 174 C3
Willacy Lane End Lancs 202 F5
Willand Devon 27 E8
  Som 27 E11
Willand Moor Devon 27 E8
Willard's Hill E Sus 38 C2
Willaston Ches W 167 G11
  Ches W 182 F4
  Shrops 149 B11
Willen M Keynes 103 C7
Willenhall W Mid 133 D9
  W Mid 119 B7
Willerby E Yorks 208 G6
  N Yorks 217 D10
Willersey Glos 99 C11
Willersley Hereford 96 B6
Willesborough Kent 54 E4
Willesborough Lees Kent 54 E4
Willesden London 67 C8
Willesleigh Devon 40 G5
Willesley Wilts 61 B11
Willett Som 42 G6

Willett Som 42 G6
Willey Shrops 132 D3
  Warks 135 G9
Willey Green Sur 50 C2
Willhayne Som 28 E4
Williamhope Borders 261 C10
Willamscot Oxon 101 B9
Williams's Green Suff 107 C9
Williamslee Borders 270 G6
Williamstown Rhondda 77 G8
Willian Herts 104 E4
Willicote Pastures
  Worcs 100 B3
Willingale Essex 87 D9
Willingcott Devon 40 E3
Willingdon E Sus 23 E7
Willingham Cambs 123 C8
  Suff 143 G8
Willingham by Stow
  Lincs 188 E5
Willingham Green
  Cambs 124 G2
Willington Bedford 104 B2
  Derbys 152 D5
  Durham 233 D9
  Kent 53 C9
  T&W 243 C8
Willington Corner
  Ches W 167 B8
Willington Quay T&W 243 D8
Willisham Suff 125 G11
Willisham Tye Suff 125 G11
Willitoft E Yorks 207 F10
Williton Som 42 E5
Willoughbridge Staffs 168 G3
Willoughby Lincs 191 G7
  Warks 119 D10
Willoughby Hills Lincs 174 F4
Willoughby-on-the-Wolds
  Notts 154 D2
Willoughby Waterleys
  Leics 135 E11
Willoughton Lincs 188 C6
Willowbank Bucks 66 B5
Willow Green Ches W 183 F10
Willow Holme Cumb 239 F9
Willows Gtr Man 195 F8
Willows Green Essex 88 B2
Willsbridge S Glos 61 E7
Willslock Staffs 151 C11
Willstone Shrops 131 D9
Willsworthy Devon 12 E6
Wilmcote Warks 118 F3
Wilmington Bath 61 G7
  Devon 15 B10
  E Sus 23 E8
  Kent 68 E4
Wilmington Green E Sus 23 D8
Wilminstone Devon 12 F5
Wilmslow Ches E 184 E4
Wilmslow Park Ches E 184 E4
Wilnecote Staffs 134 C4
Wilney Green Norf 141 G11
Wilpshire Lancs 203 G9
Wilsden W Yorks 205 F7
Wilsden Hill W Yorks 205 F7
Wilsford Lincs 173 G8
  Wilts 46 B6
  Wilts 46 F6
Wilsham Devon 41 D9
Wilshaw W Yorks 196 F6
Wilsic S Yorks 187 B9
Wilsill N Yorks 214 G3
Wilsley Green Kent 53 F9
Wilsley Pound Kent 53 F9
Wilsom Hants 49 F8
Wilson Hereford 97 G11
  Leics 153 E8
Wilsontown S Lanark 269 D9
Wilstead Bedford 103 C11
Wilsthorpe Derbys 153 C9
  Lincs 155 G11
Wilstone Herts 84 C6
Wilstone Green Herts 84 C6
Wilthorpe S Yorks 197 F10
Wilton Borders 261 G11
  Cumb 219 C10
  Hereford 97 C11
  N Yorks 217 C7
  Redcar 225 B11
  Wilts 46 G5
  Wilts 63 G9
Wilton Park Bucks 85 G7
Wiltown Devon 27 D11
  Som 28 C5
Wimbish Essex 105 D11
Wimbish Green Essex 106 D2
Wimblebury Staffs 151 G10
Wimbledon London 67 E8
Wimble Hill Hants 49 D10
Wimblington Cambs 139 E8
Wimbolds Trafford
  Ches W 182 F6
Wimborne Minster
  Dorset 18 B6
Wimborne St Giles
  Dorset 31 F8
Wimbotsham Norf 140 B2
Wimpole Cambs 104 B6
Wimpson Soton 32 E5
Wimpstone Warks 100 B4
Wincanton Som 30 B2
Winceby Lincs 174 B4
Wincham Ches W 183 F11
Winchburgh W Loth 279 G11
Winchcombe Glos 99 F10
Winchelsea E Sus 38 D6
Winchelsea Beach E Sus 38 D6
Winchester Hants 33 B7
Winchet Hill Kent 53 E8
Winchfield Hants 49 C9
  Hants 53 B8
Winchmore Hill Bucks 84 G6
  London 86 G4
Wincle Ches E 169 B7
Wincobank S Yorks 186 C5
Winder Cumb 219 B10
Windermere Cumb 221 F8
Winderton Warks 100 C6
Windhill Highld 300 E5
  S Yorks 198 G5
Windhouse Shetland 312 D6
Wind Hill Cumb 210 C5
Windle Hill Ches W 182 F5
Windlehurst Gtr Man 185 D7
Windlesham Sur 66 G2
Windley Derbys 170 F4
Windmill Corn 5 B7
  Flint 181 G11
  Wilts 61 B11

Windmill Hill Bristol 60 E5
  E Sus 23 C10
  Halton 183 E9
  Kent 69 F10
  Som 28 D4
  Worcs 197 D11
Windrush Glos 81 C11
Windsor N Lincs 199 E10
  Windsor 66 D3
Windsoredge Glos 80 E4
Windsor Green Suff 125 G7
Windwhistle Som 28 F5
Windy Arbour Warks 118 C5
Windydoors Borders 261 B10
Windygates Fife 287 G7
Windy Hill Wrex 166 E3
Windy Nook T&W 243 E7
Windywalls Borders 263 C7
Windy-Yett E Ayrs 267 E9
  N Sus 36 C2
Winestead E Yorks 201 C9
Winewall Lancs 204 E4
Winfarthing Norf 142 F2
Winford IoW 21 E7
  N Som 60 F4
Winforton Hereford 96 B5
Winfrith Newburgh
  Dorset 18 E2
Wing Bucks 103 G7
  Rutland 137 C7
Wingate Durham 234 D4
Wingates Gtr Man 195 F7
  Northumb 252 D4
Wingerworth Derbys 170 B5
Wingfield C Beds 103 F10
  Suff 126 B4
  S Yorks 186 B6
Wingfield Green Suff 126 B4
Wingfield Park Derbys 170 E5
Wingham Kent 55 B9
Wingmore Kent 55 D7
Wingrave Bucks 84 B5
Winkburn Notts 172 D2
Winkfield Brack 66 E2
Winkfield Place Brack 66 E2
Winkfield Row Brack 65 E11
Winkhill Staffs 169 E9
Winkhurst Green Kent 52 D3
Winkleigh Devon 25 F10
Winksley N Yorks 214 E5
Winkton Dorset 19 B8
Winlaton T&W 242 E5
Winlaton Mill T&W 242 E5
Winless Highld 310 D7
Winllan Powys 148 E4
Winmarleigh Lancs 202 D5
Winmarleigh Moss
  Lancs 202 D4
Winnal Hereford 97 E10
Winnal Common Hereford 97 E9
Winnall Hants 33 B7
  Worcs 116 D6
Winnard's Perch Corn 5 C8
Winnersh Wokingham 65 E9
Winnington Ches W 183 G10
  Staffs 150 B4
Winnington Green
  Shrops 149 G6
Winnothdale Staffs 169 G8
Winscales Cumb 228 F6
Winscombe N Som 44 B2
Winsdon Hill Luton 103 G11
Winsford Ches W 167 B10
  Som 42 G2
Winsham Devon 40 F3
  Som 28 F4
Winshill Staffs 152 E5
Winsh-wen Swansea 57 B7
Winskill Cumb 231 D7
  Hants 49 D7
Winslade Devon 24 D5
  Hants 49 D7
Winsley N Yorks 214 G4
  Wilts 61 G10
Winslow Bucks 102 F5
  Worcs 116 B6
Winslow Mill Hereford 98 D2
Winson Glos 81 D9
Winsor Green W Mid 133 F10
  Som 32 E4
Winstanley Gtr Man 194 G5
Winstanleys Gtr Man 194 F5
Winster Cumb 221 G8
  Derbys 170 C2
Winston Durham 224 B2
  Suff 126 E3
Winstone Glos 81 D7
Winston Green Suff 126 E3
Winswell Devon 25 D7
Winterborne Bassett
  Wilts 62 E6
Winterborne Came
  Dorset 17 D10
Winterborne Clenston
  Dorset 30 G4
Winterborne Herringston
  Dorset 17 D9
Winterborne Houghton
  Dorset 30 G4
Winterborne Kingston
  Dorset 18 B3
Winterborne Monkton
  Dorset 17 D9
Winterborne Muston
  Dorset 18 B3
Winterborne Stickland
  Dorset 30 G4
Winterborne Tomson
  Dorset 18 B3
Winterborne Whitechurch
  Dorset 30 G4
Winterborne Zelston
  Dorset 18 B3
Winterbourne Kent 54 B5
  S Glos 60 C6
  W Berks 64 E3
Winterbourne Abbas
  Dorset 17 C8
Winterbourne Bassett
  Wilts 62 E6
Winterbourne Dauntsey
  Wilts 47 G7
Winterbourne Down
  S Glos 61 D7
Winterbourne Earls Wilts 47 G7
Winterbourne Gunner
  Wilts 47 G7
Winterbourne Monkton
  Wilts 62 E6
  Dorset 17 D9
Winterbourne Steepleton
  Dorset 17 D8
Winterbourne Stoke
  Wilts 46 E5
Winterbrook Oxon 64 D6

Winterburn N Yorks.....204 B4
Winterfield Bath.......45 B7
Winter Gardens Essex..69 C9
Winterhay Green Som...28 D5
Winterhead N Som.....44 B2
Winterley Ches E.......168 D2
Wintershill Hants......33 D8
Winterton N Lincs.....200 C2
Winterton-on-Sea Norf 161 F9
Winthorpe Lincs........175 B9
  Notts.........172 D4
Winton Bmouth.........19 C7
  Cumb.............222 C5
  E Sus.............23 E8
  Gtr Man...........23 B8
  N Yorks...........225 F8
Wintringham N Yorks...217 E7
Winwick Cambs........138 G2
  Northants.......120 C2
  Warr............183 C10
Winwick Quay Warr....183 C10
Winyard's Gap Dorset...29 F7
Winyates Worcs.......117 D11
Winyates Green Worcs 117 D11
Wirksworth Derbys....170 E4
Wirksworth Moor
  Derbys...........170 E4
Wirswall Ches E.......167 G8
Wisbech Cambs.......139 B9
Wisbech St Mary Cambs 139 B8
Wisborough Green
  W Sus............35 B8
Wiseton Notts.........188 D2
Wishanger Glos........80 D6
Wishaw N Lanark......268 C5
  Warks...........134 E3
Wisley Sur............50 B5
Wispington Lincs......190 G2
Wissenden Kent........54 E2
Wissett Suff..........127 B7
Wistanstow Shrops....131 F8
Wistanswick Shrops...150 D3
Wistaston Ches E......167 E11
Wistaston Green
  Ches E...........167 E11
Wiston Pembs.........73 B8
  S Lanark........259 C11
  W Sus...........35 E10
Wiston Mains S Lanark 259 C11
Wistow Cambs........138 G5
  Leics...........136 D2
  N Yorks.........207 F7
Wiswell Lancs.........203 F10
Witcham Cambs.......139 G9
Witchampton Dorset...31 F7
Witchford Cambs.....123 B10
Witcombe Som........29 C7
Withacott Devon......24 D6
Witham Essex.........88 C4
Witham Friary Som....45 E8
Witham on the Hill
  Lincs............155 F11
Witham St Hughs Lincs 172 C5
Withcall Lincs........190 E3
Withdean Brighton....36 F4
Witherenden Hill E Sus 37 B10
Withergate Norf......160 D5
Witheridge Devon.....26 E4
Witheridge Hill Oxon..65 C7
Witherley Leics.......134 D6
Withermarsh Green
  Suff.............107 D11
Withern Lincs........190 E6
Withernsea E Yorks...201 B10
Withersdale Street Suff 142 G5
Withersdane Kent.....54 D5
Withersfield Suff.....106 B3
Witherslack Cumb....211 C8
Witherwack T&W.....243 F9
Withial Som..........44 F5
Withiel Corn..........5 B9
Withiel Florey Som....42 G3
Withielgoose Corn....5 B10
Withielgoose Mills Corn 5 B10
Withington Glos......81 B8
  Gtr Man.........184 C5
  Hereford........97 C11
  Shrops..........149 G11
  Staffs...........151 B10
Withington Green
  Ches E...........184 G4
Withington Marsh
  Hereford........97 C11
Withleigh Devon......26 E6
Withnell Lancs........194 C6
Withnell Fold Lancs...194 C6
Withybed Green Worcs 117 C10
Withybrook Som......45 D7
  Warks...........135 G8
Withybush Pembs.....73 B7
Withycombe Som......41 F11
  Som.............42 E4
Withycombe Raleigh
  Devon...........14 E6
Withyditch Bath......45 B8
Withyham E Sus......52 F3
Withy Mills Bath.....45 B7
Withymoor Village
  W Mid...........133 F8
Withypool Som.......41 F10
Withystakes Staffs....169 F7
Withywood Bristol....60 F5
Witley Sur............50 F2
Witnells End Worcs...132 G5
Witnesham Suff......126 G3
Witney Oxon.........82 C5
Wittensford Hants....32 E3
Wittering Pboro......137 C11
Wittersham Kent.....38 B5
Witton Angus........293 F7
  Norf.............142 B6
  W Mid...........133 E11
  Worcs...........117 E7
Witton Bridge Norf...160 C6
Witton Gilbert Durham 233 B10
Witton Hill Worcs.....116 E5
Witton-le-Wear Durham 233 E9
Witton Park Durham..233 E9
Wiveliscombe Som....27 B9
Wivelrod Hants.......49 F7
Wivelsfield E Sus......36 C5
Wivelsfield Green E Sus 36 C5
Wivenhoe Essex......107 G10
Wivenhoe Cross Essex 107 G10
Wiveton Norf.........177 E8
Wix Essex............108 F3
Wixams Bedford......103 C10
Wixford Warks.......117 G11
Wixhill Shrops.......149 D11
Wixoe Suff...........106 C4
Woburn C Beds.......103 D8

Woburn Sands
  M Keynes........103 D8
Wofferwood Common
  Hereford.........116 G3
Wokefield Park W Berks.65 F7
Woking Sur...........50 B4
Wokingham Wokingham.65 F10
Wolborough Devon.....14 G3
Woldhurst W Sus......22 C5
Woldingham Sur......51 B11
Woldingham Garden Village
  Sur..............51 B11
Wold Newton E Yorks..217 E10
  NE Lincs.........190 B2
Wolfclyde S Lanark....260 B2
Wolferd Green Norf...142 D5
Wolferlow Hereford...116 E3
Wolferton Norf.......158 D3
Wolfhampcote Warks 119 D10
Wolfhill Perth........286 D5
Wolf's Castle Pembs...91 F9
Wolfsdale Pembs......91 G8
Wolfsdale Hill Pembs..91 G8
Woll Borders.........261 E11
Wollaston Northants..121 E8
  Shrops..........148 G6
  W Mid...........133 G7
Wollaton Nottingham.153 B10
Wollerton Shrops.....150 C2
Wollerton Wood Shrops.150 C2
Wollescote W Mid.....133 G8
Wollrig Borders.......261 E11
Wolsingham Durham..233 D7
Wolstanton Staffs.....168 F5
Wolstenholme
  Gtr Man.........195 D11
Wolston Warks.......119 B8
Wolsty Cumb.........238 G4
Wolterton Norf.......160 C3
Wolvercote Oxon.....83 D7
Wolverham Ches W...182 F6
Wolverhampton W Mid 133 D8
Wolverley Shrops.....149 C9
  Worcs...........116 B6
Wolverstone Devon...27 G10
Wolverton Hants......48 B5
  Kent.............55 E9
  M Keynes........102 C6
  Shrops..........131 F9
  Warks...........118 E4
  Wilts............45 G9
Wolverton Common
  Hants............48 B5
Wolvesnewton Mon...79 F7
Wolvey Warks........135 F8
Wolvey Heath Warks..135 F8
Wolviston Stockton...234 F5
Womaston Powys.....114 E5
Wombleton N Yorks...216 C3
Wombourne Staffs....133 E7
Wombridge Telford...150 G3
Wombwell S Yorks....197 G11
Womenswold Kent....55 C8
Womersley N Yorks...198 D4
Wonastow Mon.......79 C7
Wonderstone N Som..43 B10
Wonersh Sur.........50 D4
Wonford Devon......14 C4
Wonson Devon........13 D9
Wonston Dorset......30 F2
  Hants...........48 F3
Wooburn Bucks......66 B2
Wooburn Green Bucks..66 B2
Wood Pembs..........91 G7
  Som.............28 D4
Woodacott Devon.....24 F5
Woodacott Cross Devon 24 F5
Woodale N Yorks.....213 D10
Woodbank Argyll.....255 F7
  Ches W..........182 G5
Woodbastwick Norf...160 F6
Woodbeck Notts......188 F3
Wood Bevington
  Warks...........117 G11
Woodborough Notts..171 F10
  Wilts............46 B6
Woodbridge Dorset...30 D5
  Dorset..........30 E2
  Glos.............81 C8
  Northumb.......253 F7
  Suff.............108 B5
Woodbridge Walk Suff 108 B5
Wood Burcote Northants 102 B3
Woodburn Common
  Bucks...........66 B2
Woodburn Moor Bucks..84 G6
Woodbury Devon......14 D6
Woodbury Salterton
  Devon...........14 D6
Woodchester Glos....80 E4
Woodchurch Kent....54 G2
  Mers............182 D3
Woodcock Wilts......45 E11
Woodcock Heath
  Staffs...........151 D11
Woodcock Hill Herts..85 G9
  W Mid...........133 G10
Woodcombe Som......42 D3
Woodcote Oxon.......33 G9
  Telford..........150 F5
Woodcote Green
  Worcs...........117 C8
Woodcott Hants......48 C2
Woodcroft Glos.......79 F8
Woodcutts Dorset....31 D7
Wood Dalling Norf...159 D11
Woodditton Cambs...124 F3
Woodeaton Oxon.....83 C8
Wood Eaton Staffs....150 F6
Wooden Pembs........73 D10
Woodend C Beds......219 C10
  Cumb...........220 F3
  Cumb...........229 F10
  Highld..........300 C5
  N Yorks.........43 E7
  Som.............44 F4
  S Yorks.........198 F4
  W Loth..........279 F11
  W Sus...........22 B4
Wood End Bedford....103 B10
  Bedford.........121 D11
  Bedford.........121 F11
  Bucks...........102 E5
  C Beds..........103 C9
  Gtr Man.........196 F2
  Hereford........98 C2
  Herts............104 F6

Wood End continued
  Warks...........118 C2
  Warks...........134 D4
  Warks...........134 F5
  Windsor..........66 E2
  W Mid...........133 C8
  W Mid...........135 G7
Wood Enderby Lincs..174 C2
Woodend Green Essex 105 F11
  Northants.......102 B2
Wood End Green London.66 C5
Woodfalls Wilts.......31 C11
Woodfield Glos........80 F2
  Oxon............101 G11
  S Ayrs...........257 E8
Wood Field Sur.......51 B7
Woodford Corn.......24 E2
  Devon...........8 E5
  Glos.............79 F11
  Gtr Man.........184 E5
  London..........86 G6
  Northants.......121 B9
  Plym.............7 D10
  Som.............42 F5
  Som.............44 E4
Woodford Bridge London 86 G6
Woodford Green London.86 G6
Woodford Halse
  Northants.......119 C10
Woodford Wells London 86 G6
Woodgate Devon......27 D10
  Norf.............159 F10
  W Mid...........133 G9
  W Sus...........22 C6
  Worcs...........117 D9
Wood Gate Staffs.....152 D3
Woodgate Hill Gtr Man 195 E10
Woodgates End Essex 105 F11
Woodgates Green
  Worcs...........116 C2
Woodgate Valley
  W Mid...........133 G10
Woodgreen Hants.....31 D11
  Oxon............82 C5
Wood Green Essex....86 E6
  London..........86 G4
  Norf.............142 E4
  W Mid...........133 D9
  W Sus...........116 D6
Woodhall Herts.......86 C2
  Invclyd..........276 G6
  N Yorks.........207 G8
  N Yorks.........223 G9
Woodhall Hills
  W Yorks.........205 F10
Woodhall Spa Lincs...173 C11
Woodham Bucks......84 B2
  Durham.........233 F11
  Sur.............66 G4
Woodham Ferrers Essex..88 F3
Woodham Mortimer
  Essex...........88 E4
Woodham Walter Essex..88 D4
Woodhatch Sur......51 D9
Woodhaven Fife.....287 E8
Wood Hayes W Mid...133 C8
Woodhead Aberds...303 F7
  Staffs...........169 G9
Woodheads Borders..271 F10
Woodhey Gtr Man....195 D9
  Mers............182 D4
Woodhey Green Ches E..167 E10
Woodhill Essex.......88 E3
  N Som...........60 D3
  Shrops..........132 G4
  Shrops..........148 E5
  Som.............28 B5
Woodhorn Northumb..253 F7
Woodhouse Cumb....211 C10
  Cumb...........219 E9
  Leics...........47 D11
  Leics...........153 F10
  N Lincs.........199 F9
  S Yorks.........186 D6
  W Yorks.........196 G6
  W Yorks.........197 C11
  W Yorks.........205 E8
  W Yorks.........205 F11
Wood House Lancs....203 C10
Woodhouse Down S Glos..60 B6
Woodhouse Eaves
  Leics...........153 G10
Woodhouse Green
  Staffs...........168 C6
Woodhouselee Midloth.270 C4
Woodhouselees
  Dumfries........239 C9
Woodhouse Mill
  S Yorks.........186 D6
Woodhouse Park
  Gtr Man.........184 D4
Woodhouses Ches W..183 F8
  Cumb...........239 G8
  Gtr Man.........184 C3
  Gtr Man.........196 G2
  Staffs...........133 B11
  Staffs...........152 F3
Woodhurst Cambs....122 B6
Woodingdean Brighton..36 F5
Woodington Hants....32 C4
Woodkirk W Yorks....197 C10
Woodlake W Sus......18 C3
Woodland Cumb.......210 B4
  Devon...........8 D5
  Devon...........8 B2
  Durham.........233 F7
  Kent............54 E6
Woodland Head Devon 13 B11
Woodlands Aberds...293 D9
  Aberds..........293 D9
  Aberds..........303 G8
  Dorset..........31 F9
  Dumfries........238 B3
  Gtr Man.........184 B2
  Hants...........32 E4
  Highld..........300 C5
  Kent............68 G5
  London..........67 D7
  N Yorks.........206 C2
  Som.............43 E7
  Som.............44 F4
  S Yorks.........198 F4
  Wokingham.......65 G9
  W Yorks.........196 B5
Woodlands Common
  Dorset..........31 F9
Woodlands Park
  Windsor.........65 D11
Woodlands St Mary
  W Berks.........63 E10
Woodlane Shrops.....150 D3
  Staffs...........152 E2
Wood Lane Shrops....149 C8
  Staffs...........168 E4
Wood Lanes Ches E...184 E6

Woodleigh Devon......8 F4
Woodlesford W Yorks 197 B11
Woodley Gtr Man.....184 C6
  Wokingham.......65 E9
Woodley Green
  Wokingham.......65 E9
Woodleys Oxon.......82 B6
Woodlinkin Derbys...170 F6
Woodloes Park Warks 118 D6
Woodmancote Glos....80 F3
  Glos.............81 D8
  Glos.............99 F9
  Glos.............170 C5
  W Sus...........22 B3
  W Sus...........36 E2
Woodmancott Hants..48 E5
Woodmansey E Yorks 209 F7
Woodmansgreen W Sus..34 B5
Woodmansterne Sur..51 B9
Woodmanton Devon..15 G7
Wood Norton Norf...159 D10
  Worcs...........99 B10
Woodplumpton Lancs 202 G6
Woodram Som.........28 D2
Woodrising Norf.....141 C9
Wood Road Gtr Man..195 E9
Woodrow Bucks......84 F6
  Cumb...........229 B10
  Dorset..........30 E3
  Dorset..........30 F2
  Worcs...........117 B7
  Worcs...........117 D11
Wood Row W Yorks...197 B11
Woods Hereford......96 B5
Wood's Corner E Sus..23 B11
Woodsden Kent.......53 G9
Wood Seats S Yorks...186 B4
Woodseaves Shrops...150 C3
  Staffs...........150 D5
Woodsetts S Yorks...187 E9
Woodsfield Worcs....98 B6
Woodsfold Lancs.....202 F5
Woodsford Dorset....17 C11
Wood's Green E Sus...52 G6
Woodside Aberdeen...293 C11
  Aberds..........303 E10
  Bedford.........121 G11
  Brack...........66 E2
  Ches E...........85 B9
  Ches E...........167 C10
  Derbys..........170 G5
  Dumfries........238 B2
  Durham.........233 F9
  Fife.............287 G8
  Fife.............287 G7
  Hants...........20 C2
  Herts............85 E10
  Herts............86 D2
  Hrtlpl...........234 D5
  London..........67 F10
  N Som...........60 C3
Woodside Green Essex..87 B8
  Kent............54 C2
Woodside of Arbeadie
  Aberds..........293 D9
Woodside Park London..86 G3
Woods Moor Gtr Man..184 D6
Woodspeen W Berks...64 F2
Woodspring Priory
  N Som...........59 F10
Wood Stanway Glos..99 E11
Woodstock Kent......70 G2
  Oxon............82 B6
  Pembs...........91 F10
Woodston Pboro......138 D3
Wood Street Norf....161 E7
  Sur.............50 C3
Wood Street Village Sur..50 C3
Woodthorpe Derbys..187 G7
  Leics...........153 F10
  Lincs...........190 E6
  Notts...........171 G9
  York............207 D7
Woodton Norf........142 E6
Woodtown Devon.....24 C6
  Devon...........25 D7
Woodvale Mers.......193 E10
Woodville Derbys....152 F6
  Kent............30 C4
Woodville Feus Angus..287 C10
Woodwall Green Staffs 150 C5
Wood Walton Cambs..138 G4
Woodway Oxon.......64 C4
Wood Yard W Mid....135 G7
Woodwell Northants..121 B9
Woodworth Green
  Ches E...........167 D9
Woodyates Dorset....31 D8
Woody Bay Devon.....41 D7
Woofferton Shrops...115 D10
Wookey Som..........44 D4
Wookey Hole Som....44 D4
Wool Dorset.........18 D2
Woolacombe Devon..40 E3
Woolage Green Kent..55 D8
Woolage Village Kent..55 C8
Woolaston Glos......79 E9
Woolaston Common Glos 79 E9
Woolaston Slade Glos..79 E9
Woolaston Woodside
  Glos.............79 E9
Woolavington Som...43 E10
Woolbeding W Sus...34 C5
Wooldale W Yorks....197 F7
Wooler Northumb....263 D11
Woolfall Heath Mers..182 C6
Woolfardisworthy Devon 26 F4
Woolfardisworthy or
  Woolsery Devon..24 C4
Woolfords Cottages
  S Lanark.........269 D10
Woolford's Water Dorset 29 F11
Woolgarston Dorset..18 E5

Woolgreaves W Yorks 197 D10
Woolhampton W Berks..64 F5
Woolhope Hereford...98 D2
Woolhope Cockshoot
  Hereford.........98 D2
Woolland Dorset.....30 F3
Woollard Bath.......60 G6
Woollaston Staffs....151 F7
Woollensbrook Herts..86 C5
Woolley Bath........61 F8
  Cambs...........122 C3
  Corn............24 D3
  Derbys..........170 C5
  W Yorks.........197 E10
Woolley Bridge Gtr Man 185 B8
Woolley Green Wilts..61 G10
  Windsor..........65 C11
Woolmer Green Herts..86 B3
Woolmere Green Worcs 117 E9
Woolmersdon Som...43 G9
Woolminstone Som...28 F6
Woolpack Corner Kent..53 F11
Woolpit Suff.........125 E9
Woolpit Green Suff...125 E9
Woolpit Heath Suff...125 E9
Woolridge Glos......98 G6
Wool's Bridge Dorset..31 F9
Woolscott Warks.....119 D9
Woolsery or
  Woolfardisworthy
  Devon...........24 C4
Woolsgrove Devon...26 G3
Woolsington T&W....242 D5
Woolstanwood Ches E 167 D11
Woolstaston Shrops..131 D9
Woolsthorpe Lincs...155 E8
Woolsthorpe by Belvoir
  Lincs............154 C6
Woolsthorpe-by-
  Colsterworth Lincs 155 E8
Woolston Corn.......6 B5
  Devon...........8 G4
  Shrops..........131 B8
  Shrops..........148 G6
  Som.............29 B10
  Som.............32 G6
  Soton...........32 E6
  Warr............183 D10
Woolston Green Devon..8 B5
Woolstone Glos......99 E8
  M Keynes........103 D7
  Oxon............63 B9
Woolton Mers........182 D6
Woolton Hill Hants..64 G2
Woolvers Hill N Som..59 G11
Woolverstone Suff...108 D3
Woolverton Som......45 C9
Woolwell Devon.......7 C10
Woolwich London....68 D2
Woolwich Ferry London 68 D2
Woonton Hereford...115 G10
  Hereford.........115 G7
Wooperton Northumb 264 E2
Wooplaw Borders....271 G9
Woore Shrops........168 G2
Wootten Green Suff..126 C4
Wootton Bedford....103 B10
  Hants...........19 B10
  Hereford.........97 D11
  Hereford.........114 G6
  IoW.............20 C6
  Kent............55 D8
  N Lincs.........200 D5
  Northants.......120 F5
  Oxon............82 B6
  Oxon............83 D7
  Shrops..........115 B9
  Shrops..........148 D6
  Staffs...........150 D6
  Staffs...........169 F10
Wootton Bourne End
  Bedford.........103 B10
Wootton Bridge IoW..20 C6
Wootton Broadmead
  Bedford.........103 C10
Wootton Common IoW..20 C6
Wootton Courtenay Som 42 E2
Wootton Fitzpaine Dorset 16 B3
Wootton Green C Beds..103 C9
  W Mid...........118 B4
Wootton Rivers Wilts..63 G7
Wootton St Lawrence
  Hants............48 C5
Wootton Wawen Warks 118 E3
Worbarrow Dorset...18 F3
Worcester Worcs.....116 G6
Worcester Park London..67 F8
Wordsley W Mid.....133 F7
Wordwell Suff.......124 C6
Worgret Dorset......18 D4
Work Orkney.........314 E4
Workhouse Common
  Norf............161 E7
Workhouse End Bedford 121 F7
Workhouse Green Suff 107 D8
Workington Cumb....228 F5
Worksop Notts.......187 F9
Worlaby Lincs.......190 F4
  N Lincs.........200 E4
Worlds End Hants....33 E10
World's End W Berks..64 E2
World's End Bucks....84 D5
  London..........86 F4
  Suff.............125 F9
Worle N Som.........59 G11
Worlebury N Som....59 G10
Worleston Ches E....167 D11
Worley Glos.........80 F4
Worlingham Suff....143 F8
Worlington Devon...26 G3
  Suff.............124 C3
Worlingworth Suff...126 D4
Wormald Green
  N Yorks.........214 G6
Wormbridge Hereford..97 E8
Wormbridge Common
  Hereford.........97 E8
Wormegay Norf......158 G2
Wormelow Tump
  Hereford.........97 E9
Wormhill Derbys.....185 G10
Wormingford Essex..107 E8
Worminghall Bucks..83 D10
Wormington Glos....99 D10
Worminster Som.....44 E5
Wormiston Ho Fife...287 F7
Wormit Fife.........287 E7
Wormleighton Warks 119 G8
Wormley Herts.......86 D5
  Sur.............50 F2
Wormley West End Herts 86 D5
Worms Ash Worcs....117 C8
Wormshill Kent......53 B11
Worms Hill Kent.....53 F8
Wormsley Hereford..97 B8
Worplesdon Sur.....50 C3
Worrall S Yorks......186 C4
Worrall Hill Glos.....79 C10
Worsbrough S Yorks.197 G11
Worsbrough Bridge
  S Yorks.........197 G11
Worsbrough Common
  S Yorks.........197 F10
Worsbrough Dale
  S Yorks.........197 G11
Worsham Oxon.......82 C3
Worsley Gtr Man.....195 G8
Worsley Brow Gtr Man 194 F5
Worsley Mesnes
  Gtr Man.........194 G5
Worstead Norf.......160 D6
Worsthorne Lancs....204 G3
Worston Devon.......7 E11
  Lancs............203 E11
Worswell Devon......7 F10
Worten Kent.........54 E3
Worth Kent..........55 B10
  Som.............44 D4
  W Sus...........51 F9
Wortham Suff.......125 B11
Worthen Shrops.....130 C6
Worthenbury Wrex..166 F6
Worthing Norf.......159 F9
  W Sus...........35 G10
Worthington Leics...153 E8
Worth Matravers Dorset 18 F5
Worthy Som..........41 D11
Worthybrook Mon...79 C7
Worting Hants.......48 C6
Wortley Glos........80 G3
  S Yorks.........186 B4
  W Yorks.........197 B9
Worton N Yorks......223 G9
  Oxon............83 C7
  Wilts...........46 B3
Wortwell Norf.......142 G5
Wotherton Shrops...130 C5
Wothorpe Pboro.....137 B10
Wotter Devon........7 C11
Wotton Glos.........80 B4
  Sur.............50 E6
Wotton-under-Edge
  Glos.............80 G3
Wotton Underwood
  Bucks...........83 B11
Woughton on the Green
  M Keynes........103 D7
Woughton Park
  M Keynes........103 D7
Wouldham Kent......69 G8
Woundale Shrops....132 E5
Wrabness Essex......108 E3
Wraes Aberds........302 F5
Wrafton Devon.......40 F3
Wragby Lincs........189 F10
  W Yorks.........198 D2
Wragholme Lincs....190 B5
Wramplingham Norf..142 B2
Wrangaton Devon.....8 D3
Wrangbrook W Yorks..198 E3
Wrangham Aberds...302 F6
Wrangle Lincs.......174 E6
Wrangle Bank Lincs..174 E6
Wrangle Lowgate Lincs 174 E6
Wrangle Low Ground
  Lincs............174 E6
Wrangway Som.......28 C4
Wrantage Som.......28 C4
Wrawby N Lincs......200 F4
Wraxall Dorset......29 G9
  N Som...........60 E4
  Som.............44 F6
Wray Lancs..........212 F2
Wray Common Sur...51 C9
Wraysbury Windsor..66 E4
Wrayton Lancs.......212 E2
Wrea Green Lancs....202 G3
Wreaks End Cumb....210 B4
Wreath Cumb.........28 B4
Wreay Cumb.........230 B4
  Cumb...........230 G4
Wrecclesham Sur....49 D10
Wrekenton T&W.....243 F7
Wrelton N Yorks.....216 B4
Wrenbury Ches E....167 F9
Wrenbury cum Frith
  Ches E...........167 F9
Wrench Green N Yorks 217 B9
Wreningham Norf...142 D3
Wrentham Suff......143 G9
Wrenthorpe W Yorks 197 C10
Wrentnall Shrops....131 C8
Wressle E Yorks......207 G10
  N Lincs.........200 F3
Wrestlingworth C Beds 104 B5
Wretham Norf.......141 F8
Wretton Norf........140 D3
Wrexham Wrex......166 E4
Wreyland Devon......13 E11
Wribbenhall Worcs..116 B5
Wrickton Shrops.....132 F2
Wrightington Bar Lancs 194 E4
Wrights Green Warr..183 B10
Wright's Green Essex..87 B8
Wrinehill Staffs.......168 F3
Wringsdown Corn....12 D2
Wrington N Som.....60 G3
Wrinkleberry Devon..24 C4
Writhlington Bath...45 C8
Writtle Essex........87 D11
Wrockwardine Telford 150 G2
Wrockwardine Wood
  Telford..........150 G4
Wroot N Lincs.......199 G8
Wrose W Yorks......205 F9
Wrotham Kent.......52 B6
Wrotham Heath Kent..52 B6
Wroughton Swindon..62 C6
Wroxall IoW.........21 F7
  Warks...........118 C4
Wroxeter Shrops.....131 B11
Wroxham Norf.......160 F6
Wroxton Oxon.......101 C8
Wyaston Derbys.....169 G11
Wyatt's Green Essex..87 F9

Wybers Wood NE Lincs 201 F8
Wyberton Lincs......174 G4
Wyboston Bedford...122 F3
Wybunbury Ches E...168 F2
Wychbold Worcs.....117 D8
Wych Cross E Sus.....52 G2
Wychnor Staffs......152 F3
Wychnor Bridges Staffs 152 F3
Wyck Hants..........49 F9
Wyck Rissington Glos 100 G3
Wycliffe Durham.....224 C2
Wycoller Lancs......204 F4
Wycomb Leics.......154 E5
Wycombe Marsh Bucks..84 G5
Wyddial Herts.......105 E7
Wydra N Yorks......205 C10
Wye Kent............54 D5
Wyebanks Kent......54 C2
Wyegate Green Glos..79 D9
Wyesham Mon.......79 C8
Wyfordby Leics......154 F5
Wyke Dorset.........30 B3
  Shrops..........132 C2
  Sur.............50 E2
  W Yorks.........197 B7
Wyke Champflower Som 45 F8
Wykeham Lincs.......156 D5
  N Yorks.........216 C6
  N Yorks.........217 C9
Wyken Shrops........132 E5
  W Mid...........135 G7
Wyke Regis Dorset...17 F9
Wykey Shrops........149 E7
Wykin Leics.........135 D8
Wylam Northumb....242 E4
Wylde Hereford......115 D9
Wylde Green W Mid..134 E2
Wyllie Caerph........77 G11
Wylye Wilts..........46 F4
Wymans Brook Glos..99 G8
Wymbush M Keynes...102 D6
Wymering Ptsmth....33 F10
Wymeswold Leics....154 E2
Wymington Bedford..121 E9
Wymondham Leics...155 F7
  Norf............142 C2
Wymondley Bury Herts 104 F4
Wymott Lancs........194 C4
Wyndham Bridgend...76 G6
Wyndham Park V Glam 58 E5
Wynds Point Hereford 98 C5
Wynford Eagle Dorset 17 B7
Wynn's Green Hereford 98 B2
Wynyard Village
  Stockton........234 F4
Wyre Piddle Worcs...99 B9
Wysall Notts.........154 D2
Wyson Hereford......115 D10
Wythall Worcs.......117 B11
Wytham Oxon........83 D7
Wythburn Cumb.....220 C6
Wythenshawe Gtr Man 184 D4
Wythop Mill Cumb....229 F9
Wyton Cambs........122 C5
  E Yorks.........209 G9
Wyverstone Suff.....125 D10
Wyverstone Green
  Suff............125 D10
Wyverstone Street
  Suff............125 D10
Wyville Lincs........155 D7
Wyvis Lodge Highld..300 B4

Y

Yaddlethorpe N Lincs 199 F11
Yafford IoW.........20 E4
Yafforth N Yorks.....224 G6
Yalberton Torbay.....9 D7
Yalding Kent.........53 C7
Yanley N Som........60 F5
Yanworth Glos.......81 D9
Yapham E Yorks......207 C11
Yapton W Sus........35 G7
Yarberry N Som......44 B2
Yarborough NE Lincs 201 F7
Yarbridge IoW.......21 D8
Yarburgh Lincs......190 C5
Yarcombe Devon.....28 F2
Yard Som............42 F5
Yardhurst Kent......54 E3
Yardley W Mid......134 F2
Yardley Gobion
  Northants.......102 C5
Yardley Hastings
  Northants.......121 F7
Yardley Wood W Mid 118 B2
Yardro Powys........114 F4
Yarford Som.........28 B2
Yarhampton Worcs..116 D5
Yarhampton Cross
  Worcs...........116 D5
Yarkhill Hereford....98 C2
Yarlet Staffs.........151 D8
Yarley Som..........44 D4
Yarlington Som......29 B11
Yarlside Cumb.......210 F4
Yarm Stockton......225 C8
Yarmouth IoW.......20 D3
Yarnacott Devon.....40 G6
Yarnbrook Wilts.....45 C11
Yarnfield Staffs......151 C7
Yarningale Common
  Warks...........118 D3
Yarnscombe Devon..25 C9
Yarnton Oxon........83 C7
Yarpole Hereford....115 E9
Yarrow Borders......261 E9
  Northumb.......250 F6
  Som.............43 E10
Yarrow Feus Borders..261 E8
Yarrowford Borders..261 E10
Yarsop Hereford.....97 B8
Yarwell Northants...137 D11
Yate S Glos..........61 C8
Yate Rocks S Glos....61 C8
Yateley Hants........65 G10
Yatesbury Wilts......62 E5
Yattendon W Berks..64 E5
Yatton Hereford.....115 D8
  Hereford.........98 B2
  N Som...........60 G2
Yatton Keynell Wilts..61 D11
Yaverland IoW.......21 D8
Yawthorpe Lincs.....188 C5
Yaxham Norf........159 G10
Yaxley Cambs........138 E2
  Suff............126 C2
Yazor Hereford......97 B8
Y Bala / Bala Gwyn..147 B8
Y Bont Faen / Cowbridge
  V Glam..........58 E3

Y Borth / Borth Ceredig 128 E2
Yeabridge Som.......28 D6
Yeading London......66 C6
Yeadon W Yorks.....205 E10
Yealand Conyers Lancs 211 E10
Yealand Redmayne
  Lancs............211 E10
Yealand Storrs Lancs 211 D9
Yealmbridge Devon...7 E11
Yealmpton Devon.....7 E11
Yearby Redcar.......235 G8
Yearngill Cumb......229 C8
Yearsley N Yorks.....215 E11
Yeaton Shrops.......149 F8
Yeaveley Derbys.....169 G11
Yedingham N Yorks..217 D7
Yelden Bedford......121 D10
Yeldersley Hollies
  Derbys..........170 G2
Yelford Oxon.........82 E5
Yelland Devon.......40 G3
  Devon...........25 E8
Yelling Cambs.......122 E5
Yelsted Kent........69 G10
Yelvertoft Northants 119 B11
Yelverton Devon......7 B10
  Norf............142 C5
Yenston Som.........30 C2
Yeoford Devon.......13 B11
Yeolmbridge Corn....12 D2
Yeo Mill Devon......26 C4
Yeo Vale Devon......24 C6
Yeovil Som...........29 D9
Yeovil Marsh Som....29 D8
Yeovilton Som.......29 C8
Yerbeston Pembs.....73 D9
Yesnaby Orkney......314 E2
Yetlington Northumb 252 B2
Yetminster Dorset...29 E9
Yett N Lanark........268 D5
Yettington Devon....15 D7
Yetts o' Muckhart Clack 286 G4
Yew Green Warks....118 D4
Yewhedges Kent......54 B3
Yew Tree Gtr Man....185 B7
  W Mid...........133 D10
Yewtree Cross Kent...55 E7
Y Fali / Valley Anglesey 178 F3
Y Felinheli / Port Dinorwic
  Gwyn............163 B8
Y Ffôr / Pforb Gwyn...145 B7
Y Gors Ceredig......112 B2
Y Gribyn Powys......129 E8
Yieldshields S Lanark 269 E7
Yiewsley London.....66 C5
Yinstay Orkney......314 E5
Y Mwmbwls / The Mumbles
  Swansea.........56 D6
Ynus-tawelog Swansea 75 D10
Ynys Gwyn...........145 B11
Ynysboeth Rhondda..77 F9
Ynysddu Caerph......77 G11
Ynysforgan Swansea..57 B7
Ynysgyfflog Gwyn....146 G2
Ynyshir Rhondda......77 G8
Ynys-isaf Powys......76 C3
Ynyslas Ceredig......128 E2
Ynysmaerdy Neath...57 B8
  Rhondda.........58 C4
Ynysmeudwy Neath..76 D2
  Neath............76 D2
Ynys Tachwedd Ceredig 128 E2
Ynystawe Swansea...75 E11
Ynyswen Powys......76 C4
  Rhondda.........77 F7
Ynysybwl Rhondda...77 G9
Ynysygwas Neath....57 C9
Yockenthwaite N Yorks 213 D8
Yockleton Shrops....149 G7
Yodercott Devon.....27 E9
Yokefleet E Yorks....199 C10
Yoker W Dunb.......267 B10
Yonder Bognie Aberds 302 E5
Yondertown Devon...7 D11
Yopps Green Kent....52 C6
York Lancs..........203 G10
  York............207 C7
Yorkletts Kent.......70 G5
Yorkley Glos.........79 D10
Yorkley Slade Glos...79 D10
York Town Sur.......65 G11
Yorton Shrops.......149 E10
Yorton Heath Shrops 149 E10
Yottenfews Cumb....219 D10
Youlgrave Derbys....170 C2
Youlthorpe E Yorks..207 B11
Youlton N Yorks.....215 G9
Youngsbury Herts....86 B5
Young's End Essex...88 B2
Young Wood Lincs...189 G10
Yoxall Staffs.........152 F2
Yoxford Suff.........127 D7
Y Pîl / Pyle Bridgend..57 E10
Yr Hôb / Hope Flint..166 D4
Ysbyty Cynfyn Ceredig 112 B5
Ysbyty Ifan Conwy..164 F4
Ysbyty Ystwyth Ceredig 112 C4
Ysceifiog Flint.......181 G11
Ysgeibion Denb......165 D9
Yspitty Carms.......56 B5
Ystalyfera Neath.....76 D3
Ystrad Rhondda......77 F7
Ystrad Aeron Ceredig 111 F10
Ystradfellte Powys...76 C4
Ystradffin Carms.....94 D5
Ystradgynlais Powys..76 C3
Ystradmeurig Ceredig 112 D4
Ystrad-mynach Caerph 77 G10
Ystradowen Carms...76 C2
  V Glam..........58 D4
Ystrad Uchaf Powys..129 C11
Ystumtuen Ceredig..112 B4
Ythanbank Aberds...303 F9
Ythanwells Aberds...302 F6
Ythsie Aberds........303 F8
Y Tymbl / Tumble Carms 75 C8
Y Waun / Chirk Wrex..148 B5

Z

Zeal Monachorum Devon 26 G2
Zeals Wilts..........45 G9
Zelah Corn...........4 E6
Zennor Corn..........1 B5
Zoar Corn............3 F7
Zouch Notts.........153 E10

County and unitary authority boundaries

Ordnance Survey National Grid

The blue lines which divide the Navigator map pages into squares for indexing match the Ordnance Survey National Grid and correspond to the small squares on the boundary map below. Each side of a grid square measures 10km on the ground.

The National Grid 100-km square letters and kilometre values are indicated for the grid intersection at the outer corners of each page. For example, the intersection SE6090 at the upper right corner of page 215 is 60km East and 90km North of the south-west corner of National Grid square SE.

Using GPS with Navigator mapping

Since Navigator Britain is based on Ordnance Survey mapping, and rectified to the National Grid, it can be used with in-car or handheld GPS for locating identifiable waypoints such as road junctions, bridges, railways and farms, or assessing your position in relation to any of the features shown on the map.

On your receiver, choose British Grid as the location format and for map datum select Ordnance Survey (this may be described as Ord Srvy GB or similar, or more specifically as OSGB36). Your receiver will automatically convert the latitude/longitude co-ordinates transmitted by GPS into compatible National Grid data.

Positional accuracy of any particular feature is limited to 50–100m, due to the limitations of the original survey and the scale of Navigator mapping.

For further information see www.gps.gov.uk

Greater London

1 City and County of the City of London
2 Hackney
3 Tower Hamlets
4 Southwark
5 Lambeth
6 Wandsworth
7 Hammersmith and Fulham
8 Royal Borough of Kensington and Chelsea
9 City of Westminster
10 Camden
11 Islington
12 Haringey
13 Waltham Forest
14 Newham
15 Greenwich
16 Lewisham
17 Merton
18 Richmond upon Thames
19 Hounslow
20 Ealing
21 Brent
22 Barnet
23 Enfield
24 Redbridge
25 Barking and Dagenham
26 Havering
27 Bexley
28 Bromley
29 Croydon
30 Sutton
31 Kingston upon Thames
32 Hillingdon
33 Harrow

1 Central Scotland

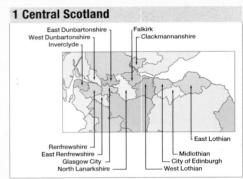

2 Northern England

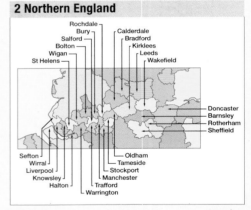

3 West Midlands

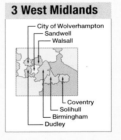

4 South Wales and Bristol area

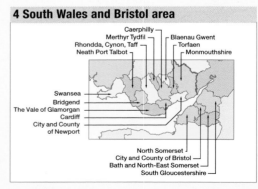

5 Thames Valley

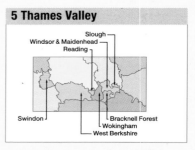

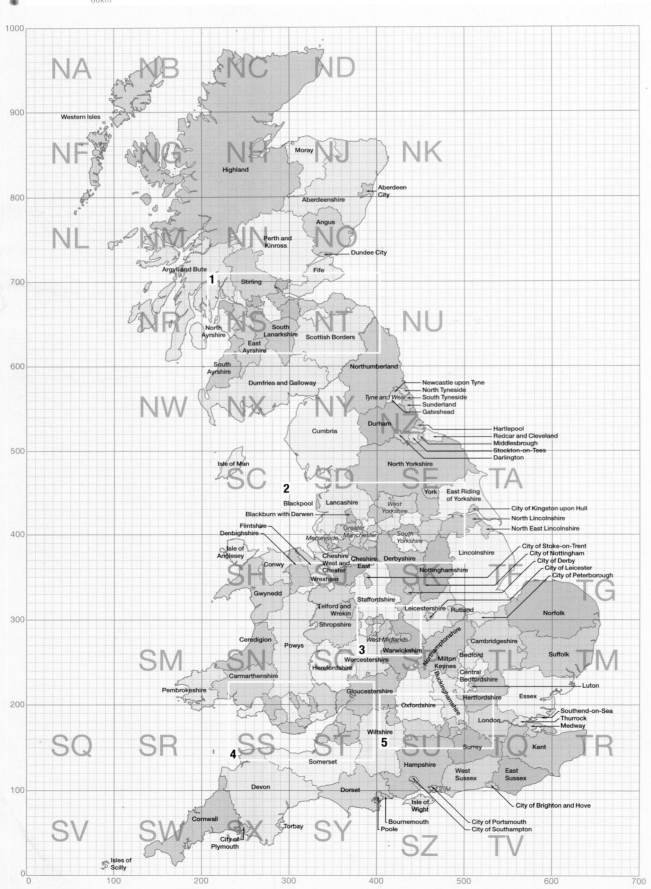